CURRENT LAW STATUTES ANNOTATED

1978

VOLUME 2

AUSTRALIA
The Law Book Co. Ltd.
Sydney : Melbourne : Brisbane

CANADA AND U.S.A.
The Carswell Company Ltd.
Agincourt, Ontario

INDIA
N. M. Tripathi Private Ltd.
Bombay

ISRAEL
Steimatzky's Agency Ltd.
Jerusalem : Tel Aviv : Haifa

MALAYSIA : SINGAPORE : BRUNEI
Malayan Law Journal (Pte.) Ltd.
Singapore

NEW ZEALAND
Sweet & Maxwell (N.Z.) Ltd.
Wellington

PAKISTAN
Pakistan Law House
Karachi

CURRENT LAW
STATUTES
ANNOTATED
1978

VOLUME 2

GENERAL EDITOR
PETER ALLSOP, M.A.
Barrister

ASSISTANT GENERAL EDITOR
CLAIRE BOOTH, LL.B.
Solicitor

LONDON
SWEET & MAXWELL   STEVENS & SONS

EDINBURGH
W. GREEN & SON

1978

Published by
SWEET & MAXWELL LIMITED
and STEVENS & SONS LIMITED
of 11 New Fetter Lane, London,
and W. GREEN & SON LIMITED
of St. Giles Street, Edinburgh,
and printed in Great Britain by
The Eastern Press Limited
London and Reading

ISBN 0 421 25830 6

CONTENTS

CHRONOLOGICAL TABLE

STATUTES

VOLUME ONE

c. 1. Participation Agreements Act 1978.
  2. Commonwealth Development Corporation Act 1978.
  3. Refuse Disposal (Amenity) Act 1978.
  4. Local Government (Scotland) Act 1978.
  5. Northern Ireland (Emergency Provisions) Act 1978.
  6. Employment Subsidies Act 1978.
  7. Consolidated Fund Act 1978.
  8. Civil Aviation Act 1978.
  9. Gun Barrel Proof Act 1978.
  10. European Assembly Elections Act 1978.
  11. Shipbuilding (Redundancy Payments) Act 1978.
  12. Medical Act 1978.
  13. Education (Northern Ireland) Act 1978.
  14. Housing (Financial Provisions) (Scotland) Act 1978.
  15. Solomon Islands Act 1978.
  16. Trustee Savings Banks Act 1978.
  17. Internationally Protected Persons Act 1978.
  18. Export Guarantees and Overseas Investment Act 1978.
  19. Oaths Act 1978.
  20. Tuvalu Act 1978.
  21. Co-operative Development Agency Act 1978.
  22. Domestic Proceedings and Magistrates' Courts Act 1978.
  23. Judicature (Northern Ireland) Act 1978.
  24. Theatres Trust (Scotland) Act 1978.
  25. Nuclear Safeguards and Electricity (Finance) Act 1978.
  26. Suppression of Terrorism Act 1978.
  27. Home Purchase Assistance and Housing Corporation Guarantees Act 1978.
  28. Adoption (Scotland) Act 1978.
  29. National Health Service (Scotland) Act 1978.
  30. Interpretation Act 1978.
  31. Theft Act 1978.

5

Contents

MEASURES

INDEX OF SHORT TITLES

References are to chapter numbers of 1978

Index of Short Titles

Finance Act 1978 *

(1978 c. 42)

ARRANGEMENT OF SECTIONS

PART I

CUSTOMS AND EXCISE

PART II

VALUE ADDED TAX

PART III

INCOME TAX, CORPORATION TAX AND CAPITAL GAINS TAX

CHAPTER I

GENERAL

* Annotations by J. F. Avery Jones, M.A., LL.B., Solicitor; Christopher Cant, B.A., Barrister; David Goy, LL.M., Barrister; Nigel Thomas, LL.B., Barrister.

CHAPTER II

CAPITAL GAINS

CHAPTER III

PROFIT SHARING SCHEMES

PART IV

CAPITAL TRANSFER TAX

PART V

MISCELLANEOUS AND SUPPLEMENTARY

An Act to grant certain duties, to alter other duties, and to amend the law relating to the National Debt and the Public Revenue, and to make further provision in connection with Finance.

[31st July 1978]

General Note

This Act received the Royal Assent on July 31, 1978, and came into force on that date.

For Parliamentary debates, see *Hansard*, H.C. Vol. 948, cols. 1651, 1671; Vol. 949, cols. 792, 923, 1188, 1321; Vol. 950, cols. 258, 389; H.L. Vol. 395, cols. 46, 321, 650.

Abbreviations

F.A. 1965	= Finance Act 1965, c. 25.
C.A.A. 1968	= Capital Allowances Act 1968, c. 3.
I.C.T.A. 1970	= Income and Corporations Taxes Act 1970, c. 10.
F.A. 1972	= Finance Act 1972, c. 41.
F.A. 1974	= Finance Act 1974, c. 30.
F.A. 1975	= Finance Act 1975, c. 7.
F. (No. 2) A. 1975	= Finance (No. 2) Act 1975, c. 45.
F.A. 1976	= Finance Act 1976, c. 40.
F.A. 1977	= Finance Act 1977, c. 36.

PART I

CUSTOMS AND EXCISE

Tobacco products duty

1.—(1) In the case of any cigarette having a tar yield of not less than 20 mg. the Table in section 4 (1) of the Finance Act 1976 (excise duty on tobacco products) shall have effect as if the rate of duty in paragraph 1 were increased by £2·25 per thousand cigarettes.

(2) The Commissioners may make regulations—

(*a*) prescribing how the tar yield of cigarettes is to be determined for the purposes of this section;

(*b*) without prejudice to section 4 (2) of the said Act of 1976, enabling the whole or any part of the additional duty imposed by this section to be remitted or repaid in such cases as may be specified in the regulations or determined by the Commissioners and subject to such conditions as they see fit to impose.

(3) For the purposes of section 6 of the said Act of 1976 (power to alter rates of duty) the increase specified in subsection (1) above shall be treated as a rate of duty separate from that applying apart from the increase; and in section 2 (2) of the Finance Act 1977 (calculation of duty in case of cigarettes more than 9 cm. long) for the words " For the purposes of paragraph 1 in the Table in the said section 4 (1) " there shall be substituted the words " For the purposes of the references to a thousand cigarettes in paragraph 1 in the Table in section 4 (1) of the Finance Act 1976 and in section 1 (1) of the Finance Act 1978 ".

(4) This section shall come into force on 4th September 1978.

GENERAL NOTE

This is a new tax in that it imposes a special surcharge on cigarettes having a tar yield of not less than 20 mg. The intention is to put up the price of a packet of 20 such cigarettes by about 7p so as to discourage persons from smoking high tar yield cigarettes. It is not intended to raise the revenue yield.

The surcharge does not comply with the steps being taken by the EEC to harmonise tobacco duties but has been allowed by agreement until December 1980.

The test to determine the tar yield will be set out in full in the regulations to be published by the Commissioners—it has been stated in the Standing Committee debates that the test will not be set out by referring to another document as has been the case with certain tests regarding duties on petrol. These regulations will be subject to annulment by either House of Parliament in accordance with s. 306 (2) Customs and Excise Act 1952.

Subs. (2) (b) expressly confers on the Commissioners power to grant concessions. The imposition of this duty takes effect from September 4, 1978.

Repayment of excise duty on beer etc.

2.—(1) The Commissioners may by regulations provide for excise duty charged on liquor to which this subsection applies and which is used as an ingredient in the production or manufacture of—

(a) any beverage of an alcoholic strength not exceeding 2° of proof; or

(b) any such article (other than a beverage) as the Commissioners may determine having regard to the alcoholic content thereof,

to be repaid subject to such conditions as may be imposed by or under the regulations.

This subsection applies to beer and to wine, made-wine and cider imported into the United Kingdom.

(2) The Commissioners may by regulations provide for excise duty charged on imported wine which is converted into vinegar to be repaid subject to such conditions as may be imposed by or under the regulations.

GENERAL NOTE

This section enables the Commissioners to make regulations to provide for the repayment of excise duty paid on imported beer, wine, made-wine and cider in certain circumstances. The Commissioners already have this power in respect of beer, wine, made-wine and cider produced in the United Kingdom.

Warehousing regulations

3. In section 16 (2) of the Finance (No. 2) Act 1975 (warehousing regulations) after paragraph (d) there shall be inserted—

" (e) enabling the Commissioners to allow goods to be removed from warehouse without payment of duty in such circumstances and subject to such conditions as they may determine; ".

GENERAL NOTE

This section has been included to remove any doubts as to the validity of reg. 8 (7) of the Warehousing Regulations 1975 (S.I. 1975 No. 1789). The history of the difficulty is that s. 89 of the Customs and Excise Act 1952 conferred on the Commissioners authority to permit the removal of goods from warehouses without the payment of duty for any purpose other than home use (e.g. for the purpose of exporting the goods or removing them to another warehouse). When s. 89 was wholly replaced by s. 16 (2) of the Finance (No. 2) Act 1975, no reference was made to this power and consequently doubts have arisen as to the validity of the new regulations dealing with this. This section removes those doubts.

Control of movement of goods

4.—(1) The Commissioners may by regulations impose conditions and restrictions as respects—

(a) the movement of imported goods between the place of importation and a place approved by the Commissioners for the clearance out of charge of such goods; and

(b) the movement of goods intended for export between a place approved by the Commissioners for the examination of such goods and the place of exportation.

(2) The regulations may in particular—

(a) require the goods to be moved within such period and by such route as may be specified by or under the regulations;

(b) require the goods to be carried in a vehicle or container complying with such requirements and secured in such manner as may be so specified; and

(c) prohibit, except in such circumstances as may be so specified, any unloading or loading of the vehicle or container or any interference with its security.

(3) If any person contravenes or fails to comply with any regulation or any requirement imposed by or under the regulations, that person and the person then in charge of the goods shall each be liable to a penalty of £500 and any goods in respect of which the offence was committed shall be liable to forfeiture.

GENERAL NOTE

It is intended that regulations will be introduced in accordance with this section to deal with the transit of goods between inland clearance depots and ports. At present there are no draft regulations and the intended regulations are being considered by the Joint Customs Consultation Committee. It is anticipated that the regulations will be available next January.

The regulations will deal with such matters as the security of the vehicles used, the route to be used and preventing the mixing of imported goods with other goods. The intention is to prevent tampering with the goods before the duty has been imposed.

Penalty for removing seals etc.

5.—(1) Where, in pursuance of any power conferred by the customs and excise Acts or of any requirement imposed by or under those Acts, a seal, lock or mark is used to secure or identify any goods for any of the purposes of those Acts and—

(a) at any time while the goods are in the United Kingdom or within the limits of any port or on passage between ports in the United Kingdom, the seal, lock or mark is wilfully and prematurely removed or tampered with by any person; or

(b) at any time before the seal, lock or mark is lawfully removed, any of the goods are wilfully removed by any person,

that person and the person then in charge of the goods shall each be liable to a penalty of £500; and for the purposes of this subsection goods in a ship or aircraft shall be deemed to be in the charge of the master of the ship or commander of the aircraft.

(2) Where, in pursuance of any Community requirement or practice which relates to the movement of goods between countries or of any international agreement to which the United Kingdom is a party and which so relates,—

(a) a seal, lock or mark is used (whether in the United Kingdom or elsewhere) to secure or identify any goods for customs or excise purposes; and

(b) at any time while the goods are in the United Kingdom, the seal, lock or mark is wilfully and prematurely removed or tampered with by any person,

that person and the person then in charge of the goods shall each be liable to a penalty of £500.

(3) This section shall be treated for all purposes as included in Part II of the Customs and Excise Act 1952 and section 70 of that Act, which is superseded by this section, shall cease to have effect.

GENERAL NOTE

This section supersedes s. 70 of the Customs and Excise Act 1952 and relaxes its provisions in two respects. The section concerns penalties imposed for tampering with seals in relation to the movement of imported and exported goods.

Previously the seals had to be attached by a Customs and Excise officer. Now the seals may be attached by a "reputable trader" in accordance with the EEC regulations. This is to save time.

In addition, the person liable to pay a penalty if there had been any tampering with a seal was the person responsible for the goods. This has now been changed to cover in addition the person who actually tampers with the seal.

Anti-dumping measures on ECSC products

6.—(1) In relation to any product covered by the ECSC treaty, the Secretary of State may by order make such provision as appears to him to be appropriate for the purpose of giving effect to any Recommendation or other Community obligation arising under that treaty and relating to the imposition, amendment, suspension, revocation or annulment of anti-dumping measures, that is to say, measures for affording protection against dumping or the granting of bounties or subsidies by countries which are not members of the Coal and Steel Community.

(2) Without prejudice to the generality of the power conferred by subsection (1) above, so far as may be necessary for giving effect to a Community obligation, an order under that subsection may, in circumstances specified in the order,—

(a) require the provision of security of an amount determined under the order by way of provisional duty;

(b) provide for the collection of the whole or a particular proportion of any amount so secured;

(c) charge a duty of customs; and

(d) make provisions of the order applicable to goods imported into the United Kingdom or another member State before the order comes into force;

and the power to make an order under that subsection includes power to vary or revoke an order previously made in the exercise of that power and shall be exercisable by statutory instrument which shall be subject to annulment in pursuance of a resolution of the Commons House of Parliament.

(3) Where the application or amount of any charge imposed by an order under subsection (1) above depends on some factor other than the country of origin, the Commissioners may require the importer of any goods to state such facts as they may think necessary in order to determine the duty chargeable on those goods; and if any facts so required are not stated, the duty chargeable shall be determined on the basis that the facts are such as the Commissioners may determine.

(4) Section 9 of the Finance Act 1961 (the regulator) shall not apply to any duty chargeable on goods by virtue of subsection (1) above, and any such duty shall be in addition to any other duty of customs for the time being chargeable on those goods.

(5) Subject to subsections (6) and (7) below, after the passing of this Act, the powers conferred on the Secretary of State by the Customs Duties (Dumping and Subsidies) Act 1969 (in the following provisions of this section referred to as " the 1969 Act ") shall not be exercisable except in relation to products covered by the ECSC Treaty and then only in cases where the imposition of a duty under that Act to protect an industry within the United Kingdom is compatible with Community obligations; and, to the limited extent that it remains operative by virtue of this subsection, the 1969 Act shall have effect—

(a) subject to the amendments in Schedule 1 to this Act; and (*b*) subject to such amendments as the Secretary of State may specify by order made by statutory instrument, being amendments which appear to him to be necessary or desirable to take account of any international agreement to which the United Kingdom is a party.

(6) No order shall be made under subsection (5) above unless a draft of it has been laid before Parliament and approved by a resolution of each House, and the power to make such an order—

(*a*) does not extend to the provisions of sections 1 (1) and (3), 7 (1), 8, 9 (1) and (2) and 10 of the 1969 Act (which relate to the charge and levy of duty); and

(*b*) is without prejudice to the power to make amendments of enactments under section 2 (2) of the European Communities Act 1972 (for the purpose of implementing Community obligations).

(7) Nothing in subsection (5) above shall affect—

(*a*) the continued operation of any order made under the 1969 Act which is in force at the passing of this Act (notwithstanding that it may relate to goods which are not products covered by the ECSC Treaty); or

(*b*) the exercise, in relation to any such order as is referred to in paragraph (*a*) above, of any power conferred by section 10 (3) or section 15 (4) of the 1969 Act to vary or remove a duty having effect by virtue of the order or to vary or revoke the order itself.

(8) After subsection (6) of section 5 of the European Communities Act 1972 (power to make provision by regulations as regards reliefs from import duties) there shall be inserted the following subsection—

" (6A) The reference in subsection (6) above to import duties includes a reference—

(*a*) to duties charged by an order under subsection (1) of section 6 of the Finance Act 1978; and

(*b*) to duties under the Customs Duties (Dumping and Subsidies) Act 1969, as that Act has effect by virtue of subsection (5) of that section ";

and any reference to import duties in regulations made under the said subsection (6) before as well as after the passing of this Act shall be construed accordingly.

(9) So much of Part I of Schedule 3 to the European Communities Act 1972 as provides for the repeal of the 1969 Act from a date to be appointed by the Secretary of State shall cease to have effect.

GENERAL NOTE

This section is concerned with the dumping of general iron and steel products in the Community. Prior to the passing of this Act there were two separate methods of passing anti-dumping measures. The British Government could unilaterally impose such measures in accordance with the Customs Duties (Dumping and Subsidies) Act 1969 (which applied to matters dealt with by the Treaty of Paris). Alternatively measures could be passed by the EEC Commission (in accordance with the Treaty of Rome). The effect of this section is to increase the effectiveness of the enforcement of the EEC anti-dumping provisions but to limit the scope of the unilateral power of the British Government.

By subs. (5) the powers under the 1969 Act can only be exercised in relation to products covered by the European Coal and Steel Community Treaty and only in so far as any such measure is compatible with the United Kingdom's obligations to the EEC. Before a measure under the 1969 Act can be effective it must have been approved by both the House of Commons and the House of Lords (subs. (6)).

The provisions for putting into effect EEC anti-dumping provisions have been made more effective by enabling the Secretary of State to comply with any EEC

Recommendation or obligation by Order. Examples of the anti-dumping measures that may be adopted are included in subs. (2) and include the charging of additional duty or the taking of a security. It is possible for a retrospective charge to be imposed in accordance with subs. (2) (*d*) and no time limit has been expressly included. There is a time limit however contained in art. 4 of Recommendation 3004/77/ECSC which provides that " duty may be assessed on products which were entered for consumption not more than 90 days prior to the date of application of provisional measures."

One of the reasons for introducing this section was the free movement of goods within the Community. It was considered that there was a danger that the goods being dumped could enter the Community in one State and then be moved to another State within the Community.

Gaming licence duty in Scotland

7.—(1) For the purpose of determining the amount of the duty chargeable under section 14 of the Betting and Gaming Duties Act 1972 on a gaming licence in respect of premises in Scotland for a period beginning after 31st March 1978 the rateable value of any lands and heritages shall be ascertained in accordance with the following provisions of this section in any case where a rateable value is shown for them in the valuation roll for the time being in force and either a lower value or no value was shown for them in the valuation roll in force on 31st March 1978.

(2) Where the rateable value of any lands and heritages falls to be ascertained in accordance with this section, then—

(*a*) if a rateable value was shown for them in the valuation roll in force on 31st March 1978, their rateable value shall be taken to be the value so shown, but subject to paragraph (*b*) below;

(*b*) if, since the value so shown was entered in that valuation roll, there has been a material change of circumstances affecting the value of the lands and heritages, their rateable value shall be taken to be the value determined under this section as the rateable value which would have been shown for them in that valuation roll if the change had been given effect to in that roll;

(*c*) if no value was shown for the lands and heritages in the valuation roll in force on 31st March 1978, their rateable value shall be taken to be the value determined under this section as the value that would have been so shown if, at the time of the valuation for the purposes of that roll, the premises in respect of which the licence is to be granted had been in existence and all relevant circumstances had been the same as at the time when the value of the lands and heritages is determined under this section.

(3) Any determination under this section shall be made by the Commissioners after consultation with the assessor appointed under the Local Government (Scotland) Act 1973 for the valuation area concerned; but the person to whom the licence is to be or has been granted may, by notice in writing given to the Commissioners not later than four weeks after the date on which the determination is notified to him, require the determination to be referred to the arbitration of a referee appointed by the Lord President of the Court of Session, the decision of which referee shall be final and conclusive.

(4) A person appointed as a referee under subsection (3) above shall not be an officer of any government department.

(5) If the amount of duty chargeable is reduced in consequence of a decision of a referee appointed under this section, any amount overpaid shall be repaid.

(6) In this section " material change of circumstances " has the meaning assigned to it by section 37 (1) of the Local Government (Scotland) Act 1975.

GENERAL NOTE

Due to the revaluation of rateable values in Scotland at the beginning of April this year it has become necessary to introduce this section to ensure that the gaming licence duty is not heavier in Scotland than elsewhere in the United Kingdom. The amount of the duty payable is based on the rateable value of the casino or building used for gaming purposes.

As a result of this section the gaming licence duty will be determined in Scotland by reference to a notional rateable value which shall be the rateable value of the building as at March 31, 1978, or what that value would have been had the building then been on the valuation roll. In the case of a building on the valuation roll at that date but in respect of which there has been a subsequent material change the notional rateable value is that which would have appeared on the roll on March 31, 1978, if account had been taken of the change.

The notional rateable value will, when necessary, be determined by consultations between the Commissioners and the assessor for the particular valuation area. There is a right of appeal to a referee appointed by the Lord President of the Court of Session. The right must be exercised within four weeks of notification of the Commissioners determination.

Vehicles excise duty: Great Britain

8.—(1) For section 7 (2) of the Vehicles (Excise) Act 1971 there shall be substituted—

" (2) A mechanically propelled vehicle shall not be chargeable with any duty under this Act by reason of its use by or for the purposes of a person (' a disabled person ') suffering from a physical defect or disability or by reason of its being kept for such use if—

(a) it is registered under this Act in the name of that person; and

(b) he has obtained, or is eligible for, a grant under paragraph 2 of Schedule 2 to the National Health Service Act 1977 in relation to that vehicle or is in receipt of a mobility allowance; and

(c) no other vehicle registered in his name under this Act is exempted from duty under this subsection or section 7 of the Finance Act 1971;

and for the purposes of this subsection a vehicle shall be deemed to be registered in the name of a disabled person in receipt of a mobility allowance if it is registered in the name of a person appointed pursuant to regulations under the Social Security Act 1975 to exercise any of his rights or powers or in the name of a person nominated for the purposes of this subsection by the disabled person or by a person so appointed."

(2) So much of section 13 of the Finance Act 1976 as excludes a person entitled to a mobility allowance from the exemption from duty conferred by section 7 of the Finance Act 1971 shall cease to have effect.

(3) In section 7 of the Finance Act 1971 after paragraph (c) there shall be inserted the words " and

(d) no vehicle exempted from duty under section 7 (2) of the Vehicles (Excise) Act 1971 is (or by virtue of that provision is deemed to be) registered in his name under that Act."

(4) Section 26 (1) (c) of the Vehicles (Excise) Act 1971 (offences in respect of licence, etc.) shall apply also to any document in the form of a licence which in pursuance of regulations made under that Act is issued in respect of a vehicle exempted from duty under the provisions mentioned in subsections (1) and (3) above; and section 26 (2) (a) of that Act (false declarations in connection with applications for a licence)

shall apply also in relation to any declaration required by any such regulations to be made in respect of any vehicle so exempted.

(5) This section shall come into force on 1st December 1978.

GENERAL NOTE

By s. 13 of the Finance Act 1976 the exemption from vehicles excise duty given to disabled persons was restricted so that a disabled person could not be entitled to both the exemption and a mobility allowance. This restriction is now removed by this section and a disabled person in receipt of a mobility allowance can from December 1, 1978, also claim the benefit of the exemption in respect of one car only.

Vehicles excise duty: Northern Ireland

9.—(1) For section 7 (2) of the Vehicles (Excise) Act (Northern Ireland) 1972 there shall be substituted—

" (2) A mechanically propelled vehicle shall not be chargeable with any duty under this Act by reason of its use by or for the purposes of a person (' a disabled person ') suffering from a physical defect or disability or by reason of its being kept for such use if—

(*a*) it is registered under this Act in the name of that person; and

(*b*) he has obtained, or is eligible for, a grant under Article 30 (3) of the Health and Personal Social Services (Northern Ireland) Order 1972 in relation to that vehicle or is in receipt of a mobility allowance; and

(*c*) no other vehicle registered in his name under this Act is exempted from duty under this subsection or subsection (2A);

and for the purposes of this subsection a vehicle shall be deemed to be registered in the name of a disabled person in receipt of a mobility allowance if it is registered in the name of a person appointed pursuant to regulations under the Social Security (Northern Ireland) Act 1975 to exercise any of his rights or powers or in the name of a person nominated for the purposes of this subsection by the disabled person or by a person so appointed.".

(2) So much of section 13 of the Finance Act 1976 as excludes a person entitled to a mobility allowance from the exemption from duty conferred by section 7 (2A) of the said Act of 1972 shall cease to have effect.

(3) In the said section 7 (2A) after paragraph (*b*) there shall be inserted the words " and

(*c*) no vehicle exempted from duty under subsection (2) is (or by virtue of that subsection is deemed to be) registered in his name under this Act.".

(4) Section 26 (*c*) of the said Act of 1972 (offences in respect of licence, etc.) shall apply also to any document in the form of a licence which in pursuance of regulations made under that Act is issued in respect of a vehicle exempted from duty under section 7 (2) or (2A) of that Act.

(5) This section shall come into force on 1st December 1978.

GENERAL NOTE

This section has the same effect for Northern Ireland as s. 8 has for the remainder of the United Kingdom.

Continuation of powers under Finance Act 1961, s. 9

10. The period after which orders of the Treasury under section 9 of the Finance Act 1961 may not be made or continue in force (which, by virtue of section 13 of the Finance Act 1977, was extended until the end of August 1978) shall extend until the end of August 1979 or such later date as Parliament may hereafter determine.

GENERAL NOTE

S. 9 of the Finance Act 1961 confers on the Treasury power to adjust by addition or deduction a liability to duty or right to drawback rebate or allowance by a prescribed percentage not exceeding 10 per cent. of the amount payable or allowable. This power is to be exercised if it appears expedient to the Treasury with a view to regulating the balance between demand and resources in the United Kingdom.

This section provides that no such order can be made by the Treasury before the end of August 1979 or such later date as Parliament may hereafter determine.

PART II

VALUE ADDED TAX

Registration

11.—(1) In paragraph 1 of Schedule 1 to the Finance Act 1972 (liability to be registered)—

(a) in the provisions before the Table, for " £7,500 " (in both places) there shall be substituted " £10,000 " and

(b) in the second column of the Table for " 2,625 ", " 4,500 ", " 6,375 " and " 7,500 " there shall be substituted respectively " 3,500 ", " 6,000 ", " 8,500 " and " 10,000 ";

and in section 20 (1) of that Act (registration of local authorities) for "£7,500 " (in both places) there shall be substituted " £10,000 ".

(2) In paragraph 2 of the said Schedule (termination of liability to be registered) for " £6,000 " (in both places) there shall be substituted " £8,500 " and for " £1,875 " there shall be substituted " £2,500 ".

(3) After paragraph 10 of that Schedule (cancellation of registration) there shall be inserted—

" 10A. Where a registered person who has at any time ceased to be liable to be registered by virtue of paragraph 2 of this Schedule has before that time failed or subsequently fails to make any return or account for or pay any tax as required by or under this Act, the Commissioners may, if they think fit, cancel his registration with effect from such date as they may determine."

(4) In paragraph 11 of that Schedule (discretionary registration) the existing provisions shall become sub-paragraph (1) and after those provisions there shall be inserted—

" (2) Where the Commissioners refuse to act or to continue to act on a request made by a person under sub-paragraph (1) (b) above, they shall give him written notice of their decision and of the grounds on which it was made.";

and in section 40 (1) of the said Act of 1972 (appeals) after paragraph (g) there shall be inserted—

" (gg) any refusal to act or to continue to act on a request under paragraph 11 (1) (b) of Schedule 1 to this Act; ".

(5) Subsection (1) above shall be deemed to have come into force on 12th April 1978 but shall apply also for determining whether a person was liable to be registered before that day if the date from which his registration would take effect in accordance with the said Schedule 1 is after 11th April 1978.

(6) Subsection (2) above shall be deemed to have come into force on 1st July 1978.

GENERAL NOTE

Subs. (1)

The limits of taxable supplies for registration are increased to £3,500, £6,000, £8,500 and £10,000 for one, two, three and four quarters respectively, or £10,000 per annum from April 12, 1978 (subs. (5)).

Subs. (2)

The limits of taxable supplies for deregistration are increased to £8,500 per annum or £2,500 per quarter for two years, or to prospective supplies of less than £8,500 in the following year, from July 1, 1978 (subs. (6)).

Subs. (3)

This enables Customs and Excise to clear the register of people who are not liable to be registered under the new deregistration limits, who fail to make returns or pay tax.

Subs. (4)

Where Customs and Excise refuse voluntary registration of a person who is below the limits for registration, they must give the reason for their decision, which can be appealed against to the VAT Tribunal.

Bad debt relief

12.—(1) Where—

    (*a*) a person has supplied goods or services for a consideration in money and has accounted for and paid tax on that supply; and

    (*b*) the person liable to pay any outstanding amount of the consideration has become insolvent,

then, subject to subsection (2) and to regulations under subsection (3) below, the first-mentioned person shall be entitled, on making a claim to the Commissioners, to a refund of the amount of tax chargeable by reference to the outstanding amount.

(2) A person shall not be entitled to a refund under this section unless—

    (*a*) he has proved in the insolvency and the amount for which he has proved is the outstanding amount of the consideration less the amount of his claim;

    (*b*) the value of the supply does not exceed its open market value; and

    (*c*) in the case of a supply of goods, the property in the goods has passed to the person to whom they were supplied.

(3) Regulations under this section may—

    (*a*) require a claim to be made at such time and in such form and manner as may be specified by or under the regulations;

    (*b*) require a claim to be evidenced and quantified by reference to such records and other documents preserved for such period, not exceeding three years from the making of the claim, as may be so specified;

    (*c*) make provision for determining what amount (if any) is the outstanding amount of the consideration in particular cases such as those involving part payment or mutual debts;

    (*d*) require the repayment of a refund under this section where any requirement of the regulations is not complied with or where the claimant subsequently proves for an amount which, taken with the amount for which he has previously proved, exceeds the amount mentioned in subsection (2) (*a*) above; and

    (*e*) make different provision for different circumstances.

(4) For the purposes of this section—

    (*a*) an individual becomes insolvent if—

        (i) in England, Wales, Northern Ireland or the Isle of

Man, he is adjudged bankrupt or the court makes an order for the administration in bankruptcy of his estate; or

(ii) in Scotland, an award of sequestration of his estates is made or he signs a trust deed for behoof of his creditors or a judicial factor is appointed under section 163 of the Bankruptcy (Scotland) Act 1913 to divide his insolvent estate among his creditors; and

(*b*) a company becomes insolvent if, in the United Kingdom or the Isle of Man, it is the subject of a creditors' voluntary winding up or the court makes an order for its winding up and the circumstances are such that it is unable to pay its debts;

and as respects insolvencies in Scotland this section shall have effect as if for references to proving in the insolvency there were substituted references to taking such steps as may be specified by regulations made under this section.

(5) In section 40 (1) of the Finance Act 1972 (appeal to VAT tribunal) after paragraph (*k*) there shall be inserted—

" (*l*) a claim for a refund under section 12 of the Finance Act 1978."

(6) This section applies where the person liable to pay the outstanding amount of the consideration becomes insolvent after 1st October 1978.

GENERAL NOTE

For the first time relief for bad debts is introduced for VAT, apart from the effective relief under the retailer's schemes which are based on cash receipts. Relief is, however, limited to those cases where the debtor is insolvent, *i.e.* bankrupt or in compulsory or creditors' voluntary liquidation (subs. (4)). VAT must have been accounted for and paid by the creditor for relief to be claimed. Presumably a trader whose input tax exceeds his output tax has still paid the output tax for this purpose. The relief is claimed from Customs and Excise in the manner set out in regulations to be made under subs. (3).

Subs. (2)

Three conditions apply to the claim. First, that only the VAT exclusive amount of the debt has been proved for in the insolvency. Customs and Excise will not, in practice, prove for this VAT as ordinary insured creditors in the insolvency. Secondly, the value does not exceed open market value (defined in F.A. 1972, s. 10). Thirdly, in the case of a supply of goods, that the property in the goods has passed. This will include cases of hire purchase and where property in the goods has been reserved by the seller's conditions of sale until payment is made.

Subs. (3)

No regulations have yet been made.

Subs. (4)

There is an appeal to the VAT Tribunal against refusal of a claim under this section.

Subs. (5)

It should be noted that the *insolvency* must occur after October 1, 1978, for the section to apply, but subject to that the debt can have been incurred earlier.

PART III

INCOME TAX, CORPORATION TAX AND CAPITAL GAINS TAX

CHAPTER I

GENERAL

Charge of income tax for 1978–79

13. Income tax for the year 1978–79 shall be charged at the basic rate of 33 per cent.; and—

   (*a*) in respect of so much of an individual's total income as does not exceed £750 at the rate of 25 per cent.;

   (*b*) in respect of so much of an individual's total income as exceeds £8,000 at such higher rates as are specified in the Table below; and

   (*c*) in respect of so much of the investment income included in an individual's total income as exceeds £1,700 at the additional rates of 10 per cent. for the first £550 of the excess and 15 per cent. for the remainder;

except that in the case of an individual who shows that, at any time within that year, his age or that of his wife living with him was sixty-five years or more, paragraph (*c*) above shall have effect with the substitution for the references to £1,700 and £550 of references to £2,500 and £500 respectively.

TABLE

Part of excess over £8,000						*Higher rate*
The first £1,000	...	...	...	...	...	40 per cent.
The next £1,000	...	...	...	...	...	45 per cent.
The next £1,000	...	...	...	...	...	50 per cent.
The next £1,500	...	...	...	...	...	55 per cent.
The next £1,500	...	...	...	...	...	60 per cent.
The next £2,000	...	...	...	...	...	65 per cent.
The next £2,500	...	...	...	...	...	70 per cent.
The next £5,500	...	...	...	...	...	75 per cent.
The remainder	...	...	...	...	...	83 per cent.

GENERAL NOTE

In addition to the basic rate of tax being reduced from 34 per cent. to 33 per cent., a new lower rate of 25 per cent. has been introduced to apply to the first £750 of taxable income (see also s. 14 below).

The section provides for entry into the higher rates of tax to be raised by £2,000 to £8,000 and also modifies in certain respects the bands of taxable income chargeable at the higher rates. The maximum rate of tax is now reached at £24,000, £2,000 higher than in 1977–78.

Modifications are made to the thresholds for the surcharge on investment income so as to raise the general threshold to the 10 per cent. rate from £1,500 to £1,700 and the threshold to the 15 per cent. rate from £2,000 to £2,250. For those over 65 the thresholds are to go up from £2,000 to £2,500 for the 10 per cent. rate and from £2,500 to £3,000 for the 15 per cent. rate.

Lower rate income tax

   14.—(1) In paragraph (*a*) of subsection (1) of section 32 of the Finance Act 1971 (income tax charged at basic and other rates) for the words " income not falling within paragraph (*b*) below " there shall be substituted the words " income not falling within paragraph (*aa*) or (*b*) below "; and after that paragraph there shall be inserted—

   " (*aa*) in respect of so much of an individual's total income as does not exceed such amount as Parliament may determine, at such lower rate or rates as Parliament may determine; and ".

   (2) After subsection (1) of that section there shall be inserted—

   " (1A) In the case of a husband whose total income includes relevant earned income of his wife—

   (*a*) the income chargeable in accordance with paragraph (*aa*) of subsection (1) of this section shall be—

(i) so much of his total income, other than relevant earned income of his wife, as does not exceed the amount referred to in that paragraph; and

(ii) so much of the relevant earned income of his wife as does not exceed that amount; and

(*b*) if there are two or more such rates as are referred to in that paragraph, those rates shall be applied separately to the income mentioned in sub-paragraph (i) and the income mentioned in sub-paragraph (ii) above,

and any provision charging income tax in accordance with that paragraph shall have effect accordingly.

(1B) For the purposes of subsection (1A) of this section earned income of the wife has the same meaning as for the purposes of sub-section (2) of section 8 of the Taxes Act and relevant earned income of the wife means so much of her earned income as exceeds the relief available in respect of it under that subsection.

(1C) Where income tax at the basic rate has been borne on income chargeable at a lower rate any necessary repayment of tax shall be made on the making of a claim.

(1D) Except where the context otherwise requires, references in the Income Tax Acts to a rate or rates lower or higher than the basic rate are references to any such rate or rates as are mentioned in paragraph (*aa*) or (*b*) of subsection (1) of this section respectively."

(3) The enactments mentioned in Schedule 2 to this Act shall have effect with the amendments there specified, being amendments consequential on the provisions of this section.

GENERAL NOTE

This section provides for a lower rate of income tax than basic rate. It amends F.A. 1972, s. 32, so that there will now be lower, basic and higher rates of income tax. It is intended that the lower rate shall be 25 per cent. and shall be charged on the first £750 of an individual's taxable income.

There are special rules applicable when an individual's total income includes taxable earned income of that individual's wife. In such a case the wife's taxable earned income is separated from the remainder of the individual's total income and each is separately charged at the lower rate of income tax.

If the basic rate of tax has been paid on income which is only subject to lower rate tax it will be necessary to make a claim for repayment of the difference.

The administrative changes resulting from the introduction of this new lower rate of tax are dealt with in the Inland Revenue Press Releases dated April 11, 1978, and headed " Pay As You Earn: Income Tax changes for 1978–79 " and that dated July 11, 1978, and headed " Tax Rebates This Month " (see Part 6).

Charge of corporation tax for financial year 1977

15. Corporation tax shall be charged for the financial year 1977 at the rate of 52 per cent.

GENERAL NOTE

The corporation tax rate remains constant.

Rate of advance corporation tax for financial year 1978

16. The rate of advance corporation tax for the financial year 1978 shall be thirty-three sixty-sevenths.

GENERAL NOTE

This has been changed whilst the Finance Bill was passing through Parliament. It originally was thirty-three sixty-sixths (which was the same as the last tax year— F.A. 1977, s. 19).

Corporation tax: other rates and fractions

17.—(1) The fraction by which, under section 93 (2) of the Finance Act 1972, chargeable gains are to be reduced before they are for the purposes of corporation tax included in the profits of an authorised unit trust or investment trust shall, as from 1st April 1977, be twenty-one twenty-sixths instead of the fraction specified in section 27 (1) of the Finance Act 1976.

(2) The small companies rate for the financial year 1977 shall be 42 per cent., and for that year the fraction mentioned in subsection (2) of section 95 of the said Act of 1972 (marginal relief for small companies) shall be one-seventh.

(3) For the financial year 1977 and subsequent financial years subsection (3) of the said section 95 shall have effect with the substitution for any reference to £40,000 of a reference to £50,000 and with the substitution for any reference to £65,000 of a reference to £85,000.

(4) Where by virtue of subsection (3) above the said section 95 has effect with different relevant amounts in relation to different parts of the same accounting period, those parts shall be treated for the purposes of that section as if they were separate accounting periods, and the profits and income of the company for that period (as defined in that section) shall be apportioned between those parts.

GENERAL NOTE

Subs. (1) reduces the charge to tax on chargeable gains made by Investment and Unit Trusts so that the effective rate of tax on such gains as from April 1, 1977, is 10 per cent. as opposed to the previous rate of 17½ per cent. This is intended to be in line with the new relief for gains realised by individuals provided for in s. 44 below.

The small companies rate remains at 42 per cent. but the applicability of the relief is increased. For the financial year 1977 the rate applies to companies with profits not exceeding £50,000 as opposed to £40,000 in 1976. Marginal relief is given to companies with profits of up to £85,000 as opposed to £65,000. In consequence of the changes in the limits, the fraction by reference to which marginal relief is given is altered from four twenty-fifths to one-seventh.

Relief for interest: limit for 1978–79

18. In paragraph 5 (1) of Schedule 1 to the Finance Act 1974 (limit on relief for interest on certain loans for the purchase or improvement of land) the references to £25,000 shall have effect for the year 1978–79 as well as for previous years of assessment.

GENERAL NOTE

Despite attempts to increase the limits imposed on interest relief in the case of loans for the purchase or improvement of land it remains at £25,000.

Alteration of personal reliefs

19.—(1) In section 8 of the Taxes Act (personal reliefs)—
　　(*a*) in subsection (1) (*a*) (married) for " £1,455 " there shall be substituted " £1,535 ";
　　(*b*) in subsection (1) (*b*) (single) and (2) (wife's earned income relief) for " £945 " there shall be substituted " £985 ";
　　(*c*) in subsection (1A) (age allowance) for " £1,975 " and " £1,250 " there shall be substituted " £2,075 " and " £1,300 " respectively;
　　(*d*) in subsection (1B) (income limit for age allowance) for " £3,500 " there shall be substituted " £4,000 ".

(2) In section 12 of that Act (allowance for female housekeeper)—
> (a) the word " female ", wherever it occurs, shall be omitted;
> (b) in subsection (1) (ii) after the word " above " there shall be inserted the words " or the relative is a man who has claimed and been allowed that higher relief ".

(3) In section 13 (a) of that Act (allowance where claimant's mother or other female relative takes charge of his brother or sister)—
> (a) for the words " either his mother, being a widow or a person living apart from her husband, or some other female relative " there shall be substituted the words " a relative ";
> (b) the words " mother or other " shall be omitted.

(4) In section 14 (2) and (3) of that Act (additional relief for widows and others in respect of children) for " £510 " there shall be substituted " £550 ".

(5) In section 17 of that Act (allowance for services of daughter) for the word " daughter " there shall be substituted the words " son or daughter " and the like amendment shall be made in sections 18 (5) and 39 (1) (d) of that Act (which contain references to the allowance under section 17).

(6) In section 18 of that Act (relief for blind persons)—
> (a) in subsection (1) (a) and (b) for the words " throughout the year a registered blind person " there shall be substituted the words " a registered blind person for the whole or part of the year ";
> (b) in subsection (2) (b) for the words " throughout the year both he and his wife were registered blind persons " there shall be substituted the words " he was a registered blind person for the whole or part of the year and his wife was also a registered blind person for the whole or part of the year ";
> (c) subsections (3) and (4) shall be omitted.

GENERAL NOTE

Subs. (1) increases the married man's allowance by £80 to £1,535 and the single person's allowance and wife's earned income allowance by £40 to £985. The age allowances are increased by £100 for a married person and by £50 for a single person.

Subss. (2) (3) and (5) operate to relax the conditions that have to be satisfied in order for the personal reliefs referred to to be obtained by eliminating any discrimination between the sexes.

The additional personal allowance referred to in subs. (4) is increased by £40 to ensure that the position of one parent families is kept in line with that of two parent families.

The personal relief for blind persons given by I.C.T.A. 1970, s. 18, is now to be available to a person who is or whose wife is registered as blind for only a part of a year of assessment (subs. (6)). Registration as blind throughout the year is no longer necessary.

Child tax allowances and benefits in respect of children

20.—(1) Except in the case of a child to whom section 25 or 26 of the Finance Act 1977 applies, the appropriate amount to be deducted from the claimant's total income under subsection (1) of section 10 of the Taxes Act (children) for the year 1978–79 shall, instead of being determined in accordance with subsection (3) of that section, be determined in accordance with subsection (2) below.

(2) The appropriate amount for the child shall vary according to the age of the child at the commencement of the year of assessment, and, subject to subsection (5) of the said section 10—
> (a) for a child shown by the claimant to have been then over the age of sixteen, shall be £165;

(*b*) for a child not so shown, but shown by the claimant to have been then over the age of eleven, shall be £135;

(*c*) in any other case, shall be £100.

(3) For the year 1978–79 and subsequent years of assessment subsection (5) of the said section 10 shall have effect with the substitution for " £350 " (in both places) and " £235 " of " £500 " and " £385 " respectively.

(4) Section 23 (3) of the said Act of 1977 (£52 of certain benefits in respect of children to be exempt from income tax for the year 1977–78) shall have effect also in relation to the year 1978–79 but with the substitution for " £52 " of " £80 ".

(5) Section 25 of the said Act of 1977 (tax allowances in the year 1977–78 for children living abroad) shall have effect also in relation to years of assessment after that year.

GENERAL NOTE

This is a further step in the process of phasing out child tax allowances which was started with F.A. 1977, s. 24. Unlike that section this section draws no distinction between the first child in a family and the other children.

The relevant child tax allowances for the tax year 1978–79 are now:

Children over 16—£165 instead of £261 for the first child and £235 for other children;

Children over 11 but 16 or under—£135 instead of £231 for the first child and £205 for the others;

Children 11 or under—£100 instead of £196 for the first child and £120 for the others.

These amounts will not apply in the case of children living abroad (to which the rules contained in F.A. 1977, s. 25, continue to apply) or to students.

For the tax year 1978–79 and subsequent years these allowances will be reduced if the child is entitled to income exceeding certain limits. The allowances will not be affected if the child is not (i) entitled to investment income exceeding £115 so long as that child's earned income does not exceed £385 (previously £235); or (ii) entitled to income exceeding £500 (previously £350).

In the case where the child's income exceeds these limits the child tax allowance will be reduced by the excess amount.

Child benefits continue to be exempt from income tax under F.A. 1977, s. 23 (1). Certain benefits specified in subsections of that section are taxable but only to the extent that they exceed £80 (as opposed to £52 in the tax year 1977–78).

Maintenance payments

21. In section 15 (1) of the Finance Act 1974 (the first £1,500 of any amounts paid as maintenance payments not to be investment income) the words " the first £1,500 of " shall be omitted.

GENERAL NOTE

Maintenance payments are now wholly exempt from liability to the investment income surcharge.

Tax repayments to wives

22.—(1) Where in any year of assessment tax has been deducted under section 204 of the Taxes Act (pay as you earn) from the earned income of a wife and, apart from this section, a repayment of tax for that year would fall to be made to her husband in consequence of an assessment under Schedule E, so much of the repayment as is attributable to the tax so deducted shall be made to her and not to him.

(2) The amount of a repayment attributable to tax deducted as mentioned in subsection (1) above is the excess (if any) of the total net tax so deducted in the year of assessment over the tax chargeable on the

wife's relevant earned income included in her husband's total income for that year after allowing—

    (a) any relief for that year under section 19 of the Taxes Act in respect of any payment made by her of the kind mentioned in paragraph 14A of Schedule 4 to the Finance Act 1976 (retirement benefits schemes); and

    (b) any relief for that year to which her husband is entitled under any other provision of the Income Tax Acts to the extent to which it cannot be allowed because his income, exclusive of her earned income, is insufficient;

but that amount shall not exceed the aggregate of the amounts repayable for that year in respect of the total net tax deducted in that year under the said section 204 from the income of the wife and the income of her husband.

(3) Where in consequence of an assessment under Schedule E any amount is repayable under this section to the wife of the person on whom the assessment is made the inspector shall notify both of them of his determination of that amount and, subject to subsection (4) below, an appeal shall lie against the determination as if it were a decision on a claim.

(4) Any appeal under subsection (3) above shall be to the General Commissioners for the division in which the spouses reside or, if they reside in different divisions, for the division in which one of them resides, as the Board may direct, or if neither resides in Great Britain to the Special Commissioners; and on any such appeal by one of the spouses the other shall have the same rights as an appellant, including any right to require the statement of a case for the opinion of the court.

(5) Where in a case to which this section applies the amount repaid to a wife or her husband exceeds the amount properly due to that person the excess shall be recoverable from that person as if it were unpaid tax.

(6) The Board may make regulations—

    (a) modifying subsection (2) above in relation to such cases as may be specified in the regulations;

    (b) modifying section 47 of the Finance (No. 2) Act 1975 (repayment supplement) in relation to cases in which a repayment falls to be made under this section;

and any such regulations shall be made by statutory instrument subject to annulment in pursuance of a resolution of the House of Commons.

(7) This section does not apply to any repayment for a year of assessment—

    (a) for which the husband is chargeable to income tax at a rate or rates higher than the basic rate; or

    (b) for which any earned income of the wife has been assessed otherwise than under Schedule E.

(8) For the purposes of this section earned income of a wife has the same meaning as for the purposes of subsection (2) of section 8 of the Taxes Act and relevant earned income of a wife means so much of her earned income as exceeds the relief available in respect of it under that subsection.

(9) References in this section to the total net tax deducted in any year under section 204 of the Taxes Act are references to the total income tax deducted during that year by virtue of regulations made under that section less any income tax repaid by virtue of any such regulations.

(10) This section applies to any repayment made after the passing of this Act.

GENERAL NOTE

This section is designed to ensure that any repayments of tax paid in respect of a wife's Schedule E income should be repaid to the wife rather than to her husband. It does not apply to tax paid under any Schedule other than Schedule E nor does it apply where there is in a year a liability to the higher rate of tax on the total joint income (see subs. (7)). In these cases a wife can secure that any repayment goes direct to her by opting for separate assessment or, with regard to her earned income, for separate taxation.

Subss. (2) (8) and (9) contain the rules to determine how much of a repayment is attributable to the wife's earnings. It is stated to be the amount of the difference between the total tax deducted from her income (under the P.A.Y.E. system) less the total tax due in respect of her income after allowing:

    (i) the wife's earned income relief;

    (ii) superannuation payments made by the wife;

    (iii) other deductions to which the husband is entitled to the extent that they cannot be set off against his income.

A determination by an Inspector of the amount of a repayment attributable to a wife's earnings can be appealed against (subs. (3)).

For a general statement giving the background to this section, see the Inland Revenue Press Release of June 29, 1978 (see Part 6).

Benefits in kind: threshold from 1979–80

23.—(1) In section 69 (1) (*b*) and (3) (*a*) of the Finance Act 1976 (definition of director's or higher-paid employment for purposes of tax on benefits in kind) for " £7,500 " there shall be substituted " £8,500 ".

(2) This section applies for the year 1979–80 and subsequent years of assessment.

GENERAL NOTE

This increases the limit at which the stricter benefits-in-kind provisions operate. For the tax year 1977–78 the limit is £5,000. This is increased by Finance Act 1977, s. 35 (3) to £7,500 with effect for the year 1978–79. This section takes effect in the tax year 1979–80. This will mean that the number of persons caught by these provisions will remain at about 400,000 it is estimated by the Revenue.

Payments for loss of employment etc.

24.—(1) In section 188 (3) of the Taxes Act and paragraph 3 of Schedule 8 to that Act (tax on excess over £5,000 of payments for loss of employment etc.) for " £5,000 ", wherever it occurs, there shall be substituted " £10,000 ".

(2) In paragraph 4 of the said Schedule 8 (lump sum received or receivable under superannuation scheme or fund to be deducted in calculating relief) the existing provisions shall become sub-paragraph (1) and at the end there shall be inserted—

" (2) In sub-paragraph (1) (*c*) above the reference to a lump sum receivable by the holder includes a reference to a lump sum that would be receivable by him if he had exercised or refrained from exercising (with any necessary consent) any option or other right conferred on him by the rules of the scheme or fund."

(3) Subsection (1) above has effect in relation to any payment which by virtue of section 187 (4) of the Taxes Act is treated as income received on or after 6th April 1978; and where under the proviso to section 188 (3) of that Act the sum there mentioned falls to be deducted from one or more payments treated as income received before, and one or more payments treated as income received on or after, that date only £5,000 of that sum shall be deducted from the first-mentioned payment or payments.

(4) Subsection (2) above has effect in relation to any payment which by virtue of the said section 187 (4) is treated as income received on or after 17th May 1978.

GENERAL NOTE

" Golden handshakes," taxable pursuant to I.C.T.A., s. 187, have in the past been taxed only if they exceed £5,000. This limit is raised by subs. (1) so that for payments treated as income received after April 6, 1978 (see subs. (3)), they will be taxable only if they exceed £10,000.

Subs. (2) is concerned with "the standard capital superannuation benefit" defined in Sched. 8, I.C.T.A., under which where there is a payment to which s. 187 applies, other than a payment of compensation for loss of office, then the excess of "the standard capital superannuation benefit" over what, by virtue of subs. (1), is now £10,000, is tax free. In determining the amount of "the standard capital superannuation benefit" a deduction must be made for any sum "received or receivable" pursuant to the provision of certain superannuation schemes. Subs. (2) enlarges this deduction, and thus operates to limit the relief, so that it includes payments that would have been receivable had the employee exercised or refrained from exercising any right or option.

Life policies etc.

25. The enactments mentioned in Schedule 3 to this Act (which relate to relief in respect of premiums payable under life policies etc.) shall have effect subject to the amendments made by that Schedule.

Retirement annuities

26.—(1) The Board may, if they think fit, and subject to any conditions they think proper to impose, approve an annuity contract under section 226 of the Taxes Act (approval of retirement annuity contracts) notwithstanding that the contract provides that the individual by whom it is made may require a sum representing the value of his accrued rights thereunder to be paid by the person with whom it is made to such other person as he may specify, that sum to be applied as the premium or other consideration under an annuity contract made between the individual and that other person and approved by the Board under that section.

(2) References in subsection (1) above to the individual by whom the contract is made include references to any widow, widower or dependant having accrued rights under the contract.

(3) Where in pursuance of any such provision as is mentioned in subsection (1) above of an annuity contract approved under section 226 of the Taxes Act, or of a corresponding provision of a contract approved under section 226A (1) (*a*) of that Act (contracts for dependants), a sum representing the value of accrued rights under one contract (" the original contract ") is paid by way of premium or other consideration under another contract (" the substituted contract "), any annuity payable under the substituted contract shall be treated as earned income of the annuitant to the same extent that an annuity payable under the original contract would have been so treated.

(4) In section 230 (7) of the Taxes Act (purchased life annuities, other than retirement annuities), there shall be added at the end of paragraph (*b*) the words " to any annuity payable under a substituted contract within the meaning of section 26 (3) of the Finance Act 1978, or ".

(5) In section 323 (4) of the Taxes Act (pension business), for the words from " , being a contract " onwards in paragraph (*a*) there shall be substituted the words " (being a contract approved by the Board under that section), or any substituted contract within the meaning of section 26 (3) of the Finance Act 1978 ".

GENERAL NOTE

Before the introduction of this section, in order for a retirement annuity contract to be approved by the Revenue for the purposes of I.C.T.A., s. 226, annuities payable under the contract could only be paid to the individual taking out the contract, to his or her widow or widower, or to his or her dependants. Subs. (1) allows a contract to be approved even though it allows a person having accrued rights under the contract to nominate another person to take the benefit of such rights. The benefit can only be taken in the form of a new annuity contract for the benefit of the nominated person (a " substituted contract ").

Payments under a " substituted contract " will enjoy broadly the same tax treatment as payments made under the original contract. Thus they will qualify as earned income to the extent to which payments under the original contract would have done (subs. (3) and see also s. 226 (1), I.C.T.A.). Again, as is the position with the original contract, a " substituted contract " will not qualify as a purchased life annuity for the purposes of I.C.T.A., s. 230 (s. 5 (4)).

Relief for individuals carrying on trade etc. partly abroad

27.—(1) The provisions of this section and Part I of Schedule 4 to this Act shall have effect for affording relief from tax for the year 1978–79 and subsequent years of assessment to an individual who in a year of assessment—

    (a) is resident in the United Kingdom; and

    (b) is carrying on a trade, profession or vocation in respect of which he is within the charge to income tax under Case I or Case II of Schedule D; and

    (c) is absent from the United Kingdom on at least thirty qualifying days;

and in that Schedule and the following provisions of this section any reference to a trade includes a reference to a profession or vocation and any reference to Case I of Schedule D includes a reference to Case II of that Schedule.

(2) For the purposes of subsection (1) above and Part I of Schedule 4 to this Act, a qualifying day, in relation to an individual carrying on a trade, is a day of absence from the United Kingdom—

    (a) which he devotes substantially to the activities of the trade; or

    (b) which is one of at least seven consecutive days on which he is absent from the United Kingdom for the purposes of the trade and which (taken as a whole) he devotes substantially to the activities of the trade; or

    (c) on which he is travelling wholly and exclusively for the purposes of the trade.

(3) If an individual carries on more than one trade and a day of absence from the United Kingdom would be a qualifying day in relation to his carrying on two or more of those trades taken together, but not in relation to his carrying on any particular trade, it shall be treated as a qualifying day for the purposes specified in subsection (2) above.

(4) In relation to an individual who carries on a trade as a member of a partnership to which section 153 of the Taxes Act applies (partnerships controlled abroad), a day shall not be treated as a qualifying day in relation to any trade or trades carried on by the partnership unless it would be so treated if references in paragraphs (a) to (c) of subsection (2) above to the trade carried on by the individual were restricted to the trading operations of the partnership within the United Kingdom.

(5) An individual shall not be entitled to relief under this section in respect of absence on qualifying days in a year of assessment unless a claim for the relief is made before the expiry of the period of two years beginning at the end of that year of assessment.

(6) For the purposes of this section an individual shall not be regarded as absent from the United Kingdom on any day unless he is

absent at the end of it; nor shall an individual be regarded as absent from the United Kingdom at any time when he is on board a vessel or aircraft engaged on—

(*a*) a voyage or journey beginning and ending in the United Kingdom (but exclusive of any part of it which begins or ends outside the United Kingdom); or

(*b*) any part beginning and ending in the United Kingdom of a voyage or journey which begins or ends outside the United Kingdom.

(7) For the purposes of this section, any area designated under section 1 (7) of the Continental Shelf Act 1964 shall be treated as part of the United Kingdom.

(8) In consequence of the provisions of this section and of Part I of Schedule 4 to this Act, the amendments in Part II of that Schedule shall have effect.

GENERAL NOTE

This section extends the tax relief already given to employees who are resident in the United Kingdom but work abroad (F.A. 1977, Sched. 7), to self-employed persons and members of partnerships. It is the stated intention that the new relief is to broadly follow the provisions applying to employees, in fact there are a number of important differences which apply adversely to self-employed persons.

The relief is to take effect for the tax year 1978–79 and applies to a taxpayer who is resident in the United Kingdom and assessed to income tax under Case I or II of Schedule D. It will not, therefore, apply to persons who carry on a trade or profession wholly abroad as the income from these will be assessed under Case V.

The relief is not, however, related to the profits earned by the taxpayer whilst abroad (as is the case with employees) but is calculated on a time-apportionment. In the case where the income of the taxpayer from work carried out whilst abroad exceeds his income from work in the United Kingdom this method of calculation is disadvantageous. Further the self-employed person (unlike an employee) can never become entitled to claim 100 per cent. relief as opposed to 25 per cent. relief.

To qualify the taxpayer satisfying the above conditions must be absent for 30 (and not the 60 originally required in the Finance Bill) qualifying days from the United Kingdom. There is no need for these to be consecutive days.

The basic definition of a qualifying date contained in subs. (2) is the same as for employees (para. 2 (2), Sched. 7, F.A. 1977). It is necessary that the taxpayer should be absent from the United Kingdom at the end of the day for it to count as a qualifying day (as with employees—para. 6, Sched. 7, F.A. 1977). Subs. (6) contains a further restriction that a person is not to be treated as absent from the United Kingdom if engaged on a trip, or any part of a trip, beginning and ending in the United Kingdom save that any part of the trip which begins or ends outside the United Kingdom may be taken into account.

For the purposes of this relief the United Kingdom includes any area designated under Continental Shelf Act 1964, s. 1 (7), which will include the United Kingdom sectors in the North Sea. Divers will not be entitled to the 25 per cent. relief under this section.

Partnerships controlled from abroad are treated separately under subs. (4). A member of such a partnership will only be entitled to this relief in respect of days of absence from the United Kingdom concerning the trading operations of the partnership carried on in the United Kingdom and not those carried on abroad.

However in respect of persons carrying on two or more trades for deciding whether days of absence from the United Kingdom are qualifying days the trades are in practice treated as one trade (subs. (3)).

Any claim for this relief must be made within two years of the end of the year of assessment to which the absence relates. The amount of relief and method of computation is determined in accordance with the rules set out in Sched. 4.

It should be noted that unlike employees, no allowance is to be made in respect of the expense of the wife and children of the taxpayer travelling to stay with him abroad (contrast with F.A. 1977, s. 32, in respect of reimbursements by employers to employees for such expenditure).

Farming and market gardening: relief for fluctuating profits

28.—(1) Subject to the provisions of this section, a person who is or has been carrying on a trade of farming or market gardening in the United Kingdom may claim that subsection (2) or (3) below shall have effect in relation to his profits from that trade for any two consecutive years of assessment if his profits for either year do not exceed such part of his profits for the other year as is there specified.

(2) If the claimant's profits for either year do not exceed seven-tenths of his profits for the other year or are nil, his profits for each year shall be adjusted so as to be equal to one-half of his profits for the two years taken together or, as the case may be, for the year for which there are profits.

(3) If the claimant's profits for either year exceed seven-tenths but are less than three-quarters of his profits for the other year, his profits for each year shall be adjusted by adding to the profits that are lower and deducting from those that are higher an amount equal to three times the difference between them less three-quarters of those that are higher.

(4) No claim shall be made under this section—

(a) in respect of any year of assessment before a year in respect of which a claim has already been made under this section; or

(b) in respect of a year of assessment in which the trade is (or by virtue of section 154 (1) of the Taxes Act is treated as) set up and commenced or permanently discontinued.

(5) Any adjustment under this section shall have effect for all the purposes of the Income Tax Acts (including any further application of this section where the second of any two years of assessment is the first of a subsequent pair) except that—

(a) subsection (2) above shall not prevent a person obtaining relief under those Acts for a loss sustained by him in any year of assessment;

(b) any adjustment under this section shall be disregarded for the purposes of section 118 (1) (b) of the Taxes Act (adjustment of assessments on discontinuance of trade) and of computing relevant income for the purposes of Schedule 5 to the Finance Act 1976 (stock relief); and

(c) where, after a claim has been made under this section in respect of the profits for any two years of assessment the profits for both or either of those years are adjusted for any other reason, this section shall have effect as if the claim had not been made but without prejudice to the making of a further claim in respect of those profits as so adjusted.

(6) This section applies to the profits of a trade carried on by a person in partnership as it applies to the profits of a sole trader except that—

(a) the profits to which the claim relates shall be those chargeable in accordance with section 152 of the Taxes Act; and

(b) any claim in respect of those profits shall be made jointly by all the partners who are individuals;

and where during the years of assessment to which the claim relates there is a change in the persons engaged in carrying on the trade but a notice is given under section 154 (2) of the Taxes Act the claim shall be made jointly by all the persons who are individuals and have been engaged in carrying on the trade at any time during those years.

Where a person who is required by this subsection to join in making a claim has died, this subsection shall have effect as if it required his personal representatives to join in making the claim.

(7) In this section references to profits from a trade for a year of assessment are references to the profits or gains from that trade which are chargeable to income tax for that year before—

(a) any deduction for losses sustained in any year of assessment;

(b) any deduction or addition for capital allowances or charges (not being allowances or charges given or made by deduction or addition in the computation of profits or gains);

(c) any deduction or addition for any relief or charge under Schedule 5 to the Finance Act 1976.

(8) Any claim under this section shall be made by notice in writing given to the inspector not later than two years after the end of the second of the years of assessment to which the claim relates but any such further claim as is mentioned in subsection (5) (c) above shall not be out of time if made before the end of the year of assessment following that in which the adjustment is made.

(9) Where a person makes a claim under this section in respect of any year of assessment, any claim by him for relief for that year under any other provision of the Income Tax Acts—

(a) shall not be out of time if made before the end of the period in which the claim under this section is required to be made; and

(b) if already made, may be revoked or amended before the end of that period;

but no claim shall by virtue of this subsection be made, revoked or amended after the determination of the claim under this section.

(10) There shall be made all such alterations of assessments or repayments of tax (whether in respect of such profits as are mentioned in subsection (1) above or of other income of the person concerned) as may be required in consequence of any adjustment under this section.

(11) Nothing in this section shall be construed as applying to profits chargeable to corporation tax.

(12) This section applies where the first of the two years mentioned in subsection (1) above is the year 1977–78 or a subsequent year of assessment.

GENERAL NOTE

This section provides for the averaging of profits made by farmers and market gardeners carrying on a trade in the United Kingdom. The relief applies for income tax purposes generally and thus can apply to individuals, trustees or partnerships (as to partnerships, see subs. (6)). It does not apply to companies (see subs. (11)).

Subs. (2)

Where in any two consecutive years of assessment the profit made in one of the years is less than 70 per cent. of the profit made in the other year the profits chargeable for each of those years can, on a claim being made, be altered to the average of the two years' profits. " Profits " for this purpose are determined before relief is given for capital allowances, stock relief and losses (see subs. (7)). A claim for the relief must be made within two years of the end of the second year of assessment (see subs. (8)).

While the averaging is done over two years the averaged profit for year two can provide the basis on which the profits for years two and three are averaged. If for example the profits chargeable in year one are £10,000 and those in year two £6,000, the farmer can average the profits and pay tax on £8,000 for each of the two years. If the profits in year three are £4,000 the profits of years two and three can then be averaged to £6,000. This will not, however, affect the averaged profit for year one.

Subs. (3)

This subsection provides a marginal relief where the difference between profits in two consecutive years is between 25 and 30 per cent. of the higher figure. The

amount by reference to which relief is given in this situation is three times the
difference between the lower figure of profit and 75 per cent. of the higher figure.
This amount to be added to the lower figure and reduced from the higher figure.

Subs. (4)
Averaging is not permitted in respect of the first or last year in which a trade
is carried on (including a cessation on a change of partners without an election
for continuance).

Subs. (5)
Relief under this section can operate to convert a year in which a loss is
made into a period of profit. A year in which a loss is made is treated as a
period of nil profit for the purposes of the relief and thus while a period of loss
can be converted into a period of profit, losses are not reflected in the averaging
calculation. The availability of loss relief is therefore unaffected (see subs. (5) (*a*)).

Subs. (12)
The first two years in which this relief can apply are 1977–78 and 1978–79.

Divers and diving supervisors

29.—(1) Where the duties of an employment which are performed by
a person in the United Kingdom or a designated area consist wholly or
mainly—

(*a*) of taking part, as a diver, in diving operations concerned with the
exploration or exploitation of the seabed, its subsoil and their
natural resources; or

(*b*) of acting, in relation to any such operations, as a diving
supervisor;

the Income Tax Acts shall have effect as if the performance by that
person of those duties constituted the carrying on by him of a trade
within Case I of Schedule D; and accordingly Schedule E shall not apply
to the emoluments from the employment so far as attributable to his
performance of those duties.

(2) In this section " designated area " means any area designated
under section 1 (7) of the Continental Shelf Act 1964.

(3) In paragraph 2 (*b*) of Schedule 15 to the Finance Act 1973
(information about emoluments paid or payable in respect of duties
performed in connection with exploration or exploitation activities) for
the words " emoluments paid or payable in respect of duties " there
shall be substituted the words " emoluments or other payments paid or
payable in respect of duties or services ".

(4) This section applies for the year 1978–79 and subsequent years of
assessment; and where the duties of a person's employment fall within
subsection (1) above at the beginning of that year this section shall apply
as if the trade mentioned in that subsection had been set up and commenced by him at the beginning of that year.

GENERAL NOTE
This section has the effect of assessing divers and diving supervisors to income
tax under Schedule D rather than Schedule E. Although employed persons for
tax purposes they are to be treated as self-employed. This was introduced with the
divers and supervisors concerned in the exploration and exploitation of North Sea
oil in mind.

It means that their income will not be subject to tax at source under the PAYE
system and they will be entitled to the benefit of the less stringent rules concerning
allowable deductions.

By virtue of the amendment in subs. (3) a holder of a licence under Petroleum
(Production) Act 1934 may still be required to give details of payments to divers
and supervisors upon the service of a notice by the Revenue. This provision takes

effect for the tax year 1978–79 and any person qualifying for this treatment at the start of the tax year can take advantage of the opening years rules if he so wishes.

Further relief for losses in early years of trade

30.—(1) Where an individual carrying on a trade sustains a loss in the trade in—

    (*a*) the year of assessment in which it is first carried on by him; or

    (*b*) any of the next three years of assessment,

he may, by notice in writing given within two years after the year of assessment in which the loss is sustained, make a claim for relief under this section.

(2) Subject to the provisions of this section, relief shall be given from income tax on an amount of the claimant's income equal to the amount of the loss, being income for the three years of assessment last preceding that in which the loss is sustained, taking income for an earlier year before income for a later year.

(3) Relief shall not be given for the same loss or the same portion of a loss both under this section and under any other provision of the Income Tax Acts.

(4) Relief shall not be given under this section in respect of a loss sustained in any period unless it is shown that the trade was carried on throughout that period on a commercial basis and in such a way that profits in the trade (or, where the carrying on of the trade forms part of a larger undertaking, in the undertaking as a whole) could reasonably be expected to be realised in that period or within a reasonable time thereafter.

(5) Relief shall not be given under this section in respect of a loss sustained by an individual in a trade if—

    (*a*) at the time when it is first carried on by him he is married to and living with another individual who has previously carried on the trade; and

    (*b*) the loss is sustained in a year of assessment later than the third year of assessment after that in which the trade was first carried on by the other individual.

(6) For the purposes of this section an individual carries on a trade whether he does so solely or in partnership; and (except as respects the computation of profits or gains and losses) an individual continues to carry on the same trade notwithstanding a change in the persons engaged in carrying it on if he is engaged in carrying it on immediately before and immediately after the change.

(7) Subject to subsections (8) and (9) below, the following enactments (which contain ancillary provisions relating to relief under section 168 of the Taxes Act) shall have effect as if references to that section included references to this section—

    (*a*) sections 168 (3), (4), (5) and (7), 169 (other than subsection (10)) and 474 (1) of the Taxes Act;

    (*b*) section 23 (2) of the Finance Act 1974;

    (*c*) paragraph 3 (1) of Schedule 2 to the Social Security Act 1975;

    (*d*) section 13 (2) of the Oil Taxation Act 1975;

    (*e*) sections 36 (9) and 41 of, and paragraph 6 of Schedule 5 to, the Finance Act 1976.

(8) In its application by virtue of subsection (7) above, section 169 of the Taxes Act shall have effect with the following modifications—

    (*a*) in subsection (3) for the words from " are those for the year of assessment " onwards there shall be substituted the words " are those for the year of loss, relief shall not be given by reference to those allowances in respect of an amount greater than the amount non-effective in that year ";

(b) in subsection (6) for the words " in the case of allowances for the following year, in taxing the trade for that following year " there shall be substituted the words " in the case of allowances for any later year, in taxing the trade for that later year ";

(c) in subsection (8) for the words " the year for which the claim is made " there shall be substituted the words " the year of loss ".

(9) In its application by virtue of subsection (7) above paragraph 6 of Schedule 5 to the Finance Act 1976 shall have effect with the following modifications—

(a) in sub-paragraph (4) for the words from " is that for the year of assessment " onwards there shall be substituted the words " is that for the year of loss, effect shall not be given to that relief in respect of an amount greater than the amount unused in that year ";

(b) in sub-paragraph (7) for the words " the year for which the claim is made " there shall be substituted the words " the year of loss ".

(10) This section applies, with the necessary modifications, in relation to a profession or vocation as it applies in relation to a trade.

(11) This section applies where the year in which the loss is sustained is the year 1978–79 or a later year of assessment.

GENERAL NOTE

This section provides for a carry back relief for initial trading losses of unincorporated businesses. Its introduction is an incentive for new businesses to be carried on by individuals directly rather than through the medium of companies in any case where losses in the first few years are anticipated.

Losses made in the first year in which a trade is carried on or in any of the next three years of assessment can be carried back on a claim being made. The carry back is permitted for three years from the year in which the loss is made. Thus, while a loss made in the first year in which a trade is carried on can be carried back to a year beginning three years before the year in which the trade is commenced, a loss made in the last year in which the relief is available can only be carried back to the year in which the trade is commenced. Losses carried back can be set against general income. By s. 168 (4), I.C.T.A. 1970, being made applicable by subs. (7), the set off will primarily be against earned income.

It is noteworthy that on the carry back relief is to be given so far as possible against income for earlier years rather than against income for later years (see subs. (2)). This is intentional. The relief is particularly designed to assist people who leave employment to start their own businesses. Such people are likely to have had more income in earlier years when they were still in employment than after they had started their own businesses. If relief is obtained for a year when income was substantial the relief will, by virtue of the progressive nature of income tax, be more substantial.

The relief is applicable not only to trading losses but also losses sustained in a profession or vocation (subs. (10)).

Dealings in commodity futures: withdrawal of loss relief

31.—(1) Relief shall not be given to any person under section 168 or 177 (2) of the Taxes Act or section 30 above (set-off of trading losses against general income) in respect of a loss sustained in a trade of dealing in commodity futures if—

(a) the loss was sustained in a trade carried on in partnership and that person or one or more of the other partners was a company; and

(b) a scheme has been effected or arrangements have been made (whether by the partnership agreement or otherwise) such that the sole or main benefit that might be expected to accrue to that person from his interest in the partnership was the obtaining of a reduction in tax liability by means of such relief as aforesaid.

(2) Where relief has been given in a case to which this section applies it shall be withdrawn by the making of an assessment under Case VI of Schedule **D**.

(3) This section applies whether the loss was sustained before or after the passing of this Act but not where the scheme was effected or the arrangements were made wholly before 6th April 1976.

GENERAL NOTE

This section is an anti-avoidance provision concerned with dealings in commodity futures by a trading partnership which includes a company as one of its members. The intention with those dealings was for one of the members to withdraw from the partnership once a loss up to an agreed amount had been incurred thereby obtaining the benefit of a loss relief.

Any such scheme that was entered into with the intention that the sole or main benefit to accrue would be the reduction in a tax liability and which was not completed before April 6, 1976, will be caught by this section. In such cases the benefit is lost by the making of an assessment under Case VI, Schedule D. The section operates retrospectively and pre-dates even the parliamentary announcement on this matter.

Sale of land with right to repurchase: restriction of relief

32.—(1) Sections 83 and 134 of the Taxes Act (which give a person relief from tax where he has paid a premium or certain other sums in respect of land) shall have effect with the following amendments, being amendments excluding from the relief cases falling within section 82 of that Act (under which the sum paid is the purchase price of land bought on terms providing for its reconveyance).

(2) In section 83—
- (*a*) in subsection (1) (*a*) for " 81 or 82 " there shall be substituted " or 81 ";
- (*b*) in subsections (1), (2) and (3) the words " estate or interest " (wherever they occur) shall be omitted;
- (*c*) subsections (4) (*b*) (iii) and (6) shall be omitted.

(3) In section 134—
- (*a*) in subsection (1) (*a*) for " 81 or 82 " there shall be substituted " or 81 ";
- (*b*) subsection (1) (iii), together with the word " and " immediately preceding it, shall be omitted;
- (*c*) in subsection (2) the words " estate or interest " shall be omitted;
- (*d*) subsection (7) shall be omitted and in subsections (1) and (2) for " (7) " there shall be substituted " (6) ".

(4) Subsection (2) above applies where the amount chargeable on the superior interest has become or would have become chargeable to tax under section 82 after 2nd December 1976; and subsection (3) above applies where the amount chargeable has become or would have become chargeable to tax under that section after that date.

GENERAL NOTE

This section is intended to counteract a scheme under which arrangements were made to sell an interest in land with provision for it to be recovered later at a reduced price. The object of the scheme was to produce large sums qualifying for relief under I.C.T.A., s. 83 or s. 134.

The Government first announced its intention to legislate against this scheme on December 3, 1976, hence the amending provisions of this section operate from that date. In broad terms the section eliminates from the relief provided by s. 83 or s. 134 cases where the original charge to tax, in respect of which relief under those provisions was claimed, arose under I.C.T.A., s. 82.

Deduction rate for sub-contractors in the construction industry

33. Section 69 (4) of the Finance (No. 2) Act 1975 (which requires deductions to be made from payments to certain sub-contractors in the construction industry) shall have effect in relation to payments made on or after 6th November 1978 with the substitution for the words " 34 per cent." of the words " 33 per cent.".

General Note
This reduction in the deduction rate applicable to payments to certain sub-contractors in the construction industry is in line with the reduction in the basic rate of income tax for 1978-79.

Exemption for community land transactions

34.—(1) In computing the profits or losses for corporation tax purposes of—
(a) an authority within the meaning of section 1 of the Community Land Act 1975 other than a local authority;
(b) a joint board established under section 2 of that Act; or
(c) a body corporate established under section 50 of that Act, the items included and the transactions recorded in any accounts or records kept by the authority, joint board or body corporate under section 43 of that Act shall be disregarded.

(2) This section shall be deemed to have come into force on 6th April 1976.

General Note
Under s. 43, Community Land Act 1975, the Secretary of State with the approval of the Treasury, can direct authorities to keep accounts and records of their land dealings (see the Community Land Accounts (England) Directions 1975 in Community Land Circular 2 (No. 128/75)). The primary purpose of the accounts was to facilitate the division of a "community land surplus account" between the Exchequer, other authorities with a deficit and the authority concerned. This section will exclude from corporation tax the income arising from activities of those Community Land Tax Act authorities who are not already exempt as local authorities. It has been included to exempt the Welsh Land Authority and new town corporations.

Close companies: relevant income

35.—(1) In paragraph 9 (3) of Schedule 16 to the Finance Act 1972 (apportionment of income of close companies: relevant maximum and minimum amounts for calculating relevant income of trading company) for " £15,000 " and " £5,000 ", in both places, there shall be substituted respectively " £75,000 " and " £25,000 ".

(2) In paragraph 9 (4) of that Schedule (associated company to be disregarded for purposes of paragraph 9 (3)) for the words " which has not carried on any trade or business at any time in that accounting period " there shall be substituted the words " which was not a trading company, or has not carried on any trade, at any time in that accounting period ".

(3) In paragraph 10 (3) (b) of that Schedule (calculation of distributable investment income) for " £500 " there shall be substituted " £1,000 ".

(4) This section has effect for any accounting period ending after 26th October 1977.

General Note
Subs. (1)
This subsection increases very substantially the exemption limit for apportionment of trading income of a close company. Instead of estate or trading income

being regarded as nil if, after corporation tax, it is less than £5,000 in an accounting period, it is to be regarded as nil if it does not exceed £25,000. The effect of this increase is that a trading company with no associated company, with estate or trading income not exceeding £45,402 before tax need not concern itself about apportionment of its undistributed income.

Abatement of estate or trading income now takes place where the income, after tax, is between £25,000 and £75,000. If, therefore, estate or trading income after tax is say £55,000 in a company's accounting period it can be abated by one-half of the difference between £55,000 and £75,000 (*i.e.* £10,000). This would leave the estate or trading income as £45,000 for apportionment purposes.

Subs. (2)

The reliefs from apportionment referred to in subs. (1) are split if a company has associated companies. This subsection amends the previous position so that companies are to be treated as associated only if they are both "trading companies" (as defined in para. 11 (1) of Sched. 16) and have carried on a trade or business at some time in the period. The previous position was that a company, albeit principally an investment company, was treated as associated if it engaged in an insignificant amount of trading in the period.

Subs. (3)

Instead of all investment income being distributable reduced by whichever is the less of 10 per cent. of estate or trading income or £500, the reference to £500 is now to be £1,000.

Close companies: acquisition of trades

36.—(1) Part II of Schedule 16 to the Finance Act 1972 (provisions for determining relevant income etc. of close companies) shall have effect subject to the amendments in Schedule 5 to this Act, being amendments to allow account to be taken, in certain cases, of the requirements of a company for the acquisition of a trade or of an interest in a trading company or in a company which is a member of a trading group.

(2) The amendments in Schedule 5 to this Act have effect with respect to accounting periods ending on or after 11th April 1978, irrespective of whether the acquisition takes place before or after that date.

GENERAL NOTE

The rules contained in Sched. 5 ease the apportionment rules governing close companies by taking into account the cost of acquiring (i) a trade, or (ii) an interest in a trading company, or (iii) an interest in a company which is a member of a trading group.

In the debate on this provision in the Standing Committee the point was raised as to whether this should be extended to the costs of acquiring a business of a professional or vocational nature. There is considerable doubt as to whether or not a company can in fact carry on a profession or vocation. The Revenue gave an undertaking that it would not seek to disallow any acquisition on the ground that it was a profession or vocation.

A further assurance was given that "first business loans" (*i.e.* loans raised at the commencement of a business) are within the terms of this relief.

The view was also stated in the debates that the Revenue consider that if 50 per cent. or more of the shares of a company are acquired, the purchaser is in fact acquiring the trade carried on by the company. This point does not arise with this section as the cost of acquiring an interest in a company if it is a trading company or a member of a trading group is covered, as well as the costs of acquiring a trade.

Capital allowances: long leases

37.—(1) Subject to the provisions of this section, where expenditure has been incurred on the construction of a building or structure and a long lease of that building or structure is granted out of an interest therein which is, within the meaning of Chapter I of Part I of the Capital

Allowances Act 1968, the relevant interest in relation to that expenditure, that Chapter shall, if the lessor and lessee so elect, have effect as if—

(a) the grant of the lease were a sale of the relevant interest by the lessor to the lessee at the time when the lease takes effect;

(b) any capital sum paid by the lessee in consideration for the grant of the lease were the purchase price on the sale; and

(c) the interest out of which the lease is granted had at that time ceased to be, and the interest granted by the lease had at that time become, the relevant interest in relation to that expenditure.

(2) Any election under this section shall have effect in relation to all the expenditure in relation to which the interest out of which the lease is granted is the relevant interest and which relates to the building or structure or (if more than one) the buildings or structures which are the subject of the lease.

(3) Any election under this section shall be by notice in writing to the inspector given within two years after the date on which the lease takes effect; and all such adjustments shall be made, whether by discharge or repayment of tax or by further assessments, as may be required for giving effect to the election.

(4) In this section " long lease " means a lease the duration of which (ascertained according to section 84 (1), (2) and (3) of the Taxes Act) exceeds fifty years; and any question whether a lease is a long lease shall be determined without regard to section 13 (3) of the said Act of 1968 (options for renewal).

(5) Section 11 (3) of the said Act of 1968 (under which the creation of a lease does not affect the continuance of a relevant interest) shall have effect subject to subsection (1) (c) above.

(6) This section does not apply where—

(a) the lessor and lessee are connected with each other within the terms of section 533 of the Taxes Act; or

(b) it appears that the sole or main benefit which may be expected to accrue to the lessor from the grant of the lease and the making of an election is the obtaining of a balancing allowance under section 3 of the said Act of 1968;

but paragraph (a) above shall not prevent the application of this section where the lessor is a body discharging statutory functions and the lessee a company of which it has control.

(7) The Tax Acts shall have effect as if this section were contained in Chapter I of Part I of the said Act of 1968.

(8) This section applies where the time when the lease takes effect is on or after 15th February 1978.

GENERAL NOTE

This section enables a lessee who has paid a premium for a lease of more than 50 years of an industrial building to qualify for industrial buildings allowance following a joint election with the lessor. In such a case the lessee will be deemed to have purchased " the relevant interest " so as to qualify for relief in accordance with s. 5, C.A.A. 1968.

One of the main purposes behind the introduction of this section is to cover the case where a public body, such as a local authority, grants a lease of a factory to a taxpayer where the relevant interest for the purposes of capital allowances is not transferred to the taxpayer. In such a case the public body would have the benefit of a capital allowance but, as it does not pay tax, would have no use for it. This section allows the parties to agree in such a case that the taxpayer should have the allowance. The section is not limited to the grant of leases by public bodies but applies generally.

The section applies where the lease takes effect on or after February 15, 1978. This was the date on which the Government announced its intention to introduce the relief.

Capital allowances: hotels

38.—(1) Chapter I of Part I of the Capital Allowances Act 1968 shall apply in relation to a qualifying hotel as if it were an industrial building or structure; but the provisions of that Chapter shall have effect in relation to any such hotel with the modifications specified in Schedule 6 to this Act.

(2) A qualifying hotel is a hotel the accommodation in which is in a building or buildings of a permanent nature and which complies with the following requirements—

(a) that it is open for at least four months in the season; and

(b) that during the time when it is open in the season—

(i) it has at least ten letting bedrooms;

(ii) the sleeping accommodation offered at the hotel consists wholly or mainly of letting bedrooms; and

(iii) the services provided for guests normally include the provision of breakfast and an evening meal, the making of beds and the cleaning of rooms.

(3) In subsection (2) above " the season " means April, May, June, July, August, September and October; and for the purposes of that subsection a letting bedroom is a private bedroom available for letting to the public generally and not normally in the same occupation for more than one month.

(4) Subject to subsection (5) below, any question whether a hotel complies with the requirements in subsection (2) (a) and (b) above at any time in a person's chargeable period or its basis period shall be determined—

(a) if the hotel has been in use for the purposes of the trade carried on by that person or by such a lessee as is mentioned in section 1 (3) of the said Act of 1968 throughout the twelve months ending with the last day of that chargeable period or its basis period, by reference to those twelve months;

(b) if the hotel was first used as aforesaid on a date after the beginning of those twelve months, by reference to the twelve months beginning with that date;

but a hotel shall not by virtue of this subsection be treated as complying with those requirements at any time in a chargeable period or its basis period after it has ceased altogether to be used.

(5) Where, during the twelve months mentioned in paragraph (a) of subsection (4) above, a hotel had fewer than ten letting bedrooms until a date which was too late for it to qualify by reference to those twelve months, it may instead qualify under paragraph (b) of that subsection by reference to the twelve months beginning with that date as if it had then first been used.

(6) For the purposes of this section—

(a) there shall be treated as included in a qualifying hotel any building (whether or not on the same site as any other part of the hotel) which is provided by the person carrying on the hotel for the welfare of workers employed in the hotel and is in use for that purpose; and

(b) where a qualifying hotel is carried on by an individual, whether alone or in partnership, there shall be treated as excluded from the hotel any accommodation which, during the time when the hotel is open in the season, is normally used as a dwelling by that person or by any member of his family or household.

(7) The Tax Acts shall have effect as if this section and Schedule 6 to this Act were contained in Chapter I of Part I of the said Act of 1968.

(8) This section applies in relation to expenditure incurred after 11th April 1978; and expenditure shall not be treated for the purposes of this subsection as having been incurred after the date on which it was in fact incurred by reason only of section 1 (6) or 5 (1) of the said Act of 1968.

General Note

This section allows certain expenditure on hotels to be deductible as a capital allowance in certain circumstances. This objective is achieved by treating a " qualifying hotel " as an industrial building or structure. As a consequence expenditure incurred for the construction, extension or structural alteration of a qualifying hotel will qualify as a capital allowance giving a right to an initial allowance of 20 per cent. and an annual writing down allowance of four per cent. on the straight line basis.

To be a qualifying hotel the building must satisfy the following requirements:

(i) a hotel of a permanent nature;
(ii) be open for at least four months between a season running from April to October;
(iii) have available during this time 10 private bedrooms for letting to the public generally which are not usually let to one person for periods longer than one month;
(iv) sleeping accommodation offered consists wholly or mainly of bedrooms;
(v) services including breakfast, evening meals, making of beds and cleaning rooms.

These conditions must be satisfied during a 12-month period ending with the last day of the relevant chargeable period or basis period or, if the business started at a later date than the commencement of that 12-month period, during the 12-month period from the commencement of the business. In a case where the hotel originally had fewer than 10 letting bedrooms but increased the bedrooms available to that number then the relevant 12-month period may run from the date at which 10 letting bedrooms were first available.

Any expenditure incurred in respect of a building for the purpose of providing for the welfare of those working at a qualifying hotel will be covered by this section. It is not necessary that the building should be on the same site as the hotel. Excluded from such treatment is any expenditure relating to a part of the hotel normally occupied between April and October by the claimant or any member of his family or household.

This treatment applies only to expenditure incurred after April 11, 1978. Expenditure incurred before the start of a business or before its acquisition will not be treated as incurred at a later date than that at which it was actually incurred despite ss. 1 (6) and 5 (1) Capital Allowance Act 1968. Sched. 6 applies to modify the application of the rules regarding capital allowances to expenditure covered by this section.

Capital allowances: agricultural and forestry buildings and works

39.—(1) In subsection (1) of section 68 of the Capital Allowances Act 1968 (writing-down allowances for agricultural and forestry buildings and works) for the words from " writing-down allowances shall be made to him " onwards there shall be substituted the words " there shall be made to him—

(a) for the chargeable period related to the incurring of that expenditure, an initial allowance of an amount equal to one-fifth of that expenditure; and
(b) during a writing-down period of eight years beginning with that period, writing-down allowances of an aggregate amount equal to four-fifths of that expenditure."

(2) After subsection (3) of that section there shall be inserted—

" (3A) A person in making a claim by virtue of this section as it applies for income tax purposes in respect of the chargeable period mentioned in paragraph (a) of subsection (1) above may require the initial allowance to be reduced to a specified amount, and a company may by notice in writing given to the inspector not later than two years after the end of that period disclaim the initial allowance or require it to be so reduced; and

(*a*) where the initial allowance is not claimed or, in the case of a company, is disclaimed, the period and amount mentioned in paragraph (*b*) of that subsection shall be ten years and the whole amount of the expenditure; and

(*b*) where the initial allowance is reduced, that period and amount shall be a fraction of the period of ten years and of the whole amount of the expenditure equal to the fraction of the whole amount of the expenditure that remains after deducting the part covered by the initial allowance."

(3) In subsection (4) of that section for the words " an allowance " there shall be substituted the words " a writing-down allowance ".

(4) In section 74 of the said Act of 1968 after subsection (5) there shall be inserted—

" (6) All such assessments and adjustments of assessments shall be made as are necessary to give effect to any notice given by a company under section 68 (3A) of this Act ".

(5) This section applies in relation to expenditure incurred after 11th April 1978.

GENERAL NOTE

In the past, allowances for expenditure on agricultural buildings and works have been given at 10 per cent. per annum over 10 years. This section provides for a new initial allowance of 20 per cent. Together with the writing down allowance this will enable 30 per cent. of expenditure to qualify for relief in the year in which it is incurred. Unless the initial allowance is not wholly claimed all expenditure will now be written off over eight years.

Subs. (2) provides for the voluntary waiver or reduction of the initial allowance but where this occurs the writing down allowance is given over a longer period. If it is waived entirely the writing down allowance is given over 10 years.

Capital allowances: sports grounds

40.—(1) If a person carrying on a trade has since the passing of the Safety of Sports Grounds Act 1975 incurred expenditure in respect of a sports stadium used for the purposes of the trade, then, if—

(*a*) at the time when the expenditure was incurred the stadium was of the description specified in subsection (1) of section 1 of that Act but no designation order under that section had come into operation in respect of the stadium; and

(*b*) the expenditure was incurred in taking steps which the local authority for the area in which the stadium is situated certify would have fallen within subsection (1) (*a*) or (*b*) of section 49 of the Finance (No. 2) Act 1975 (relief for safety expenditure at a designated sports stadium) if such an order had then been in operation and a safety certificate had then been issued or applied for,

subsection (1) of the said section 49 shall have effect in relation to the expenditure as it has effect in relation to the expenditure mentioned in that subsection.

(2) All such adjustments shall be made by discharge or repayment of tax as may be required for giving effect to the relief available under this section for expenditure incurred before the passing of this Act.

(3) Any disclaimer or claim under section 41 (3) of the Finance Act 1971 in respect of the relief available under this section for expenditure incurred before the passing of this Act, and any claim for relief (or additional relief) under any other provision of the Tax Acts which is

made in consequence of the relief available under this section for such expenditure, shall not be out of time if made within twelve months after the passing of this Act.

(4) Any provision of regulations made under section 6 (1) (*b*) of the Safety of Sports Grounds Act 1975 (power of local authorities to charge fees) shall, with the necessary modifications, apply to the issue of a certificate for the purposes of this section as it applies to the issue of a safety certificate.

(5) In this section " sports stadium ", " safety certificate " and " local authority " have the same meaning as in the said Act of 1975;

(6) The Tax Acts shall have effect as if this section were contained in Chapter I of Part III of the Finance Act 1971.

GENERAL NOTE

This section provides a relaxation to the conditions that have to be satisfied before expenditure on people's safety in sports stadiums can qualify for capital allowances pursuant to s. 49, F. (No. 2) A. 1975. For relief to be obtained under s. 49 expenditure must be incurred to comply with the terms of a safety certificate issued for the stadium under the Safety of Sports Grounds Act 1975 or be referable to the issue of such a certificate. A certificate is only required, however, if a stadium has been subject to a designation order. This section allows relief to be obtained, even in the absence of such an order, if, had such an order been made, relief under s. 49 would have been available.

Date for payment of tax for 1977-78

41.—(1) Where income tax under Schedule A, Schedule D or Schedule E was charged for the year 1977–78 by an assessment in the case of which the amount of tax charged was adjusted, after the issue of the notice of assessment and before the passing of this Act, so as to give effect to any of the provisions of the Finance (Income Tax Reliefs) Act 1977, any tax charged by the assessment which became due and payable—

(*a*) in the case of tax under Schedule A or Schedule D, before the expiration of a period of thirty days beginning with the date of notification of the adjustment; or

(*b*) in the case of tax under Schedule E, before the expiration of a period of fourteen days beginning with the date of the collector's application for payment next following notification of the adjustment,

shall be treated as having become due and payable at the expiration of that period.

(2) This section does not apply where the adjustment was made on the determination of an appeal, whether by the Commissioners or by agreement under section 54 (1) of the Taxes Management Act 1970.

GENERAL NOTE

The F. (Income Tax Reliefs) A. 1977 increased certain personal allowances for the tax year 1977–78 and exempted any general increase taking effect in that year in social security and other pensions and allowances. As a result of the passing of that Act it may have been necessary for the Revenue to serve notices of adjustment if assessments had already been made on a taxpayer. The intention of this section is to change the date at which tax becomes payable in such an event. It will apply if (i) a taxpayer has been assessed to tax under Sched. A, D or E; (ii) by virtue of the assessment tax became due and payable in the case of an assessment under Sched. A or D before the expiry of 30 days from the date of the notification of the adjustment or in the case of an assessment under Sched. 5 before the expiry of 14 days from the date of the collector's application for payment pursuant to the notice of adjustment.

As a result of this section tax assessed in such circumstances will now become due and payable at the expiry of the above periods unless the adjustment resulted from the hearing of an appeal

Deduction of tax from payments of interest in 1978–79

42. Section 522 of the Taxes Act (effect of reduction in basic rate on deduction of tax from payments of interest) shall apply as if a resolution having statutory effect under the Provisional Collection of Taxes Act 1968 and providing for the charging of income tax as specified in section 13 above had been passed immediately before the passing of this Act; and the proviso to paragraph (b) of the said section 522 shall apply to any over-deduction to be made good in consequence of this section as if the reference to the passing of the Act imposing the tax were a reference to a date one month after the passing of this Act.

GENERAL NOTE

The basic rate of income tax for 1978–79, as originally proposed by the Government, was 34 per cent. but was reduced during the course of the Finance Bill's passage through Parliament to 33 per cent. This section is concerned with making allowance for any overdeduction of tax from payments of interest made by companies before the passing of this Act but after the commencement of the tax year 1978–79. The section modifies s. 522, I.C.T.A., so that it can apply. Thus, any overdeductions made can be made good by a reduction in the tax to be deducted from the next payment of interest.

For the practice to be followed generally in relation to overdeductions of tax from interest, annuities and other annual payments, see Inland Revenue Press Statement July 7, 1978.

Repayment of tax paid under Police Regulations

43.—(1) The Board shall repay to police authorities any tax paid by those authorities by reason of the regulations mentioned in subsection (2) below (which required police authorities to discharge any tax liability of members of police forces arising in consequence of the provision of free accommodation); and no person other than a police authority shall be entitled to any repayment or credit in respect of tax paid as aforesaid unless he has made an application in that behalf to the Board or an inspector before the coming into force of this section.

(2) The regulations referred to above are—

   (a) Regulation 30A of the Police Regulations 1952;

   (b) Regulation 40A of the Police (Scotland) Regulations 1956;

   (c) any regulation subsequently in force and corresponding to either of those mentioned above.

(3) Subsection (1) above shall also apply to tax paid by the Ministry of Home Affairs for Northern Ireland or the Police Authority for Northern Ireland by reason of Article 8A of the Royal Ulster Constabulary Allowances (Rent and Compensatory Grant) Order 1963 or of any corresponding provision subsequently in force, but any tax so paid by the Ministry shall be repaid to the Authority.

(4) This section shall be deemed to have come into force on 7th July 1978.

GENERAL NOTE

In so far as under the regulations referred to police authorities are required to discharge any tax liabilities of members of police forces arising in consequence of providing them with living accommodation, the Inland Revenue is now required to repay the tax paid by those authorities.

CHAPTER II
CAPITAL GAINS

Relief for gains less than £9,500

44.—(1) An individual shall not be chargeable to capital gains tax for a year of assessment if his taxable amount for that year does not exceed £1,000.

(2) If an individual's taxable amount for a year of assessment exceeds £1,000 but does not exceed £5,000, the amount of capital gains tax to which he is chargeable for that year shall be 15 per cent. of the excess over £1,000.

(3) If an individual's taxable amount for a year of assessment exceeds £5,000, the amount of capital gains tax to which he is chargeable for that year shall not exceed £600 plus one-half of the excess over £5,000.

(4) For the purposes of this section an individual's taxable amount for a year of assessment is the amount on which he is chargeable under section 20 (4) of the Finance Act 1965 for that year but—

(a) where the amount of chargeable gains less allowable losses accruing to an individual in any year of assessment does not exceed £1,000, no deduction from that amount shall be made for that year in respect of allowable losses carried forward from a previous year or carried back from a subsequent year in which the individual dies; and

(b) where the amount of chargeable gains less allowable losses accruing to an individual in any year of assessment exceeds £1,000, the deduction from that amount for that year in respect of allowable losses carried forward from a previous year or carried back from a subsequent year in which the individual dies shall not be greater than the excess.

(5) Where in a year of assessment—

(a) the amount of chargeable gains accruing to an individual does not exceed £1,000; and

(b) the aggregate amount or value of the consideration for all the disposals of assets made by him (other than disposals gains accruing on which are not chargeable gains) does not exceed £5,000,

a statement to the effect of paragraphs (a) and (b) above shall, unless the inspector otherwise requires, be sufficient compliance with any notice under section 8 of the Taxes Management Act 1970 requiring the individual to make a return of the chargeable gains accruing to him in that year.

(6) Schedule 7 to this Act shall have effect as respects the application of this section to husbands and wives, personal representatives and trustees.

(7) The following provisions, namely—

(a) section 21 of the said Act of 1965 (alternative charge to tax); and

(b) section 57 of the Finance Act 1971 (exemption for small disposals),

shall cease to have effect.

(8) For the percentages specified in—

(a) section 112 (3) (b) and (c) of the Finance Act 1972 (unit trusts; reduction of tax liability); and

(b) section 113 of that Act (unit trusts: reduced rate of tax),

there shall be substituted " 10 per cent.".

(9) Subsections (1) to (6), (7) (b) and (8) (b) above apply for the year 1977–78 and subsequent years of assessment, subsection (7) (a) above applies for the year 1978–79 and subsequent years of assessment and subsection (8) (a) above applies to gains accruing on disposals after 5th April 1979.

GENERAL NOTE

This section abolishes the small disposals exemption (with effect for the tax year 1977–78) and the alternative charge for chargeable gains accruing to individuals (allowing assessments under Sched. D Case VI though this will not take effect until the tax year 1978–79). In their place is a new exemption (taking effect for the tax year 1977–78) whereby:

(i) a taxable amount of less than £1,000 in a year—free of tax;

(ii) a taxable amount in a year between £1,000 and £5,000—subject to 15 per cent.

(iii) over £5,000—capital gains tax can not exceed half excess of amount over £5,000 plus £600.

The relief in respect of taxable amounts exceeding £5,000 will only be beneficial up to £9,500.

In respect of losses carried forward from previous years, no deductions are made if the chargeable gains reduced by the losses for the year of assessment result in the taxable amount being less than £1,000. Where the taxable amount exceeds £1,000 the extent of the losses carried forward deducted will equal that excess. This, therefore, saves the allowable losses for future years.

A full return of an individual's chargeable gains need not be made if the taxable amount does not exceed £1,000 and the aggregate consideration for his disposals in that year are not greater than £5,000. [There are special rules regarding returns for husbands and wives living together.]

Subs. (8) reduces the rate of capital gains tax on chargeable gains accruing to unit trusts for exempt unit holders and funds in court from 17½ per cent. to 10 per cent. with effect for the year 1977–78.

Similarly the maximum tax credit available to persons disposing of units in unit trusts and shares in investment trusts will be reduced from 17½ per cent. to 10 per cent. but only in respect of gains accruing on disposals after April 5, 1979.

Sched. 7 contains special rules relating to husbands and wives, personal representatives, and trustees. It should be noted that there is no provision allowing for the carrying forward of any unutilised part of the relief.

Chattel exemption

45.—(1) In subsections (1), (3) and (5) (*b*) and (*c*) of section 30 of the Finance Act 1965 (chattels sold for £1,000 or less) for the words " one thousand pounds " there shall be substituted " £2,000 ".

(2) For subsection (2) of that section there shall be substituted—

" (2) Where the amount or value of the consideration for the disposal of an asset which is tangible movable property exceeds £2,000, there shall be excluded from any chargeable gain accruing on the disposal so much of it as exceeds five-thirds of the difference between—

(*a*) the amount or value of the consideration; and

(*b*) £2,000."

(3) In subsection (4) of that section for the word " tax " there shall be substituted the words " chargeable gains ".

(4) In subsection (5) (*b*) of that section for the words " the limitation on the amount of tax in subsection (2) of this section shall be to half the difference " there shall be substituted the words " the part of any chargeable gain that is excluded from it under subsection (2) of this section shall be so much of the gain as exceeds five-thirds of the difference ".

(5) In sections 12 (2) (*b*) and 25 (7) of the Taxes Management Act 1970 (information about chargeable gains) for " £1,000 " there shall be substituted " £2,000 ".

(6) This section applies for the year 1978–79 and subsequent years of assessment; and subsections (2) to (4) above apply also for the year 1977–78 but as if for any reference in the substituted subsection (2) to £2,000 there were substituted a reference to £1,000.

GENERAL NOTE

The exemption given to disposals of tangible movables by F.A. 1965, s. 30, if the consideration for the disposal does not exceed £1,000 is increased to £2,000 with effect for the year 1978–79.

The marginal relief for disposals exceeding that figure has also been altered. At present the amount of tax chargeable must not exceed one half of the excess. With effect for the tax year 1977–78 this has been changed. The relief now applies by excluding part of the chargeable gain rather than limiting the tax bill. So much of the chargeable gain is excluded as exceeds five-thirds of the excess of the consideration.

Relief for gifts of business assets

46.—(1) If, after 11th April 1978, an individual (in this section referred to as " the transferor ") makes a disposal, otherwise than under a bargain at arm's length, to a person resident or ordinarily resident in the United Kingdom (in this section referred to as " the transferee ") of—

(a) an asset which is, or is an interest in, an asset used for the purposes of a trade, profession or vocation carried on by the transferor or by a company which is his family company, or

(b) shares or securities of a trading company which is the transferor's family company,

then, subject to subsection (2) below, the provisions of subsection (3) below shall apply in relation to the disposal if a claim for relief under this section is made by the transferor and the transferee.

(2) Subsection (3) below does not apply in relation to a disposal if,—

(a) in the case of a disposal of an asset, any gain accruing to the transferor on the disposal is (apart from this section) wholly relieved under section 34 of the Finance Act 1965 (transfer of business on retirement); or

(b) in the case of a disposal of shares or securities, the proportion determined under subsection (3) (b) of that section of any gain accruing to the transferor on the disposal is (apart from this section) wholly relieved under that section.

(3) Where a claim for relief is made under this section in respect of a disposal—

(a) the amount of any chargeable gain which, apart from this section, would accrue to the transferor on the disposal, and

(b) the amount of the consideration for which, apart from this section, the transferee would be regarded for the purposes of capital gains tax as having acquired the asset or, as the case may be, the shares or securities,

shall each be reduced by an amount equal to the held-over gain on the disposal.

(4) Part I of Schedule 8 to this Act shall have effect for extending the relief provided for by virtue of subsections (1) to (3) above in the case of agricultural property and for applying it in relation to settled property, and, in consequence of the provisions of this section and of that Part, section 55 of the Finance (No. 2) Act 1975 (relief from tax on chargeable gains in respect of agricultural property, etc.) shall not apply in relation to a disposal of an asset after 11th April 1978.

(5) Subject to Part II of Schedule 8 to this Act (which provides for reductions in the held-over gain in certain cases) and subsection (6) below, the reference in subsection (3) above to the held-over gain on a disposal is a reference to the chargeable gain which would have accrued on that disposal apart from subsection (3) above and (in appropriate cases) section 34 of the Finance Act 1965, and in subsection (6) below that chargeable gain is referred to as the unrelieved gain on the disposal.

(6) In any case where—

(a) there is actual consideration (as opposed to the consideration equal to the market value which is deemed to be given by virtue of section 22 (4) of the Finance Act 1965) for a disposal in respect of which a claim for relief is made under this section, and

(*b*) that actual consideration exceeds the sums allowable as a deduction under paragraph 4 of Schedule 6 to that Act,

the held-over gain on the disposal shall be the amount by which the unrelieved gain on the disposal exceeds the excess referred to in paragraph (*b*) above.

(7) Subject to subsection (8) below, in this section and Schedule 8 to this Act—

(*a*) " family company " and " trading company " have the same meaning as in section 34 of the Finance Act 1965; and

(*b*) " trade ", " profession " and " vocation " have the same meaning as in the Income Tax Acts.

(8) In this section and Schedule 8 to this Act in determining whether a company is a trading company for the purposes of this section and that Schedule, the expression " trade " shall be taken to include the occupation of woodlands where the woodlands are managed by the occupier on a commercial basis and with a view to the realisation of profits.

GENERAL NOTE

This section provides a roll-over relief when the assets of a business (including one carried on by a partnership) or shares in a family trading company are disposed of other than for full consideration. This is intended to ease the tax burden on the transfer of a business from, say, one generation of a family to the next.

To qualify for this relief there must be:

(i) a disposal made by an individual (the transfer) after April 11, 1978;

(ii) it is not made as part of a bargain at arm's length;

(iii) the " transferee " is both resident and ordinarily resident in the United Kingdom;

(iv) the disposal concerns either (*a*) assets (or interests in them) of a business carried on by the transferor or his family company or (*b*) shares or securities in the transferor's family trading company.

(v) the chargeable gain on the disposal is not wholly relieved by reason of any retirement relief available to the transferor.

For these purposes, " family company " has the same meaning as in F.A. 1965, s. 34 (as amended by s. 48 below) which means the transferor must have the right to exercise at least 25 per cent. of the company's voting rights or 51 per cent. are exercisable by the transferor and his family and at least 5 per cent. by the transferor.

In the case of a disposal satisfying these requirements the amount of the chargeable gain accruing to the transferor and the amount of the consideration deemed to have been given by the transferee shall be reduced by the " held-over gain."

This sum (subject to Sched. 8) equals the chargeable gain reduced by the excess of the actual consideration given over the allowable deductions in accordance with F.A. 1965, Sched. 6, para. 4. It, therefore, postpones the payment of the capital gains tax until a disposal of the particular asset or shares for full consideration. Both agricultural property not used for the purposes of a trade and settled property are dealt with separately in Sched. 8.

For the purposes of this relief the occupation of woodlands if the occupier manages them on a commercial basis and with a view to the realisation of profits is to be treated as a trade (see I.C.T.A. 1970, s. 111).

Replacement of business assets

47.—(1) For subsection (9) of section 33 of the Finance Act 1965 (replacement of business assets: relief where person carries on two trades) there shall be substituted the following subsection—

" (9) This section shall apply in relation to a person who, either successively or at the same time, carries on two or more trades as if both or all of them were a single trade."

(2) After the said subsection (9) there shall be inserted the following subsection—

" (9A) In relation to a case where—

(a) the person disposing of, or of his interest in, the old assets and acquiring the new assets, or an interest in them, is an individual, and

(b) the trade or trades in question are carried on not by that individual but by a company which, both at the time of the disposal and at the time of the acquisition referred to paragraph (a) above, is his family company, within the meaning of section 34 below,

any reference in the preceding provisions of this section to the person carrying on the trade (or the two or more trades) includes a reference to that individual."

(3) This section applies where the acquisition of, or of the interest in, the new assets takes place after 11th April 1978.

GENERAL NOTE

This section eases the restrictions on the roll-over relief applicable on the replacement of business assets in two respects.

(i) Two trades: A person carrying on two or more trades whether at the same time or one after the other is now to be treated as if carrying on a single trade. It is no longer necessary that the trades should be concerned with the same goods or services.

(ii) Family trading companies: Relief will now be available where the assets (or interests) are sold and acquired by an individual but the trade is carried on by a family trading company of the individual, e.g. a farm is owned by an individual but actually farmed by a family company he controls. Relief will now be available on the sale of the farm and acquisition of a new farm. This relaxation will not apply if the land or other asset is owned by a company or trustees but the trade is actually carried on by the individual.

These relaxations will apply to cases where the acquisition of the asset (or interest) takes place after April 11, 1978. It is immaterial when the old asset (or the interest in it) was sold.

Transfer of business on retirement

48.—(1) For subsection (1) of section 34 of the Finance Act 1965 (relief for capital gains tax purposes on gains accruing on the transfer of a business on retirement) there shall be substituted the following subsections—

" (1) If an individual who has attained the age of 60 years—

(a) disposes by way of sale or gift of the whole or part of a business, or

(b) disposes by way of sale or gift of shares or securities of a company,

and throughout a period of at least one year ending with the disposal the relevant conditions have been fulfilled, relief shall be given under this section in respect of gains accruing to him on the disposal.

(1A) For the purposes of subsection (1) above the relevant conditions are fulfilled at any time if at that time,—

(a) in the case of a disposal falling within paragraph (a) of that subsection, the business in question is owned either by the individual or by a company with respect to which the following conditions are at that time fulfilled, namely,—

(i) it is a trading company;

(ii) it is the individual's family company; and

(iii) he is a full-time working director of it; and

(b) in the case of a disposal falling within paragraph (b) of that subsection, either the conditions in sub-paragraphs (i) to (iii) of paragraph (a) above are fulfilled with respect to the company in question or the individual owns the business which, at the time of the disposal, is owned by the company;

and in relation to a particular disposal the period, up to a maximum of 10 years, which ends with the disposal and throughout which the relevant conditions are fulfilled is in this section referred to as ' the qualifying period '.

(1B) The amount available for relief under this section shall be—

(a) in the case of an individual who has attained the age of 65 years, the relevant percentage of £50,000; and

(b) in the case of an individual who has not attained that age, the relevant percentage of the aggregate of £10,000 for every year by which his age exceeds 60 and a corresponding part of £10,000 for any odd part of a year;

and for the purpose of this subsection ' the relevant percentage ' means a percentage determined according to the length of the qualifying period on a scale rising arithmetically from 10 per cent. where that period is precisely one year to 100 per cent. where it is ten years."

(2) Subsection (3) of that section (which relates to relief in the case of a transfer of shares or securities in a family trading company) shall be amended as follows:—

(a) in paragraph (b) (which, on a disposal of shares or securities, specifies the proportion of the gains by reference to which relief is allowed) for the words " the value of the company's assets (including cash) " there shall be substituted the words " the value of the company's chargeable assets "; and

(b) at the end of the subsection there shall be added the words " and for the purposes of paragraph (b) above every asset is a chargeable asset except one, on the disposal of which by the company at the time of the disposal of the shares or securities, no chargeable gain would accrue ".

(3) In subsection (4) of that section (application of relief) for the words " subsection (1) above " there shall be substituted the words " this section " and the words " within that subsection " shall be omitted.

(4) In subsection (6) of that section, in paragraph (b) of the definition of " family company " for the words " seventy-five per cent." there shall be substituted the words " fifty-one per cent." and for the words " ten per cent." there shall be substituted the words " five per cent.".

(5) This section applies with respect to any disposal which takes place after 11th April 1978.

GENERAL NOTE

This section amends the relief from capital gains tax available on the transfer of a business on retirement.

It changes both the amount of relief and the conditions that have to be satisfied to qualify for the relief.

To qualify the following conditions must be satisfied:

(a) the individual making the disposal must be 60 years of age or over (as before);

(b) there must be a disposal by way of sale or gift (as before);

(c) the disposal must be either (i) the whole or part of a business (which includes an interest in a partnership in the view of the Revenue as expressed in the Standing Committee debates) which is owned by the individual or a family trading company of which the individual is a full-time director, or (ii) shares or securities of a family trading company of which the individual is a full-time director;

(d) the above conditions have been satisfied for a period of one year ending with the date of the disposal. Before there was a strict requirement that the conditions be satisfied for a 10-year period (see *Davenport* v. *Hasslacher* [1977] 1 W.L.R. 869).

The definition of family company contained in F.A. 1965, s. 34 (*b*), has been relaxed so that if not less than 51 per cent. of the voting rights of the company are exercisable by the individual or a member of his family and not less than 5 per cent. by the individual (as opposed to 75 per cent. and 10 per cent. before) the company qualifies as a family company.

The amount of relief available is dependent upon the age of the individual and the length of time that the above conditions have been satisfied in the years immediately preceding the disposal up to a maximum of 10 (known as the qualifying period). It seems that this must be a continuous period, not allowing for interruptions when not all the conditions were satisfied.

An individual over 65 (previously entitled to £20,000 relief) is now entitled to the relevant percentage of £50,000. A person aged between 60 and 65 is entitled to the relevant percentage of £10,000 (previously £2,000) for each year over 60 and a corresponding part of £10,000 for any odd part of that year.

The relevant percentage is

$$\frac{\text{qualifying period}}{10} \times 100 \text{ per cent.}$$

For example, a farmer aged 66 sells his farm having satisfied all the conditions for five years. The relevant percentage will be

$$\frac{5}{10} \times 100 = 50 \text{ per cent.}$$

The relief will be £50,000 × 50 per cent. = £25,000.

This represents a considerable relaxation of the rules regarding retirement relief.

There has also been an amendment to the manner in which the part of the chargeable gains accruing on a disposal of shares in a family company which qualifies for this relief is calculated.

Before this amendment the proportion used to be:

$$\frac{\text{value of chargeable business assets of company}}{\text{value of company's assets (including cash)}}$$

Now the proportion will be:

$$\frac{\text{value of chargeable business assets of company}}{\text{value of chargeable assets of company}}$$

This excludes assets of the company from the calculation which are not chargeable to capital gains tax, such as cash.

All these amendments apply to disposals after April 11, 1978.

Relief in respect of loans to traders

49.—(1) In this section " a qualifying loan " means a loan in the case of which—

(*a*) the money lent is used by the borrower wholly for the purposes of a trade carried on by him, not being a trade which consists of or includes the lending of money; and

(*b*) the borrower is resident in the United Kingdom; and

(*c*) the borrower's debt is not a debt on a security as defined in paragraph 5 of Schedule 7 to the Finance Act 1965;

and for the purposes of paragraph (*a*) above money used by the borrower for setting up a trade which is subsequently carried on by him shall be treated as used for the purposes of that trade.

(2) In subsection (1) above references to a trade include references to a profession or vocation; and where money lent to a company is lent by it to another company in the same group, being a trading company, that subsection shall apply to the money lent to the first-mentioned company as if it had used it for any purpose for which it is used by the other company while a member of the group.

(3) If, on a claim by a person who has made a qualifying loan, the inspector is satisfied that—

  (a) any outstanding amount of the principal of the loan has become irrecoverable; and

  (b) the claimant has not assigned his right to recover that amount; and

  (c) the claimant and the borrower were not each other's spouses, or companies in the same group, when the loan was made or at any subsequent time,

Part III of the said Act of 1965 shall have effect as if an allowable loss equal to that amount had accrued to the claimant when the claim was made.

(4) If, on a claim by a person who has guaranteed the repayment of a loan which is, or but for subsection (1) (c) above would be, a qualifying loan, the inspector is satisfied that—

  (a) any outstanding amount of, or of interest in respect of, the principal of the loan has become irrecoverable from the borrower; and

  (b) the claimant has made a payment under the guarantee (whether to the lender or a co-guarantor) in respect of that amount; and

  (c) the claimant has not assigned any right to recover that amount which has accrued to him (whether by operation of law or otherwise) in consequence of his having made the payment; and

  (d) the lender and the borrower were not each other's spouses, or companies in the same group, when the loan was made or at any subsequent time and the claimant and the borrower were not each other's spouses, and the claimant and the lender were not companies in the same group, when the guarantee was given or at any subsequent time,

the said Part III shall have effect as if an allowable loss had accrued to the claimant when the payment was made; and the loss shall be equal to the payment made by him in respect of the amount mentioned in paragraph (a) above less any contribution payable to him by any co-guarantor in respect of the payment so made.

(5) Where an allowable loss has been treated under subsection (3) or (4) above as accruing to any person and the whole or any part of the outstanding amount mentioned in subsection (3) (a) or, as the case may be, subsection (4) (a) is at any time recovered by him, the said Part III shall have effect as if there had accrued to him at that time a chargeable gain equal to so much of the allowable loss as corresponds to the amount recovered.

(6) For the purposes of subsection (5) above, a person shall be treated as recovering an amount if he (or any other person by his direction) receives any money or money's worth in satisfaction of his right to recover that amount or in consideration of his assignment of the right to recover it; and where a person assigns such a right otherwise than by way of a bargain made at arm's length he shall be treated as receiving money or money's worth equal to the market value of the right at the time of the assignment.

(7) No amount shall be treated under this section as giving rise to an allowable loss or chargeable gain in the case of any person if it falls to be

taken into account in computing his income for the purposes of income tax or corporation tax.

(8) Where an allowable loss has been treated as accruing to a person under subsection (4) above by virtue of a payment made by him at any time under a guarantee—

(a) no chargeable gain shall accrue to him otherwise than under subsection (5) above; and

(b) no allowable loss shall accrue to him under the said Part III,

on his disposal of any rights that have accrued to him (whether by operation of law or otherwise) in consequence of his having made any payment under the guarantee at or after that time.

(9) References in this section to an amount having become irrecoverable do not include references to cases where the amount has become irrecoverable in consequence of the terms of the loan, of any arrangements of which the loan forms part, or of any act or omission by the lender or, in a case within subsection (4) above, the guarantor.

(10) In this section "spouses" means spouses who are living together (construed in accordance with section 45 (3) of the said Act of 1965), " trading company " has the meaning given by paragraph 11 of Schedule 16 to the Finance Act 1972 and " group " shall be construed in accordance with section 272 of the Taxes Act.

(11) Subsection (3) above applies where the loan is made after 11th April 1978 and subsection (4) above applies where the guarantee is given after that date.

GENERAL NOTE

This section permits a claim to be made for an allowable loss by a lender or guarantor (but not to persons interested under a contract of indemnity) if a loan becomes irrecoverable. The following conditions must be satisfied:

(a) the money lent must be used for, or in setting up, a trade (which includes a profession or vocation) other than the lending of money. By virtue of subs. (2) the relief is extended to the case where the borrower is a company which lends the money borrowed to another member of the group;

(b) the borrower is resident in the United Kingdom;

(c) the loan is not a secured debt (within F.A. 1965, Sched. 7, para. 5);

(d) the amount has become irrecoverable;

(e) the right to recover it has not been assigned;

(f) the loan was not made between spouses or companies in the same group;

(g) the loss is not included in the claimant's accounts for the purposes of income or corporation tax;

(h) in the case of a claim by a guarantor the guarantor must have made a payment under the guarantee and the guarantor and the borrower must not be spouses or companies in the same group;

(i) in the case of a claim by the lender the loan must have been made after April 11, 1978, and in the case of a guarantor the guarantee must have been made after April 11, 1978, though the loan may have been made before then.

It would seem that no claim can be made by a person to whom the right has been assigned, as opposed to the original lender.

Any amount subsequently recovered after a claim pursuant to this provision is to be treated as a chargeable gain (under subs. (6) there is extended meaning given to recovery).

Relief for private residences

50.—(1) In section 29 of the Finance Act 1965 (relief for private residences) after subsection (4) there shall be inserted—

" (4A) If at any time during an individual's period of ownership of a dwelling-house or part of a dwelling-house he—

(a) resides in living accommodation which is for him job-related within the meaning of paragraph 4A of Schedule 1 to the Finance Act 1974; and (*b*) intends in due course to occupy the dwelling-house or part of a dwelling-house as his only or main residence,

this section shall apply as if the dwelling-house or part of a dwelling-house were at that time occupied by him as a residence."

(2) The new subsection (4A) set out above applies where the time referred to in that subsection is after the passing of this Act.

GENERAL NOTE

The addition of this subsection in F.A. 1965, s. 29, ensures that the private residence relief conferred by that section for the purposes of capital gains tax shall not be affected if the individual ceases (or does not start) to occupy his dwelling-house (or part of it) for the following reasons, provided that he intends to occupy it in due course.

The occupation must be prevented because he is occupying living accommodation provided by reason of his or his spouse's employment because (i) it is necessary to enable performance of the duties of employment; or (ii) enables the better performance of those duties and is customary; or (iii) is part of special security arrangements, there being a special threat to the employee's security.

(There are special rules contained in para. 4A (4)–(6) of Sched. 1, F.A. 1974, if the employer is a company and the employee is a director.)

This provision only applies to periods occurring after the passing of the Act.

Part disposals of land

51.—(1) In paragraph 10 (3) (*a*) and (*b*) of Schedule 19 to the Finance Act 1969 (roll-over relief for gain on part disposal of land where consideration does not exceed £2,500) for " £2,500 " there shall be substituted "£10,000 ".

(2) This section applies with respect to any disposal after 5th April 1978.

GENERAL NOTE

This increases the relief available on a part disposal of land from £2,500 to £10,000 in respect of disposals after April 5, 1978.

Alteration of dispositions taking effect on death

52.—(1) For section 24 (11) of the Finance Act 1965 (deeds of family arrangement, etc.) there shall be substituted—

" (11) Subject to subsections (12) and (13) of this section, where within the period of two years after a person's death any of the dispositions (whether effected by will, under the law relating to intestacy or otherwise) of the property of which he was competent to dispose are varied, or the benefit conferred by any of those dispositions is disclaimed, by an instrument in writing made by the persons or any of the persons who benefit or would benefit under the dispositions—

(*a*) the variation or disclaimer shall not constitute a disposal for the purposes of this Part of this Act; and

(*b*) this section shall apply as if the variation had been effected by the deceased or, as the case may be, the disclaimed benefit had never been conferred.

(12) Subsection (11) of this section does not apply to a variation unless the person or persons making the instrument so elect by written notice given to the Board within six months after the date of the instrument or such longer time as the Board may allow.

(13) Subsection (11) of this section does not apply to a variation or disclaimer made for any consideration in money or money's worth other than consideration consisting of the making of a variation or disclaimer in respect of another of the dispositions.

(14) Subsection (11) of this section applies whether or not the administration of the estate is complete or the property has been distributed in accordance with the original dispositions."

(2) This section applies in relation to any variation or disclaimer made after the passing of this Act.

GENERAL NOTE

This changes the exemption given to what are commonly called family arrangements. It has been made to bring into line this exemption with that given for capital transfer tax purposes by s. 68.

The exemption operates if:

    (i) within two years after a death (as before);
    (ii) there is a variation of the dispositions the property of which the deceased was competent to dispose or a disclaimer of a benefit conferred by such a disposition (previously this section did not cover disclaimers);
    (iii) by an instrument in writing (this used to require " a deed of family arrangement " or similar instrument);
    (iv) made by any or all of the beneficiaries or potential beneficiaries. (This would seem to exclude any other persons being made parties to the arrangement.)

The effect is that the variation or disclaimer is not a disposal but instead it is treated as if the deceased had made the variation or not conferred the benefit disclaimed.

It is made clear that an arrangement involving consideration other than the redistribution of the property disposed of by the deceased will not qualify for the exemption. However, it would seem that it will not matter that any of the parties to the variation have prior to the variation received a benefit from the property. This is a point that the Revenue has previously taken but the new subs. (14) would seem to exclude such a point now. The same cannot be true of disclaimers in that under the general law the taking of a benefit presents a disclaimer.

To obtain the benefit of this exemption all the parties to the instrument must so elect within six months of its date (presumably the date of execution) or such longer time as allowed by the Board. This election must be unanimous otherwise the variation or disclaimer will be a disposal. Previously the operation of the exemption was automatic.

CHAPTER III

PROFIT SHARING SCHEMES

Approved profit sharing schemes: appropriated shares

53.—(1) The provisions of this section apply where, after 5th April 1979, the trustees of a profit sharing scheme which has been approved in accordance with Part I of Schedule 9 to this Act appropriate shares—

    (a) which have previously been acquired by the trustees, and
    (b) as to which the conditions in Part II of that Schedule are fulfilled,
to an individual who participates in the scheme.

(2) In this Chapter references to an approved scheme are references to a scheme approved as mentioned in subsection (1) above, and in relation to such a scheme—

    (a) any reference to a participant is a reference to an individual to whom the trustees of the scheme have appropriated shares; and
    (b) subject to section 57 below, any reference to a participant's shares is a reference to the shares which have been appropriated to him by the trustees of an approved scheme.

(3) Notwithstanding that, by virtue of such an appropriation of shares as is mentioned in subsection (1) above, the beneficial interest in the shares passes to the participant to whom they are appropriated—

(*a*) the value of the shares at the time of the appropriation shall be treated as not being income of his chargeable to tax under Schedule E; and

(*b*) he shall not be chargeable to income tax under that Schedule by virtue of section 79 (4) of the Finance Act 1972 (share incentive schemes) in respect of an increase in the market value of the shares or by virtue of section 67 of the Finance Act 1976 (employee shareholdings) in any case where the shares are appropriated to him at an under value within the meaning of that section.

(4) Any reference in this Chapter to the initial market value of any of a participant's shares is a reference to the market value of those shares determined,—

(*a*) except where paragraph (*b*) below applies, on the date on which the shares were appropriated to him; and

(*b*) if the Board and the trustees of the scheme agree in writing, on or by reference to such earlier date or dates as may be provided for in the agreement.

(5) Notwithstanding anything in the approved scheme concerned or in the trust instrument or in section 54 below, for the purposes of capital gains tax a participant shall be treated as absolutely entitled to his shares as against the trustees.

(6) Where the trustees of an approved scheme acquire any shares as to which the conditions in Part II of Schedule 9 to this Act are fulfilled and, within the period of eighteen months beginning with the date of their acquisition, those shares are appropriated in accordance with the scheme—

(*a*) section 16 of the Finance Act 1973 (additional rate tax on certain income accumulated under a trust) shall not apply to income consisting of dividends on those shares received by the trustees; and

(*b*) any gain accruing to the trustees on the appropriation of those shares shall not be a chargeable gain;

and, for the purpose of determining whether any shares are appropriated within that period of eighteen months, shares which were acquired at an earlier time shall be taken to be appropriated before shares of the same class which were acquired at a later time.

(7) The Board may by notice in writing require any person to furnish to them, within such time as the Board may direct (but not being less than thirty days), such information as the Board think necessary for the purposes of their functions under this Chapter, including, in particular, information to enable the Board—

(*a*) to determine whether to approve a scheme or withdraw an approval already given; and

(*b*) to determine the liability to tax, including capital gains tax, of any participant in an approved scheme.

(8) In the Table in section 98 of the Taxes Management Act 1970 (failure to make returns, furnish information etc.) the following shall be added in the first column—

" Section 53 (7) of the Finance Act 1978 ".

GENERAL NOTE

Chap. III of the Act is concerned with the establishment of " profit sharing schemes " able to qualify for certain tax reliefs. In broad terms the legislation follows method III of the Inland Revenue's consultative document concerning such schemes published on February 2, 1978. It is important to note that the legislation only has effect as from April 5, 1979.

A profit sharing scheme can only qualify for the reliefs if it is " approved " by the Revenue as satisfying the conditions of Pt. I of Sched. 9 to this Act. Under this Schedule the scheme must provide for the establishment of a body of trustees who, out of moneys paid to them by the company concerned, acquire shares (satisfying the conditions of Pt. II of Sched. 9), for allocation to employees (satisfying the conditions of Pt. III of Sched. 9). Payments made by the company concerned will be deductible for corporation tax purposes if certain conditions are met (see s. 60). Shares allocated in accordance with a scheme will not be taxable as the income of the employee at the time of allocation nor will any subsequent increase in the value of the shares be taxable under F.A. 1972, s. 79 (4) (see s. 53 (3)). Charges may be levied on a disposal of the shares by reference to their value at the time of appropriation (and not, if greater, their value at the time of disposal). No charge is levied on a disposal later than 10 years after the allocation of the shares. For disposals before that time a percentage of value is brought into charge which diminishes the longer the shares are held (see the definition of " the appropriate percentage " in s. 54 (7)).

To ensure that the legislation is not simply used to give relief to the higher paid, there is a ceiling to the value of shares that can be allocated to any one individual in any one tax year. Shares allocated to one individual in any one year cannot exceed £500 in value (see Sched. 9, para. 1 (3)).

S. 53, apart from generally introducing the new provisions, provides specifically:

- (i) for the Schedule E relief (subs. (3));
- (ii) for the definition of " the initial market value " which is important as being the value by reference to which charges to tax may be levied on subsequent disposals of the shares (subs. (4)); and
- (iii) for shares allocated to employees to be regarded as owned by them for capital gains tax purposes despite their being in fact held by trustees on the conditions specified in s. 54 (1) (subs. (5)).

In addition subs. (6) provides for relief from additional rate income tax for the trustees of a scheme on dividends accruing from shares prior to appropriation so long as the shares are in fact appropriated within 18 months from their acquisition. After appropriation any dividends paid will form part of the income of the employee (see Sched. 9, para. 14 (*a*)) and whether or not higher rate tax or the investment income surcharge is payable will depend upon the employee's general tax position. It is to be noted that subs. (6) gives no general income tax relief to the trustees. Thus, if payments made to the trustees are deposited by them in a bank, the trustees will be liable in respect of any interest paid to them to both the basic and additional rate of tax.

Subs. (6) further provides that no capital gains tax charge should arise to the trustees on an appropriation of shares but again only so long as the appropriation takes place within 18 months from acquisition.

S. 53 makes no mention of the capital transfer tax position of the trust. This is because in most cases relief should be available from any potential charge pursuant to the provisions of F.A. 1975, Sched. 5, para. 17.

The period of retention, the release date and the appropriate percentage

54.—(1) No scheme shall be approved as mentioned in subsection (1) of section 53 above unless the Board are satisfied that, whether under the terms of the scheme or otherwise, every participant in the scheme is bound in contract with the company concerned—

- (*a*) to permit his shares to remain in the hands of the trustees throughout the period of retention; and
- (*b*) not to assign, charge or otherwise dispose of his beneficial interest in his shares during that period; and
- (*c*) if he directs the trustees to transfer the ownership of his shares to him at any time before the release date, to pay to the trustees before the transfer takes place a sum equal to income tax at the basic rate on the appropriate percentage of the locked-in value of the shares at the time of the direction; and
- (*d*) not to direct the trustees to dispose of his shares at any time before the release date in any other way except by sale for the

best consideration in money that can reasonably be obtained at the time of the sale.

(2) Any obligation imposed on a participant by virtue of subsection (1) above shall not prevent the participant from—

(a) directing the trustees to accept an offer for any of his shares (in this paragraph referred to as " the original shares "), if the acceptance or agreement will result in a new holding, as defined in paragraph 4 of Schedule 7 to the Finance Act 1965 (roll-over relief for capital gains tax purposes in cases of reconstructions, amalgamations, etc.), being equated with the original shares for the purposes of capital gains tax; or

(b) directing the trustees to agree to a transaction affecting his shares or such of them as are of a particular class, if the transaction would be entered into pursuant to a compromise, arrangement or scheme applicable to or affecting—

    (i) all the ordinary share capital of the company in question or, as the case may be, all the shares of the class in question; or

    (ii) all the shares, or shares of the class in question, which are held by a class of shareholders identified otherwise than by reference to their employment or their participating in an approved scheme; or

(c) directing the trustees to accept an offer of cash, with or without other assets, for his shares if the offer forms part of a general offer which is made to holders of shares of the same class as his or of shares in the same company and which is made in the first instance on a condition such that if it is satisfied the person making the offer will have control of that company, within the meaning of section 302 of the Taxes Act; or

(d) agreeing, after the expiry of the period of retention, to sell the beneficial interest in his shares to the trustees for the same consideration as, in accordance with subsection (1) (d) above, would be required to be obtained for the shares themselves.

(3) If, in breach of his obligation under paragraph (b) of subsection (1) above, a participant assigns, charges or otherwise disposes of the beneficial interest in any of his shares, then, as respects those shares, he shall be treated for the purposes of this Chapter as if, at the time they were appropriated to him, he was ineligible to participate in the scheme; and section 58 below shall apply accordingly.

(4) In this Chapter " the period of retention ", in relation to any of a participant's shares, means the period beginning on the date on which they are appropriated to him and ending on the fifth anniversary of that date or, if it is earlier,—

(a) the date on which the participant ceases to be an employee or director of a relevant company by reason of injury or disability or on account of his being dismissed by reason of redundancy, within the meaning of the Redundancy Payments Act 1965 or the Contracts of Employment and Redundancy Payments Act (Northern Ireland) 1965; or

(b) the date on which the participant reaches pensionable age, as defined in Schedule 20 to the Social Security Act 1975; or

(c) the date of the participant's death.

(5) In subsection (4) (a) above, " relevant company " means the company concerned or, if the scheme in question is a group scheme, a participating company; and in the application of subsection (4) (a) above

to a participant in a group scheme, the participant shall not be treated as ceasing to be an employee or director of a relevant company until such time as he is no longer an employee or director of any of the participating companies.

(6) In this Chapter " the release date ", in relation to any of a participant's shares, means the fifteenth anniversary of the date on which the shares were appropriated to him.

(7) Subject to section 58 (4) below, for the purposes of provisions of this Chapter charging an individual to income tax under Schedule E by reason of the occurrence of an event relating to any of his shares, any reference to " the appropriate percentage " in relation to those shares shall be determined according to the time of that event, as follows:—

(a) if the event occurs during the period of retention of the shares, the appropriate percentage is 100 per cent.;

(b) if the event occurs after the expiry of the period of retention and before the seventh anniversary of the date on which the shares were appropriated to the participant, the appropriate percentage is 50 per cent.; and

(c) if the event occurs on or after the seventh anniversary of that date and before the tenth anniversary of it, the appropriate percentage is 25 per cent.

GENERAL NOTE

Shares allocated under a scheme must remain in the hands of the trustees for " the period of retention " which is normally five years from the date of allocation save that it is a shorter period if the employee has died, has reached pensionable age, or has left the employment of the company in the circumstances referred to in subs. (4) (a). After the expiry of " the period of retention " but prior to " the release date "—10 years from the date of allocation—the shares can be transferred to the employee but only on his making to the trustees the appropriate payment (subs. (1) (c)). On any disposal of the shares prior to " the release date," charges under Schedule E will arise on their disposal.

Subs. (7) defines " the appropriate percentage " which is important for the purposes of the charge under Schedule E levied by s. 55 where shares subject to a scheme are disposed of prior to " the release date."

Disposal of scheme shares

55.—(1) If the trustees dispose of any of a participant's shares at any time before the release date or, if it is earlier, the date of the participant's death, then, subject to subsections (3) and (4) below, the participant shall be chargeable to income tax under Schedule E for the year of assessment in which the disposal takes place on the appropriate percentage of the locked-in value of the shares at the time of the disposal.

(2) Subject to sections 57 and 58 (6) below, any reference in this Chapter to the locked-in value of any of a participant's shares at any time shall be construed as follows:—

(a) if prior to that time the participant has become chargeable to income tax by virtue of section 56 below on a percentage of the amount or value of any capital receipt (within the meaning of that section) which is referable to those shares, the locked-in value of the shares is the amount by which their initial market value exceeds the amount or value of that capital receipt or, if there has been more than one such receipt, the aggregate of them; and

(b) in any other case, the locked-in value of the shares is their initial market value.

(3) Subject to subsection (4) below if, on a disposal of shares falling within subsection (1) above, the proceeds of the disposal are less than the locked-in value of the shares at the time of the disposal, subsection (1) above shall have effect as if that locked-in value were reduced to an amount equal to the proceeds of the disposal.

(4) If, at any time prior to the disposal of any of a participant's shares, a payment was made to the trustees to enable them to exercise rights arising under a rights issue, then, subject to subsection (5) below, subsections (1) and (3) above shall have effect as if the proceeds of the disposal were reduced by an amount equal to that proportion of that payment or, if there was more than one, of the aggregate of those payments which, immediately before the disposal, the market value of the shares disposed of bore to the market value of all the participant's shares held by the trustees at that time.

(5) For the purposes of subsection (4) above—

    (*a*) no account shall be taken of any payment to the trustees if or to the extent that it consists of the proceeds of a disposal of rights arising under a rights issue; and

    (*b*) in relation to a particular disposal the amount of the payment or, as the case may be, of the aggregate of the payments referred to in that subsection shall be taken to be reduced by an amount equal to the total of the reduction (if any) previously made under that subsection in relation to earlier disposals;

and any reference in subsection (4) or paragraph (*a*) above to the rights arising under a rights issue is a reference to rights conferred in respect of a participant's shares, being rights to be allotted, on payment, other shares in the same company.

(6) Where the disposal referred to in subsection (1) above is made from a holding of shares which were appropriated to the participant at different times, then, in determining for the purposes of this Chapter—

    (*a*) the initial market value and the locked-in value of each of those shares, and

    (*b*) the percentage which is the appropriate percentage in relation to each of those shares,

the disposal shall be treated as being of shares which were appropriated earlier before those which were appropriated later.

(7) If at any time the participant's beneficial interest in any of his shares is disposed of, the shares in question shall be treated for the purposes of this Chapter as having been disposed of at that time by the trustees for (subject to subsection (8) below) the like consideration as was obtained for the disposal of the beneficial interest; and for the purpose of this subsection there is no disposal of the participant's beneficial interest if and at the time when—

    (*a*) in England and Wales or Northern Ireland that interest becomes vested in any person on the insolvency of the participant or otherwise by operation of law, or

    (*b*) in Scotland, that interest becomes vested in a judicial factor, in a trustee on the participant's sequestrated estate or in a trustee for the benefit of the participant's creditors.

(8) If—

    (*a*) a disposal of shares falling within subsection (1) above is a transfer to which section 54 (1) (*c*) above applies, or

    (*b*) the Board is of opinion that any other disposal falling within that subsection is not at arm's length and accordingly direct that this subsection shall apply, or

    (*c*) a disposal of shares falling within that subsection is one

which is treated as taking place by virtue of subsection (7)
above and takes place within the period of retention,
then for the purposes of this Chapter the proceeds of the disposal shall
be taken to be equal to the market value of the shares at the time of the
disposal.

(9) In subsection (5) above " shares ", in the context of shares
allotted or to be allotted on a rights issue, includes securities and rights
of any description.

GENERAL NOTE
This section provides for the Schedule E charge on a disposal of the allocated
shares before " the release date " or, if earlier, the date of the employee's death.
The charge is levied on " the appropriate percentage " of the " locked-in value " of
the shares. Locked-in value is defined as " the initial market value " (s. 53 (4))
of the shares save where a capital receipt has been received by the employee prior to
the date of the disposal (which will itself be brought into charge—see s. 56) or
where the proceeds of sale of the shares are less than what would otherwise be
taken to be their locked-in value. Increases in value of the shares after allocation
are not brought into charge.

A charge can be levied whether the trustees of the scheme dispose of the allocated
shares or the employee disposes of his beneficial interest in those shares (see
subs. (7)). In addition a charge arises even if the transfer made prior to the
release date is from the trustees to the employee. In this latter case in order to
determine the extent of any charge arising, the shares are regarded as being
disposed of at market value (subs. (8)).

Capital receipts in respect of scheme shares

56.—(1) Subject to the provisions of this section if, in respect of or by
reference to any of a participant's shares, the trustees become entitled,
before the release date, to receive any money or money's worth (in this
section referred to as a " capital receipt "), the participant shall be
chargeable to income tax under Schedule E for the year of assessment
in which the entitlement arises on the appropriate percentage (determined as at the time when the trustees become so entitled) of the amount
or value of the receipt.

(2) Money or money's worth is not a capital receipt for the purposes
of this section if or, as the case may be, to the extent that—

   (a) it constitutes income in the hands of the recipient for the purposes
       of income tax; or

   (b) it consists of the proceeds of a disposal falling within section 55
       above; or

   (c) it consists of new shares within the meaning of section 57 below.

(3) If, pursuant to a direction given by or on behalf of the participant
or any person in whom the beneficial interest in the participant's shares
is for the time being vested, the trustees—

   (a) dispose of some of the rights arising under a rights issue, as
       defined in section 55 (5) above, and

   (b) use the proceeds of that disposal to exercise other such rights,

the money or money's worth which constitutes the proceeds of that
disposal is not a capital receipt for the purposes of this section.

(4) If, apart from this subsection, the amount or value of a capital
receipt would exceed the sum which, immediately before the entitlement
to the receipt arose, was the locked-in value of the shares to which the
receipt is referable, subsection (1) above shall have effect as if the
amount or value of the receipt were equal to that locked-in value.

(5) Subsection (1) above does not apply in relation to a receipt if the
entitlement to it arises after the death of the participant to whose shares
it is referable.

General Note
Capital distributions received in respect of allocated shares before "the release date" give rise to a charge to tax under Schedule E in the same way as a charge would arise on a disposal of the shares before that date. The charge is levied on the amount received save where it exceeds the "locked-in value" (as defined in s. 55) when it is limited to the "locked-in value." Any charge arising under this section reduces the possible charge that could be levied under s. 55 on a disposal of the shares (see s. 55 (2) (a)).

Company reconstructions, amalgamations etc.

57.—(1) This section applies where there occurs in relation to any of a participant's shares (in this section referred to as " the original holding ") a transaction (in this section referred to as a " company reconstruction ") which results in a new holding, as defined in paragraph 4 of Schedule 7 to the Finance Act 1965 (roll-over relief for capital gains tax purposes in cases of reconstructions, amalgamations, etc.), being equated with the original holding for the purposes of capital gains tax.

(2) Where an issue of shares of any of the following descriptions (in respect of which a charge to income tax arises) is made as part of a company reconstruction, those shares shall be treated for the purposes of this section as not forming part of the new holding, that is to say,—

(a) redeemable shares or securities issued as mentioned in section 233 (2) (c) of the Taxes Act (issues not wholly for new consideration);

(b) share capital issued in circumstances such that section 234 (1) of the Taxes Act applies (bonus issue following repayment of share capital); and

(c) share capital to which section 34 of the Finance (No. 2) Act 1975 applies (stock dividends).

(3) In this section—

(a) " new shares " means shares comprised in the new holding which were issued in respect of, or otherwise represent, shares comprised in the original holding; and

(b) " the corresponding shares ", in relation to any new shares, means those shares in respect of which the new shares are issued or which the new shares otherwise represent.

(4) Subject to the following provisions of this section, references in this Chapter to a participant's shares shall be construed, after the time of the company reconstruction, as being or, as the case may be, as including references to any new shares, and, for the purposes of this Chapter—

(a) a company reconstruction shall be treated as not involving a disposal of shares comprised in the original holding;

(b) the date on which any new shares are to be treated as having been appropriated to the participant shall be that on which the corresponding shares were appropriated; and

(c) the conditions in Part II of Schedule 9 to this Act shall be treated as fulfilled with respect to any new shares if they were (or were treated as) fulfilled with respect to the corresponding shares.

(5) In relation to shares comprised in the new holding, subsection (2) of section 55 above shall apply as if the references in that subsection to the initial market value of the shares were references to their locked-in value immediately after the company reconstruction, which shall be determined as follows : —

(a) ascertain the aggregate amount of the locked-in value immediately before the reconstruction of those shares comprised in the original holding which had at that time the same locked-in value; and

(b) distribute that amount pro rata among—

(i) such of those shares as remain in the new holding, and

      (ii) any new shares in relation to which those shares are
        the corresponding shares,
      according to their market value immediately after the re-
construction;
and paragraph (*a*) of that subsection shall apply only to capital receipts
after the date of the reconstruction.

    (6) For the purposes of this Chapter if, as part of a company
reconstruction, trustees become entitled to a capital receipt, within the
meaning of section 56 above, their entitlement to the capital receipt shall
be taken to arise before the new holding comes into being and, for the
purposes of subsection (5) above, before the date on which the locked-in
value of any shares comprised in the original holding falls to be
ascertained.

    (7) In the context of a new holding, any reference in this section to
shares includes securities and rights of any description which form part
of the new holding for the purposes of Part III of the Finance Act 1965.

GENERAL NOTE
    This section provides for the consequences of company reconstructions (*e.g.*
where there are bonus issues of shares or where there are share for share exchanges
on company takeovers) in order to:
    (i) ensure that they will not be treated as involving disposals of the original
        shares so as to give rise to a possible charge under s. 55; and
    (ii) equate the possible charge under s. 55 or s. 56 on disposals of the new
        shares to that which would have arisen on disposals of the original
        holding.
Company reconstructions involving bonus issues of shares which give rise to an
income tax charge are not treated as " new shares " for the purpose of this section
(subs. (2)). Thus no charges under s. 55 or s. 56 can arise on their disposal.

Excess or unauthorised shares

    58.—(1) If the total of the initial market values of all the shares
which are appropriated to an individual in any one year of assessment
(whether under a single approved scheme or under two or more such
schemes) exceeds £500, subsections (4) to (7) below shall apply to the
excess shares, that is to say, any share which caused that limit to be
exceeded and any share appropriated after that limit was exceeded.

    (2) For the purposes of subsection (1) above, if a number of shares
is appropriated to an individual at the same time under two or more
approved schemes, the same proportion of the shares appropriated at that
time under each scheme shall be regarded as being appropriated before
the limit of £500 is exceeded.

    (3) If the trustees of an approved scheme appropriate shares to an
individual at a time when he is ineligible to participate in the scheme by
virtue of Part III of Schedule 9 to this Act, the following provisions of
this section shall apply in relation to those shares, and in those provisions
those shares are referred to as " unauthorised shares ".

    (4) For the purposes of any provision of this Chapter charging an
individual to income tax under Schedule E by reason of the occurrence
of an event relating to any of his shares—
    (*a*) the appropriate percentage in relation to excess or unauthorised
        shares shall in every case be 100 per cent.; and
    (*b*) without prejudice to section 55 (6) above, the event shall be
        treated as relating to shares which are not excess or unauthorised
        shares before shares which are.

    (5) Excess or unauthorised shares which have not been disposed of
before the release date or, if it is earlier, the date of the death of the
participant whose shares they are shall be treated for the purposes of this

Chapter as having been disposed of by the trustees immediately before the release date or, as the case may require, the date of the participant's death, for a consideration equal to their market value at that time.

(6) The locked-in value at any time of any excess or unauthorised shares shall be their market value at that time.

(7) Where there has been a company reconstruction to which section 57 above applies, a new share (within the meaning of that section) shall be treated as an excess or unauthorised share if the corresponding share (within the meaning of that section) or, if there was more than one corresponding share, each of them was an excess or unauthorised share.

P.A.Y.E. deduction of tax

59.—(1) Subject to subsections (3) and (4) below, where the trustees of an approved scheme receive a sum of money which constitutes (or forms part of)—

(a) the proceeds of a disposal of shares falling within section 55 (1) above, or

(b) a capital receipt, within the meaning of section 56 above,

the trustees shall pay out of that sum of money to the company specified in subsection (2) below an amount equal to that on which income tax is payable in accordance with the section in question; and the company shall then pay over that amount to the participant but in so doing shall make a P.A.Y.E. deduction.

(2) The company to which the payment mentioned in subsection (1) above is to be made is the company—

(a) of which the participant is an employee or director at the time the trustees receive the sum of money referred to in that subsection, and

(b) whose employees are at that time eligible (subject to the terms of the scheme and to Schedule 9 to this Act) to be participants in the approved scheme concerned,

and if there is more than one company which falls within paragraphs (a) and (b) above, such one of those companies as the Board may direct.

(3) Where the trustees of an approved scheme receive a sum of money to which subsection (1) above applies but—

(a) there is no company which falls within paragraphs (a) and (b) of subsection (2) above, or

(b) the Board is of opinion that it is impracticable for the company which falls within those paragraphs (or, as the case may be, any of them) to make a P.A.Y.E. deduction and accordingly direct that this subsection shall apply,

then, in paying over to the participant the proceeds of the disposal or the capital receipt, the trustees shall make a P.A.Y.E. deduction in respect of an amount equal to that on which income tax is payable as mentioned in subsection (1) above as if the participant were a former employee of the trustees.

(4) Where the trustees of an approved scheme receive a sum of money to which subsection (1) above applies and the Board direct that this subsection shall apply—

   (a) the trustees shall make the payment mentioned in that subsection to the company specified in the Board's direction; and

   (b) that company shall pay over that amount to the participant but in so doing shall make a P.A.Y.E. deduction, and for that purpose if the participant is not an employee of that company he shall be treated as a former employee;

but no such direction shall be given except with the consent of the trustees, the company or companies (if any) specified in subsection (2) above and the company specified in the direction.

(5) Where in accordance with this section any person is required to make a P.A.Y.E. deduction in respect of any amount, that amount shall be treated for the purposes of section 204 of the Taxes Act (pay as you earn) and any regulations made under that section as an amount of income payable to the recipient and assessable to income tax under Schedule E, and accordingly such deduction shall be made as is required by those regulations.

(6) Where, in connection with a transfer of a participant's shares to which paragraph (c) of subsection (1) of section 54 above applies, the trustees receive such a sum as is referred to in that paragraph, that sum shall be treated for the purposes of the Income Tax Acts—

   (a) as a sum deducted by the trustees pursuant to a requirement to make a P.A.Y.E. deduction under subsection (3) above; and

   (b) as referable to the income tax to which, as a result of the transfer, the participant is chargeable by virtue of section 55 above.

(7) Unless the Board otherwise direct, in the application of this section to a sum of money which constitutes (or forms part of) the proceeds of a disposal of, or a capital receipt referable to, excess or unauthorised shares, within the meaning of section 58 above, the trustees shall determine the amount of the payment mentioned in subsection (1) above or, as the case may be, the amount of the P.A.Y.E. deduction to be made under subsection (3) above as if the shares were not excess shares.

General Note

This section provides for charges to tax levied in respect of shares allocated under profit sharing schemes to be met so far as possible by deduction of tax at source through the operation of the P.A.Y.E. system.

In so far as a charge arises on a transfer of shares by the trustees to an employee prior to " the release date " the payment made by the employee pursuant to s. 54 (1) (c) is treated as a credit against tax due from him (subs. (6)).

Schedule D deduction of payments to trustees

60.—(1) Any sum expended by the company concerned or, in the case of a group scheme, by a participating company in making a payment to the trustees of an approved scheme shall be included—

   (a) in the sums to be deducted in computing for the purposes of Schedule D the profits or gains of a trade carried on by that company, or

   (b) if that company is an investment company within the meaning of section 304 of the Taxes Act or a company in the case of which that section applies by virtue of section 305 of that Act, in the sums to be deducted as expenses of management in computing the profits of the company for the purposes of corporation tax,

if, and only if, one of the conditions in subsection (2) below is fulfilled.

(2) The conditions referred to in subsection (1) above are—

(a) that before the expiry of the relevant period the sum in question is applied by the trustees in the acquisition of shares for appropriation to individuals who are eligible to participate in the scheme by virtue of their being or having been employees or directors of the company making the payment; and

(b) that the sum is necessary to meet the reasonable expenses of the trustees in administering the scheme.

(3) For the purposes of subsection (2) (a) above, " the relevant period " means the period of nine months beginning on the day following the end of the period of account in which the sum in question is charged as an expense of the company incurring the expenditure or such longer period as the Board may allow by notice in writing given to that company.

(4) For the purposes of this section, the trustees of an approved scheme shall be taken to apply sums paid to them in the order in which the sums are received by them.

GENERAL NOTE

Payments by companies to the trustees of a scheme are deductible for corporation tax purposes only if either:

(a) the payment is within nine months applied to acquire shares for allocation; or

(b) the payment is necessary to meet administration expenses.

Unless one or other of these conditions can be satisfied no deduction is permissible even though had this section not been introduced a deduction could have been obtained.

Interpretation and construction

61.—(1) In this Chapter—

" the appropriate percentage ", in relation to any shares, shall be construed in accordance with section 54 (7) above;

" approved scheme " shall be construed in accordance with section 53 (2) above;

" the company concerned " has the meaning assigned to it by paragraph 1 (1) of Schedule 9 to this Act;

" group scheme " and, in relation to such a scheme, " participating company " have the meaning assigned by paragraph 1 (2) of that Schedule;

" initial market value ", in relation to any shares, shall be construed in accordance with section 53 (4) above;

" locked-in value ", in relation to any shares, shall be construed in accordance with section 55 (2) above;

" market value ", in relation to any shares, means their market value as determined in accordance with Part III of the Finance Act 1965 (capital gains tax);

" participant " shall be construed in accordance with section 53 (2) (a) above;

" the period of retention " has the meaning assigned to it by section 54 (4) above;

" the release date " has the meaning assigned to it by section 54 (6) above;

" shares " includes stock;

" the trust instrument ", in relation to an approved scheme, means the instrument referred to in paragraph 1 (3) (c) of Schedule 9 to this Act; and

" the trustees ", in relation to an approved scheme or a participant's shares, means the body of persons for the establishment of which the scheme must provide as mentioned in paragraph 1 (3) of Schedule 9 to this Act.

(2) Any provision of this Chapter with respect to—

(a) the order in which any of a participant's shares are to be treated as disposed of for the purposes of this Chapter, or

(b) the shares in relation to which an event is to be treated as occurring for any such purpose,

shall have effect notwithstanding any direction given to the trustees with respect to shares of a particular description or to shares appropriated to the participant at a particular time.

(3) For the purposes of capital gains tax—

(a) no deduction shall be made from the consideration for the disposal of any shares by reason only that an amount determined under this Chapter is chargeable to income tax;

(b) any charge to income tax by virtue of section 56 above shall be disregarded in determining whether a distribution is a capital distribution within the meaning of paragraph 3 of Schedule 7 to the Finance Act 1965; and

(c) nothing in any such provision as is referred to in subsection (2) above shall affect the rules applicable to the computation of a gain accruing on a part disposal of a holding of shares or other securities which were acquired at different times.

GENERAL NOTE

Subs. (3) has the important effect that any charge to capital gains tax arising on a disposal of shares allocated under a profit sharing scheme is unaffected by an income tax charge being raised on the same disposal pursuant to s. 55.

PART IV

CAPITAL TRANSFER TAX

Reduction of tax

62.—(1) For the Tables in section 37 (3) of the Finance Act 1975 (rates of tax) there shall be substituted the Tables in Schedule 10 to this Act.

(2) Subsection (1) above applies to any chargeable transfer made after 26th October 1977.

(3) Where a person who has made a chargeable transfer on or before the said 26th October dies after that date and within three years of the transfer, additional tax shall be chargeable by reason of his death only if, and to the extent that, it would have been so chargeable if the first of the new Tables had applied to that transfer.

(4) Where the rate of tax applicable to a capital distribution made after the said 26th October falls to be determined under sub-paragraph (2) of paragraph 7 of Schedule 5 to the said Act of 1975 by reference to a relevant transfer made on or before that date, the amount of tax referred to in paragraph (a) of that sub-paragraph shall be calculated as if the second of the new Tables had applied to that transfer.

(5) Where the value of any trees or underwood has been left out of account under Schedule 9 to the said Act of 1975 in determining the value transferred by the chargeable transfer made on a death on or before the said 26th October and tax is chargeable under paragraph 2 of that Schedule on a disposal of the trees or underwood after that date, the rate or rates mentioned in paragraph 3 of that Schedule shall be determined as if the first of the new Tables had applied to that transfer.

(6) Where tax is chargeable under section 78 of the Finance Act 1976 (works of art etc.) by reason of a chargeable event occurring after the said 26th October and the rate or rates at which it is charged fall to be determined under the provisions of section 79 (1) (*b*) (ii) or 81 (4) (*b*) of that Act by reference to a death which occurred, or a settlement which ceased to exist, on or before that date, those provisions shall have effect as if the new Tables had been in force at the time of the death or when the settlement ceased to exist.

(7) Any question whether any, and if so what, tax is repayable or ceases to be payable by virtue of subsection (1) (*a*) of section 87 of the said Act of 1976 (mutual transfers) shall, where—

(*a*) the donor's transfer was on or before the said 26th October; and

(*b*) the donee's transfer is after that date,

be determined as if the new Tables had applied to the donor's transfer; but this subsection shall not be construed as affecting the amount of tax which, under subsection (3) of that section, falls to be taken into account in calculating the cancelled value.

(8) In subsection (2) above the reference to a chargeable transfer made after the said 26th October does not include a reference to any chargeable transfer which by virtue of section 114 (2) of the said Act of 1976 (transfers reported late) is treated as made after that date but was in fact made on or before it.

GENERAL NOTE

This section puts into effect the reduction in the rates of tax announced by the Chancellor on October 26, 1977. The threshold is increased and the starting point of each taxable band is raised; the size of each band and the tax rates are unchanged. The new Tables are set out in Sched. 10 to the Act and the charges apply to any chargeable transfer made after October 26, 1977.

Subs. (2)

This refers to the occasion where a person dies within three years of making a chargeable transfer and additional tax becomes payable under the provisions of F.A. 1975, s. 25 (4). This subsection now provides that any additional tax which becomes payable on a death shall be charged according to the first of the new Tables where the original transfer was made on or before October 26, 1977, and the transferor dies after that date but within three years.

Subs. (4)

This refers to a capital distribution made after October 26, 1977, where the rate of tax applicable is determined under the provisions of F.A. 1975, Sched. 5, para. 7 (2) with reference to a relevant transfer made after October 26, 1977. This subsection provides that the second of the new Tables shall be used to calculate the amount of tax payable on such capital distribution.

Subs. (5)

This refers to the disposal of trees or underwood after October 26, 1977, and where an election was made to the effect that the value of the trees and underwood should be left out of account under the provisions of F.A. 1975, Sched. 9, in determining the value transferred by the chargeable transfer made on a death on or before October 26, 1977. On a disposal after that date tax is chargeable at the rate or rates determined under the provisions of F.A. 1975, Sched. 9, para. 3, and for this purpose the first of the new Tables shall apply.

Subs. (6)

Again this is an amendment consequent upon the changes in the rates of tax and refers to F.A. 1976, s. 78, which defines a chargeable event which may arise after a conditional exemption for works of art, etc., has been granted. Where the chargeable event occurs after October 26, 1977, and the conditional exemption was granted on a death or the termination of a settlement before that date then the rate or rates of tax applicable to the chargeable event which fall to be determined under F.A. 1976, s. 79 (1) (*b*) (ii) or s. 81 (4) (*b*) are to be calculated as if the new Tables were applicable at the date the conditional exemption was granted.

Subs. (7)

This refers to the mutual transfer provisions of F.A. 1976, ss. 86 and 87, under which, on the donee making a transfer back to the donor, any tax paid by the donor originally is repaid. The effect of this subsection is that where a transfer is made by a donor before October 26, 1977, and the transfer back made by the donee is after that date (but within the time limit set by ss. 86 and 87) the donor may only claim relief on the basis of the new Tables which will result in the donor obtaining less relief because the transfer back (as compared to the original transfer) is calculated at a tax rate with an increased threshold and starting points for the bands.

Subs. (8)

This restricts the effect of s. 62 (2) of the Act (which implements the new Tables). The new Tables will not apply to a chargeable transfer which by virtue of F.A. 1976, s. 114 (2), is treated as made after October 26, 1977, but was in fact made on or before that date. S. 114 deals with the case where the transfers of value are made and tax on the second transfer is accepted by the Board in full satisfaction before the first transfer is reported or discovered by the Board. S. 114 (2) provides that the earlier transfer shall be treated as if it had been made on the date on which it was discovered or, if the later transfer is made on death, immediately before the later transfer.

Exemption limit for transfers to non-domiciled spouses

63.—(1) In paragraph 1 (2) and (3) of Schedule 6 to the Finance Act 1975 (exemption limit for transfers to non-domiciled spouse) for " £15,000 " there shall be substituted " £25,000 ".

(2) This section applies to any transfer of value made after 26th October 1977.

General Note

This increases the exemption limit for transfers to non-domiciled spouses from £15,000 to £25,000 by amending F.A. 1975, Sched. 6, para. 1 (2) and (3). This section applies to any transfer of value made after 26 October, 1977.

Further relief for business property

64.—(1) Schedule 10 to the Finance Act 1976 (relief for business property) shall be amended as follows.

(2) In sub-paragraph (1) of paragraph 2 for the words " 30 per cent." there shall be substituted the words " the appropriate percentage " and after that sub-paragraph there shall be inserted—

" (1A) The appropriate percentage is—
> (*a*) in the case of property falling within paragraph 3 (1) (*a*) or (*b*) below, 50 per cent.;
> (*b*) in the case of property falling within paragraph 3 (1) (*bb*) below, 20 per cent.;
> (*c*) in the case of property falling within paragraph 3 (1) (*c*) below, 30 per cent."

(3) In paragraph 3 (1) after paragraph (*b*) there shall be inserted—

" (*bb*) shares in a company which do not fall within paragraph (*b*) above and are not quoted on a recognised stock exchange; and ".

(4) After paragraph 3 (1) there shall be inserted—

" (1A) Shares in or securities of a company do not fall within sub-paragraph (1) (b) above if—

  (a) they would not have been sufficient, without other property, to give the transferor control of the company immediately before the transfer; and

  (b) their value is taken by virtue of paragraph 9A of Schedule 10 to the Finance Act 1975 to be less than the value previously determined."

(5) At the end of paragraph 4 there shall be inserted—

" (5) Sub-paragraph (1) (b) above does not apply to shares falling within paragraph 3 (1) (bb) above; but where such shares owned by the transferor immediately before the transfer would under any of the provisions of paragraphs 4 to 7 of Schedule 7 to the Finance Act 1965 be identified with other shares previously owned by him his period of ownership of the first-mentioned shares shall be treated for the purposes of sub-paragraph (1) (a) above as including his period of ownership of the other shares."

(6) In paragraph 1 for the words " the amount transferred " there shall be substituted the words " the value transferred "; and in that paragraph (and section 73 (b) of the said Act of 1976) the words " made " and " treated as made " shall be omitted.

(7) Subsection (6) above shall be deemed always to have had effect and the other provisions of this section shall apply where the transfer of value is made after 26th October 1977.

GENERAL NOTE

This section amends F.A. 1976, Sched. 10, which provides for relief for business property.

Subs. (2)

This amends F.A. 1976, Sched. 10, para. 2 (1) by deleting the words " 30 per cent." and inserting a new sub-paragraph, F.A. 1976, Sched. 10, para. 2 (1A), which introduces the new rates for business relief.

The new rates are 50 per cent. for controlling shareholdings and interests in unincorporated businesses, 20 per cent. for minority shareholdings in unquoted companies and 30 per cent. for any land or building, machinery or plant which was used wholly or mainly for the purposes of a business carried on by a company controlled by the transferor or by a partnership of which the transferor was then a partner.

Subs. (3)

This inserts a new sub-para. 3 (1) (bb). This sub-paragraph defines the relevant business property to which the new 20 per cent. business relief applies, namely a minority shareholding in an unquoted company.

Subs. (4)

This subsection restricts the definition of control and refers to shares or securities of a company which are not by themselves sufficient, without other property, to give the transferor control of the company and their value is taken by virtue of F.A. 1975, Sched. 10, para. 9A, to be less than the value previously determined.

This paragraph gives relief where a holding of property owned by the deceased will be halved having regard to any other property affecting its value (*e.g.* an interest in possession under a settlement on related property) and within three years of death is sold by qualifying sale and the sale proceeds are less than the value on death, having regard to the other holdings. In such circumstances the shares or securities do not fall within F.A. 1975, Sched. 10, para. 3 (1) (b) (namely shares which give the transferor control of the company and thus attract 50 per cent. business relief.).

Subs. (5)

This adds a new sub-para. (5) to Sched. 10, para. 4 which provides that para. 4 (1) (b) shall not apply to para. 3 (1) (bb) (minority shareholdings in unquoted companies). Para. 4 provides for a minimum period of ownership which qualifies the property for inclusion within the term " relevant business property." This subsection provides that in the case of a minority shareholding the two-year period of ownership shall be deemed to be fulfilled if before acquiring the minority shareholding the transferor owned shares which could be identified with the minority shareholding under the provisions of F.A. 1965, Sched. 7, paras. 4 to 7, and taken together he held both holdings for two years. These provisions are concerned with company reorganisation, amalgamations, etc., and provide that where there is a reorganisation of the company's share capital and the original shares are replaced by a new holding, no disposal shall be deemed to have been made and that both holdings shall be regarded as one asset.

Further relief for woodlands

65.—(1) In paragraph 3 of Schedule 9 to the Finance Act 1975 (basis and rate of tax chargeable on disposal where value of trees or underwood has been left out of account under that Schedule) the existing provisions shall become sub-paragraph (1) and at the end there shall be inserted—

" (2) Where, if the value of the trees or underwood had not been left out of account in determining the value transferred on the death of the person in question—

(a) it would have been taken into account in determining the value of any relevant business property for the purposes of relief under Schedule 10 to the Finance Act 1976 in relation to the transfer of value made on his death; or

(b) it would have been so taken into account if that Schedule had then been in force,

the amount on which tax is chargeable under this paragraph shall be reduced by 50 per cent."

(2) This section applies to disposals after 26th October 1977.

GENERAL NOTE

This amends Sched. 9, para. 3 (1), by adding a new sub-para. (2) to para. 3. This provides that where an election has been made to defer a charge to tax on the transfer of trees or underwood, business relief will be available on the subsequent disposal so long as business relief would have been available when the election was made to defer the charge. The relief will be at the rate of 50 per cent. and will apply to disposals from October 26, 1977.

Definition of control of company

66.—(1) In sub-paragraph (7) of paragraph 13 of Schedule 4 to the Finance Act 1975 (under which a person is treated as controlling a company if he controls a majority of the votes capable of being exercised on all questions, or on any particular question, affecting the company) the words " or on any particular question " shall be omitted but after paragraph (b) there shall be inserted " and

(c) where a company has shares or securities of any class giving powers of voting limited to either or both of the following—

(i) the question of winding up the company;

(ii) any question primarily affecting shares or securities of that class,

the reference in the preceding provisions of this sub-paragraph to all questions affecting the company as a whole shall be read as a reference to all such questions except any in relation to which those powers are capable of being exercised."

(2) Subsection (1) above applies both for the purposes of the said paragraph 13 (payment of tax by instalments) and for the purposes of the provisions to which the said sub-paragraph (7) applies by virtue of—

(a) paragraph 3 (7) or 4 (b) or (bb) of Schedule 8 to the said Act of 1975 (relief for agricultural property);

(b) paragraph 13 (2) of Schedule 10 to the Finance Act 1976 (relief for business property); or

(c) section 49 (6) of the Finance Act 1977 (excluded property).

(3) This section does not affect the operation of the said paragraph 13 or of the provisions mentioned in subsection (2) above .in relation to any transfer of value made before 20th April 1978.

GENERAL NOTE

This section amends F.A. 1975, Sched. 4, para. 13 (7) which provides that a person is treated as controlling a company if he controls a majority of the votes capable of being exercised on all questions or any particular question affecting the company. This section is intended to prevent the situation where shares could be created which had voting rights on a particular question and whereby the holder of those shares could be said to have control of the company. Subs. (1) adds a new sub-para. (c) to F.A. 1975, Sched. 4, para. 13 (7); this was included at Report Stage because the scope of the original clause was too wide. The new sub-paragraph permits the existence of shares with voting rights which if their powers of voting are limited to a winding up or if the powers primarily affect shares or securities of that class then the existence of these shares are excluded from consideration, thus leaving the person holding the remainder of the shares within the definition of control of the company.

Employee trusts

67.—(1) Subject to the provisions of this section, a transfer of value made by an individual who is beneficially entitled to shares in a company is an exempt transfer to the extent that the value transferred is attributable to shares in or securities of the company which become comprised in a settlement if the trusts of the settlement are of the description specified in paragraph 17 (1) of Schedule 5 to the Finance Act 1975 and the persons for whose benefit the trusts permit the settled property to be applied include all or most of the persons employed by or holding office with the company.

(2) Subsection (1) above does not apply unless at the date of the transfer, or at a subsequent date not more than one year thereafter, both the following conditions are satisfied, that is to say—

(a) the trustees—

(i) hold more than one half of the ordinary shares in the company; and

(ii) have powers of voting on all questions affecting the company as a whole which if exercised would yield a majority of the votes capable of being exercised thereon; and

(b) there are no provisions in any agreement or instrument affecting the company's constitution or management or its shares or securities whereby the condition in paragraph (a) above can cease to be satisfied without the consent of the trustees.

(3) Where the company has shares or securities of any class giving powers of voting limited to either or both of the following—

(a) the question of winding up the company;

(b) any question primarily affecting shares or securities of that class,

the reference in subsection (2) (a) (ii) above to all questions affecting the company as a whole shall be read as a reference to all such questions except any in relation to which those powers are capable of being exercised.

(4) Subject to subsection (5) below, subsection (1) above does not apply if the trusts permit any of the settled property to be applied at any time (whether during any such period as is referred to in the said paragraph 17 (1) or later) for the benefit of—

(a) a person who is a participator in the company mentioned in subsection (1) above; or

(b) any other person who is a participator in any close company that has made a disposition whereby property became comprised in the same settlement, being a disposition which but for section 90 of the Finance Act 1976 would have been a transfer of value; or

(c) any other person who has been a participator in the company mentioned in subsection (1) above or in any such company as is mentioned in paragraph (b) above at any time after, or during the ten years before, the transfer of value mentioned in subsection (1) above; or

(d) any person who is connected with any person within paragraph (a), (b) or (c) above.

(5) The participators in a company who are referred to in subsection (4) above do not include any participator who—

(a) is not beneficially entitled to, or to rights entitling him to acquire, 5 per cent. or more of, or of any class of the shares comprised in, its issued share capital; and

(b) on a winding-up of the company would not be entitled to 5 per cent. or more of its assets;

and in determining whether the trusts permit property to be applied as mentioned in that subsection, no account shall be taken of any power to make a payment which is the income of any person for any of the purposes of income tax, or would be the income for any of those purposes of a person not resident in the United Kingdom if he were so resident.

(6) Subsection (5) of section 90 of the said Act of 1976 (interpretation) shall have effect in relation to this section as it has effect in relation to that section.

(7) The enactments mentioned in Schedule 11 to this Act (which contain other provisions about employee trusts) shall have effect with the amendments there specified, being amendments consequential on the provisions of this section and Chapter III of Part III above and amendments bringing those enactments into conformity with those provisions.

(8) Subsections (1) to (6) above apply in relation to transfers of value made on or after 11th April 1978.

GENERAL NOTE

This section eases the conditions which have to be met to secure exemption for a gift of shares or securities in a company by an individual to an employee trust within the definition of F.A. 1975, Sched. 5, para. 17 (1). The relief will now apply where the trustees hold more than one-half of the ordinary shares of the company and have the power of voting control over the company. The trustees therefore need no longer substantially acquire all the shares nor need the individual give up all his holding in the company.

Subs. (2) (a) (ii)

This requires that the trustees have powers of voting on all questions affecting the company as a whole which if exercised would yield a majority of the votes capable of being exercised thereon. This is subject to s. 67 (3).

Subs. (2) (*b*)

This subsection requires that there should be no provisions in any agreement or instrument which would deprive the trustees of the employee trust of their voting control or one-half of the shares.

Subs. (3)

This subsection is similar to s. 66 (1). It was included at the Report Stage of the Act because the scope of the original clause, *i.e.* cl. 54 (2) (*a*) (ii), was too wide. The new subsection permits a shareholding to qualify under s. 67 (2) (*a*) (ii) (definition of control of a company) where there are in existence other shares with voting rights so long as the powers of these shares are limited to voting on a winding up or on questions primarily affecting shares or securities of that class.

Subs. (4)

This subsection, which is subject to s. 67 (5), restricts the class of beneficiaries who are entitled to benefit under an employee trust.

Subs. (5)

This provision excludes from the restrictions imposed by s. 66 (4) any participator in a company who is not beneficially entitled to, or rights entitling him to acquire, 5 per cent. or more of, or of any class of the shares comprised in, its issued share capital and on a winding up would not be entitled to 5 per cent. or more of the company's assets. These provisions take effect from April 11, 1978.

Alteration of dispositions taking effect on death

68.—(1) Subject to the provisions of this section, where within the period of two years after a person's death any of the dispositions (whether effected by will, under the law relating to intestacy or otherwise) of the property comprised in his estate immediately before his death are varied, or the benefit conferred by any of those dispositions is disclaimed, by an instrument in writing made by the persons or any of the persons who benefit or would benefit under the dispositions—

(*a*) the variation or disclaimer shall not be a transfer of value; and

(*b*) Part III of the Finance Act 1975 shall apply as if the variation had been effected by the deceased or, as the case may be, the disclaimed benefit had never been conferred.

(2) Subsection (1) above does not apply to a variation unless an election to that effect is made by written notice given to the Board within six months after the date of the instrument, or such longer time as the Board may allow, by—

(*a*) the person or persons making the instrument; and

(*b*) where the variation results in additional tax being payable, the personal representatives;

but personal representatives may decline to join in an election only if no, or no sufficient, assets are held by them in that capacity for discharging the additional tax.

(3) Subsection (1) above does not apply to a variation or disclaimer made for any consideration in money or money's worth other than consideration consisting of the making, in respect of another of the dispositions, of a variation or disclaimer to which that subsection applies.

(4) Where a variation to which subsection (1) above applies results in property being held in trust for a person for a period which ends not more than two years after the death, Part III of the said Act of 1975 shall apply as if the disposition of the property that takes effect at the end of the period had had effect from the beginning of the period; but this subsection shall not affect the application of that Part in relation to any distribution or application of property occurring before that disposition takes effect.

(5) For the purposes of subsection (1) above the property comprised in a person's estate includes any excluded property but not any property to which he is treated as entitled by virtue of paragraph 3 (1) of Schedule 5 to the said Act of 1975; and that subsection applies whether or not the administration of the estate is complete or the property concerned has been distributed in accordance with the original dispositions.

(6) In paragraph 25 (4) of Schedule 4 to the said Act of 1975 (effect of certificates of discharge) after the words " shall not affect any further tax " there shall be inserted the words " that may afterwards be shown to be payable by virtue of section 47 of this Act or section 68 of the Finance Act 1978 or ".

(7) Subsections (1) to (5) above apply to a variation or disclaimer made on or after 11th April 1978 and as respects any such variation or disclaimer supersede section 47 (1) and (2) of the said Act of 1975; and subsection (6) above applies where the further tax is shown to be payable on or after that date.

GENERAL NOTE
This section redefines the provisions dealing with deeds of family arrangement and with disclaimers of legacies and other interests in a deceased person's estate. This section will, from April 11, 1978, supersede s. 47 (1) and (2) of F.A. 1975. Instruments therefore which have been entered into before April 11 will continue to be governed by the existing legislation. The main changes which are proposed are that tax treatment accorded under s. 47 will apply to any written instrument made within two years of death and varying or disclaiming a benefit under a disposition of property forming part of a deceased person's estate. The rule will apply even though the person giving up his interest in the property had taken some benefit from it or taken possession of it and the variations will not be limited in favour of members of the family or beneficiaries under the will. The section also covers agreements approved by the courts such as under the Variation of Trusts Act 1958.

Subs. (2)
This subsection allows the parties to an instrument which falls within s. 68 to elect within six months whether they wish the instrument to be dealt with according to the section or as a transfer of value. Some beneficiaries may find it advantageous to have such deeds treated as lifetime transfers.

Subs. (3)
This limits to some extent the scope of subs. (1) where there is a variation or disclaimer made for a consideration (other than a consideration consisting of dispositions, variations or disclaimers to which subs. (1) applies).

Subs. (4)
This subsection prevents a double charge to CTT where an interest in possession is terminated under a variation to which subs. (1) applies.

Subs. (5)
This subsection provides that for the purposes of subs. (1) a person's estate shall include excluded property (such as a reversionary interest : see F.A. 1975, s. 24 (3)) but excludes property to which he (that is the testator or intestate) is entitled under F.A. 1975, Sched. 5, para. 3 (1) (a person beneficially entitled to an interest in possession). This means that a s. 68 variation or disclaimer cannot apply to an interest in possession to which the testator or intestate was entitled such as an interest *pur autre vie* or an annuity. The second part of the subsection makes it clear that a beneficiary may vary a disposition after the property concerned has been distributed to him and the administration of the estate was complete.

Sales of interests under settlements

69.—(1) In section 22 (2) of the Finance Act 1975 and paragraph 4 (5) of Schedule 5 to that Act (exemptions where settled property reverts to settlor unless the settlor had acquired a reversionary interest for a consideration in money or money's worth) for the words " unless the settlor had acquired " there shall be substituted the words " unless the settlor or his spouse had acquired ".

(2) In paragraph 6 of the said Schedule 5 (charge on capital distributions of settled property) after paragraph (6A) there shall be inserted—

" (6B) Neither sub-paragraph (6) nor sub-paragraph (6A) above applies where, at or before the time when the payment is made to the person concerned or that person becomes entitled to the interest, as the case may be, an interest under the settlement is or has been acquired for a consideration in money or money's worth by—

(a) that person; or

(b) that person's spouse; or

(c) where that person is the settlor's widow or widower, the settlor."

(3) At the end of paragraph 14 (5) of the said Schedule 5 (transitional relief available only if beneficiary is an individual who is domiciled in the United Kingdom at the time the capital distribution is made) there shall be inserted the words " and who has not at or before that time acquired an interest under the settlement for a consideration in money or money's worth directly or indirectly from a person not so domiciled."

(4) In sub-paragraph (4A) of paragraph 15 of Schedule 6 to that Act (restrictions on exemptions from tax) for the words " paragraphs 1 and 10 to 13 above do not apply " there shall be substituted the words " paragraph 1 above does not apply " and the words " or body " (in both places) shall be omitted.

(5) After the said sub-paragraph (4A) there shall be inserted—

" (4B) Paragraphs 10 to 13 above do not apply in relation to any property if—

(a) immediately before the time when it becomes the property of the exempt body it is comprised in a settlement; and

(b) at or before that time, an interest under the settlement is or has been acquired for a consideration in money or money's worth by that or another exempt body.

In this sub-paragraph " exempt body " means a charity, political party or other body within the said paragraphs 10 to 13 and for the purposes of this sub-paragraph there shall be disregarded any acquisition from a charity, political party or body within paragraphs 10 to 12."

(6) For the purposes of section 22 (2) and (3) of the said Act of 1975, paragraphs 4 (5) and (6), 6 (6B) and 14 (5) of the said Schedule 5 and paragraph 15 (4A) and (4B) of the said Schedule 6, a person shall be treated as acquiring an interest for a consideration in money or money's worth if he becomes entitled to it as a result of transactions which include a disposition for such consideration (whether to him or another) of that interest or of other property.

(7) Where a person becomes entitled to an interest in possession in settled property as a result of a disposition for a consideration in money or money's worth, any question whether and to what extent the giving of the consideration is a transfer of value or chargeable transfer shall be determined without regard to paragraph 3 (1) of the said Schedule 5.

(8) Subsections (1) to (5) above apply where the acquisition of the interest is after 11th April 1978, subsection (6) above applies where the person concerned becomes entitled to the interest after that date and subsection (7) above applies where the person concerned becomes entitled to the interest after 13th June 1978.

GENERAL NOTE

This makes a number of amendments to the provisions concerning the relief given where settled property reverts to the settlor or is given to charities. The avoidance schemes made use of exemptions in the legislation by means of contingent interests and sales of contingent interests whereby an exempt person would be able to transfer a benefit thus avoiding capital transfer tax.

Subs. (2)

This subsection provides that the exemption from the discretionary trust charges which were available under Sched. 5, para. 6 (6) and (6A), cannot be claimed if the interest under the settlement has been acquired for a consideration in money or money's worth. This provision therefore brings discretionary trusts into line with those settlements where property subject to an interest in possession reverts to the settlor.

Subs. (3)

This subsection provides that if any person domiciled in the United Kingdom acquires an interest under a settlement for a consideration in money or money's worth from a person domiciled outside the United Kingdom then the transitional relief for distributions from discretionary trusts will not apply to the person who so acquires that interest.

Subs. (5)

This deprives an exempt body of the exemptions set out in F.A. 1975, Sched. 6, paras. 10 to 13, where the exempt body has purchased an interest in settled property unless the acquisition is from a charity, political party or any other exempt property within F.A. 1975, Sched. 6, paras. 10 to 13.

Subs. (6)

This subsection extends the effect of the section to the situation where an interest under a settlement is acquired indirectly.

Subs. (7)

This subsection seeks to stop an avoidance device whereby short-term interests are created and sold for sums well in excess of their real value but because a beneficiary is, under F.A. 1975, Sched. 5, para. 3 (1), treated as beneficially entitled to the whole of the property no capital transfer tax becomes payable.

Subs. (8)

This subsection provides the relevant dates for the implementation of the various subsections.

Charge on termination of discretionary trust

70.—(1) In paragraph 6 of Schedule 5 to the Finance Act 1975 (charge on capital distributions of settled property) after sub-paragraph (2) there shall be inserted—

" (2A) Where the whole or any part of the property comprised in a settlement ceases to be comprised in that settlement (otherwise than by virtue of any payment or transfer of assets made by the trustees) at a time when no interest in possession subsists in the property or that part, then, if

(*a*) sub-paragraph (2) above does not apply; but

(*b*) a person at that time becomes entitled to (or immediately thereafter has) an interest in the property or part which would be an interest in possession if held beneficially by an individual,

a capital distribution shall be treated as being made out of the property or that part of the property; and the amount of the distribution shall be taken to be equal to the value at that time of the property or that part of it."

(2) In sub-paragraph (5) of the said paragraph 6 after the words " sub-paragraph (2) " there shall be inserted the words " or (2A) ".

(3) In paragraph 11 (8) of the said Schedule 5 for the words " paragraph 6 (2) or (3) " there shall be substituted the words " paragraph 6 (2), (2A) or (3) ".

(4) At the end of paragraphs 10 (2), 11 (1A), 12 (2) and 13 (1A) of Schedule 6 to the said Act of 1975 (exceptions from charge where settled property is given to a charity etc.) there shall be added the words " and paragraph 6 (2A) of that Schedule shall not apply."

(5) In section 47 (1A) of the said Act of 1975 (exclusion of charge in case of property settled by will on discretionary trusts) for the words " paragraphs 6 (2) or 15 (3) " and " paragraphs 6 (2) and 15 (3) " there shall be substituted respectively the words " paragraph 6 (2), (2A) or 15 (3) " and " paragraphs 6 (2), (2A) and 15 (3) ".

(6) This section shall be deemed to have come into force on 11th April 1978.

GENERAL NOTE

This clause provides for a charge to be made under F.A. 1975, Sched. 5, para. 6, where property ceases to be settled in a discretionary trust and a body such as a non-close company becomes absolutely entitled to it. This is an anti-avoidance measure.

Protective trusts

71.—(1) In paragraph 18 of Schedule 5 to the Finance Act 1975 (protective trusts) for sub-paragraphs (2) and (3) there shall be substituted—

" (2) For the purposes of capital transfer tax—

    (a) there shall be disregarded the failure or determination, before the end of the trust period, of trusts to the like effect as those specified in paragraph (i) of the said section 33 (1); and

    (b) the principal beneficiary shall be treated as beneficially entitled to an interest in possession in any property which is for the time being held on trusts to the like effect as those specified in paragraph (ii) of the said section 33 (1)."

(2) This section shall be deemed to have come into force on 11th April 1978 and applies if the failure or determination of the trusts is after that date; but no capital distribution shall be treated as made by virtue of paragraph 15 (3) of the said Schedule 5 by reason only of the coming into force of this section.

GENERAL NOTE

This section amends F.A. 1975, Sched. 5, para. 18 (protective trusts), by substituting a new sub-para. (2) for sub-paras. (2) and (3). The effect of this section is that where there is a failure or determination of a protective trust which normally would create a discretionary trust under the terms of the Trustee Act 1925, s. 33 (1) (ii), now for the purposes of capital transfer tax such a failure or determination of the protective trusts shall be disregarded and the principal beneficiary shall be treated as continuing to enjoy an interest in possession in the property even though there is, under the terms of s. 33 (1) (ii), a discretionary trust in existence. This is believed to be an anti-avoidance provision aimed at preventing a scheme whereby CTT on the termination of interests in possession could be mitigated. The section applies to the failure or determination of the trusts after April 11, 1978.

Government securities in foreign ownership

72.—(1) In paragraph 3 of Schedule 7 to the Finance Act 1975 (certain government securities to be excluded property if person beneficially entitled is domiciled and ordinarily resident abroad) after sub-paragraph (2) there shall be inserted—

" (2A) Where, by the same disposition, property has ceased to be comprised in one settlement and has become comprised in another, sub-paragraph (2) above shall, in its application to the second settlement, be construed as requiring the matters there stated to be shown both in relation to the property comprised in that settlement and in relation to the property that was comprised in the first settlement.

(2B) Paragraph 24 (5) of Schedule 5 to this Act shall apply for the purposes of sub-paragraphs (1) (*b*) and (2) above as it applies for the purposes of that Schedule."

(2) This section shall be deemed to have come into force on 20th April 1978 and the new sub-paragraph (2A) set out above applies where the disposition mentioned in that sub-paragraph is on or after that date.

GENERAL NOTE

The section is an anti-avoidance measure aimed at an avoidance scheme which exploited the exemption for Government securities which are free of tax while in foreign ownership. The scheme was implemented by means of non-resident companies and settlements. F.A. 1975, Sched. 5, para. 24 (5), which treats participators in a close company as beneficially entitled to any interest in possession in settled property to which the company is entitled, was hitherto restricted in its application to Sched. 5 but now by s. 72 (1) it will also apply for the purposes of Sched. 7, para. 3 (1) (*b*).

Life policies and deferred annuity contracts

73.—(1) In paragraph 11 of Schedule 10 to the Finance Act 1975 (valuation of life policies and deferred annuity contracts in connection with transfer of value), for sub-paragraph (2) there shall be substituted—

" (2) Sub-paragraph (1) above does not apply in the case of the transfer of value which a person makes on his death or of any other transfer of value which does not result in the policy or contract ceasing to be part of the transferor's estate."

(2) This section applies where the transfer of value is made on or after 11th April 1978.

GENERAL NOTE

This is again an anti-avoidance provision aimed at preventing avoidance in valuing associated endowment and term life policies by amending F.A. 1975, Sched. 10, para. 11 (1). The clause provides that the valuation rule in para. 11 (1) is not to apply in cases where a transfer does not result in the policy ceasing to be part of the transferor's estate; or where the transfer of value is made on death.

Increase in value of settled property by omission to exercise a right

74.—(1) In section 20 (7) of the Finance Act 1975 (omission to exercise right to count as disposition if it increases the value of another person's estate) after the words " of another person's estate " there shall be inserted the words " or of settled property in which no interest in possession (within the meaning of Schedule 5 to this Act) subsists ".

(2) This section applies where the disposition under the said section 20 (7) is on or after 11th April 1978.

GENERAL NOTE

This clause amends F.A. 1975, s. 20 (7), and extends its scope by providing that a charge to tax will arise where there is an omission to exercise a right which results in the value of the property subject to a discretionary trust being increased in value.

PART V

MISCELLANEOUS AND SUPPLEMENTARY

National insurance surcharge

75.—(1) In section 1 (1) of the National Insurance Surcharge Act 1976 (surcharge of 2 per cent. on secondary Class 1 contributions) for the words " 2 per cent. " there shall be substituted the words " $3\frac{1}{2}$ per cent.".

(2) This section has effect in relation to any contribution in respect of earnings which are paid on or after 2nd October 1978.

GENERAL NOTE

This increases the surcharge imposed on employers in respect of Class 1 contributions (see s. 4 of the Social Security Act 1975 and s. 1 of the National Insurance Surcharge Act 1976) from 2 per cent. to $3\frac{1}{2}$ per cent.

Development land tax

76. Section 13 of the Development Land Tax Act 1976 shall have effect and shall be deemed always to have had effect as if the date in subsection (1) of that section were 31st March 1980.

GENERAL NOTE

S. 13 of the Development Land Tax Act 1976 provides for a reduced rate of development land tax of $66\frac{2}{3}$ per cent. to apply to the first £150,000 of development value realised in a financial year. As the section was originally drafted the reduced rate was to cease to apply after the close of the financial year ending March 31, 1979. This section extends the operation of the reduced rate so that it will apply for one more year.

Disclosure of information to tax authorities in other member States

77.—(1) No obligation as to secrecy imposed by statute or otherwise shall preclude the Commissioners of Inland Revenue or an authorised officer of those Commissioners from disclosing to the competent authorities of another member State any information required to be so disclosed by virtue of the Directive of the Council of the European Communities dated 19th December 1977 No. 77/799/EEC.

(2) Neither the Commissioners nor an authorised officer shall disclose any information in pursuance of the said Directive unless satisfied that the competent authorities of the other State are bound by, or have undertaken to observe, rules of confidentiality with respect to the information which are not less strict than those applying to it in the United Kingdom.

(3) Nothing in this section shall permit the Commissioners of Inland Revenue or an authorised officer of those Commissioners to authorise the use of information disclosed by virtue of the said Directive other than for the purposes of taxation or to facilitate legal proceedings for failure to observe the tax laws of the receiving State.

GENERAL NOTE

The Directive referred to applies to income tax, corporation tax, capital gains tax, petroleum revenue tax and development land tax, and requires exchange of information enabling the other Member States to effect a current assessment. It provides for exchange of information on request (art. 2), automatic exchange of information (arts. 1 and 3) and spontaneous exchange of information in certain listed circumstances (art. 4). It should be noted that this section relates only to information *required* to be disclosed by virtue of the Directive. Art. 2 provides that a State need not comply with a request for information if it appears that the requesting

State has not exhausted its own usual sources of information. It appears that the U.K. is obliged to require this to be done in all cases, because only then would the information be required to be disclosed.

Subs. (2)

This follows art. 7 (2) under which a State is not obliged to provide information unless the receiving State undertakes the same degree of confidentiality as the providing State. It would appear to be unnecessary, and indeed was not in the original Bill, because, unless the undertaking is given, there would be no requirement to disclose the information, and therefore disclosure would not be permitted under subs. (1). The Financial Secretary at the Report Stage said that this subsection was added by way of clarification in view of the concern which had been expressed: *Hansard,* H.C. Vol. 953, col. 1880.

Subs. (3)

This follows art. 7 (3) under which the State providing the information may permit it to be used for purposes other than those laid down in the Directive if it could be used in the providing State for similar purposes. This, therefore, limits the Inland Revenue's power under that provision.

Local loans

78.—(1) Loans in pursuance of section 3 of the National Loans Act 1968 may be made by the Public Works Loan Commissioners, in addition to any loans made by them under section 55 of the Finance Act 1975, but the aggregate of—

(a) the commitments of the Commissioners outstanding at any time in respect of undertakings entered into by them to grant such loans; and

(b) the advances in respect of such loans made by them under this section up to that time,

shall not exceed £3,000 million or such greater amount as may be specified in an order under subsection (2) below.

(2) The Treasury may, on not more than three occasions, by order made by statutory instrument increase or further increase the limit imposed by subsection (1) above by such sum not exceeding £3,000 million as may be specified in the order.

(3) No order shall be made under this section unless a draft of it has been laid before and approved by a resolution of the Commons House of Parliament.

GENERAL NOTE

This increases the limit on local authority loan from £2,000 to £3,000 million with the possibility of increasing the limit by a further £3,000 million by statutory instrument approved by a resolution of the House of Commons.

It was stated in the Standing Committee debates that the first of the local loans (Increase of Limit) Orders will be placed before the Commons early next year.

Pre-consolidation amendments

79. The enactments specified in Schedule 12 to this Act shall have effect subject to the amendments specified in that Schedule, being amendments designed to facilitate, or otherwise desirable in connection with, the consolidation of the customs and excise Acts.

Short title, interpretation, construction and repeals

80.—(1) This Act may be cited as the Finance Act 1978.

(2) In this Act " the Taxes Act " means the Income and Corporation Taxes Act 1970.

(3) In this Act—
  (a) Part I (except sections 8 and 9) shall be construed as one with the Customs and Excise Act 1952;
  (b) Part II shall be construed as one with Part I of the Finance Act 1972;
  (c) Part III, so far as it relates to income tax, shall be construed as one with the Income Tax Acts, so far as it relates to corporation tax shall be construed as one with the Corporation Tax Acts and so far as it relates to capital gains tax, shall be construed as one with Part III of the Finance Act 1965;
  (d) Part IV shall be construed as one with Part III of the Finance Act 1975.

(4) Except so far as the context otherwise requires, any reference in this Act to any enactment shall be construed as a reference to that enactment as amended, and as including a reference to that enactment as applied, by or under any other enactment, including this Act.

(5) The enactments mentioned in Schedule 13 to this Act (which include spent enactments) are hereby repealed to the extent specified in the third column of that Schedule, but subject to any provision at the end of any Part of that Schedule.

SCHEDULES

Section 6   SCHEDULE 1

AMENDMENTS OF CUSTOMS DUTIES (DUMPING AND SUBSIDIES) ACT 1969

1. In section 1 (charge of anti-dumping duties) in subsection (5) (description of goods chargeable with duty: limitation by reference to persons by whom goods are produced) after the word " produced " there shall be inserted the words " or supplied " and after the word " production " there shall be inserted the words " or supply ".

2. In section 2 (relief where margin of dumping lower than duty) in subsection (4) (period within which application for relief is to be made) for the words " six months " there shall be substituted the words " three months ".

3. In section 3 (ascertainment of export price from country of origin) in subsection (1) (rules where goods are wholly produced in country of origin) for the words from " if " to " shall " there shall be substituted the words " shall, subject to section 5 (3) below ".

4.—(1) In section 4 (ascertainment of fair market price in country of origin) in subsection (1) (rules where goods are wholly produced in country of origin) for the words from " if " to " shall " there shall be substituted the words " shall, subject to section 5 (3) below ".

(2) In subsection (3) of that section (cases in which the ordinary rule for the ascertainment of the fair market price does not apply) after the word " can " there shall be inserted the word " appropriately ".

(3) In subsection (4) of that section (ascertainment of fair market price where goods are subject to a government trading monopoly) for the words from " either " to the end of the subsection there shall be substituted the words " with subsection (2) above, the fair market price shall be determined by the Secretary of State—
  (a) in accordance with subsection (3) above, or
  (b) by reference to such other price as he considers appropriate (making any necessary adjustments to ensure comparability),
according as the Secretary of State considers appropriate."

5.—(1) In section 5 (meaning of country of origin) in subsection (1) for the words from " in relation " to the end of the subsection there shall be substituted the words " shall be determined in accordance with the rules on the common definition of the concept of origin which are for the time being applicable in accordance with any Community instrument for the purposes of the uniform application of the Common Customs Tariff ".

(2) Subsection (2) of that section shall be omitted.

(3) In subsection (3) of that section—
    (*a*) for the words " under subsection (2) " there shall be substituted the words " in accordance with subsection (1) ";
    (*b*) after the word " then " there shall be inserted the words " for the purpose of determining in accordance with section 3 or section 4 above "; and
    (*c*) the words from " shall be determined " to " except that " shall be omitted.

6. In section 6 (determination of export price and fair market price in country of exportation) for the words " in the case of goods wholly produced in one country " there shall be substituted the words " in a case where section 5 (3) above does not apply ".

7. In section 10 (additional provisions as to duties and reliefs) subsections (2) and (5) shall be omitted.

8. Section 11 (drawback on exportations) and section 12 (other reliefs relating to exportations) shall be omitted.

9. In section 13 (construction of references to production of goods, etc.) in subsection (1) the words " growing or " shall be omitted.

10. In section 14 (power to require information from importers) subsections (1) and (3) shall be omitted.

GENERAL NOTE

This Schedule makes a number of amendments to the Customs Duties (Dumping and Subsidies) Act 1969.

In para. 1, the amendment enables anti-dumping measures to be restricted in operation not only to goods from particular producers but also to goods supplied by particular persons.

Para. 2 restricts the time in which an importer may make a claim for relief under s. 2 of the 1969 Act to three instead of six months.

Paras. 3 to 6 amend the rules for determining the fair market price in the country of origin of the goods being dumped in the United Kingdom. It now confers on the Secretary of State a power to determine such price in his absolute discretion when the goods are subject to a government trading monopoly.

Section 14   SCHEDULE 2

LOWER RATE INCOME TAX

1. In section 30 (3) of the Taxes Act for the words " were charged at the basic rate to the exclusion of any other rate " there shall be substituted the words " not charged at a lower rate were charged at the basic rate to the exclusion of any higher or additional rate ".

2. In section 34 (1) (iii) of the Taxes Act after the words " shall be treated " there shall be inserted the words " as income which is not chargeable at a rate lower than the basic rate and ".

3. In section 36 (1) of the Taxes Act for the words " were chargeable at the basic rate to the exclusion of any other rate " there shall be substituted the words " not chargeable at a lower rate were chargeable at the basic rate to the exclusion of any higher or additional rate ".

4. In section 287 (1) (*c*) of the Taxes Act for the words from " notwithstanding " to " total income " there shall be substituted the words " the income included by virtue of paragraph (*a*) above in his total income shall be treated as income which is not chargeable at a rate lower than the basic rate and, notwithstanding that paragraph,".

5. In section 343 (3) of the Taxes Act—
    (*a*) in paragraph (*c*) for the words before " those amounts " there shall be substituted the words " any amounts paid or credited in respect of any such dividends or interest shall be treated as income which is not chargeable at a rate lower than the basic rate and, in computing the total income of an individual entitled thereto,"; and
    (*b*) in paragraph (i) of the proviso after the words " the basic rate " there shall be inserted the words " or any lower rate ".

6. In section 399 (4) (*c*) of the Taxes Act after the words " shall be treated " there shall be inserted the words " as income which is not chargeable at a rate lower than the basic rate and ".

7. In section 400 (3) of the Taxes Act after the words " the basic rate " there shall be inserted the words " or any lower rate ".

8. In section 403 (1) of the Taxes Act for the words " were charged at the basic rate to the exclusion of any other rate " there shall be substituted the words " not charged at a lower rate were charged at the basic rate to the exclusion of any higher or additional rate ".

9. In section 422 (2) of the Taxes Act after the words " the basic rate ", where first occurring, there shall be inserted the words " or any lower rate " and after the words " total income " there shall be inserted the words " not chargeable at a lower rate ".

10. In section 424 (c) of the Taxes Act for the words " to the exclusion of any other rate " there shall be substituted the words " not chargeable at a lower rate to the exclusion of any higher or additional rate ".

11. In section 430 (1) of the Taxes Act for the words " were chargeable at the basic rate to the exclusion of any other rate " there shall be substituted the words " not chargeable at a lower rate were chargeable at the basic rate to the exclusion of any higher or additional rate ".

12. In section 457 (1) of the Taxes Act for the words " were charged at the basic rate to the exclusion of any other rate " there shall be substituted the words " not charged at a lower rate were charged at the basic rate to the exclusion of any higher or additional rate ".

13. In section 458 (1) of the Taxes Act for the words " were charged at the basic rate to the exclusion of any other rate " there shall be substituted the words " not charged at a lower rate were charged at the basic rate to the exclusion of any higher or additional rate ".

14. In paragraph 2 (2) of Schedule 7 to the Finance Act 1971 for the words " were charged at the basic rate to the exclusion of any other rate " there shall be substituted the words " not charged at a lower rate were charged at the basic rate to the exclusion of any higher or additional rate ".

15. In section 87 of the Finance Act 1972—

    (a) in subsection (5) (c) after the words " shall be treated " there shall be inserted the words " as income which is not chargeable at a rate lower than the basic rate and "; and

    (b) in subsection (6) for the words " were charged at the basic rate to the exclusion of any other rate " there shall be substituted the words " not charged at a lower rate were charged at the basic rate to the exclusion of any higher or additional rate ".

16. In Schedule 16 to the Finance Act 1972—

    (a) in paragraph 5 (2) (d) after the words " shall be treated " there shall be inserted the words " as income which is not chargeable at a rate lower than the basic rate and "; and

    (b) in paragraph 5 (6A) for the words " were chargeable at the basic rate to the exclusion of any other rate " there shall be substituted the words " not chargeable at a lower rate were chargeable at the basic rate to the exclusion of any higher or additional rate ".

17. In section 44 of the Finance Act 1973 for the words " were chargeable at the basic rate to the exclusion of any other rate " there shall be substituted the words " not chargeable at a lower rate were chargeable at the basic rate to the exclusion of any higher or additional rate ".

18. In paragraph 19 (1A) of Schedule 2 to the Finance Act 1975 for the words " were chargeable at the basic rate to the exclusion of any other rate " there shall be substituted the words " not chargeable at a lower rate were chargeable at the basic rate to the exclusion of any higher or additional rate ".

19. In section 34 (4) (c) of the Finance (No. 2) Act 1975 after the words " shall be treated " there shall be inserted the words " as income which is not chargeable at a rate lower than the basic rate and ".

GENERAL NOTE

These paragraphs make a number of amendments consequent upon the creation of the lower rate of income tax in addition to basic and higher rates.

Finance Act 1978

SCHEDULE 3

LIFE POLICIES ETC.

Preliminary

1. In this Schedule references to any paragraphs not otherwise identified are references to paragraphs of Schedule 4 to the Finance Act 1976 (premium relief for the year 1979–80 and subsequent years of assessment).

Time of payment

2. The said Schedule 4 shall have effect as if any premium or part of a premium which is paid otherwise than in the year of assessment in which it becomes due and payable were paid in that year.

Contracts for deferred annuities

3. In paragraph 1 (preliminary) for the words from "and" onwards there shall be substituted the words " 'Schedule 1' means Schedule 1 to that Act and, unless the context otherwise requires, 'contract' means a contract for a deferred annuity".

Personal accident insurance

4. After paragraph 2 there shall be inserted—

"2A.—(1) A policy which evidences a contract of insurance to which sub-paragraph (2) below applies shall not be a qualifying policy within the meaning of Schedule 1 unless it also evidences a contract falling within subsection (2) (*a*) of section 83 of the Insurance Companies Act 1974.

(2) This sub-paragraph applies to contracts of insurance against risks of persons dying as a result of an accident or an accident of a specified class, not being contracts falling within subsection (2) (*b*) of the said section 83."

Non-resident members of armed forces, etc.

5. After paragraph 5 there shall be inserted—

"5A. Paragraphs 4 (2) and 5 above shall apply in relation to an individual who is not resident in the United Kingdom but is—

(*a*) a member of the armed forces of the Crown;

(*b*) the wife of such a member; or

(*c*) a woman serving in any of the capacities mentioned in section 366 (3),

as if the individual were so resident."

Limit on deductions

6. Paragraph 6 (limit on deductions authorised under paragraph 5) shall be omitted.

Payments to friendly societies and industrial assurance companies

7.—(1) In paragraph 13 (1) (premiums to which the paragraph applies) after the words "a policy is issued" there shall be inserted the words "or a contract is made" and after the word "policy", in the third place where it occurs, there shall be inserted the words "or contract".

(2) In paragraph 13 (4) (increases made in pursuance of regulations to be disregarded) for the words from "section 332" to "Finance Act 1975" there shall be substituted—

"(*a*) section 100 of the Stamp Act 1891 and the heading "Policy of Life Insurance" in Schedule 1 to that Act;

(*b*) section 332 of and paragraph 4 of Schedule 1 to the Taxes Act;

(*c*) section 7 (6) of the Finance Act 1975; and

(*d*) paragraph 11 (3) above; ".

Relief in respect of certain payments

8.—(1) In paragraph 14 (notices excluding the application of paragraph 5) after the word "policy" there shall be inserted the words "or contract."

(2) The provisions of that paragraph as so amended shall become sub-paragraph (1) and after those provisions there shall be inserted—

" (2) Where the application of paragraph 5 above is so excluded in relation to any payments, the relief (if any) to which the person by whom the payments are made is entitled under section 19 shall be given to him under paragraph 15 below."

9. After paragraph 14 there shall be inserted—

" 14A. Where a person is entitled to relief under section 19 in respect of—

(*a*) a payment to which section 220 (1) applies;

(*b*) a payment to which section 23 of the Finance Act 1970 applies; or

(*c*) a payment made pursuant to a retirement benefits scheme or fund in the case of which payments made by the employer are exempted from the operation of section 220 (1) by section 221 (1) (*b*) or (*c*), (2) or (4) or would be so exempted if the employer were a body corporate,

paragraph 5 above shall not apply but the like relief shall be given to him under paragraph 15 below."

Regulations

10. In paragraph 16 (2) (regulations for carrying Schedule into effect) the provisions of paragraph (*a*) shall become paragraph (*ab*) and for the words from the beginning to " may provide " there shall be substituted the words " Regulations under this paragraph shall be made by statutory instrument and, without prejudice to the generality of sub-paragraph (1) above, may provide—

(*a*) for the furnishing of such information by persons by whom premiums are payable as may be necessary for determining whether they are entitled to make deductions under paragraph 5 above and for excluding the operation of that paragraph in relation to payments made by persons who fail to comply with the regulations;

(*aa*) for rounding to a multiple of one new penny or one new half-penny as appears to the Board appropriate any payment which, after a deduction authorised under paragraph 5 above, is not such a multiple;".

Part payments to friendly societies

11.—(1) Where—

(*a*) a person is entitled to relief under section 19 of the Taxes Act in respect of part only of a payment made to a registered friendly society; and

(*b*) the insurance or contract was made by the society in the course of tax exempt life or endowment business (as defined in section 337 (3) of that Act),

Schedule 4 to the Finance Act 1976 shall not apply with respect to that relief but there shall be deducted from his total income an amount equal to one-half of that part of the payment.

(2) This paragraph applies for the year 1979–80 and subsequent years of assessment.

Part payments to trade unions

12.—(1) Where a person makes a payment to a trade union (as defined in section 2 (1) of the Trade Union Act 1913), and part of that payment is attributable to the provision of superannuation, life insurance or funeral benefits, he shall be entitled to relief under section 19 of the Taxes Act in respect of that part of the payment.

(2) Where a person is entitled to any such relief as aforesaid in respect of part of a payment made to a trade union, the said Schedule 4 shall not apply with respect to that relief but there shall be deducted from his total income an amount equal to one-half of that part of the payment.

(3) This paragraph applies for the year 1979–80 and subsequent years of assessment.

Certification of qualifying policies

13.—(1) Paragraph 11 of Schedule 1 to the Taxes Act (certification of qualifying policies) shall be amended as follows—

(*a*) in sub-paragraph (1) the words " Subject to sub-paragraph (3) below " shall be omitted and for the words " within three months of the date of issue" there shall be substituted the words "within three months of receipt of a request in writing by the policy holder";

(b) in sub-paragraph (2) for the words "the said sub-paragraph (3)" there shall be substituted the words "sub-paragraph (3) below" and for the words "within three months of the making of the variation" there shall be substituted the words "within three months of receipt of a request in writing by the policy holder"; and

(c) in sub-paragraph (3) the words from the beginning to "receipt of the request; and" shall be omitted.

(2) This paragraph applies where the qualifying policy is issued or varied after 5th April 1979.

GENERAL NOTE

Sched. 4 to the F.A. 1976 contains provisions to the effect that for 1979–80 and subsequent years life assurance relief will be given by the policyholder making a percentage reduction in the premium he pays rather than by obtaining a deduction in computing his final liability to tax. This Schedule contains provisions modifying in certain respects Sched. 4. Particular points to note are as follows:

(1) Accident insurance is taken out of the new system save where the policy concerned also provides life assurance or annuity cover (para. 4).

(2) Para. 6 of Sched. 4 precluded a deduction where premiums payable in a year exceed £1,500. This limit is now eliminated (para. 6). Life assurance relief remains limited to premiums not exceeding one-sixth of total income (see s. 21 (1), I.C.T.A.). If the relief by deduction exceeds the relief in fact available assessments to make good the excess can be made by an Inspector (para. 15, Sched. 4, F.A. 1976).

(3) Payments made pursuant to certain superannuation schemes are excluded from the new system (para. 9). Relief for such payments will be given in the manner directed by para. 15 of Sched. 4, F.A. 1976, broadly, it can be anticipated as relief has been given in the past.

Section 27   SCHEDULE 4

SCHEDULE D: RELIEF FOR ABSENCE ON BUSINESS ABROAD

PART I

COMPUTATION OF THE RELIEF

1. In any year of assessment the relief to which an individual carrying on a trade is entitled on a claim made under section 27 of this Act shall be determined by reference to such proportion of his relevant income from the trade for that year as, in accordance with paragraph 3 below, is attributable to the days in that year which are qualifying days in relation to his carrying on of that trade.

2.—(1) Subject to sub-paragraph (2) below, any reference in this Schedule to an individual's relevant income from a trade is a reference to the income from that trade in respect of which he is chargeable to income tax under Case I of Schedule D; and any reference to his relevant income from a trade for a particular year of assessment is a reference to the income in respect of which he is so chargeable for that year.

(2) In relation to any year of assessment, the references in sub-paragraph (1) above to the income from a trade in respect of which an individual is chargeable to income tax are references to the income from that trade—

(a) after making any deduction in respect of an allowance which, under section 70 of the Capital Allowances Act 1968, falls to be made as a deduction in charging the profits or gains of that trade;

(b) after making any addition in respect of any charge which, by virtue of section 70 (6) of that Act, falls to be made for purposes of income tax on those profits or gains;

(*c*) after making any deduction or set-off in respect of an allowance, the amount of which falls to be given by way of discharge or repayment of tax under section 71 of that Act and which arises from activities or that trade;

(*d*) after allowing for any deduction or addition falling to be made by virtue of any provision of Schedule 5 to the Finance Act 1976 (relief for increase in value of trading stock and work in progress) in respect of any relief or charge attributable to that trade; and

(*e*) before taking account of any set-off or reduction of income by virtue of any of sections 168, 171 and 174 of the Taxes Act or section 30 of this Act in respect of losses.

3.—(1) For the purposes of this Schedule, for any year of assessment in which there are qualifying days in relation to an individual carrying on a trade, the proportion of the individual's relevant income from the trade for that year which is attributable to those qualifying days is the proportion which the number of those days bears to 365 or, if the individual was not carrying on the trade throughout that year of assessment, to the number of days in the part of that year in which he was carrying on the trade.

(2) A day which would not be a qualifying day apart from subsection (3) of section 27 of this Act shall be treated for the purposes of this Schedule as divided equally between the two or more trades referred to in that subsection, so that in relation to each of those trades the day counts as a fraction of a qualifying day.

4.—(1) Where for any year of assessment an individual is entitled to relief as mentioned in paragraph 1 above, a sum equal to one-quarter of that proportion of his relevant income from the trade which is referred to in that paragraph shall be deducted from or set off against the amount of the profits or gains on which he is chargeable to income tax for that year under Case I of Schedule D in respect of that trade.

(2) The deduction or set-off to be made by virtue of sub-paragraph (1) above shall be made—

(*a*) after taking account of any such deduction, addition or set-off as falls within paragraphs (*a*) to (*d*) of sub-paragraph (2) of paragraph 2 above; and

(*b*) before taking account of any such set-off or reduction of income as is referred to in paragraph (*e*) of that sub-paragraph.

5.—(1) The provisions of this paragraph apply where a claim for any year of assessment made under section 27 of this Act relates (in whole or in part) to a trade carried on by an individual as a member of a partnership.

(2) With respect to the trade carried on by the individual in partnership, any reference in paragraphs 1, 3 and 4 above to his relevant income from the trade shall be construed as a reference to his share of the profits of the partnership from the trade.

(3) For the purposes of this Schedule, an individual's share of the profits of a partnership from a trade for any year of assessment means, subject to sub-paragraph (4) below, the share which is attributed to him for income tax purposes of the profits of the partnership from that trade which are chargeable to income tax under Case I of Schedule D for that year.

(4) Paragraphs (*a*) to (*e*) of sub-paragraph (2) of paragraph 2 above shall apply with respect to the reference in sub-paragraph (3) above to the share attributed to an individual for income tax purposes of the profits of a partner-ship from a trade as they apply with respect to the references in sub-paragraph (1) of that paragraph to the income from a trade in respect of which an individual is chargeable to income tax.

6. Where, by virtue of section 154 of the Taxes Act (change in persons carry-ing on a trade), a trade is treated as having been discontinued for the purpose of computing tax, it shall also be so treated for the purposes of this Schedule.

PART II

CONSEQUENTIAL PROVISIONS

7. At the end of paragraph (*c*) of sub-paragraph (2) of paragraph 31 of Schedule 5 to the Finance Act 1976 (which excludes certain deductions etc. in

computing " relevant income " for the purposes of the provisions of that Act relating to relief for increases in the value of trading stock and work in progress) there shall be added the words " and

(*d*) no account shall be taken of any deduction falling to be made by virtue of section 27 of and Schedule 4 to the Finance Act 1978 ".

8. In sub-paragraph (2) of paragraph 3 of Schedule 2 to the Social Security Act 1975 and the Social Security (Northern Ireland) Act 1975 (which excludes certain reliefs in computing the profits or gains in respect of which Class 4 contributions are payable under that Act) after paragraph (*c*) there shall be inserted the following paragraph:—

" (*cc*) section 27 of and Schedule 4 to the Finance Act 1978 (relief for absence on business abroad) ".

GENERAL NOTE

This Schedule sets out the method by which the relief given by s. 27 is computed. The amount of the relief is calculated as

$$\frac{\text{number of qualifying days}}{365} \times \frac{25}{100} \times \text{relevant income.}$$

The relevant income is the particular taxpayer's income arising from the trade or profession in the year of assessment from which has been deducted or added any appropriate amounts relating to capital allowances (para. 2 (2) (*a*) (*b*) and (*c*) concerning ss. 70 and 71, Capital Allowances Act 1968), stock relief and trading (or professional) losses.

The relevant income is the income in respect of which the individual is chargeable for the year during which he is abroad. It means that the exemption is being applied to income actually earned in a previous year—normally the accounting period ending in the 12-month period preceding the year of assessment.

It does not (as with employees) attempt to connect the relief with the actual profits earned by the work carried out abroad. The amount of the relief compares unfavourably with the relief given to employees who are entitled to deduct 25 per cent. of the emoluments attributable to duties performed abroad (F.A. 1977, Sched. 7, para. 4) though the prima facie test is to apportion the emoluments for the year on a time basis.

In the case of a qualifying day related to more than one trade or profession it is split equally between the trades or professions.

If the taxpayer is a member of a partnership then these rules are applied to his share of the net profits of the partnership.

The amount of the relief is deducted from the taxpayer's income after the prior deduction of capital allowances and stock relief but before the deduction of any trading or professional losses.

Section 36 SCHEDULE 5

RELEVANT INCOME OF CLOSE COMPANIES—AMENDMENTS OF FINANCE ACT 1972, SCHEDULE 16, PART II

1. At the end of paragraph 8 of Schedule 16 to the Finance Act 1972 (determination of relevant income for the purpose of apportioning the income of close company among participators) there shall be added the following sub-paragraphs:—

" (3) In arriving at the relevant income for any accounting period of a company which is a trading company or a member of a trading group, regard shall be had not only to the current requirements of the company's business and to such requirements necessary or advisable for the maintenance or development of that business as fall within sub-paragraph (2) (*a*) above, but also to any other requirements necessary or advisable for the acquisition of a trade or of a controlling interest in a trading company or in a company which is a member of a trading group by virtue of paragraph 11 (2) (*a*) below; but for this purpose paragraph 12A below shall apply.

(4) For the purposes of sub-paragraph (3) above, the acquisition of a controlling interest in a company means the acquisition, whether on a single

occasion or otherwise, of such ordinary share capital of that company as enables the acquiring company to exercise the greater part of the voting power in that company.

(5) For the purposes of sub-paragraph (3) above the requirements of a company's business which are necessary or advisable for such an acquisition as is mentioned in that sub-paragraph include such requirements as are necessary or advisable for—

> (a) the redemption or repayment of any share or loan capital or debt (including any premium thereon) issued or incurred in or towards payment for that acquisition, or issued or incurred for the purpose of raising money to be applied in or towards payment therefor, or

> (b) meeting any obligations of the company in respect of that acquisition,

so far as any sum so expended or applied, or intended to be expended or applied, does not fall to be treated for the purposes of this Schedule as a distribution by the company."

2. After paragraph 12 of Schedule 16 to the Finance Act 1972 there shall be inserted the following paragraph—

" 12A.—(1) Paragraph 8 (3) above shall not apply to—

> (a) the acquisition of a trade, or of an asset to be used in a trade, or of an interest in any such asset, which at the date of the acquisition or at any time within one year previously was owned by an associated company of the acquiring company; or

> (b) the intended acquisition of a trade, or of such an asset or interest as is referred to in paragraph (a) above, which, at the end of the accounting period for which the acquiring company's relevant income is to be ascertained, is owned by a company which is then an associated company of the acquiring company;

and where the trade, asset or interest was, or is, in part owned as mentioned above, paragraph 8 (3) above shall not apply with respect to that part.

(2) Paragraph 8 (3) above shall not apply to—

> (a) the acquisition of shares which at the date of the acquisition or at any time within one year previously were owned by an associated company of the acquiring company or by a person who then had control of the acquiring company; or

> (b) the intended acquisition of shares which at the end of the accounting period for which the acquiring company's relevant income is to be ascertained are owned by a company which is then an associated company of the acquiring company or by a person who has control of the acquiring company;

and where shares were, or are, in part owned as mentioned above, paragraph 8 (3) above shall not apply with respect to that part.

(3) Paragraph 8 (3) above shall not apply to—

> (a) the acquisition of shares in a company which immediately before the acquisition or at any time within one year previously was an associated company of the acquiring company; or

> (b) the intended acquisition of shares in a company which, at the end of the accounting period for which the acquiring company's relevant income is to be ascertained, is an associated company of the acquiring company.

(4) Section 302 (1) of the Taxes Act (definition of an associated company for the purposes of close companies legislation)—

> (a) shall not apply for the purposes of paragraph (a) of sub-paragraphs (1), (2) and (3) above; and

> (b) shall apply for the purposes of paragraph (b) of each of those sub-paragraphs with the omission of the words " or at any time within one year previously ".

(5) For the purposes of paragraph (a) of sub-paragraphs (1), (2) and (3) above, another company is an associated company of the acquiring company if—

> (a) the acquiring company controlled that other company or that other company controlled the acquiring company either at the date of the acquisition of the trade, asset or interest or at any time within one year previously; or

> (b) a person who had control of the acquiring company at that date also

controlled that other company either at that date or at any time within one year previously.

(6) In ascertaining for the purposes of sub-paragraphs (2) and (5) above or for the purposes of section 302 (1) of the Taxes Act as it applies for the purposes of paragraph (*b*) of sub-paragraphs (1), (2) and (3) above, whether any person has control of a company—

    (*a*) there shall be left out of account for the purposes of section 302 (2) (*c*) of the Taxes Act (under which a person may have control of a company by reason of his rights in the event of winding up) the rights of another company as loan creditor in respect of a debt incurred or redeemable loan capital issued in connection with the acquisition from that company of any trade, any asset to be used in a trade, or any interest in any such asset;

    (*b*) paragraph (*a*) of subsection (3) of section 303 of the Taxes Act (definition of " associate ") shall have effect as if the reference to a partner of a participator were omitted;

    (*c*) that paragraph and paragraph (*b*) of that subsection shall have effect as if the expression " relative " did not have the meaning assigned to it by subsection (4) of that section but meant husband or wife or, in the case of a director of the company, husband or wife or any child or remoter issue who is an infant; and

    (*d*) paragraph (*c*) of the said subsection (3) (persons who are " associates " by virtue of their interests in trusts, etc.) shall have effect as if the reference to any other person interested were a reference (and a reference only) to the trustees or to the personal representatives as defined in section 432 (4) of the Taxes Act.

(7) For the purposes of this paragraph the time of acquisition of a trade, asset or interest, or shares, acquired under a contract shall be—

    (*a*) the time at which the contract is made, or

    (*b*) if the contract is conditional (and in particular if it is conditional on the exercise of an option) the time at which the condition is satisfied,

and not, if different, the time at which the trade, asset, interest or shares is or are conveyed or transferred.

(8) For the purposes of sub-paragraph (3) of paragraph 8 above there shall be regarded as income available for distribution and not as having been applied, or as being applicable, to such requirements of a company's business as may be necessary or advisable for such an acquisition as is mentioned in that sub-paragraph any sum expended or applied, or intended to be expended or applied, as mentioned in paragraph (*a*) (iv) or paragraph (*b*) of sub-paragraph (1) of paragraph 12 above; and sub-paragraphs (2) and (3) of that paragraph shall apply for the purposes of this sub-paragraph as they apply for the purposes of that paragraph."

GENERAL NOTE

The provisions of this Schedule ease the apportionment rules applicable to close companies. Previously it was only possible to take into account the current needs of the company and its requirements for the maintenance and development of business, in determining the amount of relevant income which the Revenue might treat as having been apportioned. Now it is possible to take into account in the case of trading companies or members of a trading group such of the requirements of such a company as are necessary or advisable for:

    (i) the acquisition of a trade;

    (ii) the acquisition of a controlling interest in a trading company or a company which is a member of a trading company. This acquisition need not be effected by a single transaction but may consist of a number of separate acquisitions.

To have acquired " a controlling interest " the acquiring company must be entitled by reason of its ordinary share capital to the greater part of the voting power in the acquired company. Presumably this does not necessarily mean a simple majority of the ordinary shares but must depend on the various classes of shares of the company and the rights each class confers.

These provisions enable the cost of acquiring the first business of the company or any subsequent unconnected businesses to be taken into account.

As is usual, certain anti-avoidance provisions are included so that the following acquisitions are excluded from the relaxation of the apportionment rules:

(i) acquisitions from an associated company of the acquiring company;

(ii) acquisitions of a trade, asset to be used in a trade, interest in such an asset, or shares which at any time within one year prior to the acquisition was owned by an associated company or in the case of shares, by a person who then controlled the acquiring company;

(iii) the intended acquisition of a trade, asset (or interest therein) or shares which at the end of the accounting period in which account is to be taken of the requirements of the intended acquisition is owned by an associated company or, in the case of shares, by a person who then controls the acquiring company;

(iv) the acquisition (or intended acquisition) of shares in a company which is associated with the acquiring company at the date of acquisition or at any time during the year preceding the acquisition (or at the end of the accounting period in which account is taken of the requirements for the intended acquisition).

These new sub-paragraphs have their own definition of " associated company " as regards (i) (ii) and (iv) (save as regards intended acquisitions) above. As regards (iii) and (iv) (in respect of intended acquisitions only) the definition contained in s. 302 (1), I.C.T.A. 1970, applies, subject to the amendment contained in the new para. 12A (4) (b) of Sched. 16, F.A. 1972. However, the two definitions seem to be almost identical. It is the meaning of control contained in ss. 302 and 303, I.C.T.A. 1970, which has been amended in certain respects.

Section 38　　　　　　SCHEDULE 6

CAPITAL ALLOWANCES: HOTELS

Initial allowances

1. In section 1 (2) of the Capital Allowances Act 1968 for the reference to one-half of the capital expenditure there shall be substituted a reference to one-fifth of that expenditure.

Writing-down allowances

2. Section 2 (3) of the said Act of 1968 shall apply to any sale (whether or not the building is then a qualifying hotel) which is an event to which section 3 (1) of that Act applies.

Balancing allowances and balancing charges

3. Subsection (1) of section 3 of the said Act of 1968 shall apply on the occurrence of any such event as is there mentioned not only while the building is a qualifying hotel but also after it has ceased to be one; but where two or more such events occur during a period when the building is not a qualifying hotel that subsection shall not apply on the occurrence of any of those events except the first.

4. Where, after a building has ceased to be a qualifying hotel otherwise than on the occurrence of an event to which subsection (1) of the said section 3 applies, a period of two years elapses in which it is not a qualifying hotel and without the occurrence of any such event, that section and the other provisions of Chapter I of Part I of the said Act of 1968 shall have effect as if—

(a) the relevant interest in the building had been sold at the end of that period; and

(b) the net proceeds of the sale were equal to the price which that interest would then have fetched if sold in the open market.

5. The proviso to subsection (4) of the said section 3 shall apply to any sale (whether or not the building is then a qualifying hotel) which is an event to which subsection (1) of that section applies.

6. Where a balancing allowance or balancing charge falls to be made in the case of a building which has ceased to be a qualifying hotel and the circumstances are such as are mentioned in paragraph (a) or (b) of subsection (2) of section 12 of the said Act of 1968, the allowance or charge shall be made as provided in that subsection.

Temporary disuse

7. Paragraph 4 above has effect subject to section 12 (1) of the said Act of 1968; but a building shall not by virtue of that section be deemed to continue to be a qualifying hotel for more than two years after the end of the chargeable period or its basis period in which it falls temporarily out of use.

Eligible expenditure

8. References in Chapter I of Part I of the said Act of 1968 to expenditure on the construction of a building or structure shall not include references to expenditure incurred in taking any such steps as are mentioned in section 17 of the Finance Act 1974 or section 15 of the Finance Act 1975 (expenditure on fire safety).

Definitions

9. None of the provisions of section 7 of the said Act of 1968 except subsections (4) and (9) shall be construed as applying to a qualifying hotel.

GENERAL NOTE

This Schedule modifies the application of the rules concerning capital allowances to expenditure on qualifying hotels.

Para. 1. Provides that the initial allowance is only 20 per cent. and not 50 per cent.

Para. 2. Ensures that if the qualifying hotel is sold after the expenditure is incurred the remaining allowance is recalculated over what remains of a 25-year period from the time when building first used.

Paras. 3 to 7. A balancing allowance or charge, whichever is appropriate, shall arise on the first occurrence of any event specified in C.A.A. 1968, s. 3 (1) (*e.g.* sale of hotel, its destruction or determination of lease of hotel if applicable), or the expiry of a two-year period from the date when the hotel ceased to be a qualifying hotel. In the latter event it is as if the relevant interest in the qualifying hotel had been sold for the price which it would have fetched on the open market.

A hotel which has ceased to be a qualifying hotel for two years shall not for the purposes of capital allowances be treated as temporarily disused.

Para. 8. Any expenditure on a hotel incurred to obtain a fire certificate under Fire Precautions Act 1974 is not covered by this section but will instead qualify for a 100 per cent. allowance under F.A. 1974, s. 17, and F.A. 1975, s. 15.

Section 44 SCHEDULE 7

RELIEF FOR GAINS LESS THAN £9,500

Preliminary

1. In this Schedule references to any subsections not otherwise identified are references to subsections of section 44 of this Act.

Husband and wife

2.—(1) For any year of assessment during which a married woman is living with her husband subsections (1) to (4) shall apply to them as if the amounts of £1,000, £5,000 and £600 were divided between them—

    (*a*) in proportion to their respective taxable amounts for that year (disregarding for this purpose paragraphs (*a*) and (*b*) of subsection (4)); or

    (*b*) where the aggregate of those amounts does not exceed £1,000 and allowable losses accruing to either of them in a previous year are carried forward from that year, in such other proportion as they may agree.

(2) Sub-paragraph (1) above shall also apply for any year of assessment during a part of which (being a part beginning with 6th April) a married woman is living with her husband but—

(*a*) her taxable amount for that year shall not include chargeable gains or allowable losses accruing to her in the remainder of the year; and

(*b*) subsections (1) to (4) shall apply to her (without the modification in sub-paragraph (1) above) for the remainder of the year as if it were a separate year of assessment.

3.—(1) For any year of assessment during which or during a part of which (being a part beginning with 6th April) the individual is a married man whose wife is living with him and in relation to whom paragraph 3 (1) of Schedule 10 to the Finance Act 1965 applies subsection (5) shall apply as if—

(*a*) the chargeable gains accruing to him in the year included those accruing to her in the year or the part of the year; and

(*b*) all the disposals of assets made by her in the year or the part of the year were made by him.

(2) Subsection (5) shall not apply for any year of assessment during which or during a part of which (being a part beginning with 6th April)—

(*a*) the individual is a married man whose wife is living with him but in relation to whom the said paragraph 3 (1) does not apply; or

(*b*) the individual is a married woman living with her husband.

Personal representatives

4. For the year of assessment in which an individual dies and for the two next following years of assessment, subsections (1) to (5) shall apply to his personal representatives as they apply to an individual.

Trustees

5.—(1) For any year of assessment during the whole or part of which settled property is held on trusts which secure that, during the lifetime of a mentally disabled person or a person in receipt of attendance allowance, any of the property which is applied, and any income arising from the property, is applied only or mainly for the benefit of that person, subsections (1) to (5) shall apply to the trustees of the settlement as they apply to an individual.

(2) In this paragraph "mentally disabled person" means a person who by reason of mental disorder within the meaning of the Mental Health Act 1959 is incapable of administering his property or managing his affairs and "attendance allowance" means an allowance under section 35 of the Social Security Act 1975 or the Social Security (Northern Ireland) Act 1975.

6.—(1) For any year of assessment during the whole or part of which any property is settled property, not being a year of assessment for which paragraph 5 (1) above applies, subsections (1) to (5) shall apply to the trustees of a settlement as they apply to an individual but with the following modifications.

(2) In subsections (1), (4) and (5) for "£1,000" there shall be substituted "£500".

(3) For subsections (2) and (3) there shall be substituted—

"(2) If an individual's taxable amount for a year of assessment exceeds £500 the amount of capital gains tax to which he is chargeable for that year shall not exceed one-half of the excess."

(4) In subsection (5) for "£5,000" there shall be substituted "£2,500".

(5) This paragraph applies where the settlement was made before 7th June 1978.

GENERAL NOTE

This Schedule applies the new capital gains tax relief for gains less than £9,500 (s. 44) to husbands and wives, personal representatives and trustees.

Husbands and wives. The relief given by s. 44 cannot be claimed by both the husband and wife if during the relevant year of assessment they are living together. Instead it is divided between them. The division will be in proportion to their respective taxable amounts taking into account for these purposes only, any losses carried forward from previous years. This is subject to one qualification in the case where their taxable amounts together do not exceed £1,000 and one or both of them has carried forward losses from previous years. In such a case they can agree to divide the relief amongst them in such proportions as they decide.

The government was not prepared to allow each spouse to be entitled to the full relief as it was felt this would result in transfers between spouses to obtain the maximum advantage from the relief.

In any year of assessment in which the spouses cease to live together for the purposes of this relief, the part of the year for which they are not living together is treated as a separate year of assessment as regards the wife.

Personal Representatives. The relief may be claimed by a personal representative but only in respect of the year of assessment in which the deceased died and the two years of assessment following that one.

Trusts. The relief will apply in the same manner as for individuals to trusts providing that the capital and income is applied " only or mainly " for the benefit of a person who is mentally disabled or in receipt of an attendance allowance during that person's lifetime.

As regards other trusts the first £500 taxable amount will not be charged to capital gains tax, and thereafter the tax will be limited to one-half the excess of the taxable amount over £500.

The relief will not apply to settlements created after June 6, 1978, whether or not for the benefit of a mentally disabled person or one in receipt of an attendance allowance.

Section 46   SCHEDULE 8

RELIEF FOR GIFTS OF BUSINESS ASSETS

PART I

AGRICULTURAL PROPERTY AND SETTLED PROPERTY

Agricultural property

1.—(1) This paragraph applies where—
    (*a*) after 11th April 1978 there is a disposal of an asset which is, or is an interest in, agricultural property within the meaning of Schedule 8 to the Finance Act 1975 (capital transfer tax relief for agricultural property), and
    (*b*) apart from this paragraph, the disposal would not fall within paragraph (*a*) of subsection (1) of section 46 of this Act (in this Part of this Schedule referred to as " the principal section ") by reason only that the agricultural property is not used for the purposes of a trade carried on as mentioned in that paragraph.

(2) Where this paragraph applies, subsection (1) of the principal section shall apply in relation to the disposal if the circumstances are such that a reduction in respect of the asset—
    (*a*) is made under Schedule 8 to the Finance Act 1975 in relation to a chargeable transfer taking place on the occasion of the disposal; or
    (*b*) would be so made if there were a chargeable transfer on that occasion and a claim were duly made under that Schedule.

Settled property

2.—(1) If, after 11th April 1978, a trustee is deemed, by virtue of subsection (3) or subsection (4) of section 25 of the Finance Act 1965 (settled property) to have disposed of, and immediately reacquired—
    (*a*) an asset which is, or is an interest in, an asset used for the purposes of a trade, profession or vocation carried on by the trustee or by a relevant beneficiary, or
    (*b*) shares or securities of a trading company as to which not less than 25 per cent. of the voting rights are exercisable by the trustee at the time of the disposal and reacquisition,

subsection (3) of the principal section shall apply in relation to the disposal if a claim for relief under that section is made by the trustee.

(2) Where subsection (3) of the principal section applies by virtue of sub-paragraph (1) above—

(a) a reference to the trustee shall be substituted for the reference in paragraph (a) of that subsection to the transferor and for the reference in paragraph (b) thereof to the transferee; and

(b) subsection (6) of that section shall not apply.

(3) In paragraph (a) of sub-paragraph (1) above, "relevant beneficiary" means—

(a) where the disposal is deemed to occur by virtue of subsection (3) of section 25 of the Finance Act 1965, a beneficiary who had an interest in possession in the settled property immediately before the disposal; and

(b) where the disposal is deemed to occur by virtue of subsection (4) of that section on the termination of a life interest in possession, the beneficiary whose interest it was.

(4) Paragraph 1 above shall apply in relation to paragraph (a) of sub-paragraph (1) above as it applies in relation to paragraph (a) of subsection (1) of the principal section and references in paragraph 1 above to subsection (1) of the principal section shall be construed accordingly.

PART II

REDUCTIONS IN HELD-OVER GAIN

Application and interpretation

3.—(1) The provisions of this Part of this Schedule apply in cases where a claim for relief is made under section 46 of this Act.

(2) In this Part of this Schedule—

(a) "the principal provision" means subsection (1) of section 46 of this Act or, as the case may require, sub-paragraph (1) of paragraph 2 above;

(b) "shares" includes securities;

(c) "the transferor" and "the transferee" have the same meaning as in section 46 of this Act, except that, in a case where paragraph 2 above applies, each of those expressions refers to the trustee mentioned in that paragraph; and

(d) "unrelieved gain", in relation to a disposal, has the same meaning as in section 46 (6) of this Act.

(3) Any reference in this Part of this Schedule to a disposal of an asset is a reference to a disposal which falls within paragraph (a) of the principal provision and any reference to a disposal of shares is a reference to a disposal which falls within paragraph (b) of that provision.

(4) In relation to a disposal of an asset or of shares, any reference in the following provisions of this Part of this Schedule to the held-over gain is a reference to the held-over gain on that disposal as determined under subsection (5) or, as the case may be, subsection (6) of section 46 of this Act (taking account, where paragraph 2 above applies, of sub-paragraph (2) (b) of that paragraph).

Reductions peculiar to disposals of assets

4. If, in the case of a disposal of an asset, the asset was not used for the purposes of the trade, profession or vocation referred to in paragraph (a) of the principal provision throughout the period of its ownership by the transferor, the amount of the held-over gain shall be reduced by multiplying it by the fraction of which the denominator is the number of days in that period of ownership and the numerator is the number of days in that period during which the asset was so used.

5. If, in the case of a disposal of an asset, the asset is a building or structure and, over the period of its ownership by the transferor or any substantial part of that period, part of the building or structure was, and part was not, used for

the purposes of the trade, profession or vocation referred to in paragraph (*a*) of the principal provision, there shall be determined the fraction of the unrelieved gain on the disposal which it is just and reasonable to apportion to the part of the asset which was so used, and the amount of the held-over gain (as reduced, if appropriate, under paragraph 4 above) shall be reduced by multiplying it by that fraction.

Reduction peculiar to disposal of shares

6.—(1) If, in the case of a disposal of shares, the chargeable assets of the company whose shares are disposed of include assets which are not business assets, the amount of the held-over gain shall be reduced by multiplying it by the fraction of which the denominator is the market value of the whole of the company's chargeable assets on the date of the disposal and the numerator is the market value of the company's chargeable business assets on that date.

(2) For the purposes of this paragraph—

  (*a*) an asset is a business asset in relation to a company if it is or is an interest in an asset used for the purposes of a trade, profession or vocation carried on by the company; and

  (*b*) an asset is a chargeable asset in relation to a company at any time if, on a disposal of it at that time, a chargeable gain would accrue to the company.

Reduction where gain partly relieved by retirement relief

7.—(1) If, in the case of a disposal of an asset,—

  (*a*) the disposal is of a chargeable business asset and is comprised in a disposal of the whole or part of a business in respect of gains accruing on which the transferor is entitled to relief under section 34 of the Finance Act 1965 (transfer of business on retirement), and

  (*b*) apart from this paragraph, the held-over gain on the disposal (as reduced, where appropriate, under the preceding provisions of this Part of this Schedule) would exceed the amount of the chargeable gain which, apart from section 46 of this Act, would accrue on the disposal,

the amount of that held-over gain shall be reduced by the amount of the excess.

(2) In sub-paragraph (1) above "chargeable business asset" has the same meaning as in section 34 of the Finance Act 1965.

(3) If, in the case of a disposal of shares,—

  (*a*) the disposal is or forms part of a disposal of shares in respect of the gains accruing on which the transferor is entitled to relief under section 34 of the Finance Act 1965, and

  (*b*) apart from this paragraph, the held-over gain on the disposal (as reduced, where appropriate, under paragraph 6 above) would exceed an amount equal to the relevant proportion of the chargeable gain which, apart from section 46 of this Act, would accrue on the disposal,

the amount of that held-over gain shall be reduced by the amount of the excess.

(4) In sub-paragraph (3) above, "the relevant proportion," in relation to a disposal falling within paragraph (*a*) of that sub-paragraph, means the proportion determined under subsection (3) (*b*) of section 34 of the Finance Act 1965 in relation to the aggregate sum of the gains which accrue on that disposal.

GENERAL NOTE

This Schedule is concerned with the relief conferred by s. 46 relating to disposals of business assets (including shares or securities in family trading companies) for less than full consideration.

Para. 1. This extends the relief to cover disposals for less than full consideration of agricultural property which is not used for the purposes of a trade so long as it does (or would if the disposal had been a chargeable transfer) qualify for capital transfer tax relief under F.A. 1975, Sched. 8.

Para. 2. This extends the roll-over relief to settled property in certain circumstances. It will apply whenever there is a deemed disposal under F.A. 1965, s. 25 (3) (on a person becoming absolutely entitled) or F.A. 1965, s. 25 (4) (termination of a life interest in possession) occasioning a deemed disposal and reacquisition by the trustees.

To qualify in the case of a deemed disposal of an asset (or interest in an asset) it must have been used in a trade carried on by the trustee or beneficiary interested in possession immediately prior to the date of the deemed disposal. In the case of shares in a trading company the trustee at the date of the deemed disposal must have had the right to exercise not less than 25 per cent. of the voting rights.

The amount rolled over shall be the whole of the chargeable gain accruing on the deemed disposal.

Agricultural property not being used to carry on a trade which is subject to a settlement will be within the roll-over relief in the same circumstances as non-settled agricultural property (see para. 1).

Paras. 3 *to* 7. These paragraphs apply to reduce the held-over gains in certain circumstances.

As regards disposals of assets (or interests in assets) there will be a reduction in the following cases:

(*a*) if the asset (or interest) has not been used for the purposes of the trade during the whole of the transferor's period of ownership. Then the held-over gain is reduced by $\dfrac{\text{number of days used in trade}}{\text{number of days owned by transferor}}$ whilst owned by transferor;

(*b*) if a building or structure is used partly for the purposes of the trade and partly for other purposes then there will be an apportionment of the chargeable gain on a just and reasonable basis;

(*c*) if part of the chargeable gain is relieved by the application of the retirement relief when the disposal of the asset (or interest) is comprised in the disposal of a whole or part of a business.

As regards shares and securities there will be a reduction in the following cases:

(*a*) if certain of the chargeable assets of the company are not assets used for the purposes of the trade carried on by the company. Then the held-over gain will be reduced by $\dfrac{\text{market value of chargeable business assets}}{\text{market value of all chargeable assets}}$;

(*b*) if part of the chargeable gain is relieved by the application of the retirement relief.

SCHEDULE 9

PROFIT SHARING SCHEMES

PART I

APPROVAL OF SCHEMES

1.—(1) On the application of a body corporate (in this Schedule referred to as "the company concerned") which has established a profit sharing scheme which complies with sub-paragraphs (3) and (4) below, the Board, subject to section 54 of this Act, shall approve the scheme—

(*a*) if they are satisfied as mentioned in paragraph 2 below; and

(*b*) unless it appears to them that there are features of the scheme which are neither essential nor reasonably incidental to the purpose of providing for employees and directors benefits in the nature of interests in shares.

(2) Where the company concerned has control of another company or companies, the scheme may be expressed to extend to all or any of the companies of which it has control; and in this Schedule a scheme which is expressed so to extend is referred to as a "group scheme" and, in relation to a group scheme, the expression "participating company" means the company concerned or a company of which for the time being the company concerned has control and to which for the time being the scheme is expressed to extend.

(3) The scheme must provide for the establishment of a body of persons resident in the United Kingdom (in this Schedule referred to as "the trustees")—

(*a*) who, out of moneys paid to them by the company concerned or, in the case of a group scheme, a participating company, are required by the scheme to acquire shares in respect of which the conditions in Part II of this Schedule are fulfilled; and (*b*) who are under a duty to appropriate shares acquired by them to individuals who participate in the scheme, not being individuals who are ineligible by virtue of Part III of this Schedule; and

(*c*) whose functions with respect to shares held by them are regulated by a trust which is constituted under the law of a part of the United Kingdom and the terms of which are embodied in an instrument which complies with the provisions of Part IV of this Schedule.

(4) The scheme must provide that the total of the initial market values of the shares appropriated to any one participant in a year of assessment will not exceed £500.

(5) An application under sub-paragraph (1) above shall be made in writing and contain such particulars and be supported by such evidence as the Board may require.

2.—(1) The Board must be satisfied that at any time every person who—

(*a*) is then a full-time employee or director of the company concerned or, in the case of a group scheme, a participating company, and

(*b*) has been such an employee or director at all times during a qualifying period, not exceeding five years, ending at that time, and

(*c*) is chargeable to tax in respect of his office or employment under Case I of Schedule E,

will then be eligible, subject to Part III below, to participate in the scheme on similar terms.

(2) For the purposes of sub-paragraph (1) above, the fact that the number of shares to be appropriated to the participants in a scheme varies by reference to the levels of their remuneration, the length of their service or similar factors shall not be regarded as meaning that the participants are not eligible to participate in the scheme on similar terms.

3.—(1) If, at any time after the Board have approved a scheme,—

(*a*) a participant is in breach of any of his obligations under paragraphs (*a*), (*c*) and (*d*) of subsection (1) of section 54 of this Act, or

(*b*) there is, with respect to the operation of the scheme, any contravention of any provision of Chapter III of Part III of this Act, the scheme itself or the terms of the trust referred to in paragraph 1 (3) (*c*) above, or

(*c*) any shares of a class of which shares have been appropriated to participants receive different treatment in any respect from the other shares of that class, in particular, different treatment in respect of—

    (i) the dividend payable,

    (ii) repayment,

    (iii) the restrictions attaching to the shares, or

    (iv) any offer of substituted or additional shares, securities or rights of any description in respect of the shares, or

(*d*) the Board cease to be satisfied as mentioned in paragraph 2 above, the Board may, subject to sub-paragraph (3) below, withdraw the approval with effect from that time or from such later time as the Board may specify.

(2) If, at any time after the Board have approved a scheme, an alteration is made in the scheme or the terms of the trust referred to in paragraph 1 (3) (*c*) above, the approval shall not have effect after the date of the alteration unless the Board have approved the alteration.

(3) It shall not be a ground for withdrawal of approval of a scheme that shares which have been newly issued receive, in respect of dividends payable with respect to a period beginning before the date on which the shares were issued, treatment which is less favourable than that accorded to shares issued before that date.

4. If the company concerned is aggrieved by—

(*a*) the failure of the Board to approve a scheme,

(*b*) the failure of the Board to approve an alteration as mentioned in paragraph 3 (2) above, or

(*c*) the withdrawal of approval,

the company may, by notice in writing given to the Board within thirty days from the date on which it is notified of the Board's decision, require the matter to be determined by the Special Commissioners who shall hear and determine the matter in like manner as an appeal.

Part II

Conditions as to the Shares

5. The shares must form part of the ordinary share capital of—
   (*a*) the company concerned; or
   (*b*) a company which has control of the company concerned; or
   (*c*) a company which either is or has control of a company which—
       (i) is a member of a consortium owning either the company concerned or a company having control of that company; and
       (ii) beneficially owns not less than three-twentieths of the ordinary share capital of the company so owned.

6. The shares must be either—
   (*a*) shares of a class quoted on a recognised stock exchange; or
   (*b*) shares in a company which is not under the control of another company.

7. The shares must be—
   (*a*) fully paid up; and
   (*b*) not redeemable; and
   (*c*) not subject to any restrictions other than restrictions which attach to all shares of the same class.

8. Except where the shares are in a company whose ordinary share capital, at the time of the acquisition of the shares by the trustees, consists of shares of one class only, the majority of the issued shares of the same class must be held by persons other than—
   (*a*) persons who acquired their shares in pursuance of a right conferred on them or an opportunity afforded to them as a director or employee of the company concerned or any other company and not in pursuance of an offer to the public; and
   (*b*) trustees holding shares on behalf of persons who acquired their beneficial interests in the shares in pursuance of such a right or opportunity as is mentioned in paragraph (*a*) above.

Part III

Individuals Ineligible to Participate

9. An individual shall not be eligible to have shares appropriated to him under the scheme at any time unless he is at that time or was within the preceding eighteen months a director or employee of the company concerned or, if the scheme is a group scheme, a participating company.

10. An individual shall not be eligible to have shares appropriated to him under the scheme at any time if in that year of assessment shares have been appropriated to him under another approved scheme established by the company concerned or by—
    (*a*) a company which controls or is controlled by that company or which is controlled by a company which also controls that company, or
    (*b*) a company which is a member of a consortium owning that company or which is owned in part by that company as a member of a consortium.

11.—(1) An individual shall not be eligible to have shares appropriated to him under the scheme at any time if at that time he has, or at any time within the preceding twelve months he had, a material interest in a close company which is—
    (*a*) the company whose shares are to be appropriated; or
    (*b*) a company which has control of that company or is a member of a consortium which owns that company.

(2) Sub-paragraph (1) above shall apply in relation to a company which would be a close company but for—
    (*a*) paragraph (*a*) of subsection (1) of section 282 of the Taxes Act (exclusion of companies not resident in the United Kingdom); or
    (*b*) section 283 of the Taxes Act (exclusion of certain companies with quoted shares).

(3) For the purpose of this paragraph—
    (*a*) " close company " has the meaning assigned to it by section 282 of the Taxes Act; and
    (*b*) subsection (6) of section 285 of the Taxes Act (interest paid to directors and directors' associates) shall have effect, with the substitution of a

reference to 25 per cent. for any reference therein to 5 per cent., for the purpose of determining whether a person has or had a material interest in a company.

PART IV

PROVISIONS AS TO THE TRUST INSTRUMENT

12. The trust instrument shall provide that, as soon as practicable after any shares have been appropriated to a participant, the trustees will give him notice in writing of the appropriation—

(a) specifying the number and description of those shares; and

(b) stating their initial market value.

13.—(1) The trust instrument must contain a provision prohibiting the trustees from disposing of any shares, except as mentioned in section 54 (2) (a) of this Act, during the period of retention (whether by transfer to the participant or otherwise).

(2) The trust instrument must contain a provision prohibiting the trustees from disposing of any shares after the end of the period of retention except—

(a) pursuant to a direction given by or on behalf of the participant or any person in whom the beneficial interest in his shares is for the time being vested; and

(b) by a transaction which would not involve a breach of the participant's obligation under paragraph (c) or paragraph (d) of subsection (1) of section 54 of this Act.

14. The trust instrument must contain a provision requiring the trustees—

(a) subject to their obligations under section 59 of this Act and to any such direction as is referred to in section 56 (3) of this Act, to pay over to the participant any money or money's worth received by them in respect of, or by reference to, any of his shares, other than money's worth consisting of new shares within the meaning of section 57 of this Act; and

(b) to deal only pursuant to a direction given by or on behalf of the participant (or any such person as is referred to in paragraph 13 (2) (a) above) with any right conferred in respect of any of his shares to be allotted other shares, securities or rights of any description.

15. The trust instrument must impose an obligation on the trustees—

(a) to maintain such records as may be necessary to enable the trustees to carry out their obligations under section 59 of this Act; and

(b) where the participant becomes liable to income tax under Schedule E by reason of the occurrence of any event, to inform him of any facts relevant to determining that liability.

PART V

INTERPRETATION

16. In this Schedule "control" shall be construed in accordance with section 534 of the Taxes Act.

17. For the purposes of this Schedule a company is a member of a consortium owning another company if it is one of not more than five companies which between them beneficially own not less than three-quarters of the other company's ordinary share capital and each of which beneficially owns not less than one-twentieth of that capital.

GENERAL NOTE

This Schedule sets out the various conditions that have to be met before a profit sharing scheme can give rise to the tax advantages for employees specified in s. 53. Particular points to note are as follows:

1. Para. 1 (2) makes specific provision for a " group scheme " so that a controlling company can set up a single scheme for its own employees and those of a company or companies under its control.

2. Shares subject to a scheme must not be subject to restrictions not attaching to all shares of the same class (para. 7). This condition is not breached, however, if the shares are newly issued merely because they do not rank for dividends with respect to profits earned prior to issue (para. 3 (3)).

3. So long as there is only a single class of ordinary shares in the company in which the scheme's shares are held, it does not matter what percentage of such shares are held subject to the scheme. In other cases the percentage must never exceed 50 (para. 8).

4. The shares appropriated need not necessarily be in the company setting up the scheme (para. 5) although it must be related to it, but must be in a quoted company or one not under the control of any other company (para. 6).

5. Employees able to participate in the scheme can be limited to those who have been employed by the company concerned for a limited period of time. This period must not exceed five years (para. 2 (1) (b)).

6. All qualifying employees must participate in the scheme on similar terms (para. 2 (1)). Taking into account the provision in para. 2 (2) this would appear to mean that employees of similar status who have worked for the company for similar periods must be treated similarly. While the position is not altogether clear, appropriation dependent on performance would not appear to be possible.

7. An individual is not eligible ·to participate in the scheme if he has a material interest (more than a 25 per cent. interest) in the company whose shares are to be appropriated, in a company controlling that company, or in a company which is a member of a consortium owning that company (para. 11) unless the relevant company is non-close (see para. 11 (2) which widens the definition of close company for this purpose).

8. The scheme must provide that the total of the " initial market values " (as defined in s. 53 (4)) of the shares appropriated to any one participant in a year does not exceed £500 (para. 1 (4)).

9. The trust instrument must contain a provision to the effect that all dividends paid in respect of the allocated shares will be paid by the trustees to the person to whom the shares have been allocated (para. 14 (a)).

Section 62

SCHEDULE 10

RATES OF CAPITAL TRANSFER TAX
FIRST TABLE

Portion of value		Rate of tax
Lower limit £	Upper limit £	Per cent.
0	25,000	Nil
25,000	30,000	10
30,000	35,000	15
35,000	40,000	20
40,000	50,000	25
50,000	60,000	30
60,000	70,000	35
70,000	90,000	40
90,000	110,000	45
110,000	130,000	50
130,000	160,000	55
160,000	510,000	60
510,000	1,010,000	65
1,010,000	2,010,000	70
2,010,000	—	75

SECOND TABLE

Portion of value		Rate of tax
Lower limit £	Upper limit £	Per cent.
0	25,000	Nil
25,000	30,000	5
30,000	35,000	$7\frac{1}{2}$
35,000	40,000	10
40,000	50,000	$12\frac{1}{2}$
50,000	60,000	15
60,000	70,000	$17\frac{1}{2}$
70,000	90,000	20
90,000	110,000	$22\frac{1}{2}$
110,000	130,000	$27\frac{1}{2}$
130,000	160,000	35
160,000	210,000	$42\frac{1}{2}$
210,000	260,000	50
260,000	310,000	55
310,000	510,000	60
510,000	1,010,000	65
1,010,000	2,010,000	70
2,010,000	—	75

Section 67

SCHEDULE 11

EMPLOYEE TRUSTS

The Finance Act 1975

1.—(1) In paragraph 17 (4) of Schedule 5 to the Finance Act 1975 for paragraph (*b*) there shall be substituted—

" (*b*) in a case where the employment in question is employment by a close company, a person who is a participator in relation to that company and either—
(i) is beneficially entitled to, or to rights entitling him to acquire, not less than 5 per cent. of, or of any class of the shares comprised in, its issued share capital; or
(ii) would, on a winding-up of the company, be entitled to not less than 5 per cent. of its assets; "

and after paragraph (*b*) there shall be inserted the words " but if the trusts are those of a profit sharing scheme approved under the Finance Act 1978, paragraph (*b*) of this sub-paragraph does not preclude the application of sub-paragraph (3) (*c*) above in relation to any appropriation of shares in pursuance of the scheme."

(2) This amendment applies in relation to any payment out of the settled property made on or after 11th April 1978.

The Finance Act 1976

2.—(1) In section 56 of the Finance Act 1976 for subsection (1) there shall be substituted—

" (1) Where—
(*a*) a close company within the meaning of section 90 below disposes of an asset to trustees in circumstances such that the disposal is a disposition which by virtue of that section is not a transfer of value for the purposes of capital transfer tax; or
(*b*) an individual disposes of an asset to trustees in circumstances such that the disposal is an exempt transfer by virtue of section 67 of the Finance Act 1978,

Part III of the Finance Act 1965 (capital gains tax) shall have effect in relation to the disposal in accordance with subsections (2) and (3) below."

(2) In subsection (6) of that section for the words from " any participator who " to " assets " there shall be substituted the words " any participator who—
(*a*) is not beneficially entitled to, or to rights entitling him to acquire, 5 per cent. or more of, or of any class of the shares comprised in, its issued share capital; and

(b) on a winding-up of the company would not be entitled to 5 per cent. or more of its assets;"

and at the end there shall be inserted the words "or, if the trusts are those of a profit sharing scheme approved under the Finance Act 1978, of any power to appropriate shares in pursuance of the scheme."

(3) These amendments apply in relation to any disposal made on or after 11th April 1978.

3.—(1) In section 90 of the said Act of 1976, subsection (2) shall be omitted and in subsection (3) for the words " subsections (1) and (2) above do not apply " there shall be substituted the words " subsection (1) above does not apply ".

(2) In subsection (4) of that section for the words from " any participator who " to " assets " there shall be substituted the words " any participator who—

(a) is not beneficially entitled to, or to rights entitling him to acquire, 5 per cent. or more of, or of any class of the shares comprised in, its issued share capital; and

(b) on a winding-up of the company would not be entitled to 5 per cent. or more of its assets;"

and at the end there shall be inserted the words "or, if the trusts are those of a profit sharing scheme approved under the Finance Act 1978, of any power to appropriate shares in pursuance of the scheme."

(3) These amendments apply in relation to any disposition made on or after 11th April 1978.

GENERAL NOTE

This puts into effect the consequential amendments which are made necessary by the changes introduced by s. 67. They bring the enactments mentioned in this Schedule into line with these provisions.

Section 79

SCHEDULE 12

CUSTOMS AND EXCISE CONSOLIDATION AMENDMENTS

Alcoholic liquors

1.—(1) Part IV of the Customs and Excise Act 1952 (in this Schedule referred to as " the 1952 Act ") shall be amended in accordance with the following provisions of this paragraph.

(2) For the words " duty ", " duties " or " duty-paid ", wherever occurring, there shall be substituted the words " excise duty ", " excise duties " or " excise duty-paid " respectively.

(3) Sub-paragraph (2) above does not apply where the word " duty " or " duties " occurs in the expression " excise duty ", " duty of excise ", " excise duties ", " duties of excise ", " customs duty ", " duties of customs " or " duty-free " or to sections 167 to 170 but—

(a) in section 115 (2) (returns), for the words " customs or excise duties " there shall be substituted the words " excise duties ";

(b) in section 137 (3) (declarations), for the words " duties of customs " there shall be substituted the words " excise duty ";

(c) in section 144 (1) (fortifying wine), for the words " duty-free spirits " there shall be substituted the words " spirits which are free of excise duty ";

(d) in section 161 (4) (selling spirits), for the words " duty of customs or excise " there shall be substituted the words " excise duty ";

(e) in sections 162 (1) and 164 (1) (misdescribing spirits), for the words " either the customs duty or the excise duty " there shall be substituted the words " the excise duty "; and

(f) in section 165 (b) (deemed spirits), after the word " being " there shall be inserted the word " imported " and for the words " customs duty " there shall be substituted the words " excise duty ".

(4) In sections 103 (1) and (4), 137 (1) and 138 after the word " drawback " there shall be inserted the words " of excise duty ".

(5) In section 140 (2) (wine and made-wine regulations) after the word " person " there shall be inserted the words " contravenes or ".

(6) In sections 171 (1) and 172 (1) (gravity and strengths), the words "this Act" shall be substituted for the words "the customs and excise Acts" and the same words shall be substituted for the words "the said Acts" in sections 171 (3) and 172 (4).

2. In section 1 (5) of the Finance Act 1964 (unfit spirituous goods), for the words "the customs Acts" there shall be substituted the words "the charge of excise duty on spirits".

3. In section 14 (5) of the Finance (No. 2) Act 1975 (wine), after the words "grapes or" there shall be inserted the word "of".

4. In section 15 (6) of the Finance (No. 2) Act 1975 (made-wine), after the words "black beer" there shall be inserted the words "(as defined in section 2 (5) of the Finance Act 1964)".

5. In section 2 (6) of the Finance Act 1976 (cider regulations), after the word "person" there shall be inserted the words "contravenes or".

Matches and mechanical lighters

6.—(1) In section 220 of the 1952 Act (matches), the words "excise duty" shall be substituted for the word "duty" in subsection (1) (c) and for the words "duty of customs or excise" in subsection (3).

(2) In section 221 of the 1952 Act (mechanical lighters)—

    (a) the words "excise duty" shall be substituted for the word "duty" in subsection (1) and for the words "duty of customs or excise" in subsections (2) and (4); and

    (b) the words "and the component parts of any such mechanical lighters" and "or component parts thereof" in subsection (2) shall be omitted.

(3) In section 222 of the 1952 Act (lighters), there shall be omitted, in subsection (1) (a), the words from "(other" to "flint)", in subsection (2), the words "Subject to the next following subsection" and subsection (3).

Tobacco products

7.—(1) In section 7 of the Finance Act 1963, in subsection (2), for the word "tobacco" in the definition there shall be substituted the words "tobacco products" and, in subsection (4), after the word "aircraft" there shall be inserted the words "hovercraft (within the meaning of the Hovercraft Act 1968)" and for the words "tobacco is" there shall be substituted the words "tobacco products are".

(2) In section 6 (4) of the Finance Act 1976, the words "the order" shall be substituted for the words "an order".

Hydrocarbon oil

8. In sections 1 (1), 2 (3) and 21 (3) of the Hydrocarbon Oil (Customs & Excise) Act 1971 (interpretation, etc.), the words "this Act and the Act of 1952" shall be substituted for the words "the customs and excise Acts", in section 3 (1) the words "the Act of 1952" shall be substituted for the words "the excise Acts" and in paragraph 2 (1) of Schedule 5 the words "this Act or the Act of 1952" shall be substituted for the words "the customs or excise Acts".

Collection and management of, and certain reliefs from, duties

9. In section 37 (1) of the 1952 Act (Channel Island goods) the proviso shall be omitted and the words "duty of customs" preceding the proviso shall be construed as not including any duty other than a duty of customs.

10. In section 43 of the 1952 Act (antiques, etc.), for the words preceding paragraph (a) there shall be substituted the words "The Commissioners may allow. the delivery without payment of duty on importation".

11. In section 80 (1) of the 1952 Act (warehoused goods) in paragraph (c), after the word "goods" there shall be inserted the words "manufactured or produced in the United Kingdom".

12. In section 85 (1) of the 1952 Act (deficiency in warehoused goods), for the words "this Act," there shall be substituted the words "the customs and excise Acts".

13. In section 259 (1) of the 1952 Act (composite goods), for the words "a duty of customs" and "duty" there shall be substituted the words "excise duty" and in section 5 of and Schedule 2 to the Finance Act 1957 the following amendments shall be made—

(a) in section 5, for the words " customs duties " there shall be substituted the words " excise duties " and for the words " customs and excise " there shall be substituted the word " excise ";

(b) in Schedule 2, for the words " duty of customs " in paragraph 1 (1) and the words " duty of customs or excise " in paragraph 4 (1) there shall be substituted the words " duty of excise " and for the words " customs duties " in paragraph 3 there shall be substituted the words " excise duties "; and

(c) the following provisions in Schedule 2 shall be omitted, namely, in paragraph 1 (2) the words from " and for the purposes " to the end, paragraph 1 (3), paragraph 2 and paragraph 4 (2) (b).

14. In section 263 of the 1952 Act (lost or destroyed goods relief), in subsection (1), for the word " shall " there shall be substituted the word " may ".

15. In section 272 (1) of the 1952 Act (duty-free goods for Her Majesty's ships), for the words " customs or excise duty " there shall be substituted the words " excise duty ".

This paragraph shall come into operation on such day as the Commissioners of Customs and Excise may appoint by order made by statutory instrument.

16. In section 285 (2) (b) of the 1952 Act (imprisonment in default), for the words " such a non-payment or default as aforesaid " there shall be substituted the words " non-payment of that penalty or default of a sufficient distress to satisfy the amount of that penalty ".

17. In section 287 of the 1952 Act (application of penalties), for the words from " customs or excise Acts " to " those Acts " there shall be substituted the words " customs and excise Acts, after paying any such compensation or costs as are mentioned in section 114 of the Magistrates' Courts Act 1952 to persons other than the Commissioners ".

18. After section 306 of the 1952 Act there shall be inserted the following section—

" Directions

306A. Directions given under any provision of this Act may make different provision for different circumstances and may be varied or revoked by subsequent directions thereunder."

Terminology

19.—(1) In section 307 (1) of the 1952 Act the following amendments shall be made, namely—

(a) for the definition of " customs Acts " and " excise Acts " there shall be substituted the following definition—

" the customs and excise Acts " means this Act and any other enactment for the time being in force relating to customs or excise;

(b) the definitions of " excise trade " and " excise trader " shall be omitted but there shall be inserted in the appropriate places in alphabetical order the following definitions—

" excise licence trade " means a trade or business for the carrying on of which an excise licence is required;

" revenue trader " means any person carrying on a trade or business subject to any of the revenue trade provisions of the customs and excise Acts, whether or not that trade or business is an excise licence trade, and includes a registered club;

" the revenue trade provisions of the customs and excise Acts " means—

(a) the provisions of the customs and excise Acts relating to the protection, security, collection or management of the revenues derived from the duties of excise on goods produced or manufactured in the United Kingdom;

(b) the provisions of the customs and excise Acts relating to any activity or facility for the carrying on or provision of which an excise licence is required; and

(c) the provisions of the Betting and Gaming Duties Act 1972 (so far as not included in paragraph (b) above);

(c) the following definition shall be inserted in the appropriate place in alphabetical order—

"prohibited or restricted goods" means goods of a class or description of which the importation, exportation or carriage coastwise is for the time being prohibited or restricted under or by virtue of any enactment;

(d) for the definition of "holiday" there shall be substituted the following definition—

"holiday", in relation to any part of the United Kingdom, means any day that is a bank holiday in that part of the United Kingdom under the Banking and Financial Dealings Act 1971, Christmas Day, Good Friday and the day appointed for the purposes of customs and excise for the celebration of Her Majesty's birthday.

(2) Subject to sub-paragraphs (3) and (5) below, any reference in any enactment or instrument to the customs Acts or excise Acts shall be construed as a reference to the customs and excise Acts (as defined in sub-paragraph (1) above).

(3) In the following provisions of Part IX of the 1952 Act, namely sections 244 (1), 245 (2), 246, 247 (1) and 248 (1), for the words "the excise Acts" there shall be substituted the words "the revenue trade provisions of the customs and excise Acts".

(4) In section 34 the reference in subsection (1) to the 1952 Act or any enactments relating to customs and the reference in subsection (4) to any such enactments shall be construed as a reference to the customs and excise Acts (as defined in sub-paragraph (1) above).

(5) In section 73 of the 1952 Act, for the words "the customs Acts" there shall be substituted the words "any provision of the customs and excise Acts relating to imported goods or prohibited or restricted goods" and in section 79 (1) of that Act, for the words from "this Act" onwards there shall be substituted the words "the customs and excise Acts".

(6) Any reference in any enactment or instrument to an excise trade or an excise trader shall be construed as a reference to an excise licence trade or a revenue trader (as defined in sub-paragraph (1) above).

(7) The following provisions relating to customs clearance or charge shall be amended as provided in this sub-paragraph, that is to say—

(a) in sections 17 (1), 22 (1) and 310 (1) (a) of the 1952 Act and in section 11 (10) of the Finance Act 1966, for the words "from customs charge" there shall be substituted the words "out of charge" and in the definition of "importer" in section 307 (1) of the 1952 Act the word "customs" shall be omitted;

(b) in section 25 (1) of the 1952 Act for the words "customs clearance is given therefrom" there shall be substituted the words "clearance outwards is given";

(c) in section 294 (5) of the 1952 Act for the words "customs charge" there shall be substituted the words "customs and excise charge"; and

(d) in section 6 (4) of the Import Duties Act 1958, for the words "customs control" there shall be substituted the words "customs and excise control".

(8) In any enactment or instrument, for the expressions "customs airport" and "customs station", there shall be substituted the expressions "customs and excise airport" and "customs and excise station".

Miscellaneous

20. In section 309 (3) of the 1952 Act (Isle of Man) for the words "there shall be payable" there shall be substituted the words "a like duty of excise shall be payable" and the words from "such part" to the end shall be omitted.

21. It is hereby declared that in section 17 (1) of the Finance Act 1972 (application of the 1952 Act etc. to V.A.T.) the reference to the 1952 Act includes a reference to any enactments replacing or re-enacting Parts V and VI of that Act and the reference to enactments relating to customs generally is a reference to enactments relating generally to customs or excise duties on imported goods.

22. It is hereby declared that in section 6 (5) of the European Communities Act 1972 (application of the 1952 Act etc. to agricultural levies), the reference to the 1952 Act does not include a reference to Part IV or sections 219 to 222 of that Act and the reference to statutory provisions relating to customs generally is a reference to statutory provisions relating generally to customs or excise duties on imported goods.

23. It is hereby declared that the references in section 8 (3) of the Finance (No. 2) Act 1975 to the customs Acts and excise Acts is a reference to—
   (a) the 1952 Act (including the amendments made to section 257 of that Act by section 9 of the Finance Act 1977); and
   (b) any other enactment which relates to customs or excise and which was in force at the end of 1975;
but the said section 8 (3) shall not apply for the interpretation of the words " customs " or " excise " in any amendments made by the foregoing provisions of this Schedule.

24.—(1) Sections 27, 28 (2), (7) and (8), 31 (5), (6), (8), (9) and (11), 32 (1) and 61 of the Criminal Law Act 1977 shall extend to Northern Ireland for the purpose of any pecuniary or other penalties which may be imposed under the relevant provisions of the customs and excise Acts and so shall so much of Schedule 5 as excludes offences under the 1952 Act from the operation of the said section 28 (2).

(2) In the application of section 27 of the Criminal Law Act 1977 to Northern Ireland by virtue of sub-paragraph (1) above—
   (a) the reference in subsection (1) of that section to section 108 of the Magistrates' Courts Act 1952 shall be construed as a reference to section 64 of the Magistrates' Courts Act (Northern Ireland) 1964; and
   (b) the references in subsections (1) and (3) of that section to a magistrates' court shall be construed as references to a court of summary jurisdiction.

(3) In sub-paragraph (1) above " the relevant provisions of the customs and excise Acts " means the 1952 Act, section 10 of the Import Duties Act 1958, section 11 of the Finance Act 1966 and the Hydrocarbon Oil (Customs & Excise) Act 1971.

(4) The repeal in section 283 (2) (a) of the 1952 Act effected by section 65 (5) of and Schedule 13 to the Criminal Law Act 1977 shall also extend to Northern Ireland but not in relation to offences under sections 45 (1), 56 (2) or 304 of the 1952 Act committed as mentioned in section 26 (3) of the Misuse of Drugs Act 1971.

25. In section 5 of the Import Duties Act 1958 (reliefs from import duties) after subsection (1) there shall be inserted the following subsection :—
   " (1A) In this section and in section 6 below ' import duty ' includes duty charged under the Customs Duties (Dumping and Subsidies) Act 1969 and under section 6 (1) of the Finance Act 1978."

26. In section 13 (4) of the Import Duties Act 1958 and in section 15 (2) of the Customs Duties (Dumping and Subsidies) Act 1969 (beginning of 28 day period for orders), for the words " twenty-eight days after ", there shall be substituted the words " the period of 28 days beginning with ".

Section 80   SCHEDULE 13

REPEALS

PART I

CUSTOMS AND EXCISE

Chapter	Short title	Extent of repeal
9 & 10 Geo. 5. c. 32.	The Finance Act 1919.	Section 8. Section 38 (1).
15 & 16 Geo. 6 & 1 Eliz. 2. c. 44.	The Customs and Excise Act 1952.	In section 37 (1), the proviso. Section 70. In section 221 (2), the words " and the component parts of any such mechanical lighters " and the words " or component parts thereof ". In section 222, in subsection (1) (a), the words from " (other " to " flint) ", in subsection (2) the words " Subject to the next following subsection " and subsection (3). In section 248 (2), the words " manufacturer of glucose or saccharin ".

CUSTOMS AND EXCISE—*continued*

Chapter	Short title	Extent of repeal
15 & 16 Geo. 6 & 1 Eliz. 2. c. 44—*cont.*	The Customs and Excise Act 1952—*cont.*	In section 249 (5), the words "manufacturers of glucose or saccharin". In section 307 (1), the definitions of "excise trade", "excise trader", "tobacco" and "tobacco refuse" and, in the definition of "importer", the word "customs". Section 308 (1) and (2). In section 309, in subsection (3), the words from "such part" to the end and, in subsection (5), the words "customs or". Section 311. Schedule 8.
1 & 2 Eliz. 2. c. 34	The Finance Act 1953.	In section 3 (3) the words from "other" to "domestic use".
5 & 6 Eliz. 2. c. 49	The Finance Act 1957.	In Schedule 2, in paragraph 1 (2) the words from "and for the purposes" to the end, paragraph 1 (3), paragraph 2 and paragraph 4 (2) (*b*).
6 & 7 Eliz. 2. c. 6.	The Import Duties Act 1958.	In section 5 (1), the words from "which" to the end.
1964 c. 92.	The Finance (No. 2) Act 1964.	Sections 3 to 6. Schedules 1 and 2.
1966 c. 18.	The Finance Act 1966.	Section 7.
1969 c. 16.	The Customs Duties (Dumping and Subsidies) Act 1969.	In section 5, subsection (2) and in subsection (3) the words from "shall be determined" to "except that". Section 10 (2) and (5). Sections 11 and 12. In section 13 (1) the words "growing or". Section 14 (1) and (3).
1971 c. 12.	The Hydrocarbon Oil (Customs & Excise) Act 1971.	In paragraph 4 of Schedule 1, the words from "or, in Northern Ireland" to the end.
1972 c. 41.	The Finance Act 1972.	Section 128 (1).
1972 c. 68.	The European Communities Act 1972.	In Part I of Schedule 3 the entry relating to the Customs Duties (Dumping and Subsidies) Act 1969. In Schedule 4, paragraph 2 (4).
1976 c. 40.	The Finance Act 1976.	Section 13.
1977 c. 36.	The Finance Act 1977.	Section 13.

1. The repeals in the Customs Duties (Dumping and Subsidies) Act 1969 take effect subject to section 6 (7) of this Act.

2. The repeals in the Finance Act 1972 and the Finance Act 1976 take effect on 1st December 1978.

PART II

VALUE ADDED TAX

Chapter	Short title	Extent of repeal
1975 c. 45.	The Finance (No. 2) Act 1975	Section 19 (2).
1977 c. 36.	The Finance Act 1977.	Section 15.

PART III

INCOME TAX

Chapter	Short title	Extent of repeal
1970 c. 10.	The Income and Corporation Taxes Act 1970.	In section 12 the word " female " wherever it occurs. In section 13 (*a*) the words " mother or other ". Section 18 (3) and (4). In section 83, in subsections (1), (2) and (3) the words " estate or interest " (wherever they occur), subsection (4) (*b*) (iii) and subsection (6). In section 134, subsection (1) (iii) (together with the word " and " immediately preceding it), in subsection (2) the words " estate or interest " and subsection (7). In Schedule 1, in paragraph 11, in sub-paragraph (1) the words " Subject to sub-paragraph (3) below " and in sub-paragraph (3) the words from the beginning to " receipt of the request; and ".
1974 c. 30.	The Finance Act 1974.	In section 15 (1) the words " the first £1,500 of ".
1976 c. 40.	The Finance Act 1976.	In Schedule 4, paragraph 6.
1977 c. 36.	The Finance Act 1977.	Section 21. In section 22, in subsection (1), paragraphs (*a*), (*b*) and (*d*) and in paragraph (*c*) the words from " for " (where it first occurs) to " respectively, and ", and in subsection (3) the words from the beginning to " ; and ". Section 24. Section 26((5). Section 28. In section 35 (3) the words after the semi-colon.
1977 c. 53.	The Finance (Income Tax Reliefs) Act 1977.	Section 1.

1. The repeals in sections 83 and 134 of the Income and Corporation Taxes Act 1970 take effect as mentioned in section 32 (4) of this Act.

2. The repeal in Schedule 1 to the said Act of 1970 applies where the qualifying policy is issued or varied after 5th April 1979.

3. The repeals in Schedule 4 to the Finance Act 1976 and in section 35 (3) of the Finance Act 1977 have effect for the year 1979–80 and subsequent years of assessment.

4. The repeals in section 22 of the Finance Act 1977 do not affect the construction of the remainder of that section.

PART IV

CAPITAL GAINS

Chapter	Short title	Extent of repeal
1965 c. 25.	The Finance Act 1965.	In section 20 (3), the words "Subject, in the case of an individual, to the next following section ". Section 21. In Schedule 10, in paragraph 13 the words "section 21 of this Act or ".
1966 c. 18.	The Finance Act 1966.	In Schedule 10, paragraph 2 (3).
1970 c. 10.	The Income and Corporation Taxes Act 1970.	Section 265 (3) (*b*). In Schedule 15, in paragraph 11, in Part II of the Table the entry relating to section 21 (2) of the Finance Act 1965.
1971 c. 68.	The Finance Act 1971.	Section 57. Schedule 11.
1972 c. 41.	The Finance Act 1972.	In section 112 (3) (*c*), the words "(or would have been chargeable apart from section 21 of the Finance Act 1965) ". In section 119 (2) (*a*), the words "but not for the purposes of section 57 of the Finance Act 1971 (exemption or relief for small disposals) ".
1974 c. 30.	The Finance Act 1974.	Section 34.
1975 c. 45.	The Finance (No. 2) Act 1975.	Section 55.
1976 c. 40.	The Finance Act 1976.	Section 51. Section 52 (2) and (4). In section 56 (2) (*a*), the words "(but not for the purposes of section 57 of the Finance Act 1971) ".
1977 c. 36.	The Finance Act 1977.	Section 44.

1. The repeals in the Finance Act 1971, in section 119 (2) (*a*) of the Finance Act 1972 and in the Finance Act 1976 (except section 52 (2)) and the repeal of section 44 (2) of the Finance Act 1977 have effect for the year 1977–78 and subsequent years of assessment.

2. The repeals in the Finance Act 1966, the Finance Act 1974 and the Finance (No. 2) Act 1975 have effect in relation to disposals after 11th April 1978.

3. The repeal of section 44 (1) of the Finance Act 1977 does not affect gains accruing on disposals before 6th April 1979.

4. The other repeals mentioned above have effect for the year 1978–79 and subsequent years of assessment.

PART V
CAPITAL TRANSFER TAX

Chapter	Short title	Extent of repeal
1975 c. 7.	The Finance Act 1975.	Section 47 (1), (2) and (5). In Schedule 4, in paragraph 13 (7) the words " or on any particular question ". In Schedule 6, in paragraph 15 (4A) the words " or body " (in both places).
1976 c. 40.	The Finance Act 1976.	In section 73 (*b*) the words " made " and " treated as made ". In section 90, subsection (2), in subsection (3) (*a*) the words " or, as the case may be, the company whose shares are disposed of " and in subsection (3) (*c*) the words " or, as the case may be, the disposition of its shares ". In Schedule 10, in paragraph 1 the words " made " and " treated as made ", in paragraph 3 (1) (*b*) the word " and " and paragraph 9. In Schedule 14, paragraph 19.

1. The repeal of subsections (1) and (2) of section 47 of the Finance Act 1975 does not affect any variation or disclaimer made before 11th April 1978, and the repeal of subsection (5) of that section does not affect any deed or instrument made as provided by that subsection.

2. The repeal in paragraph 13 (7) of Schedule 4 to that Act has effect subject to section 66 (3) of this Act.

3. The repeal in Schedule 6 to that Act applies where the acquisition of the interest is after 11th April 1978.

4. The repeals in section 90 of the Finance Act 1976 do not affect dispositions made before 11th April 1978.

Independent Broadcasting Authority Act 1978

(1978 c. 43)

An Act to extend until 31st December 1981 the period during which television and local sound broadcasting services are to be provided by the Independent Broadcasting Authority and to exclude section 4 (2) and (5) of the Independent Broadcasting Authority Act 1973 in relation to proceedings in Parliament and proceedings of local authorities and committees and joint committees of local authorities.   [31st July 1978]

General Note

This Act extends until December 31, 1981, the period during which television and local sound broadcasting services are to be provided.

S. 1 extends the duration of the Independent Broadcasting Authority's function until December 31, 1981; s. 2 excludes s. 4 (2) and (5) of the Independent Broadcasting Authority Act 1973 respecting proceedings in Parliament; s. 3 contains the short title. The Act extends to Northern Ireland.

The Act received the Royal Assent on July 31, 1978, and came into force on that date.

For parliamentary debates see *Hansard,* H.C. Vol. 947, col. 661, Vol. 950, col. 1028; H.L. Vol. 393, col. 277, Vol. 395, col. 321.

Extension of duration of Authority's function

1. In section 2 (1) of the Independent Broadcasting Authority Act 1973 (which, as amended by the Independent Broadcasting Authority (No. 2) Act 1974, provides that it shall be the function of the Independent Broadcasting Authority to provide television and local sound broadcasting services until 31st July 1979) for the words " 31st July 1979 " there shall be substituted the words " 31st December 1981 ".

Exclusion of 1973 s. 4 (2) and (5) as respects proceedings in Parliament and proceedings of local authorities etc.

2.—(1) Nothing in section 4 (2) and (5) of the said Act of 1973 (of which subsection (2) provides for the exclusion from programmes broadcast by the said Authority of the opinions of the Authority and any programme contractor, and of certain persons connected with the Authority or such a contractor, about matters of political or industrial controversy or relating to current public policy and of which subsection (5) provides for the exclusion from such programmes of certain religious matter and of certain publicity for charitable or benevolent institutions) shall apply to a programme broadcast by the said Authority so far as the programme consists of proceedings in either House of Parliament or proceedings of a local authority, a committee of a local authority or a joint committee of two or more local authorities.

(2) In the preceding subsection " local authority " means any of the following bodies, namely, a local authority within the meaning of the Local Government Act 1972, a local authority within the meaning of the Local Government (Scotland) Act 1973, a district council in Northern Ireland, the Common Council of the City of London and, without prejudice to the effect of the said Act of 1972, the Inner London Education Authority.

Short title and extent

3.—(1) This Act may be cited as the Independent Broadcasting Authority Act 1978.

(2) It is hereby declared that this Act extends to Northern Ireland.

(3) Her Majesty may by Order in Council direct that any provision of this Act shall extend to the Isle of Man or any of the Channel Islands with such adaptations and modifications, if any, as may be specified in the Order; and any Order in Council under this subsection may be revoked or varied by a subsequent Order in Council.

Employment Protection (Consolidation) Act 1978 *

(1978 c. 44)

ARRANGEMENT OF SECTIONS

PART I

PARTICULARS OF TERMS OF EMPLOYMENT

PART II

RIGHTS ARISING IN COURSE OF EMPLOYMENT

* Annotations by Brian Bercusson, LL.M., Ph.D., Lecturer in Laws, Queen Mary College, University of London.

An Act to consolidate certain enactments relating to rights of employees arising out of their employment; and certain enactments relating to the insolvency of employers; to industrial tribunals; to recoupment of certain benefits; to conciliation officers; and to the Employment Appeal Tribunal.

[31st July 1978]

General Note

The collection in the Employment Protection (Consolidation) Act 1978 of most of the legislation on individual employment enacted since 1963 shows how much of that law is concerned with absence from or termination of employment. The labour law consolidated here mainly affects workers out of employment—unemployment law, a cynic might call it. For it purports to protect the *employment of workers,* not workers *in* employment. This can be shown by a simple summary of the Act's provisions.

The Act is divided into nine Parts, following the chronology of employment. Part I is concerned with the first stages: written particulars and itemised pay statements (11 sections). Part II is headed: Rights Arising in Course of Employment— guarantee payments, suspension on medical grounds, trade union membership and activities, time off work (21 sections). Part III is concerned with maternity benefits (16 sections). Parts IV to VII are concerned with matters of termination (notice and written reasons), dismissal (unfair and redundancy) and insolvency (79 sections). Part VIII provides the machinery for resolution of disputes relating to employment, and Part IX has miscellaneous and supplemental provisions (9 and 24 sections respectively).

In sum: there are 79 sections (Parts IV to VII) on termination, dismissal and insolvency, and another 33 on matters involving absence from work (seven on guarantee payments, four on suspension on medical grounds, six on time off and 16 on maternity)—a total of 112 sections (70 per cent. of the Act's provisions). And what else does the statute law consolidated here contain besides these aspects relating to workers away from or out of work? There are seven sections on a written statement of particulars, four on itemised pay statements, and another four on trade union membership and activities—a total of 15 sections (less than 10 per cent. of the total in the Act).

The enactment of legislation concerned with termination of employment has been designated by Sir Otto Kahn-Freund as the most noteworthy and important extension of regulatory legislation in the field of labour law (*Labour and the Law*, 1977, p. 26). Its limitations are no less noteworthy. As it operates in practice, as will be shown in the following Notes, it serves only to mitigate some of the economic consequences of lack of work. To achieve security of employment and control of work opportunities and stability, workers cannot rely on the law—for it provides only meagre monetary compensation to those who are prevented by the employer or otherwise cannot continue working.

To protect themselves while *in* employment, most workers, through their autonomous collective organisations, have succeeded in negotiating collective agreements on wages, hours and conditions of work. On matters concerned with termination and absence from employment, there are only the beginnings of collective industrial practice in this form. It would be hazardous to attempt to forecast whether collective bargaining will come to dominate this area as it has the substantive terms of employment. Some control over the terms of work was only achieved after a struggle of many decades. And the last dozen years in particular has witnessed a ceaseless effort by employers, through the State, to wrest back this control. Any similar power over security of employment will not be ceded any more willingly. The law on termination of employment (see the Notes to Parts V and VI) may be seen more as an intervention to maintain managerial control than to protect workers' employment security.

Labour lawyers must be concerned not only with statutory provisions and tribunal and court decisions, but also with the rights of workers and duties of employers established in industrial practice. These Notes try to reflect this by referring extensively to this practice, as well as to the developments in common law and statutory construction of tribunals and courts. Lawyers tend to focus their attention exclusively on what these bodies say. But it will often be of equal or greater importance to their clients for them to be aware of the collective custom and practice prevalent in British industry on such matters as, *e.g.* sick pay, discipline, union membership agreements, flexibility arrangements, etc.

For the impact of employment legislation on its own has been confirmed as relatively limited. One study of 301 manufacturing establishments employing 50–5,000 people concluded that the Employment Protection Act 1975 had little effect on industrial relations practice so far as managers were concerned. Only unfair dismissal appears to have made a mark—primarily by encouraging the reform or formalisation of disciplinary and dismissal procedures (less than a half of 1 per cent. of those leaving employment make unfair dismissal applications; about 1 in 100 small firms—as defined in the Bolton report (1972)—are likely to be faced with an unfair dismissal application in the course of a year; about 1 in 300 are likely to be faced with a hearing on such a complaint, and about 1 in 1,000 are likely to have to pay unfair dismissal compensation; the median award of unfair dismissal compensation in the first quarter of 1978 was £408).

As regards other individual employment rights: guarantee payments and maternity benefits—these were rarely mentioned by the employers surveyed. Indeed, in the area of redundancy, it was shown that *not* the statutory provisions of the Employment Protection Act 1975, but voluntary redundancy schemes, were the significant factor, *i.e.* negotiated practices and procedures (see W. W. Daniel and E. Stilgoe, *The Impact of Employment Protection Laws* (Policy Studies Institute), 1978).

A survey of small firms, employing less than 50 people, carried out for the Department of Employment by the Opinion Research Centre reiterated these findings. Published in 1978, the survey showed up the lack of impact—save for some effects of the unfair dismissal provisions. But only 2 per cent. of employers complained of employment legislation being the main difficulty. (*Cf.* the claim of the Smaller Firms Council of the C.B.I. as to the excessive onerousness of " the sheer volume and complexity " of legislation on small firms.) But the Department of Employment Survey showed 55 per cent. of employers interviewed admitting that they made no effort to keep up to date with changes in employment law, and none able to answer correctly the factual questions put to them about the law.

Of course, there are other employment laws, the impact of which may be appreciable. Thus in the study of larger firms, a majority of employers felt that the Health and Safety at Work, etc., Act 1974 *had* had a favourable impact in terms of safety consciousness and co-operation. The unique mechanism of enforcement (safety representatives) may hold some lessons for employment law generally.

One illustration of how extra-legal factors can fundamentally affect the impact of the legal rights consolidated here is, as elsewhere, the spread of insurance coverage. Thus, there now exists an insurance policy whereby, for £8 per employee, an employer can be covered against awards of compensation, the legal costs of defending claims—and even be provided with advice on procedures affecting employees. The policy even makes it a condition of claims under the policy for insured employers to follow a set of rules and procedures in handling dismissal so as to avoid unnecessary litigation. The rules do follow the trends of decisions handed down by tribunals and the courts.

On the other side, with total trade union membership in the United Kingdom now over 50 per cent. of the working population, many employees benefit from the legal services offered by trade unions. Full-time officials frequently represent their members in negotiations over dismissal or before industrial tribunals. However, the manpower of the British trade union movement will not allow for the burden of such legal practice. One industrial tribunal case for a single member may take days of preparation and a day or more to present—and what of the other 3,000 members and other activities and duties?

One solution proposed, for union members, is the negotiation through collective bargaining of a fringe benefit whereby the employee's legal costs would be borne by an insurance company. Such prepaid legal services benefits have already been negotiated by unions in North America, where they cover legal advice and representation on a whole range of non-employment matters giving rise to legal disputes. Alternatively, lay officials of trade unions could be given the requisite intensive training to equip them to take up many of the legal problems which arise, up to and including the appearance before the industrial tribunal. The ACAS Code of Practice on Time Off for Trade Union Duties and Activities expressly requires employers to allow such officials reasonable time off with pay to appear on behalf of constituents before an industrial tribunal (para. 13 (*e*)).

The rights of individual employees will be affected also by legislation other than that consolidated here. Apart from the obvious requirements of the Sex Discrimination Act 1975, the Equal Pay Act 1970 and the Race Relations Act 1976—there are, among the most recent, for example (as of June 1, 1978), the rights of the employee inventor to his invention, whatever the terms of the employment contract, under the Patents Act 1977; or (as of February 1, 1978), the liability of employers for personal injury or death as a result of negligence which cannot be excluded under the Unfair Contract Terms Act 1977. Then there are the implications of the Pearson Commission Report on Civil Liability and Compensation for Personal Injury.

A new and potent source of future legislation is the trend towards harmonisation of law through the EEC. The most recent effect, perhaps, was engendered by the Draft Fifth Directive on Company Law (1972), encouraging the participation of employees in the management of companies. The Report of the Committee of Inquiry on Industrial Democracy (The Bullock Report, Cmnd. 6706 (1977)) has already led to the publication of a White Paper (Cmnd. 7291 (1978)) on directors' duties to have regard to the interests of the company's employees (and see cl. 46 of the Companies Bill 1978 currently before Parliament). Further effects may be expected to result from the EEC Council Directive 77/187/EEC of February 14, 1977, on the approximation of the laws of Member States relating to the safeguarding of employees' rights in the event of transfers of undertakings, businesses or parts of businesses. Other EEC proposals would lead to fundamental changes in dismissals law and conflicts of law as it affects employment.

Finally, the Notes which follow offer an analytical view of many of the decisions of tribunals and courts. This analysis is designed to draw out the policy implications of these decisions and their likely effects on the practice of employers, trade unions and workers. The judgments are often explicitly predicated on the tribunal's or the court's view of what constitutes " reasonable," " fair," " just and equitable " or simply desirable industrial practice. The views put forward are derived from the political convictions of those making the decisions—their acceptance of the conventional wisdom as to the need for authoritarian control and inequality of reward in the relationships between employees and employers. It is vital to have a clear appreciation of these views because of their importance in the development of common law and statutory interpretation. The Notes scrutinise the decisions from the point of view of the interests of employees, which this legislation is designed to protect.

Northern Ireland

Most of the provisions of this legislation are to be found in the Industrial Relations (Northern Ireland) Order 1976 (S.I. 1976 No. 1043 (N.I. 16)) and the Industrial Relations (No. 2) (Northern Ireland) Order 1976 (S.I. 1976 No. 2147 (N.I. 28)). The equivalent of ACAS is the Labour Relations Agency (see also the Labour Relations Agency (Additional Functions) Order (Northern Ireland) 1977 (S.I. 1977 No. 177)). And see s. 157 of this Act. Northern Ireland is not otherwise covered: s. 160 (3).

See also the Employment Protection (Offshore Employment) Order 1976 (S.I. 1976 No. 766).

Commencement

Virtually all of the Act's provisions came into force on November 1, 1978 (and the rest on January 1, 1979)—s. 160 (2).

Abbreviations

1965	=	Redundancy Payments Act 1965.
1972	=	Contracts of Employment Act 1972.
TULRA	=	Trade Union and Labour Relations Act 1974.
1975	=	Employment Protection Act 1975.

Parliamentary Debates

See *Hansard*, H.L. Vol. 394, cols. 988 and 1307; Vol. 395, cols. 321 and 768; H.C. Vol. 954, col. 1103.

Table of Derivations

CONTRACTS OF EMPLOYMENT ACT 1963

1963	1978
Sch. 1,	
para. 1 (2)	Sch. 13, para. 21
para. 6	s. 22

INDUSTRIAL TRAINING ACT 1964

1964	1978
s. 12 (1)	s. 128
(2B) (3)	Sch. 9, paras. 9, 10

REDUNDANCY PAYMENTS ACT 1965

1965	1978	1965	1978	1965	1978
s. 1	s. 81	s. 10	s. 92	s. 20 (1)	Sch. 13, para. 15
2	82	11	ss. 96, 154 (1)	(2)	s. 144
3 (1) (2)	83	12	s. 97	(3)	Sch. 13, para. 14
(3)–(8)	84	13	94	21	s. 101
(9) (10)	90	13A	95	22	93
4 (1)	85	14	98	23	150
(2)	ss. 85, 90	15 (1)	Sch. 15, para. 12	24, 24A	Sch. 13, para. 12
(3)–(5)	s. 83	(2)–(4)	s. 142	25 (1) (2)	s. 153
5 (1) (2)	87	16 (1)	Repealed	(3)	81
(2A)	Sch. 14, para. 7 (1)	(2)	s. 144	(4) (5)	140
(3)	s. 153	(3)	146 (1)	26	s. 103
6 (1)	88	(4) (5)	99	ss. 27–29	Repealed
(2)	90	(6)	149	s. 30	s. 104
(3)–(5)	88	(7)	154	31	105
7	89	(8)	ss. 149, 154	32	106
8 (1)	81	17 (1) (2)	s. 141	33	107
(2)	151	(3)–(8)	Sch. 13, para. 14	34 (1)	108
(3)–(4)	Sch. 13, para. 11	18	s. 102	(2)	ss. 108, 128
9 (1)	ss. 91, 128	19	100	(3) (4)	s. 108
(2) (*a*)	s. 151				
(*b*)	91				
(3)	91				

REDUNDANCY PAYMENTS ACT 1965—*cont.*

SUPERANNUATION (MISCELLANEOUS PROVISIONS) ACT 1967

NATIONAL LOANS ACT 1968

SUPERANNUATION ACT 1972

CONTRACTS OF EMPLOYMENT ACT 1972

Contracts of Employment Act 1972—*cont.*

1972	1978
s. 13 (3) (4)	Sch. 15, paras. 1, 2
(5)	...Sch. 13, paras. 21–23
(6)	...Sch. 15, para. 4
Sch. 1, paras. 1–4C	Sch. 13, paras. 1–7
para. 5 (1)	Sch. 13,
(2)	para. 9
Sch. 1—*cont.*	
para. 5A	..Sch. 13, para. 10
paras. 6, 7	Sch. 13, para. 15
para. 8	...Sch. 13, para. 16
para. 9	...Sch. 13, para. 17
para. 10 (1)	Sch. 13, para. 18
(2)	s. 153
Sch. 1—*cont.*	
para. 10A	.Sch. 13, para. 19
para. 11	..Sch. 13, para. 24
Sch. 2	......Sch. 3
para. 1 (1)	
(b)	s. 152
(2)	Sch. 14, para. 7 (1)

National Health Service (Scotland) Act 1972

1972	1978
Sch. 6,	
para. 130	.Sch. 5

National Health Service Reorganisation Act 1973

1973	1978
Sch. 4,	
para. 106	.Sch. 5

Social Security Act 1973

1973	1978
Sch. 27,	
para. 55	.. s. 103
para. 56	.. 105
para. 58	.. 113
para. 59	.. 115

Employment and Training Act 1973

1973	1978
Sch. 2,	
Pt. I,	
para. 15	Sch. 9, paras. 9, 10

Trade Union and Labour Relations Act 1974

1974	1978
s. 26	......s. 154
30	 153
(1)	...ss. 57, 146 (2) (3)
Sch. 1,	
para. 4 (1)	ss. 54, 129
(2)	s. 54
para. 5	
(1)–(3)	55
(4)	Repealed
(5) (6)	s. 55
para. 6	
(1)–(3)	57
(4)–(6)	58
(7)	59
(8)	57
(9)	ss. 58, 153
para. 7	
(1)–(3)	s. 62
(4)	67
(5)	62
para. 8	...Repealed
Sch. 1—*cont.*	
para. 9	
(1) (a)	s. 57
(b)	ss. 57, 146 (1)
(c)	Repealed
(d)	s. 144
(e) (f)	Repealed
(2) (3)	s. 141
para. 10	.. 64
para. 11 (1)	64
(2) (3)	149
para. 12 (a)	Sch. 15, para. 10 (1)
(b)	s. 142
para. 13	.. 65
para. 14	.. 66
para. 15	.. 63
para. 16	.. 128
para. 17 (1)	67
(2) (3)	Repealed
para. 18	..Sch. 9, para. 2
Sch. 1—*cont.*	
para. 20	
(1)–(3)	s. 75
(4)	154
para. 21	Sch. 9,
(1)–(3A)	para. 1
(4) (4A)	s. 67
(5)–(6)	Sch. 9, para. 1
paras. 22–25	Sch. 9, paras. 4–7
para. 26 (1)	Repealed
(2)–(5)	s. 134
para. 27	.. 80
para. 30 (1)	151
(1A)	Sch. 13, para. 11
(2)	s. 151
(3) (4)	Sch. 13, para. 20
para. 32	.. s. 140
para. 33	.. 138
Sch. 4, para. 7	Sch. 15, para. 4

SOCIAL SECURITY (CONSEQUENTIAL PROVISIONS) ACT 1975

1975	1978
Sch. 2,	
para. 21 ..	s. 105
para. 22 ..	113
para. 23 ..	115

CRIMINAL PROCEDURE (SCOTLAND) ACT 1975

1975	1978
s. 298B (1) .	ss. 104, 107

SOCIAL SECURITY PENSIONS ACT 1975

1975	1978
s. 30 (5) ...	ss. 1, 11

EMPLOYMENT PROTECTION ACT 1975

1975	1978	1975	1978	1975	1978
s. 22 (1) (2)	s. 12	s. 51	s. 61	s. 75 (1) ...	Sch. 14,
(3) ...	143	52	153		para. 7 (1)
23	13	53	23		
24 (1) (2)	14	54	24	(2) ...	Sch. 14,
(3) ...	Sch. 14,	55 (1) (2)	25		para. 7 (2)
	para. 7 (1)	(3) (4)	Sch. 9,	(3) ...	Sch. 14,
(4) ...	s. 14,		para. 2		para. 7 (1)
	Sch. 14,	56	s. 26	(4)–(6)	Sch. 14,
	para. 7(1)	57 (1) (2)	27		para. 8
(5) ...	s. 153	(3) ...	Sch. 16,	(7) (8)	s. 73
25	15		para. 22	76	74
26	16	(4)–(8)	s. 27	77	76
27	17	58 (1)–(3)	28	78	77
28	18	(4) ...	Sch. 16,	79	78
29 (1)–(3)	19		para. 22	80 (1)–(3)	79
(4) ...	64	(5) ...	s. 28	(4) ...	Sch. 9,
30 (1) ...	143	59	29		para. 8
(2) (3)	20	60	30	81	s. 8
31 (1) ...	21	61 (1)–(4)	31	82	9
(2) ...	Sch. 14,	(5) ...	Sch. 14,	83	10
	para. 7 (1)		para. 7 (1)	84	11
(3) (4)	s. 21	(6) ...	s. 153	85	152
(5) ...	153	(7)–(13)	31	86	148,
32	22	62 (a) (b)	32		Sch. 14,
33	61	(c) ...	152		para. 8
34 (1)–(5)	60	63	121	87	s. 135
(6) ...	Sch. 15,	64	122	88	136
	para. 10 (2)	65	123	108 (1) ..	ss. 128, 129
(7) ...	s. 65	66	124	(2)–(8)	s. 133
35	33	67	125	109 (1)–(5)	131
36	34	68	126	(6) ..	Sch. 9,
37 (1)–(4)	35	69	127		para. 1
(5) ...	Sch. 14,	70 (1)–(5)	53	(7)–(9)	s. 131
	para. 7 (1)	(6) ...	Sch. 14,	110	150
38	s. 36		para. 7 (1)	112 (1) ..	Sch. 16,
39	37	71 (1) ...	s. 68		para. 19 (2)
41	38	(2)–(7)	69	(2) (3)	s. 132
42	39	(8) (9)	70	(4) ..	Sch. 16,
43	40	72 (1)–(4)	71		para. 19(1)
44	41	(5) ...	68	(5)–(8)	s. 132
45	42	(6) ...	71	117	155
46	43	(7) ...	Sch. 14,	118	140
47	44		para. 7 (1)	119 (2) ..	146 (1)
48 (1) ...	45	(8) ...	Sch. 14,	(4) ...	144
(2) ...	ss. 45, 153		para. 8	(5) (6)	141
(3) ...	s. 153	73	s. 72	(7) ..	143
(4) (5)	45	74 (1)–(3)	73	(8)–	
(6) ...	46	(4) ...	Sch. 13,	(11)	146 (4)–(7)
49	47		para. 11	(12)–	
50 (1) ...	ss. 56, 86	(5)–(7)	s. 73	(13)	144
(2) ...	s. 33			(15)–	
				(16)	149

EMPLOYMENT PROTECTION ACT 1975—*cont.*

TRADE UNION AND LABOUR RELATIONS (AMENDMENT) ACT 1976

SUPPLEMENTARY BENEFITS ACT 1976

RACE RELATIONS ACT 1976

DOCK WORK REGULATION ACT 1976

1976	1978
s. 14 (1) (2)	s. 145
(3)	...ss. 145, 151
(4)	... s. 105
(5) (6)	145
(7) ...	149
(8) ...	145
15 (1) ...	145

SOCIAL SECURITY (MISCELLANEOUS PROVISIONS) ACT 1977

1977	1978
s. 16	s. 132

REDUNDANCY REBATES ACT 1977

1977	1978
s. 1 (1) (2)	. Sch. 6, para. 13
(3)	s. 154
(4)	Sch. 6, para. 13
Sch.	Sch. 6, para. 13

CRIMINAL LAW ACT 1977

1977	1978
s. 28 (2)	...ss. 104. 107
Sch. 11,	
para. 5	...ss. 104, 107

HOUSE OF COMMONS (ADMINISTRATION) ACT 1978

1978	1978
Sch. 2,	
para. 4 ...	s. 4
para. 5 ...	139

REDUNDANCY PAYMENTS (VARIATION OF REBATES) ORDER 1977

1977	1978
Art. 3	Sch. 6, paras. 1, 2, 8, 11
4	Sch. 6, para. 12

EMPLOYMENT PROTECTION (VARIATION OF LIMITS) ORDER 1977

1977	1978
Art. 2	ss. 15, 122, Sch. 14, para. 8
3 (1) ...	Sch. 15, para. 6
(2) ...	Sch. 15, para. 15 (2)
(3)–(5)	Sch. 15, para. 16

PART I

PARTICULARS OF TERMS OF EMPLOYMENT

Written particulars of terms of employment

Written particulars of terms of employment

1.—(1) Not later than thirteen weeks after the beginning of an employee's period of employment with an employer, the employer shall give to the employee a written statement in accordance with the following provisions of this section.

(2) An employer shall in a statement under this section—

(*a*) identify the parties;

(*b*) specify the date when the employment began;

(c) state whether any employment with a previous employer counts as part of the employee's continuous period of employment, and, if so, specify the date when the continuous period of employment began.

(3) A statement under this section shall contain the following particulars of the terms of employment as at a specified date not more than one week before the statement is given, that is to say—

(a) the scale or rate of remuneration, or the method of calculating remuneration,

(b) the intervals at which remuneration is paid (that is, whether weekly or monthly or by some other period),

(c) any terms and conditions relating to hours of work (including any terms and conditions relating to normal working hours),

(d) any terms and conditions relating to—

(i) entitlement to holidays, including public holidays, and holiday pay (the particulars given being sufficient to enable the employee's entitlement, including any entitlement to accrued holiday pay on the termination of employment, to be precisely calculated),

(ii) incapacity for work due to sickness or injury, including any provision for sick pay,

(iii) pensions and pension schemes,

(e) the length of notice which the employee is obliged to give and entitled to receive to determine his contract of employment, and

(f) the title of the job which the employee is employed to do;

Provided that paragraph (d) (iii) shall not apply to the employees of any body or authority if the employees' pension rights depend on the terms of a pension scheme established under any provision contained in or having effect under an Act of Parliament and the body or authority are required by any such provision to give to new employees information concerning their pension rights, or concerning the determination of questions affecting their pension rights.

(4) Subject to subsection (5), every statement given to an employee under this section shall include a note—

(a) specifying any disciplinary rules applicable to the employee, or referring to a document which is reasonably accessible to the employee and which specifies such rules;

(b) specifying, by description or otherwise—

(i) a person to whom the employee can apply if he is dissatisfied with any disciplinary decision relating to him; and

(ii) a person to whom the employee can apply for the purpose of seeking redress of any grievance relating to his employment,

and the manner in which any such application should be made;

(c) where there are further steps consequent upon any such application, explaining those steps or referring to a document which is reasonably accessible to the employee and which explains them; and

(d) stating whether a contracting-out certificate is in force for the employment in respect of which the statement is given.

(5) The provisions of paragraphs (a) to (c) of subsection (4) shall not apply to rules, disciplinary decisions, grievances or procedures relating to health or safety at work.

(6) The definition of week given by section 153 (1) does not apply for the purposes of this section.

DERIVATION

1972, s. 4 (1), (2), (2A); 1975, Sched. 16, Part II, paras. 4, 5, 6; Social Security Pensions Act 1975 (c. 60), s. 30 (5).

GENERAL NOTE

Subs. (1)

Exclusions. Certain classes of employment are excluded from the benefits of this section: see ss. 138 (1), 139 (1), 141 (1), 145 (1) and 146 (1).

An employer need not give a written statement until 13 weeks have passed after the beginning of employment. So many temporary, casual or seasonal workers will never benefit from these provisions. But some (though perhaps as few as 6 per cent.) of these workers acquire their temporary employment through an agency—particularly clerical/office machinist and secretarial employees. These will benefit from reg. 9 (6) of the Conduct of Employment Agencies and Employment Businesses Regulations 1976, made under the Employment Agencies Act 1973. The agency must issue *immediately on engagement* of such a worker who is to be supplied to a hirer a written statement containing full details of the terms and conditions. Failure to comply may lead to withdrawal of the agency's licence—a powerful sanction. This statement does not constitute the contractual terms, but is only written evidence of them (for details see 7 I.L.J. 84 (1978)). Again, other "temps" who return to work sporadically for the same employer may gradually accumulate the 13 weeks—see Note to s. 3 (1).

Terms stated. The written particulars required to be stated must include all the categories specified in the following subsections. Terms regarding these matters may be *implied* from custom and practice, collective agreements, etc. They must, however, be made express in the statement (unless there are no terms at all (s. 2 (1), or reference is made to another document (s. 2 (3)). Other requirements for the supply of information to employees are in the Code of Practice (1972), paras. 60–62.

Statement or contract. The problems faced by workers with regard to this subsection differ somewhat from those with which lawyers and judges are preoccupied. The latter are concerned with the legal question: statement or contract? For while there is no doubt that the provision was *not* intended to secure written contracts for workers (see the exclusion in s. 5), there has been a tendency by lawyers and judges, tempted as a result of the uncertainties of unwritten contracts, to seize upon the *written statement* of particulars as the *written contract*. Signature of the statement by one or both of the parties has only added to the irresistibility of the temptation (*e.g.* in *Gascol Conversions Ltd.* v. *Mercer* [1974] I.C.R. 420, the employee's signature was the decisive factor to Orr and Lawton L.JJ. in transforming the document in question into a contract).

But there exist judicial statements to the contrary: *e.g.* Lord Parker in *Turriff Construction Ltd.* v. *Bryant* (1967) 2 K.I.R. 659; and as to the effect of signature, Lord Denning in *Secretary of State for Employment* v. *ASLEF (No. 2)* [1972] 2 Q.B. 455. And where a direct transformation of statement to contract has seemed too robust, the objective of resolving judicial uncertainty has been achieved by attaching to the statement the status of almost incontrovertible proof of the terms of the (unwritten) contract—virtually estopping a denial of its terms (*e.g.* *Smith* v. *Blandford Gee Cementation Co. Ltd.* [1970] 3 All E.R. 154, where the employer was estopped from denying what was said in the written statement; *W.P.M. Retail Ltd.* v. *Lang* [1978] I.R.L.R. 243 (E.A.T.), where the employer's failure to pay an agreed bonus was not treated as a variation of the contract; rather the employer was still bound, and the employee's continuing to work over two years was not a waiver of his rights—he was still entitled to his accumulated unpaid bonus payments). Lawyers' problems ought not unduly to confuse the ends of legislation, here simply to provide workers with information as to their terms of employment, and not to resolve judicial difficulties.

The Department of Employment Guide to the Contracts of Employment Act 1972 (the predecessor to this section) advises the employee not to " put his signature to any form of words which might imply agreement with the terms and conditions stated," since the signature might bind him regardless of other terms agreed orally (para. 6). Employees are advised, if asked to sign, to " confirm that they are only being asked to sign for *receipt* of the written statement " (para. 50).

Consequences of the contract analysis. Designation of the statement as a " contract " has the consequence for a worker of denying him the right under s. 11

to refer questions to an industrial tribunal. There are two steps to this conclusion. The first is because s. 5 excluded the right to a written statement where the contract complies with the conditions laid down there. Questions arising as to that contract could only be taken to a county court—a slower, more expensive and less expert a forum for employment disputes. The second step is illustrated by *Construction Industry Training Board* v. *Leighton* [1978] I.R.L.R. 60 (E.A.T.). There Kilner Brown J. simply classified the written statement as a contract and rejected a reference questioning its accuracy: for an industrial tribunal to do so would be to "exercise the power of the Civil Courts to declare what a contract meant or to rectify an error manifest in an otherwise binding contract."

Forms of compliance. Recent research (see 6 I.L.J. 133 (1977)) indicated that of the employers surveyed many did comply with the requirement to provide written particulars of terms of employment, at least to some extent. There remains the large number who did not comply: the problem of workers' ignorance of their own terms of employment remains unsolved by the law. But of those employers who *do* comply, the *forms* of compliance are many: there is a myriad of documents purporting to comply, ranging from letters of appointment, offers of employment on specified terms, documents intended to be written statements of particulars and others intended to be written contracts—*both* of which might be headed: "Contracts of Employment Act 1972," and follow the pattern of terms laid down by the legislation; and numerous other documents, complete and incomplete as to employment terms, headed by various titles: Contract, Statement of Particulars, Terms of Employment, Conditions of Work, etc., sometimes requiring signature of either or both parties and sometimes not.

Legalistic analysis of forms of compliance. Given the extremely varied forms of response by employers to the legislation, the lawyer's approach is as follows: he attempts to classify the various documents into one of the categories: contract/ statement of particulars. Then, as a matter of discretion—if contract, parol evidence may be allowed to amplify (though not contradict) it, and doctrines of mistake, misrepresentation, intention to create legal relations, etc. may be relevant. If a statement of particulars, evidence is allowed to amplify or contradict it, and doctrines of, *e.g.* estoppel may apply. Either way, written documents are in this way given some primary role, and employees are usually at a disadvantage in this respect. The documents are invariably drawn up by the employer—the employee only "consents." As Sir Otto Kahn-Freund says: "This is the reality of things, in the language of the law that reality is concealed. There the unilateral rule- and decision-making power of management is presented as based on a 'contract,' on the free will of the employer and the employee" (*Labour and the Law* (1977), p. 12). Employers with superior bargaining power and access to professional expertise on personnel management and legal advice naturally exploit these resources in drafting statements—geographical mobility or job flexibility clauses in employment documents are usually a good illustration of this.

Realistic analysis of forms of compliance. An alternative approach would seek to redress this imbalance: any evidence as to terms of employment would be allowed, including, without any special significance, any written documents, whatever their nature. The key-stone of this approach would be collective custom and practice. There is, of course, the problem of class-bias in judges' perceptions of such custom and practice. *E.g. Burroughs Machines Ltd.* v. *P. Timmoney* [1977] I.R.L.R. 404, where a document entitled "Particulars of Terms of Employment pursuant to s. 4 of the Contracts of Employment Act 1963 (as amended)" referred to a collective agreement providing for a "guaranteed week," save in the event of industrial action involving "federated" employers. The employer in question subsequently left the federation, and the occasion arose where a claim for guaranteed pay was made in circumstances of industrial action involving the employer himself—by then no longer a "federated" employer. The Court of Session in Scotland held that there was no written contract; the collective agreement's provisions could not be incorporated "word for word" into the contract of employment; and that "common sense" dictated that the "guaranteed week" provision be conditioned by the provision in favour of the employer in the event of industrial action on his premises. So although the employee was *not* engaged in the industrial action, and the employer *was* a party to it, it was "common sense" to the judge that the employee should bear the financial consequences.

Despite this hazard to workers, the realistic analysis probably is better suited to employees' circumstances. At the least, it avoids the practical problems for workers of forced signing of documents and maintaining adequate records over long periods, such written records being conclusive. It also avoids having to rely on the legal vagaries of doctrines of estoppel, misrepresentation, mistake, intent to create legal relations, incorporation of collective agreements (see Note to s. 2 (3)), etc. The dangers of employers' manipulating custom and practice at work can be met by the weapon of trade union organisation and action. This is more reliable than the legal weapons of estoppel, etc. in the tribunals and courts, used there to avoid the consequences of an otherwise binding and adverse written document. The requirement of the written statement of particulars would be retained to fulfil its original purpose—written information for employees—but no more.

Subs. (2)

Continuous employment in fact. It is not usual for employment with a previous employer to be counted as continuous with that of a new employer. Whatever the needs of the employee who has worked for many years in an industry, the fact of the change in the legal identity of the employer may serve to deny him the benefits of his long service. Continuity is essential in order to qualify for many legal rights.

Continuous employment in law. Ironically, s. 151 (2) provides that proceedings under s. 1 are not covered by the presumption that employment during any period was continuous. As regards other rights subject to a minimum continuous employment requirement, there was explicit provision as to the operation of such a presumption of continuity (see *e.g.* 1965, s. 9 (2) (*a*); 1974, Sched. 1, para. 30 (2); 1975, s. 126 (5)), while as regards the Contracts of Employment Act 1972 there was omitted such a presumption (1972, s. 1 (5)). But s. 151 (2) makes the anomaly even more blatant by specifically excluding this right from the benefit of the presumption.

In any event, a new employer has at least the obligation to inform the employee as to the position with regard to continuous employment—though the exact meaning of s. 2 (1), statement of a negative, is difficult to determine in this context.

Statutory continuous employment. As a matter of law, however, a change of employer does not break continuity of employment in the following circumstances defined in Sched. 13, paras. 17–18:

   (a) if a trade or business or an undertaking is transferred from one employer to another;

   (b) if by or under an Act of Parliament one corporate body is substituted for another as the employer;

   (c) if on the death of an employer, the personal representatives or trustees of the deceased take on the employee;

   (d) if there is a change in the partners, personal representatives or trustees who employ the employee;

   (e) if an employee is taken into the employment of another employer who at the time of the change is an associated employer (for definition of "associated employer," see s. 153 (4)).

The last category of transfers from one associated employer to another applies to cases both of an employer transferring the employee concerned, *e.g.* in a redundancy situation, and also to where the employee himself transfers on his own initiative. In both cases continuity of employment is maintained; in the latter case even if the employers concerned are ignorant of the transfer. And, as one industrial tribunal has held, even if there was an interval between leaving the one company and joining the other (*Binns* v. *Versil Ltd.* [1975] I.R.L.R. 273).

Subs. (3)

Remuneration. "Remuneration" is not defined in this statute, but in the Prices and Charges (Notification of Increases and Information) Order 1977 (S.I. 1977 No. 1281), it is defined in para. 16 (2) as follows:

   "'remuneration,' in relation to any employee, includes any benefit, facility or advantage, whether in money or otherwise, provided by the employer or by some other person under arrangements with the employer, whether for the employee or otherwise, by reason of the fact that the employer employs him."

In *Palmanor Ltd.* v. *Cedron* [1978] I.R.L.R. 303 (E.A.T.), the "tronc," tips paid to staff by customers and shared out by the employees themselves, was held part of the employee's remuneration, though not remuneration payable by the employer within (now) Sched. 14, para. 3 (3), although the employee was told at the time of hiring that he would be paid £30 net and would get between £60 and £80 in tips.

Fringe benefits. Details should be provided not only of wages or salary, but also of every type of fringe benefit. Recent research estimates that non-pay benefits of all kinds now make up between 10 per cent. and 30 per cent. of a company's labour costs on average. The major categories of fringe benefits are:

(a) private social welfare payments: superannuation, group life insurance, sickness payments, industrial accident payments, ex gratia and goodwill payments;

(b) payments in kind (net cost to employers for goods provided free or below cost), *e.g.* food, drink and fuel;

(c) subsidised services to employees (net cost to employers of medical services, canteens, housing, removal, transport to and from work, clothing and recreational facilities);

(d) provision for redundancy (statutory and voluntary payments to employees);

(e) paid holidays.

The average level of aggregate benefits in *manufacturing* industries rose by 106 per cent. between 1968 and 1973, while over the same period wages and salaries increased by an average 77 per cent. Benefits as a proportion of wages increased from an average of 13·6 per cent. to 14·4 per cent. over this period (see 15 B.J.I.R. 396 (1977)). A B.I.M. survey shows that over the past year or so it is the Government's pay guidelines that have had the most important single influence on the development by firms of fringe benefits policy: 48 per cent. of 400 companies investigated made major changes as a consequence of the pay policy.

What are " particulars " of remuneration? Just how particular the " particulars " of remuneration need be has been minimised recently by Kilner Brown J. in *Construction Industry Training Board* v. *Leighton* [1978] I.R.L.R. 60 (E.A.T.). The document constituting the statement of particulars specified a figure for salary which was expressly stated to include a cost of living supplement. The employee challenged the statement's accuracy (under now s. 11) on the basis that his particulars of remuneration were in fact the figure stated *plus* the cost of living supplement. The judge refused to hear the application on the ground that " every particular required by the statutory provisions was included in the contract of employment." The dispute as to the supplement was " an entirely peripheral matter. . . . It certainly was not fundamental. Of course it was important in Mr. Leighton's view."

But if inaccuracy is not a ground for challenging particulars given in the statement, the whole statutory purpose of providing information is undermined— for presumably one may imply that " particulars " means " accurate and correct " particulars. This view is borne out by *W.P.M. Retail Ltd.* v. *Lang* [1978] I.R.L.R. 243 (E.A.T.), where an assumption of jurisdiction under (now) s. 11 to determine a dispute as to entitlement to bonus pay was upheld by the E.A.T.; and by *Hodges* v. *Probert* [1976] I.R.L.R. 28 (Q.B.D.), where the court dealt with an application under (now) s. 11 to determine what the particulars *ought* to have been when they were disputed by the parties to the contract of employment.

Intervals of payment. It is interesting to speculate on the possibility that terms might exist, by implication, in a contract as to how frequently or when *increases* in remuneration must be paid. In *F. C. Gardner Ltd.* v. *Beresford* [1978] I.R.L.R. 63 (E.A.T.), the employee concerned claimed constructive dismissal on grounds that other employees had received pay increases but she had not received an increase for two years. In response to the employee's contention that it must be an implied term that an employer will not treat his employee arbitrarily, capriciously or inequitably in matters of remuneration, Phillips J. said: " No doubt, it is reasonable in most circumstances to infer a term something on those lines." He then added: " If the employers were deliberately singling her out for special treatment, inferior to that given to everybody else and they were doing it arbitrarily, capriciously and inequitably, if they did victimise in that sense, one could . . . say that she had a good claim, even under the new (contract) test."

Basic hours and overtime. According to the 1977 New Earnings Survey, in April 1977 the average weekly hours worked was for full-time adult men, 43 hours, and for women, 37·5 hours. These figures include respectively 4·1 hours overtime for men and 0·5 hours overtime for women. So, excluding overtime, all men worked 38·9 hours a week compared with 37 hours by women. These averages conceal the differences between manual and non-manual workers. Basic hours, excluding over-time, of non-manual men were 37·3; of manual men, 39·9; of non-manual women, 36·4; of manual women, 38·4. Non-manual workers worked less than a third of the overtime worked by manual workers, men and women.

While most workers were, therefore, on a basic working week below 40 hours, the overtime component served to put them over that total—and its economic significance is shown by the fact that overtime earnings made up 13·7 per cent. of the total earnings of manual men (and in some groups of workers, *e.g.* baking, over 25 per cent. of earnings come from overtime; in others, *e.g.* municipal busmen, over 20 per cent.), though only 2·9 per cent. of the earnings of non-manual men. Overtime varies, particularly for women, depending on the state of the economy. In the year up to April 1977, overtime hours worked by all men rose by 0·3 hours to 4·1, and by all women, by 0·1 to 0·5 hours.

The length of the working week is currently high on the list of bargaining demands by trade unions; *e.g.* the Ford claim put in has demanded a reduction to 35 hours. The Post Office Engineering Union has already reached a provisional agreement to reduce the working week of 125,000 telephone engineers from 40 to 37½ hours, to be implemented from December 1, 1978. The union's commitment is still to a 35-hour week.

These figures give some substance to the legal problems often discussed of whether overtime is obligatory, and the effect of variations in contractual terms or the written statement of particulars (see s. 4).

Obligatory overtime. The written statement must, therefore, with regard to overtime, state the terms according to which it is to be worked. That is, terms related to compulsory overtime, either where an amount has been agreed upon by the parties, or where the employer has the contractual right to require the employee to work overtime hours if he so orders. A recent survey of 192 organisations employing more than 500,000 people showed nearly a quarter of the organisations requiring compulsory overtime from some of their employees; 75 per cent. of these required more than four hours a week, and 25 per cent. eight hours a week or more.

" Normal working hours," those where the employee is obliged to work and the employer obliged to employ him, may include a period when the employee is paid at " overtime " rates—Sched. 14, Pt. I. Usually, however, the " normal working hours " will not be paid at overtime rates. Interestingly, while the courts have upheld as contractually binding the *employer's* right unilaterally to require overtime working, they remain reluctant to accept a right in the *employee* to have overtime working provided to him. This is the case even where employees may have worked regular overtime for many years *and* there exists a local agreement providing for fixed overtime. Nonetheless, the courts will seize on any excuse—a contrary pro-vision in a national agreement, a particular of the written statement (see, *e.g. Gascol Conversions Ltd.* v. *Mercer* [1974] I.C.R. 420) to deny that employers are bound to provide overtime working to their employees. This peculiar stance is more easily understood in the context of the fluctuations of overtime with the state of the economy: perhaps the judges are concerned that employers be obliged to provide overtime when " economic efficiency " (the " national interest ") does not require it. The loss of earnings to the worker is a lesser consideration, of a sectional nature. Indeed, workers get the worst of both worlds from the courts, for they have also held that even compulsory overtime—where the employer has the unilateral right to demand overtime working—is not part of " normal working hours " (on which compensation for redundancy and unfair dismissal (the basic award) is based): *Tarmac Roadstone Holdings Ltd.* v. *Peacock* [1973] I.C.R. 273, where the worker had regularly worked 57 hours a week, seven days a week, for 10 years, but had his redundancy payment calculated on the 40-hour nationally agreed work-week.

To overcome these problems, workers should ensure that their statements of particulars provide: (1) no overtime to be compulsory on the employee; or (2) if there is to be compulsory overtime worked, it must be obligatory on the employer as well, *i.e.* guaranteed overtime; and (3) any regular overtime worked is to be included in the " normal working hours."

Non-working hours. Apart from terms relating to basic working hours and overtime, the written statement will often contain provisions as to meal breaks (often unpaid), tea breaks (more usually manual than non-manual workers), washing and changing times (sometimes paid), and other non-working hours.

Shift-work. Details must be provided of any working patterns, *e.g.* shift-working.

The survey of 192 organisations referred to above found that 65 per cent. of the organisations operate some form of shift-working for some employees. It has been estimated that more than one-third of industrial workers are on shifts.

For example, Barclays Bank reached an agreement with the National Union of Bank Employees (NUBE) on longer working hours for its major branch at the Brent Cross Shopping Centre. As of July 22, 1978, the branch is open from 9.30 a.m. to 8 p.m. Monday to Friday, and 9 a.m. to 6 p.m. on Saturdays. In return, working hours of the staff are to be cut from 35 to 33 in the week in which they work on a Saturday, and also in the following week. In addition, a shift premium will be paid of 21 per cent. with a minimum annual payment of £321 and a maximum of £1,065.

Patterns of working hours. Other patterns, where they exist, need also to be spelled out, *e.g. flexible working hours*—an arrangement whereby employees may begin and end work at times of their choice provided they are all present at certain core-times and that within a settlement period of a week or month they work the total number of hours agreed. Of a work force of 18 million men and women in full-time employment, it is estimated that about 500 organisations with about 100,000 employees are operating flexible working hours. A *compressed working week* involves the full complement of normal weekly hours being worked, but in less than five full days. *Staggered working hours* are sometimes adopted to alleviate traffic congestion problems.

" Off-duty " or " extra " hours of work. Finally, it may be noted that hours of work should include all hours worked which are necessary to the performance of contractual obligations; *e.g.* in *Lake* v. *Essex County Council* [1978] I.R.L.R. 24 (E.A.T.), a part-time teacher had a contract which specified that her hours of work were 19 hours and 25 minutes a week. The E.A.T. held that since she *had* to do work essential to the proper performance of her job (preparation and marking—contractual duties) which in practice *exceeded* the specified amount of time, these " off-duty " working hours fell to be included in the contractual hours of work. Her contract/written statement should, therefore, have reflected the true position. This case, where the employee *has* to work longer than stipulated in the contract, is apparently not the same as where the employee merely *in practice* works more than the specified number of hours. In the latter case, tribunals will look only to the contract—see *ITT Components (Europe) Ltd.* v. *Y. Kolah* [1977] I.R.L.R. 53 (E.A.T.). There is obviously scope for much argument as to which of these two constructions applies to any given situation.

Holidays and holiday pay. The *Social Action Programme* drawn up by the EEC Commission in October 1973 contained, among other things, a Recommendation to Member States to adopt the principle of four calendar weeks as the minimum paid holiday entitlement by December 31, 1978. There is, in the U.K., as yet no general right to holidays. In practice, as a matter of contract, many employees get a minimum annual holiday of four weeks' annual leave after one year's employment, plus eight public holidays, additional days after long service, or even occasional one-off holidays for, *e.g.* key years (after 25 years' service) or additional days on an age basis to supplement service related days. Holiday pay is the largest fringe benefit in terms of levels and also as a proportion of wages and salaries. In 1968 it formed 7 per cent. of pay, and 8·8 per cent. in 1973.

Still, many workers are relatively badly off, *e.g.* manual workers in the ready mixed concrete industry, under a settlement which took effect from February 17, 1978, had their annual holiday entitlement increased only by two days to three weeks and three days a year—the additional days to be taken at a time to be decided by the employer. Timing of holidays is often controlled: many organisations limit the amount of holiday that can be taken on any one occasion (often only 10 days). In certain circumstances, extended leave may be allowed, *e.g.* to visit relatives abroad. But all depends on contract: in *Tucker* v. *British Leyland Motor Corp. Ltd.* [1978] I.R.L.R. 493, a county court held that the company could not transfer the statutory holidays to another time without the employee's consent—there was no contractual right, express or implied, to do so.

Holiday pay entitlement on termination is specifically to be singled out for attention in the statement of particulars (see also rights during the period of notice: Sched. 3, para. 2 (1) (*c*)). Accrued holiday entitlement needs be the subject of contractual provision, *e.g.* the 1978 National Engineering Agreement provides that in future new employees taken on after January 1 each year are to be entitled to annual holidays with pay proportional to the length of service in the remainder of the year. That agreement also replaces the system of accumulated holiday credits with an arrangement to pay average, 40-hour earnings during holidays: " The individual normal average 40-hour earnings shall be the normal level of remuneration received by the individual per normal 40-hour working week, but will exclude overtime payments and payments on an occasional basis, *e.g.* Christmas bonus. It will include shift allowances, nightshift allowance, individual merit rates, and other payments made as part of regular weekly earnings." Special provisions apply to the pay of shift workers and workers on PBR (payment by results). Additional special provisions cover the entitlement of the employee who is absent sick at the time of the annual holiday shut-down.

Sickness and sick pay. Terms and conditions (but note the change from " provisions " to " provision for sick pay " in s. 1 (3) (*d*) (ii)) under this heading should cover two principal aspects: sickness benefit schemes, and continuation of employment in the event of prolonged ill-health. In practice, only the first tends to be the subject of coverage in statements of particulars and even written contracts.

Despite the isolated decision in *Orman* v. *Saville Sportswear Ltd.* [1960] 1 W.L.R. 1055, the judges have proved incapable of implying a general common law duty on employers to stand by their employees in ill-health—the duty of fidelity impliedly owed by employees not being reciprocal in this instance. On the contrary, the common law regards the contract of employment as a commercial matter: if labour is defective, then payment is not required. Payment is for work done and hang the inhumanity. So workers in ill-health must rely on what they have succeeded in negotiating for themselves in their contracts.

The hardship is enormous in scale: during 1976, certificated sickness accounted for the loss of some 350 million working days, costing the taxpayer over £312 million in social security benefits (*cf.* six million working days lost through industrial disputes). Yet the variation in workers' protection is equally enormous. A Department of Health and Social Security survey of occupational sick pay schemes in 1974 found marked differences between the schemes for non-manual and manual employees, *e.g.* 25 per cent. of full-time men and 21 per cent. of full-time women receive between 13 and 26 weeks' sick pay. But there are considerable variations according to type of work. While 27 per cent. of non-manual men receive 52 weeks' sick pay or over, 25 per cent. of manual men receive only four weeks or less. Again, take-up of benefits is another matter. Ministry of Pensions and Ministry of Labour surveys in 1964 showed that in 1961 only about a fifth of the male workers incapacitated by sickness actually received employers' sick pay, though just over 50 per cent. were covered by some provision. Then there is the variation between regions: sick pay schemes most frequently are found in the South East and are least common in the West Midlands and Wales.

Sickness benefit provisions to be included in the written statement are of various types, most commonly a direct payment by employer to employee during the period of absence The employee's entitlement is to be paid for a specified number of days or weeks or months during a year, or some longer period. Alternative methods used by some employers are assurance schemes—benefits being paid by the insurance company, or Friendly Society schemes—with both employer and employee making contributions.

A shocking finding of the above-mentioned DHSS survey of 1974 was that in a substantial minority of cases, both the duration and amount of sick pay is at the employer's discretion. This finding was confirmed in a recent survey of 30 top British organisations: the 20 largest private sector employers and the 10 largest nationalised industries (see Industrial Relations Review and Report, No. 152 (May 1977)). Management was found in many cases to have complete discretion in the payment of benefits—sometimes to the extent of expressly stating the scheme not to be contractual at all; *e.g.* the Bass Charrington staff scheme, and the W.D. and H.O. Wills scheme (part of the Imperial Group). It should be considered whether the inclusion of such schemes in a written statement of terms might have implications which undermine their purportedly non-contractual nature.

The details of the terms and conditions in the written statement governing sickness benefit schemes cover such matters as:

(i) coverage of injuries as well as sickness. Employees should beware that some employers require reimbursement of sick/accident pay if the worker should get some injury compensation;

(ii) deduction of State National Insurance sickness benefit—unfortunately the norm in the schemes, though not all employers do this (*e.g.* Ford and the British Gas Corporation). Where there is no *express* term as to deduction of National Insurance benefits, however, the decision in *Marrison* v. *Bell* [1939] 2 K.B. 187 would seem to indicate that N.I. benefits are a *supplement* to any sick pay, intended to cover the exceptional expenses that arise in time of ill-health. Married women paying less than the full rate of N.I. contributions often had the *full* benefit deducted from sick pay unless they had safeguarded their position. But see now the Social Security Pensions Act 1975, ss. 3 and 18 which abolish both the married woman's right to opt out of full contributions and the lower rate of sickness and unemployment benefit. And finally, arrangements need be made to cover the position affecting pension contributions during illness, both during and after the expiry of the benefit payments;

(iii) length of service qualification for sick pay entitlement. Most manual workers have to wait some time before they become entitled. Yet these workers stand the greatest risk at their kind of work, and also have the highest chance of suffering early in their jobs. The DHSS survey found that 58 per cent. of full-time men and 48 per cent. of full-time women were required to qualify through service for sick pay coverage—most commonly a period of six months;

(iv) like N.I. sickness benefits, some sick pay schemes provide for "waiting" periods before entitlement, though again mostly manual workers are affected by this contractual liability. The DHSS survey found 70 per cent. of full-time men and 86 per cent. of full-time women *not* required to serve any "waiting days." But, *e.g.* British Steel industrial grades must wait two weeks; two days for British Rail workers; and 10 days for Thorn Consumer Electronics employees. Arrangements may exist for payments to cover these "waiting days" should the illness last a specified time. And recurrence of illness after a short time may not be subject to the "waiting days" qualification;

(v) requirements as to notification and medical certification usually exist: payment is often dependent upon it. Sometimes the employer takes the power to require the employee to be examined by a nominated doctor;

(vi) provisions as to sickness in special circumstances, *e.g.* holidays, where some agreements provide for benefit to be paid and holiday entitlement to be taken after recovery, subject to limits for long-term illness, as in the National Engineering Agreement. Sickness during strikes or lay-off may also be dealt with by special provisions;

(vii) some schemes may specify categories of cases which do not qualify; *e.g.* intentional self-injury, that arising from sports, alcoholism or drugs, etc. Certain categories of employees may be excluded wholesale, *e.g.* part-timers. Of some interest is the exclusion of pregnancy-related illness which some schemes do. Assuming that the sick pay scheme is *not* contractual (*i.e.* is discretionary, as many schemes are) and so s. 6 (6) of the Sex Discrimination Act 1975 does not prevent a claim, it would seem arguable that such an exclusion amounted to discrimination on grounds of sex under ss. 1 (1) (*a*) and 5 (3) of the 1975 Act. For pregnancy is exclusively associated with women, and men in similar circumstances, *i.e.* incapable of work through physical disability, are being treated differently—that is, are eligible for sick pay. In *Roberts* v. *BICC Ltd.* [1976] I.R.L.R. 404, an industrial tribunal held that an exclusion in a sick pay scheme specifying that "absence due to *maternity* or *confinement* does not qualify for benefit" did not apply to the case of a woman off work as a result of pregnancy complications. "Pregnancy" was a different phase from maternity, and was thus not excluded by the words of the exclusion clause. Unfortunately, the tribunal rejected the argument that the clause was discriminatory, giving the somewhat obscure reason that: "To argue over the physiological differences between men and women in the context of pregnancy and childbirth is as irrelevent as it is unproductive" (*sic*).

Normally, the terms relating to incapacity do not deal with prolonged illness, though British Aluminium operates a scheme for staff that when normal sick pay entitlement has expired, 50 per cent. of basic salary up to retirement if necessary is paid. But the many decisions of the Employment Appeal Tribunal and the courts on dismissal for ill health probably suffice to make certain terms relating to prolonged illness a matter of contractual implication. Examples would be the employer's obligation to make reasonable efforts to, first inform himself about the state of the employee's health (*Patterson* v. *Messrs. Bracketts* [1977] I.R.L.R. 137 (E.A.T.) ; then to look for alternative employment should the employee be disabled through illness (*Todd* v. *North Eastern Electricity Board*) [1975] I.R.L.R. 130). The written statement of particulars, which must include *any* terms and conditions under this heading should include details of these implied contractual obligations—if only to ensure that the employer is aware of them.

Pensions and pension schemes. Since the written statement must contain " any terms and conditions relating to pensions and pension schemes," the employee needs be informed not only of any benefits he is entitled to, but also whether he is eligible to join the scheme, and if so how and under what conditions.

Social welfare payments, mainly pensions, are the second most important category of fringe benefit in industry (after holiday pay), comprising 4·2 per cent. of pay in 1968 and 4·8 per cent. in 1973. A 1960 Glasgow University survey showed that about 66 per cent. of companies operated pension schemes and 50 per cent. gave long-service payments. A 1968 Department of Employment survey reported that in manufacturing, 72 per cent. of employers made payments into pension funds for employees. Occupational pension schemes cover about 11 million employees, and eight million of these will get at least half final salary on retirement. But these schemes have grievous faults—they are very uneven in their incidence, many workers are not covered, especially lower-paid workers and women in particular (see 5 I.L.J. 54 (1976)). They have little redistributive effect on wealth in this country. Hence the growth of State pension schemes—see the proviso to this subsection and also subs. (4) (*d*).

Notice of termination. The statutory minimum periods of notice required to be given by both employer and employee to each other are specified in s. 49, though these only apply after a qualifying period of four weeks. For rights of the employee during the period of notice, see Sched. 3.

The length of notice specified in the written statement may remove doubts arising in situations where this term is not otherwise expressed, but is rather implied into the contract or fixed by custom (though obviously the statement is still open to challenge on either of these grounds). But the general rule at common law is that, in the absence of any term, express or implied or customary, the period of notice is presumed to be of " reasonable " length. The judges' assessment of " reasonableness " is, as usual, determined by their social and political prejudices, not by workers' needs. Here the applicable prejudice relates to the social hierarchy of jobs: the higher a person's occupational status, the longer a period of notice will be deemed to be reasonable.

Problems associated with a failure by the employer to supply detailed written particulars as to notice are aggravated by this criterion of " reasonableness." In *I. G. Cuthbertson* v. *AML Distributors* [1975] I.R.L.R. 228, the employee was dismissed with one month's notice. Not having been issued with a written statement, he referred the matter to the industrial tribunal, claiming he was entitled to " reasonable " notice, and in the circumstances this was three months. The tribunal responded by a useless gesture: it declared that the notice requirement *was* one of " reasonable notice," but refused to specify what amount was " reasonable "—this question of fact had to be determined by the courts, to whom the frustrated employee was referred.

Notice provision in written statements needs to be carefully phrased to take account of any relevant dismissals procedures (assuming these can be incorporated into contracts of employment (see Note to subs. (4) (*a*)). Such procedures may contain " status quo " provisions which in practice extend the length of notice periods beyond the formal time periods often specified (see generally 4 I.L.J. 131 (1975), *E.g.* the nationally agreed procedure for the avoidance of disputes in the engineering industry, which became operative on April 5, 1976, provides in para. 5 (*b*):

" *Where notice of dismissal is given* (other than instant dismissal), it is open to the dismissed person to contest that dismissal, and if necessary, to call through the union for an external Conference, and in such a case the *person will remain an employee of the company*·until such time as either agreement is reached, or the procedure is exhausted."

It seems that in practice if the notice has expired *before* the procedure has been exhausted, the employee is expected to continue working.

Title of the job. When this particular was required to be included in the written statement by the amendment in the Employment Protection Act 1975 (Sched. 16, Pt. II, para. 4), most commentators considered it to be of minimal importance. Titles such as " Grade 2 operative " were thought to be acceptable. But it cannot be too strongly emphasised that a grade is almost the direct contradiction of a title. Grading is a function of job evaluation schemes; titles are a function of crafts, skills, qualifications, duties. Yet provision of a job analysis or specification, let alone a job description, was not thought to be required. It was pointed out that the title stated might affect unfair dismissal issues—by pointing to the nature of the work which the employee was contractually bound to perform. But it was generally thought that the title was irrelevant to matters such as work description, status and the place where work was to be performed.

In annotations to the amendment in the Employment Protection Act 1975, it was noted that " questions of job definition and geographical mobility have frequently arisen in claims before tribunals and it remains to be seen how much detail will be held to be entailed in the concept of ' title of the job '." The industrial tribunals, unfortunately, did not rise to the challenge; *e.g.* in *Churcher* v. *Weyside Engineering (1926) Ltd.* [1976] I.R.L.R. 402 there was a dispute with the employer putting forward the title " Planner and associated duties " and the employee submitting " Senior Planning Engineer." In true Solomonic fashion, the tribunal resolved that the title of the job be " Planning Engineer."

Obviously, the less specific the content of the title, the less useful it will be in fulfilling the Act's function of keeping the worker informed. It would be consistent with the intention of the legislation, therefore, to provide to the worker under this heading as much information as possible as to the work he has agreed to do for the employer.

This Act has taken what appears to be a major step in this direction by providing a definition of " job " in s. 153 (1). It " means the nature of the work which he is employed to do in accordance with his contract and the capacity and place in which he is so employed." As a result, it would appear to be required that the " title of the job " relate to all *three* requirements in sufficient particularity: the *nature* of the work, the *capacity* of the employee and the *place* in which he is employed.

Previously, there was no definition of " job " applicable to this legal requirement. The present definition is, however, identical to that used in *two* other contexts, both concerning reinstatement or re-engagement following absence or dismissal. First, in s. 48 (2) (*a*)' of the Employment Protection Act 1975 (now s. 45 (1) of this Act): the right of an employee absent on maternity leave to return to work " in the job in which she was employed under the original contract of employment " (this last phrase defined further in s. 52 of the 1975 Act—now s. 153 (1) of this Act). Second, in the Trade Union and Labour Relations Act 1974 (T.U.L.R.A.), Sched. 1, para. 7 (5) (*c*) (now s. 62 (4) (*c*) of this Act), concerning the re-engagement of a striker either " in the job which he held immediately before the date of dismissal or in a different job." For the purposes of that amendment to T.U.L.R.A., this definition of " job " was inserted into the interpretation section (s. 30 (1) of T.U.L.R.A.) by the 1975 Act, Sched. 16, Pt. III, para. 7 (4). In addition, one may note T.U.L.R.A., Sched. 1, para. 21 (3A), again amended by the 1975 Act, Sched. 16, Pt. III, para. 19 (now Sched. 9, para. 1 (4) of this Act)—which concerns the costs of adjournment arising from an employer's failure to adduce evidence as to " the availability of the job from which the complainant was dismissed, or, as the case may be, which she held before her absence." *All* these contexts are now covered by the definition of " job " in s. 153 (1) of this Act.

The amount of detail required to be included to provide particulars of the " title of the job " remains uncertain, though the scope to be covered—nature, capacity and place—is not. What is clear from the *other* contexts in which the word is used is that the " job " is an individual artefact clearly distinguishable from employment in general. The other contexts distinguish the " job " in question from—in s. 62 (4) (*c*), " a different job which would be reasonably suitable," and in s. 45 (3), " alternative employment." So the title of the job must suffice to distinguish it clearly from other " different," " alternative " jobs.

It is interesting to note other phrases used in the law which emphasise the individuality of a " job," *e.g.* " position " (defined in s. 153 (1)) is similarly individual, referring to status, nature of the work and terms and conditions of employment (the word is used in s. 57 (4) (*b*)—qualifications of the employee; s. 59—redundancy: " similar " positions implies a degree of generality; and s. 64 (1) (*b*)—retirement: again a note of generality. *Cf.* " descriptions " of employees—used in s. 65 (2) (*c*): availability of dismissals procedure agreement, again a note of generality; and *cf.* T.U.L.R.A., s. 28 (1) (*a*)—descriptions of workers in the definition of trade union imported by s. 153 (1). Again, " employees of the same class " in s. 58 (3) (*a*), or that in the definition of union membership agreement (T.U.L.R.A., s. 30 (1) imported by s. 153 (1))—" employees of an identifiable class "—the word " class " again connoting generality. Or lastly, just " duties of employment " as in the definition of " trade dispute " in T.U.L.R.A., s. 29 (1) (*c*), imported by s. 153 (1).

The need to analyse the generality or specificity of the phrase " title of the job " springs from the considerable practical consequences which will flow from one or the other approach. The ramifications are clear: a *general* approach would benefit employers by allowing them to define job titles broadly, thus gaining flexibility, shifting the employee from one type or place of work to another as the need arises. Taken to its extreme, job " titles " are here reduced to grades of a job evaluation scheme. This disregards the workers' duties, skills, the " nature of the work and the capacity . . . in which he is employed " and reduces him to a point on a numbered scale. This cannot be allowed to go unchallenged. The consequences for workers might be to undermine traditional craft skills by dilution, to threaten bargaining strength by allowing for flexibility and confining wage claims to re-gradings of a finite amount determined by the employer's scheme, and to endanger jobs by letting interchangeability enable several " jobs " to be carried out by one worker.

So conversely, a *precise* approach to " job title " benefits workers by making clear what the nature, capacity and place of employment is, and ensuring that the employer cannot add on duties, increase responsibilities, or transfer him without his consent to this variation of the contract, *i.e.*, it renders negotiable what would otherwise be a unilateral power of the employer. The interpretation of " title of the job " is therefore of the first importance. A precise approach will ensure that every employee has a statement describing an identifiable job of his own. This may, effectively, become a title to, and not only of his job.

Subs. (4)

Disciplinary rules. This requirement was introduced by the 1975 Act's amendments to the Contracts of Employment Act 1972. It made it obligatory for employers to have disciplinary rules reduced to written form. It has been pointed out that employers here are probably not given the option, which exists as regards other parts of the written statement, to state that there are no particulars to be entered (s. 2 (1)). It has, therefore, forced many employers to consider for perhaps the first time the adequacy of their existing disciplinary systems, and naturally trade unions and workers have been affected by this process of either revision of old Works Rules or the drawing up of new ones.

But such is the dominance of the managerial perspective that many basic questions arising from this provision are not considered by lawyers or others. Two such fundamental issues are: (1) *how* is the content of " disciplinary rules " discovered and reduced to writing; *how* does one determine which are the *contractual* rules of discipline. And (2) what is the *scope* of " disciplinary rules applicable to the employee " ?

As regards the first of these issues, the Code of Practice on Disciplinary Practice and Procedures in Employment (issued pursuant to s. 6 (1) and (8) of the 1975 Act, and which came into effect on June 20, 1977) is instructive. Para. 5, though obviously imbued with the managerial perspective, is quite subtle: the initiative for establishing rules " normally " lies with management, but *acceptance* by employees is *necessary* for them to be fully *effective*. So: " Management should therefore aim to secure the involvement of employees . . . when formulating new or revising existing rules . . . trade union officials may or may not wish to participate in the formulation of the rules."

What is evinced here is an appreciation—essential to the person seeking to understand the nature of *contractual terms of employment* relating to discipline— of the different ways in which these terms may be determined. A number of possibilities exist. First, by management prerogative alone: the production of uncontested books of Works Rules. Second, by management and unions jointly agreeing on the contents of such a Works Rules book. This is relatively uncommon, though certain areas such as health and safety rules may be agreed, *e.g.* TASS advises safety committees on which its members are represented to " participate in drawing up work safety rules" (yet note the irony of subs. (5)). Third, and usually ignored by those wedded to managerialism, is where these formal written books of Works Rules are in *practice* either revised, subverted, subjected to exceptions or in effect supplanted by the informal rules of custom and practice. *The degree to which Rule Books reflect terms of employment relating to discipline will vary depending on the strength and aggressiveness of workers and the counter-responses of line management or supervisors anxious to allow concessions in order to secure co-operation in maintaining production.* A fourth way of fixing terms relating to discipline is unilateral workers' control, as is the case with *e.g.* workers controlling manning levels in dock work, or in the printing industry. (See generally (1976) 5 I.L.J. 164.)

So the lawyer seeking to advise as to what rules of discipline apply—either in a specific case of disciplinary action or a general reconsideration of the Works Rules—must look at *all* these possibilities. Most judges and lawyers will, being what they are, opt for managerialism and certainty and assert the employer's formal book of Works Rules as the source of the law of discipline, putting forward evidence of signed receipts, posting on notice boards, or even trade union consent. Workers' representatives must be prepared to oppose these assertions with evidence of *other* rules of discipline, which *more accurately* reflect how the formal written rules have been modified, altered or even supplanted by custom and practice on the shop floor. Such evidence would come from oral testimony of workers, precedents, and perhaps even written notes of how certain formal Works Rules are to be " interpreted." Many claims of " unfair dismissal " arise where management attempts to enforce a disciplinary rule which nobody on the shop floor considers to be binding—it having been waived or fallen into disuse or " interpreted " into something quite different. Tribunals and courts occasionally realise this, though they rarely stipulate the " real " rule. They prefer to uphold the " formal " rule and condemn management for applying it arbitrarily or capriciously in the past. Tribunals do not usually challenge the content of rules, only the procedure of applying them.

In fact, therefore, this requirement of providing the employee with a note specifying disciplinary rules should be fulfilled only by reducing to writing the custom and practice of discipline, not the formal rules. But it requires little experience to realise how difficult a task this is. Workers are reluctant to crystallise their position. Either they are strong and well organised, so they have little to gain and stand to lose by formalisation, thus prejudicing themselves from further gains; or, where they are weak, such a crystallisation would reflect management's strength. On the other side, senior management would often refuse to endorse junior management's accommodations. Lawyers must remain aware of these problems, and bear them in mind when determining the content of disciplinary rules.

The second issue, the *scope* of disciplinary rules, is also more complex than most lawyers realise. It too is not resolved simply by referring to a book of Works Rules in any particular place. As it was put in the above cited article: " What is a disciplinary issue depends in part on what management care to treat as such. This itself will depend on the interest they have in controlling any particular aspect of employee behaviour and on their use, habitual or otherwise, of disciplinary rules to control behaviour. But it will also depend on whether employees collectively allow an issue to be treated as an individual one. This in turn will depend in part on their bargaining interests, strength and history."

Two examples will illustrate the complexity of the issues pinpointed here. First, whether management *choose* to treat certain behaviour as a disciplinary matter. Take absenteeism: is it a subject for disciplinary rules? Most employers deal with it as such, and are frequently considerably put out when their inadequate record-keeping results in unfair dismissal compensation being awarded. But other employers deal with absenteeism by measures other than disciplinary rules: *e.g.* restructuring work often helps to cut down absenteeism, as in development of team work; the introduction of flexible working hours means people who simply don't come in rather than arrive late are not absent; the introduction of special leave allowances, so that employees will be able to take leave to, *e.g.* go to a funeral, and not just be absent because of " illness "; or employers may offer positive incentives for good attendance—bonuses. Such methods may reduce absenteeism to a point where it ceases to become a matter governed by discipline.

The second example illustrates the case where *employees will not allow* a matter to be governed by discipline. The Code of Practice provides that rules drawn up should, among others, be those " necessary for the efficient and safe performance of work " (para. 6). In workplaces where craft tradition is strong, work standards may not be determined by the employer and enforced through discipline. Rather the workers' organisations set both the standards and the means of enforcement. Even more common is the case of worker regulated manning levels. This aspect of " efficiency " is also determined by the collective organisation, which may allow for days off, regulation of overtime levels, etc. Management is not permitted to implement disciplinary rules in this area. An example which is increasingly at the fore is rules governing employers' security checks. Unions are insisting on the right to have representatives present and powers to intervene where " personal and/or irrelevant questions are put "—USDAW advice to members. Staff at St. Andrew's Hospital, Bow, in East London, went on strike when an innocent member's flat was searched for hospital goods by police. Another example is rules governing secrecy. NUBE is currently challenging such rules in the banking sector—they may in any event clash with the disclosure of information requirements now embodied in legislation.

So lawyers must beware of accepting formal Works Rules at their face value. Often they are to be supplemented by informal practices which belie their literal meaning, even to the extent of supplanting them. Or they may be formalities only, not in practice implemented at all, or very rarely, their subject-matter being regulated by the workers autonomously. The implications of this for the written note required by this subsection are, therefore, obviously complex.

Remedy. The *formal* remedy where the employer fails to provide a note of the disciplinary rules, or where rules are included which are questioned as not complying with the requirements of the law, is that s. 11 allows for a reference to an industrial tribunal. But in *practice* the sanction for failure lies in claims for unfair dismissal compensation on grounds of inadequacies in the employer's disciplinary rules. These focus on such aspects as whether the employee was in fact notified of the rule (as the subsection requires him to be) ; and whether the rules were clear that the behaviour in question was subject to discipline, with an unambiguous penalty attached to breach of the rule. Failure in these respects implies a breach of the Code of Practice, especially paras. 2 to 8 and 14. And the result of this, as the Code itself says (para. 4), may be a successful claim for unfair dismissal.

Reasonably accessible. A final point on disciplinary rules: the absolute require- ment that the document be " reasonably accessible " contrasts with s. 2 (3), which provides as an alternative the requirement that the employee should have " reasonable opportunities of reading [it] in the course of his employment." The simplest form of compliance would be to supply copies of the Works Rules, or display them on a notice board. Still, there is scope here for differences of interpretation as to how much access is reasonable: clearly copies locked in drawers, not available outside of working hours, or their consultation being subject to permission of management might be deemed not to comply. One wonders whether there is a requirement that consultation be allowed every time a difference arises as to discipline. The employee concerned (and his representative) obviously need to know the details of the rules on such occasions (see Note to s. 2 (3)).

Disciplinary and grievance procedures. As subs. (4) (*a*) makes it mandatory to have disciplinary rules written down, so subs. (4) (*b*) (i) obliges employers to provide an appeals procedure on disciplinary matters. These may be fused with grievance procedures, which are also made mandatory by subs. (4) (*b*) (ii) (but see the Code of Practice, para. 16).

An example of such a fused procedure is that between the TGWU and the Hotel Bristol, Piccadilly, part of the Trafalgar House Group, covering all weekly paid staff. Disciplinary arrangements provide for verbal and written warnings, investigation and hearing. But at any stage an employee can appeal against disciplinary action through the grievance procedure, a five-stage procedure with time limits on all stages. It leads ultimately to ACAS conciliation if no agreement is reached, and provides that no industrial action will be taken until the procedure is exhausted. This last point raises two inter-related issues: first, the effect of this no-strike clause on the contracts of employment—see T.U.L.R.A., s. 18 (4). Secondly, whether the existence of such a clause implies a contractual right, should the pro- cedure be exhausted without agreement, of the workers to take industrial action. At least it might preclude the employer from invoking any discipline should employees take industrial action at the conclusion of the procedure.

The Code of Practice introduces further obligations, *e.g.* employees must be told at the time of a disciplinary action of the right to appeal, how to make it and to whom (para. 13). The old Code of Practice, upheld in numerous cases, provided that the right of appeal should, wherever practicable, be to a level of management not previously involved (para. 132 (iii)). Note that the obligations in subs. (4) (*b*) only cover a single stage procedure, further steps not being mandatory under subs. (4) (*c*).

Contracting-out certificate. Employers who had occupational pension schemes had to decide, after consulting the recognised trade unions, whether or not to contract out of the new earnings-related part of the State pension scheme which commenced on April 1, 1978. A condition for being able to get a contracting-out certificate is that the employee gets at least as much in occupational pension as he would from his additional component under the State scheme. The consequence of a failure by employers to secure a contracting-out certificate is that employees would have to pay both the contributions to the occupational scheme *and* the higher National Insurance contributions required by the new scheme.. Hence the requirement in s. 30 (5) of the Social Security Pensions Act 1975 that the note as to the existence of a certificate be provided. Any questions as to this requirement cannot, however, be referred to an industrial tribunal under s. 11 (4) (*b*). Rather it must go to the Occupational Pensions Board on a reference by the Secretary of State (Social Security Pensions Act 1975, ss. 30 (5), 60 (2)).

Subs. (5)

Health and safety rules and procedures. It is not at all clear why this exclusion was made. The GMWU pointed out in its comments on the absence of health and safety matters from the Code of Practice: " In our experience, a substantial number of disciplinary matters arise in connection with health and safety." One need only consider disputes arising when workers consider some machine or substance dangerous and the employer refuses to do anything to eliminate the risk on grounds of cost or lost production. Agreed rules and procedures would be just as useful here as in other matters. It is not clear that the employer's duties to provide information under the Health and Safety at Work etc. Act 1974, s. 2 (2) (*c*) and (3), will cover this gap.

Even so, the exclusion is not unambiguous. The 1974 Act also covers the welfare of employees. So rules, etc., relating to welfare must be supplied in the written statement. There is obviously a problem over aspects of health and safety that spills over into other areas. The most obvious case is that of rules, etc., governing smoking. Does the obligation in s. 1 apply only to those rules as they apply to matters unconnected with health and safety at work—*i.e.* the section applies if public hygiene, or the employer's image or efficiency is at stake; but not if the health and safety of the workers is at stake?

Subs. (6)

Week. What definition does apply? Seven days? Five days? The normal working week (Sched. 13)? But see s. 3. It is relevant to calculating, *e.g.* the 13 weeks within which the employer must supply the written statement (subs. (1)); and the terms to be not more than one week old (subs. (3)). The Contracts of Employment Act 1972 did not define " week," and this Act is thus faithful to its source. *Cf.* the definition of week in Sched. 13, para. 24 (1), reproducing the 1972 Act's Sched. 1, para. 11 (1).

Supplementary provisions relating to statements under s. 1

2.—(1) If there are no particulars to be entered under any of the heads of paragraph (*d*) of subsection (3) of section 1, or under any of the other provisions of section 1 (2) and (3), that fact shall be stated.

(2) If the contract is for a fixed term, the statement given under section 1 shall state the date when the contract expires.

(3) A statement given under section 1 may, for all or any of the particulars to be given by the statement, refer the employee to some document which the employee has reasonable opportunities of reading in the course of his employment or which is made reasonably accessible to him in some other way.

(4) If not more than six months after the termination of an employee's period of employment, a further period of employment is begun with the same employer, and the terms of employment are the same, no statement need be given under section 1 in respect of the second period of employment, but without prejudice to the operation of subsection (1) of section 4 if there is a change in the terms of employment.

DERIVATION

1972, s. 4 (3) to (6).

GENERAL NOTE

Subs. (1)

No particulars to be stated. An employer who states outright that there are not any terms of employment, express or implied, under one or other of the headings listed, needs be careful. The widespread practices with regard to many items will frequently allow for argument as to the existence of some understood practice as to, *e.g.* sick pay, holidays, geographical mobility, etc. Workers should bear in mind that the employer's denial in the statement of any such terms can always be contested. The formulation of the denial may be significant: the statement "there is no sick pay or holidays" is different from "there are no terms agreed relating to sick pay or holidays." The latter might simply reflect disagreement as to what the terms are, but to acknowledge that some provision is to be made. But even the former can be challenged as simply inaccurate.

By implication, it is argued that the employer cannot say there are no particulars relating to the matters in s. 1 (4)—he *must* supply a note specifying disciplinary rules, and grievance and appeal procedures. Para. 120 of the 1972 Code of Practice, still in force, supports this: each employee "must be told" how he can seek redress for grievances.

Subs. (2)

Fixed term contracts. There are numerous problems as to what is a "fixed term" contract in law to which this subsection applies. Does it include contracts which allow for termination by notice prior to the end of the fixed term? One decision from the Court of Appeal provides an affirmative answer: *Dixon* v. *British Broadcasting Corporation, The Times*, October 6, 1978. Does it include various probationary contracts which contain a fixed probationary period? The answer is not yet clear. See the Note to s. 142 for further discussion.

Date of expiry. Perhaps the most problematic situation arises when employees are employed for a fixed period, but the date of termination is not normally specified. Employment is terminated by the occurrence of specified external events. Thus in *Wiltshire County Council* v. *Guy* [1978] I.R.L.R. 301 (E.A.T.), a part-time teacher ceased to work at the end of the academic year whenever her courses finished. No actual date was agreed for the expiry of the contract, but the E.A.T. nonetheless held that she was employed under a contract for a fixed term.

Subs. (3)

Reference to documents. It is thought to be common for an employer to discharge his obligation by referring employees to documents—as where the employment is covered by a collective agreement fixing the particulars listed in s. 1. But a survey of employers in light industry in North-East London showed that this is not always the case ((1977) 6 I.L.J. 133). 80 per cent. of the employers interviewed complied with the law in some form, and of these, 78 per cent. claimed to have provided *full* particulars *without* reference to secondary documents. Those who did not provide full particulars but rather referred to secondary documents tended to have a predominantly white-collar workforce. So the common expectation that employers would avoid the burden, and employees miss the benefits of a direct supply of information was not borne out by this research. It showed that manual workers were found to be less likely to be fobbed off with a reference elsewhere. But where this did occur, the anticipated results followed: the survey disclosed a high level of ignorance among employees of such secondary documents—collective agreements, works rules, etc—even when clear reference was made to them. Again manual workers seemed *more* aware of these secondary sources than white-collar workers.

Accessibility. Ignorance would seem to contradict the logic of the law's requirements that the document be reasonably accessible to the employee or that he have reasonable opportunities of reading it in the course of his employment. But experience triumphs over logic, or over law anyway. Display on a notice board might satisfy the needs of an employee for information, but the above mentioned survey found that in some cases there were very few or only one copy available for a large number of employees spread over a number of sites. This would not seem to satisfy the requirement as to " reasonable " accessibility. As to the scope of " reasonable opportunities of reading " the document, the time off provisions of s. 28 might help trade union members. But *cf.* T.U.L.R.A., s. 18 (4) (*c*)—no-strike clauses in collective agreements must be " reasonably accessible at his place of work to the worker to whom it applies and . . . available for him to consult during working hours." But the phrase " in the course of his employment " will unnerve anybody familiar with industrial injuries compensation claims.

Legal interpretation of collective agreements. Problems can arise when the particulars resulting from reference to a collective agreement are assumed to have contractual status. Collective agreements do not always lend themselves to the formal construction expected of written contracts of employment. For problems which can result from the automatic incorporation of collective agreements by a reference in the statement of particulars, see the differing judgments of the E.A.T. and the Court of Session in *Burroughs Machines Ltd.* v. *Timmoney* [1976] I.R.L.R. 343 (E.A.T.) ; [1977] I.R.L.R. 404 (Ct. of Sess.). The collective agreement was not to be incorporated word for word; rather the court should use its " common sense."

Subs. (4)

Seasonal or recurring employment. Provision is here made for seasonal employers. They benefit although the employee may have been away for up to six months. Yet employees away from work also have needs, and long serving workers may lose their documents/statements of particulars. A right to require periodic reissuings of written statements would alleviate much of the difficulty. But this subsection automatically exempts the employer regardless of the employee's need.

Certain hours of employment to be disregarded.

3.—(1) Subject to the following provisions of this section, no account shall be taken under section 1 of employment during any period when the hours of employment are normally less than sixteen hours weekly.

(2) If the employee's relations with his employer cease to be governed by a contract which normally involves work for sixteen hours or more weekly and become governed by a contract which normally involves employment for eight hours or more, but less than sixteen hours, weekly, the employee shall nevertheless for a period of twenty-six weeks (computed in accordance with subsection (3)) be treated for the purposes of subsection (1) as if his contract normally involved employment for sixteen hours or more weekly.

(3) In computing the said period of twenty-six weeks no account shall be taken of any week—

(*a*) during which the employee is in fact employed for sixteen hours or more;

(*b*) during which the employee takes part in a strike (as defined in paragraph 24 of Schedule 13) or is absent from work because of a lock-out (as so defined) by his employer; or

(*c*) during which there is no contract of employment but which, by virtue of paragraph 9 (1) of Schedule 13, counts in computing a period of continuous employment.

(4) An employee whose relations with his employer are governed by a contract of employment which normally involves employment for eight hours or more, but less than sixteen hours, weekly shall nevertheless, if he has been continuously employed for a period of five years

or more, be treated for the purposes of subsection (1) as if his contract normally involved employment for sixteen hours or more weekly.

DERIVATION
  1972, s. 4 (7) to (10) ; 1975, Sched. 16, Part II, paras. 7, 8.

GENERAL NOTE
Subs. (1)
  Part-timers. This exclusion of part-time workers is particularly unfortunate since in many cases they do not in practice receive many of the benefits available to full-time workers. Surveys indicate that they are often on lower basic rates, do not benefit from overtime, are excluded from sick pay and pension schemes, and do not get the same holiday entitlements. Since practice does vary so greatly in the treatment of part-timers, their need for information is as great as that of full-time employees.
  Discrimination against women workers. It should be noted that compared with about 3,500,000 part-time women workers (over a third of all U.K. women workers), fewer than 700,000 men do part-time jobs. So less favourable treatment of women part-timers with regard to non-contractual benefits might very well fall within the definition of indirect discrimination in s. 1 (1) (*b*) of the Sex Discrimination Act 1975. Employment legislation itself thus indirectly discriminates against women workers—see the general exclusions effected by Sched. 13, paras. 3–7. Furthermore, the decision of the E.A.T. in *Dugdale* v. *Kraft Foods Ltd.* [1977] I.C.R. 48 indicates that unequal treatment on the grounds of hours worked is not by itself a sufficiently material difference to justify a lower rate of pay under the Equal Pay Act 1970, s. 1 (4).
  Thirteen weeks continuous employment. The right to a written statement in s. 1 does *not* require a 13 week period of *continuous* employment (*cf.* other rights which explicitly require continuity, *e.g.* guarantee payments, s. 143 (1) ; medical suspension payments, s. 143 (2) ; maternity benefits, s. 33 (3) (*b*) ; minimum period of notice, s. 49 (1), etc.). Instead, weeks may be accumulated to form an aggregate total of 13.
  This section specifies which weeks count towards the 13 weeks total, and the standard process of calculation in Sched. 13 is not applicable. This subsection ensures that periods of employment during which less than 16 hours weekly are normally worked, while they do not *count*, do not breach continuity of employment either (*cf.* Sched. 13, para. 2).
  Employers must supply the statement "not later than 13 weeks after the beginning of the employee's period of employment." No account is to be taken of periods where less than 16 hours is normally worked—hence the *commencement* of the 13 week period only occurs when the 16 plus hours weekly period begins. But once begun, the 13 week period begins to accumulate—even if the total of 13 weeks is accumulated over a longer period due to periods of employment of less than 16 hours weekly (and this is less likely due to the effect of subs. (2)). There is no stopping and starting again. This is confirmed by the omission from this subsection of the additional sentence at the end of s. 4 (7) of the 1972 Act which it replaced. That read as follows: " and this section shall apply to an employee who at any time comes or ceases to come within the exception in this subsection *as if a period of employment terminated or began at that time."* The implication of this omission is that even if the employee ceases to work for a short period altogether (*i.e.* zero hours of work weekly), should employment at 16 plus hours weekly recommence, the previous weeks will count towards the 13 week total aggregate (*cf.* Sched. 13, para. 7). Thus temporary or casual or part-time workers who are engaged sporadically by the same employer may eventually become informed of their terms of employment as s. 1 requires.

Subs. (2)
  Eight hour weeks covered. This provides special protection to employees whose normal weekly hours are reduced to below 16, but not less than 8. In effect, the alteration is rendered ineffective as regards the employee's right to a written statement under s. 1. For the weeks will still count (up to 26 weeks) so as to reach the mandatory point of 13 weeks. (This might not be so if a longer qualification period was needed, and the ordinary provisions of Sched. 13, para. 5 applied.)

Subs. (3)

Weeks to count towards the 13 *week period.* In one sense this subsection is wholly unnecessary, since there is no need for more than 13 of the 26 weeks' grace period, so resort to the extensions by way of the weeks covered in (*a*) to (*c*) is irrelevant. The equivalent for other rights requiring qualification periods is Sched. 13, para. 5 (2).

But in another sense it might be argued that the weeks falling within categories (*a*) to (*c*) do not count *either* as falling within the 26 week period, *or in any other sense*. So, *e.g.* a worker having his normal weekly hours reduced below 16, but above 8, might in fact work more than 16 hours in one week. This week, it is argued, does not count toward the 26 weeks' grace period (subs. (3) (*a*)), but is it to count towards the 13 week qualification period? Again, it will not interfere with the accumulation of the 13 weeks, only extend it still further. Still, it would seem absurd if a 16 hour week did not count towards the 13 weeks where an 8 hour week did. So a strict interpretation of the phrase " in computing the said period of 26 weeks " is to be desired to exclude that result.

Subs. (4)

It is a measure of the law's myopia that it can solemnly provide for an employee who has worked for over five years to be granted only then the right to be given information as to his terms of employment (*cf.* Sched. 13, para. 6).

Changes in terms of employment

4.—(1) If after the date to which a statement given under section 1 relates there is a change in the terms of employment to be included, or referred to, in that statement the employer shall, not more than one month after the change, inform the employee of the nature of the change by a written statement and, if he does not leave a copy of the statement with the employee, shall preserve the statement and ensure that the employee has reasonable opportunities of reading it in the course of his employment, or that it is made reasonably accessible to him in some other way.

(2) A statement given under subsection (1) may, for all or any of the particulars to be given by the statement, refer the employee to some document which the employee has reasonable opportunities of reading in the course of his employment, or which is made reasonably accessible to him in some other way.

(3) If, in referring in the statement given under section 1 or under subsection (1) of this section to any such document, the employer indicates to the employee that future changes in the terms of which the particulars are given in the document will be entered up in the document (or recorded by some other means for the information of persons referring to the document), the employer need not under subsection (1) inform the employee of any such change if it is duly entered up or recorded not later than one month after the change is made.

(4) Where, after an employer has given to an employee a written statement in accordance with section 1—

(*a*) the name of the employer (whether an individual or a body corporate or partnership) is changed, without any change in the identity of the employer, or

(*b*) the identity of the employer is changed, in such circumstances that, in accordance with section 139 (7) or paragraph 17 or paragraph 18 of Schedule 13, the continuity of the employee's period of employment is not broken,

and (in either case) the change does not involve any change in the terms (other than the names of the parties) included or referred to in the statement, then, the person who, immediately after the change, is the employer shall not be required to give to the employee a statement in accordance with section 1, but, subject to subsection (5), the change shall be treated as a change falling within subsection (1) of this section.

(5) A written statement under this section which informs an employee of such a change in his terms of employment as is referred to in subsection (4) (*b*) shall specify the date on which the employee's continuous period of employment began.

DERIVATION

1972, s. 5; 1975, Sched. 16, Pt. II, para. 9; House of Commons (Administration) Act 1978, Sched. 2, para. 4.

GENERAL NOTE

Subs. (1)

Practice. The research referred to in the Note to s. 1 (1) showed, perhaps surprisingly, that a high proportion of employers surveyed complied with this section and provided written statements of changes to their employees.

Employee must consent to change. The notification required here is of an agreed change. The common law rule is that an employer cannot change terms of employment without the consent of the employee. So merely informing the employee by a written statement is not conclusive of the existence of an *agreed* change in the terms. Unfortunately, the legal bias against workers often transforms the *knowledge* of a powerless worker into binding consent. This, despite the fact that many strikes arise precisely out of a change by management in the conditions of work which has not been and is not agreed to by the workers. One wonders what, if any, role is played by the written statement in the struggle for control over work regulation.

Status quo clauses. In practice, the potential conflict can be defused by a negotiated status quo clause, though this may only defer the problem. *E.g.* a national procedure agreement between British Leyland Truck and Bus Division and four unions (TASS, APEX, ACTSS and ASTMS) representing white-collar staff, finalised on September 6, 1977, provides that where there is any disagreement over *changes in working practices*, etc., the status quo will apply until agreement is achieved. A new agreement, effective from May 31, 1978, between the EEF and TASS contains the following clause: " Except by agreement between the parties, *general alterations* in salaries and alterations in working conditions which are the subject of agreements officially entered into or which are recognised by the employers and employees concerned, shall not be given effect to until the appropriate procedure provided in this agreement has been exhausted."

In the absence of such express status quo clauses, workers may be able to utilise the 1972 Code of Practice, para. 52 of which provides: " Major changes in working conditions should not be made by management without prior discussion with employees or their representatives." Again, the new Code of Practice on Disciplinary Practice and Procedures provides that new rules are to be introduced " only after reasonable notice " (para. 20).

Contractual mobility and flexibility clauses. A change in the *terms*, covered by this section, does not *necessarily* result from actual changes in, *e.g.* the nature of the work done or the place where it is to be done—as many workers have found to their dismay. No written notification is required in that case. So, *e.g.* Barclays Bank have a clause relating to geographical mobility in their General Rules Book: " Every member of the staff must be willing to serve at any office of the Bank as may be required and will serve the bank faithfully, diligently and to the best of his or her ability." There is a flexibility agreement between Govan Shipbuilders Ltd. and a joint negotiating committee representing certain white collar staff of October 1977 which provides: " All members of Secretarial Service Centres will perform any secretarial duties allocated to them by either the Controller of Secretarial Services or other supervisor whether or not they normally carry out this duty."

Statement of change not necessarily binding. But where the employer has not got the right in the contract, if he tries to alter rates of pay, hours of work, or the status or grade of the employee—he must obtain the employee's consent before the change can have any legal effect. So just as the *absence* of a statement does not mean that no change in the work is possible, so the *existence* of a statement does not mean that it is agreed and thus binding. Workers would be well advised, where this is practical and if possible through their union, to respond in writing denying the validity of or rejecting any unilateral changes notified by management in accordance with this section. In *Simmonds* v. *Dowty Seals Ltd.* [1978] I.R.L.R. 211 (E.A.T.), the original statement of terms provided for day working, but the worker and employer agreed to change to night working—though nothing was put in writing. After four years on nights only, the employee agreed to work for two weeks on days, but put it in writing that this was an exceptional case. When the employer tried later to order him back to permanent days, the E.A.T. held that they could not change the terms without his consent. He had actually written to them that the change to days was for two weeks only and exceptional. So he never agreed to any change on a permanent basis.

Notification in writing. Where consent has been obtained the section applies and the employee must be notified in writing within one month. While the employer need not give the employee a copy—and research has shown disturbingly that some employers *keep* the only copy—employees are advised to secure one.

Changes allowing for unfair dismissal claims. Apart from the intrinsic significance of changes in terms of employment to the employee, such changes when initiated by the employer have a vital bearing on the legal options open to the worker if he rejects the change. These are: to acquiesce, to claim damages for breach of contract, or to treat the employer's action as a repudiation—effectively a constructive dismissal. This last is now of paramount importance following the Court of Appeal's decision in *Western Excavating (ECC) Ltd.* v. *Sharp* [1978] I.R.L.R. 27. Now only fundamental breaches of contract by the employer allow an employee to claim constructive dismissal. The bearing of a statement issued under this section on the question remains as yet unexamined in the courts.

Subs. (2)

See the Note to s. 2 (3) which is substantially identical.

Subs. (3)

One statement is all. This transforms the employer's obligation to keep the employee informed with up to date notice of the state of his contractual rights and obligations into a potentially one-off exercise. An employer can in his initial statement refer to the document (collective agreement) as the source of the terms and go on to indicate that all future changes would be entered there. That would end all the direct communication required by the law on this score.

The research referred to in the Note to s. 1 (1) found that in practice barely any of the employers surveyed (light industry in North-East London) took this one-off step. Most of them provided written statements of the changes, usually " full particulars." But *Burroughs Machines Ltd.* v. *Timmoney* [1977] I.R.L.R. 404 illustrates the other mode of compliance. The employee had a contract which referred to the engineering industry agreement and stated that " the company undertakes to ensure that all alterations will be duly recorded within one month of any change." When he disaffiliated from the E.E.F., the employer notified the unions and the appropriate amendments were made in the relevant documents. The Court of Session held that none of the alterations affected the terms relating to the guaranteed week claimed by the employee, and that the act of the company in resigning from the federation " had and could have had no effect whatever upon the contract of employment between the company and the (employee)." One can only conclude that the original reference to the engineering agreement, which allowed exemptions from payment to " federated " employers was at least misleading, for non-federated employers were apparently also exempted, as the employee lost his claim.

Even non-binding changes can hurt. In a number of cases tribunals have held that changes negotiated by a trade union and included in a collective agreement could be incorporated into the contract of employment by a statement referring to the agreement. But even in cases where it has been held that, for one reason or another, the negotiated change did *not* bind the employee (*e.g.* the employee concerned was not a union member (*Ellis* v. *Brighton Co-operative Society* [1976] I.R.L.R. 419 (E.A.T.) ; or the employee had resigned from the union (*Singh* v. *B.S.C.* [1974] I.R.L.R. 131)), still, a refusal by the employee to accept the negotiated change was fatal in practice. The employer has been allowed to " fairly " dismiss the employee in these circumstances for non-cooperation. Trade unions must, therefore, ensure that employees who oppose agreements are not left entirely to the tender mercies of the employer—and the tribunals.

Subs. (4)

Change of employer's name. As with s. 2 (4), employers are exempted from having to issue statements, in this case where there is a change in name, transfer to an associated employer (Sched. 13, para. 18) or certain House of Commons staff are involved (s. 139 (7)). But the change in the identity of the parties (s. 1 (2) (a)) still needs be notified under s. 4 (1) within one month of the change. Such notification should not be undervalued. Many employees are woefully ill-informed as to the precise identity of their legal employer, particularly in complex corporate or administrative structures. A mistake can frequently cause delay in claims.

Subs. (5)

This is merely to re-assure employees of their unbroken continuity, which is in law secured by the provisions referred to in subs. (4) (b).

Exclusion of certain contracts in writing

5. Sections 1 and 4 shall not apply to an employee if and so long as the following conditions are fulfilled in relation to him, that is to say—

(a) the employee's contract of employment is a contract which has been reduced to writing in one or more documents and which contains express terms affording the particulars to be given under each of the paragraphs in subsection (3) of section 1, and under each head of paragraph (d) of that subsection;

(b) there has been given to the employee a copy of the contract (with any variations made from time to time), or he has reasonable opportunities of reading such a copy in the course of his employment, or such a copy is made reasonably accessible to him in some other way; and

(c) such a note as is mentioned in section 1 (4) has been given to the employee or he has reasonable opportunities of reading such a note in the course of his employment or such a note is made reasonably accessible to him in some other way:

Provided that if at any time after the beginning of an employee's period of employment these conditions cease to be fulfilled in relation to him, the employer shall give the employee a written statement under section 1 not more than one month after that time.

DERIVATION
1972, s. 6.

GENERAL NOTE

Written statement or written contract. There is occasional difficulty in practice in distinguishing a written statement under s. 1 from a written contract such as is referred to here. The difficulty has given rise to the issues discussed in the Note to s. 1 (1)—whether to treat the statement as the contract, or conclusive evidence of its terms. The statement might have all the trappings of a written contract, save that it would be headed " Contracts of Employment Act 1972 "—which would appear to give it the character of a mere statement.

A written contract might be different in not having *all* the information required of a statement, in particular, s. 1 (2), especially s. 1 (2) (c). It should be noted that each and every condition stipulated in (a) to (c) must be fulfilled. If any item of information is lacking, then the whole of the requirements in s. 1 come into effect. The applicability of ss. 2–4 is unstated, but perhaps assumed.

Power of Secretary of State to require further particulars

6. The Secretary of State may by order provide that section 1 shall have effect as if such further particulars as may be specified in the order were included in the particulars to be included in a statement under that section, and, for that purpose, the order may include such provisions amending section 1 (1), (2) and (3) as appear to the Secretary of State to be expedient.

DERIVATION
1972, s. 7 (1), (2).

GENERAL NOTE
No such order has yet been made. Note the protection of the requirements as to notification of disciplinary rules and procedures (s. 1 (4)) from amendment by the Secretary of State.

Power to vary number of weekly hours of employment necessary to qualify for rights

7.—(1) The Secretary of State may by order provide that this Part and Schedule 13 shall have effect as if—

    (a) for each of the references to sixteen hours in section 3 and in paragraphs 3 to 7 of Schedule 13 there were substituted a reference to such other number of hours less than sixteen as may be specified in the order; and

    (b) as if for each of the references to eight hours in section 3 and in paragraphs 6 and 7 of Schedule 13 there were substituted a reference to such other number of hours less than eight as may be specified in the order:

(2) An order under subsection (1) shall not be made unless a draft of the order has been laid before Parliament and approved by resolution of each House.

DERIVATION
1972, s. 10 (1), (4); 1975, Sched. 16, Pt. II, para. 11.

GENERAL NOTE
Note the provision in s. 10 (2) of the 1972 Act (an amendment of the 1975 Act) which allowed for retrospective effect of such an order. It is not reproduced here.

No order has yet been made.

Itemised pay statements

Right to itemised pay statement

8. Every employee shall have the right to be given by his employer at or before the time at which any payment of wages or salary is made to him an itemised pay statement, in writing, containing the following particulars, that is to say—

    (a) the gross amount of the wages or salary;

    (b) the amounts of any variable and, subject to section 9, any fixed deductions from that gross amount and the purposes for which they are made;

    (c) the net amount of wages or salary payable; and

    (d) where different parts of the net amount are paid in different ways, the amount and method of payment of each part-payment.

DERIVATION
1975, s. 81.

GENERAL NOTE
The Payment of Wages Act 1960 enabled employers to pay wages by cheque rather than cash. S. 2 (4) to (8) of that Act provided for written pay statements to be given to employees where this was done. The provisions here generalised this requirement for the benefit of all employees as regards any form of payment

of wages. Once again, however, certain classes of employment are excluded: ss. 138 (3), 141 (2), 144 (2), (4), 146 (1), (2) and notably (4)—part-time workers. The now superfluous provisions of the 1960 Act were repealed by the 1975 Act.

As only gross and net amounts are required to be specified, workers may not be informed as to details of their basic rates, shift premia, overtime payments, etc. So, *e.g.* piece-workers are not given the opportunity to assess their wage packets. Any deductions made will, of course, have to comply with the requirements of the Truck Acts 1831–1940.

In *Milsom* v. *Leicestershire County Council* [1978] I.R.L.R. 433, an industrial tribunal held that a reference to " miscellaneous deduction/payment " did not give sufficient particulars of the purposes for which the deduction was made to meet the requirements of (*b*).

Standing statement of fixed deductions

9.—(1) A pay statement given in accordance with section 8 need not contain separate particulars of a fixed deduction if it contains instead an aggregate amount of fixed deductions, including that deduction, and the employer has given to the employee, at or before the time at which that pay statement is given, a standing statement of fixed deductions, in writing, which contains the following particulars of each deduction comprised in that aggregate amount, that is to say—

    (*a*) the amount of the deduction;

    (*b*) the intervals at which the deduction is to be made; and

    (*c*) the purpose for which it is made,

and which, in accordance with subsection (4), is effective at the date on which the pay statement is given.

(2) A standing statement of fixed deductions may be amended, whether by addition of a new deduction or by a change in the particulars or cancellation of an existing deduction, by notice in writing, containing particulars of the amendment, given by the employer to the employee.

(3) An employer who has given to an employee a standing statement of fixed deductions shall, within the period of twelve months beginning with the date on which the first standing statement was given and at intervals of not more than twelve months thereafter, re-issue it in a consolidated form incorporating any amendments notified in accordance with subsection (2).

(4) A standing statement of fixed deductions shall become effective, for the purposes of subsection (1), on the date on which it is given to the employee and shall cease to have effect on the expiration of the period of twelve months beginning with that date, or, where it is re-issued in accordance with subsection (3), the expiration of the period of twelve months beginning with the date on which it was last re-issued.

DERIVATION
    1975, s. 82.

GENERAL NOTE
    Fixed deductions might include, *e.g.* union contributions under a check-off agreement, or payments under an attachment-of-earnings court order. The aggregate amount of fixed deductions cannot include variable deductions—so where amounts deducted change from week to week in accordance with earnings, they must be itemised separately, as required by s. 8 (*b*). Even where wages are usually fixed, any change may bring alterations in the amounts of various fixed deductions, requiring an amendment notice under subs. (2), to be incorporated in the consolidated statements under subs. (3).

Power to amend ss. 8 and 9

   10. The Secretary of State may by order—

      (*a*) vary the provisions of sections 8 and 9 as to the particulars which must be included in a pay statement or a standing statement of fixed deductions by adding items to or removing items from the particulars listed in those sections or by amending any such particulars; and

(*b*) vary the provisions of section 9 (3) and (4) so as to shorten or extend the periods of twelve months referred to in those subsections, or those periods as varied from time to time under this section.

DERIVATION

1975, s. 83.

GENERAL NOTE

No order has yet been made.

Enforcement of rights under Part I

References to industrial tribunals

11.—(1) Where an employer does not give an employee a statement as required by section 1 or 4 (1) or 8, the employee may require a reference to be made to an industrial tribunal to determine what particulars ought to have been included or referred to in a statement so as to comply with the requirements of the relevant section.

(2) Where—

(*a*) a statement purporting to be a statement under section 1 or 4 (1), or

(*b*) a pay statement, or a standing statement of fixed deductions, purporting to comply with section 8 or 9 (1),

has been given to an employee, and a question arises as to the particulars which ought to have been included or referred to in the statement so as to comply with the requirements of this Part, either the employer or the employee may require that question to be referred to and determined by an industrial tribunal.

(3) Where a statement under section 1 or 4 (1) given by an employer to an employee contains such an indication as is mentioned in section 4 (3), and

(*a*) any particulars purporting to be particulars of a change to which that indication relates are entered up or recorded in accordance with that indication, and

(*b*) a question arises as to the particulars which ought to have been so entered up or recorded,

either the employer or the employee may require that question to be referred to and determined by an industrial tribunal.

(4) In this section, a question as to the particulars which ought to have been included—

(*a*) in a pay statement, or in a standing statement of fixed deductions, does not include a question solely as to the accuracy of an amount stated in any such particulars;

(*b*) in a note under section 1 (4), does not include any question whether the employment is, has been or will be contracted-out employment for the purposes of Part III of the Social Security Pensions Act 1975.

(5) Where, on a reference under subsection (1), an industrial tribunal determines particulars as being those which ought to have been included or referred to in a statement given under section 1 or 4 (1) the employer

shall be deemed to have given to the employee a statement in which those particulars were included, or referred to, as specified in the decision of the tribunal.

(6) On determining a reference under subsection (2) (*a*), an industrial tribunal may either confirm the particulars as included or referred to in the statement given by the employer, or may amend those particulars, or may substitute other particulars for them, as the tribunal may determine to be appropriate; and the statement shall be deemed to have been given by the employer to the employee in accordance with the decision of the tribunal.

(7) On determining a reference under subsection (3), an industrial tribunal may either confirm the particulars to which the reference relates, or may amend those particulars or may substitute other particulars for them, as the tribunal may determine to be appropriate; and particulars of the change to which the reference relates shall be deemed to have been entered up or recorded in accordance with the decision of the tribunal.

(8) Where on a reference under this section an industrial tribunal finds that an employer has failed to give an employee any pay statement in accordance with section 8 or that a pay statement or standing statement of fixed deductions does not, in relation to a deduction, contain the particulars required to be included in that statement by that section or section 9 (1)—

(*a*) the tribunal shall make a declaration to that effect; and
(*b*) where the tribunal further finds that any unnotified deductions have been made from the pay of the employee during the period of thirteen weeks immediately preceding the date of the application for the reference (whether or not the deductions were made in breach of the contract of employment), the tribunal may order the employer to pay the employee a sum not exceeding the aggregate of the unnotified deductions so made.

In this subsection " unnotified deduction " means a deduction made without the employer giving the employee, in any pay statement or standing statement of fixed deductions, the particulars of that deduction required by section 8 or 9 (1).

(9) An industrial tribunal shall not entertain a reference under this section in a case where the employment to which the reference relates has ceased unless an application requiring the reference to be made was made before the end of the period of three months beginning with the date on which the employment ceased.

DERIVATION
1972, s. 8; 1975, s. 84; Social Security Pensions Act 1975 (c. 60), s. 30 (5).

GENERAL NOTE
Subss. (1)–(3)
Remedies. In the one claim for breach of s. 8 referred to in the Note to that section, the employee was awarded £25.

The remedy for failure to supply written particulars (ss. 1 and 4 (1)) is even more unsatisfactory than the usual individual complaint mechanism provided, and in practice it is little used. In the first quarter of 1978, applications to industrial tribunals totalled 9,689 in England and Wales and 1,291 in Scotland. Only 1 per cent. arose out of rights (including rights to a minimum period of notice) set out in the Contracts of Employment Act 1972—which is replaced by these provisions. Wedderburn in 1971 calculated that only 53 of 7,689 cases heard by tribunals in 1968 came under this heading.

The reasons for this inadequacy are not hard to find. The authors of the research into the workings of these provisions referred to in the Note to s. 1 (1) have commented: " It is perhaps ironical that in an age of widespread collective bargaining, if an employer of, say, 5,000 employees fails to provide written statements, the only recourse the work-force has is by way of individual complaint to a tribunal. It is not open to a trade union or a group of employees to bring a group action, and although there is, of course, the possibility of a ' test case,' contacts with local trade union officials suggest that a successfully brought ' test case ' does not always produce a response on the part of the employer towards the rest of the work-force. Sometimes many cases have to be brought " (6 I.L.J. 133, at 138–9 (1977)). So workers do well to rely, as with other legal rights, not on their legal remedies, but on their own industrial strength to secure the employer's compliance.

Jurisdiction of tribunals. Even where the tribunal does determine the correct particulars, it has not the power as yet to enforce those terms. (See subss. (5) and (6) for the effect of the determination.) This can only be done by applying to the ordinary courts—with all the delay and expense that entails. See, *e.g. Cuthbertson* v. *AML Distributors* [1975] I.R.L.R. 228, described in the Note to s. 1 (3)—*Notice of termination.* In *Construction Industry Training Board* v. *Leighton* [1978] I.R.L.R. 60 (E.A.T.) Kilner Brown J. was reduced to moral exhortation: the employer should by *ex gratia* payment provide the benefit declared owing to the employee. The case is significant for its perceived limits of the remedy. The E.A.T. declared it would not allow claims to clear up only " one small area of misunderstanding between the parties "—particularly where this might be usurping the functions of the courts. Whether this " de minimis " approach is desirable is questionable indeed. Particularly where, as was the case, it was conceded that the employee thought it was an important issue.

The problem of lack of jurisdiction could be cured at least in part by the Lord Chancellor exercising his powers under s. 131, and a first draft Order has been drawn up and, at the time of writing, is being considered. But the power is limited to transferring matters which are connected to termination or to other proceedings already before the industrial tribunal (s. 131 (3)). Since it has been held that *ex*-employees can proceed under this section (as long as they are within the three-month limit of subs. (9)), the problem of dual jurisdiction will not affect them should the tribunal's powers be extended to cover claims outstanding on termination. But this would still not help the employee in *Leighton's* case, who had not been terminated, and whose claim was held to be outside the boundaries of permissible claims.

Subs. (4)

Questions excluded. Subs. (4) (*a*) differs slightly from s. 84 (3) of the 1975 Act which merely excluded certain questions relating to " a statement." This has been amplified here to cover *both* pay statements *and* a standing statement of fixed deductions.

Even as it stands, however, the subsection seems to imply that a question relating not *solely* to an amount, but rather such a question accompanied by one relating to particulars, as allowed by subs. (2), may be referred to the tribunal. Since the particulars to be supplied under ss. 8 and 9 include specific statements as to amounts which must be accurate, it is logical that a question as to particulars may include one relating to the accuracy of the amounts stated.

Subs. (8)

Presumably, to be useful, the declaration will include answers to questions relating to both the employer's failure to give particulars, and where applicable, his failure to give accurate amounts.

Claims. Where the employer deducts excessive amounts, the employee is now to have two alternative claims: under his contract and under the provisions of this subsection. Where the employer simply fails to note, or erroneously specifies the amount, not in breach of contract, the only claim lies under this subsection (though the Lord Chancellor may remedy this duplication by exercising his powers under s. 131). So, *e.g.* where the statement includes a lump sum of fixed deductions, but either no standing statement under s. 9 has been given, or it is inaccurate, the employee may accordingly be awarded a sum totalling all fixed deductions over 13 weeks or to the extent that some fixed deduction was unnotified.

PART II

RIGHTS ARISING IN COURSE OF EMPLOYMENT

Guarantee payments

Right to guarantee payment

12.—(1) Where an employee throughout a day during any part of which he would normally be required to work in accordance with his contract of employment is not provided with work by his employer by reason of—

    (a) a diminution in the requirements of the employer's business for work of the kind which the employee is employed to do, or

    (b) any other occurrence affecting the normal working of the employer's business in relation to work of the kind which the employee is employed to do,

he shall, subject to the following provisions of this Act, be entitled to be paid by his employer a payment, referred to in this Act as a guarantee payment, in respect of that day, and in this section and sections 13 and 16—

    (i) such a day is referred to as a " workless day ", and

    (ii) " workless period " has a corresponding meaning.

(2) In this section and sections 13 to 17, " day " means the period of twenty-four hours from midnight to midnight, and where a period of employment begun on any day extends over midnight into the following day, or would normally so extend, then—

    (a) if the employment before midnight is, or would normally be, of longer duration than that after midnight, that period of employment shall be treated as falling wholly on the first day; and

    (b) in any other case, that period of employment shall be treated as falling wholly on the second day.

DERIVATION

    1975, s. 22 (1) (2).

GENERAL NOTE

    Origins and significance. With the enactment of the provisions in the Employment Protection Act 1975, Britain finally recognised the principle of the guaranteed week already accepted by the other members of the EEC. At the time of passage, it was estimated that this might be the most expensive provision in the 1975 Act— one estimate put the cost at £80m. (see the Report of Standing Committee F on the Employment Protection Bill, 11th Sitting, June 17, 1975, at col. 551). To allow employers to prepare for this expense, the Government did not bring the provisions into effect until February 1, 1977.

    In fact, as recently pointed out in the *Department of Employment Gazette* (June 1978, p. 658 at 660), the insignificant general impact of these provisions could have been predicted from the information collected on short-time working and temporary lay-offs during the period 1974–77. Both have been very rare. The three-day week in the 1974 power crisis was the only widespread instance. Otherwise the practice was concentrated in particular industries such as textiles. These observations were made by W. W. Daniel, whose research on the effects of employment protection laws in manufacturing industry (firms employing 50–5,000 people, 81 per cent. of the workforce in the sector) disclosed that 83 per cent. of managements evaluated the effect of guarantee payment legislation as being nil.

    Guarantee payments and social security provisions. The right to guarantee payments turns out in practice to be another exercise, albeit particularly galling, whereby under the guise of protecting workers, the State effectively harasses them. Workers are hereby to be deprived of the National Insurance Unemployment Benefits they were previously entitled to—see Note to s. 15 (1) for details. This is accomplished through the interworking of these provisions with those contained in various social security regulations. The result will serve to increase workers' problems, not alleviate them.

In the *absence* of any provision for guarantee payments, workers laid-off used to be entitled to social security payments, mainly unemployment benefit. During the first three days of lay-off, however, no benefit was payable. The enactment of provisions for guarantee payment might, therefore, seem a way of re-establishing the employee's benefit during these first three days (the three-day waiting period was a measure dropped by the National Insurance Act 1946, s. 11, but reintroduced by the Social Security Act 1971, s. 7—now the Social Security Act 1975, s. 14 (3)). The amount of daily guarantee payment, in fact, is roughly equivalent (when taxed) to the daily unemployment benefit entitlement (untaxed). To summarise: the effect of the guarantee payment provisions could be to provide payment for the first three days of lay-off. Thereafter, any such payments would be effectively set-off against unemployment benefit (see s. 132 (2)). But at least workers' earnings could have been protected to some extent during these first days of lay-off. (No doubt this could have been achieved in an infinitely simpler fashion by dropping the three-day waiting period for unemployment benefit.)

Regulations make it clear that the protection of workers was far from the intention of these provisions. Reg. 7 (1) (*d*) (i) of the Social Security (Unemployment, Sickness and Invalidity Benefits) Regulations (S.I. 1975 No. 564, as amended by S.I. 1976 No. 677) provides that "a day shall not be treated as a day of unemployment in relation to any person if it is a day in respect of which there is payable to that person—a guarantee payment" under s. 22 of the Employment Protection Act 1975 (now this section). The result is that workers who are entitled to guarantee payments from their employer *cannot receive unemployment benefit for the first eight days of the lay-off* (five days' guarantee payment plus three days' waiting period). Instead of the established and familiar machinery for collecting unemployment benefit, workers will now have to rely on their employers' willingness and efficiency in paying out five days' guarantee pay in any quarter. If the employer fails to comply, the worker has to process his claim through the Industrial Tribunal (or take collective action). He only qualifies for unemployment benefit after eight days of lay-off. Meanwhile he may have to subsist on supplementary benefit.

In practice, therefore, the procedure will be as follows: a worker is laid-off. He may or may not be entitled to and claim and receive a guarantee payment. He should apply for one if there is the slightest chance. If refused, he should apply immediately for unemployment benefit. The insurance officer must then decide either that after the three-day waiting period is over benefit is to be paid; or he must decide that the employee *is* entitled to guarantee payment—so benefit is only to be paid after eight days' lay-off. The insurance officer will normally inquire of the employer about the position. If the employer says no payment is owed, then the officer must decide whether the employer is correct or not and dispose of the claim for unemployment benefit accordingly—within 14 days. If he takes the view that the employer is wrong in denying payment, he will refuse payment until eight days have elapsed. The employee's only course then is to claim the guarantee payment from the employer within three months of the lay-off (s. 17). The worker is thus made dependent on his employer's readiness to pay up at the time of the lay-off. The State can refuse to pay up and force the worker to take legal proceedings to get his due. In this way the State has effectively transferred the burden of paying unemployment benefit to the employer—and given the worker the arduous task of enforcing payment of the benefit through the Industrial Tribunal.

It could easily be foreseen that this additional question of eligibility for guarantee payment would complicate the decisions of insurance officers. Payment of unemployment benefit would consequently be delayed if not actually denied. In two cases already reported the claim followed the Department's refusal to pay benefit because of an alleged entitlement. In one case (*Robinson* v. *Claxton & Garland (Teesside) Ltd.* [1977] I.R.L.R. 159), the Department was correct, and the worker eventually got his £6 guarantee payment, albeit seven weeks after the appropriate day of lay-off. In the other case (*Clemens* v. *Peter Richards Ltd.* [1977] I.R.L.R. 332) the Department was wrong, and three and a half months after she was denied unemployment benefit an industrial tribunal held that she was *not* in fact entitled to a guarantee payment.

The legal provisions, therefore, seem designed more for the protection of the National Insurance Fund than for workers. This is confirmed by the provisions of the Employment Protection (Recoupment of Unemployment Benefit and Supplementary Benefit) Regulations 1977 (S.I. 1977 No. 674). These erect a complex administrative structure whose purpose is to protect the State, while the worker, whose need is both more immediate and greater, will have to suffer the delays and errors which are inevitable (see the Note to s. 17 (3)).

Collective agreements and the law. The law on guarantee payments illustrates again the yawning chasm which divides workers who have to rely on the law for their rights from those who rely on themselves. It is estimated by the Department of Employment that there exist guaranteed pay arrangements at national level covering several million workers in various industries. The mechanism of Sched. 11 to the Employment Protection Act 1975 would allow for their extension to millions more. Yet in the 18 months up to the end of July 1978 only a very few claims were made for the legal entitlement. In the *Industrial Relations Law Reports* up to September 1978, only 11 cases are reported—10 in the Industrial Tribunals and the first Employment Appeal Tribunal decision. Of these, only one was reported successful—a Mr. Robinson was awarded £6 (*Robinson* v. *Claxton & Garland (Teesside) Ltd.* [1977] I.R.L.R. 159). Even if one multiplied by 1,000 the number of unreported claims and by 10,000 the amount of guarantee pay awarded so far, the results of the legal process would remain insignificant beside that achieved by workers' autonomous action. Lawyers should adjust their attention accordingly to the entitlements under collective agreements, rather than under the provisions of the legislation. The law *is* important, but only as the backdrop against which the collective struggle is waged. With regard to guarantee payments, the legislative requirements assume their importance: (a) by virtue of their being adopted instead of pre-existing collectively agreed standards; (b) as the floor from which negotiations are conducted to achieve improvements; or (c) as a standard against which other arrangements are measured for the purposes of exemption under s. 18. The Notes that follow attempt to understand the law in light of the infinitely more important industrial practice.

New scheme of compensation. Finally, a new compensation scheme for short-time working has been proposed in a consultative document issued by the Department of Employment in early 1978. It attempts to avoid the dispersion of workers through redundancies in times of lack of full-time work by topping up their pay to a certain and specified proportion—for example, 75 per cent., or even 100 per cent. on a temporary basis, the money to come from a Government-employer financed fund. This would remedy the inadequacies experienced already in the low level of guarantee payments secured by law. These proposals, if enacted, would take the form of a Bill to amend the Employment Protection Act.

Subs. (1)

Excluded classes of employment. Certain classes of employment are expressly excluded from the right to guarantee payment—see ss. 138 (3), 141 (2), 143 (1) (3) (4), 144 (2), 145 (2) and 146 (1) (2). S. 143 (3) and (4) excludes employees hired for a period of less than 12 weeks, unless more than 12 weeks are actually worked. The anomalous position may arise, therefore, of two employees being hired, A permanently and B for less than the 12 weeks, both of whom actually work over 12 weeks. If employee A is laid off on the day before the 12 weeks expire (but after four weeks have elapsed—s. 143 (1)), he is entitled to a guarantee payment. But it is not clear if employee B laid off in similar circumstances is so entitled. It would seem right that, although he only becomes eligible to claim after 12 weeks, his benefits should be preserved in the same way as A's. For other cases of possible exclusion, see s. 18.

S. 143 (1) requires four weeks' continuous employment to qualify for a payment, but some agreements (*e.g.* Biscuit Industry, Hosiery Trade, Building and Footwear Manufacture) do not specify any service qualification. Three of the first four exempted schemes under s. 18 had no service qualification. This section also has the effect, by virtue of Sched. 13, or excluding employees whose normal hours of work are below 16 per week. A claim failed, *inter alia*, on this ground in *Mailway (Southern) Ltd.* v. *Willsher* [1978] I.R.L.R. 322 (E.A.T.). Kilner Brown J. explicitly rejected the suggestion that the law be given a meaning consonant with social practice, and held that it was " obvious that casual workers were never intended to be given this privilege." Perhaps the judge ought to be put on notice that negotiators are increasingly providing for part-timers to be covered by the guaranteed week (*e.g.* the agreement of the Cadbury Schweppes Tea and Foods Group and TGWU and Guarantee Payments (Exemption) (No. 5) Order 1977 (S.I. 1977 No. 902) dated May 24, 1977, provided for part-time workers to be entitled to guarantee payments on the same principles as full-timers in the Footwear Industry).

"*Required to work.*" Tribunals appear in some cases to be adopting the law's managerial perspective and interpreting " required to work " as being followed by the words " by the employer," rather than by " contract of employment "—which indicates the employee's consent. So where employers have *enforced* a reduction in the working week due to various circumstances clearly envisaged by (*a*) and (*b*) —despite employee protests and industrial action—industrial tribunals have held that no guarantee payment entitlement exists as the employee is not " required to work " during the whole of the week: there has been a " consensual variation " of the contract (*Daley* v. *Strathclyde Regional Council* [1977] I.R.L.R. 414; *Clemens* v. *Peter Richards Ltd.* [1977] I.R.L.R. 332). The opposite result has been reached in other tribunal decisions. Since such changes are normally a temporary measure until business improves, it would seem arguable that: (a) the employee is still required to work a full week generally, albeit not for this temporary period of short-time working; (b) any change in terms which served to deprive the employee of his right to a guarantee payment would be void under s. 140 (1).

Hopefully, when the E.A.T. comes to decide the issue they will take notice of the fact that most collective agreements provide for a guaranteed *weekly* minimum— *i.e.* the provisions provide a basic minimum weekly payment regardless of whether the lay-off is for one or more days *or parts* of a day—a few hours off a shift or a few days. If the total hours worked gives less than the minimum, the guarantee applies. To take the legislation's *method of calculating* a daily guaranteed payment as the sole principle underlying the whole of the law would be to clash with widely accepted industrial practice; *e.g.* the Engineering Industry Agreement which provides for some one and a quarter million workers a weekly guaranteed minimum 40-hour rate. Of the first four schemes to gain exemption under s. 18, three were guaranteed week arrangements.

"*Throughout a day any part of which.*" Appreciation of the common industrial practice would also help the E.A.T. to decide the question whether employees are entitled to guarantee payments where the employer has not provided work during any part of the day when the employee would normally be required to work. (Normal working hours are calculated in accordance with Sched. 14—see s. 152. They may include hours paid at overtime rates (Sched. 14, para. 2)). The phrasing is ambiguous: is the phrase " not provided with work " intended to refer to only the entire day or also a part of the day? To permit the employer to avoid payment in the latter case would be to allow blatant evasion of the Act by giving employers the opportunity to require workers to attend for only a few hours instead of laying them off as would normally have been the case. By sending them home early, the employer would have evaded the application of the principle of the guaranteed week laid down in this section. Since the provision applies to cases where employees work 16 hours a week or even less (s. 143 (1) and Sched. 13), it was clearly envisaged that the failure to provide work for only a few hours a day could invoke the principle. To allow the employer to evade the principle where he fails to provide work to employees for part of the day when they would normally be required to work would be to open a major loophole in the provision, one which is not available in weekly guaranteed pay agreements.

The circumstances in which the right to a guarantee payment applies resemble in part (subs. (1) (*a*)) the description of lay-off given in the provisions on redundancy payments (s. 81 (2) (*b*)) and may eventually allow for a redundancy payment claim (s. 88). But subs. (1) (*b*) makes it clear that many more circumstances may give rise to a claim for guarantee payments: natural disasters, equipment failures, cuts in essential services or trade disputes and industrial action (not excluded by s. 13 (1)) —but apparently one industrial tribunal thought that an employer's insistence on closing on a Jewish holiday was not an " occurrence " within subs. (1) (*b*)—*North* v. *Pavleigh Ltd.* [1977] I.R.L.R. 461.

Lay-off and dismissal. Finally, workers should bear in mind that lay-off may automatically amount to a dismissal unless either the employer has a contractual right of unilateral suspension—a rarity in the case of salaried staff and not altogether easy to establish in the case of hourly-paid workers—or the employee chooses to waive the employer's breach of contract. Whether it also amounts to an *unfair* dismissal is, however, dependent on additional factors. But there is no requirement here that the employee be " ready, willing and available " in order to claim the payment where there is a failure to provide work (subject to the provision in s. 13 (2) (*a*) and especially s. 13 (2) (*b*)). So some collective agreements allow for employees to receive some sick pay during lay-off—Findus Ltd. and the TGWU and the GMWU. On the other hand, in the case of the annual holiday shut-down, employees ready and willing to work have been denied by industrial tribunals a guarantee payment because they were not " required to work " within the meaning of the subsection.

Subs. (2)
Provision is made here for the position of shift-workers. It is estimated that more than a third of all industrial workers are now on shift.

General exclusions from right under s. 12

13.—(1) An employee shall not be entitled to a guarantee payment in respect of a workless day if the failure to provide him with work occurs in consequence of a trade dispute involving any employee of his employer or of an associated employer.

(2) An employee shall not be entitled to a guarantee payment in respect of a workless day if—

   (*a*) his employer has offered to provide alternative work for that day which is suitable in all the circumstances whether or not work which the employee is under his contract employed to perform, and the employee has unreasonably refused that offer; or

   (*b*) he does not comply with reasonable requirements imposed by his employer with a view to ensuring that his services are available.

DERIVATION
1975, s. 23.

DEFINITIONS
" Trade dispute " is defined by s. 153 (1) as having the meaning given by s. 29 of TULRA.
" associated employer " is defined in s. 153 (4).

GENERAL NOTE
Subs. (1)
Collective bargaining and trade dispute disqualification. At the time the Employment Protection Act 1975 was passed, surveys by the Department of Employment of existing collective agreements which provide for guarantee payments showed that nearly all of them bar payment in the event of strike action by the company's own employees. But it was found that there were as many agreements which take into account lay-offs due to strikes as there were those which are set aside in the event of lay-off being due to a strike; *i.e.* half made an allowance for payment of some sort of guarantee payment even in the event of a dispute. The agreements which provided greater benefits than those conferred by the Act will continue to do so. Others will be void to the extent that they exclude or limit the rights under s. 12 (s. 140 (1), subject to s. 140 (2) (*a*)). For example, the National Engineering Agreement still provides for a guaranteed week unless the strike causing the lay-off is in a federated establishment. A federated employer will nevertheless be liable to pay the statutory guarantee payment to employees laid off in consequence of a dispute with another federated employer, despite the Engineering Agreement, unless the struck firm is an associated employer. Unions may therefore have increased to some extent their bargaining power *vis-à-vis* associations of employers. A strike in a selected firm could cause massive shut-downs in the rest of the industry. Nonetheless, other employers would be obliged to make guarantee payments unless they were associated employers.

Social Security and trade dispute disqualification. On the other hand, the disqualification for guarantee payment is even wider and more arbitrary than the notorious "trade dispute disqualification" for social security benefits (s. 19 (1) of the Social Security Act 1975, and s. 8 of the Supplementary Benefits Act 1976). The latter at least allows the employee to escape disqualification if he can prove that he has nothing to do with the dispute. S. 111 of the Employment Protection Act 1975 recognised the unfairness of that disqualification in certain circumstances by easing the severity of the test. Why then has an even harsher test been adopted to disqualify workers from guarantee payment who may have nothing to do with the circumstances leading to their lay-off? Employees may be disqualified from guarantee payment in consequence of a trade dispute in circumstances where they are held to be entitled to social security benefits as not barred by the trade dispute disqualification. The interaction of guarantee payments and social security benefit is discussed in more detail in the Note to s. 15 (1).

Trade dispute suspension clauses in collective agreements. It has been noted that while the exclusion here is wider than that for social security benefits, it is narrower than a number of collectively agreed provisions for suspension of negotiated guarantee payments in the circumstances of a trade dispute. In those cases, s. 140 (1) operates to render the wider exclusion void, but this is subject to s. 140 (2) (*a*)—agreements specifically exempted under s. 18. And here we find a rather alarming development: of the first 16 exempted agreements, 14 have provisions for trade dispute suspension which are as wide or *wider* than that of this subsection. (For text of the agreements, see *Encyclopedia of Labour Relations Law*, Pt. 4.) *E.g.* Guarantee Payment (Exemption) Orders Nos. 10 and 13 of 1977 and 15 of 1978 all provide that the benefit will not be payable "where there is no work due to industrial action within the plant *or outside the plant but within the industry by any group of workers covered by this Agreement or in membership of Unions signatory to this Agreement.*" Orders 10 and 15 were between the GMWU and SOGAT and respectively the Fibreboard Packing Case Employers' Association and the British Carton Association. Order 13 involved the TGWU as well as the other two unions and on the employers' side, the Multiwall Sack Manufacturers Employers' Association. Again, the Agreements contained in Orders 1, 2, 3 and 12 of 1977 allow the employer to suspend payment where he cannot provide work due to collective action "taken by *any* employees employed under the Agreement"— the agreements negotiated by organisations in the civil engineering, demolition, building and refractory users industries respectively. So, if there are several sub-contractors working, *e.g.* on a building site and one goes on strike, the other sub-contractors may escape liability for any guarantee payment even though they are not associated employers.

Other agreements contain even wider exclusion clauses. It seems clear that employers see in guaranteed pay agreements ways of putting pressure on employees (and unions) to avoid industrial action. This is obviously the case in the non-exempt agreement negotiated by Leyland with 11 unions representing 102,000 hourly paid employees in 34 plants which provided earnings security in return for production continuity. Coming into force in November 1977 were provisions for a full shift guarantee and improved lay-off and job security provisions—but subject to the loss of these benefits for individuals involved in unconstitutional industrial action during any one quarter (the quarters aligning with those in s. 15 (2)). It will be remembered that similar "penalty clauses" were the subject of a strike at Ford's in 1969.

Unions negotiating exempted agreements must feel that the benefits obtained compensate for the wider suspension clauses. But it should be noted, first, that two of the exempted agreements do contain *narrower* trade dispute suspension clauses: both were negotiated in 1977 by the National Union of the Footwear, Leather and Allied Trades with respectively the British Footwear Manufacturers' Federation (Order No. 5) and the Cut Sole Associates—British Leather Federation (Order No. 9). The suspension only operates: "in the event of any employees in a department or a factory taking part in a strike," and applies only "to all employees in *the* factory."

Secondly, it should be noted that many *non*-exempted agreements also provide benefits in circumstances which would be barred by this subsection; *e.g.* an agreement in the Drug and Fine Chemicals Industry has *no provision* for *immediate* suspension in the event of a strike. This can only occur *after* specified notice has been given *and* the workers' representatives are consulted.

Industrial tribunals' interpretations. Finally, even the best agreement could be undermined by narrow legal interpretations. It will be necessary to monitor the tribunals' approach to this subsection. Thus cases have held that a trade dispute which is *not* caught by this subsection *is* an " occurrence " within s. 12 (1) (*b*) so as to allow for guarantee payment; that, *e.g.* the Ulster Workers Strike of May 1977 was a *political* dispute, not a " trade dispute " within the meaning of s. 29 of TULRA, so that workers laid off as a consequence were *not* excluded by this subsection from claiming. But on the other hand, industrial tribunals have been prepared to accept that where a strike is only *one* factor in causing a lay-off, the workers should still suffer loss of guaranteed pay. So a strike which would *not* have caused a lay-off *but for* other factors, was still held to " cause " the lay-off, and as a result no entitlement—*Thomson* v. *Priest* (*Lindley*) *Ltd.* [1978] I.R.L.R. 99.

Subs. (2)

Alternative work suitable for a lay-off. In the original Employment Protection Bill 1975, this subsection was identical to what is now s. 20 (2). However, the wording of subs. (2) (*a*) was amended in Committee, though it appears not to have changed in substance. It does illustrate, however, that the *circumstances due to which* alternative employment is offered may vary in such ways as to affect the *criteria* both for the suitability of the work offered, and for the reasonableness of the employee's response. Contrast subs. (2) (*a*) here with s. 82 (5) which concerns an offer of alternative employment in a redundancy situation. The wording of each of these two sections regarding alternative employment is different, but both envisage some difference from the work required under the previous contract of employment. The criteria as to the suitability of employment and reasonableness of response used in the threatened permanent redundancy case, however, may not be appropriate to where there is only a temporary lay-off. For example, it could be said that under the pressure of a threatened redundancy an employee might be prepared to accept certain work which he ought not to be obliged to perform otherwise. In any event, it is clear that before being disqualified, two tests have to be satisfied: is the work suitable and was the employee reasonable. The objective circumstances of the work and the subjective circumstances of the employee must both be taken into account.

The Act does not specifically state what the terms of employment are to be if the employee accepts alternative work. It should be clear that in order to qualify as " suitable," the terms of employment should provide at least for payment at a rate not less than that which would be payable were no alternative work available and which the employee would therefore receive under the Act without performing any work at all. The point is reinforced where the employee accepts alternative work where he would be justified in reasonably refusing it. He should not be made to suffer for this.

Industrial practice—collective agreements. Again, industrial practice illuminates the issues presented by the subsection. Thus all but one of the first 16 agreements exempted under s. 18 provide for some degree of mandatory flexibility in order to qualify for guarantee payment. The degree of flexibility, however, covers a wide range—and the legal requirement in this subsection presumably falls somewhere on this spectrum. Thus in some cases workers must be willing to perform " *suitable* alternative work " (Order No. 1—Civil Engineering); or " *reasonable* alternative work " (Order Nos. 5 and 9—Footwear and Leather Manufacture). But in both the latter two cases union officers must be consulted in case of difficulty in interpreting what is reasonable alternative work.

In Order No. 4 (Wire and Wire Rope Manufacturing), if " reasonable alternative work " is undertaken, payment is to be at the *higher* of the two rates (the original or the alternative job). In some agreements there is an *occupational* qualification: the employee must be willing to perform work " in any other suitable demolition or dismantling industry occupation " (Order No. 2); or in " any other suitable building industry occupation " (Order No. 3). Both these also require movement to " any other job, site or shop where work is available," and similar geographical mobility is required in the agreement negotiated by the unions with the Refractory Users' Federation (Order No. 12). Some degree of occupational mobility is entailed in the clause in the Steeplejack and Lightning Conductor Engineering Industry (Order No. 6): employees must perform work " in any other suitable occupation," but not as much as in the Papermaking and Boardmaking Industry (Order No. 7), which allows for álternative work " in any department or in connection with any process within the establishment." Another group of agreements in similar industries (No. 10, Fibreboard Packing Cases; No. 13, Multiwall Sack Manufacturers; and No. 15, Carton Manufacturing) all require employees to "perform such work as is required, either in his own or an alternative job." Interestingly, a voluntary, non-exempt agreement, covering 12,500 workers in the Glass Container Industry makes it a condition of the guarantee that the employee "perform in the normal way any services, whether within or temporarily outside his usual occupation which in the circumstances he could reasonably be required to perform."

Exempt agreements negotiated with subsidiaries of General Mills Inc. (U.S.A.) explicitly provide for employees to "work flexibly so as to maintain a balanced work force. When this results in an employee being required to accept work at a lower grade (*e.g.* machine minder to work as a packer) the higher rate of pay will be maintained for up to six weeks" (Smith's Food Group and the TGWU, Order No. 8; and in the agreement Order No. 14 (Tudor Food Products and GMWU), the flexibility clause explicitly provides for acceptance of a change of shift, as well as a lower grade of work—again at higher basic rates preserved for up to six weeks. A final interesting contrast is provided by two exempted agreements negotiated by the same company with two unions, one general and one craft union. In both cases the company, Henry Wiggin & Co. Ltd., does not expressly require employees to accept suitable alternative work. But in the case of the agreement negotiated with the GMWU (Order No. 11), where the lack of work arises out of "the refusal of *another* employee to perform any work he is temporarily assigned to do," the employee may lose part or all of his entitlement under the agreement. This last provision is, however, *absent* in the agreement negotiated with the EETPTU (Order No. 16); *i.e.* there is no obligation to accept alternative work in order to qualify.

Industrial tribunals' interpretation. Some industrial tribunals exhibit the law's managerial outlook and insensitivity to workers' interests in interpreting this subsection. Thus in *Purdy* v. *Willowbrook International Ltd.* [1977] I.R.L.R. 388, the union representative's contention that the alternative work was unsuitable because it was outside the employee's normal trade was rejected. The industrial tribunal held there were "no good grounds for declining the offer." He had done the work previously, had the necessary skill and the Act envisaged work being suitable "even though it is work which the employee is not under his contract employed to do"—a matter the industrial tribunal failed to notice is not necessarily the same as the union representative's contention.

The legal perspective is well illustrated by the industrial tribunals' interpretation of subs. (2) (*b*). In *Meadows* v. *Faithful Overalls Ltd.* [1977] I.R.L.R. 330, the worker concerned arrived at 7.50 a.m. on a cold February morning to find the factory temperature below the permitted minimum. While management rushed about trying to get oil supplies, for the heating fuel had run out, the women workers waited in the canteen with hot tea. This had happened on a number of previous occasions of heating failure, and during the waiting time for the temperature to rise the women were paid only their basic rate, though they were on piece-work. After one and a half hours, about 9.30 a.m. the women started to go home. They were asked to wait until 9.45 a.m. when the fuel was supposed to arrive. It did not. When it did eventually arrive after 10 a.m., they had gone home. The industrial tribunal's approach was simply to evaluate the reasonableness of *management's belief* that in fact the oil would shortly arrive. Without regard to the workers' position—two hours in the cold, loss of piece rates—it was held that management's belief was reasonable, the requirement that the workers should stay was *therefore* [*sic*] reasonable, and the claim was dismissed. Perhaps the E.A.T. should take a more objective view and not be satisfied to base the legal rights of workers entirely on management's beliefs.

Calculation of guarantee payment

14.—(1) Subject to the limits set by section 15, the amount of a guarantee payment payable to an employee in respect of any day shall be the sum produced by multiplying the number of normal working hours on that day by the guaranteed hourly rate, and, accordingly, no guarantee payment shall be payable to an employee in whose case there are no normal working hours on the day in question.

(2) Subject to subsection (3), the guaranteed hourly rate in relation to an employee shall be the amount of one week's pay divided by—

(*a*) the number of normal working hours in a week for that employee when employed under the contract of employment in force on the day in respect of which the guarantee payment is payable; or

(*b*) where the number of such normal working hours differs from week to week or over a longer period, the average number of such hours calculated by dividing by twelve the total number of the employee's normal working hours during the period of twelve weeks ending with the last complete week before the day in respect of which the guarantee payment is payable; or

(*c*) in a case falling within paragraph (*b*) but where the employee has not been employed for a sufficient period to enable the calculation to be made under that paragraph, a number which fairly represents the number of normal working hours in a week having regard to such of the following considerations as are appropriate in the circumstances, that is to say,—

(i) the average number of normal working hours in a week which the employee could expect in accordance with the terms of his contract;

(ii) the average number of such hours of other employees engaged in relevant comparable employment with the same employer.

(3) If in any case an employee's contract has been varied, or a new contract has been entered into, in connection with a period of short-time working, subsection (2) shall have effect as if for the reference to the day in respect of which the guarantee payment is payable there was substituted a reference to the last day on which the original contract was in force.

DERIVATION
1975, s. 24 (1), (2), (4).

GENERAL NOTE
Subs. (1)
   Normal working hours on the day in question. The Act attempts to provide calculations for every contingency: normal working hours (Sched. 14, Pt. I), average weekly hours (Sched. 14, para. 4 (3) or s. 14 (2) (*b*) and (*c*)), a week's pay (Sched. 14, Pt. II), the average hourly rate of remuneration (Sched. 14, para. 4 (4)) and the guaranteed hourly rate (subs. (2)). Unfortunately, it seems to overlook one central question: when an employer has laid-off an employee for a day or part of a day, how is one to decide if there are any " normal working hours on the day in question " ? True, Sched. 14, Pt. I speaks of normal working hours fixed " in a week or other period." The number is to be so fixed, presumably, in the contract of employment. But this instrument may not stipulate the " normal working hours on that day " for which a guarantee payment is claimed. The question of what are the normal working hours in a day is not answered in the Act.
   Where the number is stipulated in the contract of employment, there is no problem. Otherwise, the answer may lie in simple common sense, *i.e.* a division of normal weekly hours (if these can be calculated in accordance with Sched. 14, Pt. I) or of the average weekly hours (calculated in accordance with Sched. 14, para. 4 (3) or subs. (2) (*b*) and (*c*)) by the number of days, average or normal (there is no method of calculating these in the Act, but one would assume a method similar to that used in the Act: the number fixed in the contract (normal) or the number of days worked over a 12-week period divided by 12 (average), *cf.* the same method used in calculating the maximum number of days for which a payment may be made in any three-month period: s. 15 (3)). One would thus emerge with a normal or average number of working hours in a day. If the employer failed to provide work for a day or part of a day, the guarantee payment would be calculated as specified in the subsection. Even where the normal working hours in a day have

been determined, there are at least two situations which may cause problems. First, where the employee concerned works on different days every week. How is one to know whether there are "normal working hours in that day" for which a guarantee payment is claimed? On the one hand, it should not be assumed that the employer may determine the days each week unilaterally, as this would allow for evasion of payment. On the other hand, to assume that the *employee* determines *unilaterally* the days of work each week does not accord with the realities of the employment relationship.

Remarkably enough, in *Mailway (Southern) Ltd.* v. *Willsher* [1978] I.R.L.R. 322 (E.A.T.) Kilner Brown J. found that a woman worker who, due to having children, worked irregular hours—but *in accordance with the need of the employers*—was not even an "employee" and hence disqualified from claiming. This despite the obvious statutory attempt at provision for such a case in subs. (2) (*b*). This result would seem an obvious candidate for rethinking along the lines of the Court of Appeal's guidelines, disregarded explicitly there by Kilner Brown J., that words used by Parliament should be given a meaning consonant with social justice.

A solution to the problem of calculating the guarantee payment due should depend on a review of the facts: was the failure to provide work on a particular day due to factors mentioned in s. 12 (1), or was it in accordance with the normal schedule of working, erratic as that is? Secondly, where there is a system of flexitime in operation: are there "normal working hours" in any day? Are the "core hours" relevant? Or is the calculation of the average number of working hours a solution?

Collective agreements. Most of the exempted agreements which replace the statutory provisions provide for payment at the basic rate of pay (*e.g.* Nos. 7, 11, 16), though some make express provision for the inclusion of a shift differential where applicable (Nos. 8, 14) and others go on to expressly exclude bonus, overtime and plus payments from the calculation (Nos. 10, 13, 15). Two agreements negotiated in the Footwear and Leather Industries, however, provide for a guarantee only of 75 per cent. of the employee's average earnings—and further detailed consideration of the calculation of earnings for piece workers is provided in the agreements (Nos. 5, 9). On the other hand, the agreement negotiated between the Refractory Users Federation and the GMWU, TGWU and UCATT guaranteed weekly earnings as follows: (a) Standard Hourly Rate; (b) Joint Board Supplement, and (c) Guaranteed Minimum Bonus (No. 12). And the non-exempt agreement covering 12,500 workers in the Glass Container industry, effective from May 1, 1976, provided for the payment of the hourly job rate, but also for there to be added to this for the purposes of calculation "one-fortieth of any flat supplementary payment approved by the N.J.I.C., but which has not been consolidated into rates." Even better is the agreement in the Drug and Fine Chemicals Industry, which provides for normal earnings to be guaranteed which "includes basic rate, job rate, bonus, shift differential and weekend premiums. Bonus payments which fluctuate shall be averaged over an appropriate period."

Subs. (2)

It should be noted that the guaranteed hourly rate is not necessarily the same as the basic hourly rate payable under the contract of employment. It may include an overtime element, depending on whether overtime hours are included in the "normal working hours" (Sched. 14, Pt. I) used to calculate a week's pay (Sched. 14, Pt. II). For the purposes of calculating a "week's pay," the calculation date is the last day on which the original contract was in force—Sched. 14, para. 7 (1) (*a*).

Subs. (3)

This would seem to confirm that if there is a lengthy period of short-time working, as in an extended recession, the employee may be entitled to guarantee payments every three months (see s. 15 and the identical provisions in s. 15 (4)).

But in two reported cases to date, industrial tribunals have evaded this provision. In both instances, employers *unilaterally* reduced the work-week each time under protest from the employees concerned—a breach of contract by the employer which the industrial tribunals held had been "accepted" by the employees who had bowed under pressure and continued working. Although a claim for guaranteed pay would seem the statute's clear intention for this situation, both times the industrial tribunals evaded this by saying that the employee was not "required to work" (*after* the employers' unilateral change) and thus no claim could be made under s. 12 (*Daley* v. *Strathclyde Regional Council* [1977] I.R.L.R. 414; *Clemens* v. *Peter Richards Ltd.* [1977] I.R.L.R. 332). Attention to the words of s. 12, " normally be required to work," and regard to this subsection and s. 15 (4) would indicate the opposite result, which it is hoped the E.A.T. will affirm. The argument by the industrial tribunal in *Daley* that the change was " not a short-term or temporary one " should not affect the issue. The subsection's reference to a " period of short-time working " does not stipulate that the " period " be short; whether it is " temporary " should be the subject of strict proof by the employer.

It appears that where an employee accepts alternative work in accordance with s. 13 (2) (*a*) on a short-time basis, his entitlement to a guaranteed payment in respect of workless days is unaffected and is calculated by reference to the rates of his old job. Presumably, being laid-off from the alternative employment might entitle him to a separate and additional guarantee payment, based on the new job's rate of pay.

Limits on amount of and entitlement to guarantee payment

15.—(1) The amount of a guarantee payment payable to an employee in respect of any day shall not exceed £6·60.

(2) An employee shall not be entitled to guarantee payments in respect of more than the specified number of days in any one of the relevant periods, that is to say, the periods of three months commencing on 1st February, 1st May, 1st August and 1st November in each year.

(3) The specified number of days for the purposes of subsection (2) shall be, subject to subsection (4),—

   (*a*) the number of days, not exceeding five, on which the employee normally works in a week under the contract of employment in force on the day in respect of which the guarantee payment is claimed; or

   (*b*) where that number of days varies from week to week or over a longer period, the average number of such days, not exceeding five, calculated by dividing by twelve the total number of such days during the period of twelve weeks ending with the last complete week before the day in respect of which the guarantee payment is claimed, and rounding up the resulting figure to the next whole number; or

   (*c*) in a case falling within paragraph (*b*) but where the employee has not been employed for a sufficient period to enable the calculation to be made under that paragraph, a number which fairly represents the number of the employee's normal working days in a week, not exceeding five, having regard to such of the following considerations as are appropriate in the circumstances, that is to say,—

      (i) the average number of normal working days in a week which the employee could expect in accordance with the terms of his contract;

      (ii) the average number of such days of other employees engaged in relevant comparable employment with the same employer.

(4) If in any case an employee's contract has been varied, or a new contract has been entered into, in connection with a period of short-time working, subsection (3) shall have effect as if for the references to the day in respect of which the guarantee payment is claimed there were substituted references to the last day on which the original contract was in force.

(5) The Secretary of State may vary any of the limits referred to in this section, and may in particular vary the relevant periods referred to in subsection (2), after a review under section 148, by order made in accordance with that section.

DERIVATIONS

1975, s. 25; 1977 Order (No. 2), Art. 2.

GENERAL NOTE

Subs. (1)

Guaranteed payments and unemployment benefits. As mentioned in the Note to s. 12 (1), the State has by the provision of guarantee payments increased workers' problems by making it more unlikely that their legal entitlement in the event of lay-off—either through guarantee payments or unemployment benefits—will actually be paid. But to add insult to injury, even if prompt payment of guarantee payment is made, the benefits derived under these new provisions will often be less, and sometimes substantially less, than before they were implemented. This is a function of the low level of payments provided for in this subsection.

It need hardly be said that unless guarantee payments are maintained at a reasonable level, the principle of the guaranteed week will be undermined and many who hoped to benefit will be bitterly disillusioned. At the level stipulated, workers taking hom more than £36·25 for an ordinary 40-hour week will receive a maximum of £7·25 a day in guarantee payment (Employment Protection (Variation of Limits) Order 1978 (S.I. 1978 No. 1777), effective on February 1, 1979). Those in even lower-paid jobs will be receiving even less (calculated according to s. 14). Both, however, will be restricted to five days of payment at that rate in any three-month period (subss. (2) and (3)). The maximum payments to which an employee may become entitled under this provision will amount to £36·25 or less in the three-month period.

In practice, however, but for guarantee payments, workers laid-off would frequently be better off. Those who are in fact laid-off for *only three days or less* in any three-month period will, in most cases, be better off. But for each day after the initial three days, a worker laid-off will frequently be receiving on a *daily* basis *less* than he would be entitled to by way of social security benefits. When cumulated over a maximum five-day period, *i.e.* days four to eight of lay-off, the extent of this deficiency will often outweigh the payments of the first three days, and sometimes substantially so. This is evident from the following calculations.

As of November 13, 1978, the rate of unemployment benefit was increased to £15·75 a week for single people and £25·50 for married couples (even more with children and supplementary benefit). Instead of this daily *tax-free* payment on all days after the third day, the worker will now receive a *maximum* payment of £7·25 per day for the first five days—and this £36·25 is *taxable.* For days six, seven and eight, he receives nothing (the waiting days). Only on day nine does he begin getting his social security unemployment benefit. So the total of eight days is a maximum £36·25—*taxed.* The total for unemployment benefit over the same period would be five days (days four to eight) × £4·25 (married couple's benefit over six days) = £21·25 *untaxed.* If one takes into account workers with families and factors such as tax rebates, the likelihood is that the level of social security benefits will cumulatively exceed by an ever larger margin the benefits of guarantee payments. The effect of the provisions on guarantee payments *at their present levels* is, therefore, to deprive many workers of their larger national insurance entitlement. This position can only be cured by the Secretary of State under subs. (5). The Note on that subsection indicates that there is not much ground for optimism on that score.

Collectively agreed guaranteed week provisions are the only way to effectively secure workers against this hazard, and trade unions have been active in pursuing these. A stimulus, if one is needed, was provided by the fact that improvements in guaranteed pay provisions were permitted *outside* the incomes policy limits of Phase II.

As a final point it may be noted that there is added to this subsection in this Act the indefinite article " a " before the words " guarantee payment." Speculation at this stage, and perhaps later, may be fruitless.

Subs. (2)

These particular dates were chosen as a matter of administrative convenience to avoid the end of periods coinciding with Christmas, Easter and the summer holidays, when large numbers of job-seekers and students have to be coped with by unemployment officers. The fixing of limits in this fashion, however, is bound to produce arbitrary results; if an employee is laid-off for, say, two months just before any of the dates, he is likely to receive twice the payments he would have received had he been laid-off just afterwards (though not much in terms of real gain —see the Note to subs. (1) above).

Subs. (3)

Although the maximum number of days is five, it will be less if the average or normal number of days worked in a week is less. The calculations are the same as those laid down for average and normal hours in s. 14 (2). Thus in *Trevethan* v. *Sterling Metals Ltd.* [1977] I.R.L.R. 416, day shift workers working a five-day 40-hour week were entitled to five days guaranteed pay, but night shift workers in the same plant working a four-night 40-hour week were entitled to only four days guarantee pay. The argument that the different shifts should have the same entitlement was, the industrial tribunal said, " at first sight . . . a sensible and superficially attractive proposition, but on closer examination it is not supported by the provisions of the Act."

Subs. (4)

See the Note to s. 14 (3) which is substantially identical.

Subs. (5)

When the Employment Protection Bill consultative document was published in late 1974, the level of payment was limited to £25 in any 13-week period (paras. 3–6). Only some six months later, when the Bill was published in March 1975, this limit was already raised to £30 in any three-month period. When the Bill became law in November 1975, some eight months later, the level was still £30 every three months, and this provision was not brought into effect for another 14 months—February 1977. The Employment Protection (Variation of Limits) Order 1977 (S.I. 1977 No. 2031) dated December 6, 1977, increased the limit on the amount of guarantee pay payable to an employee in respect of any day from £6 to £6·60 and the Employment Protection (Variation of Limits) Order 1978 (S.I. 1978 No. 1777), effective February 1, 1979, further increased this to £7·25 per day. The maximum number of days was left unchanged at five. This increase is far behind the rate of inflation over this period. See the list of factors to be considered by the Secretary of State in s. 148 (2).

Supplementary provisions relating to guarantee payments

16.—(1) Subject to subsection (2), a right to a guarantee payment shall not affect any right of an employee in relation to remuneration under his contract of employment (in this section referred to as " contractual remuneration ").

(2) Any contractual remuneration paid to an employee in respect of a workless day shall go towards discharging any liability of the employer to pay a guarantee payment in respect of that day, and conversely any guarantee payment paid in respect of a day shall go towards discharging any liability of the employer to pay contractual remuneration in respect of that day.

(3) For the purposes of subsection (2), contractual remuneration shall be treated as paid in respect of a workless day—

    (*a*) where it is expressed to be calculated or payable by reference to that day or any part of that day, to the extent that it is so expressed; and

    (*b*) in any other case, to the extent that it represents guaranteed remuneration, rather than remuneration for work actually done, and is referable to that day when apportioned rateably between that day and any other workless period falling within the period in respect of which the remuneration is paid.

(4) The Secretary of State may by order provide that in relation to any description of employees the provisions of sections 12 (2), 14 and 15 (3) (as originally enacted or as varied under section 15 (5)) and of subsections (1) to (3), and, so far as they apply for the purposes of

those provisions, the provisions of Schedule 14 shall have effect subject to such modifications and adaptations as may be prescribed by the order.

DERIVATIONS
    1975, s. 26.

GENERAL NOTE
Subs. (1)
    Identical provisions are to be found in this Act concerning other rights, *e.g.* s. 21 (2), s. 27 (5), s. 31 (10) and s. 35 (3). These rights are not to prejudice an employee in any way with regard to his contractual remuneration.

Subs. (2)
    Again, similar provisions are to be found relating to other statutory liabilities imposed on employers, *e.g.* s. 21 (3), s. 27 (6), s. 31 (11) and s. 35 (4).
    In practice, employers have tended to apply their own agreed arrangements for guarantee pay. Then, if the requirements under the Act are not fully offset by this payment, the Act's provisions are applied. This is the position recommended by the E.E.F. to its members with regard to the guaranteed pay terms agreed in that industry.
    Only remuneration specifically allocated as payment " in respect of a workless day " counts towards off-setting the employer's statutory liability. Ordinary remuneration paid in consequence of other contractual terms is not affected, as provided in subs. (1). This is reaffirmed by subs. (3) which requires such remuneration to be expressed as calculated or payable by reference to the workless day in question, and only to the extent that it is so expressed may it be set off.
    Statements by the Minister of State, Department of Employment (Mr. A. Booth) in Committee indicate that the intended effect of this subsection was that where the statutory liability of the employer was offset by virtue of his contractual obligation to the employee in respect of a workless day, that day was not to count towards the maximum number of days to be calculated in accordance with s. 15 (3). The view appears justified since the calculation of specified days is only made when " the guarantee payment is claimed." It also follows from the general prohibition of certain contractual provisions in s. 140 (1). While specially defined contractual remuneration may be set off against sums payable under s. 12, contractual arrangements cannot exclude or limit the future rights of the employee (s. 140 (1) (*a*) or preclude him from making a future complaint under s. 17 (s. 140 (1) (*b*)). As long as the employee opts for payment via the contractual obligation of the employer, he has not claimed his statutory right and the day does not count.

Subs. (3)
    This illustrates the need for the remuneration paid for a workless day under a contract to be clearly referable to that day. It covers the particular case of a collective agreement containing a scheme based on guaranteeing a minimum weekly wage (*e.g.* the Engineering Industry Agreement: employees are " assured of earnings equivalent to their time rate of 40 hours "). If the employee works only three days in the week, but earns enough to exceed that minimum, he will not qualify for any contractual remuneration but will still be able to claim a statutory payment for the two days when he is not provided with work. The problem arises when the employee in that situation earns below the guaranteed weekly minimum. The difference owed him under his contract is not paid in respect of any particular workless day, but in respect of a workless period—the rest of the week. This subsection provides, therefore, that this be treated as " apportioned rateably " for the remainder of the week, and be set-off accordingly against any claim for a guarantee payment for any day in that period. Employees will have to judge whether, in light of future lay-off prospects, they should use one of their specified number of days. If used in these circumstances, some of the payment will be lost through set-off, whereas a possible later claim where the minimum had been exceeded would benefit from the full payment.
    Again, as stated in the Note to subs. (2), any day for which only contractual remuneration is paid and no claim is made under s. 12 does not count towards the specified number of days available.

Complaint to industrial tribunal

17.—(1) An employee may present a complaint to an industrial tribunal that his employer has failed to pay the whole or any part of a guarantee payment to which the employee is entitled.

(2) An industrial tribunal shall not entertain a complaint relating to a guarantee payment in respect of any day unless the complaint is presented to the tribunal before the end of the period of three months beginning with that day or within such further period as the tribunal considers reasonable in a case where it is satisfied that it was not reasonably practicable for the complaint to be presented within the period of three months.

(3) Where an industrial tribunal finds a complaint under subsection (1) well-founded, the tribunal shall order the employer to pay the complainant the amount of guarantee payment which it finds is due to him.

DERIVATION
  1975, s. 27.

GENERAL NOTE
Subs. (1)

Given the maximum entitlement to guarantee payments laid down in s. 15, even in the best of circumstances—a lay-off period coinciding with the end of one three-month period lasting for 10 working days during which there is payable no contractual remuneration—the largest claim which can be made to an industrial tribunal is for £72·50. In the vast majority of cases, where less than these optimum conditions apply, the claim will amount to a few pounds only. This will make it barely worthwhile for the employee to pursue it to the industrial tribunal. It will hardly ever justify any but a very large and determined employer making an appearance before the industrial tribunal to defend itself against such miniscule claims. It will almost always be cheaper to settle the claim without the trouble of a hearing. In fact, as pointed out in the Note to s. 12 (1), very few complaints have been made. Many workers are covered by collectively agreed benefits which easily off-set those in the statute. Those not so covered are often ignorant of their existence, of the mechanism of enforcement, or unable for other practical reasons to utilise the legal remedy.

Subs. (2)

Similar provisions are to be found relating to complaints to industrial tribunals for other rights granted by this Act, *e.g.* ss. 22 (2), 24 (2), 30 (1), 31 (7), 36 (2), 43 (5) and 67 (2).

Subs. (3)

This task of the industrial tribunal is rendered considerably more complicated by the Employment Protection (Recoupment of Unemployment Benefit and Supplementary Benefit) Regulations 1977 (S.I. 1977 No. 674) dated April 7, 1977, which came into effect on May 9, 1977. The entitlement to guarantee payments interacts with social security provisions in a complicated manner (see Notes to s. 12 (1) and s. 15 (1)). The end result is that the industrial tribunal, when assessing its award, must disregard any unemployment or supplementary benefits which have been paid to or claimed by the employee during the period beginning with his potential entitlement and up to the time of the industrial tribunal's award. These social security benefits, paid or claimed, constitute an element which may be recouped by the D.H.S.S. Industrial tribunals will have to exercise great care in ensuring accurate calculation of social security benefit, as employees may be affected since the employer can only pay that part of the award not covered by a D.H.S.S. potential recoupment notice. An employee whose benefits are erroneously calculated too high may find the award of payment to him diminished by that amount, though he never received the benefits calculated.

Exemption orders

18.—(1) If at any time there is in force a collective agreement, or a wages order, whereby employees to whom the agreement or order relates have a right to guaranteed remuneration and on the application of all the parties to the agreement or, as the case may be, of the council or Board making the order, the appropriate Minister, having regard to the provisions of the agreement or order, is satisfied that section 12 should not apply to those employees, he may make an order under this section excluding those employees from the operation of that section.

(2) In subsection (1), a wages order means an order made under any of the following provisions, that is to say—

(*a*) section 11 of the Wages Councils Act 1959;

(*b*) section 3 of the Agricultural Wages Act 1948;

(*c*) section 3 of the Agricultural Wages (Scotland) Act 1949.

(3) In subsection (1), " the appropriate Minister " means—

(*a*) as respects a collective agreement or such an order as is referred to in subsection (2) (*a*) or (*c*), the Secretary of State;

(*b*) as respects such an order as is referred to in subsection (2) (*b*), the Minister of Agriculture, Fisheries and Food.

(4) The Secretary of State shall not make an order under this section in respect of an agreement unless—

(*a*) the agreement provides for procedures to be followed (whether by arbitration or otherwise) in cases where an employee claims that his employer has failed to pay the whole or any part of any guaranteed remuneration to which the employee is entitled under the agreement, and that those procedures include a right to arbitration or adjudication by an independent referee or body in cases where (by reason of an equality of votes or otherwise) a decision cannot otherwise be reached; or

(*b*) the agreement indicates that an employee to whom the agreement relates may present a complaint to an industrial tribunal that his employer has failed to pay the whole or any part of any guaranteed remuneration to which the employee is entitled under the agreement;

and where an order under this section is in force in respect of such an agreement as is described in paragraph (*b*) an industrial tribunal shall have jurisdiction over such a complaint as if it were a complaint falling within section 17.

(5) Without prejudice to section 154 (4), an order under this section may be varied or revoked by a subsequent order thereunder, whether in pursuance of an application made by all or any of the parties to the agreement in question, or, as the case may be, by the council or Board which made the order in question, or without any such application.

DERIVATION
    1975, s. 28.

GENERAL NOTE
Subs. (1)

Exempted agreements. Guarantee Payments (Exemption) (No. 16) Order 1978 (S.I. 1978 No. 429) was dated March 14, 1978, and made by the Secretary of State for Employment. The 15 other exempted agreements may be found in S.I. 1977 Nos. 156, 157, 158, 208, 902, 1096, 1158, 1322, 1349, 1522, 1523, 1583, 1601, 2032 and S.I. 1978 No. 153.

To whom do exempted agreements relate? In each case there was, as required by the subsection, a collective agreement or wages order in force. " In force " presumably means no more than " in existence " as the employee's right to guaranteed remuneration will depend on the incorporation of terms into his individual contract, and this does not depend on the enforceability of the collective agreement. This point creates problems arising from agreements which are granted exemption. Following the words of the subsection, the statutory instrument provides that s. 12 shall not apply to " any person who is an employee to whom an exempted agreement relates." The agreements themselves, however, often specify simply that they apply to " employees " (Nos. 8, 10, 13, 15) ; " hourly rated employees " (Nos. 11, 14, 16) ; " operatives in the employment of an employer " (Nos. 2, 3, 6) ; or more detailed descriptions of workers, *e.g.* Bricklayers, Masons, Labourers (No. 12).

The question arises: to whom do these agreements " relate " ? To all employees in the industry; only to employers, members of the organisations, or employees, members of trade unions party to the agreements; to employers and trade union members who while not members of the organisations concerned nonetheless abide by its terms? Some agreements are slightly more explicit, *e.g.* Nos. 5 and 9— " employee under a contract of service with an employer in the Boot and Shoe/Cut Sole Industry who is *subject to* the provisions of the National Agreement "; or No. 7—" all employees/permanent full-time workers *covered by* the National Agreement in the Papermaking and Boardmaking Industry." The question as to whom these agreements " relate " remains. And it is critical; if, *e.g.* a non-member of the employers' organisation is *not exempt*, but does in practice follow the agreement, he will be subject to and his employees will benefit from *both* the statutory and the collectively agreed benefits. If he tried to dissociate himself from the agreement, he might be required to observe it as a consequence of a claim under Sched. 11 to the Employment Protection Act 1975. If he tried to bring himself under the exemption, he would face the problem of not having access to the disputes machinery provided under the agreement—which often incorporates machinery provided by the organisation (see Note to subs. (4)). In effect, therefore, employees not covered by the exemption orders, but who fall within the scope of the agreements contained in them, may well benefit from both agreed and statutory provisions. (As regards this problem in statutory dismissals procedures agreements, see s. 65 (2) (*f*)).

Exempted agreements not less favourable? Nothing is said about whether the exempted agreement must contain terms not less favourable than the statutory provisions (*cf.* s. 65 (2) (*d*)). S. 140 (2) (*a*) would allow for such agreements to exclude or limit the operation of these provisions. In practice, as indicated by Mr. Albert Booth, then Minister of State for Employment, when the Employment Protection Bill 1975 was going through Committee, any relative disadvantages compared to the statutory scheme would be expected to be balanced by advantages over that scheme in other respects. For example, the statutory provisions only deny benefit if the employee has worked less than four weeks, has already had five days' benefit in the three-month period, has unreasonably refused suitable alternative employment, or where the lay-off was caused by a trade dispute described in s. 13 (1). Most of the agreements exempted so far do not go beyond these provisions. But, *e.g.* Nos. 5 and 9 covering the Footwear and Cut Sole Industries suspend the guarantee payment, *inter alia*, " in the event of a breakdown of machinery, fire, flood, or stoppage of fuel or power supply." In Nos. 10, 13 and 15, in the Fibreboard Packing Case, Multiwall Sack and Carton Manufacturing Industries, there is a clause of the exempt agreement which provides, " where circumstances arise outside the control of management and employees of such a nature as to make payment under this Agreement impracticable then benefit will not be payable." The unions presumably felt, and the Secretary of State agreed, that these suspension clauses were compensated for by other provisions of the Agreement. But since there is nothing which prevents employees covered by non-exempt collective agreements from choosing whichever of their rights, statutory or contractual, will benefit them more, there would not seem to be much incentive for a union to be a party to an application to obtain an exemption.

Subs. (4)

Disputes machinery under exempted agreements. Half of the 16 agreements exempted so far have provisions clearly falling under subs. (4) (*b*)—Nos. 10, 13 and 15 provide that the sole remedy for disputes is to be obtained from an industrial tribunal, while Nos. 7, 8, 11, 14 and 16 provide for a voluntary procedure in addition or as an option to complaining to an industrial tribunal. Two other agreements, Nos. 1 and 3, allow that disputes: " may, at the option of the claimant, be referred to A.C.A.S. and/or an industrial tribunal *in the event of no decision* by the (joint Civil

Engineering/Building Industry) Board." And for the Demolition Industry, Order No. 2 provides that " disputes arising under this Rule shall, in the event of no decision by the Board, *and in that event only,* be referred by the Board to the A.C.A.S. for adjudication." Order No. 12 also provides for A.C.A.S. to appoint an arbitrator in the event of a failure to agree through the voluntary procedure.

The latter four agreements would seem, despite their references to industrial tribunals in the case of Nos. 1 and 3, to come under subs. (4) (*a*), since there appears to be a necessary resort to voluntary machinery prior to going to the industrial tribunal or A.C.A.S. This raises a problem already canvassed in the Note to subs. (1)—where the collective agreement is ambiguous as to coverage, it might be argued that it only " relates " to members of the organisations negotiating it— trade unions or employers' associations. In four exempted agreements (Nos. 4, 5, 6, 9) the only remedy available involves using a voluntary procedure set up by the parties—and in which only representatives of the organisations concerned are involved. Only in the case of Order No. 4 is provision explicitly made that, instead of the voluntary procedure: " if the claimant is not a member of a trade union party to this Agreement (the dispute) may be referred to an industrial tribunal." The question arises, therefore, whether there are workers and employers to whom the agreement " relates," yet who may be subject to procedures agreed and decisions made by organisations of which they are not members. Since non-membership in this context is not often taken with good grace, difficulties may very well arise.

Two further points may be borne in mind. First, where the industrial tribunal does hear a complaint from an employee covered by an exempt agreement, it will determine the entitlement in accordance with the terms of that agreement—not the Act. Voluntary procedures involving the negotiators themselves would probably be better qualified to adjudicate on questions of ambiguity, etc. Secondly, where the agreement provides for voluntary dispute settlement under subs. (4) (*a*), there is omitted the possibility of appeal to the E.A.T. under s. 136 (1) (*e*).

Subs. (5)

The Order may be varied or revoked without any application. Revocation or variation might be anticipated where, *e.g.* the statutory limits have been improved by Order (s. 15 (5)), where the agreement was found by the employees to be less satisfactory than expected, or in any general change of circumstances.

Suspension from work on medical grounds

Right to remuneration on suspension on medical grounds

19.—(1) An employee who is suspended from work by his employer on medical grounds in consequence of—

(*a*) any requirement imposed by or under any provision of any enactment or of any instrument made under any enactment, or

(*b*) any recommendation in any provisions of a code of practice issued or approved under section 16 of the Health and Safety at Work etc. Act 1974,

which is a provision for the time being specified in Schedule 1 shall, subject to the following provisions of this Act, be entitled to be paid by his employer remuneration while he is so suspended for a period not exceeding twenty-six weeks.

(2) For the purposes of this section and sections 20 to 22 and 61, an employee shall be regarded as suspended from work only if, and so long as, he continues to be employed by his employer, but is not provided with work or does not perform the work he normally performed before the suspension.

(3) The Secretary of State may by order add provisions to or remove provisions from the list of specified provisions in Schedule 1.

DERIVATION

    1975, s. 29 (1) to (3).

GENERAL NOTE

Subs. (1)

Excluded classes of employment. For classes of employment excluded from this provision, see ss. 138 (3) ; 141 (2) ; 143 (2), (3) ; 144 (2) ; 145 (2) ; 146 (1) and (2).

Suspension, dismissal and contract. The section certainly does not confer any right on the employer to suspend an employee on medical grounds. The employer's power to suspend depends on the contract of employment, which may or may not allow suspension in these circumstances. Note that the duty to supply a written statement under s. 1 expressly excludes the requirement that disciplinary rules and procedures relating to health and safety be stated (s. 1 (5)). Further, if the employer actually *dismisses* an employee on medical grounds, s. 64 (2) provides that even after only four weeks' employment, a complaint of unfair dismissal may be made, instead of the usual 26 weeks' qualification.

What are " medical grounds " ? The key question which defines the scope of the potential benefit under this section is: in what circumstances is an employee deemed to be suspended " on medical grounds." S. 20 (1) excludes workers who are incapable of work through illness or injury. It follows that employees suspended under this section need not be ill, although they are suspended " on medical grounds."

The provision can only refer to circumstances where, due to a *potential* danger to the employee's health (medical condition) he is prevented from working and in consequence is suspended. The suspension could be said to be " on medical grounds," *i.e.* is consequent on a potential danger to health. Only certain types of dangers, however, qualify as a " medical ground " for the purposes of this entitlement: those covered by either subs. (1) (*a*) or (*b*). So in practice, the dangers could arise from, *e.g.* lead compounds in a factory employing women or young people (Factories Act 1961, s. 75 (2)), or a faulty machine or a dangerous chemical process. In each case the potential threat to health might lead to an Employment Medical Adviser (see the Employment Medical Advisory Service Act 1972) or a factory inspector ordering the cessation of the danger—by stopping to employ women or young people, by shutting down the machine or halting the process. In each case the workers denied employment would be entitled to the benefits of this section—*if* the action was in consequence of either subs. (1) (*a*) or (*b*).

Finally, a question arises as to whether, *e.g.* E.E.C. Council Directive 77/576/EEC of July 25, 1977, O.J. L229/12 of September 7, 1977, on the approximation of laws, regulations and administrative provisions of the Member States relating to the provision of safety signs at places of work, would qualify under subs. (1) (*a*) to be included in Sched. 1.

Subs. (2)

The provision of work *other* than that which the employee performed before the suspension does not mean that the employee is not to be regarded as " suspended "— he still is from his original job: see Note to s. 20 (2).

Subs. (3)

The Government apparently does not intend that the provisions of all Codes of Practice issued or approved under s. 16 of the Health and Safety at Work, etc. Act 1974 will be covered by provisions included in Sched. 1. Since the enactment of the Employment Protection Act 1975, only the Radioactive Substances (Road Transport Workers) (Great Britain) (Amendment) Regulations 1975 have been added as a result of the Employment Protection (Medical Suspension) Order 1976 (S.I. 1976 No. 659). (Yet these are not specified in Sched. 1.)

General exclusions from right under s. 19

20.—(1) An employee shall not be entitled to remuneration under section 19 in respect of any period during which he is incapable of work by reason of disease or bodily or mental disablement.

(2) An employee shall not be entitled to remuneration under section 19 in respect of any period during which—

   (*a*) his employer has offered to provide him with suitable alternative work, whether or not work which the employee is under his contract, or was under the contract in force before the suspension, employed to perform, and the employee has unreasonably refused to perform that work; or

(*b*) he does not comply with reasonable requirements imposed by his employer with a view to ensuring that his services are available.

DERIVATION

1975, s. 30 (2) (3).

GENERAL NOTE

Subs. (1)

This might seem to exclude workers who are physically incapable of performing work. But where an employee is suspended because of a legal requirement, *e.g.* he possesses or acquires certain disabling characteristics or contracts a certain disease or condition which makes it unlawful for him to do certain work—then he may still be physically capable of *some* work. Subs. (2) appears to confirm this— the employee may be incapable of doing the work which he was required to do under his contract, but may be required to perform other suitable work. It would seem that in some circumstances of physical incapacity, the employee is nevertheless entitled to claim—particularly, one would have thought, where the disease or disability was contracted in the performance of his work. All the more so, where there is nothing physically wrong with him, but some legal requirement leads to suspension as work is not available—the employee is entitled to claim.

If employees are suspended solely because of physical incapacity, they must rely on any sickness benefits accruing under their contracts of employment (to be specified in the written statement of particulars—s. 1 (3) (*d*) (ii)) and any social security benefits.

Subs. (2)

Cf. the differences in wording with s. 13 (2), and see the Note on it. Here again the circumstances may dictate different criteria as to the suitability of alternative work and the reasonableness of any employee's refusal. Also, if the suspended employee accepts alternative work, he should not suffer for it in terms of any reduction in the level of his terms of employment.

Presumably, the acceptance of alternative work does not mean that the suspension is no longer in force—in s. 19 (2) the words " he normally performed before the suspension " qualify both " not provided with work " and " does not perform the work." Otherwise, it could be argued that the suspension had in fact become a dismissal.

As is the case with other similar provisions, the employee faced with an offer of suitable alternative employment is placed by the law at a fatal disadvantage *vis-à-vis* the employer. The employee stands to lose all if he " unreasonably " rejects " suitable alternative work," hence the pressure is on him to accept whatever the employer offers. The employer for his part may choose to offer what he likes— for even if the work offered is grossly unsuitable, the worker's only *legal* remedy is to go to the industrial tribunal, and the result is the employer having to pay only what he would have had to pay if the employee had simply been suspended in the first place. So he stands to lose nothing by an offer of unsuitable work. Workers usually consider methods other than the legal process to combat such employer practices; *e.g.* the employees' trade union must be consulted on the appropriateness of the offer, and may have to consent to it (see the Agreements referred to in the Note to s. 13 (2)).

Calculation of remuneration

21.—(1) The amount of remuneration payable by an employer to an employee under section 19 shall be a week's pay in respect of each week of the period of suspension referred to in subsection (1) of that section, and if in any week remuneration is payable in respect only of part of that week the amount of a week's pay shall be reduced proportionately.

(2) Subject to subsection (3), a right to remuneration under section 19 shall not affect any right of an employee in relation to remuneration under his contract of employment (in this section referred to as " contractual remuneration ").

(3) Any contractual remuneration paid by an employer to an employee in respect of any period shall go towards discharging the employer's liability under section 19 in respect of that period, and conversely any payment of remuneration in discharge of an employer's liability under section 19 in respect of any period shall go towards discharging any obligation of the employer to pay contractual remuneration in respect of that period.

DERIVATION
    1975, s. 31 (1), (3), (4).

GENERAL NOTE
Subs. (1)
    For definition of a week's pay, see Sched. 14, Pt. II. The calculation date is the day before the suspension begins—para. 7 (1) (*b*). " Week " is defined in s. 153 (1).

Subs. (3)
    Cf. ss. 16 (2), 27 (6), 31 (11) and 35 (4) which are substantially identical, except that the words used here are " discharging any obligation of the employer " instead of " discharging any liability of the employer." Similarly, a question arises here as to whether a day or other period, during which the remuneration owed under s. 19 is set-off by an employer's existing contractual obligation, is to count towards the 26 weeks maximum period specified in s. 19 (1). If the employee does not seek to enforce his statutory right but relies on his contractual rights, is he thereby to be deprived of some of his entitlement? If the answer under s. 16 (2) was no, the answer here should be consistent.

Complaint to industrial tribunal

22.—(1) An employee may present a complaint to an industrial tribunal that his employer has failed to pay the whole or any part of remuneration to which the employee is entitled under section 19.

(2) An industrial tribunal shall not entertain a complaint relating to remuneration under section 19 in respect of any day unless the complaint is presented to the tribunal before the end of the period of three months beginning with that day, or within such further period as the tribunal considers reasonable in a case where it is satisfied that it was not reasonably practicable for the complaint to be presented within the period of three months.

(3) Where an industrial tribunal finds a complaint under subsection (1) well-founded the tribunal shall order the employer to pay the complainant the amount of remuneration which it finds is due to him.

DERIVATION
    1975, s. 32.

GENERAL NOTE
    Though claims for remuneration due under s. 19 will frequently be for modest amounts and therefore not justify an employer going to the expense of defending himself against a complaint before an industrial tribunal (see the Note to s. 17), the maximum claim of 26 weeks' remuneration is potentially substantial. As yet, however, there is no claim reported in the I.R.L.R.s. Whether this betokens compliance by employers or ignorance by workers is unknown.

Trade union membership and activities

23.—(1) Subject to the following provisions of this section, every employee shall have the right not to have action (short of dismissal) taken against him as an individual by his employer for the purpose of—

(a) preventing or deterring him from being or seeking to become a member of an independent trade union, or penalising him for doing so; or

(b) preventing or deterring him from taking part in the activities of an independent trade union at any appropriate time, or penalising him for doing so; or

(c) compelling him to be or become a member of a trade union which is not independent.

(2) In this section " appropriate time ", in relation to an employee taking part in any activities of a trade union, means time which either—

(a) is outside his working hours, or

(b) is a time within his working hours at which, in accordance with arrangements agreed with, or consent given by his employer, it is permissible for him to take part in those activities;

and in this subsection " working hours ", in relation to an employee, means any time when, in accordance with his contract of employment, he is required to be at work.

(3) The provisions of subsection (4) shall have effect in relation to an employee—

(a) of the same class as employees for whom it is the practice in accordance with a union membership agreement to belong to a specified independent trade union or to one of a number of specified independent trade unions; or

(b) not of the same class as described in paragraph (a) but of the same grade or category as such employees as are referred to in that paragraph.

(4) In relation to such an employee the right conferred by subsection (1) (b) in relation to the activities of an independent trade union shall extend to activities on the employer's premises only if that union is a specified union.

(5) For the purposes of this section a trade union—

(a) shall be taken to be specified for the purposes of, or in relation to, a union membership agreement if it is specified in the agreement or is accepted by the parties to the agreement as being the equivalent of a union so specified; and

(b) shall also be treated as so specified if—

(i) the Advisory, Conciliation and Arbitration Service has made a recommendation for recognition of that union covering the employee in question which is operative within the meaning of section 15 of the Employment Protection Act 1975; or

(ii) the union has referred a recognition issue covering that employee to the Advisory, Conciliation and Arbitration Service under section 11 of the said Act of 1975 and the Service has not declined to proceed on the reference under section 12 of that Act, the union has not withdrawn the reference, or from the reference, and the issue has not been settled or reported on under that section.

(6) An employee who genuinely objects on grounds of religious belief to being a member of any trade union whatsoever shall have the right

not to have action (short of dismissal) taken against him by his employer for the purpose of compelling him to belong to a trade union.

(7) In this section, unless the context otherwise requires, references to a trade union include references to a branch or section of a trade union.

DERIVATION

1975, s. 53.

GENERAL NOTE

Subs. (1)

Action (short of dismissal). Dismissal for the purposes described here is declared unfair by s. 58. The scope of activity covered by the phrase " action (short of dismissal) " is not limited by any definition in the Act. It obviously includes forms of disciplinary action—suspension, transfer to less desirable work (see, *e.g. Robb* v. *Leon Motor Services Ltd.* [1978] I.R.L.R. 26 (E.A.T.)), demotion, withholding of bonuses, denial of pension benefits—in so far as these are permitted by the contract of employment. It *now* also includes *omissions*—see the definition of " action," formerly in TULRA, s. 30 (1), now imported into this Act, s. 153 (1). So, *e.g.* a failure by the employer to promote would fall within the prohibited sphere (see *Nassé* v. *Science Research Council* [1978] I.R.L.R. 352 (C.A.).

Threats. Bristow J. has hinted strongly (*Brassington* v. *Cauldon Wholesale Ltd.* [1977] I.R.L.R. 479 (E.A.T.)), though without deciding the issue, that *threats* (*e.g.* to close a business and dismiss the workforce if the company was required to recognise the union) might not amount to " action " prohibited by this subsection. The " formidable argument " to this effect by the judge consists of a dubious analogy with the distinction in s. 25 (2) between industrial action and threatening to take such, and the argument that " [D]ismissal is action, not threat "—though we are here concerned with action (*short* of dismissal). Where art thou, *Rookes* v. *Barnard*, in this our hour of need? Bristow J.'s approach is founded upon his conception that " the object of Parliament in conferring upon employees the (s. 23) right was clearly to discourage employers from unfairly trying to prevent union activity in their undertaking." The sporting theory of justice apparently might allow for employers " fairly "—through threats—to prevent union activity.

Law and the struggle for control at the workplace. Crude forms of anti-trade union activity are indulged in only by less sophisticated employers. This section was clearly intended to combat the more subtle methods of preventing or deterring the spread of trade unionism. The employer does not rely only on his superior position *vis-à-vis* the employee in an employment relationship governed by the ostensibly egalitarian individual contract. His position as owner and controller of the means of production—the power of property at the point of production and often outside it—enables him to take many actions *outside* that employment relationship which will prevent or deter trade unionism. But the law here prohibits only actions which will affect the employee's trade unionism *in the context* of the individual employment relationship, not in the broader arena of anti-union activity.

This narrower power of the employer in the context of the individual employment relationship to take action (short of dismissal) to prevent or deter trade unionism derives from two areas of the relationship which he controls by law: the first is his control over the workers' time (thus, *e.g.* in the Agreement between the Unions and Vauxhall Motors Ltd., dated June 1974, the chapter on Works Standards is called: " We Sell Our Time ") ; and the second, his control over the place of work, by virtue of property ownership.

The prohibition in this section on anti-trade union actions was regarded in its previous incarnation in the Industrial Relations Act 1971, s. 5, as being essentially a defence of the employee to specific actions of the employer which denied him certain benefits as a consequence of his trade union allegiance. The legal word which best described that defensive situation was discrimination. That was the word on which most litigation under the 1971 Act centred. The Court of Appeal has confirmed that s. 23 deals with such " discrimination " (*Nassé* v. *Science Research Council* [1978] I.R.L.R. 352).

But the emphasis is not *only* the defensive one of prohibiting actions of the employer which single out the individual employee for the purpose of denying him some tidbit from the employer's table. Rather the section prohibits any action which prevents or deters him from allegiance to a trade union. The velvet glove of bribery is prohibited, but so is the mailed fist of coercion. The employer's control over the employee's time and place of work, which in the past enabled him to actively combat trade unions, is vested in him by virtue of the contract of employment and the ownership of property. The employee now has a right with which to fight back—the statutory right not to have action (short of dismissal) taken against him as an individual by his employer for the purposes described in (a) to (c). Moreover, it is a right of offence. Where the employee seeks to do anything described in (a) to (c), the employer may take some action in return. Any action which the employer takes in response which prevents or deters the employee is prohibited.

Activities of an independent trade union. In considering the scope of the activities of trade unionists protected by this section, Phillips J. indicated the following general approach as correct (*Dixon* v. *West Ella Developments Ltd.* [1978] I.R.L.R. 151 (E.A.T.)) : " [the section] was intended, and must have been intended, to discourage employers from penalising participation in activities of a fairly varied kind, and that . . . should be reasonably and not too restrictively, interpreted." Generally speaking, employees may seek to recruit other employees (*Brennan* v. *Ellward* (*Lancs.*) *Ltd.* [1976] I.R.L.R. 378 (E.A.T.)), form a union branch (*Lyon* v. *St. James' Press* [1976] I.R.L.R. 215 (E.A.T.)), simply talk of trade union matters (*Zucker* v. *Astrid Jewels Ltd.* [1978] I.R.L.R. 385 (E.A.T.)), attend union meetings (*Miller* v. *Rafique* [1975] I.R.L.R. 70), sell papers or distribute literature, collect subscriptions or post notices.

Unquestionably, they are entitled to carry on these activities outside the employer's premises and outside working hours—any action of the employer which sought to deter or prevent them would obviously be prohibited by the section, if not by the general law. But a conflict may occur when the employee carries on these activities *on* the employer's premises or *in* working time. Heretofore, the rights of contract and property frequently enabled the employer to effectively subdue employees who were brave enough to make the attempt. Henceforth, the assertion of such rights by the employer for the purpose of such intimidation will be prohibited to the extent specified in the section. As the Minister of State, Department of Employment, pointed out in Committee—employers may not now ban recruiting during lunch hours or handing out leaflets in canteens. Other actions considered as being prohibited were the refusal of a right to stick a notice on a notice board or denial of the facility to advertise the meetings of the organisation (see Standing Committee F on the Employment Protection Bill 1975, 16th Sitting, June 26, 1975, at cols. 846 and 836–837, *per* Mr. A. Booth).

Activities of trade union officials and members. In practice, the activities of trade unionists will differ, as is appreciated by ss. 27–28, depending on whether the employee is a *member* or an *official* of a trade union (see the definition of " official " in s. 153 (1), referring to TULRA, s. 30 (1)). With regard to ordinary *members*, Phillips J. in *Dixon* (cited above) asserted that it was " strongly " arguable that seeking the advice of a union representative on the shop floor, and seeking to *apply* approved union practice fell, in certain circumstances, within the scope of protected activities (though there remains the question whether these activities were carried out at the " appropriate time "—see Note to subs. (2)). The danger that rears its head here is the tendency of some judges to insist on a close connection between the union member's action and the union machinery. They insist that trade *unionists'* activity is not necessarily trade *union* activity—and if the workers concerned are just " trouble makers " they will not be protected. Judges' definitions of " trouble makers " are, needless to say, extremely subjective. Workers should try, therefore, to associate themselves with the union as closely as possible in any activity. The irony here—and in labour law generally—is that in those cases they rarely need to rely on the law.

Union officials (shop stewards, office representatives, etc.) are obviously involved in a wider range of protected trade union activities. Phillips J. in *Marley Tile Co. Ltd.* v. *Shaw* [1978] I.R.L.R. 238 (E.A.T.) appeared to consider that such activities of a shop steward as taking up a member's grievance, seeing and pressing for a meeting with the employers, telephoning a full-time union official, and calling together members for a meeting during working hours—all these were protected activities, provided, again, that they took place at an " appropriate time."

Judges' attitudes to trade union activity. The judges seem prepared to acknowledge that trade union members have a right to apply union practice, and shop stewards to, *e.g.* call shopfloor meetings during working hours. But it is inevitable that judges will differ in *their* views of what is acceptable from what trade unionists consider to be accepted practice; *e.g.* in *Robb* (cited above) the steward was transferred to other work because he was " over-enthusiastic " in carrying out his trade union duties. Phillips J. held there was no claim: the action short of dismissal was because of the steward's " over-enthusiasm," not his trade union activities. Again, in *Marley Tile Co. Ltd.* (cited above) the steward was sacked for, among other things, calling a workplace meeting to discuss management's refusal to recognise his credentials. Phillips J. upheld the steward's action, but warned that this was a case of " only a short meeting, and there is no evidence that their coming together caused any disorganisation or difficulty, or that their duties were disrupted. Circumstances might well be different where what was done was with the intention of disrupting the production process."

Statements of this kind are reminiscent of those made by the House of Lords when it attempted to resolve the conflict between a similar statutory provision and the strict legal rights of the employer (*Post Office* v. *Crouch* [1974] 1 W.L.R. 89). The N.I.R.C.'s decision that the latter prevailed to the virtual extinction of the former was specifically overruled (p. 95G). But the House went on to throw its weight almost entirely behind the rights of the employer. The rights of workers and unions given in the statute (the Industrial Relations Act 1971, s. 5) were acceptable, but only as " minor infringements " of the employer's strict legal rights which do them no real harm." As such they could be tolerated, as long as the employer was as a consequence not obliged to incur expense or submit to any substantial inconvenience (pp. 96H–97A). It might have been hoped that this restrictive interpretation of a union's function would not survive its author, the late Lord Reid— for the subsequent enactment of this section does not adopt his narrow view. Still, in *Zucker* (cited above), Phillips J. expressly approved one aspect of the House of Lords' judgment of Lord Reid—that working hours did not include paid lunch breaks.

It may be too optimistic to hope that judges can rise above the view that employees and unions are more than mere encumbrances on the employer's legal rights, to be tolerated but restricted. Decisions which allow employees to be " fairly " dismissed when they, *e.g.* contacted their union and a factory inspector over an asbestos dust hazard (*Dixon*); or complained about the " Shops and Offices Act " poster not being properly displayed (*Gardner* v. *Peeks Retail Ltd.* [1975] I.R.L.R. 244) are bad enough. But worse is the attitude that comes out in judgments like that of Kilner Brown J. in *City of Birmingham District Council* v. *Beyer* [1977] I.R.L.R. 211 (E.A.T.): a blacklisted trade unionist had to resort to a false name to get a job, and was then sacked when recognised. The judge not only denied him any remedy for unfair dismissal, but went on to tell him that " he has only himself to blame," and advised him that " What he ought to do is to swallow his pride and apologise and ask the (employer) to give him another chance." Last, but not least, he is told that he has not been " sufficiently humble." The response of trade unionists to such attitudes is unprintable.

Time and place. The section does define the right granted the employee in relation to time—only " appropriate time " is covered by the right (see subs. (2)). But it should be noted that no restriction is imposed in terms of place. On the contrary, subs. (4) makes express provision for the right to take part in trade union activities to " extend to activities on the employer's premises." The employer's purchase of the employee's time by the contract of employment is held sacred, but his other principal means of control—ownership of the place of production—is restricted by the section. To allow the employer to ban such activity as is envisaged by subs. (1) (*a*) to (*c*) would emasculate the employee's statutory right. To enable him, because of the fact that he is acting on his own property, to do anything he wishes even though this may have the effect of preventing or deterring as described in subs. (1) would be to deny the provisions any force. The attempt by the N.I.R.C. to thus interpret a similar provision was rejected. The effect of the present provision, therefore, is twofold: first, it gives employees a positive right to engage in activities on the employer's premises pertaining to the descriptions in subs. (1) (*a*) to (*c*); and secondly, it prohibits any actions by the employer, previously justified by virtue of his contractual and property rights, which could have the effects described in subs. (1) (*a*) to (*c*).

Independent trade unionists only. *Cf.* s. 5 of the Industrial Relations Act 1971, especially s. 5 (2) (*c*) which is not re-enacted here. As in the 1971 Act the rights were limited to potential members of registered trade unions (s. 61 (3)), so in this Act the rights are limited to members or potential members of "independent" trade unions (see definition in s. 153 (1)). Organisations of workers not clearly independent would be well advised to register under s. 8 of TULRA and s. 8 of the 1975 Act in order to protect members and aspirants. Otherwise, doubts might arise which could only be resolved when a complaint was lodged under s. 24. The proceedings might then be stayed as required by s. 8 (12) of the 1975 Act, while the Certification Officer decided the question of "independence" (which requires registration—s. 8 (4)).

Exclusions. Finally, even then certain classes of employment are excluded from the benefits of this provision—see ss. 138 (3), 141 (2), 144 (2), and 146 (1) (2).

Subs. (2)

"Appropriate time" is defined for similar purposes in s. 58 (2) which concerns dismissal relating to trade union membership (but note the difference in one word: the article "*the*" is used instead of "*any* activities of a trade union." *Cf.* s. 77 (10) where the definition of "appropriate time" for the purposes of interim relief against unfair dismissal is that of this subsection.

Becoming a trade union member. It would appear that, *e.g.* employees seeking to become members of a union (subs. (1) (*a*)) are not to be restricted to "appropriate time." There is, of course, a great difference between the activities of seeking to form a union or join one, and the activities of day-to-day union business. The Act seems to extend special protection to the former. So even where the employee seeks to join a union *outside* the "appropriate time," he may be protected to some extent. Once a member, however, he must restrict his activities to the "appropriate time."

Employer's implied consent to activities. While it is clear from the definition that the right to take part in union activities *during* working hours depends entirely on the consent of the employer, this consent need not be expressly or formally given. It can be *implied* from various circumstances. This is the principle which emerged from the vital decision in *Marley Tile Co. Ltd.* v. *Shaw* [1978] I.R.L.R. 238 (E.A.T.). Speaking for the unanimous tribunal, Phillips J. rejected the argument that express consent or express arrangements for trade union activities during working hours are needed. He said: "this legislation must be construed against the background of industry as it is organised in practice." Where unions are not *fully* recognised by management, there is unlikely to be such formal arrangements—yet scope will even then normally be given to shop stewards to carry out their functions. So the Act protects trade union activities during working hours where such informal arrangements can be *implied*: "It is implied by the basic willingness of the management to work together with the union." So, *e.g.* raising grievances on behalf of members is protected activity even during working hours.

This view was expressly confirmed in *Zucker* v. *Astrid Jewels Ltd.* [1978] I.R.L.R. 385 (E.A.T.). There it was found that the employers had impliedly consented to allow employees to talk of trade union matters while working at their machines (since they were allowed to converse generally). So subject to reversal by higher authority, this seems now to be the law.

Withdrawal of implied consent. An important issue is whether this implied consent to take part in trade union activities during working hours can be revoked on specific occasions. So while the shop steward might generally be allowed to function, on one specific occasion he might be ordered not to carry out his duties. Has consent thus been withdrawn so that the statutory protection no longer applies?

It need hardly be stressed that this is fundamental—if employers can unilaterally withdraw the protection at will, much of the benefit will be lost to workers. The *Marley Tile Co. Ltd.* case is interesting on this point. A majority of the E.A.T. (Phillips J. and one member) agreed that the shop steward's "summoning of the meeting of the maintenance men and the telephoning of the (full time official) *did* take place at an appropriate time . . . because . . . the implied consent of management arising out of *the general relationship of management and union in a factory* must, we would have thought, in real industrial relations terms, allow for some unusual situations where the shop steward would wish to inform his members during working hours of an unexpected development" (my emphasis). But a different majority (Phillips J. and the other member) explicitly denied that express consent was forthcoming on that specific occasion. On the contrary, the employers had remained silent in the face of the steward's activity and " the meeting ended suddenly and on a sour note." So consent could not be deduced from their silence. *Nonetheless, consent was to be implied from the general relationship.* This is more than a " silence is not consent " case. Even an indication of dissent by the employer (the " sour note ") did not revoke the protection of the Act.

Industrial action. In contrast, in *Brennan* v. *Ellward (Lancs.) Ltd.* [1976] I.R.L.R. 378 (E.A.T.) Phillips J. held that " appropriate time " " cannot extend to the activities of employees in suddenly downing tools and leaving the premises in order to consult their union officials elsewhere, and wherever they may happen to be." Here they had been warned that they would be dismissed if they left the site in the middle of the work to go and consult the union. The distinction with *Marley Tile Co. Ltd.*, it is submitted, seems to be in whether the workers are engaged in legitimate discussions or inquiries, or whether they are engaged in industrial action. In the *Marley Tile Co. Ltd.* case, the employer may not withdraw the Act's protection where industrial relations practice allows for such activity. In *Brennan,* the court simply would not countenance legislative protection for industrial action (remember in the *Marley Tile Co. Ltd.* case Phillips J. stipulated that " circumstances might well be different where what was done was with the intention of disrupting the production process "). There is, of course, no statutory provision excluding industrial action from coverage by this section (as there is in s. 28 (2) for example). And see *Winnett* v. *Seamarks Brothers Ltd.* [1978] I.R.L.R. 387 (E.A.T.).

Industrial relations v. *the contract approach.* Vain though the hope may be (in light of *Western Excavating (E.C.C.) Ltd.* v. *Sharp* [1978] I.R.L.R. 27 (C.A.), the industrial relations approach evinced in the cases cited above is to be preferred to the strict legal contractual approach. The latter is found in some previous cases; *e.g. Robb* v. *Leon Motor Services Ltd.* [1978] I.R.L.R. 26 (E.A.T.), where the terms of the employee's contract were examined to see if they could be held to infer consent by the employer (there was a reference to trade union activities at the appropriate time). But perhaps this was because, as Phillips J. said " there is no doubt that (the) union was not recognised by the employers." *Cf. Miller* v. *Rafique* [1975] I.R.L.R. 70, where the employer's initial consent *was* held to be a term of the contract, and could not be unilaterally revoked.

If the employment protection laws were to be forced into the straitjacket of contract law, the only hope at *law* for workers would be implied terms under the new " changing social conditions " test. See for an example in the time off during working hours context, *Warner* v. *Barbers Stores* [1978] I.R.L.R. 110 (E.A.T.), where the E.A.T. stated that " it is true that in these days there is either an express or implied term in many contracts of employment that there should be reasonable time off in an emergency." In practice, workers will usually opt for self-reliance, not the law.

Working hours. The issue of consent is central to trade union activity during working hours. But " working hours " are themselves the subject of definition in this subsection. In *Zucker* v. *Astrid Jewels Ltd.* [1978] I.R.L.R. 385 (E.A.T.), Phillips J. re-asserted the authority of *Post Office* v. *U.P.W.* [1974] I.R.L.R. 23 (H.L.). So an employee is not necessarily required to be at work merely because he is on the premises or even when he is on the premises during a time when he is being paid. So, ordinarily, tea-breaks, lunch breaks, etc., are times when employees are paid, but are not required to be at work. The employer's consent is not, therefore, needed for trade union activities on his premises at these times.

The judgment of Kilner Brown J. in *City of Birmingham District Council* v. *Beyer* [1977] I.R.L.R. 211 (E.A.T.) has been referred to in the Note to subs. (1). It was decided there that the union activity protected by this section " could not conceivably refer to activities outside and before the employment began." The industrial tribunal at first instance had thought it quite conceivable. So the judge asserted that the employer was free to sack the employee who had previously engaged actively in trade union activities, and for his pains been put on an employers' blacklist—he only obtained employment in the case in question by resorting to a false name. The judge in a burst of candour exclaimed: " there is no place on earth where it is correct to say that a man has a right to a job "; and " there is nothing in the legislation which we have to administer which lays down that an employer may not refuse to employ a man unless he has reasonable grounds for refusing. This may come about one day, but it is not the law at present." (One awaits with interest this judge's decisions in cases involving the closed shop and race or sex discrimination.) The judge's sympathy with an employer's right to reject workers on anti-union grounds seems to have misled him here, a case of dismissal, not refusal to employ. One hopes, therefore, that the courts may adopt a different view as to whether *only* union activities after employment has commenced are protected.

Subss. (3) and (4)

Closed shop. The rights conferred by this section are restricted where there is a union membership agreement to certain employees described in subs. (3) (*a*) and (*b*) (for further definition see that of "union membership agreement" in s. 153 (1), which refers to TULRA, s. 30 (5A), so reproducing the effect of s. 126 (4) of the 1975 Act). As mentioned above, the right of employees to take part in activities on the employer's premises is here confirmed (subs. (4)). Employees who are dissatisfied with their union may have difficulty in agitating to get rid of it—they will be unprotected if they discard their union membership, which will in addition be grounds for dismissal where there is a closed shop. But this is subject to there being a "practice"—which raises considerable difficulties of proof—see Note to s. 58 (3).

Subs. (5)

Multi-union recognition. This provision attempts to ensure that employees are protected in a situation where one powerful union obtains a closed shop agreement where other unions are either accepted in the workplace ((*a*)) or have been recommended for recognition by A.C.A.S. ((*b*) (i)) or potentially may be ((*b*) (ii)). The A.C.A.S. recommendation must be "operative"—see s. 15 (1) of the 1975 Act. Where a union is neither accepted, nor recommended or in the process of being recommended for recognition, the union membership agreement operates to allow the employer to do acts otherwise prohibited by the section. Subs. (5) (*b*) (ii) is somewhat loosely drafted so that it would appear that a union whose reference had been declined by the A.C.A.S. could instantly make another so as to remain within the subsection and thus protect its members. Whether a court would uphold this view should an employee claim a remedy under s. 24 remains to be seen.

It is singularly unfortunate that there exists with regard to *dismissal* for trade union activities a substantially similar provision to this subsection, but which is worded in slightly but crucially different form—see s. 58 (4). As employees here are to be protected against various acts of the employer, so there they were to be protected against dismissal. However, the equivalent of subs. (5) (*a*) is absent, and the equivalent of subs. (5) (*b*) (i) differs in that it omits the words "of that union" which are present here—thus apparently allowing any union to benefit where the employee in question is covered by a recommendation regarding any other union.

Subs. (6)

See the substantially identical provision in s. 58 (3).

Complaint to industrial tribunal

24.—(1) An employee may present a complaint to an industrial tribunal on the ground that action has been taken against him by his employer in contravention of section 23.

(2) An industrial tribunal shall not entertain a complaint under subsection (1) unless it is presented to the tribunal before the end of the period of three months beginning with the date on which there occurred the action complained of, or where that action is part of a series of similar actions, the last of those actions, or within such further period as the tribunal considers reasonable in a case where it is satisfied that it was not reasonably practicable for the complaint to be presented within the period of three months.

(3) Where the tribunal finds the complaint well-founded it shall make a declaration to that effect and may make an award of compensation, calculated in accordance with section 26, to be paid by the employer to the employee in respect of the action complained of.

DERIVATION
  1975, s. 54.

GENERAL NOTE
  The inadequacy of compensation as a remedy is brought home particularly in the case envisaged in subs. (2) of repeated actions by the employer, the final one of which is the determinant of the limitation period. Where the employer has been consistently in breach of the section, the remedy is not the obvious one of an order requiring him to cease and desist from his prohibited action, but rather an order of compensation to the employee. The common law's traditional perception of employment rights as matters of individual concern only are applied even where, as is most obviously the case here, the infringement is a matter of collective concern. Trade union rights are the subject of the employer's prohibited activity, yet the remedy aims solely at individual compensation. In the case of breach of the individual contract of employment this is more comprehensible than where it is a question of violation of statutory provisions granting essentially collective rights in pursuit of a clear policy of encouraging collective bargaining. The employer may continue to victimise the worker at will—he will simply have to pay for it in the traditional manner. The fact that an employer may " buy " himself out of a trade union is not lost on workers. The consequence is that, whenever possible, workers will rely on their own industrial strength to protect themselves from such anti-trade union discrimination. The cases which reach industrial tribunals will be those where this self-reliance is inadequate to deal with the powerful and intransigent employer.

Supplementary provisions relating to complaints under s. 24

  25.—(1) On a complaint under section 24 it shall be for the employer to show—
  (*a*) the purpose for which action was taken against the complainant; and
  (*b*) that the purpose was not such a purpose as is referred to in section 23 (1) (*a*) to (*c*) or (6).

  (2) In determining on a complaint under section 24, any question as to whether action was taken by the complainant's employer or the purpose for which it was taken, no account shall be taken of any pressure which, by calling, organising, procuring or financing a strike or other industrial action, or threatening to do so, was exercised on the employer to take the action complained of, and that question shall be determined as if no such pressure had been exercised.

DERIVATION
  1975, s. 55 (1) (2).

GENERAL NOTE
  Subs. (1)
  Burden of proof. The Court of Appeal in *Nassé* v. *Science Research Council* [1978] I.R.L.R. 352 has confirmed that, unlike cases of discrimination on the ground of sex or race, in the words of Lord Denning: " The burden of proof is . . . on the employer in the case of discrimination on the ground of trade union activities " (para. 36). The employee needs show that the action (short of dismissal) took place. Thereafter, it is for the employer to show the purpose for which the action was taken, and that it was not one prohibited by s. 23. The employer will have to show both that the purpose was not one within s. 23 (1) (*a*) to (*c*), and also that it did not prevent or deter or compel as there envisaged.
  Disclosure of confidential documents. But the burden of proof is often *only* a procedural formality. The employee will usually be faced with an employer asserting a legitimate purpose for the action. The employee will, therefore, effectively be faced with the task of disproving the employer's alleged purpose and disclosing the real anti-union purpose. To this end, documentation may well be crucial.
  Unfortunately, the *Nassé* case (cited above) has restricted disclosure of " confidential " documentation to very rare cases, as a last resort, where the chairman of

the industrial tribunal decides it is in the interests of justice, the public interest, that it should be disclosed. As in other cases of public interest, however, the judicial definition is hopelessly subjective and, alas, conventionally biased towards employers. So Lord Denning warns that disclosure of anti-trade union confidences " might lead to much disturbance and unrest " (para. 44); and Lawton L.J. that " it might cause a strike; and for a certainty it would cause difficulties for the foreman " (para. 50).

It is, perhaps, unfortunate that the issue arose in a case where it was lumped together with issues of disclosure in cases of sex discrimination and race discrimination. Thus Lord Denning clearly regarded his denial of confidential documents as justified by virtue of its balancing the " immense powers already granted by Parliament to the statutory Commissions " (Equal Opportunity Commission; Commission for Racial Equality) (para. 42). Nothing of the sort exists to protect trade unionists from anti-union discrimination—but Lord Denning felt free to dismiss the problem by saying: " the trade unions can look after their side " (para. 25). While part of the conventional wisdom, it should not go unchallenged.

Most revealing, however, is Lord Denning's insistence on " fairness, too, to the public services and industrial concerns of this country. They have to cope with the problems of discrimination, and should be trusted to deal with them fairly " (para. 46). This is nonsense: it is the *workers* who have to cope with the problems; the employers *create* them. And if the employers could be trusted, the legislation would not be necessary.

Action against non-union employees. During the Committee stage considering the predecessor to this provision in the Employment Protection Bill 1975, the Government undertook to amend s. 23 (6) which, it was argued, effectively required employers to show a negative—*i.e.* that the employee had no such genuine religious belief. No amendment was produced, however, and accordingly it would seem that employers will have to establish both that the purpose was not to compel the employee to join the trade union and also that the employee had no such belief. (See the discussion in Standing Committee F on the Employment Protection Bill, 17th Sitting, June 26, 1975, cols. 893–896.)

Anti-union action to safeguard national security. Replacing the former s. 55 (3) and (4) of the 1975 Act, there is special provision in Sched. 9, para. 2, for complaints under this section where the action (short of dismissal) taken is said to be " for the purpose of safeguarding national security." The law does not blush from identifying anti-union activity with safeguarding national security. The dangers posed by such activity may, it seems, be of various grades. Some lead to dismissal, but others, lesser dangers, only to action short of dismissal. In either event the embarrassing questions raised by these provisions are not to be canvassed before industrial tribunals. Perhaps we might have begun to witness the use of these provisions now that ASTMS has declared its interest in recruiting in the armed forces. The Ministry of Defence has already taken the step of banning any advertising promoting such recruitment in military magazines. But the otherwise defenceless military is protected from this threat by s. 138 (3).

Reasonableness in the circumstances. A final point: there is no express requirement, as in s. 57 (3), that the employer should have acted reasonably in the circumstances, though such a requirement may be understood to be implicit.

Subs. (2)

   Cf. s. 63.

Assessment of compensation on a complaint under s. 24

26.—(1) The amount of the compensation awarded by a tribunal on a complaint under section 24 shall be such amount as the tribunal considers just and equitable in all the circumstances having regard to the infringement of the complainant's right under section 23 by the employer's action complained of and to any loss sustained by the complainant which is attributable to that action.

(2) The said loss shall be taken to include—

   (a) any expenses reasonably incurred by the complainant in consequence of the action complained of, and (*b*) loss of any benefit which he might reasonably be expected to have had but for that action.

(3) In ascertaining the said loss the tribunal shall apply the same rule concerning the duty of a person to mitigate his loss as applies to damages recoverable under the common law of England and Wales or of Scotland, as the case may be.

(4) In determining the amount of compensation to be awarded under subsection (1), no account shall be taken of any pressure as is referred to in section 25 (2), and that question shall be determined as if no such pressure had been exercised.

(5) Where the tribunal finds that the action complained of was to any extent caused or contributed to by any action of the complainant it shall reduce the amount of the compensation by such proportion as it considers just and equitable having regard to that finding.

DERIVATION

1975, s. 56.

GENERAL NOTE

Subs. (1)

Compensation for loss and infringement. When the Employment Protection Bill 1975 was first published, the Government not only provided simply the inadequate remedy of compensation (see Note to s. 24), but based it *solely* on the *loss* suffered by the employee—a basis rejected by the Government as inadequate for unfair dismissal in another part of the Bill. This retrograde step was, however, remedied at the Report Stage when the provision was amended to provide for compensation *not only* for loss, but *also* for the employer's infringement of the complainant's rights under s. 23.

However, no directions (apart from those in subss. (4) and (5)) are given to the tribunal as to how to go about calculating the compensation payable for the employer's illegal act, as opposed to that payable for the loss caused to the employee (for which see subss. (2) and (3)). In *Brassington* v. *Cauldon Wholesale Ltd.* [1977] I.R.L.R. 479 (E.A.T.), the industrial tribunal awarded only one day's pay—to compensate the workers concerned for their travelling expenses and subsistence while attending the hearing that determined their complaint. This result was quashed by the E.A.T. which asserted that compensation should cover not *only* expenses (subs. (2) (*a*)) but any benefit lost (subs. (2) (*b*)). But the change noted in the previous paragraph—the reference to compensation by reason of the *infringement itself*—was rejected as being of no account: " so for infringement of the [s. 23] right, compensation for the employee, not a fine on the employer, however tactfully wrapped up, is the basis of the discretionary monetary award " (para. 22). Bristow J. went on to instance certain compensable injuries: " the stress engendered by such a situation might easily cause injury to health "; the frustration of the " deep and sincere wish to join a union, with all the benefits of help and advice which that might entail " (para. 33). A trade unionist would not know whether to laugh or cry at this. An approach based on quasi-religious feeling is apparent elsewhere: see Kilner Brown J.'s reference to " preaching the gospel " of trade unionism in *City of Birmingham District Council* v. *Beyer* [1977] I.R.L.R. 211 (E.A.T.); Phillips J.'s characterisation of the shop steward as having " all the over-enthusiasm of a recent convert " in *Robb* v. *Leon Motor Services Ltd.* [1978] I.R.L.R. 26 (E.A.T.). It is perhaps amusing, but not realistic, to approach the questions raised by the provisions in this way.

Parallel with other statutory remedies. Instead, certain factors should be brought to the attention of the tribunals. For example, a provision substantially identical to the one here is found in s. 30 (2) relating to compensation for an employer's failure to allow time off for trade union activities and trade union and public duties as required by ss. 27–29. Thus, for instance, compensation is to be awarded for violation of the statute and for loss consequent on that violation where an employer denies an employee time off to take part in certain trade union activities (s. 28 (1)). It is obvious that where the employer's violation is in addition one falling within s. 23 (1)—*i.e.* for the purpose of deterrence or prevention—the compensation payable will be even higher.

This example indicates, perhaps, the kinds of factors the tribunals should be taking into account. For it is clear that the violation envisaged by s. 23 is of a familiar type. It is the equivalent of dismissal for trade union membership or activities on the different level of action (short of dismissal). For guidance as to the appropriate remedies one need seek no further than the equivalent remedies for unfair dismissal in such circumstances. As prescribed in ss. 68–76, an equivalent procedure would be as follows: the tribunal would first ask the employer if he is willing to withdraw from his action where this is appropriate. If he does, the tribunal may simply award an amount which consists of benefits lost to the employee in the interim (ss. 68–69). If the employer does not fully withdraw, the tribunal would award compensation as it sees fit (s. 71 (1)). If the employer refuses to revoke his illegal action, the tribunal would make an award of compensation consisting of: (i) a special sum because of the special and illegal purpose of the employer's action—denial of trade union rights (s. 71 (2) (*b*) (i) and (3) (*a*)); (ii) another award of compensation calculated to parallel the " basic award " granted under s. 73; and (iii) compensation for loss caused due to the employer's illegal act (see Note to subs. (2)). Unlike the provisions governing unfair dismissal, there is no maximum to the amount which may be awarded under this section. This is an indication of the seriousness of the violation envisaged—an employer intimidating his employee in this way is attacking the basis of collective bargaining on which the system of industrial relations in the U.K. is built and on which the entire Act is premised. Tribunals are to be encouraged to provide every incentive to employers not to act in that manner.

Subs. (2)

It is, of course, illusory to hope to assess such loss with any degree of precision. Too many variables and intangibles are involved. Certain benefits denied: demotion, suspension, bonuses, pensions, are relatively easily quantifiable. But how does one assess other rewards of trade unionism? In a clause dropped from the original Employment Protection Bill 1975, various criteria were suggested, *inter alia*, for inclusion: (cl. 50 (3))

" (*a*) the extent (if any) to which his terms and conditions of employment are or were less favourable than they might reasonably have been expected to be if he (or he and other employees of the same employer) had not been so prevented or deterred, and

(*b*) any advice or assistance (whether by representing him in negotiations or other dealings with his employer or otherwise) which might have been given to him by that trade union, any opportunities for training or education or other benefit of which he has been deprived, and any handicaps to which he may reasonably be expected to be subject in seeking future employment, by reason of his having been so prevented or deterred."

How these were to be quantified in money terms was left to the discretion of the tribunal. Clearly the assessment which must be made will be contentious.

Subs. (3)

This is identical to the provisions relating to unfair dismissal compensation in s. 74 (4).

Subs. (4)

Cf. s. 74 (5) which is substantially identical.

Subs. (5)

Cf. s. 74 (6) which is substantially identical.

Time off work

Time off for carrying out trade union duties

27.—(1) An employer shall permit an employee of his who is an official of an independent trade union recognised by him to take time off, subject to and in accordance with subsection (2), during the employee's working hours for the purpose of enabling him—

(a) to carry out those duties of his as such an official which are concerned with industrial relations between his employer and any associated employer, and their employees; or

(b) to undergo training in aspects of industrial relations which is—
  (i) relevant to the carrying out of those duties; and
  (ii) approved by the Trades Union Congress or by the independent trade union of which he is an official.

(2) The amount of time off which an employee is to be permitted to take under this section and the purposes for which, the occasions on which and any conditions subject to which time off may be so taken are those that are reasonable in all the circumstances having regard to any relevant provisions of a Code of Practice issued by the Advisory, Conciliation and Arbitration Service under section 6 of the Employment Protection Act 1975.

(3) An employer who permits an employee to take time off under this section for any purpose shall, subject to the following provisions of this section, pay him for the time taken off for that purpose in accordance with the permission—

(a) where the employee's remuneration for the work he would ordinarily have been doing during that time does not vary with the amount of work done, as if he had worked at that work for the whole of that time;

(b) where the employee's remuneration for that work varies with the amount of work done, an amount calculated by reference to the average hourly earnings for that work.

(4) The average hourly earnings referred to in subsection (3) (b) shall be the average hourly earnings of the employee concerned or, if no fair estimate can be made of those earnings, the average hourly earnings for work of that description of persons in comparable employment with the same employer or, if there are no such persons, a figure of average hourly earnings which is reasonable in the circumstances.

(5) Subject to subsection (6), a right to be paid any amount under subsection (3) shall not affect any right of an employee in relation to remuneration under his contract of employment (in this section referred to as " contractual remuneration ").

(6) Any contractual remuneration paid to an employee in respect of a period of time off to which subsection (1) applies shall go towards discharging any liability of the employer under subsection (3) in respect of that period, and conversely any payment of any amount under subsection (3) in respect of a period shall go towards discharging any liability of the employer to pay contractual remuneration in respect of that period.

(7) An employee who is an official of an independent trade union recognised by his employer may present a complaint to an industrial tribunal that his employer has failed to permit him to take time off as required by this section or to pay him the whole or part of any amount so required to be paid.

DERIVATIONS
1975, s. 57 (1) (2) (4)—(8).

GENERAL NOTE
Subs. (1)
  Excluded classes of employment. This section came into effect on April 1, 1978. Certain classes of employment are excluded wholesale from this most important right—see ss. 138 (3); 141 (2); 144 (2); 146 (1) (2) and most importantly s. 146 (4), which deprives many part-time workers (mostly women) of the benefit of union representation.

" Officials." " Official " is defined by s. 153 (1) as having the same meaning as in TULRA, s. 30 (1). Thus anybody who is elected or appointed to be a representative of the members of an " independent " trade union (see final paragraph of the Note to s. 23 (1)) in accordance with the union's rules qualifies for this right to time off during " working hours " (defined in s. 32 (1) (*b*)). Examples would be shop stewards, staff representatives, branch secretaries, and safety representatives appointed under s. 2 (4) of the Health and Safety at Work, etc. Act 1974. The T.U.C.'s Guide on Time Off advises that the provisions for paid time off " extend to conference delegates, trainee delegates, National Executive Committee members, Regional/District Committee members and to members of all other policy committees within unions," as well as delegates to T.U.C. bodies, Trades Councils, and Industrial Training Boards, Health and Safety Advisory Committees, regional Economic Planning Committees, Sector Working Parties, Economic Development Committees and trade union members nominated or appointed to other bodies concerned with industrial matters. To give some idea of the scope of these provisions, there are over 11 million trade union members in Great Britain, and perhaps as many as 300,000 of these act as lay officials for their union.

" Recognised " trade unions. Only officials of " recognised " trade unions are entitled to time off under this section. " Recognised " is defined in s. 32 (1) (*a*) and (2) in terms formally identical to those in s. 62 (*a*) of the Employment Protection Act 1975 (in turn deriving from the definition of " recognition " in s. 11 (2) of that Act). Under the Employment Protection Act 1975, s. 126 (1), the term " collective bargaining " became a term of art. As defined here in s. 32 (2), it is confined to instances of negotiation over specific issues—those relating to or connected with one or more of the matters specified in s. 29 (1) of TULRA. The implication is that issues, apart from those in s. 29 (1), will not in themselves qualify a trade union as " recognised " for the purposes of collective bargaining over those issues, and thus enable officials of that trade union to become eligible for the right to time off contained in this section.

There are many arguments for not confining collective bargaining to the issues specified in s. 29 (1) of TULRA (see those in the Note to s. 11 (2) of the Employment Protection Act 1975 in the *Encyclopedia of Labour Relations Law*). The implications of such a restrictive definition are evident in cases concerning the right of a " recognised " trade union to be consulted over proposed redundancies under s. 99 (1) of the 1975 Act. An exemplar of these is *Joshua Wilson and Bros. Ltd.* v. *U.S.D.A.W.* [1978] I.R.L.R. 120 (E.A.T.). Reviewing the cases, Kilner Brown J. points to the issues of collective bargaining specified in s. 29 (1) of TULRA and concludes, " that there has to be clear and unequivocal evidence of one or more of these matters before an industrial tribunal should find in fact that there was recognition " (para. 5).

The " clear and unequivocal evidence " required for recognition need not be a formal act, oral or in writing. In *Joshua Wilson and Bros Ltd.* (above) the following features of the employer-trade union relationship were observed: the employees concerned were members of the trade union; the employers followed the relevant J.I.C. Agreement; the company had allowed the union representative to put up a notice publicising a wage increase agreed by the J.I.C.; the union representative had been consulted over changes with regard to allocation of duties; he had been permitted to collect union dues on the company's premises; and there was evidence of direct consultation between management and the area organiser of the union over security and discipline. Taken together, all these matters amounted to recognition by the company of the union. All these matters were within the issues specified in s. 29 (1) of TULRA. If that definition is to confine this section, other contacts between the trade union and the employer could not be invoked to support a contention that the union had been recognised.

Duties. This requirement of " recognition " applies *only* for the purpose of identifying the officials who are eligible for the right. Note: the right accrues to all officials of the trade union once the trade union is recognised. The *official* need not be " recognised " by the employer, only the trade union. Once the trade union is " recognised," the officials, recognised or not, have the right to time off (*cf.* s. 28 (2)). Also the scope of " recognition " does not qualify the purposes for which time off may be taken. These are defined in (*a*) and (*b*) and, subject to subs. (2), cover a potentially wide range—virtually any of his duties concerned with industrial relations affecting his employer, any associated employer and their employees. In their representational role stewards may be involved in ironing out problems over, *e.g.* discipline, grading, arrangement of working time, efficiency of working arrangements, interpretation of agreements, errors in pay, bonus payments, superiors' attitudes, union activity, provision of protective clothing, health and safety matters as well as negotiating on a host of other matters to further their members' interests and protect them from managements' power (see (1978) 16 B.J.I.R. 160–174). In addition, it would be incorrect to regard this section as restricting officials to, *e.g.* collective bargaining duties with the employer on matters which affected their members only. The duties of the official to protect and safeguard the interests of his members may require him to participate in the planning of strategy as well as negotiating sessions where groups of workers other than those he represents are concerned, but where the results of that bargaining will affect the interests of his members. Co-ordination of bargaining may require attendance at meetings of joint committees of shop stewards at a plant or of combined committees from a number of plants, union district committees or delegate conferences. As the T.U.C. Guide recommends: " the more representative work that a union representative has, the more paid time off should be given and, for example, senior stewards and convenors should be granted additional time off above that available to shop stewards."

A point should be made here about para. 13 of the Code of Practice (see Note to subs. (2)) which describes trade union officials' duties concerned with industrial relations. It states: " an official's duties are those duties pertaining to his or her role in the jointly agreed procedures or customary arrangements for consultation, collective bargaining and grievance handling, where such matters concern the employer and any associated employer and their employees." Any temptation to regard this as a definition should be resisted. The Code is designed to provide practical guidance, not legal definitions. It cannot be read as an " interpretation " section to s. 27. The flexibility of the guidance is exemplified by the fact that the purposes for which time off is to be permitted include, according to the examples given in para. 13, duties such as appearing before industrial tribunals, which might not fall within the sentence quoted above. There is no strict requirement, then, that the duties be " jointly agreed " or " customarily arranged." Just as the absence of formal agreement does not preclude time off (para. 10), so the absence of such agreement over what is included in " trade union duties " does not preclude the trade union official from taking time off to perform them.

A final point: industrial relations does not mean collective bargaining only. It is much wider than that, and might include duties which related to certain internal union affairs. Shop stewards have an organisational (*e.g.* educating the membership, recruitment) and informational (*e.g.* informing the members of branch and national business, passing on problems) side to their work, as well as representational work. Maintenance of the union as an institution at the workplace, and indeed as an effective body representing employees in relations with the employer on the whole spectrum of issues, can hardly be held to be unrelated to industrial relations between the employer and his employees. Shop stewards and other union officials, when employees, should not have to labour to maintain good industrial relations between employees and the employer on Sundays, evenings, work-breaks and moments that must be snatched from family and leisure life. They are here given the right to take the time required during working hours, and industrial relations can only benefit from the result.

Training. Training for which time off is permitted may be approved by the trade union of which the official is a member or the T.U.C. In 1976–77, the first year in which a grant was made, £400,000 was made available jointly by the Department of Employment and the Department of Education and Science to the T.U.C. towards the cost of trade union education and training by the T.U.C. and affiliated trade unions. In 1977–78 the figure was £650,000. The adequacy of this amount may be gauged by the previously mentioned number of 300,000 lay representatives eligible for such training. The T.U.C. *Guide to Paid Release for Union Training* proposes a four-stage system of trade union courses. Stage 1 (induction training) should introduce the newly elected official to his or her role and functions as a union representative; explain the arrangements for collective bargaining; the agreements that exist; and the operation of procedures and methods of handling grievances. Stage 2 (basic introductory courses) should provide officials with in-depth training in their union role; in the skills and knowledge required to conduct bargaining, and handle grievances effectively; in understanding and becoming skilled in resolving disciplinary issues and matters affecting job security; in understanding employment laws and rights at work issues; in organising a safer workplace for their members; in appreciating and using other legal rights, such as disclosure of information for bargaining purposes; and in understanding new developments in industrial relations such as the movement towards industrial democracy. Stage 3 (further training and up-dating training) provides for representatives with special responsibilities, e.g. senior representatives, representatives with standing special responsibilities on safety and pensions, company board members, and representatives appointed for short-term special duties, e.g. to examine with management the implications of introducing a new wage structure. Courses might involve acquiring knowledge about new legislation, standard management techniques, company accounts, health and safety, work-study and job evaluation —and obtaining skills required in analysing and using such information. Stage 4 would provide advanced training to key representatives: longer periods of intensive general studies on trade union and industrial relations subjects.

In addition it should be noted that a Code of Practice on Time Off for the Training of Safety Representatives came into operation on October 1, 1978. Complaints about a refusal by an employer to give a safety representative paid time off for training can be taken to an industrial tribunal in accordance with reg. 11 of the Safety Representatives and Safety Committees Regulations 1977.

Subs. (2)

Legal effect. For the legal effect of Codes of Practice, see Employment Protection Act 1975, s. 6 (11). A Code of Practice on Time Off for Trade Union Duties and Activities, prepared by A.C.A.S. and approved by both Houses of Parliament, came into operation on April 1, 1978 (the Employment Protection Code of Practice (Time Off) Order 1977 (S.I. 1977 No. 2076) ; the Employment Protection Act 1975 (Commencement No. 9) Order 1977 (S.I. 1977 No. 2075)). *Cf.* s. 29 (4) for factors to be had regard to in determining the extent of the right to time off for public duties. No code is required to be published providing " practical guidance " on the application of that right.

Collective agreements. The significance of the Code in practice will vary depending on two different contexts in which it will operate: (i) where there is a time-off/facilities agreement negotiated between employers and trade unions, and (ii) where there is no such agreement. That this is the crucial consideration is stated in the Code itself (para. 10) : " to take account of this wide variety of circumstances and problems, employers and unions should reach agreement or arrangements for handling time off in ways appropriate to their own situations. Subsequent advice in the Code should be read in the light of this *primary* point of guidance which A.C.A.S. considers *fundamental* to the proper operation of time off facilities."

A.C.A.S. modestly gives pride of place to collective bargaining—a characteristic of British auxiliary legislation in labour relations—and this will doubtless overcome the problem of statutory provision for widely differing circumstances in industry. It also has other less happy consequences, however, and these were succinctly stated by the authors of a study of the facilities for female shop-stewards in the N.H.S. and Local Authorities (R. H. Fryer *et al.* (1978) 16 B.J.I.R. 160–174) : " . . . the provisions of the Employment Protection Act, rather than making common provision, will in fact result in unequal availability of facilities to different groups of shop-stewards. In so far as local bargaining determines the level of facilities, the results of bargaining will reflect the strength and weaknesses of union organisation. Any systematic strengths or weaknesses of groups of workers or occupations will therefore tend to be reproduced in the level of facilities enjoyed by those workers " (p. 162). Inequality is the price of flexibility. The Code ratifies the status quo: as is the case in much of labour law, the law protects what the workers have already got for themselves.

Examples of union negotiated agreements: it was remarked in the B.J.I.R. article just quoted that in local government and the Health Service, the suggestions laid down by the Code of Practice for training have been normal practice for some time. The local authorities manual workers' National Agreement gives stewards the right to " all reasonable facilities for exercising their functions." They are allowed time off to carry out their duties with management permission " and then only to conduct such business as is urgent and relevant to the depot, site, job or workshop." The National Engineering Disputes Procedure, cl. 12, provides that " shop stewards shall be afforded reasonable facilities to deal with matters appropriate to be dealt with by them. In all other respects they shall conform to the same working conditions as their fellow employees, and shall act in accordance with the terms of this or any other relevant agreement, national, local or domestic."

More specific provision is possible for regular duties: *e.g.* Lesney Products allows paid time off for two-hour meetings for shop-stewards once a month, and for senior stewards twice a month. Where there is some difficulty in distinguishing union duties from internal union activities which management may argue are not covered, there can be a "block time" approach. The Post Office grants partly paid leave of up to 45 days per year for union officials to do work "which contains elements of both union business and of industrial relations." Otherwise, as in the time-off agreement concluded by the Co-operative Employers Association National Wages Board and the Joint Trade Union Committee for Retail Co-operative Employment effective from January 1, 1978, the agreement may simply allow for paid time off for both types of duties—whether "concerned with industrial relations between his employing society and its employees" or "duties *outside* the confines of the employing society"—with further specification of the outside duties covered.

No collective agreements. Of those workers who have not succeeded in negotiating time-off or facilities, the Code adds to para. 10 the following sentence: "the absence of a *formal* agreement dealing specifically with time off for trade union duties and activities should not *of itself* preclude the granting of release." In one sense, this replicates the interpretation of "recognition" discussed in the Note to subs. (1)—officials are qualified for this right even where there is no "formal" recognition of their trade union. Once entitled, the law should secure these legal rights. But the sentence shows A.C.A.S.'s awareness of the fragility in practice in face of the economic and social power of employers, and where trade union organisation is weak. Officials should certainly insist at a minimum on, *e.g.* time off to carry out the duties listed in the Code (para. 13); on some initial training "as soon as possible" after election or appointment (para. 16); on the facilities stipulated in para. 24—and these are by no means exhaustive, only guidance (see the more extensive facilities suggested in the T.U.C.'s Guide on Time-Off for Union Activities). But in the absence of bargaining power to secure these rights through agreements or arrangements, their enforcement through the industrial tribunals (subs. (7)) is unlikely to achieve the desired result.

Permission. A point should be made about the question of "permission" of the employer (ss. 27–29 each begin: "an employer shall permit . . ."). Can an employer frustrate the law by refusing the union official permission? *E.g.* where the official considered that attendance at a particular meeting was necessary. Can the employer deny him permission to attend that meeting, although he is entitled to take time off? The answer seems to be that permission is *required* of the employer under the section. An employer could only rely on the contract of employment to deny the employee his statutory right. But s. 140 (1) (*a*) declares void any contractual provision which purports to exclude or limit the operation of this section. An employer cannot refuse a union official permission to carry out the duties defined in subs. (1). This is confirmed by the Code (para. 25), which states that "the union official who seeks time off should ensure that the appropriate management representative is *informed* so far in advance as is reasonable in the circumstances." He need not await permission "though he is encouraged to 'seek agreement' for covering his work, for meetings of members during working hours, etc."—paras. 25 *et seq.*

Industrial action. Finally, there is the curious fact, as Holmes (Sherlock) would have said, of the missing s. 57 (3) of the Employment Protection Act 1975. That subsection instructed A.C.A.S. to "provide practical guidance on the circumstances in which a trade union official is to be permitted to take time off under this section in respect of duties connected with industrial action." A.C.A.S. has done so: paras. 31–33 of the Code. But there is still an explicit statutory statement of the right (implied in s. 57 (3) of the 1975 Act) of trade union officials to take time off with pay in connection with industrial action. (*Cf.* s. 28 (2) which expressly excludes activities "which themselves consist of industrial action.) The status of the Code is seen here in its most legally vulnerable light. The provision has been removed from this section and transferred to s. 6 (2) of the Employment Protection Act 1975 (see Sched. 16, para. 29 (2) (*b*)). It is to be hoped that out of sight will not mean out of mind when an official takes time off in circumstances of industrial action.

Subss. (3) *and* (4)

The calculation of contractual remuneration payable to the union official taking time off differs from the usual method endorsed by the statute contained in Sched. 14. The payment here is subject to the criteria of fairness, comparability and finally reasonableness in the circumstances, not simply the contract of employment.

Subs. (6)

Cf. ss. 16 (2), 21 (3), 31 (11) and 35 (4), which are substantially identical. Only contractual remuneration specifically allocated in respect of a period of time off to which subs. (1) applies is to be set off against the statutory payment.

Time off for trade union activities

28.—(1) An employer shall permit an employee of his who is a member of an appropriate trade union to take time off, subject to and in accordance with subsection (3), during the employee's working hours for the purpose of taking part in any trade union activity to which this section applies.

(2) In this section " appropriate trade union ", in relation to an employee of any description, means an independent trade union which is recognised by his employer in respect of that description of employee, and the trade union activities to which this section applies are—

(a) any activities of an appropriate trade union of which the employee is a member; and

(b) any activities, whether or not falling within paragraph (a), in relation to which the employee is acting as a representative of such a union,

excluding activities which themselves consist of industrial action whether or not in contemplation or furtherance of a trade dispute.

(3) The amount of time off which an employee is to be permitted to take under this section and the purposes for which, the occasions on which and any conditions subject to which time off may be so taken are those that are reasonable in all the circumstances having regard to any relevant provisions of a Code of Practice issued by the Advisory, Conciliation and Arbitration Service under section 6 of the Employment Protection Act 1975.

(4) An employee who is a member of an independent trade union recognised by his employer may present a complaint to an industrial tribunal that his employer has failed to permit him to take time off as required by this section.

DERIVATION

1975, s. 58 (1) to (3) (5).

GENERAL NOTE

Subs. (1)

Exclusions. The same classes of employment excluded from the benefits of the right granted in s. 27 are also excluded here—see ss. 138 (3); 141 (2); 144 (2); 146 (1) (2), and most importantly again s. 146 (4) which deprives many part-time workers (mostly women) of the benefits.

For the definition of trade union activity, see subs. (2); for that of " working hours," see s. 32 (1) (b).

Subs. (2)

" Recognised " trade unions. Trade union members eligible are those whose trade union is " recognised " (see Note to s. 27 (1)) in respect of employees of their description. So unlike s. 27 (1) which gives rights to all officials of a recognised trade union, regardless of the scope of recognition, only trade union members of a specific description of employees, that for whom the trade union is recognised, have the right to time off. However, as with trade union officials, once the right vests in the trade union member, it is not qualified further by the scope of the " recognition."

The scope of trade union activities is defined independently in (*a*) and (*b*), with the further exclusion of industrial action.

Trade union duties v. *Trade union activities*. There is obviously some overlap between this section and the provisions of s. 27. The scope of trade union activities *includes* the duties of a trade union official who is also an employee. The overlap would most likely be in the case envisaged by (*b*)—where the employee is acting as a union representative. Where such activities fall within the scope of s. 27 (1) (*a*) or (*b*), the time off is to be paid for. In such cases the union representative may be an " official," defined in s. 153 (1) as having the same meaning as in TULRA, s. 30 (1). *Cf.* the definition of " representative " in s. 17 (2) and s. 99 (2) of the Employment Protection Act 1975.

Definition of " trade union activities." Trade union *activities*, however, in contrast to the *duties* of a trade union official under s. 27, are not limited to industrial relations and need not be related to the employer in any way. One may contrast the provisions of s. 58 (1) (*b*), a right not to be dismissed, and s. 23 (1) (*b*), a right not to have action short of dismissal taken—for the purpose of preventing or deterring activities of an independent trade union. In neither of these sections are trade union activities defined. But here trade union activities *are* defined to include " *any* activities."

For the section intends to grant to trade union members for the first time the legal right to take part in union activities at a time when in the past such activities may have been denied them by their employer. The clear implication of this new right to take time off during working hours is that the activities may be held on the employer's premises. The employer is prohibited from preventing or deterring the participation in such activities—see the Note to s. 23 (1). The activities are conceived of as being integral to the autonomous existence of an organisation of workers. Although the *raison d'être* of a workers' organisation in a capitalist society requires that most of its activities be concerned with issues involving interaction between the employer and his employees-members of the union, not all the activities of the union are so narrowly conceived. They may range from the administrative maintenance of the organisation *per se*, to activities of social, educational and financial benefit to the membership, to active political agitation involving members. All these activities are covered, but the degree to which the section will be utilised depends on the extent of the particular organisation's vitality at the national and local levels, and also the extent to which employees are prepared to trade employment for time off for these activities without pay.

Code of Practice. The A.C.A.S. Code's guidance (paras. 21–22) on the scope of trade union activities is eloquent testimony to the blinkered vision of industrial relations pluralism. One was perhaps surprised at the limited view expressed by the Donovan Commission of the interests of trade union members (p. 309). This was criticised by the General Council in its Annual Report to the T.U.C. in 1968 (p. 409) which reminded those who needed reminding of the " wider social purposes " of trade unions. Industrial relations pluralism and its perspective, which confines trade union aspirations to only marginal changes in the existing institutions and objectives of industry and society, has been subject to trenchant criticism by Alan Fox and Richard Hyman since then. But it seems that A.C.A.S. is oblivious to this critique.

One is shocked by the extreme narrowness of the examples of trade union activities put forward in the Code: attendance at executive committee meetings or annual conferences (only senior members of trade unions would qualify for these rare absences from work), voting in union elections and maybe occasional workplace meetings where this would not adversely affect production or services. Reference to the objects of the TGWU as stated in its Rule Book is sufficient to reveal how pathetically inadequate the Code is in providing guidance to the potential activities of trade union members. The TGWU's members may pursue among others the following objects (r. 2)—(*e*) " the furtherance of political objects of any kind," *e.g.* if a TGWU branch decided to back the candidacy of any member for political office, canvassing activities by other members, and the conduct of his own election campaign by the candidate member himself, might be trade union political activities. Leyland agreed in early 1978 with 11 unions representing 102,000 hourly paid employees in 34 plants that employees who were parliamentary candidates could, at the time of the election, have three weeks' paid leave of absence. In r. 2 (*f*) " the transaction of insurance business "; 2 (*g*) " the extension of co-operative production and distribution "; 2 (*h*) " the establishment or carrying on, or participation, financial or otherwise, directly or indirectly, in the business of printing or publishing of a general newspaper or newspapers, or of books, pamphlets, or publications or of any kind of undertaking industrial or otherwise in the interest of and with the main purpose of furthering the interests of the Union or of trade unionism generally "; 2 (*i*) " the furtherance of, or participation, financial or otherwise, directly or indirectly, in the work, or purpose of any association or federal body having for its object the furthering of the interests of labour, trade unionism, or trade unionists, including the securing of a real measure of control in industry and participation by the workers in the management, in the interests of labour and the general community "; 2 (*k*) " the provision of opportunities for social intercourse and promotion of sport and social events amongst the members." It seems unlikely that industrial tribunals, if they come to adjudicate on time-off disputes concerning TGWU members, will find many " relevant " provisions in the Code to have regard to (subs. (3)).

Industrial action. There is, however, express exclusion from the right in this section of trade union activities " which themselves consist of industrial action whether or not in contemplation or furtherance of a trade dispute." " Industrial action " is not defined (*cf.* the definitions of " strike " and " irregular industrial action short of a strike " in ss. 167 (1) and 33 (4) respectively, of the Industrial Relations Act 1971). The phrase would seem not to cover activity auxiliary or accessory to the industrial action itself, *e.g.* calling, organising, procuring, financing or threatening a strike or other industrial action. It is not clear whether industrial action when compounded with other action is included in the phrase. For example, political activities are clearly permissible trade union activities since the Trade Union Act 1913 makes it lawful for trade unions to have political objectives. If union members strike to protest against increasing unemployment in response to their union's call, is this industrial action excluded from the scope of the section, whereas time off to lobby Parliament on the same issue would not be excluded? Again, might a " study session " called to debate the Government's current wages policy be permitted whereas a walk-out to protest the employer's latest offer in line with that policy might be excluded? The situation is further complicated due to the fact that the industrial action need not be connected with a trade dispute (as defined by s. 29 of TULRA). In the end one is left with no very clear idea of what trade union activities are excluded by this phrase.

Here again, there is a missing subsection—formerly s. 58 (4) which had instructed A.C.A.S. to provide practical guidance as to when a trade union member is to be permitted to take time off for trade union activities connected with industrial action (*cf.* the similar omission from the present s. 27. Similarly this provision has been transferred to s. 6 (2) of the Employment Protection Act 1975 (see Sched. 16, para. 23 (2) (*c*))—see Note to s. 27 (2)). Para. 33 of the Code illustrates A.C.A.S.'s inaccurate presentation of the law on this matter: members " may need to seek agreement of management to time off." This is hardly consistent with the *right* to time off—management's agreement is *not* needed; at most management need be informed. It should be remembered that the Code only provides guidance, not authoritative interpretation of the law. The courts provide the latter, and *miserabile dictu*, will be the final legal arbiters of the scope of the rights to time off.

Subs. (3)

See the Note to s. 27 (2) which is identical. A.C.A.S.'s task was not an enviable one; what is " reasonable in the circumstances " will usually involve a conflict between the employer's needs and those of the union members employed by him who wish to devote some part of their working lives not only to the promotion of the interests of their employer's organisation, but to those of their own. Even so, A.C.A.S.'s Code as it relates to trade union activities is better at pointing out problems than putting forward solutions. Thus, *e.g.* in para. 9, it refers to the difficulties of married women, whose domestic commitments limit the possibilities of active participation in their union. The implication is that such women workers should be the more particular beneficiaries of time off during working hours and at the workplace. But A.C.A.S. shies away from such direct expressions and adopts the apparently " neutral " stance of recommending agreements (para. 10). As stated in the Note to s. 27 (2), this appearance of neutrality masks the reality of employers' power which makes agreement on such issues unlikely. Even where trade unions can extract collective agreements, the under-representation of women even in unions where they are a majority (*e.g.* NUPE: 63 per cent. of members women, only 27 per cent. of shop-stewards women) will not obtain for women workers the benefits of these legal provisions. One can only reiterate Fryer's conclusion in 16 B.J.I.R. 160 at 166 that the Code of Practice would only overcome these difficulties of under-representation if explicit provision is made.

Time off for public duties

29.—(1) An employer shall permit an employee of his who is—

    (*a*) a justice of the peace;

    (*b*) a member of a local authority;

    (*c*) a member of any statutory tribunal;

    (*d*) a member of, in England and Wales, a Regional Health Authority or Area Health Authority or, in Scotland, a Health Board;

    (*e*) a member of, in England and Wales, the managing or governing body of an educational establishment maintained by a local education authority, or, in Scotland, a school or college council or the governing body of a central institution or a college of education; or

    (*f*) a member of, in England and Wales, a water authority or, in Scotland, river purification board,

to take time off, subject to and in accordance with subsection (4), during the employee's working hours for the purposes of performing any of the duties of his office or, as the case may be, his duties as such a member.

    (2) In subsection (1)—

    (*a*) " local authority " in relation to England and Wales includes the Common Council of the City of London but otherwise has the same meaning as in the Local Government Act 1972, and in relation to Scotland has the same meaning as in the Local Government (Scotland) Act 1973;

    (*b*) " Regional Health Authority " and " Area Health Authority " have the same meaning as in the National Health Service Act 1977, and " Health Board " has the same meaning as in the National Health Service (Scotland) Act 1972;

    (*c*) " local education authority " means the authority designated by section 192 (1) of the Local Government Act 1972, " school or college council " means a body appointed under section 125 (1) of the Local Government (Scotland) Act 1973, and " central institution " and " college of education " have the meanings assigned to them by section 145 (10) and (14) respectively of the Education (Scotland) Act 1962; and

    (*d*) " river purification board " means a board established under section 135 of the Local Government (Scotland) Act 1973.

    (3) For the purposes of subsection (1) the duties of a member of a body referred to in paragraphs (*b*) to (*f*) of that subsection are:—

    (*a*) attendance at a meeting of the body or any of its committees or sub-committees;

    (*b*) the doing of any other thing approved by the body, or anything of a class so approved, for the purpose of the discharge of the functions of the body or of any of its committees or sub-committees.

    (4) The amount of time off which an employee is to be permitted to take under this section and the occasions on which and any conditions subject to which time off may be so taken are those that are reasonable in all the circumstances having regard, in particular, to the following:—

    (*a*) how much time off is required for the performance of the duties of the office or as a member of the body in question, and how much time off is required for the performance of the particular duty;

(b) how much time off the employee has already been permitted under this section or sections 27 and 28;

(c) the circumstances of the employer's business and the effect of the employee's absence on the running of that business.

(5) The Secretary of State may by order—

(a) modify the provisions of subsection (1) by adding any office or body to, or removing any office or body from, that subsection or by altering the description of any office or body in that subsection; and

(b) modify the provisions of subsection (3).

(6) An employee may present a complaint to an industrial tribunal that his employer has failed to permit him to take time off as required by this section.

DERIVATION

1975, s. 59.

GENERAL NOTE

Subs. (1)

Exclusions. Certain classes of employment are excluded from the benefit of this section: see ss. 138 (3); 141 (2); 144 (2) (4); 146 (2) (4). Some Crown employees may also be restricted in their enjoyment of this right under s. 138 (8).

Numbers covered. The numbers of employees who may potentially benefit from these provisions are substantial, mainly in categories (a) and (b)—there are over 25,000 J.P.s and a similar number who are local authority councillors, most of whom are in employment. Of the over 30 types of statutory tribunals covered by (c), the National Insurance Local Tribunals, for example, have around 4,000 lay appointees, the Supplementary Benefit Appeals Tribunals over 1,500, Local Valuation Courts over 2,000, and, of course, the industrial tribunals themselves have over 2,000 lay members. Categories (d) and (f) cover several hundred individuals each, and category (e) will obviously apply to substantial numbers of, *e.g.* parents who are members.

Paid time off? Unlike s. 27, there is here no express provision for time off for public duties to be paid for by the employer. Since some public duties, *e.g.* J.P.s, are unpaid, or allow only for limited allowances (local authority council meetings), a refusal by the employer to pay for time off may *effectively* deny the employee the right to time off granted here. This is particularly the case where a particular public duty makes heavy demands on the employee's time. If unpaid, it would not be feasible to undertake the duty. It is, therefore, wrong to conclude that the law does *not* require payment for time off for public duties. Rather, as Slynn J. has put it, " in considering whether there has been a refusal to grant time, the industrial tribunal can look at the conditions subject to which an employer is prepared to grant time off (including conditions relating to pay) and could say that they really amounted to a refusal to allow time to be taken " (*Corner* v. *Buckinghamshire County Council* [1978] I.R.L.R. 320 (E.A.T.)).

" *Working hours* " is defined in s. 32 (1) (b).

Subs. (3)

For the purposes of para. (a), " attendance " will probably include time off to travel to and from the meeting. The wording of para. (b) is both inelegant and very wide indeed; *e.g.* in *Ratcliffe* v. *Dorset County Council* [1978] I.R.L.R. 191, the employee concerned was a member not only of the general Bournemouth Borough Council, but also of three sub-committees of that council, whose meetings added up to 48 half-days per annum (the industrial tribunal suggested, further, that there might be other things which he had not attended, but ought to, *e.g.* the installation of the Mayor). In *Emmerson* v. *Commissioners of Inland Revenue* [1977] I.R.L.R. 458, the employee was elected leader of the opposition, and thus had the right to attend every committee meeting of the Portsmouth City Council.

It may very well be that the period of preparation necessary for the proper performance of the functions of these bodies, *e.g.* reading background material, visiting sites, attending briefings, is also covered by this subsection.

Subs. (4)

Unlike ss. 27 and 28, there is no mandatory Code of Practice supplementing the provisions of this section. Instead, Parliament has itself given some guidance in this subsection as to the considerations affecting the " reasonableness" of the employee's demands and the employer's compliance. Subs. (4) (*b*) will only apply to trade union members or officials using ss. 27–28, but this section applies to all employees, whether trade union members or not. Subs. (4) (*c*) makes explicit reference to the employer's business circumstances. Presumably, for the contrary would be embarrassing for the employee concerned, his absence will have an adverse effect. This does not suffice in itself, however, to deny the worker his rights under the legislation.

Provisions as to industrial tribunals

30.—(1) An industrial tribunal shall not consider—
   (*a*) a complaint under section 27, 28 or 29 that an employer has failed to permit an employee to take time off; or
   (*b*) a complaint under section 27 that an employer has failed to pay an employee the whole or part of any amount required to be paid under that section;
unless it is presented within three months of the date when the failure occurred or within such further period as the tribunal considers reasonable in a case where it is satisfied that it was not reasonably practicable for the complaint to be presented within the period of three months.

(2) Where an industrial tribunal finds any complaint mentioned in subsection (1) (*a*) well-founded, the tribunal shall make a declaration to that effect and may make an award of compensation to be paid by the employer to the employee which shall be of such amount as the tribunal considers just and equitable in all the circumstances having regard to the employer's default in failing to permit time off to be taken by the employee and to any loss sustained by the employee which is attributable to the matters complained of.

(3) Where on a complaint under section 27 an industrial tribunal finds that the employer has failed to pay the employee the whole or part of the amount required to be paid under that section, the tribunal shall order the employer to pay the employee the amount which it finds due to him.

DERIVATION
   1975, s. 60.

GENERAL NOTE
Subs. (2)

Declarations. The E.A.T. has confirmed that an industrial tribunal " does not have the power to impose conditions upon the parties as to the way in which the time off shall be granted" (*Corner* v. *Buckinghamshire County Council* [1978] I.R.L.R. 320 (E.A.T.)). An industrial tribunal's imposition of a condition that " all days of absence over 10 should be unpaid leave " was, therefore, deleted from its decision. At most, the E.A.T. felt the industrial tribunal could consider whether the conditions imposed are unreasonable in deciding whether time off has been refused.

But one industrial tribunal dealing with time off for public duties, while conceding that it had no power to make a direction as to what time should be allowed off, still went on to suggest an amount it considered reasonable and expressed the hope that the parties would reach an agreement on the lines set out (*Ratcliffe* v. *Dorset County Council* [1978] I.R.L.R. 191). Another industrial tribunal similarly gave " a guide as to the approximate . . . amount of leave that should be granted," but went on to emphasise that it was for the parties to negotiate the exact amount (*Emmerson* v. *Commissioners of Inland Revenue* [1977] I.R.L.R. 458). The force of such " guides " or " suggestions " is likely in practice not to be very different from specific declarations.

Compensation. The original Employment Protection Bill 1975 provided compensation only for loss actually caused (cl. 54 (2)). At the Committee Stage, the Government conceded the difficulty of assessing compensation for loss suffered in the circumstances of permission being refused, and actually anticipated that it would rarely be appropriate to award any—*i.e.* there was to be no sanction at all for the employer's illegal refusal. Fortunately, this complacent benevolence towards law-breaking employers was remedied. As in s. 26 (1), compensation is now to be paid both for loss and for the employer's default in failing to permit time off to be taken. However, no indication is given as to how to go about calculating either the loss or the compensation for the default. As with s. 26, however, the provisions on compensation for unfair dismissal may provide an analogy here. Accordingly, as was suggested in the Note to s. 26 (1), the industrial tribunal may first request the employer to withdraw from his action of either refusing or failing to permit the requisite time off. If he does, the tribunal would simply award compensation for any interim benefits lost (ss. 68–69). If he does not do so fully, the tribunal may award compensation as it sees fit (s. 71 (1)). If the employer refused to revoke his illegal action, the tribunal may make an award consisting of: (i) a special sum (s. 71 (2) (*b*) (ii)), augmented when the refusal is motivated by specified factors (s. 71 (2) (*b*) (i) and (3)); and (ii) a payment paralleling the " basic award " for unfair dismissal cases (s. 73) and compensation for actual loss. This last will clearly not be easily quantifiable—see the problems pointed out with regard to a refusal to permit time off for trade union activities (Note to s. 26 (2)). Similar problems will arise when time off is refused for trade union and public duties. It should be noted that here, unlike the provisions in s. 26 and s. 74 concerning compensation for loss resulting from dismissal and action (short of dismissal), the factors of common law mitigation by and contributory fault of the employee, and industrial pressure on the employer are not necessarily to affect the tribunal's assessment.

Time off to look for work or make arrangements for training

31.—(1) An employee who is given notice of dismissal by reason of redundancy shall, subject to the following provisions of this section, be entitled before the expiration of his notice to be allowed by his employer reasonable time off during the employee's working hours in order to look for new employment or make arrangements for training for future employment.

(2) An employee shall not be entitled to time off under this section unless, on whichever is the later of the following dates, that is to say,—

(*a*) the date on which the notice is due to expire; or

(*b*) the date on which it would expire were it the notice required to be given by section 49 (1),

he will have been or, as the case may be, would have been continuously employed for a period of two years or more.

(3) An employee who is allowed time off during his working hours under subsection (1) shall, subject to the following provisions of this section, be entitled to be paid remuneration by his employer for the period of absence at the appropriate hourly rate.

(4) The appropriate hourly rate in relation to an employee shall be the amount of one week's pay divided by—

(*a*) the number of normal working hours in a week for that employee when employed under the contract of employment in force on the day when notice was given; or

(*b*) where the number of such normal working hours differs from week to week or over a longer period, the average number of such hours calculated by dividing by twelve the total number of the employee's normal working hours during the period of twelve weeks ending with the last complete week before the day on which notice was given.

(5) If an employer unreasonably refuses to allow an employee time off from work under this section, the employee shall, subject to subsection (9), be entitled to be paid an amount equal to the remuneration to which he would have been entitled under subsection (3) if he had been allowed the time off.

(6) An employee may present a complaint to an industrial tribunal on the ground that his employer has unreasonably refused to allow him time off under this section or has failed to pay the whole or any part of any amount to which the employee is entitled under subsection (3) or (5).

(7) An industrial tribunal shall not entertain a complaint under subsection (6) unless it is presented to the tribunal within the period of three months beginning with the day on which it is alleged that the time off should have been allowed, or within such further period as the tribunal considers reasonable in a case where it is satisfied that it was not reasonably practicable for the complaint to be presented within the period of three months.

(8) If on a complaint under subsection (6) the tribunal finds the grounds of the complaint well-founded it shall make a declaration to that effect and shall order the employer to pay to the employee the amount which it finds due to him.

(9) The amount—
   (a) of an employer's liability to pay remuneration under subsection (3); or
   (b) which may be ordered by a tribunal to be paid by an employer under subsection (8),
or, where both paragraphs (a) and (b) are applicable, the aggregate amount of the liabilities referred to in those paragraphs, shall not exceed, in respect of the notice period of any employee, two-fifths of week's pay of that employee.

(10) Subject to subsection (11), a right to any amount under subsection (3) or (5) shall not affect any right of an employee in relation to remuneration under the contract of employment (in this section referred to as " contractual remuneration ").

(11) Any contractual remuneration paid to an employee in respect of a period when he takes time off for the purposes referred to in subsection (1) shall go towards discharging any liability of the employer to pay remuneration under subsection (3) in respect of that period, and conversely any payment of remuneration under subsection (3) in respect of a period shall go towards discharging any liability of the employer to pay contractual remuneration in respect of that period.

DERIVATION
   1975, s. 61 (1)–(4), (7)–(13).

GENERAL NOTE
Subs. (1)
   Exclusions. Certain classes of employment are excluded from the provisions of this section—see ss. 138 (3), 141 (2), 144 (2) (4), 145 (2), 146 (1) (2). Many part-time workers will be excluded by virtue of the requirement of two years' continuous employment (subs. (2)), which is calculated according to Sched. 13 (s. 151 (1)), para. 3 of which only counts weeks of employment of 16 hours or more.
   Redundancy. For the meaning of " dismissal by reason of redundancy," s. 153 (2) refers to the terms of s. 81. But in *Dutton* v. *Hawker Siddeley Aviation Ltd.* [1978] I.R.L.R. 390 (E.A.T.), Phillips J. expressed the opinion that " [s. 31] applies to an employee who is dismissed by reason of redundancy even though, because of the offer of alternative employment, he may not be entitled to a redundancy payment, or even though for some other reason—there may be other reasons—he is not entitled to a redundancy payment. . . . The purpose [s. 31], of course, is to give opportunity to find other employment."

"*Allowed.*" The right is awkwardly phrased in terms of "entitled . . . to be allowed . . . reasonable time off," rather than simply "entitled . . . to . . . reasonable time off." The problem of an employer refusing to allow an employee his entitlement thus arises—much as it did with the entitlement "to be permitted" time off under ss. 27–29. As was stated in the Note to s. 27 (2), with regard to "permission," the employer can only rely on the contract of employment to deny the employee the right to time off to look for work—and s. 140 (1) (*a*) declares void any contractual provision which purports to exclude or limit the operation of this section. But see further the Note to subss. (5) and (6).

"*Reasonable*" *time off.* The amount of time during "working hours" (defined in s. 32 (1) (*b*)) which is "reasonable" may be assessed by reference to such factors as local unemployment, the nature of the employee's work, his individual characteristics—skill, age, dependants, etc., and other particular circumstances. The more difficult it is anticipated to be to find new employment, and the more serious the consequences of future unemployment, the more time may be held to be "reasonably" required.

Collective agreements. The law will be superfluous to the many trade union members covered by collectively agreed provisions; *e.g.* an agreement of September 16, 1976, between the London Co-operative Society and USDAW and the TGWU provides, in the event of redundancy, for employees to be entitled to reasonable time off *with pay* (*cf.* the limitations in the statutory entitlement (subs. (9)) to seek alternative employment, attend interviews and make arrangements for training for future employment. More explicit terms are to be found in an agreement of late 1978 between the shipping firm of Shaw Savill and Allison (part of the Furness Withy Group) and ASTMS. The agreement provides that notwithstanding the giving of formal notices of termination, employees will be entitled to a period of "protected employment" dating from the redundancy date. The length of the period will vary with the age of the redundant employee—from a minimum of three-quarters of a month at ages 20–23, up to 15 months at ages 51–55. Individuals on protected employment remain on the pay-roll on normal terms and conditions of employment, though they will not necessarily be required to attend for work. They remain employed until alternative jobs are found, or the maximum period has elapsed. During this period the company will seek to redeploy individuals into, or train them for, other jobs with the company or elsewhere in the Group. In the absence of internal vacancies, the company will assist in the finding of jobs elsewhere. Such provisions as these show up the meanness of the legal protection for workers threatened with the scrap-heap.

Subs. (2)

Only employees with two years' seniority qualify. This period is the same as that needed to qualify for a redundancy payment—s. 81 (4)—but that is hardly a reason for disqualifying needy employees with less than two years' employment facing the long dole queues.

Subs. (3)

The promise here of payment during the "reasonable" period of time off may be cruelly betrayed by the provisions of subs. (9), which purport to limit any entitlement to two-fifths of a week's pay (*i.e.* usually two days' pay).

Subs. (4)

Cf. s. 14 (2), which provides a substantially similar basis for the calculation of the hourly rate for guarantee payments. S. 14 (2) (*c*) is unnecessary here as the employee must have been continuously employed for two years in order to qualify (subs. (2)).

For definition of "week," see s. 153 (1).

For definition of "one week's pay," s. 152 refers to Sched. 14, Pt. II (and see para. 7 (1) (*c*) of that Schedule, which fixes the calculation date for the purposes of this section).

Subss. (5) *and* (6)

It seems that an employer may "reasonably" refuse to allow the time off which the employee is entitled to. Without any guidance from the statute, the industrial tribunals may be tempted to impose conditions on enjoyment of the right which, if not fulfilled, might allow an employer "reasonably" to refuse. This needs be naked judicial policy-making, since for once the judges cannot hide behind an implied intention of the parties—s. 140 (1) (*a*) prohibits any contractual term which excludes or limits the rights under this section. Perhaps for this reason the E.A.T. has already stamped out one industrial tribunal's attempt to make it a prerequisite of entitlement that the employee give to his employer details of his appointments or interviews. There is no reason, the E.A.T. went on to say, why time off should not be taken without any appointment having been made (*Dutton* v. *Hawker Siddeley Aviation Ltd.* [1978] I.R.L.R. 392 (E.A.T.)). Still, the industrial tribunals will bear watching and warning.

Subs. (9)

S. 31 grants the employee two benefits: "reasonable" time off (subs. (1)) and payment during his absence (subs. (3)). The latter entitlement is limited to a maximum of two-fifths of a week's pay under this subsection, *i.e.* no matter how much time off the employee is entitled to, his maximum entitlement to *paid* time off is two-fifths of a week's pay. Of course he may be entitled to further unpaid time off, if reasonable in accordance with subs. (1).

The provisions are rather ambiguous in terms of their impact. For example, if the employer gives four weeks' notice, and the employee is entitled in the circumstances to three days as a reasonable amount of time off to look for a job. Under this subsection, he is entitled, if working a five-day week, to be paid no more than two days' pay. Is he paid for the third day off? A number of possibilities exist. He may not be so entitled as his only entitlement derives from his contract of employment which may deny him wages when he is not at work. On the other hand, he *is* entitled to take the day off by virtue of the statutory provision, and this should *not* operate to deprive him of any contractual remuneration which he would otherwise be entitled to during his period of notice. S. 140 (1) (*a*) may operate to ensure that the employee is not forced to choose between his statutory and contractual rights. Where he *is* statutorily entitled to payment during his absence, this payment is not to affect his contractual remuneration (subss. (10) and (11)). *A fortiori,* where he is *not* to be paid for his statutory entitlement to time off, otherwise the statutory right would be worthless for the employee could have simply stayed away from work and forfeited his wages during the period of notice. The statute is supposed to augment his rights during the period of notice, not deprive him of one of them—the right to be paid. A possible compromise might be that if the employee takes time off without pay during the period of notice, he should be entitled to his full period of notice payments by working out the period of notice even where this would extend the termination date beyond that initially envisaged by the notice.

Subs. (11)

Cf. the substantially identical provisions in ss. 16 (2), 21 (3) and 35 (4). As in the three of these, relating to guarantee payments, payments during periods of suspension and during maternity leave, the question arises here whether the payment for a day on which an employee is absent but entitled nonetheless to contractual remuneration should count towards the maximum entitlement, here under subs. (9). Consistently with the other provisions, it would seem not.

Provisions supplementary to ss. 27 to 31

32.—(1) For the purposes of sections 27 to 31—

    (*a*) a trade union shall be treated as recognised not only if it is recognised for the purposes of collective bargaining, but also if the Advisory, Conciliation and Arbitration Service has made a recommendation for recognition which is operative within the meaning of section 15 of the Employment Protection Act 1975; and

    (*b*) the working hours of an employee shall be taken to be any time when, in accordance with his contract of employment, he is required to be at work.

(2) In subsection (1)—

    " collective bargaining " means negotiations related to or connected with one or more of the matters specified in section 29 (1) of the Trade Union and Labour Relations Act 1974;

" recognised " means recognised by an employer, or two or more associated employers, to any extent for the purposes of collective bargaining.

DERIVATION

1975, ss. 62 (*a*) (*b*) ; 126 (1).

GENERAL NOTE
Subs. (1)

For a substantially identical provision to (*a*), see s. 106 (1) of the Employment Protection Act 1975. "Working hours" is defined in the same way in s. 23 (2).

Subs. (2)

"Collective bargaining" is defined in the same way in s. 126 (1) of TULRA.

"Recognised" is derived from the meaning of "recognition" given in s. 11 (2) of the Employment Protection Act 1975.

PART III

MATERNITY

General Note to Part IV

The number of women employed in the United Kingdom rose from 8,891,000 in June 1973 (39·2 per cent. of the total employees in employment) to an estimated 9,281,000 (41 per cent. of the total) in June 1977. Many of these women workers do not differ in their work patterns from male workers, as was summarised in a recent Department of Employment Manpower Paper: "more women are now married, they marry younger and live longer; child-bearing is normally compressed into a short period relatively early in life. Many women now have the opportunity . . . of working continuously for 20 or 30 years." The Equal Opportunities Commission has recently pointed out that data from the new Earnings Survey shows that four out of five of the people earning the lowest 10 per cent. of incomes are women. In 1976, 43·2 per cent. of women working full-time earned less than £40 a week; only 5·2 per cent. of men were in the same position. The Equal Opportunities Commission points out that poverty and the low level of women's incomes are the result of large numbers of women in low paid sectors of industry; discrimination against women in social security; and most pertinent to the provisions of Pt. III— lack of social facilities to back up women in the dual role of breadwinner and wife and mother. The Commission urged employers to take a new look at ways of minimising the disruption of women's careers caused by childbirth and childcare. But the results of such urging have been meagre. The latest report, published in November 1978, based on a survey of 575 of Britain's largest companies, finds the survey results largely disappointing: at most, employers had tried to avoid *unlawful* discrimination, but *positive* steps, *e.g.* the provision of day-care facilities were rare.

Maternity provisions are, however, one area where companies are tempted to take an initiative. The motivation is hardly philanthropic, however, but more that (a) pay policy does not limit maternity provisions (which are deemed to be related to job security), and (b) they are relatively inexpensive—the take-up rate is low. Many women who give birth cease to work, though this perhaps is a consequence of lack of maternity provisions and will change with the new provisions. Still, what evidence there is from workplaces where maternity provisions have been made available indicates a low take-up rate. This may be explicable because the agreements, relating usually only to maternity pay and leave, do not resolve the fundamental difficulty of childcare. For examples from collective agreements, see the Notes below.

This part (ss. 33–48), the right not to be dismissed on grounds of pregnancy (s. 60) and the protection against the employer's failure to permit the woman to return to work after confinement (s. 56) were part of the attempt in the Employment Protection Act 1975 to remedy a striking gap in the labour laws of the United Kingdom all the more visible when contrasted with the laws of other members of the EEC: its failure to protect women in employment during pregnancy and after confinement. An I.L.O. Convention on this matter has existed since 1919 and was further revised in 1952. It has not yet been acceded to by the United Kingdom. In the Standing Committee on the Employment Protection Bill 1975 the Government accepted that the proposed provisions did not equal the standards of the I.L.O. Convention. It failed to provide all the benefits required, such as leave before and after birth and guaranteed payments during this period, protection against dismissal and reinstatement, nursing break provisions for returning mothers, the possible extension of maternity leave because of problems, and lighter work during pregnancy and afterwards special safeguards for health. Under the Health and Safety at Work, etc. Act 1974, however, employers do have a duty to take all reasonable steps to ensure the health and safety of pregnant employees, and this may involve certain alterations in the employee's duties where these entail exposure to pressure, heat or required, *e.g.* lifting heavy weights. As far as the Employment Protection Act is concerned, however, the Government admitted that the proposals laid down only a minimum standard.

Still, even this minimum has had its effect, *e.g.* over the first 10 months during which the maternity pay provisions have been in force (April 6, 1977–January 31, 1978), some 46,287 women have received maternity pay from their employers for which rebate has been paid from the Maternity Fund.

Women on tribunals. The future of maternity benefits will depend in practice on the extent to which trade unions, particularly those with many or even a majority of women members, fight for provisions to be made in collective agreements safeguarding them. As to the statutory provisions, their influence is subject to the deficiencies of enforcement by complaint through industrial tribunals. Apart from the inherent difficulties of women using this process, the industrial tribunals themselves are male-dominated bodies. The proportion of women on the lay panels from which members are appointed is about 20 per cent., whereas women are about 40 per cent. of the working population. For an illustration of the effect of this, see the Note to s. 48.

General provisions

Rights of employee in connection with pregnancy and confinement

33.—(1) An employee who is absent from work wholly or partly because of pregnancy or confinement shall, subject to the following provisions of this Act,—

(*a*) be entitled to be paid by her employer a sum to be known as maternity pay; and

(*b*) be entitled to return to work.

(2) Schedule 2 shall have effect for the purpose of supplementing the following provisions of this Act in relation to an employee's right to return to work.

(3) An employee shall be entitled to the rights referred to in subsection (1) whether or not a contract of employment subsists during the period of her absence but, subject to subsection (4), she shall not be so entitled unless—

(*a*) she continues to be employed by her employer (whether or not she is at work) until immediately before the beginning of the eleventh week before the expected week of confinement;

(*b*) she has at the beginning of that eleventh week been continuously employed for a period of not less than two years; and

(*c*) she informs her employer (in writing if he so requests) at least twenty-one days before her absence begins or, if that is not reasonably practicable, as soon as reasonably practicable,—

(i) that she will be (or is) absent from work wholly or partly because of pregnancy or confinement, and

(ii) in the case of the right to return, that she intends to return to work with her employer.

(4) An employee who has been dismissed by her employer for a reason falling within section 60 (1) (*a*) or (*b*) and has not been re-engaged in accordance with that section, shall be entitled to the rights referred to in subsection (1) of this section notwithstanding that she has thereby ceased to be employed before the beginning of the eleventh week before the expected week of confinement if, but for that dismissal, she would at the beginning of that eleventh week have been continuously employed for a period of not less than two years, but she shall not be entitled to the right to return unless she informs her employer (in writing if he so requests), before or as soon as reasonably practicable after the dismissal takes effect, that she intends to return to work with him.

In this subsection " dismiss " and " dismissal " have the same meaning as they have for the purposes of Part V.

(5) An employee shall not be entitled to either of the rights referred to in subsection (1) unless, if requested to do so by her employer, she produces for his inspection a certificate from a registered medical practitioner or a certified midwife stating the expected week of her confinement.

(6) The Secretary of State may by order vary the periods of two years referred to in subsections (3) and (4), or those periods as varied from time to time under this subsection, but no such order shall be made unless a draft of the order has been laid before Parliament and approved by resolution of each House of Parliament.

DERIVATION

1975, s. 35; s. 50 (2).

GENERAL NOTE

Subs. (1)

Exclusions. For classes of employment excluded from this provision, see ss. 138 (3), 141 (2), 144 (2), 146 (1) (2). Many part-time workers will be excluded by virtue of the requirement of two years' continuous employment (subs. (3) (*b*)), which is calculated according to Sched. 13 (s. 151 (1)), para. 3 of which only counts weeks of employment of 16 hours or more.

Qualification for the rights. Compare the qualification for the rights listed here—absence from work " wholly or partly because of pregnancy or confinement "—with the qualification for the same rights in the event of dismissal before the 11th week prior to confinement in subs. (4) (referring to s. 60 (1) (*a*) or (*b*))—and see the Note to subs. (4). S. 60 (1) refers to dismissal on ground of pregnancy or " any other reason connected with pregnancy." Presumably the qualification for the same rights would aspire to as little discrepancy as possible between women " absent " and women " dismissed." (But see *Elegbede* v. *Wellcome Foundation Ltd.* [1977] I.R.L.R. 383.)

Collective agreements. The two statutory rights here granted are supplemented in practice by collective agreements or various trade unions' bargaining proposals. The supplementary provisions which employees may benefit from in addition to these may either be (1) of the same kind, only more beneficial; or (2) add benefits of various new kinds. A few examples will illustrate the relative poverty of entitlement allowed for in the statute.

A number of trade unions have drawn up model maternity agreements to be guides for their negotiators. These stipulate various benefits for pregnant women workers going far beyond the statute's maternity provisions, *e.g.* the right to visit her doctor and clinic for pre-natal check-ups without loss of pay (TASS, ASTMS, APEX, GMWU); changes in working arrangements may be negotiated to alleviate difficulties caused by pregnancy, *e.g.* different starting and finishing times to ease travel, a shorter working week with normal average earnings to be maintained (TASS, GMWU). ASTMS makes special provision for temporary job moves without loss of pay where health is at risk. To provide for after-birth child-care difficulties, TASS and the GMWU encourage the following: at least temporary part-time work for a period; alteration of hours if previously hours worked were unsocial; 10 days' paid concessionary leave per annum during the first five years of the child's life where the health or the care of the child requires it. TASS goes on to allow for these child-care provisions to "apply to male employees with paternal responsibilities." Paternity leave is also an aim: TASS, ASTMS and GMWU asking for 10 days' paid leave (APEX—six days), and TASS and GMWU go on to ask for another five days where the mother's medical condition warrants it—such leave not to count against either holiday or sick pay entitlement.

These model aspirations have already been effected in a number of agreements, *e.g.* ASTMS have agreed with Longman Publishing that during the first four weeks of return the employee can work a three-day week and secure full weekly pay; and the same union agreed with Containerlink for redeployment provisions to apply if the old job adversely affects the domestic circumstances of returners. The Phillips Industries Group Policy provides for attempts to be made to alleviate any difficulties associated with the later stages of pregnancy, *e.g.* by reducing overtime, lifting or travel, and greater flexibility of hours where this helps. Paternity leave is also spreading: various agreements provide for leave from up to five days (British Institute of Management and APEX; Wilson & Whitworth Publishing and NUJ; G.L.C. (Staff); Independent Broadcasting Authority and Association of Broadcasting and Allied Staff (the B.B.C. only gives two days)), 10 days (Galleon Roadchef and GMWU, Norfolk Capital Hotels and TGWU, GMWU) or even up to 15 days (Penguin Books and ASTMS).

The significance of collective agreements—the terms of which will usually be incorporated into individual contracts of employment—is particularly great as regards the right to return to work. For s. 48 allows an employee to take advantage of either contractual or statutory rights so as to produce a composite right of the most favourable aspects of both types of provision.

Subs. (2)

Thus Sched. 2 supplements the provisions not only of Pt. III, but also those relating to unfair dismissal proceedings: ss. 56, 60–61, and redundancy proceedings —s. 86.

Subs. (3)

The contract of employment during absence. The question of whether the contract of employment subsists during the period of absence is not determined by the statute. As a matter of contract, it depends on the intentions of the parties (and see below as to the impact of collective agreements) as to whether the contract is suspended, though still in existence during the absence, or whether it is terminated and renewed only upon return to work. A presumption that the contract continues to exist where the employee indicates her intention to return to work (subs. (3) (*c*) (ii)), is implicit in the provisions of Sched. 13, para. 10 (Maternity) of which counts all the weeks of absence as being part of a period *of employment*, notwithstanding the fact that fewer than the statutory minimum hours are worked.

Where the contract terminates or is suspended *after* the 11th week before confinement (see subs. (3) (*a*)), it does not affect the statutory rights here, but it might better protect employees if it continued, albeit suspended in operation, in existence. Benefits from the longer period of employment in terms of *statutory* rights are secured by Sched. 13, but there may be gains in terms of *contractual* benefits—holidays and sick pay, as well as the contractual period of notice if the employee was not permitted to return to work, *e.g.* the employee may absent herself from work during the period of 11 weeks before confinement, sending in medical certificates, and claiming entitlement under the firm's sick pay scheme. More importantly, there may be life insurance or pension considerations attached to the contract of employment which will be affected by termination, often to the employee's detriment. For various other statutory purposes, her continuity of employment is expressly preserved by s. 56.

Collective agreements. A number of collective agreements and trade union model guides aim to secure contractual benefits during the period of absence. The model agreements produced by TASS, the GMWU and ASTMS all expressly provide that during the period of maternity leave the employee's contract is to continue unbroken, and the period of leave is to count towards calculating seniority, sickness and holiday entitlement. TASS and the GMWU even propose that the employees should have the option to commute all or part of their holiday entitlement accrued during the period of maternity leave. ASTMS specifies that maternity leave should not affect pension eligibility and benefits, and APEX proposes that there should be no loss of pension, seniority, status or promotion rights and benefits.

Various collective agreements have implemented such trade union aspirations. The United Biscuits Agreement with USDAW provides that during the period of absence service shall be regarded as continuous for the purposes of pension, sickness benefit, annual holiday entitlement and holiday pay accrual. The GMWU's agreement with Galleon Roadchef provides for annual increments, sick pay and holiday entitlements to accrue during the period of leave. At Co-operative Laundries the agreement provides for the period of absence to be deemed to be contributory service for the purposes of membership of the pension scheme. In the public sector, the G.L.C. (Staff) Agreement allows for the leave period to count for incremental purposes, and the IBA (Staff) allow for accrual of holidays, sick leave, pension rights and salary progression. The N.J.C. for Water Service Staffs Agreement provides that absences of up to 12 months because of maternity would not break continuity, but not more than six months of such absence would count for reckonable service. The B.B.C. will allow annual leave to remain unaltered only if maternity leave is under 18 weeks. Many companies, for reasons of administrative convenience (*e.g.* membership of employee in the pension fund) allow for the contract to continue, albeit suspended, in cases where employees are eligible to return to work. The contract is not regarded as terminated until (*e.g.* in W. D. & H. O. Wills), the 29th week after confinement if the employee has not returned. The Boots Company provides that if the employee does not exercise her right to return, she is considered to have left on the last day of work before the absence.

Finally, some agreements do not allow for the simpler options, where the contract is not terminated, of allowing benefits either to accumulate or not. Rather they have detailed provisions on the effect of absence on various benefits, particularly sick pay. The TASS and GMWU model agreements simply provide that *illness* related to pregnancy should be treated as normal sickness absence.

The APEX model agreement advises that maternity/paternity leave should not be reckonable against sick pay or holiday entitlement. As ASTMS points out in making the same point, otherwise a woman having a baby is likely to use up all her sick leave entitlement for the whole year, and if she gets 'flu afterwards, she would be unable to claim sick pay. The Post Office makes maternity leave an integral part of its sick pay scheme: illness and maternity leave count together towards a maximum six months' annual entitlement. Metal Box have a similar scheme and the N.J.C. Agreement for Gas Staffs and Senior Officers provides for the period of absence for maternity leave to rank against any period of sick pay entitlement under the Staff Sick Pay Scheme. Other employers treat maternity illness under the sick pay scheme only up to the beginning of official maternity leave (usually the 11th week before confinement)—the N.H.S., Heinz, Cadbury Schweppes Moreton Factory.

Absence before the 11th *week.* The contract *must* subsist, however, up to the beginning of the 11th week before confinement. The 11-week period was predetermined by the payment of maternity allowance by the Department of Health and Social Security. The only exception to this requirement is in the provisions of subs. (4), see Note. Problems are, therefore, bound to arise where a pregnant woman absents herself from work.

Now *absence* by itself does *not* operate to deny the woman her rights. But the temptation exists for industrial tribunals (and employers) to regard absence for reasons of pregnancy as tantamount to *termination/resignation* by the woman. And where this takes place *before* the 11th week, her ceasing to be employed will lead to a loss of her rights.

Two arguments and one fact combat this tendency. The arguments apply: first, where there is an agreement between the employer and employee that the woman will absent herself from work because of pregnancy (*e.g.* the woman reports that her doctor advises absence, and the employer concurs); secondly, where either side unilaterally decides on the absence. The fact is the existence of company practice or collective agreements which determine the issue. As regards the first argument, absence should be presumed *not* to terminate the contract, but only to suspend its operation. This is particularly evident where the woman (and employer) have evinced the *intention* that the woman should return to work after confinement. This way the woman continues to be employed and complies with this subsection, even if she absents herself from work *prior* to the 11th week before confinement. But in *Williams & Co.* v. *Secretary of State for Employment*

[1978] I.R.L.R. 235, an industrial tribunal refused to accept that employment had not terminated 13 weeks before confinement despite the *employer's* contention that the contract of employment *was* continuing and he was willing for the absent employee to return to her job at any time. The industrial tribunal accepted the argument that the right was *statutory* and independent of *contract*—but seems to have failed to notice the point of basic dependence noted here. The Department of Employment's refusal to pay a rebate to the employer from the Maternity Fund was upheld, despite the industrial tribunal's reluctance to reach this decision.

As regards the second argument, absence constituting termination will often be the result of the employee's purporting to resign or the employer dismissing her. With regard to the former, the E.A.T. has held that an employee's general statement of intention *not* to avail herself of her rights but in due course to leave employment is *not* an effective notice terminating her contract of employment. Such notice to be effective must be more specific as to actual date of termination (*Hughes* v. *Gwynedd Area Health Authority* [1977] I.R.L.R. 436 (E.A.T.)). All the more so, a notice of intention to be absent but to *claim* rights, including the right to return, should not be interpreted as a resignation. The E.A.T. even left it open for future decision as to whether *effective* resignations terminating *before* the 11th week are binding and irrevocable. So notice of intention to be absent will not be resignation unless it is quite specific: more likely, when absence actually occurs before the 11th week it will be open to imply merely suspension, or it may be that other provisions of the contract apply (unpaid leave, sickness provisions, the employer's own maternity policy)—but the employee continues in employment.

Apart from these two arguments, the *fact* of a clear employer policy or a collectively agreed procedure will often determine the issue in practice. ASTMS' policy on negotiating maternity agreements points out the need for flexibility on this question of leaving before or after the 11th week. Two factors are important. First, the payment of National Insurance Maternity Benefits which commences 11 weeks before the birth is forfeited while the woman remains in paid employment. Secondly, the woman may be under pressure to leave before the 11th week for health reasons—and a good maternity agreement should allow for transfer to an easier job in such a case or the safeguarding of all maternity benefits if the woman has to leave off working altogether. As was pointed out earlier, it might be most beneficial to the employee in these circumstances to stay away from work and, by sending in the medical certificates, benefit from any sick pay schemes applicable to her.

A number of company procedures should operate to avoid difficulties for the employee unwittingly leaving too early. The Boots Company provides for an interview as soon as the employee's pregnancy is known, and in the interview the employee is advised of her rights and made aware of the significance of leaving before the 11th week. A similar procedure operates at Cadbury Schweppes Moreton factory, which employs about 2,000 women. Phillips Industries Group Policy requires the employee to notify her superior as soon as pregnancy is confirmed, and again an interview follows.

If absence prior to the 11th week is a consequence of dismissal (see the meaning in s. 55), then either subs. (4) or the protection made available to pregnant women by s. 60 (Unfair Dismissal) will apply, and the latter's remedy should compensate for loss of any maternity benefits. Any dismissal prior to the 11th week should, of course, take account of the minimum periods of notice in s. 49, and their impact as regards the effective date of termination—*cf.* s. 55 (5) (not, unfortunately, applicable to the maternity provisions).

Two years' qualification period. The presumption of continuity applies—s. 151 (2), and see Sched. 13 for the rules as to computing periods of employment (s. 151 (1)).

Many collective agreements—both agreed and proposed by trade unions—provide for much shorter periods of qualification, *e.g.* TASS' Model Maternity Agreement specifies that eligibility depends on 12 months' continuous employment; ASTMS suggests a one-year qualifying period, but expressly states this should not preclude an initial demand that there should be no qualifying period. The GMWU Maternity Proposals are to apply in full to women who have completed 12 months' continuous service—but in the case of women with less than 12 months, it is proposed that negotiations should still provide for suitable arrangements if the women wish to return to work. APEX's Model Agreement for negotiators applies to all women employees, irrespective of service. When one reviews actual agreements concluded, many in the public sector only require one year's service qualification (*e.g.* British Gas, Local Government, N.H.S., Post Office) while in the private sector the periods vary: *e.g.* Heinz (Harlesden Factory) and TGWU and other trade unions—one year; Penguin Books and ASTMS—one year; London and Manchester Assurance and ASTMS—two years; Longman Publishing and ASTMS—21 months; and Wilson & Whitworth Publishing and NUJ—10 months. Sometimes the longer the period of service, the greater the benefits with regard to paid leave—*e.g.* Galleon Roadchef and GMWU.

Another issue is up to what point in time is the qualifying period to be calculated? The Act specifies two years up to the beginning of the 11*th week before* the expected week of confinement. But, for example, the TASS and ASTMS model agreements specify a 12-month period up to the expected date of *confinement*. The N.J.C. for Local Government Scheme requires 12 months' continuous service at the *date of application* for maternity leave—as does the agreement in the N.H.S. General Whitley Council. And the N.J.C. for Water Service Staffs agreement covers female employees with at least 12 months' continuous service *at the date of commencement* of the maternity leave.

21 *days' notice.* The requirement of three weeks' notice is now stated as being 21 days' notice. Subs. (3) (*c*) was amended by the Government at the Report Stage of the Employment Protection Bill 1975 to ensure that the right to maternity *pay* would not be dependent on the employee informing her employer of her intention to return to work.

Two possibilities exist which might prejudice the rights of the pregnant employee to return. First, where she actually expresses her intention *not* to return; and secondly, where she says nothing and the inference is drawn that she does not intend to return.

Conversely, of course, an expressed intention to return will satisfy the requirements of the Act—and this expression need not be in writing (unless the employer so requests). And again, an inference may be drawn from the employee's behaviour or other facts (*e.g.* she has other children who have not prevented her from working) which might suffice to satisfy the requirement.

Since there is nothing in the Act which provides that a statement, express or inferred, of intention *not* to return is binding, it seems to be open to the woman employee to *change her mind.* Providing she has fulfilled the other conditions (*e.g.* worked up to the 11th week before confinement) she can at any time express her intention to return and the right to return then comes into being. This view was said by Phillips J. in *Hughes* v. *Gwynedd Area Health Authority* [1977] I.R.L.R. 436 (E.A.T.) to have " a good deal to commend it." Only if the woman has actually *resigned,* to take effect before the 11th week begins, may she be precluded from claiming her right.

The problems of whether the woman has given notice may be avoided, at least so far as the employer is concerned, by a personnel policy which provides for interviews with pregnant employees or requires them to fill out forms giving their intentions. Trade unions should ensure that women members are properly advised and represented in the circumstances. One possible method of avoiding the dangers of this notice requirement is for employers to give the employee the option of stating that she is not sure whether she intends to return to work, in which case the company indicates that they will be prepared to keep her job open provided she confirms her intention by a certain date after her confinement. Given the pressures of the months immediately following the birth of a child, one would expect perhaps a minimum three to four months would be the period required before the mother might set up a routine which would enable her to formulate her future employment plans.

Timeliness. The requirement of timeliness—21 days before the absence begins— is subject to reasonable practicality. Judges should appreciate the position of a pregnant woman in her seventh month of pregnancy, carrying extra weight, more tired and subject to the emotional pressures of the tremendous experience she is about to undergo. The requirement here, and even more the argument that a woman has " resigned " from her job before the 11th week, should be interpreted in light of these factors. Phillips J. showed an understanding of these in *Hughes* when he envisaged the possibility that women might resign in error, in ignorance of their rights, without full understanding, and without discussion with their husbands and those able to advise them. Such resignations might not be binding, he said, in certain conditions. And, one hopes, the timeliness requirement would be interpreted

in that light. In any event, the practical effect may be mitigated by s. 34 (4)—
see the Note on that subsection.

Subs. (4)

Dismissal before the 11th week. Periods when the employee has been absent from
work wholly or partly because of pregnancy or confinement count in the qualification
period of two years up to the 11th week before confinement (Sched. 13, para.
9 (1) (*d*)). Therefore, periods of absence due to dismissal as envisaged here also
count in calculating any qualifying period.

According to this subsection, it would seem that an employee dismissed under
s. 60 (1) (*a*) or (*b*), and not re-engaged in accordance with s. 60, is entitled to the
rights of maternity pay and to return to work *whether the dismissal is fair or
unfair.* For a dismissal under s. 60 (1) (*a*) or (*b*) without re-engagement may be
fair or unfair. It will depend on, *e.g.* whether the failure to re-engage was due to
there being no suitable available vacancy or its being offered (s. 60 (2)). So if
the dismissal is *fair*—she retains her rights under subs. (1); all the more so, one
would have thought, if she was *unfairly* dismissed.

Under the original new cl. 2 inserted by the Government at the Committee Stage
of the Employment Protection Bill 1975, *only* an employee *fairly* dismissed was
to have these rights. An employee *unfairly* dismissed would presumably have been
compensated for her loss in a claim for unfair dismissal. But unless the words
" re-engaged in accordance with " are interpreted as to *exclude* the possibility of *unfair*
dismissal, this subsection would seem to give an employee dismissed under s. 60 (1) (*a*)
or (*b*) a choice of two options. Either to proceed under the procedures in ss. 45–47,
in order to obtain compensation even when short-circuited by the employer's unfair
dismissal, or to proceed on a claim for unfair dismissal—s. 60.

The remedies differ in their relative merits as far as the employee is concerned,
e.g. the unfair dismissal claim needs to be made within three months of dismissal—
s. 67 (2). If the remedy is sought under ss. 45–47, the employee can wait for some
considerable time after confinement before commencing her action. Again the
position where a redundancy occurs may differ—compare s. 45 (3): employee is
entitled to a suitable alternative vacancy, and the position in the law of unfair
dismissal in a redundancy situation—see *Vokes Ltd.* v. *Bear* [1974] I.C.R. 1.

It should be remembered that a claim for unfair dismissal may be made under
s. 60 in circumstances where no rights under this section have been lost, *e.g.* because
the employee was continuously employed for less than the requisite two years.
Presumably, however, a sum may be awarded for the loss of *potential* maternity
benefits, much as under the previous law damages were awarded for loss of
potential redundancy rights.

One unfortunate consequence of these provisions is that to the layman it may
appear confusing that an employee has been *fairly* sacked under s. 60—yet nonetheless retains her rights under this section to maternity pay and to return to work.
It will be necessary to avoid the deterrent effect of this rather confusing terminology.

Maternity pay

Maternity pay

34.—(1) Maternity pay shall be paid in respect of a period not
exceeding, or periods not exceeding in the aggregate, six weeks during
which the employee is absent from work wholly or partly because of
pregnancy or confinement (in this section and sections 35 and 36 referred
to as the payment period or payment periods).

(2) An employee shall not be entitled to maternity pay for any
absence before the beginning of the eleventh week before the expected
week of confinement, and her payment period or payment periods shall
be the first six weeks of absence starting on or falling after the beginning
of that eleventh week.

(3) The Secretary of State may by order vary the periods of six weeks
referred to in subsections (1) and (2), or those periods as varied from
time to time under this subsection, but no such order shall be made

unless a draft of the order has been laid before Parliament and approved by resolution of each House of Parliament.

(4) Where an employee gives her employer the information required by section 33 (3) (*c*) or produces any certificate requested under section 33 (5) after the beginning of the payment period or the first of the payments periods, she shall not be entitled to maternity pay for any part of that period until she gives him that information or certificate, but on giving him the information or, as the case may be, producing the certificate, she shall be entitled to be paid in respect of that part of the period or periods which fell before the giving of the information or the production of the certificate.

DERIVATION
1975, s. 36.

GENERAL NOTE
Subs. (1)

Six weeks in the aggregate. The entitlement to the six weeks' pay does not require the six weeks to be consecutive, as long as they amount in the aggregate to six. So an employee may choose to intersperse her six weeks of absence with periods of work, *e.g.* beginning with the 11th week before confinement, two weeks could be taken on paid leave of maternity absence, and then a few weeks of work, followed by the final four weeks of paid leave.

Maternity pay in collective agreements. Collective agreements are usually more generous in the quantity of maternity pay to which employees are entitled. In the public sector, paid maternity leave may be for an extended period of almost full pay, followed by a further period on half pay, *e.g.* the local government N.J.C. Scheme provides for the first four weeks at full and a further 14 weeks at half pay; similar provisions apply at British Gas, the G.L.C., N.H.S. and the University Clerical and Administrative Staff. In the private sector, ASTMS has an agreement with Penguin Books for 16 weeks' leave at full pay and eight weeks at half pay, and with London & Manchester Assurance, for 24 weeks at 90 per cent. of weekly pay. The GMWU with Galleon Roadchef provides for the period of fully paid maternity leave to rise from two weeks after one year's service, to 20 weeks after seven years' service. Payment is, however, often subject to conditions—see Note to subs. (2).

Subs. (2)

Lump sum or weekly payment. There is no requirement as to how the maternity pay is to be paid out—weekly, monthly or in a lump sum. The Department of Employment's view is that payment of a lump sum at the *end* of six weeks would be contrary to the intention of the Act. Certainly, if the contract of employment continues to exist (albeit suspended)—the normal intervals of payment should be observed. There is nothing to prevent the employer from paying the lump sum of six weeks' pay at the beginning of the period of absence.

Conditions to payment in collective agreements. Unlike the statutory entitlement, payment of negotiated maternity pay above a certain level of payments is often conditional upon the employee returning to work—particularly in the public sector. So part of the payments to staff at British Gas, the G.L.C., in local government, the N.H.S. and the Post Office is withheld until three months after the employee returns to work. This seems to be less common in the private sector—*e.g.* the Galleon Roadchef and GMWU agreement provides for payment whether or not the employee returns. But others do provide for *repayment* of part if the employee does not return for a specified period, *e.g.* Penguin Books and ASTMS: employees who return for less than five months must repay maternity pay proportionately.

Subs. (4)

This seems to conflict to some extent with the requirement of timeliness of the information given under s. 33 (3) (*c*). According to that section, the information must be given " at least 21 days before her absence begins, or if that is not reasonably practicable, as soon as reasonably practicable." Yet here the information is being given *after* the beginning of the payment period, *i.e.* according to subs. (1), after absence has begun. It would seem that an employee can obtain retrospective maternity payment even though she is late in informing the employer as required by

s. 33 (3) (c). The alternative view, that the requirement of s. 33 (3) (c) operates to exclude payment where the information is not notified in time, would render this subsection meaningless. Given that an extension of the 21-day period in s. 33 (3) (c) is possible where giving the information is not reasonably practicable, whereas the retrospective entitlement in this subsection is absolute (" she shall be entitled "), it would seem that the timeliness requirement of s. 33 (3) (c) is made much more flexible than it appears.

The question then arises whether this result, flowing from a subsection relating only to maternity pay, affects the requirement of timeliness as it relates to the giving of information for the purposes of the right to return to work in s. 33 (3) (c) (i) and (ii). Is the flexibility of the first requirement of timeliness consistent with or different from the second? After all, the same provision applies to both rights.

Calculation of maternity pay

35.—(1) The amount of maternity pay to which an employee is entitled as respects any week shall be nine-tenths of a week's pay reduced by the amount of maternity allowance payable for the week under Part I of Schedule 4 to the Social Security Act 1975, whether or not the employee in question is entitled to the whole or any part of that allowance.

(2) Maternity pay shall accrue due to an employee from day to day and in calculating the amount of maternity pay payable for any day—

> (a) there shall be disregarded Sunday or such other day in each week as may be prescribed in relation to that employee under section 22 (10) of the Social Security Act 1975 for the purpose of calculating the daily rate of maternity allowance under that Act; and

> (b) the amount payable for any other day shall be taken as one-sixth of the amount of the maternity pay for the week in which the day falls.

(3) Subject to subsection (4), a right to maternity pay shall not affect any right of an employee in relation to remuneration under any contract of employment (in this section referred to as " contractual remuneration ").

(4) Any contractual remuneration paid to an employee in respect of a day within a payment period shall go towards discharging any liability of the employer to pay maternity pay in respect of that day, and conversely any maternity pay paid in respect of a day shall go towards discharging any liability of the employer to pay contractual remuneration in respect of that day.

DERIVATION
  1975, s. 37 (1) to (4).

GENERAL NOTE
Subs. (1)
  Maternity pay and national insurance benefits. In 1977 employees became entitled to an earnings-related supplement on top of their maternity allowance. The figure of nine-tenths of a week's pay was introduced as it was calculated that roughly one-tenth would be earnings-related supplement. Only the flat-rate allowance is deducted from the employer's payment—*not* the supplement. So the employer is required to top up the State benefits payable regardless of the level of contributions paid. Together with earnings-related supplement, employees should get approximately full pay (less the employer's and employee's National Insurance contributions).
  Maternity pay and tax. The Department of Employment Guide now stipulates that maternity pay is taxable. Where a contract of employment is in existence at the date of payment of the maternity pay, the employer should deduct tax under normal P.A.Y.E. arrangements. With effect from April 6, 1978, where the contract of employment was terminated before the date of payment *no tax* should be deducted by the employer. The employee should, however, show the payment as

untaxed income in her (or her husband's) return of income to the Inland Revenue.

Calculation of a week's pay. A week's pay is defined in Sched. 14, Pt. II. The calculation date for a week's pay for the purposes of maternity pay is defined in para. 7 (1) (*d*)—the last day on which the employee worked. Certain questions arise here—where the employee has taken another job, following her acceptance of an offer made under s. 60 (2) and (3), her week's pay is to be calculated as that of her new job. This, even though, as provided in s. 60 (3) (*c*), the terms of her new employment may be rather less favourable than those of her old job. This may be a source of some apparent injustice, as a woman who refuses the offer of a new job may benefit from a higher maternity payment than a woman who accepts it (as to the right of refusal—see the Note to s. 60 (3)). One wonders why the calculation date was not made the last day on which the employee worked under the " original contract of employment" (as defined in s. 153 (1)). *Cf.* the basis of compensation for the other right—the right to return to work (Sched. 2, para. 2 (5)).

Subs. (3)

This is substantially identical to ss. 16 (1), 21 (2), 27 (5) and 31 (10). These rights are not to prejudice an employee in any way with regard to her contractual remuneration.

Subs. (4)

Again, similar provisions are to be found in ss. 16 (2), 21 (3), 27 (6) and 31 (11). Again, the question arises as to whether a day or other period during which maternity pay is payable but is set-off by the employer's existing contractual obligation is to count towards the six-week period of entitlement. The payment periods are specified in s. 34 (2) as the first six weeks of absence, but it is clear that this may be broken up into periods totalling in the aggregate six weeks but spread over a longer period. If the employee does not seek to enforce her statutory rights but relies on contractual rights, is she thereby to be deprived of some of her entitlement? With respect to previous similar benefits, it was thought not (see the Notes to ss. 16 (2) and 21 (3)).

Complaint to industrial tribunal

36.—(1) A complaint may be presented to an industrial tribunal by an employee against her employer that he has failed to pay her the whole or any part of the maternity pay to which she is entitled.

(2) An industrial tribunal shall not entertain a complaint under subsection (1) unless it is presented to the tribunal before the end of the period of three months beginning with the last day of the payment period or, as the case may be, the last of the payment periods, or within such further period as the tribunal considers reasonable in a case where it is satisfied that it was not reasonably practicable for the complaint to be presented within the period of three months.

(3) Where an industrial tribunal finds a complaint under subsection (1) well-founded, the tribunal shall order the employer to pay the complainant the amount of maternity pay which it finds is due to her.

DERIVATION
1975, s. 38.

GENERAL NOTE

Despite the large number of women who have received maternity pay (46,287 for which rebate had been paid in the 10 months from April 6, 1977, to January 31, 1978), only a tiny number of complaints have reached tribunals. In 1978, up to November, there were two cases reported in the Industrial Relations Law Reports— one on maternity pay and one on maternity leave. In 1977, another three on maternity leave, plus one which went on appeal and was reported in 1978. The reasons for this have not yet been discovered.

Maternity Pay Fund

37.—(1) The Secretary of State shall continue to have the control and management of the Maternity Pay Fund established under section 39 of the Employment Protection Act 1975, and payments shall be made out of that fund in accordance with the following provisions of this Part and section 156 (1).

(2) The Secretary of State shall prepare accounts of the Maternity Pay Fund in such form as the Treasury may direct and shall send them to the Comptroller and Auditor General not later than the end of the month of November following the end of the financial year to which the accounts relate; and the Comptroller and Auditor General shall examine and certify every such account and shall lay copies thereof, together with his report thereon, before Parliament.

(3) Any money in the Maternity Pay Fund may from time to time be paid over to the National Debt Commissioners and invested by them, in accordance with such directions as may be given by the Treasury, in any such manner as may be specified by an order of the Treasury for the time being in force under section 22 (1) of the National Savings Bank Act 1971.

DERIVATION
1975, s. 39.

GENERAL NOTE
Cf. s. 103 which contains substantially similar provisions with regard to the Redundancy Fund.

Advances out of National Loans Fund

38.—(1) Subject to the provisions of subsections (2) to (4), the Treasury may from time to time advance out of the National Loans Fund to the Secretary of State for the purposes of the Maternity Pay Fund such sums as the Secretary of State may request; and any sums advanced to the Secretary of State under this section shall be paid into the Maternity Pay Fund.

(2) The aggregate amount outstanding by way of principal in respect of sums advanced to the Secretary of State under subsection (1) shall not at any time exceed £4 million, or such larger sum, not exceeding £10 million, as the Secretary of State may by order made with the consent of the Treasury determine.

(3) No order under subsection (2) shall be made unless a draft of the order has been laid before Parliament and approved by resolution of each House of Parliament.

(4) Any sums advanced to the Secretary of State under subsection (1) shall be re-paid by the Secretary of State out of the Maternity Pay Fund into the National Loans Fund in such manner and at such times, and with interest thereon at such rate, as the Treasury may direct.

DERIVATION
1975, s. 41.

GENERAL NOTE
Cf. s. 109 which contains substantially identical provisions with regard to the Redundancy Fund.

Maternity pay rebate

39.—(1) Subject to any regulations made under this section, the Secretary of State shall pay out of the Maternity Pay Fund to every employer who makes a claim under this section and who, being liable to pay, has paid maternity pay to an employee, an amount equal to the full amount of maternity pay so paid (in this section and sections 42 and 43 referred to as a " maternity pay rebate ").

(2) The Secretary of State may if he thinks fit, and if he is satisfied that it would be just and equitable to do so having regard to all the relevant circumstances, pay such a rebate to an employer who makes a claim under this section and who has paid maternity pay to an employee in circumstances in which, by reason of the time limit provided for in section 36 (2) a complaint by the employee has been dismissed, or would not be entertained, by an industrial tribunal.

(3) For the purposes of subsections (1) and (2), a payment of contractual remuneration by an employer shall be treated as a payment of maternity pay to the extent that, by virtue of section 35 (4),—

(*a*) it extinguishes the employer's liability to pay maternity pay; or

(*b*) in a case falling within subsection (2), it would extinguish that liability if a complaint by the employee were not time-barred as described in that subsection.

(4) The Secretary of State shall make provision by regulations as to the making of claims for maternity pay rebates under this section and such regulations may in particular—

(*a*) require a claim to be made within such time limit as may be prescribed; and

(*b*) require a claim to be supported by such evidence as may be prescribed.

DERIVATION
1975, s. 42.

GENERAL NOTE
Subs. (1)

The appropriate Regulations are the Maternity Pay (Rebate) Regulations 1977 (S.I. 1977 No. 322) which came into operation on April 6, 1977. Claims for rebate from the Maternity Pay Fund are dealt with through Redundancy Payments Offices, which will provide employers with the necessary forms MP1 and MP1(R). During the first 21 weeks of operation from April 6 to August 31, 1977, the Fund paid out 12,000 payments.

Subs. (2)

Ex gratia payments made by employers to their employees in the circumstances described here may, therefore, be reimbursed by the Secretary of State. Effectively, the Secretary of State is making the payments through the medium of the employer from moneys in the Fund. Since the payment depends on the initiative of the employer, perhaps payment which is " just and equitable " ought not to depend entirely on the employer's goodwill.

Subs. (3)

Rebates may be paid to compensate an employer for payments made in accordance with a contractual term negotiated between himself and the employee which are equivalent to the statutory right to maternity pay and which, in accordance with s. 35 (4), extinguish it. The rebate is payable out of the Fund. Nonetheless, the employee or trade union negotiating with a hard-bargaining employer should consider that the employer granting maternity pay to this extent may be conceding little by it, for the cost is borne by the Fund which spreads it evenly across all employers, not solely on firms and industries employing women of child-bearing age.

Subs. (4)

The Regulations prescribe a time limit of six months beginning with the day on which the payment (*i.e.* a lump sum), or where there is more than one, the final payment, is made, or within such further period as the Secretary of State may allow. The Secretary of State can ask for such documents as are required to support the claim—and note in particular reg. 5 (2)—" every claim for a rebate shall be accompanied by a receipt signed by the employee concerned evidencing the payment by the employer to that employee of the maternity pay to which the claim relates."

Payments to employees out of Maternity Pay Fund

40.—(1) Where an employee claims that her employer is liable to pay her maternity pay and—

  (*a*) that she has taken all reasonable steps (other than proceedings to enforce a tribunal award) to recover payment from the employer; or

  (*b*) that her employer is insolvent (as defined in section 127 for the purposes of sections 122 to 126);

and that the whole or part of the maternity pay remains unpaid, the employee may apply to the Secretary of State under this section.

(2) If the Secretary of State is satisfied that the claim is well-founded the Secretary of State shall pay the employee out of the Maternity Pay Fund the amount of the maternity pay which appears to the Secretary of State to be unpaid.

(3) A payment made by the Secretary of State to an employee under this section shall, for the purpose of discharging any liability of the employer to the employee, be treated as if it had been made by the employer.

DERIVATION
    1975, s. 43.

GENERAL NOTE
    Cf. s. 106 (1) and (2) which contains similar provisions with regard to redundancy claims from an insolvent employer.

Unreasonable default by employer

41.—(1) Where the Secretary of State makes a payment to an employee in respect of unpaid maternity pay in a case falling within section 40 (1) (*a*) and it appears to the Secretary of State that the employer's default in payment was without reasonable excuse, the Secretary of State may recover from the employer such amount as the Secretary of State considers appropriate, not exceeding the amount of maternity pay which the employer failed to pay.

(2) Where a sum is recovered by the Secretary of State by virtue of this section that sum shall be paid into the Maternity Pay Fund.

DERIVATION
    1975, s. 45.

GENERAL NOTE
    Cf. s. 106 (3) and (4) which contains similar provisions with regard to the Secretary of State's recourse against an employer who has failed to pay a redundancy claim.

Supplementary provisions relating to employer's insolvency

42.—(1) Where the Secretary of State makes a payment to an employee under section 122 (which provides for payments out of the Redundancy Fund in respect of certain debts where an employer is insolvent) and that payment, in whole or in part, represents arrears of pay, then, in ascertaining for the purpose of section 40 the amount of any unpaid maternity pay, section 35 (4) shall apply as if the arrears of pay in question had been duly paid by the employer to the employee in accordance with the contract of employment.

(2) Where the Secretary of State makes a payment to an employee out of the Redundancy Fund under section 122 which, if it had been made by the employer to the employee, would have attracted a maternity pay rebate from the Maternity Pay Fund in accordance with section 39,

then, the Secretary of State shall make a payment out of the Maternity Pay Fund into the Redundancy Fund of an amount corresponding to the amount of rebate which would have been so payable.

DERIVATION
  1975, s. 45.

Complaints and appeals to industrial tribunal

43.—(1) A person who has—

  (*a*) made a claim for a maternity pay rebate under section 39, in a case to which subsection (1) of that section applies; or
  (*b*) applied for a payment under section 40,

may, subject to subsection (5), present a complaint to an industrial tribunal that—

  (i) the Secretary of State has failed to make any such payment; or
  (ii) any such payment made by the Secretary of State is less than the amount which should have been paid.

(2) Where an industrial tribunal finds that the Secretary of State ought to make any such payment or further payment, it shall make a declaration to that effect and shall also declare the amount of any such payment which it finds the Secretary of State ought to make.

(3) An employer who has made a claim for a maternity pay rebate under section 39, in a case to which subsection (2) of that section applies, may, subject to subsection (5), appeal to an industrial tribunal on the ground that—

  (*a*) the Secretary of State has refused to pay a maternity pay rebate; or
  (*b*) any rebate paid by the Secretary of State is less than the amount which should have been paid,

and if on any such appeal the tribunal is satisfied that it is just and equitable having regard to all the relevant circumstances that a maternity pay rebate should be paid or, as the case may be, finds that a further payment by way of rebate should be made, the tribunal shall determine accordingly, and the Secretary of State shall comply with the determination.

(4) Where the Secretary of State determines that an amount is recoverable from an employer under section 41, the employer may, subject to subsection (5), appeal to an industrial tribunal; and if on any such appeal the tribunal is satisfied that no amount should be recovered from the employer, or that a lesser or greater amount should be recovered (but in any case not exceeding the amount of maternity pay which the employer failed to pay) the tribunal shall determine accordingly and the amount, if any, so determined shall be the amount recoverable from the employer by the Secretary of State.

(5) An industrial tribunal shall not entertain a complaint or appeal under this section unless it is presented to the tribunal within the period of three months beginning with the date on which the relevant decision of the Secretary of State was communicated to the complainant or appellant or within such further period as the tribunal considers reasonable in a case where it is satisfied that it was not reasonably practicable for the complaint or appeal to be presented within the period of three months.

DERIVATION
  1975, s. 46.

GENERAL NOTE
  Cf. s. 108, and particularly s. 108 (4) which contains similar provisions relating to redundancy rebate claims.

Provisions as to information

44.—(1) Where an application is made to the Secretary of State by an employee under section 40, the Secretary of State may require—

(a) the employer to provide him with such information as the Secretary of State may reasonably require for the purpose of determining whether the employee's application is well-founded; and

(b) any person having the custody or control of any relevant records or other documents to produce for examination on behalf of the Secretary of State any such document in that person's custody or under his control which is of such a description as the Secretary of State may require.

(2) Any such requirement shall be made by a notice in writing given to the person on whom the requirement is imposed and may be varied or revoked by a subsequent notice so given.

(3) If a person refuses or wilfully neglects to furnish any information or produce any document which he has been required to furnish or produce by a notice under this section he shall be liable on summary conviction to a fine not exceeding £100.

(4) If any person in making a claim under section 39 or an application under section 40 or in purporting to comply with a requirement of a notice under this section knowingly or recklessly makes any false statement he shall be liable on summary conviction to a fine not exceeding £400.

DERIVATION
    1975, s. 47.

GENERAL NOTE
    Cf. s. 107 which creates similar offences in redundancy claims, and imposes heavier penalties. See s. 138 (1) which excludes Crown employment from the application of this section, but see s. 138 (5).

Right to return to work

Right to return to work

45.—(1) The right to return to work of an employee who has been absent from work wholly or partly because of pregnancy or confinement is, subject to the following provisions of this Act, a right to return to work with her original employer, or, where appropriate, his successor, at any time before the end of the period of twenty-nine weeks beginning with the week in which the date of confinement falls, in the job in which she was employed under the original contract of employment and on terms and conditions not less favourable than those which would have been applicable to her if she had not been so absent.

(2) In subsection (1) " terms and conditions not less favourable than those which would have been applicable to her if she had not been so absent " means, as regards seniority, pension rights and other similar rights, that the period or periods of employment prior to the employee's absence shall be regarded as continuous with her employment following that absence.

(3) If an employee is entitled to return to work in accordance with subsection (1), but it is not practicable by reason of redundancy for the employer to permit her so to return to work she shall be entitled, where there is a suitable available vacancy, to be offered alternative employment with her employer (or his successor), or an associated employer, under a new contract of employment complying with subsection (4).

(4) The new contract of employment must be such that—
   (a) the work to be done under the contract is of a kind which is both suitable in relation to the employee and appropriate for her to do in the circumstances; and
   (b) the provisions of the new contract as to the capacity and place in which she is to be employed and as to the other terms and conditions of her employment are not substantially less favourable to her than if she had returned to work in accordance with subsection (1).

DERIVATION
   1975, s. 48 (1) (2) (4) (5).

GENERAL NOTE
   The right to return to work only lasts for 29 weeks after the week of confinement (subject to s. 47 exceptions). One must be very sceptical of the value of this right. It amounts to a right to return to work whilst encumbered by a child less than eight months old. This is next to no right at all given the current lack of child-care facilities. To make it a reality there would have to be something in the law to require, or at least encourage, the provision of such facilities which would make a return to work possible. As it is, there is nothing to make employers provide facilities which would enable women to reclaim their jobs, and nothing is said about publicly provided schemes which would make the legal right effective. Local authority and private nursery facilities for child-care are almost non-existent, particularly those which cater for babies under two years. Some trade unions are committed to attempting to provide some measure of aid to mothers trying to cope with the double burden of child-care and work—see, e.g. the provisions in the model collective agreements cited in the Note to s. 33 (1) (*Collective agreements*). But as it stands, the legal right is largely a rhetorical exercise.

Subs. (1)
   In the original Employment Protection Bill 1975, cl. 42 (1) gave the employee the right to return to work in " the occupation in which she was employed under the original contract of employment." In the recast right to return to work contained in new cl. 4 introduced at the Committee Stage, this was changed from " occupation " to " job," but " job " was not defined. This appeared to narrow the scope of the right of the returning employee to her previous job only. In the Act, however, " job " is defined in s. 153 (1). It is not clear whether that definition expands the area of possible jobs to which the returning employee now has a right so as to include, e.g. jobs which are of the same nature, and in the same place and capacity. Whatever may be the precise meaning, it is clear that it can only expand the rights of the employee, i.e. she may be entitled to claim either her old job or some other essentially identical one. There is nothing which allows her employer to refuse the old job and offer another. His right to offer alternative employment is limited to the circumstances described in subs. (3). If he makes an offer of another " job," the employee may accept it, or ignore it and proceed to invoke the remedies provided by s. 46.
   At least two obstacles stand in the way of a woman's returning to do the same work she was doing before she left to have a baby. The first is a consequence of legal definition of " job." If this is legally defined in the contract of employment so as to cover a wide range of posts or types of work (e.g. clerical assistant, machine operative), or to cover a wide geographical area (e.g. work in any establishment of the employer)—the employer will be within his rights if he requires her to return to any of these posts or places. They are her " original job " as defined in law, whatever may be the worker's understanding of the right to return to work. This hazard can be combated by insisting on precise job descriptions and striking out wide flexibility or mobility clauses. The provision in s. 1 (3) (*f*) for a job title to be provided may help—see the Note on that subsection above (*Title of the job*). And see the attitude of the industrial tribunal in the case cited below—*Edgell*.
   The second potential obstacle is the attitude of industrial tribunals to the woman's right to return. This may be illustrated by *Edgell* v. *Lloyd's Register of Shipping* [1977] I.R.L.R. 463, where the woman asked for her post back again, and

the employer gave her another post of the same grade but with different duties and responsibilities. This was due to an administrative re-organisation which had been carried out in her absence.

To this case the industrial tribunal responded as follows:

"This is one of the elements of course which the learned draftsmen of the Act did not think about. They appear to think that businesses remain static and their organisation remains the same over an indefinite period. Of course any company or any employer is allowed to carry out such re-organisations and change their administration to suit the requirements of their business. *It is not our duty as a tribunal to question the right of management to manage.* All we are here to do is to be quite certain that an employer when carrying out those changes acts justly and fairly to the employee" (para. 10).

To the woman's arguments that her rights were based on the definition of "job"—including "nature of the work" and "capacity"—the industrial tribunal replied: "This is not an exercise in theology or semantics." Her claim was dismissed.

If industrial tribunals are going to allow managements the power to change the job offered under the aegis of an unchallengeable "management prerogative"—the outlook for returning mothers is grim. For there is nothing here which allows an employer to deny the employee her old job because it is not "practicable" for him to take her back, or because he has hired a replacement (*cf.* the provisions on reinstatement and re-engagement for unfair dismissal—ss. 69 (5) (*b*), 69 (6) (*b*) and 70 (1)). (Contrast *McFadden* v. *Greater Glasgow Passenger Transport Executive* [1977] I.R.L.R. 327, where the industrial tribunal rejected the employer's argument that giving the returning mother a supernumerary post instead of her old established clerical position was permitted. Many of the old terms were applicable but certain others (status, her own desk, security of employment) were not. Cutbacks in her employer's expenditure were not a justification.)

Subs. (2)

It is not clear if the period of absence itself counts as part of the continuous employment so as to make the period prior to it continuous with the period following it. Presumably it does, as this is the case as regards other statutory aspects of employment (Sched. 13, para. 10) and to interpret it otherwise would be to set up two separate and conflicting standards for computing continuity. *Cf.* s. 33 (4) which allows for a period of absence prior to the 11th week before confinement to count in calculating the two-year qualifying period. This definition of "terms and conditions" applicable upon the woman's return to work would seem to include any improvements from which she would have benefited but for her absence. *Cf.* the definition of reinstatement in s. 69 (3). For provisions in collective agreements which safeguard rights dependent on seniority, see the Note to s. 33 (3) (*Collective agreements*).

Subs. (3)

Cf. s. 60 (2) where any employee dismissed for pregnancy may be offered a suitable vacancy with her employer or his successor, but not with an associated employer as here. Why there should be this inconsistency in the treatment of dismissal before and after the pregnancy is not explained. The original Employment Protection Bill 1975 was consistent in allowing for an offer to be made by an associated employer where she was dismissed prior to confinement (c. 38 (2)).

Failure to make such an offer as is referred to here is automatically to be treated as an unfair dismissal (Sched. 2, para. 2 (2)). If there is redundancy and no vacancy exists, the employee may claim a redundancy payment (s. 46, referring to s. 86, and Sched. 2, Pt. II).

Subs. (4)

Cf. the similar provisions relating to an offer of alternative employment in s. 60 (3) (*b*) and (*c*), and see the Note on that subsection. But here there appears to be less justification for an employer offering somewhat less favourable terms, as there might be in offering such terms to a pregnant employee. Therefore, a refusal by a returning employee to accept the offer is even less likely to be unreasonable. An employer dismissing her in those circumstances is likely to be acting unreasonably and unfairly, and see the special provisions regulating unfair dismissals in these circumstances in Sched. 2, Pt. I (applicable by virtue of s. 46).

Enforcement of rights under s. 45

46. The remedies of an employee for infringement of either of the rights mentioned in section 45 are those conferred by or by virtue of the provisions of sections 47, 56 and 86 and Schedule 2.

DERIVATION
1975, s. 48 (6).

Exercise of right to return to work

47.—(1) An employee shall exercise her right to return to work by notifying the employer (who may be her original employer or a successor of that employer) at least seven days before the day on which she proposes to return of her proposal to return on that day (in this section referred to as the " notified day of return ").

(2) An employer may postpone an employee's return to work until a date not more than four weeks after the notified day of return if he notifies her before that day that for specified reasons he is postponing her return until that date, and accordingly she will be entitled to return to work with him on that date.

(3) Subject to subsection (4), an employee may—

> (a) postpone her return to work until a date not exceeding four weeks from the notified day of return, notwithstanding that that date falls after the end of the period of twenty-nine weeks mentioned in section 45 (1); and
>
> (b) where no day of return has been notified to the employer, extend the time during which she may exercise her right to return in accordance with subsection (1), so that she returns to work not later than four weeks from the expiration of the said period of twenty-nine weeks;

if before the notified day of return or, as the case may be, the expiration of the period of twenty-nine weeks she gives the employer a certificate from a registered medical practitioner stating that by reason of disease or bodily or mental disablement she will be incapable of work on the notified day of return or the expiration of that period, as the case may be.

(4) Where an employee has once exercised a right of postponement or extension under subsection (3) (a) or (b), she shall not again be entitled to exercise a right of postponement or extension under that subsection in connection with the same return to work.

(5) If an employee has notified a day of return but there is an interruption of work (whether due to industrial action or some other reason) which renders it unreasonable to expect the employee to return to work on the notified day of return, she may instead return to work when work resumes after the interruption or as soon as reasonably practicable thereafter.

(6) If no day of return has been notified and there is an interruption of work (whether due to industrial action or some other reason) which renders it unreasonable to expect the employee to return to work before the expiration of the period of twenty-nine weeks referred to in section 45 (1), or which appears likely to have that effect, and in consequence the employee does not notify a day of return, the employee may exercise her right to return in accordance with subsection (1) so that she returns to work at any time before the end of the period of fourteen days from the end of the interruption notwithstanding that she returns to work outside the said period of twenty-nine weeks.

(7) Where the employee has either—

> (a) exercised the right under subsection (3) (b) to extend the period during which she may exercise her right to return; or

  (*b*) refrained from notifying the day of return in the circumstances
    described in subsection (6),

the other of those subsections shall apply as if for the reference to the
expiration of the period of twenty-nine weeks there were substituted a
reference to the expiration of the further period of four weeks or, as the
case may be, of the period of fourteen days from the end of the interruption of work.

  (8) Where—

    (*a*) an employee's return is postponed under subsection (2) or
      (3) (*a*), or

    (*b*) the employee returns to work on a day later than the notified
      day of return in the circumstances described in subsection (5),

then, subject to subsection (4), references in those subsections and in
sections 56 and 86 and Schedule 2 to the notified day of return shall be
construed as references to the day to which the return is postponed or,
as the case may be, that later day.

DERIVATION
  1975, s. 49.

GENERAL NOTE
Subs. (1)
  This is presumably subject to the Public Health Act 1936, s. 205 of which
prohibits the employment of women in a factory or workshop within four weeks of
giving birth. Other than the power of postponement in subs. (2), an employer
has no power to refuse to allow the employee to return to work. Such a refusal
would be a dismissal and subject to a claim for unfair dismissal—s. 56, or
redundancy—s. 86.
  " One week " in the Employment Protection Act 1975 has been transformed into
seven days here.

Subs. (2)
  Clearly the reasons of the employer must be given before the employee's notified
day of return, not the employer's postponed date.

Subs. (3)
  There is nothing stated in the section about whether an employee may change her
mind after having given a notification to her employer about a proposed return to
work. Certainly it would seem justifiable for an employee, where medical reasons
required it, to extend her period of maternity leave beyond four weeks after a
notified day of return, as long as the eventual day of return did not go beyond
33 weeks from the week of confinement.
  One may contrast these provisions with the unlimited amount of time allowed
where there has been an interruption of work rendering it unreasonable to expect
the employee to return (subss. (5) and (6)). Events affecting the employee's
health and welfare are subject to time limits; those affecting the employer's enterprise
are not.

Subss. (5) *and* (6)
  What is an interruption of work which renders it unreasonable to expect the
employee to return to work? The subsections imply that an interruption caused by
industrial action may render it unreasonable to expect a return—an indirect and
rather ungracious recognition that blacklegging is undesirable.
  The employee has the option of returning in these circumstances. If she chooses
not to, she may, where a day of return has already been notified, return as soon as
reasonably practicable after the interruption (though, as already mentioned, there
would seem to be nothing to prevent her from changing her mind and giving a later
day of proposed return). Where there has been no notification of a day of return,
she may return at any time before 14 days after the end of the interruption, even
where this exceeds the 29-week limit on maternity leave. Presumably, this extension
would affect a determination of " reasonably practicable " where there had been a
notified day of return. It appears, therefore, that if, consequent on an anticipated

lengthy interruption, the employee makes plans for a holiday, for example, or takes another temporary job, she should have a reasonable period of time to complete her alternative arrangements. There may be problems in deciding when " work resumes after the interruption " or when the " end of the interruption " occurs—particularly in the circumstances of industrial action which is not wholly successful.

Contractual right to return to work

48.—(1) An employee who has a right both under the Act and under a contract of employment, or otherwise, to return to work, may not exercise the two rights separately but may in returning to work take advantage of whichever right is, in any particular respect, the more favourable.

(2) The provisions of sections 45, 46, 47, 56 and 86 and paragraphs 1 to 4 and 6 of Schedule 2 shall apply, subject to any modifications necessary to give effect to any more favourable contractual terms, to the exercise of the composite right described in subsection (1) as they apply to the exercise of the right to return conferred solely by this Part.

DERIVATION
   1975, Sched. 3, para. 5.

GENERAL NOTE
   This provision could be very useful to employees in situations where the circumstances were such that contractual rights were to some extent more and in other respects less favourable, *e.g.* where the contract gave a longer period of post-natal leave, but did not require the employer to allow the employee to return to her original job; or where there were no provisions regarding postponement of the return beyond the limits specified in the contract, as is provided in the Act (s. 47 (5)). The more favourable of each aspect, contractual or statutory, could be selected to form an enforceable composite right.
   As always, however, much depends on whether the tribunals will accede to this right or narrow it down by restrictive interpretation. The first decision of the E.A.T. leaves one pessimistic. In *Bovey* v. *The Board of Governors of the Hospital for Sick Children* [1978] I.R.L.R. 241 (E.A.T.) a *full-time* physiotherapist Grade 1 took maternity leave, but before going on leave she *agreed* to return to work as a *part-time* physiotherapist on the *basic grade*. On her return she sought to select the most favourable aspects of her statutory and contractual rights—to return to her original job (Physiotherapist Grade 1), as per the statute; and to work part-time, as per the agreement. The E.A.T. denied her this right on a number of grounds: (1) " a contract of employment " in s. 48 (1) means the contract under which she worked when she departed, so the agreement to return is not covered by this subsection—but there is no warrant for such a narrow interpretation; (2) anyway, the agreement to return to work part-time was " merely a collateral agreement," again not within the terms of the Act—but collateral agreements may be legally enforceable, and Mrs. Bovey did in fact return to work under it; (3) " There must be a limit to the extent to which the right in question, to return to work, can be sub-divided so as to identify the particular respects in which it is more favourable." Here the right to work part-time on the basic grade was held indivisible—but it is submitted that there is nothing to support the principle—the Act does say " in any particular respect," and here the facts were eminently suited to such sub-division.
   The real reason for the decision is the E.A.T.'s view that it would " produce an absurdity." This seemed to rely on two approaches. First, and somewhat peculiar, was eugenics. Phillips J. repeatedly referred to the " strange " result of the combination of rights, a " mulish " and " illegitimate " progeny. Maternity rights provoke peculiar responses.
   But secondly, it was stated that the two lay members of the tribunal were " convinced that if assent were given to this proposition and it were applied generally in industry, it would have most unfortunate and inconvenient consequences." The E.A.T. did not elaborate, but clearly referred to the conclusion of the industrial tribunal at first instance that if the employee was to be allowed to utilise a composite right " no employer could ever safely offer a woman the opportunity of employment on a part-time basis on different terms as to remuneration

as this might lead to a claim similar to that now advanced on behalf of Mrs. Bovey. The tribunal would be extremely reluctant unless compelled by the clear language of the statute to come to a decision which might deprive a mother who had previously filled a full-time appointment of the opportunity of an offer of part-time employment which might be beneficial to her " ([1977] I.R.L.R. 417).

The result is, in true paternalist fashion, that the E.A.T. has denied women statutory rights to allow for the *possible* exercise of employers' benevolence. So long as they cannot demand their rights, they may be allowed to benefit from employers' goodwill. Perhaps the E.A.T. should have noted the agreed facts before the industrial tribunal at first instance, which included the statement that the employers here " for reasons which *seem good and sufficient to them,* do not employ Senior Physiotherapists Grade 1 on a part-time basis at Great Ormond Street Hospital, although there *are* part-time physiotherapists *on that grade* at other hospitals within the N.H.S., and there *is* an established national hourly rate of pay for *part-time* staff *on that grade* " (my italics). Rather than resort to dubious statutory interpretation to avoid what they characterised as an absurdity, the E.A.T. might have backed up the woman here in her battle against the absurdity—by requiring the hospital to do what other hospitals had done and follow established practice.

A final point made by the E.A.T. will confirm doubts as to the capacity of all-male tribunals to decide questions of maternity rights. Referring to the woman's right to take advantage of whichever right is in any particular respect *the more favourable* the E.A.T. asked " who is to judge what are ' the more favourable ' (terms) ; that is to say, is it objective or is it according to the circumstances of the employee? For example, is part-time employment more favourable? And so on; it depends on what one wants, one supposes." One awaits with trepidation a tribunal's view of what is " objectively " more favourable to women seeking to return to work.

Part IV

Termination of Employment

Rights of employer and employee to a minimum period of notice

49.—(1) The notice required to be given by an employer to terminate the contract of employment of a person who has been continuously employed for four weeks or more—

(a) shall be not less than one week's notice if his period of continuous employment is less than two years;

(b) shall be not less than one week's notice for each year of continuous employment if his period of continuous employment is two years or more but less than twelve years; and

(c) shall be not less than twelve weeks' notice if his period of continuous employment is twelve years or more.

(2) The notice required to be given by an employee who has been continuously employed for four weeks or more to terminate his contract of employment shall be not less than one week.

(3) Any provision for shorter notice in any contract of employment with a person who has been continuously employed for four weeks or more shall have effect subject to the foregoing subsections, but this section shall not be taken to prevent either party from waiving his right to notice on any occasion, or from accepting a payment in lieu of notice.

(4) Any contract of employment of a person who has been continuously employed for twelve weeks or more which is a contract for a term certain of four weeks or less shall have effect as if it were for an indefinite period and, accordingly, subsections (1) and (2) shall apply to the contract.

(5) It is hereby declared that this section does not affect any right of either party to treat the contract as terminable without notice by

reason of such conduct by the other party as would have enabled him so to treat it before the passing of this Act.

(6) The definition of week given by section 153 (1) does not apply for the purposes of this section.

DERIVATION

1972, s. 1 (1) to (4) ; 1975, Sched. 16, Pt. II, paras. 1, 2, 3.

GENERAL NOTE

Exclusions. Certain classes of employment are excluded from the benefits of this right—ss. 138, 139, 141 (1), 143 (3) (*b*) (but see ss. 143 (4), 144 (1), 145 (1). Part-time employees may be excluded by virtue of the requirement of four weeks' continuous employment in subs. (1)—see Sched. 13, paras. 3 *et seq.* And note the absence of a presumption of continuous employment due to s. 151 (2).

Contractual notice. The position at common law as to notice of termination of a contract of employment is discussed in the Note to s. 1 (3) (*Notice of Termination*).

Notice and security of employment. While sometimes referred to as protecting *security* of employment, the section does nothing of the kind. It merely gives a brief respite to a worker faced with the agonies of unemployment. No worker after more than 12 years' work is going to feel secure or protected when told in January that he is to be dismissed in March. The section does not give the employee any financial benefit—he still has to work during the period of notice (though, *e.g.* if he is not provided with work, he is still entitled to be paid—s. 50 and Sched. 3, para. 2 (1) (*a*)). It just postpones the forthcoming problem of finding work by giving a period of time to look for it—outside working hours (though see s. 31 in the case of a redundancy). The law will provide security of employment not by giving a few weeks' grace, but by ensuring that the employee has a job—by giving him back his old one where the dismissal is unfair (and see the limitations on the legal remedies for unfair dismissals in ss. 68 *et seq.*), or by providing him with another one—which is not yet the law.

Statutory notice and other legal rights. The length of the period of notice is important with respect to other legal rights—and the statutory minimum period is in particular significant. *E.g.* s. 55 (5)—effective date of termination for purposes of unfair dismissal to be on expiry of statutory minimum period and not before; s. 122 (3) (*b*)—recovery of pay from Secretary of State where the employer is insolvent; s. 85—employee giving notice before expiry of the employer's redundancy notice (definition of " obligatory period " in s. 85 (5)).

Subss. (1) and (2)

In certain cases this provision will increase the entitlement of an employee whose contract provides for less than the statutory minimum notice—subs. (3) (and as a fall-back—s. 140 (1)). Employees must still be wary, however, as employers, wittingly or not, may insert terms in their written contract to the effect that: " the period of notice to be given by the employer is that laid down by the Act and the employee must give notice of the same length." And (1) this will often be less than the " reasonable " period of notice to which the employee is entitled at common law (for the status of the written statement—see Note to s. 1 (1)) ; (2) under the Act the employee is only required to give one week's notice. Unlike the employer's obligation, the length of the period of notice does not increase with seniority.

Subs. (3)

Waiver of notice. The latter half of this subsection is peculiar in allowing for waiver of the right to notice. This might enable an employer to exploit his economic power to do away with notice altogether where the first half of the subsection expressly intervenes to prevent him shortening it. Still, it applies only to waiver of the right " to notice "—and so the worker cannot waive his right to payment in lieu of notice even if he waives the right to the period of notice.

Wages in lieu. It has been pointed out in the *Encyclopedia of Labour Relations Law*, para. 1–365, that s. 1 (3) gives rise to the clear implication that an employee may reject (*i.e.* refuse to accept) an offer of wages in lieu and insist on working out his period of notice. In the cases where the dismissal is contested in the industrial tribunals, the longer the employee remains at work, the easier it will be for a reinstatement to be ordered by the industrial tribunal. Two problems remain for the worker to overcome: (1) the contract may expressly provide for the employer to pay wages in lieu of notice; (2) some judges have said that the employer's unilateral summary dismissal ends the contract without any possibility of the employee's keeping it alive by refusing to accept wages in lieu and working out his notice (*I.P.C. Business Press Ltd.* v. *Gray* [1977] I.T.R. 148 (E.A.T.)).

Subs. (4)

This protects the employee from an employer who attempts to evade the provisions by a series of fixed term contracts of four weeks or less each. *Cf.* s. 143 (3) (*b*) and (4) which excludes employment under contracts for a task anticipated to last 12 weeks or less—unless it does, in fact, last more than 12 weeks.

Subs. (5)

The question of what kind of conduct gives either party the right to terminate the contract without notice—so by-passing this section—is a difficult one to answer in law and even more difficult in particular factual circumstances. Not only the law of contract governs the question—so that fundamental breach/breach of fundamental term/repudiation may be chanted to resolve the mysteries. The law of unfair dismissal also affects the right to terminate without notice—and the definitions of "gross misconduct" by an employee or conduct of the employer entitling the employee to resign are no less susceptible of easy application. Added to this, the procedural requirements of the Code of Practice on Disciplinary Practice and Procedures in Employment make the question even more difficult to answer.

Subs. (6)

So what definition does apply? The word "week" is important in computing: (1) the length of notice entitlement; (2) computation of the period of continuous employment necessary for eligibility. As regards the latter, Sched. 13 applies by virtue of s. 151 (1), and there is a definition of "week" in para. 24 (1) of that Schedule. As regards the former, however, we are left in the dark. The predecessor to this section, the Contracts of Employment Act 1972, did not define "week"—but did not expressly exclude any definition as is done here.

Rights of employee in period of notice

50.—(1) If an employer gives notice to terminate the contract of employment of a person who has been continuously employed for four weeks or more, the provisions of Schedule 3 shall have effect as respects the liability of the employer for the period of notice required by section 49 (1).

(2) If an employee who has been continuously employed for four weeks or more gives notice to terminate his contract of employment, the provisions of Schedule 3 shall have effect as respects the liability of the employer for the period of notice required by section 49 (2).

(3) This section shall not apply in relation to a notice given by the employer or the employee if the notice to be given by the employer to terminate the contract must be at least one week more than the notice required by section 49 (1).

DERIVATION

1972, s. 2 (1) to (3); 1975, Sched. 16, Pt. II, para. 1.

GENERAL NOTE

Sched. 3 ensures that the employer cannot avoid paying wages during the period of notice if the employee happens to be ill, on holiday or laid off (para. 2 (1)—though sick pay and holiday pay may be set off against these wages (para. 2 (2)).

For no apparent reason, if the employer is obliged by contract to give notice which *exceeds* the minimum by one week or more, then the section no longer applies. There seems no reason why an employer who has such a minimally longer notice obligation should escape *any* liability to pay wages under the Act if, *e.g.* the employee is off sick during the period of notice. Yet the obligation lapses even if it is the employee who has given notice.

Measure of damages in proceedings against employers

51. If an employer fails to give the notice required by section 49, the rights conferred by section 50 (with Schedule 3) shall be taken into account in assessing his liability for breach of the contract.

DERIVATION
   1972, s. 3.

GENERAL NOTE
   For details as to the employer's liability for wrongful dismissal, see M. Freedland, *The Contract of Employment* (1976), pp. 244–300. Normally the liability will be to pay the wages accruing during the period of notice. For the purposes of the provisions of Sched. 3, a week's pay is calculated according to Sched. 14, and see para. 7 (1) (e).

Statutory contracts

52. Sections 49 and 50 shall apply in relation to a contract all or any of the terms of which are terms which take effect by virtue of any provision contained in or having effect under an Act of Parliament, whether public or local, as they apply in relation to any other contract; and the reference in this section to an Act of Parliament includes, subject to any express provision to the contrary, an Act passed after this Act.

DERIVATION
   1972, s. 11 (2).

Written statement of reasons for dismissal

53.—(1) An employee shall be entitled—
   (a) if he is given by his employer notice of termination of his contract of employment;
   (b) if his contract of employment is terminated by his employer without notice; or
   (c) if, where he is employed under a contract for a fixed term, that term expires without being renewed under the same contract,
to be provided by his employer, on request, within fourteen days of that request, with a written statement giving particulars of the reasons for his dismissal.

   (2) An employee shall not be entitled to a written statement under subsection (1) unless on the effective date of termination he has been, or will have been, continuously employed for a period of twenty-six weeks ending with the last complete week before that date.

   (3) A written statement provided under this section shall be admissible in evidence in any proceedings.

   (4) A complaint may be presented to an industrial tribunal by an employee against his employer on the ground that the employer unreasonably refused to provide a written statement under subsection (1) or that the particulars of reasons given in purported compliance with that subsection are inadequate or untrue, and if the tribunal finds the complaint well-founded—
   (a) it may make a declaration as to what it finds the employer's reasons were for dismissing the employee; and
   (b) it shall make an award that the employer pay to the employee a sum equal to the amount of two weeks' pay.

   (5) An industrial tribunal shall not entertain a complaint under this section relating to the reasons for a dismissal unless it is presented to the tribunal at such a time that the tribunal would, in accordance with section 67 (2) or (4), entertain a complaint of unfair dismissal in respect of that dismissal presented at the same time.

DERIVATION
   1975, s. 70 (1) to (5).

GENERAL NOTE
Subs. (1)
   Exclusions. Certain classes of employment are excluded from this right to a written statement of reasons for dismissal—see ss. 138 (3), 141 (2), 144 (2), 145 (2), 146 (1) (2); and part-time employees who are excluded by virtue of the requirement of 26 weeks' continuous employment (subs. (2))—see Sched. 13, paras. 3 *et seq.*
   The common law, natural justice and employment. The failure of the common law to insert even a modicum of natural justice into the employment relationship is evident here in the employer's power to dismiss an employee without justifying the dismissal, even where patently unfair. The law on unfair dismissal introduced in 1971 and amended in 1974 did nothing to remedy this defect. It was finally provided for in the Employment Protection Act 1975. This section is the logical corollary to the unfair dismissal legislation.
   Written statement as evidence. The written statement of reasons for dismissal provided by the employer (only required where employment has lasted 26 weeks (subs. (2)), the same as the qualification for protection against unfair dismissal (s. 64 (1) (*a*))) is admissible in evidence before an industrial tribunal adjudicating on a complaint of unfair dismissal (subs. (3)). Similarly, in cases of wrongful dismissal brought before the tribunal (s. 131). The reasons given in the written statement are not conclusive evidence of the reasons, but an employer may be estopped from denying their truth. And if he has not told the truth, or has otherwise not adequately informed the employee of the reasons for the dismissal, this would inevitably mean that one of the essential features of disciplinary procedures (as specified in the Code of Practice—para. 10 (*f*): " provide for individuals to be informed of the complaint against them and to be given an opportunity to state their case before decisions are reached ")—had not been observed. An employee cannot defend himself against reasons which are withheld from him. Since the employee is entitled not to be unfairly or wrongfully dismissed, and may complain to the tribunal if he thinks he has been, it is common sense, if not common law, to attempt to avoid unnecessary complaints by providing the employee with the reasons for his dismissal.
   " *Dismissal.*" The doubtless intended parallel to existing legislation on unfair dismissal appears, however, to have been skewed in the definition of " dismissal " which in this section is substantially that of the Industrial Relations Act 1971, s. 23 (2), rather than the more explicitly comprehensive provision in s. 55 (2) (especially s. 55 (2) (*c*)). It is not clear if " constructive dismissal " is covered (see Lord Denning's judgment in the Court of Appeal decision in *Marriott* v. *Oxford and District Co-op. Society (No. 2)* [1970] 1 Q.B. 186). It would seem desirable that an employee dismissed for the purposes of unfair dismissal legislation should be, in the same circumstances, dismissed for the purposes of this section. If the employer has conducted himself in a way which entitled the employee to terminate, the employee should have the right to have reasons for this conduct provided to him. A simple request to the employer to explain his conduct leading to the employee's termination would suffice.
   All dismissal, unfair or otherwise. Despite its obvious connection to unfair dismissal proceedings, it is equally apparent that the right granted here is separate and distinct. The right to a written statement of reasons applies equally where the dismissal was fair. The right takes the form, as it were, of the compulsory anti-reference: a worker cannot demand that the employer supply him with a reference on leaving, but is always entitled to a reason when sacked. In *Horsley Smith & Sherry Ltd.* v. *Dutton* [1977] I.R.L.R. 172 (E.A.T.), Phillips J. spoke of the wider purpose of this section. It was not confined to providing information for use by employees in the event of an unfair dismissal: " Its social purpose goes a good deal further than that. It is to enable employees to receive, if they ask for it, a written statement of reasons for dismissal."
   Oral request and the time limit. It is clear that the request can be made orally and should, if possible, be made at the time of dismissal. Employees would be well advised, however, to put the request in writing, and retain a copy. The complaint under subs. (4) has a better chance of success if the employer is shown to have failed to reply over a long period. True, the requirement here is for the employer to reply

within 14 days. But in *Charles Lang & Sons Ltd.* v. *Aubrey* [1977] I.R.L.R. 354 (E.A.T.), Lord McDonald characterised the section as "penal" and stipulated a rigid construction of its terms. This meant that only clear indication of an unreasonable refusal would lead to a finding of liability—and a period of delay beyond the 14 days stipulated was, in his view, insufficiently clear evidence. In that case the employee claimed she had made a verbal request for reasons, and she had been dismissed on November 4 or 5, 1976. She complained of unfair dismissal on November 15, 1976, and this reached the employer on or about November 19. 21 days later they sent their reasons—on December 10. If the employer can still be excused in these circumstances, the 14-day time limit is being made a mockery. (*Cf. Keen* v. *Dymo Ltd.* [1977] I.R.L.R. 118, where an industrial tribunal in an earlier case held that to provide the reasons only one day late was sufficient to entitle the employee to his remedy under subs. (4)).

Challenging the written statement. The most the employee can do when given such an anti-reference is to challenge its truth or adequacy (subs. (4)). If it can be proven that the statement was given maliciously (a concept which includes dishonesty, the introduction of extraneous matter and ulterior purposes) the employee may be able to sustain an action for libel, though the practical and legal obstacles to successful actions are notorious.

Subs. (2)

The 26-week qualification period ends with the "last *complete* week." Yet in unfair dismissal claims, the 26-week qualification (s. 64 (1) (*a*)) calculated in accordance with Sched. 13, para. 4, includes the week when the employment began or ended even if only *part* of the week was completed (see *Coulson* v. *City of London Polytechnic* [1976] I.R.L.R. 212 (E.A.T.)). Still, in *I.P.C. Business Press Ltd.* v. *Gray* [1977] I.T.R. 148 (E.A.T.), Cumming-Bruce J. held that the two calculations should be the same as the two claims would often be brought together and should not be distinguished on such a technical ground when they related to the same dismissal. And since s. 151 (1) does provide for Sched. 14 to apply to s. 70 (2), it would seem that such an interpretation is plausible.

Subs. (4)

Objective test of reasonableness. The nature of the obligation imposed on the employer is described in greater detail here. First, the employer may not unreasonably refuse to provide a written statement. The test is clearly an objective one. This was confirmed by Phillips J. in *Daynecourt Insurance Brokers Ltd.* v. *Iles* [1978] I.R.L.R. 335 (E.A.T.) : "the decision is to be taken according to the behaviour to be expected of the reasonable employer." It is difficult to see how an employer could justify a refusal to take the simple step of providing a statement where the employee has requested one. His belief, albeit sincere, that he was justified in refusing would not suffice. Employers often consider their actions in dismissing employees to be reasonable until otherwise advised by industrial tribunals. Here the employer is required to provide a statement whether or not the dismissal is fair. Only some reason related to practicability in the particular circumstances (and the employer is given 14 days) might excuse such an omission. So in *Daynecourt* a general police request to the employer not to communicate with an employee being investigated for possible criminal prosecution was not a reasonable ground for refusing to provide reasons without more. It is clear that a *failure* to supply reasons can amount to an unreasonable refusal, though there is a question of at what stage the failure becomes a refusal. Despite Lord McDonald in *Charles Lang & Sons Ltd.* (cited above), it is submitted that the 14 days' limit stipulated is a good general guideline.

Adequacy. Secondly, the statement must be adequate. The statute does not spell out the degree of detail required. One would imagine that, *e.g.* a mere reference to one of the heads of fair dismissal in s. 57 (2) would be insufficient. Indeed, the spectrum of required detail could range from a mere description of the circumstances leading to the dismissal to one which sought additionally to provide the employee deprived of his job with an adequate explanation of the employer's justification—economic, moral, political or otherwise—for his dismissal. Some guidance was given in the first case before the E.A.T.: *Horsley Smith & Sherry Ltd.* v. *Dutton* [1977] I.R.L.R. 172. Phillips J. insisted that "No particular technicalities are involved and no particular form is required. It can be perfectly simple and straightforward. But the test which we think must be satisfied is this. The document must be of such a kind that the employee, or anyone to whom he may wish to show it, can know from reading the document itself why the employee had been dismissed."

The problems so far confronted tended to be those of form—a written statement referring to other documents or interviews is insufficient unless it by itself satisfies the test of *Horsley*. But it remains to be seen whether and how deeply the E.A.T. will examine the substance, as well as the form, of the written statement.

Truth. Finally, the statement must be true. Again, the test is an objective one. It is not a question of whether the employer was malicious in providing an untrue statement of reasons. The employee is not to suffer from the employer's error, whatever his sincerity. The right is one to be told the true reasons for dismissal, not what the employer mistakenly, through carelessness or otherwise, believes to be the reasons.

Burden of proof and remedies. Unlike a complaint of unfair dismissal, the employee has to show not only dismissal, but also, if the employer has given a statement, that it was inadequate or untrue; or if he has not, that the refusal was unreasonable. The remedy envisaged in (a)—a declaration—is obviously more pertinent to the first of these cases where the statement is alleged to be inadequate or untrue. Where there has been a simple failure to provide a statement, the employee may only want the mandatory two weeks' pay (for the calculation date— see Sched. 14, para. 7 (1) (*f*) and (*g*)). Indeed, if he is simultaneously pursuing a complaint of unfair dismissal, a declaration at that stage would be otiose. The reasons for the dismissal would have to be shown at the hearing by the employer.

Subs. (5)

This appears to envisage that a complaint under this section and for unfair dismissal will coincide since both are subject to the same limitation period. It remains to be seen whether an employee complaining under this section who obtains a declaration, after the inevitable delay in having his complaint heard, would be permitted then to complain of unfair dismissal, even though this fell out of time. Would the employer's breach not be a ground for the tribunal to hold that it was not reasonably practicable for the complaint to be brought before the end of the three-month period (s. 67 (2))? If not, the employee would be wise to present both complaints at the same time—a practice which may be anticipated will grow up in the future.

PART V

UNFAIR DISMISSAL

General Note to Part V

Origins. The rights contained in this Part of the Act were first enacted in the Industrial Relations Act 1971 (ss. 22–33, 106); retained in the Trade Union and Labour Relations Act 1974 (Sched. 1) when much of the 1971 Act was repealed; and amended extensively by the Employment Protection Act 1975 and Trade Union and Labour Relations (Amendment) Act 1976.

The notion of "unfair dismissal" has been compared with that of I.L.O. Recommendation 119, approved by the International Labour Conference in 1963 (see *Encyclopedia of Labour Relations Law*, paras. 1–381—1–382) which speaks of "unjustifiable" termination. Members of the EEC have legislation on similar lines, *e.g.* France has a concept of "abusive" dismissal; West Germany, "socially unwarranted" dismissal; and Italy, dismissals without "evidence of sufficient grounds" or without "justified motive."

Philosophical concept: justice. The concept of "fairness" in dismissal can be discussed at an abstract philosophical level. Thus, D. A. S. Jackson (*Unfair Dismissal*, 1975) refers to the elaboration of the concept by John Rawls in his theory of justice, and concludes: "The concept of 'unfair dismissal' thus delves deeper into basic morality, and is therefore operationally more exacting and fundamentally apt, than any other."

Political concept: ideology. In contrast, Richard Hyman emphasises how motions of "fairness" are used as ideological tools to achieve certain ends (*Social Values and Industrial Relations*, 1975). To perceive dismissal in terms of fairness or unfairness has certain consequences in the practice of industrial relations. As Hyman

points out: " One of the most popular concepts in the everyday vocabulary of industry
is 'fairness,' a notion which may at times inspire criticism of practices or
relationships which are perceived as inequitable and sustain workers in struggles for
redress. Yet in its conventional usage the language of fairness tends on the contrary
to contain conflict and reinforce capitalist relations of control . . . a concept with
potentially radical implications is normally conservative in its application " (*Industrial
Relations—a Marxist Introduction*, 1975, p. 146).

Lawyers, employers and workers who adopt the conventional notion of " fairness "
can and do subscribe to the existing structure of power at the workplace with only
marginal criticisms. In so far as the content of the notion of " unfair dismissal "
does not challenge the existing structure of authoritarian control and inequality of
reward in industry, it is a major ideological resource of those who benefit under
the present system—the managers of industry, the minority who own and control it,
the ruling class. For if workers and others are given the option of a law of
dismissal which does not undermine the system, then resort to *other* means of
avoiding dismissal, *e.g.* strikes which may challenge the system, is less likely to
happen.

The law and managerialism. The law of unfair dismissal contains a contradiction,
therefore, of on the one hand preserving the fundamental structure of managerial
control over the work process, while on the other hand appearing sufficiently
attractive as an avenue of redress for workers who are dismissed. The key is to
note that the law accepts the *reality* of power at the workplace, while having the
appearance of controlling or regulating that power. There is no space here to
examine this aspect of the law, but one analysis of the provisions has pointed to the
" essentially managerial perspective " of the law (B. Weekes *et al.*, *Industrial
Relations and the Limits of Law*, 1974, p. 28).

The reasons permitting dismissal include conduct, capability or redundancy. But
where a fair reason for dismissal includes a refusal to co-operate with the employer
in accepting a change in job content, hours of work, status, title or grade, place of
work, refusal to obey an order, or for certain kinds of relationships with other
employees or customers; where capability is determined by expectations of management; and redundancy is a question of the commercial judgment of the employer—
then legal fairness is simply a function of managerial needs, not those of workers.
A worker can be " fairly " dismissed in law if he is incapable of producing profit, if he
misconducts himself in the furtherance of his employer's business, or if the employer
no longer needs him and he is thus " redundant." The law's approach was summed
up by Phillips J. in *Cook* v. *Thomas Linnell & Sons Ltd.* [1977] I.R.L.R. 132
(E.A.T.) : " It is important that the operation of the legislation in relation to
unfair dismissal should not impede employers unreasonably in the efficient management of their business, which must be in the interests of all. Certainly, employees
must not be sacrificed to this need; and employers must act reasonably when
removing from a particular post an employee whom they consider to be unsatisfactory." But what about the workers?

Unfair dismissal and management. A recent study of the effects of employment
protection laws in manufacturing industry (plants employing 50–5,000 people) by
W. W. Daniel and E. Stilgoe (*The Impact of Employment Protection Laws*, P.S.I.
No. 577, June 1978) concluded that the unfair dismissal requirements of legislation
had had the most widespread impact on employers. Primarily, this had taken the
form of formalising or reforming disciplinary and dismissals procedures. The extent
of this finding needs to be appreciated: the fact that unfair dismissal had the *most
effect* reflects in the main the very *low* impact of other parts of employment
legislation. The interviews carried out by the authors of the study showed that
only 17 per cent. of managements had said the legislation had a good deal of effect,
while 41 per cent. said that it had only a little effect, and fully 42 per cent. said it
had no effect at all. So while 58 per cent. said it had some effect, most of this
impact was very limited.

Unfair dismissal and trade unions. This study also revealed that the impact of
legislation varied most between workplaces characterised by different proportions of
trade union members. Thus, in workplaces where the trade union had recognition
but less than 80 per cent. membership, 21 per cent. of management evaluated the
legislation has having a good deal of effect, though again 25 per cent. said it had no
effect. In workplaces with between 80–99 per cent. trade union membership, 23 per
cent. of management thought it had a good deal of effect, but again 44 per cent.
thought it had none. And where trade union membership was 100 per cent., only

15 per cent. of managements thought it had a good deal of effect—fully 54 per cent. said it had none. The authors of the study suggest that in the very highly organised plants procedures were likely to have pre-dated the legislation, so that its introduction had less impact.

Unfair dismissal and workers. The appearance of the law of unfair dismissal as regulating the employers' power is reinforced by the full bureaucratic panoply of claims, tribunal hearings and remedial orders. This appearance is given widespread publicity, but deserves closer examination. There is room here only for a few bare statistical bones. An analysis published in the *Department of Employment Gazette* of May 1978 (p. 555) shows about 38,000 unfair dismissal *applications* registered in each of 1976 and 1977. Of cases which proceeded to disposal in 1977 (35,389) just over one-third (36·3 per cent.) went to a tribunal hearing. Just under two-thirds (63·7 per cent.) are conciliated. Of the 63·7 per cent. which are *conciliated* the following are the outcomes: 28 per cent. of all cases are withdrawn for various reasons; 35·7 per cent. are settled; 33·2 per cent. get compensation (of these over a third get less than £100; over a half get less than £150; three-quarters get less than £300; 1·2 per cent. got £3,000 or more), 1·7 *per cent. got either reinstatement or re-engagement.*

Of the 36·3 per cent. which went to *tribunals*: just over two-thirds were dismissed (25·1 per cent.); 11·2 *per cent. of claims of unfair dismissal were upheld by industrial tribunals.* Of the 11·2 per cent. upheld, 9·3 per cent. got compensation (of those, more than half got less than £400, and just under two-thirds got less than £500; 1·9 per cent. got £3,000 or more); 0·5 *per cent. got reinstatement or re-engagement.*

Conclusion. In sum: of those 35,389 workers who, being dismissed, claimed a legal remedy and had their case disposed of by the legal machinery, *more than half got nothing* (27·5 per cent. withdrawn from conciliation; 25·1 per cent. dismissed by the industrial tribunal). Of the rest, the vast majority got compensation of less, often considerably less, than £400 (87·6 per cent. at conciliation)—about five weeks' pay at the average wage. And 2·2 per cent. (770 workers) got their jobs back of the 35,389 who lost them.

So workers' assessment of the law of unfair dismissal as it actually works goes something like this: a 50–50 chance of success overall; a 1 in 10 chance of success if you get to an industrial tribunal; most likely a few weeks' wages if you do get something; a 1 in 50 chance of getting your job back. Workers who have any other option are well advised to stay clear of the legal machinery in trying to combat unfair dismissal. Lawyers may advise their clients accordingly. Employers have little to fear.

These annotations cannot do justice to the complexity and rich detail of the law as it has been applied by the industrial tribunals. For such detail, readers are referred to the general work on *The Law of Unfair Dismissal* by S. D. Anderman, 1978. All that can be accomplished here is to make a few observations.

Right not to be unfairly dismissed

Right of employee not to be unfairly dismissed

54.—(1) In every employment to which this section applies every employee shall have the right not to be unfairly dismissed by his employer.

(2) This section applies to every employment except in so far as its application is excluded by or under any provision of this Part or by section 141 to 149.

DERIVATION
   1974, para. 4.

GENERAL NOTE
   Characteristics of applicants: industry. The *Department of Employment Gazette* of November 1977 (p. 1214) gives details of the characteristics of the employees who made an application claiming the right under this section during 1976. Three industrial groups—distribution trades (16·6 per cent.), miscellaneous services

(16 per cent.) and construction (13·9 per cent.) made up nearly half of all applications. Densely unionised industries such as coal mining and quarrying, shipbuilding and marine engineering, vehicles and gas, electricity and water, accounted for 0·1 per cent., 0·6 per cent., 0·7 per cent., 1·3 per cent. and 0·5 per cent. respectively.

Size of employer. As in previous years, there was a disproportionate number of claims from small firms: about one-fifth of all applications came from employees working in undertakings employing less than 20 employees. Just under half (48·7 per cent.) came from employees in firms employing less than 100 employees (though more than three-quarters of the total workforce is employed by concerns with more than 100 employees). Still, firms with 1,000 employees or more still accounted for 15·6 per cent. of the applications.

Age, length of service, sex, earnings. With regard to the age of applicants, over a third were under 30 and 57·9 per cent. under 40. A large proportion of applicants had a relatively short period of employment when they claimed unfair dismissal: 23·5 per cent. had been employed between six months and one year (up to March 1975 the period of qualification for protection was one year—TULRA, Sched. 1, para. 10); another 23·5 per cent. had been employed between one and two years (up to September 1974 the qualification period had been two years—Industrial Relations Act 1971, s. 28 (*a*)). Altogether, 73·4 per cent. had been employed for less than five years. Still that leaves over a quarter of employees with long service relying on the law to protect them from alleged unfair dismissal. Women, who make up almost 40 per cent. of the workforce, made up 25·1 per cent. of all applications in 1976. It is a reflection of women's weak economic position that over half of them earned less than £30 per week, and fully 83 per cent. less than £40 per week. Even with male applicants, just over a third earned £40 a week or less. The majority of applicants, in other words, came from the relatively low-paid.

For the definition of " employee "—see s. 153 (1).

Meaning of unfair dismissal

Meaning of " dismissal "

55.—(1) In this Part, except as respects a case to which section 56 applies, " dismissal " and " dismiss " shall be construed in accordance with the following provisions of this section.

(2) Subject to subsection (3), an employee shall be treated as dismissed by his employer if, but only if,—

(*a*) the contract under which he is employed by the employer is terminated by the employer, whether it is so terminated by notice or without notice, or

(*b*) where under that contract he is employed for a fixed term, that term expires without being renewed under the same contract, or

(*c*) the employee terminates that contract, with or without notice, in circumstances such that he is entitled to terminate it without notice by reason of the employer's conduct.

(3) Where an employer gives notice to an employee to terminate his contract of employment and, at a time within the period of that notice, the employee gives notice to the employer to terminate the contract of employment on a date earlier than the date on which the employer's notice is due to expire, the employee shall for the purposes of this Part be taken to be dismissed by his employer, and the reasons for the dismissal shall be taken to be the reasons for which the employer's notice is given.

(4) In this Part " the effective date of termination "—

(*a*) in relation to an employee whose contract of employment is terminated by notice, whether given by his employer or by the employee, means the date on which that notice expires;

(b) in relation to an employee whose contract of employment is terminated without notice, means the date on which the termination takes effect; and

(c) in relation to an employee who is employed under a contract for a fixed term, where that term expires without being renewed under the same contract, means the date on which that term expires.

(5) Where the notice required to be given by an employer by section 49 would, if duly given when notice of termination was given by the employer, or (where no notice was given) when the contract of employment was terminated by the employer, expire on a date later than the effective date of termination as defined by subsection (4), that later date shall be treated as the effective date of termination in relation to the dismissal for the purposes of sections 53 (2), 64 (1) (a) and 73 (3) and paragraph 8 (3) of Schedule 14.

DERIVATION

1974, para. 5 (1) to (3), (5), (6); 1975, Sched. 16, Pt. III, paras. 8, 9, 10.

GENERAL NOTE

Dismissal is termination of contract, not employment. The law of unfair dismissal chooses to focus on termination *not* of employment—but of the *contract of employment* (see P. Elias in [1978] I.L.J. 16, 101). The common-sense understanding —that a worker should be able to claim when his employment ends, and then see if it is fair or not, is rejected for the legalistic alternative. It is the contract which must terminate.

Now this might not have been too serious a defect—except that the termination of the contract must be of a particular kind in law—a " dismissal " as defined here: termination flowing from the *employer's* actions. This may be a direct termination by the employer (subs. (1) (a)) or termination by the employee but only where justified by the employer's conduct (subs. (3) (c))—called " constructive " dismissal. In all cases, *the burden is on the employee* to prove " dismissal." Since this flows from the employer's actions, he must be able to show that the employer's actions led to the dismissal. And in cases of " constructive " dismissal, this often has the effect of having to show that the employer's actions were unfair (dressed up in the language of contract—that the employer " repudiated " the contract) thus reversing the general burden of proof from the employer to the employee.

Subss. (1) and (2)

Termination but not dismissal. That "dismissal" *only* includes these legally defined cases of termination of employment means that the employee whose employment ends some other way is deprived of a remedy for unfair dismissal. Examples of termination which are not " dismissal " are, *e.g.* by what some judges see as being mutual agreement (*Lees* v. *Arthur Greaves* [1974] 2 All E.R. 393 (C.A.)), or by " frustration "—the cause of termination was an event neither party could control (see *Egg Stores (Stamford Hill) Ltd.* v. *Leibovici* [1976] I.R.L.R. 376 (E.A.T.), where Phillips J. sets out nine factors to be taken into account in deciding if the contract is " frustrated," focusing on the employer's need, not the worker's). But a termination of this kind may have just as serious consequences for the employee, and may be perceived by him as very unfair.

Termination by employer. This may be relatively straightforward—as where the employer gives notice of termination, or dismisses without notice (but see the complications catered for by subss. (3) to (5)—and for the impact of *status quo* clauses—see Notes to s. 1 (3) (*Notice of Termination*)). But problems will arise when tribunals differ from employees' views of what act constitutes termination by the employer. Tribunals seem to expect workers to accept certain behaviour which employers need not tolerate, *e.g.* in *Chesham Shipping Ltd.* v. *Rowe* [1977] I.R.L.R. 391 (E.A.T.), Phillips J. warned industrial tribunals not to misunderstand employers' words " which everybody understood were little more than abuse or something of that sort." But other cases have not condoned such behaviour (see, *e.g.* *Turner* v. *Keen* [1978] I.R.L.R. 110 (E.A.T.) for two tests of whether the employers' words terminated the contract).

Expiry of fixed term contract. The law's focus on termination of *contract* rather than of employment has led to some ungainly judicial gyrations on the question of what *is* a "fixed term contract"—as if it was relevant to the unemployed worker's needs, having been unfairly treated. So in *British Broadcasting Corp.* v. *Ioannou* [1975] I.R.L.R. 184 (C.A.) the court said that a contract for a fixed term which allowed for termination before its end by three months' notice was not a "fixed term" contract within the meaning of s. 142. It was an "apparent" fixed term contract. But the E.A.T. later held that such a contract *was* a "fixed term" contract for the purposes of *this* subsection (s. 55 (2) (*b*))—*British Broadcasting Corp.* v. *Dixon* [1977] I.R.L.R. 337 (confirmed by the Court of Appeal in *Dixon* v. *British Broadcasting Corp., The Times,* October 6, 1978, p. 22). Once the employee shows that his fixed term contract has expired, the employer has to go on to show that it was fair (see the criteria for fairness in the circumstances in *Terry* v. *East Sussex County Council* [1976] I.R.L.R. 332 (E.A.T.)).

Constructive dismissal. There are many cases where employers do not sack workers by straightforward termination of the contract (subs. (2) (*a*)). Other methods of sacking are used, *e.g.* (1) easing the worker out by harrassing him till he "leaves" or "resigns" and thus is not apparently "dismissed"—to this end the employer may use all kinds of harrassing tactics; (2) trying to change the employment—in effect, sacking the worker from his old job and taking him on in a new one—by changing his job content, status, title or grade, pay or fringe benefits, place of work, hours of work or other conditions; (3) without necessarily intending to sack the worker, the employer behaves in such a way as to make continued employment impossible. His behaviour is such that the worker need not tolerate it—and can treat himself as dismissed.

In each of the circumstances, workers will naturally turn to their trade union representatives as the first line of defence. But subs. (3) (*c*) provides a definition of dismissal which allows them to claim, or threaten to claim, if the first line of defence should fail—they can claim "constructive" dismissal.

The most difficult problem is how to decide whether the conduct of the employer entitles the worker to terminate the contract and treat himself as dismissed. From the worker's point of view, if the employer is doing any of the three things mentioned above—indirectly trying to sack him, trying to change his contract, or acting outrageously—he should be entitled to claim constructive dismissal. So the wider these categories are, the more protection he will have in his employment. Obviously, it is in the employer's interest to narrow down the scope of these categories as much as possible.

The judges are divided on the question of how to deal with this problem: what test to use in deciding whether the conduct of the employer entitled the employee to terminate the contract. Some took a broad view: *e.g.* Phillips J. in *George Wimpey & Co. Ltd.* v. *Cooper* [1977] I.R.L.R. 205 (E.A.T.)—conduct justifying termination is "of a kind which, in accordance with good industrial relations practice, no employee could reasonably be expected to accept"; or Kilner Brown J. in *Gilbert* v. *Goldstone Ltd.* [1976] I.R.L.R. 257 (E.A.T.)—the test is that of "what is reasonable in the circumstances, having regard to equity."

Other judges took a narrow legalistic view: *e.g.* Bristow J. in *Wetherall (Bond St. W. 1)* v. *Lynn* [1977] I.R.L.R. 333 (E.A.T.)—the test is the same as in the law of contract—repudiation: "where an employer so conducts himself as to show that he does not intend to be bound by the contract of employment." A good lawyer's test—but the law is for workers, not lawyers. How is the worker to know that the employer no longer intends to be bound? The lawyer's answer is—look at the contract's terms, not what is reasonable, acceptable, equitable or just. But what does the contract say? Bristow J. further added that regard must also be had to implied terms in the contract which "reflect the changes in the relationship between employer and employee as social standards change." So the lawyer's sensibility needs to be sharp to appreciate what behaviour of the employer is a breach of contract by the latest "social standards."

Later in 1977 came intervention from the Court of Appeal. In a few remarks, the Lords Justices of Appeal demolished Bristow J.'s argument (*Turner* v. *London Transport Executive* [1977] I.R.L.R. 441). Megaw L.J. strongly asserted that dismissal in the law of unfair dismissal in some respects is "quite plainly at variance with the concepts of the common law." But a still later intervention by other judges of the Court of Appeal has once again reverted to the contractual test of fundamental breach of contract and repudiatory conduct (*Western Excavating*

(*E.C.C.*) *Ltd.* v. *Sharp* [1978] I.R.L.R. 27). So the test most comprehensible and favourable to workers—reasonableness and acceptability in terms of good industrial relations practice—has been rejected for the lawyer's test of contractual repudiation. This test is both more obscure, even to lawyers and especially to workers, and narrower—so employers will benefit at the expense of workers.

Just one illustration of the legal difficulties encountered by adopting the repudiation test is the confusion as to what the consequence is in law on the contract of repudiatory conduct. Is it automatically terminated, or does it depend on whether the employee accepts the repudiation? For problems arise: when does the employment end—at the time of the employer's action or the worker's reaction? What if something happens between the repudiation and its acceptance? Who terminates the contract, the employer who repudiates or the worker who accepts it? When is the effective date of termination? (*Cf.* subs. (4)). Lawyers may well celebrate the contractual test; workers will not.

Subs. (3)

Employee shortening the period of notice. The former requirement that the employee's notice be in writing, and that it be given within the " obligatory " period —*i.e.* the statutory minimum period—of notice was abolished by the Employment Protection Act 1975, Sched. 16, Pt. III, para. 8. *Cf.* s. 85 (1) and (2).

Subs. (4)

Effective date of termination. For all those employment rights connected to dismissal which depend on a period of so many weeks' continuous employment, this subsection is crucial. For it fixes the point, the effective date of termination, from which one calculates backwards the length of the period of employment. *E.g.* the 26-week qualifying period—s. 64 (1) (*a*) ; and the period upon which the basic award of compensation is based—s. 73 (3). The definition contained here is applied generally by its inclusion in the interpretation section (s. 153 (1))—which makes one wonder why there was special need for it here. It thus applies, *e.g.* to the right to written reasons which requires a 26-week qualification period—s. 53 (2). The effective date of termination as defined here may be subject to alteration—see subss. (3) and (5). The problem is particularly acute in cases of constructive dismissal, for the contractual test of repudiation has not produced any definitive answer as to whether it is the employer's or the employee's act which fixes the date of termination.

Subs. (5)

Note that this special provision only applies for the purposes of s. 53 (2)— written statement of reasons; s. 64 (1) (*a*)—26-week qualifying period; s. 73 (3)— computation of basic award, and Sched. 14, para. 8 (3) (where an order has been made altering certain limits under s. 148—workers may be covered by the alteration under this subsection). Still other provisions in which the effective date of termination is vital (*e.g.* s. 67 (2)—complaint to be made before the end of three months beginning with the effective date of termination) will not benefit from the provisions of this subsection.

Failure to permit woman to return to work after confinement treated as dismissal

56. Where an employee is entitled to return to work and has exercised her right to return in accordance with section 47 but is not permitted to return to work, then she shall be treated for the purposes of this Part as if she had been employed until the notified day of return, and, if she would not otherwise be so treated, as having been continuously employed until that day, and as if she had been dismissed with effect from that day for the reason for which she was not permitted to return.

DERIVATION
1975, s. 50 (1).

GENERAL NOTE
See generally Notes to ss. 33 and 45–48.
Since the award of compensation recoverable under both the unfair dismissal procedure and the redundancy procedure (see s. 86) increases with the length of continuous employment, by treating an employee denied her right to return to work

as having been continuously employed until the notified day of return, a period of up to nine months may effectively be added on to her employment period (11 weeks before confinement plus 29 weeks afterwards), and even more if various extensions occur as envisaged in s. 47. This, although she will have been absent during part or all of this period. But see the exception to this in Sched. 2, para. 5.

Similar provisions affect the computation of the period of continuous employment required to qualify for these rights (see Sched. 13, paras. 9 (1) (d), (2); and 10).

General provisions relating to fairness of dismissal

57.—(1) In determining for the purposes of this Part whether the dismissal of an employee was fair or unfair, it shall be for the employer to show—

    (a) what was the reason (or, if there was more than one, the principal reason) for the dismissal, and

    (b) that it was a reason falling within subsection (2) or some other substantial reason of a kind such as to justify the dismissal of an employee holding the position which that employee held.

(2) In subsection (1) (b) the reference to a reason falling within this subsection is a reference to a reason which—

    (a) related to the capability or qualifications of the employee for performing work of the kind which he was employed by the employer to do, or

    (b) related to the conduct of the employee, or

    (c) was that the employee was redundant, or

    (d) was that the employee could not continue to work in the position which he held without contravention (either on his part or on that of his employer) of a duty or restriction imposed by or under an enactment.

(3) Where the employer has fulfilled the requirements of subsection (1), then, subject to sections 58 to 62, the determination of the question whether the dismissal was fair or unfair, having regard to the reason shown by the employer, shall depend on whether the employer can satisfy the tribunal that in the circumstances (having regard to equity and the substantial merits of the case) he acted reasonably in treating it as a sufficient reason for dismissing the employee.

(4) In this section, in relation to an employee,—

    (a) " capability " means capability assessed by reference to skill, aptitude, health or any other physical or mental quality;

    (b) " qualifications " means any degree, diploma or other academic, technical or professional qualification relevant to the position which the employee held.

DERIVATION
1974, para. 6 (1) to (3), (8), (9) (a) (b); 1974, s. 30 (1).

GENERAL NOTE
Subs. (1)

    Burden of proving a fair reason. It might be thought that a reason for dismissal was a set of facts which led to the decision to dismiss. But the tribunals have held that the decisive factor need not be the facts, but rather may be only what was in the employer's mind. The employer must show that he had a fair reason in his mind at the time when he decided on dismissal (*Devis & Sons Ltd.* v. *Atkins* [1977] I.R.L.R. 314 (H.L.)). This might be to allow a stupid, careless or bad-tempered employer to dismiss for a reason which he genuinely believes to be fair within the Act, but which is in fact wrong: *i.e.* his belief is not, in fact, correct. The judges have allowed employers to get away with this: *Trust Houses Forte Leisure Ltd.* v. *Aquilar* [1976] I.R.L.R. 251 (E.A.T.).

    Workers can, however, overcome the employer's alleged reason if they can show either (i) facts which clearly contradict the employer's stated belief at the time; or (ii) that there were no facts which supported the employer's alleged belief at the time. Either way, it is the sincerity of the employer's reasons which is being challenged: that there is no apparent basis for his stated reason, and thus it is not the real reason. So where evidence of other motives or reasons for dismissal can be shown, these too may be produced in evidence to counter the employer's stated reason.

All this amounts to a heavy burden on the employee to show that the employer's reason is false, not supported by the facts, or not sincere or genuine. The burden placed on the employer is by no means the worker's salvation. He has much to do if his claim is to succeed.

He may be helped here by the new Industrial Tribunals (Labour Relations) (Amendment) Regulations 1978 (S.I. 1978 No. 991), which amend r. 3 of the Schedule to the principal Regulations (S.I. 1974 No. 1386) to require the employer to give " sufficient particulars to show " on what grounds he is resisting the claim of unfair dismissal. If inadequate, the employee can ask for further and better particulars (r. 4). Additionally, a request for a written statement of reasons under s. 53 may elucidate further information as to the employer's reasons—and the employer may be estopped from denying those reasons at the tribunal hearing.

A reason within subs. (2). The method of determining unfairness adopted by the law is to stipulate particular fair reasons and exclude any others. As Phillips J. said in *Devis & Sons Ltd.* v. *Atkins* [1976] I.T.R. 15 (D.C.), unfair dismissal " is a form of words which could be translated as being equivalent to dismissal ' contrary to statute '." The reasons designated fair include those in subs. (2), but also others —see, *e.g.* s. 58 (3)—dismissal for refusal to join a trade union in a closed shop establishment. Certain other reasons are expressly declared unfair—*e.g.* s. 58 (trade union membership), s. 60 (pregnancy), s. 63 (pressure on the employer to be ignored), sex discrimination (Sex Discrimination Act 1975, s. 6 (2) (*b*)) and race discrimination (Race Relations Act 1976, s. 4 (2) (*c*))—though in the last two cases the burden is on the *employee* to show the unfair reason.

Some other substantial reason—employers' interests. Not surprisingly, the law in this subsection provides a catch-all category available to employers who cannot fit their reasons for dismissal into any of the others designated as fair: " some other substantial reason." And here we see something truly remarkable. Tribunals and judges have transformed this provision into an employers' charter. Through this catch-all phrase has flowed all the unchallenged political theory known as the unitary view of industrial relations, the conventional ruling class wisdom as regards business efficiency, economic necessity and interests of the organisation. It seems that this innocuous phrase contains, according to the judges, all these factors—each of them may make a dismissal fair (which would otherwise be unfair as it did not fall into the other specified categories). Where the interests of the employer require a dismissal, he may invoke one of these to cloak his interests in " fairness " under the law. And this is all the judges' doing. And even more remarkable to lawyers is that the judges have trampled underfoot the sanctity of contract. It seems that employers who *unilaterally* change terms of the contract as to wages, hours, conditions of work, etc.—a clear breach of contract where not accepted by the employee— are supported by the judges. It seems that this subsection gives employers an implied right to break contracts when it is in their interests to do so. If employees who resist are sacked, they have no remedy. (For a recent illustration of this approach, see *Hollister* v. *National Farmers' Union* [1978] I.R.L.R. 161 (E.A.T.)— " a sound business reason.") There is something even more startling to all but the most cynical labour lawyers familiar with judicial fulminations about statutes enabling trade unions to deprive individual workers of their freedom to bargain (see, *e.g.* Browne-Wilkinson L.J. in *Powley* v. *ACAS* [1977] I.R.L.R. 190 (D.C.), Lord Denning M.R. in the Court of Appeal and Lord Salmon in the House of Lords in *ACAS* v. *Grunwick Processing Laboratories Ltd.* [1978] I.R.L.R. 38). For the judges have held that, of all things, the very fact that the unilateral change had been agreed with a trade union (of which the employee was not even a member) was one of the circumstances which supported the employer's claim that he had some other substantial reason justifying dismissal (*Ellis* v. *Brighton Co-operative Society* [1976] I.R.L.R. 419 (E.A.T.)). Surely the defenders of individual liberty in the higher courts will not let that pass.

In all this there has been little in the way of defending the employee's interest— or even his contractual rights. Rarely in recent times has the power of judicial law-making been so flagrantly exploited to favour employers' interests.

Other substantial reasons. Apart from contractual changes in the employer's interests, other grounds for holding dismissals fair under the cover of "some other substantial reason" exist. They tend to parallel the above description, *e.g.* where the employer's major customer threatens to withdraw unless the employee is sacked, dismissal can be fair (*Scott Packing & Warehousing Co. Ltd.* v. *Paterson* [1978] I.R.L.R. 166 (E.A.T.)); where the employer's insurance company does not accept the employee—dismissal can be fair (*Moody* v. *Telefusion Ltd.* [1978] I.R.L.R. 311 (E.A.T.)); and where the employee refused to join the union in a closed shop establishment, and further refused even to pay an amount to a charity—dismissal can be fair (*Rawlings* v. *Lionweld Ltd.* [1978] I.R.L.R. 481). But *cf.* the case of expiry of a fixed term contract—this has been held possibly to amount to some other substantial reason—but the judges have stressed the need to balance with the employer's interest of the employee in security of employment (*Terry* v. *East Sussex County Council* [1976] I.R.L.R. 332 (E.A.T.); *Cohen* v. *London Borough of Barking* [1976] I.R.L.R. 416 (E.A.T.)). It is preferable that judges attempt to balance employers' and employees' interests than that they should decide on the basis of the needs of the "business"—as if the employee's needs were thereby considered.

Reasonableness in all the circumstances. Finally, it must always be remembered that *whatever* the reason for the dismissal—including if it falls into the category of "some other substantial reason"—the employer who shows the reason must go on to satisfy the test in accordance with subs. (3)—that he acted reasonably in the circumstances.

Subs. (2)

Managerial standards of fairness. As stated in the General Note to Part V, the statutory "fair" reasons listed here reflect a managerial perspective. Thus, under the heading of "*capability or qualifications*" (see definition in subs. (4)), come two principal types of cases: whether the employee is incapacitated due to ill-health, or lacks the skill or competence to perform the work. In the former case, the question to be determined in law is "whether in all the circumstances the *employer* can be expected to wait any longer and if so, how much longer" (Phillips J. in *Spencer* v. *Paragon Wallpapers Ltd.* [1976] I.R.L.R. 373 (E.A.T.)). Again, in the latter case, it is managerial standards not those of workers (or even others) which determine incapacity: "it is sufficient that *the employer* honestly believes on reasonable grounds that the man is incapable or incompetent. It is not necessary for the employer to prove that he is in fact incapable or incompetent" (Lord Denning in *Taylor* v. *Alidair Ltd.* [1978] I.R.L.R. 82 (C.A.)).

With regard to "*conduct*" there is an enormous range of behaviour of employees which is deemed to fall within the scope of justifiable dismissal. A few headings must suffice here: refusal to co-operate with management, refusal to obey an order, insubordination, refusal to accept changes in hours of work, job content, etc., bad relationships with customers, breach of company rules.

The definition of *redundancy* itself (s. 81 (2)) refers to the "requirements of that business"—not those of the employee.

Limits on managerial reasons for dismissal. If the employer needed only to show one of the listed reasons to avoid any claim for unfair dismissal, the law would be completely useless to workers. So managerial standards of fairness are limited by the provision in subs. (3)—reasonableness. This restriction on managements' power to dismiss qualifies each of the managerial standards of this subsection in many ways. Even if it does not shift the initial and fundamental support of the law for managements' interest, it is important for employees to know of the limitations imposed by subs. (3) (see Note below). With regard to the reasons in this subsection, certain restrictions may be mentioned here, though only by way of illustration. Study of the cases is necessary—and see the detailed treatment in S. D. Anderman, *The Law of Unfair Dismissal* (1978). Above all, the law is continually developing: employees should monitor cases to ensure that any new safeguards are noted and utilised.

Capability—ill-health. Incapacity through ill-health is a common reason put forward by employers justifying dismissal. But the dismissal may be held unfair even if the employee is absent or incapable through illness if the employer fails to take certain steps. *E.g.* if he neglects to establish with some accuracy the employee's medical condition—by contacting the employee, discussing it with him, getting a physician's opinion, and if the latter's report is challenged by the employee, getting a further opinion (*Liverpool Area Health Authority (Teaching)*

Central and Southern District v. *Edwards* [1977] I.R.L.R. 471 (E.A.T.)). Or again, it may be unreasonable to dismiss an employee incapacitated from working at his normal job where instead of dismissal another job was available to be offered to him which *could* be done by the employee in question (*Merseyside & North Wales Electricity Board* v. *Taylor* [1975] I.R.L.R. 60 (Q.B.D.), applied in *Todd* v. *North East Electricity Board* [1975] I.R.L.R. 130—employee disabled by a foot condition not offered a clerical vacancy). Finally, any special circumstances in the employee's favour should be taken into account to some extent, *e.g.* if the illness or injury resulted from the employee's work or the employee had long service.

Capability—lack of skill or competence. Despite the above quoted statement of Lord Denning in *Taylor* v. *Alidair Ltd.* [1978] I.R.L.R. 82 (C.A.), there remains some doubt over whether the employer can dismiss an employee for incompetence on his belief alone—however erroneous or ill-judged. In *Taylor*, Geoffrey Lane L.J. stipulated as one question to be answered: "whether there was a reasonable ground for that belief "—and he was adamant in stating that "the question of whether that reasonableness must be judged objectively or subjectively does not arise in this case." So workers may be able to challenge employers' assessments. And apart from obvious indicators such as whether the business or department or shop as a whole was producing satisfactorily, comparisons with the work of other employees may be invoked to undermine the employers' alleged belief. But the judges do attach weight to the "objective" views of management. As Phillips J. said in *Cook* v. *Thomas Linnell & Sons Ltd.* [1977] I.R.L.R. 132 (E.A.T.): "When responsible employers have genuinely come to the conclusion over a reasonable period of time that a manager is incompetent we think that it is some evidence that he is incompetent." Still, the employer's method of coming to his assessment may be challenged. Certainly if management is itself responsible in some way for the poor performance, by, *e.g.* failing to give adequate training, supervision, support staff, working conditions, or clear instructions—the dismissal may be found unfair.

Inadequacies in the employee's performance or failures by him in that respect need not be due to what the law refers to here by lack of " capability." Kilner Brown J. has pointed this out in *Sutton & Gates (Luton) Ltd.* v. *Boxall* [1978] I.R.L.R. 486 (E.A.T.). Putting forward a narrow interpretation of incapability he said: "Cases where a person has not come up to standard through his own carelessness, negligence or maybe idleness are much more appropriately dealt with as cases of conduct or misconduct rather than of capability." He distinguished the "question of sheer incapability due to inherent incapacity to function, compared with a failure to exercise to the full such talent as is possessed." In the latter case, the employee "should be warned of it, probably several times, and be given plenty of opportunity to improve his performance." Perhaps an employer who fails to take steps to help the employee reach the designated standard may be acting unreasonably so as to make the dismissal unfair.

Finally, as with illness, an employee who is incapable of doing his job might be capable of filling an available vacancy—and a dismissal in these circumstances might be unreasonable and thus unfair. Any extenuating circumstances in the employee's favour will also affect the issue of reasonableness.

Conduct. Dismissal for misconduct is the most important case where the limitations on the employer's power to dismiss for a "fair" reason—conduct—need to be appreciated. But for these limitations, the employer might be able to dismiss an employee for a single offence of whatever nature. So the criterion of reasonableness in subs. (3) imposes at least two limitations. Dismissal for a single act of misconduct will only be allowed in very serious cases; otherwise it is unreasonable. And where ordinary misconduct is repeated, the employer must follow certain procedures before the dismissal will be upheld as fair. The Code of Practice on Disciplinary Practice and Procedures in Employment provides in para. 10 (*h*) that employers' disciplinary procedures should "ensure that, except for gross misconduct, no employees are dismissed for a first breach of discipline." While there is no elaboration of what constitutes gross misconduct, the industrial tribunals have treated certain types of actions as gross misconduct in certain circumstances, *e.g.* refusal to obey an order, violence, dishonesty, insubordination, etc. But much depends on the employer's own Works Rules on discipline. The Code provides that employers should ensure that employees know and understand disciplinary rules (para. 7), and the likely consequences of breaking the rules "and in particular they should be given a clear indication of the type of conduct which may warrant summary dismissal" (para. 8). So, *e.g.* where notices were put up to the effect that clocking other employees' cards was "a serious breach of factory regulations" rendering the offender "liable to instant dismissal," Kilner Brown J. held the dismissal unfair as the words "liable to instant dismissal" did not mean that a single offence would necessarily lead to dismissal (*Meridian Ltd.* v. *Gomersall* [1977] I.R.L.R. 125 (E.A.T.)). Even where the applicable rules stated that failing to ring a purchase up on the till was gross misconduct, and that cases of gross misconduct would *normally* result in immediate dismissal, Lord McDonald held that there was still an element of discretion left and dismissal could be found unfair (*Laws Stores Ltd.* v. *Oliphant* [1978] I.R.L.R. 251 (E.A.T.)). He added that even if the rule was stated in more mandatory terms, an industrial tribunal could still question if the employer had acted reasonably. This seems consistent with para. 14 of the Code. It should also be noted that the Code has guidance which must be taken into account by industrial tribunals on such matters as where employees are charged with or convicted of criminal offences outside employment (para. 15).

Where the act of misconduct is not serious enough to justify instant dismissal, repetition may suffice to make dismissal legally fair: *e.g.* bad language, drunkenness, carelessness, bad time-keeping, etc. But, again, much will depend on whether the employer acts reasonably: *e.g.* is even repetition of a minor offence sufficient to justify the extreme penalty of dismissal when other sanctions are available (again para. 14 of the Code must be taken into account: "when determining the disciplinary action to be taken the supervisor or manager should bear in mind the need to satisfy the test of reasonableness in all the circumstances. So far as possible account should be taken of the employee's record and any relevant factors." This last is, of course, always applicable—so, *e.g.* improvements in the employee's performance, any fault of the employer or others, or any mitigating factors should be considered.

Redundancy. It is clear that a dismissal for redundancy may be held to be an unfair dismissal—either under the special provisions of s. 59, or because it is unreasonable under subs. (3). This was restated clearly by Phillips J. in *Cox* v. *Wildt Mellor Bromley Ltd.* [1978] I.R.L.R. 157 (E.A.T.). He referred to previous cases which put the burden on the employer, and required him "to show how the employee came to be dismissed for redundancy, upon what basis the selection was made, and how it was applied in practice." The employer must be prepared in sufficient detail to deal with questions on these matters before the industrial tribunal, and "in outline at least with any general points which a reasonable employer would consider to be important in the circumstances of the case, such as efforts to find him other employment or to assist him." Failure to show these things may lead to a finding of unfair dismissal. Workers should ensure that the employers are aware of these obligations in a redundancy situation.

So if the method of selection among employee-candidates for redundancy is unfair, their dismissal may be unfair. Phillips J. was prepared even to hold that if the accepted custom and practice in the industry as to redundancy selection was unreasonable, that the employer acting on the basis of it was not likely to succeed in discharging the onus on him under subs. (3) (*Watling & Co. Ltd.* v. *Richardson* [1978] I.R.L.R. 255 (E.A.T.)).

Again, Phillips J. has stressed that, especially where redundancy is likely to be contentious, "It is very important that the employers should follow the normal practice, and the normal practice is that there should be proper consultation. Consultation with the union if possible; consultation with those who are candidates for redundancy." While failure to consult will not necessarily make the redundancy dismissal unfair, it may lead to that conclusion—as it did in the case from which this quotation was taken—*Laffin & Callaghan* v. *Fashion Industries (Hartlepool) Ltd.* [1978] I.R.L.R. 448 (E.A.T.). The obligation to consult the recognised union is laid down in s. 99 of the Employment Protection Act 1975, and that to consult employees in paras. 44–46 of the 1972 Code of Practice issued under the Industrial Relations Act 1971 (and see the other suggested measures employers should adopt to avoid or mitigate the effects of redundancies laid down in those paragraphs). The requirement of consultation was emphasised in *British United Shoe Machinery Co. Ltd.* v. *Clarke* [1977] I.R.L.R. 297 (E.A.T.). In that case Phillips J. also reiterated that the E.A.T. "has consistently followed the decision of the N.I.R.C. in *Vokes* v. *Bear Ltd.* [1973] I.R.L.R. 363 to the effect that employers when dismissing an employee for redundancy ought to make reasonable efforts to find him other employment."

Finally, as ever, a failure by the employer to consider the personal circumstances of the redundant employee may make the dismissal unfair, *e.g.* in *Forman Construction Ltd.* v. *Kelly* [1977] I.R.L.R. 469 (E.A.T.), the employer's decision to make the employee redundant without taking into consideration that he was a registered disabled person and also had longer service than some employees who were not dismissed led to the conclusion that the dismissal was unfair.

Contravention of a statute. Even where continued employment would contravene a statute (*e.g.* a driver who loses his licence), dismissal may be unfair if the employer acts unreasonably, *e.g.* in *Sandhu* v. *Department of Education and Science and Hillingdon London Borough* [1978] I.R.L.R. 208 (E.A.T.), the employer sacked a teacher declared to be unsuitable by the D.E.S.—which made it unlawful to continue to employ him as such. The E.A.T. allowed the appeal from the decision of the industrial tribunal that once it was unlawful, then it followed that it was reasonable for the employer to comply with the law. This, said the E.A.T., proceeded on too narrow a view of the requirement of subs. (3), and instead postulated that: "What a reasonable employer would have done would have been to discuss the matter with him, with the D.E.S. and see whether what had gone wrong could be put right, so that he could have a fair trial and a fair opportunity to prove himself." As with other headings considered above, it may be that a reasonable employer would search for alternative employment, or seek ways of avoiding the dismissal without contravening the statute.

Subs. (3)

Lawyers and reasonableness. The interpretation and application of this subsection constitutes a fascinating instance of legal institutions—tribunals and courts—shaping policy. As it stands, the subsection appears to give the industrial tribunal the power to determine that the dismissal is unfair, unless the employer can satisfy it that he acted reasonably. The implications of such a power are quite significant—for the first time, employees have the right to appeal to an apparently independent third party when they feel the employer's action is unreasonable and thus unfair. Yet even such a possible *post facto* reduction in management's prerogative to do as it thinks fit was too radical a concept for most lawyers—whether tribunal chairmen or judges—to accept, whatever Parliament may have intended. And those of the more independently minded tribunals who took their remit literally and began to question employers' judgment as to what was reasonable were quickly subdued.

What most lawyers declared to be the law was as follows. Under this subsection, far from tribunals being empowered to pass judgment on the employers' actions, they must *take the part of the employer* and ask if, *as the employer*, the action was reasonable. *Not* whether the tribunal as an independent arbiter thinks it was reasonable, but whether an *employer* would think it was. The standard of reasonableness was turned into that of a reasonable employer—as if the seriousness of a dog's bite should be judged by the standard of a reasonable dog. There is nothing objective about the standard of reasonableness thus put forward—unless, that is, one subscribes to the unitary view of industrial relations—that employers and employees are united in their common interest in the business enterprise and share common industrial standards. But, it need hardly be said, such a view is extremely politically contentious and has been criticised as such by industrial relations pluralists, not to mention many others.

Moreover, even when a tribunal takes the view that a reasonable *employer* would not have acted as the employer in question did, they may still be precluded from interfering with the management's decision. The judges are divided over the extent to which, even then, the tribunal's views can override those of the employer in question. The *less* management-minded—*less*, mind you, have held that there may be differences between the actions of different reasonable employers. Management has discretion—some may be harsh, others lenient—but it is not for tribunals to condemn the former by saying they are acting unreasonably. It is harsh—but fair, and not unreasonable. It is not for the tribunal to substitute its judgment for the employers.' So many tribunals have been overruled by the E.A.T. and higher courts when they condemn management's actions as unreasonable, that they will now only rarely interfere with management's substantive decisions.

This tendency is reinforced by the *more* management-minded judges' views on the matter. These judges apparently find it conceivable that the law will interfere only with the most extreme cases of unreasonable behaviour by management. As stated by Cumming-Bruce J. in *Vickers Ltd.* v. *Smith* [1977] I.R.L.R. 11 (E.A.T.), industrial tribunals may overrule management decisions not where management's decision was merely wrong, but only where: " It was so wrong, that no sensible or reasonable management could have arrived at the decision at which the management arrived." It is here seriously suggested that the law will hold as unfair only the most extremely unreasonable sorts of management action. Many judges have been wary of too firmly endorsing this extreme position, and have continued to allow industrial tribunals to intervene where management's action is only very unfair, and not positively outrageous. But for a superb attempt at reconciliation of the two views, one must look to Phillips J.'s judgment in *Watling & Co. Ltd.* v. *Richardson* [1978] I.R.L.R. 255 (E.A.T.). *Vickers Ltd.* v. *Smith* is said there to have " given rise to certain misunderstandings." While in law, the standard stated there was " accurate enough . . . it can, particularly to laymen, seem to suggest an inordinately high standards," Phillips J. reiterated the primacy of the words of the Act—now subs. (3): " The difficulty is that the words can be applied in practice in more than one way." He contrasts the " heretical " view of the standard as the " hunch of the particular industrial tribunal, which (though rarely) may be whimsical or eccentric," with the " objective standard of the way in which a reasonable employer in those circumstances in that line of business, would have behaved." Mind you, applying this *objective* standard " equally reasonable, fair, sensible and prudent employers would take different courses, one choosing ' A,' another ' B ' and another ' C '." It seems the industrial tribunal must not substitute its " hunch " for what any of the reasonable employers might do. It is submitted that Phillips J. underestimates the possibility of a standard of reasonable behaviour which is just as " objective " as the standard of the " reasonable employer "—perhaps, it may be suggested, a standard from the vantage point of the employee in the circumstances in that line of employment. If the judges opt for the standard of the reasonable employer, they must expect such political decisions to be scrutinised and subjected to criticism by other groups or classes whose interests are as a result subordinated.

Procedural reasonableness. Any *substantive* challenge by industrial tribunals to employers' views of when it is reasonable to dismiss an employee for incapacity, misconduct, redundancy, etc., is, therefore, severely constrained by the attitudes of the E.A.T. and higher courts. What does remain, and it is a valuable legal resource for workers, is to challenge employers' actions on *procedural* grounds.

The starting point is the Code of Practice on Disciplinary Practice and Procedures in Employment. Para. 10 lays down certain standards which disciplinary procedures should abide by, *e.g.* be in writing (*a*); provide for matters to be dealt with quickly (*c*); give individuals an opportunity to state their case before decisions are reached (*f*); and be accompanied by a trade union or other representative of their choice (*g*); ensure that disciplinary action is not taken until the case has been carefully investigated (*i*), etc. Para. 11 describes how the procedure should operate: facts should be established promptly through an investigation by management. If a serious case, a brief period of suspension with pay may be considered. Before decisions are made as to guilt or penalty, the employee should be given the opportunity to state his case, having been advised of his rights, including the right to be accompanied by a representative. Para. 12 outlines the procedures which should normally be observed where disciplinary action is decided upon—warnings, oral and written, including a final written warning, possible other penalties short of dismissal—though, *e.g.* suspension without pay should not be prolonged. All penalties are subject to the test of reasonableness in the circumstances (para. 14). Finally, there should be a right of appeal of which the employee should be informed (paras. 10 (*k*), 13, 16 and 17). Special procedures are needed for, *e.g.* shift workers or isolated workers, or trade union officials—shop stewards and office representatives who should never be disciplined until the case has been discussed with a senior official or full-time trade union official. Records of discipline should be kept, but provision made for them to be disregarded after a specified period of satisfactory conduct.

The significance of these standards is that the tribunals must, where they are relevant, take them into account in any unfair dismissal claim. And if the employer has not abided by them in one or more ways, this may, and often does, lead to a finding that he has acted unreasonably under subs. (3), even where he may have a fair reason under subss. (1) or (2).

The Note to subs. (2) has given some indication of this approach. Dismissals for incapability may be unfair if the employer fails to show he has adequately investigated the alleged incompetence, or has not given adequate opportunity for improvement. Dismissals for misconduct may be unfair if there is no preceding warning, incidents are not investigated, hearings are not conducted fairly, or penalties are inappropriate to the offence. Dismissals for redundancy may be unfair if consultations are not carried out or the procedure for selection is unsatisfactory.

This view of the law has been confirmed by the House of Lords decision in *Devis & Sons Ltd.* v. *Atkins* [1977] I.R.L.R. 314. Viscount Dilhorne delivering the principal speech declared: (para. 37)

"It does not follow that non-compliance with the Code necessarily renders a dismissal unfair, but I agree with the view expressed by Donaldson J. in *Earl* v. *Slater and Wheeler (Airlyne) Ltd.* [1972] I.R.L.R. 115 that a failure to follow a procedure prescribed in the Code may lead to the conclusion that a dismissal was unfair, which, if that procedure had been followed, would have been held to have been fair."

Whether the employee is entitled to compensation where the dismissal is unfair on what is sometimes call this "technical" ground, is another question—see Note to s. 74 (1).

A few illustrations from the area of misconduct will be given here: *e.g. Lees* v. *The Orchard* [1978] I.R.L.R. 20 (E.A.T.), where a shop assistant was dismissed for dishonesty, the dismissal was held unfair as the employer acted unreasonably in not investigating more carefully the allegation of misappropriation of money from the till, *e.g.* by attempting to make some contact with the customer concerned; *Bentley Engineering Co. Ltd.* v. *Mistry* [1978] I.R.L.R. 436 (E.A.T.), where a works office clerk was dismissed for fighting. The employer did investigate and took statements from witnesses. But when his case was heard by the management, the employee was not given copies of these statements nor were the witnesses or even the other party to the fight present. His dismissal was held unfair, because he did not have the opportunity to know in sufficient detail what was said against him, and so could not defend himself. *Johnson Matthey Metals Ltd.* v. *Harding* [1978] I.R.L.R. 248 (E.A.T.) involved dismissal of the employee for alleged theft of a fellow employee's watch. The employee appealed from the production manager to the local director but the latter had already discussed the matter with the former and agreed that the former's decision was appropriate. This behaviour was criticised, and led, with other factors, to a finding that the dismissal was unfair. Lawyers will recognise in these requirements similarities to the rules of natural justice applied in administrative law, and this similarity has been noted and accepted by the judges—see, *e.g.* Bristow J. in *Khanum* v. *Mid-Glamorgan Area Health Authority* [1978] I.R.L.R. 215 (E.A.T.).

Limitations on the need for procedural fairness. Workers need beware, however, that there exist limits on the need for employers to follow fair procedures. First, the Code of Practice is not law—only guidance which the industrial tribunals must take account of where relevant. But they may decide it is not relevant (*e.g. Brown* v. *Hall Advertising Ltd.* [1978] I.R.L.R. 246 (E.A.T.)); or use their discretion and simply refuse to apply it (having taken it into account), *e.g.* where the nature of the employee's conduct is said to override the necessity for compliance with the prescribed procedure—*Cardiff City Council* v. *Condé* [1978] I.R.L.R. 218 (E.A.T.); or, *e.g.* dismissal is allowed without any warnings having been given (*Retarded Children's Aid Society Ltd.* v. *Day* [1978] I.R.L.R. 128 (C.A.)).

Secondly, where the employer has failed to comply with the proper procedure, the tribunals have nonetheless held the dismissal to be fair where, it is said, the procedural omission or defect was insignificant—procedure is said to be a needless formality. In *Lowndes* v. *Specialist Heavy Engineering Ltd.* [1976] I.R.L.R. 246 (E.A.T.), Phillips J. re-affirmed that "as a general rule, a failure to follow a fair procedure, whether by warnings or by giving an opportunity to be heard before dismissal, will result in the ensuing dismissal being found to be unfair. But there will be exceptions. . . ." *Lowndes* was a case where the employee was dismissed for incompetence following five serious and costly errors, without a written warning or an opportunity to answer the complaints against him or to be represented. The E.A.T. upheld the dismissal as fair, because "though an explanation might conceivably have been produced, it was wildly unlikely that it would be." Still, it was emphasised that failures in procedure will ordinarily lead to the conclusion that the dismissal was unfair. In *Charles Letts & Co.* v. *Howard* [1976] I.R.L.R. 248 (E.A.T.), the E.A.T. put the onus on the employer to satisfy the tribunal that even if the proper, fair procedure had been carried out, it would not have made any difference. It is obvious that if the tribunals ignore failures to follow procedures, the result would be to subordinate employees' interests to the convenience of a management in a hurry.

Dismissal relating to trade union membership

58.—(1) For the purposes of this Part, the dismissal of an employee by an employer shall be regarded as having been unfair if the reason for it (or, if more than one, the principal reason) was that the employee—

(a) was, or proposed to become, a member of an independent trade union;

(b) had taken, or proposed to take, part at any appropriate time in the activities of an independent trade union; or

(c) had refused, or proposed to refuse, to become or remain a member of a trade union which was not an independent trade union.

(2) In subsection (1), " appropriate time " in relation to an employee taking part in the activities of a trade union, means time which either—

(a) is outside his working hours, or

(b) is a time within his working hours at which, in accordance with arrangements agreed with or consent given by his employer, it is permissible for him to take part in those activities;

and in this subsection " working hours ", in relation to an employee, means any time when, in accordance with his contract of employment, he is required to be at work.

(3) Dismissal of an employee by an employer shall be regarded as fair for the purposes of this Part if—

(a) it is the practice, in accordance with a union membership agreement, for employees for the time being of the same class as the dismissed employee to belong to a specified independent trade union, or to one of a number of specified independent trade unions; and

(b) the reason for the dismissal was that the employee was not a member of the specified union or one of the specified unions, or had refused or proposed to refuse to become or remain a member of that union or one of those unions;

unless the employee genuinely objects on grounds of religious belief to being a member of any trade union whatsoever, in which case the dismissal shall be regarded as unfair.

(4) For the purposes of subsection (3), a union shall be treated as specified for the purposes of or in relation to a union membership agreement (in a case where it would not otherwise be so treated) if—

(a) the Advisory, Conciliation and Arbitration Service has made a recommendation for recognition covering the employee in question which is operative within the meaning of section 15 of the Employment Protection Act 1975; or

(b) the union has referred a recognition issue (within the meaning of that Act) covering that employee to the Advisory, Conciliation and Arbitration Service under section 11 of that Act and the Service has not declined to proceed on the reference under section 12 of that Act, the union has not withdrawn the reference, or from the reference, and the issue has not been settled or reported on under that section.

(5) Any reason by virtue of which a dismissal is to be regarded as

unfair in consequence of subsection (1) or (3) is in this Part referred to as an inadmissible reason.

(6) In this section, unless the context otherwise requires, references to a trade union include references to a branch or section of a trade union.

DERIVATION

1974, para. 6 (4) to (6), (9); 1975, Sched. 16, Pt. III, paras. 11, 12; Trade Union and Labour Relations (Amendment) Act 1976 (c. 7), ss. 1 (e), 3 (5), (6).

GENERAL NOTE

Subs. (1)

No qualifications. Employees are protected from dismissal (as from action (short of dismissal)—s. 23) however short their period of employment and whatever their age if the reason is an inadmissible one—*i.e.* one of those in (a) to (c) (subs. (5) and s. 64 (3)).

Burden of proof. But unlike the case of action (short of dismissal) (s. 25 (1)), the burden of proving an inadmissible reason would appear to be on the employee (*contra* Lord Denning, dissenting, in *Smith* v. *Hayle Town Council* [1978] I.R.L.R. 413 (C.A.)). The weight of this burden, according to Lord Denning, dissenting in *Smith*, will depend in each case on the " opportunities and know-ledge with respect to the facts to be proved which may be possessed by the parties respectively." So where Smith did all he could and showed some evidence of anti-union bias—the burden shifted to the employer to prove the contrary.

A similar approach was evinced in *Goodwin Ltd.* v. *Fitzmaurice* [1977] I.R.L.R. 393 (E.A.T.), where Phillips J. asserted that the burden is on the employee, who ought to begin by submitting his case, but that save in exceptional cases, the tribunal should go on to hear what the employer has to say, for when the employer's reason is examined it may be seen not to be the true reason, and thus bolster up what at the outset seemed to be a weak case for the employee.

Principal and other reasons. In *Smith*, the employee was dismissed by a one-vote majority decision of the town council, and succeeded in proving that at least one of the councillors voted against him out of anti-union prejudice (he had just joined NALGO). Nonetheless, Eveleigh L.J., with whom Sir David Cairns agreed, held that in a corporate action, all those concerned should be considered, and since there may be other reasons that operate, the existence of some anti-union prejudice may exist without amounting to the principal reason for dismissal. So Smith had not satisfied the burden of showing the principal reason to be anti-union prejudice. So, as if the burden was not heavy enough, trade unionists need be psychologists as well.

Trade union activities. For details as to what are " activities of an independent trade union," whether of officials or members, and judicial attitudes—see the Note to s. 23 (1) above.

Subs.(2)

Appropriate time. For details as to what is an " appropriate time," including questions of *implied consent* by the employer, *withdrawal of consent*, and the case of *industrial action*—see the Note to s. 23 (2) above.

Subs. (3)

Problems in showing a " practice." " Union membership agreement " is defined in s. 30 (1) of TULRA (referred to by s. 153 (1)). Employers who wish to rely on this provision to avoid an unfair dismissal claim have their work cut out for them. First, the E.A.T. has said it is not enough just to show that there is a closed shop agreement, and that the employee was not a union member—despite the literal meaning of the words here. No, if the agreement has conditions in it, the employer must show he has satisfied those conditions. So, where he did not follow the three-stage procedure for dealing with non-union members, he cannot use this subsection. Apparently, he is also required to " establish a strict com-pliance with the terms of the union membership agreement " (*Jeffrey* v. *Laurence Scott & Electromotors Ltd.* [1977] I.R.L.R. 466 (E.A.T.)).

Secondly, despite the removal of the word " all " from the phrase which now reads " employees for the time being " by the Trade Union and Labour Relations (Amendment) Act 1976 (which received the Royal Assent on March 25, 1976), the

E.A.T. still insists that "almost all the employees of the relevant class" should have come to belong to the union. This was said to be a necessary qualification for the "practice" to be demonstrated by the employer. So where nine of 42 employees (of whom eight were claiming here) were not members, it could not be said that the provision was satisfied. A lovely "Catch 22": by refusing to join the union, a few employees could effectively prevent the employer from claiming a "practice" (*Himpfen* v. *Allied Records Ltd.* [1978] I.R.L.R. 154 (E.A.T.)).

Thirdly, in *Himpfen*, the employer had preceded his conclusion of a union membership agreement with USDAW by a general statement to his employees to the effect that they were free to join a union of their choice. When eight of the employees joined the TGWU and were subsequently sacked, they claimed unfair dismissal. The employer invoked the agreement with USDAW and the protection of this subsection's provisions. The E.A.T. held he was estopped from doing so. Having represented that the employees could join any union, they were not entitled by way of defence to bring forward the agreement. As this was the only available defence, the claim should be upheld. One awaits with interest to see when the next step will be taken, *i.e.* an estoppel by conduct is held to exist whereby employees were free to join or not to join trade unions, and thus the employer is barred from invoking the union membership agreement.

Some other substantial reason. The employer's hope may be to avoid these problems by asserting as a reason for dismissal the provision in s. 57 (1)—that refusal to join the union was some other substantial reason for dismissing the non-unionist—as was stated in *Rawlings* v. *Lionweld Ltd.* [1978] I.R.L.R. 481 (E.A.T.), and then showing that it was reasonable to do so as required by s. 57 (3).

Conscience v. *religion.* The continuing epic of *Saggers* v. *British Railways Board (No. 2)* [1978] I.R.L.R. 435 (E.A.T.) demonstrates that a man's conscience and religion may be sufficiently entangled to keep him within the terms of a section from which conscientious grounds have specifically been excluded. Indeed, *Saggers* v. *British Railways Board* [1977] I.R.L.R. 266 (E.A.T.) had the distinction of establishing that an exclusively personal but genuine belief by the employee in question could be deemed "religious" within the meaning of this provision. This seems to be the personal and genuine belief of some members of the E.A.T.

Independent Review Committee. Finally, it would not be right to omit mention of the Independent Review Committee set up by the TUC in 1976 to hear appeals from employees dismissed from their jobs as a result of having been expelled from or refused admission to a trade union where a union membership agreement operates. Chaired by Lord Wedderburn, in a little over two years the Committee received 18 complaints falling within its terms of reference and held hearings in 14 cases (see Annex to the TUC General Council Report of 1978).

Subs. (4)

Cf. s. 23 (5), and see the Note to that subsection.

Dismissal on ground of redundancy

59. Where the reason or principal reason for the dismissal of an employee was that he was redundant, but it is shown that the circumstances constituting the redundancy applied equally to one or more other employees in the same undertaking who held positions similar to that held by him and who have not been dismissed by the employer, and either—

(*a*) that the reason (or, if more than one, the principal reason) for which he was selected for dismissal was an inadmissible reason; or

(*b*) that he was selected for dismissal in contravention of a customary arrangement or agreed procedure relating to redundancy and there were no special reasons justifying a departure from that arrangement or procedure in his case,

then, for the purposes of this Part, the dismissal shall be regarded as unfair.

DERIVATION

1974, para. 6 (7).

GENERAL NOTE

Burden of proof. The employer who seeks to establish redundancy cannot avail himself of the presumption in s. 91 (2)—see Sched. 9, para. 5. But once the employer proves redundancy, the burden of showing the dismissal unfair under this section falls on the employee.

The basis of selection in law. The employee must first show that the redundancy " applied equally " to others. These others must be in the same " undertaking "— a term not defined in the Act. Since we are dealing with redundancy, the definition in s. 81 applies (s. 153 (2)), and accordingly it would seem that " undertaking " is at least as large, and probably larger, than a business or workplace. An employer may have his undertaking in various places and carry on a number of businesses. (*Cf.* the use of the word " undertaking " in the Health and Safety at Work etc. Act 1974, ss. 1 (3) and 3.)

So the employee may seek to compare himself with others in the same undertaking, but these must hold " positions similar " to his. " Position " is defined in s. 153 (1), in a way which includes status, nature of the work and terms and conditions of employment—taken as a whole.

The basis of selection in practice. A study commissioned by the Office of Population Censuses and Surveys (O.P.C.S.) and published by HMSO in 1971 (*Effects of the Redundancy Payments Act,* by S. R. Parker *et al.*) found that in the practice of the employers surveyed, there were two main bases on which selection criteria for redundancy were applied: to the establishment as a whole (32 per cent. of employers), or department by department (42 per cent. of employers). The larger the establishment, the more likely it was that the criteria would be applied department by department (p. 49).

The legal basis of selection in practice. In those cases which cannot be resolved by voluntary procedures, employees bringing claims involving this section may, therefore, be challenging the employer's application of a selection process (whether agreed with a trade union or not) based on a unit of selection smaller than that envisaged by the law. The lack of definition of the legal basis of selection, and the consequent flexibility, gives the judges and tribunals a great deal of scope in deciding whether a selection procedure has been properly carried out.

Indeed, the problems of applying criteria can be extremely complex and are almost bound to be seen as arbitrary by those suffering from the selection, *e.g.* the problems that can be created by " bumping " are notorious. If the unit of selection is wider than a department, then an employee in one department may " bump " a less senior employee in another department. The matter is further complicated when the basis for calculation of seniority is different from that of the unit of selection, *e.g.* a redundancy scheme introduced with effect from May 2, 1977, for workers with National Carriers Ltd. (NCL). Once the number of redundancies has been fixed, the most junior staff in the grade at the depot concerned will be selected. But for the calculation of service, all permanent appointed service with NCL will be used.

By way of illustration of the problem, compare the requirement now established that the employer in a redundancy situation needs look for suitable available vacancies before dismissal of an employee (see Note to s. 57 (2)—*Redundancy*). But how wide must the employer cast his net? In *Thomas & Betts Manufacturing Co. Ltd.* v. *Harding* [1978] I.R.L.R. 213 (E.A.T.), counsel relied on the parallel with this section to argue that the limitation to employees in the same undertaking who held similar positions applied also to limit the requirement to look for vacancies. Phillips J., while acknowledging that " there is force in that submission," rejected it. He did so because of " the practical problem and difficulty which lies in the way of [this] interesting submission . . . that it seems to us almost impossible to de-limit in any intelligent form the section or the grade or the area to which it would be legitimate to look. . . ." It is submitted that the same practical difficulties will exist when this section is applied. Rather, as Phillips J. went on to say: " the fact that a business may be divided into sections, or employees may be divided into different grades, or that the business may be carried on in more than one plant—are all matters of practical importance which the industrial tribunal will need to take into account. . . ." It seems, therefore, that it will be very much a matter of applying the criteria of the law to the facts of every individual situation. In *Thomas & Betts,* the employee working on " fittings," dismissed when a redundancy arose in her section, was held to have been unfairly dismissed because there were people in other parts of the business (in particular one packer) who had less service. Thus, the dismissal was unreasonable within s. 57 (3).

Inadmissible reason. Once the claimant demonstrates a unit of selection conforming to the criteria (undertaking, position), he must then go on to show discriminatory selection. Anti-trade union discrimination is deemed inadmissible (s. 58 (5)). For further discussion, see the Notes to ss. 58 and 23.

Arrangements or procedures. The burden of proving the existence of an agreed procedure or customary arrangement is on the employee. In the case of an agreed procedure, this is not too difficult. But the OPCS study cited above found that in only 15 per cent. of all establishments surveyed was there an agreement or understanding with trade unions about redundancy (p. 50).

An example of an agreed selection procedure for redundancy is that between NUBE and Lloyds and Scottish Finance (ratified December 6, 1977). The following priorities were established: (i) voluntary redundancy, which allows the company discretion to reject a volunteer; (ii) part-time staff, with those of least service leaving first; (iii) all staff aged 60 (male) and 55 (female) and over to be given the option of voluntary early retirement without actuarial deduction of pension; (iv) staff with least service in the particular area in which redundancy is being declared; (v) notwithstanding the above, consideration will be given, subject to an appeal being made, to members of staff with individual problems including disability and particular family circumstances; (vi) if staff have to accept alternative employment of a lower grade due to a redundancy exercise, salaries will not be reduced. If the salary is in excess of the maximum salary for the new job, increases or increments will not be paid as long as the salary is outwith the salary band of the new job; (vii) there may be occasions where the company must declare redundancy of a particular job classification where, therefore, the selection criteria listed (i)–(iv) cannot logically apply. There is a joint negotiating committee which acts as an appeals committee to hear objections to any redundancy selections.

Whether a customary arrangement exists may be disputed. There is no guidance in the statute as to how clear-cut and certain or how long established a " customary arrangement " need be. Indeed, it does not seem to require a bilateral nature— it may be a practice imposed by the employer on his employees. On balance, it would favour employees if the burden of showing a customary arrangement were discharged relatively easily—for the alternative is to give the employer freedom to select among redundant employees without any constraint (subject to the requirements of the Code of Practice and s. 57 (3)).

Customary arrangement and custom. Unfortunately, the Court of Appeal in *Bessenden Properties Ltd.* v. *Corness* [1974] I.R.L.R. 338 upheld the view of the NIRC that the term " customary arrangement " meant something so well known, certain and clear as to be in effect an implied agreed procedure. M. Freedland in *The Contract of Employment* (1976) (p. 15) contrasts the " archaism " in employment relationships of the common law rule that custom is imported into contract only when " reasonable, certain and notorious." The custom and practice of industry, which is of infinitely greater importance, he notes, would frequently be the opposite of " certain and notorious." Nonetheless, the Court of Appeal here again upheld the contract model, not the industrial relations model. Its judgment was cited as a model precedent by Bristow J. in *Earl of Bradford* v. *Jowett* [1978] I.R.L.R. 16 (E.A.T.).

Evidence needed. So where there was " no evidence upon which any customary arrangement or agreed procedure relating to redundancy could have been found," the High Court would not permit the industrial tribunal to uphold what it considered to be the normal rule of last-in-first-out (*British Olivetti Ltd.* v. *Kay* [1975] I.R.L.R. 29). And where there was not " any evidence in industrial practice, locally or nationally, about the importance to be attached to one of the candidates for redundancy being ' in post,' " there could not be said to be any application of this provision (*Grundy (Teddington) Ltd.* v. *Willis* [1976] I.R.L.R. 118 (E.A.T.)).

Selection in the absence of procedure or arrangement. It is clear that even where the employee has failed to satisfy the burden imposed on him by this section, the dismissal may be unfair as the employer has not satisfied the burden imposed on him by s. 57 (3)—to act reasonably in the circumstances (*Bristol Channel Ship Repairers Ltd.* v. *O'Keefe and Lewis* [1977] I.R.L.R. 13 (E.A.T.)). Thus, in *Laffin & Callaghan* v. *Fashion Industries (Hartlepool) Ltd.* [1978] I.R.L.R. 448 (E.A.T.), Phillips J. confirmed that " there was no customary arrangement or agreed procedure," but nonetheless held the dismissal unfair because "it is very important that the employers should follow the normal practice, and the normal practice is that there should be proper consultation. Consultation with the union if possible; consultation with those who are candidates for redundancy." And in *Forman Construction Ltd.* v. *Kelly* [1977] I.R.L.R. 469 (E.A.T.), Lord McDonald confirmed the absence of any procedure, but nonetheless held the dismissal unfair because the employer has not taken into account the personal characteristics of the redundant employee before dismissing him.

Agreed procedures and fairness. Finally, it may be noted that Phillips J. in *Watling & Co. Ltd.* v. *Richardson* [1978] I.R.L.R. 255 (E.A.T.) was prepared to hold unfair a dismissal which was in accordance with custom and practice in the electrical contracting business. He held that the custom and practice itself was unreasonable and that the employer had therefore not discharged the burden under s. 57 (3). But in *Clyde Pipeworks Ltd.* v. *Foster* [1978] I.R.L.R. 313 (E.A.T.), Lord McDonald held that once an agreement had been reached with the unions, the employer, as long as the method of selection was a fair one in general terms, need not further consult in carrying out his selection in accordance with the agreement.

Dismissal on ground of pregnancy

60.—(1) An employee shall be treated for the purposes of this Part as unfairly dismissed if the reason or principal reason for her dismissal is that she is pregnant or is any other reason connected with her pregnancy, except one of the following reasons—

(a) that at the effective date of termination she is or will have become, because of her pregnancy, incapable of adequately doing the work which she is employed to do;

(b) that, because of her pregnancy, she cannot or will not be able to continue after that date to do that work without contravention (either by her or her employer) of a duty or restriction imposed by or under any enactment.

(2) An employee shall be treated for the purposes of this Part as unfairly dismissed if her employer dismisses her for a reason mentioned in subsection (1) (a) or (b), but neither he nor any successor of his, where there is a suitable available vacancy, makes her an offer before or on the effective date of termination to engage her under a new contract of employment complying with subsection (3).

(3) The new contract of employment must—

(a) take effect immediately on the ending of employment under the previous contract, or, where that employment ends on a Friday, Saturday or Sunday, on or before the next Monday after that Friday, Saturday or Sunday;

(b) be such that the work to be done under the contract is of a kind which is both suitable in relation to the employee and appropriate for her to do in the circumstances; and

(c) be such that the provisions of the new contract as to the capacity and place in which she is to be employed and as to the other terms and conditions of her employment are not substantially less favourable to her than the corresponding provisions of the previous contract.

(4) On a complaint of unfair dismissal on the ground of failure to offer to engage an employee as mentioned in subsection (2), it shall be for the employer to show that he or a successor made an offer to engage her in compliance with subsections (2) and (3) or, as the case may be, that there was no suitable available vacancy for her.

(5) Section 55 (3) shall not apply in a case where an employer gives notice to an employee to terminate her contract of employment for a reason mentioned in subsection (1) (a) or (b).

DERIVATION
1975, s. 34 (1)–(5).

GENERAL NOTE
Subs. (1)

Pregnancy dismissal automatically treated as unfair. Pregnancy is not made simply an exception to the " fair " reasons for dismissal given in s. 57 (2), or stated to be within the phrase " some other substantial reason " in s. 57 (1). (*Cf.* s. 61—dismissal of replacement employee held to be such a substantial reason justifying dismissal, but may still be unfair if unreasonable—s. 57 (3).) Dismissal on grounds of pregnancy is unfair and such a dismissed employee when claiming to an industrial tribunal *is to be treated* without more as unfairly dismissed. *Cf.* the provisions of s. 58 (1) and s. 59, where dismissal is to be regarded as unfair. Unlike the case of these provisions, the tribunal is here not to have regard to otherwise relevant factors in providing a remedy to the dismissed employee (*e.g.* it seems likely that the qualifications specified in s. 64 (1) should not apply; but opinion is divided on this question and an industrial tribunal has held, without the point having apparently been argued, that the 26-week qualification does apply—*Reaney* v. *Kanda Jean Products Ltd.* [1978] I.R.L.R. 427). It is submitted that the complainant is to be treated as unfairly dismissed regardless of those provisions (though subject to the remainder of this section).

Remedies. The tribunal should proceed immediately to determine the appropriate remedies under ss. 67–76. It is submitted that this may include an additional payment where the tribunal makes an order for reinstatement or reengagement which is not complied with by the employer, and could amount to 26–52 weeks' pay (s. 71 (2) (*b*) (i) and (3) (*b*)), as dismissal for pregnancy may be an act of sex discrimination (though the contrary was decided by the tribunal in *Reaney* (above). And in *George* v. *Beecham Group* [1977] I.R.L.R. 43, the tribunal applied s. 71 (2) (*b*) (ii)).

Reasons connected with pregnancy. The scope of " any other reason connected with her pregancy " is clearly very wide and covers matters occurring after as well as before the confinement (*e.g.* miscarriage, as was the case in *George* (above) ; or post-natal illness). Not only medical matters, but social or family matters affecting her may be included, as long as they are linked with the pregnancy. The most common effects are likely to be absence somehow connected with or by reason of the pregnancy.

Employers' escape clause. The employer may escape being treated as having unfairly dismissed the employee if he can prove one of the reasons in (*a*) or (*b*). That is . not to say, of course, that proof of one of them renders the dismissal " fair " without more. The employer is simply not automatically treated as having unfairly dismissed the employee. The ordinary procedure of the unfair dismissal provisions apply, and under s. 57 (3), the employer will have to show that he acted reasonably.

Dismissal because of pregnancy. It has been held by an industrial tribunal that dismissal because of pregnancy in (*a*) and (*b*) is narrower than dismissal for any reason connected with pregnancy. So where the employee was dismissed because she was incapacitated because of hypertension brought on by her pregnancy, this incapability did not provide the employer with a defence under (*a*). The dismissal was therefore treated as unfair (*Elegbede* v. *Wellcome Foundation Ltd.* [1977] I.R.L.R. 313).

Incapability. The meaning of (*a*) is bound to give rise to disputation. It is not clear whether it covers the same ground as incapability in s. 57 (see the definition in s. 57 (4) (*a*)). One industrial tribunal has already held that the employer comes within the provision if he shows that the woman was incapable of doing a substantial part of the work (*Brear* v. *W. Wright Hudson Ltd.* [1977] I.R.L.R. 287). However, determining capability in the context of pregnancy is probably different. For example, ill-health might make a dismissal fair in certain circumstances of ordinary employment; in the context of pregnancy it would be unlikely, because of its necessarily transient nature, to be held to render the employee " incapable." In any event, the employer must act reasonably in the circumstances. Since the whole tenor of the Act is that a woman is to make her own decision as to whether she wishes to continue working while pregnant, it will be for the employer to show that she is incapable and that the dismissal is justified. Even a doctor's certificate may be insufficient for this if the woman is determined and capable.

The effect of (*b*) would seem to contradict the spirit at least of s. 19. If the employer dismisses for pregnancy, may this not be a medical ground ? In identical circumstances, a suspended employee might receive up to 26 weeks' pay. Should not at least an equivalent remedy be available for dismissal? Otherwise, an employee would be without remedy if dismissed where she could be compensated if suspended. In these circumstances, therefore, dismissal for the reason in (*b*) would almost certainly be "unreasonable." Suspension would be the reasonable response of an employer under the statutory duty. Dismissal would be unfair.

Subs. (2)

Suitable alternative employment. An offer of suitable alternative employment cannot be imposed on a pregnant employee (*e.g.* where the employer wants her to maintain a particular sexist image) unless the employer shows either (*a*) or (*b*) of subs. (1). Where it can be shown that the woman is incapable of or prohibited from doing her normal job, however, the employer, or any successor, must offer her suitable alternative employment where there is a vacancy. Failure to do so, regardless of whether the employee requested it and even where it might seem reasonable to assume that she would not want it, renders the dismissal unfair, as *per* subs. (1)— see, *e.g. Martin* v. *B.S.C. Footwear (Supplies) Ltd.* [1978] I.R.L.R. 95. The obligation is an absolute one to offer the alternative employment. Preconceptions of what the woman concerned may want or be willing to do are irrelevant. The offer must be made. The burden of proving the offer or the absence of a vacancy is on the employer (subs. (4)).

Dismissal. Unless women are adequately informed of their legal rights and how to secure them (*e.g.* by not resigning prior to the 11th week before confinement) there is likely to be some difficulty over the factual question of whether a woman employee resigned, agreed to leave, went on temporary leave, was suspended, by mutual agreement or otherwise, or was actually dismissed. The right to the offer of alternative employment where subs. (1) (*a*) or (*b*) can be shown (and also other maternity rights—see s. 33 (4) and the Note to the subsection) can only be obtained where the woman has been "dismissed."

Subject to other provisions of the Act (*e.g.* subs. (5)), the meaning of dismissal is that of s. 55. Given that the nature of the circumstances indicates only a temporary break in employment (*e.g.* as stated above, suspension is the reasonable response), an implied evidential presumption should operate that a woman does not intend permanent resignation in the event of the circumstances of subs. (1) (*a*) or (*b*). Otherwise, employers might attempt to manipulate termination interviews to establish voluntary resignation, where only temporary suspension of work was intended.

Reasonableness. To repeat a point previously made, even where the employer shows the circumstances of subs. (1) (*a*) or (*b*) and has made an offer as required here (or has failed to, because there is no suitable available vacancy), the dismissal may still be unfair as the employer may be acting unreasonably in the circumstances (s. 57 (3)). Thus, where subs. (1) (*a*) or (*b*) applies, and the employer has made an offer (complying with subs. (3)), which has been refused, the reasonable response may still be suspension, not dismissal.

Subs. (3)

Not substantially less favourable. What (*c*) means is that the new employment offered may be different since it is suitable and appropriate to the circumstances of a pregnant employee, but it may therefore be less favourable in its terms. The employer is thus obliged to consider a wide range of possible employment where available. Nothing, however, is said about the reasonableness of an employee's response to any offer which, according to (*c*), may be somewhat less favourable to her than her previous employment. A pregnant employee may, by implication therefore, be granted the right to refuse an offer of work even where it complies with the requirements (*a*) and (*b*). One justification for such a refusal may be that her maternity pay will be less if she accepts it—see Sched. 14, para. 7 (1) (*d*), and the Note to s. 35 (1). An employer dismissing her in those circumstances might still be acting unreasonably. Suspension, again, is the appropriate response.

Subs. (4)

The Act does not embody the suggestion of the Employment Protection Bill Consultative Document of 1974 that in specified circumstances the employer should be required to provide the tribunal with information about relevant vacancies in his organisation either before or at the hearing (para. 23). Since the burden of proving that there is no suitable vacancy is on the employer here, he could be obliged to disclose such information to the tribunal as will enable it to make a decision.

Subs. (5)

It is not clear why the employee had to be deprived in these circumstances of any maternity rights. It heightens the danger of contrived " resignations " mentioned in the Note to subs. (2). If the reason is that the employer had to have time prior to the dismissal taking effect to find suitable vacancies, the reply obviously is that such a drastic provision as this was scarcely necessary. It might simply have provided that the employer's defence of an offer of new employment subsisted throughout the specified period of notice, or, if necessary, barred an employee from giving notice effectively shortening the employer's notice. Either of those would be preferable to simply destroying all the employee's rights in order to safeguard a possible defence of the employer. If the employer had no alternative employment, or if the reason alleged by him under subs. (1) (*a*) or (*b*) was false, is the employee nonetheless barred from any remedy?

Dismissal of replacement

61.—(1) Where an employer—

    (*a*) on engaging an employee informs the employee in writing that his employment will be terminated on the return to work of another employee who is, or will be, absent wholly or partly because of pregnancy or confinement; and

    (*b*) dismisses the first-mentioned employee in order to make it possible to give work to the other employee;

then, for the purposes of section 57 (1) (*b*), but without prejudice to the application of section 57 (3), the dismissal shall be regarded as having been for a substantial reason of a kind such as to justify the dismissal of an employee holding the position which that employee held.

(2) Where an employer—

    (*a*) on engaging an employee informs the employee in writing that his employment will be terminated on the end of a suspension such as is referred to in section 19 of another employee; and

    (*b*) dismisses the first-mentioned employee in order to make it possible to allow the other employee to resume his original work;

then, for the purposes of section 57 (1) (*b*), but without prejudice to the application of section 57 (3), the dismissal shall be regarded as having been for a substantial reason of a kind such as to justify the dismissal of an employee holding the position which that employee held.

DERIVATION
1975, ss. 33, 51.

GENERAL NOTE
Subs. (1)

This subsection is substantially identical to subs. (2) and the comments made in the Note below apply here. In both cases, where a replacement is dismissed, presumably the provision is to have effect by virtue of its status as a statutory exception to the normal unfair dismissal procedure and not as a contractual term. If the replacement employee's rights were only to be affected by virtue of the employer's inserting a term in the contract on engaging him or her to the effect described in (*a*), then, after the 26 weeks' qualification had been achieved for protection from unfair dismissal (s. 64 (1) (*a*)), this contractual provision would not avail the employer (s. 140 (1)).

One notes with sadness the pedantic insistence on the pronoun " his " where it would have been more appropriate to use the by now legally equal " her."

Subs. (2)

The first words of (*b*) in the original Employment Protection Bill 1975 read: " is obliged to dismiss," but were changed on Report to simply " dismisses." This was a brave but futile attempt to avoid some of the difficulties which could be anticipated where an employer was put in the position of defending himself against a charge of unfair dismissal by the substitute employee. For it is easy to question whether the substitute had to be dismissed " in order to allow the other employee to resume his original work." It could be argued: (a) that changes in the economic position of the company or simply work arrangements made dismissal unnecessary; or (b) that dismissal was not necessary as another suitable job was available which the replacement could have had; or even (c) that another employee should have been dismissed in order to allow the returning worker to resume employment. This last might be rejected by an industrial tribunal given the existence of a written notice informing the substitute of the temporary nature of his employment. But at least the first two would seem to have been actually anticipated by the section, for it goes on to say that although dismissal of a replacement in these circumstances is a substantial reason justifying dismissal, it may nevertheless be unreasonable in particular circumstances. Therefore, the employer must prove that it was not only justifiable, but that he acted reasonably as well.

One example should suffice to illustrate the potential problems for an employer: if there is a last-in-first-out procedure for dismissal existing in the plant, and the replacement employee is hired, but subsequently another employee is taken on, the temporary employee may have seniority and the prior right to claim a job. Would the employer, therefore, be acting unreasonably if he dismissed the replacement where there was a less senior employee?

Dismissal in connection with a lock-out, strike or other industrial action

62.—(1) The provisions of this section shall have effect in relation to an employee who claims that he has been unfairly dismissed by his employer where at the date of dismissal—

    (a) the employer was conducting or instituting a lock-out, or

    (b) the employee was taking part in a strike or other industrial action.

(2) In such a case an industrial tribunal shall not determine whether the dismissal was fair or unfair unless it is shown—

    (a) that one or more relevant employees of the same employer have not been dismissed, or

    (b) that one or more such employees have been offered re-engagement, and that the employee concerned has not been offered re-engagement.

(3) Where it is shown that the condition referred to in paragraph (b) of subsection (2) is fulfilled, the provisions of sections 57 to 60 shall have effect as if in those sections for any reference to the reason or principal reason for which the employee was dismissed there were substituted a reference to the reason or principal reason for which he has not been offered re-engagement.

(4) In this section—

    (a) " date of dismissal " means—

        (i) where the employee's contract of employment was terminated by notice, the date on which the employer's notice was given, and

        (ii) in any other case, the effective date of termination;

    (b) " relevant employees " means—

        (i) in relation to a lock-out, employees who were directly interested in the trade dispute in contemplation or furtherance of which the lock-out occurred, and

        (ii) in relation to a strike or other industrial action, employees who took part in it; and

    (c) any reference to an offer of re-engagement is a reference to an offer (made either by the original employer or by a successor of that employer or an associated employer) to re-engage an employee, either in the job which he held immediately before the date of dismissal or in a different job which would be reasonably suitable in his case.

DERIVATION

1974, para. 7 (1)–(3), (5); 1975, Sched. 16, Pt. III, para. 13.

GENERAL NOTE

Changing attitudes to industrial action. The Employment Protection Act 1975 made a significant and decisive change in the way the law was henceforth to treat the relationship of strike activity to the employee's rights *vis-à-vis* the employer. The old statutory provisions reflected the common law view that a strike was a breach of contract: if the employee was dismissed for strike activity "the dismissal shall not be regarded as unfair" (TULRA, Sched. 1, para. 8 (2)). The only limitation on the employer's traditional right to dismiss strikers (unless based on the contract of employment) was where the employee could show that he was being discriminated against by reason of his trade union membership or activities ("an inadmissible reason").

Despite the conventional view that strike activity is illegitimate and dangerous, if not actually treason—a view frequently reflected in the common law's treatment of such activity—it has increasingly dawned on the public consciousness that such a view could be construed as representing only a bourgeois perspective prejudiced towards middle-class interests. The view has been challenged by the assertion that strike activity could also be regarded as a form of workers' self-defence and a legitimate form of promotion of working-class interests—not just Luddism and greed. The result of this challenge to the conventional wisdom may be seen in these provisions.

No longer is strike activity to be regarded without more as justifying dismissal. While, unfortunately, the law persists in denying the striker protection unless he can show some form of discrimination between himself and others (subs. (2) (*a*) and (*b*), equivalent to old para. 8 (2) (*b*) and (*c*)), once he has shown this, it is up to the employer to prove that his dismissal was fair, *i.e.* it is no longer assumed that dismissal for strike activity is fair unless it was motivated by anti-union bias. While the latter would obviously render the dismissal unfair under the new provisions as well, the law now envisages general justification for strike activity which precludes the employer from automatically dismissing the striking employee. So, *e.g.* if the employer attempts to show misconduct in striking as a "fair" reason, the tribunal will have to decide if in the circumstances the action of the employer was legitimate, whether it was reasonable in the circumstances for the employer to dismiss the striker and if he did so in a reasonable manner. The tribunal is no longer to be governed simply by the traditional legal perspective on strike activity. Other considerations and interests in defence of such activity must now be taken into account. It will be up to the complainant and those representing him to ensure that these are put forward adequately.

Further changes. The next step may be to erode the blanket immunity given to employers who dismiss all their employees for taking part in industrial action. Now that it is recognised that selective dismissal may be unfair, it is possible to consider that wholesale dismissal may be just as unfair.

Judges are fond of declaring how necessary the power fairly to dismiss is: *e.g.* Phillips J. in *Thompson* v. *Eaton Ltd.* [1976] I.R.L.R. 308 (E.A.T.)—" otherwise, an employer must always submit to the demands of strikers, go out of business or pay compensation for unfair dismissal." This position was considered by Phillips J. to be a kind of legal neutrality (*Gallagher* v. *Wragg* [1977] I.C.R. 174 (E.A.T.)).

But one can conceive of cases where it seems at the least inconsistent with existing provisions of the law to allow the employer to dismiss strikers fairly. Thus, *e.g.* a Bill introduced in the last parliamentary session (Second Reading on January 21, 1978) by Mr. I. Mikardo, M.P., would allow employees to bring an unfair dismissal claim if they have been dismissed while striking in support of an ACAS recommendation for recognition which had not been complied with by the employer.

Subs. (1)

When is an employee taking part in a strike or other industrial action? Employers who wish to defend themselves by using this provision must, therefore,

satisfy the tribunal that there was a strike, lock-out or other industrial action.
"Lock-out," " strike " and " other industrial action " are not defined. *Cf.* the
definitions in Sched. 13, para. 24. And in *Winnett* v. *Seamarks Brothers Ltd.* [1978]
I.R.L.R. 387 (E.A.T.), Slynn J. thought that employees who are not yet due to
begin work but who decide they will not work when the time comes to begin were
" taking part in strike action or other industrial action." (Is this a legacy of
Chappell v. *Times Newspapers Ltd.* [1975] I.C.R. 145 (C.A.)?)

More interesting is the problem raised by that case where the employee concerned
was a shop steward who at the time of being sacked was negotiating hard on behalf
of his members—trade union activities at an appropriate time. Slynn J. thought:
" There may be difficulty in these cases in deciding whether the dismissal was in
truth a taking part in the activities of an independent trade union, or whether it was
in truth because the employee was taking part in strike action or other industrial
action." Clearly lawful activity under statute (ss. 27–28) or under contract (*e.g.* a
refusal to work overtime which is not obligatory) should not be termed industrial
action.

Again, it should be noted that where strikers have informed the employer that
the strike is over, the employer who *then* dismisses them cannot invoke this section,
as they are no longer " taking part in a strike " (*Heath* v. *Longman* (*Meat Salesmen*)
Ltd. [1973] I.R.L.R. 214 (N.I.R.C.)).

Strike, or employer's coercive action/fundamental breach? In *Thompson* v. *Eaton
Ltd.* [1976] I.R.L.R. 308 (E.A.T.), the argument was put forward by counsel that
there was a difference between resisting coercion by the employers, and the
employees initiating coercion. The former, it was argued, would not be industrial
action. Phillips J. rejected this test of fault, for, he said, " it would be impossible
to apply in practice. It is very rare for strikes, or other industrial action, to be
wholly the fault of one side or the other." His conclusion did not quite flow from
this premise, however, since by rejecting the argument he allowed the employer to
take the benefit of the section even where he was at fault.

The most Phillips J. would do was to say of the " case where a strike or other
industrial action has been provoked, or even engineered, by the employer in some
gross manner. It seems to us very probable that in such circumstances the provisions
(of this section) would not apply." He referred also to gross misconduct of the
employer which amounted to a repudiation—so that a subsequent strike would only
occur *after* dismissal, *e.g.* in *Wilkins* v. *Cantrell & Cochrane* (*GB*) *Ltd.* [1978]
I.R.L.R. 483 (E.A.T.), Kilner Brown J. referred to the industrial tribunal's statement
that if an employer was guilty of persistent and deliberate overloading of the
employee's vehicles " they would have no hesitation whatsoever in saying that there
had been a fundamental breach of the contract. . . . "

Dismissal. But only fundamental breach of contract by the employer would
entitle the employees to regard themselves as dismissed *prior* to having taken part
in industrial action (*Western Excavating* (*E.C.C.*) *Ltd.* v. *Sharp* [1978] I.R.L.R. 27
(C.A.)). But Kilner Brown J. went on to say, citing *Simmons* v. *Hoover Ltd.* [1976]
I.R.L.R. 266 (E.A.T.), that normally it is the strikers whose act is a fundamental
breach (albeit it may be precipitated by the employer's apparently lesser breach),
and this may lead to termination by the employer: " Where the men go on strike,
then the responsibility passes back to the employer. He then has to decide whether
the strike was justified; he then has to give due warning to the strikers, and he then
has in the last resort, as in this case, to exercise his judgment in deciding whether or
not to put an end to the contract by issuing notices of dismissal." In *Simmons* v.
Hoover Ltd., the E.A.T. decisively rejected the argument that the contract of
employment was only suspended during strike action, as advocated by Lord Denning in
Morgan v. *Fry* [1968] 2 Q.B. 710.

Subs. (2)
When need the re-engagement take place? It is clear that where the relevant
employee who was re-engaged took part in the industrial action (see definition of
" relevant employee " in subs. (4) (*b*)), he may be re-engaged at any time—even
before other employees were dismissed. These other employees can still claim under
this subsection (*Frank Jones* (*Tipton*) *Ltd.* v. *Stock* [1978] I.R.L.R. 87 (H.L.)).
Again, there is no limit stated as to how long *after* the strike the employer who
re-engages a striker can be faced with other strikers claiming unfair dismissal. In
Sealey v. *Avon Aluminium Co. Ltd.* [1978] I.R.L.R. 285, an industrial tribunal
upheld claims by strikers sacked on April 5, 1977, when one of their number was

re-engaged in late August or early September of that year. See the wide definition of re-engagement in subs. (4) (c). And s. 67 (3) allows for complaint to be made three months or more after any relevant employee is offered re-engagement.

Subs. (3)
   Fair reasons for non-re-engagement. The E.A.T. has rejected the contention that some different standard applies in cases of non-re-engagement from that applicable in cases of dismissal. So where a striker's pre-strike conduct would not have justified dismissal—it could not be invoked on its own to justify non-re-engagement. While going on strike is not a sufficient reason, the E.A.T. thought that if there were not enough jobs to go around, that might be a telling reason. Another " valid matter to be considered is the loyalty of those who serve during the strike, but . . . by the same token to give carte blanche to the loyalty of those who did work is likely to cause indignation among those who out of a corresponding loyalty to their fellow workmen did not stay loyal to the management." All the circumstances needed to be looked at (*Laffin & Callaghan* v. *Fashion Industries (Hartlepool) Ltd.* [1978] I.R.L.R. 448 (E.A.T.)).
   The problem of discovering a " fair " reason for non-re-engagement where the other strikers did *not* apply for re-engagement, but only claimed for unfair dismissal, gave great concern to the industrial tribunal in *Sealey* (cited above). It was forced to the conclusion that a " failure to apply for re-engagement " was neither a fair reason within s. 57 (2) nor some other substantial reason within s. 57 (1). Consequently, as the employer could not show a fair reason—the claim was upheld.

Subs. (4)
   For definition of " effective date of termination," see s. 153 (1), which refers to s. 55 (4) and (5).

Pressure on employer to dismiss unfairly

63. In determining, for the purposes of this Part any question as to the reason, or principal reason, for which an employee was dismissed or any question whether the reason or principal reason for which an employee was dismissed was a reason fulfilling the requirements of section 57 (1) (b) or whether the employer acted reasonably in treating it as a sufficient reason for dismissing him,—
   (a) no account shall be taken of any pressure which, by calling, organising, procuring or financing a strike or other industrial action, or threatening to do so, was exercised on the employer to dismiss the employee, and
   (b) any such question shall be determined as if no such pressure had been exercised.

DERIVATION
1974, para. 15.

GENERAL NOTE
   Where employees put pressure on the employer to dismiss a worker because they objected to his attempts to organise for the TGWU, the consequent dismissal of the employee was held unfair (*Trend* v. *Chiltern Hunt Ltd.* [1977] I.R.L.R. 66 (E.A.T.)). If the employer cannot put forward any reason other than the pressure, he will have failed to satisfy the requirements of s. 57, and the claim will succeed (*Hazells Offset Ltd.* v. *Luckett* [1977] I.R.L.R. 430 (E.A.T.)).

Exclusion of section 54

Qualifying period and upper age limit

64.—(1) Subject to subsection (3), section 54 does not apply to the dismissal of an employee from any employment if the employee—
   (a) was not continuously employed for a period of not less than twenty-six weeks ending with the effective date of termination, or

(*b*) on or before the effective date of termination attained the age
which, in the undertaking in which he was employed, was the
normal retiring age for an employee holding the position which
he held, or, if a man, attained the age of sixty-five, or, if a
woman, attained the age of sixty.

(2) If an employee is dismissed by reason of any such requirement or
recommendation as is referred to in section 19 (1), subsection (1) (*a*)
shall have effect in relation to that dismissal as if for the words " twenty-
six weeks " there were substituted the words " four weeks ".

(3) Subsection (1) shall not apply to the dismissal of an employee if
it is shown that the reason (or, if more than one, the principal reason)
for the dismissal was an inadmissible reason.

DERIVATION
1974, para. 10; 1975, s. 29 (4); 1974, para. 11 (1); 1975, Sched. 16, Pt. III,
para. 15.

GENERAL NOTE
Subs. (1)
The computation of the requisite period of employment is according to Sched. 13.
Failure to give proper notice. Where the employer has failed to give the
minimum period of notice required by s. 49, s. 55 (5) operates to extend the
effective date of termination to the date on which that notice would have expired
had that notice been given. Since after four weeks every employee is entitled
under s. 49 to at least one week's notice, the result is that after 25 weeks'
employment, employees have the right to claim unfair dismissal.

An attempt to extend the provision to cases where the employer has failed to
give his contractual period of notice failed in *Fox Maintenance Ltd.* v. *Jackson*
[1977] I.R.L.R. 306 (E.A.T.). There an employee summarily dismissed would have
qualified had he received his proper contractual notice. Overruling the industrial
tribunal, Phillips J. decided that the employer should not be deprived of his right
to dismiss unfairly somebody employed less than 26 weeks if " only the accident " of
summary dismissal had occurred.

Disciplinary and status quo procedures. The " effective date of termination "
up to which a period of employment is computed is defined in s. 153 (1) as having
the meaning given by s. 55 (4) and (5). Normally, however, the effective date will
be at the expiry of the period of notice or whenever summary dismissal occurs.
Problems arise where there exist disciplinary or status quo procedures which provide
for employment to be continued until certain procedures are exhausted. In the Note
to s. 1 (3)—*Notice of termination*—reference was made to such procedures, *e.g.*
in the engineering industry.

It appears, however, that they will need to be explicit, as the judges will not
easily allow interference with the employer's common law right of summary
dismissal for, *e.g.* misconduct. Thus, in *Sainsbury Ltd.* v. *Savage* [1978] I.R.L.R.
479 (E.A.T.), Slynn J. doubted that simply a provision for appeal after dismissal
would postpone the effective date of termination. Even a procedure that provided that
pending the decision of an appeal " the employee will be suspended without pay,
but, if reinstated, will receive full back-pay for the period of suspension " was
inadequate to prevent a dismissal taking effect immediately. Employees will need
to review the wording of their existing procedures to ensure that this strict approach
does not operate to their disadvantage.

Normal retiring age. In *Nothman* v. *London Borough of Barnet* [1977] I.R.L.R.
489 (C.A.), Lawton L.J. suggested, and Lord Denning accepted, the following
meaning of " normal retiring age ": " it is the age in any particular profession at
which a person must or should retire." It is not clear whether there is a normal
retiring age for every profession, or whether it changes depending on the terms
of employment of the particular worker. But the interpretation advanced by the
E.A.T. in a number of cases (*e.g. Post Office* v. *Waddell* [1977] I.R.L.R. 344),
that the normal retiring age was when employees *usually* retired, was rejected. A
statistical approach, therefore, will not be determining. Still, it can be argued that
there is no normal retiring age in a particular case—though evidence will be needed
for this. At any rate, the normal retiring age is *not* the same as pensionable age

(*Ord* v. *Maidstone & District Hospital Management Committee* [1974] I.R.L.R. 80 (N.I.R.C.)).

Only one qualifying age limit. In *Nothman,* both the industrial tribunal and the E.A.T. had held that the law erected a double barrier—the normal retiring age *and* 60 for women, 65 for men. Kilner Brown J. castigated Parliament for enacting discriminatory legislation which to his regret he had to enforce as it was perfectly clear. But fortunately, all three judges of the Court of Appeal said it was obvious to them that the law could be interpreted to make the standard *either* 60 years of age (for women) *or* the normal retiring age, if higher. The House of Lords has confirmed the view of the Court of Appeal.

Subs. (3)

The 26-week qualification does not affect proceedings under the Sex Discrimination Act 1975 nor the Race Relations Act 1976, where an employee has been dismissed on grounds of sex or race discrimination.

Exclusion in respect of dismissal procedures agreement

65.—(1) An application may be made jointly to the Secretary of State by all the parties to a dismissal procedures agreement to make an order designating that agreement for the purposes of this section.

(2) On any such application the Secretary of State may make such an order if he is satisfied—

(*a*) that every trade union which is a party to the dismissal procedures agreement is an independent trade union;

(*b*) that the agreement provides for procedures to be followed in cases where an employee claims that he has been, or is in the course of being, unfairly dismissed;

(*c*) that those procedures are available without discrimination to all employees falling within any description to which the agreement applies;

(*d*) that the remedies provided by the agreement in respect of unfair dismissal are on the whole as beneficial as (but not necessarily identical with) those provided in respect of unfair dismissal by this Part;

(*e*) that the procedures provided by the agreement include a right to arbitration or adjudication by an independent referee, or by a tribunal or other independent body, in cases where (by reason of an equality of votes or for any other reason) a decision cannot otherwise be reached; and

(*f*) that the provisions of the agreement are such that it can be determined with reasonable certainty whether a particular employee is one to whom the agreement applies or not.

(3) Where a dismissal procedures agreement is designated by an order under this section which is for the time being in force, the provisions of that agreement relating to dismissal shall have effect in substitution for any rights under section 54; and accordingly that section shall not apply to the dismissal of an employee from any employment if it is employment to which, and he is an employee to whom, those provisions of the agreement apply.

(4) Subsection (3) shall not apply to the right not to be unfairly dismissed for any reason mentioned in subsection (1) or (2) of section 60.

DERIVATION

1974, para. 13; 1975, s. 34 (7).

GENERAL NOTE

There has as yet been no order in respect of a voluntary dismissals procedures agreement (for definition of " dismissal procedures agreement," see s. 153 (1)). For a detailed discussion of the requirements stipulated here, see S. D. Anderman, *The Law of Unfair Dismissal* (1978), App. III.

Revocation of exclusion order under s. 65

66.—(1) At any time when an order under section 65 is in force, any of the parties to the dismissal procedures agreement to which the order relates may apply to the Secretary of State for the order to be revoked.

(2) If on any such application the Secretary of State is satisfied either—

    (*a*) that it is the desire of all the parties to the dismissal procedures agreement that the order should be revoked, or

    (*b*) that the agreement has ceased to fulfil all the conditions specified in section 65 (2),

the Secretary of State shall revoke the order by a further order made under this section.

(3) Any order made under this section may contain such transitional provisions as appear to the Secretary of State to be appropriate in the circumstances, and, in particular, may direct—

    (*a*) that, notwithstanding section 65 (3), an employee shall not be excluded from his rights under section 54 where the effective date of termination falls within a transitional period which is specified in the order and is a period ending with the date on which the order under this section takes effect and shall have an extended time for presenting a complaint under section 67 in respect of a dismissal where the effective date of termination falls within that period, and

    (*b*) that in determining any complaint of unfair dismissal presented by an employee to whom the dismissal procedures agreement applies, where the effective date of termination falls within that transitional period, an industrial tribunal shall have regard to such considerations (in addition to those specified in this Part and paragraph 2 of Schedule 9) as may be specified in the order.

DERIVATION
1974, para. 14.

Remedies for unfair dismissal

Complaint to industrial tribunal

67.—(1) A complaint may be presented to an industrial tribunal against an employer by any person (in this Part referred to as the complainant) that he was unfairly dismissed by the employer.

(2) Subject to subsection (4), an industrial tribunal shall not consider a complaint under this section unless it is presented to the tribunal before the end of the period of three months beginning with the effective date of termination or within such further period as the tribunal considers reasonable in a case where it is satisfied that it was not reasonably practicable for the complaint to be presented before the end of the period of three months.

(3) Subsection (2) shall apply in relation to a complaint to which section 62 (3) applies as if for the reference to the effective date of termination there were substituted a reference to the first date on which any relevant employee was offered re-engagement (within the meaning of section 62 (4)).

(4) An industrial tribunal shall consider a complaint under this section if, where the dismissal is with notice, the complaint is presented after the notice is given notwithstanding that it is presented before the effective date of termination and in relation to such a complaint the provisions of this Act, so far as they relate to unfair dismissal, shall have effect—

(a) as if references to a complaint by a person that he was unfairly
   dismissed by his employer included references to a complaint by
   a person that his employer has given him notice in such circumstances that he will be unfairly dismissed when the notice expires;
(b) as if references to reinstatement included references to the withdrawal of the notice by the employer;
(c) as if references to the effective date of termination included
   references to the date which would be the effective date of
   termination on the expiry of the notice; and
(d) as if references to an employee ceasing to be employed included
   references to an employee having been given notice of dismissal.

DERIVATION
   1974, paras. 17 (1), 21 (4), (4A), 7 (4); 1975, Sched. 16, Pt. III, paras. 13, 16,
20, 21.

GENERAL NOTE
Subs. (1)
   In accordance with s. 140 (1), no agreement to accept, *e.g.* a severance payment
"which is a final settlement leaving you with no outstanding claims" can preclude a
claim. The agreement is void (*Council of Engineering Institutions* v. *Maddison*
[1976] I.R.L.R. 389 (E.A.T.)).

Subs. (2)
   Effective date of termination. The definition in s. 153 (1), referring to s. 55 (4)
and (5), does *not* allow for the employee to calculate the three-month period from
the end of the statutory minimum notice, as is done with regard to other rights
listed in s. 55 (5). The three months begins with the termination of the contract,
even when dismissal is summary.
   Again, the employee may present a claim during his period of notice, but before
he is terminated (subs. (4)), but, *e.g.* if notified that his contract will not be
renewed when it expires, he cannot claim until the contract has expired (*Throsby*
v. *Imperial College of Science and Technology* [1977] I.R.L.R. 337 (E.A.T.)).
   Problems again arise here concerning the effective date of termination when
there are disciplinary procedures or status quo provisions—see the Notes to s. 1 (3)
(*Notice of termination*) and s. 64 (1) (*Disciplinary and status quo procedures*). To
wait until voluntary procedures have been exhausted before presenting a claim to an
industrial tribunal will usually prove fatal *if* the contract of employment has
terminated and three months have elapsed (*Singh* v. *Post Office* [1973] I.C.R. 437
(N.I.R.C.)).
   Not reasonably practicable. This subsection has given rise to so many decisions,
and is of such significance given the relative lack of general knowledge of legal
rights—even over dismissal—in employment, that it deserves detailed treatment.
   The cases in which this subsection has been analysed give a fascinating insight
into how judges' moral preconceptions shape the meaning of words in a statute.
The original provision under Industrial Tribunals Regulations provided for a claim
to be allowed if the tribunal was "satisfied that in the circumstances it was not
practicable" for the claim to be presented within the time limit (then 28 days).
Differences between the Scottish (strict) and English (liberal) E.A.T.s arose, and the
Court of Appeal finally decided the issue in favour of the English approach in
Dedman v. *British Building and Engineering Appliances Ltd.* [1974] 1 All E.R. 520.
By a majority (Lord Denning and Scarman L.J.), the C.A. gave to the word
"practicable" what Phillips J. pointed out in *Wall's Meat Co. Ltd.* v. *Khan* [1978]
I.R.L.R. 74 (E.A.T.) was "a meaning which it would not ordinarily have." Lord
Denning said the test to be applied was whether the employee or his advisers were
at fault: "If he was not at fault, nor his advisers—so that he had just cause or
excuse for not presenting his complaint within the [period]—then it was not
practicable for him to present it within that time." So from a question of
practicability of complaint, the courts arrived at a test of fault. (Stamp L.J. in
the minority took the strict Scottish view—ignorance is no excuse for lateness; fault
is irrelevant.)
   When the wording was changed from "practicable" to "reasonably practicable"
in the Trade Union and Labour Relations Act 1974, Sched. 1, para. 21 (4)—and as

is now the case in this subsection—the judges simply asserted that the test remained the same regardless of the change in statutory language (see, *e.g.* Lord McDonald in *House of Clydesdale Ltd.* v. *Fry* [1976] I.R.L.R. 391 (E.A.T.); Cumming-Bruce J. in *Times Newspapers Ltd.* v. *O'Regan* [1977] I.R.L.R. 101 (E.A.T.); Kilner Brown J. in *Avon County Council* v. *Haywood Hicks* [1978] I.R.L.R. 118 (E.A.T.)).

Even more surprisingly, perhaps, Phillips J., in acknowledging the change in language, insisted on applying *Dedman,* but stressed that there was now no room for extra judicial *benevolence* (*Wall's Meat Co. Ltd.* v. *Khan* [1978] I.R.L.R. 74 (E.A.T.)). Since the issue was not one of practicability, but of fault, judges felt free to consider late claims according to their own moral conceptions of blame-worthiness. But in upholding the E.A.T.'s decision in the *Wall's Meat Co. Ltd.* case, both Shaw and Brandon L.JJ. in the Court of Appeal agreed that where the reason for lateness was some physical impediment (injury or illness) or absence abroad or a postal strike—this might justify allowing a claim to proceed ([1978] I.R.L.R. 499).

Criminal charges. This comes out particularly well in cases where employees are accused of dishonesty and actually prosecuted. Workers would often wait until charges are dismissed before claiming unfair dismissal—and by that time the three months' period will have elapsed. In the Court of Appeal decision in *Porter* v. *Bandridge Ltd.* [1978] I.R.L.R. 271, the majority (Stephenson and Waller L.JJ.) took the following approach: "This imposes a duty upon the applicant to show precisely why it was that he did not present his complaint. He has to satisfy the tribunal that he did not know of his rights during the whole of this period and that there was no reason why he should make inquiries or should know of his rights during that period." *Dedman* lives. Only Ormrod L.J., dissenting, urged that it was after all the statutory language, not that of the judges in *Dedman* that governed; that the change to "reasonably practicable" meant that the wording should be examined "on broader lines than the [Court of Appeal in *Dedman*] was envisaging."

Ignorance: is it an excuse? The logic of practicability is straightforward: if a worker is ignorant (a) of his rights to claim unfair dismissal, or (b) of the three-month time limit, it is not practicable for him to present a complaint within the time limit. So ignorance (*pace* Stamp L.J. in *Dedman* and the Scottish E.A.T.) is a legal excuse.

But this contradicts an established principle of English law—an ideological support (for it benefits those who are educated and informed or who have access to advice and information) and bureaucratic need (for without it much law could not be enforced)—namely, that ignorance of the law is no excuse. See, *e.g.* Kilner Brown J. in *Avon County Council* v. *Haywood Hicks* [1978] I.R.L.R. 118 (E.A.T.): "It offends our notion of common sense that an intelligent, well-educated man should be able to divorce himself from all common knowledge of the rights of employees to claim compensation and to isolate himself from all the obligations upon an employee whose contract of employment has come to an end who ought to consider his position and take all necessary action for his own benefit." The moralistic attitudes of middle-class judges transforms the legal excuse of practicability into a question of "obligations" on the employee in light of "common knowledge." Even if the worker can show that he did not know—that he was confused, had problems of unemployment, support for his family, etc.—if, by middle-class standards, he ought to have known and acted, the judges will be very reluctant to allow him the benefit of the statutory provisions. This was confirmed by the majority of the Court of Appeal in *Porter* v. *Bandridge Ltd.*

In addition, however, there is now the additional authority of the Court of Appeal in *Wall's Meat Co. Ltd.* v. *Khan* [1978] I.R.L.R. 499. Lord Denning said, *inter alia,* that although it would be the reaction of the ordinary man charged with theft to want to see what happened before making a claim—this was not an acceptable reason for saying it was not reasonably practicable. But on the wider question of ignorance of the law, the court's views were divided. Lord Denning and Brandon L.J. maintained the position that ignorance could be regarded as grounds for holding the delay to fall within the exception of "not reasonably practicable"—but *not* if the ignorance or mistaken belief arose from the fault of the employee or his advisers. Shaw L.J., to the contrary, supporting Ormrod L.J. in *Porter* v. *Bandridge Ltd.,* would not allow that fault or lack of it was relevant to determining practicability: "Good sense must reject the proposition that it is practicable to put forward a claim when the potential claimant does not know it exists; and logically it can make no difference if his ignorance is excusable or if it results from his own ineptitude or inertia."

So the position as to whether ignorance will excuse a late application seems to be that most judges of the Court of Appeal regard it as depending on the fault of the employee—but some do not regard fault as relevant. In the former case, where fault is relevant, it is a question of fact for the industrial tribunal to decide in each case as to whether the employee has been at fault in being ignorant. As to the case where the employee knew of his rights, but not of the time limit, Shaw L.J. in the *Wall's Meat Co. Ltd.* case thought this too was irrelevant—once he knew of his rights, ignorance of the time limit was no excuse. Brandon L.J. thought, however, that it was possible even then for the employee to show he was not at fault in not knowing of the time limit.

Since it will frequently come down to a question of fact for the industrial tribunal to decide as to the reasonableness of the employee's ignorance, a few generalisations about industrial tribunals' practice may be made (with the warning that they are by no means rules). It seems that where the employee has consulted solicitors or other professional advisers, he will not be able to excuse himself because he was ignorant or not informed. He will have to claim against his advisers for the damages resulting. But if he is advised wrongly by others—Citizens Advice Bureaux, Department of Employment Offices, Employment Exchange officials, etc.— he will be excused. It seems likely that trade union officials (full-time officers) will be deemed professional advisers. If lay officials—shop stewards and the like—are involved, there is less likelihood of the employee being barred.

But the above should be considered against the background of Lord Denning's comments in *Wall's Meat Co. Ltd.*, that industrial tribunals should be fairly strict in enforcing the time limit. On the other hand, Ormrod L.J.'s comment in *Porter* should be remembered: " There is no obvious reason why it should be strictly construed when the time limit is short in comparison with all other limitation periods, and the persons affected are ordinary working men and women " (para. 25).

Subs. (4)

Employees need to weigh up the advantages and disadvantages of putting the employer on notice that he faces an industrial tribunal hearing and possibly heavy damages and/or reinstatement by lodging a claim during the notice period. It may induce the employer to change his mind. On the other hand, it may undermine a trade union official's attempt at negotiating a settlement unless he gives tactical approval of the submission of a claim.

Remedies for unfair dismissal

68.—(1) Where on a complaint under section 67 an industrial tribunal finds that the grounds of the complaint are well-founded, it shall explain to the complainant what orders for reinstatement or re-engagement may be made under section 69 and in what circumstances they may be made, and shall ask him whether he wishes the tribunal to make such an order, and if he does express such a wish the tribunal may make an order under section 69.

(2) If on a complaint under section 67 the tribunal finds that the grounds of the complaint are well-founded and no order is made under section 69, the tribunal shall make an award of compensation for unfair dismissal, calculated in accordance with sections 72 to 74, to be paid by the employer to the employee.

DERIVATION

1975, s. 71 (1) ; s. 72 (5).

GENERAL NOTE

Remedies. The Employment Protection Act 1975 replaced the previous law on remedies available to employees who had been unfairly dismissed (TULRA, Sched. 1, para. 17 (2) and (3)). The remedies available under the old law, particularly those of reinstatement and re-engagement, were found to be hopelessly inadequate. This was not a result of any intrinsic defects, but solely because the industrial tribunals simply did not apply them. Thus, in 1974, 13·4 per cent. of all complainants were completely successful in their claims for unfair dismissal, yet in only 0·6 per cent. of those cases did the tribunals recommend reinstatement or re-engagement, *i.e.* six out of every 1,000 succeeded in being reinstated or re-engaged, whereas nearly 140 in every 1,000 succeeded in an unfair dismissal case. In 1974, four times as many reinstatements (12 *v.* 3) and re-engagements (232 *v.* 56) resulted from conciliation efforts as from the tribunals. (These figures are found in the Report of Standing Committee F on the Employment Protection Bill, 21st Sitting, July 3, 1975, at cols. 1098–1100.) These abysmal figures led to the extraordinary new provisions now found here. The old remedies of reinstatement and re-engagement are not fundamentally changed—the obligations on the employer remain substantially similar. But the *tribunals* are put under what is hoped will be an inescapable obligation to apply these remedies.

The figures given in the General Note to Pt. V above do not bear out any claim that much of a change has occurred. Without going into detail, the law changed on June 1, 1976, when the new provisions on remedies came into effect. The figures, if anything, show a change for the worse:

Outcome of cases: conciliated and heard by tribunals

Year		Cases conciliated			Tribunal cases		
		No.	%	% of all cases	No.	%	% of all cases
1975	Reinstatement	234		1·0	62		0·3
	Re-engagement	262		1·2	115		0·5
	Total:	496		2·2	177		0·8
1976	Reinstatement	382	1·7	1·1	102	0·8	0·3
	Re-engagement	203	0·9	0·6	78	0·6	0·2
	Total:	585	2·6	1·7	180	1·4	0·5
1977	Reinstatement	427		1·3	178		0·5
	Re-engagement	290		0·9	109		0·3
	Total:	717		2·2	287		0·8

Source: *Department of Employment Gazette*, April 1976, October 1977, May 1978.

The significance of the industrial tribunal making an order for reinstatement or re-engagement is twofold. It is the only chance the employee unfairly dismissed has of getting his job back. And in times, as at present, of high unemployment, this need hardly be over-emphasised. Secondly, if the employer fails to comply with an order to reinstate or re-engage the employee unfairly dismissed, then the compensation payable by the employer is increased over and above what would normally be awarded (s. 71).

Subs. (1)

The old law (TULRA, Sched. 1, para. 17 (2), and its predecessor, the Industrial Relations Act 1971, s. 106 (4) (*b*)) required the industrial tribunal to recommend reinstatement or re-engagement where it considered it would be " practicable and in accordance with equity." Despite this mandatory requirement, the remedy was very rarely applied. Consequently, the new procedure forcibly directs the tribunal's attention to this requirement by instructing it to publicly recite the new law, for the benefit of the complainant as well. (In fact, new questions are in the unfair dismissal claim form (Question 15 on IT Form 1) so that the complainant can state his position regarding reinstatement or re-engagement from the outset, to help ACAS in conciliation proceedings.)

Following this public recitation, the employee complainant has the opportunity of again affirming his wish to be reinstated or re-engaged or otherwise. The nature of the choice being offered him will be made much more clear and precise owing to the greater definition of these remedies as expounded by the tribunal (s. 69 (2) (3) (4) and s. 70 (2)). If he expresses a wish to be reinstated or re-engaged, the tribunal *still has discretion* to refuse to grant the remedy, but its discretion is bounded not merely by the loosely defined criteria of practicability and equity, as under the old law. Rather, the tribunal must take into account the considerations described in ss. 69 (5) (6) and 70 (1).

The entire procedure has been reshaped to provide guidance not so much for the complainant as for the tribunal. It is forcibly marched along the path of reinstatement or re-engagement as the law and the complainant directs. It is obviously the intention that tribunals will be somewhat embarrassed in failing to make an order after all this and instead resorting to an award of compensation. This, it is said almost as an aside in subs. (2), is only to be made where no order for reinstatement or re-engagement is granted.

Despite all this extraordinary new procedure, the results as indicated in the statistics above do not appear to have achieved the aim of returning many unfairly dismissed employees to their jobs.

Subs. (2)

The old law on compensation for unfair dismissal was either repealed or replaced by the Employment Protection Act 1975 (TULRA, Sched. 1, para. 19, repealed by Sched. 18 and replaced by ss. 73–76, and TULRA, Sched. 1, para. 20, replaced by new para. 20 in Sched. 16, Pt. III, para. 17). The law is now in ss. 72–76 of this Act.

The inadequacy of the old law was finally recognised. The logical consequence of the former principle of compensation (loss of the complainant attributable to the employer's fault, subject to the common law duty to mitigate) was an abysmally low level of recompense to those who had lost their jobs through the unfair and illegal action of their employer. Employees who went through the lengthy procedure usually lost (one estimate was that almost two in every three employees (62 per cent.) whose cases reach tribunals had them dismissed). Those who, after conciliation, settled with the employer for some monetary compensation received a median average of £98, while those who saw it through successfully walked away with awards of a median average of £202. (These figures are taken from B. Weekes *et al.*, *Industrial Relations and the Limits of Law* (1975), p. 17.) At the Committee Stage of the Employment Protection Bill 1975 it was confirmed that during 1974 over 60 per cent. of compensation awards for unfair dismissal was for amounts less than £300 (Standing Committee F on the Employment Protection Bill, 22nd Sitting, July 8, 1975, col. 1137). An employer could usually, therefore, get away with unfairly sacking an employee at the cost of perhaps twice or three times the wages he would have paid in lieu of notice anyway, and frequently less. Coupled with practically non-existent reinstatement and re-engagement, to talk of an employee's " legal " protection against unfair dismissal was often a bad joke. Where they could, workers relied on their own means of self-defence to protect their jobs.

The 1975 Act's solution to the failure of the old law was mainly to promote the remedies of reinstatement and re-engagement. In addition, however, the principle of compensation was fundamentally altered from one based on loss alone to one which allows for compensation over and above loss. While this change in principle was welcome, it was transparently obvious that it heralded only a minimum change in practice. For the basis of compensation over and above that of loss is the same as that for a redundancy payment—see Sched. 4, paras. 2–4, and *cf.* s. 73 (3) to (6). The result is that, in effect, the law provides for an employee unfairly dismissed to receive, additionally to his loss, the equivalent of a redundancy payment (here called the basic award). If the rationale for the basis of compensation for redundancy is obscure, the rationale for making the basis for compensation for unfair dismissal the same must be Delphic.

One may look askance at the seemingly arbitrary basis of compensation under the law. One must protest the legislation's crude proffering of the equivalent of a redundancy payment when it is common knowledge that under the law of compensation as previously interpreted the tribunals already awarded 50 per cent. of the value of the employee's accrued redundancy protection (see *Norton Tool Co. Ltd.* v. *Tewson* [1972] I.C.R. 501 (N.I.R.C.)). The legislation only offers in effect the other 50 per cent. of this accrued protection since the compensatory award is no longer to include 50 per cent. of accrued redundancy rights (s. 74 (3)). In sum, the old inadequate basis of compensation already included as only *one* of its elements 50 per cent. of the additional new element introduced by the new law. It need hardly be said that the awards under the new law could not be expected to be more than minimally above those of the old law.

The figures given in the General Note to Part V bear this out. Detailed figures on settlements in conciliation and tribunal awards may be obtained from charts in the *Department of Employment Gazette* of April 1976, October 1977 and May 1978. In percentage terms, increases appear to have been substantial. But in absolute terms, the worker ends up with the equivalent of only several weeks' wages to tide him over till he can find his next job (there has been no maximum monetary award since the change in the basis of unfair dismissal compensation on June 1, 1976: there have been 52 cases up to the end of 1977 since the inception of the right to claim unfair dismissal in which the applicant received a monetary award of over £5,000).

The following figures for the median awards given by industrial tribunals can be found in the *Department of Employment Gazette* of December 1977:

First quarter 1975	£200
Second quarter 1975	171
First quarter 1976	195
Second quarter 1976	210
First quarter 1977	350
Second quarter 1977	355

The figures for 1977 comprise awards consisting of both a basic and compensatory element. The median award in the first quarter of 1978 was £408.

In sum: the hopes for legal protection of workers who cannot defend themselves must remain with the legal remedy of reinstatement or re-engagement. Employers will have little to fear from that of compensation.

Order for reinstatement or re-engagement

69.—(1) An order under this section may be an order for reinstatement (in accordance with subsections (2) and (3)) or an order for re-engagement (in accordance with subsection (4)), as the industrial tribunal may decide, and in the latter case may be on such terms as the tribunal may decide.

(2) An order for reinstatement is an order that the employer shall treat the complainant in all respects as if he had not been dismissed, and on making such an order the tribunal shall specify—

(*a*) any amount payable by the employer in respect of any benefit which the complainant might reasonably be expected to have had but for the dismissal, including arrears of pay, for the period between the date of termination of employment and the date of reinstatement;

(*b*) any rights and privileges, including seniority and pension rights, which must be restored to the employee; and

(*c*) the date by which the order must be complied with.

(3) Without prejudice to the generality of subsection (2), if the complainant would have benefited from an improvement in his terms and conditions of employment had he not been dismissed, an order for reinstatement shall require him to be treated as if he had benefited from that improvement from the date on which he would have done so but for being dismissed.

(4) An order for re-engagement is an order that the complainant be engaged by the employer, or by a successor of the employer or by an associated employer, in employment comparable to that from which he was dismissed or other suitable employment, and on making such an order the tribunal shall specify the terms on which re-engagement is to take place including—

(*a*) the identity of the employer;

(*b*) the nature of the employment;

(*c*) the remuneration for the employment;

(*d*) any amount payable by the employer in respect of any benefit which the complainant might reasonably be expected to have had but for the dismissal, including arrears of pay, for the period between the date of termination of employment and the date of re-engagement;

(*e*) any rights and privileges, including seniority and pension rights, which must be restored to the employee; and

(*f*) the date by which the order must be complied with.

(5) In exercising its discretion under this section the tribunal shall first consider whether to make an order for reinstatement and in so doing shall take into account the following considerations, that is to say—

(*a*) whether the complainant wishes to be reinstated;

(*b*) whether it is practicable for the employer to comply with an order for reinstatement;

(*c*) where the complainant caused or contributed to some extent to the dismissal, whether it would be just to order his reinstatement.

(6) If the tribunal decides not to make an order for reinstatement it shall then consider whether to make an order for re-engagement and if so on what terms; and in so doing the tribunal shall take into account the following considerations, that is to say—

(*a*) any wish expressed by the complainant as to the nature of the order to be made;

(*b*) whether it is practicable for the employer or, as the case may be, a successor or associated employer to comply with an order for re-engagement;

(*c*) where the complainant caused or contributed to some extent to the dismissal, whether it would be just to order his re-engagement and if so on what terms;

and except in a case where the tribunal takes into account contributory fault under paragraph (*c*) it shall, if it orders re-engagement, do so on terms which are, so far as is reasonably practicable, as favourable as an order for reinstatement.

DERIVATION

1975, s. 71 (2) to (7).

GENERAL NOTE

Subss. (2) and (3)

Reinstatement—the primary remedy. The terms reinstatement and re-engagement were defined neither in TULRA where both appeared nor in the Industrial Relations Act 1971, where only the latter appeared. The tribunal's recommendation for reinstatement or re-engagement under those Acts was to be one on " reasonable " terms. Their legislative definition in this section coincides to some extent with previously conceived meanings. Reinstatement is clearly the primary remedy laid down by the law for unfair dismissal. Compensation is intended to be avoided unless numerous considerations point irrevocably in that direction—see subs. (5). In deciding whether to make an order under this section, the tribunal must first consider reinstatement (subs. (5)) and only if it does not do so does it consider re-engagement (subs. (6)).

Restitution. The definition of reinstatement includes not only the right of the employee to return to his old job with the same terms and conditions of employment and all rights and privileges intact as if the employee had been continuously employed up to the date of the order being complied with (*cf.* the right of a woman employee to return after pregnancy—s. 45 (1) and (2)), but more. Subs. (3) provides that where his old terms and conditions would have been improved had he not been dismissed, his terms of reinstatement shall be at the level of the improvement, not those of his old job. Moreover, any such improvement is to be paid retrospectively from the date of its coming into effect, for subs. (2) (*a*) provides for what is effectively reimbursement to the employee of all benefits lost during the interim period (monetary benefits, of course, and the cash equivalent of other benefits as quantified by the tribunal), subject to s. 70 (2).

The original Employment Protection Bill 1975 only provided for reimbursement of arrears of pay (including bonuses) (cl. 65 (3) (*a*)). This was considerably widened to include all benefits, monetary over and above ordinary pay, and otherwise. Indeed, there is nothing to indicate that the benefits concerned need be connected with the employment relationship, though it is most likely they will be. Still, if the employee can show that he lost a benefit as a direct consequence of the dismissal, the employer may be required to reimburse him.

In sum, the definition of reinstatement here is a far cry from simply permitting the employee to return to his old job. It is effectively to restore the employee to the position he would now be in but for the unfair dismissal by the employer— and that means that any interim benefits lost are made up and any interim improvements are retained. It does not seem that the tribunal, having decided to make an order of reinstatement after considering the factors in subs. (5) and s. 70 (1), is entitled to narrow down the remedy as defined here. Subs. (2) is in mandatory language ("shall") both as regards the terms of the employee's reinstatement in his old job and as regards his reimbursement for loss. So, *e.g.* the contributory fault of the employee may militate against his reinstatement to some degree (subs. (5) (c)), but once it is decided to reinstate him, this cannot be used to reduce his remedy. Only s. 70 (2) applies to that purpose, as regards the monetary award; the only way the tribunal can alter the old terms of employment is to improve them under subs. (3).

Consequences for the employer. Finally, when all is said and done, the fact remains that the employer has in effect emerged relatively unscathed from the entire process. He has unfairly dismissed the employee, but the only consequence will be that the employee may, after undergoing the lengthy procedure, be put in the same position as if he had not been so dismissed. The employee is not compensated for any more than what he has lost due to the dismissal, while the employer pays only losses suffered, reduced by the important factors in s. 70 (2).

This unfortunate consequence whereby the employer escaped any punishment for his unfair act and the employee was not recompensed for the infringement of his right not to be unfairly dismissed is all too familiar. For it was the case as regards the remedy of compensation awarded in 99 per cent. of the successful claims for unfair dismissal under the old law in TULRA. That situation was remedied by the 1975 Act—in addition to the compensatory award there is also to be a basic award. The deficiency remains, however, where the remedy is that of reinstatement or re-engagement. Presumably employees are to be grateful for the law having restored them to their jobs, without more.

Subs. (4)

Re-engagement. In the case of an order for re-engagement, the tribunal is given a degree of latitude in defining the terms of the order (subs. (1)). Nonetheless, although the job is different, everything else of significance in the employment relationship is to be treated as if the employee had been reinstated (*cf.* the parallel provisions of subs. (4) (*d*)–(*f*) and subs. (2) (*a*)–(*c*)). Comparability is the criterion, and while this is not the identical employment as would be the case with reinstatement, the employee is to be treated comparably. The latitude given the tribunal in specifying terms may be used to give effect, as regards re-engagement, to the provisions of subs. (3) as they affect reinstatement. That this is the case is conclusively shown by subs. (6), which requires the tribunal to specify terms of re-engagement not less favourable than would be the case in an order for reinstatement, so far as is reasonably practicable, except where the tribunal takes into account contributory fault of the complainant. In sum, subject to the last mentioned qualification, the remedy of re-engagement should be the equivalent of reinstatement. The comments made in the Notes to subss. (2) and (3) apply here as well.

Subs. (5)

Tribunal practice. Reinstatement is the primary remedy. Having upheld a complaint of unfair dismissal, the tribunal must first consider ordering it and in so doing must consider the factors stipulated here. They replaced the considerations of practicability and equity, applicable before the law changed on June 1, 1976. Up to then, having considered those factors, it emerged that the tribunals would automatically discard reinstatement or re-engagement as a remedy once the employer indicated that it was impracticable for him, *e.g.* because he had hired a permanent replacement. Very few tribunals questioned the employer's right to do so and most simply turned to the remedy of compensation. As explained above, the consequence was an abysmally low number of reinstatements and re-engagements, and the law now contained in these sections is the result of the attempt to reform this practice.

Matters to be considered—wish of the employee. The provisions of this subsection (paralleled closely by those of subs. (6) regarding re-engagement) are, therefore, of the utmost importance. Though not expressed to be in any order of priority, it would seem that factor (*a*) is of paramount importance. Having been unfairly dismissed, the wish of the wronged employee should prevail over the convenience of the unfair employer (factor (b)), unless mitigated by some contributory fault (factor (c)). The primary significance of factor (a) is reinforced by the fact that, unlike the old law, the tribunal may not order this remedy unless the employee so wishes (s. 68 (1)). It is his wish that makes this primary remedy possible, and given the background to and logic of the remedies proposed in these sections, this wish should be respected.

Practicability. Factor (b) appears to be the equivalent of the criterion of practicability contained in the old law. Given that it was the previous interpretation of this criterion that led to the wholesale revamping of the law, it would be folly to accede to this apparent equivalence. To do so would render the entire exercise futile. One must attempt to interpret this criterion without regard to a former view which rendered the remedy a nullity. Thus, for example, one notes that the qualification is " practicable," and not " reasonably practicable " (which appears in subs. (6)). The distinction in terms of how onerous is the duty is well known from the area of law concerned with health and safety at work. The former (e.g. in s. 4 of the Factories Act 1961—the duty to properly ventilate factory premises) is not an absolute standard, to be complied with even where totally impracticable, but nevertheless imposes a very strong onus on the employer to comply with the duty (in our case, the order for reinstatement or re-engagement). In contrast, the latter (used throughout the Health and Safety at Work, etc. Act 1974) is much more a matter of judgment in each case, with the normal standards of " responsible employers " being used as a yardstick.

In interpreting practicability under the old law on reinstatement, the judges tended to adopt the less strict standard of " reasonable practicability " in the circumstances, instead of considering whether it was only just less than totally impracticable for the employer to comply with a recommendation for reinstatement or re-engagement. Under the standard in the new law, mere inconvenience and even substantial difficulty should not suffice to excuse an employer from carrying out an order which could practicably be complied with. Henceforth, nothing less should move a tribunal considering whether an unfair employer should be ordered to reinstate an employee. (S. 70 (1) deals with the particular circumstances of the employee having been replaced.)

Contributory fault. Factor (c), it is evident from the last lines of subs. (6), is equivalent to " contributory fault " on the part of the complainant, and may roughly coincide with the old criterion of " equity." Given a finding of unfair dismissal and that the remedy of reinstatement does no more than restore him to his original position, without anything to compensate him for his ordeal, it would seem that only in extraordinary cases would a tribunal allow the fault of the employee to determine the question, overruling factors (a) and (b). The logical consequence of the procedure culminating in a finding of unfair dismissal is that the fault of the employee, if any, was one meriting not dismissal but some other lesser sanction. The employer should not be allowed to benefit from his wrongful application of the extreme disciplinary sanction of dismissal to prevent reinstatement.

Will anything change? Having said all this, one must confess to some pessimism as to whether the judges will be moved by argument based on the need to protect employees. Thus, in an early case considering this provision, Kilner Brown J. took his guidance from the judgment of Scarman L.J. in *Dedman* v. *British Building and Engineering Appliances Ltd.* [1973] I.R.L.R. 379 (C.A.)—a case where the word " practicable " was transformed into a question of fault (see the Note to s. 67 (2)—*Not reasonably practicable*)—see *Meridian Ltd.* v. *Gomersall* [1977] I.R.L.R. 425 (E.A.T.). And in *Enessy Co. SA t/a The Tulchan Estate* v. *Minoprio* [1978] I.R.L.R. 489 (E.A.T.), Lord McDonald introduced the view that different considerations applied to small employers with few staff than applied to factories or substantial organisations: " Where there must exist a close personal relationship as is the case here reinstatement can only be appropriate in exceptional circumstances and to enforce it upon a reluctant employer is not a course which an industrial tribunal should pursue unless persuaded by powerful evidence that it would succeed." As pointed out in the General Note to s. 54, there is a disproportionate number of claims for unfair dismissal from employees in small firms: in 1976, about one-fifth of all applications came from employees working in undertakings employing less than 20 employees. Just under half (48·7 per cent.) came from employees in firms employing less than 100 employees. So Lord McDonald's intervention could dramatically reduce the chances of reinstatement for these workers. And to take the employer's reluctance as a factor in deducing practicability—when he has been found to have acted unfairly—will disillusion many who had hoped that the new law would produce a new approach by the judges.

Subs. (6)

Considerations for re-engagement. Again, the tribunal is directed to consider reinstatement first, and only if it decides not to make such an order is it to consider re-engagement. The alternative remedy of compensation does not yet enter into the contemplated procedure. Substantially identical criteria are to be considered by the tribunal in deciding whether to order re-engagement as with reinstatement (see the Note to subs. (5)). Given the much wider scope of re-engagement, covering as it does the possibilities of employment in various comparable jobs with the employer, a successor or an associated employer, it will be even more difficult for employers to show that it was not practicable to re-engage the complainant. Re-engagement is required where practicable. The terms are to be equivalent to those of reinstatement (see subs. (2)), so far as is reasonably practicable, subject to the contributory fault of the employee ((*c*))—on which see the Note to subs. (5).

The Employment Protection Bill Consultative Document 1974 promised that: " In order to assist the tribunal to judge the practicability of reinstatement (*sic*) the employer should be required to provide the tribunal with information about relevant vacancies in his own or any associated organisation either before or at the hearing " (para. 23). The provisions of the section do not explicitly require this, but it is logical that the tribunals would consider this step in determining the question of practicability. Indeed, the provisions of Sched. 9, para. 4 envisage some penalty on the employer in certain circumstances who fails " to adduce reasonable evidence as to the availability of the job from which the complainant was dismissed . . . or of comparable or suitable employment."

Supplementary provisions relating to s. 69

70.—(1) Where in any case an employer has engaged a permanent replacement for a dismissed employee, the tribunal shall not take that fact into account in determining, for the purposes of subsection 5 (*b*) or (6) (*b*) of section 69, whether it is practicable to comply with an order for reinstatement or re-engagement unless the employer shows—

(*a*) that it was not practicable for him to arrange for the dismissed employee's work to be done without engaging a permanent replacement; or

(*b*) that he engaged the replacement after the lapse of a reasonable period, without having heard from the dismissed employee that he wished to be reinstated or re-engaged, and that when the employer engaged the replacement it was no longer reasonable for him to arrange for the dismissed employee's work to be done except by a permanent replacement.

(2) In calculating for the purpose of subsection (2) (*a*) or 4 (*d*) of section 69 any amount payable by the employer, the tribunal shall take into account, so as to reduce the employer's liability, any sums received by the complainant in respect of the period between the date of termination of employment and the date of reinstatement or re-engagement by way of—

(*a*) wages in lieu of notice or ex gratia payments paid by the employer;

(*b*) remuneration paid in respect of employment with another employer;

and such other benefits as the tribunal thinks appropriate in the circumstances.

DERIVATION

1975, s. 71 (8) (9).

GENERAL NOTE
Subs. (1)

As a consequence of tribunals' habitual deference to the employer's interests in not requiring him to reinstate or re-engage a complainant, whose wishes and interests were thereby sacrificed, express provision is made here to ensure that these latter are not ignored. Indeed, the position is reversed: the employee's interest in and right to reinstatement are paramount, and the hiring of a permanent replacement by the employer is not to prejudice them unless the employer can show either (*a*) or (*b*). So, first, unless the employer can show that it was totally impracticable to hire a temporary replacement or arrange to have the work done by other employees, (*a*) will not be satisfied. Secondly, (*b*) substitutes reasonableness for practicability—though it is not clear how these two will differ in application—but only after a reasonable period has elapsed.

It is not immediately apparent how the tribunals will determine what is a " reasonable period." The employer will be aware that the employee has a right of complaint for unfair dismissal. The law fixes three months plus " such other further period as the tribunal considers reasonable " in certain circumstances (s. 67 (2)) as the maximum period of complaint. Circumstances being infinitely variable, the law obviously considers that an employee might reasonably not lodge a complaint up to the end of this period, taking into account factors affecting the employee's individual position. The extent to which an unfair employer might be allowed to shorten this period as regards the employee's primary remedy by engaging a permanent replacement is subject to " reasonableness." Inevitably a trade-off must be made by the tribunal between the interests of the employer whose position requires the hiring of a permanent replacement and the interests of the employee being reinstated. Everything said above indicates that the tribunals are being pressed to favour the latter. Thus, an employer who failed to ascertain the employee's intentions as regards complaint and wishes as regards reinstatement or re-engagement, and hired a permanent replacement even after a substantial period had elapsed, might not be permitted to avoid the remedy. For even when the employer shows (*a*) or (*b*), this is only to be taken into account and is not conclusive in determining practicability, which itself is only one of the considerations listed in s. 69 (5) and (6).

Subs. (2)

The original Employment Protection Bill 1975 included a further sub-heading which allowed for the deduction of " social security benefits " (cl. 65 (9) (*c*)). The subsection as it now stands thus differs substantially from the common law principle of calculation of damages. The tribunal need not deduct all benefits received, but only those deemed appropriate. Thus, *e.g.* the employer may not be allowed to reap the benefits of the employee's rights to social security benefits. *Cf.* the rules which apply to deduct social security benefits from the compensatory award under s. 74 (see the regulations referred to in the Note to s. 74 (1)).

Enforcement of s. 69 order and compensation

71.—(1) If an order under section 69 is made and the complainant is reinstated or, as the case may be, re-engaged but the terms of the order are not fully complied with, then, subject to section 75, an industrial tribunal shall make an award of compensation, to be paid by the employer to the employee, of such amount as the tribunal thinks fit having regard to the loss sustained by the complainant in consequence of the failure to comply fully with the terms of the order.

(2) Subject to subsection (1), if an order under section 69 is made but the complainant is not reinstated or, as the case may be, re-engaged in accordance with the order—

  (*a*) the tribunal shall make an award of compensation for unfair dismissal, calculated in accordance with sections 72 to 74, to be paid by the employer to the employee; and

  (*b*) unless the employer satisfies the tribunal that it was not practicable to comply with the order, the tribunal shall make an additional award of compensation to be paid by the employer to the employee of an amount—

(i) where the dismissal is of a description referred to in subsection (3), not less than twenty-six nor more than fifty-two weeks' pay, or

(ii) in any other case, not less than thirteen nor more than twenty-six weeks' pay.

(3) The descriptions of dismissal in respect of which an employer may incur a higher additional award in accordance with subsection (2) (*b*) (i) are the following, that is to say,—

(*a*) a dismissal which is unfair by virtue of section 58 (1) or (3);

(*b*) a dismissal which is an act of discrimination within the meaning of the Sex Discrimination Act 1975 which is unlawful by virtue of that Act;

(*c*) a dismissal which is an act of discrimination within the meaning of the Race Relations Act 1976 which is unlawful by virtue of that Act.

(4) Where in any case an employer has engaged a permanent replacement for a dismissed employee the tribunal shall not take that fact into account in determining, for the purposes of subsection (2) (*b*) whether it was practicable to comply with the order for reinstatement or re-engagement unless the employer shows that it was not practicable for him to arrange for the dismissed employee's work to be done without engaging a permanent replacement.

(5) Where in any case an industrial tribunal makes an award of compensation for unfair dismissal, calculated in accordance with sections 72 to 74, and the tribunal finds that the complainant has unreasonably prevented an order under section 69 from being complied with, it shall, without prejudice to the generality of section 74 (4), take that conduct into account as a failure on the part of the complainant to mitigate his loss.

DERIVATION

1975, s. 72 (1)–(4) (6); Race Relations Act 1976 (c. 74), Sched. 3, para. 1 (2).

GENERAL NOTE

Subs. (1)

The tribunal is to award compensation only for loss sustained by the complainant in consequence of the employer's failure to comply fully. S. 75 provides for a maximum of £5,750. The borderline between partial and total non-compliance with an order of reinstatement or re-engagement is a difficult one to discern, particularly in the case of the former. Reinstatement, as defined in s. 69 (2), envisages a total restoration of the employee to his previous position. If the employer fails to do this, he is not simply in partial non-compliance, he is not complying at all, for what he is doing amounts to re-engagement, as defined in s. 69 (4). Similar problems may arise in cases of non-compliance with an order for re-engagement where the employer's response was sufficiently different from that envisaged by the order as not to be compliance at all.

The significance of the distinction between total and partial non-compliance lies in the employee's remedy: if the latter, he gets only compensation for loss as the tribunal thinks fit. If the former, he gets compensation in accordance with subss. (2)–(4), which includes much more. Those subsections allow for extensive compensation where the non-compliance amounts to discrimination on grounds of trade unionism, race or sex. Where the employer fails to comply fully with the order on, *e.g.* such grounds, the tribunal may consider him to be in total non-compliance. Alternatively, some of the loss calculated as compensation for only partial compliance may include some element of recompense for such discrimination (on the scale envisaged by subs. (2) (*b*) (i)). Such loss might even include damages for loss of the potential compensation under subss. (2) (*a*) and (2) (*b*) (ii). The tribunals may try to establish some consistency between the remedies for partial and total non-compliance.

Subs. (2)

The broad wording of this subsection seems to confirm that the tribunal is given considerable discretion in deciding whether or not an employer has complied only partially so as to fall under the provisions in subs. (1). For where he has not acted "in accordance with the order," he is subject to this subsection. An employer who failed to comply with the order in some substantial way, or in an inacceptable (*e.g.* discriminatory) manner, might be held to fall under this sub-section. In such cases the tribunal may hold that the complainant was not reinstated or re-engaged in accordance with the order.

Samples of additional awards for non-compliance with tribunal recommendations under the old law (TULRA, Sched. 1, para. 19 (4) (*b*)) suggested extreme arbitrariness—the amounts concerned varied between 3–130 per cent. of the tribunal's original award of compensation for loss. This subsection attempts to narrow down the boundaries of this variation by fixing maximum and minimum limits.

In deciding whether an additional award under subs. (2) (*b*) is to be made, the tribunal considers only whether the employer has shown that compliance was not practicable. The tribunal will already have decided that reinstatement or re-engagement *was* practicable, having made the order (s. 69 (5) (*b*) and (6) (*b*)). It is highly unlikely that an employer could justify on subsequent events that it had since become impracticable. As in making its previous decision on practic-ability the hiring of a permanent replacement was rejected as unreasonable (s. 70 (1)), it is unlikely that the employer who since then had hired one could satisfy the tribunal that such a step was reasonable (subs. (4)).

Enessy Co. SA t/a The Tulchan Estate v. *Minoprio* [1978] I.R.L.R. 489 (E.A.T.), illustrates the problems of deciding on whether compliance has taken place. In response to the industrial tribunal's order, the employers here agreed to treat the employees as employed *up to* the date specified as the latest date of reinstatement, but declared them redundant on that date. The industrial tribunal held this to be non-compliance, and made an additional award. On appeal, Lord McDonald said he could "readily visualise circumstances where an intervening circumstance such as redundancy can make it impossible for an employer to comply" and it would be unfair to penalise the employer there. He did not advert to the employee's position, however, and did not seem to regard this as coming under the question of "practicability," since he went on to say that the employer had not satisfied the burden in (*b*) because he had not, *e.g.* interviewed the employees or discussed the future with them.

Subs. (3)

If the employer's failure to reinstate or re-engage the complainant is the result of his refusal to accept back a non-unionist where a union membership agreement has since come into effect, the employer may be protected from having to pay additional compensation under (*a*). (If the original dismissal had been for that reason, the question would never have arisen as it would be fair.) *Cf.* the possible absence of such protection for the employer when an employee returning to work after pregnancy is refused employment (Sched. 2, para. 2 (4)).

It will not be possible for the complainant to successfully claim compensation for the same loss due to discrimination both under this section and under the Race Relations Act 1976, or the Sex Discrimination Act 1975 (see s. 76). Where the compensation differs (*e.g.* here the basic award and under the Sex Discrimination Act for injury to feelings), a claim should be brought under both enactments (see s. 73 (1) (*c*)).

Subs. (5)

Where an order is made, but the complainant fails to be reinstated or re-engaged, the tribunal is to make an award under ss. 72–74 (subs. (2) (*a*)); but if the reasons for the failure are that the complainant "unreasonably prevented" compliance by the employer, the damages awarded for loss may be reduced. Three points should be noted:

  (i) no account is to be taken of the complainant's attitude or actions as regards reinstatement or re-engagement *unless* an order has been made. Since an order may only be made where the complainant wishes (s. 68 (1)), this provision only applies where the complainant apparently undergoes a change of mind after having expressed such a wish, and prevents the order being complied with. The assessment of the "reasonableness" of the employee's actions by the tribunal may be influenced by the concept of the "trial period" (s. 84 (3) and (4)). So, *e.g.* if the employee leaves (*i.e.* prevents compliance) he may still be treated as falling under subs. (2).

(ii) since only damages calculated in accordance with ss. 72–74 may be reduced, where the employee's actions have prevented compliance *only in part* by the employer, the damages assessed under subs. (1) are not affected by this subsection, though the tribunal there assesses the amount as it "thinks fit."

(iii) the parallel provisions in the old law, TULRA, Sched. 1, para. 19 (4) (*a*), provided that a refusal of an offer of reinstatement or re-engagement as recommended, if unreasonable, reduced all the damages awarded. Here such conduct affects only the compensatory award (not the basic award nor even the additional award where one is made) since only that award is subject to the duty of mitigation (s. 74 (4)).

Amount of compensation

Compensation for unfair dismissal

72. Where a tribunal makes an award of compensation for unfair dismissal under section 68 (2) or 71 (2) (*a*) the award shall consist of a basic award (calculated in accordance with section 73) and a compensatory award (calculated in accordance with section 74).

DERIVATION

1975, s. 73.

GENERAL NOTE

Awards v. *profit.* In 1973, the total amount paid in unfair dismissal compensation (awards agreed in conciliation and awarded by tribunals) was £0·9m. The gross trading profits or surplus of companies or public corporations was £10,849m. (D. A. S. Jackson, *Unfair Dismissal* (1975), Table 16, p. 66).

Maximum award. The maximum sum payable to an employee unfairly dismissed can amount to:

(i) *basic award*: (s. 73) 20 years' employment after age 41 at 1½ weeks' pay (s. 73 (3) (*a*) and (4)) at a maximum of £110 per week = £3,300, plus

(ii) *compensatory award*: (s. 74) a maximum of £5,750 (s. 75), plus

(iii) *additional award*: (s. 71 (2)) the maximum, where failure to comply with an order for reinstatement is discriminatory, is 52 weeks'· pay at £110 per week = £5,720,

a total of £14,770. (See The Employment Protection (Variation of Limits) Order 1978 (S.I. 1978 No. 1777), and The Unfair Dismissal (Increase of Compensation Limit) Order 1978 (S.I. 1978 No. 1778)—both effective February 1, 1979.)

There has been no maximum monetary award since the change in the basis of unfair dismissal compensation on June 1, 1976.

Calculation of basic award

73.—(1) The amount of the basic award shall be the amount calculated in accordance with subsections (3) to (6), subject to—

(*a*) subsection (2) of this section (which provides for an award of two weeks' pay in certain redundancy cases);

(*b*) subsection (7) (which provides for the amount of the award to be reduced where the employee contributed to the dismissal);

(*c*) subsection (8) (which provides for a minimum award of two weeks' pay in certain cases);

(*d*) subsection (9) (which provides for the amount of the award to be reduced where the employee received a payment in respect of redundancy); and

(e) section 76 (which prohibits compensation being awarded under this Part and under the Sex Discrimination Act 1975 or the Race Relations Act 1976 in respect of the same matter).

(2) The amount of the basic award shall be two weeks' pay where the tribunal finds that the reason or principal reason for the dismissal of the employee was that he was redundant and the employee—

(a) by virtue of section 82 (5) or (6) is not, or if he were otherwise entitled would not be, entitled to a redundancy payment; or

(b) by virtue of the operation of section 84 (1) is not treated as dismissed for the purposes of Part VI.

(3) The amount of the basic award shall be calculated by reference to the period, ending with the effective date of termination, during which the employee has been continuously employed, by starting at the end of that period and reckoning backwards the numbers of years of employment falling within that period, and allowing—

(a) one and a half weeks' pay for each such year of employment which consists wholly of weeks in which the employee was not below the age of forty-one;

(b) one week's pay for each such year of employment which consists wholly of weeks in which the employee was below the age of forty-one and was not below the age of twenty-two; and

(c) half a week's pay for each such year of employment which consists wholly of weeks in which the employee was below the age of twenty-two and was not below the age of eighteen.

(4) Where, in reckoning the number of years of employment in accordance with subsection (3), twenty years of employment have been reckoned no account shall be taken of any year of employment earlier than those twenty years.

(5) Where in the case of an employee the effective date of termination is after the specified anniversary the amount of the basic award calculated in accordance with subsections (3) and (4) shall be reduced by the appropriate fraction.

(6) In subsection (5) " the specified anniversary " in relation to a man means the sixty-fourth anniversary of the day of his birth, and in relation to a woman means the fifty-ninth anniversary of the day of her birth, and " the appropriate fraction " means the fraction of which—

(a) the numerator is the number of whole months reckoned from the specified anniversary in the period beginning with that anniversary and ending with the effective date of termination; and

(b) the denominator is twelve.

(7) Where the tribunal finds that the dismissal was to any extent caused or contributed to by any action of the complainant it shall, except in a case where the dismissal was by reason of redundancy, reduce the amount of the basic award by such proportion as it considers just and equitable having regard to that finding.

(8) Where the amount calculated in accordance with subsections (3) to (7) is less than the amount of two weeks' pay, the amount of the basic award shall be two weeks' pay.

(9) The amount of the basic award shall be reduced or, as the case may be, be further reduced, by the amount of any redundancy payment awarded by the tribunal under Part VI in respect of the same dismissal or of any payment made by the employer to the employee on the ground that the dismissal was by reason of redundancy, whether in pursuance of Part VI or otherwise.

DERIVATION
1975, s. 74 (1)–(3) (5)–(7); s. 75 (7) (8).

GENERAL NOTE

Subs. (2)

But where a redundancy payment is made, it may operate to reduce the basic award to below two weeks' pay (subs. (9))—otherwise, two weeks' pay will be the irreducible minimum basic award—subs. (8).

Subss. (3) *to* (6)

See the basis of calculation for a redundancy payment in Sched. 4, paras. 2–4, which is substantially identical. For a " week's pay," see Sched. 14, Pt. II. The maximum basic award is presently £110 per week (£100 per week up to February 1, 1979)—for a total of £3,300 (Employment Protection (Variation of Limits) Order 1978 (S.I. 1978 No. 1777)).

Subs. (7)

This provision was not included in the original Employment Protection Bill 1975, which allowed only for the compensatory award to be reduced (cl. 70 (6)), now s. 74 (6). This provision was only introduced at the Report Stage, and the result is that now the total amount of compensation may be reduced for contributory fault. This was the position under the pre-1975 law—TULRA, Sched. 1, para. 19 (3). The sole difference is that the basic award cannot be reduced below two weeks' pay (subs. (8)). The legal requirement of a minimum basic award aroused the righteous indignation of the House of Lords in *Devis & Sons Ltd.* v. *Atkins* [1977] I.R.L.R. 314. The moral outrage of an award to an employee whose misconduct is established eclipsed in their Lordships' eyes the fact that the dismissal in question, perpetrated by the employer, was unfair. So Lord Diplock spoke of a "veritable rogues' charter," Lord Simon of "grave injustice" and Lord Fraser expressed anxiety and the hope that the matter would receive the early attention of Parliament. As yet, no one else seems bothered. But note Lord Diplock's veiled threat as to the implications for the interpretation of what is now s. 57 (3)—which might override this obstacle to justice being achieved. Still, in *Moncrieff* (*Farmers*) v. *MacDonald* [1978] I.R.L.R. 112 (E.A.T.), Lord McDonald held that subsequently discovered dishonesty cannot affect the basic award entitlement.

As to the curious exclusion of redundancy dismissals from this provision for reduction for contributory fault—see the Note to s. 74 (3).

Calculation of compensatory award

74.—(1) Subject to sections 75 and 76, the amount of the compensatory award shall be such amount as the tribunal considers just and equitable in all the circumstances having regard to the loss sustained by the complainant in consequence of the dismissal in so far as that loss is attributable to action taken by the employer.

(2) The said loss shall be taken to include—

(*a*) any expenses reasonably incurred by the complainant in consequence of the dismissal, and

(*b*) subject to subsection (3), loss of any benefit which he might reasonably be expected to have had but for the dismissal.

(3) The said loss, in respect of any loss of any entitlement or potential entitlement to, or expectation of, a payment on account of dismissal by reason of redundancy, whether in pursuance of Part VI or otherwise, shall include only the loss referable to the amount, if any, by which the amount of that payment would have exceeded the amount of a basic award (apart from any reduction under section 73 (7) or (9)) in respect of the same dismissal.

(4) In ascertaining the said loss the tribunal shall apply the same rule concerning the duty of a person to mitigate his loss as applies to damages recoverable under the common law of England and Wales or of Scotland, as the case may be.

(5) In determining, for the purposes of subsection (1), how far any loss sustained by the complainant was attributable to action taken by the employer no account shall be taken of any pressure which, by calling,

organising, procuring or financing a strike or other industrial action, or threatening to do so, was exercised on the employer to dismiss the employee, and that question shall be determined as if no such pressure had been exercised.

(6) Where the tribunal finds that the dismissal was to any extent caused or contributed to by any action of the complainant it shall reduce the amount of the compensatory award by such proportion as it considers just and equitable having regard to that finding.

(7) If the amount of any payment made by the employer to the employee on the ground that the dismissal was by reason of redundancy, whether in pursuance of Part VI or otherwise, exceeds the amount of the basic award which would be payable but for section 73 (9) that excess shall go to reduce the amount of the compensatory award.

DERIVATION

1975, s. 76.

GENERAL NOTE
Subs. (1)

The old law, stated in TULRA, Sched. 1, para. 19 (1), was retained in substantially identical form when the remedies for unfair dismissal were recast in 1975. The maximum compensatory award remained at £5,200. It is only to be raised to £5,750 on February 1, 1979 (s. 75).

A nil award may be just and equitable. Three criteria appear in this subsection by which to measure the compensatory award: what is just and equitable in the circumstances; the loss sustained by the complainant; and the extent to which it is attributable to the employer's action. The last is further reflected in subs. (6) which allows for reduction of the award to the extent of the complainant's contributory fault.

The normal unfair dismissal claim, when upheld, will have the compensatory award determined in straightforward manner in accordance with factors relating to the employee's loss (see Note to subs. (2)). The loss is, after all, the *sole* factor mentioned to which the tribunal is to have regard. And given the failure of the industrial tribunals to apply the remedies of reinstatement/re-engagement, all an employee can hope for is usually that he recoups his losses incurred as a result of the employer's established illegal action.

But the courts have reserved to themselves the power to undermine or overlook the compensatable loss caused by the employer's unfair actions, using the " just and equitable " criterion. It has been held on the authority of the House of Lords that even where a finding is made that the employee is unfairly dismissed, it may be " just and equitable " to award nil compensation—*Devis & Sons Ltd.* v. *Atkins* [1977] I.R.L.R. 314. Thus, *e.g.* Lord Simon of Glaisdale chose to subordinate his own reading of the " natural meaning " of the words (" loss " governing " just and equitable ") to that of Viscount Dilhorne, whose reading involved " no real violence to the language."

This point had been the subject of different approaches previously by different judges in the E.A.T. *E.g.* in *Courtney* v. *Babcock & Wilcox (Operations) Ltd.* [1977] I.R.L.R. 30 (E.A.T.), Lord McDonald asserted that it was quite conceivable that a dismissal could be unfair without automatically attracting any compensation at all. In contrast, Phillips J. in *Trend* v. *Chiltern Hunt Ltd.* [1977] I.R.L.R. 66 (E.A.T.), emphasised that, while it was possible to conceive of an award of nil compensation: " Industrial Tribunals should take care to see that they do not fall into inconsistency by on the one hand finding a dismissal to be unfair while on the other denying the applicant any compensation. . . . Industrial Tribunals would be wise if they find themselves coming to such a conclusion to reconsider it in the light of the question: ' Would such a finding in truth involve a basic inconsistency '."

The inconsistency here is an obvious one—where the statute has directed the judges to find a dismissal unfair in stated circumstances, some would say it was inconsistent, if not worse, for the judge to nullify the effect of the statute by holding that in his opinion it was just and equitable to deny any remedy. Phillips J. went on to say that to reduce compensation by more than 80 per cent. " is likely to be seen as verging on the inconsistent." But Viscount Dilhorne in *Devis*

& *Sons Ltd.* v. *Atkins* said his conclusions were wrong. He could not see any inconsistency.

Compensation for " technical " unfair dismissal. A particular illustration of the above discussion as to nil awards is the case of the failure of the employer to follow a procedure stipulated in the Code of Practice (see Note to s. 57 (3)—*Procedural reasonableness*). In *Trend's* case Phillips J. agreed that it was open to an industrial tribunal which has found unfair dismissal to make a nil award " if on the evidence they are satisfied that the applicant has not suffered any loss," *i.e.* even if the employer had followed the procedure, dismissal would have resulted. It is argued, therefore, that no loss flows from the unfair action of the employer. That is to focus on the loss attributable to the action (which includes omission—s. 153 (1)) taken by the employer. Viscount Dilhorne in *Devis* seemed to think that here again it might be just and equitable to deny the employee any compensatory award.

Thus, *e.g.* in *Clyde Pipeworks Ltd.* v. *Foster* [1978] I.R.L.R. 313 (E.A.T.), the employer had failed to consult employees and their representatives in accordance with para. 46 of the 1972 Code of Practice, yet Lord McDonald in the E.A.T. held that: " even if there had been further consultation it would have made no difference to dismissal on the ground of redundancy." The compensatory award (but not the basic award) would thus be reduced to nil. *Cf. UBAF Bank Ltd.* v. *Davis* [1978] I.R.L.R. 442 (E.A.T.) where counsel for the employer relied on *Devis* and Arnold J. accepted it, but added that an award of nil compensation " would have to be, as we think, a case in which the unfairness was of a highly technical character."

Three points should be borne in mind in questions concerned with compensation for " technical " unfair dismissal.

Burden of proof of loss. First, the onus is on the employer, where the proper procedure has not been observed, to prove that " had the manner of dismissal been fair, it could and would have made no difference to the result " (Cumming-Bruce J. in *Charles Letts & Co. Ltd.* v. *Howard* [1976] I.R.L.R. 248 (E.A.T.)). Once unfair dismissal has been established, it has been held that the onus of proof in relation to loss lies on the claimant. But Phillips J. in *Barley* v. *Amey Roadstone Corp. Ltd.* [1977] I.R.L.R. 299 (E.A.T.) was emphatic in saying that when there is a failure in procedure: " it is wrong in applying the onus of proof to apply it so strictly that no claimant can hope to discharge it." Rather: " although the burden of proof lies mainly on the claimant, the evidential burden may well shift—and indeed usually will shift—to the employer once the claimant has put forward some coherent, sensible suggestion as to what the result of the failure to consult, or whatever the failure is, is likely to have been, and what would be likely to have happened had there been no failure." For, as Phillips J. said in a subsequent case (*British United Shoe Machinery Co. Ltd.* v. *Clarke* [1977] I.R.L.R. 297 (E.A.T.)), where the industrial tribunal finds the dismissal unfair: " it will be necessary for it to proceed to assess compensation, and for that purpose to make some estimate of what would have been the likely outcome had that been done which ought to have been done."

" Technical " unfairness is still unfair dismissal. Secondly, the temptation to regard " technical " unfair dismissal as somehow a lesser degree of unfairness needs be resisted. As Phillips J. put it in *Trend* v. *Chiltern Hunt Ltd.* [1977] I.R.L.R. 66 (E.A.T.) : " care must be taken lest a tendency to withhold compensation should unintentionally encourage the opinion that adherence to the Code of Practice, procedure agreements, and so on, is unimportant."

Common law unfairness and statutory unfairness. Finally, however the lawyer may rationalise, it will seem inconsistent to the layman that a dismissal can be held to be unfair, and yet no compensation be awarded, *despite loss incurred*, either because the loss is held to be inevitable anyway (and so did not flow from the employer's unfairness), or on the grounds that it is " just and equitable." All but the most confirmed common lawyers will feel uneasy at judges using their discretion to render the employee subjected to unfairness as stated by the statute to be without remedy.

Subs. (2)

Heads of damage compensatable. It was confirmed by the E.A.T. in *Tidman* v. *Aveling Marshall Ltd.* [1977] I.R.L.R. 218, that it is the duty of the industrial tribunal to inquire into the possibility of various heads of damage having been incurred by the unfairly dismissed employee. These were confirmed as being those listed in the leading case of *Norton Tool Co. Ltd.* v. *Tewson* [1972] I.R.L.R. 86 (N.I.R.C.), and include: (1) the immediate loss of wages; (2) the manner of dismissal; (3) future loss of wages, and (4) loss of protection in respect of unfair dismissal. To these heads there is a further one since added: loss of pension rights. For a list of four factors the industrial tribunals should have regard to in compensating for loss of pension rights, see *Smith, Kline & French Laboratories Ltd.* v. *Coates* [1977] I.R.L.R. 220 (E.A.T.).

Social security deductions. In accordance with s. 132 (formerly s. 112 of the Employment Protection Act 1975), regulations are now in existence requiring the employer to repay to the National Insurance Fund and the Exchequer any social security benefits paid to employees which would previously have been deducted from industrial tribunal awards. See the Employment Protection (Recoupment of Unemployment Benefit and Supplementary Benefit) Regulations 1977 (S.I. 1977 No. 674)—and see (1977) 6 I.L.J. 192.

For the impact on the employee, however, the effect of the Social Security (Unemployment, Sickness and Invalidity Benefit) Regulations (S.I. 1975 No. 564, reg. 7, as amended by S.I. 1976 No. 677) have to be appreciated. They state that any day to which the award relates is deemed *not* to be a day of unemployment. For the full implications, see (1977) 6 I.L.J. 54.

Subs. (3)

Under the pre-1975 law, the compensation for unfair dismissal included a sum intended to reimburse the employee for loss of his potential entitlement to a redundancy payment—a figure assessed arbitrarily at 50 per cent. of the value of the accrued rights being adopted. As the complainant is now to receive the equivalent of the whole of such a redundancy payment, called the basic award, this subsection rather disingenuously provides for that previous sum (50 per cent. of a redundancy payment) to be off-set by the basic award (100 per cent. of a redundancy payment)—*i.e.* in practice it will not be paid. The circumstances where a basic award is likely to be low (*e.g.* s. 73 (2)) are those where the compensation for potential loss of redundancy rights under the old law would also have been low. Where, however, the potential entitlement to redundancy payment would have exceeded the amount of the basic award (*e.g.* due to the employer's paying above the statutory minimum), the loss of this potential extra entitlement may be included in the compensatory award over and above the basic award.

The only difficulty may arise from the curious provision of s. 73 (7) which states that contributory fault is not to be considered as reducing the basic award in cases of redundancy. Under the old law the sum paid for loss of potential redundancy rights was reduced together with the rest of the loss assessed in accordance with the proportion deemed to be due to the complainant's fault (TULRA, Sched. 1, para. 19 (3)). The complainant may thus benefit under the new law where he has been at fault in a redundancy situation. For his basic award cannot be reduced (although his compensatory award can—subs. (6)). In such a redundancy situation, however, the complainant might receive a redundancy payment anyway, which would be set off entirely under both the old and the present law—so as to result in no practical difference at all. Under the old law, no loss of potential rights would be assessed, since he might get a redundancy payment; whereas under the present law, the basic award is reduced by any such payment (s. 73 (9)). Where the dismissal was for misconduct in a redundancy situation, however, the entitlement to and amount of the redundancy payment might be affected by ss. 82 (2) and 92 (3) of this Act. One must resist the temptation to examine here the complications adduced by such a situation.

Subs. (4)

The duty to mitigate contained in the common law of employment was not interpreted afresh by tribunals in light of the new circumstances of statutory protection against unfair dismissal. The old common law doctrine applied in cases of wrongful dismissal meant that an employee had to make every effort to find another job. This clearly contradicted the intention of the statutory provisions which envisaged the employee being reinstated. The tribunals tended to ignore this. It is hoped that they will at some point alert themselves to the need for a fresh look at the common law doctrine.

Subs. (6)

The principle of nil compensation again. In the Note to subs. (1) above there was described the division of opinion among the judges in the E.A.T. as to the principle of the making of a nil compensatory award. This was discussed in the context of the dual criterion in subs. (1)—" just and equitable " award *v.* loss compensation. But the issue arose more frequently where an award of compensation was reduced by 100 per cent. by some judges, while others deemed it not proper to reduce an award by more than 80 per cent. (see, *e.g.* Kilner Brown J. in *Kemp* v. *Shipton Automation Ltd.* [1976] I.R.L.R. 305 (E.A.T.)). This latter view was expressly disapproved by the House of Lords in *Devis & Sons Ltd.* v. *Atkins* [1977] I.R.L.R. 314. A number of points were made in the Note to subs. (1) which are relevant to the same principle of nil compensation and may also be applied here— but a few others are worth noting.

Contributory fault and incapability. In *Kraft Foods Ltd.* v. *Fox* [1977] I.R.L.R. 431 (E.A.T.), Kilner Brown J. said: " If an employee is incompetent or incapable and cannot, with the best will in the world, measure up to the job, it seems to us to be wrong to say that that condition of incapacity is a contributory factor to his dismissal." The implication to be derived from this statement was that, so long as the employee was incapable through lack of innate ability, it was impossible to say he contributed to his own dismissal. Contribution implied conduct controlled by the employee. In subsequent cases (*e.g. Sutton & Gates (Luton) Ltd.* v. *Boxall* [1978] I.R.L.R. 486 (E.A.T.)) Kilner Brown J. has attempted to avoid his dictum being misapplied to any but the *true* incapability case. With this reservation, one welcomes it. (But see the doubts of Phillips J. in *Moncur* v. *International Paint Co. Ltd.* [1978] I.R.L.R. 223 (E.A.T.).)

Ex gratia payments. In *UBAF Bank Ltd.* v. *Davis* [1978] I.R.L.R. 442 (E.A.T.), Arnold J. held that where an employee on dismissal is given pay in lieu of notice and an *ex gratia* payment, these sums are not to be included in the calculation of loss. Any reduction to be made is applicable to the amount lost only. So, an employer may not invoke the *ex gratia* payment in any way to reduce the amount of loss remaining after the reduction has been made.

Subs. (7)

Both the basic (s. 73 (9)) and the compensatory awards are reduced to the extent of any redundancy payment.

Limit on compensation

75.—(1) The amount of compensation awarded to a person under section 71 (1) or of a compensatory award to a person calculated in accordance with section 74 shall not exceed £5,200.

(2) The Secretary of State may by order increase the said limit of £5,200 or that limit as from time to time increased under this subsection, but no such order shall be made unless a draft of the order has been laid before Parliament and approved by a resolution of each House of Parliament.

(8) It is hereby declared for the avoidance of doubt that the limit imposed by this section applies to the amount which the industrial tribunal would, apart from this section, otherwise award in respect of the subject matter of the complaint after taking into account any payment made by the respondent to the complainant in respect of that matter and any reduction in the amount of the award required by any enactment or rule of law.

DERIVATION

1974, para. 20; 1975, Sched. 16, Pt. III, para. 17.

GENERAL NOTE

Subs. (1)

When the old law on compensation was recast in the Employment Protection Act 1975, the maximum compensatory award remained at £5,200, *i.e.* 104 weeks at the old maximum rate of £50 weekly. As of February 1, 1979, the maximum compensatory award is raised to £5,750 (the Unfair Dismissal (Increase of Compensation Limit) Order 1978 (S.I. 1978 No. 1778)). But the basic and additional awards are now calculated at the rate of £100 per week maximum (and £110 per week as of February 1, 1979 (the Employment Protection (Variation of Limits) Order 1978 (S.I. 1978 No. 1777)). In effect, therefore, if the employment is paid at the maximum rate or above, an employee's award has been progressively reduced from 104 weeks' pay (originally set by the Industrial Relations Act 1971, s. 118 (1)), down to approximately half that—about 52 weeks' pay.

Subs. (3)

This is a "for the avoidance of doubt" provision, introduced in 1975, in an attempt to raise awards from their then, and still now, low levels.

Compensation for act which is both sex or racial discrimination (or both) and unfair dismissal

76.—(1) Where compensation falls to be awarded in respect of any act both under the provisions of this Act relating to unfair dismissal and under one or both of the following Acts, namely the Sex Discrimination Act 1975 and the Race Relations Act 1976, an industrial tribunal shall not award compensation under any one of those two or, as the case may be, three Acts in respect of any loss or other matter which is or has been taken into account under the other or any other of them by the tribunal or another industrial tribunal in awarding compensation on the same or another complaint in respect of that act.

(2) Without prejudice to section 75 (whether as enacted or as applied by section 65 of the Sex Discrimination Act 1975 or section 56 of the Race Relations Act 1976) in a case to which subsection (1) applies, the aggregate of the following amounts of compensation awarded by an industrial tribunal, that is to say—

(*a*) any compensation awarded under the said Act of 1975; and
(*b*) any compensation awarded under the said Act 1976; and
(*c*) any compensation awarded under section 71(1) or, as the case may be, which is calculated in accordance with section 74;

shall not exceed the limit for the time being imposed by section 75.

DERIVATION

1975, s. 77; Race Relations Act 1976 (c. 74), Sched. 3, para. 1 (3).

GENERAL NOTE
Subs. (1)

Where the "loss or other matter" compensated differs, it will be worthwhile claiming under both Acts. See the Note to s. 71 (3).

Interim relief

Interim relief pending determination of complaint of unfair dismissal

77.—(1) An employee who presents a complaint to an industrial tribunal that he has been unfairly dismissed by his employer and that the reason for the dismissal (or, if more than one, the principal reason) was that the employee—

(*a*) was, or proposed to become, a member of a particular independent trade union; or
(*b*) had taken, or proposed to take, part at any appropriate time in the activities of a particular independent trade union of which he was or proposed to become a member;

may, subject to the following provisions of this section, apply to the tribunal for an order under the following provisions of this section.

(2) An industrial tribunal shall not entertain an application under this section unless—

   (*a*) it is presented to the tribunal before the end of the period of seven days immediately following the effective date of termination (whether before, on or after that date); and

   (*b*) before the end of that period there is also so presented a certificate in writing signed by an authorised official of the independent trade union of which the employee was or had proposed to become a member stating that on the date of the dismissal the employee was or had proposed to become a member of the union and that there appear to be reasonable grounds for supposing that the reason for his dismissal (or, if more than one, the principal reason) was one alleged in the complaint.

(3) An industrial tribunal shall determine an application under this section as soon as practicable after receiving the application and the relevant certificate, but shall, at least seven days before the date of the hearing, give the employer a copy of the application and certificate, together with notice of the date, time and place of the hearing.

(4) An industrial tribunal shall not exercise any power it has of postponing the hearing in the case of an application under this section except where the tribunal is satisfied that special circumstances exist which justify it in doing so.

(5) If on hearing an application under this section it appears to an industrial tribunal that it is likely that on determining the complaint to which the application relates the tribunal will find that the complainant was unfairly dismissed and that the reason for the dismissal (or if more than one, the principal reason) was a reason mentioned in subsection (1), the tribunal shall announce its findings and explain to both parties (if present) what powers the tribunal may exercise on an application under this section and in what circumstances it may exercise them, and shall ask the employer (if present) whether he is willing, pending the determination or settlement of the complaint—

   (*a*) to reinstate the employee, that is to say, to treat the employee in all respects as if he had not been dismissed; or

   (*b*) if not, to re-engage him in another job on terms and conditions not less favourable than those which would have been applicable to him if he had not been dismissed.

(6) In subsection (5) " terms and conditions not less favourable than those which would have been applicable to him if he had not been dismissed " means, as regards seniority, pension rights and other similar rights, that the period prior to the dismissal shall be regarded as continuous with his employment following the dismissal.

(7) If the employer states that he is willing to reinstate the employee, the tribunal shall make an order to that effect.

(8) If the employer states that he is willing to re-engage the employee in another job and specifies the terms and conditions on which he is willing to do so, the tribunal shall ask the employee whether he is willing to accept the job on those terms and conditions, and—

   (*a*) if the employee is willing to accept the job on those terms and conditions, the tribunal shall make an order to that effect; and

   (*b*) if the employee is unwilling to accept the job on those terms and conditions, then, if the tribunal is of the opinion that the refusal is reasonable, the tribunal shall make an order for the continuation of his contract of employment, but otherwise the tribunal shall make no order under this section.

(9) If, on the hearing of an application under this section, the employer fails to attend before the tribunal or he states that he is un-

willing either to reinstate the employee or re-engage him as mentioned in subsection (5), the tribunal shall make an order for the continuation of the employee's contract of employment.

(10) In this section—

" appropriate time " has the same meaning as in section 23;

" authorised official ", in relation to a trade union, means an official of the union authorised by the union to act for the purposes of this section;

and any reference to the date of dismissal is a reference—

(a) where the employee's contract of employment was terminated by notice (whether given by his employer or by him), to the date on which the employer's notice was given; and

(b) in any other case, to the effective date of termination.

(11) A document purporting to be an authorisation of an official by a trade union to act for the purposes of this section and to be signed on behalf of the union shall be taken to be such an authorisation unless the contrary is proved, and a document purporting to be a certificate signed by such an official shall be taken to be signed by him unless the contrary is proved.

DERIVATION
1975, s. 78.

GENERAL NOTE

The reason for the introduction of this remedy in the Employment Protection Act 1975 may be deduced from statistics given at the Committee Stage of that Act's passage through Parliament. These indicated that although less than 20 per cent. of all strikes due to dismissal between 1966–73 concerned workers' representatives being dismissed, their share of man-days lost through strikes increased from 17 per cent. at the beginning to over 40 per cent. at the end of that period. Additionally, while only 60 per cent. of dismissal strikes concerned only one employee dismissed, 90 per cent. of dismissal strikes concerning employee representatives concerned one employee. (Standing Committee F on the Employment Protection Bill, 30th Sitting, July 22, 1975, at col. 1632.) The obvious conclusion was that the dismissal of single shop stewards leads to most damaging strikes. To combat the problem, not of anti-trade union discrimination by employers, but of the loss of production due to industrial action caused by this discrimination, there was proposed the palliative of providing the employee in those circumstances with legal continuity of employment pending determination of his complaint by an industrial tribunal.

While lawyers may be impressed by the radical nature of this legal remedy, trade unionists are unlikely to be. Decades of harsh experience have engrained in workers the lesson that protection of themselves and particularly of their organisation at work depends not on the law or the fiat of some legal tribunal, but on their own strength *vis-à-vis* their employer. The proof of this was plain for all to see— contrast the disproportionate number of strikes over such dismissals with the number of complaints to industrial tribunals in such cases: only 27 in the six months between the end of September 1974 and the end of March 1975. Resort to tribunals is made only when the organisation of workers is so weak or the employer so strong that self-reliance would be fatal. The inducement here proffered—an order of legal continuation of the contract of employment after a specially hastened hearing (still estimated to take place only two to three weeks after the dismissal)—is not one which any shop steward worth his salt is going to wait for unless he has to. Any reduction in strike activity in such dismissal cases will be due more to union weakness and general economic factors than the availability of the new legal remedy. During the first two years since the remedy came into force (June 1, 1976), only three industrial tribunal cases were reported in the Industrial Relations Law Reports—of which two were unsuccessful.

Subs. (1)

The dismissal is one for which protection is provided by s. 58 (1) (a) and (b). For a definition of " appropriate time," subs. (10) refers to s. 23. The trade union activities concerned may be those envisaged by s. 23 (1) (*b*), s. 27, s. 28 or s. 58 (1) (*b*). The parallel has had certain unfortunate consequences, as an employee allegedly dismissed for trade union reasons in a redundancy situation (s. 59 (*a*)) has been held by an industrial tribunal not eligible to use this provision. Only first degree discrimination was said to be eligible (*Farmeary* v. *Veterinary Drug Co. Ltd.* [1976] I.R.L.R. 322).

Subs. (2)

An " authorised official " is defined in subs. (10). Any challenge to a document purporting to be such authorisation, or that a certificate is not signed by such an official must be proved by the employer (subs. (11)). The method and degree of such authorisation is left to the discretion of each particular trade union.

The certificate need only state that the employee concerned was or proposed to become a trade union member, not that he was dismissed for those reasons. The official needs also state only that there *appear* to be reasonable grounds for *supposing* that the complaint is true—not that there *are* such reasonable grounds. The certificate, therefore, is almost unchallengeable. But despite this widely drafted provision, see the numerous comments by the industrial tribunal chairman in *Farmeary* v. *Veterinary Drug Co. Ltd.* [1976] I.R.L.R. 322.

Subs. (3)

The hearing is to be " as soon as practicable," but given the need for obtaining the certificate, filing the application, processing it and sending it to the employer, plus another seven days' grace before the hearing, it is unlikely to be sooner than two to three weeks after the dismissal. In the three tribunal cases reported so far, the delays between the date of dismissal and hearing were: 18 days, 16 days and 25 days. In the E.A.T. case of *Taplin* v. *Shippam Ltd.* [1978] I.R.L.R. 450 (E.A.T.), the hearing was on July 7, 1978, and the employee was dismissed on November 25, 1977—over seven months earlier.

Subs. (5)

Is " likely " pretty good? The interim hearing differs from that determining the complaint in the normal course of events. The evidence produced may be only partial in character, for the employer may not even be present—see subs. (9) for the mandatory procedure in that event. But the uncertainty remains as to what will satisfy the requirements of this subsection—though it is clearly a standard short of that proof needed at the final determination. Thus factors which tribunals must take into account will be of some importance even though at the final hearing they are not determinants—*e.g.* Code of Practice, para. 15 (*b*)—disciplinary action taken without prior discussion with a senior trade union representative or full-time official is a breach of the Code and may help to satisfy the requisite burden of proof here.

In *Taplin* v. *Shippam Ltd.* [1978] I.R.L.R. 450 (E.A.T.), Slynn J. thought the applicant needed to show more than just a " reasonable " prospect of success, and suggested that the correct approach was whether he had established that he had a " pretty good " chance of succeeding in the final application. The industrial tribunal's criterion of " more than probable "—*i.e.* " 50 per cent. or more " was insufficiently close to the E.A.T.'s view not to be reversible. No doubt further euphemisms will be forthcoming, each as helpful as its predecessor.

In contrast to the provisions of s. 68 (1), the tribunal's making of an order for reinstatement or re-engagement depends on the employer's acquiescence (although once made, special remedies are available for breach of such an order—s. 79 (2) ; *cf.* s. 71 (1) and (2)). The remedies themselves are very sparsely defined compared to their much fuller treatment in s. 69 (2) to (4). One may assume that in practice the tribunal would not provide the employee concerned with anything less than what is there required of the employer reinstating or re-engaging him. See, *e.g.* the order made by the industrial tribunal in *Forsyth* v. *Fry's Metals Ltd.* [1977] I.R.L.R. 243.

Subs. (6)

Cf. s. 45 (2) for a parallel between re-engagement here and a woman's right to return to work after pregnancy.

Subs. (7)

It seems that the employee is presumed to desire reinstatement by virtue of his application. His wishes do not appear to be considered at the hearing, as is mandatory under s. 69 (5) (*a*). Yet in the case of re-engagement, the employee's wishes are the deciding factor, subject to their reasonableness (subs. (8)).

Subs. (8)

The employer apparently specifies the terms of re-engagement, but in order to be acceptable they must obviously fall within the definition in subs. (5) (*b*). Otherwise, the employee would in effect be required to accept these terms and denied the remedy if he unreasonably refuses. The tribunal must decide (i) whether the terms specified by the employer amount to re-engagement; and (ii) if so whether the employee has unreasonably refused them.

Orders for continuation of contract of employment

78.—(1) An order for the continuation of a contract of employment under section 77 shall be an order that the contract of employment, if it has been terminated, shall continue in force as if it had not been terminated and if not, shall on its termination, continue in force, in either case until the determination or settlement of the complaint and only for the purposes of pay or any other benefit derived from the employment, seniority, pension rights and other similar matters and for the purpose of determining for any purpose the period for which the employee has been continuously employed.

(2) Where the tribunal makes any such order it shall specify is the order the amount which is to be paid by the employer to the employee by way of pay in respect of each normal pay period or part of any such period falling between the date of the dismissal and the determination or settlement of the complaint and, subject to subsection (5), the amount so specified shall be that which the employee could reasonably have been expected to earn during that period or part, and shall be paid, in the case of a payment for any such period falling wholly or partly after the order, on the normal pay day for that period and, in the case of a payment for any past period, within a time so specified.

(3) If an amount is payable by way of pay in pursuance of any such order in respect only of part of a normal pay period the amount shall be calculated by reference to the whole period and be reduced proportionately.

(4) Any payment made to an employee by an employer under his contract of employment, or by way of damages for breach of that contract, in respect of any normal pay period or part of any such period shall go towards discharging the employer's liability in respect of that period under subsection (2), and conversely any payment under subsection (2) in respect of any period shall go towards discharging any liability of the employer under, or in respect of breach of, the contract of employment in respect of that period.

(5) If an employee, on or after being dismissed by his employer, receives a lump sum which, or part of which, is in lieu of wages but is not referable to any normal pay period, the tribunal shall take the payment into account in determining the amount of pay to be payable in pursuance of any such order.

(6) For the purposes of this section the amount which an employee could reasonably have been expected to earn, his normal pay period and the normal pay day for each such period shall be determined as if he had not been dismissed.

DERIVATION

1975, s. 79.

GENERAL NOTE

Subs. (1)

The remedy is constructed for the sole benefit of the employee—the contract is continued for the purposes of ensuring that benefits under that contract continue to accrue to the employee. Other obligations owed under the contract of employment (*e.g.* those of the employee towards the employer) are not continued in force. So, *e.g.* the employee's duty to work is terminated until there is either a revocation or variation of the order (s. 79 (1)) or a determination or settlement of the complaint.

Subs. (2)

The employee is to receive his anticipated earnings, not an amount calculated using his contractual rate of pay, hours of work, etc.

Subs. (4)

Payment of wages in lieu of notice to a dismissed employee, and any damages for wrongful dismissal are to be set off against any payments ordered under subs. (2), and vice versa. Awards of the tribunal under the statutory provisions on unfair dismissal will not be set off under this subsection (see Note to s. 79 (3)).

Subs. (5)

The intent of this subsection is to deal with cases where, *e.g.* four weeks' pay in lieu of notice being owed, the employer gives a lump sum not specifically referable to any normal pay period. Consistently with subs. (4), it seems that only that part of the lump sum which is in lieu of wages is to be set off. If the lump sum includes an amount exceeding the wages during the period of notice, this is to be considered a gratuity and not to be set off.

Supplementary provisions relating to interim relief

79.—(1) At any time between the making of an order by an industrial tribunal under section 77 and the determination or settlement of the complaint to which it relates, the employer or the employee may apply to the tribunal for the revocation or variation of the order on the ground of a relevant change of circumstances since the making of the order, and that section shall apply to the application as it applies to an application for an order under that section except that—

   (*a*) no certificate need be presented to the tribunal under subsection (2) (*b*), and no copy of the certificate need be given to the employer under subsection (3), of that section; and

   (*b*) in the case of an application by an employer, for the reference in the said subsection (3) to the employer there shall be substituted a reference to the employee.

(2) If on the application of an employee an industrial tribunal is satisfied that the employer has not complied with the terms of an order for the reinstatement or re-engagement of the employee under section 77 (7) or (8),—

   (*a*) the tribunal shall make an order for the continuation of the employee's contract of employment and section 78 shall apply to an order under this subsection as it applies to an order for the continuation of a contract of employment under section 77; and

   (*b*) the tribunal shall also order the employer to pay the employee such compensation as the tribunal considers just and equitable in all the circumstances having regard to the infringement of the employee's right to be reinstated or re-engaged in pursuance of the order under section 77 (7) or (8) and to any loss suffered by the employee in consequence of the non-compliance.

(3) If on the application of an employee an industrial tribunal is satisfied that the employer has not complied with the terms of an order for the continuation of a contract of employment, then—

(*a*) if the non-compliance consists of a failure to pay an amount by way of pay specified in the order, the tribunal shall determine the amount of pay owed by the employer to the employee on the date of the determination, and, if on that date the tribunal also determines the employee's complaint that he has been unfairly dismissed by his employer, the tribunal shall specify that amount separately from any other sum awarded to the employee; and

(*b*) in any other case, the tribunal shall order the employer to pay the employee such compensation as the tribunal considers just and equitable in all the circumstances having regard to any loss suffered by the employee in consequence of the non-compliance.

DERIVATION

1975, s. 80 (1) to (3).

GENERAL NOTE

Subs. (2)

Failure of the employer to comply wholly or in part with an order for reinstatement or re-engagement under s. 77 may lead to an application under this section, which is essentially repetitive of the s. 77 procedure, except that the order for the continuation of the contract of employment is automatic, and in addition, an award of compensation is made for (i) the employer's breach of the previous order, and (ii) any loss thereby caused to the employee. *Cf.* the remedies for breach of an order for reinstatement or re-engagement under s. 71 (1) and (2). While no limits are placed on the compensation to be awarded under this subsection, the sum will probably be consistent with the provisions of that section (especially s. 71 (2) (*b*) (i) which envisages similar circumstances of discrimination on grounds of trade unionism).

Subs. (3)

The somewhat obscurely drafted provisions of this subsection seem to envisage the following alternatives:

(*a*) following an order for continuation of his contract, the employee waits until approximately the date of the hearing which finally determines his complaint to make an application under this section, so that on the same date both the complaint and the application are dealt with. The tribunal, if satisfied of non-compliance, must then specify the amount of pay owed under its previous order to be paid to the employee separately from any other sum awarded if it should uphold the complaint of unfair dismissal (whether on grounds of the alleged anti-trade union bias or otherwise), *i.e.* it is not to be set off against any such sum nor taken into account in any way in assessing compensation (which in these circumstances may be substantial). It is apparently to be treated as extra compensation to be paid by the employer for failing to comply with the tribunal's order. *Cf.* the compensation payable for the infringement of an interim order of reinstatement or re-engagement (subs. (2) (*b*)). (If it was set off, of course, it would render the whole interim procedure a farce, as effectively there would be no reason for the unfair employer to comply.)

(*b*) (i) following an order for continuation of his contract, the employee makes another *interim* application, *i.e.* one which is decided by the tribunal before the final determination. In such a case, the tribunal would award compensation for any loss suffered due to non-compliance (*including* any amount of pay owed under the terms of the order) and, of course, maintain the order for continuation of the contract. Any further non-compliance would be subject to further interim applications or a final one as described in (a) above.

(ii) if the tribunal decides on the employee's application favourably on the date of the final determination, but determines that the dismissal was not unfair, the employer may still be ordered to pay some compensation for loss caused to the employee due to his non-compliance (*e.g.* the employee, believing himself to be still employed by order of the tribunal and entitled to payments, may not have sought alternative employment).

At least one point remains controversial: since the contract of employment is continued in existence by order in accordance with statute, may not the employee, instead of relying on alternative (b) (ii), simply sue on the contract before the industrial tribunal (see s. 78 (4))? This might seem preferable to relying on the discretion of the tribunal under (b). Since no provision is made for the employer to recover any sums paid in accordance with the tribunal's order even where the final determination is in his favour, it would seem that the reason is that the employee is contractually entitled to them.

Teachers in aided schools

Teacher in aided school dismissed on requirement of local education authority

80.—(1) Where a teacher in an aided school is dismissed by the governors or managers of the school in pursuance of a requirement of the local education authority under paragraph (*a*) of the proviso to section 24 (2) of the Education Act 1944, this Part shall have effect in relation to the dismissal as if—

(*a*) the local education authority had at all material times been the teacher's employer, and

(*b*) the local education authority had dismissed him, and the reason or principal reason for which they did so had been the reason or principal reason for which they required his dismissal.

(2) For the purposes of a complaint under section 67 as applied by this section—

(*a*) section 71 (2) (*b*) shall have effect as if for the words " not practicable to comply " there were substituted the words " not practicable for the local education authority to permit compliance "; and

(*b*) section 74 (5) shall have effect as if any reference to the employer were a reference to the local education authority.

DERIVATION
1974, para. 27; 1975, Sched. 16, Pt. III, paras. 26, 27.

PART VI

REDUNDANCY PAYMENTS

General Note

Origins. The rights contained in this Part were first enacted in the Redundancy Payments Act 1965, though extensive amendments were introduced in various pieces of legislation, most recently in the Employment Protection Act 1975, Sched. 16, Pt. I.

Policy of the legislation. The theory and policy behind the legislation has been subjected to a great deal of analysis and criticism. Thus, in the major work on *The Law of Redundancy* (1971), C. Grunfeld speaks of the " predominant purpose " and " primary aim " as being to mitigate or reduce the resistance of workers to industrial reorganisation and the redeployment of labour. He says the " paramount policy of the Act " is to enable British management to achieve what he calls the " principal end " of facilitating labour mobility. While others, *e.g.* K. W. Wedderburn (*The Worker and the Law* (1971)) regards the rationale of the Act as still shrouded in mystery, he is clear that redundancy reflects a management idea—*i.e.* " superfluity " of workers. And the law's identification with management's interests is comprehensively analysed in R. H. Fryer's lengthy critique in *Redundancy and Paternalist Capitalism* (1973), App. II.

Myths of the Redundancy Payments Act. An extract from Fryer's excellent critique is to be found in (1973) 2 I.L.J. 1, where he considers what are said to be the six myths of the 1965 Act: " namely, that the legislation provides an element of employment security; that it gives some sort of job ' property rights ' to workers; that by regulating redundancy, it restricts managerial discretion; that it compensates workers for their loss of job; that redundancy payments act as a disincentive to find alternative work; and that, irrespective of other advantages or disadvantages, it at least affords minimum cover to all who lose their job because of redundancy."

In contrast to these myths, Fryer argues that the legislation has become a positive inducement to insecurity of work by encouraging some trade union officers and workers to abandon protective attitudes to job security. As to a regulatory effect on management, the result of the Act has been to tend to take redundancy out of both conflict and the area of collective action and control by workers. The argument as to " property rights " in the job is shown not to be an appropriate analogy (and see Grunfeld who says that: " To say that a person's work should be regarded as being as good as property rights is to imply that it is no better "). As to the Act's compensating workers made redundant, any assessment must adopt criteria for adequacy; and given the minimal nature of the vast majority of compensatory payments, it must be said that the Act is little short of a deliberate deception. Figures produced by Fryer add to this picture by showing how, on the most optimistic assessment, only one-third of those dismissed in 1971 by reason of redundancy received *statutory* payments. In fact, it may have been 25 per cent. or less. Of those who did get payments, the low levels (averaging £292 in 1971, though by reason of inflation this had risen to an average of £524 in 1975 and £619 in 1977) could hardly support a view that they had a disincentive effect on workers seeking employment.

Management power and economic policy. Whatever the intended policy of the 1965 Act, there seems to be considerable evidence that its economic policy has failed. A study entitled *Effects of the Redundancy Payments Act* by S. R. Parker *et al.* (Office of Population Censuses and Surveys (O.P.C.S.), HMSO 1971) concluded that most redundancies were the consequence of economic causes, not the mobility which would lead to the desired organisational and technological changes. Another study, *The Impact of Employment Protection Laws,* by W. W. Daniel and E. Stilgoe (1978) found similarly that in a survey of about 300 employers, over 60 per cent. of redundancies were due to deficient demand for the employer's product. The result was that older marginal workers got sacked and, as a recent analysis put it: " for many older workers the mobility the Redundancy Payments Act facilitated was mobility out of the active labour force " (*Department of Employment Gazette,* September 1978, p. 1033). Of course, this effect has different significance for different groups. Thus recently a company devised a scheme providing insurance cover for management executives made redundant. For an annual premium, the policyholder gets a steady income during redundancy while looking for another job. Ordinary workers need rely on unemployment benefit.

Fryer brings out fully how the Act reinforced the primacy of business considerations and the secondary nature of the question of employment security. The protection of management's power has, therefore, been the guiding light of the courts in interpreting the Act. This was most recently reiterated by Lord Denning in *Lesney Products & Co. Ltd.* v. *Nolan* [1977] I.R.L.R. 77 (C.A.): " it is important that nothing should be done to impair the ability of employers to re-organise their work force and their times and conditions of work so as to improve efficiency. They may re-organise it so as to reduce overtime and thus to save themselves money, but that does not give the man a right to redundancy payment." The main effect of the Redundancy Payments Act was to make it easier for employers to sack workers as redundant. So in the O.P.C.S. study referred to above, 63 per cent. of managers who thought that the Act made the discharge of employees easier referred to the easing of conscience. Judges seem to be rather less conscience-stricken.

Collective agreements. Despite the encouragement of government departments (the Ministry of Labour published extensive surveys of redundancy information, advice and practice in 1961 and 1963), there does not seem to have been any major development in collective bargaining over redundancies. In the survey of the effects of the Act by the O.P.C.S. in 1971, only 15 per cent. of all establishments surveyed had " an agreement or understanding with trade unions about redundancy " (but K. W. Wedderburn (1971) cites a B.I.M. survey in 1969 which found that many companies had " policies " (usually last-in-first-out) and that one-half had schemes or agreements whereby payments exceeded the amounts payable under the Act— though half paid nothing to workers who left after " warning " and before formal notice). And while 58 per cent. of trade union officers surveyed felt that the 1965 Act had made no difference to employers' willingness to sign redundancy agreements, three-quarters thought that the Act had helped management to get workers to accept manpower changes. Indeed, this may explain the practice of employers, many of whom voluntarily pay one and a half times or twice what is required by the Act.

The next step in redundancy promotion was the provisions of what is now s. 59 (*b*), introduced first by the Industrial Relations Act 1971, s. 24 (5) (*b*) (see Note to s. 59). This was accompanied by a Code of Practice, paras. 44–46 of which laid down certain points of guidance beginning with: "Responsibility for deciding the size of the work force rests with management. But before taking the final decision to make any substantial reduction, management should consult employees or their representatives, unless exceptional circumstances make this impossible." These suggestions have been given statutory backing by the Employment Protection Act 1975, s. 99, which makes consultation mandatory when redundancies are proposed. But although some employers will have established procedures, most trade unions are unwilling to enter into agreements, preferring to emphasise and insist on job security rather than redundancy for their members. It may be noted that it was not until 1972, over six years after the Redundancy Payments Act 1965, that the public employment services were re-organised by government.

The State and redundancy law. The role of the Ministry of Labour, later Department of Employment, in promoting redundancy while failing to deal with the consequential unemployment is not the only way the State has taken an active role prejudicial to workers' interests. Many of the disputes that have arisen before industrial tribunals have arrived due to the active intervention of the Department anxious to prevent a redundancy payment being made. The Department's responsibility for the Redundancy Fund has led it countless times to intervene, contrary to the wishes of both employer and employee, and prevent any redundancy payment. Intervention to ensure that payment is made is not deemed to be an activity worthy of the Department's resources. See, *e.g. North-East Coast Shiprepairers Ltd.* v. *Secretary of State for Employment* [1978] I.R.L.R. 149 (E.A.T.).

Right to redundancy payment

General provisions as to right to redundancy payment

81.—(1) Where an employee who has been continuously employed for the requisite period—

    (*a*) is dismissed by his employer by reason of redundancy, or

    (*b*) is laid off or kept on short-time to the extent specified in subsection (1) of section 88 and complies with the requirements of that section,

then, subject to the following provisions of this Act, the employer shall be liable to pay to him a sum (in this Act referred to as a " redundancy payment ") calculated in accordance with Schedules 4, 13 and 14.

(2) For the purposes of this Act an employee who is dismissed shall be taken to be dismissed by reason of redundancy if the dismissal is attributable wholly or mainly to—

    (*a*) the fact that his employer has ceased, or intends to cease, to carry on the business for the purposes of which the employee was employed by him, or has ceased, or intends to cease, to carry on that business in the place where the employee was so employed, or

    (*b*) the fact that the requirements of that business for employees to carry out work of a particular kind, or for employees to carry out work of a particular kind in the place where he was so employed, have ceased or diminished or are expected to cease or diminish.

For the purposes of this subsection, the business of the employer together with the business or businesses of his associated employers shall be treated as one unless either of the conditions specified in this sub-section would be satisfied without so treating those businesses.

(3) In subsection (2), " cease " means cease either permanently or temporarily and from whatsoever cause, and " diminish " has a corresponding meaning.

(4) For the purposes of subsection (1), the requisite period is the period of two years ending with the relevant date, excluding any week which began before the employee attained the age of eighteen.

DERIVATION

1965, ss. 1, 48 (3), 25 (3), 8 (1) ; 1975, Sched. 16, Pt. I, paras. 1, 5 (1), 18.

GENERAL NOTE

Subs. (1)

The requisite period is two years—subs. (4).

For classes of employment excluded from the right to a redundancy payment, see ss. 82 (1), 99, 100 (2), 144 (2), 145 (3) and 146 (1).

The Department of Employment reported Redundancy Fund transactions during 1977 affecting 267,234 employees. Payments totalling £165,438,000 were made (an average payment of £619). Construction and the distribution trades were the two groups which recorded the highest numbers of redundancies. These figures should not be confused with the total numbers of actual redundancies, estimated to be between three-quarters and one million people annually. So at best only one of three or four employees made redundant receives any redundancy payment under statute.

Subs. (2)

Cessation of the business. Temporary cessation is enough to amount to redundancy (subs. (3)). Problems have arisen where employees are off sick when the business closes down. In *Scarr* v. *Goodyear & Sons Ltd.* [1975] I.R.L.R. 166, the industrial tribunal held the employee's contract had been frustrated during his absence—so though the business had ceased before he could return, he lost his entitlement as he had not been dismissed. In *Whitworth* v. *Bilabbey Ltd.* [1975] I.R.L.R. 206, an employee not informed while absent through illness about the business temporarily closing was held not dismissed when the business resumed. This although both temporary cessation and an intention to cease—if they lead to dismissal—are redundancy dismissals within the definition of this subsection.

Place of employment. For problems concerned with the question of whether the business has ceased or diminished in the place of employment—see Note to s. 1 (3) (*Title of the job*), which deals with problems of an employee's contractual obligation to change his place of work, and his right to refuse to do so.

Requirements of the business: re-organisations—redundancy v. *efficiency.* C. Grunfeld (*The Law of Redundancy* (1971), pp. 82 *et seq.*) lists and analyses a large number of categories of cases where re-organisations or changes in work of one kind or another have been held to lead to redundancies, or not so held. There seems in recent years to have been an attempt periodically by Lord Denning in the Court of Appeal to impose a general rule as to when re-organisation of the business or changes in work leading to dismissals are or are not to amount to redundancies. The criterion he puts forward is efficiency—a management view. These attempts are followed by rearguard actions led by Phillips J. insisting on the need to decide each case on its facts.

Thus, in *Johnson* v. *Nottingham Combined Police Authority* [1974] I.R.L.R. 20 (C.A.), where the change in hours of work to an alternating shift system was rejected by the employees, Lord Denning held that: " It does not automatically give rise to a right to redundancy payments. If the employer proves that it was a reorganisation so as to achieve more efficient working, a man is not entitled to redundancy payments." But in *Kykot* v. *Smith Hartley Ltd.* [1975] I.R.L.R. 372 (Q.B.D.), Phillips J. avoided that principle by holding that on the facts—the abolition of a whole night shift and a falling off of trade—there was a redundancy. He expressly overruled the industrial tribunal's reliance on *Johnson* and said: " In truth, all these cases of redundancy claims ultimately raise questions of fact and the decided cases are only of value in enunciating the principles."

In *Lesney Products & Co. Ltd.* v. *Nolan* [1977] I.R.L.R. 77 (C.A.), however, Lord Denning reaffirmed this principle in *Johnson* where there had been an abolition of an entire shift and a falling off of sales. Again, the principle was that: " an employer is entitled to reorganise his business so as to improve his efficiency "— which might not amount to a redundancy situation even where it meant changes for the employees. But again in *Robinson* v. *British Island Airways Ltd.* [1977] I.R.L.R. 477 (E.A.T.), Phillips J. was emphatic that a reorganisation could lead to redundancy. He did not resort to efficiency as the criterion. But insisted that: " What has to be done in every case is to analyse the facts and to match the analysis against the words of [s. 81] " .

This controversy over the validity of " efficiency " as allowing the employer to avoid redundancy payments is a basic illustration of some judges subscribing to conventional managerial definitions. For the reduction of a work force without reducing the work done can be described as efficiency only from the point of view of management—for productivity increases. So it is efficient for them. For the remaining workers—who have more work to do, and for those out of work—to describe the dismissals as efficient would be illogical. To further deny them redundancy payments on the grounds of this " efficiency " is to add insult to injury. But it is managerial logic these judges adopt.

Subs. (4)

Continuity of employment is determined in accordance with Sched. 13, and for the purposes of a redundancy claim, a person's employment is presumed to have been continuous, unless the contrary is shown (s. 151). The relevant date is defined in s. 90 (1)—but see s. 90 (3) where the employer fails to give the requisite minimum period of notice under s. 49 (1).

Collective agreements may allow for redundancy payments for shorter term employees, *e.g.* that between NUBE and Lloyd's and Scottish Finance allows for *ex gratia* payments of one week's pay if they have less than one year's service; two weeks if one to two years' service. The agreement between the Gas Conversion Association and the GMWU (effective February 1, 1976) covers workers with less than the two years' service required for the statutory payment, and provides for additional supplements up to a maximum of £315.

General exclusions from right to redundancy payment

82.—(1) An employee shall not be entitled to a redundancy payment if immediately before the relevant date the employee—

(a) if a man, has attained the age of sixty-five, or

(b) if a woman, has attained the age of sixty.

(2) Except as provided by section 92, an employee shall not be entitled to a redundancy payment by reason of dismissal where his employer, being entitled to terminate his contract of employment without notice by reason of the employee's conduct, terminates it either—

(a) without notice, or

(b) by giving shorter notice than that which, in the absence of such conduct, the employer would be required to give to terminate the contract, or

(c) by giving notice (not being such shorter notice as is mentioned in paragraph (b)) which includes, or is accompanied by, a statement in writing that the employer would, by reason of the employee's conduct, be entitled to terminate the contract without notice.

(3) If an employer makes an employee an offer (whether in writing or not) before the ending of his employment under the previous contract to renew his contract of employment, or to re-engage him under a new contract of employment, so that the renewal or re-engagement would take effect either immediately on the ending of his employment under the previous contract or after an interval of not more than four weeks thereafter, the provisions of subsections (5) and (6) shall have effect.

(4) For the purposes of the application of subsection (3) to a contract under which the employment ends on a Friday, Saturday or Sunday—

(a) the renewal or re-engagement shall be treated as taking effect

immediately on the ending of the employment under the previous
contract if it takes effect on or before the next Monday after that
Friday, Saturday or Sunday; and

(b) the interval of four weeks shall be calculated as if the employment
had ended on that Monday.

(5) If an employer makes an employee such an offer as is referred to
in subsection (3) and either—

(a) the provisions of the contract as renewed, or of the new contract,
as to the capacity and place in which he would be employed, and
as to the other terms and conditions of his employment, would
not differ from the corresponding provisions of the previous
contract; or

(b) the first-mentioned provisions would differ (wholly or in part)
from those corresponding provisions, but the offer constitutes an
offer of suitable employment in relation to the employee;

and in either case the employee unreasonably refuses that offer, he shall
not be entitled to a redundancy payment by reason of his dismissal.

(6) If an employee's contract of employment is renewed, or he is
re-engaged under a new contract of employment, in pursuance of such
an offer as is referred to in subsection (3), and the provisions of the
contract as renewed, or of the new contract, as to the capacity and place
in which he is employed, and as to the other terms and conditions of his
employment, differ (wholly or in part) from the corresponding provisions
of the previous contract but the employment is suitable in relation to
the employee, and during the trial period referred to in section 84 the
employee unreasonably terminates the contract, or unreasonably gives
notice to terminate it and the contract is thereafter, in consequence,
terminated, he shall not be entitled to a redundancy payment by reason
of his dismissal from employment under the previous contract.

(7) Any reference in this section to re-engagement by the employer
shall be construed as including a reference to re-engagement by the
employer or by any associated employer, and any reference in this section
to an offer made by the employer shall be construed as including a
reference to an offer made by an associated employer.

DERIVATION

1965, ss. 2, 48 (1) ; 1975, Sched. 11, Pt. I, para. 18.

GENERAL NOTE

Subs. (1)

All talk of the law's intentions as regards alleviating hardship or compensating
workers for loss of their jobs or providing some "property rights" in the job
ceases when the stipulated age is reached. Rather, since mobility is no longer in
question, the market value of the labour commodity is zero. The pill need no
longer be gilded.

Subs. (2)

Misconduct and redundancy. The difficulties of interpretation offered by this
subsection have been remarked upon by most commentators and were emphasised by
Phillips J. in *Simmons* v. *Hoover Ltd.* [1976] I.R.L.R. 266 (E.A.T.), who nonetheless
offered certain statements "with a fair amount of confidence":

" (1) s. 2 (2) operates only by way of exclusion and, accordingly, has no effect
in the case of an applicant who is not prima facie entitled to a redundancy
payment, *e.g.* where, although there is a redundancy situation, his dismissal
is not attributable wholly or mainly to redundancy but to some other cause,
such as misconduct;

(2) the requirements of (*a*), (*b*) and (*c*) of subs. (2) are presumably designed
to ensure that the employee is put on notice that he is being dismissed
otherwise than in the ordinary course of the contract;

(3) a failure to serve such a notice under (*a*), (*b*) or (*c*) prevents the employer from relying on s. 2 (2).''

Phillips J. went on to consider whether the subsection could apply where there had been one dismissal as well as where there had been two—*i.e.* a case of dismissal for redundancy followed by a dismissal for misconduct, and also a case of a single dismissal for redundancy and not explicitly for misconduct—which also satisfies the conditions of this subsection—albeit by accident. He concluded that in his judgment it applied both to the case of a single and a double dismissal.

In addition to these statements, counsel, at the E.A.T.'s request, prepared a Schedule setting out examples of the principal cases in which s. 2 might apply with the consequences that might follow. Note further s. 92 (3) which confirms the discretion enabling judges to award the whole or part of the redundancy payment.

Misconduct and strikes. The question of whether strike action will fall within this subsection as entitling the employer to dismiss (assuming it was not saved by s. 92 (1)) was considered at length in *Simmons*. By a majority (dissent by Mr. A. C. Blyghton, Legal Officer of the TGWU), the E.A.T. held that it did. The dissenting member argued powerfully that the " conduct " referred to here could not cover a strike situation *alone*—there was needed some act in addition to a strike.

The problems, therefore, tend to be greatest where questions of redundancy payments arise during or in connection with a strike—see s. 92. Phillips J. in *Simmons* concluded his judgment by advocating a clarification of the rules concerning the dismissal of strikers in a redundancy situation, as this was preferable to a restatement of the common law of obligations under a contract of employment. It is submitted that the policy underlying redundancy payments is different from that of the common law regulating the employment relationship and the relationship needs general clarification not confined only to cases of strikes and redundancy.

Subss. (3) *to* (7)

Offer of re-engagement or renewal of employment. Unlike the law prior to the amendments introduced in the Employment Protection Act 1975 (Sched. 16, Pt. I, para. 2), the offer of renewal of employment or re-engagement need not be in writing. Since the obvious and desirable purpose of the former requirement was to ensure that employees were adequately informed and given the opportunity to study the terms of their continued employment, it is not easy to justify this omission. The new provision for a trial period (s. 84) affects only an employee who has decided to accept the offer. He will still have to make the critical decision —both in terms of his future employment and of his entitlement to a redundancy payment—as to whether or not to accept the offer. The lack of written confirmation of the details may hinder him in doing so.

It is clear, however, that writing was only the formal part of the requirements placed on the employer with regard to his offer of employment. The substance of the obligation remains to ensure that the employee is given sufficient detail to enable him to make a reasonable judgment about his future employment. If the employer fails to fulfil this obligation, and the employee in consequence decided to refuse the offer, he will not be denied the redundancy payment because such a refusal is later held to be unreasonable. The employer will not have complied with the provisions of subs. (3), and the employee will be held to have been dismissed for redundancy. See *Havenhand* v. *Thos. Black Ltd.* [1968] I.T.R. 271 (D.C.), adopted in *Ramseyer Motors Ltd.* v. *Bradshaw* [1972] I.T.R. 3 (D.C.): " The object of requiring an offer in writing specifying at least those particulars of the terms of the new employment which will differ from the old, is clearly to give the employee who has been dismissed from his old employment an opportunity to consider in documentary form the terms of the new employment being offered which differ from the terms on which he has hitherto been employed, so that he may make a considered choice between accepting that employment or having to look for another job and claiming a redundancy payment with the risk involved in the latter choice that his claim will fail if he has unreasonably refused a suitable offer." The risk is no different, and in the absence of the requirement of documentary form—one would hope the courts will be even more strict in ensuring the employee faced with oral offers is given adequate opportunity to consider it before making his decision.

Unilateral changes v. *offers.* It has been suggested that these provisions coupled with those instituting the trial period (s. 84) could be exploited by employers in practice to introduce unilateral changes into the contract of employment (see Industrial Relations Legal Information Bulletin, No. 50, October 15, 1975). Such action by employers would be extremely unwise because, *inter alia*, of the legal consequences. For a unilateral change of terms is a breach of contract, and it is clear law that, if minor, the employee may claim damages, and if serious, he may treat the contract as repudiated. Even where the employee continued to work, the employer could not escape a claim for breach of contract unless the employee was shown to have " accepted " the breach (the rules of contract law on matters of fundamental breach are rather fluid). In any case, the employer could not erect the façade of an " offer " (unwritten) and a " trial period " of four weeks to show that there had been acceptance of a breach of contract (unilateral change of terms of employment). To do so he would have to establish (i) a redundancy situation affecting the employee; (ii) an offer satisfying the requirements described above; (iii) an acceptance of the offer (equivalent to the acceptance of the breach); and (iv) a conscious and conscientious trial period. It would be extremely difficult for the employer to construct all this out of implications from behaviour alone, particularly behaviour ignorant of the provisions of this legislation. (Even if it was done successfully, certain complications would inevitably result: *e.g.* s. 84 (6) would apply so that a subsequent termination within the " trial period " would relate back to the original change in employment, and the reasons for that would havé to be established.) Certainly, the mere assertion by an employer that, by virtue of these provisions an employee was deemed to accept a fundamental breach of contract after four weeks of his continuing employment would be dismissed out of hand.

Taking up the offer. Under the pre-1975 law (Redundancy Payments Act, s. 2 (3) (*b*)), a renewal or re-engagement on the same terms of employment had to be continuous with the old contract of employment. Under the new provisions (subs. (3)), as with employment on different terms, so also that on the same terms need only be taken up within four weeks of the ending of the old contract. (And see s. 84 (1)).

Suitable alternative employment—reasonable refusal. Factors which might lead to a conclusion that the new employment offered was unsuitable or the refusal of an employee reasonable are: changes in pay, in travelling time, in skill or status, etc. For an attempt to categorise the cases, see Grunfeld, *The Law of Redundancy* (1971), Chap. 5.

But the facts are determining, *e.g.* in *Dutton* v. *Hawker Siddeley Aviation Ltd.* [1978] I.R.L.R. 390 (E.A.T.), which concerned the refusal to accept a temporary transfer from a machinist's position to work as a capstan setter operator; having held an unreasonable refusal of suitable alternative employment, Phillips J. said: " Great care has to be exercised before it can be said that an employee who is skilled and with a particular trade can be required to move to some other in a case where his contract does not provide for it. But what in our judgment makes this case distinct and special is that this was a temporary arrangement, part and parcel of a system which was for the benefit of everybody concerned, arrived at after negotiation, to which everybody but he consented, which as we have said, was purely temporary, and which if he did not like it he could leave and return to his previous employment, where, if there was work for him he would get it, or, if not, he would be declared redundant."

Redundancy schemes may define in some detail where alternative work is considered suitable. One example is that introduced at National Carriers Ltd. (NCL), effective May 2, 1977:

" Factors which may be taken into account in determining what constitutes an offer of suitable alternative work in relation to the employee concerned are the skills of the employee, the nature of his previous work, earnings in his new job compared with his previous earnings and, where the new job is in a different place the difficulties which the transfer might cause.

" In determining whether the alternative employment offered is suitable in relation to the employee concerned, he should have regard to the skill, knowledge and experience of the grade in which the employee was previously employed, but consideration should also be given to the practicability of training the employee for work in other grades. The age of the employee will also be taken into account as will the hours of work compared with those in the employee's present post. Where it is evident that an employee's promotional prospects will be affected by the proposed offer, this will be regarded as a good reason for the employee to decline the alternative job offered to him.

" The comparative level of remuneration attached to the new post offered for a normal week's work (*i.e.* excluding overtime and Sunday duty) will be a relevant factor. If the earnings attached to the alternative post offered, calculated in accordance with the provisions of the Redundancy Payments Act are materially below those of the employee's present post, an employee may, with good reason, decline the offer.

" The alternative work offered should be within reasonable distance of the employee's place of residence, having regard to the availability of transport and hours of work.

" For the purpose of determining what constitutes an offer of suitable alternative work:

(a) the post must be one which would not involve an increase in the employee's present daily travelling time by an average of more than half an hour in each direction by train or public road transport provided that the total daily travelling time between the employee's home and his new place of work does not average more than an hour and a quarter in each direction.

(b) in cases where an employee already incurs travelling time in excess of an average of an hour and a quarter in each direction, a reasonable offer would be one which would not involve him in any travelling in excess of that already incurred; and

(c) special consideration will be given to cases falling under (b) above where it can be shown that, whilst additional travelling to that already incurred is not involved, difficulties in travelling will be experienced, *e.g.* an employee working in an urban area with a direct train service who is transferred to a rural area with indirect transport services.

" Travelling time for this purpose will include:
—waiting time en route arising from making train or bus connections.
—waiting time for first train or bus service following completion of turn of duty."

Other collective agreements will provide special protection for employees taking up alternative work, *e.g.* retention of previous basic rates, or subsidised travel.

Dismissal by employer

83.—(1) In this Part, except as respects a case to which section 86 applies, " dismiss " and " dismissal " shall, subject to sections 84, 85 and 93, be construed in accordance with subsection (2).

(2) An employee shall be treated as dismissed by his employer if, but only if,—

(a) the contract under which he is employed by the employer is terminated by the employer, whether it is so terminated by notice or without notice, or

(b) where under that contract he is employed for a fixed term, that term expires without being renewed under the same contract, or

(c) the employee terminates that contract with or without notice, in circumstances (not falling within section 92 (4)) such that he is entitled to terminate it without notice by reason of the employer's conduct.

DERIVATION
1965, s. 3 (1), (2) ; 1975, Sched. 16, Pt. I, para. 3.

GENERAL NOTE
Subs. (2)
This is substantially identical to the definition of dismissal for the purposes of unfair dismissal—s. 55 (2), and see the Note to that subsection.
Voluntary redundancy. The section perceives redundancy in terms exclusively of dismissal by the employer—but the dismissal may be considerably softened where the employees concerned volunteer for redundancy. The Code of Practice

itself stipulates that should redundancy become necessary, management should "consider introducing schemes for voluntary redundancy," etc. (para. 46 (ii)). And many collective agreements similarly prescribe that certain steps be taken prior to dismissals being effected—including calling for volunteers, often as the final step of a selection procedure.

Advance warning. Where the employers give advance warning of impending redundancy, and as a consequence employees leave to find or take up other jobs, the legal position may be characterised as: (1) no dismissals—employee has terminated his own employment; (2) dismissal—the employer's advance warning is tantamount to notice of dismissal (though a specific date or event may need to be stated); (3) dismissal—the employer's action entitles the employee to terminate without notice.

The leading authority of the High Court decision in *Morton Sundour Fabrics Ltd.* v. *Shaw* [1967] I.T.R. 84 adopted the first solution. The second, however, has been upheld by a number of industrial tribunals on particular facts distinguishable from the leading authority. The third, however, is unlikely to be adopted in light of the "contract" test enunciated by the Court of Appeal in *Western Excavating (ECC) Ltd.* v. *Sharp* [1977] I.R.L.R. 25. The shock of redundancy is not appreciated sufficiently by those well-cushioned from the dole queue. (And see the extraordinary provision in s. 92 (4).)

Renewal of contract or re-engagement

84.—(1) If an employee's contract of employment is renewed, or he is re-engaged under a new contract of employment in pursuance of an offer (whether in writing or not) made by his employer before the ending of his employment under the previous contract, and the renewal or re-engagement takes effect either immediately on the ending of that employment or after an interval of not more than four weeks thereafter, then, subject to subsections (3) to (6), the employee shall not be regarded as having been dismissed by his employer by reason of the ending of his employment under the previous contract.

(2) For the purposes of the application of subsection (1) to a contract under which the employment ends on a Friday, Saturday or Sunday—

(*a*) the renewal or re-engagement shall be treated as taking effect immediately on the ending of the employment if it takes effect on or before the Monday after that Friday, Saturday or Sunday, and

(*b*) the interval of four weeks referred to in that subsection shall be calculated as if the employment had ended on that Monday.

(3) If, in a case to which subsection (1) applies, the provisions of the contract as renewed, or of the new contract, as to the capacity and place in which the employee is employed, and as to the other terms and conditions of his employment, differ (wholly or in part) from the corresponding provisions of the previous contract, there shall be a trial period in relation to the contract as renewed, or the new contract (whether or not there has been a previous trial under this section).

(4) The trial period shall begin with the ending of the employee's employment under the previous contract and end with the expiration of the period of four weeks beginning with the date on which the employee starts work under the contract as renewed, or the new contract, or such longer period as may be agreed in accordance with the next following subsection for the purpose of retraining the employee for employment under that contract.

(5) Any such agreement shall—

(*a*) be made between the employer and the employee or his representative before the employee starts work under the contract as renewed or, as the case may be, the new contract;

(*b*) be in writing;

(*c*) specify the date of the end of the trial period; and

(*d*) specify the terms and conditions of employment which will apply in the employee's case after the end of that period.

(6) If during the trial period—

    (*a*) the employee, for whatever reason, terminates the contract, or gives notice to terminate it and the contract is thereafter, in consequence, terminated; or

    (*b*) the employer, for a reason connected with or arising out of the change to the renewed, or new, employment, terminates the contract, or gives notice to terminate it and the contract is thereafter, in consequence, terminated,

then, unless the employee's contract of employment is again renewed, or he is again re-engaged under a new contract of employment, in circumstances such that subsection (1) again applies, he shall be treated as having been dismissed on the date on which his employment under the previous contract or, if there has been more than one trial period, the original contract ended for the reason for which he was then dismissed or would have been dismissed had the offer (or original offer) of renewed, or new, employment not been made, or, as the case may be, for the reason which resulted in that offer being made.

(7) Any reference in this section to re-engagement by the employer shall be construed as including a reference to re-engagement by the employer or by any associated employer, and any reference in this section to an offer made by the employer shall be construed as including a reference to an offer made by an associated employer.

DERIVATION
    1965, ss. 3 (3) to (8), 48 (1) ; 1975, Sched. 16, Pt. I, paras. 3, 18.

GENERAL NOTE
    Length and extension of trial period. The trial period comes into effect automatically upon employment on new terms as to capacity and place and other terms and conditions and lasts for a period of four weeks. It may, however, be lengthened for purposes of retraining by agreement with the employee or his representative—which should encourage collective bargaining on this score. The period of trial in practice available to an employee may last longer due to collectively agreed provisions. Thus, *e.g.* an agreement between APEX and the Decca Group provides that: " An employee who is transferred to alternative employment and who later wishes to leave for any reason, must do so within a period of six months and must be able to show reasonable cause as to why he/she found the alternative employment unsuitable." The statutory trial period may be capable of further extension, as indicated by Phillips J. in *Air Canada* v. *Lee* [1978] I.R.L.R. 392 (E.A.T.), where the duration of the trial period is not specified by the employer. Where there is no effort by the employer to terminate the contract, where the only dismissal is when the employee makes up her mind—albeit well in excess of the four-week period—that she does not accept the new employment—then the employee is treated as dismissed for redundancy. Not that the trial period can last forever. But if the employers do not make inquiries as to what the employee is going to do, the employee may extend the period to a reasonable length before announcing her decision.

    Termination during trial period. Many complications arise where the employment is terminated during the trial period. Thus, although an employee can terminate the trial period " for whatever reason " and will be held to have been dismissed as of the date his original contract ended and for the reason that it ended (*i.e.* redundancy), nonetheless, if he terminates the trial period unreasonably, he loses his redundancy payment (s. 82 (6)). He is, however, carefully protected from any loss of rights during his trial period. If the employer terminates the contract for whatever reason, the termination is treated as if on the date of the ending of the original contract and for the reason it was then ended. So, *e.g.* if the employee is dismissed for misconduct during the trial period, he may still be treated as redundant. This is obviously so as not to prejudice his redundancy rights during the trial period, otherwise he might stand to lose them during what need to be only a temporary deferment of a redundancy situation.

Interestingly, however, although the employee is treated as if dismissed for redundancy (or the original reason) whatever the reason for his termination during the trial period, this is only for the purposes of Pt. VI of this Act. Thus, if he is *unfairly dismissed* during the trial period, he might not be precluded from a claim on that score. Otherwise an employer would derive protection for unfair acts from a provision designed only to protect the employee's eligibility for a redundancy payment. The employee's entitlement to awards for both redundancy and unfair dismissal, however, is tempered by the provisions of s. 73 (9).

Finally, although the trial period is only for four weeks, the new contract of which it is the testing period may itself provide for a period of notice, and consequently, the employee will be entitled to this period of notice even if it entails employment during a period following the four-week period.

The effect of s. 90 (1) (*d*) is that the relevant date for the purposes of a claim for a redundancy payment (see the provisions of s. 101) is the date of the actual dismissal, but for any other purposes, is the date of the original dismissal for redundancy. Why there should be such a distinction is not explained.

Employee anticipating expiry of employer's notice

85.—(1) The provisions of this section shall have effect where—
- (*a*) an employer gives notice to an employee to terminate his contract of employment, and
- (*b*) at a time within the obligatory period of that notice, the employee gives notice in writing to the employer to terminate the contract of employment on a date earlier than the date on which the employer's notice is due to expire.

(2) Subject to the following provisions of this section, in the circumstances specified in subsection (1) the employee shall, for the purposes of this Part, be taken to be dismissed by his employer.

(3) If, before the employer's notice is due to expire, the employer gives him notice in writing—
- (*a*) requiring him to withdraw his notice terminating the contract of employment as mentioned in subsection (1) (*b*) and to continue in the employment until the date on which the employer's notice expires, and
- (*b*) stating that, unless he does so, the employer will contest any liability to pay to him a redundancy payment in respect of the termination of his contract of employment,

but the employee does not comply with the requirements of that notice, the employee shall not be entitled to a redundancy payment by virtue of subsection (2) except as provided by subsection (4).

(4) Where, in the circumstances specified in subsection (1), the employer has given notice to the employee under subsection (3), and on a reference to a tribunal it appears to the tribunal, having regard both to the reasons for which the employee seeks to leave the employment and those for which the employer requires him to continue in it, to be just and equitable that the employee should receive the whole or part of any redundancy payment to which he would have been entitled apart from subsection (3), the tribunal may determine that the employer shall be liable to pay to the employee—
- (*a*) the whole of the redundancy payment to which the employee would have been so entitled, or
- (*b*) such part of that redundancy payment as the tribunal thinks fit.

(5) In this section—
- (*a*) if the actual period of the employer's notice (that is to say, the period beginning at the time when the notice is given and ending at the time when it expires) is equal to the minimum period which (whether by virtue of any enactment or otherwise) is required to be given by the employer to terminate

the contract of employment, " the obligatory period ", in relation to that notice, means the actual period of the notice;

(b) in any other case, " the obligatory period ", in relation to an employer's notice, means that period which, being equal to the minimum period referred to in paragraph (a), expires at the time when the employer's notice expires.

DERIVATION
1965, s. 4.

GENERAL NOTE
A trap. One trap which may operate to deny the employee his payment arises where he gives his counter-notice (note—in writing) outside the obligatory period of notice, as defined in subs. (5). This trap was eliminated by the Employment Protection Act 1975, as it affected the law of unfair dismissal—see s. 55 (3). Its existence here is anomalous, but dangerous.

Collective agreements. Collective agreements have improved, hardly a difficult task, on these provisions. Thus, a recent agreement between Shaw Savill and Albion (part of the Furness Withy Group) and ASTMS provides that an employee should be given about three months', and not less than two months' notice before the date on which the work requirement ceases (the "redundancy date"). Employees are entitled to a period of protected employment dating from the redundancy date calculated on the basis of age—but the employee may terminate his employment at any time after the redundancy date on giving one week's notice in writing.

Another agreement, reached on September 16, 1976, between the London Co-operative Society and USDAW and the TGWU provides that management will agree to workers leaving their jobs early without loss of any redundancy pay, but excluding payment for unexpired notice, subject to satisfying the employer that they have starting dates for other employment. NUBE reached an agreement, ratified on December 6, 1977, with Lloyd's and Scottish Finance that allowed that the employee might request early release in writing and if the company did not object, then the right to redundancy was not affected.

Employees leaving early. The problem remains of the legal difficulties of employees who upon advance warning of a redundancy situation leave their employment to find other work. The case of *Morton Sundour Fabrics Ltd.* v. *Shaw* [1967] I.T.R. 84 is authority for the proposition that employees leaving in such circumstances are not dismissed—see the Note to s. 83 (2).

Failure to permit woman to return to work after confinement treated as dismissal

86. Where an employee is entitled to return to work and has exercised her right to return in accordance with section 47 but is not permitted to return to work, then she shall be treated for the purposes of the provisions of this Part as if she had been employed until the notified day of return, and, if she would not otherwise be so treated, as having been continuously employed until that day, and as if she had been dismissed with effect from that day for the reason for which she was not permitted to return.

DERIVATION
1975, s. 50 (1).

GENERAL NOTE
See generally ss. 33, 45–48 (especially s. 45 (3) and (4)), and the Notes to those sections. *Cf.* s. 56, which is substantially similar, and the Note to it.

Lay-off and short-time

87.—(1) Where an employee is employed under a contract on such terms and conditions that his remuneration thereunder depends on his being provided by the employer with work of the kind which he is employed to do, he shall, for the purposes of this Part, be taken to be laid off for any week in respect of which, by reason that the employer does not provide such work for him, he is not entitled to any remuneration under the contract.

(2) Where by reason of a diminution in the work provided for an employee by his employer (being work of a kind which under his contract the employee is employed to do) the employee's remuneration for any week is less than half a week's pay, he shall for the purposes of this Part be taken to be kept on short-time for that week.

DERIVATION
   1965, s. 5 (1), (2) ; 1975, Sched. 16, Pt. I, para. 4.

GENERAL NOTE
   The operation of these provisions may be affected by the proposals contained in the consultative document issued by the Department of Employment in early 1978: " Compensation for Short-Time Working." This proposes a permanent scheme whereby employees put on short-time should be paid a proportion of their normal gross pay, the employers to be reimbursed in part by a new Short-Time Working Fund financed by contributions from employers and the Exchequer. In addition, a temporary arrangement is proposed under which employers would be fully reimbursed where the Department of Employment was satisfied that the short-time working was introduced instead of redundancy, and there were good prospects of returning to full-time work. The document suggested that 75 per cent. of normal gross pay be paid to workers, and it is thought that about 420,000 workers would be thus helped, of whom 390,000 would be workers whose employers would be entitled to a full refund. If enacted, these provisions would further complicate the position with regard to guarantee payments and unemployment benefit (see the Note to s. 15 (1)).

Subs. (1)
   Lay-off or dismissal? It is clear that unless the employer has the right under the contract of employment to lay-off an employee without dismissing him, any such unilateral suspension by the employer without the employee's consent would be a repudiation of the contract and hence a dismissal. The employee could then claim either 'unfair dismissal or a redundancy payment. See, *e.g. Jewell* v. *Neptune Concrete Ltd.* [1975] I.R.L.R. 147.
   Contractual guarantee payments. The inter-action with *contractual* guarantee payment provisions needs be noted. It was held by the N.I.R.C. in *Powell Duffryn Wagon Co. Ltd.* v. *House* [1974] I.T.R. 46 that as long as the workers were entitled to be paid their fall-back rate, they could not be laid off within the meaning of this subsection because they would still be entitled to a payment. The distinction was drawn between lay-off in common industrial language and lay-off as defined in the Act. But Sir John Donaldson did agree that if the right to a guaranteed wage was temporarily suspended (*i.e.* contractual variation as opposed to waiver by the employee), the result would be that there was no entitlement. The conclusion that follows is that this would be a statutory lay-off—and this view was adopted by the industrial tribunal in *Hulse* v. *Harry Perry* [1975] I.R.L.R. 181.
   Time workers and piece-workers. The industrial tribunal in *Hulse* also took the view that the N.I.R.C. had thus held that the statute applied to time workers as well as piece workers (despite the dicta of Parker L.C.J. in *Hanson* v. *Wood* (*Abingdon Process Engravers*) [1968] I.T.R. 46 (D.C.).

Subs. (2)
   Again, the implications of guaranteed wage agreements might be to preclude employees utilising this provision if the employee is guaranteed at least half a week's pay (see the agreements cited in the Notes to ss. 12 *et seq.*). A week's pay is calculated in accordance with Sched. 14, Pt. II.

Right to redundancy payment by reason of lay-off or short-time

88.—(1) An employee shall not be entitled to a redundancy payment by reason of being laid off or kept on short-time unless he gives notice in writing to his employer indicating (in whatsoever terms) his intention to claim a redundancy payment in respect of lay-off or short-time (in this Act referred to as a " notice of intention to claim ") and, before the service of that notice, either—

    (a) he has been laid off or kept on short-time for four or more consecutive weeks of which the last before the service of the notice ended on the date of service thereof or ended not more than four weeks before that date, or

    (b) he has been laid off or kept on short-time for a series of six or more weeks (of which not more than three were consecutive) within a period of thirteen weeks, where the last week of the series before the service of the notice ended on the date of service thereof or ended not more than four weeks before that date.

  (2) Where an employee has given notice of intention to claim,—

    (a) he shall not be entitled to a redundancy payment in pursuance of that notice unless he terminates his contract of employment by a week's notice which (whether given before or after or at the same time as the notice of intention to claim) is given before the end of the period allowed for the purposes of this paragraph (as specified in subsection (5) of section 89), and

    (b) he shall not be entitled to a redundancy payment in pursuance of the notice of intention to claim if he is dismissed by his employer (but without prejudice to any right to a redundancy payment by reason of the dismissal):

Provided that, if the employee is required by his contract of employment to give more than a week's notice to terminate the contract, the reference in paragraph (a) to a week's notice shall be construed as a reference to the minimum notice which he is so required to give.

  (3) Subject to subsection (4), an employee shall not be entitled to a redundancy payment in pursuance of a notice of intention to claim if, on the date of service of that notice, it was reasonably to be expected that the employee (if he continued to be employed by the same employer) would, not later than four weeks after that date, enter upon a period of employment of not less than thirteen weeks during which he would not be laid off or kept on short-time for any week.

  (4) Subsection (3) shall not apply unless, within seven days after the service of the notice of intention to claim, the employer gives to the employee notice in writing that he will contest any liability to pay to him a redundancy payment in pursuance of the notice of intention 'o claim.

DERIVATION
    1965, s. 6 (1), (3) to (5).

GENERAL NOTE
Subs. (3)
    For a recent illustration of where the employer failed to satisfy the tribunal (a) that it was reasonably to be expected that employment would be available within four weeks of the employee's notice, and (b) that it would last for not less than 13 weeks—see *Hulse* v. *Harry Perry* [1975] I.R.L.R. 181.
    And see the conclusive presumption in s. 89 (1).

Supplementary provisions relating to redundancy payments in respect of lay-off or short-time

  89.—(1) If, in a case where, an employee gives notice of intention to claim and the employer gives notice under section 88 (4) (in this section referred to as a " counter-notice "), the employee continues or has continued, during the next four weeks after the date of service of the notice of intention to claim, to be employed by the same employer, and he is or has been laid off or kept on short-time for each of those weeks, it shall be conclusively presumed that the condition specified in subsection (3) of section 88 was not fulfilled.

(2) For the purposes of both subsection (1) of section 88 and sub-section (1) of this section, it is immaterial whether a series of weeks (whether it is four weeks, or four or more weeks, or six or more weeks) consists wholly of weeks for which the employee is laid off or wholly of weeks for which he is kept on short-time or partly of the one and partly of the other.

(3) For the purposes mentioned in subsection (2), no account shall be taken of any week for which an employee is laid off or kept on short-time where the lay-off or short-time is wholly or mainly attributable to a strike or a lock-out (within the meaning of paragraph 24 of Schedule 13) whether the strike or lock-out is in the trade or industry in which the employee is employed or not and whether it is in Great Britain or elsewhere.

(4) Where the employer gives a counter-notice within seven days after the service of a notice of intention to claim, and does not withdraw the counter-notice by a subsequent notice in writing, the employee shall not be entitled to a redundancy payment in pursuance of the notice of intention to claim except in accordance with a decision of an industrial tribunal.

(5) The period allowed for the purposes of subsection (2) (*a*) of section 88 is as follows, that is to say,—

(*a*) if the employer does not give a counter-notice within seven days after the service of the notice of intention to claim, that period is three weeks after the end of those seven days;

(*b*) if the employer gives a counter-notice within those seven days, but withdraws it by a subsequent notice in writing, that period is three weeks after the service of the notice of withdrawal;

(*c*) if the employer gives a counter-notice within those seven days and does not so withdraw it, and a question as to the right of the employee to a redundancy payment in pursuance of the notice of intention to claim is referred to a tribunal, that period is three weeks after the tribunal has notified to the employee its decision on that reference.

(6) For the purposes of paragraph (*c*) of subsection (5) no account shall be taken of any appeal against the decision of the tribunal, or of any requirement to the tribunal to state a case for the opinion of the High Court or the Court of Session, or of any proceedings or decision in consequence of such an appeal or requirement.

DERIVATION
  1965, s. 7.

The relevant date

90.—(1) Subject to the following provisions of this section, for the purposes of the provisions of this Act so far as they relate to redundancy payments, " the relevant date ", in relation to the dismissal of an employee—

(*a*) where his contract of employment is terminated by notice, whether given by his employer or by the employee, means the date on which that notice expires;

(*b*) where his contract of employment is terminated without notice, means the date on which the termination takes effect;

(*c*) where he is employed under a contract for a fixed term and that term expires as mentioned in subsection (2) (*b*) of section 83, means the date on which that term expires;

(*d*) where he is treated, by virtue of subsection (6) of section 84, as having been dismissed on the termination of his employment under a previous contract, means—

(i) for the purposes of section 101, the date which is the relevant date as defined by paragraph (*a*), (*b*) or (*c*) in relation to the renewed, or new, contract, or, where there has been more than one trial period under section 84, the last such contract; and

(ii) for the purposes of any other provision, the date which is the relevant date as defined by paragraph (*a*), (*b*) or (*c*) in relation to the previous contract, or, where there has been more than one trial period under section 84, the original contract; and

(*e*) where he is taken to be dismissed by virtue of section 85 (2), means the date on which the employee's notice to terminate his contract of employment expires.

(2) " The relevant date ", in relation to a notice of intention to claim or a right to a redundancy payment in pursuance of such a notice,—

(*a*) in a case falling within paragraph (*a*) of subsection (1) of section 88, means the date on which the last of the four or more consecutive weeks before the service of the notice came to an end, and

(*b*) in a case falling within paragraph (*b*) of that subsection means the date on which the last of the series of six or more weeks before the service of the notice came to an end.

(3) Where the notice required to be given by an employer to terminate a contract of employment by section 49 (1) would, if duly given when notice of termination was given by the employer, or (where no notice was given) when the contract of employment was terminated by the employer, expire on a date later than the relevant date as defined by subsection (1), then for the purposes of section 81 (4) and paragraph 1 of Schedule 4 and paragraph 8 (4) of Schedule 14, that later date shall be treated as the relevant date in relation to the dismissal.

DERIVATION

1965, ss. 3 (9), 4 (2), 6 (2), (3), (10) ; 1975, Sched. 16, Pt. I, para. 3.

Reference of questions to tribunal

91.—(1) Any question arising under this Part as to the right of an employee to a redundancy payment, or as to the amount of a redundancy payment, shall be referred to and determined by an industrial tribunal.

(2) For the purposes of any such reference, an employee who has been dismissed by his employer shall, unless the contrary is proved, be presumed to have been so dismissed by reason of redundancy.

(3) In relation to lay-off or short-time, the questions which may be referred to and determined by an industrial tribunal, as mentioned in subsection (1), shall include any question whether an employee will become entitled to a redundancy payment if he is not dismissed by his employer and he terminates his contract of employment as mentioned in subsection (2) (*a*) of section 88; and any such question shall for the purposes of this Part be taken to be a question as to the right of the employee to a redundancy payment.

DERIVATION

1965, s. 9 (1), (2) (*b*), (3).

GENERAL NOTE
Subs. (1)

In the first quarter of 1978, applications to industrial tribunals totalled 9,689 in England and Wales and 1,291 in Scotland, of which 7 per cent. dealt with redundancy payments and a further 4 per cent. with both unfair dismissal and redundancy payments (80 per cent. dealt with unfair dismissal). The figures from previous years tend to be about the same, ranging from 7–9 per cent. of the total number of applications (in 1977 there were a total of 41,995 applications). But this should be seen in contrast to the numbers of employees to whom payments are made (those in respect of whom rebates were paid to employers were: in 1975—340,215; in 1974—182,161; in 1973—176,919; in 1972—297,120, and in 1971—370,306).

Subs. (2)

The presumption comes to the aid of the employee: (1) where no evidence is offered as to the reason for dismissal; (2) where there is an even balance of evidence for and against a finding of redundancy, the balance is resolved in favour of the employee; and (3) where the redundancy is only a contributory factor, the employee will succeed since the employer must prove that the dismissal is attributable " wholly or mainly " to redundancy (s. 81 (2)).

Special provisions as to termination of contract in cases of misconduct or industrial dispute

92.—(1) Where at any such time as is mentioned in subsection (2), an employee who—

(a) has been given notice by his employer to terminate his contract of employment, or

(b) has given notice to his employer under subsection (1) of section 88,

takes part in a strike, in such circumstances that the employer is entitled, by reason of his taking part in the strike, to treat the contract of employment as terminable without notice, and the employer for that reason terminates the contract as mentioned in subsection (2) of section 82, that subsection shall not apply to that termination of the contract.

(2) The times referred to in subsection (1) are—

(a) in a case falling within paragraph (a) of that subsection any time within the obligatory period of the employer's notice (as defined by section 85 (5)), and

(b) in a case falling within paragraph (b) of subsection (1), any time after the service of the notice mentioned in that paragraph.

(3) Where at any such time as is mentioned in subsection (2) an employee's contract of employment, otherwise than by reason of his taking part in a strike, is terminated by his employer in the circumstances specified in subsection (2) of section 82, and is so terminated as mentioned therein, and on a reference to an industrial tribunal it appears to the tribunal, in the circumstances of the case, to be just and equitable that the employee should receive the whole or part of any redundancy payment to which he would have been entitled apart from section 82 (2), the tribunal may determine that the employer shall be liable to pay to the employee—

(a) the whole of the redundancy payment to which the employee would have been so entitled, or

(b) such part of that redundancy payment as the tribunal thinks fit.

(4) Where an employee terminates his contract of employment without notice, being entitled to do so by reason of a lock-out by his employer, section 83 (2) (c) shall not apply to that termination of the contract.

(5) In this section " strike " and " lock-out " each has the meaning given by paragraph 24 of Schedule 13.

DERIVATION
    1965, ss. 10, 56 (1).

GENERAL NOTE
Subs. (1)
    The operation of this subsection in conjunction with s. 82 (2) was the subject of detailed consideration in *Simmons* v. *Hoover Ltd.* [1976] I.R.L.R. 266 (E.A.T.). It deals, said Phillips J., with the man who has been dismissed (in circumstances such that he is entitled to a redundancy payment) who later goes on strike. The argument that it also applied to the case of a man who is dismissed for redundancy when already on strike was rejected. There must be two dismissals: an earlier one for redundancy followed by a dismissal for striking.
    The E.A.T. by a majority, held that at common law an employer was entitled to dismiss summarily an employee who refused to do any work which he was engaged to do—and that this included a strike. They noted that the intention of this provision was " to neutralise the effect of a strike or lock-out upon the right of an employee to receive a redundancy payment, in some cases. So it might be thought that it was not intended that the action of employees in going on strike was to be caught by [s. 82 (2)]. Accordingly, we have wondered whether such action fell within the words ' employee's conduct.' On reflection, however, in the view of the majority any doubt is set at rest by the terms of [s. 92 (1)]. This subsection deals with the case of a man prima facie entitled to a redundancy payment who subsequently goes on strike, and is dismissed by his employer for that reason ' as mentioned in subs. (2) of [s. 82].' It is provided that in these circumstances that subsection is not to apply to his dismissal. In other words, the effect of [s. 92 (1)] in those circumstances is to save the employee from the exclusion imposed by [s. 82 (2)]." See for further comment the Note to s. 82 (2).

Subs. (3)
    Again, in *Simmons* v. *Hoover Ltd.* [1976] I.R.L.R. 266 (E.A.T.) it was held that this subsection also required there to be two dismissals, *i.e.* an earlier one followed by a dismissal for misconduct during the currency of the notice of termination.

Implied or constructive termination of contract
    93.—(1) Where in accordance with any enactment or rule of law—
        (*a*) any act on the part of an employer, or
        (*b*) any event affecting an employer (including, in the case of an individual, his death),
operates so as to terminate a contract under which an employee is employed by him, that act or event shall for the purposes of this Part be treated as a termination of the contract by the employer, if apart from this subsection it would not constitute a termination of the contract by him and, in particular, the provisions of sections 83, 84 and 90 shall apply accordingly.
    (2) Where subsection (1) applies, and the employee's contract of employment is not renewed, and he is not re-engaged under a new contract of employment, so as to be treated, by virtue of section 84 (1), as not having been dismissed, he shall, without prejudice to section 84 (6), be taken for the purposes of this Part to be dismissed by reason of redundancy if the circumstances in which his contract is not so renewed and he is not so re-engaged are wholly or mainly attributable to one or other of the facts specified in paragraphs (*a*) and (*b*) of section 81 (2).
    (3) For the purposes of subsection (2), section 81 (2) (*a*), in so far as it relates to the employer ceasing or intending to cease to carry on the business, shall be construed as if the reference to the employer included a reference to any person to whom, in consequence of the act or event in question, power to dispose of the business has passed.
    (4) In this section, any reference to section 84 (1) includes a reference to that subsection as applied by section 94 (2) or as so applied and (where appropriate) modified by section 95 (2), and where section 84 (1)

applies as so modified the references in subsection (2) of this section to renewal of or re-engagement under a contract of employment shall be construed as including references to renewal of or re-engagement in employment otherwise than under a contract of employment.

DERIVATION

1965, s. 22; 1975, Sched. 16, Pt. I, para. 10.

GENERAL NOTE

Subs. (1)

Grunfeld (pp. 49–55) gives details of the three principal situations covered by this provision: death of the employer (and see the additional provisions in Sched. 12, Pt. III), the dissolution of a partnership and the receivership or winding up of a company. Where the employer is insolvent, the employee may apply to the Secretary of State for payment—s. 106.

In circumstances of, *e.g.* long-term illness, there is the possibility in law that an employee who seeks to return to work may be refused his job on the grounds of redundancy, but it is argued that he is not dismissed but rather the contract is terminated by " frustration." Since there is here required an act on the part of the employer ((*a*))—employees might be in difficulty. But see the tests of " frustration " laid down by the N.I.R.C. in *Marshall* v. *Harland & Wolff* [1972] I.R.L.R. 90, and industrial tribunals have held that employees " absent from illness for lengthy periods are dismissed " (see, *e.g.* *Maxwell* v. *Walter Howard Designs Ltd.* [1975] I.R.L.R. 77).

Change of ownership of business

94.—(1) The provisions of this section shall have effect where—

(*a*) a change occurs (whether by virtue of a sale or other disposition or by operation of law) in the ownership of a business for the purposes of which a person is employed, or of a part of such a business, and

(*b*) in connection with that change the person by whom the employee is employed immediately before the change occurs (in this section referred to as " the previous owner ") terminates the employee's contract of employment, whether by notice or without notice.

(2) If, by agreement with the employee, the person who immediately after the change occurs is the owner of the business, or of the part of the business in question, as the case may be (in this section referred to as " the new owner "), renews the employee's contract of employment (with the substitution of the new owner for the previous owner) or re-engages him under a new contract of employment, sections 84 and 90 shall have effect as if the renewal or re-engagement had been a renewal or re-engagement by the previous owner (without any substitution of the new owner for the previous owner).

(3) If the new owner offers to renew the employee's contract of employment (with the substitution of the new owner for the previous owner) or to re-engage him under a new contract of employment, subsections (3) to (6) of section 82 shall have effect, subject to subsection (4), in relation to that offer as they would have had effect in relation to the like offer made by the previous owner.

(4) For the purposes of the operation, in accordance with subsection (3), of subsections (3) to (6) of section 82 in relation to an offer made by the new owner—

(*a*) the offer shall not be treated as one whereby the provisions of the contract as renewed, or of the new contract, as the case may be, would differ from the corresponding provisions of the contract as in force immediately before the dismissal by reason only that the new owner would be substituted for the previous owner as the employer, and

(b) no account shall be taken of that substitution in determining whether the refusal of the offer was unreasonable or, as the case may be, whether the employee acted reasonably in terminating the renewed, or new, employment during the trial period referred to in section 84.

(5) The preceding provisions of this section shall have effect (subject to the necessary modifications) in relation to a case where—

(a) the person by whom a business, or part of a business, is owned immediately before a change is one of the persons by whom (whether as partners, trustees or otherwise) it is owned immediately after the change, or

(b) the persons by whom a business, or part of a business, is owned immediately before a change (whether as partners, trustees or otherwise) include the person by whom, or include one or more of the persons by whom, it is owned immediately after the change,

as those provisions have effect where the previous owner and the new owner are wholly different persons.

(6) Sections 82 (7) and 84 (7) shall not apply in any case to which this section applies.

(7) Nothing in this section shall be construed as requiring any variation of a contract of employment by agreement between the parties to be treated as constituting a termination of the contract.

DERIVATION
1965, ss. 13, 48 (2) ; 1975, Sched. 16, Pt. I, paras. 7, 18.

GENERAL NOTE
For a definition of " business," see s. 153 (1). And *cf.* the provisions of Sched. 13, para. 17.

The definition of " business " in s. 153 (1) does not suffice to guide claimants as to whether the business has been transferred so as to disentitle them to a redundancy payment. Grunfeld (pp. 180 *et seq.*) gives detailed guidance on how the courts and tribunals have dealt with this problem.

An increasingly common difficulty arises where there is a substantial transfer of assets and it is disputed that in law a " business " has been transferred. In *Woodhouse* v. *Peter Brotherhood Ltd.* [1972] 3 W.L.R. 215, the Court of Appeal, reversing the N.I.R.C., held that if the new owner does not take over the business as a going concern but only takes over the physical assets using them in a *different* business, then the employee is entitled to a redundancy payment from the outgoing owner (*per* Lord Denning M.R.). This was applied in *Crompton* v. *Truly Fair (International) Ltd.* [1975] I.R.L.R. 250 (Q.B.D.), so that a sale of the lease of a factory was held to be a transfer of physical assets, not the transfer of a business. But in *Hector Powe Ltd.* v. *Melon* [1978] I.R.L.R. 258 (E.A.T.), Lord McDonald distinguished *Woodhouse*, saying, *inter alia*, that on the facts before him there was no material difference between the type of work carried on immediately before and immediately after the transfer—so the workers were not entitled to claim. The fate of workers wishing to safeguard or claim their redundancy rights falls to be decided on such questions of " law."

Transfer to Crown employment

95.—(1) Section 94 shall apply to a transfer of functions from a person not acting on behalf of the Crown (in this section referred to as the transferor) to a government department or any other officer or body exercising functions on behalf of the Crown (in this section referred to as the transferee) as that section applies to a transfer of a business, but with the substitution for references to the previous owner and new owner of references to the transferor and transferee respectively.

(2) In so far as the renewal or re-engagement of the employee by the transferee is in employment otherwise than under a contract of employment—

    (*a*) references in section 94 (and in sections 82 (4) to (6), 84 and 90 as they apply by virtue of that section) to a contract of employment or to the terms of such a contract shall be construed as references to employment otherwise than under such a contract and to the terms of such employment; and

    (*b*) references in subsection (4) of section 94, as modified by subsection (1) of this section, to the substitution of the transferee for the transferor shall be construed as references to the substitution of employment by the transferee otherwise than under a contract of employment for employment by the transferor under such a contract.

DERIVATION

    1965, s. 13A; 1975, s. 120 (2).

Exemption orders

96.—(1) If at any time there is in force an agreement between one or more employers or organisations of employers and one or more trade unions representing employees, whereby employees to whom the agreement applies have a right in certain circumstances to payments on the termination of their contracts of employment, and, on the application of all the parties to the agreement, the Secretary of State, having regard to the provisions of the agreement, is satisfied that section 81 should not apply to those employees, he may make an order under this section in respect of that agreement.

(2) The Secretary of State shall not make an order under this section in respect of an agreement unless the agreement indicates (in whatsoever terms) the willingness of the parties to it to submit to an industrial tribunal such questions as are mentioned in paragraph (*b*) of subsection (3).

(3) Where an order under this section is in force in respect of an agreement—

    (*a*) section 81 shall not have effect in relation to any employee who immediately before the relevant date is an employee to whom the agreement applies, but

    (*b*) section 91 shall have effect in relation to any question arising under the agreement as to the right of an employee to a payment on the termination of his employment, or as to the amount of such a payment, as if the payment were a redundancy payment and the question arose under this Part.

(4) Any order under this section may be revoked by a subsequent order thereunder, whether in pursuance of an application made by all or any of the parties to the agreement in question or without any such application.

DERIVATION

    1965, s. 11.

GENERAL NOTE

Subs. (1)

    So far only two agreements have been the subject of an order by the Secretary of State—see S.I. 1969 No. 207 (the Centrax Group); and S.I. 1970 No. 354 (electricity supply). S. 140 (2) (*f*) protects the provisions of the agreements so concluded from being void should any of their provisions conflict with those of the Act.

Claims as to extension of terms and conditions

97.—(1) A claim under paragraph 1 of Schedule 11 to the Employment Protection Act 1975 (claims as to recognised terms and conditions and general level of terms and conditions) may be reported to the Advisory, Conciliation and Arbitration Service in accordance with that Schedule, and may be referred by the Service to the Central Arbitration Committee, and the Committee may make an award under that Schedule, notwithstanding that the terms and conditions which it is claimed that the employer is not observing consist of or include terms and conditions as to payments to be made to employees in the circumstances specified in paragraph (*a*) or paragraph (*b*) of section 81(1) or in similar circumstances, and that provision for redundancy payments is made by this Act.

(2) Where a claim which is reported to the Advisory, Conciliation and Arbitration Service under the said paragraph 1 is founded upon recognised terms and conditions and relates to an agreement in respect of which an order under section 96 is for the time being in force, and the Central Arbitration Committee makes an award in pursuance of that claim, section 96 (3) shall have effect in relation to all persons in respect of whom the employer is required by that award to observe the recognised terms and conditions, whether they are persons to whom section 96 (3) would apply apart from this subsection or not.

DERIVATION

    1965, s. 12; 1975, Sched. 16, Pt. I, para. 6.

GENERAL NOTE

Subs. (1)

    The potential of Sched. 11 to the Employment Protection Act 1975 is again illustrated here. Redundancy agreements between employers and workers can be extended or their benefits spread to cover other workers. So, *e.g.* the Agreement between the Gas Conversion Association and the GMWU which improves redundancy payments above the statutory minimum could be extended by a Sched. 11 claim for recognised terms to all workers in the industry. Or the agreement between Hector Powe Tailoring and Pierre Cardin and USDAW increasing the statutory limits by 40 per cent. might be extended using the " general level " claim under Sched. 11 to other workers in retail tailoring establishments.

    An interesting point arises from agreements or terms extended which include any provisions which make payments conditional or otherwise exclude or limit the benefits allowed. According to s. 140 (1), such provisions are void (unless the agreement concerned is one referred to by subs. (2)). So a composite right could emerge from a Sched. 11 claim of the more favourable aspects of the agreement or terms extended, and those of the Act.

Exclusion or reduction of redundancy payment on account of pension rights

98.—(1) The Secretary of State shall by regulations make provision for excluding the right to a redundancy payment, or reducing the amount of any redundancy payment, in such cases as may be prescribed by the regulations, being cases in which an employee has (whether by virtue of any statutory provision or otherwise) a right or claim (whether legally enforceable or not) to a periodical payment or lump sum by way of pension, gratuity or superannuation allowance which is to be paid by reference to his employment by a particular employer and is to be paid, or to begin to be paid, at the time when he leaves that employment or within such period thereafter as may be prescribed by the regulations.

(2) Provision shall be made by any such regulations for securing that the right to a redundancy payment shall not be excluded, and that the amount of a redundancy payment shall not be reduced, by reason of any right or claim to a periodical payment or lump sum, in so far as

that payment or lump sum represents such compensation as is mentioned in section 118 (1) and is payable under a statutory provision, whether made or passed before, on or after the passing of this Act.

(3) In relation to any case where, under section 85 or 92 or 110, an industrial tribunal determines that an employer is liable to pay part (but not the whole) of a redundancy payment, any reference in this section to a redundancy payment, or to the amount of a redundancy payment, shall be construed as a reference to that part of the redundancy payment, or to the amount of that part, as the case may be.

DERIVATION
1965, s. 14.

GENERAL NOTE
Subs. (1)
See the Redundancy Payments Pensions Regulations 1965 (S.I. 1965 No. 1932).

Public offices, etc.

99.—(1) Without prejudice to any exemption or immunity of the Crown, section 81 shall not apply to any person in respect of any employment which—

(a) is employment in a public office for the purposes of section 38 of the Superannuation Act 1965, or

(b) whether by virtue of that Act or otherwise, is treated for the purposes of pensions and other superannuation benefits as service in the civil service of the State, or

(c) is employment by any such body as is specified in Schedule 5.

(2) Without prejudice to any exemption or immunity of the Crown, section 81 shall not apply to any person in respect of his employment in any capacity under the Government of an overseas territory (as defined by section 114).

DERIVATION
1965, s. 16 (4), (5); Superannuation Act 1972 (c. 11), Sched. 6, para. 54.

Domestic servants

100.—(1) For the purposes of the application of the provisions of this Part to an employee who is employed as a domestic servant in a private household, those provisions (except section 94) shall apply as if the household were a business and the maintenance of the household were the carrying on of that business by the employer.

(2) Without prejudice to section 146 (1), section 81 shall not apply to any person in respect of employment as a domestic servant in a private household, where the employer is the father, mother, grandfather, grandmother, stepfather, stepmother, son, daughter, grandson, granddaughter, stepson, stepdaughter, brother, sister, half-brother, or half-sister of the employee.

DERIVATION
1965, s. 19.

Claims for redundancy payments

101.—(1) Notwithstanding anything in the preceding provisions of this Part, an employee shall not be entitled to a redundancy payment unless, before the end of the period of six months beginning with the relevant date—

(a) the payment has been agreed and paid, or

(b) the employee has made a claim for the payment by notice in writing given to the employer, or

(c) a question as to the right of the employee to the payment, or as to the amount of the payment, has been referred to an industrial tribunal, or

(d) a complaint relating to his dismissal has been presented by the employee under section 67.

(2) An employee shall not by virtue of subsection (1) lose his right to a redundancy payment if, during the period of six months immediately following the period mentioned in that subsection, the employee—

(a) makes such a claim as is referred to in paragraph (b) of that subsection,

(b) refers to a tribunal such a question as is referred to in paragraph (c) of that subsection, or

(c) makes such a complaint as is referred to in paragraph (d) of that subsection,

and it appears to the tribunal to be just and equitable that the employee should receive a redundancy payment having regard to the reason shown by the employee for his failure to take any such step as is referred to in paragraph (a), (b) or (c) of this subsection within the period mentioned in subsection (1), and to all the other relevant circumstances.

DERIVATION

1965, s. 21; 1975, Sched. 16, Pt. I, para. 9.

GENERAL NOTE

Subs. (1)

After the relevant date. The "relevant date" is defined in s. 90. So compliance with (a) to (d) before the relevant date is premature and was not allowed in *Watts* v. *Rubery Owen Conveyancer Ltd.* [1977] I.R.L.R. 112 (E.A.T.).

Claims of right v. *claims as to amount.* This subsection was characterised by Phillips J. in *The Bentley Engineering Co. Ltd.* v. *Crown and Miller* [1976] I.R.L.R. 146 (Q.B.D.), who noted that: "it is not like the ordinary limitation provision which merely bars the remedy; the effect is to extinguish the remedy." He interpreted (a) as referring to a claim as to a right to a payment, and thus not affecting a claim as to the *amount* of a payment. So where the claimant established (a)—that there had been agreed a payment, albeit not the payment being claimed some two years after the dismissal—the latter claim as to amount could not be barred by the subsection.

Claim by notice in writing. It may be noted that once a claim has been made in accordance with (b)—to the employer—there is no requirement anywhere that the subsequent complaint to the industrial tribunal must follow within any particular period of time. This was confirmed by Phillips J. in *Price* v. *Smithfield & Zwanenberg Group Ltd.* [1978] I.R.L.R. 80 (E.A.T.). He said that the test of whether (b) had been complied with required one to look at the circumstances, which could allow for the incorporation of some earlier oral conversation—though this approach had dangers. So a letter "without prejudice," and stating that payment was sought only if the matter was not voluntarily settled still satisfied the requirements of (b).

Subs. (2)

This was added by the Employment Protection Act 1975, Sched. 16, Pt. I, para. 9, and allows the industrial tribunal to exercise its discretion within a six-month period *following* the initial six-month period. *Cf.* the discretion granted by s. 67 (2).

Written particulars of redundancy payment

102.—(1) On making any redundancy payment, otherwise than in pursuance of a decision of a tribunal which specifies the amount of the payment to be made, the employer shall give to the employee a written statement indicating how the amount of the payment has been calculated.

(2) Any employer who without reasonable excuse fails to comply with subsection (1) shall be guilty of an offence and liable on summary conviction to a fine not exceeding £20.

(3) If an employer fails to comply with the requirements of sub-section (1), then (without prejudice to any proceedings for an offence under subsection (2)) the employee may by notice in writing to the employer require him to give to the employee a written statement complying with those requirements within such period (not being less than one week beginning with the day on which the notice is given) as may be specified in the notice; and if the employer without reasonable excuse fails to comply with the notice he shall be guilty of an offence under this subsection and liable on summary conviction—

(a) if it is his first conviction of an offence under this subsection, to a fine not exceeding £20, or

(b) in any other case, to a fine not exceeding £100.

DERIVATION
  1965, s. 18.

Redundancy Fund

Establishment and maintenance of fund

103.—(1) The Secretary of State shall continue to have the control and management of the Redundancy Fund established under section 26 of the Redundancy Payments Act 1965 (in this Part referred to as " the fund "), and payments shall be made out of the fund in accordance with the provisions of sections 104 to 109 and 156 and Part VII.

(2) The Secretary of State shall prepare accounts of the fund in such form as the Treasury may direct, and shall send them to the Comptroller and Auditor General not later than the end of the month of November following the end of the financial year to which the accounts relate; and the Comptroller and Auditor General shall examine and certify the accounts and shall lay copies thereof, together with his report thereon, before Parliament.

(3) Any moneys forming part of the fund may from time to time be paid over to the National Debt Commissioners and by them invested, in accordance with such directions as may be given by the Treasury, in such manner as may be specified by an order of the Treasury for the time being in force under section 22 (1) of the National Savings Bank Act 1971.

DERIVATION
  1965, s. 26; Social Security Act 1973 (c. 38), Sched. 27, para. 55.

GENERAL NOTE
  The Redundancy Fund is maintained by contributions paid by employers as part of the National Insurance contribution (and see s. 109). The balance of the Fund at February 3, 1978, was + £33·1 m., whereas on December 30, 1977, it was + £28·4 m., on December 26, 1975, + £1·6 m., on December 28, 1973, it was + £9·2 m., on December 28, 1972, − £5·9 m. and on December 27, 1968, − £16·2 m.

Redundancy rebates

104.—(1) Subject to the provisions of this section, the Secretary of State shall make a payment (in this Part referred to as a " redundancy rebate ") out of the fund to any employer who—

(a) is liable under the foregoing provisions of this Part to pay, and has paid, a redundancy payment to an employee, or

(b) under an agreement in respect of which an order is in force under section 96, is liable to make, and has made, a payment to an employee on the termination of his contract of employment, or

(c) by virtue of any award made by the Central Arbitration Committee as mentioned in section 97 (2) in relation to an agreement in respect of which such an order is in force, is liable to make, and has made, a payment to an employee on the termination of his contract of employment.

(2) No redundancy rebate shall be payable by virtue of this section in a case falling within paragraph (b) or paragraph (c) of subsection (1) if the employee's right to the payment referred to in that paragraph arises by virtue of a period of employment (computed in accordance with the provisions of the agreement in question) which is less than one hundred and four weeks.

(3) The Secretary of State may if he thinks fit pay a redundancy rebate to an employer who has paid an employee a redundancy payment in circumstances in which, owing to section 101, the employee had no right to, and the employer had no liability for, the payment, if the Secretary of State is satisfied that it would be just and equitable to do so having regard to all the relevant circumstances.

(4) The amount of any redundancy rebate shall (subject to subsection (7)) be calculated in accordance with Schedule 6.

(5) The Secretary of State shall make provision by regulations as to the making of claims for redundancy rebates; and any such regulations may in particular—

(a) require any claim for a redundancy rebate to be made at or before a time prescribed by the regulations;

(b) in such cases as may be so prescribed, require prior notice that such a claim may arise to be given at or before a time so prescribed, so however that, where the claim would relate to an employer's payment in respect of dismissal, the regulations shall not require the notice to be given more than four weeks before the date on which the termination of the contract of employment takes effect; and

(c) for the purpose of determining the right of any person to, and the amount of, any redundancy rebate, require a person at any time when he makes a claim or gives prior notice as mentioned in paragraph (a) or paragraph (b) to provide such evidence and such other information, and to produce for examination on behalf of the Secretary of State documents in his custody or under his control of such descriptions, as may be determined in accordance with the regulations.

(6) In relation to any case where, under section 85 or 92 or 110, an industrial tribunal determines that an employer is liable to pay part (but not the whole) of a redundancy payment, the reference in subsection (1) (a) to a redundancy payment shall be construed as a reference to that part of the redundancy payment.

(7) If any employer who, in accordance with subsection (1), would be entitled to a redundancy rebate fails to give prior notice as required by any such regulations in accordance with paragraph (b) of subsection (5) and it appears to the Secretary of State that he has so failed without reasonable excuse, the Secretary of State may, subject to section 108, reduce the amount of the rebate by such proportion (not exceeding one-tenth) as appears to the Secretary of State to be appropriate in the circumstances.

(8) Any person who—

(a) in providing any information required by regulations under this section, makes a statement which he knows to be false in a material particular, or recklessly makes a statement which is false in a material particular, or

(b) produces for examination in accordance with any such regulations a document which to his knowledge has been wilfully falsified,

shall be guilty of an offence.

(9) A person guilty of an offence under subsection (8) shall be liable on summary conviction to a fine not exceeding the prescribed sum or to imprisonment for a term not exceeding three months or both, or on conviction on indictment to a fine or to imprisonment for a term not exceeding two years or both.

(10) In subsection (9) above " the prescribed sum " means—

(a) in England and Wales, the prescribed sum within the meaning of section 28 of the Criminal Law Act 1977 (that is to say, £1,000 or another sum fixed by order under section 61 of that Act to take account of changes in the value of money);

(b) in Scotland, the prescribed sum within the meaning of section 289B of the Criminal Procedure (Scotland) Act 1975 (that is to say, £1,000 or another sum fixed by an order made under section 289D of that Act for that purpose).

DERIVATION

1965, s. 30; 1975, Sched. 16, Pt. I, para. 12; Criminal Procedure (Scotland) Act 1975 (c. 21), s. 289B (1); Criminal Law Act 1977 (c. 45), s. 28 (2), Sched. 11, para. 5.

GENERAL NOTE

See also the Redundancy Rebates Act 1977. The amount of rebate currently payable to an employer who has made a redundancy payment is 41 per cent. (Redundancy Payments (Variation of Rebates) Order 1977 (S.I. 1977 No. 1321).

The total cost to the Redundancy Fund of rebates to employers was estimated as the following: 1977–78: £82·1 m.; 1978–79: £75·5 m.; 1979–80: £68·5 m. Of this, a substantial proportion was paid direct to employees under the provisions of s. 106 —see the Note to that section.

Subs. (1)

As to when the employer is liable so as to make the rebate payable, see the Court of Appeal decision in *Secretary of State for Employment* v. *Globe Elastic Thread Co. Ltd.* [1978] I.R.L.R. 417. But see the limitation stated by the E.A.T. in *North East Coast Ship Repairers Ltd.* v. *Secretary of State for Employment* [1978] I.R.L.R. 149.

Subs. (7)

Cf. the provisions of s. 104 of the Employment Protection Act 1975 which provided for similar reductions in rebate where the employer failed to notify proposed redundancies. From March 8, 1976, to March 31, 1977, action was taken to reduce the rebate under s. 104 in 169 cases. The total sum of those reductions was approximately £15,500—an average penalty of £91·70.

Payments out of fund to employers in other cases

105.—(1) The Secretary of State may make payments out of the fund to employers in respect of employees to whom this section applies.

(2) This section applies to employees to whom, by virtue of section 144 (2), 145 or 149, section 81 does not apply.

(3) The Secretary of State may determine the classes of employees to whom this section applies in respect of whom payments are to be made by virtue of this section, and, with the approval of the Treasury, may determine the amounts of the payments which may be so made in respect of any class of such employees.

(4) The payments made to an employer by virtue of this section shall not, in respect of any period, exceed the amount appearing to the Secretary of State to be equal to the amount paid into the fund from the appropriate employment protection allocation (under section 134 of the Social Security Act 1975) from all secondary Class 1 contributions paid by that employer under Part I of that Act.

DERIVATION
  1965, s. 31; Social Security Act 1973, Sched. 27, para. 56; Social Security (Consequential Provisions) Act 1975 (c. 18), Sched. 2, para. 21; 1975, Sched. 16, Pt. I, para. 13; Dock Work Regulation Act 1976 (c. 79), s. 14 (4).

Payments out of fund to employees

106.—(1) Where an employee claims that his employer is liable to pay to him an employer's payment, and either—
  (a) that the employee has taken all reasonable steps (other than legal proceedings) to recover the payment from the employer and that the employer has refused or failed to pay it, or has paid part of it and has refused or failed to pay the balance, or
  (b) that the employer is insolvent and that the whole or part of the payment remains unpaid,
the employee may apply to the Secretary of State for a payment under this section.

(2) If on an application under this section the Secretary of State is satisfied—
  (a) that the employee is entitled to the employer's payment;
  (b) that either of the conditions specified in subsection (1) is fulfilled; and
  (c) that, in a case where the employer's payment is such a payment as is mentioned in paragraph (b) or paragraph (c) of section 104 (1), the employee's right to the payment arises by virtue of a period of employment (computed in accordance with the provisions of the agreement in question) which is not less than one hundred and four weeks,
the Secretary of State shall pay to the employee out of the fund a sum calculated in accordance with Schedule 7, reduced by so much (if any) of the employer's payment as has been paid.

(3) Where the Secretary of State pays a sum to an employee in respect of an employer's payment—
  (a) all rights and remedies of the employee with respect to the employer's payment, or (if the Secretary of State has paid only part of it) all his rights and remedies with respect to that part of the employer's payment, shall be transferred to and vest in the Secretary of State; and
  (b) any decision of an industrial tribunal requiring the employer's payment to be paid to the employee shall have effect as if it required that payment, or, as the case may be, that part of it which the Secretary of State has paid, to be paid to the Secretary of State;
and any moneys recovered by the Secretary of State by virtue of this subsection shall be paid into the fund.

(4) Where the Secretary of State pays a sum under this section in respect of an employer's payment, then (subject to the following provisions of this subsection) section 104 shall apply as if that sum had been paid by the employer to the employee on account of that payment; but if, in a case falling within paragraph (a) of subsection (1), it appears to the Secretary of State that the refusal or failure of the employer to pay

the employer's payment, or part of it, as the case may be, was without reasonable excuse, the Secretary of State may, subject to section 108, withhold any redundancy rebate to which the employer would otherwise be entitled in respect of the employer's payment, or may reduce the amount of any such rebate to such extent as the Secretary of State considers appropriate.

(5) For the purposes of this section an employer shall be taken to be insolvent if—

(a) he has become bankrupt or has made a composition or arrangement with his creditors or a receiving order is made against him;

(b) he has died and an order has been made under section 130 of the Bankruptcy Act 1914 for the administration of his estate according to the law of bankruptcy, or by virtue of an order of the court his estate is being administered in accordance with the rules set out in Part I of Schedule 1 to the Administration of Estates Act 1925; or

(c) where the employer is a company, a winding-up order has been made with respect to it or a resolution for voluntary winding-up has been passed with respect to it, or a receiver or manager of its undertaking has been duly appointed, or possession has been taken, by or on behalf of the holders of any debentures secured by a floating charge, of any property of the company comprised in or subject to the charge.

(6) In the application of this section to Scotland, for paragraphs (a), (b) and (c) of subsection (5) there shall be substituted the following paragraphs:—

(a) an award of sequestration has been made on his estate, or he has executed a trust deed for his creditors or entered into a composition contract;

(b) he has died and a judicial factor appointed under section 163 of the Bankruptcy (Scotland) Act 1913 is required by the provisions of that section to divide his insolvent estate among his creditors; or

(c) where the employer is a company, a winding-up order has been made or a resolution for voluntary winding-up is passed with respect to it or a receiver of its undertaking is duly appointed.

(7) In this section " legal proceedings " does not include any proceedings before an industrial tribunal, but includes any proceedings to enforce a decision or award of an industrial tribunal.

DERIVATION

1965, s. 32; 1975, Sched. 16, Pt. I, paras. 14, 15.

GENERAL NOTE

For a discussion, see Grunfeld, pp. 254 et seq.

The total cost to the Redundancy Fund of payments direct to employees under these provisions where the employer fails to make a payment was estimated as follows (the figures in brackets are the estimated amounts of rebates to employers during the same period): 1977–78: £14·6 m. (£67·5 m.); 1978–79: £14 m. (£61·5 m.); 1979–80: £12·5 m. (£56 m.). Clearly a substantial proportion of the Redundancy Fund (between one-fifth and one-quarter) goes to payments directly to employees.

For details of the calculation of payments to employees out of the Redundancy Fund, see Sched. 7.

Supplementary provisions relating to applications under s. 106

107.—(1) Where an employee makes an application to the Secretary of State under section 106, the Secretary of State may, by notice in writing given to the employer, require the employer to provide the

Secretary of State with such information, and to produce for examination on behalf of the Secretary of State documents in his custody or under his control of such descriptions, as the Secretary of State may reasonably require for the purpose of determining whether the application is well-founded.

(2) If any person on whom a notice is served under this section fails without reasonable excuse to comply with a requirement imposed by the notice, he shall be guilty of an offence and liable on summary conviction to a fine not exceeding £100.

(3) Any person who—

(a) in providing any information required by a notice under this section, makes a statement which he knows to be false in a material particular, or recklessly makes a statement which is false in a material particular, or

(b) produces for examination in accordance with any such notice a document which to his knowledge has been wilfully falsified,

shall be guilty of an offence under this subsection.

(4) A person guilty of an offence under subsection (3) shall be liable on summary conviction to a fine not exceeding the prescribed sum or to imprisonment for a term not exceeding three months or both, or on conviction on indictment to a fine or to imprisonment for a term not exceeding two years or both.

(5) In subsection (4) above " the prescribed sum " means—

(a) in England and Wales, the prescribed sum within the meaning of section 28 of the Criminal Law Act 1977 (that is to say, £1,000 or another sum fixed by order under section 61 of that Act to take account of changes in the value of money);

(b) in Scotland, the prescribed sum within the meaning of section 289B of the Criminal Procedure (Scotland) Act 1975 (that is to say, £1,000 or another sum fixed by an order made under section 289D of that Act for that purpose).

DERIVATION
1965, s. 33; Criminal Procedure (Scotland) Act 1975 (c. 21), s. 289B (1); Criminal Law Act 1977 (c. 45), s. 28 (2), Sched. 11, para. 5.

References and appeals to tribunal relating to payments out of fund

108.—(1) Subsections (2) and (3) shall have effect where—

(a) a claim is made for a redundancy rebate on the grounds that an employer is liable to pay, and has paid, an employer's payment, or prior notice that such a claim may arise is given in accordance with regulations made under section 104 (5) (b), or

(b) an application is made to the Secretary of State for a payment under section 106, where it is claimed that an employer is liable to pay an employer's payment.

(2) Where any such claim or application is made or such prior notice is given, there shall be referred to an industrial tribunal—

(a) any question as to the liability of the employer to pay the employer's payment;

(b) in a case falling within paragraph (a) of subsection (1), any question as to the amount of the rebate payable in accordance with Schedule 6;

(c) in a case falling within paragraph (b) of subsection (1), any question as to the amount of the sum payable in accordance with Schedule 7.

(3) For the purposes of any reference under subsection (2), an

employee who has been dismissed by his employer shall, unless the
contrary is proved, be presumed to have been so dismissed by reason of
redundancy.

(4) Where, in any case to which section 104 (3) applies, the Secretary
of State refuses to pay a redundancy rebate, the employer may appeal
to an industrial tribunal; and if on any such appeal the tribunal is
satisfied that it is just and equitable having regard to all the relevant
circumstances that a redundancy rebate should be paid, the tribunal shall
determine accordingly, and the Secretary of State shall comply with any
such determination of a tribunal.

(5) In any case where the Secretary of State withholds, or reduces
the amount of, a redundancy rebate in pursuance of section 104 (7) or
section 106 (4), the employer may appeal to an industrial tribunal; and
if on any such appeal the tribunal is satisfied—

(a) in a case where the rebate was withheld, that it should be paid
in full, or should be reduced instead of being withheld, or

(b) in a case where the rebate was reduced, that it should not be
reduced, or should be reduced by a smaller or larger proportion
than that which the Secretary of State has applied,

the tribunal shall determine accordingly, and the Secretary of State
shall comply with any such determination.

DERIVATION
1965, s. 34; 1975, Sched. 16, Pt. I, para. 16.

Financial provisions relating to the fund

109.—(1) Subject to the following provisions of this section, the
Treasury may from time to time advance out of the National Loans
Fund to the Secretary of State for the purposes of the fund such sums
as the Secretary of State may request; and any sums advanced to the
Secretary of State under this section shall be paid into the fund.

(2) The aggregate amount outstanding by way of principal in respect
of sums advanced to the Secretary of State under this section shall not
at any time exceed £16 million or such larger sum not exceeding £40
million as the Secretary of State may by order made with the consent
of the Treasury determine.

(3) Any sums advanced to the Secretary of State under this section
shall be repaid by the Secretary of State out of the fund into the
National Loans Fund in such manner and at such times, and with
interest thereon at such rate, as the Treasury may direct.

(4) An order shall not be made under this section unless a draft of
the order has been laid before Parliament and approved by resolution
of each House of Parliament.

DERIVATION
1965, s. 35 (1) (2) (4) (7); National Loans Act 1968 (c. 13), s. 5 (1), Sched. 1;
1975, Sched. 16, Pt. I, para. 17.

Miscellaneous and supplemental

Strike during currency of employer's notice to terminate contract

110.—(1) The provisions of this section shall have effect where, after
an employer has given notice to an employee to terminate his contract of employment (in this section referred to as a " notice of
termination ")—

(a) the employee begins to take part in a strike of employees of the
employer, and

(*b*) the employer serves on him a notice in writing (in this section referred to as a " notice of extension ") requesting him to agree to extend the contract of employment beyond the time of expiry by an additional period comprising as many available days as the number of working days lost by striking (in this section referred to as " the proposed period of extension ").

(2) A notice of extension shall indicate the reasons for which the employer makes the request contained in the notice, and shall state that unless either—

(*a*) the employee complies with the request, or

(*b*) the employer is satisfied that, in consequence of sickness, injury or otherwise, he is unable to comply with it, or that (notwithstanding that he is able to comply with it) in the circumstances it is reasonable for him not to do so,

the employer will contest any liability to pay him a redundancy payment in respect of the dismissal effected by the notice of termination.

(3) For the purposes of this section an employee shall be taken to comply with the request contained in a notice of extension if, but only if, on each available day within the proposed period of extension, he attends at his proper or usual place of work and is ready and willing to work, whether he has signified his agreement to the request in any other way or not.

(4) Where an employee on whom a notice of extension has been served—

(*a*) complies with the request contained in the notice, or

(*b*) does not comply with it, but attends at his proper or usual place of work and is ready and willing to work on one or more (but not all) of the available days within the proposed period of extension,

the notice of termination shall have effect, and shall be deemed at all material times to have had effect, as if the period specified in it had (in a case falling within paragraph (*a*)) been extended beyond the time of expiry by an additional period equal to the proposed period of extension or (in a case falling within paragraph (*b*)) had been extended beyond the time of expiry up to the end of the day (or, if more than one, the last of the days) on which he so attends and is ready and willing to work; and section 50 and Schedule 3 shall apply accordingly as if the period of notice required by section 49 were extended to a corresponding extent.

(5) Subject to subsection (6), if an employee on whom a notice of extension is served in pursuance of subsection (1) does not comply with the request contained in the notice, he shall not be entitled to a redundancy payment by reason of the dismissal effected by the notice of termination, unless the employer agrees to pay such a payment to him notwithstanding that the request has not been complied with.

(6) Where a notice of extension has been served, and on a reference to an industrial tribunal it appears to the tribunal that the employee has not complied with the request contained in the notice and the employer has not agreed to pay a redundancy payment in respect of the dismissal in question, but that the employee was unable to comply with the request, or it was reasonable for him not to comply with it, as mentioned in subsection (2) (*b*) the tribunal may determine that the employer shall be liable to pay to the employee—

(*a*) the whole of any redundancy payment to which the employee would have been entitled apart from subsection (5), or

(*b*) such part of any such redundancy payment as the tribunal thinks fit.

(7) The service of a notice of extension, and any extension, by virtue of subsection (4) of the period specified in a notice of termination,—

(*a*) shall not affect any right either of the employer or of the employee to terminate the contract of employment (whether before, at or after the time of expiry) by a further notice or without notice, and

(*b*) shall not affect the operation of sections 81 to 102 in relation to any such termination of the contract of employment.

(8) In this section any reference to the number of working days lost by striking is a reference to the number of working days in the period beginning with the date of service of the notice of termination and ending with the time of expiry which are days on which the employee in question takes part in a strike of employees of the employer.

(9) In this section, " strike " has the meaning given by paragraph 24 of Schedule 13, " time of expiry ", in relation to a notice of termination, means the time at which the notice would expire apart from this section, " working day ", in relation to an employee, means a day on which, in accordance with his contract of employment, he is normally required to work, " available day ", in relation to an employee, means a working day beginning at or after the time of expiry which is a day on which he is not taking part in a strike of employees of the employer, and " available day within the proposed period of extension " means an available day which begins before the end of that period.

DERIVATION

1965, ss. 40, 56 (1).

GENERAL NOTE

In practice this provision is highly unlikely to be utilised. A strike in the circumstances of a redundancy situation is likely to render relationships incompatible with further employment. The result of an employee failing to comply with this obligation is to deny him his redundancy payment (subs. (5))—*cf.* the refusal of suitable alternative employment, where the employee is at least given the right to a reasonable refusal (s. 82 (5) and (6)).

Payments equivalent to redundancy rebates in respect of civil servants, etc.

111.—(1) The provisions of this section shall have effect with respect to employment of any of the following descriptions, that is to say—

(*a*) any such employment as is mentioned in paragraph (*a*), paragraph (*b*) or paragraph (*c*) of subsection (1) of section 99 whether as originally enacted or as modified by any order under section 149 (1);

(*b*) any employment remunerated out of the revenue of the Duchy of Lancaster or the Duchy of Cornwall;

(*c*) any employment remunerated out of the Queen's Civil List;

(*d*) any employment remunerated out of Her Majesty's Privy Purse.

(2) Where the Secretary of State is satisfied that a payment has been, or will be, made in respect of the termination of any person's employment of any description specified in subsection (1), and that the payment has been, or will be, so made to or in respect of him—

(*a*) in accordance with the Superannuation Act 1965, as that Act continues to have effect by virtue of section 23 (1) of the Superannuation Act 1972,

(*b*) in accordance with any provision of a scheme made under section 1 of the Superannuation Act 1972, or

(*c*) in accordance with any such arrangements as are mentioned in subsection (3),

the Secretary of State shall pay the appropriate sum out of the fund to the appropriate fund or authority.

(3) The arrangements referred to in paragraph (*c*) of subsection (2) are any arrangements made with the approval of the Minister for the Civil Service for securing that payments by way of compensation for loss of any such employment as is mentioned in subsection (1) will be made—

    (*a*) in circumstances which in the opinion of the Minister for the Civil Service correspond (subject to the appropriate modifications) to those in which a right to a redundancy payment would have accrued if section 81 had applied, and

    (*b*) on a scale which in the opinion of the Minister for the Civil Service, taking into account any sums which are payable as mentioned in subsection (2) (*a*) or (*b*) to or in respect of the person losing the employment in question, corresponds (subject to the appropriate modifications) to that on which a redundancy payment would have been payable if section 81 had applied.

(4) For the purposes of subsection (2) the appropriate sum is the sum appearing to the Secretary of State to be equal to the amount of the redundancy rebate which would have been payable under section 104 if such a right as is mentioned in paragraph (*a*) of subsection (3) had accrued, and such a redundancy payment as is mentioned in paragraph (*b*) of subsection (3) had been payable and had been paid.

(5) Any accounts prepared by the Secretary of State under section 103 (2) shall show as a separate item the aggregate amount of sums paid under subsection (2) during the period to which the accounts relate.

(6) In this section " the appropriate fund or authority "—

    (*a*) in relation to employment of any description falling within paragraph 7 of subsection (1) of section 39 of the Superannuation Act 1965 (whether as originally enacted or as modified by any order under that section), means the fund out of which, or the body out of whose revenues, the employment is remunerated;

    (*b*) in relation to any employment remunerated out of the revenues of the Duchy of Lancaster, means the Chancellor of the Duchy, and, in relation to any employment remunerated out of the revenues of the Duchy of Cornwall, means such person as the Duke of Cornwall, or the possessor for the time being of the Duchy of Cornwall, appoints;

    (*c*) in relation to any employment remunerated out of the Queen's Civil List or out of Her Majesty's Privy Purse, means the Civil List or the Privy Purse, as the case may be; and

    (*d*) in any other case, means the Consolidated Fund.

DERIVATION

    1965, s. 41; Superannuation Act 1972 (c. 11), Sched. 6, para. 55; Minister for the Civil Service Order 1968 (S.I. 1968 No. 1656).

References to tribunal relating to equivalent payments

    112.—(1) This section applies to any such payment as is mentioned in subsection (3) of section 111 which is payable in accordance with any such arrangements as are mentioned in that subsection.

    (2) Where the terms and conditions (whether constituting a contract of employment or not) on which any person is employed in any such employment as is mentioned in subsection (1) of section 111 include provision—

    (*a*) for the making of any payment to which this section applies, and

    (*b*) for referring to a tribunal any such question as is mentioned in the following provisions of this subsection, any question as to the right of any person to such a payment in respect of that employment, or as to the amount of such a payment shall be referred to and determined by an industrial tribunal.

DERIVATION

1965, s. 42.

Employment under Government of overseas territory

113.—(1) Where the Secretary of State is satisfied that, in accordance with any such arrangements as are mentioned in subsection (3), a payment has been, or will be, made in respect of the termination of a person's employment in any capacity under the Government of an overseas territory (in this section referred to as " the relevant Government "), and that in respect of the whole or part of the period during which that person was in that employment, employer's contributions were paid in respect of him, the Secretary of State shall pay the appropriate sum out of the fund to such other fund or authority as may be designated in that behalf by the relevant Government.

(2) The reference in subsection (1) to employer's contributions is a reference to secondary Class 1 contributions paid in respect of the person in question by persons who were in relation to him secondary Class 1 contributors by virtue of section 4 (4) (*a*) of the Social Security Act 1975, and in relation to any period before 6th April 1975, to employer's contributions within the meaning of the National Insurance Act 1965.

(3) The arrangements referred to in subsection (1) are any arrangements made by or on behalf of the relevant Government for securing that payments by way of compensation for loss of employment in the capacity in question will be made—

    (*a*) in circumstances which in the opinion of the Secretary of State correspond (subject to the appropriate modifications) to those in which a right to a redundancy payment would have accrued if section 81 had applied, and

    (*b*) on a scale which in the opinion of the Secretary of State corresponds (subject to the appropriate modifications) to that on which a redundancy payment would have been payable if that section had applied.

(4) For the purposes of subsection (1) the appropriate sum (subject to subsection (5)) is the sum appearing to the Secretary of State to be equal to the amount of the redundancy rebate which would have been payable under section 104 if such a right as is mentioned in paragraph (*a*) of subsection (3) had accrued, and such a redundancy payment as is mentioned in paragraph (*b*) of that subsection had been payable and had been paid.

(5) Where it appears to the Secretary of State that such contributions as are mentioned in subsection (1) were paid in respect of part (but not the whole) of the period of employment in question, the rebate which would have been payable as mentioned in subsection (4) shall be calculated as if the employment had been limited to that part of the period.

(6) Any accounts prepared by the Secretary of State under section 103 (2) shall show as a separate item the aggregate amount of sums paid under subsection (1) during the period to which the accounts relate.

DERIVATION

1965, s. 43 (1)–(5) ; Social Security Act 1973 (c. 38), Sched. 27, para. 58; Social Security (Consequential Provisions) Act 1975 (c. 18), Sched. 2, para. 22.

Meaning of " Government of overseas territory "

114.—In this Part " overseas territory " means any territory or country outside the United Kingdom; and any reference to the Government of an overseas territory includes a reference to a Government constituted for two or more overseas territories and to any authority established for the purpose of providing or administering services which are common to, or relate to matters of common interest to, two or more such territories.

DERIVATION
   1965, s. 43 (6).

Application of Part VI to employment not under contract of employment

115.—(1) This section applies to employment of any description which—

(*a*) is not employment under a contract of service or of apprenticeship, and

(*b*) is not employment of any description falling within paragraphs (*a*) to (*d*) of section 111 (1),

but is employment such that secondary Class 1 contributions are payable under Part I of the Social Security Act 1975 in respect of persons engaged therein.

(2) The Secretary of State may by regulations under this section provide that, subject to such exceptions and modifications as may be prescribed by the regulations, this Part and the provisions of this Act supplementary thereto shall have effect in relation to any such employment of a description to which this section applies as may be so prescribed as if—

(*a*) it were employment under a contract of employment, and

(*b*) any person engaged in employment of that description were an employee, and

(*c*) such person as may be determined by or under the regulations were his employer.

(3) Without prejudice to the generality of subsection (2), regulations made under this section may provide that section 105 shall apply to persons engaged in any such employment of a description to which this section applies as may be prescribed by the regulations, as if those persons were employees to whom that section applies.

DERIVATION
   1965, s. 49; Social Security Act 1973, Sched. 27, para. 59; Social Security (Consequential Provisions) Act 1975, Sched. 2, para. 23.

GENERAL NOTE
   See Redundancy Payments Office Holders Regulations 1965 (S.I. 1965 No. 2007); Redundancy Payments Office Holders (Scotland) Regulations 1966 (S.I. 1966 No. 1436).

Provision for treating termination of certain employments by statute as equivalent to dismissal

116.—(1) The Secretary of State may by regulations under this section provide that, subject to such exceptions and modifications as may be prescribed by the regulations, the provisions of this Part shall have effect in relation to any person who, by virtue of any statutory provisions,—

(*a*) is transferred to, and becomes a member of, a body specified in those provisions, but (*b*) at a time so specified ceases to be a member of that body unless before that time certain conditions so specified have been fulfilled,

as if the cessation of his membership of that body by virtue of those provisions were dismissal by his employer by reason of redundancy.

(2) The power conferred by subsection (1) shall be exercisable whether membership of the body in question constitutes employment within the meaning of section 153 or not; and, where that membership does not constitute such employment, that power may be exercised in addition to any power exercisable by virtue of section 115.

DERIVATION
   1965, s. 50.

GENERAL NOTE

See the Redundancy Payments Termination of Employment Regulations 1965 (S.I. 1965 No. 2022).

Employees paid by person other than employer

117.—(1) This section applies to any employee whose remuneration is, by virtue of any statutory provision, payable to him by a person other than his employer.

(2) For the purposes of the operation, in relation to employees to whom this section applies, of the provisions of this Part and Schedule 13 specified in column 1 of Schedule 8, any reference to the employer which is specified in column 2 of Schedule 8 shall be construed as a reference to the person responsible for paying the remuneration.

(3) In relation to employees to whom this section applies, section 119 shall have effect as if—

(*a*) any reference in subsection (1) or subsection (2) of that section to a notice required or authorised to be given by or to an employer included a reference to a notice which, by virtue of subsection (2), is required or authorised to be given by or to the person responsible for paying the remuneration;

(*b*) in relation to a notice required or authorised to be given to that person, any reference to the employer in paragraph (*a*) or paragraph (*b*) of subsection (2) of that section were a reference to that person; and

(*c*) the reference to the employer in subsection (5) of that section included a reference to that person.

(4) In this section and in Schedule 8, " the person responsible for paying the remuneration " means the person by whom the remuneration is payable as mentioned in subsection (1).

DERIVATION
   1965, s. 51.

Statutory compensation schemes

118.—(1) This section applies to any statutory provision which was in force immediately before 6th December 1965, whereby the holders of such situations, places or employments as are specified in that provision are, or may become, entitled to compensation for loss of employment, or for loss or diminution of emoluments or of pension rights, in consequence of the operation of any other statutory provision referred to therein.

(2) The Secretary of State may make provision by regulations for securing that where apart from this section a person is entitled to

compensation under a statutory provision to which this section applies, and the circumstances are such that he is also entitled to a redundancy payment, the amount of the redundancy payment shall be set off against the compensation to which he would be entitled apart from this section; and any statutory provision to which any such regulations apply shall have effect subject to the regulations.

DERIVATION
  1965, s. 47.

GENERAL NOTE
  See the Redundancy Payments Statutory Compensation Regulations 1965 (S.I. 1965 No. 1988).

Provisions as to notices

119.—(1) Any notice which under this Part is required or authorised to be given by an employer to an employee may be given by being delivered to the employee, or left for him at his usual or last-known place of residence, or sent by post addressed to him at that place.

(2) Any notice which under this Part is required or authorised to be given by an employee to an employer may be given either by the employee himself or by a person authorised by him to act on his behalf, and, whether given by or on behalf of the employee,—

  (a) may be given by being delivered to the employer, or sent by post addressed to him at the place where the employee is or was employed by him, or

  (b) if arrangements in that behalf have been made by the employer, may be given by being delivered to a person designated by the employer in pursuance of the arrangements, or left for such a person at a place so designated, or sent by post to such a person at an address so designated.

(3) In the preceding provisions of this section, any reference to the delivery of a notice shall, in relation to a notice which is not required by this Part to be in writing, be construed as including a reference to the oral communication of the notice.

(4) Any notice which, in accordance with any provision of this section, is left for a person at a place referred to in that provision shall, unless the contrary is proved, be presumed to have been received by him on the day on which it was left there.

(5) Nothing in subsection (1) or subsection (2) shall be construed as affecting the capacity of an employer to act by a servant or agent for the purposes of any provision of this Part, including either of those subsections.

DERIVATION
  1965, s. 53.

Offences

120.—(1) Where an offence under this Part committed by a body corporate is proved to have been committed with the consent or connivance of, or to be attributable to any neglect on the part of, any director, manager, secretary or other similar officer of the body corporate or any person who was purporting to act in any such capacity, he as well as the body corporate shall be guilty of that offence and shall be liable to be proceeded against and punished accordingly.

(2) In this section " director ", in relation to a body corporate established by or under any enactment for the purpose of carrying on

under national ownership any industry or part of an industry or undertaking, being a body corporate whose affairs are managed by its members, means a member of that body corporate.

DERIVATION
  1965, s. 52.

PART VII

INSOLVENCY OF EMPLOYER

Priority of certain debts on insolvency

121.—(1) An amount to which this section applies shall be treated for the purposes of—

(a) section 33 of the Bankruptcy Act 1914;

(b) section 118 of the Bankruptcy (Scotland) Act 1913; and

(c) section 319 of the Companies Act 1948;

as if it were wages payable by the employer to the employee in respect of the period for which it is payable.

(2) This section applies to any amount owed by an employer to an employee in respect of—

(a) a guarantee payment;

(b) remuneration on suspension on medical grounds under section 19;

(c) any payment for time off under section 27 (3) or 31 (3);

(d) remuneration under a protective award made under section 101 of the Employment Protection Act 1975.

DERIVATION
  1975, s. 63.

GENERAL NOTE
Subs. (1)

Under legislation, unpaid wages owed by an insolvent employer are treated as preferential debts. The preference extends, however, only to debts accruing during the four months preceding the date of the receiving order, and is subject to a maximum sum of £800 per employee. (The maximum sum was increased from £200 to £800 by the Insolvency Act 1976.) Employees affected by the insolvency of their employer have been estimated to number in recent years some 30,000–40,000 annually, with claims oustanding of some £4m. Where claims fall outside the statutory limits, the arrears of pay owed rank as ordinary debts. Even where any sums can be recovered, the process may take years. With the addition to the preferred debts of the amounts specified in subs. (2), these limits may become even more out-dated and unrealistic. Some of the sums owed may have been payable over a period of time exceeding four months, and thus may be partly denied by the cut-off limits. As the claim under s. 122 against the Secretary of State only covers debts in respect of periods considerably shorter than four months (s. 122 (3)), the preferential status of these debts may be significant, though the £800 limit works to off-set this difference in practice.

Those sections concerned with purely financial bankruptcy (ss. 121–127) do not apply to the Crown (s. 138 (1)), but see s. 138 (5).

Subs. (2)

Unlike the original Employment Protection Bill 1975 (cl. 57 (2) (c)), this section does not specifically include among the preferred debts sums owed as maternity pay, since this need is effectively provided for by the provision in s. 40 (1) (b).

Employee's rights on insolvency of employer

122.—(1) If on an application made to him in writing by an employee the Secretary of State is satisfied—

(a) that the employer of that employee has become insolvent; and

(b) that on the relevant date the employee was entitled to be paid the whole or part of any debt to which this section applies,

the Secretary of State shall, subject to the provisions of this section, pay the employee out of the Redundancy Fund the amount to which in the opinion of the Secretary of State the employee is entitled in respect of that debt.

(2) In this section the " relevant date " in relation to a debt means the date on which the employer became insolvent or the date of the termination of the employee's employment, whichever is the later.

(3) This section applies to the following debts:—

(a) any arrears of pay in respect of a period or periods not exceeding in the aggregate eight weeks;

(b) any amount which the employer is liable to pay the employee for the period of notice required by section 49 (1) or (2) or for any failure of the employer to give the period of notice required by section 49 (1);

(c) any holiday pay in respect of a period or periods of holiday, not exceeding six weeks in all, to which the employee became entitled during the twelve months immediately preceding the relevant date;

(d) any basic award of compensation for unfair dismissal (within the meaning of section 72);

(e) any reasonable sum by way of reimbursement of the whole or part of any fee or premium paid by an apprentice or articled clerk.

(4) For the purposes of subsection (3) (a), any such amount as is referred to in section 121 (2) shall be treated as if it were arrears of pay.

(5) The total amount payable to an employee in respect of any debt mentioned in subsection (3), where the amount of that debt is referable to a period of time, shall not exceed £100 in respect of any one week or, in respect of a shorter period, an amount bearing the same proportion to £100 as that shorter period bears to a week.

(6) The Secretary of State may vary the limit referred to in subsection (5) after a review under section 148, by order made in accordance with that section.

(7) A sum shall be taken to be reasonable for the purposes of subsection (3) (e) in a case where a trustee in bankruptcy or liquidator has been or is required to be appointed if it is admitted to be reasonable by the trustee in bankruptcy or liquidator under section 34 of the Bankruptcy Act 1914 (preferential claims of apprentices and articled clerks), whether as originally enacted or as applied to the winding up of a company by section 317 of the Companies Act 1948.

(8) Subsection (7) shall not apply to Scotland, but in Scotland a sum shall be taken to be reasonable for the purposes of subsection (3) (e) in a case where a trustee in bankruptcy or liquidator has been or is required to be appointed if it is admitted by the trustee in bankruptcy or the liquidator for the purposes of the bankruptcy or winding up.

(9) The provisions of subsections (10) and (11) shall apply in a case where one of the following officers (hereinafter in this section referred to as the " relevant officer ") has been or is required to be appointed in connection with the employer's insolvency, that is to say, a trustee in bankruptcy, a liquidator, a receiver or manager, or a trustee under a composition or arrangement between the employer and his creditors or under a trust deed for his creditors executed by the employer; and in this subsection " liquidator " and " receiver " include the Official Receiver in his capacity as a provisional liquidator or interim receiver.

(10) Subject to subsection (11), the Secretary of State shall not in such a case make any payment under this section in respect of any debt until he has received a statement from the relevant officer of the amount of that debt which appears to have been owed to the employee on the relevant date and to remain unpaid; and the relevant officer shall, on request by the Secretary of State, provide him, as soon as reasonably practicable, with such a statement.

(11) Where—

  (a) a period of six months has elapsed since the application for a payment under this section was received by the Secretary of State, but no such payment has been made;

  (b) the Secretary of State is satisfied that a payment under this section should be made; and

  (c) it appears to the Secretary of State that there is likely to be further delay before he receives a statement about the debt in question,

then, the Secretary of State may, if the applicant so requests or, if the Secretary of State thinks fit, without such a request, make a payment under this section, notwithstanding that no such statement has been received.

DERIVATION
  1975, s. 64; 1977 Order (No. 2), art. 2.

GENERAL NOTE
Subs. (1)
  Cf. s. 40 (1) (b) relating to maternity pay, and s. 106 (1) (b) relating to redundancy payments.
  An application may be made any time after the employer has become insolvent, and there is no limitation period on applications. But payment may not be made by the Secretary of State until six months after the application, unless the " relevant officer " has made a statement of the amount of the debt owed (subs. (9)–(11)). For the definition of insolvency and its limitations, see s. 127 (1) and (2), and the Note to that section.
  Certain classes of employment are excluded from this section (ss. 141 (2), 144 (2) (4), 145 (2), 146 (1) (2)), as are workers who are not " employees " (see the definition in s. 153 (1)).

Subs. (2)
  The consequence of this provision will be to complicate further the situation described in the Note to subs. (3) below, where the preferred debt owed to the employee under s. 121 or other enactments coincides only in part with the amounts specified in subs. (3). An employee dismissed only after insolvency may claim as a preferred debt sums owed before the date of the receiving order, but may claim against the Secretary of State for sums owed both after the insolvency but before the termination and before the insolvency as well—as described in the Note to subs. (3).

Subs. (3)
  The specification of only certain debts as being recoverable, and then only up to certain limits, is difficult to justify on any rational grounds as well as giving rise to some potentially hideous complications. It would have simplified matters immensely to provide for the recompense of all debts owed to the employee by his insolvent employer arising out of the employment relationship. In the result here, certain anomalies are inevitable: *e.g.* as regards debts arising from an award of compensation for unfair dismissal, the compensatory award (s. 74) is covered in part by (a) to (c); the basic award (s. 73) is covered *in toto* by (d); but the additional award under s. 71 (2) (b) is not covered at all. Again, the debts qualifying for preferential treatment under s. 121 (2) are to be recoverable (subs. (4)), but only in part as subject to the limit of subs. (3) (a).
  Some decisions have further limited the potential of this section. Thus, in *Fox*

Brothers (Clothes) Ltd. v. *Bryant* [1978] I.R.L.R. 485 (E.A.T.), Kilner Brown J. doubted " very much if there can be an unfair dismissal in the case of a properly conducted entry into liquidation." So, if this be correct, the provision in subs. (3) (*d*) seems otiose. And in *Secretary of State for Employment* v. *Wilson* [1977] I.R.L.R. 483 (E.A.T.), Phillips J. characterised the rights given in this section against the Secretary of State as being no better than those the employee has against the employer. Therefore, subs. (3) (*b*) was interpreted as barring recovery of any amount where the employee suffered no damage as a consequence of the employer's breach.

Complications arise in the relationship of this section to s. 121 which treats certain debts owed employees as preferred. Do the amounts treated as preferred necessarily coincide with the amounts recoverable from the Secretary of State? There are three possibilities: (i) where the preferred debt does not exceed the amounts specified in this subsection, the two clearly coincide and if the employee is not paid by the " relevant officer " (subs. (9)), he should recover the sums owed through application to the Secretary of State; (ii) where the preferred debt exceeds the amounts specified in this subsection, part of it may still coincide with the sums recoverable from the Secretary of State; *e.g.* (*b*); (iii) but where the preferred debt exceeds the amounts specified in this subsection, some of it may not coincide with the amount specified here, *e.g.* because it relates to periods exceeding eight or six weeks though not more than four months, and is still not over £800. For instance, a claim for certain bonus payments over a period of 12 weeks prior to insolvency— (*a*) only covers eight weeks whereas the debt is preferred over the full 12 weeks, as long as it does not exceed £800.

It seems that where the preferred debt overlaps the amounts recoverable from the Secretary of State, the employee has the rather complex option of exploiting his special position as a preferred creditor up to the maximum limits, and then claiming as much of the remainder as is permissible under s. 122. This may be of real value where the employee is owed, *e.g.* a sum of money which accrued slowly over several months. For the last four months, he may claim as a preferred creditor up to £800. For any remaining sum owed which accrued during that period, as well as for sums accruing previously, he may claim additionally the amounts specified in this subsection. It will be important, of course, that the application to the Secretary of State specifies the relevant debts and time periods to which the claim relates, as otherwise the Secretary of State may usurp the employee's preferred creditor position (s. 125 (1) and (2)). As long as the claim is specific as to the times when the debts accrued, the Secretary of State should not be entitled to pick and choose which debt he takes over so as to benefit from the employee's preferred position. The words " in the opinion of the Secretary of State " in subs. (1) were inserted only to provide for exceptional cases where no statement under subs. (10) is forthcoming and records and information are not available in the normal way. The remainder of the debt not covered by either s. 121 or s. 122 or otherwise preferred, will be recoverable by the employee from the insolvent employer on the ordinary basis. For the definition of " holiday pay," see s. 127 (3).

Subs. (4)

It is not clear precisely how the separate debts referred to in s. 121 (2) (*a*)–(*d*) owed by the employer are to be treated as arrears of pay. Each of the payments to be made under those headings may be referable to different weeks over a considerable period of time and it would obviously contradict the purpose of the section if any week during which some payment under any of these headings was owed counted as one of the maximum aggregate of eight weeks. It would be much preferable to interpret this subsection as meaning that each of the different types of debt owed under s. 121 (2) was to be treated separately as arrears and was subject to a separate maximum of eight weeks of payment in the aggregate. This was the effect of the provision in the original Employment Protection Bill 1975 (cl. 58 (2) (*f*)) which appears to have been unfortunately translated in an ambiguous fashion into this separate subsection.

Subs. (5)

A question arises as to whether the debts payable by the Secretary of State as specified in subs. (3) are subject to a limit of £110 per week for each debt or £110 per week when all the debts have been lumped together. The subsection is ambiguous, but logic, consistency and above all commercial convenience would seem to indicate the former interpretation. For in themselves the debts listed in s. 121 (2) and s. 122 (3) (*a*)–(*d*) and (*e*) are not subject to any such limitation individually, and s. 122 (3) (*d*) is limited on its own to a maximum of £110 per week (Sched. 14, para. 8 (1) (*b*)). The parallel provision requiring the Secretary of State to take over from the insolvent employer in the case of redundancy payments provides for a £110 per week limit on that debt alone (raised from £100 by the Employment Protection (Variation of Limits) Order 1978 (S.I. 1978 No. 1777)), and in the case of default on payment of maternity pay there is no such limit (s. 40 (1) (*b*)).

As pointed out, the various debts listed may have accrued in different weeks, and if all were to be bunched together when falling in any one week, the result might be that part of some of them would not be payable by the Secretary of State in some weeks while the whole was paid in others. The remainder would still be owed by the employer, either as preferred or ordinary debts, but the resulting complications in calculating these would be hideous indeed. One does not envy the task of the employee-creditor, the " relevant official " (subs. (9)), or the Secretary of State who takes over the rights of the employee (s. 125 (1)) in respect of only that part of the debt calculated to have been paid, if such a limitation as is proposed by the latter interpretation is adopted. For concentrated in that £110 might be sums from any of the nine different types of debts in amounts which vary from week to week. It is obviously far simpler and in accordance with the logic and intent of the provision that where the Secretary of State takes over the debts listed here, he pays each of them subject to the £110 limit on each, rather than create the hideous hodgepodge of amalgamated debts which would result from an overall £110 limit.

The limit was raised from £100 to £110 by the Employment Protection (Variation of Limits) Order 1978 (S.I. 1978 No. 1777), with effect from February 1, 1979, for every insolvency which occurs after that date.

Payment of unpaid contributions to occupational pension scheme

123.—(1) If, on application made to him in writing by the persons competent to act in respect of an occupational pension scheme, the Secretary of State is satisfied that an employer has become insolvent and that at the time that he did so there remained unpaid relevant contributions falling to be paid by him to the scheme, the Secretary of State shall, subject to the provisions of this section, pay into the resources of the scheme out of the Redundancy Fund the sum which in his opinion is payable in respect of the unpaid relevant contributions.

(2) In this section " relevant contributions " means contributions falling to be paid by an employer in accordance with an occupational pension scheme, either on his own account or on behalf of an employee; and for the purposes of this section a contribution of any amount shall not be treated as falling to be paid on behalf of an employee unless a sum equal to that amount has been deducted from the pay of the employee by way of a contribution from him.

(3) The sum payable under this section in respect of unpaid contributions of an employer on his own account to an occupational pension scheme shall be the least of the following amounts—

(*a*) the balance of relevant contributions remaining unpaid on the date when he became insolvent and payable by the employer on his own account to the scheme in respect of the twelve months immediately preceding that date;

(*b*) the amount certified by an actuary to be necessary for the purpose of meeting the liability of the scheme on dissolution to pay the benefits provided by the scheme to or in respect of the employees of the employer;

(*c*) an amount equal to ten per cent. of the total amount of remuneration paid or payable to those employees in respect of the twelve months immediately preceding the date on which the employer became insolvent.

(4) For the purposes of subsection (3) (*c*), " remuneration " includes

holiday pay, maternity pay and any such payment as is referred to in section 121 (2).

(5) Any sum payable under this section in respect of unpaid contributions on behalf of an employee shall not exceed the amount deducted from the pay of the employee in respect of the employee's contributions to the occupational pension scheme during the twelve months immediately preceding the date on which the employer became insolvent.

(6) The provisions of subsections (7) to (9) shall apply in a case where one of the following officers (hereafter in this section referred to as the " relevant officer ") has been or is required to be appointed in connection with the employer's insolvency, that is to say, a trustee in bankruptcy, a liquidator, a receiver or manager, or a trustee under a composition or arrangement between the employer and his creditors or under a trust deed for his creditors executed by the employer; and in this subsection " liquidator " and " receiver " include the Official Receiver in his capacity as a provisional liquidator or interim receiver.

(7) Subject to subsection (9), the Secretary of State shall not in such a case make any payment under this section in respect of unpaid relevant contributions until he has received a statement from the relevant officer of the amount of relevant contributions which appear to have been unpaid on the date on which the employer became insolvent and to remain unpaid; and the relevant officer shall, on request by the Secretary of State provide him, as soon as reasonably practicable, with such a statement.

(8) Subject to subsection (9), an amount shall be taken to be payable, paid or deducted as mentioned in subsection (3) (*a*) or (*c*) or subsection (5), only if it is so certified by the relevant officer.

(9) Where—

   (*a*) a period of six months has elapsed since the application for a payment under this section was received by the Secretary of State, but no such payment has been made;

   (*b*) the Secretary of State is satisfied that a payment under this section should be made; and

   (*c*) it appears to the Secretary of State that there is likely to be further delay before he receives a statement or certificate about the contributions in question,

then, the Secretary of State may, if the applicants so request or, if the Secretary of State thinks fit, without such a request, make a payment under this section, notwithstanding that no such statement or certificate has been received.

DERIVATION

   1975, s. 65.

GENERAL NOTE

Subs. (1)

   The same classes of employment are excluded from this section as from s. 122 (see ss. 141 (2), 144 (2) (4), 145 (2), 146 (1) (2). The definition of " occupational pension scheme " in s. 127 (3) ensures that only " employees," and not all workers benefiting from such schemes are protected.

Subs. (2)

   The substance of the latter half of this subsection is reiterated in subs. (5)— what was described by the then Minister of State, Department of Employment (Mr. A. Booth) as a " belt and braces situation " (Standing Committee F on the Employment Protection Bill, 20th Sitting, July 3, 1975, at col. 1046).

Subs. (3)

The three alternatives provided for here were devised to avoid unduly heavy demands being made on the Redundancy Fund through schemes devised by unscrupulous employers on the verge of bankruptcy granting large benefits to their employees. Employers contributing to the Fund are thus protected, albeit possibly at the expense of the employees, who would only be protected by alternative (*b*).

Complaint to industrial tribunal

124.—(1) A person who has applied for a payment under section 122 may, within the period of three months beginning with the date on which the decision of the Secretary of State on that application was communicated to him or, if that is not reasonably practicable, within such further period as is reasonable, present a complaint to an industrial tribunal that—

(a) the Secretary of State has failed to make any such payment; or

(b) any such payment made by the Secretary of State is less than the amount which should have been paid.

(2) Any persons who are competent to act in respect of an occupational pension scheme and who have applied for a payment to be made under section 123 into the resources of the scheme may, within the period of three months beginning with the date on which the decision of the Secretary of State on that application was communicated to them, or, if that is not reasonably practicable, within such further period as is reasonable, present a complaint to an industrial tribunal that—

(a) the Secretary of State has failed to make any such payment; or

(b) any such payment made by him is less than the amount which should have been paid.

(3) Where an industrial tribunal finds that the Secretary of State ought to make a payment under section 122 or 123, it shall make a declaration to that effect and shall also declare the amount of any such payment which it finds the Secretary of State ought to make.

DERIVATION
1975, s. 66.

Transfer to Secretary of State of rights and remedies

125.—(1) Where, in pursuance of section 122, the Secretary of State makes any payment to an employee in respect of any debt to which that section applies—

(a) any rights and remedies of the employee in respect of that debt (or, if the Secretary of State has paid only part of it, in respect of that part) shall, on the making of the payment, become rights and remedies of the Secretary of State; and

(b) any decision of an industrial tribunal requiring an employer to pay that debt to the employee shall have the effect that the debt or, as the case may be, that part of it which the Secretary of State has paid, is to be paid to the Secretary of State.

(2) There shall be included among the rights and remedies which become rights and remedies of the Secretary of State in accordance with subsection (1) (*a*) any right to be paid in priority to other creditors of the employer in accordance with—

(a) section 33 of the Bankruptcy Act 1914;

(b) section 118 of the Bankruptcy (Scotland) Act 1913; and

(c) section 319 of the Companies Act 1948,

and the Secretary of State shall be entitled to be so paid in priority to any other unsatisfied claim of the employee; and in computing for the purposes of any of those provisions any limit on the amount of sums to be so paid any sums paid to the Secretary of State shall be treated as if they had been paid to the employee.

(3) Where in pursuance of section 123 the Secretary of State makes any payment into the resources of an occupational pension scheme in respect of any contributions to the scheme, any rights and remedies in respect of those contributions belonging to the persons competent to act in respect of the scheme shall, on the making of the payment, become rights and remedies of the Secretary of State.

(4) Any sum recovered by the Secretary of State in exercising any right or pursuing any remedy which is his by virtue of this section shall be paid into the Redundancy Fund.

DERIVATION
    1975, s. 67.

GENERAL NOTE
    Where the amounts specified in an employee's application to the Secretary of State under s. 122 overlap with parts of the debt given preferential status under the enactments referred to here, the Secretary of State becomes, to the extent of the overlap, the preferred creditor in place of the employee. As explained in the Note to s. 122 (3), it may thus again be in the interests of the employee in certain circumstances to avoid any overlap by using up the full extent of his preferred status before claiming as much of the remainder as possible under s. 122. The price paid by the employee for his claim to the Secretary of State under s. 122 is that the remainder of the debt owed by the employer to him will be paid in circumstances where the Secretary of State has become an additional creditor, perhaps even a preferred one, thus diminishing the likelihood of the employee's being fully repaid. Circumstances could arise where the remaining assets of an employer after preferred claims by the employee had been satisfied, went to the Redundancy Fund, instead of satisfying the remainder of the employee's claim. Still, if the employee has extracted the full extent of his preferred debt from the Secretary of State under s. 122, it would seem that at least nothing of the preferential status of the employee remains for the benefit of the Secretary of State, and through him the Redundancy Fund.

Power of Secretary of State to obtain information in connection with applications

126.—(1) Where an application is made to the Secretary of State under section 122 or 123 in respect of a debt owed, or contributions to an occupational pension scheme falling to be made, by an employer, the Secretary of State may require—

(*a*) the employer to provide him with such information as the Secretary of State may reasonably require for the purpose of determining whether the application is well-founded; and

(*b*) any person having the custody or control of any relevant records or other documents to produce for examination on behalf of the Secretary of State any such document in that person's custody or under his control which is of such a description as the Secretary of State may require.

(2) Any such requirement shall be made by notice in writing given to the person on whom the requirement is imposed and may be varied or revoked by a subsequent notice so given.

(3) If a person refuses or wilfully neglects to furnish any information or produce any document which he has been required to furnish or produce by a notice under this section he shall be liable on summary conviction to a fine not exceeding £100.

(4) If a person, in purporting to comply with a requirement of a notice under this section, knowingly or recklessly makes any false statement he shall be liable on summary conviction to a fine not exceeding £400.

DERIVATION
1975, s. 68.

Interpretation of ss. 122 to 126

127.—(1) For the purposes of sections 122 to 126, an employer shall be taken to be insolvent if, but only if, in England and Wales,—

(a) he becomes bankrupt or makes a composition or arrangement with his creditors or a receiving order is made against him;

(b) he has died and an order is made under section 130 of the Bankruptcy Act 1914 for the administration of his estate according to the law of bankruptcy, or by virtue of an order of the court his estate is being administered in accordance with rules set out in Part I of Schedule 1 to the Administration of Estates Act 1925; or

(c) where the employer is a company, a winding up order is made or a resolution for voluntary winding up is passed with respect to it, or a receiver or manager of its undertaking is duly appointed, or possession is taken, by or on behalf of the holders of any debentures secured by a floating charge, of any property of the company comprised in or subject to the charge.

(2) For the purposes of sections 122 to 126, an employer shall be taken to be insolvent if, but only if, in Scotland,—

(a) an award of sequestration is made on his estate or he executes a trust deed for his creditors or enters into a composition contract;

(b) he has died and a judicial factor appointed under section 163 of the Bankruptcy (Scotland) Act 1913 is required by that section to divide his insolvent estate among his creditors; or

(c) where the employer is a company, a winding-up order is made or a resolution for voluntary winding up is passed with respect to it or a receiver of its undertaking is duly appointed.

(3) In sections 122 to 126—

" holiday pay " means—

(a) pay in respect of a holiday actually taken; or

(b) any accrued holiday pay which under the employee's contract of employment would in the ordinary course have become payable to him in respect of the period of a holiday if his employment with the employer had continued until he became entitled to a holiday;

" occupational pension scheme " means any scheme or arrangement which provides or is capable of providing, in relation to employees in any description of employment, benefits (in the form of pensions or otherwise) payable to or in respect of any such employees on the termination of their employment or on their death or retirement;

and any reference in those sections to the resources of such a scheme is a reference to the funds out of which the benefits provided by the scheme are from time to time payable.

DERIVATION
1975, s. 69.

GENERAL NOTE

The limitation of the rights in Pt. VII to insolvency as defined in this section confines the benefits to those workers whose employers' default coincides with bankruptcy or winding-up proceedings. It does not affect the all too common occurrence of a small firm or company simply ceasing to trade without actually becoming insolvent. Employees face considerable difficulties in such a case. Proceedings in the industrial tribunal or a county court will often result in an order which the employer cannot comply with, and the procedure of putting the employer through bankruptcy or winding-up proceedings is not practical. The remedy given in s. 122 would have been of greatest value in these circumstances.

PART VIII

RESOLUTION OF DISPUTES RELATING TO EMPLOYMENT

Industrial tribunals

Industrial tribunals

128.—(1) The Secretary of State may by regulations make provision for the establishment of tribunals, to be known as industrial tribunals, to exercise the jurisdiction conferred on them by or under this Act or any other Act, whether passed before or after this Act.

(2) Regulations made wholly or partly under section 12 of the Industrial Training Act 1964 and in force immediately before the date on which this section comes into force shall, so far as so made, continue to have effect as if they had been made under subsection (1), and tribunals established in accordance with such regulations shall continue to be known as industrial tribunals.

(3) Schedule 9, which makes provision, among other things, with respect to proceedings before industrial tribunals, shall have effect.

(4) Complaints, references and appeals to industrial tribunals shall be made in accordance with regulations made under paragraph 1 of Schedule 9.

DERIVATION

1974, para. 16; Industrial Training Act 1964 (c. 16), s. 12 (1); 1965, ss. 9 (1), 34 (2); 1972, s. 8 (7) (8); 1975, s. 108 (1).

GENERAL NOTE

For the lengthy list of the appropriate Regulations governing the practice and procedure of industrial tribunals, see the *Encyclopedia of Labour Relations Law*, Pt. 4A.

There is no fixed total number of industrial tribunals since each tribunal is convened, as required, from a panel of chairmen and two panels of lay members. On average 74 tribunals currently sit in Great Britain every working day. 72 full-time chairmen, including two women (3 per cent.) have been appointed for England and Wales by the Lord Chancellor and nine full-time chairmen, including one woman (11 per cent.) have been appointed for Scotland by the Lord President. There are 2,448 lay members of whom 494 (20 per cent.) are women. 1,137 (46 per cent.) appointments have been made by the TUC and an identical number and proportion on the nomination of the CBI. The total cost of industrial tribunals in the financial year 1976–77 was estimated at £5½ m.

The following are the numbers of cases referred to industrial tribunals and heard by them in each year since 1965, involving all jurisdictions, and the number of tribunal hearings involving unfair dismissal cases in 1973–75 and 1977:

Year	Cases referred	Cases heard	Unfair dismissal
1965 ⎫		500	
1966 ⎬	10,759	5,356	
1967	12,456	8,496	
1968	10,673	8,591	
1969	10,679	7,726	
1970	11,336	8,632	
1971	9,514	7,383	
1972	14,827	7,745	
1973	14,517	7,188	3,996
1974	16,448	6,857	3,380

Year	Cases referred	Cases heard	Unfair dismissal
1975	35,897	12,518	8,729
1976	47,673	19,234	
1977	46,961	18,962	12,842

Source: *Department of Employment Gazette,* April 1977, July 1978.

The proportional distribution of applications to industrial tribunals according to the jurisdictions conferred on them is reflected in the figures for the first quarter of 1978 (January 1–March 31). There were 9,689 applications registered in England and Wales and 1,291 in Scotland. Of these, 80 per cent. were under TULRA (Pt. V of this Act), 7 per cent. under the Redundancy Payments Act 1965 (Pt. VI of this Act), and 4 per cent. under both Acts. 3 per cent. were made under the Employment Protection Act 1975 (Pts. I (ss. 8–10) ; II, III, IV (s. 53) and VII of this Act), 1·5 per cent. under the Equal Pay Act 1970, 1 per cent. under each of the Race Relations Act 1976 and the Contracts of Employment Act 1972 (Pts. I (ss. 1–7) and IV (ss. 49–52) of this Act) and 0·5 per cent. under the Sex Discrimination Act 1975. The remaining proportion of applications were made under various other Acts—the Selective Employment Payments Compensation Regulations, Industrial Training Act, Health and Safety at Work, etc. Act—which are within the scope of the industrial tribunals. There was also a small number of unclassified applications.

80 per cent. of industrial tribunal hearings are completed within one day and 95 per cent. within two days. 96 per cent. of tribunal decisions are unanimous. Though the parties are still only legally represented in a minority of cases, the proportion is increasing. An unpublished Government study based on statistics of a selected sample of over 600 cases in mid-1974 showed that applicants were represented by a lawyer in 20 per cent. of cases, respondents in 37 per cent. of cases. A more recent survey covering four weeks in October 1977 showed some 33 per cent. of employees and 49 per cent. of employers legally represented at industrial tribunal hearings.

Remedy for infringement of certain rights under this Act

129. The remedy of an employee for infringement of any of the rights conferred on him by sections 8 and 53 and Parts II, III, V and VII shall, if provision is made for a complaint or for the reference of a question to an industrial tribunal, be by way of such complaint or reference and not otherwise.

DERIVATION
    1975, s. 108 (1) ; 1974, para. 4 (1).

Jurisdiction of referees to be exercised by tribunals

130.—(1) There shall be referred to and determined by an industrial tribunal any question which by any statutory provision is directed (in whatsoever terms) to be determined by a referee or board of referees constituted under any of the statutory provisions specified in Schedule 10 or which is so directed to be determined in the absence of agreement to the contrary.

(2) The transfer of any jurisdiction by this section shall not affect the principles on which any question is to be determined or the persons on whom the determination is binding, or any provision which requires particular matters to be expressly dealt with or embodied in the determination, or which relates to evidence.

DERIVATION
    1965, s. 44.

Power to confer jurisdiction on industrial tribunals in respect of damages, etc., for breach of contract of employment

131.—(1) The appropriate Minister may by order provide that on any claim to which this section applies or any such claim of a description specified in the order, being in either case a claim satisfying the relevant condition or conditions mentioned in subsection (3), proceedings for the recovery of damages or any other sum, except damages or a sum due in respect of personal injuries, may be brought before an industrial tribunal.

(2) Subject to subsection (3), this section applies to any of the following claims, that is to say—

    (*a*) a claim for damages for breach of a contract of employment or any other contract connected with employment;

    (*b*) a claim for a sum due under such a contract;

    (*c*) a claim for the recovery of a sum in pursuance of any enactment relating to the terms or performance of such a contract;

being in each case a claim such that a court in England and Wales or Scotland, as the case may be, would under the law for the time being in force have jurisdiction to hear and determine an action in respect of the claim.

(3) An order under this section may make provision with respect to any such claim only if it satisfies either of the following conditions, that is to say—

    (*a*) it arises or is outstanding on the termination of the employee's employment; or

    (*b*) it arises in circumstances which also give rise to proceedings already or simultaneously brought before an industrial tribunal otherwise than by virtue of this section;

or, if the order so provides, it satisfies both those conditions.

(4) Where on proceedings under this section an industrial tribunal finds that the whole or part of a sum claimed in the proceedings is due, the tribunal shall order the respondent to the proceedings to pay the amount which it finds due.

(5) Without prejudice to section 154 (3), an order under this section may include provisions—

    (*a*) as to the manner in which and time within which proceedings are to be brought by virtue of this section; and

    (*b*) modifying any other enactment.

(6) Any jurisdiction conferred on an industrial tribunal by virtue of this section in respect of any claim shall be exercisable concurrently with any court in England and Wales or in Scotland, as the case may be, which has jurisdiction to hear and determine an action in respect of the claim.

(7) In this section—

    " appropriate Minister ", as respects a claim in respect of which an action could be heard and determined in England and Wales, means the Lord Chancellor and, as respects a claim in respect of which an action could be heard and determined by a court in Scotland, means the Secretary of State;

    " personal injuries " includes any disease and any impairment of a person's physical or mental condition;

and any reference to breach of a contract includes a reference to breach of—

    (*a*) a term implied in a contract by or under any enactment or otherwise;

    (*b*) a term of a contract as modified by or under any enactment or otherwise; and

    (*c*) a term which, although not contained in a contract, is incorporated in the contract by another term of the contract.

(8) No order shall be made under this section unless a draft of the order has been laid before Parliament and approved by resolution of each House of Parliament.

DERIVATION
    1975, s. 109 (1)–(5) (7)–(9).

GENERAL NOTE
Subs. (1)

The ministerial power to confer jurisdiction on industrial tribunals came into being on January 1, 1976. At the time of writing no such Order has yet been published, but it is understood that a draft Order has been drawn up and is being considered by interested parties prior to being laid before Parliament. For the definition of " appropriate Minister " and " personal injuries," see subs. (7). The provisions of this section merely define the scope of the Order-making power. The Order itself will specify in greater detail the sorts of claims which may become the subject of proceedings before a tribunal.

Subs. (2)

" Breach of contract " is rather obviously explained in subs. (7). Examples of contracts " connected with employment " given by the Government at the Committee Stage of the Employment Protection Bill 1975 were those granting an employee returning after pregnancy the right to her job where her old contract had ceased to exist (envisaged by the provisions of s. 48), and a contract to treat previous employment as continuous. Presumably the Order will provide further elucidation. As described in (*a*)–(*c*), most claims arising out of disputes in the employment relationship are included (but see the limitations imposed by subs. (3)).

Subs. (3)

These conditions serve to exclude the possibility of industrial tribunals having jurisdiction in many claims otherwise falling within the descriptions of subs. (2) (*a*)–(*c*). For example, all claims arising during the existence of the contract of employment—a simple dispute over holiday pay—will not usually fall within these conditions. Their intention seems to be to include only those cases where an employee would be forced otherwise to divide his remedy between an industrial tribunal and a court. Where a claim arises on dismissal or in connection with other rights under this Act, the employee will not therefore have to pursue his remedies in two different places. It does not appear to be the intention to allow tribunals a jurisdiction outside these special circumstances.

Subs. (5)

Might this power include the modification of legislation on legal aid in civil proceedings to allow for its provision in claims before tribunals where it would have been available had the claim come before a court?

Subs. (6)

In certain cases the availability of legal aid before a court may influence the decision as to whether to bring proceedings in a court rather than before a tribunal. But see subs. (5).

Recoupment of certain benefits

Recoupment of unemployment benefit and supplementary benefit

132.—(1) This section applies to payments which are the subject of proceedings before industrial tribunals, and which are—
    (*a*) payments of wages or compensation for loss of wages; or
    (*b*) payments, by employers to employees, under Part II, III or V or section 53 or in pursuance of an award under section 103 of the Employment Protection Act 1975; or
    (*c*) payments, by employers to employees, of a nature similar to, or for a purpose corresponding to the purpose of, such payments as are mentioned in paragraph (*b*);
and to payments of remuneration in pursuance of a protective award under section 101 of the said Act of 1975.

(2) The Secretary of State may by regulations make provision with respect to payments to which this section applies for all or any of the following purposes—

(a) enabling the Secretary of State to recover from an employer, by way of total or partial recoupment of unemployment benefit or supplementary benefit, a sum not exceeding the amount of the prescribed element of the monetary award or, in the case of a protective award, the amount of the remuneration;

(b) requiring or authorising the tribunal to order the payment of such a sum, by way of total or partial recoupment of either benefit, to the Secretary of State instead of to the employee;

(c) requiring the tribunal to order the payment to the employee of only the excess of the prescribed element of the monetary award over the amount of any unemployment benefit or supplementary benefit shown to the tribunal to have been paid to the employee, and enabling the Secretary of State to recover from the employer, by way of total or partial recoupment of the benefit, a sum not exceeding that amount.

(3) Without prejudice to subsection (2), regulations under that subsection may—

(a) be so framed as to apply to all payments to which this section applies or one or more classes of those payments, and so as to apply both to unemployment benefit and supplementary benefit or only to one of those benefits;

(b) confer powers and impose duties on industrial tribunals, on the Supplementary Benefits Commission and on insurance officers and other persons;

(c) impose, on an employer to whom a monetary award or protective award relates, a duty to furnish particulars connected with the award and to suspend payments in pursuance of the award during any period prescribed by the regulations;

(d) provide for an employer who pays a sum to the Secretary of State in pursuance of this section to be relieved from any liability to pay the sum to another person;

(e) confer on an employee who is aggrieved by any decision of the Commission as to the total or partial recoupment of supplementary benefit in pursuance of the regulations (including any decision as to the amount of benefit) a right to appeal against the decision to an Appeal Tribunal constituted in accordance with the Supplementary Benefits Act 1976 and for that purpose apply section 15 (2) and (3) of that Act (appeals) with or without modifications;

(f) provide for the proof in proceedings before industrial tribunals (whether by certificate or in any other manner) of any amount of unemployment benefit or supplementary benefit paid to an employee; and

(g) make different provision for different cases.

(4) Where in pursuance of any regulations under subsection (2) a sum has been recovered by or paid to the Secretary of State by way of total or partial recoupment of unemployment benefit or supplementary benefit—

(a) section 119 (1) and (2) of the Social Security Act 1975 (repayment of benefit revised on review) shall not apply to the unemployment benefit recouped; and

(b) sections 18 and 20 of the Supplementary Benefits Act 1976 (recovery of expenditure on supplementary benefits from persons liable for maintenance and recovery in cases of misrepresentation or non-disclosure) shall not apply to the supplementary benefit recouped.

(5) Any amount found to have been duly recovered by or paid to the Secretary of State in pursuance of regulations under subsection (2) by way of total or partial recoupment of unemployment benefit shall be paid into the National Insurance Fund.

(6) In this section—

" monetary award " means the amount which is awarded or ordered to be paid, to the employee by the tribunal or would be so awarded or ordered apart from any provision of regulations under this section;

" the prescribed element ", in relation to any monetary award, means so much of that award as is attributable to such matters as may be prescribed by regulations under subsection (2);

" supplementary benefit " has the same meaning as in the Supplementary Benefits Act 1976; and

" unemployment benefit " means unemployment benefit under the Social Security Act 1975.

DERIVATION

1975, s. 112 (2) (3) (5)–(8) ; Supplementary Benefits Act 1976 (c. 71), Sched. 7, para. 40 ; Social Security (Miscellaneous Provisions) Act 1977 (c. 5), s. 16.

GENERAL NOTE

For a detailed discussion of the significance of these provisions in relation to guarantee payments and unfair dismissal compensation, see the Notes to ss. 15 (1) and 74 (2). These provisions came into force on January 1, 1976.

For regulations made under subs. (2), see the Employment Protection (Recoupment of Unemployment Benefit and Supplementary Benefit) Regulations 1977 (S.I. 1977 No. 674). These are detailed provisions. They enable the Secretary of State to recover from an employer sums paid by way of unemployment and supplementary benefit out of a prescribed part of an amount awarded by an industrial tribunal in certain proceedings brought by an employee against an employer. They apply to unfair dismissal, failure to make guarantee payments, failure to make payments in respect of remuneration for periods of medical suspension from work and protective awards. The amount prescribed in the regulations as the amount available for the purpose of recouping benefit is the amount due under the award in respect of the period for which benefit has been or is likely to have been paid. The amount recouped cannot exceed the amount of benefit actually paid. An employee may give notice in writing that he questions the correctness of the determination as to amount, and there is then a determination as to the amount. There is a right of appeal against that to the relevant statutory authorities.

Conciliation officers

General provisions as to conciliation officers

133.—(1) The provisions of subsections (2) to (6) shall have effect in relation to industrial tribunal proceedings, or claims which could be the subject of tribunal proceedings,—

(*a*) arising out of a contravention, or alleged contravention, of any of the following provisions of this Act, that is to say, sections 8, 12, 19, 23, 27, 28, 29, 31, 33 and 53; or

(*b*) arising out of a contravention, or alleged contravention, of section 99 or 102 of the Employment Protection Act 1975 or of a provision of any other Act specified by an order under subsection (7) as one to which this paragraph applies; or

(*c*) which are proceedings or claims in respect of which an industrial tribunal has jurisdiction by virtue of an order under section 131.

(2) Where a complaint has been presented to an industrial tribunal, and a copy of it has been sent to a conciliation officer, it shall be the duty of the conciliation officer—

    (*a*) if he is requested to do so by the complainant and by the person against whom the complaint is presented, or

    (*b*) if, in the absence of any such request, the conciliation officer considers that he could act under this subsection with a reasonable prospect of success,

to endeavour to promote a settlement of the complaint without its being determined by an industrial tribunal.

(3) Where at any time—

    (*a*) a person claims that action has been taken in respect of which a complaint could be presented by him to an industrial tribunal, but

    (*b*) before any complaint relating to that action has been presented by him,

a request is made to a conciliation officer (whether by that person or by the person against whom the complaint could be made) to make his services available to them, the conciliation officer shall act in accordance with subsection (2) as if a complaint has been presented to an industrial tribunal.

(4) Subsections (2) and (3) shall apply, with appropriate modifications, to the presentation of a claim and the reference of a question to an industrial tribunal as they apply to the presentation of a complaint.

(5) In proceeding under subsection (2) or (3) a conciliation officer shall, where appropriate, have regard to the desirability of encouraging the use of other procedures available for the settlement of grievances.

(6) Anything communicated to a conciliation officer in connection with the performance of his functions under this section shall not be admissible in evidence in any proceedings before an industrial tribunal, except with the consent of the person who communicated it to that officer.

(7) The Secretary of State may by order—

    (*a*) direct that further provisions of this Act be added to the list in subsection (1) (*a*);

    (*b*) specify a provision of any other Act as one to which subsection (1) (*b*) applies.

DERIVATION
    1975, s. 108 (2)–(8).

GENERAL NOTE
Subs. (1)
    Cf. the similar provisions of s. 134.

At December 1, 1976, 212 persons were in posts as conciliation officers at ACAS—all of them full-time. The south-east regional office of ACAS, which covers a working population of about 8 million from the Wash to the Isle of Wight, is now the Service's busiest office. Each working day it handles nearly 400 inquiries by telephone or letter from employers, trade unions and individuals on all aspects of industrial relations. In a year this represents about a third of all ACAS' regional work throughout the country. About 80 per cent. of inquiries concern unfair dismissal (see s. 134).

The new statutory rights for individuals in the Employment Protection Act 1975 produced only 905 cases received by ACAS for conciliation in 1976. The single largest number concerned written statements of the reasons for dismissal—which were almost universally associated with unfair dismissal cases. Of the 481 cases completed during 1976, 147 (31 per cent.) were settled by ACAS, 10 (2 per cent.) were settled privately, and 132 (27 per cent.) were withdrawn. 192 (40 per cent.) were referred to tribunals for hearing.

Subs. (2)

An agreement not to pursue remedies granted by the Act as a consequence of conciliation may be binding: s. 140 (2) (*e*). And see *Duport Furniture Products Ltd.* v. *Moore, The Times,* October 18, 1978 (E.A.T.).

Functions of conciliation officers on complaint under s. 67

134.—(1) Where a complaint has been presented to an industrial tribunal under section 67 by a person (in this section referred to as the complainant) and a copy of it has been sent to a conciliation officer, it shall be the duty of the conciliation officer—

> (*a*) if he is requested to do so by the complainant and by the employer against whom it was presented, or
>
> (*b*) if, in the absence of any such request, the conciliation officer considers that he could act under this section with a reasonable prospect of success,

to endeavour to promote a settlement of the complaint without its being determined by an industrial tribunal.

(2) For the purpose of promoting such a settlement, in a case where the complainant has ceased to be employed by the employer against whom the complaint was made,—

> (*a*) the conciliation officer shall in particular seek to promote the reinstatement or re-engagement of the complainant by the employer, or by a successor of the employer or by an associated employer, on terms appearing to the conciliation officer to be equitable; but
>
> (*b*) where the complainant does not wish to be reinstated or re-engaged, or where reinstatement or re-engagement is not practicable, and the parties desire the conciliation officer to act under this section, he shall seek to promote agreement between them as to a sum by way of compensation to be paid by the employer to the complainant.

(3) Where at any time—

> (*a*) after the complainant has ceased to be employed by an employer, in circumstances where the employee claims that he was unfairly dismissed, but
>
> (*b*) before any complaint relating to that claim has been presented by the claimant under section 67,

a request is made to a conciliation officer (whether by the employer or by the employee) to make his services available to them, the conciliation officer shall act in accordance with subsections (1) and (2) as if a complaint had been presented in pursuance of that claim.

(4) In proceeding under subsections (1) to (3), a conciliation officer shall where appropriate have regard to the desirability of encouraging the use of other procedures available for the settlement of grievances.

(5) Anything communicated to a conciliation officer in connection with the performance of his functions under this section shall not be admissible in evidence in any proceedings before an industrial tribunal, except with the consent of the person who communicated it to that officer.

Derivation

1974, para. 26 (2) (3) (4) (4A) (5); 1975, Sched. 16, Pt. III, paras. 24, 25.

General Note

Cf. the similar provisions of s. 133, and the Notes to that section.

Subs. (1)

During 1976, ACAS received 38,107 cases of alleged unfair dismissal for conciliation, as compared with 29,100 in 1975. 36,562 cases were completed during the year. Of those, 11,636 (32 per cent.) were settled by conciliation, another 1,323 (4 per cent.) were settled privately, and 7,440 (20 per cent.) were withdrawn. Of all those dealt with, 56 per cent. were cleared without reference to the tribunal. The remaining 16,163 cases (44 per cent.) were forwarded to the tribunal for hearing. (For details as to the outcome of conciliation—see the Note to Pt. V.)

Subs. (2)

An agreement not to pursue remedies granted by the Act as a consequence of conciliation may be binding: s. 140 (2) (*e*). In *Duport Furniture Products Ltd.* v. *Moore, The Times,* October 18, 1978 (E.A.T.), Kilner Brown J. confirmed that the use of COT 3 to record an agreement was the necessary action taken by a conciliation officer in accordance with s. 140 (2) (*e*) and so the employee concerned was not entitled to bring a claim of unfair dismissal before the industrial tribunal.

Subs. (5)

The effect of this provision was considered in *Grazebrook* v. *Wallens* [1973] I.C.R. 256, where it was said that: " It is not intended to render evidence inadmissible which could have been given if there had been no communication to the conciliation officer. . . . The test is whether evidence exists in an admissible form apart from evidence based upon such communication to the conciliation officer."

Employment Appeal Tribunal

Employment Appeal Tribunal

135.—(1) The Employment Appeal Tribunal established under section 87 of the Employment Protection Act 1975 shall continue in existence by that name for the purpose of hearing appeals under section 136.

(2) The Employment Appeal Tribunal (in this Act referred to as " the Appeal Tribunal ") shall consist of—

(*a*) such number of judges as may be nominated from time to time by the Lord Chancellor from among the judges (other than the Lord Chancellor) of the High Court and the Court of Appeal;

(*b*) at least one judge of the Court of Session nominated from time to time by the Lord President of that Court; and

(*c*) such number of other members as may be appointed from time to time by Her Majesty on the joint recommendation of the Lord Chancellor and the Secretary of State.

(3) The members of the Appeal Tribunal appointed under subsection (2) (*c*) shall be persons who appear to the Lord Chancellor and the Secretary of State to have special knowledge or experience of industrial relations, either as representatives of employers or as representatives of workers (within the meaning of the Trade Union and Labour Relations Act 1974).

(4) The Lord Chancellor shall, after consultation with the Lord President of the Court of Session, appoint one of the judges nominated under subsection (2) to be President of the Appeal Tribunal.

(5) No judge shall be nominated a member of the Appeal Tribunal except with his consent.

(6) The provisions of Schedule 11 shall have effect with respect to the Appeal Tribunal and proceedings before the Tribunal.

DERIVATION
   1975, s. 87.

GENERAL NOTE
Subs. (1)

Comparison of the E.A.T. with the N.I.R.C. is inevitable, and certainly many of the provisions of ss. 135–136 of and Sched. 11 to this Act are similar to those of ss. 99, 114–115 of and Pts. II and V of Sched. 3 to the Industrial Relations Act

1971. In an illuminating article in (1978) 7 I.L.J. 137, the former President of the E.A.T., Mr. Justice Phillips points out that the Industrial Relations Act itself drew heavily on the Restrictive Practices Act 1956 which set up the Restrictive Practices Court. He notes that that court was primarily concerned with deciding questions of fact and opinion rather than law.

The most important difference between the E.A.T. and the N.I.R.C. is evident from the former's title: it is exclusively an appeal tribunal—it has no original jurisdiction of its own. Also, unlike the National Industrial Relations Court, the co-operation of trade unions and employers will in practice be required for its ordinary operation (Sched. 11, para. 16). By refusing to co-operate (i.e. by refusing consent for proceedings to be heard save before the E.A.T. consisting of a judge and members representing both sides of industry, and instructing representatives not to accept appointment) either employers' or workers' organisations could paralyse the normal operation of the E.A.T. The N.I.R.C. only narrowly escaped this sort of paralysis by a last-minute amendment of the relevant provisions of the Industrial Relations Bill.

Subs. (2)

In an article in the *Department of Employment Gazette* of March 1977 (p. 218), Phillips J. stated that the E.A.T. aimed to have three judges in London at any one time from a panel of six or seven—himself on a full-time basis and the others in sessions of six weeks at a time. Due to the shortage of High Court judges, he considered that in the long term, amendment to the legislation enabling Circuit Judges to sit on the E.A.T. might solve the problem.

In Scotland, the E.A.T. is operated by Lord McDonald, a judge of the Court of Session.

Subs. (3)

Unlike the N.I.R.C., the E.A.T. may have no " independent " members. All appointees are to have had experience as representatives of employers or workers. In practice, the result will probably be that ordinary workers and employers are excluded in favour of union officials and representatives of employers' organisations. (But note the reference to TULRA—which was not present in s. 87 (3) of the Employment Protection Act 1975.)

Once appointed, lay members are to act as independent uncommitted lay judges—they are not to support one side or the other and are to be totally objective and impartial—though they have equal voting power with the judge. So an appeal tribunal consisting predominantly of laymen decides questions of law. Yet in practice unanimity is the rule. Of the 891 appeals heard in the first 21 months of its experience (the E.A.T. was set up on March 30, 1976), the number in which there was a disagreement was less than 20, and the number in which the judge was in a minority was three. In *Marley Tile Co. Ltd.* v. *Shaw* [1978] I.R.L.R. 238 (E.A.T.), Phillips J. stated that where the expert members of the E.A.T. were not in agreement upon a matter which is particularly within their competence to decide, it seemed to him the correct approach was to come down in favour of affirming the decision appealed from, especially where the expert members of the industrial tribunal were in agreement.

Appeals to Tribunal from industrial tribunals and Certification Officer

136.—(1) An appeal shall lie to the Appeal Tribunal on a question of law arising from any decision of, or arising in any proceedings before, an industrial tribunal under, or by virtue of, the following Acts—

(a) the Equal Pay Act 1970;
(b) the Sex Discrimination Act 1975;
(c) the Employment Protection Act 1975;
(d) the Race Relations Act 1976;
(e) this Act.

(2) The Appeal Tribunal shall hear appeals on questions of law arising in any proceedings before, or arising from any decision of, the Certification Officer under the following enactments—

(a) sections 3, 4 and 5 of the Trade Union Act 1913;
(b) section 4 of the Trade Union (Amalgamations, etc.) Act 1964.

(3) The Appeal Tribunal shall hear appeals on questions of fact or law arising in any proceedings before, or arising from any decision of, the Certification Officer under the following enactments—

(*a*) section 8 of the Trade Union and Labour Relations Act 1974;

(*b*) section 8 of the Employment Protection Act 1975.

(4) Without prejudice to section 13 of the Administration of Justice Act 1960 (appeal in case of contempt of court), an appeal shall lie on any question of law from any decision or order of the Appeal Tribunal with the leave of the Tribunal or of the Court of Appeal or, as the case may be, the Court of Session,—

(*a*) in the case of proceedings in England and Wales, to the Court of Appeal;

(*b*) in the case of proceedings in Scotland, to the Court of Session.

(5) No appeal shall lie except to the Appeal Tribunal from any decision of an industrial tribunal under the Acts listed in subsection (1) or from any decision under the enactments listed in subsections (2) and (3) of the Certification Officer appointed under section 7 of the Employment Protection Act 1975.

DERIVATION

    1975, s. 88; Race Relations Act 1976 (c. 74), Sched. 3, para. 1 (4).

GENERAL NOTE

Subs. (1)

    Statistics of appeals. According to figures given by Phillips J. in (1978) 7 I.L.J. 137, during the first 21 months of its experience (from March 30, 1976), the E.A.T. received 1,527 appeals, of which 891 proceeded to a hearing. The proportion of appeals from industrial tribunals is a little over 4 per cent. Far and away the largest class of appeals concerned cases of unfair dismissal, and within that class, the largest type of appeal concerned the questions posed by s. 57 (3).

    A more detailed breakdown of appeals over the first 12 months of its existence (March 30, 1976–March 31, 1977) is available from the *Department of Employment Gazette* of May 1977 (p. 442). This shows a total of 883 appeals, of which 199 were withdrawn before hearing and 443 disposed of on hearing (241 remaining outstanding at March 31, 1977). Of the 443 appeals disposed of on hearing, 235 were dismissed (53 per cent.), 86 were allowed (19·4 per cent.), 120 were remitted (27 per cent.) and two were withdrawn.

    Of the total of 883 appeals, 679 were under TULRA, 92 under the Redundancy Payments Act 1965, and a further 16 combined the two. 56 were under the Equal Pay Act 1970, and only 14 under the Employment Protection Act 1975. The rest (Sex Discrimination Act, Contracts of Employment Act, and various combined claims) accounted for 26 appeals.

    Questions of law and politics. In his Notes on the E.A.T. in (1978) 7 I.L.J. 137, Phillips J. makes some fascinating comments on how the E.A.T. has gone about defining its own approach to " what is a question of law? " He puts forward three categories of cases falling into this field.

    First, a question of the construction of a statute. He concedes that there is usually more than one answer—and forthrightly declares that in deciding which answer to uphold as the law he values highly the expert members' views of how the different answers will work in practice—the advantages and disadvantages of rival interpretations. This should lay to rest the long standing debate as to the relevance of policy to determining questions of law. For what is or is not the most desirable practice is eminently a question of policy.

    Secondly, a ground of appeal lies where there is no evidence to support the industrial tribunal's basic findings of fact. And again, Phillips J. points out the tendency of the expert members to respond more to appeals on this ground— since " being expert in the field the facts speak more loudly to them, perhaps, than to the judge." Again, industrial relations experience more than legal knowledge is clearly one factor in deciding what is a question of law.

    But it is in the third case that the political implications of deciding what is a question of law come out most clearly. That is where the appellant argues that the decision of the industrial tribunal is so unreasonable that it must be wrong.

Phillips J. makes the necessary genuflection towards the common law authorities (favouring the speech of Lord Radcliffe in *Edwards* v. *Bairstow* [1956] A.C. 14). But he gives as the formula adopted by the E.A.T. the following: " if we, that is the judge, the representative of the employers and the representative of the workers, are individually and collectively satisfied that the decision is ' wrong,' judged by the standards of good industrial practice, we feel justified in saying that the decision is a contrary one, and is wrong in point of law " (p. 140).

So good industrial practice is a powerful signpost to saying a question of law exists on which an appeal may be based. And, to repeat a point already made— the political orientation of the sitting judges and members will determine what is good industrial practice. That this is denied outright by judges and others should not reflect on its accuracy. For, Phillips J. says in the same I.L.J. article that " it can scarcely be thought to be straying into the field of politics to observe that (the system of labour law) is remarkably lop-sided. . . . Thus there is a complete withdrawal of the law from the field of industrial disputes, and trade unions in many respects remain outside the law." The increasing frequency with which injunctions are being handed out to employers in industrial disputes makes one doubt that statement—and one must wonder what effect the views expressed have on decisions upon claims of unfair dismissal arising out of industrial action (see Notes to s. 62).

Subs. (3)

The E.A.T. early decided that there was no general right of appeal against a decision of the Certification Officer under s. 8 of the Employment Protection Act 1975 (*General and Municipal Workers Union* v. *Certification Officer* [1977] 1 All E.R. 771), thus eliminating a large number of possible appeals under this heading.

Subs. (4)

Although a superior court of record headed by a judge, the E.A.T. has only the powers of the body or officer appealed from, and its decision or award has only the same effect and is enforced in the same manner as that body's or officer's decision or award (see Sched. 11). It would seem that, prima facie, it has not the power to enforce its judgments by order, as could the NIRC. It was argued at the Committee Stage of the Employment Protection Bill 1975, however, that such powers are in effect granted to the E.A.T. by para. 22, particularly by virtue of the phrase " all other matters incidental to its jurisdiction." This, it was said, included the enforcement of awards. Thus, para. 23 envisages fines for contempt. The Government insisted that while the E.A.T. could punish for contempt of itself, it could not do so for refusal to comply with any order—and the orders of the E.A.T. were not enforceable in that sense (see the debate in the report of Standing Committee F on the Employment Protection Bill, 23rd Sitting, July 8, 1975, cols. 1223–1230).

PART IX

MISCELLANEOUS AND SUPPLEMENTAL

Extension of employment protection legislation

Power to extend employment protection legislation

137.—(1) Her Majesty may by Order in Council provide that—
  (*a*) the provisions of this Act; and
  (*b*) any legislation (that is to say any enactment of the Parliament of Northern Ireland and any provision made by or under a Measure of the Northern Ireland Assembly) for the time being in force in Northern Ireland which makes provision for purposes corresponding to any of the purposes of this Act,
shall, to such extent and for such purposes as may be specified in the Order, apply (with or without modification) to or in relation to any person in employment to which this section applies.

(2) This section applies to employment for the purposes of any activities—

    (*a*) in the territorial waters of the United Kingdom; or

    (*b*) connected with the exploration of the sea bed or subsoil or the exploitation of their natural resources in any area designated by order under section 1 (7) of the Continental Shelf Act 1964; or

    (*c*) connected with the exploration or exploitation, in a foreign sector of the continental shelf, of a cross-boundary petroleum field.

(3) An Order in Council under subsection (1)—

    (*a*) may make different provision for different cases;

    (*b*) may provide that all or any of the enactments referred to in subsection (1), as applied by such an Order, shall apply to individuals whether or not they are British subjects and to bodies corporate whether or not they are incorporated under the law of any part of the United Kingdom (notwithstanding that the application may affect their activities outside the United Kingdom);

    (*c*) may make provision for conferring jurisdiction on any court or class of court specified in the Order, or on industrial tribunals, in respect of offences, causes of action or other matters arising in connection with employment to which this section applies;

    (*d*) without prejudice to the generality of subsection (1) or of paragraph (*a*), may provide that the enactments referred to in subsection (1), as applied by the Order, shall apply in relation to any person in employment for the purposes of such activities as are referred to in subsection (2) in any part of the areas specified in paragraphs (*a*) and (*b*) of that subsection;

    (*e*) may exclude from the operation of section 3 of the Territorial Waters Jurisdiction Act 1878 (consents required for prosecutions) proceedings for offences under the enactments referred to in subsection (1) in connection with employment to which this section applies;

    (*f*) may provide that such proceedings shall not be brought without such consent as may be required by the Order;

    (*g*) may, without prejudice to the generality of the power under subsection (1) to modify the enactments referred to in that subsection in their application for the purposes of this section, modify or exclude the operation of sections 141 and 144 or paragraph 14 of Schedule 13 or of any corresponding provision in any such Northern Irish legislation as is referred to in subsection (1) (*b*).

(4) Any jurisdiction conferred on any court or tribunal under this section shall be without prejudice to jurisdiction exercisable apart from this section by that or any other court or tribunal.

(5) In subsection (2) above—

    " cross-boundary petroleum field " means a petroleum field that extends across the boundary between a designated area and a foreign sector of the continental shelf;

    " foreign sector of the continental shelf " means an area which is outside the territorial waters of any State and within which rights are exercisable by a State other than the United Kingdom with respect to the sea bed and subsoil and their natural resources;

    " petroleum field " means a geological structure identified as an oil or gas field by the Order in Council concerned.

DERIVATION
   1975, s. 127 (1) (c)–(g), (2)–(4).

GENERAL NOTE
   In relation to subs. (2) (a) and (b), see the Employment Protection (Offshore Employment) Order 1976 (S.I. 1976 No. 766), as amended by the Employment Protection (Offshore Employment) (Amendment) Order 1977 (S.I. 1977 No. 588), which applies, with exceptions and modifications, the provisions of the Acts contained in subs. (1) (a)–(f) of this section to or in relation to powers in certain employments in British Territorial Waters and designated areas of the Continental Shelf. The order does not extend to areas adjacent to Northern Ireland. There are transitional provisions relating to ss. 99 and 100 of the Employment Protection Act 1975.

Crown employment

Application of Act to Crown employment

138.—(1) Subject to the following provisions of this section, Parts I (so far as it relates to itemised pay statements), II, III (except section 44), V, VIII and this Part and section 53 shall have effect in relation to Crown employment and to persons in Crown employment as they have effect in relation to other employment and to other employees.

(2) In this section, subject to subsections (3) to (5), " Crown employment " means employment under or for the purposes of a government department or any officer or body exercising on behalf of the Crown functions conferred by any enactment.

(3) This section does not apply to service as a member of the naval, military or air forces of the Crown, or of any women's service administered by the Defence Council, but does apply to employment by any association established for the purposes of the Auxiliary Forces Act 1953.

(4) For the purposes of this section, Crown employment does not include any employment in respect of which there is in force a certificate issued by or on behalf of a Minister of the Crown certifying that employment of a description specified in the certificate, or the employment of a particular person so specified, is (or, at a time specified in the certificate, was) required to be excepted from this section for the purpose of safeguarding national security; and any document purporting to be a certificate so issued shall be received in evidence and shall, unless the contrary is proved, be deemed to be such a certificate.

(5) For the purposes of Parts I (so far as it relates to itemised pay statements), II, III (except section 44 (3) and (4)), V, VII (except section 126 (3) and (4)), VIII and this Part and section 53, none of the bodies referred to in Schedule 5 shall be regarded as performing functions on behalf of the Crown and accordingly employment by any such body shall not be Crown employment within the meaning of this section.

(6) For the purposes of the application of the provisions of this Act in relation to employment by any such body as is referred to in subsection (5), any reference to redundancy shall be construed as a reference to the existence of such circumstances as, in accordance with any arrangements for the time being in force as mentioned in section 111 (3), are treated as equivalent to redundancy in relation to such employment.

(7) For the purposes of the application of the provisions of this Act in relation to Crown employment in accordance with subsection (1)—
   (a) any reference to an employee shall be construed as a reference to a person in Crown employment;

(b) any reference to a contract of employment shall be construed as a reference to the terms of employment of a person in Crown employment;

(c) any reference to dismissal shall be construed as a reference to the termination of Crown employment;

(d) any reference to redundancy shall be construed as a reference to the existence of such circumstances as, in accordance with any arrangements for the time being in force as mentioned in section 111 (3), are treated as equivalent to redundancy in relation to Crown employment;

(e) the reference in paragraph 1 (5) (c) of Schedule 9 to a person's undertaking or any undertaking in which he works shall be construed as a reference to the national interest; and

(f) any other reference to an undertaking shall be construed, in relation to a Minister of the Crown, as a reference to his functions or (as the context may require) to the department of which he is in charge and, in relation to a government department, officer or body, shall be construed as a reference to the functions of the department, officer or body or (as the context may require) to the department, officer or body.

(8) Where the terms of employment of a person in Crown employment restrict his right to take part in—

(a) certain political activities; or

(b) activities which may conflict with his official functions,

nothing in section 29 shall require him to be allowed time off work for public duties connected with any such activities.

DERIVATION

1974, para. 33; 1975, s. 121, Sched. 16, Pt. III, paras. 33, 34.

House of Commons Staff

Provisions as to House of Commons staff

139.—(1) The provisions of Parts I (so far as it relates to itemised pay statements), II, III (except section 44), V and VIII, and this Part and section 53 shall apply to relevant members of House of Commons staff as they apply to persons in Crown employment within the meaning of section 138 and accordingly for the purposes of the application of those provisions in relation to any such members—

(a) any reference to an employee shall be construed as a reference to any such member;

(b) any reference to a contract of employment shall be construed as including a reference to the terms of employment of any such member;

(c) any reference to dismissal shall be construed as including a reference to the termination of any such member's employment;

(d) the reference in paragraph 1 (5) (c) of Schedule 9 to a person's undertaking or any undertaking in which he works shall be construed as a reference to the national interest or, if the case so requires, the interests of the House of Commons; and

(e) any other reference to an undertaking shall be construed as a reference to the House of Commons.

(2) Nothing in any rule of law or the law or practice of Parliament shall prevent a relevant member of the House of Commons staff from bringing a civil employment claim before the court or from bringing

before an industrial tribunal proceedings of any description which could be brought before such a tribunal by any person who is not such a member.

(3) In this section—

"relevant member of the House of Commons staff" means—

   (*a*) any person appointed by the House of Commons Commission (in this section referred to as the Commission) or employed in the refreshment department; and

   (*b*) any member of Mr. Speaker's personal staff;

"civil employment claim" means a claim arising out of or relating to a contract of employment or any other contract connected with employment, or a claim in tort arising in connection with a person's employment; and

"the court" means the High Court or the county court.

(4) It is hereby declared that for the purposes of the enactments applied by subsection (1) and of Part VI (where applicable to relevant members of House of Commons staff) and for the purposes of any civil employment claim—

   (*a*) the Commission is the employer of staff appointed by the Commission; and

   (*b*) Mr. Speaker is the employer of his personal staff and of any person employed in the refreshment department and not falling within paragraph (*a*);

but the foregoing provision shall have effect subject to subsection (5).

(5) The Commission or, as the case may be, Mr. Speaker may designate for all or any of the purposes mentioned in subsection (4)—

   (*a*) any description of staff other than Mr. Speaker's personal staff; and

   (*b*) in relation to staff so designated, any person;

and where a person is so designated he, instead of the Commission or Mr. Speaker, shall be deemed for the purposes to which the designation relates to be the employer of the persons in relation to whom he is so designated.

(6) Where any proceedings are brought by virtue of this section against the Commission or Mr. Speaker or any person designated under subsection (5), the person against whom the proceedings are brought may apply to the court or the industrial tribunal, as the case may be, to have some other person against whom the proceedings could at the time of the application be properly brought substituted for him as a party to those proceedings.

(7) For the purposes mentioned in subsection (4) a person's employment in or for the purposes of the House of Commons shall not, provided he continues to be employed in such employment, be treated as terminated by reason only of a change (whether effected before or after the passing of the House of Commons (Administration) Act 1978, and whether effected by virtue of that Act or otherwise) in his employer and (provided he so continues) his first appointment to such employment shall be deemed after the change to have been made by his employer for the time being, and accordingly—

   (*a*) he shall be treated for the purposes so mentioned as being continuously employed by that employer from the commencement of such employment until its termination; and

   (*b*) anything done by or in relation to his employer for the time being in respect of such employment before the change shall be so treated as having been done by or in relation to the person who is his employer for the time being after the change.

(8) In subsection (7) " employer for the time being ", in relation to a person who has ceased to be employed in or for the purposes of the House of Commons, means the person who was his employer immediately before he ceased to be so employed, except that where some other person would have been his employer for the time being if he had not ceased to be so employed, it means that other person.

(9) If the House of Commons resolves at any time that any provision of subsections (3) to (6) should be amended in its application to any member of the staff of that House, Her Majesty may by Order in Council amend that provision accordingly.

DERIVATION
    1975, s. 122 (1), (3)–(8) ; House of Commons (Administration) Act 1978, Sched. 2, para. 5.

Contracting out of provisions of Act

Restrictions on contracting out

140.—(1) Except as provided by the following provisions of this section, any provision in an agreement (whether a contract of employment or not) shall be void in so far as it purports—

(a) to exclude or limit the operation of any provision of this Act; or
(b) to preclude any person from presenting a complaint to, or bringing any proceedings under this Act before, an industrial tribunal.

(2) Subsection (1) shall not apply—

(a) to any provision in a collective agreement excluding rights under section 12 if an order under section 18 is for the time being in force in respect of it;
(b) to any union membership agreement so far as it affects the rights of an employee—
    (i) under section 23 in accordance with subsection (4) of that section;
    (ii) under section 58 in accordance with subsection (3) of that section;
(c) to any provision in a dismissal procedures agreement excluding rights under section 54 if that provision is not to have effect unless an order under section 65 is for the time being in force in respect of it;
(d) to any agreement to refrain from presenting a complaint under section 67, where in compliance with a request under section 134 (3) a conciliation officer has taken action in accordance with that subsection;
(e) to any agreement to refrain from proceeding with a complaint presented under section 67 where a conciliation officer has taken action in accordance with section 134 (1) and (2);
(f) to any provision in an agreement if an order under section 96 is for the time being in force in respect of it;
(g) to any agreement to refrain from instituting or continuing any proceedings before an industrial tribunal where a conciliation officer has taken action in accordance with section 133 (2) or (3);
(h) to any provision of an agreement relating to dismissal from employment such as is mentioned in section 142 (1) or (2).

DERIVATION
    1965, s. 25 (4) ; 1972, s. 2 (4) ; 1974, para. 32, 1975, s. 118.

Excluded classes of employment

Employment outside Great Britain

141.—(1) Sections 1 to 4 and 49 to 51 do not apply in relation to employment during any period when the employee is engaged in work wholly or mainly outside Great Britain unless the employee ordinarily works in Great Britain and the work outside Great Britain is for the same employer.

(2) Sections 8 and 53 and Parts II, III, V and VII do not apply to employment where under his contract of employment the employee ordinarily works outside Great Britain.

(3) An employee shall not be entitled to a redundancy payment if on the relevant date he is outside Great Britain, unless under his contract of employment he ordinarily worked in Great Britain.

(4) An employee who under his contract of employment ordinarily works outside Great Britain shall not be entitled to a redundancy payment unless on the relevant date he is in Great Britain in accordance with instructions given to him by his employer.

(5) For the purpose of subsection (2), a person employed to work on board a ship registered in the United Kingdom (not being a ship registered at a port outside Great Britain) shall, unless—

(a) the employment is wholly outside Great Britain, or

(b) he is not ordinarily resident in Great Britain,

be regarded as a person who under his contract ordinarily works in Great Britain.

DERIVATION

1972, s. 12 (1); 1974, para. 9 (2), (3); 1975, s. 119 (5), (6); 1965, s. 17, (1), (2).

GENERAL NOTE

There has been some difficulty over this section in a number of cases. The difficulty was in deciding whether an employee worked inside or outside Great Britain, when in fact he worked all over the place, including places outside Great Britain. This has arisen in particular with regard to workers on oil rigs (see, *e.g.* [1975] I.R.L.R. 341; [1976] I.R.L.R. 91).

The E.A.T., when it finally considered the problem, took the following view: the law is that anybody who ordinarily works outside Great Britain is not entitled to protection. In many cases, workers work both inside and outside Great Britain, that is, they *ordinarily* work both inside and outside. Since they ordinarily work outside (as well as inside) Great Britain, they are not protected. So in May 1976, in *Portec (U.K.) Ltd.* v. *H. Mogensen* [1976] I.R.L.R. 209 (E.A.T.), Bristow J. rejected a claim by a managing director who looked after the factory in Wales but also ran sales from Paris.

It is striking that this view excludes from protection many people who ordinarily work inside Great Britain (though they may also ordinarily work outside Great Britain). Using the judge's reasoning, he would be "driven" to the opposite conclusion if the statute had stated that workers may claim "if they ordinarily work inside Great Britain" (even if they also work outside). He, however, was convinced that it was the intention of Parliament to exclude people who ordinarily worked inside the U.K., so long as they committed the mistake of also working ordinarily outside it.

The E.A.T. followed the same line in October 1976: in *Wilson* v. *Maynard Shipbuilding Consultants AB* [1976] I.R.L.R. 384. Phillips J. said of a staff consultant that he did work abroad for substantial periods of time. Proportions were unimportant. Under his contract's terms he was working abroad in the ordinary performance of his contract—he was not protected. But the Court of Appeal in November 1977, a year later, overturned the E.A.T.'s point of view. They allowed an appeal by the worker in *Wilson* v. *Maynard Shipbuilding Consultants AB* [1977] I.R.L.R. 491. They said a person cannot at the same time be said to be ordinarily working both inside and outside Great Britain. They said the question is *not* to be determined by looking at the proportions of time actually spent inside or outside Great Britain. The correct approach is to look at the terms of the contract in order to ascertain *where the employee's base is to be.* The country where his base is to be is likely to be the place where he is to be treated as ordinarily working. The terms which indicate the base were said to include: (1) where his headquarters are; (2) where the travels involved in his employment begin and end; (3) where his private residence—his home—is or is expected to be; (4) where, and perhaps in what currency he is to be paid; and (5) whether he is to be subject to pay national insurance contributions in Great Britain.

Despite this guidance, Bristow J. seemed unable to resolve the problem in a way which protects employees. In *Claisse* v. *Hostetter, Stewart & Keydril Ltd.* [1978] I.R.L.R. 205 (E.A.T.), the worker lost again. Bristow J. accepted that the C.A. had told him he was wrong in *Portec,* but after consideration, he fixed the employee's base on the oil-rig, and thus left him unprotected. In *Todd* v. *British Midland Airways Ltd.* [1978] I.R.L.R. 370 (C.A.), Lord Denning reaffirmed the principle in *Wilson* and opined that it had been misapplied by the E.A.T. in *Claisse.* (For a general consideration of this and other problems, see the article by M. Forde in [1978] I.L.J. 228.)

Contracts for a fixed term

142.—(1) Section 54 does not apply to dismissal from employment under a contract for a fixed term of two years or more, where the dismissal consists only of the expiry of that term without its being renewed, if before the term so expires the employee has agreed in writing to exclude any claim in respect of rights under that section in relation to that contract.

(2) An employee employed under a contract of employment for a fixed term of two years or more entered into after 5th December 1965 shall not be entitled to a redundancy payment in respect of the expiry of that term without its being renewed (whether by the employer or by an associated employer of his), if before the term so expires he has agreed in writing to exclude any right to a redundancy payment in that event.

(3) Such an agreement as is mentioned in subsection (1) or (2) may be contained either in the contract itself or in a separate agreement.

(4) Where an agreement under subsection (2) is made during the currency of a fixed term, and that term is renewed, the agreement under that subsection shall not be construed as applying to the term as renewed, but without prejudice to the making of a further agreement under that subsection in relation to the term so renewed.

DERIVATION
 1974, para. 12 (*b*); 1965, s. 15 (2) to (4).

GENERAL NOTE
 As to what is a fixed term contract—see the Note to s. 55 (1) and (2) (*Expiry of fixed term contract*).

Minimum periods of employment

143.—(1) An employee shall not be entitled to a guarantee payment in respect of any day unless he has been continuously employed for a period of four weeks ending with the last complete week before that day.

(2) An employee shall not be entitled to remuneration under section 19 unless he has been continuously employed for a period of four weeks ending with the last complete week before the day on which the suspension begins.

(3) Subject to subsection (4)—
 (*a*) sections 12 and 19 do not apply to employment under a contract for a fixed term of twelve weeks or less; and

(b) sections 12, 19 and 49 do not apply to employment under a contract made in contemplation of the performance of a specific task which is not expected to last for more than twelve weeks.

(4) Subsection (3) does not apply where the employee has been continuously employed for a period of more than twelve weeks.

DERIVATION
1975, ss. 22 (3), 30 (1), 119 (7); 1972, s. 9 (2A); 1975, Sched. 16, Pt. II, para. 10 (a).

GENERAL NOTE
See Note to s. 12 (1) (*Excluded classes of employment*), and the General Note to s. 49 (*Exclusions*).

Mariners

144.—(1) Sections 1 to 6 and 49 to 51 do not apply to—
   (a) a person employed as a master of or a seaman on a sea-going British ship having a gross registered tonnage of eighty tons or more, including a person ordinarily employed as a seaman who is employed in or about such a ship in port by the owner or charterer of the ship to do work of a kind ordinarily done by a seaman on such a ship while it is in port, or
   (b) a person employed as a skipper of or a seaman on a fishing boat for the time being required to be registered under section 373 of the Merchant Shipping Act 1894.

(2) Sections 8 and 53 and Parts II, III and V to VII do not apply to employment as master or as a member of the crew of a fishing vessel where the employee is remunerated only by a share in the profits or gross earnings of the vessel.

(3) Section 141 (3) and (4) do not apply to an employee, and section 142 (2) does not apply to a contract of employment, if the employee is employed as a master or seaman in a British ship and is ordinarily resident in Great Britain.

(4) Sections 8, 29, 31, 122 and 123 do not apply to employment as a merchant seaman.

(5) Employment as a merchant seaman does not include employment in the fishing industry or employment on board a ship otherwise than by the owner, manager or charterer of that ship except employment as a radio officer, but, save as aforesaid, it includes employment as master or a member of the crew of any ship and as a trainee undergoing training for the sea service, and employment in or about a ship in port by the owner, manager or charterer of the ship to do work of the kind ordinarily done by a merchant seaman on a ship while it is in port.

DERIVATION
1972, s. 9 (2); 1975, s. 119 (4); 1974, para. 9 (1) (d); 1965, ss. 16 (2), 20; 1975, s. 119 (12), (13).

Dock workers

145.—(1) Sections 1 to 6 and 49 to 51 do not apply to any registered dock worker except when engaged in work which is not dock work.

(2) Sections 12, 19, 31, 53, 54, 122 and 123 do not apply to employment as a registered dock worker other than employment by virtue of which the employee is wholly or mainly engaged in work which is not dock work.

(3) Subject to subsection (4), section 81 does not apply to any person in respect of his employment as a registered dock worker, unless

it is employment by virtue of which he is wholly or mainly engaged in work which is not dock work.

(4) Subsection (3) does not apply where—

    (*a*) the person became a registered dock worker in consequence of having been employed on work which became classified;

    (*b*) at the date of the termination of his employment he has been continuously employed since a time before that work was classified; and

    (*c*) as a result of the termination he ceases to be a registered dock worker,

and, for the purposes of this subsection, Schedule 13 shall have effect subject to the provisions of the new Scheme.

(5) In this section—

    " classified " means classified as dock work for the purposes of the new Scheme by an order under section 11 of the Dock Work Regulation Act 1976;

    " dock work ", in relation to a dock worker registered under the 1967 Scheme, means the same as in that Scheme and in relation to one registered under the new Scheme means any work which, by reference to what it is or where it is done, is classified;

    " registered " means registered under the 1967 Scheme or under the new Scheme, and in relation to a worker who is registered under the Scheme, means registered in a main register thereunder, and not in an extension register;

    " the 1967 Scheme " means the Scheme made under the Dock Workers (Regulation of Employment) Act 1946 and set out, as varied, in Schedule 2 to the Dock Workers (Regulation of Employment) (Amendment) Order 1967;

    " the new Scheme " means the Scheme made and in force under section 4 of the Dock Work Regulation Act 1976.

DERIVATION
    Dock Work Regulation Act 1976 (c. 79), ss. 14 (1)–(3), (5), (6), (8), 15 (1).

Miscellaneous classes of employment

146.—(1) The following provisions of this Act do not apply to employment where the employer is the husband or wife of the employee, that is to say, sections 1, 4, 8, 53, 122 and 123 and Parts II, III, V and VI.

(2) Parts II, III, V and VII and sections 8, 9, 53 and 86 do not apply to employment under a contract of employment in police service or to persons engaged in such employment.

(3) in subsection (2), " police service " means service—

    (*a*) as a member of any constabulary maintained by virtue of any enactment, or

    (*b*) in any other capacity by virtue of which a person has the powers or privileges of a constable.

(4) Subject to subsections (5), (6) and (7), the following provisions of this Act (which confer rights which do not depend upon an employee having a qualifying period of continuous employment) do not apply to employment under a contract which normally involves employment for less than sixteen hours weekly, that is to say, sections 8, 27, 28 and 29.

(5) If the employee's relations with his employer cease to be governed by a contract which normally involves work for sixteen hours or more weekly and become governed by a contract which normally involves employment for eight hours or more, but less than sixteen hours, weekly,

the employee shall nevertheless for a period of twenty-six weeks, computed in accordance with subsection (6), be treated for the purposes of subsection (4) as if his contract normally involved employment for sixteen hours or more weekly.

(6) In computing the said period of twenty-six weeks no account shall be taken of any week—

(*a*) during which the employee is in fact employed for sixteen hours or more;

(*b*) during which the employee takes part in a strike (as defined by paragraph 24 of Schedule 13) or is absent from work because of a lock-out (as so defined) by his employer; or

(*c*) during which there is no contract of employment but which, by virtue of paragraph 9 (1) of Schedule 13, counts in computing a period of continuous employment.

(7) An employee whose relations with his employer are governed by a contract of employment which normally involves employment for eight hours or more, but less than sixteen hours, weekly shall nevertheless, if he has been continuously employed for a period of five years or more be treated for the purposes of subsection (4) as if his contract normally involved employment for sixteen hours or more weekly.

DERIVATION

(1)—1972, s. 9 (3) ; 1975, s. 119 (2), Sched. 16, Pt. II, para. 10 (*b*), Pt. III, para. 14 (*b*) ; 1974, para. 9 (1) (*b*) ; 1965, s. 16 (3).

(2), (3)—1974, s. 30 (1) ; 1975, s. 126 (1).

(4)–(7)—1975, s. 119 (8)–(11).

GENERAL NOTE

Subs. (4)

Most of the rights granted individual employees by the provisions of this Act stipulate as a condition of entitlement that the employee should have been continuously employed for a specific period. Thus, guarantee payments (four weeks, s. 143 ·(1)) ; payments during suspension on medical grounds (four weeks, s. 143 (2)) ; maternity pay and the right to return to work after pregnancy (two years, s. 33 (3) (*b*)) ; time off to look for work, etc. (two years, s. 31 (2)) ; and a written statement of reasons for dismissal (26 weeks, s. 53 (2)).

Only two individual rights granted (besides those referred to in this subsection) are not stated to be dependent on such a period of continuous employment—the right not to have action (short of dismissal) taken against one for trade union reasons (s. 23, and *cf.* the similar protection against dismissal for such reasons, also not subject to any such qualification—s. 64 (3)), and the entitlement to a protective award (s. 102 of the Employment Protection Act 1975).

The period of continuous employment is to be calculated in accordance with the provisions of Sched. 13 (s. 151 (1)). These are consistent with the provisions here (subss. (4) to (7))—see paras. 4–6.

Subs. (5)

If the employee's hours of work are changed from 16 or more weekly to between eight and 16 hours weekly, he is nonetheless to be treated as if he was employed for 16 hours weekly, but only for a period of 26 weeks. It is not clear why the arbitrary period of 26 weeks' grace is thus granted, since after five years' employment the employee qualifies again (subs. (7)). The consequence is that an employee may qualify, lose his qualification and re-qualify all within a period of one year—with extremely arbitrary results should his employer act to his detriment during one of the periods of non-qualification. This result could be avoided by interpreting the provision to mean that once qualified, an employee could not lose his qualification by changing his number of hours worked weekly. This interpretation is made explicit albeit subject to a condition in the provisions of Sched. 13, para. 7.

Another suggestion for overcoming this potential arbitrariness is through the Act's failure to stipulate which weeks are to count towards the 26-week limit. There is nothing to indicate that the employee must use them up immediately following the change in his hours of work, and the provisions of subs. (6) will frequently operate to chop up the period of 26 weeks so as to spread it over a much longer period. Consequently, one would submit that it is left to the employee's discretion to decide which weeks of his employment under 16 hours weekly count towards the 26-week maximum (and, of course, he need not reveal this to his employer). The consequences of this spreading of the 26-week period are no more arbitrary than those of any other method, and would probably lead to a greater degree of protection for the employee.

Application of ss. 1 to 4 to excluded employment

147. Sections 1 to 4 shall apply to an employee who at any time comes or ceases to come within the exceptions from those sections provided for by or under sections 3 (1), 143 to 146 and 149 as if a period of employment terminated or began at that time.

DERIVATION
1972, ss. 4 (7), 9 (4).

Supplementary provisions

Review of limits

148.—(1) The Secretary of State shall in each calendar year review—
   (*a*) the limits referred to in section 15;
   (*b*) the limit referred to in section 122 (5); and
   (*c*) the limits imposed by paragraph 8 (1) of Schedule 14 on the amount of a week's pay for the purposes of those provisions;
and shall determine whether any of those limits should be varied.

(2) In making a review under this section the Secretary of State shall consider—
   (*a*) the general level of earnings obtaining in Great Britain at the time of the review;
   (*b*) the national economic situation as a whole; and
   (*c*) such other matters as he thinks relevant.

(3) If on a review under this section the Secretary of State determines that, having regard to the considerations mentioned in subsection (2), any of those limits should be varied, he shall prepare and lay before each House of Parliament the draft of an order giving effect to his decision.

(4) Where a draft of an order under this section is approved by resolution of each House of Parliament the Secretary of State shall make an order in the form of the draft.

(5) If, following the completion of an annual review under this section, the Secretary of State determines that any of the limits referred to in subsection (1) shall not be varied, he shall lay before each House of Parliament a report containing a statement of his reasons for that determination.

(6) The Secretary of State may at any time, in addition to the annual review provided for in subsection (1), conduct a further review of the limits mentioned in subsection (1), so as to determine whether any of those limits should be varied, and subsections (2) to (4) shall apply to such a review as if it were a review under subsection (1).

DERIVATION
1975, s. 86.

GENERAL NOTE
This section follows the precedent of s. 120 of the Social Security Act 1975, which provides for annual reviews of contributions under that Act. The Redundancy Fund is financed by a 0·2 per cent. contribution paid by employers as part of Class I

contributions based on earnings between £11 and £69 a week. These earnings limits may be varied as a result of the annual review under the Social Security Act, thus affecting the income of the Redundancy Fund. Since payments due to insolvency under s. 122 and redundancy payments are financed from the Fund, it follows that the weekly earnings limit of £110 on those payments should also be reviewed annually. Other payments should be treated consistently.

The current limits are fixed by the Employment Protection (Variation of Limits) Order 1978, which came into operation on February 1, 1979.

Subs. (5)

Where the Secretary of State determines not to vary the limits, he merely lays a report before Parliament, not an order. Consequently, the matter cannot be debated as the ordinary procedure for statutory instruments would allow in the case of an order under subs. (3) varying the limits.

Subs. (6)

The Secretary of State must publish reasons for *not* varying the limits if so decided in the annual review, but not if the same decision is made in any further review. Subs. (5) does not apply to such further review.

General power to amend Act

149.—(1) Subject to the following provisions of this section, the Secretary of State may by order

(a) provide that any enactment contained in this Act which is specified in the order shall not apply to persons or to employments of such classes as may be prescribed in the order;

(b) provide that any such enactment shall apply to persons or employments of such classes as may be prescribed in the order subject, except in relation to section 54 (but without prejudice to paragraph (a)), to such exceptions and modifications as may be so prescribed;

(c) vary, or exclude the operation of, any of the following provisions of this Act, that is to say, sections 64 (1), 99, 141 (2) and (5), 143 (3) and (4), 144 (1), (2), (4) and (5), 145 (1), (2) and (3) and 146 (1) and (4) to (7);

(d) add to, vary or delete any of the provisions of Schedule 5.

(2) Subsection (1) does not apply to the following provisions of this Act, namely, sections 7, 52, 55, 57, 58, 59, 62, 63, 65, 66, 67, 75, 80, 103 to 120, 128, 134, 141 (1) and 142 (1) and Schedules 3, 9, and 13, and, in addition, paragraph (b) of subsection (1) does not apply to sections 1 to 6 and 49 to 51 and paragraph (c) of subsection (1) does not apply to section 143 as that section applies in relation to section 49.

(3) The provisions of this section are without prejudice to any other power of the Secretary of State to amend, vary or repeal any provision of this Act or to extend or restrict its operation in relation to any person or employment.

(4) No order under subsection (1) shall be made unless a draft of the order has been laid before Parliament and approved by a resolution of each House of Parliament.

DERIVATION

1965, s. 16 (6) (8); 1972, s. 9 (5) (7); 1974, para. 11 (2) (3); 1975, s. 119 (15) (16); Dock Work Regulation Act 1976 (c. 79), s. 14 (7).

Death of employee or employer

150. Schedule 12 shall have effect for the purpose of supplementing and modifying the provisions of Part I (so far as it relates to itemised pay statements), section 53 and Parts II, III, and V to VII as respects the death of an employee or employer.

DERIVATION
  1965, s. 23; 1975, s. 110.

Continuous employment

151.—(1) Subject to sections 104 (2) and 106 (2), Schedule 13 shall have effect for the purposes of this Act for ascertaining the length of an employee's period of employment and whether that employment has been continuous, and references in this Act to a period of employment shall be construed accordingly.

(2) For the purposes of any proceedings under this Act, other than proceedings for a breach of section 1, 2, 4 or 49, a person's employment during any period shall, unless the contrary is shown, be presumed to have been continuous.

DERIVATION
  1965, ss. 1 (2) (*a*); 8 (2), 1972, s. 1 (5); 1974, para. 30 (1) (2); 1975, s. 126 (5), Dock Work Regulation Act 1976 (c. 79), s. 14 (3).

Calculation of normal working hours and a week's pay

152. Schedule 14 shall have effect for the purposes of this Act for calculating the normal working hours and the amount of a week's pay of any employee.

DERIVATION
  1972, Sched. 2, para. 1 (1) (*b*); 1975, ss. 62 (*c*), 85, Sched. 5, para. 1 (1) (*b*).

Interpretation

153.—(1) In this Act, except so far as the context otherwise requires—

" act " and " action " each includes omission and references to doing an act or taking action shall be construed accordingly;

" business " includes a trade or profession and includes any activity carried on by a body of persons, whether corporate or unincorporate;

" certified midwife " means a midwife certified under the Midwives Act 1951 or the Midwives (Scotland) Act 1951;

" collective agreement " has the meaning given by section 30 (1) of the Trade Union and Labour Relations Act 1974;

" confinement " means the birth of a living child or the birth of a child whether living or dead after twenty-eight weeks of pregnancy;

" contract of employment " means a contract of service or apprenticeship, whether express or implied, and (if it is express) whether it is oral or in writing;

" dismissal procedures agreement " means an agreement in writing with respect to procedures relating to dismissal made by or on behalf of one or more independent trade unions and one or more employers or employers' associations;

" effective date of termination " has the meaning given by section 55 (4) and (5);

" employee " means an individual who has entered into or works under (or, where the employment has ceased, worked under) a contract of employment;

" employer ", in relation to an employee, means the person by whom the employee is (or, in a case where the employment has ceased, was) employed;

" employers' association " has the same meaning as it has for the purposes of the Trade Union and Labour Relations Act 1974;

" employer's payment " means a payment falling within paragraph (*a*), (*b*) or (*c*) of section 104 (1);

" employment ", except for the purposes of sections 111 to 115, means employment under a contract of employment;

" expected week of confinement " means the week, beginning with midnight between Saturday and Sunday, in which it is expected that confinement will take place;

" government department ", except in section 138 and paragraph 19 of Schedule 13, includes a Minister of the Crown;

" guarantee payment " has the meaning given by section 12 (1);

" inadmissible reason " has the meaning given by section 58 (5);

" independent trade union " means a trade union which—

    (*a*) is not under the domination or control of an employer or a group of employers or of one or more employers' associations; and

    (*b*) is not liable to interference by an employer or any such group or association (arising out of the provision of financial or material support or by any other means whatsoever) tending towards such control;

and, in relation to a trade union, " independent " and " independence " shall be construed accordingly;

" job ", in relation to an employee, means the nature of the work which he is employed to do in accordance with his contract and the capacity and place in which he is so employed;

" maternity pay " has the meaning given by section 33 (1);

" Maternity Pay Fund " means the fund referred to in section 37;

" maternity pay rebate " has the meaning given by section 39;

" notice of intention to claim " has the meaning given by section 88;

" notified day of return " has the meaning given by section 47 (1) and (8);

" official ", in relation to a trade union, has the meaning given by section 30 (1) of the Trade Union and Labour Relations Act 1974;

" original contract of employment ", in relation to an employee who is absent from work wholly or partly because of pregnancy or confinement, means the contract under which she worked immediately before the beginning of her absence or, if she entered into that contract during her pregnancy by virtue of section 60 (2) or otherwise by reason of her pregnancy, the contract under which she was employed immediately before she entered into the later contract or, if there was more than one later contract, the first of the later contracts;

" position ", in relation to an employee, means the following matters taken as a whole, that is to say, his status as an employee, the nature of his work and his terms and conditions of employment;

" Redundancy Fund " means the fund referred to in section 103;

" redundancy payment " has the meaning given by section 81 (1);

" redundancy rebate " has the meaning given by section 104;

" relevant date ", for the purposes of the provisions of this Act which relate to redundancy payments, has the meaning given by section 90;

" renewal " includes extension, and any reference to renewing a contract or a fixed term shall be construed accordingly;

" statutory provision " means a provision, whether of a general or a special nature, contained in, or in any document made or issued under, any Act, whether of a general or special nature;

" successor " has the meaning given by section 30 (3) and (4) of the Trade Union and Labour Relations Act 1974;

" trade dispute " has the meaning given by section 29 of the said Act of 1974;

" trade union " has the meaning given by section 28 of the said Act of 1974;

" union membership agreement " has the meaning given by section 30 (1) of the said Act of 1974 and " employees ", in relation thereto, has the meaning given by section 30 (5A) of that Act;

" week " means, in relation to an employee whose remuneration is calculated weekly by a week ending with a day other than Saturday, a week ending with that other day, and in relation to any other employee, a week ending with Saturday.

(2) References in this Act to dismissal by reason of redundancy, and to cognate expressions, shall be construed in accordance with section 81.

(3) In sections 33, 47, 56, 61 and 86 and Schedule 2, except where the context otherwise requires, " to return to work " means to return to work in accordance with section 45 (1), and cognate expressions shall be construed accordingly.

(4) For the purposes of this Act, any two employers are to be treated as associated if one is a company of which the other (directly or indirectly) has control, or if both are companies of which a third person (directly or indirectly) has control; and the expression " associated employer " shall be construed accordingly.

(5) For the purposes of this Act it is immaterial whether the law which (apart from this Act) governs any person's employment is the law of the United Kingdom, or of a part of the United Kingdom, or not.

(6) In this Act, except where otherwise indicated—

    (*a*) a reference to a numbered Part, section or Schedule is a reference to the Part or section of, or the Schedule to, this Act so numbered, and

    (*b*) a reference in a section to a numbered subsection is a reference to the subsection of that section so numbered, and

    (*c*) a reference in a section, subsection or Schedule to a numbered paragraph is a reference to the paragraph of that section, subsection or Schedule so numbered, and

    (*d*) a reference to any provision of an Act (including this Act) includes a Schedule incorporated in the Act by that provision.

(7) Except so far as the context otherwise requires, any reference in this Act to an enactment shall be construed as a reference to that enactment as amended or extended by or under any other enactment, including this Act.

DERIVATION

1965, ss. 5 (3), 25 (1) (2), 36 (5) (6), 48 (4), 56, Sched. 1, para. 9, Sched. 4, para. 11, Sched. 6, para. 3; 1972, ss. 11 (1), 12 (2), Sched. 1, para. 10 (2); 1974, s. 30, Sched. 1, para. 6 (9) (*c*); 1975, ss. 24 (5), 31 (5), 48 (2) (3), 52, 61 (6), 126, Sched. 4, para. 8 (*b*), Sched. 16, Pt. I, para. 18, Pt. II, para. 19, Pt. III, para. 7 (2) (3) (4); Trade Union and Labour Relations (Amendment) Act 1976 (c. 7), s. 3 (3) (4).

Orders, rules and regulations

154.—(1) Any power conferred by any provision of this Act to make an order (other than an Order in Council or an order under section 65 or 66) or to make rules or regulations shall be exercisable by statutory instrument.

(2) Any statutory instrument made under any power conferred by

this Act to make an Order in Council or other order or to make rules or regulations, except—

(*a*) an instrument required to be laid before Parliament in draft; and

(*b*) an order under section 18,

shall be subject to annulment in pursuance of a resolution of either House of Parliament.

(3) Any power conferred by this Act which is exercisable by statutory instrument shall include power to make such incidental, supplementary or transitional provisions as appear to the authority exercising the power to be necessary or expedient.

(4) An order made by statutory instrument under any provision of this Act may be revoked or varied by a subsequent order made under that provision.

This subsection does not apply to an order under section 96 but is without prejudice to subsection (4) of that section.

DERIVATION

1965, ss. 11 (4), 16 (7) (8), 35 (6) (7), Sched. 1, para. 5 (5) (6), Sched. 4, para. 21A (3); Superannuation (Miscellaneous Provisions) Act 1967 (c. 28), s. 9 (4); 1972, ss. 7 (2) (3), 9 (6) (7), 10 (3) (4); 1974, s. 26, Sched. 1, para. 20 (4); 1975, s. 123, Sched. 16, Pt. I, paras. 21, 34, Pt. II, para. 11; 1977, s. 1 (3).

Offences by bodies corporate

155.—(1) Where an offence under section 44 or 126 committed by a body corporate is proved to have been committed with the consent or connivance of, or to be attributable to any neglect on the part of, any director, manager, secretary or other similar officer of the body corporate, or any person who was purporting to act in any such capacity, he as well as the body corporate shall be guilty of that offence and shall be liable to be proceeded against and punished accordingly.

(2) Where the affairs of a body corporate are managed by its members, subsection (1) shall apply in relation to the acts and defaults of a member in connection with his functions of management as if he were a director of the body corporate.

DERIVATION

1975, s. 117.

Payments into the Consolidated Fund

156.—(1) There shall be paid out of the Maternity Pay Fund into the Consolidated Fund sums equal to the amount of any expenses incurred by the Secretary of State in exercising his functions under this Act relating to maternity pay.

(2) There shall be paid out of the Redundancy Fund into the Consolidated Fund sums equal to the amount of any expenses incurred—

(*a*) by the Secretary of State in consequence of Part VI, except expenses incurred in the payment of sums in accordance with any such arrangements as are mentioned in section 111 (3);

(*b*) by the Secretary of State (or by persons acting on his behalf) in exercising his functions under sections 122 to 126.

(3) There shall be paid out of the Redundancy Fund into the Consolidated Fund such sums as the Secretary of State may estimate in accordance with directions given by the Treasury to be the amount of any expenses incurred by any government department other than the Secretary of State in consequence of the provisions of sections 103 to 109.

DERIVATION
1975, s. 124 (3) (4); 1965, s. 55 (5) (6); National Loans Act 1968 (c. 13),
Sched. 1.

Northern Ireland

157.—(1) If provision is made by Northern Irish legislation (that is
to say by or under a Measure of the Northern Ireland Assembly) for
purposes corresponding to any of the purposes of this Act, except
sections 1 to 7 and 49 to 51, the Secretary of State may, with the
consent of the Treasury, make reciprocal arrangements with the appropriate Northern Irish authority for co-ordinating the relevant provisions
of this Act with the corresponding provisions of the Northern Irish
legislation, so as to secure that they operate, to such extent as may be
provided by the arrangements, as a single system.

(2) For the purpose of giving effect to any such arrangements the
Secretary of State shall have power, in conjunction with the appropriate
Northern Irish authority—

    (a) where the arrangements relate to the provisions of this Act
        relating to maternity pay, to make any necessary financial
        adjustments between the Maternity Pay Fund and any fund
        established under Northern Irish legislation; and

    (b) where the arrangements relate to Part VI or to sections 122 to
        126, to make any necessary financial adjustments between the
        Redundancy Fund and the Northern Ireland Redundancy Fund.

(3) The Secretary of State may make regulations for giving effect in
Great Britain to any such arrangements, and any such regulations may
make different provision for different cases, and may provide that the
relevant provisions of this Act shall have effect in relation to persons
affected by the arrangements subject to such modifications and
adaptations as may be specified in the regulations, including provision—

    (a) for securing that acts, omissions and events having any effect
        for the purposes of the Northern Irish legislation shall have a
        corresponding effect for the purposes of this Act (but not so as to
        confer a right to double payment in respect of the same act,
        omission or event); and

    (b) for determining, in cases where rights accrue both under this
        Act and under the Northern Irish legislation, which of those
        rights shall be available to the person concerned.

(4) In this section " the appropriate Northern Irish authority "
means such authority as may be specified in that behalf in the Northern
Irish legislation.

DERIVATION
1975, s. 128; 1965, s. 58.

The Isle of Man

158.—(1) If an Act of Tynwald is passed for purposes similar to the
purposes of Part VI, the Secretary of State may, with the consent of
the Treasury, make reciprocal arrangements with the appropriate Isle
of Man authority for co-ordinating the provisions of Part VI with the
corresponding provisions of the Act of Tynwald so as to secure that they
operate, to such extent as may be provided by the arrangements, as a
single system.

(2) For the purpose of giving effect to any such arrangements, the
Secretary of State shall have power, in conjunction with the appropriate
Isle of Man authority, to make any necessary financial adjustments
between the Redundancy Fund and any fund established under the
Act of Tynwald.

(3) The Secretary of State may make regulations for giving effect in Great Britain to any such arrangements, and any such regulations may provide that Part VI shall have effect in relation to persons affected by the arrangements subject to such modifications and adaptations as may be specified in the regulations, including provision—

   (*a*) for securing that acts, omissions and events having effect for the purposes of the Act of Tynwald shall have a corresponding effect for the purposes of Part VI (but not so as to confer a right to double payment in respect of the same act, omission or event); and

   (*b*) for determining, in cases where rights accrue both under this Act and under the Act of Tynwald, which of those rights shall be available to the person concerned.

(4) In this section " the appropriate Isle of Man authority " means such authority as may be specified in that behalf in an Act of Tynwald.

DERIVATION
1965, s. 57.

Transitional provisions, savings, consequential amendments and repeals

159.—(1) The transitional provisions and savings in Schedule 15 shall have effect but nothing in that Schedule shall be construed as prejudicing section 38 of the Interpretation Act 1889 (effect of repeals).

(2) The enactments specified in Schedule 16 shall have effect subject to the amendments specified in that Schedule.

(3) The enactments specified in the first column of Schedule 17 are hereby repealed to the extent specified in column 3 of that Schedule.

Citation, commencement and extent

160.—(1) This Act may be cited as the Employment Protection (Consolidation) Act 1978.

(2) This Act, except section 139 (2) to (9) and the repeals in section 122 of the Employment Protection Act 1975 provided for in Schedule 17 to this Act, shall come into force on 1st November 1978, and section 139 (2) to (9) and those repeals shall come into force on 1st January 1979.

(3) This Act, except sections 137 and 157 and paragraphs 12 and 28 of Schedule 16, shall not extend to Northern Ireland.

SCHEDULES

Section 19   SCHEDULE 1

PROVISIONS LEADING TO SUSPENSION ON MEDICAL GROUNDS

1. The Paints and Colours Manufacture Regulations 1907.   S.R. & O. 1907 No. 17... Reg. 5.

2. The Yarn (Dyed by Lead Compounds) Heading Regulations 1907.   S.R. & O. 1907 No. 616   Reg. 4.

3. The Vitreous Enamelling Regulations 1908.   S.R. & O. 1908 No. 1258 Reg. 10.

4. The Tinning of Metal Hollow-ware, Iron Drums and Harness Furniture Regulations 1909.   S.R. & O. 1909 No. 720   Reg. 6.

5. The Lead Smelting and Manufacture Regulations 1911.   S.R. & O. 1911 No. 752   Reg. 13.

6. The Lead Compounds Manufacture Regulations 1921.	S.R. & O. 1921 No. 1443	Reg. 11.
7. The Indiarubber Regulations 1922.	S.R. & O. 1922 No. 329	Reg. 12.
8. The Chemical Works Regulations 1922.	S.R. & O. 1922 No. 731	Reg. 30.
9. The Electric Accumulator Regulations 1925.	S.R. & O. 1925 No. 28...	Reg. 13.
10. The Lead Paint Regulations 1927.	S.R. & O. 1927 No. 847	Reg. 6.
11. The Pottery (Health and Welfare) Special Regulations 1950.	S.I. 1950 No. 65 ...	... Reg. 7.
12. The Factories Act 1961.	1961 c. 34 ...	... Section 75 (2) (including that section as extended by section 128).
13. The Ionising Radiations (Unsealed Radioactive Substances) Regulations 1968.	S.I. 1968 No. 780	... Regs. 12 and 33.
14. The Ionising Radiations (Sealed Sources) Regulations 1969.	S.I. 1969 No. 808	... Regs. 11 and 30.
15. The Radioactive Substances (Road Transport Workers) (Great Britain) Regulations 1970.	S.I. 1970 No. 1827	... Reg. 14.

DERIVATION
1975, Sched. 2.

Section 33

SCHEDULE 2

SUPPLEMENTARY PROVISIONS RELATING TO MATERNITY

PART I

UNFAIR DISMISSAL

Introductory

1. References in this Part to provisions of this Act relating to unfair dismissal are references to those provisions as they apply by virtue of section 56.

Adaptation of unfair dismissal provisions

2.—(1) Section 57 shall have effect as if for subsection (3) there were substituted the following subsection:—

" (3) Where the employer has fulfilled the requirements of subsection (1), then, subject to sections 58 (1), 59, 60 and 62, the determination of the question whether the dismissal was fair or unfair, having regard to the reason shown by the employer, shall depend on whether the employer can satisfy the tribunal that in the circumstances (having regard to equity and the substantial merits of the case) he would have been acting reasonably in treating it as a sufficient reason for dismissing the employee if she had not been absent from work.".

(2) If in the circumstances described in section 45 (3) no offer is made of such alternative employment as is referred to in that subsection, then the dismissal which by virtue of section 56 treated as taking place shall, notwithstanding anything in section 57 or 58, be treated as an unfair dismissal for the purposes of Part V of this Act.

(3) The following references shall be construed as references to the notified day of return, that is to say—

(*a*) references in Part V of this Act to the effective date of termination;

(*b*) references in sections 69 and 70 to the date of termination of employment.

(4) The following provisions of this Act shall not apply, that is to say, sections 55, 58 (3), 64 (1), 65, 66, 73 (5) and (6), 141 (2), 142 (1), 144 (2), 145 (2) and

146 (1), paragraph 11 (1) of Schedule 13, paragraphs 7 (1) (*f*) to (*i*) and (2) and 8 (3) of Schedule 14 and paragraph 10 of Schedule 15.

(5) For the purposes of Part II of Schedule 14 as it applies for the calculation of a week's pay for the purposes of section 71 or 73, the calculation date is the last day on which the employee worked under the original contract of employment.

PART II

REDUNDANCY PAYMENTS

Introductory

3. References in this Part to provisions of this Act relating to redundancy are references to those provisions as they apply by virtue of section 86.

Adaptation of redundancy payments provisions

4.—(1) References in Part VI of this Act shall be adapted as follows, that is to say—

(*a*) references to the relevant date, wherever they occur, shall be construed, except where the context otherwise requires, as references to the notified day of return;

(*b*) references in sections 82 (4) and 84 (1) to a renewal or re-engagement taking effect immediately on the ending of employment under the previous contract or after an interval of not more than four weeks thereafter, shall be construed as references to a renewal or re-engagement taking effect on the notified day of return or not more than four weeks after that day; and

(*c*) references in section 84 (3) to the provisions of the previous contract shall be construed as references to the provisions of the original contract of employment.

(2) Nothing in section 86 shall prevent an employee from being treated, by reason of the operation of section 84 (1), as not having been dismissed for the purposes of Part VI of this Act.

(3) The following provisions of this Act shall not apply, that is to say, sections 81 (1) (*b*), 82 (1) and (2), 83 (1) and (2), 85, 87 to 89, 90 (3), 92, 93, 96, 110, 144 (2), 146 (1) and 150, paragraph 4 of Schedule 4, Schedule 12 and paragraphs 7 (1) (*j*) and (*k*) and 8 (4) of Schedule 14.

(4) For the purposes of Part II of Schedule 14 as it applies for the calculation of a week's pay for the purposes of Schedule 4, the calculation date is the last day on which the employee worked under the original contract of employment.

Prior redundancy

5. If, in proceedings arising out of a failure to permit an employee to return to work, the employer shows—

(*a*) that the reason for the failure is that the employee is redundant; and

(*b*) that the employee was dismissed or, had she continued to be employed by him, would have been dismissed, by reason of redundancy during her absence on a day earlier than the notified day of return and falling after the beginning of the eleventh week before the expected week of confinement,

then, for the purposes of Part VI of this Act the employee—

(i) shall not be treated as having been dismissed with effect from the notified day of return; but

(ii) shall, if she would not otherwise be so treated, be treated as having been continuously employed until that earlier day and as having been dismissed by reason of redundancy with effect from that day.

PART III

GENERAL

Dismissal during period of absence

6.—(1) This paragraph applies to the dismissal of an employee who is under this Act entitled to return to work and whose contract of employment continues to subsist during the period of her absence but who is dismissed by her employer during that period after the beginning of the eleventh week before the expected week of confinement.

(2) For the purposes of sub-paragraph (1), an employee shall not be taken to be dismissed during the period of her absence if the dismissal occurs in the course of the employee's attempting to return to work in accordance with her contract in circumstances in which section 48 applies.

(3) In the application of Part V of this Act to a dismissal to which this paragraph applies, the following provisions shall not apply, that is to say, sections 58 (3), 64, 65, 66, 141 (2), 144 (2), 145 and 146 (1).

(4) Any such dismissal shall not affect the employee's right to return to work, but—

    (*a*) compensation in any unfair dismissal proceedings arising out of that dismissal shall be assessed without regard to the employee's right to return; and

    (*b*) that right shall be exercisable only on her repaying any redundancy payment or compensation for unfair dismissal paid in respect of that dismissal, if the employer requests such repayment.

Power to amend or modify

7.—(1) The Secretary of State may by order amend the provisions of this Schedule and section 48 or modify the application of those provisions to any description of case.

(2) No order under this paragraph shall be made unless a draft of the order has been laid before Parliament and approved by a resolution of each House of Parliament.

DERIVATION
1975, Sched. 3, paras. 1 to 4, 6, 7.

Section 50   SCHEDULE 3

RIGHTS OF EMPLOYEE IN PERIOD OF NOTICE

Preliminary

1. In this Schedule the "period of notice" means the period of notice required by section 49 (1) or, as the case may be, section 49 (2).

Employments for which there are normal working hours

2.—(1) If an employee has normal working hours under the contract of employment in force during the period of notice, and if during any part of those normal working hours—

    (*a*) the employee is ready and willing to work but no work is provided for him by his employer; or

    (*b*) the employee is incapable of work because of sickness or injury; or

    (*c*) the employee is absent from work in accordance with the terms of his employment relating to holidays,

then the employer shall be liable to pay the employee for the part of normal working hours covered by paragraphs (*a*), (*b*) and (*c*) a sum not less than the amount of remuneration for that part of normal working hours calculated at the average hourly rate of remuneration produced by dividing a week's pay by the number of normal working hours.

(2) Any payment made to the employee by his employer in respect of the relevant part of the period of notice whether by way of sick pay, holiday pay or otherwise, shall go towards meeting the employers' liability under this paragraph.

(3) Where notice was given by the employee, the employer's liability under this paragraph shall not arise unless and until the employee leaves the service of the employer in pursuance of the notice.

Employments for which there are no normal working hours

3.—(1) If an employee does not have normal working hours under the contract of employment in force in the period of notice the employer shall be liable to pay the employee for each week of the period of notice a sum not less than a week's pay.

(2) Subject to sub-paragraph (3), the employer's obligation under this paragraph shall be conditional on the employee being ready and willing to do work of a reasonable nature and amount to earn a week's pay.

(3) Sub-paragraph (2) shall not apply—

(a) in respect of any period during which the employee is incapable of work because of sickness or injury, or

(b) in respect of any period during which the employee is absent from work in accordance with the terms of his employment relating to holidays,

and any payment made to an employee by his employer in respect of such a period, whether by way of sick pay, holiday pay or otherwise, shall be taken into account for the purposes of this paragraph as if it were remuneration paid by the employer in respect of that period.

(4) Where the notice was given by the employee, the employer's liability under this paragraph shall not arise unless and until the employee leaves the service of the employer in pursuance of the notice.

Sickness or industrial injury benefit

4.—(1) The following provisions of this paragraph shall have effect where the arrangements in force relating to the employment are such that—

(a) payments by way of sick pay are made by the employer to employees to whom the arrangements apply, in cases where any such employees are incapable of work because of sickness or injury, and

(b) in calculating any payment so made to any such employee an amount representing, or treated as representing, sickness benefit or industrial injury benefit is taken into account, whether by way of deduction or by way of calculating the payment as a supplement to that amount.

(2) If during any part of the period of notice the employee is incapable of work because of sickness or injury, and—

(a) one or more payments, by way of sick pay are made to him by the employer in respect of that part of the period of notice, and

(b) in calculating any such payment such an amount as is referred to in sub-paragraph (1) (b) is taken into account as therein mentioned,

then for the purposes of this Schedule the amount so taken into account shall be treated as having been paid by the employer to the employee by way of sick pay in respect of that part of that period, and shall go towards meeting the liability of the employer under paragraph 2 or paragraph 3 accordingly.

Absence on leave granted at request of employee

5. The employer shall not be liable under the foregoing provisions of this Schedule to make any payment in respect of a period during which the employee is absent from work with the leave of the employer granted at the request of the employee (including any period of time off taken in accordance with section 27, 28, 29 or 31).

Notice given before a strike

6. No payment shall be due under this Schedule in consequence of a notice to terminate a contract given by an employee if, after the notice is given and on or before the termination of the contract, the employee takes part in a strike of employees of the employer.

In this paragraph " strike " has the meaning given by paragraph 24 of Schedule 13.

Termination of employment during period of notice

7.—(1) If, during the period of notice, the employer breaks the contract of employment, payments received under this Schedule in respect of the part of the period after the breach shall go towards mitigating the damages recoverable by the employee for loss of earnings in that part of the period of notice.

(2) If, during the period of notice, the employee breaks the contract and the employer rightfully treats the breach as terminating the contract, no payment shall be due to the employee under this Schedule in respect of the part of the period of notice falling after the termination of the contract.

DERIVATION
1972, Sched. 2, subst. 1975, Sched. 5.

Section 81   SCHEDULE 4

CALCULATION OF REDUNDANCY PAYMENTS

1. The amount of a redundancy payment to which an employee is entitled in any case shall, subject to the following provisions of this Schedule, be calculated by reference to the period, ending with the relevant date, during which he has been continuously employed.

2. Subject to paragraphs 3 and 4, the amount of the redundancy payment shall be calculated by reference to the period specified in paragraph 1 by starting at the end of that period and reckoning backwards the number of years of employment falling within that period, and allowing—

(a) one and a half weeks' pay for each such year of employment which consists wholly of weeks (within the meaning of Schedule 13) in which the employee was not below the age of forty-one;

(b) one week's pay for each such year of employment (not falling within the preceding sub-paragraph) which consists wholly of weeks (within the meaning of Schedule 13) in which the employee was not below the age of twenty-two; and

(c) half a week's pay for each such year of employment not falling within either of the preceding sub-paragraphs.

3. Where, in reckoning the number of years of employment in accordance with paragraph 2, twenty years of employment have been reckoned, no account shall be taken of any year of employment earlier than those twenty years.

4.—(1) Where in the case of an employee the relevant date is after the specified anniversary, the amount of the redundancy payment, calculated in accordance with the preceding provisions of this Schedule, shall be reduced by the appropriate fraction.

(2) In this paragraph " the specified anniversary ", in relation to a man, means the sixty-fourth anniversary of the day of his birth, and, in relation to a woman, means the fifty-ninth anniversary of the day of her birth, and " the appropriate fraction " means the fraction of which—

(a) the numerator is the number of whole months, reckoned from the specified anniversary, in the period beginning with that anniversary and ending with the relevant date, and

(b) the denominator is twelve.

5. For the purposes of any provision contained in Part VI whereby an industrial tribunal may determine that an employer shall be liable to pay to an employee either—

(a) the whole of the redundancy payment to which the employee would have been entitled apart from another provision therein mentioned, or

(b) such part of that redundancy payment as the tribunal thinks fit,

the preceding provisions of this Schedule shall apply as if in those provisions any reference to the amount of a redundancy payment were a reference to the amount of the redundancy payment to which the employee would have been so entitled.

6. The preceding provisions of this Schedule shall have effect without prejudice to the operation of any regulations made under section 98 whereby the amount of a redundancy payment, or part of a redundancy payment, may be reduced.

7. Where the relevant date does not occur on a Saturday, any reference in the preceding provisions of this Schedule to the relevant date shall be construed as a reference to the Saturday immediately following the date.

DERIVATION
1965, Sched. 1, paras. 1–4, 6–9; 1975, Sched. 16, Pt. I, paras. 19, 20, 22.

Section 99   SCHEDULE 5

NATIONAL HEALTH SERVICE EMPLOYERS

1. A Regional Health Authority, Area Health Authority, special health authority, Health Board or the Common Services Agency for the Scottish Health Service.

2. The Dental Estimates Board.

3. Any joint committee constituted under section 13 (8) of the National Health Service (Scotland) Act 1972.

4. The Public Health Laboratory Service Board.

DERIVATION

1965, Sched. 3; National Health Service Reorganisation Act 1973 (c. 32), Sched. 4, para. 106; National Health Service (Scotland) Act 1972 (c. 58), Sched. 6, para. 130.

Section 104   SCHEDULE 6

CALCULATION OF REDUNDANCY REBATES

PART I

REBATES IN RESPECT OF REDUNDANCY PAYMENTS

1. Subject to sections 104 (7) and 108 and to the following provisions of this Part, the amount of any redundancy rebate payable in respect of a redundancy payment shall be calculated by taking the number of years of employment by reference to which the redundancy payment falls to be calculated in accordance with Schedule 4 and allowing—

   (a) 123/200 of one week's pay for each year of employment falling within sub-paragraph (a) of paragraph 2 of that Schedule;
   (b) 41/100 of one week's pay for each year of employment falling within sub-paragraph (b) of that paragraph; and
   (c) 41/200 of one week's pay for each year of employment falling within sub-paragraph (c) of that paragraph.

2. Where the amount of the redundancy payment, calculated in accordance with paragraphs 1, 2 and 3 of Schedule 4, is reduced by virtue of paragraph 4 of that Schedule, the amount of the rebate shall be 41/100 of the amount of the redundancy payment as so reduced.

3.—(1) The provisions of this paragraph shall have effect in relation to any case where—

   (a) under section 85, 92 or 110 an industrial tribunal is empowered to determine that an employer shall be liable to pay to an employee either the whole or part of the redundancy payment to which the employee would have been entitled apart from another provision therein mentioned, and
   (b) the tribunal determines that the employer shall be liable to pay part (but not the whole) of that redundancy payment.

(2) There shall be ascertained what proportion that part of the redundancy payment bears to the whole of it (in this paragraph referred to as "the relevant proportion").

(3) There shall also be ascertained what, in accordance with the preceding provisions of this Part, would have been the amount of the redundancy rebate payable in respect of that redundancy payment if the employer had been liable to pay the whole of it.

(4) Subject to paragraph 4, the amount of the rebate payable in that case shall then be an amount equal to the relevant proportion of the amount referred to in sub-paragraph (3).

4. Where the amount of a redundancy payment or part of a redundancy payment is reduced in accordance with regulations made under section 98,—

   (a) the proportion by which it is so reduced shall be ascertained, and
   (b) the amount of any redundancy rebate calculated by reference to that payment shall be reduced by that proportion.

PART II

REBATES IN RESPECT OF OTHER PAYMENTS

Introductory

5. The provisions of this Part shall have effect for the purpose of calculating the amount of any redundancy rebate payable in respect of an employer's payment which is not a redundancy payment or part of a redundancy payment (in this Part referred to as "the agreed payment").

6. In this Part "the agreement", in relation to the agreed payment, means the agreement referred to in paragraph (*b*) or paragraph (*c*) of section 104 (1) by reference to which that payment is payable; and "the relevant provisions of the agreement" means those provisions of the agreement which relate to either of the following matters, that is to say—

(*a*) the circumstances in which the continuity of an employee's period of employment is to be treated as broken, and

(*b*) the weeks which are to count in computing a period of employment.

7. In this Part any reference to the amount of the relevant redundancy payment, in relation to the agreed payment, shall be construed as a reference to the amount of the redundancy payment which the employer would have been liable to pay to the employee if—

(*a*) the order referred to in paragraph (*b*) of subsection (1) of section 104, or (as the case may be) the order and the award referred to in paragraph (*c*) of that subsection, had not been made;

(*b*) the circumstances in which the agreed payment is payable had been such that the employer was liable to pay a redundancy payment to the employee in those circumstances;

(*c*) in relation to that redundancy payment, the relevant date had been the date on which the termination of the employee's contract of employment is treated for the purposes of the agreement as having taken effect; and

(*d*) in so far as the relevant provisions of the agreement are inconsistent with the provisions of Schedule 13 as to the matters referred to in sub-paragraphs (*a*) and (*b*) of paragraph 6, those provisions of the agreement were substituted for those provisions of that Schedule;

and "the assumed conditions" means the conditions specified in sub-paragraphs (*a*) to (*d*) of this paragraph.

Method of calculation

8. Subject to sections 104 (7) and 108, and to the following provisions of this Part, the amount of any redundancy rebate payable in respect of the agreed payment shall be an amount calculated as follows, that is to say, by taking the number of years of employment by reference to which the amount of the relevant redundancy payment would fall to be calculated in accordance with Schedule 4 (as that Schedule would have applied if the assumed conditions were fulfilled), and allowing—

(*a*) 123/200 of one week's pay for each such year of employment falling within sub-paragraph (*a*) of paragraph 2 of that Schedule;

(*b*) 41/100 of one week's pay for each such year of employment falling within sub-paragraph (*b*) of that paragraph; and

(*c*) 41/200 of one week's pay for each such year of employment falling within sub-paragraph (*c*) of that paragraph.

9. For the purposes of paragraph 8, Schedule 13 shall have effect as if paragraphs 11 (2), 12 and 14 were omitted.

10. Where the amount of the agreed payment is less than the amount of the relevant redundancy payment—

(*a*) the proportion which it bears to the amount of the relevant redundancy payment shall be ascertained, and

(*b*) the amount of the rebate shall (except as provided by the next following paragraph) be that proportion of the amount calculated in accordance with the preceding provisions of this Part of this Schedule.

11. Where the amount of the relevant redundancy payment calculated in accordance with paragraphs 1, 2 and 3 of Schedule 4 would (if the assumed conditions were fulfilled) have been reduced by virtue of paragraph 4 of that Schedule, the amount of the rebate shall be 41/100 of the amount of the relevant redundancy payment as so reduced.

Savings

12.—(1) This Schedule shall have effect in relation to redundancy rebates of a kind specified in sub-paragraph (2), as if—

(*a*) in paragraphs 1 and 8, for the reference to 123/200, 41/100 and 41/200 there were substituted a reference to 3/4, 1/2 and 1/4 respectively, and

(*b*) in paragraphs 2 and 11 for each reference to 41/100 there were substituted a reference to 1/2.

(2) The redundancy rebates referred to in sub-paragraph (1) are—
    (a) any rebate payable in respect of the whole or part of a redundancy payment in relation to which the relevant date is or would but for the operation of section 90 (3) be earlier than 14th August 1977;
    (b) any rebate payable in respect of a payment to an employee on the termination of his contract of employment which is paid—
        (i) in pursuance of an agreement in respect of which an order under section 96 is in operation; or
        (ii) in pursuance of an award made under Schedule 11 to the Employment Protection Act 1975 in connection with such an agreement,
where, under the agreement in question, the employee's contract is treated for the purposes of the agreement as having been terminated on a date earlier than 14th August 1977.

Power to modify paragraphs 1, 2, 8 and 11

13.—(1) The Secretary of State may from time to time by order modify this Schedule—
    (a) by substituting for the three fractions of a week's pay for the time being specified in sub-paragraphs (a), (b) and (c) of paragraphs 1 and 8 one of the other sets of three fractions specified in the following Table; and
    (b) by substituting for the fraction for the time being specified in paragraphs 2 and 11 for the purpose of calculating the amount of the rebates in respect of reduced payments the like fraction as, by virtue of paragraph (a) is substituted for the fraction in paragraphs 1 (b) and 8 (b)

TABLE

	Fraction in paragraphs 1 (a) and 8 (a)	Fraction in paragraphs 1 (b), 2, 8 (b) and 11	Fraction in paragraphs 1 (c) and 8 (c)
1	21/40	7/20	7/40
2	123/200	41/100	41/200
3	27/40	9/20	9/40
4	3/4	1/2	1/4
5	33/40	11/20	11/40
6	9/10	3/5	3/10
7	39/40	13/20	13/40
8	21/20	7/10	7/20
9	9/8	3/4	3/8
10	6/5	4/5	2/5

In this Table—
    (a) the three fractions specified in paragraph 2 are those which, at the passing of this Act, are specified in sub-paragraphs (a), (b) and (c) of paragraphs 1 and 8;
    (b) the second of the fractions specified in paragraph 2 is the fraction which, at the passing of this Act, is specified in paragraphs 2 and 11.

(2) No order shall be made under sub-paragraph (1) unless a draft thereof has been laid before and approved by a resolution of each House of Parliament.

DERIVATION
    Paras. 1, 2—1965, Sched. 5, paras. 2, 3; 1977 Order, art. 3.
            3–7—1965, Sched. 5, paras. 4 to 8.
              8—1965, Sched. 5, para. 9; 1977 Order, art. 3.
        9, 10—1965, Sched. 5, paras. 10, 11.
        11—1965, Sched. 5, para. 12; 1977 Order, art. 3.
        12—1977 Order, art. 4.

Section 106   SCHEDULE 7

CALCULATION OF PAYMENTS TO EMPLOYEES OUT OF REDUNDANCY FUND

1.—(1) Where the employer's payment is a redundancy payment, the sum referred to in section 106 (2) is a sum equal to the amount of that payment.

(2) Where, in a case falling within section 104 (6), the employer's payment is part of a redundancy payment, the sum referred to in section 106 (2) is a sum equal to the amount of that part of the payment.

2.—(1) The provisions of this paragraph shall have effect for the purpose of determining the sum referred to in section 106 (2) in relation to an employer's payment which is not a redundancy payment or part of a redundancy payment.

(2) Paragraphs 6 and 7 of Schedule 6 shall have effect for the purposes of this paragraph as they have effect for the purposes of Part II of that Schedule; and in the application of those paragraphs in accordance with this sub-paragraph the employer's payment in relation to which the sum referred to in section 106 (2) falls to be determined shall be taken to be the agreed payment.

(3) In relation to any such employer's payment, the sum in question shall be a sum equal to—

(*a*) the amount of the employer's payment, or

(*b*) the amount of the relevant redundancy payment,

whichever is the less.

DERIVATION
1965, Sched. 6, paras. 1, 2.

Section 117	SCHEDULE 8

EMPLOYEES PAID BY VIRTUE OF STATUTORY PROVISION BY PERSON OTHER THAN EMPLOYER

Provision of Act	*Reference to be construed as reference to the person responsible for paying the remuneration*
Section 81 (1) ...	The second reference to the employer.
Section 85 (3) ...	The reference to the employer in paragraph (*b*).
Section 85 (4) ...	The last reference to the employer.
Section 88 (4) ...	The reference to the employer.
Section 89 (1) ...	The first reference to the employer.
Section 89 (4) and (5)	The references to the employer.
Section 92 (3) ...	The second reference to the employer.
Section 98 (3) ...	The reference to the employer.
Section 101 (1) ...	The reference to the employer.
Section 102	The references to the employer.
Section 104	The references to the employer.
Section 106	The references to the employer.
Section 107 (1) ...	The reference to the employer.
Section 108 (1), (2), (4) and (5) ...	The references to the employer.
Section 110 (2) ...	The third reference to the employer.
Section 110 (5) and (6)	The reference to the employer.
Schedule 13, paragraph 12 (3) ...	The references to the employer.

DERIVATION
1965, Sched. 8.

Section 128	SCHEDULE 9

INDUSTRIAL TRIBUNALS

Regulations as to tribunal procedure

1.—(1) The Secretary of State may by regulations (in this Schedule referred to as " the regulations ") make such provision as appears to him to be necessary or expedient with respect to proceedings before industrial tribunals.

(2) The regulations may in particular include provision—

(a) for determining by which tribunal any appeal, question or complaint is to be determined;

(b) for enabling an industrial tribunal to hear and determine proceedings brought by virtue of section 131 concurrently with proceedings brought before the tribunal otherwise than by virtue of that section;

(c) for treating the Secretary of State (either generally or in such circumstances as may be prescribed by the regulations) as a party to any proceedings before an industrial tribunal, where he would not otherwise be a party to them, and entitling him to appear and to be heard accordingly;

(d) for requiring persons to attend to give evidence and produce documents, and for authorising the administration of oaths to witnesses;

(e) for granting to any person such discovery or inspection of documents or right to further particulars as might be granted by a county court in England and Wales or, in Scotland, for granting to any person such recovery or inspection of documents as might be granted by the sheriff;

(f) for prescribing the procedure to be followed on any appeal, reference or complaint or other proceedings before an industrial tribunal, including provisions as to the persons entitled to appear and to be heard on behalf of parties to such proceedings, and provisions for enabling an industrial tribunal to review its decisions, and revoke or vary its orders and awards, in such circumstances as may be determined in accordance with the regulations;

(g) for the appointment of one or more assessors for the purposes of any proceedings before an industrial tribunal, where the proceedings are brought under an enactment which provides for one or more assessors to be appointed.

(h) for the award of costs or expenses, including any allowances payable under paragraph 10 other than allowances payable to members of industrial tribunals or assessors;

(i) for taxing or otherwise settling any such costs or expenses (and, in particular, in England and Wales, for enabling such costs to be taxed in the county court); and

(j) for the registration and proof of decisions, orders and awards of industrial tribunals.

(3) In relation to proceedings on complaints under section 67 or any other enactment in relation to which there is provision for conciliation, the regulations shall include provision—

(a) for requiring a copy of any such complaint, and a copy of any notice relating to it which is lodged by or on behalf of the employer against whom the complaint is made, to be sent to a conciliation officer;

(b) for securing that the complainant and the employer against whom the complaint is made are notified that the services of a conciliation officer are available to them; and

(c) for postponing the hearing of any such complaint for such period as may be determined in accordance with the regulations for the purpose of giving an opportunity for the complaint to be settled by way of conciliation and withdrawn.

(4) In relation to proceedings under section 67—

(a) where the employee has expressed a wish to be reinstated or re-engaged which has been communicated to the employer at least seven days before the hearing of the complaint; or

(b) where the proceedings arise out of the employer's failure to permit the employee to return to work after an absence due to pregnancy or confinement,

regulations shall include provision for requiring the employer to pay the costs or expenses of any postponement or adjournment of the hearing caused by his failure, without a special reason, to adduce reasonable evidence as to the availability of the job from which the complainant was dismissed, or, as the case may be, which she held before her absence, or of comparable or suitable employment.

(5) Without prejudice to paragraph 2, the regulations may enable an industrial tribunal to sit in private for the purpose of hearing evidence which in the opinion of the tribunal relates to matters of such a nature that it would be against the

interests of national security to allow the evidence to be given in public or of hearing evidence from any person which in the opinion of the tribunal is likely to consist of—

(a) information which he could not disclose without contravening a prohibition imposed by or under any enactment; or

(b) any information which has been communicated to him in confidence, or which he has otherwise obtained in consequence of the confidence reposed in him by another person; or

(c) information the disclosure of which would, for reasons other than its effect on negotiations with respect to any of the matters mentioned in section 29 (1) of the Trade Union and Labour Relations Act 1974 (matters to which trade disputes relate) cause substantial injury to any undertaking of his or in which he works.

(6) The regulations may include provision authorising or requiring an industrial tribunal, in circumstances specified in the regulations, to send notice or a copy of any document so specified relating to any proceedings before the tribunal, or of any decision, order or award of the tribunal, to any government department or other person or body so specified.

(7) Any person who without reasonable excuse fails to comply with any requirement imposed by the regulations by virtue of sub-paragraph (2) (d) or any requirement with respect to the discovery, recovery or inspection of documents so imposed by virtue of sub-paragraph (2) (e) shall be liable on summary conviction to a fine not exceeding £100.

National security

2.—(1) If on a complaint under section 24 or 67 it is shown that the action complained of was taken for the purpose of safeguarding national security, the industrial tribunal shall dismiss the complaint.

(2) A certificate purporting to be signed by or on behalf of a Minister of the Crown, and certifying that the action specified in the certificate was taken for the purpose of safeguarding national security, shall for the purposes of sub-paragraph (1) be conclusive evidence of that fact.

Payment of certain sums into Redundancy Fund

3. Any sum recovered by the Secretary of State in pursuance of any such award as is mentioned in paragraph 1 (2) (h) where the award was made in proceedings in pursuance of Part VI of this Act shall be paid into the Redundancy Fund.

Exclusion of Arbitration Act 1950

4. The Arbitration Act 1950 shall not apply to any proceedings before an industrial tribunal.

Presumption as to dismissal for redundancy

5. Where in accordance with the regulations an industrial tribunal determines in the same proceedings—

(a) a question referred to it under sections 81 to 102, and

(b) a complaint presented under section 67,

section 91 (2) shall not have effect for the purposes of the proceedings in so far as they relate to the complaint under section 67.

Right of appearance

6. Any person may appear before an industrial tribunal in person or be represented by counsel or by a solicitor or by a representative of a trade union or an employers' association or by any other person whom he desires to represent him.

Recovery of sums awarded

7.—(1) Any sum payable in pursuance of a decision of an industrial tribunal in England or Wales which has been registered in accordance with the regulations shall, if a county court so orders, be recoverable by execution issued from the county court or otherwise as if it were payable under an order of that court.

(2) Any order for the payment of any sum made by an industrial tribunal in Scotland may be enforced in like manner as a recorded decree arbitral.

(3) In this paragraph any reference to a decision or order of an industrial tribunal—

    (*a*) does not include a decision or order which, on being reviewed, has been revoked by the tribunal, and

    (*b*) in relation to a decision or order which, on being reviewed, has been varied by the tribunal, shall be construed as a reference to the decision or order as so varied.

Constitution of tribunals for certain cases

8. An industrial tribunal hearing an application under section 77 or 79 may consist of a President of Industrial Tribunals, the chairman of the tribunal or a member of a panel of chairmen of such tribunals for the time being nominated by a President to hear such applications.

Remuneration for presidents and full-time chairmen of industrial tribunals

9. The Secretary of State may pay such remuneration as he may with the consent of the Minister for the Civil Service determine to the President of the Industrial Tribunals (England and Wales), the President of the Industrial Tribunals (Scotland) and any person who is a member on a full-time basis of a panel of chairmen of tribunals which is appointed in accordance with regulations under subsection (1) of section 128.

Remuneration etc. for members of industrial tribunals and for assessors and other persons

10. The Secretary of State may pay to members of industrial tribunals and to any assessors appointed for the purposes of proceedings before industrial tribunals such fees and allowances as he may with the consent of the Minister for the Civil Service determine and may pay to any other persons such allowances as he may with the consent of that Minister determine for the purposes of, or in connection with, their attendance at industrial tribunals.

Pensions for full-time presidents or chairmen of industrial tribunals

11.—(1) The Secretary of State may from time to time make to the Minister for the Civil Service, as respects any holder on a full-time basis of any of the following offices established by regulations under section 128 who is remunerated, apart from any allowances, on an annual basis, namely—

    (*a*) President of the Industrial Tribunals (England and Wales);

    (*b*) President of the Industrial Tribunals (Scotland);

    (*c*) member of a panel of chairmen so established,

a recommendation that the Minister shall pay to that holder (hereafter in this paragraph referred to as " the pensioner") out of moneys provided by Parliament an annual sum by way of superannuation allowance calculated in accordance with sub-paragraph (3).

(2) No such allowance shall be payable unless—

    (*a*) the pensioner is at the time of his retirement over the age of seventy-two or, where he retires after fifteen years' service, over the age of sixty-five; or

    (*b*) the Secretary of State is satisfied by means of a medical certificate that at the time of the pensioner's retirement the pensioner is, by reason of infirmity of mind or body, incapable of discharging the duties of his office and that the incapacity is likely to be permanent.

(3) The said annual sum shall be a sum not exceeding such proportion of the pensioner's last annual remuneration (apart from any allowances) as in the following Table corresponds with the number of the pensioner's completed years of relevant service.

TABLE

Years of service				Fraction of remuneration
Less than 5	...	...	...	six-fortieths
5	...	...	...	ten-fortieths
6	...	...	...	eleven-fortieths
7	...	...	...	twelve-fortieths
8	...	...	...	thirteen-fortieths
9	...	...	...	fourteen-fortieths
10	...	...	...	fifteen-fortieths
11	...	...	...	sixteen-fortieths
12	...	...	...	seventeen-fortieths
13	...	...	...	eighteen-fortieths
14	...	...	...	nineteen-fortieths
15 or more	...	...	...	twenty-fortieths

(4) In this paragraph the expression "relevant service" means service on a full-time basis as holder of any of the offices referred to in sub-paragraph (1) (including such service remunerated otherwise than on an annual basis) or service in any such other capacity under the Crown as may be prescribed by regulations made by the Minister for the Civil Service; and regulations under this sub-paragraph—

(a) may be made generally or subject to specified exceptions or in relation to specified cases or classes of case and may make different provision for different cases or classes of cases; and

(b) may provide that in calculating relevant service either the whole of a person's prescribed service of any description shall be taken into account or such part thereof only as may be determined by or under the regulations.

(5) The decision of the Minister shall be final on any question arising as to—

(a) the amount of any superannuation allowance under sub-paragraph (1); or

(b) the reckoning of any service for the purpose of calculating such an allowance.

(6) Sections 2 to 8 of the Administration of Justice (Pensions) Act 1950 (which provide for the payment of lump sums on retirement or death and of widows' and children's pensions in the case of persons eligible for pensions for service in any of the capacities listed in Schedule 1 to that Act) shall have effect as if—

(a) the capacity of holder on a full-time basis of any of the offices referred to in sub-paragraph (1) were listed in the said Schedule 1; and

(b) in relation to that capacity the expression "relevant service" in the said sections 2 to 8 had the meaning assigned by sub-paragraph (4); and

(c) in relation to such a holder of such an office, any reference in the said section 2 to his last annual salary were a reference to his last annual remuneration apart from allowances.

(7) Where the rate of the superannuation allowance payable to any person under subparagraph (1) is or would be increased by virtue of regulations made under sub-paragraph (4) in respect of relevant service in some capacity other than as holder of one of the offices referred to in sub-paragraph (1), and a pension payable to him wholly in respect of service in that other capacity would have been paid and borne otherwise than out of moneys provideed by Parliament, any pension benefits paid to or in respect of him as having been the holder of such an office shall, to such extent as the Minister for the Civil Service may determine, having regard to the relative length of service and rate of remuneration in each capacity, be paid and borne in like manner as that in which a pension payable to him wholly in respect of service in that other capacity would have been paid and borne.

(8) In this paragraph the expression "pension" includes any superannuation or other retiring allowance or gratuity, and the expression "pensionable" shall be construed accordingly, and the expression "pension benefits" includes benefits payable to or in respect of the pensioner by virtue of sub-paragraph (6).

DERIVATION

Para.

1—1974, para. 21 (1)–(3A), (5), (5A), (6) ; 1975, s. 109 (6), Sched. 16, Pt. III, paras. 18, 19, 22, 23.

2—1975, s. 55 (3), (4) ; 1974, para. 18.

3—1965, s. 46 (6).

4—1974, para. 22.

5—1974, para. 23.

6—1974, para. 24.

7—1974, para. 25.

8—1975, s. 80 (4).

Paras. 9, 10—Industrial Training Act 1964 (c. 16), s. 12 (2B), (3) ; 1965, s. 46 (5) ; Employment and Training Act 1973 (c. 50), Sched. 2, Pt. I, para. 15 ; Minister for the Civil Service Order 1971 (S.I. 1971 No. 2099).

Para.

11—Superannuation (Miscellaneous Provisions) Act 1967 (c. 28), s. 9 ; Minister for the Civil Service Order 1968 (S.I. 1968 No. 1656).

Section 130   SCHEDULE 10

STATUTORY PROVISIONS RELATING TO REFEREES AND BOARDS OF REFEREES

1. Regulations under section 37 of the Coal Industry Nationalisation Act 1946.

2. Regulations under section 67 of the National Insurance Act 1946.

3. Regulations under section 68 of the National Health Service Act 1946, and orders under section 11 (9) or section 31 (5) of that Act.

4. Regulations under section 67 of the National Health Service (Scotland) Act 1947.

5. Regulations under Schedule 5 to the Fire Services Act 1947.

6. Regulations under section 101 of the Transport Act 1947.

7. Subsections (3) and (5) of section 54 of the Electricity Act 1947, and regulations under section 27 of the Electricity Act 1957.

8. Regulations under section 140 of the Local Government Act 1948, and such regulations as applied by any local Act, whether passed before or after this Act.

9. Regulations under subsection (1) or subsection (2) of section 60 of the National Assistance Act 1948.

10. Rules under section 3 of the Superannuation (Miscellaneous Provisions) Act 1948.

11. Subsections (3) and (5) of section 58 of the Gas Act 1948, and regulations under section 60 of that Act.

12. Subsection (4) of section 6 of the Commonwealth Telegraphs Act 1949 and regulations under that section.

13. Regulations under section 25 of the Prevention of Damage by Pests Act 1949.

14. Regulations under section 42 of the Justices of the Peace Act 1949.

15. Regulations under section 27 or section 28 of the Transport Act 1953.

16. Regulations under section 24 of the Iron and Steel Act 1953.

17. Regulations under section 12 of the Electricity Reorganisation (Scotland) Act 1954.

18. Orders under section 23 of the Local Government Act 1958 and regulations under section 60 of that Act.

19. Regulations under section 1 of the Water Officers Compensation Act 1960.

20. Regulations under section 18 (6) of the Land Drainage Act 1961.

21. Subsection (6) of section 74 of the Transport Act 1962 and orders under that section, regulations under section 81 of that Act, and paragraph 17 (3) of Schedule 7 to that Act.

22. Orders under section 84 of the London Government Act 1963 and regulations under section 85 of that Act.

23. Regulations under section 106 of the Water Resources Act 1963.

DERIVATION

1965, Sched. 7.

SCHEDULE 11

EMPLOYMENT APPEAL TRIBUNAL

PART I

PROVISIONS AS TO MEMBERSHIP, SITTINGS, PROCEEDINGS AND POWERS

Tenure of office of appointed members of Appeal Tribunal

1. Subject to paragraphs 2 and 3, a member of the Appeal Tribunal appointed by Her Majesty under section 135 (2) (*c*) (in this Schedule referred to as an "appointed member") shall hold and vacate office as such member in accordance with the terms of his appointment.

2. An appointed member may at any time resign his membership by notice in writing addressed to the Lord Chancellor and the Secretary of State.

3.—(1) If the Lord Chancellor, after consultation with the Secretary of State, is satisfied that an appointed member—

    (*a*) has been absent from sittings of the Appeal Tribunal for a period longer than six consecutive months without the permission of the President of the Tribunal; or

    (*b*) has become bankrupt or made an arrangement with his creditors; or

    (*c*) is incapacitated by physical or mental illness; or

    (*d*) is otherwise unable or unfit to discharge the functions of a member;

the Lord Chancellor may declare his office as a member to be vacant and shall notify the declaration in such manner as the Lord Chancellor thinks fit; and thereupon the office shall become vacant.

(2) In the application of this paragraph to Scotland for the references in sub-paragraph (1) (*b*) to a member's having become bankrupt and to a member's having made an arrangement with his creditors there shall be substituted respectively references to a member's estate having been sequestrated and to a member's having made a trust deed for behoof of his creditors or a composition contract.

Temporary membership of Appeal Tribunal

4. At any time when the office of President of the Appeal Tribunal is vacant, or the person holding that office is temporarily absent or otherwise unable to act as President of the Tribunal, the Lord Chancellor may nominate another judge nominated under section 135 (2) (*a*) to act temporarily in his place.

5. At any time when a judge of the Appeal Tribunal nominated by the Lord Chancellor is temporarily absent or otherwise unable to act as a judge of that Tribunal, the Lord Chancellor may nominate another person who is qualified to be nominated under section 135 (2) (*a*) to act temporarily in his place.

6. At any time when a judge of the Appeal Tribunal nominated by the Lord President of the Court of Session is temporarily absent or otherwise unable to act as a judge of the Appeal Tribunal, the Lord President may nominate another judge of the Court of Session to act temporarily in his place.

7. At any time when an appointed member is temporarily absent or otherwise unable to act as a member of the Appeal Tribunal, the Lord Chancellor and the Secretary of State may jointly appoint a person appearing to them to have the qualifications for appointment as such a member to act temporarily in his place.

8.—(1) At any time when it appears to the Lord Chancellor that it is expedient to do so in order to facilitate in England and Wales the disposal of business in the Appeal Tribunal, he may appoint a qualified person to be a temporary additional judge of the Tribunal during such period or on such occasions as the Lord Chancellor thinks fit.

(2) In this paragraph "qualified person" means a person qualified for appointment as a puisne judge of the High Court under section 9 of the Supreme Court of Judicature (Consolidation) Act 1925 or any person who has held office as a judge of the Court of Appeal or of the High Court.

9. A person appointed to act temporarily in place of the President or any other member of the Appeal Tribunal shall, when so acting, have all the functions of the person in whose place he acts.

10. A person appointed to be a temporary additional judge of the Appeal Tribunal shall have all the functions of a judge nominated under section 135 (2) (*a*).

11. No judge shall be nominated under paragraph 5 or 6 except with his consent.

Organisation and sittings of Appeal Tribunal

12. The Appeal Tribunal shall be a superior court of record and shall have an official seal which shall be judicially noticed.

13. The Appeal Tribunal shall have a central office in London.

14. The Appeal Tribunal may sit at any time and in any place in Great Britain.

15. The Appeal Tribunal may sit, in accordance with directions given by the President of the Tribunal, either as a single tribunal or in two or more divisions concurrently.

16. With the consent of the parties to any proceedings before the Appeal Tribunal, the proceedings may be heard by a judge and one appointed member, but, in default of such consent, any proceedings before the Tribunal shall be heard by a judge and either two or four appointed members, so that in either case there are equal numbers of persons whose experience is as representatives of employers and whose experience is as representatives of workers.

Rules

17.—(1) The Lord Chancellor, after consultation with the Lord President of the Court of Session, shall make rules with respect to proceedings before the Appeal Tribunal.

(2) Subject to those rules, the Tribunal shall have power to regulate its own procedure.

18. Without prejudice to the generality of paragraph 17 the rules may include provision—

(a) with respect to the manner in which an appeal may be brought and the time within which it may be brought;

(b) for requiring persons to attend to give evidence and produce documents, and for authorising the administration of oaths to witnesses;

(c) enabling the Appeal Tribunal to sit in private for the purpose of hearing evidence to hear which an industrial tribunal may sit in private by virtue of paragraph 1 of Schedule 9.

19.—(1) Without prejudice to the generality of paragraph 17 the rules may empower the Appeal Tribunal to order a party to any proceedings before the Tribunal to pay to any other party to the proceedings the whole or part of the costs or expenses incurred by that other party in connection with the proceedings, where in the opinion of the Tribunal—

(a) the proceedings were unnecessary, improper or vexatious, or

(b) there has been unreasonable delay or other unreasonable conduct in bringing or conducting the proceedings.

(2) Except as provided by sub-paragraph (1), the rules shall not enable the Appeal Tribunal to order the payment of costs or expenses by any party to proceedings before the Tribunal.

20. Any person may appear before the Appeal Tribunal in person or be represented by counsel or by a solicitor or by a representative of a trade union or an employers' association or by any other person whom he desires to represent him.

Powers of Tribunal

21.—(1) For the purpose of disposing of an appeal the Appeal Tribunal may exercise any powers of the body or officer from whom the appeal was brought or may remit the case to that body or officer.

(2) Any decision or award of the Appeal Tribunal on an appeal shall have the same effect and may be enforced in the same manner as a decision or award of a body or officer from whom the appeal was brought.

22.—(1) The Appeal Tribunal shall, in relation to the attendance and examination of witnesses, the production and inspection of documents and all other matters incidental to its jurisdiction, have the like powers, rights, privileges and authority—

(a) in England and Wales, as the High Court,

(b) in Scotland, as the Court of Session.

(2) No person shall be punished for contempt of the Tribunal except by, or with the consent of, a judge.

23.—(1) In relation to any fine imposed by the Appeal Tribunal for contempt of the Tribunal, section 14 of the Criminal Justice Act 1948 and section 47 of the Criminal Justice Act 1967 (which relate to fines imposed and recognizances forfeited at certain courts) shall have effect as if in those provisions any reference to the Crown Court included a reference to the Tribunal.

(2) A magistrates' court shall not remit the whole or any part of a fine imposed by the Appeal Tribunal except with the consent of a judge who is a member of the Tribunal.

(3) This paragraph does not extend to Scotland.

Staff

24. The Secretary of State may appoint such officers and servants of the Appeal Tribunal as he may determine, subject to the approval of the Minister for the Civil Service as to numbers and as to terms and conditions of service.

PART II

SUPPLEMENTARY

Remuneration and allowances

25. The Secretary of State shall pay the appointed members of the Appeal Tribunal, the persons appointed to act temporarily as appointed members, and the officers and servants of the Tribunal such remuneration and such travelling and other allowances as he may with the approval of the Minister for the Civil Service determine.

26. A person appointed to be a temporary additional judge of the Appeal Tribunal shall be paid such remuneration and allowances as the Lord Chancellor may, with the approval of the Minister for the Civil Service, determine.

Pensions, etc.

27. If the Secretary of State determines, with the approval of the Minister for the Civil Service, that this paragraph shall apply in the case of an appointed member, the Secretary of State shall pay such pension, allowance or gratuity to or in respect of that member on his retirement or death or make that member such payments towards the provision of such a pension, allowance or gratuity as the Secretary of State may with the like approval determine.

28. Where a person ceases to be an appointed member otherwise than on his retirement or death and it appears to the Secretary of State that there are special circumstances which make it right for him to receive compensation, the Secretary of State may make him a payment of such amount as the Secretary of State may, with the approval of the Minister for the Civil Service, determine.

DERIVATION
1975, Sched. 6.

Section 150   SCHEDULE 12

DEATH OF EMPLOYEE OR EMPLOYER

PART I

GENERAL

Introductory

1. In this Schedule " the relevant provisions " means Part I (so far as it relates to itemised pay statements), section 53 and Parts II, III, V. VI and VII of this Act and this Schedule.

Institution or continuance of tribunal proceedings

2. Where an employee or employer has died, tribunal proceedings arising under any of the relevant provisions may be instituted or continued by a personal representative of the deceased employee or, as the case may be, defended by a personal representative of the deceased employer.

3.—(1) If there is no personal representative of a deceased employee, tribunal proceedings arising under any of the relevant provisions (or proceedings to enforce a tribunal award made in any such proceedings) may be instituted or continued on behalf of the estate of the deceased employee by such person as the industrial tribunal may appoint being either—

(a) a person authorised by the employee to act in connection with the proceedings before the employee's death; or

(b) the widower, widow, child, father, mother, brother or sister of the deceased employee,

and references in this Schedule to a personal representative shall be construed as including such a person.

(2) In such a case any award made by the industrial tribunal shall be in such terms and shall be enforceable in such manner as may be provided by regulation made by the Secretary of State.

4.—(1) Subject to any specific provision of this Schedule to the contrary, in relation to an employee or employer who has died—

(a) any reference in the relevant provisions to the doing of anything by or in relation to an employee or an employer shall be construed as including a reference to the doing of that thing by or in relation to any personal representative of the deceased employee or employer; and

(b) any reference in the said provisions to a thing required or authorised to be done by or in relation to an employee or employer shall be construed as including a reference to any thing which, in accordance with any such provision as modified by this Schedule (including sub-paragraph (a)), is required or authorised to be done by or in relation to any personal representative of the deceased employee or employer.

(2) Nothing in this paragraph shall prevent references in the relevant provisions to a successor of an employer from including a personal representative of a deceased employer.

Rights and liabilities accruing after death

5. Any right arising under any of the relevant provisions as modified by this Schedule shall, if it had not accrued before the death of the employee in question, nevertheless devolve as if it had so accrued.

6. Where by virtue of any of the relevant provisions as modified by this Schedule a personal representative of a deceased employer is liable to pay any amount and that liability had not accrued before the death of the employer, it shall be treated for all purposes as if it were a liability of the deceased employer which had accrued immediately before his death.

PART II

UNFAIR DISMISSAL

Introductory

7. In this Part of this Schedule "the unfair dismissal provisions" means Part V of this Act and this Schedule.

Death during notice period

8. Where an employer has given notice to an employee to terminate his contract of employment and before that termination the employee or the employer dies, the unfair dismissal provisions shall apply as if the contract had been duly terminated by the employer by notice expiring on the date of the death.

9. Where the employee's contract of employment has been terminated by the employer and by virtue of section 55 (5) a date later than the effective date of termination as defined by subsection (4) of that section is to be treated as the effective date of termination for the purposes of certain of the unfair dismissal

provisions, and before that later date the employee or the employer dies, section 55 (5) shall have effect as if the notice referred to in that subsection as required to be given by the employer would have expired on the date of the death.

Remedies for unfair dismissal

10. Where an employee has died, then, unless an order for reinstatement or re-engagement has already been made, section 69 shall not apply; and accordingly if the industrial tribunal finds that the grounds of the complaint are well-founded the case shall be treated as falling within section 68 (2) as a case in which no order is made under section 69.

11. If an order for reinstatement or re-engagement has been made and the employee dies before the order is complied with—

  (a) if the employer has before the death refused to reinstate or re-engage the employee in accordance with the order, section 71 (2) and (3) shall apply and an award shall be made under section 71 (2) (b) unless the employer satisfies the tribunal that it was not practicable at the time of the refusal to comply with the order;

  (b) if there has been no such refusal, section 71 (1) shall apply if the employer fails to comply with any ancillary terms of the order which remain capable of fulfilment after the employee's death as it would apply to such a failure to comply fully with the terms of an order where the employee had been reinstated or re-engaged.

Part III

Redundancy Payments: Death of Employer

Introductory

12. The provisions of this Part shall have effect in relation to an employee where his employer (in this Part referred to as " the deceased employer ") dies.

13. Section 94 shall not apply to any change whereby the ownership of the business, for the purposes of which the employee was employed by the deceased employer, passes to a personal representative of the deceased employer.

Dismissal

14. Where by virtue of subsection (1) of section 93 the death of the deceased employer is to be treated for the purposes of Part VI of this Act as a termination by him of the contract of employment, section 84 shall have effect subject to the following modifications:—

  (a) for subsection (1) there shall be substituted the following subsection—

    " (1) If an employee's contract of employment is renewed, or he is re-engaged under a new contract of employment, by a personal representative of the deceased employer and the renewal or re-engagement takes effect not later than eight weeks after the death of the deceased employer, then, subject to subsections (3) and (6), the employee shall not be regarded as having been dismissed by reason of the ending of his employment under the previous contract.";

  (b) in subsection (2), paragraph (a) shall be omitted and in paragraph (b) for the words " four weeks " there shall be substituted the words " eight weeks ";

  (c) in subsections (5) and (6), references to the employer shall be construed as references to the personal representative of the deceased employer.

15. Where by reason of the death of the deceased employer the employee is treated for the purposes of Part VI of this Act as having been dismissed by him, section 82 shall have effect subject to the following modifications—

  (a) for subsection (3) there shall be substituted the following subsection—

    " (3) If a personal representative of the deceased employer makes an employee an offer (whether in writing or not) to renew his contract of employment, or to re-engage him under a new contract of employment, so that the renewal or re-engagement would take effect not later than eight weeks after the death of the deceased employer the provisions of subsections (5) and (6) shall have effect.";

(*b*) in subsection (4), paragraph (*a*) shall be omitted and in paragraph (*b*) for the words "four weeks" there shall be substituted the words "eight weeks";

(*c*) in subsection (5), the reference to the employer shall be construed as a reference to the personal representative of the deceased employer.

16. For the purposes of section 82 as modified by paragraph 15—

(*a*) an offer shall not be treated as one whereby the provisions of the contract as renewed, or of the new contract, as the case may be, would differ from the corresponding provisions of the contract as in force immediately before the death of the deceased employer by reason only that the personal representative would be substituted as the employer for the deceased employer, and

(*b*) no account shall be taken of that substitution in determining whether the refusal of the offer was reasonable, or, as the case may be, whether the employee acted reasonably in terminating the renewed, or new, employment during the trial period referred to in section 84.

Lay-off and short-time

17. Where the employee has before the death of the deceased employer been laid off or kept on short-time for one or more weeks, but has not given to the deceased employer notice of intention to claim, then if after the death of the deceased employer—

(*a*) his contract of employment is renewed, or he is re-engaged under a new contract by a personal representative of the deceased employer, and

(*b*) after the renewal or re-engagement, he is laid off or kept on short-time for one or more weeks by the personal representative of the deceased employer,

the provisions of sections 88 and 89 shall apply as if the week in which the deceased employer died and the first week of the employee's employment by the personal representative were consecutive weeks, and any reference in those sections to four weeks or thirteen weeks shall be construed accordingly.

18. The provisions of paragraph 19 or (as the case may be) paragraph 20 shall have effect where the employee has given to the deceased employer notice of intention to claim, and—

(*a*) the deceased employer has died before the end of the next four weeks after the service of that notice, and

(*b*) the employee has not terminated the contract of employment by notice expiring before the death of the deceased employer.

19. If in the circumstances specified in paragraph 18 the employee's contract of employment is not renewed by a personal representative of the deceased employer before the end of the next four weeks after the service of the notice of intention to claim, and he is not re-engaged under a new contract by such a personal representative before the end of those four weeks, section 88 (1) and (2) and (in relation to subsection (1) of that section) section 89 (2) and (3) shall apply as if—

(*a*) the deceased employer had not died, and

(*b*) the employee had terminated the contract of employment by a week's notice (or, if under the contract he is required to give more than a week's notice to terminate the contract, he had terminated it by the minimum notice which he is so required to give) expiring at the end of those four weeks,

but sections 88 (3) and (4) and 89 (1) and (4) shall not apply.

20.—(1) The provisions of this paragraph shall have effect where, in the circumstances specified in paragraph 18, the employee's contract of employment is renewed by a personal representative of the deceased employer before the end of the next four weeks after the service of the notice of intention to claim, or he is re-engaged under a new contract by such a personal representative before the end of those four weeks, and—

(*a*) he was laid off or kept on a short-time by the deceased employer for one or more of those weeks, and

(*b*) he is laid off or kept on short-time by the personal representative for the week, or for the next two or more weeks, following the renewal or re-engagement.

(2) Where the conditions specified in sub-paragraph (1) are fulfilled, sections 88 and 89 shall apply as if—

(a) all the weeks for which the employee was laid off or kept on short-time as mentioned in sub-paragraph (1) were consecutive weeks during which he was employed (but laid off or kept on short-time) by the same employer, and

(b) each of the periods specified in paragraphs (a) and (b) of subsection (5) of section 89 were extended by any week or weeks any part of which was after the death of the deceased employer and before the date on which the renewal or re-engagement took effect.

Continuity of period of employment

21. For the purposes of this application, in accordance with section 100 (1), of any provisions of Part VI of this Act in relation to an employee who was employed as a domestic servant in a private household, any reference to a personal representative in—

(a) this Part of this Schedule, or

(b) paragraph 17 of Schedule 13,

shall be construed as including a reference to any person to whom, otherwise than in pursuance of a sale or other disposition for valuable consideration, the management of the household has passed in consequence of the death of the deceased employer.

PART IV

REDUNDANCY PAYMENTS: DEATH OF EMPLOYEE

22.—(1) Where an employer has given notice to an employee to terminate his contract of employment, and before that notice expires the employee dies, the provisions of Part VI of this Act shall apply as if the contract had been duly terminated by the employer by notice expiring on the date of the employee's death.

(2) Where the employee's contract of employment has been terminated by the employer and by virtue of section 90 (3) a date later than the relevant date as defined by subsection (1) of that section is to be treated as the relevant date for the purposes of certain provisions of Part VI of this Act, and before that later date the employee dies, section 90 (3) shall have effect as if the notice referred to in that subsection as required to be given by an employer would have expired on the employee's death.

23.—(1) Where an employer has given notice to an employee to terminate his contract of employment, and has offered to renew his contract of employment, or to re-engage him under a new contract, then if—

(a) the employee dies without having either accepted or refused the offer, and

(b) the offer has not been withdrawn before his death,

section 82 shall apply as if for the words "the employee unreasonably refuses" there were substituted the words "it would have been unreasonable on the part of the employee to refuse".

(2) Where an employee's contract of employment has been renewed, or he has been re-engaged under a new contract of employment, and during the trial period the employee dies without having terminated or having given notice to terminate the contract, subsection (6) of that section shall apply as if for the words from "and during the trial period" to "terminated" there were substituted the words "and it would have been unreasonable for the employee, during the trial period referred to in section 84, to terminate or give notice to terminate the contract".

24. Where an employee's contract of employment has been renewed, or he has been re-engaged under a new contract of employment, and during the trial period he gives notice to terminate the contract but dies before the expiry of that notice, sections 82 (6) and 84 (6) (a) shall have effect as if the notice had expired and the contract had thereby been terminated on the date of the employee's death.

25.—(1) Where, in the circumstances specified in paragraphs (a) and (b) of subsection (1) of section 85, the employee dies before the notice given by him under paragraph (b) of that subsection is due to expire and before the employer has given him notice under subsection (3) of that section, subsection (4) of that section shall apply as if the employer had given him such notice and he had not complied with it.

(2) Where, in the said circumstances, the employee dies before his notice given under section 85 (1) (*b*) is due to expire but after the employer has given him notice under subsection (3) of section 85, subsections (3) and (4) of that section shall apply as if the circumstances were that the employee had not died, but did not comply with the last-mentioned notice.

26.—(1) Where an employee has given notice of intention to claim and dies before he has given notice to terminate his contract of employment and before the period allowed for the purposes of subsection (2) (*a*) of section 88 has expired the said subsection (2) (*a*) shall not apply.

(2) Where an employee, who has given notice of intention to claim, dies within seven days after the service of that notice, and before the employer has given a counter-notice, the provisions of sections 88 and 89 shall apply as if the employer had given a counter-notice within those seven days.

(3) In this paragraph " counter-notice " has the same meaning as in section 89 (1).

27.—(1) In relation to the making of a claim by a personal representative of a deceased employee who dies before the end of the period of six months beginning with the relevant date, subsection (1) of section 101 shall apply with the substitution for the words " six months ", of the words " one year ".

(2) In relation to the making of a claim by a personal representative of a deceased employee who dies after the end of the period of six months beginning with the relevant date and before the end of the following period of six months, subsection (2) of section 101 shall apply with the substitution for the words " six months ", of the words " one year ".

28. In relation to any case where, under any provision contained in Part VI of this Act as modified by this Schedule, an industrial tribunal has power to determine that an employer shall be liable to pay to a personal representative of a deceased employee either—

(*a*) the whole of a redundancy payment to which he would have been entitled apart from another provision therein mentioned, or

(*b*) such part of such a redundancy payment as the tribunal thinks fit,

any reference in paragraph 5 to a right shall be construed as including a reference to any right to receive the whole or part of a redundancy payment if the tribunal determines that the employer shall be liable to pay it.

DERIVATION

1975, Sched 12; 1965, Sched. 4, am. 1975, Sched. 16, Pt. I, paras. 23–34.

Para.　　1—

2—1975, Sched. 12, para. 2.

3—1975, Sched. 12, para. 3; 1965, Sched. 4, para. 21A (1), (2).

4—1975, Sched. 12, para. 4; 1965, Sched. 4, paras. 14, 21.

5—1975, Sched. 12, para. 5; 1965, Sched. 4, para. 22 (1).

6—1975, Sched. 12, para. 6; 1965, Sched. 4, para. 15.

Paras.　7–11—1975, Sched. 12, paras. 8 to 12.

12–21—1965, Sched. 4, paras. 1 to 5, 7 to 10, 13.

22–28—1965, Sched. 4, paras. 16 to 20, 22 (2).

Section 151　　　　　SCHEDULE 13

COMPUTATION OF PERIOD OF EMPLOYMENT

Preliminary

1.—(1) Where an employee's period of employment is, for the purposes of any enactment (including any enactment contained in this Act), to be computed in accordance with this Schedule, it shall be computed in weeks, and in any such enactment which refers to a period of employment expressed in years, a year means fifty-two weeks (whether continuous or discontinuous) which count in computing a period of employment.

(2) For the purpose of computing an employee's period of employment (but not for any other purpose), the provisions of this Schedule apply, subject to paragraph 14, to a period of employment notwithstanding that during that period the employee was engaged in work wholly or mainly outside Great Britain or was excluded by or under this Act from any right conferred by this Act.

2. Except so far as otherwise provided by the following provisions of this Schedule, any week which does not count under paragraphs 3 to 13 breaks the continuity of the period of employment.

Normal working weeks

3. Any week in which the employee is employed for sixteen hours or more shall count in computing a period of employment.

Employment governed by contract

4. Any week during the whole or part of which the employee's relations with the employer are governed by a contract of employment which normally involves employment for sixteen hours or more weekly shall count in computing a period of employment.

5.—(1) If the employee's relations with his employer cease to be governed by a contract which normally involves work for sixteen hours or more weekly and become governed by a contract which normally involves employment for eight hours or more, but less than sixteen hours, weekly and, but for that change, the later weeks would count in computing a period of employment, then those later weeks shall count in computing a period of employment or, as the case may be, shall not break the continuity of a period of employment, notwithstanding that change.

(2) Not more than twenty-six weeks shall count under this paragraph between any two periods falling under paragraph 4, and in computing the said figure of twenty-six weeks no account shall be taken of any week which counts in computing a period of employment, or does not break the continuity of a period of employment, otherwise than by virtue of this paragraph.

6.—(1) An employee whose relations with his employer are governed, or have been from time to time governed, by a contract of employment which normally involves employment for eight hours or more, but less than sixteen hours, weekly shall nevertheless, if he satisfies the condition referred to in sub-paragraph (2), be treated for the purposes of this Schedule (apart from this paragraph) as if his contract normally involved employment for sixteen hours or more weekly, and had at all times at which there was a contract during the period of employment of five years or more referred to in sub-paragraph (2) normally involved employment for sixteen hours or more weekly.

(2) Sub-paragraph (1) shall apply if the employee, on the date by reference to which the length of any period of employment falls to be ascertained in accordance with the provisions of this Schedule, has been continuously employed within the meaning of sub-paragraph (3) for a period of five years or more.

(3) In computing for the purposes of sub-paragraph (2) an employee's period of employment, the provisions of this Schedule (apart from this paragraph) shall apply but as if, in paragraphs 3 and 4, for the words "sixteen hours" wherever they occur, there were substituted the words "eight hours".

7.—(1) If an employee has, at any time during the relevant period of employment, been continuously employed for a period which qualifies him for any right which requires a qualifying period of continuous employment computed in accordance with this Schedule, then he shall be regarded for the purposes of qualifying for that right as continuing to satisfy that requirement until the condition referred to in sub-paragraph (3) occurs.

(2) In this paragraph the relevant period of employment means the period of employment ending on the date by reference to which the length of any period of employment falls to be ascertained which would be continuous (in accordance with the provisions of this Schedule) if at all relevant times the employee's relations with the employer had been governed by a contract of employment which normally involved employment for sixteen hours or more weekly.

(3) The condition which defeats the operation of sub-paragraph (1) is that in a week subsequent to the time at which the employee qualified as referred to in that sub-paragraph—

(a) his relations with his employer are governed by a contract of employment which normally involves employment for less than eight hours weekly; and

(b) he is employed in that week for less than sixteen hours.

(4) If, in a case in which an employee is entitled to any right by virtue of sub-paragraph (1), it is necessary for the purpose of ascertaining the amount of his

entitlement to determine for what period he has been continuously employed, he shall be regarded for that purpose as having been continuously employed through-out the relevant period.

Orders under section 7

8. The foregoing provisions of this Schedule shall have effect subject to any order made under section 7 and an order under that section shall affect the operation of this Schedule as respects periods before the order takes effect as well as respects later periods.

Periods in which there is no contract of employment

9.—(1) If in any week the employee is, for the whole or part of the week—

(a) incapable of work in consequence of sickness or injury, or

(b) absent from work on account of a temporary cessation of work, or

(c) absent from work in circumstances such that, by arrangement or custom, he is regarded as continuing in the employment of his employer for all or any purposes, or

(d) absent from work wholly or partly because of pregnancy or confinement,

that week shall, notwithstanding that it does not fall under paragraph 3, 4 or 5, count as a period of employment.

(2) Not more than twenty-six weeks shall count under paragraph (a) or, subject to paragraph 10, under paragraph (d) of sub-paragraph (1) between any periods falling under paragraph 3, 4 or 5.

Maternity

10. If an employee returns to work in accordance with section 47 after a period of absence from work wholly or partly occasioned by pregnancy or confine-ment, every week during that period shall count in computing a period of employ-ment, notwithstanding that it does not fall under paragraph 3, 4 or 5.

Intervals in employment where section 55 (5) or 84 (1) or 90 (3) applies

11.—(1) In ascertaining, for the purposes of section 64 (1) (a) and of section 73 (3), the period for which an employee has been continuously employed, where by virtue of section 55 (5) a date is treated as the effective date of termination which is later than the effective date of termination as defined by section 55 (4), the period of the interval between those two dates shall count as a period of employment notwithstanding that it does not otherwise count under this Schedule.

(2) Where by virtue of section 84 (1) an employee is treated as not having been dismissed by reason of a renewal or re-engagement taking effect after an interval, then, in determining for the purposes of section 81 (1) or Schedule 4 whether he has been continuously employed for the requisite period, the period of that interval shall count as a period of employment except in so far as it is to be disregarded under paragraphs 12 to 14 (notwithstanding that it does not other-wise count under this Schedule).

(3) Where by virtue of section 90 (3) a date is to be treated as the relevant date for the purposes of section 81 (4) which is later than the relevant date as defined by section 90 (1), then in determining for the purposes of section 81 (1) or Schedule 4 whether the employee has been continuously employed for the requisite period, the period of the interval between those two dates shall count as a period of employment except in so far as it is to be disregarded under para-graphs 12 to 14 (notwithstanding that it does not otherwise count under this Schedule).

Payment of previous redundancy payment or equivalent payment

12.—(1) Where the conditions mentioned in sub-paragraph (2) (a) or (2) (b) are fulfilled in relation to a person, then in determining, for the purposes of section 81 (1) or Schedule 4, whether at any subsequent time he has been continuously employed for the requisite period, or for what period he has been continuously employed, the continuity of the period of employment shall be treated as having been broken—

(a) in so far as the employment was under a contract of employment, at the date which was the relevant date in relation to the payment mentioned in sub-paragraph (2) (*a*) or, as the case may be, sub-paragraph (2) (*b*); or

(*b*) in so far as the employment was otherwise than under a contract of employment, at the date which would have been the relevant date in relation to that payment had the employment been under a contract of employment,

and accordingly no account shall be taken of any time before that date.

(2) Sub-paragraph (1) has effect—

(*a*) where—

(i) a redundancy payment is paid to an employee, whether in respect of dismissal or in respect of lay-off or short-time; and

(ii) the contract of employment under which he was employed (in this section referred to as " the previous contract ") is renewed, whether by the same or another employer, or he is re-engaged under a new contract of employment, whether by the same or another employer; and

(iii) the circumstances of the renewal or re-engagement are such that, in determining for the purposes of section 81 (1) or Schedule 4 whether at any subsequent time he has been continuously employed for the requisite period, or for what period he has been continuously employed, the continuity of his period of employment would, apart from this paragraph, be treated as not having been broken by the termination of the previous contract and the renewal or re-engagement; or

(*b*) where—

(i) a payment has been made, whether in respect of the termination of any person's employment or in respect of lay-off or short-time, either in accordance with any provisions of a scheme under section 1 of the Superannuation Act 1972 or in accordance with any such arrangements as are mentioned in section 111 (3); and

(ii) he commences new, or renewed, employment; and

(iii) the circumstances of the commencement of the new, or renewed, employment are such that, in determining for the purposes of section 81 (1) or Schedule 4 whether at any subsequent time he has been continuously employed for the requisite period, or for what period he has been continuously employed, the continuity of his period of employment would, apart from this paragraph, be treated as not having been broken by the termination of the previous employment and the commencement of the new, or renewed, employment.

(3) For the purposes of this paragraph, a redundancy payment shall be treated as having been paid if—

(*a*) the whole of the payment has been paid to the employee by the employer, or, in a case where a tribunal has determined that the employer is liable to pay part (but not the whole) of the redundancy payment, that part of the redundancy payment has been paid in full to the employee by the employer, or

(*b*) the Secretary of State has paid a sum to the employee in respect of the redundancy payment under section 106.

Certain weeks of employment to be disregarded for purposes of Schedule 4

13. In ascertaining for the purposes of Schedule 4 the period for which an employee has been continuously employed, any week which began before he attained the age of eighteen shall not count under this Schedule.

Redundancy payments: employment wholly or partly abroad

14.—(1) In computing in relation to an employee the period specified in section 81 (4) or the period specified in paragraph 1 of Schedule 4, a week of employment shall not count if—

(*a*) the employee was employed outside Great Britain during the whole or part of that week, and

(*b*) he was not during that week, or during the corresponding contribution week,—

(i) where the week is a week of employment after 1st June 1976, an employed earner for the purposes of the Social Security Act 1975 in respect of whom a secondary Class 1 contribution was payable under that Act; or

(ii) where the week is a week of employment after 6th April 1975 and before 1st June 1976, an employed earner for the purposes of the Social Security Act 1975; or

(iii) where the week is a week of employment before 6th April 1975, an employee in respect of whom an employer's contribution was payable in respect of the corresponding contribution week;

whether or not the contribution mentioned in paragraph (i) or (iii) of this sub-paragraph was in fact paid.

(2) For the purposes of the application of sub-paragraph (1) to a week of employment where the corresponding contribution week began before 5th July 1948, an employer's contribution shall be treated as payable as mentioned in sub-paragraph (1) if such a contribution would have been so payable if the statutory provisions relating to national insurance which were in force on 5th July 1948 had been in force in that contribution week.

(3) Where by virtue of sub-paragraph (1) a week of employment does not count in computing such a period as is mentioned in that sub-paragraph, the continuity of that period shall not be broken by reason only that that week of employment does not count in computing that period.

(4) Any question arising under this paragraph whether—

(a) an employer's contribution was or would have been payable, as mentioned in sub-paragraph (1) or (2), or

(b) a person was an employed earner for the purposes of the Social Security Act 1975 and if so whether a secondary Class 1 contribution was payable in respect of him under that Act,

shall be determined by the Secretary of State; and any legislation (including regulations) as to the determination of questions which under that Act the Secretary of State is empowered to determine (including provisions as to the reference of questions for decision, or as to appeals, to the High Court or the Court of Session) shall apply to the determination of any question by the Secretary of State under this paragraph.

(5) In this paragraph "employer's contribution" has the same meaning as in the National Insurance Act 1965, and "corresponding contribution week", in relation to a week of employment, means a contribution week (within the meaning of the said Act of 1965) of which so much as falls within the period beginning with midnight between Sunday and Monday and ending with Saturday also falls within that week of employment.

(6) The provisions of this paragraph shall not apply in relation to a person who is employed as a master or seaman in a British ship and is ordinarily resident in Great Britain.

Industrial disputes

15.—(1) A week shall not count under paragraph 3, 4, 5, 9 or 10 if in that week, or any part of that week, the employee takes part in a strike.

(2) The continuity of an employee's period of employment is not broken by a week which does not count under this Schedule, and which begins after 5th July 1964 if in that week, or any part of that week, the employee takes part in a strike.

(3) Sub-paragraph (2) applies whether or not the week would, apart from sub-paragraph (1), have counted under this Schedule.

(4) The continuity of the period of employment is not broken by a week which begins after 5th July 1964 and which does not count under this Schedule, if in that week, or any part of that week, the employee is absent from work because of a lock-out by the employer.

Reinstatement after service with the armed forces, etc.

16.—(1) If a person who is entitled to apply to his former employer under Part II of the National Service Act 1948 (reinstatement in civil employment) enters the employment of that employer not later than the end of the six month period mentioned in section 35 (2) (b) of that Act, his previous period of employment with that employer (or if there was more than one such period, the last of those periods) and the period of employment beginning in the said period of six months shall be treated as continuous.

(2) The reference in this paragraph to Part II of the National Service Act 1948 includes a reference to that Part of that Act as amended, applied or extended by any other Act passed before or after this Act.

Change of employer

17.—(1) Subject to this paragraph and paragraph 18, the foregoing provisions of this Schedule relate only to employment by the one employer.

(2) If a trade or business or an undertaking (whether or not it be an undertaking established by or under an Act of Parliament) is transferred from one person to another, the period of employment of an employee in the trade or business or undertaking at the time of the transfer shall count as a period of employment with the transferee, and the transfer shall not break the continuity of the period of employment.

(3) If by or under an Act of Parliament, whether public or local and whether passed before or after this Act, a contract of employment between any body corporate and an employee is modified and some other body corporate is substituted as the employer, the employee's period of employment at the time when the modification takes effect shall count as a period of employment with the second-mentioned body corporate, and the change of employer shall not break the continuity of the period of employment.

(4) If on the death of an employer the employee is taken into the employment of the personal representatives or trustees of the deceased, the employee's period of employment at the time of the death shall count as a period of employment with the employer's personal representatives or trustees, and the death shall not break the continuity of the period of employment.

(5) If there is a change in the partners, personal representatives or trustees who employ any person, the employee's period of employment at the time of the change shall count as a period of employment with the partners, personal representatives or trustees after the change, and the change shall not break the continuity of the period of employment.

18. If an employee of an employer is taken into the employment of another employer who, at the time when the employee enters his employment is an associated employer of the first-mentioned employer, the employee's period of employment at that time shall count as a period of employment with the second-mentioned employer and the change of employer shall not break the continuity of the period of employment.

Crown employment

19.—(1) Subject to the following provisions of this paragraph, the provisions of this Schedule shall have effect (for the purpose of computing an employee's period of employment, but not for any other purpose) in relation to Crown employment and to persons in Crown employment as they have effect in relation to other employment and to other employees, and accordingly, except where the context otherwise requires, references to an employer shall be construed as including a reference to the Crown.

(2) In this paragraph, subject to sub-paragraph (3), "Crown employment" means employment under or for the purposes of a government department or any officer or body exercising on behalf of the Crown functions conferred by any enactment.

(3) This paragraph does not apply to service as a member of the naval, military or air forces of the Crown, or of any women's service administered by the Defence Council, but does apply to employment by any association established for the purposes of the Auxiliary Forces Act 1953.

(4) In so far as a person in Crown employment is employed otherwise than under a contract of employment, references in this Schedule to an employee's relations with his employer being governed by a contract of employment which normally involves employment for a certain number of hours weekly shall be modified accordingly.

(5) The reference in paragraph 17 (2) to an undertaking shall be construed as including a reference to any function of (as the case may require) a Minister of the Crown, a government department, or any other officer or body performing functions on behalf of the Crown.

Reinstatement or re-engagement of dismissed employee

20.—(1) Regulations made by the Secretary of State may make provision—

(*a*) for preserving the continuity of a person's period of employment for the purposes of this Schedule or for the purposes of this Schedule as applied by or under any other enactment specified in the regulations, or

(*b*) for modifying or excluding the operation of paragraph 12 subject to the recovery of any such payment as is mentioned in sub-paragraph (2) of that paragraph,

in cases where, in consequence of action to which sub-paragraph (2) applies, a dismissed employee is reinstated or re-engaged by his employer or by a successor or associated employer of that employer.

(2) This sub-paragraph applies to any action taken in relation to the dismissal of an employee which consists—

(*a*) of the presentation by him of a complaint under section 67, or

(*b*) of his making a claim in accordance with a dismissal procedures agreement designated by an order under section 65, or

(*c*) of any action taken by a conciliation officer under section 134 (3).

Employment before the commencement of Act

21. Save as otherwise expressly provided, the provisions of this Schedule apply to periods before it comes into force as they apply to later periods.

22. If, in any week beginning before 6th July 1964, the employee was, for the whole or any part of the week, absent from work—

(*a*) because he was taking part in a strike, or

(*b*) because of a lock-out by the employer,

the week shall count as a period of employment.

23. Without prejudice to the foregoing provisions of this Schedule, any week which counted as a period of employment in the computation of a period of employment in accordance with the Contracts of Employment Act 1972 whether for the purposes of that Act, the Redundancy Payments Act 1965, the Trade Union and Labour Relations Act 1974 or the Employment Protection Act 1975, shall count as a period of employment for the purposes of this Act, and any week which did not break the continuity of a person's employment for the purposes of those Acts shall not break the continuity of a period of employment for the purposes of this Act.

Interpretation

24.—(1) In this Schedule, unless the context otherwise requires,—

" lock-out " means the closing of a place of employment, or the suspension of work, or the refusal by an employer to continue to employ any number of persons employed by him in consequence of a dispute, done with a view to compelling those persons, or to aid another employer in compelling persons employed by him, to accept terms or conditions of or affecting employment;

" strike " means the cessation of work by a body of persons employed acting in combination, or a concerted refusal or a refusal under a common understanding of any number of persons employed to continue to work for an employer in consequence of a dispute, done as a means of compelling their employer or any person or body of persons employed, or to aid other employees in compelling their employer or any person or body of persons employed, to accept or not to accept terms or conditions of or affecting employment;

" week " means a week ending with Saturday.

(2) For the purposes of this Schedule the hours of employment of an employee who is required by the terms of his employment to live on the premises where he works shall be the hours during which he is on duty or during which his services may be required.

DERIVATION

1972, Sched. 1, am. 1975, Sched. 16, Pt. II, paras. 12 to 19.

Paras. 1–7—1972, Sched. 1, paras. 1 to 4C.

Para.   8—1972, s. 10 (2).

9—1972, Sched. 1, para. 5 (1), (2).

10—1972, Sched. 1, para. 5A.

Para.   11—1974, Sched. 1, para. 30 (1) (A); 1975, s. 74 (4); 1965, s. 8 (3),
                (3A), (4), Sched. 1, para. 1 (1) (*b*) (*c*); 1975, Sched. 16, Pt. I,
                paras. 5, 19, 20, Pt. III, para. 29.
        12—1965, ss 24, 24A; 1975, s. 20 (3).
        13—1965, Sched. 1, para. 1 (1) (*a*).
        14—1965, ss. 17 (3)–(8), 20 (1), (3); 1975, Sched. 16, Pt. I, para. 8.
        15—1972, Sched. 1, paras. 6, 7.
        16—1972, Sched. 1, para. 8.
        17—1972, Sched. 1, para. 9.
        18—1972, Sched. 1, para. 10.
        19—1972, Sched. 1, para. 10A; 1975, s. 120 (1).
        20—1974, para. 30 (3), (4); 1975, Sched. 16, Pt. III, para. 30.
        21—Contracts of Employment Act 1963 (c. 49), Sched. 1, para. 1 (2);
                1972, s. 13 (5).
        22—Contracts of Employment Act 1963 (c. 49), Sched. 1, para. 6; 1972,
                s. 13 (5).
        23—1972, s. 13 (5).
        24—1972, Sched. 1, para. 11.

Section 152   SCHEDULE 14

CALCULATION OF NORMAL WORKING HOURS AND A WEEK'S PAY

PART I

NORMAL WORKING HOURS

1. For the purposes of this Schedule the cases where there are normal working
hours include cases where the employee is entitled to overtime pay when employed
for more than a fixed number of hours in a week or other period, and, subject to
paragraph 2, in those cases that fixed number of hours shall be the normal working
hours.
    2. If in such a case—
        (*a*) the contract of employment fixes the number, or the minimum number,
                of hours of employment in the said week or other period (whether or
                not it also provides for the reduction of that number or minimum in
                certain circumstances), and
        (*b*) that number or minimum number of hours exceeds the number of hours
                without overtime,
that number or minimum number of hours (and not the number of hours without
overtime) shall be the normal working hours.

PART II

A WEEK'S PAY

Employments for which there are normal working hours

3.—(1) This paragraph and paragraph 4 shall apply if there are normal
working hours for an employee when employed under the contract of employment
in force on the calculation date.
    (2) Subject to paragraph 4, if an employee's remuneration for employment in
normal working hours, whether by the hour or week or other period, does not vary
with the amount of work done in the period, the amount of a week's pay shall be
the amount which is payable by the employer under the contract of employment
in force on the calculation date if the employee works throughout his normal
working hours in a week.
    (3) Subject to paragraph 4, if sub-paragraph (2) does not apply, the amount
of a week's pay shall be the amount of remuneration for the number of normal
working hours in a week calculated at the average hourly rate of remuneration
payable by the employer to the employee in respect of the period of twelve weeks—
        (*a*) where the calculation date is the last day of a week, ending with that
                week;

(*b*) in any other case, ending with the last complete week before the calculation date.

(4) References in this paragraph to remuneration varying with the amount of work done include references to remuneration which may include any commission or similar payment which varies in amount.

4.—(1) This paragraph shall apply if there are normal working hours for an employee when employed under the contract of employment in force on the calculation date, and he is required under that contract to work during those hours on days of the week or at times of the day which differ from week to week or over a longer period so that the remuneration payable for, or apportionable to, any week varies according to the incidence of the said days or times.

(2) The amount of a week's pay shall be the amount of remuneration for the average weekly number of normal working hours (calculated in accordance with sub-paragraph (3)) at the average hourly rate of remuneration (calculated in accordance with sub-paragraph (4)).

(3) The average number of weekly hours shall be calculated by dividing by twelve the total number of the employee's normal working hours during the period of twelve weeks—
(*a*) where the calculation date is the last day of a week, ending with that week;
(*b*) in any other case, ending with the last complete week before the calculation date.

(4) The average hourly rate of remuneration shall be the average hourly rate of remuneration payable by the employer to the employee in respect of the period of twelve weeks—
(*a*) where the calculation date is the last day of a week, ending with that week;
(*b*) in any other case, ending with the last complete week before the calculation date.

5.—(1) For the purpose of paragraphs 3 and 4, in arriving at the average hourly rate of remuneration only the hours when the employee was working, and only the remuneration payable for, or apportionable to, those hours of work, shall be brought in; and if for any of the twelve weeks mentioned in either of those paragraphs no such remuneration was payable by the employer to the employee, account shall be taken of remuneration in earlier weeks so as to bring the number of weeks of which account is taken up to twelve.

(2) Where, in arriving at the said hourly rate of remuneration, account has to be taken of remuneration payable for, or apportionable to, work done in hours other than normal working hours, and the amount of that remuneration was greater than it would have been if the work had been done in normal working hours, account shall be taken of that remuneration as if—
(*a*) the work had been done in normal working hours and
(*b*) the amount of that remuneration had been reduced accordingly.

(3) For the purpose of the application of sub-paragraph (2) to a case falling within paragraph 2, sub-paragraph (2) shall be construed as if for the words " had been done in normal working hours ", in each place where those words occur, there were substituted the words " had been done in normal working hours falling within the number of hours without overtime ".

Employments for which there are no normal working hours

6.—(1) This paragraph shall apply if there are no normal working hours for an employee when employed under the contract of employment in force on the calculation date.

(2) The amount of a week's pay shall be the amount of the employee's average weekly remuneration in the period of twelve weeks—
(*a*) where the calculation date is the last day of a week, ending with that week;
(*b*) in any other case, ending with the last complete week before the calculation date.

(3) In arriving at the said average weekly rate of remuneration no account shall be taken of a week in which no remuneration was payable by the employer to the employee and remuneration in earlier weeks shall be brought in so as to bring the number of weeks of which account is taken up to twelve.

The calculation date

7.—(1) For the purposes of this Part, the calculation date is,—
(*a*) where the calculation is for the purposes of section 14, the day in

respect of which the guarantee payment is payable, or, where an employee's contract has been varied, or a new contract entered into, in connection with a period of short-time working, the last day on which the original contract was in force;

(b) where the calculation is for the purposes of section 21, the day before that on which the suspension referred to in section 19 (1) begins;

(c) where the calculation is for the purposes of section 31, the day on which the employer's notice was given;

(d) where the calculation is for the purposes of section 35, the last day on which the employee worked under the contract of employment in force immediately before the beginning of her absence;

(e) where the calculation is for the purposes of Schedule 3, the day immediately preceding the first day of the period of notice required by section 49 (1) or, as the case may be, section 49 (2);

(f) where the calculation is for the purposes of section 53 or 71 (2) (b) and the dismissal was with notice, the date on which the employer's notice was given;

(g) where the calculation is for the purposes of section 53 or 71 (2) (b) but sub-paragraph (f) does not apply, the effective date of termination;

(h) where the calculation is for the purposes of section 73 and by virtue of section 55 (5) a date is to be treated as the effective date of termination for the purposes of section 73 (3) which is later than the effective date of termination as defined by section 55 (4), the effective date of termination as defined by section 55 (4);

(i) where the calculation is for the purposes of section 73 but section 55 (5) does not apply in relation to the date of termination, the date on which notice would have been given had the conditions referred to in sub-paragraph (2) been fulfilled (whether those conditions were in fact fulfilled or not);

(j) where the calculation is for the purposes of section 87 (2), the day immediately preceding the first of the four or, as the case may be, the six weeks referred to in section 88 (1);

(k) where the calculation is for the purposes of Schedule 4 and by virtue of section 90 (3) a date is to be treated as the relevant date for the purposes of certain provisions of this Act which is later than the relevant date as defined by section 90 (1), the relevant date as defined by section 90 (1);

(l) where the calculation is for the purposes of Schedule 4 but sub-paragraph (k) does not apply, the date on which notice would have been given had the conditions referred to in sub-paragraph (2) been fulfilled (whether those conditions were in fact fulfilled or not).

(2)   The conditions referred to in sub-paragraphs (1) (i) and (l) are that the contract was terminable by notice and was terminated by the employer giving such notice as is required to terminate that contract by section 49 and that the notice expired on the effective date of termination or on the relevant date, as the case may be.

Maximum amount of week's pay for certain purposes

8.—(1) Notwithstanding the preceding provisions of this Schedule, the amount of a week's pay for the purpose of calculating—

(a) an additional award of compensation (within the meaning of section 71 (2) (b)) shall not exceed £100;

(b) a basic award of compensation (within the meaning of section 72) shall not exceed £100;

(c) a redundancy payment shall not exceed £100;

(2) The Secretary of State may after a review under section 148 vary the limit referred to in sub-paragraph (1) (a) or (b) or (c) by an order made in accordance with that section.

(3) Without prejudice to the generality of the power to make transitional provision in an order under section 148, such an order may provide that it shall apply in the case of a dismissal in relation to which the effective date of termination for the purposes of this sub-paragraph, as defined by section 55 (5), falls after the order comes into operation, notwithstanding that the effective date of

termination, as defined by section 55 (4), for the purposes of other provisions of this Act falls before the order comes into operation.

(4) Without prejudice to the generality of the power to make transitional provision in an order under section 148, such an order may provide that it shall apply in the case of a dismissal in relation to which the relevant date for the purposes of this sub-paragraph falls after the order comes into operation, notwithstanding that the relevant date for the purposes of other provisions of this Act falls before the order comes into operation.

Supplemental

9. In any case in which an employee has not been employed for a sufficient period to enable a calculation to be made under any of the foregoing provisions of this Part, the amount of a week's pay shall be an amount which fairly represents a week's pay; and in determining that amount the tribunal shall apply as nearly as may be such of the foregoing provisions of this Part as it considers appropriate, and may have regard to such of the following considerations as it thinks fit, that is to say—

(a) any remuneration received by the employee in respect of the employment in question;

(b) the amount offered to the employee as remuneration in respect of the employment in question;

(c) the remuneration received by other persons engaged in relevant comparable employment with the same employer;

(d) the remuneration received by other persons engaged in relevant comparable employment with other employers;

10. In arriving at an average hourly rate or average weekly rate of remuneration under this Part account shall be taken of work for a former employer within the period for which the average is to be taken if, by virtue of Schedule 13, a period of employment with the former employer counts as part of the employee's continuous period of employment with the later employer.

11. Where under this Part account is to be taken of remuneration or other payments for a period which does not coincide with the periods for which the remuneration or other payments are calculated, then the remuneration or other payments shall be apportioned in such manner as may be just.

12. The Secretary of State may by regulations provide that in prescribed cases the amount of a week's pay shall be calculated in such manner as the regulations may prescribe.

DERIVATION

Paras. 1–6   —1975, Sched. 4, paras. 1–6.

    7 (1)—1975, ss. 24 (3), (4), 31 (2), 37 (5), 61 (5); 1972, Sched. 2, para. 1 (2); 1975, ss. 75 (3), 75 (1), 70 (6), 72 (7); 1965, s. 5 (2A), Sched. 1, para. 5 (1), (3); 1975, Sched. 5, para. 1 (2), Sched. 16, Pt. I, paras. 4, 21.

    (2)—1975, s. 75 (2); 1965, Sched. 1, para. 5 (2); 1975, Sched. 16, Pt. I, para. 21.

    8   —1975, ss. 75 (4)–(6), 72 (8), 86; 1965, Sched. 1, para. 5 (4), (5), (7); 1975, Sched. 16, Pt. I, para. 21; 1977 Order (No. 2), art. 2.

    9   —1975, Sched. 4, para. 7.

    10   —1975, Sched. 4, para. 8 (a).

    11, 12   —1975, Sched. 4, paras. 9, 10.

Section 159   SCHEDULE 15

Transitional Provisions and Savings

General

1. So far as anything done or treated as done under or for the purposes of any enactment repealed by this Act could have been done under a corresponding

provision of this Act it shall not be invalidated by the repeal but shall have effect as if done under or for the purposes of that provision.

2. Where any period of time specified in an enactment repealed by this Act is current immediately before the corresponding provision of this Act comes into force, this Act shall have effect as if the corresponding provision had been in force when that period began to run.

3. Nothing in this Act shall affect the enactments repealed by this Act in their operation in relation to offences committed before the commencement of this Act.

4. Any reference in an enactment or document, whether express or implied, to—

    (a) an enactment which is re-enacted in a corresponding provision of this Act;

    (b) an enactment replaced or amended by a provision of the Employment Protection Act 1975 which is re-enacted in a corresponding provision of this Act;

    (c) an enactment in the Industrial Relations Act 1971 which was re-enacted with or without amendment in a corresponding provision in Schedule 1 to the Trade Union and Labour Relations Act 1974 and that corresponding provision is re-enacted by a corresponding provision of this Act;

shall, except so far as the context otherwise requires, be construed as, or as including, a reference to the corresponding provision of this Act.

5. Paragraphs 1 to 4 have effect subject to the following provisions of this Schedule.

Guarantee payments

6. Section 15 (1) shall have effect in relation to any day before 1st February 1978 as if for " £6·60 " there were substituted " £6 ".

Maternity pay

7. No employee is entitled to receive maternity pay in respect of a payment period or payment periods beginning before 6th April 1977.

Termination of employment

8. Sections 49 and 50 apply in relation to any contract made before the commencement of this Act.

Unfair dismissal

9.—(1) The repeal by this Act of the provisions relating to unfair dismissals of the Employment Protection Act 1975, of Schedule 1 to the Trade Union and Labour Relations Act 1974 and of the Trade Union and Labour Relations (Amendment) Act 1976 shall not have effect in relation to dismissals where the effective date of termination is earlier than 1st October 1976 and, accordingly, those provisions shall continue to apply to such dismissals as they applied thereto before this Act came into force.

(2) Without prejudice to the generality of sub-paragraph (1), the provisions of paragraphs 17 (2) and (3) and 19 of Schedule 1 to the said Act of 1974 shall, notwithstanding the repeal of those provisions by the Employment Protection Act 1975, continue to apply to dismissals where the effective date of termination falls before 1st June 1976.

(3) Where the notice required to be given by an employer to terminate a contract of employment by section 49 (1) would, if duly given when notice of termination was given by the employer, or (where no notice was given) when the contract of employment was terminated by the employer, expire on a date later than the effective date of termination as defined by section 55 (4), that later date shall be treated as the effective date of termination for the purposes of sub-paragraphs (1) and (2).

10.—(1) Section 54 does not apply to a dismissal from employment under a contract for a fixed term of two years or more, where the contract was made before 28th February 1972 and is not a contract of apprenticeship, and the dismissal consists only of the expiry of that term without its being renewed.

(2) Sub-paragraph (1) in its application to an employee treated as unfairly dismissed by virtue of subsection (1) or (2) of section 60 shall have effect as if for the reference to 28th February 1972 there were substituted a reference to 1st June 1976.

Redundancy

11.—(1) The repeal by this Act of any provision of the Redundancy Payments Act 1965 and of any enactment amending that Act shall not have effect in relation to dismissals and to lay-off and short-time where the relevant date falls before 1st June 1976, and, accordingly, a person's entitlement to or the computation of a redundancy payment or the reference of questions to industrial tribunals concerning such entitlement or computation in cases where the relevant date falls before 1st June 1976 shall continue to be determined as if this Act were not in force.

(2) Where the notice required to be given by an employer to terminate a contract of employment by section 49 would, if duly given when notice of termination was given by the employer, or (where no notice was given) when the contract of employment was terminated by the employer, expire on a date later than the relevant date as defined by section 90 (1), that later date shall be treated as the relevant date for the purposes of sub-paragraph (1).

12. Section 81 shall not apply to an employee who immediately before the relevant date (within the meaning of section 90) is employed under a contract of employment for a fixed term of two years or more, if that contract was made before 6th December 1965 and is not a contract of apprenticeship.

13. Sections 104 and 107 shall have effect in relation to an offence committed before 17th July 1978 as if—

(*a*) for each reference to the prescribed sum in subsection (9) of section 104 and subsection (4) of section 107 there were substituted a reference to £100, and

(*b*) subsection (10) of section 104 and subsection (5) of section 107 were omitted.

14. Schedule 5 shall have effect as if there were added at the end the following paragraph—

" 5. The Boards of Governors of the hospitals specified in Schedule 1 to the National Health Service (Preservation of Boards of Governors) Order 1974.".

This paragraph shall cease to have effect on 22nd February 1979 or, if the said Order of 1974 is revoked on an earlier date, on that date.

Insolvency

15.—(1) Subject to sub-paragraph (2), the provisions of sections 122 and 123 shall apply in relation to an employer who becomes insolvent (within the meaning of section 127) after 19th April 1976, and shall in such a case apply to any debts mentioned in section 122 and to any unpaid relevant contribution (within the meaning of section 123), whether falling due before or after that date.

(2) Section 122 shall have effect in relation to any case where the employer became insolvent before 1st February 1978 as if for each reference to £100 there were substituted a reference to £80.

Calculation of a week's pay

16. Paragraph 8 of Schedule 14 shall have effect—

(*a*) for the purpose of calculating an additional award of compensation in any case where the date by which the order for re-instatement or re-engagement was required to be complied with fell before 1st February 1978;

(*b*) for the purpose of calculating a basic award of compensation in any case where the effective date of determination (as defined by subsection (5) of section 55 or, if the case is not within that subsection, by subsection (4) of that section) fell before 1st February 1978;

(*c*) in relation to a claim for a redundancy payment, where the relevant date fell before 1st February 1978,

as if for each reference to £100 were substituted a reference to £80.

Computation of period of continuous employment

17. For the purposes of the computation of a period of continuous employment falling to be made before 1st February 1977—

    (*a*) paragraphs 3 and 4 of Schedule 13 shall have effect as if for the word " sixteen " there were substituted the word " twenty-one ", and

    (*b*) paragraphs 5, 6 and 7 of that schedule shall not apply.

Legal proceedings

18. Notwithstanding the repeal of any enactment by this Act, the Employment Appeal Tribunal and the industrial tribunals may continue to exercise the jurisdiction conferred on them by or under any enactment which is repealed by this Act with respect to matters arising out of or in connection with the repealed enactments.

House of Commons staff

19. Section 122 of the Employment Protection Act 1975 shall, until 1st January 1979, have effect as if it applied the enactments which are mentioned in subsection (1) of section 139 of this Act to relevant members of the House of Commons staff (within the meaning of the said section 122).

DERIVATION

Paras. 1–3	— —
4	—1975, Sched. 17, para. 18; 1974, Sched. 4, para. 7; 1972, s. 13 (6).
5	— —
6	—1977 Order (No. 2), art. 3 (1).
7	—Employment Protection Act 1975 (Commencement No. 4) Order 1976 (S.I. 1976 No. 530); Employment Protection Act 1975 (Commencement No. 5) Order 1976 (S.I. 1976 No. 1379).
8	—1972, s. 13 (2).
9	—1975, Sched. 17, para. 7.
10 (1)	—1974, para. 12 (*a*).
(2)	—1975, s. 34 (6).
11	—1975, Sched. 17, para. 16.
12	—1965, s. 15 (1).
13	— —
14	—National Health Service (Preservation of Boards of Governors) Order 1974 (S.I. 1974 No. 281).
15 (1)	—1975, Sched. 17, para. 8.
(2)	—1977 Order (No. 2), art. 3 (2).
16	—1977 Order (No. 2), art. 3 (3) (4) (5).
17	—1975, Sched. 17, para. 17.
18	— —

Section 159   SCHEDULE 16

CONSEQUENTIAL AMENDMENTS

House of Commons Offices Act 1846 (9 & 10 *Vict. c.* 77)

1. In section 5 of the House of Commons Offices Act 1846, after the words " Employment Protection Act 1975 " there are inserted the words " the Employment Protection (Consolidation) Act 1978 ".

Trade Union Act 1913 (2 & 3 *Geo.* 5. *c.* 30)

2. In section 5A of the Trade Union Act 1913, for the words " section 88 (2) of the Employment Protection Act 1975 " there are substituted the words " section 136 (2) of the Employment Protection (Consolidation) Act 1978 ".

Iron and Steel Act 1949 (12, 13 & 14 *Geo.* 6. *c.* 72)

3.—(1) In section 40 of the Iron and Steel Act 1949, in subsection (3), for the words from " a tribunal " to the end there are substituted the words " an industrial tribunal.".

(2) In section 41 of the said Act of 1949, in subsection (3), for the words from " a tribunal" to the end are substituted the words " an industrial tribunal ".

Industrial Training Act 1964 (*c.* 16)

4.—(1) In section 4 (7) of the Industrial Training Act 1964, for the words from " a tribunal" to " Act " there are substituted the words " an industrial tribunal ".

(2) For subsection (1) of section 12 of the said Act of 1964 there is substituted the following subsection—

" (1) A person assessed to levy imposed under this Act may appeal to an industrial tribunal.".

Trade Unions (*Amalgamations, etc.*) *Act* 1964 (*c.* 24)

5. In section 4 (8) of the Trade Union (Amalgamations, etc.) Act 1964, for the words " section 88 (2) of the Employment Protection Act 1975 " there are substituted the words " section 136 (2) of the Employment Protection (Consolidation) Act 1978 ".

Transport Act 1968 (*c.* 73)

6. In section 135 (4) (*b*) of the Transport Act 1968, for the words from " a tribunal " to the end there are substituted the words " an industrial tribunal.".

Transport (*London*) *Act* 1969 (*c.* 35)

7.—(1) In section 37 (4) (*b*) of the Transport (London) Act 1969, for the words from " a tribunal" to the end there are substituted the words " an industrial tribunal.".

(2) In paragraph 6 of Schedule 2 to the said Act of 1969, for the words " paragraph 10 (3) of Schedule 1 to the Contracts of Employment Act 1963 and section 8 (2) of the Redundancy Payments Act 1965, for the purposes of those Acts " there are substituted the words " section 151 (1) of and paragraph 17 (3) of Schedule 13 to the Employment Protection (Consolidation) Act 1978, for the purposes of that Act ".

Post Office Act 1969 (*c.* 48)

8. In paragraph 33 of Schedule 9 to the Post Office Act 1969—
  (*a*) in sub-paragraph (1) for the words " sections 1 and 2 of the Contracts of Employment Act 1963, Schedule 1 " there are substituted the words " sections 49 and 50 and Part VI of the Employment Protection (Consolidation) Act 1978, Schedule 13 ", for the words " the said Act of 1963 " there are substituted the words " the said Act of 1978 "; and for the words " twenty-one hours " there are substituted the words " sixteen hours ";
  (*b*) in sub-paragraph (2), for the words " Schedule 1 to the said Act of 1963 " there are substituted the words " Schedule 13 to the said Act of 1978 ";
  (*c*) in sub-paragraph (3), for the words " 7 of Schedule 2 to the said Act of 1963 " there are substituted the words " 10 of Schedule 14 to the said Act of 1978 " and for the words from " paragraph 10 " to the end there are substituted the words " Schedule 13 to that Act shall be construed as a reference to that Schedule as it has effect by virtue of sub-paragraph (1) above.";
  (*d*) in sub-paragraph (4), for the words " the said Act of 1963 " and " Schedule 1 " there are substituted respectively the words " the said Act of 1978 " and " Schedule 13 ";
  (*e*) at the end there is added the following sub-paragraph—
      " (6) This paragraph applies notwithstanding the provisions of section 99 of the Employment Protection (Consolidation) Act 1978.".

Income and Corporation Taxes Act 1970 (*c.* 10)

9.—(1) In section 412 (6) of the Income and Corporation Taxes Act 1970, for the words " section 32 of the Redundancy Payments Act 1965 " there are substituted the words "section 106 of the Employment Protection (Consolidation) Act 1978".

(2) In section 412 (7) of the said Act of 1970—

    (*a*) for the words "Part II of the Redundancy Payments Act 1965" there are substituted the words "the Employment Protection (Consolidation) Act 1978";

    (*b*) for the words "section 30 (2) of the Redundancy Payments Act 1965" there are substituted the words "section 104 (2) of the Employment Protection (Consolidation) Act 1978";

    (*c*) for the words "Schedule 5 to the Redundancy Payments Act 1965" there are substituted the words "Schedule 6 to the Employment Protection (Consolidation) Act 1978";

    (*d*) for the words "Redundancy Payments Act 1965" in paragraph (*c*) of the said section 412 (7), there are substituted the words "the Employment Protection (Consolidation) Act 1978".

Atomic Energy Authority Act 1971 (*c.* 11)

10.—(1) In subsection (1) of section 10 of the Atomic Energy Authority Act 1971, for the words "section 22 of the Redundancy Payments Act 1965" there are substituted the words "section 93 of the Employment Protection (Consolidation) Act 1978".

(2) In subsection (2) of the said section 10—

    (*a*) for the words "section 4 of the Contracts of Employment Act 1963" there are substituted the words "sections 1 to 4 of the Employment Protection (Consolidation) Act 1978";

    (*b*) for the words "subsection (8) of that section", in both places where they occur, there are substituted the words "section 5 of the said Act of 1978";

    (*c*) for the words "the said section 4" there are substituted the words "the said sections 1 to 4".

(3) In subsection (3) of the said section 10—

    (*a*) for the words "Section 4A (1) of the Contracts of Employment Act 1963" there are substituted the words "Section 11 of the Employment Protection (Consolidation) Act 1978";

    (*b*) for the words "section 4" there are substituted the words "sections 1 to 4".

(4) In subsection (4) of the said section 10—

    (*a*) for the words from the beginning to "Redundancy Payments Act 1965" there are substituted the words "For the purposes of Schedule 13 to the said Act of 1978 (computation of period of employment)";

    (*b*) for the words "paragraph 10" there are substituted the words "paragraph 17".

Tribunals and Inquiries Act 1971 (*c.* 62)

11. In section 13 of the Tribunals and Inquiries Act 1971, the following subsection is inserted after subsection (1)—

"(1A) Subsection (1) of this section shall not apply in relation to proceedings before industrial tribunals which arise under or by virtue of any of the enactments mentioned in section 136 (1) of the Employment Protection (Consolidation) Act 1978.".

Civil Aviation Act 1971 (*c.* 75)

12.—(1) In paragraph 1 of Schedule 9 to the Civil Aviation Act 1971—

    (*a*) in sub-paragraph (1) for the words "sections 1 and 2 of the Contracts of Employment Act 1963, Schedule 1" there are substituted the words "sections 49 and 50 and Part VI of the Employment Protection (Consolidation) Act 1978, Schedule 13", for the words "the said Act of 1963" there are substituted the words "the said Act of 1978"; and for the words "twenty-one hours" there are substituted the words "sixteen hours";

(b) in sub-paragraph (2), for the words "Schedule 1 to the said Act of 1963" there are substituted the words "Schedule 13 to the said Act of 1978".

(c) in sub-paragraph (3), for the words "7 of Schedule 2 to the said Act of 1963" there are substituted the words "10 of Schedule 14 to the said Act of 1978" and for the words from "paragraph 10" to the end there are substituted the words "Schedule 13 to that Act shall be construed as a reference to that Schedule as it has effect by virtue of sub-paragraph (1) above.";

(d) in sub-paragraph (4), for the words "the said Act of 1963" and "Schedule 1" there are substituted respectively the words "the said Act of 1978" and "Schedule 13";

(e) at the end there is added the following sub-paragraph—
   "(6) This paragraph applies notwithstanding the provisions of section 99 of the Employment Protection (Consolidation) Act 1978.".

(2) In paragraph 4 of the said Schedule 9—
(a) for the words "paragraph 10 (2) of Schedule 1 to the Contracts of Employment Act 1963 and section 13 (1) of the Redundancy Payments Act 1965" there are substituted the words "section 94 (1) of and paragraph 17 (2) of Schedule 13 to the Employment Protection (Consolidation) Act 1978";

(b) for the words "the said section 13 (1)" there are substituted the words "the said section 94 (1)";

(c) for the words from "the said Act of 1963" to "Act of 1965" there are substituted the words "the said paragraph 17 (2) and the references to the said section 94 (1)", and after the words "a reference" there are inserted the words "to paragraph 10 (2) of Schedule 1".

Transport Holding Company Act 1972 (c. 14)

13.—(1) In section 2 (3) (c) of the Transport Holding Company Act 1972, for the words from "a tribunal" to the end there are substituted the words "an industrial tribunal.".

(2) In section 2 (7) of the said Act of 1972, for the words "a tribunal established under section 12 of the Industrial Training Act 1964" there are substituted the words "an industrial tribunal".

Finance Act 1972 (c. 41)

14. In paragraph 1 (b) of Part V of Schedule 12 to the Finance Act 1972, for the words "Redundancy Payments Act 1965" there are substituted the words "Employment Protection (Consolidation) Act 1978".

British Library Act 1972 (c. 54)

15. In paragraph 13 (3) (a) of the Schedule to the British Library Act 1972, for the words "the Acts of 1963 and 1965" there are substituted the words "the Employment Protection (Consolidation) Act 1978".

Gas Act 1972 (c. 60)

16. In section 36 (5) of the Gas Act 1972, for the words from "a tribunal" to the end there are substituted the words "an industrial tribunal.".

Health and Safety at Work etc. Act 1974 (c. 37)

17. The following subsection is inserted in section 80 of the Health and Safety at Work etc. Act 1974 after subsection (2)—
   "(2A) Subsection (1) above shall apply to provisions in the Employment Protection (Consolidation) Act 1978 which re-enact provisions previously contained in the Redundancy Payments Act 1965, the Contracts of Employment Act 1972 or the Trade Union and Labour Relations Act 1974 as it applies to provisions contained in Acts passed before or in the same Session as this Act.".

Trade Union and Labour Relations Act 1974 (c. 52)

18. In section 8 (7) of the Trade Union and Labour Relations Act 1974, for the words "section 88 (3) of the Employment Protection Act 1975" there are substituted the words "section 136 (3) of the Employment Protection (Consolidation) Act 1978".

Social Security Act 1975 (c. 14)

19.—(1) In section 114 of the Social Security Act 1975, the following subsection is inserted after subsection (2)—

"(2A) It is hereby declared for the avoidance of doubt that the power to make regulations under subsection (1) above includes power to make regulations for the determination of any question arising as to the total or partial recoupment of unemployment benefit in pursuance of regulations under section 132 of the Employment Protection (Consolidation) Act 1978 (including any decision as to the amount of benefit.".

(2) In section 139 of the said Act of 1975, after subsection (2) there is inserted the following subsection—

"(2A) Subsection (1) above does not apply to regulations made under this Act and contained in a statutory instrument which states that the regulations provide only that a day in respect of which there is payable a particular description of any payment to which section 132 of the Employment Protection (Consolidation) Act 1978 (recoupment of unemployment and supplementary benefits) applies shall not be treated as a day of unemployment for the purposes of entitlement to unemployment benefit.".

Sex Discrimination Act 1975 (c. 65)

20.—(1) In section 65 (2) of the Sex Discrimination Act 1975, for the words "paragraph 20 of Schedule 1 to the Trade Union and Labour Relations Act 1974" there are substituted the words "section 75 of the Employment Protection (Consolidation) Act 1978".

(2) In section 75 (5) (c) of the said Act of 1975 for the words "paragraph 21 of Schedule 1 to the Trade Union and Labour Relations Act 1974." there are substituted the words "paragraph 1 of Schedule 9 to the Employment Protection (Consolidation) Act 1978.".

Scottish Development Agency Act 1975 (c. 69)

21. In paragraph 6 of Schedule 3 to the Scottish Development Agency Act 1975, for sub-paragraphs (a), (b) and (c) there are substituted the words "the Employment Protection (Consolidation) Act 1978".

Welsh Development Agency Act 1975 (c. 70)

22. In paragraph 7 of Schedule 2 to the Welsh Development Agency Act 1975, for sub-paragraphs (a), (b) and (c) there are substituted the words "the Employment Protection (Consolidation) Act 1978".

Employment Protection Act 1975 (c. 71)

23.—(1) The Employment Protection Act 1975 shall be amended in accordance with the following provisions of this paragraph.

(2) In section 6 (2)—

  (a) the words from "in relation to" to "that is to say" shall be omitted;
  (b) for the words "section 57 below; and" there are substituted the words "section 27 of the Employment Protection (Consolidation) Act 1978, including guidance on the circumstances in which a trade union official is to be permitted to take time off under that section in respect of duties connected with industrial action; and";
  (c) for the words "section 58 below" there are substituted the words "section 28 of the said Act of 1978, including guidance on the question whether,

and the circumstances in which, a trade union member is to be permitted to take time off under that section for trade union activities connected with industrial action.".

(3) In section 8 (9), for the words " section 88 (3) below " there are substituted the words " section 136 (3) of the Employment Protection (Consolidation) Act 1978 ".

(4) In section 102 (4), for the words " Schedule 2 to the Contracts of Employment Act 1972 " there are substituted the words " Schedule 3 to the Employment Protection (Consolidation) Act 1978 ", and for the words " section 1 (1) " there are substituted the words " section 49 (1) ".

(5) In section 104 (1) (a), for the words " section 30 (1) of the Redundancy Payments Act 1965 " there are substituted the words " section 104 (1) of the Employment Protection (Consolidation) Act 1978 ".

(6) In section 106 (3), for the words from the beginning to " Redundancy Payments Act 1965 " there are substituted the words " Schedule 14 to the Employment Protection (Consolidation) Act 1978 shall apply for the calculation of a week's pay for the purposes of section 102 above, and, for the purposes of Part II of that Schedule, the calculation date is—

    (a) in the case of an employee who was dismissed before the date on which the protective award was made, the date which by virtue of paragraph 7 (1) (k) or (l) of the said Schedule 14 ".

(7) In section 108 (1), for the words " paragraph 21 of Schedule 1 to the 1974 Act " there are substituted the words " paragraph 1 of Schedule 9 to the Employment Protection (Consolidation) Act 1978 ".

(8) In section 119 (1), for the words " Parts II and IV of this Act apply " there are substituted the words " Part IV of this Act applies ".

(9) In section 119, the following subsection is added at the end—

    " (17) Schedule 13 to the Employment Protection (Consolidation) Act 1978 and, so far as they modify that Schedule, any order under section 7 of that Act and any regulations under paragraph 20 of that Schedule, shall have effect for the purposes of this section in determining for what period an employee has been continuously employed; and, for the purposes of any proceedings brought under or by virtue of this Act, a person's employment during any period shall, unless the contrary is shown, be presumed to have been continuous.".

(10) In section 121 (5), for the words " Schedule 3 to the Redundancy Payments Act 1965 " there are substituted the words " Schedule 5 to the Employment Protection (Consolidation) Act 1978 ".

(11) In section 121 (6) and (7), for the words " section 41 (3) of the Redundancy Payments Act 1965 " there are substituted the words " section 111 (3) of the Employment Protection (Consolidation) Act 1978 ".

(12) In section 125 (1) for the words from the beginning to " Part III of that Schedule " there are substituted the words " The provisions of the 1974 Act specified in Part III of Schedule 16 to this Act ".

(13) In section 126 (1), for the words " paragraph 5 of Schedule 1 to the 1974 Act " there are substituted the words " section 55 of the Employment Protection (Consolidation) Act 1978 ".

New Towns (Amendment) Act 1976 (c. 68)

24. In section 13 of the New Towns (Amendment) Act 1976—

    (a) in subsection (5), for the words " Schedule 1 to the Contracts of Employment Act 1972 " there are substituted the words " Schedule 13 to the Employment Protection (Consolidation) Act 1978 ";

    (b) in subsection (6), for the words " section 13 of the Redundancy Payments Act 1965 " there are substituted the words " section 94 of the Employment Protection (Consolidation) Act 1978 ".

Race Relations Act 1976 (c. 74)

25.—(1) The Race Relations Act 1976 shall be amended in accordance with the following provisions of this paragraph.

(2) In section 56 (2) for the words " paragraph 20 of Schedule 1 to the Trade Union and Labour Relations Act 1974 " there are substituted the words " section 75 of the Employment Protection (Consolidation) Act 1978 ".

(3) In section 66 (7) for the words " paragraph 21 of Schedule 1 to the Trade Union and Labour Relations Act 1974 " there are substituted the words " paragraph 1 of Schedule 9 to the Employment Protection (Consolidation) Act 1978 ".

(4) In paragraph 11 of Schedule 2—

> (a) In sub-paragraph (3) for the words " the Redundancy Payments Act 1965 " there are substituted the words " Part VI of the Employment Protection (Consolidation) Act 1978 ";
>
> (b) for sub-paragraph (4) (a) and (b) there is substituted the following paragraph—
>
>> " (a) the Employment Protection (Consolidation) Act 1978 except Part VI of that Act; ".

Development of Rural Wales Act 1976 (c. 75)

26. In both paragraph 6 of Schedule 2 and paragraph 6 of Schedule 6 to the Development of Rural Wales Act 1976, for sub-paragraphs (a), (b) and (c) there are substituted the words " the Employment Protection (Consolidation) Act 1978 ".

Dock Work Regulation Act 1976 (c. 79)

27.—(1) In section 14 (7) of the Dock Work Regulation Act 1976 for the words " subsections (1), (5) and (6) above " there are substituted the words " subsection (6) above ".

(2) In paragraph 17 (1) of Schedule 1 to the said Act of 1976, for the words " Schedule 1 to the Contracts of Employment Act 1972 " there are substituted the words " Schedule 13 to the Employment Protection (Consolidation) Act 1978 ".

Aircraft and Shipbuilding Industries Act 1977 (c. 3)

28. In both section 49 (10) and section 50 (3) (b) of the Aircraft and Shipbuilding Industries Act 1977, for the words " a tribunal established under section 12 of the Industrial Training Act 1964 or, as the case may require " there are substituted the words " an industrial tribunal or, as the case may require, a tribunal established under ".

Social Security (Miscellaneous Provisions) Act 1977 (c. 5)

29. In section 18 of the Social Security (Miscellaneous Provisions) Act 1977—

> (a) in subsection (1) (c), for " Act 1975 " there shall be substituted " (Consolidation) Act 1978 ";
>
> (b) in subsection (2) (a), for the words " section 43 of the Employment Protection Act 1975 " there are substituted the words " section 40 of the Employment Protection (Consolidation) Act 1978 ";
>
> (c) in subsection (2) (b), for " 64 (3) (a) " and " 45 (1) " there are substituted " 122 (3) (a) " and " 42 (1) " respectively;
>
> (d) in subsection (2) (e), for the words " that Act " there are substituted the words " the Employment Protection Act 1975 ".

New Towns (Scotland) Act 1977 (c. 16)

30. In section 3 (6) of the New Towns (Scotland) Act 1977 for paragraphs (a), (b) and (c) there are substituted the words " Parts I, IV, V and VI of the Employment Protection (Consolidation) Act 1978 ".

Housing (Homeless Persons) Act 1977 (c. 48)

31. In section 14 (4) of the Housing (Homeless Persons) Act 1977—

> (a) in paragraph (a), for the words " section 13 of the Redundancy Payments Act 1965 " there are substituted the words " section 94 of the Employment Protection (Consolidation) Act 1978 ";

(b) in paragraph (b), for the words "Schedule 1 to the Contracts of Employment Act 1972" there are substituted the words "Schedule 13 to the said Act of 1978", and the words "sections 1 and 2 of" shall cease to have effect.

National Health Service Act 1977 (c. 49)

32. In paragraph 13 (1) (b) of Schedule 14 to the National Health Service Act 1977, the reference to paragraph 106 of Schedule 4 to the National Health Service Reorganisation Act 1973 shall cease to have effect, and, accordingly, for that reference to paragraph 106 there is substituted a reference to paragraph 107 of the said Schedule 4.

Scotland Act 1978 (c. 51)

33. In section 33 of the Scotland Act 1978—
  (a) in subsection (1), for paragraphs (a) and (b) there is substituted the following paragraph—
      "(a) Parts I (so far as it relates to itemised pay statements), II, III (except section 44), V, VIII and IX and section 53 of the Employment Protection (Consolidation) Act 1978; and",
  and for the words "section 121 of the Employment Protection Act 1975" there are substituted the words "section 138 of the Employment Protection (Consolidation) Act 1978";
  (b) in subsection (2), for the words "paragraph 21 (5) (c) of Schedule 1 to the Act of 1974" there are substituted the words "paragraph 1 (5) (c) of Schedule 9 to the Employment Protection (Consolidation) Act 1978".

House of Commons (Administration) Act 1978 (c. 36)

34. In Paragraph 1 of Schedule 2 to the House of Commons (Administration) Act 1978, after the words "the Employment Protection Act 1975" there are inserted the words "and section 139 of the Employment Protection (Consolidation) Act 1978".

Section 159   SCHEDULE 17

REPEALS

Chapter	Short title	Extent of repeal
1964 c. 16.	Industrial Training Act 1964.	Section 12 (2B), (3) and (4).
1965 c. 62.	Redundancy Payments Act 1965.	Sections 1 to 26. Sections 30 to 44. Sections 46 to 55 except section 55 (6) (b). Sections 56 to 58. In section 59, subsection (2) and in subsection (3) the words "except the last preceding section". Schedules 1 to 9.
1967 c. 17.	Iron and Steel Act 1967.	In section 31, in subsection (3), paragraph (c) and all the words following paragraph (c), and subsections (4) (b) and (6).
1967 c. 28.	Superannuation (Miscellaneous Provisions) Act 1967.	Section 9.
1968 c. 13.	National Loans Act 1968.	In Schedule 1, the paragraph relating to the Redundancy Payments Act 1965.

SCHEDULE 17—*continued*

Chapter	Short title	Extent of repeal
1969 c. 8.	Redundancy Rebates Act 1969.	The whole Act.
1969 c. 48.	Post Office Act 1969.	In Schedule 9, paragraph 34.
1970 c. 41.	Equal Pay Act 1970.	Section 2 (7).
1971 c. 75.	Civil Aviation Act 1971.	In Schedule 9, paragraph 2.
1972 c. 11.	Superannuation Act 1972.	In Schedule 6, paragraphs 54 and 55.
1972 c. 53.	Contracts of Employment Act 1972.	The whole Act.
1972 c. 54.	British Library Act 1972.	In paragraph 13 (2) of the Schedule, the definition of " the Act of 1963 ".
1972 c. 58.	National Health Service (Scotland) Act 1972.	In Schedule 6, paragraph 130.
1973 c. 32.	National Health Service Reorganisation Act 1973.	In Schedule 4, paragraph 106.
1973 c. 38.	Social Security Act 1973.	In Schedule 27, paragraphs 54 to 59.
1973 c. 50.	Employment and Training Act 1973.	In Schedule 2 in Part I, paragraph 15.
1974 c. 52.	Trade Union and Labour Relations Act 1974.	In section 1 (2), paragraphs (*b*) and (*c*) and, in paragraph (*d*), the references to sections 146, 148, 149, 150 and 151 of the 1971 Act. In section 30 (1), the definitions of " dismissal procedures agreement ", " position " and " job ". In Schedule 1, paragraphs 4 to 16, 17 (1), 18, 20 to 27 and 30, in paragraph 32, sub-paragraphs (1) (*b*) and (2) (*b*) to (*e*) and, in paragraph 33, sub-paragraphs (3) (*c*) and (*d*) and (4A). In Schedule 3, paragraph 16. In Schedule 4, paragraphs 1, 3 and 6 (4).
1975 c. 18.	Social Security (Consequential Provisions) Act 1975.	In Schedule 2, paragraphs 19 to 23.
1975 c. 60.	Social Security Pensions Act 1975.	Section 30 (5).
1975 c. 71.	Employment Protection Act 1975.	Part II except section 40. Section 108 (2) to (8). Section 109. Section 112. In section 118 (2), in paragraph (*a*) the words " section 22 above or " and " section 28 or, as the case may be ," and paragraphs (*b*) and (*c*). In section 119— subsection (2); in subsection (3) the figures from " 22 " to " 70 "; in subsection (4) the figures from " 22 " to " 81 "; in subsection (5), the figures from " 22 " to " 81 "; in subsection (7) the figures " 22 " and " 29 "; subsections (8) to (11); in subsection (12) the figures from " 59 " to " 81 ". Section 120. In section 121— in subsection (1), the reference to sections 47 and 63 to 69; in subsection (5), the reference to sections 47 (3) and (4) and 68 (3) and (4); subsection (8).

Chapter	Short title	Extent of repeal
1975 c. 71—cont.	Employment Protection Act 1975—*cont.*	In section 122 (1), the words "Schedule 1 to the Contracts of Employment Act 1972 and Parts I and II of Schedule 1 to the 1974 Act"; and in paragraph (*d*), the words "paragraph 21 (5) (*c*) of Schedule 1 to the 1974 Act and". In section 122, subsection (3), in subsection (4) the definition of "civil employment claim" and in subsection (5) the words from "and of the Redundancy" to "employment claim". In section 123 (2) (*b*) the words "28 or". In section 124, subsections (2) to (4). In section 126— in subsection (1), the definitions of "guarantee payment" and "maternity pay"; subsections (3) and (5). In section 127— in subsection (1), paragraphs (*c*) and (*d*); in subsection (3) (*g*), the words from "the following" to "also of". In section 128— in subsection (1), the words "or of the 1974 Act so far as it relates to unfair dismissal" and "and the 1974 Act"; subsection (2); in subsection (3), the words "and the relevant provisions of the 1974 Act" in both places where they occur, and the words "or the relevant provisions of the 1974 Act". Section 129 (2). Schedules 2 to 6. In Schedule 12— in paragraph 1, the words from "and" to the end; paragraphs 8 to 12. In Schedule 16— Parts I and II; in Part III, paragraphs 8 to 30 and 34; in Part IV, paragraph 14. In Schedule 17, paragraphs 7 to 10, 16 and 17.
1976 c. 7.	Trade Union and Labour Relations (Amendment) Act 1976.	Section 1 (*e*). Section 3 (5) and (6).
1976 c. 68.	New Towns (Amendment) Act 1976.	In section 13 (5), the words "sections 1 and 2 of".
1976 c. 71.	Supplementary Benefits Act 1976.	In Schedule 7, paragraph 40.
1976 c. 74.	Race Relations Act 1976.	In Schedule 3, paragraphs 1 (2), (3) and (4).
1976 c. 79.	Dock Work Regulation Act 1976.	In section 14, subsections (1) to (5) and in subsection (6), paragraph (*a*) and so much of paragraph (*b*) as relates to sections 22, 29, 61, 64, 65 and 70 of the Employment Protection Act 1975. In Schedule 1, paragraph 17 (2).
1977 c. 5.	Social Security (Miscellaneous Provisions) Act 1977.	Section 16.

SCHEDULE 17—*continued*

Chapter	Short title	Extent of repeal
1977 c. 22.	Redundancy Rebates Act 1977.	The whole Act.
1977 c. 38.	Administration of Justice Act 1977.	Section 6. Section 32 (11).
1977 c. 48.	Housing (Homeless Persons) Act 1977.	In section 14 (4) (b), the words " sections 1 and 2 of ".

Statute Law (Repeals) Act 1978

(1978 c. 45)

ARRANGEMENT OF SECTIONS

An Act to promote the reform of the statute law by the repeal, in accordance with recommendations of the Law Commission and the Scottish Law Commission, of certain enactments which (except in so far as their effect is preserved) are no longer of practical utility; and to facilitate the citation of statutes.

[**31st July 1978**]

General Note

This Act received the Royal Assent on July 31, 1978, and came into force on that date.

For parliamentary debates, see *Hansard*, H.L. Vol. 390, col. 1979; Vol. 391, col. 1160; Vol. 395, col. 321; H.C. Vol. 954, col. 1104.

Northern Ireland

The Act extends to Northern Ireland.

Repeals and associated amendments

1.—(1) The enactments mentioned in Schedule 1 to this Act are hereby repealed to the extent specified in column 3 of that Schedule.

(2) The enactments mentioned in Schedule 2 to this Act are, in consequence of certain of the repeals made by this Act, hereby amended as provided by that Schedule.

Citation of Acts

2. Schedule 3 to this Act shall have effect to facilitate the citation of the Acts of Parliament mentioned in it.

Extent

3.—(1) This Act extends to Northern Ireland.

(2) Her Majesty may by Order in Council provide that the repeal by this Act of any enactment specified in the Order shall on a date so specified extend to any of the Channel Islands or the Isle of Man.

Short title

4. This Act may be cited as the Statute Law (Repeals) Act 1978.

SCHEDULES

SCHEDULE 1

Section 1

REPEALS

PART I

ADMINISTRATION OF JUSTICE

Chapter	Short title	Extent of repeal
6 Geo. 4. c. 62.	Poor Prisoners (Scotland) Act 1825.	The whole Act.
6 & 7 Will. 4. c. 43.	Judicial Ratifications (Scotland) Act 1836.	The whole Act.
32 & 33 Vict. c. 68.	Evidence Further Amendment Act 1869.	The whole Act except as it applies to Northern Ireland.
34 & 35 Vict. c. 42.	Citation Amendment (Scotland) Act 1871.	The whole Act.
40 & 41 Vict. c. 43.	Justices Clerks Act 1877.	Section 10.
45 & 46 Vict. c. 42.	Civil Imprisonment (Scotland) Act 1882.	Section 8.
15 & 16 Geo. 5. c. 49.	Supreme Court of Judicature (Consolidation) Act 1925.	In Schedule 4, the paragraph beginning with the words " For the purposes ".
12, 13 & 14 Geo. 6 c. 27.	Juries Act 1949.	Sections 30 and 35 (3). The whole Act except as it applies to Scotland.
12, 13 & 14 Geo. 6. c. 101.	Justices of the Peace Act 1949.	Section 45 (4). Section 46 (2). In Schedule 7, Parts I and III.
14 Geo. 6. c. 27.	Arbitration Act 1950.	Section 43.
15 & 16 Geo. 6 & 1 Eliz. 2. c. 55.	Magistrates' Courts Act 1952.	In Schedule 4, in Part III, paragraph 3. In Schedule 5, the entry relating to the County Police Act 1840, and in the entry relating to the Summary Jurisdiction Act 1857 the word " eight ".
2 & 3 Eliz. 2. c. 36.	Law Reform (Limitation of Actions, &c.) Act 1954.	The whole Act.
2 & 3 Eliz. 2. c. 37.	Superannuation (President of Industrial Court) Act 1954.	The whole Act.
7 & 8 Eliz. 2. c. 22.	County Courts Act 1959.	In section 89 (3), the words " county borough ". In section 147 (2), the words from " notwithstanding " to " 1968 ".
8 & 9 Eliz. 2. c. 65.	Administration of Justice Act 1960.	In section 18 (4), the words from " but " onwards. In Schedule 3, the entry relating to the Criminal Justice Act 1948.

SCHEDULE 1—*continued*

Chapter	Short title	Extent of repeal
10 & 11 Eliz. 2. c. 15.	Criminal Justice Administration Act 1962.	Section 19. Schedule 1. In Schedule 4, the entry relating to the South Staffordshire Stipendiary Justice Act 1899.
1964 c. 42.	Administration of Justice Act 1964.	Section 31. In section 37 (4), the words " section 8 (5) of this Act " (where they first occur) and paragraph (*a*). In section 41 (6), the words " section 31 and ". In Schedule 3, paragraphs 8 and 12 (3).
1965 c. 45.	Backing of Warrants (Republic of Ireland) Act 1965.	Section 9 (2).
1969 c. 58.	Administration of Justice Act 1969.	In section 7 (2), in subsection (3) added to section 89 of the County Courts Act 1959, the words " county borough ". Sections 25 (2), 26 (2) and (3), 27 (2), (4), (5), (6) and (7), 28 and 35 (2). Schedule 2.

PART II

CHARITIES

Chapter or number	Title or short title	Extent of repeal
11 Geo. 3. c. 10 (1771).	An Act for carrying into Execution an Agreement made between Peter Burrell, Esquire, Surveyor-general of His Majesty's Lands, and the Trustees of Morden College, in the County of Kent, for enabling His Majesty, His Heirs and Successors, to grant Leases of Maidenstone Hill, in the Parish of East Greenwich in the County of Kent to the said Trustees, upon the Terms mentioned in the said Agreement; and for impowering the said Trustees to increase the Salaries and Pensions of the Treasurer, Chaplain, and poor Merchants, in the said College.	The whole Act.
8 & 9 Eliz. 2. c. 58.	Charities Act 1960.	Section 49 (2) (*a*) and (*b*).

Church Assembly Measure

Chapter or number	Title or short title	Extent of repeal
1958 No. 1.	Church Funds Investment Measure 1958.	In section 5, in subsections (1) and (2) the words " the Minister of Education or ", and in subsection (3) the words " said Minister or ", and in the case of each subsection the references substituted for those words by article 3 (2) of the Secretary of State for Education and Science Order 1964 and article 6 (4) of the Transfer of Functions (Wales) Order 1970.

PART III

CONSTITUTIONAL LAW

Chapter	Short title	Extent of repeal
6 Anne c. 41.	Succession to the Crown Act 1707.	Section 26.
56 Geo. 3. c. 98.	Consolidated Fund Act 1816.	Section 14.
9 Eliz. 2. c. 6.	Ministers of the Crown (Parliamentary Secretaries) Act 1960.	In section 4 (1), the words from " being amendments " onwards. Section 5. In Schedule 1, the entry relating to the Ministry of National Insurance Act 1944.
10 & 11 Eliz. 2. c. 30.	Northern Ireland Act 1962.	Section 25 (1) (*b*). In section 29 (2), the words from " other " to " section ".
1975 c. 24.	House of Commons Disqualification Act 1975.	In Part II of Schedule 1, the entry relating to the Appellate Tribunal constituted under the provisions of the National Service Act 1948 relating to conscientious objectors. In Part III of Schedule 1, the entry relating to the Chairman or Deputy Chairman of a Local Tribunal constituted under the provisions of the National Service Act 1948 relating to conscientious objectors and the entry relating to the Chairman or Reserve Chairman of a Military Service (Hardship) Committee constituted under Schedule 3 to that Act.

PART IV

DUCHY OF CORNWALL

Chapter	Title or short title	Extent of repeal
11 Hen. 7. c. 34 (1495).	An Acte for the assurering of certayne lands to the Prynce of Wales.	The whole Act.

SCHEDULE 1—*continued*

Chapter	Title or short title	Extent of repeal
50 Geo. 3. c. 6 (1810).	An Act to enable his Royal Highness George Prince of Wales, to grant Leases of certain Lands and Premises called Prince's Meadows, in the Parish of Lambeth, in the County of Surrey, Parcel of His said Royal Highnesses's Duchy of Cornwall, for the purpose of building thereon.	The whole Act.
52 Geo. 3. c. 123.	Duchy of Cornwall Act 1812.	The whole Act except sections 6 to 9.
1 & 2 Vict. c. 101.	Duchies of Lancaster and Cornwall (Accounts) Act 1838.	In the title, the words from " revive " to " and to ". The preamble. Section 1.
7 & 8 Vict. c. 105.	Duchy of Cornwall (No. 2) Act 1844.	The whole Act except sections 39, 40, 53 to 70 and 92 and the Schedules. In section 92, the definitions of " Oath " and " Conventionary Tenant ".
11 & 12 Vict. c. 83.	Assessionable Manors Award Act 1848.	The whole Act except sections 6 and 14.
21 & 22 Vict. c. 109.	Cornwall Submarine Mines Act 1858.	The preamble. Sections 1, 2, 7 and 9.
23 & 24 Vict. c. 53.	Duchy of Cornwall Act 1860.	The whole Act.

PART V

EDUCATION

Chapter	Title or short title	Extent of repeal
10 Geo. 2. c. 19 (1736).	An Act for the more effectual preventing the unlawful playing of Interludes within the Precincts of the two Universities in that Part of *Great Britain* called *England*, and the Places adjacent; and for explaining and amending so much of the [Act 9 Geo. 2. c. 23] as may affect the Privilege of the said Universities, with respect to licensing Taverns, and all other Publick Houses within the Precincts of the same.	The whole Act.
56 Geo. 3. c. 136 (1816).	An Act to enable His Majesty to grant certain Lands, Tenements, and Hereditaments, escheated and devolved to His Majesty by the Dissolution of Hertford College, in the University of Oxford, and the Site of the said College	The whole Act.

SCHEDULE 1—*continued*

Chapter	Title or short title	Extent of repeal
56 Geo. 3. c. 136 (1816)—*cont.*	and Buildings thereon, to the Chancellor, Masters and Scholars of the said University, in Trust for the Principal and other Members of Magdalen Hall, for the Purpose of their removing to such Site; and to enable the said Chancellor, Masters and Scholars of the said University, and the President and Scholars of Saint Mary Magdalen College, to do all necessary Acts for such Removal.	
4 & 5 Vict. c. 38.	School Sites Act 1841.	Sections 15 and 19.
19 & 20 Vict. c. xvii.	Cambridge Award Act 1856.	In section 11, the words "Tenth George the Second Chapter Nineteen, and ".
7 Edw. 7. c. 43.	Education (Administrative Provisions) Act 1907.	The whole Act.
13 & 14 Geo. 5. c. 33.	Universities of Oxford and Cambridge Act 1923.	Sections 2 to 4.
7 & 8 Geo. 6. c. 31.	Education Act 1944.	Section 107. In section 120, subsection (2); and in the proviso to subsection (3), the words from " and Part II " onwards. In Schedule 8, Part I except the entries relating to sections 10 and 96 of the Children and Young Persons Act 1933; and Part II.
8 & 9 Geo. 6. c. 37.	Education (Scotland) Act 1945.	In Schedule 4, the entries relating to the Unemployment Insurance Act 1935, sections 32, 50 and 65 of the Children and Young Persons (Scotland) Act 1937 and the Factories Act 1937.
9 & 10 Geo. 6. c. 50.	Education Act 1946.	Sections 8 (4) and 15. In Schedule 2, in Part I, the entry relating to section 86 of the Education Act 1944.
11 & 12 Geo. 6. c. 40.	Education (Miscellaneous Provisions) Act 1948.	Section 13. In Schedule 1, in Part I, the entry relating to section 48 (3) of the Education Act 1944; and in the entry relating to section 116 of that Act the paragraph beginning with " In the provision ".
1 & 2 Eliz. 2. c. 33.	Education (Miscellaneous Provisions) Act 1953.	Sections 13 and 19.
10 & 11 Eliz. 2. c. 12.	Education Act 1962.	Section 11. In section 12 (1), the words from " and ' the Scottish Act of 1946 ' " onwards. In section 14, subsection (3); and subsection (5) except the words " this Act shall not extend to Scotland ".
10 & 11 Eliz. 2. c. 47.	Education (Scotland) Act 1962.	In section 142 (1), the words from " or under " to " 1935 ".
1964 c. 82.	Education Act 1964	Sections 3 and 4. In section 5, in subsection (2) the words from " (except " to " thereof) "; subsection (3); in subsection (4) the words from " in " to " Wales "; and subsection (6) except the words " this Act shall not extend to Scotland ".

Chapter	Title or short title	Extent of repeal
1965 c. 3.	Remuneration of Teachers Act 1965.	Section 6. In section 9 (4), the words " except section 6 thereof ".

PART VI
ELECTIONS

Chapter	Short title	Extent of repeal
42 & 43 Vict. c. 75.	Parliamentary Elections and Corrupt Practices Act 1879.	In section 2, the words from " Every certificate " onwards.
47 & 48 Vict. c. 70.	Municipal Elections (Corrupt and Illegal Practices) Act 1884.	The whole Act.
49 & 50 Vict. c. 57.	Parliamentary Elections (Returning Officers) Act (1875) Amendment Act 1886.	The whole Act.
7 & 8 Geo. 5. c. 64.	Representation of the People Act 1918.	In section 21 (3), the words from " and the " onwards. Section 42. Schedule 6.
4 & 5 Geo. 6. c. 3.	Local Elections and Register of Electors (Temporary Provisions) Act 1940.	The whole Act.
7 & 8 Geo. 6. c. 2.	Local Elections and Register of Electors (Temporary Provisions) Act 1943.	The whole Act.
8 & 9 Geo. 6. c. 5.	Representation of the People Act 1945.	The whole Act.
11 & 12 Geo. 6. c. 65.	Representation of the People Act 1948.	Section 55 (1). In section 74, in subsection (1) the words from " and with respect " onwards; and in subsection (3) the words " or by the said Schedule ". Section 75 (1). In section 77 (1), the definitions of " electoral area ", " local government election ", and " parish ". Section 78 (3). In section 80, subsections (2), (5) and (6), proviso (*c*) to subsection (7), and subsections (8), (9) and (10).
7 & 8 Eliz. 2. c. 22.	County Courts Act 1959.	In Schedule 10, in Part II, paragraph 6. Section 205 (5) (*e*).

PART VII
ELECTRICITY SUPPLY

Chapter	Short title	Extent of repeal
16 & 17 Geo. 5. c. 51.	Electricity (Supply) Act 1926.	In Schedule 6, the entry relating to section 1 of the Electricity (Supply) Act 1919, and in the entry relating to section 15 of that Act the words " by the Lord Chief Justice, or in Scotland " and " the Minister of Health (or, in the case of Scotland,".

Schedule 1—*continued*

Chapter	Short title	Extent of repeal
6 & 7 Geo. 6. c. 32.	Hydro-Electric Development (Scotland) Act 1943.	In section 14 (2), the words " or the growing produce thereof ".
10 & 11 Geo. 6. c. 54.	Electricity Act 1947.	In Schedule 4, in Part I, the entries relating to sections 29 and 31 of the Electricity (Supply) Act 1919 and section 3 of the Electricity Supply (Meters) Act 1936.
2 & 3 Eliz. 2. c. 60.	Electricity Reorganisation (Scotland) Act 1954.	In section 10 (2), the words from " and accordingly " onwards. Section 13. In Schedule 1, in Part II, the entries relating to sections 49 and 53 of the Electricity Act 1947.
5 & 6 Eliz. 2. c. 48.	Electricity Act 1957.	Section 39.
1972 c. 17.	Electricity Act 1972.	Sections 3 and 4 (3). The Schedule.

PART VIII

EMPLOYMENT

Chapter	Short title	Extent of repeal
2 & 3 Vict. c. 71.	Metropolitan Police Courts Act 1839.	Section 37.
10 & 11 Geo. 5. c. 65.	Employment of Women, Young Persons and Children Act 1920.	In the preamble, the words " and Part III " and " women and ". In section 1, in subsection (3), the words " or woman " and the words " and Part III respectively "; and in subsection (6), paragraph (*e*). In section 3 (1), the word " women ". In section 4, the definition of " woman "; and in the definition of " industrial undertaking " the words " and women " and the words " and III ". In the Schedule, Part III.
25 & 26 Geo. 5. c. 8.	Unemployment Insurance Act 1935.	The whole Act.
26 Geo. 5 & 1 Edw. 8. c. 22.	Hours of Employment (Conventions) Act 1936.	Section 1 (3).
1 & 2 Geo. 6. c. 8.	Unemployment Insurance Act 1938.	The whole Act.
8 & 9 Eliz. 2. c. 18.	Local Employment Act 1960.	The whole Act.
1963 c. 19.	Local Employment Act 1963.	The whole Act.
1966 c. 34.	Industrial Development Act 1966.	In section 16, subsections (1) and (2); and in subsection (3) the words from " and no grant " onwards. Sections 20 and 21.
1969 c. 44.	National Insurance Act 1969.	The whole Act.
1972 c. 5.	Local Employment Act 1972.	Section 22 (2). In Schedule 3, the entries relating to the Town and Country Planning Act 1962. Schedule 4.

Act of Parliament of Northern Ireland

Chapter	Short title	Extent of repeal
1969 c. 6 (N.I.)	Mines Act (Northern Ireland) 1969.	In Schedule 4, in paragraph 14, the word " women ".

PART IX

FINANCE

Chapter	Short title	Extent of repeal
54 Geo. 3. c. 92.	Probate and Legacy Duties (Ireland) Act 1814.	The whole Act.
56 Geo. 3. c. 98.	Consolidated Fund Act 1816.	Section 18.
5 & 6 Vict. c. 82.	Stamp Duties (Ireland) Act 1842.	The whole Act.
16 & 17 Vict. c. 59.	Stamp Act 1853.	Section 20.
22 & 23 Vict. c. 21.	Queen's Remembrancer Act 1859.	Section 15. The Schedule.
31 & 32 Vict. c. 88.	Court of Chancery and Exchequer Funds (Ireland) Act 1868.	The whole Act.
53 & 54 Vict. c. 21.	Inland Revenue Regulation Act 1890.	Sections 10, 14, 15, 23 and 33. In section 35 (1), the words from "and order" to the end of the subsection. Sections 38 (2) and 40.
7 & 8 Geo. 5. c. 31.	Finance Act 1917.	Section 34.
8 & 9 Geo. 5. c. 15.	Finance Act 1918.	Section 42.
9 & 10 Geo. 5. c. 37.	War Loan Act 1919.	Section 3 (1).
22 & 23 Geo. 5. c. 51.	Sunday Entertainments Act 1932.	Section 2.
9 & 10 Geo. 6. c. 82.	Cable and Wireless Act 1946.	Sections 1 (2) and (3), 2, 4 (1), (2) and (3), 5, 6 and 7 (*b*). Schedules 1, 2 and 3
10 & 11 Geo. 6. c. 40.	Industrial Organisation and Development Act 1947.	Section 10.
12, 13 & 14 Geo. 6. c. 20.	Cinematograph Film Productions (Special Loans) Act 1949.	In section 9, subsection (1), and in subsection (2), the words "save as provided in subsection (1) of this section".
12, 13 & 14 Geo. 6. c. 47.	Finance Act 1949.	Section 15.
6 & 7 Eliz. 2. c. 11.	Isle of Man Act 1958.	Section 1 (4).
9 & 10 Eliz. 2. c. 36.	Finance Act 1961.	In section 11 (1), the words "and guns".
1966 c. 18.	Finance Act 1966.	Sections 29 and 53 (6).
1972 c. 19.	Sunday Cinema Act 1972.	Sections 1, 3 and 4. The Schedule.

Act of Parliament of Ireland

35 Geo. 3. c. 28 (Ir.).	Collection of Revenue Act (Ireland) 1795.	The whole Act.

PART X

FISHERIES AND HARBOURS

Chapter	Title or short title	Extent of repeal
23 Hen. 8. c. 8 (1531).	An Acte for the amendinge and mayntenance of the havens and portes of Plymouth, Dertmouth, Tynmouth, Falmouth and Fowey in the Counties of Devon and Cornwall.	The whole Act.

SCHEDULE 1—*continued*

Chapter	Title or short title	Extent of repeal
27 Hen. 8. c. 23 (1535).	An Acte for the preservation of the Havens and Portes in the Counties of Devon and Cornwall.	The whole Act.
30 Geo. 2. c. 21 (1757).	An Act for the more effectual Preservation and Improvement of the Spawn and Fry of Fish in the River of Thames and Waters of Medway; and for the better regulating the Fishery thereof.	The whole Act.
22 & 23 Vict. c. 29 (1859).	An Act to repeal a certain Toll levied upon Fishing Vessels passing the Nore.	The whole Act.
24 & 25 Vict. c. 47.	Harbours and Passing Tolls, &c. Act 1861.	Parts II and III. Sections 21, 44, 48, 54 and 56 to 64. Schedules 1 and 3.
26 & 27 Vict. c. 114.	Salmon Fishery (Ireland) Act 1863.	The whole Act.
31 & 32 Vict. c. 123.	Salmon Fisheries (Scotland) Act 1868.	In section 34, the words from the beginning to " Provided, that ".
3 Edw. 7. c. 31.	Board of Agriculture and Fisheries Act 1903.	Section 1 (5).
3 & 4 Eliz. 2. c. 7.	Fisheries Act 1955.	Sections 3 (1), 4 and 6 (1).
1964 c. 72.	Fishery Limits Act 1964.	Section 3 (2).

PART XI

HIGHWAYS

Chapter	Title or short title	Extent of repeal
9 Hen. 5. St. 2. c. 11 (1421).	For the Repair of bridges at Burford and Culhamford between Abingdon and Dorchester.	The whole Act.
2 & 3 Vict. c. 47.	Metropolitan Police Act 1839.	Section 10.
10 Edw. 7 & 1 Geo. 5. c. 7.	Development and Road Improvement Funds Act 1910.	Section 3.
1 Edw. 8 & 1 Geo. 6. c. 5.	Trunk Roads Act 1936.	In section 6 (7), the words from " and subsection (1) " to " conveniences " and the word " respectively ". Section 12 (7), (8) and (11). In Schedule 2, the entry relating to section 3 of the Bridges Act 1929. In Schedule 4, paragraph 8. In Schedule 5, paragraphs 3 and 5 to 9.
9 & 10 Geo. 6. c. 30.	Trunk Roads Act 1946.	Section 9.
14 Geo. 6. c. 39.	Public Utilities Street Works Act 1950.	In section 33 (2), the words from the beginning to the word " and " immediately following paragraph (*d*). In Schedule 5, the entries relating to the Metropolis Management Act 1855, the Metropolis Gas Act 1860, the Local Government Act 1888 and the Public Health (Scotland) Act 1897.

SCHEDULE 1—*continued*

Chapter	Title or short title	Extent of repeal
14 & 15 Geo. 6. c. 25.	Supplies and Services (Defence Purposes) Act 1951.	The whole Act.
6 & 7 Eliz. 2. c. 30.	Land Powers (Defence) Act 1958.	Section 1 (3).
8 & 9 Eliz. 2. c. 63.	Road Traffic and Roads Improvement Act 1960.	Section 22 (1).

PART XII

LOCAL GOVERNMENT AND HOUSING

Chapter	Short title	Extent of repeal
34 & 35 Vict. c. 70.	Local Government Board Act 1871.	In section 2, the words from "vested in" (where they first occur) to "Acts, or "; the words from "or vested in or imposed on Her" to "said schedule" and the words from "and except" onwards. In section 7, the words "according to circumstances" and "the Poor Law Board "; and the words from "or Her" onwards. In the Schedule, in Part I, the entries relating to the Registration of Births, Deaths, and Marriages enactments and the Public Improvements enactment.
46 & 47 Vict. c. 18.	Municipal Corporations Act 1883.	Section 12. In section 25 (2), the words "and of the other parts of this Act". Section 27.
50 & 51 Vict. c. 55.	Sheriffs Act 1887.	In Schedule 2, the words "or of her franchises" and the words "or of his franchises".
51 & 52 Vict. c. 41.	Local Government Act 1888.	In section 79 (3), the word "administrative". Section 82. Section 87 (2) and (4). In section 100, the definitions of "county", "entire county", "administrative county", "borough", "quarter sessions borough", "parliamentary county", "parliamentary election", "parliamentary voters", "existing", "district council", "county district" and "urban authority"; the words from "where an area" to "county rate"; the definitions of "property", "expenses" and "costs"; the paragraph relating to the costs of petty sessions; and the definition of "the divisions of Lincolnshire". Section 109.
56 & 57 Vict. c. 73.	Local Government Act 1894.	In section 21, paragraph (1). Section 25 (1). In section 26 (7), the words from "and the" onwards. Sections 32, 35, 66 and 71.

SCHEDULE 1—*continued*

Chapter	Short title	Extent of repeal
56 & 57 Vict. c. 73—*cont.*	Local Government Act 1894—*cont.*	In section 75 (2), the definitions of " parochial elector ", " election ", " trustees ", " parochial charity ", " county ", " county council ", " elementary school " and " prescribed ". Section 84.
11 & 12 Geo. 6. c. 26.	Local Government Act 1948.	In section 94, in subsection (2) the words " for England and Wales or, as the case may be," (in both places), and in subsection (4) paragraph (*a*). In section 100, in subsection (1), the words from " rating authorities " to " for the benefit of ". In section 100, in subsection (1), the words " the Minister ", where they first occur, and the words from " or the Minister " to " are concerned". In section 110, the words " the Minister and as respects Scotland,". Section 143.
11 & 12 Geo. 6. c. 29.	National Assistance Act 1948.	Section 58.
3 & 4 Eliz. 2. c. 24.	Requisitioned Houses and Housing (Amendment) Act 1955.	The whole Act.
5 & 6 Eliz. 2. c 56.	Housing Act 1957.	In Schedule 10, the entry relating to the Requisitioned Houses and Housing (Amendment) Act 1955.
6 & 7 Eliz. 2. c. 33.	Disabled Persons (Employment) Act 1958.	In the Schedule, in paragraph 1 (1) (*d*), the words " and fifty-eight ".
6 & 7 Eliz. 2. c. 55.	Local Government Act 1958.	In section 56 (1), the word " county " in " county district ". Section 61. In section 63 (1), the words from the beginning to " of this Act ". In section 64, the words " an order or rules or ". In section 66, in subsection (1), the definitions of " Act of 1955 ", " Area Board ", " borough ", " joint board ", " Minister ", " appropriate Minister ", " parish " and " relevant expenditure "; in subsection (2), the words "Parts II to IV of ", the words " county borough or county " and the words from " and in the said " onwards; and subsection (3). In section 67, proviso (*f*). In Schedule 8, paragraphs 27 and 28, and in paragraph 35 the words " 19 " and " 27 ".
8 & 9 Eliz. 2. c. 20.	Requisitioned Houses Act 1960.	The whole Act.
10 & 11 Eliz. 2. c. 50.	Landlord and Tenant Act 1962.	Section 2 (2).
10 & 11 Eliz. 2. c. 56.	Local Government (Records) Act 1962.	Section 7 (2).
1963 c. 33.	London Government Act 1963.	In section 1 (6), the words from " (and " to " 1933) " and the words from " and the council " onwards. Section 8 (2). Section 62 (3). In Schedule 2, paragraph 31 (i) and (ii).
1966 c. 42.	Local Government Act 1966.	Section 37. In section 39, the words from " and the power " onwards.

Schedule 1—*continued*

Chapter	Short title	Extent of repeal
1966 c. 42— *cont.*	Local Government Act 1966—*cont.*	In section 41 (1), in the definition of " local authority ", the words " county borough ".
1968 c. 46.	Health Services and Public Health Act 1968.	In section 45 (5), in paragraph (*b*), the words " and 58 ".
1970 c. 42.	Local Authority Social Services Act 1970.	In Schedule 1, the entry relating to section 58 of the National Assistance Act 1948.
1972 c. 66.	Poisons Act 1972	In section 11 (2), in paragraph (*a*) of the definition of " local authority ", the words " county borough ".
1972 c. 70.	Local Government Act 1972.	In section 88 (2), the words from the beginning to " council " (where first occurring). In Schedule 2, paragraphs 6 (4), 7 (3) and 8 and Part II.
1973 c. 65.	Local Government (Scotland) Act 1973.	Section 171 (3).
1977 c. 42.	Rent Act 1977.	In Schedule 23, paragraph 21.

Part XIII

Museums and Galleries

Chapter	Short title	Extent of repeal
29 & 30 Vict. c. 83.	National Gallery Enlargement Act 1866.	The whole Act, except sections 1, 3, 16, 17, 20 and 29.
30 & 31 Vict. c. 41.	National Gallery Enlargement Act 1867.	The whole Act.
52 & 53 Vict. c. 25.	National Portrait Gallery Act 1889.	The whole Act.
1 Edw. 7. c. 16.	National Gallery (Purchase of Adjacent Land) Act 1901.	The whole Act.
22 & 23 Geo. 5. c. 34.	British Museum Act 1932.	Section 2 (2).
1963 c. 24.	British Museum Act 1963.	Section 13 (3).

Part XIV

Property

Chapter	Title or subject	Extent of repeal
11 Hen. 7. c. 35 (1495).	(Lands assured to Duke of York).	The whole Act.
11 Hen. 7. c. 36 (1495).	(Estates of Duchess of Bedford).	The whole Act.
11 Hen. 7. c. 37 (1495).	(Estates of Marquis of Dorset and Wife).	The whole Act.
11 Hen. 7. c. 39 (1495).	(Estates of Earl of Suffolk).	The whole Act.
11 Hen. 7. c. 40 (1495).	(Estates of Earl of Surrey).	The whole Act.
12 Hen. 7. c. 8 (1496).	(Feoffments made by the King).	The whole Act.

Chapter	Title or subject	Extent of repeal
19 Hen. 7. c. 26 (1503).	(Prince of Wales).	The whole Act.
19 Hen. 7. c. 29 (1503).	(Monastery of Syon).	The whole Act.
19 Hen. 7. c. 30 (1503).	Partition of Lands: Barkley and Earl of Surrey).	The whole Act.
19 Hen. 7. c. 33 (1503).	(Estate of Lord Wells).	The whole Act.
3 Hen. 8. c. 16 (1511).	(Estates of Earl of Surrey).	The whole Act.
3 Hen. 8. c. 18 (1511).	(Grant to William Compton).	The whole Act.
4 Hen. 8. c. 10 (1512).	(Grant to Earl and Countess of Devon).	The whole Act.
4 Hen. 8. c. 11 (1512).	(Countess of Devon and Hugh Conway).	The whole Act.
4 Hen. 8. c. 12 (1512).	(Countess of Devon and William Knyvet).	The whole Act.
4 Hen. 8. c. 13 (1512).	(Estates of Earl of Surrey).	The whole Act.
5 Hen. 8. c. 9 (1513).	The Creacion of the Duke of Norfolk.	The whole Act.
5 Hen. 8. c. 10 (1513).	The Creacion of the Duke of Suffolk.	The whole Act.
5 Hen. 8. c. 11 (1513).	The Creacion of the Erle of Surrey.	The whole Act.
5 Hen. 8. c. 14 (1513).	An Acte concernyng the Dourey of the Countesse of Oxford.	The whole Act.
5 Hen. 8. c. 18 (1513).	An Acte concernyng Sir Edwarde Poynynges.	The whole Act.
6 Hen. 8. c. 19 (1514).	Ratificacion of the Kings graunte made to the Duke of Norfolk.	The whole Act.
6 Hen. 8. c. 20 (1514).	Ratificacion of the Kings letters patents to the Duke of Suffolk.	The whole Act.
6 Hen. 8. c. 23 (1514).	Thassuraunce of the titles of the Kings Manour of Hanworth.	The whole Act.
14 & 15 Hen. 8. c. 18 (1523).	Thacte concernying the Kynges Honour of Beuleu.	The whole Act.
14 & 15 Hen. 8. c. 24 (1523).	(Sale of land to Sir William Compton).	The whole Act.
14 & 15 Hen. 8. c. 25 (1523).	(Sale of land to Thomas Kitson).	The whole Act.
14 & 15 Hen. 8. c. 26 (1523).	(Sale of land to Sir Richard Sacheverell).	The whole Act.
14 & 15 Hen. 8. c. 27 (1523).	(Grant to Lord Marny).	The whole Act.
14 & 15 Hen. 8. c. 30 (1523).	(Grant to Earl of Northumberland).	The whole Act.
14 & 15 Hen. 8. c. 31 (1523).	(Grants to Sir Andrew Windsor and Anthony Windsor).	The whole Act.
14 & 15 Hen. 8. c. 33 (1523).	(Grant to Earl of Shrewsbury).	The whole Act.
14 & 15 Hen. 8. c. 34 (1523).	(Jointure of Elizabeth Talboys).	The whole Act.
21 Hen. 8. c. 22 (1529).	An Acte for thassuraunce of dyvers Mannors Landes and Tenements to Thomas Duke of Norfolk, and theires males of his bodye lawfullie begotten.	The whole Act.

Chapter	Title or subject	Extent of repeal
21 Hen. 8. c. 26 (1529).	An Acte for thassuraunce of certaine Landes to Elizabeth Duches of Norfolk duringe hir life and after hir decease to Thomas Duke of Norfolk hir housbonde for ever and his heires.	The whole Act.
22 Hen. 8. c. 17 (1530).	An Acte concernyng the Duke of Rychemond.	The whole Act.
22 Hen. 8. c. 19 (1530).	An Acte concernyng of certen Londs to the Heyres of Syr William Fyloll.	The whole Act.
22 Hen. 8. c. 21 (1530).	An Acte of Exchaung betwene the Kyngs Highnes and the heyres of the Lord Marques Mountegue.	The whole Act.
22 Hen. 8. c. 22 (1530).	An Acte concernyng certen Anuytes graunted oute of the Bysshopriche of Wynchester.	The whole Act.
22 Hen. 8. c. 23 (1530).	An Acte concernyng the assuraunce of the Joyntor of the Lady Dorathie Countesse of Derby.	The whole Act.
23 Hen. 8. c. 21 (1531).	An Acte concernyng an Exchaung of certeyn londz betwene the Kings Highnes & the Abbot of Westminster.	The whole Act.
23 Hen. 8. c. 22 (1531).	An Acte concernyng an Exchaung of Londz betwene the Kyngs Highnes & the Master Fellowes & Scolers of Crystes Colledg in Cambrydg.	The whole Act.
23 Hen. 8. c. 23 (1531).	An Acte concernyng an Exchaung of Londz betwene the Kyngs Highnes & the Abbot of Waltham of Holy Crosse.	The whole Act.
23 Hen. 8. c. 24 (1531).	An Acte concernying an Exchaung of certen Londz betwene the Kyngz Highnes & the Provost of Eton.	The whole Act.
23 Hen. 8. c. 25 (1531).	An Acte concernyng an Exchaung of Londz betwene the Kyngs Highnes & the Abbot of Seynt Albones.	The whole Act.
23 Hen. 8. c. 26 (1531).	An Acte concernyng the Exchaung of certen Londz betwene the Kyngz Highnes & the Lord of Seynt Johns.	The whole Act.
23 Hen. 8. c. 27 (1531).	An Acte concernyng an Exchaung of Landz betwene the Kyngs Highnes & the Pryour of Shene.	The whole Act.

SCHEDULE 1—*continued*

Chapter	Title or subject	Extent of repeal
23 Hen. 8. c. 28 (1531).	An Acte concernyng an Exchaunge of Londs betwene the Kyngs Highnes the Duke of Rychemond & the Lorde Lumley.	The whole Act.
23 Hen. 8. c. 29 (1531).	An Acte concernyng the Assuraunce of certen Londz unto Henry Erle of Surrey in consyderacyon of his Maryage.	The whole Act.
23 Hen. 8. c. 30 (1531).	An Acte concernyng the Manour of Hunsdon from hensforth to be called the Honoure of Hunesdon.	The whole Act.
23 Hen. 8. c. 31 (1531).	An Acte concernyng the Assuraunce of the Joynture of the Lady Elizabeth Countes of Wiltshyre.	The whole Act.
23 Hen. 8. c. 32 (1531)	An Acte concernyng the Award made by the Kyngs Highnes of Coopcenory unto the heyres generall of the Erle of Oxford.	The whole Act.
23 Hen. 8. c. 33 (1531).	An Acte concernyng the Assuraunce of the Joyntures of the Lady Anne & the Lady Elizabeth Counteses of Oxford.	The whole Act.
24 Hen. 8. c. 14 (1532).	An Acte concernyng the Assuraunce of certen Londs unto Walter Wallsh and Dame Elizabeth his wyff late the wyff of Syr Wyllyam Compton knyght decessed.	The whole Act.
25 Hen. 8. c. 23 (1533).	An Acte concernyng the Towne of Plymmouthe.	The whole Act.
25 Hen. 8. c. 24 (1533).	An Acte of Exchaung of certen Londz betwene the Duke of Norfolk & the heyres generall of the Erle of Oxford.	The whole Act.
25 Hen. 8. c. 26 (1533).	An Acte concernyng an Exchaung of certeyn Londs betwene the Kyngs Highnes & the Abbott of Walltham.	The whole Act.
25 Hen. 8. c. 30 (1533).	An Acte betwene the Kyngz Highnes the Duke of Rychemond & the Lord Lumley.	The whole Act.
25 Hen. 8. c. 31 (1533).	An Acte concernyng the assuraunce of the Maner of Pyssowe to the Kings Highnes and his heires.	The whole Act.
25 Hen. 8. c. 33 (1533).	An Acte concernyng the Assuraunce of Christ Churche in London to the Kyngs Highnes and to his heires.	The whole Act.

Schedule 1—*continued*

Chapter	Title or subject	Extent of repeal
26 Hen. 8. c. 20 (1534).	An Acte concernyng the assurance of certen Londz unto Thomas Duke of Norfolk & others.	The whole Act.
26 Hen. 8. c. 21 (1534).	An Acte concernyng the assuraunce of certen Londes unto the Duke of Rychemond and his heires.	The whole Act.
26 Hen. 8. c. 24 (1534).	An Acte of exchaunge betwene the Kyng and Thabbott of Waltham.	The whole Act.
27 Hen. 8. c. 29 (1535).	An Acte concernyng the assuraunce of the Maner of Grenes Norton to the Kyngs Highnes and his heires.	The whole Act.
27 Hen. 8. c. 30 (1535).	An Acte concernyng the assuraunce of certen Londs to the Lady Elizabeth Vaulx in recompense of her Joynture.	The whole Act.
27 Hen. 8. c. 31 (1535).	An Acte concernyng the assuraunce of certen Londs to the Kyngs Highnes and his heyres late apperteynyng unto John Tuchet Knyght Lorde Awdeley.	The whole Act.
27 Hen. 8. c. 32 (1535).	An Acte conteynyng the concord and agrement betwene the Erle of Rutlond & the Cyte of Yorke and others.	The whole Act.
27 Hen. 8. c. 33 (1535).	An Acte concernyng an exchaunge of certen Londs betwene the Kyngs Highnes the Duke of Norfolk & the Priour & Covent of Thetford.	The whole Act.
27 Hen. 8. c. 34 (1535).	An Acte concernyng an exchaunge of certen Londs betwene the Kyngs Highnes and the Archebisshop of Canterburye.	The whole Act.
27 Hen. 8. c. 36 (1535).	An Acte concernyng the assuraunce of the Lady Elianour Clyffordes Joynture.	The whole Act.
27 Hen. 8. c. 37 (1535).	An Acte concernyng the Kyngs gracyouse pardon graunted unto the Duke of Suffolk.	The whole Act.
27 Hen. 8. c. 38 (1535).	An Acte concernyng an exchaunge of certen londs betwene the Kyngs Highnes the Duke of Suffolk and Therle of Northumberland.	The whole Act.

SCHEDULE 1—*continued*

Chapter	Title or subject	Extent of repeal
27 Hen. 8. c. 39 (1535).	An Acte concernyng the assuraunce of the Duke of Suffolk place in Southwerk to the Kyngs Highnes and his Heyres; and concernyng also the assuraunce of Norwiche place unto the Duke of Suffolk and his Heires.	The whole Act.
27 Hen. 8. c. 40 (1535).	An Acte conteynyng an agreament betwene Charles Duke of Suffolk and Sir Crystofer Wylloughby.	The whole Act.
27 Hen. 8. c. 43 (1535).	An Acte betwene Syr Pers Dutton & others.	The whole Act.
27 Hen. 8. c. 44 (1535).	An Acte concernyng the partycyon of Londs betwene the heyres of the Lord Broke.	The whole Act.
27 Hen. 8. c. 45 (1535).	An Acte concernyng the assuraunce of all the Temporaltyes belonging unto the Bisshoppriche of Norwiche unto the Kings Highnes and his heires.	The whole Act.
27 Hen. 8. c. 46 (1535).	An Acte concernyng the particyon of certen Londs betwene the Lord Thomas Howard and Sir Thomas Ponyngs Knyght.	The whole Act.
27 Hen. 8. c. 47 (1535).	An Acte concernyng thassuraunce of the possessyons of the Erle of Northumberland to the Kyngs Highnes & his Heyres.	The whole Act.
27 Hen. 8. c. 48 (1535).	An Acte concernyng the assuraunce of certen Londs unto Sir Thomas Awdeley Knight Lorde Chauncellour of Englond and his heyres	The whole Act.
27 Hen. 8. c. 49 (1535).	An Acte concernyng the Assuraunce of a voyde plotte of grounde being in Chepe in London to the Mayer and Comynaltye of the sayd Cyte of London and their Successours.	The whole Act.
27 Hen. 8. c. 50 (1535).	An Acte concernyng the assuraunce of the maner of Halying to the Kyngs Highnes and his heires.	The whole Act.
27 Hen. 8. c. 51 (1535).	An Acte concernying the Assuraunce of the Lordship and Maner of Collyweston to the Quenes Grace for terme of her lyffe.	The whole Act.

SCHEDULE 1—*continued*

Chapter	Title or subject	Extent of repeal
27 Hen. 8. c. 52 (1535)	An Acte concernyng an exchaunge of L o n d s betwene the Kyngs Highnes and the Presydent and Scolers of Corpus Christi College in the Universyte of Oxford.	The whole Act.
27 Hen. 8. c. 53 (1535).	An Acte concernyng an exchaung of L o n d s betwene the Kyngs Highnes and the Prior and Covent of Marten Abbaye.	The whole Act.
27 Hen. 8. c. 54 (1535).	An Acte concernyng the assuraunce of c e r t e n Londs unto Sir Arthure Darcy Knyght & his heyres.	The whole Act.
27 Hen. 8. c. 55 (1535).	An Acte concernyng the assuraunce of c e r t e n Londs unto Anne Fittzwilliam in recompence of her Joynture.	The whole Act.
27 Hen. 8. c. 56 (1535).	An Acte concernyng the assuraunce of c e r t e n Londs unto the Lord William Howarde for terme of his lyffe.	The whole Act.
27 Hen. 8. c. 57 (1535).	An Acte concernying the assuraunce of c e r t e n Londs unto Thomas Pope.	The whole Act.
27 Hen. 8. c. 58 (1535).	An Acte adnullyng aswell a Dede of Feoffement as also an I n d e n t u r e fraudeilently made by Sir T h o m a s More Knight of his purchased Londs in Chelseth or ellswhere in the Countye of Middlesex.	The whole Act.
27 Hen. 8. c. 61 (1535).	An Acte concernyng the assuraunce of the Maner of Bromhill to the Kyngs Highnes and unto his heyres.	The whole Act.
28 Hen. 8. c. 19 (1536).	An Acte concernyng the assuraunce of the Maner or Hyde of Southwark unto the Kyngs Highnes his heyres and Successours, late belongyng to the Monastery or House of Seynt Savyour of Barmondesey.	The whole Act.
28 Hen. 8. c. 20 (1536).	An Acte concernying the assuraunce of certeyn L o n d e s unto Dame Grace, wyfe unto Sir Henry Parker sonne and heyre apparaunt unto H e n r y Lord Morley, in recompence of her Joynture.	The whole Act.

SCHEDULE 1—*continued*

Chapter	Title or subject	Extent of repeal
28 Hen. 8. c. 21 (1536).	An Acte concernyng an exchaunge of certyn Londes betwene the Kyngs Highnes and the Lord Pryour of Seynt Johns Jerusalem in Englond and his Co-brethern.	The whole Act.
28 Hen. 8. c. 22 (1536).	An Acte concernyng the assuraunce of certen Londs unto the Kyngs Highnes somtyme belongyng to the Erldom of Warwike.	The whole Act.
28 Hen. 8. c. 25 (1536).	An Acte concernyng the assuraunce of certen Londs unto Sir Edward Seymor Knyght Vicount Beauchamp.	The whole Act.
28 Hen. 8. c. 26 (1536).	An Acte concernyng assuraunce of a messuage and certen Londs in Kewe unto Sir Edward Semer Vicount Beauchamp, & to the Lady Anne his Wyfe.	The whole Act.
28 Hen. 8. c. 28 (1536).	An Acte concernyng the assuraunce of the moitie of Ricardes Castell unto John Onley and unto his heires.	The whole Act.
28 Hen. 8. c. 29 (1536).	An Acte concernyng an exchaunge of certen Londs betwene the Kyngs Highnes and the Abbott of Westminster, for Covent Gardeyn.	The whole Act.
28 Hen. 8. c. 30 (1536).	An Acte concernyng the assuraunce of Stanton Barrey to the Kyngs Highnes and his heyres.	The whole Act.
28 Hen. 8. c. 32 (1536).	An Acte concernyng the assuraunce of certen Londs unto the Kyngs Highnes and his heyres from Sir William Essex Sir Hugh Vaughan William Jenyns & others.	The whole Act.
28 Hen. 8. c. 33 (1536).	An Acte concernyng an exchaung betwene the Kyngs Highnes and the Bisshop of Duresme for Duresme Place.	The whole Act.
28 Hen. 8. c. 34 (1536).	An Acte concernyng the assuraunce of Bayneyards Castell unto the Duke of Richemond and unto his heyres.	The whole Act.
28 Hen. 8. c. 35 (1536).	An Acte concernyng an exchaunge of certen Londs bethweyne the Kyngs Highnes and the Lord Sandes.	The whole Act.

Chapter	Title or subject	Extent of repeal
28 Hen. 8. c. 36 (1536).	An Acte ratefyeng of an Awarde made by the Kyngs Highnes betwene Syr Adryan Fortescue and Syr Walter Stoner.	The whole Act.
28 Hen. 8. c. 37 (1536).	An Acte concernyng a mariage to be hadd betwene Richard Deveroux sonne and heyre apparaunt of W a l t e r Deveroux Knyght Lorde Ferres and Lady Dorothie doughter unto the Erle of Huntyngton.	The whole Act.
28 Hen. 8. c. 38 (1536).	An Acte concernyng the assuraunce of the Maners of Parysgarden Hyde and others to the Quenys Grace.	The whole Act.
28 Hen. 8. c. 39 (1536).	An Acte concernying the assuraunce of c e r t e n Londs unto the Kyngs Majestie and unto his heires somtyme belongyng unto the Erldome of Marche.	The whole Act.
28 Hen. 8. c. 40 (1536).	An Acte concernyng the assuraunce of the Maner of Kyrtelyng unto Edward Northe and his heires.	The whole Act.
28 Hen. 8. c. 41 (1536).	An Acte concernyng the assuraunce of the Maner of Birmyngeham to the Kyngs Highnes and his heyres.	The whole Act.
28 Hen. 8. c. 42 (1536).	An Acte concernyng an Exchaunge of c e r t e n Londes betwene the Kyngs Highnes the Abbott of Abyngdon and others.	The whole Act.
28 Hen. 8. c. 43 (1536).	An Acte concernyng the Assuraunce of c e r t e n Londs unto Thomas Jermyn and his heyres.	The whole Act.
28 Hen. 8. c. 44 (1536).	An Acte concernyng the assuraunce of the Maner of Haselyngfeld unto the Priour and Covent of Charter House nyghe London and to there successours for ever.	The whole Act.
28 Hen. 8. c. 46 (1536).	An Acte concernyng the assuraunce of c e r t e n Londs unto Thomas Hatclyff Squyer & unto his heires.	The whole Act.
28 Hen. 8. c. 47 (1536).	An Acte concernyng the assuraunce of c e r t e n Londs unto John Gostwyke and his heires.	The whole Act.

Schedule 1—*continued*

Chapter	Title or subject	Extent of repeal
28 Hen. 8. c. 48 (1536).	An Acte concernyng a mariage to be hadd and solemnyzed betwene the Lord Bulbeke sonne and heyre apparaunt unto the Erle of Oxford and the Lady Dorathie eldest Daughter of the Erle of Westmoreland.	The whole Act.
28 Hen. 8. c. 49 (1536).	An Acte concernyng an Exchaunge of Londs betwene the K y n g s Highnes and the Abbot and Covent of Westminster.	The whole Act.
28 Hen. 8. c. 50 (1536).	An Acte concernyng an exchaung of L o n d s betwene the Kings Highnes, the Archebisshop of Caunterburye, and Thomas Crumwell Esquyre the Kyngs chieff Secretory.	The whole Act.
28 Hen. 8. c. 51 (1536).	An Acte concernyng thassuraunce of certayn Londs unto the Lady Katheryn Duches of Suffolk, in recompence of her Jointure.	The whole Act.
31 Hen. 8. c. 5 (1539).	An Acte whereby the M a n o r of Hampton Courte is made an Honor.	The whole Act.
33 Hen. 8. c. 26 (1541).	A Bill towching thannihilating off certayne conveyances devised by Sir Jhon Shelton.	The whole Act.
33 Hen. 8. c. 37 (1541).	An Acte touchinge the Honor of Ampthill.	The whole Act.
33 Hen. 8. c. 38 (1541).	An Acte concerninge the Honor of Grafton.	The whole Act.
34 & 35 Hen. 8. c. 21 (1542).	An Acte for the confirmacon of letters patents notwithstanding mysnaming of any thing conteyned in the same.	The whole Act.
37 Hen. 8. c. 18 (1545).	An Acte for the ereccon of the Honors of Westminster Kingeston St. Osithes & Donyngton.	The whole Act.
2 & 3 Edw. 6. c. 12 (1548).	An Acte for the assuraunce to the Tenantes of Grauntes and Leases made of the Duke of Somersetts d e m e n e Londs.	The whole Act.
21 Jas. I. c. 30 (1623).	An Acte for the assuring of a Messuag called Yorke Howse & other T e n e m e n t s to the Kinge, and for other Lands to the Archbysshopp of Yorke in liewe thereof.	The whole Act.

SCHEDULE 1—*continued*

Chapter	Title or subject	Extent of repeal
3 Chas. 1. c. 6 (1627).	An Act for the establishing of the Estates of the tenants of Bromfeild and Yale in the Countie of Denbigh and of the Tenures Rens and Services thereuppon reserved according to a late Composicion made for the same with the Kings most Excellent Majestie then Prince of Wales.	The whole Act.
11 Will. 3. c. 2 (1698).	An Act for granting an Aid to His Majesty by Sale of the forfeited and other Estates and Interests in Ireland and by a Land Tax in England for the severall Purposes therein mentioned.	The whole Act.
3 & 4 Anne c. 4 (1704).	An Act for the better enabling Her Majesty to grant the Honor and Mannor of Woodstock with the Hundred of Wooton to the Duke of Marlborough and his Heires in Consideration of the eminent Services by him performed to Her Majestye and the Publick.	The whole Act.
7 Anne c. 29 (1708).	An Act for the Relief of the Earl of Clanriccard (lately called Lord Bophin) of the Kingdom of Ireland in relation to his Estate and for the more effectual selling or setting the Estate of the said Earl to Protestants.	The whole Act.
28 Geo. 2. c. 54 (1755).	An Act to enable the Reverend William Markham, Doctor of Laws, and Thomas Salter, Esquire, to build Houses, and open a Square in and upon a certain Piece of Ground called Dean's Yard, Westminster, and several Pieces of Ground contiguous thereto.	The whole Act.
31 Geo. 2. c. 16 (1757)	An Act to enforce and render more effectual [the Act 25 Geo. 2. c. 41].	The whole Act.
2 Geo. 3. c. 17 (1762).	An Act for Relief of the Vassals of the several Estates which are or may be annexed to the Crown, by virtue of [the Act 25 Geo. 2. c. 41], and for carrying the	The whole Act.

Chapter	Title or subject	Extent of repeal
2 Geo. 3. c. 17 (1762)—*cont.*	Purposes of the said Act more effectually into Execution; and for enforcing and carrying into Execution so much of [the Act 1 Geo. 3. c. 19] as relates to the paying and discharging the Wadsetts affecting the Estate of Lovat.	
10 Geo. 3. c. 13 (1770).	An Act for enabling His Majesty to grant the Inheritance in Fee Simple of the Manor of Cosham, in the County of Wilts, with the Rights, Members, and Appurtenances thereof, now held, under a Demise by Letters Patent under the Seal of His Majesty's Court of Exchequer, in Trust for Paul Methuen Esquire, unto the said Paul Methuen, and his Heirs, upon a full and adequate Consideration to be paid for the same.	The whole Act.
11 Geo. 3. c. 56 (1771).	An Act for divesting out of the Crown, and to vest in Gerald Fitzgerald of Rathrone, in the County of Meath, in the Kingdom of Ireland, Esquire, and his Heirs, the Reversion in Fee of and in several Lands in Ireland therein mentioned.	The whole Act.
12 Geo. 3. c. 19 (1772).	An Act to enable His Majesty to grant certain Houses in Fenchurch Street and Addle Street, in the City of London, escheated to the Crown by the Death of Lieutenant-general John Brown, without Heir, unto Frederick Montagu Esquire, and his Heirs, upon the Trusts therein mentioned.	The whole Act.
12 Geo. 3. c. 35 (1772).	An Act for enabling Their Majesties to enfranchise Copyhold Lands holden of the Manor of Richmond, in the County of Surrey, and for enabling His Majesty to shut up a Lane leading from Richmond Green to the River Thames, and to sell and exchange certain Lands within the Manors of Richmond and Wimbledon.	The whole Act.

SCHEDULE 1—*continued*

Chapter	Title or subject	Extent of repeal
12 Geo. 3. c. 43 (1772).	An Act for vesting Ely House, in Holbourn, in His Majesty, His Heirs and Successors, and for applying the Purchase-money, with another Sum therein mentioned, in the purchasing of a Freehold Piece of Ground in Dover Street, and in the building and fitting up another House thereon, for the future Residence of the Bishops of Ely, and the Surplus to the Benefit of the See; and for other Purposes therein mentioned.	The whole Act.
12 Geo. 3. c. 44 (1772).	An Act to enable His Majesty to grant the Reversion or Remainder in Fee-simple, now vested in His Majesty, of and in an Annual or Fee-farm Rent of One hundred and thirteen pounds, One of the several Fee-farm Rents granted to the Right Honourable Edward, heretofore Earl of Sandwich, by His late Majesty King Charles the Second, unto the Honourable James Archibald Stuart, and his Heirs, upon a full and adequate Considera-tion to be given by him, or His Heirs, for the same.	The whole Act.
12 Geo. 3. c. 59 (1772).	An Act for vesting in His Majesty certain Heredi-taments at Richmond, in the County of Surrey, belonging to Catharine Viscountess Fitzwilliam, and held by Lease from the Crown; and for vesting the Freehold and Inheritance of cer-tain Leasehold and Copyhold Hereditaments at Richmond aforesaid in Trustees, and their Heirs, in Trust for the said Catharine Vis-countess Fitzwilliam, as a Part of the Compen-sation for the same, and for other Purposes therein mentioned.	The whole Act.
17 Geo. 3. c. 17 (1776).	An Act for dividing the Chase of Enfield, in the	The whole Act.

SCHEDULE 1—*continued*

Chapter	Title or subject	Extent of repeal
17 Geo. 3. c. 17 (1776)—*cont.*	County of Middlesex; and for other Purposes therein mentioned.	
18 Geo. 3. c. 61 (1778).	An Act for repealing certain Provisions in Two Acts [namely 1 Anne c. 26 and 1 Anne Stat. 2. c. 18].	The whole Act.
23 Geo. 3. c. 61 (1783).	An Act for vesting in Henry Earl of Pembroke, his Heirs and Assigns, for ever, the Fee-simple and Inheritance of the Hundred of Kynswardston, and certain Lands and Hereditaments in the Parishes of Great Bedwyn and Burbage, in the County of Wilts; and for settling other Lands and Hereditaments in lieu thereof to the same Uses.	The whole Act.
25 Geo. 3. c. 98 (1785).	An Act to enable His Majesty to grant the Inheritance of certain Lands, Tenements, and Hereditaments, situate in or near North Scotland Yard, in the County of Middlesex, in Exchange for the Inheritance of certain Buildings or Barracks, and Land adjoining thereto, and also of certain Ground contiguous to Tinmouth Castle, in the County of Northumberland, belonging to the Duke of Northumberland, or for such further or other Compensation as shall be a full Consideration for the same; and also to impower the said Duke to make such Exchange.	The whole Act.
26 Geo. 3. c. 27 (1786).	An Act for authorising the Lord Chief Baron, and remanet Barons of the Court of Exchequer in Scotland, out of the unappropriated Money arising from the forfeited and lately annexed Estates in Scotland, to pay a certain Sum to the Society in Scotland for propagating Christian Knowledge for the Purposes, and under the Conditions therein mentioned.	The whole Act.

SCHEDULE 1—*continued*

Chapter	Title or subject	Extent of repeal
28 Geo. 3. c. 63 (1788).	An Act for charging several Estates in the Counties of Northumberland, Cumberland, and Durham, settled upon the late Charles Radcliffe deceased, for Life, with Remainder to his First and other Sons, in Tail Male, with the Payment of a clear yearly Rent Charge of Two thousand five hundred Pounds, payable to the Grandson of the said Charles Radcliffe, the Right Honourable Anthony James Earl of Newburgh, and the Heirs Male of his Body to be begotten.	The whole Act.
30 Geo. 3. c. 51 (1790).	An Act for divesting out of the Crown the Reversion in Fee of and in certain Hereditaments, heretofore the Estate of Sir Roger Strickland Knight, deceased, in Catterick and Tunstall, in the County of York; and for vesting the same in the several Persons entitled to the said Hereditaments; and for extinguishing and destroying a certain Term of One hundred Years, for which the said Hereditaments were limited in Trust for His late Majesty King George the First, His Heirs and Successors.	The whole Act.
32 Geo. 3. c. 24 (1792).	An Act to repeal so much of [the Act 27 Geo. 3. c. 22] as relates to the Sale of the House in the Privy Garden, heretofore used as an Office for the Commissioners of the Lottery; and to enable His Majesty to grant the said Premises.	The whole Act.
33 Geo. 3. c. 46 (1793).	An Act for vesting in His Majesty certain forfeited Estates in Ireland, subject to the Disposition of the Parliament of Ireland.	The whole Act.
35 Geo. 3. c. 40 (1795).	An Act to enable His Majesty to grant to the Right Honourable John Earl of Upper Ossory in the Kingdom of Ireland, Baron Upper Ossory, of Ampthill, in	The whole Act.

SCHEDULE 1—*continued*

Chapter	Title or subject	Extent of repeal
35 Geo. 3. c. 40 (1795)—*cont.*	the County of Bedford, His Heirs and Assigns, in Fee Simple, all the Estate, Right, Title, and Interest, remaining in His Majesty, in and upon the Haye or Walk of Farming Woods, in the Forest of Rockingham, in the County of Northampton, and also the Reversion of certain Offices, Rents, and other Hereditaments in the said County of Northampton, to which the said Earl of Upper Ossory is entitled for Three Lives, under a Grant from His present Majesty, upon a full and adequate Consideration to be paid for the same.	
36 Geo. 3. c. 62 (1796).	An Act to enable His Majesty to grant to John Earl of Westmorland, His Heirs and Assigns, in Fee Simple, all the Estate, Right, Title, and Interest, remaining in His Majesty in and upon the Hayes or Walks of Sulehay Fermes, and Shortwood, and Morebay, in the Forest of Rockingham, in the County of Northampton, upon a full and adequate Consideration to be paid for the same.	The whole Act.
36 Geo. 3. c. 63 (1796).	An Act to enable His Majesty to grant to Henry Earl of Exeter, his Heirs and Assigns, in Fee Simple, all the Estate, Right, Title and Interest, remaining in His Majesty in and upon the Haye or Walk of Westhay, in the Forest of Rockingham, in the County of Northampton, upon a full and adequate Consideration to be paid for the same.	The whole Act.
37 Geo. 3. c. 47 (1797).	An Act for discharging the Estates of John Yeldham Esquire, from certain Demands of the Crown, upon the Conditions therein mentioned.	The whole Act.
44 Geo. 3. c. 25 (1804).	An Act to enable His Majesty to grant the Inheritance, in Fee	The whole Act.

Chapter	Title or subject	Extent of repeal
44 Geo. 3. c. 25 (1804)—*cont.*	Simple, of certain Manors, Messuages, Lands and Hereditaments, in the Parishes of Byfleet, Weybridge, Walton, Walton Leigh, and Chertsey, in the County of Surrey, to His Royal Highness Frederick Duke of York and Albany, for a valuable Consideration.	
45 Geo. 3. c. 116 (1805).	An Act for enabling His Majesty to grant a certain Creek, called Chelson Bay, otherwise Shilston Bay, in or near the Parish of Plympton Saint Mary, in the County of Devon; and for vesting the same, for a valuable Consideration, in the Right Honourable Lord Boringdon, and his Heirs.	The whole Act.
47 Geo. 3. Sess. 2. c. 77 (1807).	An Act for confirming Articles of Agreement for an Exchange of Lands between His Majesty and David Jebb Esquire, in the Parish of Egham, in the County of Surrey.	The whole Act.
52 Geo. 3. c. 124 (1812).	An Act for vesting in His Majesty, His Heirs and Successors, certain Lands or Grounds, formerly Part of the Wastes of the Manor of Sandhurst, in the County of Berks, freed and discharged of Commonable and other Rights.	The whole Act.
55 Geo. 3. c. 188 (1815).	An Act for enabling His Majesty to grant to John Francis Erskine of Mar Esquire, and his Heirs and Assigns, the Feu Duties and Quit Rents arising in the Lordship of Stirling, in Discharge of a Debt of greater Value created upon the said Feu Duties by a Grant from His Majesty King George the First.	The whole Act.
57 Geo. 3. c. 129 (1817)	An Act for vesting in His Majesty a certain Part of the Open Commons and Waste Lands within the Manor or Royalty of Rialton and Retraighe alias Reterth in the Parish of Saint Columb Major, in the County of Cornwall.	The whole Act.

SCHEDULE 1—*continued*

Chapter	Title or subject	Extent of repeal
4 Geo. 4. c. 75 (1823).	An Act for enabling His Majesty to inclose Part of Kew Green, and for dividing and extinguishing Rights of Common over certain Lands in the Parish of Kew, in the County of Surrey.	The whole Act.
1 & 2 Will. 4. c. 50 (1831).	An Act to enable the Commissioners of His Majesty's Treasury to make a Conveyance of Fresh Wharf in the City of London.	The whole Act.
5 & 6 Vict. c. 78 (1842).	An Act for effecting an Exchange between Her Majesty and the Provost and College of Eton.	The whole Act.
6 & 7 Vict. c. 19 (1843).	An Act to empower the Commissioners of Her Majesty's Woods to appropriate to Building Purposes the Area of Thatched House Court, and to widen and improve Little Saint James's Street, in the Parish of Saint James Westminster.	The whole Act.
8 & 9 Vict. c. 104 (1845).	An Act to empower the Commissioners of Her Majesty's Woods to appropriate to building Purposes the Area of Darby Court, in the Parish of Saint James Westminster.	The whole Act.
21 & 22 Vict. c. 36 (1858).	An Act for releasing the Lands of the Commissioners for the Exhibition of 1851, upon the Repayment of Monies granted in aid of their Funds.	The whole Act.

PART XV

RAILWAYS

Chapter	Title or short title	Extent of repeal
31 Geo. 2. c. 22 (Pr.). (1757).	An Act for establishing Agreements, made between Charles Brandling Esquire, and other Persons, Proprietors of Lands, for laying down a Waggon Way, in order for the better supplying the Town and Neighbourhood of Leeds, in the County of York, with Coals.	The whole Act.

SCHEDULE 1—*continued*

Chapter	Title or short title	Extent of repeal
19 Geo. 3. c. 11 (1779).	An Act for rendering more beneficial [the Act 31 Geo. 2. c. 22].	The whole Act.
33 Geo. 3. c. 86 (1793).	An Act for amending and enlarging the Powers of Two Acts [namely, 31 Geo. 2. c. 22. 19 Geo. 3. c. 11].	The whole Act.
43 Geo. 3. c. xii (1803).	An Act for amending and enlarging the Powers of several Acts [namely 31 Geo. 2. c. 22, 19 Geo. 3. c. 11 and 33 Geo. 3. c. 86].	The whole Act.
5 & 6 Vict. c. 55.	Railway Regulation Act 1842.	Section 20, including that section as applied by any other enactment.
46 & 47 Vict. c. 34.	Cheap Trains Act 1883.	The whole Act, including the Act as applied by any other enactment.
11 & 12 Geo. 5. c. 55.	Railways Act 1921.	Section 14. In section 68, in subsection (1) the proviso, and subsection (3). Section 70 (2). In section 71 (1), the proviso. Section 86 (2). Schedules 3 and 9.
13 & 14 Geo. 5. c. 27.	Railway Fires Act (1905) Amendment Act 1923.	Section 4.
12, 13 & 14 Geo. 6. c. 11.	Railway and Canal Commission (Abolition) Act 1949.	Sections 6 and 7.
1 & 2 Eliz. 2. c. 13.	Transport Act 1953.	Section 24.
10 & 11 Eliz. 2. c. 46.	Transport Act 1962.	In section 57 (3) (*b*), the words " and section twenty-four of the Transport Act 1953 ".

PART XVI

RELIGIOUS DISABILITIES

Chapter	Short title	Extent of repeal
31 Geo. 3. c. 32	Roman Catholic Relief Act 1791.	The whole Act.
10 Geo. 4. c. 7.	Roman Catholic Relief Act 1829.	The preamble. Sections 2, 5 and 11. In section 16, the words from " or any office ", where they first occur, to " within this realm ". Sections 23 and 24.
30 & 31 Vict. c. 75.	Office and Oath Act 1867.	The whole Act.

SCHEDULE 1—*continued*

PART XVII

MISCELLANEOUS

Chapter	Title or short title	Extent of repeal
33 Hen. 8. c. 35 (1541).	The Bill for the Conduyettes at Gloucester.	The whole Act.
31 Geo. 2. c. 25 (1757).	An Act for establishing a free Market for the Sale of Corn and Grain within the City or Liberty of Westminster.	The whole Act.
32 Geo. 2. c. 61 (1758).	An Act for discharging the Inhabitants of the Town of Manchester, in the County Palatine of Lancaster, from the Custom of grinding their Corn and Grain, except Malt, at certain Water Corn Mills in the said Town, called the School Mills; and for making a proper Recompence to the Feoffees for such Mills.	The whole Act.
17 Geo. 3. c. 24 (1776).	An Act for expediting the Sale of Estates in Scotland belonging to the York Buildings Company, for the Relief of their Creditors.	The whole Act.
24 Geo. 3. Sess. 1. c. 19 (1783).	An Act for settling the Rates for the Carriage of Passengers and Goods for Hire to and from the Isle of Wight.	The whole Act.
39 Geo. 3. c. 34.	Partridges Act 1799.	The whole Act.
1 & 2 Vict. c. 43.	Dean Forest (Mines) Act 1838.	In section 56, the words from " subject to " to " signified as aforesaid ".
32 & 33 Vict. c. 10.	Colonial Prisoners Removal Act 1869.	In section 2, the words " or within British India ".
35 & 36 Vict. c. 94.	Licensing Act 1872.	Section 39.
38 & 39 Vict. c. 55.	Public Health Act 1875.	In Schedule 5, in Part III, in the paragraph relating to section 35 of the Act 35 & 36 Vict. c. 79 the words from " under " (where it first occurs) to " same, and "; and the paragraphs relating to section 37 of that Act.
52 & 53 Vict. c. 30.	Board of Agriculture Act 1889.	In Part II of Schedule 1, the entries relating to the London (City) Tithes Act 1879, the Commonable Rights Compensation Act 1882, the Allotments Act 1887, the Public Schools (Eton College Property) Act 1873, the Improvement of Lands (Ecclesiastical Benefices) Act 1884 and the Settled Lands Acts (Amendment) Act 1887.
63 & 64 Vict. c. 15.	Burial Act 1900.	The whole Act.
2 Edw. 7. c. 8.	Cremation Act 1902.	In sections 2 and 3, the definition of " burial authority ".
8 & 9 Geo. 5. c. 59.	Termination of the Present War (Definition) Act 1918.	The whole Act.

Schedule 1—*continued*

Chapter	Title or short title	Extent of repeal
9 & 10 Geo. 5 c. 20.	Scottish Board of Health Act 1919.	In Schedule 1, paragraphs 2 and 3.
10 & 11 Geo. 5. c. 5.	War Emergency Laws (Continuance) Act 1920.	The whole Act.
15 & 16 Geo. 5. c. 19.	Trustee Act 1925.	Section 69 (3). Schedule 1.
15 & 16 Geo. 5. c. 61.	Allotments Act 1925.	Section 3 (2).
24 & 25 Geo. 5. c. 36.	Petroleum (Production) Act 1934.	In the Schedule, the entries relating to the licences dated 16th December 1930 and 20th July 1931.
10 & 11 Geo. 6. c. 39.	Statistics of Trade Act 1947.	Section 19 (3).
14 & 15 Geo. 6. c. 39.	Common Informers Act 1951.	In the Schedule, the entry relating to the Partridges Act 1799.
15 & 16 Geo. 6 & 1 Eliz. 2. c. 31.	Cremation Act 1952.	Section 4.
4 & 5 Eliz. 2. c. 19.	Friendly Societies Act 1955.	Section 5.
4 & 5 Eliz. 2. c. 48	Sugar Act 1956.	Section 18 (7) and (8). Section 34. In section 35, subsection (1), and in subsection (2) the definition of " the Government ".
6 & 7 Eliz. 2. c. 70.	Slaughterhouses Act 1958.	The whole Act.
1964 c. 26.	Licensing Act 1964.	In Schedule 14, paragraphs 5 and 7.
1965 c. 36.	Gas Act 1965.	In section 28 (4), the proviso. Section 31 (2).
1965 c. 56.	Compulsory Purchase Act 1965.	In Schedule 6, the entry relating to the Local Government Act 1933.
1971 c. 17.	Industry Act 1971.	Section 1. In section 3 (2), the words " I or " and paragraph (*a*). Schedule 1. In Schedule 2, Part I, and in Part II the entries relating to the House of Commons Disqualification Act 1957 and the Transport Act 1968.
1971 c. 40.	Fire Precautions Act 1971.	In section 28 (5), the proviso.
1971 c. 66.	Friendly Societies Act 1971.	Section 11 (6).
1976 c. 16.	Statute Law (Repeals) Act 1976.	In Schedule 2, in Part I, in the entry relating to the Inebriates Act 1898, the words " and the Licensing (Scotland) Act 1959, section 160 ".
1976 c. 66.	Licensing (Scotland) Act 1976.	In section 50 (2), the words from " and an application " onwards.
1977 c. 49.	National Health Service Act 1977.	In Schedule 14, in paragraph 13 (1) (*b*), the word " 48 ". In Schedule 15, paragraphs 11 and 68.

Section 1

SCHEDULE 2

Amendments

School Sites Act 1841

1. In the proviso to section 14 of the School Sites Act 1841 for the words from " without " to the end substitute " unless the Secretary of State consents ".

School Grants Act 1855

2. In section 1 of the School Grants Act 1855 for the words from "the consent" to "writing" substitute "the Secretary of State gives his written consent".

Public Records Act (Northern Ireland) 1923

3.—(1) Section 12 of the Public Records Act (Northern Ireland) 1923 shall be renumbered so as to become section 12 (1) of that Act.

(2) The following subsection shall be added at the end of the resulting subsection, and shall accordingly be section 12 (2) of the said Act of 1923:—

"(2) Without prejudice to the foregoing provisions of this section, the provisions of this Act shall have effect in relation to copies of calendars prepared as mentioned in section 27 (5) of the Administration of Justice Act 1969 which have been removed to the Public Record Office in Northern Ireland, either before the commencement of that Act or in pursuance of a direction given under section 27 of that Act as they have effect in relation to Northern Ireland records.".

Section 2   SCHEDULE 3

CITATION OF ACTS

1. The Acts specified below (none of which has hitherto had a short title) may respectively be cited by short titles assigned to them in column 3.

Chapter	Title	Short title
1 Mar. Sess. 3 c. 4.	An Acte for thestablishing of thoffice of the L. Steward of the Quenes Majesties most Honourable Housholde.	The Lord Steward Act 1554.
52 Geo. 3. c. 123.	An Act for amending and enlarging the Powers of an Act passed in the Fiftieth Year of His Present Majesty, to enable His Royal Highness the Prince of Wales to grant Leases of certain Lands and Premises called Prince's Meadows, in the Parish of Lambeth in the County of Surrey, Parcel of His said Royal Highness's Duchy of Cornwall, for the purpose of building thereon.	The Duchy of Cornwall Act 1812.
17 & 18 Vict. c. 93.	An Act for the Exchange of the Office in Somerset House of the Duchy of Cornwall for an Office to be erected in Pimlico on the Hereditary Possessions of the Crown.	The Duchy of Cornwall Office Act 1854.

2.—(1) In the Short Titles Act 1896, in Schedule 1 in column 3 against the Act 5 Geo. 4. c. 82, for the words "The Clerk of Parliaments Act 1824" substitute the words "The Clerk of the Parliaments Act 1824".

(2) A corresponding change shall be made in any existing citation of that Act, but without prejudice to the validity of any citation not so amended.

Employment (Continental Shelf) Act 1978

(1978 c. 46)

An Act to make provision for the application of certain enactments
to employment connected with the exploration or exploitation
of areas of the continental shelf adjacent to areas designated
under the Continental Shelf Act 1964.   [31st July 1978]

General Note

This Act provides for the application of certain enactments to employment
connected with the continental shelf.

S. 1 states that the Employment Protection Act 1975, s. 127, shall apply to
employment connected with the exploration or exploitation of a petroleum field in
the continental shelf; s. 2 contains definitions; s. 3 gives the short title.

The Act received the Royal Assent on July 31, 1978, and came into force on
that date.

For parliamentary debates see *Hansard*, H.C. Vol. 949, col. 1184; Vol. 951, col.
95; Vol. 952, col. 1222; H.L. Vol. 394, cols. 313, 1677; Vol. 395, col. 651.

Powers to apply employment legislation

1.—(1) The employment to which section 127 of the Employment
Protection Act 1975 (power to extend employment legislation by Order
in Council) applies shall include employment for the purposes of any
activities connected with the exploration or exploitation, in a foreign
sector of the continental shelf, of a cross-boundary petroleum field.

(2) In relation to employment concerned with the exploration or
exploitation of a cross-boundary petroleum field, the powers to make
Orders in Council under—

(*a*) section 10 (5) of the Sex Discrimination Act 1975, and

(*b*) section 8 (5) of the Race Relations Act 1976,

in respect of designated areas shall be exercisable also in respect of
foreign sectors of the continental shelf.

Interpretation

2. In section 1 above—

"cross-boundary petroleum field" means a petroleum field that
extends across the boundary between a designated area and
a foreign sector of the continental shelf;

"designated area" means an area designated under section 1 (7)
of the Continental Shelf Act 1964;

"foreign sector of the continental shelf" means an area which
is outside the territorial waters of any State and within which
rights are exercisable by a State other than the United Kingdom with respect to the sea bed and subsoil and their natural
resources;

"petroleum field" means a geological structure identified as
an oil or gas field by the Order in Council concerned.

Short title

3. This Act may be cited as the Employment (Continental Shelf)
Act 1978.

Civil Liability (Contribution) Act 1978 *

(1978 c. 47)

ARRANGEMENT OF SECTIONS

An Act to make new provision for contribution between persons who are jointly or severally, or both jointly and severally, liable for the same damage and in certain other similar cases where two or more persons have paid or may be required to pay compensation for the same damage ; and to amend the law relating to proceedings against persons jointly liable for the same debt or jointly or severally, or both jointly and severally, liable for the same damage.   [31st July 1978]

General Note

Abbreviations

" The 1935 Act "	=	Law Reform (Married Women and Tortfeasors) Act 1935 (as amended by s. 1 (4) Fatal Accidents Act 1959).
" Report "	=	The Law Commission Report No. 79, ' Law of Contract, Report on Contribution,' March 9, 1977 (H.M.S.O.).
" Working Paper "	=	The Law Commission Working Paper No. 59, ' Contribution,' May 15, 1975 (H.M.S.O.).
" Senate ' Comments ' "	=	Memorandum submitted to the Law Commission, following publication of the Working Paper, by the Senate of the Inns of Court and the Bar.
" Contribution "	=	See below (" Introduction ").
P	=	Plaintiff
D1	=	First defendant sued by P. Throughout these annotations, D1 will represent the party seeking to recover contribution.
D2	=	Second defendant. D2 will represent the party from whom contribution is being sought. In the contribution proceedings D1 *v.* D2, D1 is a plaintiff and D2 a defendant.

* Annotations by D. M. Morgan, B.A., Lecturer-in-Law, University of East Anglia.

Introduction

"'Contribution'—a technical term in the law—is used to describe the distribution of the burden of financial responsibility among a number of persons responsible, in one way or another, for causing the damage which has to be compensated " *per* Lord Scarman (H.L. Deb. Vol. 395, No. 115, col. 247).

The common law rules of contribution—which cannot be the subject of detailed consideration here—generally would not permit one defendant who was held responsible for causing loss or injury to a plaintiff to recover by way of contribution any of the damages which he was required to pay from any other person similarly responsible to the injured party, unless they were liable to a " common demand " (*e.g.* joint lessees) (*Kendall* v. *Hamilton* (1879) 4 App.Cas. 504 (contract), which can itself be traced back to the complementary rule in tort, *Merryweather* v. *Nixan* (1799) 8 T.R. 186). The philosophy which lay behind these rules being that " no man [*i.e.* D1] can claim damages [from D2] when the root of the damages he claims is his own wrong " (*per* Lord Dunedin, *Weld-Blundell* v. *Stephens* [1920] A.C. 956 at 976). This rule was abolished in respect of tort by s. 6 of the 1935 Act, following a recommendation to that effect by the Law Revision Committee in their *Third Interim Report* (1934; Cmd. 4637, para. 7). In that same report, the Committee opined that if the resulting legislation was found to work satisfactorily for tort, then consideration should be given to extending the proposed reform to other areas of the law.

Background to the Act

On July 12, 1971, The Law Society and the General Council of the Bar drew the attention of the Law Commission to the " remedying of defects in the law of an isolated nature (which nevertheless may be of general importance) where no separate Bill is merited," and which they considered to be unsatisfactory. In para. 4 of their Memorandum, they noted that:

" Co-contractors and co-tortfeasors may claim contribution from one another but not where each of the two . . . is liable for breach of his separate contract. An extension of s. 6 of the Law Reform (Married Women and Tortfeasors) Act 1935 could be made."

The same situation also applied where both or one of the wrongdoers was a guarantor, surety, trustee or executor, although where appropriate, the terms of the relevant contract could ensure that one wrongdoer could recover an indemnity or contribution short of a complete indemnity from another wrongdoer. Nonetheless, the scope which was allowed by the law for wrongdoers other than tortfeasors left some intractable problems in the law of contribution.

The Law Commission Report (paras. 5–7) gave two examples of this. The first is taken from the reported case of *McConnell* v. *Lynch-Robinson* [1957] N.I. 70, arising under s. 16 (1) (c) of the Law Reform (Miscellaneous Provisions) Act (Northern Ireland) 1937, which is to the same effect as s. 6 (1) (c) of the 1935 Act.

P engaged D1, an architect, to draw plans and supervise the building work of a new house for P. *By a separate contract*, P engaged D2 to undertake the work. D2 in breach of contract, failed to damp course the house properly and D1, in breach of contract, failed to notice this error. P was forced to spend a substantial amount of money to rectify this, and sued D1. D1 failed to have D2 joined as a third party in the proceedings as it was held that P's claim lay in contract and not tort, and contractual contribution could only be ordered where D1 and D2 were liable *to the same demand* (*Deering* v. *Earl of Winchelsea* (1787) 2 Bos.Pul. 270).

An example of the second type of situation in which the problem arises might be where P's house falls down. Two persons are at fault, the architect (D1) who has breached his contract, and the local authority (D2) whose building inspector negligently approved the work for the house. D1 is in breach of contract, D2 is a tortfeasor. The 1935 Act applies only to two (or more) persons liable as tortfeasors, therefore, again, no contribution could be sought by D1 from D2.

These situations have long been regarded as gaps in the common law, although much of the harshness has been mitigated by Rules of the Supreme Court (*e.g.* R.S.C. Ords. 13, r. 1, and 19, r. 2; Ord. 14 r. 8; Ord. 81 rr. 1, 5) and generous interpretations by the courts. The Law Commission had also felt that this was an area of law which should be examined (see *First Programme* (1965) Law Com. No. 1; *Seventh Annual Report* (1972), Law Com. No. 50, para. 52), and they took the opportunity to do so in their 59th Working Paper entitled " Contribution."

This was followed by their Report (No. 79, 1977), which finally gave rise to a Bill, introduced into Parliament as a Private Member's Bill. Lord Scarman, welcoming the Bill into the House of Lords, indicated that the area of law which it was seeking to reform was "technical and archaic," and although of more obvious importance to practitioners,

> "... can be welcomed by the jurist because it makes a modest step towards breaking down conceptual differences of the law and emphasises that what matters in the law is function, that is, the achievement of justice."

(H.L. Deb., Vol. 395, No. 115, col. 250)

As is quite common nowadays, the Law Commission appended a Draft Bill to their report (Appendix C), but this has not been wholly accepted in the resultant legislation. This is important for two reasons. Firstly, as the Notes to individual sections will attempt to demonstrate, the final Act is not without its difficulties of interpretation, and at one point (see below, s. 1 (5)) the wording of the subsection may have produced a completely different result from that which was intended. Secondly, the Act does not go as far as some individuals and organisations would have liked. Two examples may be given. S. 2 (3) (*b*) deals with the effect on the contribution proceedings between D1 and D2 of the contributory negligence of P. Again, as will be seen from the Notes, the Law Commission's proposal was considered to be a second-best alternative. They had not felt able to recommend their preferred solution to this problem, because of the supposed effects which this might have had on other areas of law, particularly "discharge by breach" in the law of contract. The Senate did not agree. They noted in their "Comments" the Law Commission's provisional view (which is preferred in the Act), that contribution and contributory negligence should be dealt with separately. They continued, (para. 3):

> "We are not convinced that this is right. Both principles are concerned with the apportionment of loss or liability *and in practice both frequently fall to be considered in the same action.* The apportionment of liability for a plaintiff's loss, whether as between him and the defendant or defendants, on the one hand, or as between two or more defendants, on the other hand, appears to us to be no more than two facets of the same basic principle."

Their view, however, has not been accepted (see below, Notes to s. 2 (3)).

The second point at which the Act may lack comprehensiveness is with respect to foreign judgments. Cl. 2 of the original Bill, before amendment by the Standing Committee, made similar provision for contribution proceedings, D1 *v.* D2, where D1 had been ordered or agreed to pay P, in an external judgment, award or settlement (where neither P nor D1 need have been U.K. nationals). The Law Commission had not addressed themselves to the question, and this difficult and complex area had been introduced on Government advice. The Confederation of British Industry, in a letter to the promoter of the Bill, Mr. Geoffrey Pattie, M.P., had pointed out that the case for dealing with foreign judgments and the consequences of them was outweighed by the considerations against. They referred in particular to the negotiations currently taking place about the enforcement of judgments within the European Community as between the United Kingdom and America. The Lord Chancellor's Department was also known to be of the view that the inclusion of foreign judgments was unnecessary for the successful implementation of the main purposes of the Bill, and the clause was withdrawn during the Committee proceedings.

One final comment is appropriate here. The Law Commission rejected the ideas that any reform of the law of contribution should be initiated completely afresh without regard to s. 6 of the 1935 Act and the experience which that has afforded, and that the law of civil liability as a whole should be codified in the form presented by the Irish Civil Liability Act 1961, (No. 41 of 1961). In their Working Paper they gave their reasons for this (at para. 11).

First, Part III of the Irish Act (ss. 11–46), which is entitled "Concurrent Faults," deals with many procedural problems already covered by Rules of the Supreme Court, albeit in a different manner. Additionally, some provisions of the Irish law on contributory negligence (Irish Act, ss. 34–42) differ from those in England, Wales and Northern Ireland. Secondly, the Law Commission's opinion was that some provisions of the Irish Act detrimentally affect the position of P when there is more than one wrongdoer whom he may sue (*e.g.* s. 35 (1) (*g*) of the Irish Civil Liability Act 1961; *cf.* "Report," paras. 71–73). They considered that "any change in the law of contribution that reduced the present rights of the plaintiff would be retrograde" ("Report," para. 11 (d); cf. Law Revision Cttee., *Third Interim Report* (1934, Cmd. 4637, para. 12: "We suggest that in any amendment it should be made clear that the plaintiff is not to be obliged to sue more than one joint-tortfeasor, and is still to be entitled to recover the whole of his damages from anyone [sic] of the joint tortfeasors")).

Finally, and of greatest importance to the Law Commission, was the existence of the framework of contribution provided by s. 6 of the 1935 Act. Their conclusion, which most commentators would support, is that the provisions of the Act have worked well over the last 40 years, and therefore formed a suitable base for the extension of statutory rights of contribution.

The Bill received widespread support throughout its legislative passage, and despite the several observations made above is a welcome reform of the law. However, as has been mentioned, it appears not to be without its difficulties, and these will be explored below.

Content of the Act

S. 1 sets out the circumstances in which one person who is or may be liable in respect of damage may recover contribution from another similarly liable. S. 2 provides for the assessment of contribution in the proceedings brought under s. 1. S. 3 abolishes the residue of the common law rule that judgment obtained against D1 bars further action against D2 and s. 4 restates in broader terms the effect of s. 6 (1) (b) of the 1935 Act, which dealt with separate actions against separate defendants, and disincentives there provided to adopt this course of action. S. 5 details the Act's applicability to the Crown and s. 6 is the Interpretation section. S. 7 provides for certain savings and s. 8 extends the application of the Act to Northern Ireland, which had not initially been proposed. S. 9 and Scheds. 1 and 2 deal with the consequential amendments and repeals. S. 10 indicates the short title, commencement and extent of the Act.

Commencement

The Act, which received its Royal Assent on July 31, 1978, is to come into force on January 1, 1979 (s. 10 (2)). Nothing in the Act is to affect any case where the debt or damage in question occurred before the commencement date (s. 7(1)), and no contribution proceedings may be brought under the Act for breach of any obligation assumed before the Act comes into force (s. 7 (2)).

Extent

The Act, which is extended to Northern Ireland by provision of s. 8, does not extend to Scotland, except in so far as provided for in s. 1 (5) and (6).

Parliamentary debates

See H.L. Vol. 395, cols. 10, 245–255, 804–805; H.C. Vol. 943, col. 1925; Vol. 953, col. 2017; H.C. (Stand.Com. C), cols. 1–68.

Proceedings for contribution

Entitlement to contribution

1.—(1) Subject to the following provisions of this section, any person liable in respect of any damage suffered by another person may recover contribution from any other person liable in respect of the same damage (whether jointly with him or otherwise).

(2) A person shall be entitled to recover contribution by virtue of subsection (1) above notwithstanding that he has ceased to be liable in respect of the damage in question since the time when the damage occurred, provided that he was so liable immediately before he made or was ordered or agreed to make the payment in respect of which the contribution is sought.

(3) A person shall be liable to make contribution by virtue of subsection (1) above notwithstanding that he has ceased to be liable in respect of the damage in question since the time when the damage occurred, unless he ceased to be liable by virtue of the expiry of a period of limitation or prescription which extinguished the right on which the claim against him in respect of the damage was based.

(4) A person who has made or agreed to make any payment in bona fide settlement or compromise of any claim made against him in respect of any damage (including a payment into court which has been accepted) shall be entitled to recover contribution in accordance with this section without regard to whether or not he himself is or ever was liable in respect of the damage, provided, however, that he would have been liable assuming that the factual basis of the claim against him could be established.

(5) A judgment given in any action brought in any part of the United Kingdom by or on behalf of the person who suffered the damage in question against any person from whom contribution is sought under this section shall be conclusive in the proceedings for contribution as to any issue determined by that judgment in favour of the person from whom the contribution is sought.

(6) References in this section to a person's liability in respect of any damage are references to any such liability which has been or could be established in an action brought against him in England and Wales by or on behalf of the person who suffered the damage; but it is immaterial whether any issue arising in any such action was or would be determined (in accordance with the rules of private international law) by reference to the law of a country outside England and Wales.

GENERAL NOTE
Subs. (1)
The most obvious feature of this subsection, which introduces the "entitlement to contribution" is that the provisions of the Act extend only to those persons "jointly . . . or otherwise" liable for the same *damage,* thus leaving the existing common law rules for the recovery of joint *debts* unaltered. A common law right of indemnity may be created either by a contractual provision (see, *e.g. Arthur White (Contractors)* v. *Tarmac Civil Engineering* [1967] 1 W.L.R. 1508), or may be founded in quasi-contract. Such a case arises under a contract of guarantee, where D1 guarantees the liability of D2 to make payment to P. D2 defaults on his payment and D1 claims an indemnity from D2.

> "The essence of the rule is that there is a liability for the same debt resting on [D1] and [D2] and [D1] has been legally compelled to pay, but [D2] gets the benefit of the payment, because his debt is discharged, either entirely or *pro tanto,* whereas [D2] is primarily liable to pay as between himself and [D1]": *per* Lord Wright, *Brook's Wharf & Bull Wharf* v. *Goodman Bros.* [1937] 1 K.B. 534, 544 (cited "Working Paper," para. 16).

A similar situation arises where D1 claims in quasi-contract or equity a contribution from D2 which falls short of a complete indemnity. Here D1 must show that he and D2 are liable for the same debt, but that he (D1) has paid more than equity should require him to do. Here, the role of the court is to see that, "if, as between several persons or properties all equally liable at law *to the same demand,* it would be equitable that the burden should fall in a certain way, the court will so far as possible, having regard to the solvency of the different parties, see that, if that burden is placed inequitably by the exercise of the legal right, its incidence should be afterwards readjusted": *per* Clauson L.J., *Whitham* v. *Bullock* [1939]2 K.B. 81, 85.

These rules led to three particular difficulties, in that they could only be invoked where:
  (i) the liability was to the same (or common) demand—which in so far as it applies to damages is abolished by the present Act (s. 6 (1));
  (ii) the loss which was suffered by P could only be apportioned equally, and not equitably as between D1 and D2, unless, "the balance of responsibility is so

heavily tipped against D2 that a complete indemnity is justified " (" Report," para. 28, citing *Robertson* v. *Southgate* (1847) 6 Hare 536). Again, in respect of damages, this is removed by s. 6 (1) of the present Act;

(iii) judgment in favour of P against D1 barred any further action against D2. This was abolished by s. 6 (1) (*a*) of the 1935 Act in respect of defendant tortfeasors, and is abolished in respect of *both* damage and debts by s. 3 of the instant legislation.

In so far as the rules apply to debts, the rules relating to common demand and equal not equitable apportionment are not affected by this Act. The comments received by the Law Commission indicated that the rules noted above could work inequitably in relation to damages, hence the reforms introduced by the Act, but that as far as debts were concerned, they were thought to work reasonably well (see *Report*, paras. 28–29). However, there was not general agreement on this point, as may be conveniently illustrated by an example taken from the Senate " Comments ": " D1 and D2 are trustees of a will. D1 has been chosen because he is an old friend of the family. D2 is an accountant and, unlike D1, will benefit from a professional trustee charging clause in the will. It appears to us unjust that (as the law stands at present) liability for an honest, but erroneous, investment decision will, as between D1 and D2, lie on them equally " (para. 4. *Cf. Bahin* v. *Hughes* (1886) 31 Ch.D. 390).

In so far as these rules apply between co-trustees, the rule of equal contribution also applies (*Chillingworth* v. *Chambers* [1896] 1 Ch. 685; *Robinson* v. *Harkin* [1896] 2 Ch. 415), even where one of the co-trustees is a so-called passive trustee (*Bahin* v. *Hughes* (above)). This general rule is subject to three exceptions, namely (i) where the breach of trust has been committed on the advice of a solicitor-trustee (*Lockhart* v. *Reilly* (1856) 25 L.J.Ch. 697); (ii) where one trustee alone has received money into his own hands and made use of it to his benefit (*Bahin* v. *Hughes* (at p. 395)); (iii) where a trustee is also a beneficiary (*Chillingworth* v. *Chambers* (above)). In so far as these rules apply to damages, they are modified by the 1978 Act (ss. 1 (1), 6 (1)), but again, where a breach of trust incurs a debt for which the trustees are held liable, the former common law rules will still apply. As the Senate noted: " We also think that the same flexible rule (introduced by s. 2 (1) of the present Act) should apply to debts as well as damages. We see no good reason for distinguishing between the two " (*op. cit.* para. 4).

One further aspect of s. 1 (1) which is not specifically dealt with in that subsection is the same problem which arose under the interpretation of s. 6 (1) (*c*) of the 1935 Act. S. 1 (1) does not specify the time at which the liability which gives rise to the damage complained of must have arisen in order to give rise to contribution proceedings between D1 and D2, and it is submitted that s. 6 (1) is of no particular help on this question. It was suggested on debate that this is implicitly dealt with in subss. (2) and (3), and a proposed amendment to subs. (1) which would have brought it back to the solution proposed by the Law Commission (see Draft Bill, cl. 3 (1)) was defeated. Cl. 3 (1) of the Draft Bill provided: " Subject to the following provisions of this section, any person who is liable in respect of any damage suffered by another person *at the time when the damage in question occurs* may recover contribution from any other person who is liable in respect of the same damage *at that time* (whether jointly with him or otherwise)."

The italicised words have been omitted from the final Act, and subss. (2) and (3) have taken their place. It is submitted that although there were cogent reasons for this change of drafting, the position now achieved may not in fact be a different way of achieving the Law Commission's proposal, as was the suggestion on debate (see Stand.Com.C. cols. 1–24). (This one provision occupied more of the Committee's attention than any other single item.) This submission will be explored below (see notes to subss. (3) and (5), and the present annotations will deal only with the matter arising under subs. (1).

The explanatory notes provided by the Law Commission to their proposed cl. 3 (1) indicated that:

" Apart from extending the ambit of statutory contribution beyond tortfeasors, it makes it plain that whether a person is liable is to be determined at the time when the damage occurs. Thus a person seeking to recover contribution does not cease to be able to do so because his liability has been discharged by payment or compromise. Similarly a person from whom contribution is sought does not cease to be under an obligation to contribute because the claim against him by [P] is or has been held to be statute-barred or has been dismissed for want of prosecution." (Appendix C, cl. 3, Explanatory Note 3.)

Thus, the whole intention of what is now contained in s. 1 (1)–(3) of the 1978 Act was to overcome the wording of s. 6 (1) (c) of the 1935 Act, where similar problems had arisen over the issue of the time for ascertaining the liability of the party from whom contribution is sought (*i.e.* D2). S. 6 (1) (c) provided: " . . . any tortfeasor liable in respect of that damage may recover contribution from any other tortfeasor *who is, or would, if sued have been*, liable in respect of the same damage."

The difficulties had arisen over the interpretation to be given to the words " or would, if sued have been held liable." As Lord Keith of Avonholme pointed out in *Wimpey (George) & Co.* v. *B.O.A.C.* [1955] A.C. 169, 195, the wording of the section " . . . contemplates the possibility of an action by an injured party against a person liable as a joint tortfeasor and at the same time regards him as having been sued by the injured party in a hypothetical action in the past." The wording had been interpreted to mean that D2 would have been shown to be liable if sued by P " at the time most favourable to the plaintiff " (*per* Lord Reid in *Wimpey* at p. 190), or if sued " at any time " (*per* McNair J. in *Harvey* v. *O'Dell* [1958] 2 Q.B. 78, 109).

What the draftsmen wanted to avoid was the problem which had occurred, under s. 6 (1) (c) of the 1935 Act, whereby a cesser of liability after the damage had occurred, as between P and D2 (whether on limitation, dismissal for want of prosecution, or admission of liability by D1; the latter having been successfully argued by D2 as defeating a claim for contribution where D2 showed that neither he nor D1 were in fact liable; hence D1 could not recover a contribution (*J. P. Corry & Co.* v. *Clarke* [1967] N.I. 62)) could defeat D1's claim for contribution. The wording of s. 1 (2) and (3) is an attempt to avoid this type of difficulty, but whether it has been successful is, it is submitted, unclear (see below subss. (3) and (5)).

An example of a situation which *is* saved by the adoption of the present wording, which could have given rise to difficulties if the time for ascertaining liability arose at the time when the damage occurred, might be as follows:

P makes a contract with D2 which gives rise to liability on the formation of the contract. P is injured through the breach of contract and tortious action by D1 10 years later. The occurrence of the damage may in these circumstances be after the liability of D2 has ceased, whereas D1's liability arises only on the sufferance of damage by P. If liability and damage had to coincide as between D1 and D2, D1 may have found his entitlement to contribution defeated by a requirement that liability for the damage caused by D2's breach of contract occurred after D2's liability had ceased (for example, in a contractual provision limiting D2's liability to a specified period of time, assuming that this was held valid under the Unfair Contract Terms Act 1977, where applicable). This difficulty is avoided (see s. 1 (2) and (3)), by requiring there to be only some overlap in the liabilities of D1 and D2, and not a coincidence.

Subs. (2)

S. 1 (2) sets out the circumstances in which D1 will be entitled to claim contribution from D2. Notwithstanding that D1's liability has ceased to P, whether through judgment, settlement, or compromise within the limitation period—as between P and D1—if he was so liable immediately before his liability ceased he may recover a contribution. The proviso to the subsection is quite clear. (For example, if D1 settles or compromises a claim with P beyond the limitation period between P and D1, then he is *not* entitled to claim a contribution from D2.)

Subs. (3)

This provision, which sets out D2's liability to make a contribution to D1 is, it is submitted, the subject of clumsy drafting when read in the context of the rest of s. 1. This is enlarged on in the notes to s. 1 (5), suffice it for the present to indicate the *proposed* effect of s. 1 (3). The raison d'etre of the subsection is to overcome the problems encountered under s. 6 (1) (c) of the 1935 Act where D2 could show that his liability to P had been extinguished. The decision of the

House of Lords in *Wimpey* v. *B.O.A.C.* [1955] A.C. 169 was to the following effect: P sued D2. His claim was held statute-barred and was dismissed. P then successfully sued D1. D1 claimed a contribution from D2 who successfully pleaded that he had been held *not liable* in earlier proceedings, and therefore was not a tortfeasor " held liable " within the meaning of s. 6 (1) (c). The Court of Appeal, in *Hart* v. *Hall & Pickles* [1969] 1 Q.B. 405, distinguished *Wimpey*, and held that the same reasoning did not apply where P. *v.* D2 had been dismissed for want of prosecution.

The purported effect of s. 1 (3) is to reverse the decision in *Wimpey*, and to provide that other than where D2 has defeated P's claim " on the merits of the case " (see s. 1 (5)), his successful defence to P's action shall not operate as a bar to contribution proceedings. The proviso to this is that it shall be a defence to D2 in the contribution proceedings to show that the period of limitation or prescription for D1's contribution action (two years from the date of ascertainment of D1's liability, Limitation Act 1963, s. 4) has expired. It is not specified in the Act whether D1's action against D2 may also be dismissed for want of prosecution where D1 has been guilty of culpable delay in bringing the proceedings, but this would appear to be only reasonable (*cf. Slade & Kempton (Jewellery)* v. *N. Kayman* [1969] 1 W.L.R. 1285).

Subs. (4)

The purpose of this subsection is to overcome the difficulty created by the Court of Appeal's judgment in *Stott* v. *West Yorkshire Road Car Co.* [1971] 2 Q.B. 651. Its effect is to allow D1 to sue D2 for contribution even though he has made an out of court settlement or compromise with P, providing that the facts giving rise to D1's liability can be established. (The final wording of the subsection is somewhat curious. Amendment No. 23 (Stand.Com.C. col. 25), which was defeated, would have provided that the facts must give rise to a cause of action between P and D1 even though P may have been unable to *prove* D1 liable.) The difficulty posed by *Stott* was that the court sanctioned an out-of-court settlement as giving D1 an entitlement to recover from D2, obviously wishing to encourage such settlements, but also indicated that D1 would have to show that

(i) D2 was liable for the damage to P;

(ii) D1 *would have been liable* if P had sued him to judgment.

In *Stott*, D1 had not admitted liability, whereas in *Corry & Co.* v. *Clarke* [1967] N.I. 62, D1 had so admitted. The same problem arose in respect of each. D2 may have in his possession evidence of his *own* liability which would show that D1 was *not* liable. Thus D1 would not satisfy the second of the two requirements of *Stott*. The effect would be that D1, whose liability to P has not been established, has made a payment to P whereas D2, whose liability has been established, has made neither payment to P nor a contribution to D1. (Could D1 recover under the common law of restitution?: *cf. Kiddle* v. *Lovett* (1885) 16 Q.B.D. 605.) The subsection removes this anomaly, providing only that the settlement or compromise between P and D1 can be shown to have been made " bona fide." This, it appears, is not to be interpreted as " reasonable " (the wording used by s. 22 of the Irish Civil Liability Act, which deals with the same point), but is directed towards " collusive settlements " (*e.g. Corvi* v. *Ellis*, 1969 S.L.T. 350) and not to the quantum of the settlement. It was suggested that one of the main motivations behind the proviso was to exclude foreign law settlements in which case the wording of the section would not appear sufficiently wide. Matters which may be of importance here include the circumstances in which the settlement was made and the relationship between the settling parties, but not the amount of the settlement, which is not binding or conclusive in proceedings between D1 and D2 (see, *inter alia, Stott*).

However, this provision, when suggested by the Law Commission, was not universally welcomed. The Senate indicated (*op. cit.,* para. 8) that as far as claims in tort were concerned, no particular problems appear to have arisen; " In practice [for D2] to question D1's liability (as envisaged by *Stott*), will but rarely prove a fruitful avenue for exploration . . ."

In relation to claims in contract, however, the Senate thought that this provision was totally undesirable. " The factors which persuade D1 to settle a claim in contract are more likely to be extraneous to the strict legal issues than will usually be the case in tort. Take the case of *McConnell* v. *Lynch-Robinson* itself [see above,

" Background to the Act "]. Thus P may be an important client of D1 and one with whom it is politic for D1 to come promptly to terms. Further, there is in a commercial situation greater scope for collusion or the exertion of economic weight than in tort. We therefore consider it essential that in contract cases D2 should be able to avail himself, as against D1 of any legal or evidential point which D1 could have but—for whatever reason—did not, use against P."

There appears to be some force in this argument, and whether the requirement of bona fides is sufficient to protect D2 from such matters may be open to doubt. Clearly, where a settlement is being proposed by D1, on which he subsequently intends to found contribution proceedings, it will usually be advisable for him to ensure that D2 is kept fully aware of this fact. This does not, of course, overcome the possibility that subsequent to making the settlement, D1 may discover the existence of D2, thus leaving the precise ambit of s. 1 (4) to the courts.

One problem with which the Act does not, rather anomalously, deal also remains a problem at common law. Generally, it deals with the effect of a release of one of the defendants. Specifically, it may be seen by way of an example.

Example: D2 settles or makes a compromise with P, for £2,000, in the form of a " covenant not to sue " (for the importance of this, see below on the effect of a *release*, and *cf.* s. 3 of the Act). P, in a subsequent action against D1 recovers in full £5,000. Can D1 then sue D2 for further contribution?

S. 17 (1) of the Irish Civil Liability Act 1961 retains in force the old English common law rule that release of or accord with one concurrent wrongdoer discharges all the others if that release or accord indicates such an intention. The point is expressly left open by the silence of the 1978 Act. S. 1 (4) merely deals with the situation of a defendant settlor being entitled to recover contribution. S. 1 (3) indicates that D2 shall still remain liable to contribute " notwithstanding that he has ceased to be liable in respect of the damage."

It is submitted that this does not entirely cover the point at issue here. A release of one joint wrongdoer releases all the others, even though this was not the intention of the parties for P's cause of action is regarded as indivisible and release of one extinguishes the right on which that cause is based. (*Nicholson* v. *Revill* (1836) 4 A. & E. 675 (contract); *Duck* v. *Mayeu* [1892] 2 Q.B. 511 (tort)). A release has to be distinguished from a " covenant not to sue," which simply prevents the right of action against the defendant with whom the plaintiff makes the covenant (*Hutton* v. *Eyre* (1815) 6 Taunt. 289 (contract); *Duck* v. *Mayeu* (*supra*) (tort)). That this is still thought to be good law has been recently affirmed: *Cutler* v. *McPhail* [1962] 2 Q.B. 292, at 298.

The same rules as apply to releases also used to apply to judgment against one joint wrongdoer, even if that judgment was unsatisfied (*Kendall* v. *Hamilton* (1879) 4 App.Cas. 504 (contract), *Brinsmead* v. *Harrison* (1871) L.R. 7 C.P. 547 (tort)). The rule applied only to joint, and not joint and several contractors (*Blyth* v. *Fladgate* [1891] 1 Ch. 337 (*per* Stirling J. at 353)) based on the complementary rule in tort that it applied only to joint tortfeasors (*Brinsmead* v. *Harrison* (above)). These rules for judgment were modified in relation to tort by s. 6 (1) (*a*) of the 1935 Act which is extended by s. 3 of the 1978 Act to other causes of action (see below, s. 3, notes).

However, the wording of s. 6 (1) (*a*) of the 1935 Act and s. 3 of the 1978 Act refer only to " judgments," and not to releases, hence the importance, noted in the example given above, of the settlement taking the form of a " covenant not to sue," and not a full release. Lord Denning has gone as far as to suggest that the rule regarding release is obsolete (*Bryanston Finance* v. *de Vries* [1975] Q.B. 703 at 723), and the courts have shown their dislike of the doctrine of release by holding that a reservation of rights (*i.e.* a " covenant not to sue ") can be implied (*Gardiner* v. *Moore* [1969] 1 Q.B. 55). Release, therefore, it would appear, still operates to bar an action by P against other wrongdoers (cf. Salmond, " *Law of Torts*," 17th ed. (1977) p. 443, footnote 68). Release, however, does not appear to bar an action by D1 for contribution in proceedings against D2. This was implicit in *Stott* v. *West Yorkshire Road Car Co.* [1971] 2 Q.B. 651, and now expressly provided for in s. 1 (4) of the present Act. But can this work in reverse and protect D2 from proceedings to make a contribution to D1 in the example noted above? The principle of contribution is that D2 should not be so protected, but this would defeat the object of D2 making a compromise with P. In America, the Uniform Act was specifically amended to ensure that a tortfeasor who settles in good faith is exempt from liability to contribute. The obvious effect of this was to encourage settlements. The Tasmanian Tortfeasors and Contributory Negligence Act 1954 provides a compromise, such that P's claim against other defendants is reduced, not by the amount paid by D2, but by what would have been D2's proper share (s. 3 (3)). (This assumes a larger importance when placed in the perspective of s. 4 of the 1978 Act which, so far as it applies to judgments, modifies the former provisions of s. 6 (1) (b) of the 1935 Act, to remove the rule that the amount recovered in the first judgment set a ceiling on further awards. Of course, this is merely to argue by analogy, for we are here concerned only with a release). There appears to be no case directly in point to solve the particular problem of D2's continuing liability, for s. 1 (3) was introduced ostensibly to deal with the limitation point discussed in the Notes to that subsection. As Fleming, *The Law of Torts*, 5th ed. (1978) p. 245 puts it: "In the absence of . . . a specific statutory mandate (contra U.S.A. and Tasmania), the question boils down to whether the courts would not feel bound to the view that a tortfeasor's liability to contribution remains as unaffected by a subsequent release as by effluxion of time." (The case of *Calderwood* v. *Nom.Def.* [1970] N.Z.L.R. 296 which he then cites as authority for the contrary view, he rightly criticises (*ibid.* footnote 11), and is now covered by s. 1 (3) of the 1978 Act).

Given these difficulties, it is to be regretted that neither the Law Commission nor the draftsmen considered the recommendation of the Senate ("Comments," para. 6): "We think it is a time to examine the rule that the release of one joint wrongdoer or contractor releases the others. Our provisional view is that the rule should also be abolished. This would rid the law of the highly technical—and, we feel, unmeritorious—distinction between a release and an agreement not to sue." There is, it is submitted, much force in this.

Judgment is no longer a bar to any action (s. 3), and neither judgment nor release affects the contribution proceedings (s. 1 (2), (3), (4)). However, if D2 makes a "covenant not to sue" with P rather than a release, D1 is not relieved of his liability to P, may subsequently be sued, and may recover a contribution from D2 (s. 1 (2) (3)). If, however, D2 makes a compromise with P which is seen as a full release, P cannot sue D1, and D2 may recover a contribution from D1. Caveat emptor!

Subs. (5)

The purported effect of this subsection is to provide a saving in respect of the provision introduced by s. 1 (3) of the Act (see above). The whole problem of what the Law Commission called "Double Jeopardy" was examined in paras. 60–67 of its Report. The question to be answered is if P sues D2 first, and then D1, should D1 be able to re-open any questions which the earlier case decided—for example, if D2 is found not liable for the damage suffered by P, should D1 be able, perhaps through adducing new evidence not available to P, to raise a fresh investigation of D2's liability? It has always been accepted that such subsequent proceedings do not form an example of res judicata; the contribution proceedings are a cause of action sui generis, and not dependent on the initial wrong for their implementation. The answer which s. 1 (5) gives to this question is that a "judgment . . . shall be conclusive in the proceedings for contribution as to any issue determined by that judgment in favour of [D2]."

Clearly, the intention of the Act is to avoid the situation which arose in *Wimpey*, to the effect that if P v. D2 was barred for limitation then D1 could not successfully sue D2 for contribution if D1 had subsequently been ordered to pay P. The reason for this is that D2, in the terms of s. 6 (1) (c) of the 1935 Act, was not a "tortfeasor who is, or would if sued have, been liable in respect of the same damage." This has been limited (see *Hart* v. *Hall & Pickles* [1969] 1 Q.B. 405, 411, 412), indicating that D2 should in such circumstances only have a defence to D1 where he has previously defeated P's claim "on the merits" of the case. The Law Commission's Draft Bill, cl. 3 (7) recommended the adoption of these words: "In any proceedings for contribution under this section the fact that a person has been held not liable in respect of any damage in any action brought by or on behalf of the person who incurred it shall be conclusive evidence that he was not liable in respect of the damage at the time when it occurred, provided that the judgment in his favour rested on a determination of the merits of the claim against him in respect of the damage (and not for example, on the fact that the action was brought after the expiration of any period of limitation applicable thereto)."

The present section provides that a judgment given in any part of the U.K. (thus including Scottish judgments) "shall be conclusive . . . as to any issue determined by that judgment in favour of . . . [D2]." It is submitted that this is neither as satisfactory as the Law Commission's proposal, nor, indeed, is it as secure from attack.

The subsection is phrased in mandatory terms "shall be conclusive," and not simply as to the issue of liability, but as to "any issue" determined. S. 1 (3) provides that D2 shall be liable to contribute notwithstanding that he has otherwise ceased to be so liable. But what is this liability? S. 6 (1) (see below) indicates that liability is to be established if the person who suffered it " . . . *is* entitled to recover compensation from him in respect of that damage." Take the following example. P sues D2; his claim fails because it is statute-barred. D2 *was once* liable to P, but no longer *is*, in other words he is *not liable* to compensate P. That is the order of the court (see, *inter alia, Lake* v. *Lake* [1955] P. 336), the reasons given do not form part of the judgment. The fact (if established) that D2 was once liable is not relevant. This therefore constitutes "an issue determined by that judgment in favour of D2," and is conclusive in his favour (s. 1 (5)). S 1 (3) provides that contributions may be sought from D2 "notwithstanding that he has ceased to be liable." D2 has not "ceased to be liable," he has been found *not* liable; P is *not* "entitled to recover compensation from him in respect of that damage" (s. 6 (1)), and D2 is therefore *not* "liable in respect of any damage for the purposes of this Act" (s. 6 (1)).

It is perhaps to be hoped that this interpretation, which is not strained, is not correct. It does not appear to be subject to the principle *generalia specialibus non derogante*, nor does it appear as a conflict of statutory interpretation between s. 1 (3), s. 1 (5) and s. 6 (1), nor would s. 1 (6) appear to offer an alternative to this solution (see below). If the above interpretation is correct, the wording which has been adopted by the draftsmen has, it is respectfully submitted, failed to achieve the desired objective. Indeed, it has had completely the reverse effect. If it remains open to a court to do so, it is to be hoped that some applications of the mischief rule may be applied to apparently inconsistent provisions. See Cross, "*Statutory Interpretation*" (1976), pp. 101–3. Nil desperandum!

Subs. (6)

This purports to define "liability" for the purposes of s. 1, as liability (see s. 6 (1)) which has or "could be established. . . .". It does not appear to cover the problem posed at s. 1 (5) (above), for liability could not be established if a defendant were sued beyond the period of limitation. To have afforded this escape to the difficulties of s. 1 (5), the relevant wording would have had to be "which has or could have been established. . . ."

Assessment of contribution

2.—(1) Subject to subsection (3) below, in any proceedings for conbution under section 1 above the amount of the contribution recoverable from any person shall be such as may be found by the court to be just and equitable having regard to the extent of that person's responsibility for the damage in question.

(2) Subject to subsection (3) below, the court shall have power in any such proceedings to exempt any person from liability to make contribution, or to direct that the contribution to be recovered from any person shall amount to a complete indemnity.

(3) Where the amount of the damages which have or might have been awarded in respect of the damage in question in any action brought in England and Wales by or on behalf of the person who suffered it against the person from whom the contribution is sought was or would have been subject to—

  (*a*) any limit imposed by or under any enactment or by any agreement made before the damage occurred;

  (*b*) any reduction by virtue of section 1 of the Law Reform (Contributory Negligence) Act 1945 or section 5 of the Fatal Accidents Act 1976; or

(c) any corresponding limit or reduction under the law of a country outside England and Wales;

the person from whom the contribution is sought shall not by virtue of any contribution awarded under section 1 above be required to pay in respect of the damage a greater amount than the amount of those damages as so limited or reduced.

GENERAL NOTE
Subs. (1)

The provisions of s. 2 (1) remove the vestiges of the rule that contribution between joint wrongdoers who cause damage to P must be divided equally rather than equitably. The section adopts the wording of s. 6 (2) of the 1935 Act, that contribution may now be assessed on the basis of what the court decides to be " just and equitable, having regard to the extent of that person's responsibility for the damage in question." The interpretation of the words in the 1935 Act indicate that both the blameworthiness and the extent to which the act is directly connected with the damage are material in considering the apportionment of damage between D1 and D2 (*per* Lord Pearce, *The Miraflores and The Abadesa* [1967] A.C. 826, 845) and it is clear that neither causation nor culpability is to be the sole test. Most commentators appear to agree that what is important is that the court, taking a " common sense view of the facts" (Street, *Torts,* 6th ed. (1976) p. 450), " determine the degree of responsibility " (*Weaver* v. *Commercial Process Co.* (1947) 63 T.L.R. 466) which each defendant bears for the damage (*cf. Collins* v. *Hertfordshire County Council* [1947] K.B. 598, which suggests causation as the proper test. But see Chapman (1948) 64 L.Q.R. 26: " Causation is difficult enough; degrees of causation would really be a nightmare "). It should be noted that the same provisions do not apply to jointly incurred debts, so that the rule of equal contribution between debtors still applies, despite a Senate recommendation to the contrary.

Subs. (2)

The court, as under the 1935 Act, may contemplate D1 as being entitled to a complete indemnity from D2. An example is provided by *Adamson* v. *Jarvis* (1827) 4 Bing. 66, where an auctioneer sued by P in conversion was held entitled to a complete indemnity from D2, who purported to be, but was not in fact the owner of goods entered in the auction. The most (in) famous example of indemnity is, however, between master and servant, as illustrated by *Lister* v. *Romford Ice and Cold Storage* [1957] A.C. 555 (which, in fact, left open the point of whether an indemnity could have been given under the 1935 Act). It may be thought unfortunate that the particular relationship of employer-employee was not exempted from this provision in the statute, although some protection is afforded to the negligent employee by the decision of the Court of Appeal in *Morris* v. *Ford Motor Co.* [1973] Q.B. 792, that an agreement between employer and employee in an industrial setting, where subrogation against employees was unrealistic, contained an implied term excluding the employer's rights of subrogation.

Rights of indemnity may be provided by statute (for example s. 40 (2) of the Civil Aviation Act 1949) and s. 7 (3) (*a*) of this Act makes a specific saving in respect of express or implied contractual or other rights to indemnity.

Subs. (3)

This subsection provides that where D2's liability is subject to an upper limit by virtue of statute or an agreement made between D2 and P prior to the occurrence of the damage, or where P's damages are reduced under the statutory provisions regarding the contributory negligence of P *vis-à-vis* D2, then D2's liability to make a contribution to D1 shall be limited in accordance with the agreement or the damages so reduced.

The difficulties of legislating these particular provisions engaged the Law Commission in both its " Working Paper " and " Report " in detailed considerations of the possible alternative solutions open to them, and although a broad consensus of opinion was achieved with respect to " upper limits " (clauses regulating the payment of damages), different answers were favoured on the question of the effect of the plaintiff's contributory negligence. These two areas may call for greater investigation here.

(a) *Limitation of liability*

Where the contribution proceedings arising under the present Act are " mixed," *i.e.* where, for example, D1 is a contractor and D2's liability lies in tort, several important differences between the respective laws of contract and tort are pertinent to the problems of contribution.

As between any plaintiff, contractor and contractor/tortfeasor the rights and obligations which flow from the contract between P and D1 may differ widely from contract to contract, due to the existence, for example, of waivers of liability or limitations of liability by virtue of a liquidated damages clause. Additionally, although this may not arise frequently in practice, the innocent party to a broken contract may have remedies other than a claim for damages on the breach of contract. It could be argued that the existence of such matters, as between P and D1, should not affect the determination of proceedings between D1 and D2; since contribution is itself a device for adjusting the equities between D1 and D2, each should be able to benefit proportionally from the presence of the other. This presents one difficulty, and is a familiar problem in contribution issues: whether D1 should be worse off as a result of the existence of D2 than if D1's breach of obligation had alone caused damage to P. The Law Commission, however, clearly saw that D1's rights of contribution are derivative from P's original rights against D1, and are not independent rights (" Report," paras. 68–74). It is not appropriate here to consider fully whether this view is necessarily correct; it is, however, submitted that as far as contribution proceedings between tortfeasors and " mixed " contribution proceedings are concerned, D1's rights against D2 should be seen as rights *sui generis*, the only nexus between the defendants being the injury which they inflicted on P. In contribution proceedings between parties who have both contracted with P, the relationship may be somewhat different.

The Law Commission proposed three solutions to this problem, none of which embraced the possibility of disregarding the limitation clause in the contribution proceedings. Their preference, which finds statutory preference, was that the loss should be divided equally between D1 and D2 (assuming the court to have found both 50 per cent. to blame), subject to the limitation on D1's overall liability set by the clause in the contract or provision in the statute. The whole balance would then fall on D2 (see Law Commission " Report," paras. 70–74, for their example of this mechanism working in practice).

(b) *Contributory negligence as a defence*

This becomes a particularly important issue in " mixed," contractual or breach of trust contribution cases, because it raises the question, which the Law Commission and now the present Act have chosen to avoid, of the extent to which contributory negligence is a defence to causes of action other than in tort. The argument put forward by Williams, *Joint Torts and Contributory Negligence* (1951), that " fault," as defined in s. 4 of the Law Reform (Contributory Negligence) Act 1945, includes all negligence, whether tortious or contractual, and all other acts or omissions giving rise to liability in tort, thus making the defence available in (*e.g.*) contract claims, has found some judicial and statutory favour (see *Sayers* v. *Harlow Urban District Council* [1958] 1 W.L.R. 623; *Artingstoll* v. *Hewen's Garage* [1973] R.T.R. 197, 201; *De Meza* v. *Apple* [1974] 1 Lloyd's Rep. 508 (where the point was expressly left open on appeal [1975] 1 Lloyd's Rep. 498); para. 19 of Sched. 1 to the Trade Union and Labour Relations Act 1974 (claims for compensation for unfair dismissal); *cf.* s. 34 (1) of the Irish Civil Liability Act 1961). This being the case, the problems raised by contributory negligence are similar to those posed by a limitation of liability clause. The Law Commission recommended, however, that what appeared to them to be the most satisfactory solution, to allow contributory negligence to be pleaded as a partial defence to breach of contract, could not be introduced without a consequential reform in the law of contributory negligence itself (" Report," para. 30). There would also be repercussions in the substantive law of contract, for example, in relation to " discharge by breach " and the assessment of *quantum* of damage, and they felt obliged to follow an alternative course. Their view was not shared by the Senate, who commented (" Comments," para. 3): " The provisional view expressed by the Law Commission is that contribution and contributory negligence should be dealt with separately and that the reform of the law of contributory negligence raises questions of principle which are largely irrelevant to the present study. We are not convinced that this is right. Both principles are concerned with the apportionment of loss or liability and in practice both frequently fall to be considered in the same action. The apportionment of liability for a plaintiff's loss, whether as between him and the defendant or defendants, on the one hand, or as between two or more defendants, on the other hand, appears to us to be no more than two facets of the same basic problem."

However, this sensible view did not prevail, and the Law Commission's solution may be indicated by way of an example (" Report," para. 76) : P purchases a car from D1. The car has defective lights, and while driving one night, the lights suddenly go out, and P negligently drives into an obstacle, negligently left in the road by D2. *Vis-à-vis* D2, is 60 per cent. to blame. D1 and D2 are held equally liable. P suffers £1,000 loss.

The damages are to be divided equally between D1 and D2, subject to P's 60 per cent. blameworthiness *vis-à-vis* D2, if D2 had been sued alone (£1,000, for which if D2 is 40 per cent. liable = £400). D2's contribution is therefore limited to a ceiling of £400, which he pays, and D1 pays £600. The justification for this approach is that D1 if sued alone for breach of contract could have been held liable for all or none of the £1,000 damage, but it is submitted that this ignores the whole basis of the contribution proceedings, which arise because D1's breach of contract was *not* the sole cause of the total loss.

Proceedings for the same debt or damage

Proceedings against persons jointly liable for the same debt or damage

3. Judgment recovered against any person liable in respect of any debt or damage shall not be a bar to an action, or to the continuance of an action, against any other person who is (apart from any such bar) jointly liable with him in respect of the same debt or damage.

GENERAL NOTE

S. 3 extends the provision of s. 6 (1) (a) of the 1935 Act to all other causes of action other than tort, abolishing the common law rules that judgment was a bar to further action. The words " or to the continuance of an action," which do not appear in the 1935 Act, were inserted to avoid any possible doubt that such proceedings should not be affected by judgment in another action, as to which doubts had been expressed by Lord Denning M.R. in *Bryanston Finance* v. *de Vries* [1975] Q.B. 703, 722.

This is the only section of the Act which has any effect on proceedings for debts, as opposed to damage. This has been fully considered at s. 1(above).

Successive actions against persons liable (jointly or otherwise) for the same damage

4. If more than one action is brought in respect of any damage by or on behalf of the person by whom it was suffered against persons liable in respect of the damage (whether jointly or otherwise) the plaintiff shall not be entitled to costs in any of those actions, other than that in which judgment is first given, unless the court is of the opinion that there was reasonable ground for bringing the action.

GENERAL NOTE

This section replaces s. 6 (1) (b) of the 1935 Act but extends those provisions to all causes of action and removes the " sanction in damages " previously found in s. 6 (1) (b) of the 1935 Act, which used the award of damages in the first action brought by P as a ceiling for the award of damages in subsequent actions. One of the reasons behind introducing the sanction into the 1935 Act was that juries could not be relied on to assess damages in the same way (Law Reform Committee, *Third Interim Report* (1934), Cmd. 4637, para. 11; " Report," paras. 40–41). That difficulty has now largely passed, and with the possibilities of injustice which s. 6 (1) (b) of the 1935 Act was thought to represent, its abolition is a welcome reform. The " sanction in costs " remains as a way of encouraging consolidated actions, and Rules of the Supreme Court can be used to prevent the following situation from arising:

P *v.* D1   judgment (unsatisfied)
D1 *v.* D2   contribution
P *v.* D2   judgment

i.e. D1 has claimed contribution without paying P. D2 must here insist on payment by D1 to P before D2 pays D1, and can invoke the discretion of the court to stay execution of the judgment P *v.* D2 until P is paid by D1. See R.S.C., Ord. 47, r. 1 (1) (*a*).

An attempt was made in Standing Committee to introduce a new cl. 1 which would have provided that payment by D2 to D1 would have been a bar to subsequent proceedings against him by P. This clause was withdrawn, on the assurance that the Rules Committee would be asked to propose an amendment to Ord. 47, r. 1 (1) (*a*), which would deal specifically with contribution proceedings, to the effect that a person seeking enforcement of an award made in contribution proceedings could not do so without the leave of the court.

Supplemental

Application to the Crown

5. Without prejudice to section 4 (1) of the Crown Proceedings Act 1947 (indemnity and contribution), this Act shall bind the Crown, but nothing in this Act shall be construed as in any way affecting Her Majesty in Her private capacity (including in right of Her Duchy of Lancaster) or the Duchy of Cornwall.

Interpretation

6.—(1) A person is liable in respect of any damage for the purposes of this Act if the person who suffered it (or anyone representing his estate or dependants) is entitled to recover compensation from him in respect of that damage (whatever the legal basis of his liability, whether tort, breach of contract, breach of trust or otherwise).

(2) References in this Act to an action brought by or on behalf of the person who suffered any damage include references to an action brought for the benefit of his estate or dependants.

(3) In this Act " dependants " has the same meaning as in the Fatal Accidents Act 1976.

(4) In this Act, except in section 1 (5) above, " action " means an action brought in England and Wales.

GENERAL NOTE
Subs. (1)

This is the core of the Act, which extends the provisions introduced in respect of tortfeasors by the 1935 Act, to encompass other joint or otherwise wrongdoers (s. 1 (1)), whatever the basis of their legal liability, " whether tort, breach of contract, breach of trust or otherwise " or a mixture of any two or more of those. This will enable problems such as those posed by the Law Commission in their Report, paras. 5–7, to be overcome. It may be thought that these wider provisions will themselves give rise to some particular problems, discussed by the Law Commission's Working Paper at paras. 46–56. Two of these have already been dealt with, " Upper Limits " and contributory negligence, but the Law Commission observed two other areas of potential difficulty.

(a) *Remoteness of damage*

The Law Commission's conclusion (" Working Paper," para. 47) was that differences in the rules relating to remoteness of damage, particularly in respect of contract and tort, were unlikely to cause any practical difficulties. This was supported by bodies who submitted comments on the Working Paper, reinforcing the Law Commission's observation that even the 1935 Act had required tortfeasors to be liable for the *same* damage, and that contribution proceedings may only found a claim "in respect of the items [of damage] common to the two claims" (Working Paper, para. 47). This is adopted by s. 1 (1) of the 1978 Act, which provides that the defendants must be responsible for the same (*i.e.* same items of) damage.

(b) *Limitation of actions.*

The Law Commission concluded in their Report (para. 32), that no recommendations for change were called for in respect of limitation periods. The Limitation Acts do not apply in the same way to all defendants. For example, an action must be brought for fraud within six years of the discovery of the fraud, except for a fraudulent breach of trust, on which no time limit is set (*cf.* s. 2 (1) (*a*) and s. 26 of the Limitation Act 1939 with s. 19 (1) (*a*)).

Other difficulties were noted by the Law Commission ("Working Paper," para. 48), namely:

  (i) time starts to run for a breach of contract from the date of the breach, whereas in some torts it runs from the date of the damage;
 (ii) special periods of limitation are set for actions on certain kinds of contracts, *e.g.* art. 49, Sched. 1 to the Uniform Laws on International Sales Act 1967;
(iii) similarly, certain torts have special periods of limitation, *e.g.* different limitation periods applied to claims in tort against D1 and D2 in *George Wimpey & Co.* v. *B.O.A.C.*.[1955] A.C. 169.

At the time of publication of the Law Commission's Report, the Law Reform Committee was considering the whole question of periods of limitation, and their report "Law Reform Committee, Twenty-first Report. Final Report on the Limitation of Actions" (1977) Cmnd. 6923, was presented to Parliament in May 1977. They considered the Law Commission's Report in the general context of procedural problems, and they too felt that no suitable reforms could be recommended: "We are not convinced that the present law often causes hardship. That it can do so, as can limitation in other cases, must be admitted . . ." (Cmnd. 6923; para. 5: 10), but they saw no advantage in "tinkering" with the law to deal with the few practical difficulties which their research had indicated may occur. They also felt that the problem posed by the Law Commission in their Working Paper, paras. 31–35, was also extremely unlikely to arise in practice, and as a result, the optimism voiced by the Senate in their "Comments" ("We do not understand that s. 4 of the Limitation Act causes any particular difficulties, or works unjustly, in practice. We do not therefore think that any change is called for here. . . . We . . . think that in practice the difficulties spoken of are more theoretical than real " para. 10), was endorsed.

Subs. (3)

"*Fatal Accidents Act* 1976." Claims under the Fatal Accident Acts may be made on behalf of the deceased's spouse, parent, grandparent, child, grandchild, brother, sister, uncle, aunt, and—in the case of the last four relatives—their issue. Relationships by marriage are treated as blood relationships, a legally adopted child is treated as a natural child and an illegitimate child is treated as the legitimate child of his mother and reputed father. "Half" and "step" relationships are treated as full relationships.

Cf. the recommendation of the Pearson Commission (Royal Commission on Civil Liability and Compensation for Personal Injury (1978) Cmnd. 7054—1, para. 404) that the law in England, Wales and Northern Ireland, should be brought into line with that provided for in Scotland by the Damages (Scotland) Act 1976, Sched. 1 to which provides that the following shall be entitled to claim as a dependant:

  (*a*) any person who immediately before the deceased's death was the spouse of the deceased;
  (*b*) any person who was a parent or child of the deceased;
  (*c*) any person not falling within para. (*b*) above who was accepted by the deceased as a child of his family;
  (*d*) any person who was an ascendant or descendant (other than a parent or child) of the deceased;
  (*e*) any person who was, or was the issue of, a brother, sister, uncle or aunt of the deceased; and
  (*f*) any person who, having been a spouse of the deceased, had ceased to be so by virtue of a divorce.

Savings

7.—(1) Nothing in this Act shall affect any case where the debt in question became due or (as the case may be) the damage in question occurred before the date on which it comes into force.

(2) A person shall not be entitled to recover contribution or liable to make contribution in accordance with section 1 above by reference to any liability based on breach of any obligation assumed by him before the date on which this Act comes into force.

(3) The right to recover contribution in accordance with section 1 above supersedes any right, other than an express contractual right, to recover contribution (as distinct from indemnity) otherwise than under this Act in corresponding circumstances; but nothing in this Act shall affect—

(*a*) any express or implied contractual or other right to indemnity; or

(*b*) any express contractual provision regulating or excluding contribution;

which would be enforceable apart from this Act (or render enforceable any agreement for indemnity or contribution which would not be enforceable apart from this Act).

General Note

Subss. (1) and (2) deal merely with transitional matters and have no substantive effect. The Act will come into force on January 1, 1979 (s. 10 (2)), and for the purposes of subss. (1) and (2) that is the date by which those provisions are to be construed.

Subs. (3)

Subs. (3) substantially reproduces material previously contained in s. 6 (4) (*c*) 1935 Act. Provision (*a*) express or implied contractual rights of indemnity, ensure that the Law Commission's conclusion on these matters is implemented ("Report," para. 26); so that if D2 has a right of indemnity against D1, the contribution proceedings are not to be successful. (The principles of indemnity are cast fairly widely, and are discussed in the Report at paras. 16–17.) S. 7 (3) (*b*) is consequent upon the provisions of s. 2 (3) (*a*).

Any express contractual right of contribution is specifically excluded from the provisions of the Act by s. 7 (3) (see, *e.g. Arthur White (Contractors)* v. *Tarmac Civil Engineering* [1967] 1 W.L.R. 1508).

Application to Northern Ireland

8. In the application of this Act to Northern Ireland—

(*a*) the reference in section 2 (3) (*b*) to section 1 of the Law Reform (Contributory Negligence) Act 1945 or section 5 of the Fatal Accidents Act 1976 shall be construed as a reference to section 2 of the Law Reform (Miscellaneous Provisions) Act (Northern Ireland) 1948 or Article 7 of the Fatal Accidents (Northern Ireland) Order 1977;

(*b*) the reference in section 5 to section 4 (1) of the Crown Proceedings Act 1947 shall be construed as a reference to section 4 (1) of that Act as it applies in Northern Ireland;

(*c*) the reference in section 6 (3) to the Fatal Accidents Act 1976 shall be construed as a reference to the Fatal Accidents (Northern Ireland) Order 1977;

(*d*) references to England and Wales shall be construed as references to Northern Ireland; and

(*e*) any reference to an enactment shall be construed as including a reference to an enactment of the Parliament of Northern Ireland and a Measure of the Northern Ireland Assembly.

Consequential amendments and repeals

9.—(1) The enactments specified in Schedule 1 to this Act shall have effect subject to the amendments set out in that Schedule, being amendments consequential on the preceding provisions of this Act.

(2) The amendments specified in Schedule 2 to this Act are hereby repealed to the extent specified in column 3 of that Schedule.

Short title, commencement, and extent

10.—(1) This Act may be cited as the Civil Liability (Contribution) Act 1978.

(2) This Act shall come into force on 1st January next following the date on which it is passed.

(3) This Act, with the exception of paragraph 1 of Schedule 1 thereto, does not extend to Scotland.

SCHEDULES

SCHEDULE 1

Consequential Amendments

The Law Reform (Contributory Negligence) Act 1945

1. For section 5 (*b*) of the Law Reform (Contributory Negligence) Act 1945 (application to Scotland) there shall be substituted—

"(*b*) section 3 of the Law Reform (Miscellaneous Provisions) (Scotland) Act 1940 (contribution among joint wrongdoers) shall apply in any case where two or more persons are liable, or would if they had all been sued be liable, by virtue of section 1 (1) of this Act in respect of the damage suffered by any person."

The Public Utilities Street Works Act 1950

2. In section 19 (4) of the Public Utilities Street Works Act 1950 (indemnity in respect of damage by execution of works)—

(*a*) for the words " within the meaning of the Law Reform (Married Women and Tortfeasors) Act 1935 " there shall be substituted the words " suffered by the authority as a result of a tort "; and

(*b*) for the words " section six of that Act " there shall be substituted the words " section 1 of the Civil Liability (Contribution) Act 1978 ".

The Statute of Limitations (Northern Ireland) 1958

3. For section 10 of the Statute of Limitations (Northern Ireland) 1958 there shall be substituted the following section—

" Time-limit for claiming contribution

10.—(1) Where under section 1 of the Civil Liability (Contribution) Act 1978 any person becomes entitled to a right to recover contribution in respect of any damage from any other person, no action to recover contribution by virtue of that right shall be brought after the end of the period of two years from the date on which that right accrued.

(2) For the purposes of this Act the date on which a right to recover contribution in respect of any damage accrues to any person (in this subsection referred to as " the relevant date ") shall be ascertained as follows, that is to say—

(*a*) if the person in question is held liable in respect of that damage by a judgment given in any civil proceedings, or an award made on any arbitration, the relevant date shall be the date on which the judgment is given, or the date of the award, as the case may be;

(*b*) if, in any case not falling within the preceding paragraph, the person in question makes or agrees to make any payment to one or more persons in compensation for that damage (whether he admits any liability in respect of the damage or not), the relevant date shall be the earliest date on which the amount to be paid by him is agreed between him (or his representative) and the person (or each of the persons, as the case may be) to whom the payment is to be made;

and for the purposes of this subsection no account shall be taken on any judgment or award given or made on appeal in so far as it varies the amount of damages awarded against the person in question."

4. In section 8 (*e*) (iii) of that Act, and in section 50 (9) of that Act (as substituted by Article 4 (3) of the Limitation (Northern Ireland) Order 1976), for the words " by a tortfeasor under section 16 of the Law Reform (Miscellaneous Provisions) Act (Northern Ireland) 1937 " there shall be substituted the words " under section 1 of the Civil Liability (Contribution) Act 1978 ".

The Carriage by Air Act 1961

5.—(1) In section 4 (1) of the Carriage by Air Act 1961 (limitation of liability) paragraph (*a*) shall be omitted.

(2) In section 5 (2) of that Act, for the word " tortfeasors " there shall be substituted the words " persons liable for any damage to which the Convention relates ".

The Limitation Act 1963

6. For section 4 of the Limitation Act 1963 (time-limit for claiming contribution between tortfeasors) there shall be substituted the following section:—

" Time-limit for claiming contribution

4.—(1) Where under section 1 of the Civil Liability (Contribution) Act 1978 any person becomes entitled to a right to recover contribution in respect of any damage from any other person, no action to recover contribution by virtue of that right shall (subject to subsection (3) of this section) be brought after the end of the period of two years from the date on which that right accrued.

(2) For the purposes of this section the date on which a right to recover contribution in respect of any damage accrues to any person (in this subsection referred to as " the relevant date ") shall be ascertained as follows, that is to say—

(*a*) if the person in question is held liable in respect of that damage by a judgment given in any civil proceedings, or an award made on any arbitration, the relevant date shall be the date on which the judgment is given, or the date of the award, as the case may be;

(*b*) if, in any case not falling within the preceding paragraph, the person in question makes or agrees to make any payment to one or more persons in compensation for that damage (whether he admits any liability in respect of the damage or not), the relevant date shall be the earliest date on which the amount to be paid by him is agreed between him (or his representative) and the person (or each of the persons, as the case may be) to whom the payment is to be made;

and for the purposes of this subsection no account shall be taken of any judgment or award given or made on appeal in so far as it varies the amount of damages awarded against the person in question.

(3) Sections 22 (1) and 26 of the Limitation Act 1939 (which make provision for cases of disability, fraud and mistake) shall each have effect as if any reference therein to that Act included a reference to subsection (1) of this section, and section 2 (1) of the Limitation (Enemies and War Prisoners) Act 1945 shall be amended by adding at the end of the definition of " statute of limitation " the words " subsection (1) of section 4 of the Limitation Act 1963 ".

(4) In this section references to an action and to section 22 (1) or section 26 of the Limitation Act 1939 shall be construed as including references respectively to an arbitration and to the said section 22 (1) or, as the case may be, section 26 as applied to arbitrations by section 27 (1) of that Act; and subsections (3) to (7) of section 27 (which relate to the application of that Act to arbitrations) shall apply for the purposes of this section."

The Carriage of Goods by Road Act 1965

7. In section 5 (1) of the Carriage of Goods by Road Act 1965 (exclusion, as respects carriers, of the general law with respect to contribution between persons liable for the same damage), for the words from " section 6 (1) (c) " to " Northern Ireland) 1937 " there shall be substituted the words " section 1 of the Civil Liability (Contribution) Act 1978 ".

The Carriage by Railway Act 1972

8. In section 6 (2) of the Carriage by Railway Act 1972 (special provision with respect to actions against railway undertakings), for the words " section 6 (1) (a) of the Law Reform (Married Women and Tortfeasors) Act 1935 " there shall be substituted the words " section 3 of the Civil Liability (Contribution) Act 1978 ".

Section 9 (2)

SCHEDULE 2

REPEALS

Chapter	Short Title	Extent of Repeal
25 & 26 Geo. 5 c. 30.	The Law Reform (Married Women and Tortfeasors) Act 1935.	Section 6.
1 Edw. 8 & 1 Geo. 6. c. 9 (N.I.).	The Law Reform (Miscellaneous Provisions) Act (Northern Ireland) 1937.	Section 16.
8 & 9 Geo. 6. c. 28.	The Law Reform (Contributory Negligence) Act 1945.	Section 1 (3). In section 1 (5) the words " or contributions ".
10 & 11 Geo. 6. c. 44.	The Crown Proceedings Act 1947.	Section 4 (2) (including that section as it applies in Northern Ireland).
1948 c. 23 (N.I.).	The Law Reform (Miscellaneous Provisions) Act (Northern Ireland) 1948.	Section 2 (3). In section 2 (5) the words " or contributions ".
1958 c. 10 (N.I.).	The Statute of Limitations (Northern Ireland) 1958.	Section 74 (5).
7 & 8 Eliz. 2. c. 65.	The Fatal Accidents Act 1959.	Section 1 (4).
1959 c. 18 (N.I.).	The Fatal Accidents Act (Northern Ireland) 1959.	Sections 1 (4) and 3 (1).
9 & 10 Eliz. 2. c. 27.	The Carriage by Air Act 1961.	Section 4 (1) (a).
10 & 11 Eliz. 2. c. 43.	The Carriage by Air Act (Supplementary Provisions) Act 1962.	In section 3 (1), the words from " paragraph " to " and in ".
1964 c. 1 (N.I.).	The Limitation Act (Northern Ireland) 1964.	Section 4.
1972 c. 33.	The Carriage by Railway Act 1972.	Section 6 (6) (a).
S.I. 1977/1251 (N.I. 18.).	The Fatal Accidents (Northern Ireland) Order 1977.	In Schedule 1, paragraph 1 (2).

Homes Insulation Act 1978

(1978 c. 48)

An Act to provide for local authority grants towards the thermal insulation of dwellings.   **[31st July 1978]**

General Note

This Act provides for local authority grants towards thermal insulation of dwelling-houses.

S. 1 provides for grants to be made by local authorities towards the cost of thermal insulation of dwellings in accordance with schemes to be made by the Secretary of State; s. 2 relates to the financing of such grants; s. 3 relates to Northern Ireland; s. 4 gives the short title.

The Act received the Royal Assent on July 31, 1978, and came into force on that date.

For parliamentary debates see *Hansard*, H.C. Vol. 950, col. 951; Vol. 952, col. 888; H.L. Vol. 394, col. 1652; Vol. 395, col. 782.

Grants for thermal insulation

1.—(1) In accordance with such schemes as may be prepared and published by the Secretary of State and laid by him before Parliament, local authorities shall make grants towards the cost of works undertaken to improve the thermal insulation of dwellings in their areas.

(2) Schemes under this Act shall from time to time specify—

> (*a*) the insulation works for which grant is to be available and the descriptions of dwellings which are to qualify; and

> (*b*) the persons from whom applications are to be entertained in respect of different dwellings and categories of dwellings.

(3) The first such scheme shall be for the improved insulation of roof spaces and water supply; and the grant available under this scheme shall be, for any dwelling, 66 per cent. of the cost of the works qualifying for grant or £50, whichever is the lesser amount.

The Secretary of State may by order alter that percentage or money sum, or both.

(4) Under other schemes, the grant shall be such percentage of the cost of the works so qualifying, or such money sum (whichever is the lesser amount), as the Secretary of State may prescribe by order for each scheme.

(5) A scheme other than the first may provide—

> (*a*) for grants to be made only to those applying on grounds of special need; or

> (*b*) to be made, in the case of those so applying, on a higher scale prescribed by the order under subsection (4).

(6) For this purpose " special need " is to be determined by reference to such matters personal to the applicant as may be prescribed by the scheme, particularly age, disability, bad health and inability without under hardship to finance the cost of the works.

(7) In the administration of this Act, local authorities shall comply with any directions given to them by the Secretary of State (after consulting their representative organisations), particularly in matters relating to—

> (*a*) the way in which applications for grant are to be dealt with, and the priorities to be observed between applicants and different categories of applicants; and

(b) the means of authenticating applications, so that grant is only given in proper cases, and of ensuring that the works are carried out to any standard specified in the applicable scheme.

(8) The local authorities to make grants under this Act are—

(a) in Greater London—

(i) as regards dwellings in a general improvement area or housing action area declared by the Greater London Council under the Housing Acts, that Council, and

(ii) otherwise, London borough councils and the Common Council of the City of London;

(b) elsewhere in England and Wales, district councils and the Council of the Isles of Scilly; and

(c) in Scotland, islands and district councils.

(9) "By order" means by order made by statutory instrument with Treasury approval, and

(a) an order under section 1 (3) or (4) may be varied or revoked by a subsequent order under the subsection; and

(b) orders under either subsection shall be subject to annulment in pursuance of a resolution of the House of Commons.

Finance

2.—(1) Finance for the making of grants under this Act shall be provided to local authorities from time to time by the Secretary of State; and a local authority is not required, nor has power by virtue of this Act, to make grants in any year beyond those for which the Secretary of State has notified them that finance is committed for that year in respect of the authority's area.

(2) The Secretary of State shall, with Treasury approval, pay such sums as he thinks reasonable in respect of administration expenses incurred by local authorities in operating this Act.

(3) Any sums required by the Secretary of State for financing grants under this Act, or for making contributions under subsection (2) above, shall be paid out of money provided by Parliament.

Northern Ireland

3.—(1) An Order in Council under paragraph 1 (1) (b) of Schedule 1 to the Northern Ireland Act 1974 (legislation for Northern Ireland in the interim period) which states that it is made only for purposes corresponding to those of sections 1 and 2 of this Act—

(a) shall not be subject to paragraph 1 (4) and (5) of that Schedule affirmative resolution of both Houses of Parliament); but

(b) shall be subject to annulment by resolution of either House.

Citation and extent

4.—(1) This Act may be cited as the Homes Insulation Act 1978.

(2) Subject to section 3, this Act does not extend to Northern Ireland.

Community Service by Offenders (Scotland) Act 1978

(1978 c. 49)

An Act to make provision as respects the performance of unpaid work by persons convicted or placed on probation in Scotland; and for connected purposes.   **[31st July 1978]**

General Note

This Act provides for the performance of unpaid work by convicted persons or persons on probation in Scotland.

S. 1 sets out the circumstances in which the court may make a community service order; s. 2 states the contents of such an order and sets out to whom copies are to be sent; s. 3 sets out the obligations of the person to whom the order relates; s. 4 relates to procedure on the failure of an offender to comply with an order; s. 5 provides for amendment and revocation of community service orders; s. 6 deals with such orders relating to persons residing in England and Wales; s. 7 amends the Criminal Procedure (Scotland) Act 1975, ss. 183 and 384, to provide for community service orders; s. 8 provides for such an order to be made after failing to comply with a probation order; s. 9 inserts s. 27A into the Social Work (Scotland) Act 1968 relating to grants for community service orders; s. 10 empowers the Secretary of State to make rules regulating work under community service orders or probation orders; s. 11 states that the Secretary of State shall lay an annual report before Parliament on the working of such orders; s. 12 contains definitions; s. 13 contains financial provisions; s. 14 contains amendments; s. 15 gives the short title. The Act extends to Scotland only.

The Act received the Royal Assent on July 31, 1978, and shall come into force on a date to be appointed by the Secretary of State.

For parliamentary debates see *Hansard*, H.C. Vol. 949, col. 1363; Vol. 951, col. 846; H.L. Vol. 394, col. 290; Vol. 395, col. 321.

Community service orders

1.—(1) Subject to the provisions of this Act, where a person of or over 16 years of age is convicted of an offence punishable by imprisonment, other than an offence the sentence for which is fixed by law, the court may, instead of dealing with him in any other way, make an order (in this Act referred to as " a community service order ") requiring him to perform unpaid work for such number of hours (being in total not less than forty nor more than two hundred and forty) as may be specified in the order.

(2) A court shall not make a community service order in respect of any offender unless—

   (a) the offender consents;

   (b) the court has been notified by the Secretary of State that arrangements exist for persons who reside in the locality in which the offender resides, or will be residing when the order comes into force, to perform work under such an order;

   (c) the court is satisfied, after considering a report by an officer of a local authority about the offender and his circumstances, and, if the court thinks it necessary, hearing that officer, that the offender is a suitable person to perform work under such an order; and

   (d) the court is satisfied that provision can be made under the arrangements mentioned in paragraph (b) above for the offender to perform work under such an order.

(3) A copy of the report mentioned in subsection (2) (c) above shall be supplied to the offender or his solicitor.

(4) Before making a community service order the court shall explain to the offender in ordinary language—

   (a) the purpose and effect of the order and in particular the obligations on the offender as specified in section 3 of this Act;

   (b) the consequences which may follow under section 4 of this Act if he fails to comply with any of those requirements; and

   (c) that the court has under section 5 of this Act the power to review the order on the application either of the offender or of an officer of the local authority in whose area the offender for the time being resides.

(5) The Secretary of State may by order direct that subsection (1) above shall be amended by substituting, for the maximum or minimum number of hours specified in that subsection as originally enacted or as subsequently amended under this subsection, such number of hours as may be specified in the order; and an order under this subsection may specify a different maximum or minimum number of hours for different classes of case.

(6) An order under subsection (5) above shall be made by statutory instrument, but no such order shall be made unless a draft of it has been laid before, and approved by a resolution of, each House of Parliament; and any such order may be varied or revoked by a subsequent order under that subsection.

(7) Nothing in subsection (1) above shall be construed as preventing a court which makes a community service order in respect of any offence from—

   (a) imposing any disqualification on the offender;

   (b) making an order for forfeiture in respect of the offence;

   (c) ordering the offender to find caution for good behaviour.

Further provisions about community service orders

2.—(1) A community service order shall—

   (a) specify the locality in which the offender resides or will be residing when the order comes into force;

   (b) require the local authority in whose area the locality specified under paragraph (a) above is situated to appoint or assign an officer (referred to in this Act as " the local authority officer ") who will discharge the functions assigned to him by this Act; and (*c*) state the number of hours of work which the offender is required to perform.

(2) Where, whether on the same occasion or on separate occasions, an offender is made subject to more than one community service order, or to both a community service order and a probation order which includes a requirement that that offender shall perform any unpaid work, the court may direct that the hours of work specified in any of those orders shall be concurrent with or additional to those specified in any other of those orders, but so that at no time shall the offender have an outstanding number of hours of work to perform in excess of the maximum provided for in section 1 (1) of this Act.

(3) Upon making a community service order the court shall—

(*a*) give a copy of the order to the offender;

(*b*) send a copy of the order to the director of social work of the local authority in whose area the offender resides or will be residing when the order comes into force; and

(*c*) where it is not the appropriate court, send a copy of the order (together with such documents and information relating to the case as are considered useful) to the clerk of the appropriate court.

Obligations of persons subject to community service orders

3.—(1) An offender in respect of whom a community service order is in force shall—

(*a*) report to the local authority officer and notify him without delay of any change of address or in the times, if any, at which he usually works; and

(*b*) perform for the number of hours specified in the order such work at such times as the local authority officer may instruct.

(2) Subject to section 5 (1) of this Act, the work required to be performed under a community service order shall be performed during the period of twelve months beginning with the date of the order; but, unless revoked, the order shall remain in force until the offender has worked under it for the number of hours specified in it.

(3) The instructions given by the local authority officer under this section shall, so far as practicable, be such as to avoid any conflict with the offender's religious beliefs and any interference with the times, if any, at which he normally works or attends a school or other educational establishment.

Failure to comply with requirements of community service orders

4.—(1) If at any time while a community service order is in force in respect of any offender it appears to the appropriate court, on evidence on oath from the local authority officer, that that offender has failed to comply with any of the requirements of section 3 of this Act (including any failure satisfactorily to perform the work which he has been instructed to do), that court may issue a warrant for the arrest of that offender, or may, if it thinks fit, instead of issuing a warrant in the first instance issue a citation requiring that offender to appear before that court at such time as may be specified in the citation.

(2) If it is proved to the satisfaction of the court before which an offender appears or is brought in pursuance of subsection (1) above that he has failed without reasonable excuse to comply with any of the requirements of the said section 3, that court may—

(*a*) without prejudice to the continuance in force of the order, impose on him a fine not exceeding £50;

(b) revoke the order and deal with that offender in any manner in which he could have been dealt with for the original offence by the court which made the order if the order had not been made; or

(c) subject to section 1 (1) of this Act, vary the number of hours specified in the order.

Amendment and revocation of community service orders, and substitution of other sentences

5.—(1) Where a community service order is in force in respect of any offender and, on the application of that offender or of the local authority officer, it appears to the appropriate court that it would be in the interests of justice to do so having regard to circumstances which have arisen since the order was made, that court may—

(a) extend, in relation to the order, the period of twelve months specified in section 3 (2) of this Act;

(b) subject to section 1 (1) of this Act, vary the number of hours specified in the order;

(c) revoke the order; or

(d) revoke the order and deal with the offender for the original offence in any manner in which he could have been dealt with for that offence by the court which made the order if the order had not been made.

(2) If the appropriate court is satisfied that the offender proposes to change, or has changed, his residence from the locality for the time being specified under section 2 (1) (a) of this Act to another locality and—

(a) that court has been notified by the Secretary of State that arrangements exist for persons who reside in that other locality to perform work under community service orders; and

(b) it appears to that court that provision can be made under those arrangements for him to perform work under the order;

that court may, and on the application of the local authority officer shall, amend the order by substituting that other locality for the locality for the time being specified in the order; and the provisions of this Act shall apply to the order as amended.

(3) Where the court proposes to exercise its powers under subsection (1) (a), (b) or (d) above otherwise than on the application of the offender, it shall issue a citation requiring him to appear before the court and, if he fails to appear, may issue a warrant for his arrest.

Community service orders relating to persons residing in England or Wales

6.—(1) Where a court is considering the making of a community service order under section 1 (1) of this Act and it is satisfied that the offender has attained the age of 17 years and resides, or will be residing when the order comes into force, in England or Wales, then—

(a) the said section 1 shall have effect as if for paragraphs (b) and (d) of subsection (2) there were substituted the following paragraphs—

" (b) the court has been notified by the Secretary of State that arrangements exist for persons who reside in the petty sessions area in which the offender resides, or will be residing when the order comes into force, to perform work under community service orders made under section 14 of the Powers of Criminal Courts Act 1973;

(d) it appears to that court that provision can be made under the arrangements mentioned in paragraph (b) above for

       him to perform work under the order made under sub-
       section (1) above; ";

(b) the order shall specify that the unpaid work required to be performed by the order shall be performed under the arrangements
mentioned in section 1 (2) (b) of this Act as substituted by
paragraph (a) above.

(2) Where a community service order has been made under the said
section 1 (1) and—

    (a) the appropriate court is satisfied that the offender has attained
the age of 17 years and proposes to reside or is residing in
England or Wales;

    (b) that court has been notified by the Secretary of State that
arrangements exist for persons who reside in the petty sessions
area in which the offender proposes to reside or is residing to
perform work under community service orders made under
section 14 of the Powers of Criminal Courts Act 1973; and

    (c) it appears to that court that provision can be made under those
arrangements for him to perform work under the order made
under the said section 1 (1),

it may amend the order by specifying that the unpaid work required to
be performed by the order shall be performed under the arrangements
mentioned in paragraph (b) of this subsection.

(3) Schedule 1 to this Act shall have effect in relation to a community service order made or amended by virtue of this section.

Requirement that probationer shall perform unpaid work

7. In each of sections 183 and 384 of the 1975 Act (probation)—

    (a) in subsection (4) after word " considers " there shall be
inserted " (a) " and at the end of the subsection there shall
be added the words " or (b) where the probation order is to
include such a requirement as is mentioned in subsection (5A)
below, conducive to securing or preventing the aforesaid
matters ";

    (b) after subsection (5) there shall be inserted the following sub-
section—

        " (5A) Without prejudice to the generality of subsection
(4) above, where a court which is considering making a probation order—

        (a) is satisfied that the offender is of or over 16 years of
age and has committed an offence punishable with
imprisonment and that the conditions for the making of
a community service order under the Community Service by Offenders (Scotland) Act 1978 specified in
paragraphs (a) and (b) of section 1 (2) of that Act
have been met;

        (b) has been notified by the Secretary of State that
arrangements exist for persons who reside in the
locality where the offender resides, or will be residing
when the order comes into force, to perform unpaid
work as a requirement of a probation order; and

        (c) is satisfied that provision can be made under the
arrangements mentioned in paragraph (b) above for
the offender to perform unpaid work under the
probation order,

    it may include in the probation order, in addition to any other
requirements, a requirement that the offender shall perform
unpaid work for such number of hours (being in total not less

than forty nor more than two hundred and forty) as may be specified in the probation order; and the said Act of 1978 shall apply to a probation order including such a requirement as it applies to a community service order, but as if—

> (i) subsections (1), (2) (*b*) and (*d*) and (4) (*b*) of section 1 and sections 4 and 6 were omitted;
>
> (ii) in section 1 (5) for the words " subsection (1) above " there were substituted the words " subsection (5A) of section 183 or, as the case may be, 384 of the 1975 Act "; and
>
> (iii) any other necessary modifications were made.";

(*c*) in subsection (6) for " or (5) " there shall be substituted " (5) or (5A)".

Community service order may be made after failure to comply with requirement of probation order

8. In each of sections 186 (2) and 387 (2) of the 1975 Act (failure to comply with requirement of probation order), at the end there shall be added—

" ; or

> (*d*) without prejudice to the continuance in force of the probation order, in a case where the conditions required by the Community Service by Offenders (Scotland) Act 1978 are satisfied, make a community service order, and the provisions of that Act shall apply to such an order as if the failure to comply with the requirement of the probation order were in respect of which the order had been made."

Grants in respect of community service facilities

9. After section 27 of the Social Work (Scotland) Act 1968 there shall be inserted the following section—

" Grants in respect of community service facilities

27A. The Secretary of State may make to a local authority grants of such amount and subject to such conditions as he may with the consent of the Treasury determine in respect of expenditure incurred by the authority in providing a service for the purposes mentioned in paragraph (*b*) of section 27 (1) of this Act in relation to persons mentioned in sub-paragraph (iii) of that paragraph.".

Rules

10.—(1) The Secretary of State may make rules for regulating the performance of work under community service orders or probation orders which include a requirement that the offender shall perform unpaid work.

(2) Without prejudice to the generality of subsection (1) above, rules under this section may—

(*a*) limit the number of hours' work to be done by a person under such an order on any one day;

(*b*) make provision as to the reckoning of time worked under such orders;

(*c*) make provision for the payment of travelling and other expenses in connection with the performance of work under such orders;

(*d*) provide for records to be kept of the work done by any person under such an order.

(3) Rules under this section shall be made by statutory instrument subject to annulment in pursuance of a resolution of either House of Parliament.

Annual reports to be laid before Parliament

11. The Secretary of State shall lay before Parliament each year, or incorporate in annual reports he already makes, a report of the working of community service orders.

Interpretation

12.—(1) In this Act—
    " the 1975 Act " means the Criminal Procedure (Scotland) Act 1975;
    " the appropriate court" means—
        (*a*) where the relevant community service order has been made by the High Court, the High Court;
        (*b*) in any other case, the court having jurisdiction in the locality for the time being specified in the order under section 2 (1) (*a*) of this Act, being a sheriff or district court according to whether the order has been made by a sheriff or a district court, but in a case where the order has been made by a district court and there is no district court in that locality, the sheriff court;
    " local authority " means a regional or islands council.
  (2) Except where the context otherwise requires, expressions used in this Act and in the 1975 Act shall have the same meanings in this Act as in that Act.
  (3) Except where the context otherwise requires, any reference in this Act to any enactment is a reference to it as amended, and includes a reference to it as extended or applied, by or under any other enactment, including this Act.

Financial provisions

13. There shall be defrayed out of money provided by Parliament any increase attributable to the provisions of this Act·in the sums payable out of such money under any other Act.

Minor and consequential amendments

14. The enactments specified in Schedule 2 to this Act shall have effect subject to the amendments there specified, being minor amendments and amendments consequential on the provisions of this Act.

Short title, commencement and extent

15.—(1) This Act may be cited as the Community Service by Offenders (Scotland) Act 1978.
  (2) This Act shall come into force on such a day as the Secretary of State may appoint by order made by statutory instrument; and different days may be appointed under this subsection for different provisions of this Act or for different purposes, or for the purposes of the same provision in relation to different classes of case.
  (3) Any order under subsection (2) above may make such transitional provision as appears to the Secretary of State to be expedient in connection with the provisions thereby brought into force.
  (4) Subject to subsection (5) below, this Act extends to Scotland only.
  (5) Section 6 (3) and this section and paragraphs 2, 3 and 5 of Schedule 1 extend to England and Wales.

SCHEDULES

SCHEDULE 1

COMMUNITY SERVICE ORDERS MADE OR AMENDED BY VIRTUE OF
SECTION 6

1. Section 1 (4) of this Act shall apply to a community service order made by virtue of section 6 of this Act as if—

(*a*) in paragraph (*a*) for the reference to section 3 of this Act there were substituted a reference to section 15 of the Powers of Criminal Courts Act 1973;

(*b*) in paragraph (*b*) for the reference to section 4 of this Act there were substituted a reference to section 16 of the said Act of 1973 as applied by paragraph 3 below and to paragraph 4 below;

(*c*) for paragraph (*c*) there were substituted the following paragraph—

" (*c*) the powers of the magistrates' court under section 17 of the said Act of 1973 as applied by paragraph 5 of Schedule 1 to this Act and of the court in Scotland under paragraph 6 of that Schedule.".

2. Subsection (1) (*a*) and (*b*) and (3) (*b*) and (*c*) of section 2 and sections 3 to 5 of this Act shall not apply to a community service order made or amended by virtue of the said section 6; but, subject to paragraphs 3 and 5 below, section 14 (4) and sections 15 to 17 of the said Act of 1973 shall apply to the order as if it were a community service order made under the said section 14.

3. Section 16 of the said Act of 1973 shall have effect in relation to an order made or amended by virtue of the said section 6 as if for subsections (3) to (7) there were substituted the following subsection—

" (3) If it is proved to the satisfaction of the magistrates' court before which an offender appears or is brought under this section that he has failed without reasonable excuse to comply with any of the requirements of section 15 of this Act, the court may, without prejudice to the continuance of the order, impose on him a fine not exceeding £50 or issue a summons requiring him to appear before the court in Scotland by which the order was made.".

4. A court in Scotland before which an offender has been required under section 16 (3) of the said Act of 1973 (as substituted by paragraph 3 above) to appear may—

(*a*) if he fails to so appear, issue a warrant for his arrest;

(*b*) in relation to the community service order, exercise the powers conferred on an appropriate court by section 4 (2) of this Act.

5. Section 17 of the said Act of 1973 shall have effect in relation to an order made or amended by virtue of the said section 6 as if—

(*a*) for subsections (2) to (4) there were substituted the following subsection—

" (2) Where, on the application of the offender or the relevant officer, it appears to a magistrates' court acting for the petty sessions area for the time being specified in the order that it would be in the interests of justice (having regard to circumstances which have arisen since the order was made or amended, as the case may be, by virtue of section 6 of the Community Service by Offenders (Scotland) Act 1978) that the order should be revoked or that the offender should be dealt with in some other manner for the offence in respect of which the order was made, the magistrates' court shall refer the case to the court in Scotland by which the order was made.";

(*b*) in subsection (7), the words " or (2) " were omitted.

6. A court in Scotland to which a case relating to a community service order has been referred under section 17 (2) of the said Act of 1973 (as substituted by paragraph 5 above) may, in relation to that order, exercise the powers conferred on an appropriate court by section 5 (1) (*b*), (*c*) or (*d*) of this Act:

Provided that, where the court proposes to exercise the powers conferred on an appropriate court by paragraph (*b*) or (*d*) of the said section 5 (1), it shall issue a citation requiring the offender to appear before it.

7. Where an offender who has been required under the proviso to paragraph 6 above to appear before a court in Scotland fails to do so, that court may issue a warrant for his arrest.

8. The court by which a community service order is made or amended by virtue of the said section 6 shall send three copies of the order to the clerk to the justices

for the petty sessions area specified therein, together with such documents and information relating to the case as it considers likely to be of assistance to the court acting for that petty sessions area.

<table>
<tr><td>Section 14</td><td>SCHEDULE 2</td></tr>
</table>

MINOR AND CONSEQUENTIAL AMENDMENTS

The Social Work (Scotland) Act 1968 (c. 49)

1. In section 27 (supervision of persons put on probation or released from prisons etc.)—
   (a) at the end of subsection (1) (b) (ii) add " and (iii) without prejudice to sub-paragraphs (i) and (ii) above, persons in the area who are subject to a community service order under the Community Service by Offenders (Scotland) Act 1978 or a probation order which includes a requirement that the offender shall perform unpaid work ";
   (b) for the words " probation scheme " wherever they occur substitute " probation and community service scheme."

The Criminal Procedure (Scotland) Act 1975 (c. 21)

2. In section 188 (1) (probation orders relating to persons residing in England or Wales), after " Act " insert " (not being a probation order including a requirement that the offender shall perform unpaid work)."

3. In section 389 (1) (probation orders relating to persons residing in England or Wales), after " Act " insert " (not being a probation order including a requirement that the offender shall perform unpaid work) ".

Inner Urban Areas Act 1978 *

(1978 c. 50)

ARRANGEMENT OF SECTIONS

An Act to make provision as respects inner urban areas in Great Britain in which there exists special social need; to amend section 8 of the Local Employment Act 1972; and for connected purposes. **[31st July 1978]**

General Note

The Inner Urban Areas Act 1978 received the Royal Assent on July 31, 1978. With the exception of s. 12, the Act extends to Scotland. It does not extend to Northern Ireland. The purpose of the Act is to give effect to some of the proposals contained in the White Paper *Policy for the Inner Cities* (Cmnd. 6845), published in June 1977.

Many of the inner areas surrounding the centres of our cities suffer, in a marked way and to an unacceptable extent from economic decline, physical decay and adverse social conditions. This economic decline is manifested by a loss of jobs, a high rate of unemployment, distortion in the population structure and in some cities, by extensive areas of disused land and buildings. The Inner Area Studies of parts of Liverpool, Birmingham, Lambeth and West Central Scotland (commissioned by the Government) underlined the erosion of inner area economies and the shortage within such areas of private investment which might assist the process of regeneration.

* Annotations by Victor Moore, LL.M., Senior Lecturer in Law, University of Reading.

The main thrust of the Act is to extend the powers of selected local authorities to assist industry so that it is encouraged to maintain existing operations in inner urban areas and, where possible, to extend them.

All local authorities have existing powers to encourage industrial growth. Under the Local Authorities (Land) Act 1963, for example, local authorities may make advances towards the cost of any building erected on land bought or leased from them. Again, under the Local Government Act 1972, an authority can offer an initial rent concession on the grant of a lease if the terms of the lease as a whole constitute the best terms that can reasonably be obtained. Also, some authorities have Private Act powers to extend their ability to assist industry. Under s. 262 of the Local Government Act 1972, however, powers in Private Acts dating from before April 1, 1974, will lapse (unless renewed) in 1979 or 1984.

In order to sustain existing employment and generate new, the Inner Urban Areas Act 1978, provides for the following additional powers to be given to selected authorities (each to be called a " designated district authority "), drawn from the two major tiers of local government, namely, county and district:—

(a) power to make loans of up to 90 per cent. on commercial terms for the acquisition of land and for carrying out building and site works (s. 2) ;

(b) power to give loans or grants towards the cost of setting up common ownership or co-operative enterprises (s. 3) ; and

(c) power to declare " improvement areas," either industrial or commercial in character, in which authorities can make loans or grants for environmental improvements and give grants for the conversion and improvement of industrial or commercial buildings (ss. 5 and 6).

In addition to the above powers, selected local authorities will be able, if the Secretary of State so directs, to adopt a local plan for an area before the structure plan for that area has been approved, provided the local plan is generally in line with the draft structure plan (s. 12).

The Act also provides the following three extra powers for other selected local authorities who have entered into an arrangement with the Secretary of State or other Ministers (under s. 7), for determining the action to be taken to alleviate conditions giving rise to special social need in any inner urban area:

(d) loans (which may be interest free for up to two years) for site preparation and the installation of services (s. 9) ;

(e) grants to assist with rents paid by firms taking new leases of industrial or commercial premises (s. 10) ; and

(f) grants towards loan interest paid on land and buildings by small firms employing under 50 staff (s. 11).

Parliamentary debates

For parliamentary debates see *Hansard*, H.L. Vol. 392, col. 603; Vol. 393, col. 681; Vol. 394, cols. 578 and 1312; Vol. 395, col. 794; H.C. Vol. 943, col. 1686; Vol. 948, cols. 1393 and 1517; Vol. 954, col. 1036.

Commencement

The Act came into force on July 31, 1978.

Designated districts

Designation of districts by Secretary of State

1.—(1) If the Secretary of State is satisfied—

(*a*) that special social need exists in any inner urban area in Great Britain; and

(*b*) that the conditions which give rise to the existence of that need could be alleviated by the exercise of the powers conferred by this Act,

he may by order specify any district which includes the whole or any part of that area as a designated district for the purposes of this Act.

(2) In this Act " designated district authority ", in relation to a designated district, means the council of that district or the council of the county or region which includes that district.

Definitions
  " county ": s. 17 (1).
  " designated district ": ss. 1 (1), 17 (1).
  " designated district authority ": ss. 1 (2), 17 (1).
  " district ": s. 17 (1).

General Note
   Under this section, if the Secretary of State is satisfied that special social need
exists in any inner urban area in Great Britain and that the conditions giving rise
to it could be alleviated by the use of powers under the Act, he may, by order,
specify the district which includes the whole or part of that area as a " designated
district." The designated district authorities are then the relevant district council
and the county council. In Scotland, the appropriate regional council, and in
Greater London the Greater London Council and the appropriate London Borough
Council, will also be designated district authorities where relevant.
   The Act does not spell out the criteria to be used by the Secretary of State in
selecting the districts to be designated. In a written answer to a Parliamentary
question on June 13, 1978, however, the Secretary of State said:
   " In determining the selection of . . . districts to be designated under the Inner
Urban Areas Bill, I have to make a judgment about the scale, intensity and con-
centration of the problems of individual districts."
   " Every urban area has a different combination of social and economic stress.
In some districts there are small areas of intense deprivation and dereliction while
in others problems are more evenly distributed. In some areas housing and social
difficulties predominate; in others unemployment is the main problem. I have had
to consider statistical data, much of which is only available for complete districts,
as well as other evidence."
   He then set out a table for those districts which he proposed to designate as
soon as the Bill received the Royal Assent, the basic data used in each case to
assess need. The table shows that the data includes under social/demographic
factors, matters such as estimated population loss or gain, serious overcrowding,
new commonwealth population, single parent families and pensioners. Economic
factors include unemployment, socio-economic groups on low incomes and day pupils
taking free meals. Physical factors include households lacking basic amenities and
derelict land (see H.C. Vol. 951, col. 468).

Subs. (1)
   Any order made under this subsection shall be made by statutory instrument,
the instrument being subject to the negative resolution procedure of either House
of Parliament (s. 15 (2)).

Loans for acquisition of or works on land
   2.—(1) Where a designated district authority are satisfied that—
     (a) the acquisition by any person of land situated within the
         designated district or within the same county or region as the
         designated district; or
     (b) the carrying out by any person of any works on land so
         situated,
would benefit the designated district, they may make a loan to that person
for the purpose of enabling him to acquire that land or, as the case
may be, carry out the works; but the council of a designated district
shall not make a loan as respects land situated in the same county or
region as that district without first consulting the council of the district
in which the land is situated.
   (2) A loan under this section, together with interest thereon, shall
be secured by a mortgage of the land or, in Scotland, by a standard
security over the land.
   (3) The amount of the principal of a loan under this section shall
not exceed—
     (a) in the case of a loan made for the purpose of enabling a person
         to acquire land, 90 per cent. of the value of the security;

(*b*) in the case of a loan made for the purpose of enabling a person to carry out works, 90 per cent. of the value which it is estimated the security will bear when the works have been carried out.

(4) Subject to subsection (5) below, a loan under this section shall carry interest either—

(*a*) at a rate not less than one quarter per cent. greater than the rate which, on the date of acceptance of the offer to make the loan, is the rate for the time being determined by the Treasury in accordance with section 5 of the National Loans Act 1968 in respect of local loans made on the security of local rates on that date and for the same period as the loan; or

(*b*) at such other rate as the Secretary of State may fix in the case of a loan.

In this subsection " local loans " and " made on the security of local rates " have the same meanings as in section 6 (2) of the said Act of 1968.

(5) Where, on the date of acceptance of an offer to make a loan under this section, there are two or more rates of interest for the time being determined by the Treasury as mentioned in subsection (4) above, the reference in that subsection to the rate so determined shall be read as a reference to such one of those rates as may be specified in a direction given by the Treasury for the purposes of this section; and the Treasury shall cause any such direction to be published in the London and Edinburgh Gazettes as soon as may be after giving it.

(6) A mortgage or standard security securing a loan under this section shall be taken at the time when the loan is made or, in the case of a loan made for the purpose of enabling a person to carry out works on land belonging to the authority in pursuance of an agreement whereby the land—

(*a*) will be sold or leased to him; or

(*b*) in Scotland, will be sold, leased or feued to him,

if the works are carried out to the authority's satisfaction, at the time when the land is sold, leased or feued to him in pursuance of that agreement.

(7) A mortgage or standard security securing a loan under this section shall include provision—

(*a*) for repayment being made, subject to paragraphs (*c*) and (*d*) below, within such period, not exceeding thirty years, as may be specified in the mortgage or standard security;

(*b*) for repayment being made, subject to paragraphs (*c*) and (*d*) below, either by instalments of principal or by an annuity of principal and interest combined;

(*c*) that, in the event of any of the conditions subject to which the loan is made not being complied with, the balance for the time being unpaid shall become repayable on demand by the authority;

(*d*) that the said balance, or such part thereof as may be provided for in the mortgage or standard security, may, in any event other than that specified in paragraph (*c*) above, be repaid on any conditions as may be specified in the mortgage or standard security after one month's written notice of intention to repay has been given to the authority;

(*e*) where repayment is to be made by an annuity of principal and interest combined, for determining the amount by which the annuity or the life of the annuity is to be reduced when a part of the loan is paid off otherwise than by way of an instalment of the annuity.

DEFINITIONS

" county ": s. 17 (1).
" designated district ": ss. 1 (1), 17 (1).
" designated district authority ": ss. 1 (2), 17 (1).
" district ": s. 17 (1).
" land ": s. 17 (1).

GENERAL NOTE

This section gives power to designated district authorities to make loans to any person for the acquisition of land or the carrying out of works on land. The amount of the principal of any loan so made must not exceed 90 per cent. of the value of the land. The loan must also be subject to the other terms and conditions prescribed in this section.

Before a district council for a designated district makes a loan in relation to land outside its own area, it must first consult the council for the district in which that land is situated.

Loans and grants for establishing common ownership and co-operative enterprises

3.—(1) Where a designated district authority are satisfied that the establishment by any persons of a body which is intended to meet the requirements of—

(*a*) paragraphs (*a*) to (*c*) of subsection (1) of section 2 of the Industrial Common Ownership Act 1976 (common ownership enterprises); or

(*b*) paragraphs (*a*) and (*b*) of subsection (2) of that section (co-operative enterprises),

would benefit the designated district, they may make a loan or a grant or both to those persons for the purpose of enabling them to establish that body.

(2) The Secretary of State may, either generally or with respect to particular cases, give directions as to the making of loans and grants under this section and, in particular, as to the imposition of conditions.

(3) Subject to subsection (2) above, a designated district authority, in making a loan or a grant under this section, may impose such conditions as they may think fit and may, in particular, impose a condition requiring the repayment of all or any part of the loan or grant—

(*a*) if any other condition is not complied with; or

(*b*) in such other circumstances as they may specify.

DEFINITIONS

" designated district ": ss. 1 (1), 17 (1).
" designated district authority ": ss. 1 (2), 17 (1).

GENERAL NOTE

This section gives power to designated district authorities to make loans or grants or both to persons wishing to establish a common ownership or co-operative enterprise intended to meet relevant requirements of the Industrial Common Ownership Act 1976. It is intended that the power be used mainly to provide financial assistance for professional, administrative and related expenses attendant upon the establishment of such an enterprise. Once established, other powers given to designated district authorities under the Act (*e.g.* under s. 2), may be exercised in favour of the enterprise.

The power is subject to the right of the Secretary of State to give directions as to how it is to be exercised. In addition, the designated district authority may impose conditions in giving any financial assistance.

Improvement areas

Declaration of and changes in improvement areas

4.—(1) The provisions of the Schedule to this Act shall have effect as respects the procedure for declaring areas to be, and for making changes in, improvement areas.

(2) In this Act " improvement area ", in relation to a designated district authority, means an area declared to be such an area by that authority.

DEFINITIONS
" designated district authority ": ss. 1 (2), 17 (1).
" improvement area ": ss. 4 (2), 17 (1).

GENERAL NOTE
This section and the Schedule to the Act enables any designated district authority to declare an area an " improvement area." The procedure for the declaration of such an area, for making changes to such an area and the functions of the Secretary of State with regard thereto are contained in the Schedule.

In order for an area to be declared an " improvement area," the designated district authority must be satisfied that the area is predominantly an industrial or a commercial area or both or that the area would be predominantly such if it were developed in accordance with the development plan, and that the conditions within it could be improved by the exercise of powers conferred by ss. 5 and 6.

For the powers of designated district authorities with regard to works on land situated within an " improvement area " see ss. 5 and 6.

Loans and grants for improving amenities

5.—(1) Where a designated district authority are satisfied that the carrying out by any person of any works mentioned in subsection (2) below on land situated within an improvement area would benefit that area, they may make a loan or a grant or both to that person for the purpose of enabling him to carry out those works.

(2) The works referred to in subsection (1) above are as follows—
(*a*) the construction of fencing or walls;
(*b*) landscaping and the planting of trees, shrubs and plants;
(*c*) the clearance or levelling of land;
(*d*) the cleansing of watercourses, whether natural or artificial, or the reclamation of land covered with water;
(*e*) the cleaning, painting, repair or demolition of structures or buildings; and
(*f*) the construction of parking spaces, access roads, turning heads or loading bays.

(3) Subsections (2) and (3) of section 3 above shall apply in relation to the making of loans or grants under this section as they apply in relation to the making of loans or grants under that section.

DEFINITIONS
" designated district authority ": ss. 1 (2), 17 (1).
" improvement area ": ss. 4 (2), 17 (1).
" land ": s. 17(1).

GENERAL NOTE
This section enables a designated district authority to make loans or grants for the environmental improvements specified in subs. (2) on land situated within an improvement area where the authority is satisfied the work would benefit that area.

Although no limit is placed by the Act on the financial assistance that may be given by the designated authority, the Secretary of State may give directions and he may impose conditions on the giving of assistance, as may the designated district authority.

Grants for converting or improving buildings

6.—(1) Where a designated district authority are satisfied that the carrying out by any person of any works mentioned in subsection (2) below on land situated within an improvement area would benefit that area, they may make a grant to that person for the purpose of enabling him to carry out those works.

(2) The works referred to in subsection (1) above are as follows—

(a) the conversion, extension, improvement or modification of industrial or commercial buildings; and

(b) the conversion of other buildings into industrial or commercial buildings.

(3) The amount of a grant under this section shall not exceed—

(a) 50 per cent. of the cost of carrying out the works; or

(b) £1,000, or such other amount as may be specified in an order made by the Secretary of State, for each job which, in the opinion of the authority, is likely to be created or preserved as a result of the carrying out of the works,

whichever is the less.

An order under this subsection may make different provision for different designated districts.

(4) Subsections (2) and (3) of section 3 above shall apply in relation to the making of grants under this section as they apply in relation to the making of grants under that section.

(5) In this section "industrial or commercial building" means a building in use or intended for use for industrial or commercial purposes.

DEFINITIONS

"designated district authority": ss. 1 (2), 17 (1).

"improvement area": ss. 4 (2), 17 (1).

"industrial or commercial building": s. 6 (5).

"land": s. 17 (1).

GENERAL NOTE

This section enables a designated district authority to make grants for the conversion and improvement of industrial or commercial buildings on land situated within an improvement area where the authority is satisfied the work would benefit that area. The amount of the grant is not to exceed the lesser of (a) 50 per cent. of the cost of the works, or (b) £1,000 or such other amount prescribed by the Secretary of State, for each job created or preserved by the carrying out of the works.

The Secretary of State may give directions as to the making of grants. He may also impose conditions on their making, as may the designated district authority.

Subs. (3)

Any order made by the Secretary of State shall be made by statutory instrument, it being subject to the negative resolution procedure of either House of Parliament (s. 15 (2)).

Arrangements for determining action

Power to enter into arrangements

7.—(1) If the Secretary of State is or Ministers are satisfied that special social need exists in any inner urban area in Great Britain and that the conditions which give rise to the existence of that need are such that a concerted effort should be made to alleviate them, he or they may, as respects any district which includes the whole or any part of that area, enter into arrangements with—

(a) the council of that district or the council of the county or region which includes that district or both; and

(b) such other person or persons (if any) as may appear to him or them appropriate,

being arrangements for determining, by consultation between the parties, the action to be taken (whether in the district or not) for the purpose of alleviating those conditions.

(2) Where each of two or more districts includes the whole or any part of any inner urban area as respects which the Secretary of State is or Ministers are satisfied as mentioned in subsection (1) above, arrangements under that subsection may take the form of a single set of arrangements covering both or all of those districts.

(3) In this section " Ministers " means the Secretary of State and any other Minister or Ministers of the Crown; and in subsection (1) above " action " includes the exercise of functions under this or any other Act (whenever passed) including, in particular, functions (whether of Ministers or councils) relating to planning or the compulsory acquisition of land.

DEFINITIONS
"action": s. 7 (3).
"county": s. 17 (1).
"district": s. 17 (1).
"Ministers": s. 7 (3).

GENERAL NOTE
This section provides that the Secretary of State (and other Ministers) may enter into arrangements with local authorities and other persons, both in designated districts and other areas, where he is (or they are) satisfied that conditions giving rise to the existence of special social need are such that concerted action should be made to alleviate them.

The action referred to includes the exercise of functions under the Act or under any other Act including, in particular, functions relating to planning or the compulsory acquisition of land (subs. (3)).

The purpose of the section appears to be to give Ministers specific statutory authority to participate in the action mentioned, where their participation might otherwise be regarded as being in conflict with their statutory duties in relation to such action.

Special areas

Orders specifying special areas

8.—(1) Where any arrangements have been entered into under section 7 (1) above as respects a designated district, the Secretary of State may, subject to subsection (3) below, by order specify the whole or any part of that district as an area as respects which the powers conferred by sections 9, 10 and 11 below shall be exercisable by the designated district authority, or, as the case may be, either or both of the designated district authorities with whom he has entered into those arrangements.

(2) In this Act an area so specified in relation to a designated district authority is referred to, in relation to that authority, as a " special area ".

(3) The Secretary of State shall not make an order under subsection (1) above enabling a designated district authority to exercise the powers conferred by sections 9, 10 and 11 below as respects a special area except with the consent of that authority.

DEFINITIONS
"designated district": ss. 1 (1), 17 (1).
"designated district authority": ss. 1 (2), 17 (1).
"special area": ss. 8 (2), 17 (1).

GENERAL NOTE

This section provides that where arrangements are made with a designated district authority under s. 7, the Secretary of State may specify the whole or part of the designated district as a "special area." Within such an area, the powers given to designated district authorities by ss. 9, 10 and 11 may be exercised.

Loans for site preparation

9.—(1) Where a designated district authority are satisfied that the carrying out by any person of any works mentioned in subsection (2) below on land situated within a special area would benefit that area, they may make a loan to that person for the purpose of enabling him to carry out those works.

(2) The works referred to in subsection (1) above are as follows—
  (a) the demolition of structures or buildings;
  (b) the removal of foundations;
  (c) the clearance of land;
  (d) the levelling of land;
  (e) the construction of access roads; and
  (f) the provision of sewers or drains.

(3) Where a designated district authority are satisfied that the carrying out by any statutory undertakers or other authority of any works for the provision of electricity, gas, water or sewerage services for land situated within a special area would benefit that area, they may make a loan to any person for the purpose of enabling him to make any payments required as a condition of the carrying out of those works.

(4) Subject to subsections (5) and (6) below, subsections (2) to (7) of section 2 above shall apply in relation to loans made under this section as they apply in relation to loans made under that section for the purpose of enabling a person to carry out works.

(5) In making a loan under this section, an authority may agree, if they think fit, that no interest shall be payable in respect of, and no repayments of principal shall be required within, such period beginning with the making of the loan and not exceeding two years as the authority may determine.

(6) The Secretary of State may, either generally or with respect to particular cases, give directions as to the making of loans under this section and, in particular, as to the imposition of conditions.

DEFINITIONS
  " designated district authority ": ss. 1 (2), 17 (1).
  " land ": s. 17 (1).
  " special area ": ss. 8 (2), 17 (1).

GENERAL NOTE

This section provides that designated district authorities may make loans for site preparation and the installation of services in special areas.

The loans may be free of interest and the repayment of principal may be delayed for a period of up to two years. Furthermore, the Secretary of State may give directions with regard to the making of loans. Subject to these provisions, the loan must comply with the terms and conditions prescribed in s. 2 (2) to (7).

Grants towards rent

10.—(1) Where a designated district authority are satisfied that the taking by any person of a lease of a building which—
  (a) is intended for use for industrial or commercial purposes; and
  (b) is situated within a special area,
would benefit that area, they may, in respect of such period and by such instalments as they may determine, make a grant to that person towards the rent payable under that lease.

(2) Subsections (2) and (3) of section 3 above shall apply in relation to the making of grants under this section as they apply in relation to the making of grants under that section.

DEFINITIONS
" designated district authority ": ss. 1 (2), 17 (1).
" special area ": ss. 8 (2), 17 (1).

GENERAL NOTE
This section gives a designated district authority power to make grants towards rents of industrial or commercial premises in special areas. The grants are payable to persons taking the lease. The Secretary of State may give directions as to the making of grants and may require the authority to impose conditions on them.

Grants towards loan interest

11.—(1) Where—
　　(a) a designated district authority are satisfied that the acquisition by a small firm of land situated within a special area, or the carrying out by such a firm of any works on land so situated, would benefit the special area; and
　　(b) a loan is made to the firm (whether by the authority or by any other person) for the purpose of enabling it to acquire that land or, as the case may be, carry out those works,
the authority may, in respect of such period and by such instalments as they may determine, make a grant to the firm towards the interest payable in respect of that loan.

(2) Subsections (2) and (3) of section 3 above shall apply in relation to the making of grants under this section as they apply in relation to the making of grants under that section.

(3) In this section " small firm " means an industrial or commercial undertaking which has no more than fifty employees.

DEFINITIONS
" designated district authority ": ss. 1 (2), 17 (1).
" land ": s. 17 (1).
" small firm ": s. 11 (3).
" special area ": ss. 8 (2), 17 (1).

GENERAL NOTE
This section enables a designated district authority to make a grant towards the interest payable in respect of any loan made to a small firm for the acquisition of land or the carrying out of works on land situated within a special area. A small firm is defined as an industrial or commercial undertaking with no more than 50 employees.
The Secretary of State may give directions as to the making of grants. He may also impose conditions on their making, as may the designated district authority.

Miscellaneous

Adoption of local plans

12.—(1) Where a local planning authority have prepared a local plan for the whole or any part of a designated district and the Secretary of State has not approved the structure plan so far as it relates to the area of that local plan, the authority may, if the Secretary of State so directs, adopt the local plan (and take such preliminary steps as are mentioned in section 12 (2) of the Town and Country Planning Act 1971) notwithstanding—
　　(a) that the structure plan has not been approved as aforesaid; and

(b) in the case of a district planning authority, that they have not obtained a certificate under section 14 (5) or (7) of that Act (certificate that local plan conforms generally to approved structure plan);

but before adopting the local plan, the authority shall make such modifications to it (if any) as may be necessary to make it conform generally to the structure plan as it stands for the time being.

(2) Where—

(a) a local planning authority have prepared or are proposing to prepare a local plan for the whole or any part of a designated district;

(b) the Secretary of State has approved the structure plan so far as it relates to the area of that local plan or proposed local plan;

(c) the Secretary of State has directed under section 10 (1) of the said Act of 1971 (alteration of structure plans) that proposals for alterations to the structure plan so far as it relates to the area of that local plan or proposed local plan should be submitted to him for approval; and

(d) proposals for those alterations have not been submitted to the Secretary of State, or have been submitted to the Secretary of State but have not been approved by him,

the Secretary of State may direct that such of the provisions of that Act mentioned in subsection (3) below as are applicable shall have effect as respects that local plan or proposed local plan as if proposals for those alterations had been so submitted and so approved or, as the case may be, so approved.

(3) The provisions of the said Act of 1971 referred to in subsection (2) above are as follows—

(a) section 11 (9) (proposals in local plan to conform generally to structure plan as it stands for the time being) and paragraph 11 (4) (a) of Schedule 4 (corresponding provision for Greater London); and

(b) section 14 (2) and (5) to (7) (local plan to conform, and certificate that it does conform, generally to approved structure plan).

(4) Before giving a direction under subsection (1) or subsection (2) above, the Secretary of State shall consult—

(a) the county planning authority whose area includes and the district planning authority whose area consists of the designated district; or

(b) in the case of a designated district in Greater London, the Greater London Council and the London borough council whose area consists of that district.

(5) This section shall apply in relation to a district (other than a designated district) as respects which arrangements have been entered into under section 7 (1) above as it applies in relation to a designated district.

(6) This section does not extend to Scotland.

DEFINITIONS
" designated district ": ss. 1 (1), 17 (1).

GENERAL NOTE
This section enables certain local authorities in England and Wales to adopt a local plan in advance of the approval or alteration of a structure plan, if the Secretary of State, after consultation with the appropriate authorities, so directs. The local authorities that may be subject to such a direction are those who have prepared a local plan for the whole or any part of a " designated district," and those who have prepared a local plan for the whole or part of a " non-designated " district and

who have entered into an arrangement with the Secretary of State or a Minister under the provisions of s. 7. The purpose of this provision is to reduce the risk of delay in developing an area with serious inner problems where the " old-style " development plan is out of date and a local plan for the area has been prepared but cannot be adopted until the structure plan for the area has been approved. Before adopting the local plan, the local planning authority must make such modifications to it as are necessary to ensure that it conforms generally to the structure plan as that plan stands for the time being.

Power to incur expenditure for certain purposes not otherwise authorised

13. The powers conferred by this Act on designated district authorities shall be in addition to that conferred on them by section 137 (1) of the Local Government Act 1972 or section 83 (1) of the Local Government (Scotland) Act 1973 (power of local authorities to incur expenditure for certain purposes not authorised by any other enactment); and accordingly those sections shall have effect as if this Act had not been enacted.

DEFINITIONS
   " designated district authority ": ss. 1 (2), 17 (1).

GENERAL NOTE
   This section declares that the powers conferred by the Act do not affect the general power conferred by s. 137 (1) of the Local Government Act 1972 or s. 83 (1) of the Local Government (Scotland) Act 1973 for local authorities to incur expenditure for the benefit of their area up to the product of a two penny rate.

Grants towards acquisition of or works on derelict and other land in Greater London

14. In subsection (4) of section 8 of the Local Employment Act 1972 (grants towards the cost of acquiring or carrying out works on derelict or other land) the following shall be inserted after the definition of " the appropriate minister ": —

> " ' county ' includes Greater London and ' district ' includes a London borough, and any reference to the council of a county or district shall be construed accordingly;".

GENERAL NOTE
   This section amends s. 8 of the Local Employment Act 1972 (grants towards acquisition of works on derelict and other land in Greater London) to enable grants under that section to be given in Greater London.

Orders and directions

15.—(1) Any order under this Act shall be made by statutory instrument, and may be varied or revoked by a subsequent order so made.

(2) A statutory instrument containing an order made under section 1 (1) or 6 (3) above shall be subject to annulment in pursuance of a resolution of either House of Parliament.

(3) It is hereby declared that any direction given under this Act may be varied or revoked by a subsequent direction so given.

Financial provisions

16. There shall be paid out of money provided by Parliament any increase attributable to this Act in the sums so payable under any other Act.

Interpretation

17.—(1) In this Act, unless the context otherwise requires—
   " county " includes Greater London and " district " includes a

London Borough, and any reference to the council of a county or district shall be construed accordingly;

" designated district " means any district specified as such a district by an order made under section 1 (1) above;

" designated district authority " has the meaning given by section 1 (2) above;

" improvement area ", in relation to a designated district authority, has the meaning given by section 4 (2) above;

" land " includes land covered with water, any interest in land and any easement, servitude or right in, to or over land;

" special area ", in relation to a designated district authority, has the meaning given by section 8 (2) above.

(2) Except so far as the context otherwise requires, any reference in this Act to an enactment shall be construed as a reference to that enactment as amended by or under any other enactment.

Short title and extent

18.—(1) This Act may be cited as the Inner Urban Areas Act 1978.

(2) This Act does not extend to Northern Ireland.

SCHEDULE

Section 4 (1)

Improvement Areas

Procedure for declaring area to be improvement area

1.—(1) Where a designated district authority are satisfied that conditions in an area within the designated district which—

   (*a*) is predominantly an industrial area, a commercial area or an industrial and commercial area; or

   (*b*) if developed in accordance with the development plan, would be predominantly such an area,

could be improved by the exercise of the powers conferred by section 5 or 6 above, the authority may, after consulting the other designated district authority, pass a resolution declaring the area to be an improvement area.

(2) A resolution under sub-paragraph (1) above shall specify the date on which it is to take effect, and that date shall not be earlier than the end of the period of three months beginning with the passing of the resolution.

(3) As soon as practicable after passing the resolution the authority shall—

   (*a*) publish a notice of the effect of the resolution identifying the area and naming a place or places where a copy of the resolution and a map on which the area is defined may be inspected at all reasonable times; and

   (*b*) send to the Secretary of State a copy of the resolution and a copy of the map.

Functions of the Secretary of State

2.—(1) If it appears to the Secretary of State appropriate he may—

   (*a*) at any time before a resolution under paragraph 1 (1) above takes effect, send to the authority a notification that all or any part of the area to which the resolution relates is not to be an improvement area;

   (*b*) at any time after a resolution under that paragraph takes effect, send to the authority a notification that all or any part of the improvement area is no longer to be such an area.

(2) A notification under sub-paragraph (1) (*a*) above shall take effect on the date on which it is received by the authority.

(3) A notification under sub-paragraph (1) (*b*) above shall specify the date on which it is to take effect, and that date shall not be earlier than the end of the period of six months beginning with the sending of the notification.

(4) As soon as practicable after receiving the notification the authority shall publish a notice of the effect of the notification naming a place or places where a copy of the notification and, in the case of a notification affecting a part only of the area, a map on which that part of the area is defined may be inspected at all reasonable times.

Termination of all or part of improvement area

3.—(1) At any time after a resolution under paragraph 1 (1) above takes effect, the authority may pass a further resolution declaring that all or any part of the improvement area is no longer to be such an area.

(2) A resolution under sub-paragraph (1) above shall take effect on the date on which it is passed.

(3) As soon as practicable after passing the resolution the authority shall—

    (*a*) publish a notice of the effect of the resolution naming a place or places where a copy of the resolution and, in the case of a resolution affecting part only of the area, a map on which that part of the area is defined may be inspected at all reasonable times; and

    (*b*) send to the Secretary of State a copy of the resolution and a copy of any map.

Publication

4. Any reference in this Schedule to publication of a notice is a reference to publication in two or more newspapers circulating in the locality, of which at least one shall, if practicable, be a local newspaper.

Savings

5. A notification under paragraph 2 (1) (*b*) above, or a resolution under paragraph 3 (1) above, shall not affect the continued operation of section 5 or 6 above in relation to any loan or grant the offer of which is accepted before the notification or resolution takes effect.

Scotland Act 1978 *

(1978 c. 51)

ARRANGEMENT OF SECTIONS

PART I

THE SCOTTISH ASSEMBLY AND EXECUTIVE

The Scottish Assembly

---

* Annotations by Professor A. W. Bradley and D. J. Christie, LL.B., Department of Constitutional and Administrative Law, University of Edinburgh.

An Act to provide for changes in the government of Scotland and in the procedure of Parliament and in the constitution and functions of certain public bodies. [31st July 1978]

General Note

Background

The Scotland Act 1978 and the Wales Act 1978 (c. 52) authorise schemes of devolution to Scotland and Wales. Together they constitute the most substantial reform to be made in the machinery of government in the United Kingdom for many years. The Royal Assent was given to the Scotland Act on July 31, 1978, but the scheme of devolution proposed by the Act will come into operation only when an order or orders to this effect have been made by the Secretary of State for Scotland (s. 83), and such orders cannot be made until after a referendum in Scotland has been held (s. 85 and Sched. 17). After that referendum has been held, the final decision on devolution will be a matter for Parliament, but if either less than 40 per cent. of the electorate have voted " Yes " or a majority of those voting have voted " No," the Secretary of State must lay before Parliament a draft Order in Council to repeal the Act (s. 85 (2)).

The immediate political background to the Act may be found in growing criticism during the 1960s of the machinery of government and in the electoral advance of the Scottish National Party from 1966 to October 1974, when 11 S.N.P. members were elected to Parliament. In 1969 the Labour Government decided that a Royal Commission on the Constitution be appointed, *inter alia*, " to examine the present functions of the central legislature and government in relation to the several countries, nations and regions of the United Kingdom " and to consider whether any changes were desirable " in those functions or otherwise in present constitutional and economic relationships." The majority report of the Commission was published in 1973 (Cmnd. 5460); it will be referred to in these notes as the Kilbrandon Report, after the name of its second chairman. Rejecting federalism and separatism, the report identified three forms of devolution (a) administrative devolution (corresponding to the existing administration of Scotland by means of the Scottish Office and the Secretary of State for Scotland); (b) executive devolution (under which a directly elected assembly in Scotland might be responsible for Scotland's domestic administration, in accordance with laws passed at Westminster); and (c) legislative devolution (under which both administrative and legislative powers would be devolved to a Scottish executive and legislature). Eight of the 13 members of the Commission favoured legislative devolution for Scotland. Notwithstanding many departures from the detailed proposals in the Kilbrandon Report, the Scotland Act 1978 embodies a scheme of legislative devolution which is based upon the majority recommendations in that report.

Two members of the Royal Commission signed a Memorandum of Dissent (Cmnd. 5460–I), which stressed the need for a uniform system of government throughout Great Britain and recommended elected assemblies for Scotland, Wales and five English regions, to be responsible for the execution of domestic policies within a framework of national laws.

The Labour Government's developing policy on devolution may be traced in a series of White Papers: *Devolution within the U.K., some alternatives for discussion,* 1974; *Democracy and Devolution, Proposals for Scotland and Wales,* Cmnd. 5732, September 1974; *Our Changing Democracy, Devolution to Scotland and Wales,* Cmnd. 6348, November 1975; and *Devolution to Scotland and Wales, Supplementary Statement,* Cmnd. 6585, August 1976. During the 1976–77 session of Parliament, the Scotland and Wales Bill (which also provided for executive devolution to Wales) began its progress through the Commons, but on February 22, 1977, the Government's " guillotine " motion for the allocation of 20 more days for the Bill's consideration in the Commons was defeated by 312–287 and the Bill thereafter made no further progress. On July 26, 1977, the Lord President of the Council made a statement of the Government's further proposals for devolution (*Hansard*, H.C. Vol. 936, col. 313).

In the 1977–78 session, the Government introduced separate Bills for Scotland and Wales and, although the Government did not have an absolute majority in the Commons, these Bills were successfully steered through Parliament. Limited time having been allocated to the Scotland Bill in the Commons, the House failed to consider many clauses of the Bill and it fell to the Lords to remedy this omission. Many but not all of the numerous amendments made by the Lords were rejected by the Commons on the recommendation of the Government.

Parliamentary debates

House of Commons: (*Hansard*, H.C.) *first reading*, Vol. 938, cols. 162–163 (November 4, 1977); *second reading*, Vol. 939, cols. 51–214 (November 14, 1977); *Comm.*, Vol. 939, cols. 1321–1484, 1534–1684; Vol. 940, cols. 267–428, 507–660, 1140–1288, 1410–1562;

Vol. 941, cols. 1446–1627, 1681–1821; Vol. 942, cols. 254–412, 470–601, 1195–1343, 1418–1556; Vol. 943, cols. 273–415, 490–626 (November 22, 23, 29, 30, December 6, 7, 1977, January 10, 11, 17, 18, 24, 25, 31, February 1, 1978); *Rept.*, Vol. 944, cols. 252–394, 450–609 (February 14, 15, 1978); *third reading*, Vol. 944, cols. 1445–1606 (February 22, 1978).

House of Lords: (*Hansard*, H.L.) *first reading*, Vol. 389, col. 234 (February 23, 1978); *second reading*, Vol. 389, cols. 1178–1353, 1365–1466 (March 14, 15, 1978); *Comm.*, Vol. 390, cols. 11–107, 114–160, 458–544, 547–614, 627–722, 728–776, 984–999, 1005–1073, 1087–1141, 1157–1171, 1176–1323, 1436–1605, 1617–1632, 1643–1709, 1739–1795; Vol. 391, cols. 178–268, 279–346, 367–440, 449–524, 791–892, 903–966, 982–1072, 1081–1146; Vol. 392, cols. 133–214, 220–299, 311–396, 408–472 (April 4, 11, 12, 18, 19, 24, 25, May 3, 4, 9, 10, 16, 17, 1978); *Rept.*, Vol. 392, cols. 1231–1310, 1313–1377, 1387–1463, 1473–1549; Vol. 393, cols. 11–166, 180–278, 291–308, 956–1057 (June 7, 8, 12, 13, 20, 1978); *third reading*, Vol. 394, cols. 378–463, 487–554 (June 29, 1978).

Commons' Consideration of Lords' Amendments: (*Hansard*, H.C.) Vol. 953, cols. 674–842; Vol. 954, cols. 49–220, 295–434 (July 6, 17, 18, 1978); *Lords' Consideration of Commons' Amendments and Reasons:* (*Hansard*, H.L.) Vol. 395, cols. 430–513, 548–605 (July 20, 1978); *Commons' Consideration of Lords' Amendments:* (*Hansard*, H.C.) Vol. 954, cols. 1593–1670 (July 26, 1978); *Lords' Consideration of Commons' Amendments and Reasons:* (*Hansard*, H.L.) Vol. 395, cols. 951–968 (July 27, 1978).

The Act in outline

The Act seeks to hand over to new Scottish institutions responsibility for much of the domestic government of Scotland, while at the same time seeking to maintain " the firm continuing framework of the United Kingdom " (*Our Changing Democracy*, Cmnd. 6348, p. 1). Legislative powers are to be devolved to a directly elected Assembly, and executive powers to a new Scottish Executive. Wide powers of administering the devolved services are conferred on the Scottish Executive, subject to control by the Assembly, but there is no comparable delegation of the power to raise revenue by taxation. The length and complexity of the Act are due mainly to two factors: (a) the elaborate detail with which the areas of devolved powers are defined; (b) the desire of the Government to establish controls and safeguards over the exercise of the devolved powers, in order to maintain the " political and economic unity " of the U.K.

Pt. I of the Act (together with Scheds. 1–6) establishes the machinery necessary for the creation of the new Assembly and the Scottish Executive. For the initial election of the Assembly, existing parliamentary constituencies will be used, each returning either two or three members according to the size of the electorate, except that Orkney and Shetland will each return one member (s. 1). For subsequent elections, existing constituencies will be divided into single-member Assembly constituencies, on the recommendation of the Boundary Commission for Scotland (s. 1 (4) and Sched. 1). Despite the recommendation in the Kilbrandon Report and the views of the House of Lords, a system of proportional representation will not be used. The Assembly will normally have a fixed life of four years (s. 2), but by a majority of two-thirds of its members the Assembly may require a dissolution within this period (s. 3). Assembly elections will be conducted according to the Representation of the People Acts as applied with modification by order of the Secretary of State for Scotland; peers resident in Scotland will be entitled to vote (s. 4). Ss. 5–16 make provision for certain essential matters relating to the procedure and composition of the Assembly, including by-elections (s. 5), the standing orders of the Assembly (s. 7), disqualifications from membership (ss. 8–11), resignation of members (s. 13), and the conferment of absolute privilege in the law of defamation upon Assembly proceedings and upon documents published by the Assembly (s. 15).

The legislative measures of the Assembly are to be known as Scottish Assembly Acts, when they have been passed by the Assembly (see s. 26) and approved by the Queen in Council. Within the Assembly's legislative competence, an Assembly Act may amend or repeal provisions made by or under an Act of Parliament (ss. 17–18). Certain important limitations upon the legislative competence of the Assembly are contained in Sched. 2; further details as to the extent of legislative powers are contained in Pt. IV of the Act and Sched. 10. By s. 19, if the Secretary of State considers that a Bill passed by the Assembly is not within the Assembly's legislative competence, or has doubts on this matter, he is to refer the question of competence to the Judicial Committee of the Privy Council; if he considers that an Assembly Bill is not compatible with the United Kingdom's EEC or other international obligations, or that legislation to implement such obligations should be passed by Parliament, he is to notify the Assembly accordingly and the Bill will not then become law.

S. 20 establishes the Scottish Executive: its members are to be the First Secretary and the other Scottish Secretaries, and these together with assistants to the Secretaries must be appointed from among members of the Assembly, except that the person appointed to exercise the functions of a law officer is not required to be a member of the Assembly (s. 20 (6)). Such of the Crown's executive powers as relate to devolved matters, and would, but for devolution, be exercisable on behalf of the Sovereign by a minister of the Crown, are to be exercisable in Scotland on behalf of the Crown by a Scottish Secretary (s. 21). Scottish Secretaries are also to exercise powers of delegated legislation concerning devolved matters which would otherwise be vested in ministers of the Crown, with Assembly procedures being substituted for existing parliamentary procedures of control (s. 22 and Sched. 3). Certain statutory powers are to be exercised by Scottish Secretaries with the consent of U.K. ministers (s. 23 and Sched. 4); other powers may be exercised both by the Secretary of State for Scotland and by a Scottish Secretary (s. 23 (3) and Sched. 5).

The Assembly's power to make standing orders regulating its own procedure (s. 7) is amplified by ss. 24–31 which, *inter alia*, require the Assembly to take account of the Crown's interest in certain classes of legislation (s. 24 and Sched. 6), to make provision for preserving order in the Assembly (s. 25), to provide for three main stages in the consideration of Assembly Bills (s. 26), to require the disclosure of members' pecuniary interests (s. 27), to provide for the reporting of Assembly debates (s. 29), and to secure the financial initiative of the Scottish Executive in financial legislation (s. 30). Moreover the Assembly has a wide power to appoint committees relating to devolved matters (s. 28). Finally, in this Part of the Act, ss. 32–34 provide for the clerk and other staff of the Assembly and for the remuneration of members of the Assembly, Scottish Secretaries and their assistants.

Pt. II of the Act governs relations between the new Scottish administration and U.K. authorities. Agency arrangements may be made for the provision of services by agreement between a Scottish Secretary, U.K. government departments and other public authorities (s. 35), and the Secretary of State may require information from Scottish Secretaries (s. 36). Orders in Council may be made amending the law in any part of the United Kingdom where this may seem necessary or expedient in consequence of any Assembly Act (s. 37). Ss. 38–41 give the Secretary of State an important group of reserve powers to intervene in matters devolved to Scotland. Thus he may decide that certain Assembly Bills affecting reserved matters should not in the public interest become law (s. 38); he may direct that executive action affecting certain reserved matters should or should not be taken (s. 39); and he may revoke delegated legislation made by the Scottish Secretary which affects reserved matters (s. 40). Whenever the Secretary of State exercises these powers to over-ride Scottish decisions, he must seek parliamentary approval for his action. The Secretary of State may also intervene to protect the special interests of the Orkney and Shetland Islands (s. 41). Industrial and economic guidelines prepared by the Secretary of State on such matters as the promotion of industrial and economic development by the Scottish Development Agency are to be binding upon the Scottish Executive (s. 42 and Sched. 7).

Pt. III (with Sched. 9) deals with financial arrangements for the devolved services. Two Scottish Funds are established—the Scottish Consolidated Fund and the Scottish Loans Fund—modelled on the U.K. counterparts. Management of these Funds is the responsibility of the Scottish administration, subject to the constitutional control exercised by the Scottish Comptroller and Auditor General (whose office is created by s. 54) and subject also to the appropriation of money by the Assembly (ss. 44–47). The main source of finance for the devolved services is to come from payments into the Scottish Funds by the Secretary of State, acting for the U.K. Government and with approval of the House of Commons (ss. 48 and 49). Borrowing and capital expenditure by the Scottish Secretaries are regulated by ss. 50–53. Separate accounting and auditing arrangements are made for the devolved services: the Scottish Comptroller and Auditor General will audit the accounts of the Scottish administration and report on them to the Assembly; and the Assembly must appoint an Accounts Committee to examine and report on these accounts (ss. 54–59).

Consisting only of three sections, Pt. IV must be read with three important schedules, Scheds. 10–12. By s. 63, the legislative competence of the Assembly extends to the matters included within 25 subject groups set out in Pt. I of Sched. 10; but Pt. I of Sched. 10 is itself subject to the later parts of the same schedule, namely Pt. II, which lists matters not included within the groups in Pt. I, and Pt. III, which tabulates a long list of statutory provisions and states expressly whether or not the matters in question are included within the groups listed in Pt. I. Sched. 11 lists matters which are within the administrative powers of the Scottish Executive but are not within the legislative competence of the Assembly. Certain reservations from the matters devolved (*e.g.* the prerogative of mercy and the conduct of relations with any country outside the U.K.) are made by s. 64.

S. 65 and Sched. 12 provide for the handling of " devolution issues " that may arise in proceedings before courts and tribunals in any part of the U.K. By " devolution issue " is meant two kinds of question: (a) whether a provision of an Assembly Act is within the legislative competence of the Assembly; (b) whether a matter on which a Scottish Secretary has acted or is proposing to act is a devolved matter. Pt. V contains miscellaneous matters. S. 66 is a response to the position that may arise after the Assembly has come into existence, when Scottish M.P.s at Westminster may vote on legislation relating to England although English M.P.s may not take part in the legislative work of the Assembly. By s. 67, civil servants working for the Scottish Executive are to be members of the U.K. civil service. S. 69 empowers a minister of the Crown to make orders affecting the composition, functioning and financing of the public bodies listed in Sched. III. S. 71 and Sched. 14 give powers of intervention to the Secretary of State in respect of certain town planning matters which otherwise are devolved to the Scottish Executive. Ss. 72–74 provide for the future ownership and control of government property used in connection with devolved functions. S. 76 authorises the making of temporary provision for the investigation of complaints of maladministration arising out of action taken by or on behalf of a Scottish Secretary.

Pt. VI, General and Supplementary, includes provisions relating to the making of orders by ministers of the Crown (s. 79), interpretation (s. 81), and the amendment of existing Acts by order of a minister of the Crown where it appears necessary or expedient in consequence of the Scotland Act 1978 (s. 82 and Sched. 16). The Scotland Act itself is not to come into operation until a day or days appointed by order of the Secretary of State (s. 83). Before the first such order is laid before Parliament a referendum of the electorate in Scotland is to be held (s. 85 and Sched. 17) but, if a general election is held first, at least three months must elapse before the referendum is held (s. 86). Within three months of the first commencement order being made to bring the Act into operation, the Secretary of State must appoint a commission to consider the future government of the Orkney and Shetland Islands (s. 84).

General Comment

The scheme of devolution proposed by the Act raises many important legal and constitutional issues upon which it is possible to make only brief comment.

(a) *The legislative supremacy of the U.K. Parliament*

When the Bill was introduced into the Commons, it began with the following clause, entitled " Effect of Act ": " The following provisions of this Act make changes in the government of Scotland as part of the U.K. They do not affect the unity of the U.K. or the supreme authority of Parliament to make laws for the U.K. or any part of it." In part this clause was inspired by s. 75, Government of Ireland Act 1920 (supreme authority of U.K. Parliament to legislate for Northern Ireland declared to be unaffected by the 1920 Act), but it was widely criticised in debate and the Commons voted to remove it from the Bill (*Hansard*, H.C. Vol. 939, col. 1402 (Nov. 22, 1977). The Government did not seek to reinstate it. On the Diceyan view that Parliament may not bind its successors, the clause was in law unnecessary because Parliament would retain full power to legislate for Scotland, whether or not an Assembly had been created with legislative powers. However, the clause might have served to discourage the development of a binding convention to the effect that Parliament should not legislate on matters that had been devolved to the Assembly.

Regarding the Scotland Act, the following propositions may be advanced: (a) that Parliament retains full legislative capacity to amend or repeal the Scotland Act and to do so at any time, whether before or after the referendum of the Scottish electorate (s. 85) and whether or not the provisions of the Act have come into effect; (b) that Parliament retains full legislative capacity on all matters affecting Scotland, whether or not they are within the legislative competence of the Assembly, and whether or not the Assembly has yet legislated on these matters. Thus Parliament will have power to amend or repeal any Assembly Acts.

The effect of s. 17 (2) must, however, be considered, by which " a Scottish Assembly Act may amend or repeal a provision made by or under an Act of Parliament " (and contrast the provision made in the Government of Ireland Act 1920, s. 6). The following propositions are also advanced: (c) that the Assembly will, within the area of its legislative competence, have power to amend or repeal Acts of Parliament passed *before* the Scotland Act 1978; (d) that the Assembly may also, within the area of its legislative competence, have power to amend or repeal Acts of Parliament passed *after* the Scotland Act 1978, but this will depend on what is held to be the intention of Parliament in passing the later Act; the later Act may be held to demonstrate an intention to amend the Scotland Act in this respect (proposition (a) above). There is therefore no legal basis for any fear of an endless game of legislative " ping-pong " developing between the Assembly and Parliament.

In relation to the legislative supremacy of Parliament, note also: (i) that the Assembly's legislative powers do not extend to amending the Scotland Act itself (s. 17 (2) and Sched. 2, para. 7) although Sched. 2, para. 7 does permit the Assembly to legislate on certain matters included in Sched. 16 as amendments to existing Acts of Parliament; (ii) that wide powers of amending Acts of Parliament by subordinate legislation are conferred by s. 37 and s. 82 (3); (iii) that, by legislating for the procedure by which certain Bills should pass through the House of Commons, s. 66 breaks new constitutional ground; but it is submitted that no court would be willing to examine whether or not the House had complied with s. 66 (*Edinburgh and Dalkeith Rly.* v. *Wauchope* (1842) 8 Cl. & F. 710; *Pickin* v. *British Railways Board* [1974] A.C. 765, and *cf.* the analogous provision made in s. 17 (4) regarding Assembly Acts).

(b) *The status of the Assembly and the Executive vis-à-vis the Crown*

Neither the Assembly nor the Executive are granted corporate personality by the Act (unlike the Welsh Assembly: Wales Act 1978, s. 1 (4)). Nor does the Act provide expressly that the Assembly and the Executive shall exercise their powers in the name of the Crown. Moreover, neither Assembly nor Executive are to have direct access to the Sovereign, the Secretary of State retaining all powers that involve advice to the Sovereign. As regards the Executive, however, s. 21 makes certain executive powers of the Sovereign exercisable in Scotland by a Scottish Secretary " on behalf of Her Majesty." Moreover, all Scottish Secretaries are to hold office at Her Majesty's pleasure (s. 20 (5)); and service as an officer or servant of a Scottish Secretary is to be service in Her Majesty's Home Civil Service (s. 67 (1)). If account is also taken of other features of the scheme (*e.g.* the arrangements for financing the Assembly and Executive, and for vesting in the First Secretary property belonging to the Secretary of State (s. 72)), there can be no doubt that Scottish Secretaries and their civil servants will be able to enjoy the immunities and privileges of Crown status. Thus, for example, the property of the First Secretary will not in law be liable to pay rates nor be subject to town planning control. The Scottish Executive will also, subject to the supervisory powers of the courts, be able to claim executive privilege in the law of evidence (formerly known as " Crown privilege "—see Sched. 6, para. 2 and note thereon). Scottish Secretaries and their civil servants will " hold office under Her Majesty " for the purpose of the Official Secrets Act 1911, s. 2 (1).

But the Act does not deal with the application of the Crown Suits (Scotland) Act 1857 and the Crown Proceedings Act 1947 to the Scottish administration. It is indeed uncertain which authority should be sued in respect of vicarious liability for the wrongful acts of Scottish Secretaries and the civil servants. The Acts of 1857 and 1947 would seem to make it necessary for litigants to sue either the Lord Advocate or the Secretary of State. The matter is one that could and should be dealt with by a minister's order under s. 82 (3), at least until the Assembly are in a position to legislate.

The position of the Assembly is less clear. Although not incorporated, it is given subsidiary powers, including power to acquire property, phrased in terms usually associated with statutory corporations (*e.g.* Local Government (Scotland) Act 1973, s. 69). The legal status of the Assembly Clerk and of the Assembly's officers and servants is complex (ss. 32, 33). For some purposes, the position of Assembly staff is made akin to that of Crown servants (s. 33) but it is not clear whether they may be regarded as holding office under the Crown for other purposes, *e.g.* under the Official Secrets Act 1911 and the Crown Proceedings Act 1947. Again an order under s. 82 (3) may be needed to clarify the matter.

(c) *Executive responsibility*

The Act provides for an elected Assembly with power to legislate on many matters concerning the internal administration of Scotland and for an Executive with both policy-making and administrative powers. Although no express provision is made for this in the Act, it is certain that the Scottish Executive will be regarded as responsible to the Assembly for its policies and executive decisions; and it is very likely that many of the conventional practices relating to Cabinet government and ministerial responsibility will be adopted in Edinburgh. But the position of the devolved administration will be far from being a carbon copy of the Whitehall/Westminster relationship.

One reason why new constitutional relationships regarding executive responsibility are likely to arise is to be found in the position of the Secretary of State for Scotland. The Act gives numerous supervisory powers of a constitutional kind to the Secretary of State in respect of the Assembly and Executive (see, *e.g.* ss. 2, 4, 6, 7, 20, 24 (with Sched. 6), 34 (2), 36, 38–42, 48–50, 72, 83). The Secretary of State will also be responsible to Parliament for matters of Scottish government that are not devolved (*e.g.* the police and other local government functions listed in Sched. 15; agricultural policy affecting Scotland; and matters concerned with the judicial system reserved by Sched. 10, Pt. II, paras. 14–19) and are not administered by U.K. or British departments (*e.g.* social security, industrial relations). The Secretary of State will also be a key figure in the allocation of finance to the new Scottish administration : it is difficult to suppose that he will not take some political interest in how the money is spent. The Act, however, makes no provision for any formal contact between the Secretary of State and the Assembly.

(d) *The allocation of legislative and executive powers*

The allocation of legislative and executive powers to the Assembly and Executive respectively is the most complex part of the Act, and one unlikely to be understood by most Assembly members and the electorate. One method of allocating powers would have been to confer a general power to legislate on the Scottish Assembly, subject to matters expressly reserved in the Act. Instead matters are devolved only if they fall within subjects listed in the Groups set out in Sched. 10, Pt. I, and are not excluded by the entries in Sched. 10, Pts. II and III. In particular it is unfortunate that subjects are included within or excluded from the legislative competence of the Assembly by reference to provisions of existing statutes, since the effect of this must be to place obstacles in the way of an Assembly which wishes to legislate comprehensively on a given subject. (*Cf. Scottish Law Commission*, Memorandum No. 32, August 1976.) Moreover the safeguarding of the U.K. Government's interests by reference to specific statutory provisions (*e.g.* on town planning, s. 71 and Sched. 14) must make it virtually impossible for the Assembly to legislate to amend those provisions, even though elsewhere in the Act legislative competence is apparently conferred on the Assembly (entry for Town and Country Planning (Scotland) Act 1972 in Sched. 10, Pt. III). Similarly, since the power to recommend to Her Majesty the appointment of the members of the Mental Health Commission is excluded from devolution (entry for Mental Health (Scotland) Act 1960 in Sched. 10, Pt. III), it is uncertain whether the Scottish Assembly's power to legislate on mental health includes power to abolish the Commission or to alter its functions.

(e) *Judicial review of Assembly Acts*

The Act makes full provision for judicial review of Assembly Acts both before enactment (s. 19) and thereafter (s. 65 and Sched. 12). While some devolution issues may be settled in the ordinary civil and criminal courts, the Act envisages a new constitutional role for the Judicial Committee of the Privy Council in interpreting and applying its provisions. The Act excludes judicial review of Assembly measures only on matters of procedure (s. 17 (4)).

Interpretation

Throughout the Act and these notes, " Assembly " refers to the Scottish Assembly (s. 81 (1)) created by s. 1; " the Secretary of State " means " one of Her Majesty's Principal Secretaries of State for the time being " (Interpretation Act 1978, s. 5 and Sched. 1, and see *Agee* v. *Lord Advocate*, 1977 S.L.T. (Notes) 54). While the duties of the Secretaries of State are in law interchangeable, it is likely that the powers vested in the Secretary of State by this Act will be exercised by the Secretary of State for Scotland.

Many sections of the Act empower the Secretary of State or a Minister of the Crown to make orders (*e.g.* s. 2 (1), s. 49 (5), s. 82 (3), s. 83 (1)). By s. 79 (1) any power to make orders conferred on a Minister of the Crown is to be exercisable by statutory instrument; and the Statutory Instruments Act 1946 therefore applies. The 1946 Act also applies to any power under this Act for the making of Orders in Council.

PART I

THE SCOTTISH ASSEMBLY AND EXECUTIVE

The Scottish Assembly

The Scottish Assembly

1.—(1) There shall be a Scottish Assembly.

(2) Subject to subsection (3) below, the initial members of the Assembly shall be returned for the areas which, at the time of their election, are constituencies for parliamentary elections in Scotland, and there shall be—

(a) three initial members for each of those areas of which the electorate is more than 125 per cent. of the electoral quota; and

(b) two initial members for each of the others.

(3) There shall be one initial member for Orkney and one for Shetland.

(4) The members of the Assembly other than the initial members shall be returned for the Assembly constituencies for the time being specified in an Order in Council under Schedule 1 to this Act and there shall be one member for each such constituency.

(5) In this section and Part III of Schedule 1 to this Act " initial members " means members elected before an election to which an Order in Council under Part I of that Schedule applies, and " electorate " and " electoral quota " have the meanings assigned to them by paragraph 14 of that Schedule.

GENERAL NOTE

This section, together with Sched. 1, makes provision for the establishment of the Scottish Assembly (subs. (1)), for the Assembly's size and composition and for the method of election of its members (subss. (2)–(5) and Sched. 1).

The Assembly is a unicameral body as recommended by the Kilbrandon Report, paras. 799–802, and proposed in *Our Changing Democracy*, para. 32. The term " Assembly " also stems from *Our Changing Democracy* although it had already been used in a less specific and more descriptive sense in the Kilbrandon Report and *Democracy and Devolution: Proposals for Scotland and Wales.*

Until such time as Assembly constituencies are created (see subs. (4) and Sched. 1, para. 5), existing parliamentary constituencies will be used as Assembly constituencies, but returning either two or three members to the Assembly according to the formula set out in subss. (2) and (3). By Sched. 1, para. 12, the number of initial members for each constituency will be specified in an order made by the Secretary of State. The two or three (as the case may be) candidates with the most votes in each parliamentary constituency will become Assembly members (see *Our Changing Democracy*, para. 32. and Sched. 1, Pt. III). This expedient, which has resulted in the separate provision in this section for " initial members " and " members," has been found necessary because of the impossibility of creating single member Assembly constituencies in the relatively short time before the first Assembly election is held. The purpose of allowing certain parliamentary constituencies to return three Assembly members is to remove the most serious instances of unfairness which stem from the marked differences in the size of electorates in Scottish parliamentary constituencies, but the formula set out in subs. (2) may well produce further instances of unfairness. If, for example, parliamentary constituency X has 126 per cent. of the electoral quota, it will be divided into three Assembly constituencies so that each Assembly member will represent 42 per cent. of the electoral quota. However, if parliamentary constituency Y has 120 per cent. of the electoral quota it will, although it is almost as large as constituency X, be divided into only two Assembly constituencies so that each Assembly member will represent 60 per cent. of the electoral quota. Although subs. (2) is essentially of a transitional nature, this potential unfairness will continue once the Assembly constituencies have been created; see Sched. 1, para. 9, which embodies substantially the same formula.

Because subs. (2) and Sched. 1, para. 9, are very similar in terms, there will be no significant change in the size of the Assembly once elections are held on the basis of Assembly constituencies; it is expected that the Assembly will have in the region of 150 members. The Kilbrandon Report, paras. 789–791, 1140, had suggested an assembly of about 100 members, while *Our Changing Democracy*, para. 32, proposed an Assembly of about 140 members, on the basis of a formula which differed from that now contained in this Act, in that a parliamentary constituency which had less than 75 per cent. of the electoral quota would become a single Assembly constituency. This proposal was not adopted because such constituencies tend to be very large in terms of geographical area; see Lord McCluskey, Solicitor-General for Scotland, *Hansard*, H.L. Vol. 390, col. 135 (April 4, 1978).

The debates in Parliament on this section were dominated by the argument whether Assembly members should be elected by the same method as M.P.s (that is, the relative majority or " first past the post " system) or by some method of proportional representation. The Kilbrandon Report had recommended the single transferable vote method of proportional representation (see paras. 779–88), but this was ruled out at an early stage in the Government's planning (see *Democracy and Devolution: Proposals for Scotland and Wales*, para. 31). An attempt made during the Committee stage in the Commons to introduce the " additional member " system of proportional representation was unsuccessful, but the Lords during its Committee stage amended the Bill to introduce a very similar system. The Commons later voted to disagree with the amendments, and the Lords gave way; *Hansard*, H.C. Vol. 939, cols. 1409–84, 1535–1606 (November 22–23, 1977); H.L. Vol. 390, cols. 42–106, 114–159, 458–544 (April 4, 5 and 11, 1978); H.C. Vol. 953, cols. 677–748 (July 6, 1978); H.L. Vol. 395, cols. 430–461 (July 20, 1978).

Subs. (2)

" *initial members.*" This term is defined in subs. (5). While the term implies that only the first members of the Assembly will be elected on the basis of this subsection, the effect of subs. (4) (and in particular the words " the members of the Assembly other than the initial members ") is that Assembly elections (including by-elections) will, if necessary, continue to be held on this basis until such time as the Assembly constituencies are created. By the House of Commons (Redistribution of Seats) Act 1958, s. 2 (1), the Boundary Commissions must undertake a general review of constituencies at intervals of not less than 10 or more than 15 years. The last such review was completed in 1969, which suggests that the Scottish Boundary Commission might well undertake the creation of Assembly constituencies as part of a general review rather than as a special operation. The same inference may also be drawn from Sched. 1, para. 1.

" *at the time of their election.*" This phrase is necessary because the parliamentary constituencies could well undergo changes in area between Assembly elections.

" *(a) three initial members . . . of the electoral quota.*" On the basis of the 1977 electoral register, the electoral quota (as defined in Sched. 1, para. 14; see subs. (5)) was approximately 53,337 and the 125 per cent. figure was approximately 64,000. On this basis, five parliamentary constituencies would return three Assembly members: East Dunbartonshire, East Kilbride, Midlothian, West Renfrewshire and West Lothian; Lord McCluskey, Solicitor-General for Scotland, *Hansard*, H.L. Vol. 390, col. 134 (April 4, 1978). The terms " electorate " and " electoral quota " are defined in Sched. 1, para. 14; see subs. (5).

Subs. (3)

Special provision for the initial members to represent Orkney and Shetland has been made because of the geographical circumstances of that constituency. Other special provisions for Orkney and Shetland are to be found in ss. 41 and 84.

Time of election and term of office of members of Assembly

2.—(1) The first ordinary election of members of the Assembly shall be held on a day appointed by order of the Secretary of State and, subject to subsection (2) below, any subsequent ordinary election shall be held on the third Thursday in March in the fourth year following that in which the previous ordinary election was held.

(2) The Secretary of State may, by order made with respect to the second or any subsequent ordinary election of members of the Assembly, appoint as a day for the holding of the election a day not more than two months earlier nor more than two months later than the day on which the election would be held apart from the order.

(3) The term of office of any member of the Assembly, whether elected at an ordinary election or otherwise, shall begin on the day on which he is elected and end with the dissolution of the Assembly.

(4) No order under this section shall be made unless a draft of it has been laid before, and approved by resolution of, each House of Parliament.

GENERAL NOTE

The normal four-year term of office of the Assembly arises from a suggestion in the Kilbrandon Report, paras. 792–798, 1140, which was accepted by the Government; see *Our Changing Democracy*, para. 35. While a three-year term, it was felt, might not be long enough to allow an Executive to implement its policies, a fixed five-year term might be too long, and allow the Assembly to become out of touch with its electorate; Lord Kirkhill, Minister of State at the Scottish Office, *Hansard*, H.L. Vol. 390, col. 586 (April 11, 1978). It was also indicated in *Our Changing Democracy*, para. 35, that the Secretary of State would be empowered to make minor adjustments to the date of an ordinary election so as to give a "" convenient " election day. This represents a compromise between the view in the Kilbrandon Report that there should be no departures at all from the fixed-term principle, and the situation regarding Parliament which may be dissolved at any time during its maximum five-year lifespan by the Queen on the advice of her Prime Minister.

Subs. (1)

It is consistent with other provisions of the Act (see s. 6, regarding the first meeting of the Assembly, and s. 7 (1), regarding the regulation of Assembly procedure until such time as the Assembly has made its own standing orders) that the Secretary of State should be empowered to fix the date of the first ordinary election.

" *ordinary election.*" This term has been adopted from local government law; see the Local Government (Scotland) Act 1973, s. 8. An ordinary election is one *due* to be held on the date prescribed by this subsection. Even if the date is advanced or postponed under subs. (2), it remains an ordinary election for the purposes of the Act.

" *the third Thursday in March.*" This date has been chosen at least in part because the new electoral register comes into force on February 16 each year: Electoral Registers Act 1949, as amended by the Electoral Registers Act 1953.

" *by order.*" By subs. (4), an order made under subs. (1) requires an affirmative resolution of both Houses of Parliament before it can be formally made. Quite apart from the argument that in principle Parliament should be able to discuss, and vote on, such an important matter as the date of the first ordinary election, it might in practice have been unwise to adopt a negative resolution procedure (as was provided for in cl. 3 of the Scotland and Wales Bill) because at least 40 days (which could span three calendar months) would have to be allowed between the laying date and the date fixed for the election (Statutory Instruments Act 1946, s. 5). Since it would be risky in the extreme to hold the election before the 40-day period had expired, an undesirable delay might have resulted.

Subs. (2)

The general objective of subs. (2) is to provide a measure of flexibility in the timing of ordinary elections by empowering the Secretary of State to vary the date by up to two months on either side of the date on which the election would normally be held according to subs. (1). While a period shorter than two months might be of little practical utility, a longer period would increase the risk of the Secretary of State being accused of altering the election date for political as opposed to purely administrative reasons. The figure of two months therefore represents a compromise between these two opposing considerations. While flexibility may seem desirable in principle, the practical value of the subsection is less certain. For example, to advance the date of an ordinary election so as to avoid a clash with a General Election would involve revealing the likely date of the latter at a far earlier time than the Government would wish, while postponement of an election in these circumstances would risk a clash with local government elections in early May.

No provision is made for a minimum interval of time between the laying of the order and the date of the election. In theory, therefore, an order postponing an election could be laid before Parliament and approved by it when the election campaign was already well advanced. Moreover, the wording of the subsection is not entirely clear, and raises the interesting question whether the power conferred on the Secretary of State by this subsection could be used to bring about successive postponements of an ordinary election. Assume that according to subs. (1) an ordinary election is due to be held on March 16. Before that date the Secretary of State makes an order under subs. (2) postponing the date of the election until May 11. Before May 11 he makes a further order under subs. (2) postponing the election until July 6, and after the second order has come into effect revokes the first order under s. 79 (2). This series of actions can be viewed in two possible ways: (a) when the second order comes into effect, there are in fact two orders because the first order is not immediately revoked. The election is then to be held on a day (July 6) which is not more than " two months later than the day [May 11] on which the election would be held apart from the [second] order ". If further postponement is permissible, then clearly there is no theoretical limit to further postponements brought about in the same way; (b) as soon as the first order is revoked, the second order is the only order to which subs. (2) could apply, and it is still necessary for the election to be held not more than two months later than the date (March 16) on which the election would be held apart from the order. Any order purporting to postpone an ordinary election beyond that period would be *ultra vires*. The Government have made clear that they do not intend ordinary elections to be capable of successive postponements, and that they reject interpretation (a). In any event, the requirement that orders made under s. 2 (2) be subject to an affirmative resolution of both Houses of Parliament (see below) is an obvious safeguard. See *Hansard*, H.L. Vol. 392, cols. 1289–1300 (June 7, 1978).

" *by order.*" By subs. (4), an order made under subs. (2) requires an affirmative resolution of both Houses of Parliament before it can be formally made. This follows from a Government defeat on the Report stage in the Lords; originally no provision was made for the laying of the order before Parliament, on the argument that the choosing of an election date was " a matter of simple administrative convenience " and that so limited was the discretion given to the Secretary of State by the subsection that there would be no justification for seeking parliamentary time for approval of the order (a negative resolution procedure being inappropriate for the same reasons as these set out above in relation to subs. (1)); moreover, the Secretary of State would be accountable to Parliament for the exercise of his power. The Lords, however, desired a more effective control; *Hansard*, H.L. Vol. 392, cols. 1300 (June 7, 1978).

Subs. (3)

For the position of Scottish Secretaries and assistants to Scottish Secretaries, see s. 20 (7).

" *ordinary election or otherwise.*" A member of the Assembly may be elected at an ordinary election, at a by-election or at an election held after premature dissolution of the Assembly (see s. 3). When this subsection is read alongside s. 3 (1) (*a*), it becomes clear that a member elected at a by-election or an election held after a premature dissolution will hold office only until the next ordinary election. Thus an Assembly elected after the premature dissolution of its predecessor would sit only until the date of the next ordinary election.

Dissolution of Assembly

3.—(1) The Assembly as constituted from time to time—

    (*a*) shall stand dissolved on the eve of any ordinary election of members; and

    (*b*) shall be dissolved by order of the Secretary of State if the Assembly resolves that it should be dissolved and, if the resolution is passed on a division, the members voting in favour of it number not less than two-thirds of the total number of members of the Assembly (including any whose seat is vacant).

(2) An order dissolving the Assembly shall require an election of members to be held on the day following the dissolution, and that day shall not be later than two months after the date of the resolution in pursuance of which the order is made.

GENERAL NOTE

Except in cases where the Assembly is dissolved prematurely under subs. (1) (*b*), it will be dissolved automatically according to the provisions of subs. (1) (*a*) immediately before the day of an ordinary election (*cf.* Local Government (Scotland) Act, s. 4 (3)). In this respect the position is the same as that of Parliament which, in the very unlikely event of it not being dissolved before the end of its maximum possible five year life, is automatically dissolved by the provisions of the Septennial Act 1715, as amended by the Parliament Act 1911. There is nothing in this section to prevent the Assembly from continuing to transact business up to the evening before election day. In practice, however, it is probable that the Assembly will adjourn for the period leading up to the election to allow its members to take part in the election campaign.

Provision for premature dissolution is made in subss. (1) (*b*) and (2). The absence of such a provision in the Scotland and Wales Bill was criticised during that Bill's Committee stage; *Hansard*, Vol. 925 H.C. Deb. cols. 579–633 (February 2, 1977). The situation envisaged was that of a Scottish Executive which, during the life of an Assembly, loses the support of the Assembly as a result of either changes in the party composition of the Assembly through by-elections or the break-up of a coalition Executive. In such circumstances it might be possible for the Assembly to nominate a new First Secretary able to form a new Executive (see s. 20 and note thereon) and such a nomination would require only a simple majority as opposed to the two-thirds majority required by subs. (1) (*b*). If, however, the Assembly is unable to produce a new Executive by this method, the case for a premature dissolution is obviously very strong. Accordingly Mr. Michael Foot, M.P., Lord President of the Council, in his statement to the House of Commons on July 26, 1977, gave a commitment that the Scotland Bill would contain a provision permitting premature dissolution; *Hansard*, H.C. Vol. 936, col. 314.

Subs. (1)

" (*a*) *shall stand dissolved on the eve of any ordinary election.*" The life of an Assembly will come to an end at midnight immediately before election day. The phrase " shall be dissolved " has not been used because the dissolution takes place automatically by the provisions of the Act, rather than by the order or resolution of any person or body.

" (*b*) *shall be dissolved by order of the Secretary of State.*" Provided that the resolution passed by the Assembly is valid, the Secretary of State is under an obligation to make the appropriate order. The intention is clearly that the initiative and responsibility for premature dissolution should lie with the Assembly. The resolution need not be preceded by the carrying of a motion of no confidence in the Executive. No provision is made for the laying of the order before Parliament; to have done so would transfer ultimate responsibility for premature dissolution from the Assembly to Parliament.

" *not less than two-thirds of the total number of members of the Assembly.*" This is the first of two provisions designed to ensure that premature dissolution takes place only in exceptional circumstances. If the requirement were for example only of a simple majority of those present and voting, it would be difficult to describe the Assembly as being of a fixed term.

Subs. (2)

" *an election.*" Elections held following a premature dissolution are not described in the Act as " ordinary elections," although, as explained below, they could exceptionally be ordinary elections. Thus members elected at such an election serve only for the remainder of the fixed term period where the election is not an ordinary election. This is the second safeguard against premature dissolution being treated as other than an exceptional occurrence.

" *two months.*" - This is the maximum permitted period between the date of the passing of the resolution and the date of the election. If, therefore, a resolution is passed within four months of the date of an ordinary election as determined by s. 2 (1), it seems that the Secretary of State could by relying on both s. 2 (2) and subs. (2) of this section advance the date of the ordinary election so as to avoid the need for such an election to follow closely upon the heels of an election held under subs. (2). Say, for example, that the resolution under subs. (1) (*b*) is passed on November 24, 1978, and that the next ordinary election is due on March 9, 1979. An ordinary election could then be held on January 18, 1979, since this is within two months of the date of the resolution (subs. (2)) and also within two months of the normal date for the next ordinary election (s. 2 (2)).

Elections to Assembly

4.—(1) The persons entitled to vote as electors at an Assembly election in any Assembly constituency shall be—

(*a*) those, who at the date of the election—

(i) have their names on such parts of the register of parliamentary electors as relate to the Assembly constituency; and

(ii) would be entitled to vote as electors at a parliamentary election in the parliamentary constituency comprising the Assembly constituency; and

(*b*) peers who, at that date—

(i) have their names on such parts of the register of local government electors as relate to the Assembly constituency; and

(ii) would be entitled to vote at a local government election in an electoral area comprised in or wholly or partly coinciding with the Assembly constituency.

(2) Subsection (1) of this section applies with the necessary modifications to the election of initial members (within the meaning of section 1 of this Act).

(3) The Secretary of State may by order make provision—

(*a*) as to the conduct of elections of members of the Assembly (including the registration of electors); and

(*b*) as to the questioning of such an election and the consequences of irregularities.

(4) An order under this section may—

(*a*) apply, with such modifications or exceptions as may be specified in it, any provision of the Representation of the People Acts, any provision of the enactments relating to returning officers, and any provision made under any enactment; and

(*b*) so far as may be necessary in consequence of any provision made by it for the registration of electors, amend any provision made by or under the Representation of the People Acts as to the registration of parliamentary electors or local government electors.

(5) An order under this section may provide for the charging of any sum on the Scottish Consolidated Fund.

(6) No election of a member of the Assembly shall be questioned except under the provisions of Part III of the Representation of the People Act 1949 as applied by an order under this section.

(7) A statutory instrument made under this section shall be subject to annulment in pursuance of a resolution of either House of Parliament.

DEFINITIONS

" electoral area ": Local Government (Scotland) Act 1973, s. 235 (1).
" enactment ": s. 83 (1).

GENERAL NOTE

This section contains the provisions governing the franchise for Assembly elections, and the conduct of such elections. Its relative brevity is achieved by the attraction, in subs. (1) (*a*), of much of the already existing law concerning the parliamentary and local government franchise, and by the provisions in subss. (3) to (6) empowering the Secretary of State to make delegated legislation which will govern the conduct of Assembly elections; statutory instruments made under these subsections may also apply existing statutory provisions with or without modification.

Subs. (1)

This subsection determines who is entitled to vote in an Assembly election, and in which Assembly constituency he may do so. The basic principle is that those entitled to vote in parliamentary elections may also vote in Assembly elections; *i.e.* those who are resident there on the qualifying date (October 10) for inclusion in the electoral register, are either British subjects or citizens of the Republic of Ireland, are at least 18 years of age, are not subject to any legal incapacity to vote and appear on the electoral register (Representation of the People Acts 1949, s. 1 (1), and 1969, s. 1). The appearance of a person's name on the electoral register is conclusive on the question whether the person is resident in the constituency on the qualifying date. The question of resident may, however, cause difficulties in cases where, for example, a person has a house in Scotland as well as in England, and wishes to vote in Assembly elections. It seems that where a person has a permanent home in two constituencies, but where one home is only incidental to a more substantive home, the former will not be taken as a " residence " for the purposes of the Representation of the People Act 1949 (*Scott* v. *Phillips*, 1974 S.L.T. 32). However, this would probably not apply in the case of a person who possessed residences in both Scotland and England, and the Scottish residence is occupied for a significant part of the year (*Sim* v. *Galt* (1892) 20 R. 84).

Separate provision is necessary for peers, since they are legally incapable of voting in parliamentary elections (see, *e.g. Earl Beauchamp* v. *Madresfield* (1872) L.R. 8 C.P. 245) although they may vote in local government elections (Representation of the People Act 1949, s. 10 (4), proviso). The parliamentary and local government registers are only notionally separate; in practice a single register is maintained (Representation of the People Act 1949, s. 7 (2)), with voters who fall into special categories (*e.g.* service voters, merchant seamen, and those entitled to vote in local government elections only) having their names marked accordingly.

" *any Assembly constituency.*" For the phrase " Assembly constituency," see s. 1 and Sched. 1. In some cases an elector may have a choice as to which Assembly constituency to vote in. This will arise if the elector appears on the parliamentary electoral register for two or more separate constituencies and is accordingly able to choose which parliamentary constituency to vote in, or—exceptionally—if the elector appears more than once on the electoral register for a single parliamentary constituency, and the entries relate to more than one Assembly constituency. Likewise peers may have a choice if they appear on the local government electoral register for electoral areas which fall within two Assembly constituencies. In other respects, however, as explained below, amendments made to this subsection have greatly restricted the opportunity for choice in voting.

" (*i*) *have their names on such parts of the register of parliamentary electors as relate to the Assembly constituency; and.*" These words were the subject of a government amendment made during the Report stage in the Commons. During the Committee stage, it had been pointed out that as the Bill stood an elector would be able to make a choice between the two or three Assembly constituencies within the parliamentary constituency in which he lived. The effect of the amendment is that an elector can vote only in the Assembly constituency in which he is registered as residing. There is, however, no possibility of plural voting since the government intend to use the power under subs. (3) to apply the Representation of the People Act 1949, s. 48, which makes it an offence to vote more than once in the same constituency or in more than one constituency; *Hansard*, H.C. Vol. 939, cols. 1655–60 (November 23, 1977), Vol. 944, cols. 509–11 (February 15, 1978).

" *parliamentary constituency comprising the Assembly constituency.*" " Comprising," in this context, appears to mean " included within." By Sched. 1, para. 6, " each Assembly constituency shall be wholly comprised in one parliamentary constituency."

" *(b)* . . . *(i) have their names on such parts of the register of local government electors as relate to the Assembly constituency; and.*" The words in subs. (1) *(b)* (i) were the subject of a Government amendment during the Report stage in the Lords. During the Committee stage, it had been pointed out that as the Bill stood, where a peer was entitled to appear more than once on the register of local government electors, he would be able to choose which Assembly constituency to vote in if the local government electoral areas to which the entries related fell within the boundaries of more than one Assembly constituency. The effect of the amendment is that the peers entitled to vote in any Assembly constituency will be those who have their name on the parts of the local government electoral register which relate to that Assembly constituency. For the reason explained above, however, there would have been no possibility of exploiting this defect to allow plural voting; *Hansard,* H.L. Vol. 390, cols. 638–642 (April 12, 1978), Vol. 392, cols. 1313–1314 (June 7, 1978).

" *electoral area comprised in or wholly or partly coinciding with the Assembly constituency.*" The wording here differs from that in subs. (1) *(a)* (ii) because, while Assembly constituencies are required to be wholly comprised within a single parliamentary constituency, Sched. 1, para. 8 states that " regard shall be had, as far as practicable, to the boundaries of local government areas." It is therefore possible that a local government electoral area will be wholly comprised within a single Assembly constituency; or that the boundaries of the electoral area and the Assembly constituency will be identical; or that the electoral area will straddle two or more Assembly constituencies. Even in this last case, however, there is no possibility of a peer being able to choose which constituency to vote in, because of the effect of subs. (1) *(b)* (i).

Subs. (2)

Until such time as the Assembly constituency boundaries have been created electors will vote either in their normal parliamentary constituencies, or (in the case of peers) in the parliamentary constituency comprising the local government electoral area in which they are entitled to vote. See s. 1 and note thereon, and Sched. 1, Pt. III.

Subss. (3) *and* (4)

The main provisions regarding the conduct of parliamentary and local government elections are contained in the Representation of the People Act 1949, Pt. III. It is clear from subs. (6) and from ss. 9 (3) and 11 (3) that it is intended to apply this part of the Act to Assembly elections, by an order made under subs. (3).

Subs. (5)

As originally drafted, this subsection provided for election costs to be a charge on the U.K. Consolidated Fund. An amendment made during the Committee stage in the Lords, however, provided for such costs to be charged upon the Scottish Consolidated Fund. The Government originally accepted the amendment as being consequential upon an earlier amendment by which the power to review the Assembly electoral arrangements and to initiate charges would have passed from Westminster to the Assembly, and in the light of this amendment it was considered logical that the responsibility for financing elections should also pass to the Assembly. Even though the earlier amendment did not survive, the amendment to this subsection remained as the Government appeared to be persuaded that the amendment would make little difference in practice; as matters now stand, it seems that the cost of elections will become a fixed item when the size of the block grant is being negotiated; *Hansard,* H.L. Vol. 390, cols. 643–645 (April 12, 1978). For the Scottish Consolidated Fund, see Pt. III.

Subs. (6)

The wording of this subsection is very similar to the Representation of the People Act 1949, s. 107 (originally the Parliamentary Elections Act 1868, s. 50) which states that " no election or return to Parliament shall be questioned except in accordance with the provisions of this Act." Prior to the 1868 Act, controverted elections were tried by the House itself, and the purpose of s. 50 was to transfer the jurisdiction of the House's election committees to the judiciary so as to ensure an impartial and informed examination of the issue. This subsection accordingly ensures that the elections of Assembly members may only be questioned by the election petition procedure under Pt. III of the 1949 Act, whereby within 21 days of the official return of the result of the election, a petition may be presented by an elector for the constituency in question, by an unsuccessful candidate or by any person claiming to have been validly nominated as a candidate. The petition is heard by an Election Court which, in the case of disputed Assembly elections, will consist of two judges of the Court of Session. The petition may raise a number of issues, including the improper conduct of the election by officials, whether the successful candidate was legally disqualified, and allegations of election offences such as unauthorised expenditure. The determination of the Election Court is, in petitions arising from parliamentary elections, communicated to the Speaker and the House of Commons then gives the appropriate directions, *e.g.* for confirming or altering the election return. In this way the form of the Commons' jurisdiction over its own composition is maintained. It may be assumed that under this Act, the Election Court's determination will be communicated to the presiding officer of the Assembly; only the presiding officer can fix the date of a by-election (s. 5 (2)) should one be necessary as a result of the Election Court's findings.

By-elections

5.—(1) Subject to subsection (4) of this section, where the seat of a member of the Assembly is vacant an election shall be held to fill the vacancy.

(2) The date of the election shall be fixed by the presiding officer of the Assembly in accordance with subsection (3) of this section.

(3) The date of the election shall be not later than three months after the occurrence of the vacancy, except that if the vacancy does not come to the notice of the presiding officer within one month of its occurrence the date of the election shall be not later than three months after the vacancy comes to his notice.

(4) The election shall not be held if the latest date for holding it would fall within the three months preceding the next election to be held in pursuance of section 2 or section 3 of this Act.

(5) For the purposes of this section a vacancy shall be deemed to have occurred on such date as may be determined under the standing orders of the Assembly, and references in this section to the presiding officer include any person for the time being performing the functions of presiding officer.

GENERAL NOTE

If, during the lifetime of an Assembly, a vacancy occurs in its membership, a by-election must be held to fill that vacancy unless the latest date for holding the by-election (calculated in accordance with subs. (3)) would fall within the three month period preceding the next ordinary election (see s. 2) or an election held after a premature dissolution (see s. 3). Vacancies may arise through the death of a member, or his resignation (see s. 13), or through his being disqualified for membership (see ss. 8–11). Normally the by-election must be held within three months of the vacancy occurring, although some flexibility on the timing of the by-election is allowed to meet exceptional or unusual situations. By contrast, there is no equivalent time-limit for the holding of by-elections to fill vacancies in the House of Commons. The justification for imposing a time-limit in relation to the Assembly is that its duration is fixed, and that it has a much smaller membership than the Commons; accordingly it was felt to be undesirable that the period of the vacancy be left to the discretion of the political parties; Lord McCluskey, Solicitor-General for Scotland, *Hansard*, H.L. Vol. 390, cols. 656–7 (April 12, 1978). See also Report of the Speaker's Conference on Electoral Law (1973, Cmnd. 5500).

Subs. (2)

"*presiding officer.*" See subs. (5) and also s. 7 (2). The fact that it is the presiding officer who is under a duty to fix the date of the by-election will, along with subs. (3), prevent by-elections being timed as a means of securing party political advantage. By contrast, when a vacancy arises in the House of Commons while it is in session, although it is the Speaker who authorises the issue of a writ for the by-election, the warrant for the issue of the writ is made on the order of the House, and by custom the necessary motion is moved by the Chief Whip of the party which held the seat before the vacancy occurred. During a recess, however, the Speaker himself may order the issue of the writ, but may only do so on receipt of a certificate from two M.P.s that a vacancy has arisen; see the Recess Elections Act 1975.

It appears that under this subsection the presiding officer may fix the date for the by-election whether the Assembly is in session or in recess (assuming that the Assembly will have sessions in the parliamentary sense). Assembly standing orders may well require proof of the existence of a vacancy (and see subs. (5) regarding the determination of the date when a vacancy is deemed to have occurred) but it does not appear to be intended that standing orders will provide for some form of official certification of a vacancy (say, along the lines of the certificate set out in the Recess Elections Act 1975, Sched. 1) without which the presiding officer would be unable to proceed. No doubt it is assumed that most vacancies will come immediately to the presiding officer's attention, while subs. (3) makes special provision for the small number which may not.

Subs. (3)

" *three months.*" There are two pointers towards the selection of this particular period; one is the recommendation of the Speaker's Conference on Electoral Law (1973), referred to above. The second is the Local Government (Scotland) Act 1973, s. 37 (1), which provides that where a casual vacancy occurs in the office of councillor, a by-election must be held within three months of the date on which the vacancy is deemed to have occurred.

" *except that . . . comes to his notice.*" This is intended to provide for the exceptional situation where a vacancy does not come immediately to the notice of the presiding officer, but the practical value of the provision is uncertain. During the Committee stage in the Lords, Lord McCluskey, Solicitor-General for Scotland, took the examples of where a vacancy arises during a recess, or where a member disappears (*e.g.* on a climbing or sailing holiday) and it is not known for a number of weeks that the member is in fact dead; *Hansard*, H.L. Vol. 390, cols. 658-9 (April 12, 1978). However, as noted already, there appears to be nothing to prevent the operation of the procedure during a recess, and the second situation will almost certainly be covered by Assembly standing orders under subs. (5). The likelihood of a delay in notification for party political advantage is slight, unless standing orders or the development of a convention provides, as with the House of Commons, that notification must be made by a member of the same party as the member whose seat has been vacated.

Subs. (5)

" *a vacancy shall be deemed to have occurred . . .*" This provision seems designed to meet the situation envisaged by the Solicitor-General and referred to above. Say a member becomes missing on a climbing holiday, and his body is not discovered for eight weeks. It would be competent for Assembly standing orders to provide that the vacancy shall be deemed to have occurred on the date of the discovery of the body, not the estimated date of the member's death.

" *references in this section to the presiding officer . . .*" This is intended to provide for the situation where the presiding officer has vacated office or is unwell, abroad, or dead.

First meeting of Assembly

6. The first meeting of the Assembly shall be held on such day and at such time and place as the Secretary of State may direct.

GENERAL NOTE

It is consistent with other provisions of the Act (see s. 2 (1), regarding the first ordinary election, and s. 7 (1), regarding the regulation of Assembly procedure until such time as the Assembly has made its own standing orders) that the Secretary of State should be empowered to make the arrangements for the Assembly's first meeting. It is intended that thereafter the Assembly should make such arrangements for itself; see *Our Changing Democracy*, para. 36.

Procedure of Assembly

7.—(1) The procedure of the Assembly shall be regulated by standing orders of the Assembly; but the Secretary of State may give directions for regulating its procedure pending the making of standing orders.

(2) The standing orders shall include provision for the election of a presiding officer from among the members of the Assembly and for his tenure of office.

GENERAL NOTE

This section should be read together with ss. 24 to 31, which contain more detailed provisions concerning Assembly standing orders. It was envisaged in *Our Changing Democracy*, para. 40, that the Secretary of State would make interim standing orders to govern Assembly procedure until such time as the Assembly made its own standing orders, and effect is given to this proposal in subs. (1); the intention is that the "directions," which will be in the form of standing orders, will be available when the Assembly comes into being; Lord McCluskey, Solicitor-General for Scotland, *Hansard*, H.L. Vol. 390, cols. 1498, 1503 (April 24, 1978), and it is possible that the directions will form the basis of the Assembly's own standing orders.

For other instances of the important role of the Secretary of State at the outset of the Assembly's life, see s. 2 (1), regarding the first ordinary election, and s. 6, regarding the first meeting of the Assembly.

Subs. (2) has been included here, rather than among the other provisions concerning standing orders in ss. 24 to 31, because the election and term of office of the presiding officer are considered to be fundamental to the operation of the Assembly, while the matters dealt with in ss. 24 to 31 are considered to be of a more general and ancillary nature; Lord Kirkhill, Minister of State at the Scottish Office, *Hansard*, H.L. Vol. 392, cols. 1319–1323 (June 7, 1978).

Subs. (2) makes no provision for the appointment of a deputy presiding officer; presumably this is left to the Assembly's discretion.

Disqualification for membership of Assembly

8.—(1) Subject to section 9 of this Act, a person is disqualified for membership of the Assembly if—

(*a*) he is disqualified for membership of the House of Commons under paragraphs (*a*) to (*e*) of section 1 (1) of the House of Commons Disqualification Act 1975; or

(*b*) is disqualified otherwise than under that Act for membership of that House or for sitting and voting in it; or

(*c*) he is a Lord of Appeal in Ordinary; or

(*d*) he holds any of the offices for the time being designated by Order in Council as offices disqualifying for membership of the Assembly; or

(*e*) he has been convicted in the United Kingdom, the Channel Islands, the Isle of Man or the Irish Republic of any offence and has had passed on him a sentence of imprisonment (whether suspended or not) for a period of not less than three months without the option of a fine and a period of less than five years has elapsed since the date of that conviction.

(2) A person who holds office as lord-lieutenant or lieutenant for any region, islands area or district in Scotland is disqualified for membership of the Assembly for any Assembly constituency comprising the whole or part of that area or district or of the part of that region in which he discharges his functions.

(3) For the purposes of subsection (1) (*e*) above the ordinary date on which the period allowed for appealing against a conviction expires or, if an appeal against a conviction is made, the date on which the appeal is finally disposed of or abandoned, shall be deemed to be the date of the conviction.

(4) Subsection (2) of this section applies with the necessary modifications to membership of the Assembly before an election to which an Order in Council under Part I of Schedule 1 to this Act applies.

(5) No recommendation shall be made to Her Majesty in Council to make an Order under this section unless a draft of the Order has been laid before and approved by a resolution of each House of Parliament, but this does not apply to an Order made by virtue of section 79 (2) of this Act if the Assembly has resolved that the Secretary of State be requested to recommend the making of the Order.

GENERAL NOTE

This section, which should be read together with ss. 9 to 11, sets out the categories of persons who will be disqualified from membership of the Assembly and contains other related provisions. The structure of the section is such that anyone not disqualified by reference to its provisions is qualified; moreover, the section disqualifies both persons affected by its provisions from being elected to the Assembly, and also members of the Assembly who become affected during the lifetime of an Assembly. It is clear, therefore, that there is no residential qualification for Assembly members, nor is there a requirement that a member be a registered elector for his constituency; *cf.* Local Government (Scotland) Act 1973, s. 29 (1).

Members of local authorities, the Welsh Assembly, the House of Commons and the Assembly of the European Communities are not precluded from membership of the Assembly. The Government accepted the view of the Kilbrandon Report, para. 1142, that dual membership of the Assembly and the U.K. Parliament should be permissible, and might even be desirable as a means of providing cross-fertilisation between one body and the other; it was also felt that to preclude dual membership by statute would be inconsistent with the stated desire to maintain the political unity of the U.K. The same consideration regarding cross-fertilisation has been applied also to the Assembly of the European Communities. Given the extremely heavy workload involved in dual membership, however, it is not anticipated that it will become a common phenomenon; *Hansard*, H.L Vol. 390, cols. 676–684 (April 12, 1978). In general this section follows *Our Changing Democracy*, para. 37, and paras. 1–8 of Appendix A. The position of peers and the clergy is dealt with in s. 9.

Subs. (1)

(*a*) The categories of persons included in paras. (*a*) to (*e*) of s. 1 (1) of the House of Commons Disqualification Act 1975 (the 1975 Act) are: the holders of judicial office (specified in Sched. 1, Pt. I, to that Act); civil servants (including the staff of the Scottish Executive (see s. 67)); members of the armed forces; members of police forces maintained by police authorities; and members of foreign legislatures outside the Commonwealth. This paragraph also attracts the 1975 Act, s. 3, which provides a number of exceptions to the disqualifications in s. 1 (1) (*c*) of that Act concerning reserve and auxiliary forces, etc.

(*b*) The grounds and nature of the disqualification referred to in this paragraph are, in outline, as follows:

aliens are disqualified from membership at common law, and by the Act of Settlement 1700, s. 3, as amended by the Status of Aliens Act 1914, and the British Nationality Act 1948;

persons under 21 *years of age* are disqualified from membership by the Parliamentary Elections Act 1695, s. 7 (applied to Scotland by the Act of Union 1707);

lunatics are disqualified at common law (the Act does not attract the Mental Health Act 1959, s. 137, which provides a procedure for unseating an M.P. who is suffering from mental illness; nor does it contain a comparable provision);

bankrupts are incapable of being elected to or sitting or voting in the House of Commons for five years after discharge, by the Bankruptcy Act 1890, s. 9, as applied to Scotland by the Bankruptcy (Scotland) Act 1913;

persons guilty of corrupt or illegal election practices under the Representation of the People Act 1949, Pt. III (to be applied under s. 4 of this Act), are disqualified in varying ways and for varying periods according to the offence committed. It may be presumed that the variations will be maintained so far as disqualification from membership of the Assembly is concerned.

(*d*) This paragraph should be read together with subs. (5). It is intended that the Orders in Council will be generally based on the same principles as the corresponding provisions of the 1975 Act, and in particular on the criteria for disqualification set out in *Our Changing Democracy*, Appendix A, para. 4: *viz.* (a) paid office holders with functions confined to Scotland who are appointed by the Scottish administration will be disqualified; (b) paid office holders in bodies appointed by the U.K. Government who are disqualified from membership of the House of Commons will also be disqualified from membership of the Assembly if the functions of the body extend to Scotland; (c) unpaid office holders will be disqualified only if they cannot perform their Assembly duties satisfactorily or if it is particularly important that they are seen to be free from political bias; if disqualification is appropriate, its territorial application will follow that for paid officers. One obvious difference between the provisions of this Act and those of the 1975 Act is that the latter contains, in Sched. 1, Pts. II and III, a detailed list of disqualifying offices; moreover s. 5 (2) of the 1975 Act provides that when the list of offices is altered by Order in Council under s. 5 (1), new copies of the Act which are printed must incorporate the amendments. The decision not to adopt the same scheme in this Act means that the public will not have ready access to an up-to-date list in a single legislative document.

(*e*) There is no equivalent statutory provision regarding disqualification from membership of the House of Commons, but the House does have the power to expel a person deemed unfit for membership. (Expulsion in these circumstances, however, does not create a disability.) Since the Assembly does not possess the same powers and privileges as the House of Commons, it was obviously thought necessary to make specific statutory provision in this area, although it is arguable that the Assembly could have claimed a power similar to that of the House of Commons under s. 14. The model taken for this paragraph is the Local Government (Scotland) Act 1973, s. 31 (1) (*c*), and it should be noted that, as in that Act, only the more serious offences will lead to disqualification from Assembly membership. Following discussion during the Committee stage in the Lords, an amendment was moved by the Government during the Report stage to make the paragraph consistent with the Rehabilitation of Offenders Act 1974. As the paragraph was originally drafted, the criterion for disqualification was whether a person was convicted " not earlier than five years before the last ordinary election." However, the last ordinary election could be almost four years earlier than the date of the conviction, so that the total period of disqualification could extend to almost nine years, *i.e.* the five-year period provided for in para. (*e*), plus the period between the date of the conviction and the last ordinary election. This was considered to be unnecessarily restrictive, and inconsistent with the Rehabilitation of Offenders Act 1974, s. 5 (2), Table A, which lays down a minimum rehabilitation period of five years. The position now is that anyone convicted in the British Isles of an offence for which he is sentenced to not less than three months' imprisonment without the option of a fine will be disqualified from membership of the Assembly until a period of five years has elapsed from the date of that conviction; *Hansard*, H.L. Vol. 390, cols. 669–676, 699–701 (April 12, 1978); Vol. 392, cols. 1325–1327 (June 7, 1978).

" *the Irish Republic.*" Convictions in the Irish Republic are also referred to in the Local Government (Scotland) Act 1973.

" *date of . . . conviction.*" This is calculated by reference to subs. (3).

Subs. (2)

This is consistent with the 1975 Act, s. 1 (2), and Sched. 1, Pt. III, by which lieutenants are barred from membership for any parliamentary constituency comprising the whole or part of the area in which they hold their office. This in turn is a reflection of the general rule that the holders of these offices should not take part in political activity within their area, but may take part in national politics or in political activities in other areas. There are, it seems, occasional departures from this rule, and it does not seem to apply at all to the Lord Provosts of the four major Scottish cities. See Local Government (Scotland) Act 1973, s. 205. This subsection should be read alongside subs. (4).

Subs. (4)

The purpose of this subsection is to apply the provisions of subs. (2) (which, unlike subs. (1), specifically refers to Assembly constituencies) to elections held before the Assembly constituencies are created. See s. 1, and note thereon, and Sched. 1.

Subs. (5)

The first Order in Council will have to be made well before the first ordinary election, since the contents of the Order will influence the selection of candidates by political parties.

The purpose of the second part of the subsection (from " but this does not apply " to the end of the sentence) is to allow an expedited method of altering the list of disqualifying offices, *e.g.* where the alteration is consequential upon an Assembly Act which creates new offices or abolishes existing offices. In these circumstances the Affirmative Resolution procedure need not be used; instead the Assembly may resolve to request the Secretary of State to recommend the making of an appropriate order under s. 79 (2).

Exceptions and power to grant relief from disqualification

9.—(1) A person is not disqualified for membership of the Assembly by reason only—

(*a*) that he is a peer, whether of the United Kingdom, Great Britain, England, Scotland or Ireland; or

(*b*) that he has been ordained or is a minister of any religious denomination.

(2) Where a person was, or is alleged to have been, disqualified for membership of the Assembly, either generally or for any Assembly constituency, on any ground other than one falling within section 8 (1) (*b*) or (*e*) of this Act and it appears to the Assembly—

(*a*) that that ground has been removed; and

(*b*) that it is proper to do so;

it may resolve that any disqualification incurred by that person on that ground shall be disregarded.

(3) A resolution under subsection (2) above shall not affect any proceedings under Part III of the Representation of the People Act 1949 as applied by an order under section 4 of this Act or enable the Assembly to disregard any disqualification which has been established in such proceedings or in proceedings under section 11 of this Act.

GENERAL NOTE

This section deals with two separate matters. Subs. (1) provides that peers and members of the clergy will not be disqualified for membership of the Assembly. This is generally based upon the Kilbrandon Report, para. 1142 (which did not, however, envisage a general relief for all clergy, but only for Church of Scotland ministers), and more particularly on *Our Changing Democracy*, Appendix A, paras. 5 and 6. Without this specific provision most peers and many members of the clergy would otherwise be disqualified by s. 8 (1) (*b*). The second part of the section, contained in subss. (2) and (3), permits the Assembly to grant relief from disqualification in certain defined circumstances. The provisions follow as closely as possible the parallel provisions in the House of Commons Disqualification Act 1975 (the 1975 Act).

Subs. (1)

" *by reason only.*" A person may be otherwise disqualified on any of the grounds set out in s. 8 (1) and (2).

" *a peer, whether of the United Kingdom, Great Britain, England, Scotland or Ireland.*" Peers of the U.K., Great Britain, England or Scotland are ineligible for membership of the House of Commons because they have a seat in the House of Lords; Irish peers, however, may by the Peerage Act 1963, s. 5, sit for any U.K. constituency.

" *has been ordained.*" This is designed to cover priests in the Roman Catholic Church and clergymen of the Church of England and the Church of Ireland, who are disqualified from membership of the House of Commons by the Roman Catholic Relief Act 1829, s. 9, and the House of Commons (Clergy Disqualification) Act 1801, s. 1. Clergy of the Episcopal Church of Scotland and of the Church in Wales are not so disqualified.

" *minister of any religious denomination.*" This is designed to cover Church of Scotland ministers, who are disqualified from membership of the House of Commons by the House of Commons (Clergy Disqualification) Act 1801, s. 1. Ministers of nonconformist churches are not, as a general rule, disqualified from membership of the House of Commons, but the breadth of the phrase used in this subsection should be adequate to remove any doubts regarding membership of the Assembly (see *Erskine May* (19th ed.) p. 43, and the 1975 Act, s. 10 (3)).

Subs. (2)

The corresponding provision in the 1975 Act is s. 6 (2), which permits the House of Commons to direct, by order, that a disqualification or alleged disqualification may be disregarded. Like the Commons, the Assembly may resolve to disregard a disqualification only if the two separate conditions in paras. (*a*) and (*b*) are satisfied; the Assembly might wish to rely on para. (*b*) and refuse relief if it were not satisfied that the disqualification arose from anything other than inadvertence. Even if the ground for disqualification is removed, a member will by s. 10 lose his seat if the Assembly does not grant relief.

" *was, or is alleged to have been.*" The use of the past tense is necessary since the Assembly cannot, because of para. (*a*), grant relief until the ground for disqualification has been removed. While under s. 10 sanctions cannot be taken against a member until his disqualification has been established beyond doubt, it is nevertheless possible for the Assembly to dispose of the matter under this section while it is still the subject of a mere allegation.

" *either generally or for any Assembly constituency.*" Some disqualifications (*e.g.* under s. 8 (2)) will arise only in relation to particular constituencies. In the absence of any provision corresponding to s. 8 (4), it does not appear that the Assembly will be able to grant relief from disqualifications in respect of particular constituencies which are incurred before Assembly constituencies are created. For the phrase " Assembly constituency," see s. 1 and Sched. 1.

" *on any ground other than one falling within section* 8 (1) (*b*) or (*e*) *of this Act.*" As originally drafted, this subsection would have enabled the Assembly to grant relief from any of the grounds of disqualification provided for in s. 8. A Government amendment moved during the Report stage in the Lords removed from the ambit of relief disqualifications other than those arising under the 1975 Act (s. 8 (1) (*b*)) and those arising from crimes for which a person has been sentenced to a prison sentence within the last five years (s. 8 (1) (*e*)). This amendment has the effect of making the ambit of relief under this subsection the same as that for the House of Commons under the 1975 Act, for the House of Commons is able to grant relief only in respect of disqualifications arising under that Act; *Hansard*, H.L. Vol. 390, cols. 701–705 (April 12, 1978); Vol. 392, cols. 324–325, 1327–1328 (June 7, 1978).

Subs. (3)

This subsection provides that decisions of an election court under the Representation of the People Act 1949, Pt. III (as applied by order under s. 4), or of the Court of Session under s. 11, shall prevail over any resolution of the Assembly under subs. (2). The corresponding provision in the 1975 Act is s. 6 (3).

Effect of disqualification

10.—(1) Subject to any resolution of the Assembly under section 9 of this Act,

    (*a*) if a person disqualified for membership of the Assembly, or for membership for a particular Assembly constituency, is elected as a member of the Assembly or, as the case may be, as a member for that constituency, his election shall be void; and

    (*b*) if a member of the Assembly becomes disqualified for membership of the Assembly or for membership for the Assembly constituency for which he is sitting, his seat shall be vacated.

(2) Subsection (1) above applies with the necessary modifications to membership of the Assembly before an election to which an Order in Council under Part I of Schedule 1 to this Act applies.

(3) The validity of any proceedings of the Assembly shall not be affected by the disqualification of any person for membership of the Assembly or for membership for any Assembly constituency.

GENERAL NOTE

This section provides in subs. (1) that where a person disqualified under s. 8 is elected to the Assembly, and no relief is granted under s. 9, his election is void; similarly, if a person becomes disqualified after his election, his seat shall be vacated by process of law. In either case, a by-election under s. 5 will follow. The corresponding provision in the House of Commons Disqualification Act 1975 is s. 6 (1). As in s. 8 (4), provision is made in subs. (2) for subs. (1) to apply with appropriate modifications with regard to elections which take place before Assembly constituencies are created. Subs. (3) provides that even if a disqualified person participates in Assembly proceedings, their validity may not be questioned for that reason.

Subs. (1)

" *Assembly constituency.*" See s. 1 and Sched. 1.

Subs. (3)

" *proceedings of the Assembly.*" See s. 81 (2).

Judicial proceedings as to disqualification

11.—(1) Any person who claims that a person purporting to be a member of the Assembly is disqualified or has been disqualified at any time since his election may apply to the Court of Session for a declarator to that effect, and the decision of the court on the application shall be final.

(2) On an application under this section the person in respect of whom the application is made shall be the defender; and the applicant shall give such security for the expenses of the proceedings, not exceeding £200, as the Court of Session may direct.

(3) An application under this section in respect of any person may be made whether the grounds on which it is made are alleged to have subsisted at the time of his election or to have arisen subsequently; but no declarator shall be made under this section in respect of any person—

(*a*) on grounds which subsisted at the time of his election, if an election petition is pending or has been tried in which his disqualification on those grounds is or was in issue; or

(*b*) on any ground, if a resolution under section 9 of this Act requires that the ground shall be disregarded.

(4) In this section " disqualified " means disqualified for membership of the Assembly or for any Assembly constituency.

GENERAL NOTE

This section corresponds to the House of Commons Disqualification Act 1975, s. 7, which gives jurisdiction to the Judicial Committee of the Privy Council to decide questions of disqualification arising under that Act, largely in replacement of the old common informer procedure whereby an outsider could sue a disqualified person for financial penalties. The Judicial Committee has no jurisdiction to make a declaration on disqualification which arises otherwise than under the 1975 Act, but there are no comparable limitations under this section on the jurisdiction of the Court of Session. S. 7 of the 1975 Act is otherwise followed in a number of important respects. Like the Judicial Committee, the Court of Session has jurisdiction whether the grounds of the disqualification existed at the time of the election or arose subsequently, subject to the two provisos (contained in subs. (3) (*a*) and (*b*)) that no declarator may be made where an election petition is pending or has already been tried (unless the application to the Court of Session is on different grounds) or where the Assembly has under s. 9 resolved that the disqualification or alleged disqualification be disregarded. The purpose of the provisos is to avoid conflicts of jurisdiction. Where a declarator is made, it would still be open to the Assembly in appropriate cases to resolve under s. 9 that the disqualification be disregarded; otherwise, the effects of disqualification as laid down in s. 10 (1) will apply.

The section seems to provide a simple alternative to the procedure by election petition under the Representation of the People Act 1949, Pt. III, although there are two significant differences. First, election petitions must be presented within 21 days of the return of the election, while under this section there is no time limit on the making of the application. Secondly, an election petition must be brought by a registered elector for the constituency in question, by an unsuccessful candidate, or by any person claiming to have been validly nominated as a candidate; under this section, however, there are no such restrictions. There are, therefore, sufficient differences between the two procedures to justify their separate existence.

Subs. (2)
" *and the applicant shall give such security for the expenses of the proceedings, not exceeding £200, as the Court of Session may direct.*" These words were the subject of a Government amendment moved during the Committee stage in the Lords. The effect of the amendment was to bring the section further into line with the 1975 Act, s. 7. It is interesting to note that the term " security " has been used, rather than the Scottish term " caution," on the grounds that " security " would be more comprehensible; Lord McCluskey, Solicitor-General for Scotland, *Hansard,* H.L. Vol. 390, cols. 706–8 (April 12, 1978). The Scottish term " expenses " was, however, inserted in place of the English term " costs " as a Government amendment during the Third Reading stage in the Lords; *Hansard,* H.L. Vol. 393, col. 378 (June 29, 1978).

Subs. (4)
" *Assembly constituency.*" See s. 1 and Sched. 1.

Members' oath of allegiance

12.—(1) A member of the Assembly shall, as soon as may be after his election, and at a meeting of the Assembly, take the oath of allegiance set out in section 2 of the Promissory Oaths Act 1868 or make the corresponding affirmation and shall not, until he has done so, take part in any other proceedings of the Assembly.

(2) If a member has not taken the oath or made the affirmation required by this section within two months of his election, or such longer period as the Assembly may have allowed before the expiration of the second month, he shall cease to be a member at the expiration of that month or longer period.

GENERAL NOTE
With certain modifications (notably the absence of any monetary penalty for sitting or voting without having taken the oath or made the affirmation) this section adopts the procedure laid down for M.P.s. An Assembly member may not participate in any other proceedings of the Assembly until he has taken the oath or made the corresponding affirmation (subs. (1)); nor, by s. 34 (5), may he be paid. Moreover, if he fails to take the oath or make the affirmation within two months of his election, or such longer period as the Assembly may determine, he shall cease to be a member and a by-election under s. 5 will have to be held (subs. (2)).

It appears that the proceedings for taking the oath or making the affirmation will have to be administered by the Clerk (see s. 32), for a difficulty will arise if it is intended that the oath be administered by the presiding officer. Subs. (1) clearly provides that a member may not take part in any other proceedings of the Assembly until he has taken the oath or made the affirmation, and the election of a presiding officer is a " proceeding of the Assembly." How, then, may members take part in the election of a presiding officer until they have taken the oath? When a new Parliament first meets at Westminster, the taking of the oath or making of the affirmation is administered by the Speaker, but not until after his election. The Parliamentary Oaths Act 1866, s. 5, (see note on subs. (2) below) expressly provides that until the Speaker has been elected penalties are not attached to participation in a debate by an M.P. who has not taken the oath.

A written record will be necessary as proof that the oath has been taken or the affirmation made.

Subs. (1)
" *the oath of allegiance set out in section 2 of the Promissary Oaths Act* 1868." The form of the oath is as follows: " I, . . ., do swear that I will be faithful and bear true allegiance to Her Majesty Queen Elizabeth, her heirs and successors, according to law. So help me God." It is likely that the oath will be taken in the customary Scottish manner, *i.e.* with uplifted hand. See Oaths Act 1978, s. 3.

" *or make the corresponding affirmation.*" A person who objects to being sworn, and stating as a ground for the objection that he has no religious belief, or that taking an oath is contrary to his religious belief, may be permitted instead to make a solemn affirmation. The form of the affirmation is as follows: " I, . . ., do solemnly, sincerely and truly declare and affirm . . ." (followed by the words of the oath, but omitting the imprecation). See Oaths Act 1978, ss. 5 and 6.

" *any other proceedings of the Assembly.*" Taking the oath, or making the affirmation, must take place at a meeting of the Assembly and will be regarded as a proceeding of the Assembly. For the phrase " proceedings of the Assembly," see s. 81 (2).

Subs. (2)

Contrast the Parliamentary Oaths Act 1866, s. 5, which provides that if an M.P. votes, or sits during a debate after the Speaker has been chosen without having made and subscribed the oath, a penalty of £500 will be imposed for every occasion he does so; in addition " his seat shall be vacated as if he were dead."

" *or such longer period . . . second month.*" Given the nature of the sanction contained in this subsection for failing to take the oath or make the affirmation, a provision of this nature seems necessary to cover the situation where, *e.g.* an elected member is too ill to participate in the proceedings, or is unavoidably absent from the country. The power to grant an extension of the two month period is discretionary, and must be exercised before the end of that period.

Resignation

13. A member of the Assembly may at any time resign his seat by giving notice in writing to the presiding officer or to any person authorised by the standing orders of the Assembly to receive the notice.

GENERAL NOTE

The straightforward procedure whereby a member of the Assembly can at any time resign his seat by giving written notice to the presiding officer or other authorised person contrasts markedly with the more complex procedure for resigning a seat in the House of Commons. It is settled that an M.P. cannot relinquish his seat, but to evade this restriction an M.P. who wishes to resign accepts an office under the Crown which disqualifies him from membership. See the House of Commons Disqualification Act 1975, s. 4.

Resignation of an Assembly seat will normally be followed by a by-election; see s. 5.

Subsidiary powers of Assembly

14. Subject to the provisions of this Act, the Assembly may do anything (whether or not involving the acquisition or disposal of any property) which is calculated to facilitate, or is conducive or incidental to, the discharge of any of its functions; and any expenses incurred under this section shall be paid out of the Scottish Consolidated Fund.

DEFINITION

" property ": s. 81 (1)

GENERAL NOTE

It is a well established principle of law that when a public authority exceeds the powers vested in it by statute, the acts done in excess of those powers are invalid as being *ultra vires.* It is equally well established that an authority's powers include not only those expressly conferred, but also those which are reasonably incidental to the express powers (see, *e.g. D. & J. Nicol* v. *Dundee Harbour Trustees,* 1915 S.C. (H.L.) 7); again, however, an act which cannot be regarded as being in exercise of an incidental power will be *ultra vires.* The purpose of this section is to avoid any doubts that the principle of incidental or implied powers applies to the Assembly.

The section is concerned solely with administrative arrangements, and has no relation to the legislative powers of the Assembly, which are conferred by separate provisions (see ss. 17 and 18 and Sched. 2, especially para. 8 thereof). It is intended to ensure that the Assembly will be free to undertake such steps as the acquisition of office accommodation, furniture and equipment, and the provision of library facilities. While the scope of the power conferred by the section may seem wide, actions taken under the authority of the section must be related to the functions of the Assembly as determined by this Act.

The section is based on the Local Government (Scotland) Act 1973, s. 69, and the key words " is calculated to facilitate, or is conducive or incidental to . . ." are drawn directly from that section, as is the word " subsidiary " in the marginal note. By contrast with the 1973 Act, however, there is no reference to the borrowing or lending of money. It is probable that s. 69 did not add anything to the implied powers which local authorities possess at common law; equally it is probable that the Assembly, as a statutory creation (albeit unique in its form), also possesses these powers, for the *ultra vires* doctrine is not confined in its operation to statutory corporations such as local authorities. This section therefore appears to be very much a precautionary measure, to put the matter of implied powers beyond question.

For the Scottish Consolidated Fund, see Pt. III.

Defamatory statements in Assembly proceedings

15.—(1) For the purposes of the law of defamation in any part of the United Kingdom—

   (a) any statement (whether oral or written) made in proceedings of the Assembly; and

   (b) the publication under the authority of the Assembly of any document;

shall be absolutely privileged.

(2) Where the publication of any document is privileged by virtue of subsection (1) (b) of this section the publication of any abstract from or summary of it which is fair and accurate is also privileged, unless the publication is proved to be made with malice.

GENERAL NOTE

The purpose of this section, according to the Government, is to confer upon the Assembly the same degree of liberty of expression as Parliament enjoys. During the Bill's stages in the House of Lords, however, it was repeatedly argued that subs. (1) (a) in particular conferred a wider immunity than Parliament at present possesses, and as a result the provision had a somewhat difficult passage through Parliament.

Erskine May states, " Freedom of speech is a privilege essential to every free council or legislature " (19th ed., p. 73). Just as the privileges of Parliament are essentially functional, in that they are " absolutely necessary for the due execution of its powers " (*Erskine May* 19th ed., p. 67) so this section was justified by the Government on the grounds that it was necessary for the effective working of the Assembly, and that it did not go further than was required for that purpose; the Assembly will be enacting legislation which would otherwise be dealt with by Parliament, and if its members were constantly at risk of defamation actions, they might be inhibited in their discussion of Bills, with the possible consequence that the content of legislation might not be fully or properly considered. The existence of legislative powers cannot, however, be the sole justification for conferment of the privilege, since liberty of expression will be of value in other aspects of the Assembly's work.

It was perhaps inevitable that M.P.s and peers should have considered the section against the background of their own privileges. In places (*e.g.* subs. (1) (a)) the words are based on an analogy with Parliament but there are, however, a number of indications that too close a comparison may be misleading. Although the courts may well be prepared to allow themselves, when interpreting the section, to be guided by Westminster rules and practices, the opportunities for so doing may be restricted if the Assembly adopts its own distinctive methods of working. Moreover, the section has deliberately not been constructed in such a way as to attract the powers, privileges and immunities of Parliament, even in the limited sphere of freedom of speech. This is in contrast to the corresponding provisions in the constitutions of former British colonies as well as to the Government of Ireland Act 1920, s. 18 (1), so that indirectly the construction of the section serves to reinforce the Assembly's subordinate nature.

While it is true that new parliamentary privileges must be created by statute rather than by resolution (see, *e.g.* Parliamentary Commissioner Act 1967, s. 10 (5), conferring absolute privilege on a complaint forwarded by an M.P. to the Parliamentary Commissioner for Administration) whatever powers and privileges the Assembly possesses must be derived from statute. Parliament possesses a number of privileges (notably freedom from arrest) which have no counterpart in this section or elsewhere in the Act; this is clearly in application of the principle that the privileges conferred should be confined to those deemed necessary to enable the Assembly to operate effectively. Likewise, the Assembly will not have any penal jurisdiction; although it will through its standing orders be able to preserve order in its proceedings, and to exclude members therefrom (see s. 25), it will not in the absence of express words be able to expel any of its members; nor will it be able to institute proceedings against outsiders. Finally, the scope of the privilege conferred by this section will be ultimately for determination by the courts, whose jurisdiction will not be fettered as it is with regard to parliamentary proceedings by Art. 9 of the Bill of Rights 1688, which provides that " freedom of speech and debate or proceedings in Parliament ought not to be impeached or questioned in any court or place outside Parliament." There is no scope for any argument that the rules governing the powers and functions of the Assembly are distinct from the general law of the land, as there is regarding the corresponding laws of Parliament. This again reinforces the subordinate nature of the Assembly, in so far as there is an obvious relationship between the principles on which the jurisdiction of the courts is admitted or restricted in matters of parliamentary privilege, and the attitude of the courts towards the traditional doctrine of parliamentary supremacy (see, *e.g. Bradlaugh* v. *Gossett* (1884) 12 Q.B.D. 271; *Pickin* v. *British Railways Board* [1974] A.C. 765).

As explained already there is obviously some justification for viewing this section against the background of parliamentary privilege, but it is more appropriate to see it only as making certain alterations to the law of defamation both in Scotland and elsewhere in the U.K. by adding to the types of statements, etc., to which absolute or qualified privilege applies. Support for this view is provided by the opening words of the section, which deserve a special emphasis. The section does not provide any immunity for Assembly members from the operation of criminal law.

Subs. (1)

" *in any part of the U.K.*" Clearly the protection given by the section would be much diminished if it only altered the law of Scotland.

" *(a) any statement (whether oral or written) made in proceedings of the Assembly.*" The most difficult phrase in this paragraph is " proceedings of the Assembly." In s. 81 (2) this phrase is declared to include " proceedings of any committee of the Assembly or of any sub-committee of such a committee." More importantly, however, the phrase has been deliberately used to attract the same meaning as the similar phrase " proceedings in Parliament " in Art. 9 of the Bill of Rights, even though that phrase has itself caused difficulties: see *Erskine May*, 19th ed., pp. 87–91. Lord McCluskey, Solicitor-General for Scotland, explained during the Third Reading stage in the Lords, " We start off with a model—the model of the Westminster Parliament. We tried to copy that in respect of the Assembly in relation to this one limited matter. The model itself is somewhat blurred and vague, the reason being that the courts have not had to consider the matter. If we make a copy of a blurred model, it is hardly surprising that we end up with a slightly blurred copy "; *Hansard*, H.L. Vol. 393, col. 384 (June 29, 1978). The alternative course of action would have been to provide a more precise definition; both the Second Report of the Joint Committee on the Publication of Proceedings in Parliament ((1969–70) H.L. 109, H.C. 261) and the Report of the Faulks Committee on Defamation (1975; Cmnd. 5909) recommended that " proceedings in Parliament " be given a statutory definition, the latter committee providing a definition in cl. 7 (6) of its draft Bill. Although it is reasonable to assume that the interpretation of " proceedings of the Assembly " will cause difficulties, the Government claimed that this would be less disadvantageous than an attempt to resolve the difficulties in respect of the Assembly alone, in advance of full consideration of the general issue of defamation by Parliament.

Drawing on the Westminster analogy (and bearing in mind that the procedures adopted by the Assembly may affect the validity of that analogy) there can be no doubt that absolute privilege will be given to oral statements made by Assembly members on the floor of the Assembly or in its committees, to oral statements made by the Assembly Clerk and officers and servants of the Assembly when acting in the course of their duties, and to oral statements made by witnesses before Assembly committees. Oral statements made outside the precincts of the Assembly (*e.g.* a conversation on Assembly business between an Assembly member and a Scottish Secretary in the latter's office) may well also be protected under this paragraph, but a purely private conversation between two Assembly members would probably not be protected, even though it took place within the Assembly precincts. Nor is it entirely clear whether statements made in the course of Assembly proceedings may be used to support a defamation action, where the cause of the action arises out of something done or said outside the Assembly. In *Church of Scientology of California* v. *Johnson-Smith* [1972] 1 All E.R. 378, it was held that what was said or done in Parliament could not be relied upon for this purpose, but particular emphasis was placed in the judgment on Art. 9 of the Bill of Rights.

So far as written statements are concerned, absolute privilege would presumably be conferred upon notices of motions, written answers to questions, and written evidence submitted by an outsider to a committee. The position regarding correspondence between a constituent and an Assembly member, between Assembly members, or between an Assembly member and a Scottish Secretary is less clear, even if the content of the correspondence is in some way related to the actual or prospective business of the Assembly, because to attract absolute privilege the statement must be made " in proceedings of the Assembly." It was here that the suggestion arose that the Assembly was being given a greater degree of liberty of expression than Parliament, in the absence of any limiting definition of the nature of the written statements to be afforded absolute privilege. In 1957, for example, the House of Commons by a very narrow majority rejected the view of its Committee of Privileges that a letter concerning a nationalised industry from an M.P. to a minister was a " proceeding in Parliament." After discussion at the Committee and Report stages in the Lords it was finally agreed during the Third Reading stage (contrary to the advice of the Government) to amend the paragraph so that it would read " any statement in proceedings of the Assembly." The House of Commons, however, rejected this amendment, Mr. John Smith M.P., Minister of State at the Privy Council Office, arguing that it would be undesirable to leave an ambiguity as to whether written statements were included or not—a somewhat weak argument given the full discussion of the matter in the House of Lords. (*Hansard*, H.L. Vol. 390, cols. 714–22 (April 12, 1978); Vol. 392, cols. 1335–45 (June 7, 1978); Vol. 393, cols. 378–90 (June 29, 1978); H.C. Vol. 953, cols. 747–78 (July 6, 1978)).

" (*b*) *the publication under the authority of the Assembly of any document.*" This paragraph corresponds to the Parliamentary Papers Act 1840, s. 1, which confers absolute privilege upon papers and reports published by or under the authority of either House of Parliament. Command Papers, however (*i.e.* papers presented to Parliament formally by command of the Sovereign, but in practice by the Government), do not receive protection from the 1840 Act although in exceptional cases the special parliamentary procedure of the motion for an unopposed return can be used to give a Command Paper the status of a parliamentary paper for the purpose of the 1840 Act. It will be open to the Assembly, if it so wishes, to devise an equivalent procedure so that absolute privilege can be given to any equivalent of Command Papers.

Subs. (2)

This subsection corresponds to the Parliamentary Papers Act 1840, s. 3, which, in the absence of malice, protects the publication of extracts from, or abstracts of, papers published by or under the authority of Parliament. Thus, for example, reports in the press of parliamentary papers are given qualified privilege, as are broadcast reports (Defamation Act 1952, s. 9) provided that they satisfy the requirements of the section. This subsection is concerned only with abstracts or summaries of documents which are absolutely privileged under subs. (1) (*b*); it is not concerned with unofficial newspapers or broadcast reports of Assembly proceedings, which will be given qualified privilege according to the terms of the Defamation Act 1952, ss. 7 and 9, as amended by Sched. 16, paras. 12–13, of this Act. (See Sched. 16, paras. 14–16, for corresponding amendments to Defamation Act (Northern Ireland) 1955).

" *which is fair and accurate.*" These words were added to the subsection during the Committee stage in the House of Lords by an amendment which was accepted by the Government. The phrase " fair and accurate " does not appear in the Parliamentary Papers Act 1840, s. 3. In favour of the amendment it was argued that the omission of the words " fair and accurate " rendered the privilege excessively wide in scope. It is arguable, however, that the amendment may in practice make little difference to the provision, since if an extract or summary was not fair and accurate, it is likely that a malicious intent could be established, *Hansard*, H.L. Vol. 390, cols. 728–735 (April 12, 1978).

" *unless the publication is proved to be made with malice.*" By the Parliamentary Papers Act 1840, s. 3, the onus of proving that the extract or summary was printed without malice lies, unusually, upon the defender. Under this subsection, however, it appears that it is for the pursuer to establish malice. This is in line with a recommendation of the Faulks Committee on Defamation, para. 226.

Corrupt practices

16. The Assembly shall be a public body for the purposes of the Prevention of Corruption Acts 1889 to 1916.

GENERAL NOTE

The three Acts of Parliament collectively referred to as the Prevention of Corruption Acts 1889 to 1916 are the Public Bodies Corrupt Practices Act 1889, the Prevention of Corruption Act 1906, and the Prevention of Corruption Act 1916. Under these Acts, it is an offence for any person corruptly to give or receive any gift or other advantage as an inducement to influence the conduct of any member, officer or servant of any public body. There has in recent years been some doubt as to the interpretation of the term " public body ", which is defined in the 1889 Act, s. 7, as amended by the 1916 Act; see *R.* v. *Manners* [1978] A.C. 43. This section makes clear beyond doubt that the Assembly is included within the meaning of that term; by contrast, however, Parliament is not so included.

Legislation

Scottish Assembly Acts

17.—(1) Subject to section 18 of this Act, the Assembly may make laws, to be called Scottish Assembly Acts.

(2) A Scottish Assembly Act may amend or repeal a provision made by or under an Act of Parliament.

(3) Proposed Scottish Assembly Acts shall be known as Bills, and a Bill shall become a Scottish Assembly Act when it has been passed by the Assembly and approved by Her Majesty in Council.

(4) The validity of any proceedings leading to the enactment of a Scottish Assembly Act shall not be called in question in any legal proceedings.

(5) Every Scottish Assembly Act shall be judicially noticed.

GENERAL NOTE
Subs. (1)

In the phrase " Subject to section 18 of this Act," there is an indication that the legislative powers of the Assembly are not unlimited, and it is necessary to read this subsection along with a number of other provisions in the Act to ascertain the scope of the powers conferred. In this respect the Act's provisions are based on two key concepts: " legislative competence," which is introduced in s. 18, is defined more fully in Sched. 2 where, in para. 1, the second key concept of " devolved matter " is encountered. This is dealt with more fully in ss. 63 and 64 of the Act (s. 81, the interpretation section, refers to s. 63), and s. 63 (2) makes a further reference (in the context of the Assembly's legislative competence) to Sched. 10, which sets out the details of the devolved matters. Essentially, therefore, the Assembly's legislative competence is defined in terms of devolved matters.

It may well be that Acts of the Scottish Assembly will be given a special citation to distinguish them from Acts of Parliament, as was the practice with the former Parliament of Northern Ireland; see Report of the Renton Committee on the Preparation of Legislation (Cmnd. 6053, 1975), paras. 18.8–18.14.

Subs. (2)

When legislative power is devolved to the Assembly, all existing Acts of Parliament and subordinate legislation applying to Scotland will continue so to apply until such time as they are superseded by Assembly Acts or subordinate legislation made under such Acts. The power to amend or repeal U.K. legislation is in general not limited to legislation in force prior to the Assembly's establishment, although it is subject to Sched. 2, para. 7 which, with limited exceptions, prevents the Assembly from amending this Act. Moreover, as noted in more detail below, Parliament could entrench its own legislation so as to prevent repeal of amendment by the Assembly. In addition, of course, the Assembly will be able to legislate regarding a devolved matter on which hitherto there has been no legislation.

It may be supposed that once the Assembly is in operation, Parliament will no longer make laws on matters falling within the Assembly's competence without the prior agreement of the Scottish administration. The Kilbrandon Report, at para. 1126, indicated that a constitutional convention should develop to this effect, and *Our Changing Democracy*, while less explicit, hinted the same at para. 51. There is, however, nothing in law to prevent Parliament from legislating on matters falling within the Assembly's legislative competence without the consent of the Scottish administration, since the legislative supremacy of Parliament remains unaffected by this Act. It is intended that such a course of action would be exceptional, but arguably Parliament would be justified in taking such a step if, for example, the Assembly declined to legislate on a matter on which legislation was necessary to give effect to an international obligation of the U.K.; Lord McCluskey, Solicitor-General for Scotland, *Hansard*, H.L. Vol. 390, cols. 989–990 (April 18, 1978).

Moreover, Parliament could, if it wished, prevent the Assembly from amending or repealing an Act of Parliament, even if its subject matter fell within the Assembly's competence, by inserting a provision in the Act to the effect that amendment or repeal would be beyond the Assembly's competence. An entrenching provision of this nature would have to be read alongside the Scotland Act, and would over-ride the provisions of this subsection to the extent of the inconsistency between them. The same result could be achieved by amendment of Sched. 10 to this Act.

Inconsistencies may arise between Acts of Parliament and Assembly Acts, although these should be exceptional; in the normal event, they will be avoided by consultation between the U.K. Government and the Scottish Executive or, if necessary, by one of a number of possible means: amendment of the Act of Parliament by the Assembly Act under this subsection; amendment of the Act of Parliament or of the Assembly Act by a further Act of Parliament; or by Order in Council under s. 37. If inconsistencies do arise, it remains to be seen whether the courts would treat both measures as having equal weight, and so apply the normal rule of construction whereby the later measure is regarded as having impliedly repealed the earlier to the extent of the inconsistency between them, or whether the courts would prefer the Act of the supreme legislature to that of the subordinate; there is no doubt that Scottish Assembly Acts are a species of subordinate legislation; see Lord Fraser of Tullybelton, *Hansard*, H.L. Vol. 389, cols. 1429–1430 (March 15, 1978). *Cf.* Government of Ireland Act 1920, s. 6 (2).

Subs. (3)

The legislature which makes Scottish Assembly Acts consists of the Assembly and of Her Majesty in Council. Given the procedures established by s. 19 for the scrutiny of Bills, and by s. 38 for moving the rejection of Bills in certain circumstances, it may be assumed that approval will be given automatically (like the Royal Assent to U.K. Bills) once a Bill has been submitted to Her Majesty in Council by the Secretary of State; see, however, s. 19 and note thereon.

" *passed by the Assembly*." The legislative procedures of the Assembly will be governed by standing orders; see s. 26.

Subs. (4)

The effect of this subsection is that an Assembly Act may not be challenged in legal proceedings on procedural grounds; for challenge on substantive grounds, see s. 65 and Sched. 12. This will apply even if, for example, the relevant standing orders of the Assembly have not been followed (see s. 26) or if there is a dispute as to the result of a vote. In this respect the position is similar to that concerning Acts of Parliament; see *Edinburgh and Dalkeith Railway Co.* v. *Wauchope* (1842) 8 Cl. & F. 710, *Pickin* v. *British Railways Board* [1974] A.C. 765 (H.L.).

Subs. (5)

The effect of this subsection is that Assembly Acts need not be proved in court proceedings. In this respect they are in the same position as Acts of Parliament;

see Interpretation Act 1978, s. 3. In the light of this provision it is perhaps curious that no provision is made either here or elsewhere in the Act for a " master copy " of an Assembly Act (comparable to that contained on the Parliament Roll) to which reference could be made in the event of any doubt or dispute as to the text. It is possible that the actual copy of the Bill approved by Her Majesty in Council could be used for this purpose; *Hansard*, H.L. Vol. 390, cols. 750–751 (April 12, 1978).

Legislative competence of Assembly

18.—(1) A Scottish Assembly Act shall be law only if or to the extent that it is within the legislative competence of the Assembly.

(2) Any question whether a provision is within the legislative competence of the Assembly shall be determined in accordance with Schedule 2 to this Act.

GENERAL NOTE

This section follows on from s. 17 (1), and should be read in conjunction with Sched. 2, which sets out the criteria according to which questions of legislative competence will be decided. It is also of importance in various other provisions of the Act, *e.g.* ss. 19, 63–65, and Scheds. 10–12.

Subs. (1)

This subsection contains a provision of principle which opens the way for judicial review of Assembly legislation after its approval, on grounds of substantive *ultra vires;* see s. 65 and Sched. 12. It also serves to emphasise that the Assembly is a subordinate legislature whose powers are limited by the Act which created it.

" *only if or to the extent that.*" These words are necessary because an Assembly Act may be beyond the Assembly's legislative competence either wholly or in respect only of certain of its provisions. Their effect is that if, say, only one provision in an Assembly Act is found to be *ultra vires*, the rest of the Act—or as much as can sensibly be severed from the offending provision—is still valid. By contrast, if a provision in an Assembly Bill is found to be *ultra vires* during the course of pre-assent judicial review, no such severance can take place, and the Bill as a whole will not be submitted to the Privy Council; see s. 19 (1) and (4).

Subs. (2)

" *a provision.*" The provision may be in an Assembly Bill or in an Assembly Act, since Sched. 2 applies in both pre- and post-assent judicial review of legislation.

Scrutiny of Assembly Bills

19.—(1) The Secretary of State shall consider every Bill passed by the Assembly and, if he is of opinion that any of its provisions is not within the legislative competence of the Assembly, he shall refer the question whether that provision is within that competence to the Judicial Committee of the Privy Council for decision and he may also do so if he is of opinion that there is sufficient doubt about it to justify the reference; but no such reference shall be made in a case falling within subsection (2) below or section 38 (3) of this Act.

(2) If, after considering a Bill in pursuance of subsection (1) above, the Secretary of State is of opinion that the Bill is not compatible with Community obligations or any other international obligations of the United Kingdom or that it provides for matters which are or ought to be provided for by or under legislation passed by Parliament and implementing any such obligation, he shall certify to the Assembly that he is of that opinion and shall not submit the Bill to Her Majesty in Council for approval.

(3) The decision of the Judicial Committee on any question referred to it under this section shall be stated in open court.

(4) If the Judicial Committee decides that any provision of a Bill is not within the legislative competence of the Assembly the Secretary of State shall not submit the Bill to Her Majesty in Council for approval; and if the Judicial Committee decides that a provision is within the legislative competence of the Assembly the decision shall be binding in all legal proceedings.

DEFINITION

" Community obligation ": European Communities Act 1972, s. 1 (2) and Sched. 1.

GENERAL NOTE

The main purpose of this section is to set out the procedure for pre-assent scrutiny of Assembly Bills. Central to the procedures provided by the section is the Secretary of State, who is placed under a duty to consider every Bill passed by the Assembly. If he is of opinion that any of the Bill's provisions are beyond the Assembly's legislative competence, he must refer the suspect provisions to the Judicial Committee of the Privy Council for a decision. He may also do so if his doubts about a provision are such as to justify such a reference. If the Judicial Committee decides that the provision or provisions in question are not within the Assembly's competence, the Bill cannot then be submitted to Her Majesty in Council for approval. If, however, the provision is decided to be within the Assembly's competence, the decision of the Judicial Committee in respect of that provision will be binding in all future legal proceedings (see s. 65 and Sched. 12, regarding post-assent judicial review of Assembly Acts). In such a case the Bill would normally be submitted to Her Majesty in Council for approval in the usual way, although the Act does not require the Secretary of State to do so; it would therefore seem that there is nothing to prevent the Secretary of State in these circumstances from moving the rejection of the Bill under s. 38.

Entirely different considerations apply if the Secretary of State is of the view that the Bill is not compatible with a Community obligation or an international obligation of the U.K., or that the matters provided for in the Bill ought instead to be, or are already, provided for in U.K. legislation implementing the obligation in question. In such cases the Secretary of State simply certifies his opinion to the Assembly, and does not submit the Bill for approval. The Judicial Committee is not involved in such cases.

There is, however, nothing in the section to prevent the Assembly from reconsidering a Bill which has not been submitted for approval, and from passing it again with such alterations as it thinks fit.

It may be assumed that the procedures created by this section will in practice be supplemented by informal consultations between the Scottish administration and the U.K. Government, from an early stage in the legislative process, and that references to the Judicial Committee will be made only in the exceptional cases where there is a genuine difference of opinion which cannot be resolved. It may be assumed also that legal advice will be available to the Secretary of State from both the Scottish and the English Law Officers as well as from his departmental legal staff, and also to the Scottish Executive from its legal personnel (see s. 20 (6)). The Assembly itself may well wish to provide legal advice to its members on matters of legislative competence (which will be particularly valuable in the field of private members' legislation, assuming that this particular aspect of Westminster legislative practice is followed by the Assembly) and to make formal provision in its standing orders for consideration of questions of legislative competence as part of its legislative process (see Lord Elwyn-Jones L.C., *Hansard*, H.L. Vol. 390, cols. 1066–8 (April 18, 1978)).

Historically, the Judicial Committee of the Privy Council has had an important role in advising the Crown on problems arising from U.K. colonies and the Commonwealth, and it has had considerable experience in dealing with constitutional questions covering the legislative competence of colonial and similar legislatures. It also has the power under the Judicial Committee Act 1833, s. 4, to give advisory opinions on matters of law when references to it are made by the Crown, but a more direct precedent can be found in the Government of Ireland Act 1920, s. 51, which gave the Judicial Committee power to decide questions of legislative validity at both the pre-enactment and post-enactment stages. There is therefore some justification for the argument of the Government (see Lord Elwyn-Jones L.C., *Hansard*, H.L. Vol. 390, cols. 1107–8 (April 18, 1978)) that in exercising its jurisdiction under this section the Judicial Committee will be exercising its traditional role. While the Act is silent on this point, it may be assumed that the arguments before the Judicial Committee on references under this section will be conducted by counsel for the Secretary of State on the one hand, and for the Scottish Executive on the other hand. Likewise, no indication is given as to whether other persons or groups (such as local government authorities, trade associations or private individuals) will also be allowed to be parties to the proceedings; their opposition to an Assembly Bill might be stronger than the Secretary of State's.

The section as a whole has had a somewhat chequered history. *Our Changing Democracy*, paras. 56–60, envisaged that at the pre-approval stage, questions of *vires* would be determined by the Government, and that a Bill containing provisions considered to be *ultra vires* would be referred back to the Assembly by the Secretary of State with a statement of reasons. This proposal was widely criticised on the grounds that an essentially legal question involving the construction of statutory provisions ought to be decided by a court, and not by a politician; and it was in response to these criticisms that in the *Supplementary Statement*, para. 12, it was indicated that doubts about the legality of an Assembly Bill would be resolved by the Judicial Committee. This section was also amended by Parliament to a considerable extent, as is explained in more detail below.

Subs. (1)

" *The Secretary of State shall consider every Bill passed by the Assembly.*" This clearly indicates that the Secretary of State will not be formally involved in the legislative process until the Bill has completed its passage through the Assembly.

" *any of its provisions.*" This may refer to, at one extreme, one particular subsection or, at the opposite extreme, the whole Bill.

" *legislative competence.*" See Sched. 2.

" *that provision.*" This indicates that however much of a Bill is in the Secretary of State's opinion beyond the Assembly's legislative competence, he is obliged to identify clearly the suspect provision or provisions for the purposes of the reference to the Judicial Committee. It is important that he does so for the purposes of subs. (4).

" *decision.*" This is a departure from the normal rule whereby the Judicial Committee does not reach a decision, but instead provides advice to the Crown. *Cf.* Northern Ireland Constitution Act 1973, s. 18.

" *and he may also do so if he is of opinion that there is sufficient doubt about it to justify the reference.*" These words permit a reference to be made to the Judicial Committee if the Secretary of State's attitude to a provision is such that he has doubts, which fall short of a firm opinion, that it is beyond the Assembly's legislative competence. The words were added by a Government amendment made during the Report stage in the Lords following discussion during the Committee stage; *Hansard*, H.L. Vol. 390, col. 1072 (April 18, 1978); Vol. 392, cols. 1375–6 (June 7, 1978).

Subs. (2)

In this subsection, Community obligations are treated as a single concept, and are dealt with in the same way as international obligations of the U.K. This in general terms follows from *Our Changing Democracy*, para. 87, where it was stated: " The Government must remain responsible for all international relations, including those concerned with our membership of the European Community . . . "

The phrase " Community obligation " is defined in the European Communities Act 1972, s. 1 (2) and Sched. 1, as follows: " any obligation created or arising by or under the Treaties, whether an enforceable Community obligation or not." It refers, in the first place, to obligations which are enforceable in U.K. law, possibly at the instance of individuals, as provided in s. 2 (1) of that Act. Secondly, it refers to obligations which are not *per se* enforceable by virtue of s. 2 (1), such as an obligation under s. 2 (2) to implement in or for the U.K. a provision of Community law which is not " directly applicable." Such obligations exist only in and by virtue of Community law, and are owed by the U.K., as a member state, to the Community under the law of which they arise. They could be enforced not by individual right of action in U.K. courts but by enforcement procedures taken under the EEC Treaty, arts. 169–72.

During the Bill's stages in the Lords, it was suggested that the two principal types of Community obligation ought not to be treated in the same way. It was generally accepted that since the responsibility for securing the implementation of international obligations and the second type of Community obligation (as outlined above) rests with the U.K. Government, and continues to do so whatever the view of any domestic court on the existence or scope of that obligation, it was right that questions of compatibility between such obligations and a provision in an Assembly Bill should be decided directly by the Government. It was argued, however, that the first type of Community obligation (as outlined above) was of an entirely different character, and that when questions of compatibility arose between obligations which arose from directly applicable provisions of Community law and a provision in an Assembly Bill, a justiciable issue arose which was entirely suitable for determination by the Judicial Committee since it was, from a legal viewpoint, essentially the same type of issue as would be referred in the event of a provision in an Assembly Bill being alleged to be outwith the Assembly's competence. It was also observed that if such issues could be referred to the Judicial Committee, there then arose the possibility of a further reference under the EEC Treaty, art. 177 to the European Court of Justice to obtain a final interpretation of the scope of the Community obligation in question. During the Report stage in the Lords, amendments were made to give effect to these arguments, but these were against the wishes of the Government whose spokesmen argued that the distinction between the two types of Community obligations was more apparent in principle than in practice, and that the amendments would create political and practical difficulties. The Commons, however, did not accept the amendment; *Hansard*, H.L. Vol. 390, cols. 119–141 (April 18, 1978); Vol. 392, cols. 1361–1374 (June 7, 1978); H.C. Vol. 953, cols. 777–778 (July 6, 1978).

" *by or under.*" These words were the subject of a minor Government amendment made during the Third Reading stage in the Lords, and recognise that Community obligations may be implemented either by Act of Parliament or by subordinate legislation under the European Communities Act 1972, s. 2 (2); *Hansard*, H.L. Vol. 393, cols. 389–390 (June 29, 1978).

Subs. (3)

This follows the Judicial Committee Act 1833, s. 3.

Subs. (4)

" *any provision of.*" Even if only a single provision in an Assembly Bill is found by the Judicial Committee to be outwith the Assembly's legislative competence, the Secretary of State is under a duty not to submit the whole Bill to Her Majesty in Council for approval; the Judicial Committee may not sever the provisions which were the subject of its decision. The Assembly would presumably then wish to give further consideration to the Bill and make such amendments to it as it thinks fit.

" *and if the Judicial Committee decides . . . in all legal proceedings.*" These words were added as a Government amendment made during the Report stage in the Lords following considerable discussion in Committee. In the absence of any provision on the binding nature of Judicial Committee decisions, it would have to be assumed that the normal principles would apply so that in post-assent review proceedings a decision of the Judicial Committee which was in point would not be binding, but only of the highest persuasive authority. The amendment is designed to promote certainty in Assembly Acts, without seriously eroding the principle of post-assent review; the decisions of the Judicial Committee will be concerned only with those provisions identified by the Secretary of State as being suspect (see subs. (1)), and it must be assumed that all the relevant arguments will have been considered; *Hansard*, H.L. Vol. 390, cols. 1163–1171, 1176–1195 (April 19, 1978); Vol. 392, cols. 1349–1354, 1377 (June 7, 1978).

Executive functions and subordinate legislation

The Scottish Executive

20.—(1) There shall be a Scottish Executive one of whose members shall be known as the First Secretary and the others as Secretaries of the Scottish Executive.

(2) Any reference in this Act or in any Act amended by or under this Act to a Scottish Secretary is a reference to the First Secretary or any of the Secretaries of the Scottish Executive.

(3) Subject to subsections (6) and (7) of this section—

   (*a*) Scottish Secretaries shall be appointed by the Secretary of State; and (*b*) the First Secretary may appoint persons to be assistants to Scottish Secretaries; and

(*c*) any person appointed under this subsection shall be appointed from among the members of the Assembly.

(4) If the Assembly has nominated one of its members for appointment as First Secretary that member shall be so appointed; and in appointing the other Scottish Secretaries the Secretary of State shall act on the advice of the First Secretary.

(5) A Scottish Secretary shall hold office at Her Majesty's pleasure and an assistant to a Scottish Secretary may be removed from office by the First Secretary.

(6) A Scottish Secretary or assistant to a Scottish Secretary who is to perform functions corresponding to functions performed by a Law Officer of the Crown may (whether or not he is to perform also other functions) be appointed notwithstanding that he is not a member of the Assembly, and may then take part in the proceedings of the Assembly but shall not vote.

(7) A person appointed (otherwise than in pursuance of subsection (6) of this section) to be a Scottish Secretary or an assistant to a Scottish Secretary shall relinquish his appointment on ceasing to be a member of the Assembly; but for this purpose a member of the Assembly shall not be treated as ceasing to be such a member on the dissolution of the Assembly if he is again elected at the election following the dissolution.

(8) A Scottish Secretary may appoint such officers and servants as he may think appropriate for the exercise of such of the powers mentioned in section 21 (1) of this Act as are for the time being exercised by him.

(9) A person appointed a Scottish Secretary shall be on appointment take the official oath set out in section 3 of the Promissory Oaths Act 1868 and (unless he has taken it on a previous occasion) the oath of allegiance set out in section 2 of that Act (or make the corresponding affirmation).

GENERAL NOTE

Provision is made in this section for the composition of the Scottish Executive, for the appointment and removal from office of its members and for the appointment of the staff who will work in the various departments of the devolved administration. In a number of respects its terms do not follow the description of the Executive given in *Our Changing Democracy*, para. 43–50, in that they leave many more matters to the discretion of the Assembly and Executive. The section deliberately provides only a bare constitutional framework for the Executive, which will gradually be filled in through the development of conventions and practices. No attempt is made to specify how the Executive will operate in practice, or the nature of its relationship with the Assembly. The Kilbrandon Report, para. 1144, suggested that the doctrines of Cabinet and ministerial responsibility should operate in broadly the same way as they do at Westminster. It is reasonable to assume that they will indeed do so, given that members of the Executive and their assistants will be members of the Assembly (with the possible exception of these appointed under subs. (6) to perform functions corresponding to those of Law Officers of the Crown), but it will be open to the Executive and the Assembly to modify and develop these doctrines in whatever way they think appropriate; indeed some modification seems inevitable given that the Assembly has considerable discretion to determine its own rules of procedure (see ss. 7 and 24–31) which may, in particular, lead to a more extensive committee structure than that at Westminster (see s. 28). The political relationship between the Scottish administration and the U.K. Government will also affect Assembly-Executive relationships.

Subs. (1)

The Executive does not possess corporate status and does not have the power to act in its own name (see s. 21). No provision is made for either a maximum or minimum size of the Executive, or for the nature and allocation of portfolios. It seems that political pressures, combined with the fact that by s. 34 the salaries of Executive members are determined by the Assembly and paid for out of the Scottish Consolidated Fund, are expected to be sufficient to prevent the Executive from expanding to an excessive size. Assistants to Scottish Secretaries (first mentioned in subs. (3) (*b*)) are not members of the Executive.

Subs. (2)

The term " Scottish Secretary " when used in this Act refers to the First Secretary or any of the Secretaries in the Executive. Thus the office of Scottish Secretary is unitary, and any Scottish Secretary may exercise the functions of any other Scottish Secretary. In this respect the office of Scottish Secretary is comparable to that of a U.K. Secretary of State; see Interpretation Act 1978, Sched. 1, and *Agee* v. *Lord Advocate*, 1977 S.L.T. (Notes) 54. However, by s. 72 (1) (*a*), property is specifically vested in the First Secretary.

Subs. (3)

Para. (*a*). Although Scottish Secretaries hold office at Her Majesty's pleasure (subs. (5)) and will be exercising powers which ultimately derive from the Crown (see s. 21), Scottish Secretaries will be appointed not by the sovereign, but by the Secretary of State. Neither here nor elsewhere in the Act is direct contact permitted between the sovereign and the Executive or Assembly, on the argument that this would be inappropriate in a devolved system of government. The Secretary of State's discretion in the matter of appointments is severely restricted by subs. (4).

Para. (*b*). Since assistants to Scottish Secretaries will not be directly exercising powers on behalf of Her Majesty (s. 21 (1)) it is appropriate that they be appointed by the First Secretary. This adds one further link to the chain of authority which by virtue of para. (*a*) already extends from the sovereign, through the Secretary of State, to the First Secretary and the other Scottish Secretaries. No provision is made for a maximum or minimum number of assistants, or for their role, for the same reasons as those set out above in relation to the size and organisation of the Scottish Executive. As already noted, assistants will not be members of the Executive; see subs. (1).

Para. (*c*). Subject to subs. (6), Scottish Secretaries and assistants must be members of the Assembly at the time of their appointment. There is no possibility of a Scottish Secretary or an assistant who loses his seat at an Assembly election being re-appointed on condition that he obtains a seat in a by-election as soon as possible. See, however, subs. (7).

Subs. (4)

As already noted, by subs. (3) (*a*), it is the Secretary of State's duty formally to appoint the First Secretary. By this subsection, he is in making that appointment under a further duty to appoint the member of the Assembly who is nominated for the office by the Assembly. It may be assumed that the method of nomination will be provided in Assembly standing orders. It may also be assumed that the nominee will be, in the opinion of the Assembly, the person best able to command the support of a majority of the Assembly. If, after an Assembly election, one political party represented in the Assembly has an absolute majority over the other parties, the leader of that party in the Assembly is certain to be nominated. If, however, no party has an absolute majority, the onus is still placed by the subsection on the members of the Assembly, and on the parties which they represent, to consult amongst each other with a view to finding a nominee; in such a case the nominee might be the leader of one of the minority parties, and he might find himself First Secretary of either a minority or a coalition Executive. Exceptionally the situation might arise where the Assembly cannot agree on a nomination. In that event (and this explains the use of the word " if " which opens the subsection) the Secretary of State must (subs. (3) (*a*)) select and appoint a First Secretary on his own initiative. Before doing so, he would to forestall any criticisms or accusations of political bias have to satisfy himself—and, indeed, the House of Commons, to which he is responsible for the decision which he takes—that the Assembly could not resolve the deadlock on its own, and to this end he would presumably feel bound to engage in consultations with the parties represented in the Assembly, along with any independent members. If the person appointed in these circumstances was rejected by the Assembly (on a vote of confidence, for example) the Assembly itself could make a nomination at that stage. Alternatively the Assembly might wish to resolve under s. (3) (1) (*b*) that it be dissolved, in order to test the opinion of the electorate; it could, moreover, take such a step at an earlier stage to prevent the Secretary of State from acting on his initiative.

Once the First Secretary has been appointed, then on the assumption that he can, if only temporarily, command the Assembly's support, he will proceed to select the other members of the Executive. By the second limb of this subsection, the Secretary of State is under a duty to act on the advice of the First Secretary. It follows, then, that the formation of a new Executive cannot take place until a First Secretary has been appointed.

Subs. (5)

In law, the fact that a Scottish Secretary holds office at Her Majesty's pleasure renders him liable to instant dismissal; the power of dismissal will be exercised on the sovereign's behalf by the Secretary of State, and presumably a convention will develop to the effect that the dismissal of Scottish Secretaries other than the First Secretary will, by corollary with the method of appointment, take place only on the advice of the First Secretary. In practice, however, it is likely that dismissals will be rare, and that Scottish Secretaries other than the First Secretary will simply resign when they are asked to do so by the First Secretary or, if it is a case of the whole Executive resigning, in the wake of the First Secretary.

It may be assumed that the First Secretary will resign if he loses a vote of confidence in the Assembly, if another party gains an absolute majority in an election, or if he loses the confidence of his party (possibly as the result of a leadership contest). In the first two cases, the rest of the Executive would be certain to resign with him. If, however, he did not resign it would be open to the Assembly under subs. (4) to nominate a new First Secretary. If by that stage the former First Secretary had still not resigned the Secretary of State would have no choice but to dismiss him, and then, as he is obliged to, appoint the new nominee.

The manner of dismissal of assistants to Scottish Secretaries, under the second limb of this subsection, is a direct corollary to their manner of appointment.

Subs. (6)

The purpose of this subsection is to ensure that the best available person can be appointed to perform the functions of a Law Officer even though he is not a member of the Assembly. The subsection also permits the allocation of additional functions, although it is not likely that such functions will be particularly extensive or important if the person appointed is not a member of the Assembly. The provision that such a person may take part in proceedings of the Assembly, but without voting, reflects S.O. 63 (1) of the House of Commons, which provides that a Lord Advocate, if he is an M.P., may attend a Scottish Standing Committee even though he is not a member of it, and can then speak but not vote.

The Act does not alter the position of the Scottish Law Officers, who remain members of the U.K. Government.

Subs. (7)

It is provided in the first limb of this subsection that Scottish Secretaries and their assistants (other than those who by virtue of subs. (6) are not members of the Assembly) will automatically relinquish their appointment when they cease, for whatever reason, to be members of the Assembly. This is clearly consistent with subs. (3) (c). However, by s. 2 (3), the term of office of Assembly members ends with the dissolution of the Assembly. Accordingly Scottish Secretaries and their assistants would be obliged to relinquish office at that time but for the second limb of this subsection, which provides that the holder of such an office who is re-elected will be regarded as having continued to be a member during the period of the election, and indeed until such time as the composition of the new Executive is settled. The purpose of this second limb is therefore to provide for continuity between successive Executives. If it should happen that a Scottish Secretary is not re-elected, his powers could, by subs. (2), be exercised by another Scottish Secretary, but no provision is made for the situation where no Scottish Secretaries are re-elected. If such an unlikely situation arose it would be possible for all the powers to be exercised by a person appointed in pursuance of subs. (6).

Subs. (8)

This subsection empowers a Scottish Secretary to appoint staff to carry out devolved executive powers; assuming that the Whitehall pattern of organisation is followed, such staff will constitute the departments of the devolved administration, the departments being headed by Scottish Secretaries. The staff will continue to be, or will become, members of the U.K. Home Civil Service; see s. 67. S. 67 (1), when read in conjunction with this subsection, appears to preclude a Scottish Secretary from appointing officers and servants who are not civil servants. While it may well have been intended that the persons appointed under this subsection will have the same relationship to a Scottish Secretary as present civil servants do to Ministers in departments of central government, it cannot be assumed that this will be the case. Moreover, the subsection seems to have been deliberately worded so as to authorise officers and servants to exercise powers themselves; their statutory function is not merely one of providing assistance and advice. This, no doubt, is with a view to avoiding challenges to a civil servant's legal authority; see, *e.g. Dalziel School Board* v. *Scotch Education Department*, 1915 S.C. 234 and *R.* v. *Skinner* [1968] 2 Q.B. 700, 707 (Widgery L.J.).

Neither this subsection nor s. 67 places any control over the ultimate size or shape of the total establishment. The Lords did make amendments imposing such controls, but these were finally rejected by the Commons, having been resisted by the Government on the ground that the Scottish administration ought to decide such matters for itself; *Hansard,* H.L. Vol. 390, cols. 1279–96 (April 19, 1978); Vol. 392, cols. 1416–28 (June 8, 1978); H.C. Vol. 953, col. 810 (July 6, 1978); H.L. Vol. 395, cols. 483–96 (July 20, 1978); H.C. Vol. 954, cols. 1593–637 (July 26, 1978); H.L. Vol. 395, cols. 951–6 (July 27, 1978).

Subs. (9)

" *the official oath set out in section 3 of the Promissory Oaths Act 1868.*" The oath will be as follows: " I, ——, do swear that I will well and truly serve Her Majesty Queen Elizabeth in the Office of [Scottish Secretary]. So help me God."

" (*unless he has taken it on a previous occasion*)." Scottish Secretaries other than those appointed in pursuance of subs. (6) will have taken the oath *qua* members of the Assembly; see s. 12.

Executive powers

21.—(1) Such of Her Majesty's executive powers as would otherwise be exercisable on behalf of Her Majesty by a Minister of the Crown shall, if they relate to devolved matters and are exercisable in or as regards Scotland, be exercisable on behalf of Her Majesty by a Scottish Secretary.

(2) The executive powers mentioned in subsection (1) of this section include any executive power conferred on a Minister of the Crown by an enactment passed or made before the passing of this Act; and a Scottish Secretary shall perform any duty which by such an enactment is imposed on a Minister of the Crown so far as it falls to be performed in or as regards Scotland and relates to a devolved matter.

DEFINITIONS

" devolved matter ": s. 81 (1), referring to s. 63.
" enactment ": s. 81 (1).
" Minister of the Crown ": s. 81 (1).
" Scottish Secretary ": s. 81 (1), referring to s. 20 (2).

GENERAL NOTE

This section identifies the executive powers which are to be exercised by Scottish Secretaries (see s. 20). It corresponds to ss. 17 and 18, which identify the legislative powers of the Assembly.

By subs. (1), the executive powers of the Scottish Secretaries are those which would otherwise be exercised by a Minister of the Crown, are exercisable in or as regards Scotland (although not necessarily exclusively) and relate to devolved matters. As regards devolved matters, reference should be made to ss. 63–64 and Scheds. 10 and 11. There is a measure of overlap between the provisions relating to legislative powers and those relating to executive powers. In both cases, the concept of a " devolved matter " is crucial; and while the matters covered in Sched. 10 relate to both legislative and executive functions, the matters referred to in Sched. 11 relate to executive competence alone. Consequently Assembly legislation will be administered by Scottish Secretaries, as will U.K. legislation which deals with matters falling within the legislative competence of the Assembly, until such time as the Assembly repeals or amends that legislation under s. 17 (2). The powers conferred by U.K. legislation set out in Sched. 11 will also be exercised by Scottish Secretaries. In all cases, it is necessary that the executive powers satisfy the requirements of this section, and their exercise is subject to the possible intervention of the Secretary of State under s. 39. Subs. (2), which does not derogate from the generality of subs. (1), is particularly concerned with the exercise of powers arising under U.K. legislation.

The scope of the powers devolved under this section is not defined with any precision, which may create difficulties in the future when, for example, the courts are asked to determine whether an act of a Scottish Secretary is *intra vires* this Act.

Subs. (1)

As originally drafted, this subsection opened with the words " Such of Her Majesty's prerogative and other executive powers . . ." The words " prerogative and other " were removed, with the Government's agreement, by an amendment made during the Report stage in the Lords; *Hansard*, H.L. Vol. 392, cols. 1445–6 (June 8, 1978). During the Third Reading stage in the Lords, after considerable discussion at the Committee and Report stages, subs. (1) was removed in its entirety and replaced by an alternative subsection, which would have confined the Scottish Secretary to executive powers conferred on Ministers under existing enactments in devolved areas. This was against the wishes of the Government, whose spokesmen argued that this would lead to a substantial diminution in the scope of the devolved executive powers. The House of Commons rejected the amendment; *Hansard*, H.L. Vol. 390, cols. 1223–41 (April 19, 1978); Vol. 392, cols. 1427–46 (June 8, 1978); Vol. 393, cols. 391–404 (June 29, 1978); H.C. Vol. 953, cols. 783–810 (June 6, 1978).

" *Such of.*" This indicates that the subsection relates only to those of Her Majesty's powers which fulfil the qualifications set out in the subsection.

" *Her Majesty's executive powers as would otherwise be exerciseable on behalf of Her Majesty by a Minister of the Crown.*" The removal of the words " prerogative and other " cannot affect the meaning of the subsection, since the phrase " executive powers " clearly includes prerogative powers derived from the common law as well as powers derived from statute. While prerogative powers are less important than statutory powers in the context of this section, they are by no means without significance; Group 25 of Sched. 10, for example, provides that compensation out of public funds for victims of crime is a devolved matter; the present Criminal Injuries Compensation scheme is not governed by statute. Mention should also be made of " general executive powers " (such as the power to enter into contracts or to hold property) which do not stem from statute but which, though they have their legal source in the common law, cannot be included under the heading " prerogative " since they are held and exercised in common with all other persons. The effect of the Lords' amendment referred to above would have prevented a Scottish Secretary from exercising these general powers.

The phrase " on behalf of " is significant, since it means that in law Scottish Secretaries are to exercise their powers on behalf of the sovereign. This may well be important in litigation involving the Scottish Executive; see the Crown Proceedings Act 1947. Moreover, it restricts the scope of the prerogative powers exercisable by a Scottish Secretary to those otherwise exercisable by a minister (that is, without the sovereign's personal intervention) and excludes the sovereign's personal prerogatives, where the sovereign acts on the advice of her ministers or at her own discretion. It seems, therefore, that the subsection gives statutory recognition to a distinction which, in the context of the central government of the U.K., rests on constitutional convention.

The concern over this subsection in the Lords (see above) stemmed from the inclusion of prerogative powers within its scope. The principal ground of criticism, it seems, was that by permitting Scottish secretaries to exercise such prerogative powers as fulfilled the qualifications laid down, the powers in question were being subsumed by statute law (by application, one assumes, of the principle applied in *Att.-Gen.* v. *De Keyser's Royal Hotel* [1920] A.C. 508). This, it was argued, was dangerous since in cases of doubt as to the scope of a Scottish Secretary's powers, the courts would be obliged to look only at the very general terms of this Act, and would be debarred from considering what the prerogative consists of other than in terms of the Act. Even if it is assumed that the courts would restrict themselves so severely in their construction of this Act, the major argument is surely fallacious. All that the subsection does is to declare that certain powers which have in the past been exercised by a minister on behalf of the sovereign will in future, in certain limited areas, be exercised on behalf of the Crown by a Scottish Secretary. Therefore it only affects the manner of the exercise of the prerogative, and leaves untouched the scope, and the form, of the prerogative powers themselves. A useful parallel can be found in the Royal Assent Act 1967, which merely regulates the manner of notification of the Royal Assent to a Bill, but does not affect the nature of that particular prerogative power.

Subordinate instruments

22.—(1) Where, by or under any Act passed before this Act, any power to make, confirm or approve orders, rules, regulations or other subordinate legislation is conferred on a Minister of the Crown, then, to the extent that—

(*a*) the power is exercisable as regards Scotland; and

(*b*) it is so exercisable exclusively with respect to a devolved matter;

it shall be exercisable by a Scottish Secretary.

(2) If the enactment conferring the power makes provision—

(*a*) for any instrument or the draft of any instrument made in the exercise of the power to be laid before Parliament or either House of Parliament; or

(*b*) for the annulment or approval of any such instrument or draft by or in pursuance of a resolution of either or both Houses of Parliament; or

(*c*) prohibiting the making of such an instrument without that approval;

then, in relation to the exercise of the power in accordance with subsection (1) above, the provision shall have effect as if any reference in it to Parliament or either House of Parliament were a reference to the Assembly.

(3) If the enactment conferring the power makes provision requiring any order (within the meaning of the Statutory Orders (Special Procedure) Act 1945) to be subject to special parliamentary procedure, then, in relation to the exercise of the power in accordance with subsection (1) above, the provision shall have effect as if it required the order to be subject to such special procedure as may be prescribed by the standing orders of the Assembly; but this subsection does not apply where the power is exercised in any of the circumstances specified in paragraphs 1 to 3 of Schedule 3 to this Act or is such a power as is mentioned in paragraph 4 of that Schedule and is exercised as mentioned in that paragraph.

(4) If the enactment conferring the power makes provision for any order made under it to be a provisional order, that is to say an order which requires to be confirmed by Act of Parliament, then, in relation to the exercise of the power in accordance with subsection (1) above, the provision shall have effect as if it required the order to be confirmed by Scottish Assembly Act.

(5) Where, by or under any Act passed before this Act, a power is conferred on a person other than a Minister of the Crown to make orders, rules, regulations or other subordinate legislation, then, in relation to any exercise of that power as regards Scotland and with respect only to a devolved matter,—

(*a*) subsection (2) above shall apply with the necessary modifications; and

(*b*) if the enactment conferring the power applies the Statutory Instruments Act 1946 as if the power were exercisable by a Minister of the Crown, that Act (as amended by Schedule 16 to this Act) shall apply as if the power were exercisable by a Scottish Secretary.

(6) **Where, by or under any Act passed before this Act, power is conferred on Her Majesty to make an Order in Council, Her Majesty may by Order in Council make provision for securing that, to the extent that the power is exercisable as regards Scotland and exclusively with respect to a devolved matter, it shall be exercisable by order and treated for the purposes of this section as if it had been conferred by that Act on a Minister of the Crown.**

(7) **No recommendation shall be made to Her Majesty in Council to make an Order under subsection (6) above unless a draft of the Order has been laid before and approved by resolution of each House of Parliament.**

DEFINITIONS

" devolved matter ": s. 81 (1), referring to s. 63.
" enactment ": s. 81 (1).
" Minister of the Crown ": s. 81 (1).
" Scottish Secretary ": s. 81 (1), referring to s. 20 (2).

GENERAL NOTE

This section contains provisions which either directly transfer (subss. (1)–(5)) or provide machinery for transferring (subss. (6)–(7)) the exercise of powers to make subordinate instruments from the U.K. Government and Parliament to the Scottish Assembly and Executive. Once the Assembly and Executive are in operation, there will be three sources of power to make subordinate instruments; (i) powers in Scottish Assembly Acts; (ii) powers in Acts of Parliament passed after this Act, *e.g.* where Parliament legislates on a devolved matter and confers the power to make subordinate instruments on a Scottish Secretary; and (iii) powers in existing Acts of Parliament which relate to devolved matters. This section is concerned solely with the third of these categories, but whatever the source of the power, a subordinate instrument made by a Scottish Secretary is subject to revocation by the Secretary of State under s. 40.

In general terms this section follows the principles laid down in ss. 17, 18 and 21 regarding legislative and executive powers, in that the powers to make subordinate instruments will be transferred only if they are exercisable (but not necessarily exclusively) as regards Scotland, and if they are exercisable exclusively with respect to a devolved matter.

It will be competent for the Assembly to create, by Assembly Act, its own code of procedure to govern the making, in relation to devolved matters, of subordinate instruments by Scottish Secretaries under Acts of Parliament and Assembly Acts. Until that legislation is passed, however, the making of instruments by Scottish Secretaries under powers conferred by U.K. Acts will be governed by the Statutory Instruments Acts 1946 as amended by Sched. 16, paras. 2–8, of this Act (see also Sched. 2, para. 7, for the power to amend Sched. 16 in this regard). The 1946 Act accordingly now refers not merely to ministers and procedures in Parliament, but also to Scottish Secretaries and procedures in the Assembly. So far as possible the amendments seek to ensure that the Assembly procedures will reflect those at Westminster. This follows *Our Changing Democracy*, para. 68 which stated : " Any procedure in the Scottish Assembly for delegated legislation under United Kingdom Acts will be required initially to correspond as closely as possible to whatever may be required in Parliament by the relevant Act; it is right that the Scottish Executive should at that stage be bound by the procedures for the control of delegated legislation which were considered to be a necessary part of the Act when it was passed." See subs. (3).

The section does not apply to the Private Legislation Procedure (Scotland) Act 1936; see s. 31 (4).

Subs. (1)

This subsection transfers to the Scottish Executive a wide range of enabling powers which already exist under Acts of Parliament and which have hitherto been exercised by a Minister of the Crown. As already noted, the limitation on the power is contained in paras. (a) and (b). S. 82 (1) provides that for the exercise of powers under this subsection, enactments and other documents which pre-date this Act are to be interpreted as if references to a Minister of the Crown were, or included, references to a Scottish Secretary.

" *power to make, confirm or approve orders, rules, regulations or other subordinate legislation.*" These words are taken from the Statutory Instruments Act 1946, s. 1 (1).

Subs. (2)

The general effect of this subsection is to require the Assembly to assume from Parliament the task of scrutinising subordinate instruments. As the subsection indicates, the manner of the scrutiny is laid down by the parent Act in each case. Paras. (*a*), (*b*) and (*c*) follow in general terms the Statutory Instruments Act 1946, ss. 4–7 and, as already noted, that Act, as amended by Sched. 16 of this Act, will apply to instruments made under the powers conferred by this section.

" *or in pursuance of a resolution of.*" These words were added by a Government amendment made during the Committee stage in the Lords, and are designed to make the paragraph resemble more accurately the terms of the Statutory Instruments Act 1946, s. 5; *Hansard*, H.L. Vol. 390, col. 1311 (April 19, 1978).

Subs. (3)

The special parliamentary procedure created by the Statutory Orders (Special Procedure) Act 1945 requires an order to which the Act applies to be laid before Parliament after approval by the appropriate minister; it then comes into effect automatically at the end of the prescribed period, provided that no petitions are submitted for its amendment and the order is not annulled by resolution of either House. If, however, a petition is presented against the order it is referred to the Lord Chairman of Committees in the House of Lords and the Chairman of Ways and Means in the House of Commons, who then make a report to their respective Houses. If within 21 days of the report no resolution of annulment has been passed in either House, the petition is referred to a Joint Committee of both Houses, and the proceedings are then similar to these for a private Bill. Provided that there is no opposition to the order, the procedure is simpler than that by way of a local or private Act of Parliament, or a provisional order.

This subsection provides that the special parliamentary procedure is to be retained in the circumstances set out in Sched. 3. In other circumstances, when the order is approved by a Scottish Secretary in accordance with subs. (1), it will be for the Assembly to lay down such special procedure as it thinks fit in its Standing Orders. The explanation for the division is that this Act devolves the power to make and confirm a number of orders which have hitherto been subject to the special parliamentary procedure. Some of these orders, however, although dealing with devolved matters, could adversely affect the interests of statutory undertakers and other bodies operating in reserved areas. Accordingly with regard to these orders the special parliamentary procedure will continue to apply.

" *where the power . . . is exercised as mentioned in that paragraph.*" The second limb of the subsection, which consists essentially of these words, was recast by a Government amendment made during the Report stage in the Lords, as a paving amendment for the reorganisation of Sched. 3; *Hansard*, H.L. Vol. 392, cols. 1473–1474 (June 8, 1978).

Subs. (4)

This subsection refers to the procedure where a provisional (or draft) order is made by a Minister, and parliamentary approval for the order is obtained by means of a Provisional Order Confirmation Bill. When the provisional order is made, if any person petitions either House of Parliament while the Bill is awaiting confirmation, the petitioner is allowed to appear before the Select Committee to which the Bill is referred, and the proceedings then follow these applicable to a private Bill.

The effect of this subsection is that where a provisional order is made by a Scottish Secretary in accordance with subs. (1), confirmation of the order will be secured through an Assembly Act. It may be assumed that Assembly Standing Orders will contain the necessary procedural rules.

See s. 31 for provisions relating to the Private Legislation Procedure (Scotland) Act 1936.

Subs. (5)

This subsection is similar in terms to subs. (1), but refers to the situation where the power to make orders, rules, regulations or other subordinate legislation is conferred on persons other than a minister of the Crown (such as a local authority or public corporation).

The purpose of the subsection is, in circumstances where the power is exercised as regards Scotland and with respect only to a devolved matter, to apply subs. (2) so that scrutiny of the instrument will be by the Assembly, not by Parliament (para. (*a*)), and also the Statutory Instruments Act 1946, as amended by Sched. 16 to this Act (para. (*b*)).

Subs. (6)

It is consistent with the other provisions of this section that the powers hitherto exercisable by Her Majesty by Order in Council should be included in the transfer to the Scottish administration of the power to make subordinate instruments, where the power is exercisable as regards Scotland and exclusively with respect to a devolved matter. The effect of this subsection is to convert the power to make Orders in Council into a power to make orders, which will be vested in a Scottish Secretary and exercised as though the parent Act vested the power in a Minister of the Crown (see subs. (1), and also the Statutory Instruments Act 1946, s. 1). The only other possible arrangement, since the Scottish Executive has no direct access to the Sovereign, would have been for the Secretary of State to act as intermediary, and to submit draft Orders after approval by the Assembly.

Relatively few powers are affected by this subsection, but see, for example, the Burial Grounds (Scotland) Act 1855, s. 5 (Sched. 10, Pt. I, Group 20) and the Development of Tourism Act 1969, ss. 17–18 (Sched. 10, Pt. I, Group 17). Since the power to make Orders in Council is being converted into a power to make orders, it is necessary that the transfer be itself made by Order in Council, and the subsection envisages the possibility of a series of Orders in Council, for this purpose.

" *Her Majesty may by Order in Council.*" The word " may " is used to leave the U.K. Government with discretion in the matter, as well as to maintain, in a formal sense, the discretion of the Queen in Council.

Powers exercisable with consent or concurrently

23.—(1) Where an enactment conferring a power on a Minister of the Crown makes provision for the exercise of the power with the concurrence or subject to the consent or approval of, or after consultation with, any other Minister of the Crown, that provision shall not apply to the exercise of the power (in accordance with section 21 or 22 of this Act) by a Scottish Secretary unless either—

(*a*) the enactment is listed in Schedule 4 to this Act, or
(*b*) the power relates to the borrowing of money outside the United Kingdom or in a currency other than sterling.

(2) Where an enactment conferring a power on a Minister of the Crown makes no such provision, but the enactment is listed in Schedule 4 to this Act, then, except as otherwise provided in that Schedule, the power shall not be exercised by a Scottish Secretary without the consent of a Minister of the Crown.

(3) Notwithstanding anything in the preceding provisions of this Act, any power under the enactments listed in Schedule 5 to this Act may be exercised both by the Secretary of State and by a Scottish Secretary.

DEFINITIONS
" enactment ": s. 81 (1).
" Minister of the Crown ": s. 81 (1).
" Scottish Secretary ": s. 81 (1), referring to s. 20 (2).

GENERAL NOTE
This section, which should be read along with Scheds. 4 and 5, deals with two separate matters. Subss. (1) and (2) determine the circumstances in which a Scottish Secretary is obliged to act with the concurrence, or subject to the consent or approval

of, or after consultation with, a Minister of the Crown. Subs. (3) determines the circumstances in which a power is exercisable by both a Scottish Secretary and the Secretary of State. Generally the section provides qualifications to the transfer of executive power to Scottish Secretaries effected by ss. 21 and 22.

The word "concurrence" used in subs. (1) has a different sense to the word "concurrently" in the marginal note to this section (and also in the heading to Sched. 5). In the former case, it denotes "agreement." In the latter case, it refers to the possibility of two persons exercising the same power, either separately or together.

Subs. (1)

This subsection is concerned with U.K. enactments which provide that in exercising a power thereby conferred, the Minister of the Crown must act with the concurrence or subject to the consent or approval of, or after consultation with, another Minister. Requirements of this nature are found primarily in three specialised areas, *viz.* in powers (i) for the control of public expenditure and borrowing by public bodies on the domestic or foreign markets, where Treasury approval is regularly required; (ii) for the numbers, and pay and pensions, of staff, where the consent of the Minister for the Civil Service is frequently required; (iii) for the protection of statutory undertakers, where the approval of the responsible Minister is regularly required.

The section provides that where the power in question is now to be exercised by a Scottish Secretary in accordance with ss. 21 and 22, the Scottish Secretary may act alone, except in the circumstances set out in paras. (*a*) and (*b*).

Subs. (2)

This subsection provides for situations where the enactment in question does not make the provision referred to in subs. (1) (that is, where hitherto the powers have been exercised on the sole responsibility of individual Ministers) but is listed in Sched. 4. In such cases, the power conferred by the enactment in question cannot be exercised by a Scottish Secretary without the consent of a Minister.

The enactments contained in Sched. 4 are principally concerned with public sector pay and pensions and with planning matters. So far as the former are concerned, the objective is to permit the U.K. Government to retain control over pay and conditions of service in the public sector and to ensure the continuance of negotiations and arrangements at a national level; see *Our Changing Democracy*, para. 161, and also s. 43 (Ministers' consent to terms and conditions of service of certain persons). As regards planning matters, certain statutory undertakers (such as British Rail) will continue to be responsible to U.K. Ministers; these are referred to in the Act as "excepted statutory undertakers" and defined in s. 81 (1). Because town and country planning is, in general, a devolved matter (Sched. 10, Pt. I, Group 6) excepted statutory undertakers are given special consideration so that their statutory duties can be taken properly into account when decisions are taken. (Special consideration of this nature is not unprecedented; see, for example, the New Towns (Scotland) Act 1968 and the Town and Country Planning (Scotland) Act 1972). In the normal event protection in planning matters will be afforded through the terms of s. 71 and Sched. 14, but more specific protection is given to excepted statutory undertakers by making the exercise of power by a Scottish Secretary subject to ministerial consent.

Subs. (3)

In only a very few areas will powers be exercisable by both a Scottish Secretary and the Secretary of State; but the enactments contained in Sched. 5 have particular features which make such exercise desirable if both a Scottish Secretary and the Secretary of State are to carry out their functions effectively. The powers relate to such matters as the conduct of research, the payment of certain grants and the designation of bodies for particular purposes. For example, a Scottish Secretary will need access to the Criminal Justice (Scotland) Act 1949, s. 75 (1) (*b*) and (3) (*f*) if he wishes to authorise expenditure on criminal research (see Sched. 10, Pt. I, Group 25). The Secretary of State may also, however, wish to authorise expenditure on criminal research since a number of matters relating to crime (*e.g.* the police) are reserved to him.

"*may be exercised both by the Secretary of State and a Scottish Secretary.*" These words indicate that the powers in question may be exercised either by a Scottish Secretary, or the Secretary of State, or both of them acting together.

Standing orders—particular provisions

Crown interests and public records

24. The standing orders of the Assembly shall include provision for securing that a Bill proposing to make any such provision as is mentioned in Schedule 6 to this Act does so expressly and not merely by implication and will not be allowed to pass unless the Crown's consent has been signified by the Secretary of State.

GENERAL NOTE

This is the first of eight sections which supplement s. 7 by making more detailed provisions concerning the content of Assembly Standing Orders.

When legislating within its area of competence, the Assembly will have the capacity to bind the Crown, but the exercise of its powers is limited in two respects by this section whenever a provision in an Assembly Bill falls within the categories listed in Sched. 6. Generally, these are provisions which affect the Crown in either its private or public capacity, and a description of them has been scheduled as an alternative to using the amorphous term " Crown " in this section. Arguably, however, the ambiguity was only transferred to the Schedule, and especially para. 5 thereof.

First, the Bill must, by the standing orders of the Assembly, state expressly that its provisions fall within the categories so listed; this goes somewhat further than the judicial approach to the interpretation of Acts of Parliament, by which an Act is presumed not to bind the Crown in the absence of express provision or necessary implication (see Crown Proceedings Act 1947, s. 40 (2) (*f*) and *Province of Bombay* v. *Municipal Corporation of Bombay* [1947] A.C. 58 (P.C.)). It is submitted, however, that despite a failure to comply with this section, an Assembly Act could still be held to bind the Crown's interests by implication.

Secondly, an Assembly Bill which contains such a provision will by standing orders, not be allowed to pass unless the Crown's consent has been signified by the Secretary of State. This in general terms corresponds to parliamentary usage whereby Bills affecting the prerogative, hereditary revenues, personal property or interests of the Crown or the Duchy of Cornwall receive the signification of the Queen's consent before they are passed; normally this takes place at the beginning of the Third Reading debate (so that account may be taken of any amendments made up to that time), but if the matters affecting the royal interests form an important part of the Bill, the consent is signified at the beginning of the Second Reading debate. The consent is expressed in terms to the effect that Her Majesty, having been informed of the purpose of the Bill, has consented to place her prerogative or interest, or both, at the disposal of Parliament for the purposes of the Bill.

As already noted, the requirement that the Crown's consent be signified to Assembly Bills in the cases covered by this section will be imposed by Assembly standing orders; it does not appear directly in this Act. If the requirement as regards any particular Bill is not adhered to, and the Bill is approved by Her Majesty in Council, s. 17 (4) will operate to prevent the resulting Act from being challenged in legal proceedings. But what is more likely is that the Secretary of State would refuse to obtain approval of the Bill from Her Majesty in Council on the ground that such a Bill cannot have passed the Assembly within the meaning of s. 17 (3). The Queen's consent for Assembly Bills will be sought through the Secretary of State and conveyed by the same means, because the Scottish Executive has no direct access to the Crown. The granting of the consent will therefore be on the advice of the Secretary of State. This raises the possibility of this section being used by the U.K. Government to block Assembly legislation without recourse to its powers under s. 38.

The reference to " public records " in the marginal note to this section is explained by Sched. 6, para. 7.

Preservation of order

25. The standing orders of the Assembly shall include provision for preserving order in the proceedings of the Assembly, and any standing order made by virtue of this section may include provision for excluding a member from such proceedings.

GENERAL NOTE

This is the second of eight sections which supplement s. 7 by making more detailed provisions concerning the content of Assembly standing orders.

Its effect is to require the Assembly to include within its standing orders provision for preserving order in its proceedings, and any standing order made under this section may also make provision for the exclusion of a member.

" *shall.*" As the Bill was originally drafted, the inclusion in standing orders of a provision to preserve order would not have been mandatory. The word " shall," along with other minor consequential changes, was introduced by an amendment, which the Government accepted, during the Committee stage in the Lords; *Hansard*, H.L. Vol. 390, cols. 1472–3 (April 24, 1978).

" *proceedings of the Assembly.*" See s. 81 (2).

" *any standing order made by virtue of this section.*" These words were introduced by a Government amendment (consequential upon the amendment referred to above) during the Report stage in the Lords. The amendment ensures that exclusion can only follow from a breach of the standing order concerning the preservation of order; *Hansard*, H.L. Vol. 392, cols. 1494–5 (June 8, 1978).

" *may.*" The word " may " is used with a view to indicating to the Assembly the general view of Parliament that it would be sensible to have a provision on this matter. The same formula appears in ss. 27 (2), 28 (1) and 31 (1); *Hansard*, H.L. Vol. 390, cols. 1484–5 (April 24, 1978). It is not intended to derogate from the generality of s. 7 (1).

" *provision for excluding a member from the Assembly.*" It will be for the Assembly to determine in any standing order it makes on this matter to determine the nature and the period of the exclusion, and also the procedures leading to the imposition of such a penalty; *cf.* House of Commons S.O.s 23–25. The Assembly will not, it seems, be able to expel any of its members, on the argument that as a statutory creation it cannot deprive a person of an office (see s. 2 (3)) in the absence of express words empowering it to do so.

Stages of Bills

26. The standing orders of the Assembly shall include provision—

    (*a*) for general debate on a Bill with an opportunity for members to vote on its general principles;

    (*b*) for the consideration of, and an opportunity for members to vote on, the details of a Bill; and

    (*c*) for a final stage at which a Bill can be passed or rejected.

GENERAL NOTE

This is the third of eight sections which supplement s. 7 by making more detailed provisions concerning the content of Assembly standing orders.

The section was added by an amendment during the Report stage in the Lords, following discussion during the Committee stage. It has a somewhat protracted history; it was envisaged in *Our Changing Democracy*, para. 54, that the various stages for handling Assembly legislation would in broad terms be determined by statute, and the Scotland and Wales Bill (cl. 26 (3)) laid down these stages in identical language to that used in the White Paper. However, in the Lord President of the Council's statement to the House of Commons on July 26, 1977, (*Hansard*, H.C. Vol. 936, cols. 313–4) it was indicated that the Assembly would be given greater scope to determine its own procedure, and in consequence of that change of policy the provision was omitted in the original draft of the Scotland Bill. In the Lords, it was argued that since the Assembly would, within the area of its competence, be making laws hitherto made by Parliament, it was right that Parliament should be able to determine at least the outlines of the legislative process in the Assembly. The Government resisted the amendment in the Lords, relying on the argument used by the Lord President of the Council, but the Commons accepted the amendment without debate on division; *Hansard*, H.L. Vol. 390, cols. 1485–1512 (April 24, 1978); Vol. 392, cols. 1495–1514 (June 8, 1978); H.C. Vol. 953, col. 815 (July 6, 1978).

The three paragraphs in the section correspond generally to the Second Reading, Committee, and Third Reading stages in Parliament, although the section does not require the Assembly to adopt these aspects of parliamentary procedure. Within the guidelines laid down by the section, it remains open to the Assembly to adopt its own legislative procedure, and in so doing it may, for example, wish to make a different use of its committees; see s. 28. (The Scotland and Wales Bill, in cl. 29 (6), had envisaged an important role for Assembly committees in examining proposals for legislation before the introduction of Bills into the Assembly.)

It will also be open to the Assembly to create separate standing orders for public and private legislation; see *Hansard*, H.L. Vol. 390, col. 1578 (April 24, 1978); Vol. 391, cols. 1044–1045 (May 10, 1978).

" *(c) for a final stage at which a Bill can be passed or rejected.*" The matter of the passing of an Assembly Bill is of particular importance for the purposes of ss. 19 (1) and 24.

Members' pecuniary interests

27.—(1) The standing orders of the Assembly shall include provision for securing that members with pecuniary interests, as defined by the standing orders, or such other interests (if any) as may be specified in the standing orders, in any matter disclose them before taking part in any proceedings dealing with that matter, and may include provision for preventing or restricting participation of such members in such proceedings.

(2) Standing orders made in pursuance of subsection (1) above may include provision for excluding members contravening them from the proceedings of the Assembly.

(3) If a member of the Assembly takes part in any proceedings in contravention of any provision made in pursuance of this section he shall be liable on summary conviction to a fine not exceeding £500.

General Note

This is the fourth of eight sections which supplement s. 7 by making detailed provisions concerning the content of Assembly standing orders.

It is intended to ensure that the Assembly will through its standing orders provide that members with interests in the matter under discussion should disclose them, so that knowledge of any influences on their conduct or behaviour will become known both to the Assembly and the public. It also empowers the Assembly to include provision for preventing or restricting the participation in Assembly proceedings of members who have interests, and lays down a penalty, enforceable in the courts, for failure to disclose them.

For the term " proceedings of the Assembly," see s. 81 (2).

Subs. (1)

" *or any other interests (if any) as may be specified in the standing orders.*" These words were added by a Government amendment made during the Third Reading stage in the Lords, following considerable discussion during the Committee and Report stages, when it was argued that to confine the provisions to pecuniary interests only was undesirably restrictive, since a member might well have interests of a non-pecuniary nature (for example, through involvement in the activities of an interest group) which might influence his behaviour as much as a pecuniary interest. Without this amendment, it might have been argued that the particularity of the provision on pecuniary interests was intended to bar the Assembly from making any provision on other interests although it is clear from the terms of the amendment (in particular, the phrase " (if any) ") that the Assembly need not make such other provision. If, however, the Assembly does exercise its power in this matter, its rules governing the disclosure of interests might be more extensive than those in the House of Commons, which are concerned primarily with pecuniary interests; *Erskine May* (19th edn.), pp. 407–412 and Appdx. II; *Hansard*, H.L. Vol. 390, cols. 1512–9 (April 24, 1978); Vol. 392, cols. 1515–23 (June 8, 1978); Vol. 394, cols. 404–6 (June 29, 1978).

" *disclose.*" It may be assumed that the standing orders will determine the manner of disclosure. So far as the House of Commons is concerned, registration in the recently introduced Register of Members' Interests is sufficient disclosure for voting purposes, but M.P.s must still declare a relevant interest in debate even if it has been registered.

Subs. (2)

This subsection was added by a Government amendment during the Third Reading stage in the Lords, following discussion during the Committee and Report stages, during which it was argued that the financial penalty provided for in subs. (3) was inadequate, since it would not by s. 8 (1) (*e*), give rise to disqualification from membership. See subs. (3) and note thereon. *Hansard*, H.L. Vol. 390, cols. 1519–25 (April 24, 1978); Vol. 392, cols. 1523–8 (June 8, 1978); Vol. 394, cols. 404–6 (June 29, 1978).

" *excluding.*" This does not mean the same as " expulsion "; see s. 25 and note thereon.

Subs. (3)

The maximum fine for the corresponding offence in the Local Government (Scotland) Act 1973, s. 38 (2), is £200; it should also be noted that this Act was passed before the Government had completed its consideration of the recommendations of the Royal Commission on Standards of Conduct in Public Life (1976; Cmnd. 6524); one of its recommendations was that the penalty for failure to disclose pecuniary interests by local government councillors should be a maximum of £400 or six months' imprisonment on summary conviction, and an unlimited fine or two years' imprisonment for conviction on indictment (para. 156).

Committees

28.—(1) The standing orders of the Assembly may include provisions for the appointment of committees with functions extending to any matter which, whether in relation to the Assembly or in relation to the Scottish Executive, is a devolved matter.

(2) In appointing members to such committees the Assembly shall secure that the balance of parties in the Assembly is as closely as practicable reflected in the membership of each such committee.

DEFINITION

" devolved matter ": s. 81 (1), referring to s. 63.

GENERAL NOTE

This is the fifth of eight sections which supplement s. 7 by making detailed provisions concerning the content of Assembly standing orders.

Its effect is to empower the Assembly to appoint committees with functions extending to any devolved matter, and to require the Assembly in appointing such committees to ensure that their membership reflects the party balance in the Assembly as a whole.

The section has had a chequered history. *Our Changing Democracy*, paras. 76–79, stated that the Assembly would have " a highly developed system of committees to advise the Executive and investigate its activities." There would, it was envisaged, be a committee corresponding to each of the main subject fields of the Executive which would be consulted by the Executive on any proposed legislation relevant to its terms of reference, and in general oversee the work of the corresponding Executive department. The relatively detailed proposals of *Our Changing Democracy* were reflected in the Scotland and Wales Bill, cl. 29, but in the light of the subsequent Government policy decision to leave the Assembly as much freedom as possible to regulate its own procedures (*cf.* s. 26) this Act, as originally drafted, contained only a very brief enabling provision. The Lords, however, made a number of amendments to the section: the appointment of committees was made mandatory (Third Reading stage), and the Assembly was further required to ensure that no committee be appointed with functions not relating to devolved matters (Third Reading stage) and that the membership of the committees appointed reflected the party balance in the Assembly (Report stage). The Government resisted each of these amendments in the Lords, but by the time of the Commons' consideration of the Lords' amendments had dropped their resistance to the third of the amendments mentioned above, which now appears as subs. (2). The other two amendments were rejected by the Commons. *Hansard*, H.L. Vol. 390, cols. 1525–47 (April 24, 1978); Vol. 392, cols. 1528–41 (June 8, 1978); Vol. 393, cols. 406–17 (June 14, 1978); H.C. Vol. 953, cols. 815–42 (July 6, 1978).

The Assembly's standing orders will not be able to empower committees to send for persons and papers in the same way as the House of Commons and the House of

Lords. The reason for the absence of such a provision is the difficulties of enforcement; Parliament's powers in this regard stem from its privileges which, as a matter of policy, have not been given to the Assembly; *cf.* s. 15. It seems that Assembly committees will have the power to require the attendance of members of the Assembly, officers and staff of the Assembly, Scottish Secretaries and their staff, and the members and officials of bodies operating directly and exclusively under the Assembly's control (Lord Kirkhill, Minister of State at the Scottish Office, *Hansard*, H.L. Vol. 390, cols. 1542–3 (April 24, 1978)) although it is by no means clear how, for example, the Assembly could enforce its wishes, particularly against civil servants.

The Accounts Committee of the Assembly is not covered by this section; see s. 58.

Subs. (1)

" *extending to any matter which is . . . a devolved matter.*" The effect of this phrase seems to be that the only limitation on the power of the Assembly regarding the subject matter of its committees is its inability to set up a committee with functions which do not extend to a devolved matter. It may certainly, therefore, set up a committee on transport, an area which is partly reserved and partly devolved. Arguably it may also set up a committee on U.K. fiscal policy (even though that is not a devolved matter) provided that the functions of such a committee extended to the implications of fiscal policy on devolved matters.

Subs. (2)

It is likely that the Assembly will follow the House of Commons in appointing a Committee of Selection.

" *parties.*" This is the only reference in the Act to political parties.

" *as closely as practicable.*" This does not mean that the committees must in terms of their party composition be an absolute microcosm of the Assembly; this may be impossible in practice if the Assembly contains parties with a very small representation. *Cf.* House of Commons S.O. 62 (2), which requires the Committee of Selection in nominating the members of a standing committee to " have regard to . . . the composition of the House."

Reporting and publishing of proceedings of the Assembly

29. The standing orders of the Assembly shall include provision for the reporting of the proceedings of the Assembly and for the publication of the reports of such proceedings.

GENERAL NOTE

This is the sixth of eight sections which supplement s. 7 by making detailed provisions concerning the content of Assembly standing orders.

This section was added during the Third Reading stage in the Lords, following discussion at the Report stage. The Government opposed the amendment in the Lords on the grounds that the Assembly ought to decide such a matter for itself. This opposition was not sustained, however, when the Lords' amendments were under consideration in the Commons; *Hansard*, H.L. Vol. 392, cols. 1541–2 (June 8, 1978); Vol. 393, cols. 417–26 (June 29, 1978).

The intention of Lord Gray, who moved the amendment, was that the Assembly should produce verbatim reports, comparable to Hansard, rather than adopt a paraphrase or minute type of reporting, but the section makes only a minimal provision and leaves the form of the reports and their publication to the discretion of the Assembly.

For the rules concerning the privilege which will attach to such reports, see s. 15 and note thereon.

Financial initiative

30. The standing orders of the Assembly shall include provision for securing that, where a Scottish Assembly Bill proposes to authorise any expenditure to be met from, or loan to be made out of, the Scottish Consolidated Fund or the Scottish Loans Fund or the release or composition of any debt owed to the Crown, the Bill cannot pass unless the authorisation has been recommended by a Scottish Secretary.

This is the seventh of eight sections which supplement s. 7 by making detailed provisions concerning the content of Assembly standing orders.

It is similar to the provisions of House of Commons S.O. 89, and thus reflects the financial procedure of the Commons, whereby a charge may not be considered unless it is proposed or recommended by the Crown. This is Erskine May's second rule of financial procedure; see *Erskine May* (19th edn.), pp. 706–8.

The section is designed to ensure that the Scottish Executive retains control over public expenditure, and that private Members' Bills (assuming that private members' legislation is permitted by the Assembly) do not result in unplanned burdens on the block grant.

For the provisions relating to the Scottish Consolidated Fund, the Scottish Loans Fund, and other financial provisions, see Pt. III.

Members of Assembly acting as additional Commissioners

31.—(1) The standing orders of the Assembly may include provision for the formation of a panel of members of the Assembly to act as additional Commissioners under the Private Legislation Procedure (Scotland) Act 1936.

(2) Where—

    (a) the Secretary of State certifies that a draft order submitted to him under section 1 of the Act of 1936 contains provisions which are within the legislative competence of the Assembly, and

    (b) Commissioners are to be appointed under section 5 of that Act for the purpose of inquiring as to the propriety of making and issuing a provisional order in the terms of the draft,

then, if a panel has been formed under subsection (1) of this section, the Chairman of Committees of the House of Lords and the Chairman of Ways and Means in the House of Commons shall appoint an additional Commissioner from that panel.

(3) A Commissioner appointed under this section shall be treated for the purposes of the Act of 1936 as if he were appointed under that Act; and subsections (7) and (8) of section 5 of that Act shall apply in relation to a Commissioner so appointed as if any reference to Parliament, or to either House of Parliament, included a reference to the Assembly.

(4) Section 22 above shall not apply to the Act of 1936.

This is the last of eight sections which supplement s. 7 by making detailed provisions concerning the content of Assembly standing orders.

The Private Legislation Procedure (Scotland) Act 1936 is concerned solely with private legislation by Parliament and requires that all matters which would otherwise be dealt with by a private Bill, in relation to Scotland, must normally be dealt with by the provisional order procedure set out in the Act, whereby applications for parliamentary powers are made by petition to the Secretary of State to issue a provisional order in accordance with the promoters' draft and modified as the Secretary of State thinks necessary. If the order is opposed, or if the Secretary of State thinks inquiry desirable, he will direct an inquiry to be held before Commissioners; usually this stage of the procedure takes place in Scotland. Hitherto there have been two parliamentary panels comprising members of each House, and also a non-parliamentary panel. If the Commissioners report against the order, the Secretary of State refuses to issue it. If the Commissioners' report is favourable, however, the Secretary of State may issue the order in the terms applied for or with modifications. The order may then be confirmed by Parliament, having been introduced as a Provisional Order Confirmation Bill.

This section provides that the Assembly may make standing orders whereby a panel of Assembly members may be formed to act as Commissioners. If such a panel is formed, it will by subs. (2) become obligatory for the Chairmen (see below) to appoint a Commissioner from that panel if the draft order contains a provision within the

Assembly's legislative competence. In other respects the procedure under the 1936 Act remains unchanged.

Other aspects of private legislation by Westminster are untouched by this Act; nor does the Act alter the present rules regarding hybrid bills at Westminster. As already noted (see s. 26) the Assembly is free to establish its own procedure on matters within its legislative competence.

Subs. (2)

" *legislative competence.*" See Sched. 2.

" *Chairman of Committees of the House of Lords and the Chairman of Ways and Means in the House of Commons.*" These words were added by a minor drafting amendment, which was accepted by the Government, during the Report stage in the Lords; *Hansard*, H.L. Vol. 392, cols. 1543–4 (June 8, 1978).

Subs. (3)

" *subsections (7) and (8) of section 5.*" By the former provision a member of either House of Parliament who has been appointed to act as a Commissioner may continue to act even though Parliament has been dissolved; the latter provision requires persons appointed as Commissioners not to have a personal or local interest in the matter of the proposed order, and to make a declaration to that effect.

Subs. (4)

This subsection was added during the Report stage in the Commons; it was considered desirable in view of the generality of s. 22 (1); *Hansard*, H.C. Vol. 944, col. 528 (February 15, 1978).

Officers of Assembly

Clerk, officers and servants of Assembly

32.—(1) There shall be a Clerk of the Assembly, who shall be appointed by the Assembly.

(2) The Clerk may, with the consent of the Assembly as to numbers, appoint persons to act as officers and servants of the Assembly, and the conditions of service of those persons shall be such as he may with the consent of the Assembly determine.

(3) There shall be paid out of the Scottish Consolidated Fund—

(a) to the Clerk and to the officers and servants appointed by him, such salaries and allowances; and

(b) to or in respect of persons who cease to hold office as Clerk or such officers or servants, such amounts by way of pensions, allowances or gratuities or by way of provision for any such benefits;

as the Assembly may from time to time determine.

(4) Any determination under subsection (3) of this section may take effect from the date on which it is made or such other date as the Assembly may specify, but not so as to diminish the sums payable for any period preceding the determination.

(5) Any functions of the Clerk of the Assembly may, if the office of Clerk is vacant or the Clerk is for any reason unable to act, be discharged by any other officer for the time being discharging the duties of the Clerk.

GENERAL NOTE

This section makes provision for the appointment of the Clerk and staff of the Assembly, who will perform duties similar to those in the departments of the House of Commons, *i.e.* the Department of the Clerk of the House, the Speaker's Department, the Department of the Sergeant at Arms, the Library Department, and the Administration Department. Neither in this section nor elsewhere in the Act, however, is specific provision made for offices corresponding to that of Counsel to the Speaker, Sergeant at Arms, and Librarian.

For the purposes of the employment legislation applied by s. 33, the employer of the Clerk and the staff of the Assembly is deemed to be the presiding officer or another person designated by him (s. 33 (4)) but the Act does not deal with all aspects of their status; nothing, for example, is said about vicarious liability for the negligent acts of Assembly staff. It appears that the staff are not civil servants, but it is not clear whether some or all of them will be recruited through the Civil Service Commission, as are members of the Department of the Clerk of the House of Commons and House of Commons Library Clerks.

Subs. (1)

This subsection provides for a Clerk to the Assembly to be appointed by the Assembly. The Clerk is given no special status, in contrast to the Clerk of the House of Commons, who is appointed by the Crown for life. Presumably the Clerk could be removed from office by resolution of the Assembly, unless the Assembly provides otherwise in his terms and conditions of service.

Subs. (2)

This subsection empowers the Clerk to appoint staff, subject to the Assembly's consent regarding numbers and conditions of service. The Assembly is left to make its own arrangements in these matters, and may choose to establish a committee for the purpose under s. 28. The salaries and conditions of service of the officers of the House of Commons and their staff are regulated by a Commission set up under the House of Commons Offices Act 1812.

Subs. (3)

This subsection provides for the payment of salaries, pensions, allowances and gratuities to the Clerk and the Assembly staff to be fixed by the Assembly and paid out of the Scottish Consolidated Fund (for which, see Pt. III). Although the Assembly is given discretion as to salary levels, the appropriation of money from the Scottish Consolidated Fund will require an order under s. 45 by a Scottish Secretary.

Subs. (4)

This subsection permits a determination by the Assembly under subs. (3) to take effect immediately, or at such time as the Assembly may specify; the effect of the second limb of the subsection is that a retrospective award may not reduce payments due up to the day when the determination is made.

Application of employment legislation to Clerk, officers and servants of Assembly

33.—(1) The following provisions, namely—

(*a*) Schedule 1 to the Contracts of Employment Act 1972;

(*b*) Part II of Schedule 1 to the Trade Union and Labour Relations Act 1974; and

(*c*) the Employment Protection Act 1975;

shall apply to the Clerk of the Assembly and to officers and servants appointed by him under section 32 of this Act as they apply to persons in Crown employment within the meaning of section 121 of the Employment Protection Act 1975.

(2) Accordingly, for the purposes of the application of the provisions mentioned in subsection (1) of this section in relation to the Clerk and any such officer or servant—

(*a*) any reference to an employee shall be construed as a reference to the Clerk or, as the case may require, such an officer or servant;

(*b*) any reference to a contract of employment shall be construed as a reference to the terms of his employment;

(*c*) any reference to dismissal shall be construed as a reference to the termination of his employment;

(*d*) the references in paragraph 21 (5) (*c*) of Schedule 1 to the Act of 1974 and section 18 (1) (*e*) of the Act of 1975 to any person's undertaking or any undertaking in which he works shall be construed as a reference to the national interest or the interests of

Scotland or, if the case so requires, the interests of the Scottish Assembly; and

(e) any other reference to an undertaking shall be construed as a reference to the Scottish Assembly.

(3) The provisions of section 1 of the Equal Pay Act 1970, Parts II and IV of the Sex Discrimination Act 1975 and Parts II and IV of the Race Relations Act 1976 shall apply to an act done by the employer of the Clerk or of an officer or servant appointed by him and to service as Clerk or such an officer or servant as they apply to an act done by, and to service for the purposes of, a Minister of the Crown, and accordingly shall so apply as if references in those provisions to a contract of employment included references to the terms of service as Clerk or such an officer or servant.

(4) For the purposes of the enactments applied by the preceding provisions of this section, the presiding officer of the Assembly shall be deemed to be the employer of the Clerk and of the officers and servants appointed by the Clerk, except that in relation to any description of such officer or servant for the time being designated by the presiding officer a person so designated shall be deemed to be the employer for those purposes or, if it is so stated in the designation, such of those purposes as are so designated.

(5) Where any proceedings are brought by virtue of this section against the presiding officer or any person designated by him, the person against whom they are brought may apply to the industrial tribunal to have some other person against whom they could have been properly brought substituted for him as a party to those proceedings.

GENERAL NOTE

This section applies to the Clerk, officers and servants of the Assembly a number of provisions in the Contracts of Employment Act 1972, the Trade Union and Labour Relations Act 1974, the Employment Protection Act 1975, the Equal Pay Act 1970, the Sex Discrimination Act 1975 and the Race Relations Act 1976.

These provisions are applied in the same general way as they apply to persons in the employment of the Crown under the Employment Protection Act 1975, s. 121 (which defines " Crown employment " for these purposes), and in particular to most of the staff of the House of Commons under s. 122. However, this section differs from s. 122 in that the Clerk of the Assembly, unlike the Clerk of the House of Commons, is given protection by the legislation.

Subs. (4)

This subsection deems the presiding officer of the Assembly (see s. 7 (2)) to be the employer for the purposes of the legislation applied by this section, but enables him to designate another person to be the employer of some or all of the staff (but not of the Clerk) for some or all of the purposes of the legislation. Thus, the person who is in practice responsible for staff matters may be put officially into that position for the purposes of the legislation, which is effective only when there is an identified employer.

Subs. (5)

This subsection enables the presiding officer, or anyone to whom he has delegated his responsibilities under subs. (4), to apply to the industrial tribunal in the event of proceedings being brought against him, for some other person to be nominated as party to the proceedings. This appears to be intended to provide a procedure which can take account of the pattern of employment in the Assembly.

Remuneration of members of Assembly, Scottish Executive etc.

Remuneration of members, etc.

34.—(1) There shall be paid to members of the Assembly, Scottish Secretaries and assistants to Scottish Secretaries such salaries and allowances as the Assembly may from time to time determine.

(2) Pending the first determination under subsection (1) of this section of any salaries and allowances for members of the Assembly their amounts shall be such as the Secretary of State may direct.

(3) The Assembly may make provision for the payment of pensions, gratuities or allowances to or in respect of persons who have ceased to be members of the Assembly, Scottish Secretaries or assistants to Scottish Secretaries.

(4) Different provision may be made under this section for different cases.

(5) Without prejudice to the period for which any salaries or allowances are payable under this section, no payment shall be made under this section to or in respect of a person required by section 12 or section 20 of this Act to take an oath or make an affirmation unless he has done so.

(6) Payments under this section shall be made out of the Scottish Consolidated Fund.

DEFINITION
" Scottish Secretary ": s. 81 (1), referring to s. 20 (2).

GENERAL NOTE
This section empowers the Assembly to determine the salaries and allowances (such as travelling allowances) to be paid to Assembly members, Scottish Secretaries and their assistants (subs. (1)). Initially, however, the Secretary of State will determine the salaries and allowances of Assembly members, and this determination will last until such time as it is altered by the Assembly (subs. (2)). It appears from a statement of Lord Kirkhill, Minister of State at the Scottish Office, that the initial determination will be no higher than the salaries and allowances of M.P.s; *Hansard*, H.L. Vol. 392, col. 1547 (June 8, 1978). The Assembly is also left free to determine the pensions and similar payments to be paid to former Assembly members, Scottish Secretaries and their assistants (subs. (3)). Subs. (4) enables the Assembly to make different provisions in different cases; thus some Scottish Secretaries could be paid more than others, for example, and Assembly members who are chairmen of committees could be given a higher salary than the ordinary " backbencher." No payment under this section may be made until the appropriate oath has been taken or affirmation made (see s. 12 for Assembly members, and s. 20 (9) for Scottish Secretaries) (subs. (5)). All payments made under this section will be from the Scottish Consolidated Fund (for which, see Pt. III) (subs. (6)).

During the Report stage in the Lords, following discussion during the Committee stage, amendments were made which would have made the Secretary of State responsible at all times for fixing the level of salaries, allowances and pensions, subject to the control of the House of Commons. It was argued that the Assembly ought not to have an unfettered right to determine these levels. The Government resisted these amendments, on the basis that the rates of remuneration, of Assembly members at least, would have to be related to the working hours of the Assembly and the work load of its members, and that these were matters for the Assembly to decide. The Commons rejected the amendments, and the Lords then gave way; *Hansard*, H.L. Vol. 390, cols. 1581–1597 (April 24, 1978); Vol. 392, cols. 1544–1549 (June 8, 1978); H.C. Vol. 954, cols. 49–88 (July 17, 1978).

PART II

RELATIONS WITH UNITED KINGDOM AUTHORITIES

Agency arrangements and information

Agency arrangements and provision of services

35.—(1) Arrangements may be made between a Scottish Secretary and any relevant authority for any functions of one of them to be discharged by, or by officers of, the other, and for the provision by one of them for the other of administrative, professional or technical services.

(2) No such arrangements for the discharge of any functions shall affect the responsibility of the authority on whose behalf the functions are discharged.

(3) In this section " relevant authority " means any department of the Government of the United Kingdom and any public or local authority or public corporation.

DEFINITION
" Scottish Secretary ": s. 81 (1), referring to s. 20 (2).

GENERAL NOTE
The purpose of this section is to enable arrangements to be made between a Scottish Secretary, on the one hand, and any relevant authority (as defined in subs. (3)), on the other hand, for one party to carry out functions or provide services on behalf of the other. As in any agency agreement, an arrangement under this section cannot be made without the consent of both parties. A provision of this nature is necessary because a person on whom a statutory duty is imposed or a power is conferred cannot delegate the exercise of that duty or power, or discharge it through any other person, without statutory authority; see, *e.g. Thomson* v. *Dundee Police Commissioners* (1887) 15 R. 164.

Precedents for a provision of this nature can be found in the Government of Ireland Act 1920, s. 63, and the Northern Ireland Constitution Act 1973, s. 11; *cf.* also Local Government (Scotland) Act 1973, s. 56.

Subs. (1)
It is clear from the words of this subsection that a two-way process is envisaged; thus, for example, a Scottish Secretary could undertake functions on behalf of a U.K. government department, and vice versa.

Subs. (2)
This subsection reflects the Latin maxim *qui facit per alium, facit per se*, and lays down the rule that responsibility for the discharge of a function remains unaltered by any arrangements made under this section. Thus if a Scottish Secretary made an arrangement with a U.K. Minister whereby the latter would discharge a function vested by law in the former, the Scottish Secretary would remain responsible in law for that function; this is an important consideration in the context of actions for breach of statutory duty. He could, moreover, exercise the function himself notwithstanding the arrangement made, and revoke the arrangement at any time; see *Huth* v. *Clarke* (1890) 25 Q.B.D. 391, *Manton* v. *Brighton Corporation* [1951] 2 K.B. 393, and *cf.* Local Government (Scotland) Act 1973, s. 56 (4). (These, however, are matters of strict law; in practice, they would presumably be subject to consultation.) Political responsibility, it is submitted, would also remain with the Scottish Secretary in these circumstances, by analogy with legal responsibility, and again it is against the Scottish Secretary that complaints of maladministration would be made.

The subsection makes no specific provision for financial responsibility, which may be presumed to be a matter for negotiation between the parties to the arrangement.

Subs. (3)
The width of the definition of " relevant authority " may be noted; by contrast, the Northern Ireland Constitution Act 1973, s. 11, permitted such arrangements only with U.K. departments.

Provision of information

36. Where it appears to the Secretary of State that any information relating to the exercise of functions by a Scottish Secretary is required for the exercise of functions by a Minister of the Crown he may request the Scottish Secretary to supply the information and the Scottish Secretary shall comply with the request.

DEFINITION
" Scottish Secretary ": s. 81 (1), referring to s. 20 (2).

GENERAL NOTE

This section empowers the Secretary of State to require a Scottish Secretary to supply any information relating to the exercise of his functions which is required by any minister. It is intended for use as essentially a reserve power, for it is envisaged that in the normal event information will be exchanged between the Scottish Executive and the U.K. Government freely and without difficulty; Mr. John Smith, M.P., Minister of State at the Privy Council Office, *Hansard,* H.C. Vol. 940, col. 1271 (December 6, 1977).

The U.K. Government might need information on devolved functions to meet requests made to it by international organisations, or if the information is relevant and necessary to the exercise of its own responsibilities (*e.g.* the calculation of the block grant). However, Scottish Secretaries are put into a subordinate position by this section, for no corresponding power is given to a Scottish Secretary to require information of a U.K. Minister, even though information on a number of matters (*e.g.* manpower policy) might be valuable to the Scottish Executive.

Cf. Local Government (Scotland) Act 1973, s. 199.

Supplementary and reserve powers

Power to make changes in law consequential on Scottish Assembly Acts

37.—(1) Her Majesty may by Order in Council make any such amendments of the law of the United Kingdom or any part of it (including any provision contained in this Act) and such further provision as appear to Her to be necessary or expedient in consequence of any provision made by or under any Scottish Assembly Act.

(2) No recommendation shall be made to Her Majesty in Council to make an Order under this section unless a draft of the Order has been laid before and approved by a resolution of each House of Parliament.

GENERAL NOTE

This section enables alterations to the law of the U.K. to be made which are necessary or expedient as a result of provisions made by or under a Scottish Assembly Act. The power is exercisable by Order in Council, and by subs. (2) the draft Order is required to be approved by both Houses of Parliament.

Although large portions of this Act are devoted to creating a dividing line between devolved and non-devolved matters, it is certain that in practice that line will not be found to be absolutely clear. This is recognised in the Act, for by Sched. 2, para. 8, the Assembly is competent to legislate with regard to non-devolved matters provided that the provision in question is merely incidental to or consequential upon other provisions, and those other provisions are within its competence. This will, for example, allow the Assembly when it is amending Acts of Parliament (as it is permitted to do by s. 17 (2)) to tidy up the U.K. legislation. There may, however, be instances where the power conferred by Sched. 2, para. 8 is inadequate for this purpose; indeed, it is possible that further substantive amendments are required after amendment of an Act by the Assembly.

This section is designed to meet this purpose without the need for an amending Act of Parliament. Although the power appears to be expressed in extremely broad terms, it is exercisable only in consequence of provisions made by or under a Scottish Assembly Act, which by s. 18 (1) must be within the legislative competence of the Assembly. This, therefore, is an important restriction on the scope of the power. A further restriction is created by the words " necessary or expedient," which the courts may well be prepared to construe narrowly; see *Daymond* v. *South West Water Authority* [1976] A.C. 609 (H.L.).

There may, however, be occasions when the powers in this section will be inadequate to secure changes in U.K. law which become necessary or desirable in consequence of Assembly legislation (or subordinate instruments made thereunder). In such an event, an Act of Parliament will be required. This applies also, of course, to amendments to this Act; the purpose of expressly permitting amendments to this Act is to allow detailed changes to be made to provisions such as the detailed list of enactments in Pt. III of Sched. 10 when these deal with matters included in the Groups in Pt. I thereof.

Precedents for a provision of this nature can be found in the Government of

Ireland Act 1920, s. 69, the Northern Ireland Constitution Act 1973, s. 39 (1), and the Local Government (Scotland) Act 1973, s. 215 (where, however, the power was exercisable by order). The National Health Service Reorganisation Act 1973, s. 57 (6) and the Pensioners' Payments and National Insurance Act 1973, s. 7, confer a power to make Orders in Council to amend the Acts for consolidation purposes; see the Renton Report on The Preparation of Legislation (Cmnd. 6053, 1975), para. 14.25.

For the Parliamentary debates on this section (including the views of Government spokesmen as to its intention) see *Hansard*, H.C. Vol. 940, cols. 1410–65 (December 7, 1977); H.L. Vol. 390, cols. 1603–5, 1618–25 (April 24–25, 1978).

See also s. 82 (3).

Power to move rejection of certain Assembly Bills

38.—(1) If it appears to the Secretary of State—

(*a*) that a Bill passed by the Assembly contains any provision which would or might affect a reserved matter, whether directly or indirectly; and

(*b*) that the enactment of that provision would not be in the public interest;

he may lay the Bill before Parliament together with a reasoned statement that in his opinion it ought not to be submitted to Her Majesty in Council.

(2) For the purposes of this section a reserved matter is one—

(*a*) which concerns Scotland (whether or not it also concerns any other part of the United Kingdom); but

(*b*) with respect to which the Scottish Assembly has no power to legislate (disregarding for this purpose paragraph 8 of Schedule 2 to this Act).

(3) If a Bill is laid before Parliament under subsection (1) of this section and within a period of twenty-eight days beginning with the day on which it is so laid, each House of Parliament resolves that the Bill shall not be submitted to Her Majesty in Council the Bill shall not be submitted to Her Majesty in Council for approval.

GENERAL NOTE

This section empowers the Secretary of State to invite Parliament to reject an Assembly Bill on the grounds that in his view it contains a provision which will or might affect a reserved matter (as defined in subs. (2)), and also that the provision, if enacted, would again in his view not be in the public interest. Parliament may then resolve that the Bill should not be submitted to Her Majesty in Council for approval (subs. (3)). S. 39 (power to prevent or require action) and s. 40 (power to revoke subordinate instruments) are somewhat similar in their terms, but this section differs from those two sections in that it does not mention incompatibility with Community or international obligations; that problem is dealt with in s. 19.

A veto of this nature was suggested in the Kilbrandon Report, paras. 765–766, as being necessary to ensure compliance with international obligations of the U.K., to prevent the adoption of policies believed to be inconsistent with the maintenance of the political and economic unity of the U.K., and generally to safeguard any other essential interest of the U.K. The involvement of Parliament in the procedure was thought to be preferable to, say, blocking the approval of a Bill by Her Majesty in Council, since it would allow the matter to be debated in a public forum. This line of reasoning was adopted in *Our Changing Democracy*, paras. 57–59, but it was envisaged there that the Bill would not be laid before Parliament until the Assembly had had an opportunity to re-consider it in the light of a reasoned statement of the Secretary of State's objections.

It would appear that the procedures created by this section are intended to permit scrutiny of Assembly Bills by Parliament on political grounds, while those created by s. 19 are intended to permit scrutiny on legal grounds by the Judicial Committee. This clear division between political and legal review is reinforced by s. 19 (1), by which a provision in a Bill laid before Parliament under this section may not be referred to the Judicial Committee; it also imposes a duty on the Secretary of State to refer to the Judicial Committee a provision which meets criteria in s. 19 for such a reference.

There is, however, nothing in the Act to prevent the Secretary of State from referring a provision in an Assembly Bill to Parliament under this section after it has been found by the Judicial Committee to be within the Assembly's legislative competence following a reference under s. 19, provided of course that the criteria for a reference under this section can be satisfied.

It is likely that, as in the case of s. 19, the procedures created by this section will in practice be supplemented by informal consultations between the Scottish administration and the U.K. Government, and that the Secretary of State and his advisers will examine Assembly Bills, and amendments thereto, and indicate the objections which will have to be met if references to Parliament are to be avoided: Lord McCluskey, Solicitor-General for Scotland, *Hansard*, H.L. Vol. 390, cols. 1651–3 (April 25, 1978). These consultations will permit the Assembly to reconsider the provision or provisions in question.

Subs. (1)

This subsection is deliberately worded so as to base the institution of the override procedures clearly upon the political judgment of the Secretary of State. Emphasis should therefore be placed upon the words " appear to," " might affect " (in para. (*a*)), " the public interest " (in para. (*b*)) and " *may* lay . . . before Parliament " (thus, even if a provision in an Assembly Bill satisfied the Secretary of State as to the criteria laid down in (*a*) and (*b*), he is still not obliged to lay it before Parliament). As a corollary, it seems that a further effect of the language will be to make it extremely difficult to challenge the decisions of the Secretary of State in court (though he will, in the normal way, be politically accountable to Parliament for the exercise of his powers under this section.) *Cf.* s. 39 (1) and (2), and s. 40 (1) and (2).

" *reasoned*." This word was added as a Government amendment during the Report stage in the Lords, following discussion during the Committee stage. The purpose of the amendment is to ensure that the Secretary of State identifies the particular points which led him to reject the Bill. This will obviously be of benefit to Parliament, but the existence of this formal requirement contrasts sharply with the purely informal notification of the U.K. Government's objections which is all the Assembly will receive before it passes the Bill, and which presumably is intended to take the place of the formal reference back to the Assembly which was envisaged in *Our Changing Democracy*. *Hansard*, Vol. 390, cols. 1629, 1644, 1651–5 (April 25, 1978); Vol. 393, cols. 12–13 (June 12, 1978).

Subs. (2)

" *reserved matter*." This concept is unique to the over-ride sections (*i.e.* this section, and ss. 39–40) and does not appear elsewhere in the Act.

" (*a*) *which concerns Scotland* (*whether or not it also concerns any other part of the United Kingdom*)." Because this paragraph is linked with para. (*b*) below, the powers under the section cannot be used in relation to a matter which concerns England and Wales, but which is a devolved matter in Scotland, with a view to protecting the English/Welsh analogue of devolved matters (*e.g.* education). Thus the powers can only be used to protect non-devolved matters which are U.K. matters, such as defence and economic policy.

" (*b*) *with respect to which* . . . *Schedule* 2 *to this Act*." As originally drafted, this paragraph referred to the " legislative competence of the Assembly," but that phrase is used elsewhere in the Act solely to describe the character of a provision in an Assembly Act or Bill, and is therefore inappropriate for use in this context. The change was made by a Government amendment during the Committee stage in the Lords; *Hansard*, H.L. Vol. 390, cols. 1661–5 (April 25, 1978). See ss. 18 and 63–64.

" (*disregarding for this purpose paragraph* 8 *of Schedule* 2 *to this Act*)." The effect of these words is that if a matter is one on which the Assembly has power to legislate solely by virtue of Sched. 2, para. 8, it is still a reserved matter for the purposes of this section.

Subs. (3)

As originally drafted, this subsection would have empowered the House of Commons, alone, and without the agreement of the House of Lords, to decide that an Assembly Bill should not be submitted for approval to Her Majesty in Council. This procedure in effect would have enabled the Commons by a second vote to override an adverse decision by the Lords and reflected the provisions of the Parliament (No. 2) Bill 1968–69 relating to subordinate legislation. The Lords, during the Committee stage, rebelled against the provision, it being argued that any alteration in the constitutional relation-ship between the Lords and the Commons ought to be made by legislation specifically designed for that purpose. The Commons subsequently accepted this and later, similar amendments; see ss. 39 (6) and 40 (5); *Hansard*, H.L. Vol. 390, cols. 1665–95 (April 25, 1978).

As a result of the amendment, the position now is that even if the Secretary of State, the U.K. Government as a whole, and the House of Commons all agree that a provision in an Assembly Bill is (to use a general, non-statutory phrase) damaging to U.K. interests, the Bill will still be submitted for approval if the Lords alone disagree with that assessment. In that situation, the only course of action open to the U.K. Government, if it wished to maintain its objections, would be an Act of Parliament.

See also s. 77, which provides that in reckoning any period for the purposes of this section, no account shall be taken of any time during which Parliament is dissolved or prorogued or during which both Houses are adjourned for more than four days.

Power to prevent or require action

39.—(1) If it appears to the Secretary of State—

(*a*) that any action proposed to be taken by or on behalf of a Scottish Secretary would or might affect a reserved matter, whether directly or indirectly, or

(*b*) that any action capable of being so taken is not proposed to be taken and that failure to take it would or might affect a reserved matter, whether directly or indirectly;

then, if it appears to him desirable in the public interest to use his powers under this subsection, he may direct that the proposed action shall not be taken or, as the case may be, that the action capable of being taken shall be taken.

(2) If it appears to the Secretary of State—

(*a*) that any action proposed to be taken by or on behalf of a Scottish Secretary would be incompatible with Community obligations or any other international obligations of the United Kingdom; or

(*b*) that any action capable of being so taken is required for the purpose of implementing any Community obligation or any other international obligation of the United Kingdom;

he may direct that the proposed action shall not be taken or, as the case may be, that the action capable of being taken shall be taken.

(3) For the purposes of this section a reserved matter is one—

(*a*) which concerns Scotland (whether or not it also concerns any other part of the United Kingdom); but

(*b*) with respect to which a Scottish Secretary has no power to act.

(4) A direction under this section may be varied or revoked by a further direction; and any such direction shall be taken to be given as soon as it is communicated to a Scottish Secretary.

(5) A direction under this section shall be binding on every Scottish Secretary.

(6) A direction under subsection (1) of this section shall cease to have effect at the expiration of a period of twenty-eight days beginning with the date on which it is given, unless before the end of that period a resolution approving it is passed by each House of Parliament; and if at any time before the end of that period either House of Parliament rejects a motion approving the direction, the direction shall cease to have effect at that time.

DEFINITIONS

" Community obligation ": European Communities Act 1972, s. 1 (2) and Sched. 2.
" Scottish Secretary ": s. 81 (1), referring to s. 20 (2).

GENERAL NOTE

This section empowers the Secretary of State to issue directions to a Scottish Secretary regarding future actions. Directions may be of two possible types: (i) of a *negative* quality, to stop a proposed action being taken by or on behalf of a Scottish Secretary; and (ii) of a *positive* quality, to require a certain action to be taken by or on behalf of a Scottish Secretary which would otherwise not be taken. The two grounds on which this intervention in decision-making by a Scottish Secretary may be supported are set out in subs. (1) and (2); by subs. (1), where the proposed action or inaction would directly or indirectly affect any " reserved matter " (defined in subs. (3)), *and* where the Secretary of State considers that his intervention would be desirable in the public interest, and by subs. (2), where the action proposed by a Scottish Secretary would be incompatible with Community or other international obligations of the U.K., *or* when action is required to implement such obligations.

In each case the intervention is governed by the phrase " if it appears to the Secretary of State," which indicates that the subjective judgment of the situation is the decisive factor. Other expressions in this section, such as " appear to him desirable in the public interest," suggest that the main control over the use of this section will be political and not judicial. Indeed, subs. (6) makes express provision for obtaining parliamentary approval of directions issued under subs. (1).

Directions made under this section may be varied or revoked by subsequent directions (subs. (4)), and are binding on all Scottish Secretaries (subs. (5)). They take effect when they are communicated to a Scottish Secretary (subs. (4)), but directions made under subs. (1) will cease to have effect after 28 days unless they have been confirmed by a resolution of each House of Parliament (subs. (6)).

No attempt is made to define or otherwise clarify the extremely wide term " action," which is used frequently in this section. Does it, for example, extend to the preparation and drafting of an Assembly Bill or subordinate instrument? Or is it intended rather to refer to an administrative decision with external consequences?

The powers of intervention granted by this section are limited to controlling the future action of a Scottish Secretary, and do not include an express power to revoke action which has already been taken; *cf.* s. 40.

Generally, this section follows the policy set out in *Our Changing Democracy*, paras. 72–75, except that the Act does not confer on the U.K. Government the power envisaged in para. 73 to resume from the Scottish administration responsibility for the devolved matter in question.

This section does not apply to certain powers exercisable by a Scottish Secretary under the Town and Country Planning (Scotland) Act 1972; see s. 71 and Sched. 14.

Subs. (1)

It seems that the main purpose of the power to issue directions under this subsection is to enable the U.K. Government to overrule a Scottish Secretary on policy grounds in circumstances when powers retained by the U.K. Government and exercisable in or as regards Scotland would otherwise be adversely affected. By relying on para. (*a*), it might be possible to use this power to stop action by a Scottish Secretary which was *ultra vires* (on the assumption that such action might well affect a reserved matter and might reasonably be supported to be injurious to the public interest), but this would involve the Secretary of State in judging the legality of the proposed action or inaction, and the intention of the Government, at least according to *Our Changing Democracy*, para. 75, was that these powers of intervention should be exercised " on grounds of policy as distinct from law." The position may be contrasted with that regarding Assembly Bills, for ss. 19 and 38 make a clear distinction between judicial review on grounds of legality and preventing the passage of Bills on political grounds. Although this Act does not expressly provide a procedure comparable to that in s. 19 whereby the Secretary of State could refer a proposed action by the Scottish Executive to the courts to test its legality, it is arguable that the Secretary of State would under general principles of law be able to do this; as was said in *Our Changing Democracy*, para. 75, " the legality of the administration's executive acts will be open to challenge in the courts just like that of the Government's own executive acts."

Although at first sight para. (*b*) appears to be the corollary of para. (*a*), it has the somewhat different purpose of enabling the Secretary of State to require a Scottish Secretary to take some action which is (by virtue of the words " capable of being so taken ") *intra vires* a Scottish Secretary, and which would assist the Secretary of State (or, indeed, any other U.K. Minister) in the exercise of his responsibilities in relation to reserved matters. However, an action which was *ultra vires* would not become *intra vires* merely because it was carried out in accordance with a direction made under this paragraph.

This paragraph was reworded, for purposes of clarity, by way of a Government amendment made during the Report stage in the Lords, following discussion during the Committee stage; *Hansard*, H.L. Vol. 390, cols. 1739–1741 (April 25, 1978); Vol. 393, cols. 13–14 (June 12, 1978).

Subs. (2)

This subsection does not distinguish between Community obligations of the U.K. and obligations which arise from " directly applicable " provision of Community law and which apply to individuals; see s. 19 (1) and note thereon. It is understandable that the U.K. Government, through the Secretary of State and subject to parliamentary approval, should be empowered to determine questions concerning its own obligations, but to adopt the same rule regarding obligations which are directly applicable to individuals could involve the Secretary of State in taking decisions on problems of Community law which might be more appropriate for a court of law and which might in any event be remitted to a court at a later stage by an individual. As in subs. (1), therefore, issues of policy and issues of law are not clearly distinguished.

Two further points may be made : first, no mention is made of Community rights, powers or liabilities (see European Communities Act, s. 2 (1)). Is it to be assumed, then, that the Secretary of State is powerless to act if, for example, a proposed action of a Scottish Secretary would be incompatible with a legal right which an individual possesses by virtue of a directly applicable provision of Community law? Secondly, in contrast to the position under subs. (1), the Secretary of State is not obliged before making a direction under this subsection to take into account whether to do so would be desirable in the public interest. Presumably it is always in the public interest that adherence to Community and international obligations should have precedence over the actions of a subordinate executive.

Subs. (3)

" *reserved matter.*" See note on s. 38 (2); this subsection is the precise counterpart to that subsection, but adapted to fit executive action.

" *(b) with respect to which a Scottish Secretary has no power to act.*" See ss. 21, 63 and 64.

Subs. (4)

" *any such direction shall be taken to be given as soon as it is communicated to a Scottish Secretary.*" It is envisaged that the direction will be communicated by a letter from the Secretary of State; Lord McCluskey, Solicitor-General for Scotland, *Hansard*, H.L. Vol. 390, cols. 1751–1752 (April 25, 1978). Arguably, in view of subs. (5), it would be more appropriate for the letter to be sent to the First Secretary rather than to the Scottish Secretary responsible for the matter in question.

Subs. (5)

The general effect of this subsection is to impose a duty on all Scottish Secretaries to follow any directions given. It is necessary, in view of s. 20 (2), to impose the duty on all Scottish Secretaries irrespective of the departmental responsibilities which they may have been given, but what is not entirely clear is the manner of the enforcement of the duty. During the Committee stage in the House of Lords, Lord McCluskey, the Solicitor-General for Scotland, indicated that it would not be possible for the Secretary of State to sue a Scottish Secretary for this purpose since they both have the status of Crown agents (*Hansard*, H.L. Vol. 390, col. 1752 (April 25, 1978)) but there is no authority for the general proposition that one agent or servant of the Crown cannot sue another. Moreover, there would surely be practical value in permitting litigation of this nature. In the U.K. there is a considerable amount of litigation between local authorities and ministers when disputes arise as to their respective powers and duties (see *Secretary of State for Education and Science* v. *Metropolitan Borough of Tameside* [1977] A.C. 1014 for a recent example), while in federal jurisdictions, litigation is used to determine disputes between federal and provincial administrations (see *e.g. Att.-Gen. for Canada* v. *Att.-Gen. for Ontario* [1937] A.C. 326). Directions may also become the subject of litigation between a Scottish Secretary and an individual, where for example the latter has an interest in adherence to the terms of a direction, or (though this situation is not entirely relevant to the rule stated in this subsection) where a

Scottish Secretary attempts to enforce an action based on a direction which the individual claims is invalid.

It must be assumed that declarator would be the only appropriate remedy in view of the Scottish Secretary's status as a Crown servant (see note on s. 20 above, and Crown Proceedings Act 1947, s. 21), but unless doubts as to the validity of the direction were raised during the course of the litigation it is arguable that a declaratory remedy might have little practical effect in view of the clear words of this subsection.

No provision is made in this section for the publication of directions, although since directions will become the legal basis for executive actions it is arguable that public knowledge of directions will be as important as public knowledge of primary and secondary legislation. The production of the direction as evidence in litigation would be covered by the Documentary Evidence Act 1868, s. 2 and Schedule, as amended by the Reorganisation of Offices (Scotland) Act 1939, s. 1 (a).

Subs. (6)

This subsection applies only to directions made under subs. (1). Subs. (2) seems to have been excluded from its provisions on the argument that Parliament should not be allowed an opportunity to interfere with the responsibility of U.K. Ministers to ensure compliance with international or EEC obligations. The position under s. 40 is comparable; see s. 40 (5).

As originally drafted, this subsection provided for a direction to be approved in certain circumstances by the House of Commons only. This possibility was removed by an amendment made during the Committee stage in the Lords; *Hansard*, H.L. Vol. 390, cols. 1753–4 (April 25, 1978). A further drafting amendment was made during the Report stage in the Lords; *Hansard*, H.L. Vol. 393, cols. 14–5 (June 12, 1978). For a fuller explanation of the background to the amendments, see note on s. 38 (3).

See also s. 77, which provides that in reckoning any period for the purposes of this section, no account shall be taken of any time during which Parliament is dissolved or prorogued or during which both Houses are adjourned for more than four days.

Power to revoke subordinate instruments

40.—(1) If it appears to the Secretary of State—

(a) that an instrument made by a Scottish Secretary under any Act of Parliament or Scottish Assembly Act affects a reserved matter, whether directly or indirectly; and

(b) that the public interest makes it desirable that he should use his powers under this subsection;

he may by order revoke the instrument.

(2) If it appears to the Secretary of State that an instrument made by a Scottish Secretary under any Act of Parliament or Scottish Assembly Act is incompatible with Community obligations or any other international obligations of the United Kingdom or provides for any matter which is or ought to be provided for in an instrument made by the Secretary of State and implementing such an obligation, he may by order revoke the instrument.

(3) For the purposes of this section a reserved matter is one which is a reserved matter for the purposes of section 39 of this Act.

(4) An order under this section may contain such consequential provisions as appear to the Secretary of State to be necessary or expedient.

(5) An order under subsection (1) of this section revoking an instrument shall not be made unless either—

(a) a draft of the order has, within the period of twenty-eight days beginning with the day on which the instrument was made, been approved by a resolution of each House of Parliament; or

(b) the order is laid before Parliament with a statement by the Secretary of State that the public interest requires it to be made without delay;

but an order made in pursuance of paragraph (b) above shall cease to have effect at the expiration of the period of twenty-eight days mentioned in paragraph (*a*) above unless before the end of that period a resolution approving it is passed by each House of Parliament; and if at any time before the end of that period either House of Parliament rejects a motion approving the order the order shall cease to have effect at that time.

(6) Where an order under subsection (1) of this section revoking an instrument ceases to have effect at any time the instrument shall after that time again have effect as if the order had not been made.

DEFINITIONS
" Community obligation ": European Communities Act 1972, s. 1 (2) and Sched. 2.
" Scottish Secretary ": s. 81 (1), referring to s. 20 (2).

GENERAL NOTE
This section entrusts the Secretary of State with a negative power to revoke a subordinate instrument made by a Scottish Secretary under an Act of Parliament or Scottish Assembly Act. The power is exercisable by order and is subject to Parliamentary approval (subs. (5)); the special procedures provided by that subsection to apply in cases of urgency should be noted.

Although the structure of the section is similar to s. 39, there are important points of difference in their terms. There is no power under this section to prevent in advance the making of a subordinate instrument (see subs. (1) (*a*)), nor to require the making of a subordinate instrument. Had the latter power been conferred it could, for example, have been used to ensure that a power to make subordinate instruments conferred by Act of Parliament, and which had already been exercised by a U.K. Minister as regards England and Wales, was also exercised as regards Scotland by a Scottish Secretary. As it is, s. 22 (1) precludes a U.K. Minister from making an instrument which could competently be made by a Scottish Secretary, subject to the specialised exception concerning the implementation of Community and international obligations: see subs. (2) and s. 64 (3).

The language of the section is, however, very similar to s. 39; there is again the clear intention that the Secretary of State's decision to make an order be based on his political judgment. (See also s. 38 (1).)

Generally the provisions of the section follow the policy set out in *Our Changing Democracy*, paras. 72–75, and in particular para. 73b.

As originally drafted, the section contained a provision (cl. 38 (7) of the Bill presented to the House of Commons) which would have made it impossible for an order made by the Secretary of State under subs. (1) to be subject to the procedure of the House of Lords for dealing with hybrid instruments (see House of Lords S.O. 216 and 216A, and Offshore Petroleum Development (Scotland) Act 1975, s. 1, on which the provision was modelled). If, for example, the Scottish Secretary's instrument were hybrid, the Secretary of State's order to revoke that instrument could in turn have that character. Had the provision been retained, an individual would have been unable to petition against a hybrid order. The purpose of the provision was to prevent the override order from being delayed for what might have been a considerable period while the procedure was followed through; the Government, however, were persuaded by the discussion during the Committee stage in the Lords that the value in allowing the individual to petition against a hybrid order outweighed the possible advantages of avoiding delay. Accordingly they did not oppose an amendment made during the Report stage in the House to remove the provision. *Hansard*, H.L. Vol. 390, cols. 1756–67 (April 25, 1978); Vol. 393, cols. 16–7 (June 12, 1978).

Subs. (1)
" *an instrument made by a Scottish Secretary.*" As noted already, the power conferred by this section may only be exercised after the instrument has been made. The Act contains no general procedural requirements as to the making of a subordinate instrument by a Scottish Secretary, so that as is the case with subordinate instruments made by a U.K. Minister it will be necessary to consult the parent Act of Parliament or Scottish Assembly Act for the procedure in each case. See note on s. 22, and Sched. 16, paras. 2–8, for amendments to the Statutory Instruments Act 1946.
" *affects a reserved matter, whether directly or indirectly.*" For the purposes of this section it is immaterial whether the instrument in *intra* or *ultra vires*; *cf.* s. 39 (1) (*a*) and see note thereon.

Subs. (2)

This subsection has two main purposes: first, it is designed to ensure that subordinate instruments made by a Scottish Secretary are compatible with Community or other international obligations of the U.K.; *cf.* s. 39 (2) (*a*), and see note on s. 39 (2). Secondly, it is designed to ensure that such instruments do not provide for matters already provided for in an instrument made by the Secretary of State, or which ought to be so provided for (see s. 64 (3)). It is curious that while s. 64 (3) refers to the making of subordinate instruments by any Minister of the Crown, this subsection refers to the Secretary of State; see, however, Interpretation Act 1978, Sched. 1.

Subs. (3)

See s. 39 (3) and note thereon.

Subs. (4)

For the phrase " necessary or expedient," see s. 37 (1) and general note on that section.

Subs. (5)

This subsection provides two separate procedures for parliamentary approval of the Secretary of State's order. In the normal event, a draft order must be approved by each House of Parliament within 28 days of it being made (see para. (*a*)). In more urgent cases, however, the Secretary of State may lay the order itself before Parliament with a statement that it is in the public interest that the order be made without delay (see para. (*b*)); in such cases the order ceases to have effect after 28 days unless it is approved by each House of Parliament; the order also ceases to have effect if a motion approving the order is rejected by either House of Parliament. See s. 77, which provides that in reckoning any period for the purposes of this section, no account shall be taken of any time during which Parliament is dissolved or prorogued or during which both Houses are adjourned for more than four days.

The procedure laid down in this subsection only applies to orders made under subs. (1). Subs. (2) seems to have been excluded from its provisions on the argument that Parliament should not be allowed an opportunity to interfere with the responsibility of U.K. Ministers to ensure compliance with international or EEC obligations. The position under s. 39 is comparable; see s. 39 (6).

As originally drafted, this subsection provided for an order to be approved in certain circumstances by the House of Commons only. This possibility was removed by an amendment made during the Committee stage in the House of Lords; *Hansard*, H.L. Vol. 390, col. 1756 (April 25, 1978). A further drafting amendment was made during the Report stage in the House of Lords; *Hansard*, H.L. Vol. 393, col. 16 (June 12, 1978). For a fuller explanation of the background to the amendment, see note on s. 38 (3).

Subs. (6)

By this subsection the instrument may be automatically brought back to life if the Secretary of State's order ceases to have effect by the operation of the procedures under subs. (5).

Orkney and Shetland

Protection of special interests of Orkney and Shetland

41. Where it appears to the Secretary of State that—

(*a*) any provision of a Bill passed by the Assembly; or

(*b*) any action proposed to be taken by or on behalf of a Scottish Secretary; or

(*c*) any instrument made by a Scottish Secretary under any Act of Parliament or Scottish Assembly Act;

would or might cause substantial detriment to the special social or economic needs and interests of the Orkney Islands or the Shetland Islands or any of their inhabitants or to the status of their councils, sections 38, 39 and 40 of this Act shall apply respectively as they would apply if that provision, action or instrument were such as is mentioned in subsection (1) (a) of section 38 or, as the case may be, 39 or 40.

GENERAL NOTE

The background to this section lies in the concern of Orkney and Shetland over the Government's proposals for a Scottish Assembly. The islands councils for these areas, which by the Local Government (Scotland) Act 1973 are single-tier local authorities and so responsible for all local government services within their areas, did not wish their status to be altered by the Assembly (see Sched. 10, Pt. I, Group 5), and were apprehensive that the Assembly might neglect their special needs, particularly as regards finance. They also desired protection for their reserve funds, which are financed by income from off-shore oil activities (see Shetland County Council Act and Orkney County Council Act 1974). These funds are used to minimise disturbance from oil-based activities on the islands, and also to prepare for the future of the islands when the oil operations are abandoned.

During the Committee stage in the Commons, Mr. Grimond, M.P. for Orkney and Shetland, succeeded in moving an amendment which provided that if in the referendum on the Act (see now s. 85) a majority in Orkney or Shetland did not wish effect to be given to the Act, the Secretary of State would lay before Parliament a draft Order providing that the Act would not apply to the area in question, or both areas; the Order would also have required the establishment of a commission to review the government of the islands. Because of the operation of the guillotine, the amendment was passed without debate (*Hansard*, H.C. Vol. 942, cols. 1547–8 (January 25, 1978)) and other related amendments were not reached.

Negotiations between the islands councils and the Government continued, however, and resulted in this section, s. 84 (which provides for a commission to examine the government of the Orkney and Shetland Islands) and the removal of the " Grimond amendment." These amendments—which were declared to be acceptable to the Government, the islands councils and Mr. Grimond—were made during the Report stage in the Lords; *Hansard*, Vol. H.L. 393, cols. 975–87 (June 20, 1978). During the Third Reading stage, this section was moved from Pt. V to its present position, which is more appropriate in view of its relationship to ss. 38–40; *Hansard*, H.L. Vol. 394, col. 431 (June 29, 1978). It is also of interest, particularly to legal geographers, that in the final preparation of the text of the Act, the Government replaced the term " Orkneys and Shetlands " in the italicised heading and the marginal note with the more accurate term " Orkney and Shetland "; this was in response to a request from the Duke of Atholl during the Third Reading debate.

The effect of this section is that the over-ride powers in ss. 38–40, which relate respectively to Assembly legislation, executive action by a Scottish Secretary, and subordinate legislation made by a Scottish Secretary, will be available to the Secretary of State where he considers that the special needs and interests of the Islands or their inhabitants, or the status of their councils, are substantially at risk. The section does not provide an absolute guarantee to the Islands, because the Secretary of State cannot intervene under ss. 38–40 unless he is satisfied that it would be in the public interest to do so; there is, therefore, the possibility of conflict between the Islands and the Secretary of State on this point.

" *status of their councils.*" The inclusion of this phrase was specifically requested by the islands councils, and is intended to protect their status as single-tier local authorities under the Local Government (Scotland) Act 1973.

Industrial and economic guidelines

Industrial and economic guidelines

42.—(1) The Secretary of State shall with the approval of the Treasury prepare guidelines—

    (a) as to the exercise by a Scottish Secretary of the powers under the Scottish Development Agency Act 1975 with respect to such of the functions of the Scottish Development Agency as relate to the promotion, financing, establishment, carrying on, growth, reorganisation, modernisation or development of industry or industrial undertakings;

(*b*) as to the exercise by a Scottish Secretary of the powers under the Highlands and Islands Development (Scotland) Acts 1965 and 1968 with respect to such of the functions of the Highlands and Islands Development Board as relate to economic development; and

(*c*) as to the exercise by a Scottish Secretary of the powers under the enactments listed in Schedule 7 to this Act so far as those powers are exercisable in relation to the disposal of premises or other land for industrial purposes by any of the bodies mentioned in subsection (2) below.

(2) The bodies referred to in subsection (1) (*c*) above are—

(*a*) the Scottish Development Agency;

(*b*) the Highlands and Islands Development Board;

(*c*) a regional, islands or district council; and

(*d*) any development corporation within the meaning of the New Towns (Scotland) Act 1968.

(3) If, by or under any Scottish Assembly Act, power is conferred—

(*a*) on any body to dispose of premises or other land for industrial purposes; and

(*b*) on a Scottish Secretary to exercise functions with respect to such a disposal by that body;

the Secretary of State may by order add that body to those specified in subsection (2) above, and the enactment conferring the power on a Scottish Secretary to the enactments listed in Schedule 7 to this Act.

(4) A Scottish Secretary shall exercise the powers with respect to which guidelines are prepared under this section so as to give effect to the guidelines.

(5) The guidelines prepared under this section shall be contained in or determined under an order of the Secretary of State.

(6) A statutory instrument made under this section shall be subject to annulment in pursuance of a resolution of either House of Parliament.

DEFINITION

" Scottish Secretary ": s. 81 (1), referring to s. 20 (2).

GENERAL NOTE

This section empowers the Secretary of State, with Treasury approval, to make guidelines governing the exercise by a Scottish Secretary of various powers in the general area of industrial and economic development. The powers in question are specified in paras. (*a*) to (*c*) of subs. (1). The guidelines will be contained in, or determined under, an order made by the Secretary of State (subs. (5)).

The provisions of the section reflect one of the central propositions of the Act, that the transfer of powers to the new organs of government should not adversely affect the economic unity of the U.K. *Our Changing Democracy* stated that the U.K. Government would continue to regulate the framework of trade so as to maintain a fair competitive balance for industry and commerce throughout the U.K. (para. 20). It was also stated that regional policies would remain a U.K. responsibility since " relative need can be assessed only by taking an overall view, and that particular areas would be precluded from drawing up their own schemes of economic support and assistance within an overall allocation, since divergences could easily distort competition in ways incompatible with a unified economy " (para. 22).

The application of this general policy to the Scottish Development Agency (S.D.A.) and the Highlands and Islands Development Board (H.I.D.B.) results in a division of responsibility for their functions between the Scottish administration and the U.K. Government. As regards the S.D.A., it was stated in *Our Changing Democracy* that its industrial functions would remain under U.K. Government control, while the Assembly would be given control over its environmental and factory building functions (except for deciding the terms of disposal of premises or land for industrial purposes, which would also remain a matter for the U.K. Government lest distortions arise through the offer of more generous financial terms than these available elsewhere in the U.K.). As a reflection of this division of responsibility, the Scottish administration and the U.K. Government would each be responsible for appointing one-half of the Agency's members, with the Secretary of State consulting the Scottish administration before appointing the chairman (paras. 138, 281). In the *Supplementary Statement*, however, it was proposed that the Scottish administration be given responsibility for appointing the Agency's members, and for all aspects of its work except the giving of selective industrial assistance under the Industry Act 1972, s. 7, which would remain the responsibility of the Secretary of State. The industrial investment functions of the Agency and the terms for disposal of land for industrial purposes would be subject to guidelines laid down by the U.K. Government (para. 20).

The allocation of responsibility for the various functions of the Agency provided for by this Act follows these policy statements and, as finally settled, may be summarised as follows:

General description of function or power	Principal provision in Scottish Development Agency Act 1975	Extent of transfer of power	Relevant provisions in this Act
1. Appointment of members	s. 1	Executive	Sched. 11, Group E, para. 9
2. Industrial investment	s. 2 (2) (*a*), (*b*), (*c*)	Executive (subject to guidelines)	Sched. 11, Group E, para. 9; s. 42 (1) (*a*) (guidelines)
3. Selective financial assistance under Industry Act 1972, s. 7	s. 5	(Reserved)	See Sched. 10, Pt. III; and *n.b.* absence of reference to these functions in Sched. 11
4. Environmental and factory building	s. 2 (2) (*d*), (*e*), (*g*), (*h*)	Legislative and executive; but as regards latter, subject to guidelines on disposal of land etc. for industrial purposes	Sched. 10, Pt. I, Group 6; s. 42 (1) (*c*), (2), Sched. 7 (guidelines). See also Sched. 10, Pt. III

As regards the H.I.D.B., *Our Changing Democracy* envisaged that responsibility for all aspects of the Board's work would be devolved, except with regard to alteration of the Board's powers and the geographical area which it covers. However, the granting of assistance to industry, fishing and agriculture would be subject to a system of guidelines and cash limits on individual projects which would be laid down by the U.K. Government and within which the Board and the Scottish administration would be able to determine their own priorities (paras. 139, 281). (This was the first and only reference to guidelines in *Our Changing Democracy*; only later was the use of that device extended in the *Supplementary Statement* to certain functions of the S.D.A., and then in the Act itself to local authorities and new town development corporations which, like the S.D.A. and the H.I.D.B., have power to dispose of land for industrial purposes).

The allocation of responsibility for the various functions of the Board provided for by this Act follows the policy set out in *Our Changing Democracy*. While no aspects of its functions fall within the scope of the Assembly's powers (Sched. 10, Pt. III), all of its functions—including the appointment of its members—become the responsibility of the Scottish Executive by Sched. 11, Group E, para. 2, except for the power to extend the Board's area under the Highlands and Islands Development

(Scotland) Act 1965, s. 1, and the power under s. 10 (4) of that Act to authorise the carrying out of works, so far as the power is exercisable in relation to excepted statutory undertakers (for which see s. 81 (1) of this Act). However, by subs. (1) (*b*) of this section, where the functions of the Board relate to economic as opposed to social development, the exercise of powers under the Act by the Scottish executive will be subject to the Secretary of State's guidelines.

It should be emphasised that the Act does not alter the scope of the powers or functions of the S.D.A. or the H.I.D.B.; rather, as already explained, it alters in certain respects the sources of Government control over these bodies by transferring supervisory powers from the Secretary of State to the Scottish Executive and, again in certain respects, by limiting the discretion conferred on the Scottish Executive through the making of guidelines under this section. The autonomy of both the S.D.A. and the H.I.D.B., however, has hitherto been limited in certain areas by directions or arrangements made by the Secretary of State (see, *e.g.* Scottish Development Agency Act 1975, s. 4, and Highlands and Islands Development (Scotland) Act 1965, ss. 2 (1) and 8 (1)), so that where such powers are transferred by this Act to the Scottish Executive, which is in turn bound by guidelines made by the Secretary of State, it is clear that the chain of control over the S.D.A. and the H.I.D.B. is now lengthened. It appears, too, that the guidelines made under this section will not differ greatly from the directions and arrangements made hitherto by the Secretary of State (Lord Kirkhill, Minister of State at the Scottish Office, *Hansard*, H.L. Vol. 391, col. 183 (May 3, 1978)), so that in practice the Scottish Executive may only have minimal discretion in formulating the content of the directions and arrangements which are issued to the S.D.A. or the H.I.D.B. In short, it may well be that the transfer of supervisory powers to the Scottish Executive is formal rather than real, and that this Act will greatly complicate the work of the S.D.A. and the H.I.D.B. and cause a blurring of responsibility for supervision of their work.

During the debates at the Committee stage in the Lords, the Government made clear that guidelines would be made under this section before the Scottish Executive assumes its powers, and that while the making of guidelines was the statutory responsibility of the U.K. Government, there would be consultation on points of detail between the U.K. Government and the Scottish Executive both before the first set of guidelines is made, and again later when changes are proposed. It was also thought that the Joint Council for Scotland suggested in the Lord President of the Council's statement on July 26, 1977 (*Hansard*, H.C. Vol. 936, col. 315) might be an appropriate vehicle for such consultation; Lord Kirkhill, Minister of State at the Scottish Office, *Hansard*, H.L. Vol. 390, cols. 1786–7 (April 25, 1978).

Subs. (1)

Para. (*a*). The guidelines to be made under this paragraph relate to the industrial investment functions of the S.D.A., and the paragraph corresponds to the Scottish Development Agency Act 1975, s. 2 (2) (*a*) and (*c*). The general purpose of the guidelines is to ensure that assistance to industry is not provided on more generous terms than those available elsewhere in the U.K. Accordingly, the S.D.A. will, through the Scottish Executive, be required to continue to operate in a commercial manner (*e.g.* by not giving unfair advantage to companies in which it has an interest), and the guidelines will cover such matters as target rates of return on investments, minimum interest rates on returns made by the S.D.A., and the criteria for making grants. (Lord Kirkhill, Minister of State at the Scottish Office, *Hansard*, H.L. Vol. 390, cols. 1783–1784 (April 25, 1978).) Reports on the " guideline functions " of the S.D.A. are to be sent to the Secretary of State as well as to the Scottish Executive, and will be laid before the Assembly as well as Parliament; see Sched. 16, para. 51.

Para. (*b*). The guidelines to be made under this paragraph will serve the same broad purpose as those under subs. (1) (*a*) with regard to the S.D.A. They will cover such matters as the criteria for giving financial assistance to industrial and commercial enterprises, the overall limits of assistance in individual cases (whether by grant or loan), and the terms of loans (Lord Kirkhill, Minister of State at the Scottish Office, *Hansard*, H.L. Vol. 390, cols. 1784–5 (April 25, 1978)). Reports on the " guideline functions " of the H.I.D.B. are, as in the case of the S.D.A., to be sent to the Secretary of State as well as to the Scottish Executive, and will be laid before the Assembly as well as Parliament; see Sched. 16, para. 20.

" *economic development.*" The Highlands and Islands Development (Scotland) Act 1965 refers to both economic and social development, but the terms are not defined in the Act, and no distinction is made between the two types of development in relation to the H.I.D.B.'s powers and functions. The H.I.D.B. has available a sum of money reserved for " non-economic or social grants " which will not be subject to guidelines made under this section, but which represents only a very small proportion of the total funds available to it, no doubt in recognition of the fact that most forms of economic development automatically bring social development in their wake. Because so many of the Board's activities are channelled into economic as opposed to purely social development, it seems that the guidelines will be far more significant in practice than the provisions of this subsection might suggest.

Para. (*c*). The purpose of this paragraph is to ensure that public bodies which are empowered to dispose of premises or other land for industrial purposes do so on terms which are comparable to those applicable elsewhere in Great Britain. The guidelines will therefore have the same general purpose as those to be made under paras. (*a*) and (*b*). The paragraph should be read alongside subss. (2) and (3), and also Sched. 7. Subs. (2) lists the public bodies covered by this paragraph, and Sched. 7 contains the enactments conferring the powers which are to be subject to guidelines. The effect of subs. (3) is that where the Assembly creates land disposal powers which are equivalent to those covered by this paragraph, the Secretary of State may by order add to the provisions of Sched. 7 and, should the public body in question be a new creation of the Assembly, to the provisions of subs. (2) also.

Subs. (4)

This subsection places a duty on a Scottish Secretary to exercise the powers covered by this section in such a way as to give effect to any guidelines which have been made. There seems to be nothing to prevent this duty from being enforced judicially, and there would certainly be value in such a procedure if, say, there were doubts as to the validity or interpretation of any guidelines (see *Laker Airways* v. *Department of Trade* [1977] 1 Q.B. 643 (C.A.)). However, in appropriate cases the Secretary of State would also be able to enforce the observance of his guidelines through s. 39 of this Act (power to prevent or require action), and it is moreover the view of the Government that in the normal event the issue of guidelines will not give rise to conflict between the Secretary of State and a Scottish Secretary; Lord Kirkhill, Minister of State at the Scottish Office, *Hansard*, H.L. Vol. 391, cols. 179–197 (May 3, 1978).

" *give effect to.*" *Cf.* Highlands and Islands Development (Scotland) Act 1965, s. 2 (1); Scottish Development Agency Act 1975, s. 4.

Subs. (5)

" *shall be contained in or determined under.*" It is intended that the principal guidelines will be published in the statutory instruments made by the Secretary of State under this section, but the effect of the words " determined under " is that some detailed material (*e.g.* relating to minimum interest rates on loans) will be subject to alteration from time to time without the need for an amending statutory instrument; *Hansard*, H.L. Vol. 390, cols. 1782–3 (April 25, 1978).

Remuneration and conditions of service

Minister's consent to terms and conditions of service of certain persons

43.—(1) A Minister of the Crown may from time to time by notice given to a Scottish Secretary specify any description of persons coinciding with or falling within a description listed in Schedule 8 to this Act.

(2) A notice under this section may specify a description of persons either generally or in relation to any of their terms and conditions of service.

(3) Where a notice under this section is in force, then notwithstanding anything in this Act, the consent of a Minister of the Crown shall not be required for the determination of the terms and conditions of service of persons of a description specified in the notice or, as the case may be, of such of those terms and conditions as are so specified.

(4) A notice under this section may be withdrawn or modified by a subsequent notice under this section.

DEFINITIONS

" Minister of the Crown " : s. 81 (1).
" Scottish Secretary " : s. 81 (1), referring to s. 20 (2)
" terms and conditions of service " : s. 81 (1).

GENERAL NOTE

This section is concerned with the terms and conditions of service of certain National Health Service staff, and of certain practitioners who provide services under arrangement with health authorities. The categories of persons affected are set out in Sched. 8, which should be read with this section.

Our Changing Democracy, para. 161, stated that the powers of the Scottish administration over pay and conditions in the devolved services could not be unlimited, because their decisions had to be related to wider considerations of national economic and pay policy. Health is in general a devolved service by virtue of Sched. 10, Pt. I, Group 1. Accordingly, s. 23 (2) together with Sched. 4 provides that a Scottish Secretary may exercise certain powers (in this context, in connection with terms and conditions of service) only with the consent of the appropriate minister. However, it was recognised that in relation to the persons covered by this section, some terms and conditions of service do affect pay, while others do not, and that separation of the two types for the purpose of this Act was not possible. Accordingly, it was felt that s. 23 (2) might operate in an unnecessarily restrictive fashion by requiring the consent of a Minister to the alteration of terms and conditions of service by a Scottish Secretary in circumstances where the alteration would not affect any pay policy currently operated by the U.K. Government.

This section therefore enables exceptions to be made to the operation of s. 23 (2). It comes into operation when a minister gives notice to a Scottish Secretary; the notice may specify any group of persons covered by or included within the categories listed in Sched. 8 (subs. (1)), and the specification may relate either to their terms and conditions of service in general or to particular aspects thereof (subs. (2)). A notice given under subs. (1) may be withdrawn or modified by a subsequent notice (subs. (4)). When a notice is in force, it will be possible for a Scottish Secretary to authorise variations in the terms and conditions of service of persons specified in the notice free from ministerial control (subs. (3)).

PART III

FINANCIAL PROVISIONS

General Note to Part III

The difficult issues relating to the public finance of devolution were examined in the Kilbrandon Report, chap. 14. The Report stressed the need to maintain the political and economic unity of the U.K., assumed that U.K. governments would continue to require powers for the centralised management of the economy and concluded that, while the main powers of taxation should continue to rest with Parliament, the devolved governments in Scotland and Wales should be able to make their own expenditure decisions within a total budget. The Report proposed an annual block grant to each devolved area, calculated by an independent exchequer board which would set the standards that the devolved services would be expected to meet and would estimate the corresponding expenditure. The block grant would thus be calculated on an expenditure basis and not with reference to sources of revenue available or assigned to the devolved governments.

The development of the Government's policy on finance may be traced in the following White Papers : *Democracy and Devolution, Proposals for Scotland and Wales*, 1974, Cmnd. 5732 (paras. 23 and 31); *Our Changing Democracy*, 1975, Cmnd. 6348 (paras. 93–112); *Devolution to Scotland and Wales, Supplementary Statement*, 1976, Cmnd. 6585 (para. 16); and *Devolution: Financing the Devolved Services*, 1977, Cmnd. 6890. In the last document, the Government explained why it favoured the system of block funds voted by Parliament and calculated on an expenditure basis to take account of both the needs of the whole U.K. and the special needs of Scotland and Wales. After examining many proposals for devolving taxation, the Government had discovered no form of taxation which could conveniently be devolved, although it was not opposed in principle to the devolved administrations having power to raise limited additional revenue to supplement the block funds (see speech by Mr. Millan, M.P., Secretary of State for Scotland, *Hansard*, H.C. Vol. 939, cols. 65–68 (November 14, 1977)). Regarding the block fund, the Government hoped that it would be possible by agreement with the devolved administrations to establish a formula relating needs in Scotland and Wales in respect of the devolved services to comparable expenditure elsewhere in the U.K., on a percentage basis; such a formula might need to be reviewed periodically, say every four years. But no such formula would be written into the devolution legislation.

Pt. III of the Act accordingly contains merely the legal framework necessary to enable block grants for expenditure on the devolved services to be paid from the U.K. Exchequer to the new Scottish Executive. It establishes machinery for making the Executive publicly accountable to the Assembly for its expenditure, but it contains no provision enabling the U.K. Government directly to control the choice of expenditure priorities within the devolved services. The block fund is to include provision for rate support for local government current expenditure, but the Scottish Executive will be responsible for deciding the amount of rate support grant (s. 68). Despite attempts made in Parliament (see *Hansard*, H.C. Vol. 941, col. 1508 (January 10, 1978); H.L. Vol. 391, col. 315 (May 3, 1978); Vol. 391, col. 402 (May 4, 1978); Vol. 393, col. 39 (June 12, 1978)), the Assembly will have no power to impose taxation, other than the power to replace rates with a local tax of substantially the same character (Sched. 2, para. 4); and the Act contains no formula governing the block grant payable to the Scottish Executive or even requiring certain considerations to be taken into account in the calculation of the grant (see *Hansard*, H.C. Vol. 944, col. 301 (February 14, 1978); H.L. Vol. 391, col. 296 (May 3, 1978); Vol. 393, col. 22 (June 12, 1978)).

According to the 1977 White Paper (Cmnd. 6890), in 1975–76 total public expenditure on the services to be devolved amounted in Scotland to £2,817 million. Taking account of other available sources of revenue (rates, borrowing by local authorities and public corporations), and assuming that devolution had already occurred, the Government calculated that the total block fund needed for Scotland in 1975–76 would have been £1,871 million. The White Paper also confirmed that in Scotland public expenditure per head of the population was considerably higher than in England: in 1975–76, Scotland had 9.3 per cent. of the population in the U.K. but received 11 per cent. of identifiable public expenditure (and see Kilbrandon Report, para. 589).

On finance as on other matters, the Act refrains from imposing a departmental system on the devolved services. However, it seems essential that the Scottish Executive should establish a finance department, headed by a Scottish Secretary responsible for finance, and that the various financial functions assigned to a Scottish Secretary in Pt. III of the Act (*e.g.* ss. 44 (2), 46 (1), 50 (1), 57 (1) (*b*)) should be performed by the same person, who will in fact if not in name be Scotland's Chancellor of the Exchequer.

An important financial provision not included in Pt. III of the Act is s. 30 (financial initiative of the Scottish Executive).

Establishment and management of Scottish Funds

Scottish Consolidated Fund and Loans Fund

44.—(1) There shall be a Scottish Consolidated Fund and a Scottish Loans Fund.

(2) A Scottish Secretary may from time to time cause sums to be transferred from one to the other of those Funds.

DEFINITION

" Scottish Secretary ": s. 81 (1), referring to s. 20 (2).

GENERAL NOTE

This section establishes a Scottish Consolidated Fund and a Scottish Loans Fund with functions which replicate those of the U.K. Consolidated Fund (established by the Consolidated Fund Act 1816) and the National Loans Fund (established by the National Loans Act 1968). The Scottish Consolidated Fund will be the channel for all the grant finance which the Scottish administration will receive from the Government; it will also be the basis for the system of expenditure control established by the Act. The existence of the Scottish Loans Fund will not mean that local and other public authorities in Scotland lose their existing borrowing powers, but public corporations which are devolved will borrow from the Scottish Loans Fund instead of the National Loans Fund (s. 60 (2) and Sched. 9).

Subs. (2)

Subject to the controls provided by later sections in this Part of the Act, day-to-day management of the Scottish Consolidated Fund and the Scottish Loans Fund will be a matter for the Scottish administration. This subsection will enable there to be a process of frequent balancing between the two funds, but daily balancing is not required (*cf.* National Loans Act 1968, s. 18); it should be unnecessary for either Fund to have recourse to short-term borrowing from outside while there are sums available in the other Fund.

Payments out of Scottish Consolidated Fund

45.—(1) No payment shall be made out of the Scottish Consolidated Fund except in accordance with credits granted on the Fund by the Scottish Comptroller and Auditor General; but this subsection does not apply to transfers under section 44 (2) of this Act.

(2) The Scottish Comptroller and Auditor General shall grant credits on the Scottish Consolidated Fund at the request of a Scottish Secretary, but shall not grant any such credit for the payment of any sum unless that sum—

(*a*) has been charged on the Fund by or under any Act of Parliament or Scottish Assembly Act; or

(*b*) is part of the sums appropriated for any purpose by an order made by a Scottish Secretary;

and no sum issued out of the Scottish Consolidated Fund on credits granted under paragraph (*a*) or (*b*) of this subsection shall be applied for any purpose other than that for which it is charged or appropriated as mentioned in that paragraph.

DEFINITION

" Scottish Secretary ": s. 81 (1), referring to s. 20 (2).

GENERAL NOTE

This section establishes the basic system for formal control of payments from the Scottish Consolidated Fund. By subs. (1) payments are to be made only in accordance with credits granted by the Scottish Comptroller and Auditor General (see s. 54), who must satisfy himself that proper authority exists for the payments before granting credits (subs. (2)). Payments made from the Fund must be used only for the purposes for which payment has been authorised (subs. (2)). This system broadly resembles that which applies to the U.K. Consolidated Fund, with three differences: (a) that only the Treasury may request payments from the U.K. Fund whereas any Scottish Secretary may in law do so in respect of the Scottish Fund; (b) that sums may be charged on the Scottish Fund either by an Act of Parliament or by a Scottish Assembly Act; and (c) that sums which are not charged on the Scottish Fund by Act must fall within the scope of an appropriation order made by a Scottish Secretary under s. 46 (1), whereas at the U.K. level an Appropriation Act is required.

Subs. (1)

Transfer payments from the Scottish Consolidated Fund to the Scottish Loans Fund under s. 44 (2) do not require to be authorised by credits granted by the Scottish Comptroller and Auditor General (*cf.* National Loans Act 1968, s. 18 (5)).

Subs. (2)

The reason for the inclusion of Acts of Parliament as a source of authority for charges upon the Scottish Consolidated Fund can be shown by examples from this Part of the Act: thus the expenses, salary and pension of the Scottish Comptroller and Auditor General are charged on the Scottish Fund (ss. 54 (8) and 55 (5)). In this connection, s. 60 (1) (*a*) is relevant, since in relation to devolved matters this allows sums already charged by existing Acts of Parliament on the U.K. Consolidated Fund to be charged instead upon the Scottish Consolidated Fund. An example would be the salary and expenses of the Health Service Commissioner for Scotland (National Health Service (Scotland) Act 1972, s. 43 (5) and see *Hansard*, H.L. Vol. 391, col. 251 (May 3, 1978)). In practice, the bulk of expenditure from the Scottish Consolidated Fund will be authorised by appropriation orders made under s. 46 (1).

Appropriation of sums forming part of Scottish Consolidated Fund and destination of receipts

46.—(1) Sums forming part of the Scottish Consolidated Fund may be appropriated only for a purpose falling within devolved matters or a purpose for which they are payable out of that Fund under this Act or any other Act of Parliament; and no order appropriating such sums shall be made by a Scottish Secretary unless a draft of the order has been laid before the Assembly and has been approved by a resolution of the Assembly.

(2) An order appropriating sums forming part of the Scottish Consolidated Fund may provide for the disposal of or the accounting for sums forming part of the receipts of any Scottish Secretary; and so far as those receipts are not so disposed of or accounted for and are not payable into the Scottish Loans Fund they shall be paid into the Scottish Consolidated Fund.

GENERAL NOTE
Subs. (1)

In place of the procedure for appropriation by Act of Parliament which is observed at Westminster, this section provides for appropriation from the Scottish Consolidated Fund to be by means of an order made by a Scottish Secretary. To ensure democratic control of the appropriation procedure, such an order is to be made only after a draft of the order has been approved by resolution of the Assembly. Presumably the details of Assembly procedure will be settled by standing orders (s. 7), but debate on the draft order may well give an opportunity for a general debate on the policies and administrative performance of the Scottish Executive, if the Westminster model is followed.

By subs. (1), sums may be appropriated from the Scottish Consolidated Fund only for devolved matters or for purposes authorised by this Act or any other Act of Parliament. The reference to devolved matters includes purposes authorised by Assembly Acts since the legislative competence of the Assembly is restricted to provisions relating to devolved matters (Sched. 2, para. 1).

By reason of the amendments made in Sched. 16, paras. 2–8, to the Statutory Instruments Act 1946, which extend that Act with modifications to subordinate instruments made by Scottish Secretaries, appropriation orders made under s. 46 (1) will be statutory instruments. S. 46 (1) lays down no period of time within which the Assembly must approve a draft appropriation order since it will obviously be in the interests of the Scottish Executive to secure the Assembly's approval in time before its money runs out.

Subs. (2)

The effect of this subsection is that receipts arising in the course of the administration of the devolved services (*e.g.* charges for services rendered) have to be accounted for but will have to be paid into the Scottish Consolidated Fund only if no other provision for dealing with them has been made by an appropriation order. It will therefore be possible for the Scottish Executive to decide that certain expenditure (*e.g.* on N.H.S. pharmaceutical or dental services) should be accounted for on a net basis. (For appropriations in aid, see Public Accounts and Charges Act 1891, s. 2 and Erskine May, *Parliamentary Practice* (19th ed.) pp. 721–2).

Payments out of Scottish Loans Fund

47.—(1) No payment shall be made out of the Scottish Loans Fund except in accordance with credits granted on the Fund by the Scottish

Comptroller and Auditor General; but this subsection does not apply to transfers under section 44 (2) of this Act.

(2) The Scottish Comptroller and Auditor General shall grant credits on the Scottish Loans Fund at the request of a Scottish Secretary, but shall not grant any such credit for the payment of any sum unless—

   (a) a Scottish Secretary has power to lend that sum; or

   (b) the sum is required for the payment of interest on, or the repayment of, sums paid into the Fund under section 49 or 50 of this Act or amounts deemed under any provision of this Act to be amounts of advances made to a Scottish Secretary; or

   (c) the sum is required for a purpose incidental to any for which credits may be granted under paragraph (a) or (b) above;

and no sum issued out of the Scottish Loans Fund on credits granted under paragraph (a) of this subsection shall be applied for any purpose other than the lending of money by a Scottish Secretary.

DEFINITION
   " Scottish Secretary ": s. 81 (1), referring to s. 20 (2).

GENERAL NOTE
   Subs. (1) makes the same provision for the Scottish Loans Fund as is made for the Scottish Consolidated Fund by s. 45 (1). Subs. (2), which is equivalent to s. 45 (2), provides that a credit may be issued for payment from the Scottish Loans Fund only if a Scottish Secretary has power to lend the sum in question; or if the sum is required to repay to the U.K. Government principal or interest due under ss. 49 or 50 or in respect of other amounts deemed to be advances to a Scottish Secretary (e.g. in the case of existing debt under s. 61); or if the sum is required for incidental purposes. Sums issued for lending by a Scottish Secretary may be used only for that purpose.

Payments into Scottish Funds out of United Kingdom Funds

Payments into Scottish Consolidated Fund out of moneys provided by Parliament

   48.—(1) The Secretary of State shall from time to time make out of moneys provided by Parliament payments into the Scottish Consolidated Fund of such sums as he may determine by order made with the consent of the Treasury.

   (2) No order under this section shall be made unless a draft of it has been laid before the House of Commons and approved by a resolution of that House; and there shall be laid before that House, together with the draft, a statement of the considerations leading to the determinations to be made by the order.

DEFINITION
   " Treasury ": Interpretation Act 1978, Sched. 1.

GENERAL NOTE
Subs. (1)
   This is probably the most important financial subsection in the whole Act since it gives authority for the financing of devolution by means of a " block fund," consisting of periodical payments made into the Scottish Consolidated Fund by the U.K. Government. Although subs. (1) is phrased in terms imposing a duty upon the Secretary of State to make these payments, its effect is to give complete discretion to the Secretary of State, with the consent of the Treasury, to decide what payments should be made to the Scottish administration to pay for the devolved services. Despite the reference to the Secretary of State and the Treasury, the sums in question will be so large and of such political importance that the necessary decisions will without doubt be taken collectively by the U.K. Government, and at the same time as similar decisions affecting Wales (Wales Act 1978, s. 44) and expenditure decisions concerning England. Subs. (1) is essentially an enabling provision and it imposes

no statutory limits or qualifications upon the making of payments. Thus the absence of any reference to the frequency of the payments means that, even though an annual basis for the making of payments is in practice adopted, there will be no obstacle to the making of supplementary payments to meet unforeseen needs, inflationary increases in the cost of services, and so on. There is no indication of how the payments are to be calculated. Nor is there any statutory requirement for prior consultation or negotiation between the Secretary of State and the Scottish Executive, although it is certain that extensive consultation will take place. Indeed, Lord Kirkhill, Minister of State at the Scottish Office, said in Parliament: " The total of devolved public expenditure, and the amount of the block fund will be negotiated between the U.K. Government and the Scottish Administration. The method of determining the block fund will have to be discussed and agreed with the Administration, but it may be possible to devise a formula approach to this also. It is the Government's intention that the consultations with the Scottish Administration will take place on a virtually continuous basis, and not as a series of disconnected, highly political confrontations "; *Hansard*, H.L. Vol. 391, col. 281 (May 3, 1978).

It was the Government's view that, while it might well be found desirable to establish a formula basis for calculating the block fund over a period of years, no such formula could or should be written into the legislation (see *Devolution: Financing the Devolved Services*, paras. 76–78). The Government also considered that the provision of information about needs and standards of public services in all parts of the U.K. might be assisted by the creation of an independent advisory body, without executive responsibilities, to assist both the U.K. Government and the devolved administrations in Scotland and Wales in the process of negotiation and consultation (para. 72).

Subject to the limitation contained in s. 46 (1) that payments from the Scottish Consolidated Fund may be appropriated only for devolved matters, the Act leaves to the Scottish Executive and Assembly complete discretion as to how the block fund is to be divided between the various devolved services. It remains to be seen whether in practice the U.K. Government will refrain from taking an interest in the detailed expenditure decisions of the Scottish administration and from seeking to influence them.

Subs. (2)

Since decisions taken under subs. (1) will have implications for all parts of the U.K., they are to take effect only when the House of Commons has approved them under the procedure set out in this subsection. As well as the draft order specifying the amount of a proposed payment into the Scottish Consolidated Fund, the Government will have to lay before the House of Commons a statement of the considerations taken into account in determining that amount. When the Bill was passing through Parliament, the Government rejected amendments seeking to include in this statement comparisons between England and Scotland of the respective levels of public expenditure per head of population (*Hansard*, H.L. Vol. 391, col. 296 (May 3, 1978); Vol. 393, col. 22 (June 12, 1978)).

Payments into Scottish Loans Fund out of National Loans Fund

49.—(1) The Secretary of State shall from time to time pay into the Scottish Loans Fund such sums as he may with the consent of the Treasury determine.

(2) The Treasury may issue to the Secretary of State such sums out of the National Loans Fund as are required to enable him to make payments under this section.

(3) Payments under this section into the Scottish Loans Fund shall be deemed to be advances made to a Scottish Secretary and shall be repayable at such times and with interest at such rates as may be determined by the Treasury; and any sums received by the Secretary of State by way of repayment or interest shall be paid into the National Loans Fund.

(4) The aggregate outstanding in respect of the principal of sums paid under subsection (1) of this section shall not exceed £500 million.

(5) The Secretary of State may from time to time by order made with

the consent of the Treasury substitute for the amount specified in sub-section (4) above such increased amount as may be specified in the order.

(6) No order shall be made under this section unless a draft of it has been laid before the House of Commons and approved by a resolution of that House.

DEFINITIONS
" Scottish Secretary ": s. 81 (1), referring to s. 20 (2).
" Treasury ": Interpretation Act 1978, Sched. 1.

GENERAL NOTE
This section lays down the procedure by which payments will be made from the National Loans Fund into the Scottish Loans Fund for the purpose of financing borrowing by the devolved public corporation and by any new public bodies which the Scottish Assembly may by Assembly Act create. The effect of s. 60 (2) and the related Sched. 9 is that existing powers of Ministers to make advances from the National Loans Fund will be converted into powers for Scottish Secretaries to make advances from the Scottish Loans Fund.

As with s. 48, decisions on aggregate public expenditure will be made by the U.K. Government while the detailed expenditure decisions within that aggregate will be a matter for the Scottish administration; the formal procedure to give effect to the public expenditure policies of the U.K. Government is contained in s. 52. By contrast with s. 48, s. 49 (4) provides for an upper limit of £500m. on the amount that may be advanced to the Scottish Loans Fund. This limit may however be increased from time to time by order (subs. (5)).

Subs. (3)
The effect of deeming payments into the Scottish Loans Funds to be advances to a Scottish Secretary is that the Scottish Secretary becomes liable to repay the loan with interest. Times of repayment and rates of interest will be determined by the Treasury (*cf.* National Loans Act 1968, s. 5).

Subs. (4)
The limit stated applies to the total of payments made under subs. (1) and does not apply to any transfer to the Scottish Loans Fund of existing debts brought about by s. 61 and Sched. 9.

Borrowing and capital expenditure

Short term borrowing by Scottish Executive

50.—(1) A Scottish Secretary may borrow in sterling temporarily, either by way of overdraft or otherwise, such sums as may appear to him required for the purpose of meeting a temporary excess of sums paid out of either of the Funds mentioned in section 44 (1) of this Act over sums paid into that Fund or for the purpose of providing a working balance in the Fund.

(2) Sums borrowed by a Scottish Secretary shall be paid into the Scottish Loans Fund or the Scottish Consolidated Fund.

(3) So far as sums required for the repayment of, or the payment of interest on, sums borrowed under this section are not paid out of the Scottish Loans Fund they shall be charged on the Scottish Consolidated Fund.

(4) The aggregate outstanding in respect of the principal of sums borrowed by Scottish Secretaries shall not exceed £75 million.

(5) The Secretary of State may from time to time by order made with the consent of the Treasury substitute for the amount specified in subsection (4) of this section such increased amount as may be specified in the order.

(6) A statutory instrument made under this section shall be subject to annulment in pursuance of a resolution of the House of Commons.

DEFINITIONS

" Scottish Secretary ": s. 81 (1), referring to s. 20 (2).
" Treasury ": Interpretation Act 1978, Sched. 1.

GENERAL NOTE

This section empowers a Scottish Secretary to borrow temporarily and in sterling, up to a stated amount (subs. (4)), sums that may be needed to meet temporary fluctuations in the cash position of the Scottish Consolidated Fund and the Scottish Loans Fund. In view of s. 44 (2), which enables sums to be transferred freely from one fund to the other, it would seem unlikely that the power of short-term borrowing from external sources will be used when there is a sufficient balance in one fund to meet the demands being made on the other.

S. 50 does not require Treasury approval to be obtained before the Scottish Secretary may exercise these borrowing powers. Treasury consent will however be needed if the limit on short-term borrowing under this section is to be raised (subs. (5)). Treasury consent will also be needed if borrowing by a Scottish Secretary is to be backed by a Treasury guarantee under s. 51.

In the absence of any other powers in the Act authorising a Scottish Secretary to borrow money, it would appear that the borrowing powers of the Scottish Executive are restricted to those conferred by s. 50 and that a Scottish Secretary could not enter into long term loans or borrow short term for long term purposes (such as the building of hospitals). The section does not however seek to define the words " temporarily " and " temporary excess " used in subs. (1).

Subs. (3)

The effect of this subsection is to charge the Scottish Consolidated Fund with repayment of principal and payment of interest in respect of sums borrowed under this section. Accordingly, no appropriation order will be required before the sums in question can be issued from the Scottish Consolidated Fund (s. 45 (2)). It will be for the Scottish Comptroller and Auditor General to satisfy himself that the borrowing powers conferred by s. 50 have not been exceeded.

Subs. (6)

The effect of this formula is to bring into operation s. 5 (1) of the Statutory Instruments Act 1946, which provides a period of 40 days within which a resolution for annulment may be passed by the House of Commons.

Treasury guarantee of sums borrowed by Scottish Executive

51.—(1) The Treasury may guarantee, in such manner and on such conditions as they think fit, the repayment of the principal of and the payment of interest on any sums borrowed by a Scottish Secretary.

(2) Immediately after a guarantee is given under this section the Treasury shall lay a statement of the guarantee before each House of Parliament; and where any sum is issued for fulfilling such a guarantee the Treasury shall as soon as possible after the end of each financial year (beginning with that in which the sum is issued and ending with that in which all liability in respect of the principal of the sum and in respect of interest thereon is finally discharged) lay before each House of Parliament a statement relating to that sum.

(3) Any sums required by the Treasury for fulfilling a guarantee under this section shall be charged on the Consolidated Fund.

(4) If any sums are issued in fulfilment of a guarantee given under this section, a Scottish Secretary shall make to the Treasury, at such time and in such manner as the Treasury may from time to time determine, payments of such amounts as the Treasury may determine in or towards repayment of the sums so issued and payments of interest, at such rate as the Treasury may from time to time determine, on what is outstanding for the time being in respect of sums so issued.

(5) Any sums payable to the Treasury under subsection (4) above shall be charged on the Scottish Consolidated Fund and any sums received by the Treasury under that subsection shall be paid into the Consolidated Fund of the United Kingdom.

DEFINITIONS
" Scottish Secretary ": s. 81 (1), referring to s. 20 (2).
" Treasury ": Interpretation Act 1978, Sched. 1.

GENERAL NOTE
This section gives authority to the Treasury, if they think fit, to guarantee the repayment of sums borrowed by a Scottish Secretary under s. 50. It does not oblige the Scottish Executive to seek Treasury guarantees in respect of its short term borrowing, nor does the granting of a Treasury guarantee affect the legal limit on the Executive's borrowing imposed by s. 50 (4). If a Treasury guarantee is granted, any sums which the Treasury has to pay are charged on the U.K. Consolidated Fund (subs. (3)) but are to be recouped from the Scottish Consolidated Fund (subs. (5)).

Limitation of capital expenditure financed by borrowing

52.—(1) In exercising his powers in relation to the bodies specified in subsection (3) of this section and his powers under section 94 of the Local Government (Scotland) Act 1973 (capital expenses) a Scottish Secretary shall endeavour to secure that the aggregate of the expenditure incurred in any financial year which is relevant capital expenditure does not exceed such amount as the Secretary of State may by order made with the consent of the Treasury determine as the limit of such expenditure for that year.

(2) For the purposes of this section only expenditure met out of borrowed money is relevant capital expenditure and, subject thereto, relevant capital expenditure is capital expenditure—

  (a) incurred by any body specified in paragraphs (c) to (j) of subsection (3) of this section, or

  (b) incurred by the British Waterways Board or the Housing Corporation and met out of money borrowed from, or with the consent of, a Scottish Secretary, or

  (c) incurred with the consent of a Scottish Secretary by local authorities or bodies formed by local authorities.

(3) The bodies referred to in subsection (1) of this section are—

  (a) the Housing Corporation;
  (b) the British Waterways Board;
  (c) the Scottish Development Agency;
  (d) the Highlands and Islands Development Board;
  (e) the Scottish Transport Group;
  (f) the Scottish Special Housing Association;
  (g) any development corporation within the meaning of the New Towns (Scotland) Act 1968;
  (h) the Central Scotland Water Development Board and any new board established under section 5 (1) of the Water (Scotland) Act 1967;
  (i) the Scottish Tourist Board;
  (j) any river purification board.

(4) If power to incur capital expenditure is conferred on any body established by or under a Scottish Assembly Act the Secretary of State may by order add that body to those specified in subsection (3) of this section and amend subsection (2) of this section accordingly.

(5) In this section " expenditure " includes the making of loans.

(6) No order under subsection (1) of this section shall be made unless a draft of it has been laid before the House of Commons and approved

by a resolution of that House; and there shall be laid before that House, together with the draft, a statement of the considerations leading to the determination to be made by the order.

(7) A statutory instrument made under subsection (4) of this section shall be subject to annulment in pursuance of a resolution of the House of Commons.

DEFINITIONS

" Scottish Secretary ": s. 81 (1), referring to s. 20 (2).
" Treasury ": Interpretation Act 1978, Sched. 1.

GENERAL NOTE

This section, together with s. 48, contains the powers which the U.K. Government will need to control the total levels of public expenditure on the devolved services in any financial year. S. 48 is concerned with the revenue which will be available to the Scottish Executive for its own expenditure. This section seeks to establish control over capital expenditure by public corporations and local authorities that is financed from borrowing and requires statutory authorisation from a Scottish Secretary. An annual limit for relevant capital expenditure will be imposed by the Secretary of State with the consent of the Treasury (subs. (1)), and this limit will require the approval of the House of Commons (subs. (6)).

Subs. (1)

This subsection does not impose an absolute obligation on the Scottish administration to keep relevant capital expenditure within the permitted limit, but an obligation on a Scottish Secretary to endeavour to secure that the limit is not exceeded. In practice, the incurring of capital expenditure does not follow immediately upon the giving of permission for such expenditure, and varying periods of delay may occur as, for example, contracts for major public works are placed. By use of s. 36 (provision of information), the U.K. Government will be able to receive regular information from the Scottish administration regarding the progress of the capital expenditure programme.

The powers of the Scottish Secretary which the section is designed to control are of two kinds: (a) powers in relation to the public corporations listed in subs. (3); and (b) powers affecting local authorities under the Local Government (Scotland) Act 1973, s. 94, which requires local authorities to seek consent of central government before incurring any liability to meet capital expenses. Under Sched. 10, Pt. I, to this Act, local government and local finance fall under Group 5 as being devolved matters. From the entry for the Local Government (Scotland) Act 1973 in Sched. 10, Pt. III, it is clear that powers under s. 94 of the 1973 Act are devolved, except in relation to the " scheduled services " (for which see, in the present Act, s. 81 (1) and Sched. 15); in brief, these are local authority services such as the police which are excluded from devolution, and for financing which the Secretary of State will remain responsible.

" Relevant capital expenditure " is defined in subs. (2); see also subs. (5).

Subs. (2)

This subsection defines " relevant capital expenditure." Only expenditure met from borrowed money comes within the definition. The British Waterways Board and the Housing Corporation are dealt with separately from the other public bodies listed in subs. (3) because they operate throughout Great Britain and require borrowing consent from a Scottish Secretary, and borrow from the Scottish Loans Fund, only in respect of their activities in Scotland. (For the devolution of housing and inland waterways, see respectively Groups 4 and 15 listed in Sched. 10, Pt. I.)

Subs. (4)

This provides that, if new public bodies with power to incur capital expenditure and to finance it by borrowing are set up by Assembly Acts the Secretary of State will be able by order to bring them within the control of this section.

Subs. (5)

This subsection is needed because the expenditure of several of the public bodies listed in subs. (3) (*e.g.* the Scottish Development Agency, and the Highlands and Islands Development Board) often takes the form of loans to individuals or companies to establish or develop private businesses.

Subs. (6)

The procedure for securing parliamentary approval of the annual limit for capital expenditure set under subs. (1) is identical with that provided for payments into the Scottish Consolidated Fund by s. 48 (2).

Subs. (7)

See note on s. 50 (6).

Rates of interest on certain loans from Scottish Loans Fund

53. Where a Scottish Secretary has power to advance any sums to a body established by or under a Scottish Assembly Act the rate of interest on any advance made in the exercise of the power shall be not less than the lowest rate determined by the Treasury under section 5 of the National Loans Act 1968 in respect of similar advances made out of the National Loans Fund on the day the advance is made.

DEFINITION

" Treasury ": Interpretation Act 1978, Sched. 1.

GENERAL NOTE

This section provides that, in respect of loans to bodies which may be set up in the future under Assembly legislation, the rate of interest must not be lower than that on similar loans made from the National Loans Fund at the same date. S. 60 (2) (b) lays down the same rule in respect of loans from the Scottish Loans Fund to existing public bodies with borrowing powers. The effect of the rule seems to be that, if the Scottish Assembly wishes to provide loans at lower rates of interest to any public body, it will have to provide specific legislative authority for this and finance the subsidy from the Scottish Consolidated Fund.

Accounts and audit

Scottish Comptroller and Auditor General

54.—(1) There shall be a Scottish Comptroller and Auditor General.

(2) The Scottish Comptroller and Auditor General shall be appointed by Her Majesty and, subject to subsection (3) of this section, shall hold office during good behaviour.

(3) The Scottish Comptroller and Auditor General—

    (a) may be relieved of office by Her Majesty at his own request; and

    (b) may be removed from office by Her Majesty if the Assembly resolves that the Secretary of State be requested to recommend the removal to Her Majesty.

(4) The Scottish Comptroller and Auditor General shall not be a member of the House of Commons or of the Scottish, Welsh or Northern Ireland Assembly.

(5) The Scottish Comptroller and Auditor General may appoint officers and servants, subject to the consent as to numbers of a Scottish Secretary.

(6) Subject to subsection (7) of this section, any functions of the Scottish Comptroller and Auditor General may be performed by an officer of his authorised by him for that purpose.

(7) An authority given under subsection (6) of this section to certify and report on accounts for the Assembly—

    (a) shall extend only to accounts in respect of which the presiding officer of the Assembly has certified to the Assembly that the Scottish Comptroller and Auditor General is unable to do so himself; and (*b*) shall cease on a vacancy arising in the office of the Scottish Comptroller and Auditor General.

(8) The expenses of the Scottish Comptroller and Auditor General shall be defrayed out of the Scottish Consolidated Fund.

GENERAL NOTE

This section provides for the creation of an office directly analogous to the existing office of Comptroller and Auditor General, created by the Exchequer and Audit Departments Act 1866. In appointing the Scottish Comptroller and Auditor General, the Crown will act on the advice of the Secretary of State, but it seems that the Secretary of State will first consult with the Scottish Executive (*Hansard*, H.L. Vol. 391, col. 391 (May 4, 1978)); or, though this seems less likely, with the Assembly (*Hansard*, H.L. Vol. 391, col. 374 (May 4, 1978)). The tenure of office of the Scottish Comptroller and Auditor General is modelled on that of his U.K. counterpart (Exchequer and Audit Departments Act 1866, s. 3). He holds office during good behaviour (subs. (2)). By subs. (3), he may be removed from office by the Crown, either at his own request (as he would presumably wish to do when he reached an appropriate age for retiring, since there seems to be no statutory retiring age: *cf.* Parliament Commissioner Act 1967, s. 1 (3), and Exchequer and Audit Departments Act 1950, s. 2 (2)) or if the Assembly resolves to request the Secretary of State to recommend the Crown to remove him. In the unlikely event of such a resolution being passed, it is submitted that (a) the Secretary of State is not under a statutory duty to comply with the Assembly's request but would of course have to defend a refusal in Parliament; (b) the Sovereign would be under a constitutional duty to comply with the Secretary of State's recommendation (*cf.* the discussion in *Hansard*, H.L. Vol. 391, cols. 367–78, 397–8 (May 4, 1978)). Since the Scottish Comptroller and Auditor General will be exercising his duties in respect of the devolved services on behalf of the Assembly, the Government resisted proposals that he should be removable from office on the resolution of both Houses of Parliament (*Hansard*, H.L. Vol. 391, cols. 369–70 (May 4, 1978)).

Subs. (2)

This form of tenure, " during good behaviour," closely resembles that on which judges of the High Court and Court of Appeal in England and Lords of Appeal in Ordinary hold their office (Supreme Court of Judicature (Consolidation) Act 1925, s. 12 (1) and Appellate Jurisdiction Act 1876, s. 6). The equivalent in Scots law is tenure *ad vitam aut culpam* (Claim of Right 1689, art. 1).

Subs. (5)

Departing from the precedent of the Exchequer and Audit Departments Act 1866, the Act does not create a department to be headed by the Scottish Comptroller and Auditor General. Instead this subsection authorises him to appoint his own staff, subject to approval as to numbers being obtained from a Scottish Secretary. Staff of the Scottish Comptroller and Auditor General will be members of the U.K. Home Civil Service (s. 67 (1)). During the Lords debate on this clause, the Government rejected a proposal that the Scottish Comptroller and Auditor General should be required to appoint qualified accountants to his staff (*Hansard*, H.L. Vol. 391, col. 381 (May 4, 1978)) and expressed the view that any radical reorganisation of government accounting and auditing procedures would have to begin at Westminster and not with the Assembly (*Hansard*, H.L. Vol. 391, col. 395 (May 4, 1978)).

Subss. (6) *and* (7)

Subs. (6) permits the Scottish Comptroller and Auditor General to delegate performance of his functions to authorised officers but subs. (7) restricts the extent of this delegation in respect of certifying and reporting on the Scottish Executive's accounts to the Assembly (*cf.* Exchequer and Audit Departments Act 1957, s. 2).

Subs. (8)

The expenses of the Scottish Comptroller and Auditor General, as well as his salary and pension (s. 55 (5)), are charged directly on the Scottish Consolidated Fund. They will therefore fall outside the Assembly's appropriation procedure (s. 45 (2) (*a*)). The U.K. Comptroller and Auditor General's salary and pension are charged on the

Consolidated Fund (Exchequer and Audit Departments Act 1950, s. 2 (4); Exchequer and Audit Departments Act 1957, s. 1 (4)) but the expenses of his department are not.

Salary and pension of Scottish Comptroller and Auditor General

55.—(1) There shall be paid to the Scottish Comptroller and Auditor General such salary as the Assembly may from time to time determine.

(2) There shall be paid to or in respect of a person who ceases to hold office as Scottish Comptroller and Auditor General such amounts by way of pensions, allowances or gratuities or by way of provision for any such benefits as the Assembly may from time to time determine.

(3) Any determination under the preceding provisions of this section may take effect from the date on which it is made or such other date as the Assembly may specify, but not so as to diminish the sums payable for any period preceding the determination.

(4) If a person ceases to be Scottish Comptroller and Auditor General and it appears to the Assembly that there are special circumstances which make it right that he should receive compensation there shall be paid to him such amount as the Assembly may determine.

(5) Any sums payable under this section shall be charged on the Scottish Consolidated Fund.

GENERAL NOTE

This section places the responsibility for determining the salary, pension and other allowances of the Scottish Comptroller and Auditor General upon the Scottish Assembly. The amounts payable may be determined retrospectively, but not so as to reduce any sums previously payable (subs. (3)). In special circumstances compensation may be paid for loss of office (subs. (4)). Sums payable in respect of salary, pension, etc. are charged on the Scottish Consolidated Fund (subs. (5)).

Access of Scottish Comptroller and Auditor General to books and documents

56. The Scottish Comptroller and Auditor General shall have free access, at all convenient times, to the books of account and other documents relating to the accounts of a Scottish Secretary and may require a Scottish Secretary to furnish him from time to time, or at regular periods, with accounts of his transactions.

DEFINITION

" Scottish Secretary " : s. 81 (1), referring to s. 20 (2).

GENERAL NOTE

This section, based on s. 28 of the Exchequer and Audit Departments Act 1866, gives the Scottish Comptroller and Auditor General the right of access to the accounts and related documents held by the Scottish administration. The right of access is conferred much more concisely than the comparable powers of the Parliamentary Commissioner for Administration, and there is no immunity for the equivalent of Cabinet documents (*cf.* Parliamentary Commissioner Act 1967, s. 8). This section also empowers the Scottish Comptroller and Auditor General to require a Scottish Secretary to provide accounts (and see s. 57).

Appropriation and other accounts and audit

57.—(1) For each financial year—

(*a*) accounts shall be prepared by Scottish Secretaries of sums paid and received by them; and

(*b*) a Scottish Secretary shall prepare an account of payments into and out of the Scottish Consolidated Fund and an account of payments into and out of the Scottish Loans Fund.

(2) The accounts prepared under subsection (1) above shall be sent to the Scottish Comptroller and Auditor General not later than the end

of November following the end of the financial year to which they relate; and he shall examine, certify and report on the accounts and lay copies of them, together with his report, before the Assembly.

DEFINITIONS

" financial year ": s. 81 (1).
" Scottish Secretary ": s. 81 (1), referring to s. 20 (2).

GENERAL NOTE

By subs. (1), all Scottish Secretaries are to prepare accounts of sums paid and received by them in each financial year, and one Scottish Secretary, presumably the Secretary in charge of finance, is to prepare accounts for the two Scottish Funds. Subs. (2) governs the submission of accounts to the Scottish Comptroller and Auditor General and lays down his general duties in respect of them. The U.K. Comptroller and Auditor General in examining appropriation accounts is required to satisfy himself " that the money expended has been applied to the purpose or purposes for which the grants made by Parliament were intended to provide and that the expenditure conforms to the authority which governs it " (Exchequer and Audit Departments Act 1921, s. 1). In practice the scope of the examination made on audit may go far beyond these formal matters.

Accounts Committee

58.—(1) The Assembly shall appoint an Accounts Committee, which shall examine and report to the Assembly on the accounts and reports laid before the Assembly by the Scottish Comptroller and Auditor General.

(2) The Accounts Committee may include one but shall not include more than one person who is a Scottish Secretary or an assistant to a Scottish Secretary.

DEFINITION

" Scottish Secretary ": s. 81 (1), referring to s. 20 (2).

GENERAL NOTE

Although the Assembly under s. 28 has power to make standing orders for the appointment of committees, the only committee which it is required to appoint is the Accounts Committee under this section. The work of the Accounts Committee will probably be modelled on that of the Public Accounts Committee of the House of Commons. By Westminster custom, the chairman of the Public Accounts Committee is always a senior member of the Opposition with ministerial experience. The Public Accounts Committee also always includes the Financial Secretary to the Treasury; hence subs. (2). Although the composition of committees appointed under s. 28 must reflect the balance of parties in the Assembly (s. 28 (2)), this requirement does not apply to the Accounts Committee.

Although this Act does not provide for the devolved services to be administered through a system of departments, it is very likely that a departmental system will develop. If the practice of Whitehall and Westminster is followed, the senior civil servant in each department will be the accounting officer of his department and will as such be expected to attend meetings of the Accounts Committee when his department's accounts are being examined.

Publication of accounts and reports under sections 57 and 58

59. The Assembly shall publish the accounts and reports received by it under sections 57 and 58 of this Act.

GENERAL NOTE

The section is self-explanatory. By virtue of s. 15 (1) (b), the contents of any documents published by the Assembly will be absolutely privileged in the law of defamation throughout the U.K.

Modification of existing enactments

Modification of enactments providing for payments into or out of Consolidated Fund or authorising advances from National Loans Fund

60.—(1) So much of any Act passed before this Act as—

    (*a*) charges any sum on the Consolidated Fund; or

    (*b*) requires or authorises the payment of any sum into or out of the Consolidated Fund; or

    (*c*) requires or authorises the payment of any sum out of moneys provided by Parliament;

shall have effect, in relation to any devolved matter, as if it provided for the sum to be charged on or, as the case may be, paid out of or into the Scottish Consolidated Fund (except to the extent that, by virtue of section 23 (3) of this Act, the sums are to be paid by or to a Minister of the Crown).

(2) So far as any power to advance money conferred by the enactments mentioned in Schedule 9 to this Act is exercisable by a Scottish Secretary—

    (*a*) any sums which for the purpose or as the result of the exercise of the power are required to be issued or paid shall, instead of being issued to the Secretary of State out of the National Loans Fund or paid to him or into that Fund, be issued to a Scottish Secretary out of the Scottish Loans Fund or, as the case may be, paid to a Scottish Secretary or into that Fund; and

    (*b*) the rate of interest on any advance made in the exercise of the power shall be not less than the lowest rate determined by the Treasury under section 5 of the National Loans Act 1968 in respect of similar advances made out of the National Loans Fund on the day the advance is made; and

    (*c*) any account relating to the sums mentioned in paragraph (*a*) above shall be sent to and audited and reported on by the Scottish Comptroller and Auditor General and his report shall be laid before and published by the Assembly.

DEFINITIONS

    " devolved matter " : s. 81 (1), referring to s. 63.

    " Minister of the Crown " : s. 81 (1).

    " Scottish Secretary " : s. 81 (1), referring to s. 20 (2).

    " Treasury " : Interpretation Act 1978, Sched. 1.

GENERAL NOTE

    The object of this section is, in respect of devolved matters, to alter provisions in existing Acts of Parliament which refer to U.K. financial machinery so that they should instead apply to the new Scottish financial machinery.

Subs. (1)

    Subs. (1) achieves this by substituting, in relation to devolved matters, references to the Scottish Consolidated Fund for references to the U.K. Consolidated Fund. (The subsection seems incomplete, however, in that it does not expressly substitute the phrase " payment . . . out of moneys provided by the Assembly " for the phrase in para. (*c*) " payment . . . out of moneys provided by Parliament." But the intention is obvious). The reference to s. 23 (3) is needed because certain statutory powers (listed in Sched. 5) are to be exercisable both by the Secretary of State and by a Scottish Secretary.

Subs. (2)

    Subs. (2) must be read together with Sched. 9, which lists a number of statutes which authorise the lending of money to public bodies by the Secretary of State; these loans have hitherto been made from the National Loans Fund. Since these powers are after devolution to be exercisable by a Scottish Secretary, payments and repayments will then be made via the Scottish Loans Fund. Para. (*b*) in subs. (2) serves the same purpose as s. 53 (Rates of interest on certain loans from Scottish Loans Fund) in relation to loans made under the statutes listed in Sched. 9. Accounts relating to loans from the Scottish Loans Fund are to be audited by the Scottish Comptroller and Auditor General (para. (*c*)).

Existing debt

Existing debt

61. Where any power to advance money conferred by the enactments mentioned in Schedule 9 to this Act is exercisable by a Scottish Secretary but was, before it became so exercisable, exercised by the Secretary of State—

(*a*) any amount payable by way of repayment of or interest on the sum advanced by the Secretary of State in the exercise of that power shall, instead of being paid to the Secretary of State and into the National Loans Fund, be paid to a Scottish Secretary and into the Scottish Loans Fund; and

(*b*) amounts equal to those which, by virtue of this section, are to be received by a Scottish Secretary in repayment of principal shall be deemed to be amounts of advances made at the coming into operation of this section to a Scottish Secretary by the Secretary of State and repayable at such times and with interest at such rates as may be determined by the Treasury; and

(*c*) any sums received by the Secretary of State by virtue of paragraph (*b*) above shall be paid into the National Loans Fund.

DEFINITIONS
" Scottish Secretary ": s. 81 (1), referring to s. 20 (2).
" Treasury ": Interpretation Act 1978, Sched. 1.

GENERAL NOTE
Like s. 60 (2), this section must be read together with Sched. 9. The Acts listed in that Schedule originally authorised the Secretary of State to make loans to certain public bodies, such as the Scottish Development Agency, the money coming from the National Loans Fund. Since these powers concern devolved matters, after devolution the loans will be made by a Scottish Secretary from the Scottish Loans Fund. The present section deals with loans issued by the Secretary of State and not repaid before the Scottish Executive begins to exercise its devolved powers. Its effect is that all payments in respect of these existing loans due after the commencement date are to be made to a Scottish Secretary and paid into the Scottish Loans Fund (para. (*a*)). The principal sums outstanding on the commencement date are to be deemed to be advances from the Secretary of State to a Scottish Secretary (para. (*b*)) and sums received in repayment of these deemed advances will be paid into the National Loans Fund (para. (*c*)). These rather complex provisions have the beneficial effect that public bodies, like the Scottish Development Agency and the Scottish Transport Group, which will have received loans before the commencement date and will receive further loans after the commencement date, will after the section comes into operation make all their payments to a single recipient, namely a Scottish Secretary.

These loans made before the commencement date will not count against the statutory limit for payments into the Scottish Loans Fund (s. 49 (4)), since that limit is confined to payments made by the Secretary of State into the Scottish Loans Fund under s. 49 (1).

Accounts by Secretary of State

Accounts by Secretary of State

62. The Secretary of State shall for each financial year prepare an account in such form and manner as the Treasury may direct of sums paid and received by him under section 49 or 61 of this Act, and send it to the Comptroller and Auditor General not later than the end of November following the year; and the Comptroller and Auditor General shall examine, certify and report on the account and lay copies of it, together with his report, before each House of Parliament.

DEFINITION

" Treasury ": Interpretation Act 1978, Sched. 1.

GENERAL NOTE

This section requires the Secretary of State to prepare annual accounts regarding sums paid and received by him under ss. 49 (payments into Scottish Loans Fund out of National Loans Fund) and 61 (existing debt). Since these payments and receipts all concern the National Loans Fund, the accounts are to be audited by the U.K. Comptroller and Auditor General and his report is to be laid in Parliament. Accounts in respect of payments into and out of the Scottish Loans Fund will be the responsibility of a Scottish Secretary and the Scottish Comptroller and Auditor General (s. 57).

PART IV

DEVOLVED MATTERS AND DETERMINATION OF QUESTIONS RELATING THERETO

General Note to Part IV

This Part of the Act, together with Scheds. 10–12, serves two purposes : (a) it defines the matters on which powers are to be devolved to the Assembly and Scottish Executive; and (b) it provides procedure enabling the courts to decide disputes as to the extent of the devolved powers. Pt. IV must however be read with other provisions of the Act, notably s. 18 and Sched. 2 (legislative competence of the Assembly), s. 19 (pre-assent scrutiny of Assembly bills) and s. 21 (executive powers).

Devolved matters

63.—(1) References in this Act to devolved matters shall be construed in accordance with the following provisions of this section, but subject to section 64 of this Act.

(2) In relation to the legislative competence of the Assembly, a devolved matter is one which is included in the Groups in Part I of Schedule 10 to this Act.

(3) In relation to the powers and duties of a Scottish Secretary, a devolved matter is—

(a) any matter included in the Groups in Part I of Schedule 10 to this Act;

(b) any matter with respect to which powers within the Groups in Schedule 11 to this Act are exercisable; and

(c) any matter with respect to which powers are exercisable by a Scottish Secretary under any other provision of this Act (including any provision contained in Schedule 16).

DEFINITION

" Scottish Secretary ": s. 81 (1), referring to s. 20 (2).

GENERAL NOTE

This section, together with s. 64 and Scheds. 10 and 11, provides an extensive and detailed description of the term "devolved matter." This term is used in several key provisions relating to the devolution of powers, notably Sched. 2, para. 1 (" . . . a provision is within the legislative competence of the Assembly if, and only if, the matter to which it relates is a devolved matter "), s. 21 (vesting of executive powers in relation to devolved matters), s. 22 (power to make subordinate instruments with respect to devolved matters), and s. 46 (appropriation from Scottish Consolidated Fund for devolved matters).

The Government of Ireland Act 1920, s. 4 (1), gave the Stormont Parliament a broad power " to make laws for the peace, order and good government of Northern Ireland," subject to matters which were expressly stated in the Act to be reserved to the U.K. Parliament. But the basis of the scheme in this Act is that only powers specified in the Act are devolved. Thus a matter which is not stated in the Act to be devolved (*e.g.* the armed forces, the postal services) is, as was said during the parliamentary debates, reserved to the U.K. Parliament " by silence " (see Lord McCluskey, *Hansard*, H.L. Vol. 391, col. 421 (May 4, 1978)). However, a matter is devolved even if it is not mentioned expressly in the Act if it falls within one of the subject groups listed in Sched. 10, Pt. I.

Subs. (2)

This subsection concerns matters within the legislative competence of the Assembly, as opposed to matters within the executive competence of the Scottish Secretaries (for which see subs. (3)). It provides that matters included within the groups specified in Sched. 10, Pt. I are within the legislative competence of the Assembly. Although subs. (2) does not refer expressly to Pts. II and III of Sched. 10, Pt. I of Sched. 10 operates subject to the later parts of the Schedule. This is made clear by the preliminary paragraph in Pt. I. This states that the matters specified in Pt. II of the Schedule are not included in the groups of devolved matters; and that, concerning the matters dealt with by the statutes listed in Pt. III, whether or not those matters are devolved or not is specified in Pt. III. It is therefore not possible by reading Sched. 10, Pt. I, alone to assume that a topic falling within one of the subject groups is devolved, since it may be excluded by later provision in Sched. 10. (Thus " social welfare " is included in Sched. 10, Pt. I, Group 2, but " social security and war pensions " are excluded from devolution by Sched. 10, Pt. II.)

" *legislative competence.*" This term is found in other related sections of the Act, notably s. 18 (with Sched. 2), s. 19 and s. 65 (with Sched. 12, para. 1 (*a*)). It means the area of substantive power to legislate conferred by the Act on the Assembly, and not to the procedure by which Assembly Acts are to be made. Indeed, as noted earlier, s. 17 (4) seeks to exclude judicial review of the procedure by which Assembly Acts are made, whereas the Act provides machinery for enabling disputed questions of legislative competence to be resolved judicially, whether these arise before or after enactment of an Assembly Act. Failure to observe procedural requirements (*e.g.* those imposed by s. 24 and Sched. 6) does not mean that an Assembly Act is outside the legislative competence of the Assembly. Similarly, the power of the Secretary of State (with parliamentary approval) to veto Bills passed by the Assembly (s. 38) does not in law cut down the legislative competence of the Assembly, although exercise of the power would obviously restrict the freedom of the Assembly to use its legislative powers to the full.

Subs. (3)

This defines devolved matters in relation to the functions of the Scottish Secretaries, who are to be responsible: (a) for all matters within the legislative competence of the Assembly; (b) for all the statutory powers of U.K. Ministers listed in Sched. 11 (but on which power to legislate is not vested in the Assembly); and (c) for other statutory powers vested in a Scottish Secretary (*e.g.* by ss. 69 and 72). It may be inferred from the Act that the Scottish Secretaries will be responsible to the Assembly for their administration of these matters, which will be financed out of the block grant provided to the Scottish administration from U.K. funds (s. 48). But certain of these powers will be subject to detailed approval by U.K. Ministers (*e.g.* s. 23 and Sched. 4), and this may detract from the direct responsibility owed by the Scottish Executive to the Assembly.

Reservations

64.—(1) The prerogative of mercy is not a devolved matter.

(2) To the extent that a matter involves the conduct of relations with any country outside the United Kingdom it is not a devolved matter.

(3) If it appears to a Minister of the Crown—

> (*a*) that the implementation of a Community obligation or any other international obligation of the United Kingdom requires the exercise of any power to make a subordinate instrument; and
>
> (*b*) that the power could be exercised by a Scottish Secretary; but
>
> (*c*) that it is desirable that it should be exercised by a Minister of the Crown,

he may exercise the power as if the matter with respect to which it is exercisable were not a devolved matter.

DEFINITIONS

" Community obligation ": see ss. 19 (2) and 39 (2) and notes thereon.
" Minister of the Crown ": s. 81 (1).
" Scottish Secretary ": s. 81 (1), referring to s. 20 (2).

GENERAL NOTE

This section makes reservations from the matters devolved by s. 63. The reservations apply to both Assembly and Executive.

Subs. (1)

The prerogative of mercy will continue to be exercised in Scotland by the Crown on the advice of the Secretary of State. Apart from the formal consideration that Scottish Secretaries are to have no direct access to the Sovereign, the reason for excluding the prerogative of mercy from devolution is that the prosecution of crimes will continue to be the task of the Lord Advocate (Sched. 10, Pt. II, para. 24); nor are the police to be devolved, although the treatment of offenders will be (Sched. 10, Pt. I, Group 25). But for the reservation made in this subsection, the entry for Group 25 (Crime) in Sched. 10, Pt. I, would have devolved the prerogative of mercy.

In Sched. 10, Pt. III, the entry for the Criminal Procedure (Scotland) Act 1975 excludes from devolution the cognate power of the Secretary of State under s. 263 of that Act to refer criminal cases after conviction to the High Court of Justiciary for the opinion of the court.

Subs. (2)

In *Our Changing Democracy*, para. 19, the Government stated that the maintenance of political unity in the U.K. required that the Government must conduct all international relations, including those flowing from membership of the EEC. This subsection excludes from the scope of devolved matters any aspect of those matters which " involves the conduct of relations with any country outside the U.K." In the Wales Act 1978, s. 28 provides that the Welsh Assembly " shall not in the exercise of its functions conduct relations with any country outside the U.K." According to the Lord Chancellor, these provisions of the Scotland Act and the Wales Act have exactly the same meaning (*Hansard*, H.L. Vol. 391, col. 1096 (May 10, 1978)). But is this necessarily the case? It is clear from the Wales Act that what is forbidden is any attempt by the Welsh Assembly itself to conduct foreign relations; the different formulation in the Scotland Act is arguably open to the interpretation that what is excluded from devolution is any aspect of devolved matters which involves the conduct of foreign relations by the Scottish Assembly and Executive *or by the U.K. Government*. On this interpretation, which would require the word " involves " to be read as " affects " or " relates to," action by the U.K. Government in negotiating a cultural treaty with Ruritania might have the effect of narrowing the scope of the powers in respect of cultural matters devolved to the Scottish administration (by Sched. 10, Pt. I, Group 3). Note that the consequences of a matter being excluded from devolution are that the Assembly may not legislate about it, nor may any money from the

Scottish Consolidated Fund be spent upon it (s. 46 (1)). Moreover, the Act itself contemplates that the powers of the Scottish administration may be used for the purpose of implementing Community or other international obligations of the U.K. (s. 64 (3)). While therefore the present subsection is capable of bearing a wider interpretation than the Wales Act 1978, s. 28, it is submitted that the view of the Lord Chancellor mentioned above is to be preferred; and that the subsection is aimed at any attempt by the Scottish Assembly or Executive to establish what might be called quasi-diplomatic relations with foreign countries.

A further difficulty in the subsection is the notion of " relations with any country outside the U.K." Do these words exclude, for example, (a) an Assembly Act authorising local authorities to spend money on " twinning " arrangements with local authorities abroad; (b) a visit abroad by an Assembly committee to study the working of regional government; or (c) a letter by a civil servant in the housing department of the Scottish Executive to a foreign company inquiring about new methods of housing construction? The effect of the subsection would indeed be drastic if it prevented the Scottish administration from having any dealings with individuals, companies or public authorities in foreign countries.

According to the Government, the subsection also excludes the conduct of relations with international organisations, at least with those which are intergovernmental, since relations with such an organisation would necessarily involve relations with other countries. On this ground the Government resisted an amendment to insert the phrase " or group of countries " into the subsection (*Hansard*, H.L. Vol. 393, col. 228 (June 13, 1978)). But difficulties could arise in respect of international organisations which were not in form intergovernmental but whose national members were in fact supported by their governments.

So far as the EEC is concerned, the Government view is that the subsection excludes any attempt by the Scottish administration to conduct relations with the EEC (*Hansard, ibid.*). But the EEC is arguably more than " a group of countries " and it is not obvious that the EEC Commission is either " a country outside the U.K." or even the government of such a country. Accordingly the subsection may not prevent the Scottish administration opening an office in Brussels for the purpose of obtaining information about the work of the EEC Commission. According to the Lord Chancellor, speaking in the context of representatives of the Scottish administration accompanying a Foreign Office delegation to talks in Brussels, " there would be nothing irregular in the Scottish Executive having somebody actually in Brussels. . . . However the actual negotiation, the carrying out or formulation of policy within the EEC is a matter in the sole responsibility and charge of the Government " (*Hansard*, H.L. Vol. 391, col. 1099 (May 10, 1978)).

Subs. (3)

This subsection enables a U.K. Minister to exercise powers of delegated legislation to implement Community or other international obligations of the U.K. even though the powers in question, so far as they relate to devolved matters, have been entrusted to a Scottish Secretary (*e.g.* under s. 22). This subsection needs to be read with s. 40 (2), which gives the Secretary of State power to revoke subordinate instruments made by a Scottish Secretary which are incompatible with Community or other international obligations. " Subordinate instrument " is not defined, but it would seem to relate to what is set out in s. 22, namely " any power to make, confirm or approve orders, rules, regulations or other subordinate legislation."

In relation to Community obligations, the entry for the European Communities Act 1972 in Sched. 16 to the present Act amends s. 2 (2) of that Act so that, by Order in Council, a Scottish Secretary may be authorised to make subordinate legislation for the purpose of implementing Community obligations and related matters. One effect of the present subsection is to enable a U.K. Minister to legislate even though such an Order in Council has been made.

Legal proceedings involving devolution issues

65. Schedule 12 to this Act shall have effect with respect to the legal proceedings and questions mentioned therein.

GENERAL NOTE

Since the legislative powers of the Assembly are limited by the Act, it follows that questions may arise in the courts as to the validity of Assembly Acts on grounds of *vires* of competence. They may also arise as to whether action by a Scottish Secretary goes outside the area of devolved executive powers. Without Sched. 12, it would have been necessary for the courts to rule on these questions of *vires* in the normal course of litigation, just as they ordinarily deal with challenges to the validity of subordinate legislation and administrative acts. In the Scotland and Wales Bill, no special provision was made for these matters but the Government later decided to include this in the Scotland Bill (Michael Foot M.P., Lord President of the Council, *Hansard*, H.C. Vol. 936, col. 313 (July 26, 1977)).

In relation to Assembly Acts, the procedure in Sched. 12 for post-assent review complements the procedure in s. 19 for pre-assent scrutiny of Assembly bills.

Notes on Sched. 12 follow the text of the Schedule.

PART V

MISCELLANEOUS

Voting of Scottish Members of Parliament

Voting of Scottish Members of Parliament

66.—(1) Subject to subsection (2) of this section, if, following the first meeting of the Scottish Assembly, a Bill to which this section applies has been passed by the House of Commons but there would not have been a majority in support of the Bill if there had been excluded from the members who voted in the division of that House on the question that the Bill be read the second time all those representing parliamentary constituencies in Scotland, that Bill shall be deemed not to have been read the second time unless after the next fourteen days on which that House has sat after the division took place that House confirms its decision that the Bill be read the second time.

(2) Subsection (1) of this section shall not come into operation unless it has been approved by a resolution of the House of Commons.

(3) This section applies to any Bill which does not relate to or concern Scotland or any part of Scotland but would, if it had related to or concerned Scotland, have been within the legislative competence of the Assembly.

GENERAL NOTE

This section seeks to resolve what has become known as the " West Lothian question," so called after the M.P. for West Lothian, Mr. Tam Dalyell, who as an opponent of the Government's proposals for devolution has persistently raised the question both inside and outside Parliament (see his book, *Devolution: The End of Britain.*) Essentially, the " West Lothian question " is as follows : when the Assembly is in operation, the matters devolved to it will cease to be the direct responsibility of Parliament, and Scottish M.P.s will no longer have any control over them. These matters will, however, still be the responsibility of Parliament as regards the rest of the U.K., and so will continue to be affected by the views and votes of Scottish M.P.s. Thus, for example, Scottish M.P.s will after devolution be able to influence education in England, but not in Scotland because education, as a devolved matter, will become subject to the control of the Assembly. English M.P.s, however, will not have any corresponding control over Scottish education. This situation has been seen by Mr. Dalyell and others as illogical and likely to create tensions between Scotland and the rest of the U.K., but clearly it is inherent in the Act and indeed in any system of legislative devolution which is introduced to only one part of a unitary state. Only by the introduction of a federal system of government could the situation be wholly avoided.

It cannot be said that the " West Lothian question " was first noticed in relation to this Act; as the Kilbrandon Report observed (see paras. 810–5), the question of Irish representation at Westminster was one of the most bitterly disputed matters in the various Irish Home Rule Bills. The expedient adopted in relation to Northern Ireland was to give its M.P.s full voting rights in the Commons, but to reduce their numbers in proportion to the electorate (see Government of Ireland Act 1920, s. 19, and House of Commons (Redistribution of Seats) Act 1949, s. 2, Sched. 2). Thus Northern Ireland would be represented by 17 M.P.s, and not 12 as at present, if each of its M.P.s represented the same number of electors as English M.P.s. The Kilbrandon Report noted that apart from reducing the level of representation in the Commons, two other possibilities had been discussed in relation to the Irish Home Rule Bills. One was to take away representation in the House of Commons entirely, but this was rejected since it would deny any voice at all in the consideration of important non-devolved matters such as defence and foreign affairs. The other possibility—termed the " in and out " principle—was to allow the M.P.s to vote on the matters reserved to Parliament, but not on the matters devoted to the Assembly operating within their area. This was considered by the Kilbrandon Report to be the most logical solution in principle, but probably unworkable in practice in view of the difficulty in defining with adequate precision the circumstances in which the M.P.s could or could not vote. Moreover, political difficulties might be created if the removal of voting rights from certain M.P.s deprived the Government of its majority in certain circumstances. The Kilbrandon Report therefore rejected both of these possibilities. It later recommended, however, that Scotland should no longer be over-represented in the House of Commons when compared with England; this would require a reduction in the number of Scottish M.P.s from 71 (see House of Commons (Redistribution of Seats) Act 1949, s. 2, Sched. 2) to about 57, allowing for special considerations in sparsely populated areas (para. 1147).

The Government, however, made an early decision that Scotland would retain its existing number of M.P.s so that " the determination of United Kingdom policies should reflect the needs and contributions of all its constituent parts " (*Democracy and Devolution: Proposals for Scotland and Wales*, paras. 32–3). Nor did the Government propose any modification of Scottish M.P.s' voting rights. Consequently, the Scotland Bill as originally drafted made no provision at all for the status or number of Scottish M.P.s after the establishment of the Assembly, and the Government made clear that it would oppose any alterations to the status quo. But during the Committee stage in the Lords, two amendments were introduced: one would have required, after the Assembly had come into operation, the appointment of a Speaker's Conference to review the level of Scottish representation in the House of Commons. This amendment was accepted by the Lords but later rejected by the Commons without discussion or vote; see *Hansard*, H.L. Vol. 392, cols. 173–208 (May 16, 1978). The second amendment, which was withdrawn after debate, was based on the " in and out " principle, and would have precluded Scottish M.P.s from voting on " any matter in respect of which legislative competence in relation to Scotland [had been] devolved to the Scottish Assembly"; *Hansard*, H.L. Vol. 392, cols. 261–89 (May 16, 1978).

The present section began life as a new clause moved during the Report stage in the Lords. It was rejected by the Commons, by the casting vote of the Deputy Speaker, but then returned to the Commons by the Lords with two amendments; these amendments had also been rejected by the Commons, and are noted below. Finally, the Commons agreed to accept the new clause by a majority of one vote; *Hansard*, H.L. Vol. 393, cols. 241–77 (June 13, 1978); H.C. Vol. 954, cols. 155–206 (July 17, 1978); H.L. Vol. 395, cols. 508–12 (July 20, 1978); H.C. Vol. 954, cols. 1637–60 (July 26, 1978). The inclusion of the section also led to an amendment to the Long Title of the Act, by the addition of the words " and in the procedure of Parliament "; *Hansard*, H.L. Vol. 393, cols. 1056–7 (June 20, 1978).

The section seeks to provide that where a Bill in the House of Commons which falls within the scope of subs. (3) receives a majority on its Second Reading only by virtue of the votes of Scottish M.P.s, a second vote will take place at least 14 days later, and only if a majority is obtained on that second vote will the Bill be deemed to have been read a second time (subs. (1)). By subs. (2), however, the section will not come into operation until it is approved by resolution of the Commons; this provision is designed to ensure that the Commons retain final control over their own legislative procedures. In effect, therefore, the section enables the procedures of the Commons to be modified; it does not alter either the number or the status of Scottish M.P.s. The purpose of allowing the 14-day period is, in the words of Earl Ferrers, " to give time for people to think again ". The section is clearly aimed at Scottish M.P.s, but only seldom are M.P.s (wherever their constituency) able to vote as completely free agents. In practice, therefore, whether the section will have any practical effect depends very much on the attitude of political parties and the activities of their Whips. It is indeed possible that if the section is brought into operation, the second vote would simply be a repeat of the first. Moreover there are, as noted below, other serious defects which suggest that the proposed cure may be less desirable than the supposed disease.

Subs. (1)

" *the first meeting of the Scottish Assembly.*" See s. 6.

" *if . . . a Bill . . . has been passed by the House of Commons.*" The effect of those words is that the modified procedure cannot come into operation until the Bill has been read a third time and passed by the Commons. Yet the remainder of this subsection implies, necessarily, that if a second vote on Second Reading is required, that vote would take place before the Bill proceeds any further. The contradiction in the subsection has arisen because as originally drafted it required the second vote to take place at the Third Reading stage, so that the inclusion of the words now under discussion fitted into the subsection. The amendment to advance the time of the second vote was made to ensure that the issue would be finally decided before detailed work on the Bill was carried out at the Committee stage, but for the subsection to make sense the reference to the Bill being passed by the Commons should have been removed when the amendment was made.

Subs. (3)

" *but would, if it had related to or concerned Scotland, have been within the legislative competence of the Assembly.*" These words were the second amendment to the section made by the Lords, and their effect is to narrow the scope of the Bills which may be subject to the operation of this section. As it stood originally, the section would have applied to all Bills which did not relate to or concern Scotland, or any part thereof, irrespective of whether the matters dealt with in the Bills were devolved to the Assembly. It was felt, however, (see Mr. Francis Pym, M.P., *Hansard*, H.C. Vol. 954, col. 160 (July 17, 1978)) that this was too wide; it would not, he argued, be appropriate to use the procedure in relation to, say, a Bill concerning the police in England and Wales because the police is not a matter on which the Assembly may legislate. If a Bill concerning the police in Scotland could be voted on by all M.P.s, there was no justification for a modified procedure in relation to Bills concerning the police in England and Wales.

The subsection makes no provision as to the resolution of disputes over whether a Bill falls within its terms. This gap is made all the more glaring by the amendment referred to above, for it is clear that elsewhere in the Act questions as to the legislative competence of the Assembly are for the most part to be decided by a court of law (see ss. 19 (1), 63–5 and Sched. 12). No provision is made for issues arising under this subsection to be referred to a court; nor would such a referral be appropriate. If, therefore, the matter is to be decided by the House of Commons itself, the question arises whether Scottish M.P.s should be allowed to vote on the issue, since their votes might well decide the issue one way or the other. For this and other reasons, the section seems to create more problems than it resolves.

Civil Servants

Status and remuneration of certain officers and servants

67.—(1) Service as an officer or servant of a Scottish Secretary or of the Scottish Comptroller and Auditor General shall be service in Her Majesty's Home Civil Service, and appointments to any position as such an officer or servant shall be made accordingly.

(2) Service in the capacity of—

> (*a*) the Registrar General of Births, Deaths and Marriages for Scotland or any officer or servant of his;

> (*b*) the Accountant of Court or any officer or servant of his;

shall continue to be service in Her Majesty's Home Civil Service.

(3) Any salary and allowances in respect of service in any such capacity as is mentioned in subsections (1) and (2) above (including contributions to any pension scheme) shall be payable out of the Scottish Consolidated Fund.

(4) A Scottish Secretary shall pay to the Minister for the Civil Service out of the Scottish Consolidated Fund such sums in respect of each financial year as the Minister for the Civil Service may determine, subject to any directions of the Treasury, as being equivalent to—

(*a*) the increase during that year of such of his liabilities as are attributable to the provision of pensions, allowances or gratuities to or in respect of persons who are or have been serving in any such capacity as is mentioned in subsections (1) and (2) above, in so far as that increase results from their service, their ceasing to serve or their suffering diminution of emoluments during that financial year; and

(*b*) the increase during that year of such of his liabilities as are attributable to the expenses to be incurred in administering those pensions, allowances or gratuities.

(5) Her Majesty may by Order in Council designate any description of person for the purposes of this section; and references in this section to an officer or servant of a Scottish Secretary shall include any person of a description so designated.

DEFINITION

" Scottish Secretary ": s. 81 (1), referring to s. 20 (2).

GENERAL NOTE

This section provides that the staff of a Scottish Secretary and the Scottish Comptroller and Auditor General (subs. (1)), the Registrar General of Births, Deaths and Marriages for Scotland, the Accountant of Court, and their staff (subs. (2)) and any person of a description designated by Order in Council under subs. (5), will be members of the home civil service, and that the expenses of maintaining them will be payable out of the Scottish Consolidated Fund (subs. (3)). Subs. (4) makes provision for the payments in respect of superannuation.

The effect of the section is that there will be no separate civil service for Scotland. This is contrary to the recommendation of the Kilbrandon Report, paras. 806–7, 1145, which considered a separate civil service to be desirable on the grounds that the Scottish administration would wish to select its own senior officials, might not be willing for personnel administration to be handled by a central government department, and would wish to be able to rely upon the undivided loyalty of its officials, especially when dealing with U.K. government departments over such matters as the block grant. The Government, however, believed that to maintain a unified service would assist consultation and co-operation between the Scottish adminiftration and U.K. government departments and doubted, in the light of experience, whether divided loyalties would arise. It envisaged potential difficulties in attracting recruits to a separate civil service which might in view of its smaller size be seen to offer a less attractive career. It believed that it would be advantageous for the Scottish administration to be able to recruit from the wider pool of a unified service, and argued that a separate Scottish civil service would require additional staff and expenditure for such matters as recruitment and training. Finally, however, the possibility was left open of altering the present arrangements in the future, following discussion between the Scottish administration and the U.K. Government. See *Our Changing Democracy*, paras. 80–5.

The consequences of retaining a unified civil service are, as regards the staff covered by this section, that the present arrangements regarding qualification, recruitment, selection and dismissal will continue (see Civil Service Order in Council, 1969) and the staff of Scottish Secretaries will be members of the same groups and classes as the staff of U.K. departments. In principle, therefore, there should be the same degree of mobility between the departments of the Scottish administration and U.K. departments as there is at present between U.K. departments. It is reasonable to assume that the present rules governing the political activities of civil servants will continue, as will the present arrangements for collective bargaining. Although the Scottish administration will be given control over the total number of its staff (see subs. (3), and s. 20 (8) and note thereon), the U.K. Government will maintain control over the levels of appointment (see Civil Service Order in Council 1969, art. 5); this, as well as the other matters referred to, will require regular consultation between the Scottish administration and the Civil Service Department.

It will be open to a Scottish Secretary to appoint civil servants on a temporary basis; these appointments are termed " period appointments " and are of less than five years' duration. Civil servants engaged on this basis are appointed on civil service terms, but unlike the holders of permanent appointments are not certificated by the Civil Service Commissioners. On this basis Scottish Secretaries will, like U.K. Ministers, be able to appoint special or political advisers. It will not be possible for a Scottish Secretary to appoint as an officer or servant a person who is not a civil servant. Although Sched. 10, Pt. II, para. 23 empowers a Scottish Secretary to determine the terms and conditions of service (for which phrase, see s. 81 (1)) of persons who are paid by him, persons who are members of Her Majesty's Home Civil Service are expressly excluded from the terms of the paragraph, which is intended to empower the engagement of consultants, for example, on a feepaying basis; see Lord McCluskey, Solicitor-General for Scotland, *Hansard*, H.L. Vol. 392, cols. 212–3 (May 16, 1978).

Despite these considerations, the position of a civil servant working within the Scottish administration may not be identical to that of one working in a U.K. department. While Civil Service Department control over grading will obviously affect the shape of Scottish departments it does not follow, especially in view of the wide terms of s. 20 (8), that the relationship between civil servants and Scottish Secretaries will be identical to that between civil servants and a Minister of the Crown. Likewise the relationship between civil servants and the Assembly has yet to be worked out, and it is possible that the Assembly, through its committee structure (see s. 28), may attempt further erosion of the traditional anonymity of the civil servant. Such a development could cause tensions within the civil service itself, as well as between the Assembly and the U.K. Government.

For the position of the Clerk and the staff of the Assembly, see ss. 32–3.

Subs. (1)

For the appointment of officers and servants of a Scottish Secretary, see s. 20 (8), and for the appointment of the officers and servants of the Scottish Comptroller and Auditor General, see s. 54 (5).

"Her Majesty's Home Civil Service." As originally drafted, the subsection contained the phrase " the home civil service of the state," which was derived from the Minister for the Civil Service Order 1968, art. 2 (1) (*a*). During the Report stage in the Lords, following discussion at the Committee stage, the Government agreed to accept amendments substituting the phrase " Her Majesty's Home Civil Service," which is derived from the Civil Service Order in Council 1969, in both this subsection and subs. (2). The amendment was made to improve the elegance of the Act rather than its substance; *Hansard*, H.L. Vol. 392, cols. 207–11 (May 16, 1978); Vol. 393, cols. 291–2 (June 13, 1978).

" appointments to any position as such an officer or servant shall be made accordingly." It is this phrase which attracts the existing regulations regarding the appointment, etc. of staff; see general note above.

Subs. (2)

The purpose of this subsection is to make clear that the Registrar General of Births, Deaths and Marriages for Scotland and the Accountant of Court, along with their staff, will continue to be civil servants. The subsection was considered necessary because by statute, the Registrar General and Accountant of Court appoint their own staff (see Registration of Births, Deaths and Marriages (Scotland) Act 1965, s. 2 (1), and Judicial Factors (Scotland) Act 1889, s. 1). In practice, however, the staff in question are recruited by the Civil Service Commission and treated as civil servants.

This subsection was added as a Government amendment during the Committee stage in the Commons, along with consequential drafting amendments to subss. (3) and (4) (*a*); *Hansard*, H.C. Vol. 942, cols. 1277–9 (January 24, 1978).

Subs. (3)

In providing that the pay and allowances of civil servants working within the Scottish Administration are payable from the Scottish Consolidated Fund, and so ultimately from the block grant, this subsection provides an indirect limitation on the number of appointments which Scottish Secretaries and others can make. For the Scottish Consolidated Fund, see Pt. III.

Subs. (4)

This subsection is concerned with payments in connection with the principal Civil Service Superannuation Scheme, established under the Superannuation Act 1972, in respect of the staff covered by subss. (1) and (2). Because pensions to these staff will be payable from the U.K. Superannuation Vote, appropriate payments have to be made from the Scottish Consolidated Fund to the Exchequer in respect of this liability; this subsection is therefore based on the same principle as subs. (3). The Minister for the Civil Service is empowered to determine the sums to be paid, subject to Treasury direction.

" *in respect of each financial year.*" As originally drafted, the corresponding phrase in the Bill was " in each financial year." The alteration was made as a Government amendment during the Report stage in the Lords in view of the practical difficulties in completing the complex calculation of payments in the financial year to which they relate.

" *their ceasing to serve or their suffering diminution of emoluments.*" As originally drafted, the Bill allowed the calculations to be based only on service during the year. These words were added as a Government amendment during the Report stage in the Lords; their effect is that the calculations may now also be based on the ending of service (*e.g.* through loss of office or premature retirement) or down-grading. For this and the immediately preceding amendment, see *Hansard*, H.L. Vol. 393, cols. 292–3 (June 13, 1978).

Subs. (5)

This subsection is intended to allow other staff to be designated as civil servants at any time in the future. It is normal practice for civil service matters to be regulated by Order in Council.

This subsection was added as a Government amendment during the Committee stage in the House of Commons; *Hansard*, H.C. Vol. 942, cols. 1277–9 (January 24, 1978).

" *description of* " and " *of a description.*" These words were the subject of a Government amendment made during the Committee stage in the Lords. As originally drafted, the subsection referred to the designation of any person, not the description of any person. The purpose of the amendment was to ensure that the references to designated persons are not construed as references to persons as individuals, but to persons described by reference to the capacity in which they perform their tasks; *Hansard*. H.L. Vol. 392, cols. 211–2 (May 16, 1978).

Rate support grants

Rate support grants

68.—(1) Grants for any financial year which, after the coming into force of this section, fall to be made under sections 2 to 6 of the Local Government (Scotland) Act 1966 to local authorities in Scotland shall be made by a Scottish Secretary out of the Scottish Consolidated Fund (instead of by the Secretary of State out of moneys provided by Parliament).

(2) In taking into consideration the matters mentioned in paragraphs (*a*) to (*d*) of subsection (3) of section 2 of the Local Government (Scotland) Act 1966 (as substituted by Schedule 2 to the Local Government (Scotland) Act 1975) a Scottish Secretary shall have regard to such considerations affecting scheduled functions as the Secretary of State may bring to his notice after consulting with such associations of local authorities as appear to him to be concerned and before the conclusion of the consultations required by that subsection.

DEFINITION

" Scottish Secretary ": s. 81 (1), referring to s. 20 (2).

GENERAL NOTE

Rate support grant is a block grant given in aid of the current expenditure of local authorities. By Sched. 10, Pt. I, Group 5, responsibility for paying rate support grant is devolved to the Scottish Executive as an aspect of local government and local finance, and the Assembly is also thereby empowered to alter the system (see also Sched. 2, para. 4 (2)).

By subs. (1), the amount of the rate support grant will be drawn on the block grant paid into the Scottish Consolidated Fund by the Secretary of State (see s. 48). In calculating the size of the block grant, the U.K. Government will therefore be required to work out a notional element for the rate support grant, based on assumptions as to the likely requirements of local authorities, less the assumed contribution made by local rates and amounts borrowed by local authorities for capital expenditure. (It is assumed that approximately 50 per cent. of the block grant will be used for rate support grant purposes; Lord McCluskey, Solicitor-General for Scotland, *Hansard*, H.L. Vol. 393, cols. 302–3 (June 13, 1978)). However, no specific elements for rate support grant purposes will be earmarked within the block grant, so that the Scottish Executive will have a discretion (which may in practice prove to be somewhat marginal) either to increase or reduce the notional element according to its own priorities.

The rate support grant will continue to be worked out in accordance with the Local Government (Scotland) Act 1966 (as amended by the Local Government (Scotland) Act 1975, Sched. 2) but the settlement will be reached after consultations between the Scottish Executive and local authorities, and not between the Secretary of State and local authorities as hitherto (subs. (1)). For these purposes, the local authorities are represented by the Convention of Scottish Local Authorities (COSLA).

The situation is however complicated by the fact that once this Act is in operation, certain functions of local authorities will be reserved to the control of central government through the Secretary of State; these functions, termed "scheduled functions" in this Act, are listed in Sched. 15; see s. 81 (1) and note thereon. By far the most important of these functions is the police, although a large portion of expenditure on the police is in any event obtained through a specific grant (see Police (Scotland) Act 1967, s. 32 and Sched. 10, Pt. II, para. 5). It is estimated that approximately 10 per cent. of the total expenditure of local authorities will be on scheduled functions (Mr. Bruce Millan, M.P., Secretary of State for Scotland, *Hansard*, H.C. Vol. 942, cols. 1292–3 (January 24, 1978)). General support for scheduled functions will, however, continue to be made through the rate support grant, which requires that the Secretary of State be involved in the process of determining the rate support grant, and such involvement would have to continue in some form even if the rate support system were altered by Assembly legislation. Subs. (2) accordingly requires a Scottish Secretary to have regard to such considerations affecting scheduled functions as the Secretary of State may bring to his notice before the conclusion of his (the Scottish Secretary's) consultations with COSLA under the Local Government (Scotland) Act 1966, s. 2 (3). It is not therefore envisaged that the Secretary of State will be involved in the main consultations between the Scottish Executive and COSLA; rather he will consult with COSLA about the scheduled functions, and then communicate the outcome to a Scottish Secretary for use in the main consultations. A Scottish Secretary is not required by subs. (2) to follow the findings of the Secretary of State; even if such a requirement were imposed, the Scottish Executive could evade it by deducting the amount in dispute from the total rate support grant or from some item in it, or by adding the amount. See *Hansard*, H.C. Vol. 942, cols. 1290–1291 (January 24, 1978).

The power of Scottish Secretaries and U.K. Ministers to make specific grants to local authorities for specific purposes is not affected by this section. Scottish Secretaries may make such grants in respect of devolved functions (such as education) by Sched. 10, Pt. I, Group 5. The power to make such grants in respect of scheduled functions is reserved to the Secretary of State by Sched. 10, Pt. II, para. 5.

Subs. (1)

"*which, after the coming into force of this section.*" These words were the subject of a Government drafting amendment made during the Report stage in the Commons; *Hansard*, H.C. Vol. 944, col. 531 (February 15, 1978).

Subs. (2)

"*the matters mentioned in paragraphs (a) to (d) of subsections (3) of section 2 of the Local Government (Scotland) Act 1966 (as substituted by Schedule 2 to the Local Government (Scotland) Act 1975).*" These matters are, in summary, as follows: (a) the rate of relevant expenditure of local authorities; (b) fluctuation in the demand for local authority services which is not under local authority control; (c) the need to develop local authority services; and (d) the current level of prices, costs and remuneration, and future variations in that level.

Public bodies

Public bodies

69.—(1) A Minister of the Crown may by order make such provision in relation to any body listed in Schedule 13 to this Act as is mentioned in subsection (2) below; and

(*a*) in relation to any body listed in Part II of that Schedule the provisions of sections 21, 22, 60, 61 and 78 of this Act shall not apply; and

(*b*) in relation to any body listed in Part I of that Schedule the order may modify or exclude any of the provisions specified in paragraph (*a*) above.

(2) The provisions that may be made by an order under this section in relation to any body are provisions—

(*a*) enabling powers to be exercised or requiring duties to be performed by a Scottish Secretary instead of by a Minister of the Crown, or by the one or by the other, or by a Scottish Secretary with the consent of a Minister of the Crown;

(*b*) requiring or authorising the appointment of additional members;

(*c*) apportioning any assets or liabilities;

(*d*) imposing, or enabling the imposition of, any limits in addition to or in substitution for existing limits;

(*e*) providing, in the case of a body listed in Part II of Schedule 13 to this Act, for the application of section 52 of this Act;

(*f*) requiring or authorising payments into or out of the Scottish Consolidated or Loans Fund (instead of or in addition to payments into or out of the Consolidated Fund of the United Kingdom or the National Loans Fund or out of moneys provided by Parliament);

(*g*) requiring payments, with or without interest, to a Minister of the Crown or into the Consolidated Fund or National Loans Fund;

and such provisions, including provisions relating to the keeping, auditing and certification of accounts and the making of reports and provisions modifying any enactment, as appear to the Minister making the order necessary or expedient in consequence of other provisions of the order or incidental or supplementary thereto.

(3) Before making an order under this section relating to any body the Minister making the order shall consult the body; and if the body is listed in Part II of Schedule 13 to this Act the order shall not be made except at the request of a Scottish Secretary.

(4) No order shall be made under this section unless a draft of the order has been laid before and approved by a resolution of each House of Parliament.

DEFINITIONS

" Minister of the Crown ": s. 81 (1).

" Scottish Secretary ": s. 81 (1), referring to s. 20 (2).

GENERAL NOTE

This section provides machinery for achieving a division of responsibility in respect of public bodies which are responsible for reserved as well as for devolved matters, most of which operate in England and Wales as well as Scotland. The bodies in question are listed in Sched. 13, which should be read in conjunction with this section. The section does not apply to public bodies (such as Health Boards) whose remit relates solely to devolved matters and which operate wholly within Scotland. Legislative competence and executive powers relating to such bodies are included among the devolved matters, and so are transferred by ss. 18, 21, 22 and 63 and by

Scheds. 2 and 10. Nor does it apply to arrangements between the Scottish Executive and a public body made under s. 35 whereby one may act as the agent of the other.

The basic effect of the section is to enable the U.K. Government to make formal adjustments to the structure, powers and duties of public bodies to which the section applies. It empowers a Minister to make an order devolving some or all of the responsibilities listed in subs. (2) to the Scottish administration (subs. (1)). Before making an order, the Minister must consult the body concerned (subs. (3)) and the order must be laid in draft before, and approved by, each House of Parliament (subs. (4)). Until the appropriate order is made, each body listed in Sched. 13 will continue to operate as it has done hitherto. In three respects the section makes separate provision according to whether the body is listed in Pt. I or Pt. II of Sched. 13. First, for those bodies listed in Pt. II, the powers which would otherwise be conferred on a Scottish Secretary by ss. 21, 22, 60, 61 and 78 of the Act are withheld (subs. (1) (a)), while for the single body listed in Pt. I (the Housing Corporation) the order may modify or exclude any of these provisions (subs. (1) (b)). Secondly, for the Pt. II bodies, the initiative rests with a Scottish Secretary to request a Minister to make an order, while for the Housing Corporation in Pt. I, the initiative is left to the Minister (subs. (4)). Thirdly, by subs. (2) (e), the order may provide for the application of s. 52 to Pt. II bodies only.

Once an order relating to Pt. II bodies has been made, it will be competent for the Assembly to legislate in respect of that body, provided of course that the matter to which the legislation relates is a devolved matter; see Sched. 2, para. 5. This power will be exercisable where, for example, the order made by the Minister confers powers or duties on a Scottish Secretary under subs. (2) (a), and the Assembly wishes to alter them. It will not, however, be possible for the Assembly to legislate so as, for example, to confer on a Scottish Secretary the power to make subordinate instruments in relation to the body in question; the effect of such legislation would be to amend subs. (1) (a), and by Sched. 2, para. 7, the amendment of this Act does not, in general, fall within the Assembly's legislative competence. This restriction does not apply to the Housing Corporation in Pt. I.

The explanation for the division between the Housing Corporation in Pt. I and the other bodies in Pt. II appears to be based upon an assumption (which is not, however, made clear on the face of this section) that the Scottish administration will require additional functions in relation to the Housing Corporation for the effective implementation of its general devolved responsibility in relation to housing (see Sched. 10, Pt. I, Group 4), while for the Pt. II bodies, the maintenance of the status quo (until such time as the making of an order is requested by a Scottish Secretary under subs. (4)) will not be a source of major inconvenience. This suggests also, by implication, that in relation to the Housing Corporation in Pt. I, the appropriate order may be made as soon as the Act takes effect and this view is reinforced by the provisions of Sched. 2, para. 5.

See *Our Changing Democracy*, paras. 155–9, and Appendix E, and *Supplementary Statement*, para. 28.

Subs. (2)

This subsection specifies the provisions which a Minister may make by an order under subs. (1). The provisions include: (i) the transfer of functions currently exercised by a Minister concerning, for example, the power to make some of the appointments to governing boards, and to issue directions on the activities of the body in Scotland; and (ii) the division of financial responsibility, so that the separate activities of the body in Scotland are financed from the Scottish Consolidated and Loans Funds, and so that the accounts of the body's activities financed from the funds are submitted to the Assembly rather than to Parliament.

For the Scottish Consolidated and Loans Funds, see Pt. III.

" (d) . . . or enabling the imposition of. . . ." These words were added by a Government amendment made during the Report stage in the Commons: *Hansard*, H.C. Vol. 944, col. 531 (February 15, 1978).

" (e) providing, in the case . . . section 52 of this Act." This paragraph was added by a Government amendment made during the Report stage in the Lords; it ensures that where the power to authorise borrowing is transferred to a Scottish Secretary, the control arrangements provided in s. 52 will apply; *Hansard*, H.L. Vol. 393, col. 306 (June 13, 1978).

Subs. (4)

As originally drafted, this subsection provided for the negative resolution procedure to be applied to an order made under this section. Following comments made in the Commons on the corresponding provision of the Wales Bill (see now the Wales Act 1978, s. 59) the Government accepted that the affirmative resolution procedure was justified; *Hansard*, H.L. Vol. 392, cols. 239–41 (May 16, 1978).

Tourism

Tourism

70.—(1) The British Tourist Authority shall cease to discharge the functions conferred on it by section 2 (1) (*a*) of the Development of Tourism Act 1969 of encouraging people living in Great Britain to take their holidays there.

(2) A Scottish Secretary may make arrangements with the British Tourist Authority for that Authority to carry on activities outside the United Kingdom for the purpose of encouraging people to visit Scotland.

DEFINITION

" Scottish Secretary ": s. 81 (1), referring to s. 20 (2).

GENERAL NOTE

By Sched. 10, Pt. I, Group 17, tourism is a devolved matter. This section makes further provision for the development of tourism in Scotland, and should be read in conjunction with Sched. 16, paras. 29–32, which amend the Development of Tourism Act 1969, notably in relation to the composition and powers of the British Tourist Authority.

Our Changing Democracy, para. 152, stated that the Scottish administration would become responsible for tourism in Scotland, including the Scottish Tourist Board. This is primarily achieved by Sched. 10, Pt. I, Group 17, and reinforced by subs. (1), which is concerned with the domestic promotion of tourism. In taking away from the British Tourist Authority its functions of encouraging people living in Great Britain to take their holidays there, the subsection ensures that the Scottish Tourist Board will now have sole responsibility for encouraging people living in Great Britain to visit Scotland.

The British Tourist Authority will retain its statutory responsibility for the overseas promotion of tourism in Scotland as well as in England and Wales, and will continue to be responsible to, and funded by, the U.K. Government. This arrangement is based ostensibly on the argument that a combined overseas promotion exercise is more likely to be effective; see *Supplementary Statement*, para. 26. However, by Sched. 10, Part I, Group 17, and Sched. 16, para. 30, the Scottish administration will also have a statutory responsibility for this aspect of tourism, so that it may make funds of its own available to the British Tourist Authority for any specific promotion projects. Subs. (2) puts beyond any doubt that might be caused by s. 64 (2) the power of the Scottish administration to enter into such arrangements with the British Tourist Authority, although agency arrangements are already authorised by s. 35. It is on s. 35 that the Scottish administration would have to rely if it wished to make arrangements with any agency other than the British Tourist Authority, although it seems that arrangements with agencies outside the U.K. would be precluded by s. 64 (2); see note thereon. The intention appears to be that the overseas promotion of tourism in Scotland should be undertaken by the British Tourist Authority.

It is also because of its increased statutory responsibilities that the Scottish Tourist Board has been given increased representation on the British Tourist Authority; see Sched. 16, para. 29. Alterations in the Authority's composition were envisaged in the *Supplementary Statement*, paras. 26–7, but the original provisions in the Bill were altered by a Government amendment during the Report stage in the House of Lords, following discussion at the Committee stage: *Hansard*, H.L. Vol. 392, cols. 439–50 (May 17, 1978); Vol. 393, cols. 1054–5 (June 20, 1978).

Planning

Planning

71. Section 39 of this Act does not apply to any action proposed to be taken or capable of being taken by a Scottish Secretary in the exercise of any of the powers specified in Part I of Schedule 14 to this Act; but the provisions of Part II of that Schedule shall have effect in relation to those powers.

DEFINITION
" Scottish Secretary ": s. 81 (1), referring to s. 20 (2).

GENERAL NOTE
As envisaged in *Our Changing Democracy*, para. 132, physical planning is in general devolved to the Scottish Assembly; see Sched. 10, Pt. I, Group 6. *Our Changing Democracy* also stated, however, in para. 133 that the Scottish administration's powers in this area would be subject to the U.K. Government's right to " call in " any particular planning issue for its decision if it affected, or could affect, a non-devolved matter such as defence. The Government's policy was explained in more detail by Lord Kirkhill, Minister of State at the Scottish Office, during the Committee stage in the Lords: " When land use disputes arise requiring a judgment as to priorities between devolved and non-devolved interests, in the last resort they can be resolved only at the level of central government since the devolved administration by its nature does not have the same authority to assess the implications for the non-devolved interests. The constituency for such interests is the entire United Kingdom and not merely Scotland." (*Hansard*, H.L. Vol. 392, col. 245 (May 16, 1978)).

This section gives effect to that policy. It is a parallel provision to s. 39 (power to prevent or require action), but expressly precludes that section from applying to the exercise of the planning powers listed in Sched. 14, Pt. I and provides that Sched. 14, Pt. II, shall apply instead when the U.K. Government wishes to intervene. In contrast to s. 39 (see subs. (6) thereof), Sched. 14 does not involve recourse to Parliament which as a political forum was not thought to be a suitable body for the determination of planning issues. Under Sched. 14, moreover, interested parties are not denied the right which they possess under normal planning procedures to express their views, which they would be if the s. 39 procedure had been adopted; Lord Kirkhill, Minister of State at the Scottish Office, *Hansard*, H.L. Vol. 392, col. 245 (May 16, 1978).

Property

Transfer of property

72.—(1) The Secretary of State shall by order provide—
  (*a*) for the transfer to and vesting in the First Secretary of property vested in the Secretary of State and appearing to him to be property used or to be used solely or mainly for the Assembly or for or in connection with the exercise of functions concerned with devolved matters; and
  (*b*) for the exercise by a Scottish Secretary of rights specified in or determined under the order to use property vested in the Secretary of State and appearing to the Secretary of State to be property used or to be used as mentioned in paragraph (*a*) above but not solely or mainly so used or to be used.

(2) Without prejudice to the power under section 37 of this Act, if a Scottish Assembly Act provides for any functions of a body listed in Schedule 13 to this Act to be no longer exercisable in Scotland, a Minister of the Crown may by order provide for the transfer of property vested in the body and used in connection with those functions and for reserving or conferring rights to use property so transferred or property excepted from the transfer.

(3) An order under subsection (1) or (2) of this section may be made with respect to any property, notwithstanding any provision (of whatever nature) which would prevent or restrict its transfer or, as the case may be, the granting of the rights concerned by other means.

(4) The preceding provisions of this section shall not apply to land acquired by the Secretary of State (whether under section 39 of the Forestry Act 1967 or otherwise) as land suitable for afforestation or for

purposes connected with forestry or as land necessarily acquired with any such land.

(5) An order under this section may be made subject to any exceptions or reservations specified in or determined under the order and may contain such consequential, incidental or supplementary provisions (including provisions for the transfer of liabilities connected with the property concerned) as appear to the Minister making the order to be necessary or expedient.

(6) A statutory instrument made under this section shall be subject to annulment in pursuance of a resolution of either House of Parliament.

DEFINITIONS

" devolved matter ": s. 81 (1), referring to s. 63.
" Minister of the Crown ": s. 81 (1).
" property ": s. 81 (1).
" Scottish Secretary ": s. 81 (1) referring to s. 20 (2).

GENERAL NOTE

This section requires the Secretary of State to make an order, which will be subject to the negative resolution procedure (subs. (6)), to transfer to the Scottish administration such property as he considers is, or will be, used for the Assembly or for the performance of devolved functions. The property will hitherto have been vested in the Secretary of State for the Environment and the Secretary of State for Scotland, and will include, for example, the Assembly buildings themselves, office accommodation for members of the Scottish Executive and their staff, hospitals, and prisons. This section is concerned solely with the *transfer* of property; for the power to acquire and dispose of land (including buildings), see s. 73.

Several minor amendments were made to the section during its passage through Parliament; see *Hansard*, H.C. Vol. 942, cols. 1339–40 (January 24, 1978).

Cf. Local Government (Scotland) Act 1973, s. 222.

Subs. (1)

Para. (*a*). This is concerned with property which the Secretary of State considers is, or will be, used entirely or principally for the Assembly, or for or in connection with the exercise of functions concerned with devolved matters. In these circumstances the property will be transferred to and vested in the First Secretary of the Scottish Executive. The vesting of property specifically in the First Secretary is an exception to the general rule that the functions of Scottish Secretaries are interchangeable; see s. 20 and note thereon.

Para. (*b*). This is concerned with property which the Secretary of State considers is, or will be, used for the purposes specified in para. (*a*) above, but not entirely or even principally so used. The property referred to in this paragraph will therefore be used only in part for devolved functions (*e.g.* office accommodation of which only one section will be used by Scottish Executive staff). In these circumstances the property is not transferred; instead, the order will confer user rights on a Scottish Secretary.

Subs. (2)

This subsection enables a U.K. Minister to deal by order with the property of public bodies listed in Sched. 13 (see s. 67 and note thereon). If the Assembly legislates so as to reduce or terminate the functions of any of these bodies in Scotland, the order made by the Minister may not only transfer the property used in connection with the functions taken away by the Assembly Act, but also retain or confer rights to use either the property transferred, or other property which is not included in the transfer. It is not competent for the Assembly itself to legislate to transfer the property of bodies to which this subsection applies; see Sched 2, para. 6.

Subs. (3)

This subsection sets aside restrictions on the transfer of property or user rights. Were it not for this subsection, it might be possible for a landlord or feudal superior to refuse to agree to the transfer; some property, for example, has hitherto been held by the Secretary of State on lease.

Subs. (4)

This subsection prevents the transfer to the Scottish administration of land, or user rights in land, which is held by the Secretary of State for forestry purposes. As originally drafted, the section would have permitted the transfer of such land, but amendments were made when it was decided that forestry should not be a devolved matter.

Subs. (5)

This subsection, which applies to orders made under subss. (1) and (2), enables a Minister to transfer property, or user rights in property, subject to such exceptions, reservations, or supplementary provisions as he considers necessary or expedient (for the phrase " necessary or expedient," see note on s. 37). This could include, for example, the reservation of user rights, or the transfer of liabilities connected with the property such as the liability to pay rent.

Acquisition and disposal of land by First Secretary

73.—(1) In relation to so much of the public service as is concerned with devolved matters the First Secretary shall have the like powers to acquire and dispose of land as are conferred on the Secretary of State by the enactments specified in subsection (2) of this section; and those enactments, and the enactments applied by them, shall have effect accordingly with the necessary modifications.

(2) The enactments referred to in subsection (1) of this section are section 2 of the Commissioners of Works Act 1852, section 103 of the Town and Country Planning (Scotland) Act 1972 and section 37 of the Community Land Act 1975, except subsection (3) of that section.

DEFINITIONS

" devolved matter ": s. 81 (1), referring to s. 63.

" enactment ": s. 81 (1).

" land ": Town and Country Planning (Scotland) Act 1972, s. 275 (1) (repeated in Community Land Act 1975, s. 6).

GENERAL NOTE

This section confers upon the First Secretary powers to acquire (compulsorily or otherwise) and dispose of land (which includes buildings) in connection with the devolved public service. The powers, which are conferred by the enactments specified in subs. (2), are the same as those exercised by the Secretary of State (in practice, the Secretary of State for the Environment through the Property Services Agency) on behalf of the U.K. Government, but the power conferred by the Community Land Act 1975, s. 37 (3), has been excluded because it is concerned with international matters.

The vesting of the powers specifically in the First Secretary of the Scottish Executive is consistent with s. 72; see note thereon.

A drafting amendment was made to subs. (1) during the Committee stage of the Commons; *Hansard*, H.C. Vol. 942, col. 1340 (January 24, 1978).

Supplementary provisions as to property vested in First Secretary

74.—(1) Any property vested in the First Secretary shall be deemed to be vested in the person for the time being holding the office of First Secretary; and in any instrument relating to any property so vested it shall be sufficient to describe the First Secretary by that title.

(2) References in any enactment passed or made before the passing of this Act to property vested in or held for the purposes of a Government department shall be construed as including references to property vested in the First Secretary or held for the purposes of a Scottish Secretary; and in relation to land so vested or held the First Secretary shall be deemed to be a Government department for the purposes of any such enactment.

(3) No stamp duty shall be chargeable on any instrument made by, to or with a Scottish Secretary.

DEFINITIONS
    " enactment ": s. 81 (1)
    " land ": Town and Country Planning (Scotland) Act 1972, s. 275 (1) (repealed in Community Land Act 1975, s. 6).
    " property ": s. 81 (1).
    " Scottish Secretary ": s. 81 (1), referring to s. 20 (2).

GENERAL NOTE
    This section is consequential upon ss. 72 and 73.

Subs. (1)
    In providing that property vested in the First Secretary shall be deemed to be vested in the person who for the time being holds that office, this subsection avoids the need for a transfer of property each time the office changes hands. This, in part, achieves the same purpose as making the First Secretary a corporation sole, but that is a concept unknown to Scots law. *Cf.* Ministers of the Crown Act 1975, s. 3.

Subs. (2)
    This subsection extends references to Crown or government property in existing legislation to include property vested in the First Secretary or held for devolved purposes. It further provides that where land is so vested or held, the First Secretary will be deemed to be a government department for the purpose of existing legislation.

Subs. (3)
    A drafting amendment was made to this subsection during the Committee stage of the Commons; *Hansard,* H.C. Vol. 942, col. 1341 (January 24, 1978).

Jury Service

Exemption from jury service

75.—(1) In Part III of Schedule 1 to the Juries Act 1974 (excusal of certain persons from jury service) after the entries under the heading " Parliament " there shall be inserted the following:

" *Scottish Assembly and Scottish Executive*
Member of Scottish Assembly.
Scottish Secretary.
Assistant to Scottish Secretary.".

(2) A person who is a member of the Assembly, a Scottish Secretary or an assistant to a Scottish Secretary shall not be liable to serve on any jury in Scotland.

DEFINITION
    " Scottish Secretary ": s. 81 (1), referring to s. 20 (2).

GENERAL NOTE
    By this section, members of the Scottish Assembly, Scottish Secretaries and assistants to Scottish Secretaries are exempted from jury service in England, Wales and Scotland. Separate provision is made for jury service in England and Wales (subs. (1)) and in Scotland (subs. (2)).
    The effect of the section is to create the same situation as exists in the House of Commons. Exemption from jury service is a privilege of the House (see *Erskine May,* 19th ed., p. 102) although in relation to England and Wales the privilege has been given statutory form in the Juries Act 1974, s. 9 and Sched. 1, Pt. III, and exemption is achieved by adding to the categories in that Schedule.
    Persons who are exempted from jury service are entitled to be excused as of right, but may nevertheless serve if they wish to do so. Specific mention is made of Scottish Secretaries and assistants to Scottish Secretaries because by s. 20 (6) it is possible to appoint to either office a person who is to perform the functions of a Law Officer but who is not a member of the Assembly.

Maladministration

Complaints of maladministration

76.—(1) Her Majesty may by Order in Council make provision, to have effect pending the making of such provision by or under any Scottish Assembly Act, for the investigation of administrative action taken by or on behalf of a Scottish Secretary, the Scottish Record Office, the Department of the Registers of Scotland or the General Register Office, Scotland.

(2) The provisions of sections 21, 22 (6), 60 and 78 of this Act shall not apply in relation to the Parliamentary Commissioner Act 1967, but an Order in Council under this section may apply, with such exceptions and modifications as appear to Her Majesty to be necessary or expedient, any of the provisions of that Act.

(3) A statutory instrument made under this section shall be subject to annulment in pursuance of a resolution of either House of Parliament.

DEFINITION

" Scottish Secretary ": s. 81 (1), referring to s. 20 (2).

GENERAL NOTE

It was envisaged in *Our Changing Democracy* that arrangements for the investigation of maladministration on the part of the Scottish administration would be made by Parliament (see para. 86 and Appendix B), and effect was given to this proposal in the Scotland and Wales Bill, cll. 93–106. However, the statement of Mr. Michael Foot, M.P., Lord President of the Council, on July 26, 1977, indicated a change in policy whereby the Assembly would be free to make its own arrangements on this matter (*Hansard*, H.C. Vol. 936, col. 314). Subs. (1) of this section clearly assumes that the Assembly will be competent to legislate for the investigation of maladministration in relation to devolved matters, but specific authority is provided by the inclusion of the Parliamentary Commissioner Act 1967 (" the 1967 Act ") (but subject to this section) in the list of enactments in Sched. 10, Pt. III. As originally drafted, the Bill did not contain this reference, it being justifiably assumed that because the Assembly was competent to legislate for any or all matters devolved to it, it was competent to legislate about maladministration in these matters. (The specific references to the " investigation of maladministration " made in Sched. 10, Pt. I, Groups 1 (Health) and 5 (Local government and local finance) are made, it seems, for the avoidance of doubt; otherwise it could have been argued, on the basis of the restrictive wording in the preliminary paragraph in Sched. 10, Pt. I—and in particular the words " if, and only if "—that maladministration was excluded since it was not an integral aspect of these matters.) This original formulation, however, ignored those matters which were the subject of executive devolution only (see s. 63 (3) (*b*) and (*c*)), and it was to correct this omission that the reference to the Parliamentary Commissioner Act 1967 was added to Sched. 10 by a Government amendment made during the Committee stage in the Lords; *Hansard*, H.L. Vol. 391, cols. 1017–8 (May 10, 1978).

The purpose of this section is to make interim arrangements for the investigation of maladministration until such time as the Assembly creates its own machinery. It provides for the provisions of the 1967 Act, modified as necessary, to be applied by Order in Council (which, by subs. (3), will be subject to the negative resolution procedure) to the investigation of administrative action taken by or on behalf of a Scottish Secretary or any of the bodies referred to in subs. (1).

Note that the term " maladministration " appears only in the marginal note and not in the text of the section itself. It may therefore be possible for the Assembly, when legislating in this area, to rely on the wide term " the investigation of administrative action " used in subs. (1) and thus extend the scope of the investigative powers presently allowed to the Parliamentary Commissioner. It will not, however, be possible for the interim Order in Council to provide for such an extension in view of the restrictive wording in subs. (2); see note thereon.

For the amendments to the 1967 Act made by this Act, see Sched. 16, paras. 22–25.

Subs. (1)

" *the investigation of administrative action taken by or on behalf of.*" This is an abbreviated version of the formula used in the 1967 Act, s. 5 (1).

" *the Scottish Record Office, the Department of the Registers of Scotland or the General Register Office, Scotland.*" These bodies are currently subject to investigation by the Parliamentary Commissioner under the 1967 Act, s. 4 and Sched. 2; however with the exception of the functions of the General Register Office regarding population censuses (see Sched. 10, Part II, para. 13), they will be dealing with devolved matters (see Sched. 10, Part I, Groups 19, 23 and 24). Specific reference to these bodies is needed because, assuming that the Scottish administration does not alter the present arrangements, their operations will not come within the jurisdiction of a Scottish Secretary.

Subs. (2)

The sections referred to in the first limb of this subsection provide, *inter alia*, for the modification of existing U.K. legislation in relation to the Assembly and the Scottish Executive. But for this subsection, these provisions would have applied to the 1967 Act by virtue of its inclusion in Sched. 10, Pt. III, but in this case the modification will be achieved by the Order in Council to be made under this section, and the modification provisions are accordingly excluded. This limb of the subsection was added by a Government amendment during the Committee stage in the Lords, in consequence of the addition of the 1967 Act to Sched. 10, Pt. III; *Hansard*, H.L. Vol. 392, cols. 292–4 (May 16, 1978).

As originally drafted, this subsection would have made it possible for the Order in Council to have added to the provisions of the 1967 Act. The word " additions " was, however, removed by a Government amendment during the Report stage in the Lords (following discussion at the Committee stage) so that now the Order may only provide for modifications or exceptions to the Act, the argument being that any additions to the legislation (*e.g.* by extending the grounds for investigation) ought to be made by Act of Parliament; *Hansard*, H.L. Vol. 392, cols. 292–4 (May 16, 1978); Vol. 393, col. 975 (June 20, 1978).

" *necessary or expedient.*" For this phrase, see s. 37 and note thereon.

Part VI

General and Supplementary

Reckoning of time for certain purposes

77. In reckoning any period for the purposes of section 38, 39 or 40 of this Act, no account shall be taken of any time during which Parliament is dissolved or prorogued or during which both Houses are adjourned for more than four days.

General Note

This section makes provision for the computation of the 28-day period for the purposes of ss. 38 (3), 39 (6) and 40 (5). See notes on these sections.

The formula in the section is taken from the Statutory Instruments Act 1946, s. 7 (1).

Modification of enactments requiring laying of reports before Parliament

78.—(1) Where any enactment passed or made before the passing of this Act makes provision for any report to be laid before Parliament or either House of Parliament and the report relates exclusively to devolved matters it shall be laid instead before the Assembly.

(2) In this section " report " includes any statement.

Definitions

" devolved matter ": s. 81 (1), referring to s. 63.

" enactment ": s. 81 (1).

GENERAL NOTE

This section provides that reports which under previous legislation have been laid before Parliament are now to be laid before the Assembly if they relate exclusively to devolved matters.

The wide interpretation given to the word " report " by subs. (2) ensures, for example, that this section will apply to the " comment " which a Scottish Secretary will be able to make to the Assembly when presenting the report of the Red Deer Commission under the Deer (Scotland) Act 1959, s. 3 (2).

Orders

79.—(1) Any power to make orders conferred by this Act on a Minister of the Crown shall be exercisable by statutory instrument.

(2) Any order made under any provision of this Act may be varied or revoked by a subsequent order made under that provision.

DEFINITION

" Minister of the Crown ": s. 81 (1).

GENERAL NOTE

Subs. (1) provides that any power to make orders conferred by this Act on a Minister of the Crown is to be exercisable by statutory instrument. It is not necessary for such a provision to be made in relation to Orders in Council, which are declared to be statutory instruments by the Statutory Instruments Act 1946, s. 1 (1) (a).

Subs. (2), however, does apply to Orders in Council as well as ministerial orders since it refers to any order made under this Act.

Expenses

80. There shall be paid out of moneys provided by Parliament any administrative expenses incurred by a Minister of the Crown under this Act and any increase attributable to this Act in the sums so payable under any other Act.

DEFINITION

" Minister of the Crown ": s. 81 (1).

GENERAL NOTE

This is a common-form provision which authorises the payment out of money provided by Parliament of any administrative expenses incurred by any Minister under this Act, or, in consequence of this Act, under any other Act. *Cf.* Local Government (Scotland) Act 1973, s. 234.

It is likely that the expenses to be met under this section will relate to transitional arrangements for the establishment of the Assembly and the Scottish Executive, such as the referendum (see s. 85), the construction and equipment of the Assembly buildings, the engagement of additional civil servants, and the first ordinary election to the Assembly. Permanent commitments will become a charge on the Scottish Consolidated Fund (for which see Pt. III) once the Assembly and the Scottish Executive are in operation.

Interpretation

81.—(1) In this Act, except where the context otherwise requires—

" Assembly " means the Scottish Assembly;

" devolved matter " has the meaning assigned to it by section 63 of this Act;

" enactment " includes an enactment of the Parliament of Northern Ireland, a Measure of the Northern Ireland Assembly, an Order in Council under section 1 (3) of the Northern Ireland (Temporary Provisions) Act 1972 or paragraph 1 of Schedule 1 to the Northern Ireland Act 1974, a Scottish Assembly Act, any instrument made by virtue of an enactment (as defined herein) and a Royal Warrant;

" excepted statutory undertakers " means—

(a) persons (other than the Scottish Transport Group and such other authority, body and undertakers as the Secretary of State may by order specify) authorised by any enactment to carry on any road transport, dock, harbour, pier or lighthouse undertaking or any undertaking for the supply of electricity, gas or hydraulic power; and

(b) the Post Office, the British Railways Board and the National Coal Board;

and for such purposes as the Secretary of State may by order specify, includes such other authority, body or undertakers as he may so specify;

" financial year " means a year ending with 31st March;

" grants to universities " does not include payments to universities by education authorities;

" the Highlands and Islands " means the Western Isles, the Shetland Islands, the Orkney Islands, the Highland Region and, in the Strathclyde Region, the district of Argyll and Bute and the Island of Arran;

" Minister of the Crown " includes the Treasury;

" navigation authority " means persons authorised by any enactment to work, maintain, conserve, improve or control any estuary, harbour or dock;

" property " includes rights and interests of any description;

" recreative activities " includes any form of sport;

" road transport undertaking " does not include a passenger transport undertaking;

" scheduled functions " means functions relating to matters listed in Schedule 15 to this Act;

" Scottish Secretary " has the meaning assigned to it by section 20 (2) of this Act; and

" terms and conditions of service " includes pensions, gratuities or allowances payable on retirement or death and compensation for loss of office or employment or loss or diminution of emoluments, or provision for such benefits.

(2) Except where the context otherwise requires, references in this Act to the proceedings of the Assembly include references to proceedings of any committee of the Assembly or of any sub-committee of such a committee.

(3) Except where the context otherwise requires, any reference in this Act to an enactment is a reference to that enactment as amended, and includes a reference to it as applied, by any other enactment.

(4) A statutory instrument made for the purposes of the definition of " excepted statutory undertakers " in subsection (1) of this section shall be subject to annulment in pursuance of a resolution of either House of Parliament.

GENERAL NOTE
Subs. (1)

" *excepted statutory undertakers.*" This definition is important for many purposes in the Act, *e.g.* s. 23 and Sched. 4. It distinguishes between statutory undertakers and other public bodies which remain the responsibility of the U.K. Government from those which will be responsible to the devolved Scottish administration. Excepted statutory undertakers are those whose functions are not connected with devolved matters.

During the Report stage in the Lords, a Government amendment was made which had the effect of (1) empowering the Secretary of State to make, by order, further exclusions to the definition; and (2) excluding from the definition bodies authorised to carry out works in relation to road transport, docks, etc. The definition now specifies only bodies authorised to carry on such undertakings; this amendment has the effect of ensuring that local authorities carrying out devolved functions would not be caught by the definition; *Hansard*, H.L. Vol. 393, cols. 988–9 (June 20, 1978).

The definition also, in the words after paras. (*a*) and (*b*), empowers the Secretary of State, by order, to add to the list of excepted statutory undertakers, for such purposes as the order may specify. Other minor amendments were made during the Report stage in the House of Commons; *Hansard*, H.C. Vol. 944, col. 532 (February 15, 1978).

Statutory instruments made for the purposes of this definition are by subs. (4) subject to the negative resolution procedure.

"*financial year.*" This term is so defined that the Scottish administration will operate to the same financial year as the U.K. Government and also Scottish local authorities; see Local Government (Scotland) Act, 1975, s. 18. *Cf.* the definition of " financial year " in the Interpretation Act 1978, Sched. 1.

"*grants to universities.*" This is so defined as to ensure that payments to universities by education authorities are not excluded from the categories of devolved matters by Sched. 10, Pt. II, para. 3.

"*the Highlands and Islands.*" Reference is made to this area in Sched. 10, Pt. II, para. 8, in the context of air services. The definition, taken from the Scottish Development Agency Act 1975, s. 21, was included by a Government amendment made during the Report stage in the Commons; *Hansard*, H.C. Vol. 944, col. 532 (February 15, 1978).

"*Minister of the Crown.*" The extension of this term to include the Treasury is necessary because by the Interpretation Act 1978, Sched. 1, Treasury powers are formally vested in the Lords Commissioners of the Treasury who are not all ministers even though they include ministers among their number. Such ministers can then sign Treasury instruments, not as ministers but as Commissioners in accordance with the Treasury Instruments (Signature) Act 1849.

"*navigation authority.*" The definition excludes canal or other inland navigation or navigable river authorities. The effect is that for the purposes of this Act a navigation authority, like an excepted statutory undertaker, has functions which are not related to devolved matters. The term " navigation authority " appears in Sched. 3.

"*property.*" The definition given to this term includes, but is not confined to, physical property such as land, buildings and possessions. See, especially, s. 72.

"*recreative activities.*" See Sched. 10, Pt. I, Group 3 and note thereon.

"*road transport undertaking.*" The definition excludes passenger transport undertakings, which are to be devolved, from the category of " excepted statutory undertakers "; see above.

"*scheduled functions.*" These are functions of local authorities which do not relate to devolved matters. They are listed in Sched. 15. The identification of these functions is important for calculating the rate support grant under s. 68, and for the making of grants for specific purposes relating to these functions; see Sched. 10, Pt. II, para. 5. The term " scheduled functions " replaces the term " reserved functions " which was used in the Bill as originally drafted; see Lord McCluskey, Solicitor-General for Scotland, *Hansard*, H.L. Vol. 392, col. 327 (May 17, 1978).

"*terms and conditions of service.*" This term, which is defined widely, is particularly important for the purposes of Sched. 4 and s. 43.

Subs. (2)

See ss. 10, 13, 15, 25, 27 and 29, and notes thereon.

Subs. (4)

See Statutory Instruments Act 1946, s. 5.

Construction and amendment of existing enactments, etc.

82.—(1) So far as may be necessary for the purpose or in consequence of the exercise by a Scottish Secretary of any executive power or of any such power as is mentioned in section 22 (1) of this Act, any enactment or other document passed or made before the passing of this Act and relating to a devolved matter shall be construed as if references to a Minister of the Crown were or included references to a Scottish Secretary.

(2) The enactments mentioned in Schedule 16 to this Act shall have effect subject to the amendments specified in that Schedule.

(3) A Minister of the Crown may by order make such amendments in any Act passed before or in the same session as this Act and in any other enactment passed or made before the passing of this Act as appear to him necessary or expedient in consequence of this Act.

(4) Where a provision of an enactment is amended or replaced by or under this Act—

  (a) that provision or the provision replacing it shall not be taken to be affected by section 21, 22, 60, 61 or 78 of this Act or subsection (1) of this section; and

  (b) the amendment or replacement shall not be taken to prejudice the effect of any of those sections or that subsection on other provisions of that enactment.

(5) A statutory instrument made under subsection (3) of this section shall be subject to annulment in pursuance of a resolution of either House of Parliament.

DEFINITIONS
  " devolved matter ": s. 81 (1), referring to s. 63.
  " enactment ": s. 81 (1).
  " Minister of the Crown ": s. 81 (1).
  " Scottish Secretary ": s. 81 (1), referring to s. 20 (2).

GENERAL NOTE
Subs. (1)
  The purpose of this subsection is to bring about the conversion of references to a Minister of the Crown for the purposes of ss. 21 and 22 (1), and also in relation to powers which are ancillary to the substantive powers transferred to a Scottish Secretary under these sections. Thus references in any existing provision to a Minister of the Crown are to be construed as if they " were or included " references to a Scottish Secretary so far as this is necessary for the purpose, or in consequence of, the transfer of power to a Scottish secretary under ss. 21 and 22 (1).
  " *for the purpose or in consequence of.*" It is these words which show that the subsection applies to ancillary as well as substantive powers.
  " *were or included.*" The words " or included " are intended to allow for the situation where it is not possible simply to transfer the function from a Minister to a Scottish Secretary because the power in question relates to both devolved and non-devolved matters, and so must be available to both the Minister and a Scottish Secretary. It is likely that this situation will arise most frequently in relation to ancillary powers.

Subs. (2)
  See notes on Sched. 16.

Subs. (3)
  This empowers a Minister of the Crown to make amendments to other U.K. legislation if it appears to him to be necessary or expedient to do so in consequence of this Act. The power is exercisable by order, and any statutory instrument made is, by subs. (5), subject to the negative resolution procedure.
  This is the last of three provisions in the Act which enable consequential amendments to be made to U.K. legislation; see also Sched. 2, para. 8, and s. 37. These two provisions, however, enable amendment to U.K. legislation to be made in the wake of Scottish Assembly legislation, while this subsection is intended to enable such amendments to be made in the wake of this Act.
  Precedents for such a provision can be found in the National Health Service (Scotland) Act 1972, s. 61, the National Health Services (Reorganisation) Act 1973, s. 54 (2), and the Local Government (Scotland) Act 1973, s. 215.
  " *in any Act, passed before or in the same session as this Act.*" The reason for the express inclusion of subsequent Acts passed in the same session as this Parliament is to overcome the presumption that a later Act cannot be amended by subordinate legislation made under an earlier Act.
  " *any other enactment passed or made before the passing of this Act.*" This refers

primarily (but not, because of the width of the term " enactment," entirely) to subordinate legislation.

" *necessary or expedient.*" This provides a significant limitation on the scope of the power conferred by this subsection; see note on s. 37.

Subs. (4)

This establishes the relationship between the specific amendments to enactments made by or under this Act, and the provisions in ss. 21, 22, 60, 61, 78 and subs. (1) of this section which, in more general terms, bring about the transfer of powers and functions to Scottish Secretaries or otherwise modify existing enactments. By para. (*a*), these provisions do not apply to any provision of an enactment which is amended or replaced by this Act (*e.g.* by Sched. 16) or under it (*e.g.* by an order made·under subs. (3)); this is because the Act or the order, as the case may be, will itself produce the result required. Thus, if the provision in its new form contains a reference to a Minister, the intention is that the reference should remain unaltered and should not, for example, be subject to the operation of subs. (1) of this section. However, by para. (*b*), the provisions do apply to other provisions of the enactment which are not amended or replaced by or under this Act.

Subs. (5)

See Statutory Instruments Act 1946, s. 5.

Commencement

83.—(1) The preceding provisions of this Act (and the Schedules relating to them) shall not come into operation until such day as the Secretary of State may by order appoint.

(2) Different days may be appointed under this section for different provisions of this Act and for different purposes of the same provision.

(3) An order under this section may contain such transitional and supplementary provisions as appear to the Secretary of State to be necessary or expedient, including provisions for expenses to be defrayed out of moneys provided by Parliament.

(4) The first order under this section shall not be made unless a draft of it has been laid before Parliament and approved by a resolution of each House of Parliament.

GENERAL NOTE

In part, the commencement provisions contained in this section are in common form, but others are of a special nature since they are consequential upon s. 85, which provides for the holding of a referendum. See, in particular, subs. (4) and s. 85 (1).

Subs. (1)

This confers upon the Secretary of State the power to appoint, by order, the days on which ss. 1–82, and their related Schedules, are to come into effect; it follows that this and succeeding sections, and their related Schedules, came into effect when the Royal Assent was granted. Orders made under this subsection are not subject to any parliamentary procedure, apart from the first commencement order (subs. (4)).

Subs. (2)

This is designed to produce the maximum possible flexibility in bringing the Act into effect. It is reasonable to assume that the first stage will be to bring the machinery for elections to the Assembly into operation, and that the first election will be followed by a transitional period during which the Assembly and the Executive will prepare for the formal transfer of powers. During this period, it is likely, for example, that the Scottish Consolidated Fund will be established, and that orders will be made under s. 69 to provide for the future of public bodies and, under s. 76, for the investigation of maladministration. The transfer of operational responsibility for devolved matters is likely to be the final stage, but even this could be phased to occur over a period of time.

Subs. (3)

This subsection would, for example, enable an order to provide that the salaries of

Assembly members shall be payable out of the U.K. Consolidated Fund until such time as the Scottish Consolidated Fund is established.

" *necessary or expedient.*" This phrase provides a significant limitation on the scope of the power conferred; see note on s. 37.

Subs. (4)

Not only is the first commencement order to be subject to an affirmative resolution of both Houses of Parliament but also, by s. 85 (1), a referendum is to be held before a draft of the order is laid.

Special provisions as to Orkney and Shetland

84.—(1) The Secretary of State shall, within three months of making the first order under section 83 of this Act, establish a commission to recommend such changes in the government of the Orkney Islands and the Shetland Islands as may be desirable.

(2) In making its recommendations the commission shall have regard, among other things, to the special social and economic needs and interests of the Islands; and the recommendations may include recommendations for making changes in this Act, including changes in the constitution and powers of the Assembly.

GENERAL NOTE

This section was included in the Act as a concession to opinion in Orkney and Shetland against the establishment of a Scottish Assembly. The background is explained in the note to s. 41.

The section requires the Secretary of State, within three months of making the first commencement order under s. 83, to establish a commission to review the government of Orkney and Shetland and to make recommendations thereon. By subs. (2), the commission may recommend changes in this Act, including changes affecting the Assembly itself. Although amendments to this Act may be recommended by the commission, this section confers no power to make any such amendments, so that an Act of the U.K. Parliament would be required for this purpose.

A commission of this nature was envisaged in the "Grimond amendment", which was made during the Committee stage in the Commons (*Hansard*, H.C. Vol. 942, cols. 1584–8 (January 25, 1978)) but which was removed from the Act during the Report stage in the Lords when this section and s. 41 were added. By the " Grimond amendment," however, a commission would have been appointed only if a majority of people in Orkney or Shetland voted in the referendum to be held under s. 85 that the provisions of the Act should not be brought into effect. Under this section, the commission will be established whatever the result of the referendum in Orkney and Shetland. See *Hansard*, H.L. Vol. 393, cols. 999–1002 (June 20, 1978).

Referendum

85.—(1) Before a draft of the first order to be made under section 83 of this Act is laid before Parliament a referendum shall be held in accordance with Schedule 17 to this Act on the question whether effect is to be given to the provisions of this Act.

(2) If it appears to the Secretary of State that less than 40 per cent. of the persons entitled to vote in the referendum have voted " Yes " in reply to the question posed in the Appendix to Schedule 17 to this Act or that a majority of the answers given in the referendum have been " No " he shall lay before Parliament the draft of an Order in Council for the repeal of this Act.

(3) If a draft laid before Parliament under this section is approved by a resolution of each House Her Majesty in Council may make an Order in the terms of the draft.

GENERAL NOTE

Neither the Kilbrandon Report nor any of the Government White Papers made any reference to the desirability or otherwise of inviting the general public to express their views on devolution through a referendum. The Scotland and Wales Bill, as originally drafted, did not contain provision for a referendum, but at the end of the Second Reading debate on the Bill the Government announced its intention that a referendum be held, and a new clause and schedule were added during the Committee stage; *Hansard*, H.C. Vol. 922, cols. 1736–7 (December 16, 1976); Vol. 925, cols. 1791, *et seq.* (February 10, 1977). The Lord President of the Council's statement to the House of Commons on July 26, 1977 affirmed the Government's commitment to a referendum once the new legislation had been passed; *Hansard*, H.C. Vol. 936, cols. 317–8.

This section, which should be read along with s. 86 and Sched. 17, provides that before the first commencement order can be made under s. 83, a referendum must be held in Scotland on the question whether effect is to be given to this Act (subs. (1)). Subs. (2) requires the Secretary of State to lay an Order before Parliament for the repeal of the Act if it appears to him that less than 40 per cent. of those entitled to vote have voted " Yes " in the referendum, or that a simple majority have voted " No." The Order must be approved by resolution of each House (subs. (3)).

Like the referendum on EEC membership in 1975 (see Referendum Act 1975), this referendum is essentially consultative and advisory in character, although its advisory nature is somewhat reduced by subs. (2) on the Secretary of State's discretion. Strictly speaking, however, it is for Parliament to decide whether the Act should be repealed, just as it is for Parliament to decide whether the first commencement order should be made under s. 83 (4).

During the Committee stage in the Lords, a new subsection was added which would have required an Order for the repeal of the Act to be laid before Parliament if both Houses had refused to pass the first commencement order under s. 84 (3). The amendment, which the Government opposed as being unnecessary, was rejected by the Commons; *Hansard*, H.L. Vol. 392, cols. 348–69 (May 17, 1978); H.C. Vol. 954, cols. 295–308 (July 18, 1978).

The Lords also removed from the Bill during the Committee stage a provision which would have empowered the House of Commons in certain circumstances to confirm a draft Order made under this section even though the House of Lords had failed to approve it. This was consistent with other similar amendments made to ss. 38–40, the " over-ride " sections. For the background to the amendment, see note on s. 38 (3). *Hansard*, H.L. Vol. 392, col. 348 (May 17, 1978).

Subs. (1)

For the detailed provisions governing the conduct of the referendum, including the wording of the ballot paper, see Sched. 17.

Subs. (2)

In its original form this subsection contained a general provision for the repeal of the Act by Order if the result of the referendum, and all the surrounding circumstances, suggested to the Secretary of State that the Act should not be brought into effect. The provision regarding the 40 per cent. threshold of " Yes " votes was introduced by an amendment made against the wishes of the Government during the Committee stage in the Commons, primarily on the argument that since implementation of the Act would effect a major constitutional change, Parliament should satisfy itself that there was a substantial degree of support for it; *Hansard*, H.C. Vol. 942, cols. 1460–542 (January 25, 1978). An attempt to restore the subsection to its original state during the Report stage in the Commons was unsuccessful; *Hansard*, H.C. Vol. 944, cols. 533–607 (February 15, 1978).

" *It it appears to the Secretary of State.*" It is for the Secretary of State to calculate what percentage of those entitled to vote have voted " Yes." The calculation will not be entirely straightforward, since an allowance will have to be made for those whose names might appear on the electoral register but who are not entitled to vote because, *e.g.* they are dead or have not reached the age of 18 by the date of referendum. Plural registration will also have to be taken into account. Once the calculation has been completed, the Secretary of State will either introduce the draft Order for repeal of the Act under this subsection or the first commencement order under s. 83 (4).

" *entitled to vote.*" For the provisions governing entitlement to vote in the referendum, see Sched. 17, para. 2.

" *or that a majority of the answers given in the referendum have been ' No '.*" These words were introduced by a Government amendment during the Committee stage in the Lords, and brought the subsection into line with the corresponding provision in the Wales Bill. The amendment will come into effect only if, despite

40 per cent. of those entitled to vote saying " Yes," over 40 per cent. vote "No." This will require a turn-out of over 80 per cent. (If the number voting " Yes " is less than 40 per cent. of those entitled to vote, the provisions of the subsection as originally drafted will apply.) *Hansard,* H.L. Vol. 392, cols. 344–8 (May 17, 1978).

Period between general election and referendum

86. If a proclamation summoning a new Parliament is made before a referendum is held in pursuance of section 85 of this Act, the referendum shall not be held earlier than three months after the date of the poll at the election of members for the new Parliament; and if an earlier date has been appointed by Order in Council under paragraph 1 of Schedule 17 to this Act, the Order shall not take effect, but without prejudice to the making of a new Order under that paragraph.

GENERAL NOTE

This section provides that if Parliament is dissolved before the referendum has been held under s. 85, a period of at least three months must elapse after the date of the ensuing general election before the referendum can take place. It also provides that if an order fixing the date of the referendum has been made under Sched. 17, para. 1 when the dissolution takes place, the order shall not take effect but may be subsequently replaced by a new order.

The section was added to the Act during the Report stage in the Commons by an amendment tabled by Mr. Dalyell, M.P., in spite of a Government assurance that there was no intention of permitting a general election campaign and the referendum campaign to coincide. The Government made a number of technical amendments to the clause during the Committee stage in the Lords. *Hansard,* H.C. Vol. 944, cols. 252–98 (February 14, 1978); H.L. Vol. 392, cols. 435–6 (May 17, 1978).

Short title

87. This Act may be cited as the Scotland Act 1978.

SCHEDULES

Section 1

SCHEDULE 1

ASSEMBLY CONSTITUENCIES

PART I

REPORTS OF BOUNDARY COMMISSION AND ORDERS IN COUNCIL

1. Where the Boundary Commission for Scotland submit to the Secretary of State a report under subsection (1) of section 2 of the Act of 1949 they shall submit with it a supplementary report showing into what Assembly constituencies Scotland should be divided in accordance with the provisions of Part II of this Schedule; and where, after the first supplementary report submitted under this paragraph, they submit a report under subsection (3) of that section, they shall submit with it a supplementary report showing into what Assembly constituencies the area to which the report relates should be divided in accordance with the provisions of Part II of this Schedule.

2. Sections 2 (4), 2 (5), and 3 of the Act of 1949 (notice of proposed report of Boundary Commission and implementation of recommendations in report) paragraphs 3 and 4 of Part III of Schedule 1 to that Act (notice of proposed recommendation and local inquiries) and section 4 of the Act of 1958 (procedure) shall apply in relation to a supplementary report made under this Schedule and a recommendation made or proposed to be made in such a report; and in those provisions as they apply by virtue of this paragraph references to constituencies shall be construed as references to Assembly constituencies and references to electors as references to electors for the Assembly.

3. Subsections (4) and (5) of section 210 of the Local Government (Scotland)

Act 1973 (attendance of witnesses at inquiries) shall apply in relation to an inquiry held in pursuance of paragraph 2 of this Schedule.

4. Nothing in paragraph 2 of this Schedule shall be taken as enabling the Secretary of State to modify any recommendation or draft Order in Council in a manner conflicting with the provisions of Part II of this Schedule.

5. An Order in Council under the provisions applied by paragraph 2 of this Schedule shall apply to the first ordinary election for the Assembly held after the Order comes into force and (subject to any further Order in Council) to any subsequent election for the Assembly, but shall not affect any earlier election or the constitution of the Assembly before the first election to which the Order applies.

Part II

Division of Scotland into Assembly Constituencies

6. Each Assembly constituency shall be wholly comprised in one parliamentary constituency.

7. The electorate of any Assembly constituency shall be as near the electorate of any other Assembly constituency comprised in the same parliamentary constituency as is practicable, having regard to paragraph 8 of this Schedule.

8. Regard shall be had, so far as practicable, to the boundaries of local government areas.

9. A parliamentary constituency the electorate of which is more than 125 per cent. of the electoral quota shall comprise three Assembly constituencies and any other parliamentary constituency shall comprise two Assembly constituencies.

10. The Boundary Commission may depart from the strict application of paragraph 8 of this Schedule if it appears to them that the departure is desirable to avoid an excessive disparity between the electorates of Assembly constituencies comprised in the same parliamentary constituency.

11. The Boundary Commission may depart from the strict application of paragraph 7 or 8 of this Schedule—

   (a) if special geographical considerations, including in particular the size, shape and accessibility of an Assembly constituency, appear to them to render the departure reasonable; or

   (b) if, taking account, so far as they reasonably can, of the inconvenience resulting from alterations of Assembly constituencies, and of any local ties which would be broken by such alterations, a departure appears to them desirable.

Part III

Return of Initial Members

12. The Secretary of State shall by order specify the areas for which, in accordance with section 1 (2) and (3) of this Act, the initial members of the Assembly are to be returned, and the order shall indicate the electoral quota and, for each of those areas, the electorate and the number of initial members to be returned.

Part IV

Interpretation

13. In Parts I and II of this Schedule—

   " electoral quota " means the number obtained by dividing the electorate by the number of parliamentary constituencies into which Scotland would be divided if effect were given to the recommendations of the Boundary Commission;

   " electorate " means the number of persons whose names, on the date specified for the purposes of this paragraph in the supplementary report of the Boundary Commission, appear on the registers of electors for the Assembly or, as the case may require, such parts of those registers as relate to the constituency or proposed constituency concerned;

" the Act of 1949 " means the House of Commons (Redistribution of Seats) Act 1949;

" the Act of 1958 " means the House of Commons (Redistribution of Seats) Act 1958.

14. In Part III of this Schedule, this paragraph and section 1 of this Act—

" electoral quota " means the number obtained by dividing the electorate (as defined in this paragraph) of Scotland by the number of parliamentary constituencies there at the time of the election of initial members; and

" electorate " means the number of persons whose names appear on the relevant registers of parliamentary electors last published before the date on which the order under paragraph 12 of this Schedule was made, the relevant registers being, as the case may require, those for the constituency concerned or those for all constituencies in Scotland.

GENERAL NOTE

PART I

This Part is primarily concerned with the procedure for creating Assembly constituencies and for making subsequent alterations to their boundaries. (Elections to the Assembly will, however, take place on the basis of parliamentary constituencies until such time as the Assembly constituencies have been created; see s. 1, and note thereon, and also paras. 5 and 12 of this Schedule.) The procedure for creating and altering Assembly constituencies is similar to that for parliamentary constituencies, and certain provisions of the House of Commons (Redistribution of Seats) Acts 1949–58 will apply. The final decisions on Assembly constituencies lie with Parliament and not the Assembly. Para. 1 obliges the Boundary Commission to submit supplementary reports to the Secretary of State along with its periodic reports under s. 2 (1) of the 1949 Act (which recommend changes in the Scottish parliamentary constituencies or state that no changes are required) and also along with any reports made under s. 2 (3) of the 1949 Act (which recommend changes in particular parliamentary constituencies). The supplementary reports are to show the Assembly constituencies into which Scotland (or, as the case may be, particular parliamentary constituencies) should be divided in accordance with Pt. II of this Schedule. Para. 2 applies to the making and implementation of these supplementary reports certain provisions of the 1949 and 1958 Acts, with appropriate modifications. S. 2 (4) is concerned with notification to the Secretary of State of the intention to make a report, and the publication of a notice to that effect in the Edinburgh Gazette. S. 2 (5) requires the Secretary of State to lay any report before Parliament, together with a draft Order in Council to give effect to the report's recommendations (any proposed modifications to the report must, by para. 4, conform to the criteria set out in para. 4 of this Schedule). S. 3 of the 1949 Act requires the Secretary of State to submit to Her Majesty for approval any Order approved by both Houses of Parliament; it also makes provision for the coming into effect of an Order in Council, but this, as regards the Assembly, is subject to the qualifications contained in para. 5 of this Schedule. (Thus an Order in Council altering Assembly constituencies does not apply to Assembly elections until the first ordinary election after the Order is in force. Subject to further Orders it applies to all subsequent elections. However, any by-elections (see s. 5) before the next ordinary election, or elections following a premature dissolution of the Assembly (see s. 3 (1) (*b*)) would take place unaffected by any Orders made since the previous ordinary election).

Paras. 3 and 4 of Pt. III of Sched. I to the 1949 Act require the Boundary Commission to publish details of its proposed recommendations and to take account of subsequent recommendations, and empower the holding of a local inquiry in respect of any constituency; s. 4 of the 1958 Act contains supplementary provisions, *e.g.* by requiring a local inquiry where 100 or more electors object to the proposed recommendations. Where a local inquiry is held, the Local Government (Scotland) Act 1973, s. 210 (4) and (5) will apply (para. 3 of this Schedule).

PART II

This Part sets out the rules which the Boundary Commission for Scotland must observe in recommending the boundaries of Assembly constituencies (as well as the Secretary of State, in modifying the Commission's recommendations). Apart from paras. 6 and 9, the rules are similar to those in Sched. 2 to the 1949 Act, as amended by the 1958 Act, for redistributing parliamentary constituencies. Thus it is already provided that parliamentary constituencies should as far as practicable follow local government boundaries (para. 4, Sched. 2, 1949 Act; see para. 8), and that the strict application of the rules may be departed from in certain cases (para. 6, Sched. 2, 1949 Act; see paras. 10 and 11). By contrast the requirement in para. 6 that every Assembly constituency should be wholly comprised within a single parliamentary constituency is absolute. The Government considered that any departure from this rule might be confusing to voters, and might also complicate the local organisation of political parties, which tends to be based on parliamentary constituencies; Lord McCluskey, Solicitor-General for Scotland, *Hansard*, H.L. Vol. 390, cols. 553–4 (April 11, 1978). However, the force of these arguments is weakened by the fact that since the reform of local government in Scotland in 1973, there have been a number of areas where the boundaries of parliamentary constituencies and local government areas do not coincide.

The purpose of para. 9 is to remove the most serious instances of unfairness which stem from the marked differences in the size of electorates in Scottish parliamentary constituencies and in particular to guard against under-representation in particularly densely populated areas; it is possible, however, that unfairness may also result where there are constituencies with electorates narrowly falling short of 125 per cent. of the electoral quota; *cf.* s. 1 (2), and general note on s. 1.

Part III

This Part of the Schedule is concerned with elections which take place before the Assembly constituencies have been created; see s. 1 (2) and (3). The order made under this paragraph must (i) specify the areas for which the initial members are to be returned; (ii) indicate the number of parliamentary electors; (iii) state whether two or three initial members are to be returned; (iv) indicate the average number of electors per parliamentary constituency (*i.e.* the " electoral quota " as defined in para. 14).

Part IV

This contains the interpretation provisions for words and phrases used in this Schedule and in s. 1. The words " electorate " and " electoral quota " have different definitions according to whether the words are used in relation to an election of initial members, or of members. The definitions are derived from the 1949 Act, Sched. 2, para. 7.

Section 18   SCHEDULE 2

Legislative Competence of Assembly

1. Subject to the following provisions of this Schedule, a provision is within the legislative competence of the Assembly if, and only if, the matter to which it relates is a devolved matter.

2. A provision is not within the legislative competence of the Assembly if it extends to any part of the United Kingdom other than Scotland.

3.—(1) Subject to sub-paragraph (2) below, a provision is not within the legislative competence of the Assembly if it would—

    (*a*) confer on any public body a power to borrow money, other than a power to borrow from a Scottish Secretary or by overdraft or temporary loan;

    (*b*) confer on any body a power to borrow money outside the United Kingdom or otherwise than in sterling;

    (*c*) confer on any body a power to guarantee a loan;

    (*d*) alter the sources from which or the methods by which a public body existing at the passing of this Act may borrow money; or

    (*e*) alter the power of a body existing at the passing of this Act to guarantee a loan.

(2) Sub-paragraphs (1) (*a*) to (1) (*c*) above do not prevent a provision from being within the legislative competence of the Assembly if the body on which it confers a power replaces directly or indirectly a body existing at the passing of this Act and the power is no different from that of the body which it replaces.

4.—(1) A provision is not within the legislative competence of the Assembly if it would impose, alter or abolish any tax.

(2) This paragraph does not prevent a provision from being within the legislative competence of the Assembly if its effect is only—

(*a*) to alter a rate levied at the passing of this Act without substantially changing its character; or

(*b*) to replace such a rate (whether or not so altered) by a local tax substantially of the same character; or

(*c*) to alter such a local tax without substantially changing its character or to replace it by a local tax substantially of the same character.

5. A provision relating to any body listed in Part II of Schedule 13 to this Act is not within the legislative competence of the Assembly if it would take effect before an order under section 69 of this Act relating to that body has come into force.

6. A provision is not within the legislative competence of the Assembly if its effect could be produced by an order under section 72 (2) of this Act.

7. A provision is not within the legislative competence of the Assembly if its effect would be to amend this Act; but nothing in this paragraph shall prevent the further amendment by a Scottish Assembly Act of any of the enactments amended by paragraphs 3 to 7, 21, 26, 30, 31, 39, 40 and 52 of Schedule 16 to this Act.

8. Paragraph 1 above does not prevent a provision from being within the legislative competence of the Assembly if it is merely incidental to or consequential on other provisions and those other provisions are within that competence.

GENERAL NOTE

This Schedule defines the scope of the Assembly's legislative powers. Paras. 1 and 2 set out two basic principles which will operate in determining those powers, and the remaining paragraphs consist of exceptions to, and refinements of, those principles. The Schedule is phrased in terms of " provisions " and thus will be applicable in both pre- and post-assent judicial review; see s. 18 (2).

Para. 1. " *devolved matter* ": see s. 81 (1), referring to s. 63.

Para. 3. This paragraph limits the Assembly's competence to legislate on borrowing powers and the guarantee of loans. The restrictions contained in sub-para. (1) (*a*), (*b*) and (*c*) are modified by sub-para. (2). For the term " Scottish Secretary " in sub-para. (1) (*a*), see s. 81 (1), referring to s. 20 (1); the funds borrowed will be drawn from the Scottish Loans Fund (for which, see Pt. III). The Assembly cannot, however, confer borrowing powers on a Scottish Secretary. The effect of sub-para. (2) is that where the Assembly establishes a new public body which replaces an existing public body either directly or indirectly, the new body may be given the same borrowing powers and powers to guarantee a loan as the old body enjoyed (including the power to borrow outside the U.K. or in a currency other than sterling). The phrase " directly or indirectly " has been included because the new public body may not be a carbon-copy of the body which it replaces.

Para. 4. Sub-para. (1) states as a general principle that the Assembly will not have legislative competence in relation to taxation; this follows *Our Changing Democracy*, paras. 94–100 and 106–8. The devolved services will be financed under a system of block funds, which will be under the control of the House of Commons; see Pt. III. Sub-para. (2), however, allows the Assembly legislative competence in respect of the local government rating system, which is made a devolved matter by Sched. 10, Pt. I, Group 5. This implements *Our Changing Democracy*, para. 110. However, the competence created in this matter by Sched. 10 is limited by this sub-paragraph to three areas: (*a*) modification of the existing rating system; (*b*) replacement of the existing rating system by a closely analogous local tax, *i.e.* one levied by local authorities and related to the occupation of property; (*c*) further modification to such a new local tax—provided that the new or altered tax has substantially the same character as a rate. Thus it would not, for example, be competent for the Assembly to replace rates by a new form of local tax such as a local income tax, since rates are based on the occupation of property. Nor would it be competent for the Assembly to assume from local authorities their power to levy rates, since this again would amount to a substantial alteration of the character of rates.

Para. 5. This paragraph should be read in conjunction with s. 69 and Sched. 13. The bodies listed in Sched. 13 are responsible for reserved as well as devolved matters, and/or operate in England and Wales as well as in Scotland. S. 69 provides machinery for allocating responsibility for these bodies, and the effect of this paragraph is that until a relevant order has been made under s. 69 the Assembly may not legislate in relation to a body listed in Sched. 13, Pt. II. Once the order has been made, however, the Assembly will be able to legislate regarding the body in question by virtue of its competence in the relevant devolved matters covered by Sched. 10, Pt. I.

Para. 6. This paragraph should be read in conjunction with s. 72 (2) and Sched. 13. The effect of s. 72 (2) is that if the Assembly abolishes or reduces the functions of a public body listed in Sched. 13, a Minister may by order transfer the property vested in the body and used for the purposes of the functions in question. (It follows from para. 5 above, of course, that the Assembly could not do so unless an order had been made under s. 69.) This paragraph therefore prevents the Assembly from legislating so as to transfer that property either to itself or to some other body.

Para. 7. This paragraph restricts the generality of s. 17 (2) by preventing the Assembly from amending this Act. The words after the semi-colon, however, which were added by a Government amendment made during the Report stage in the Commons (*Hansard*, H.C. Vol. 944, col. 607 (February 15, 1978)), create a series of minor exceptions to this rule by permitting the Assembly to make further amendments to enactments already amended by Sched. 16 and which relate to devolved matters by virtue of Sched. 10. It is not that the amendment merely avoids inconsistency between this paragraph and para. 1; the wording of para. 1 and of the first limb of this paragraph is such that were it not for the amendment, the Assembly would have been precluded from legislating on the matters dealt with in the Acts listed in Sched. 16, even though they would otherwise have been devolved matters.

Para. 8. The purpose of this paragraph is to permit the Assembly to pass legislation which lies essentially within its competence even though this involves minor intrusions into areas which are not within its competence. Thus, for example, although housing is a devolved matter (by virtue of Sched. 10, Pt. I, Group 4), Assembly legislation on housing may involve consequential amendments to the legislation on compulsory acquisition, which is not a devolved matter (Sched. 10, Pt. II, para. 6). Were it not for this paragraph, the consequential amendments could only be made by Order in Council under s. 37, or by Act of Parliament.

The paragraph seems to be intended to meet the same purpose as the well-established " pith and substance " doctrine of Commonwealth law whereby, in considering the validity of legislation, it is its pith and substance which is looked at and a marginal spill-over into invalidity is disregarded. Presumably it was thought unwise to rely on the courts unaided to adopt this doctrine with regard to Assembly legislation.

As originally drafted (when the wording was based on the Northern Ireland Constitution Act 1973, s. 5) the paragraph was criticised on the grounds that it was excessively wide in the light of its stated purpose and a Government amendment was made during the Report stage in the Lords to meet this criticism. Accordingly a provision in an Assembly Act is not within the competence of the Assembly in terms of this paragraph unless it is " merely incidental to or consequential upon " other provisions which are themselves within the Assembly's competence. *Hansard*, H.C. Vol. 940, cols. 391–424 (November 29, 1977); H.L. Vol. 390, cols. 1017–37 (April 18, 1978); Vol. 392, cols. 1354–6 (June 7, 1978).

Section 22   SCHEDULE 3

POWERS OF SCOTTISH SECRETARY TO MAKE OR CONFIRM ORDERS SUBJECT TO SPECIAL PARLIAMENTARY PROCEDURE

Circumstances in which special parliamentary procedure applies or may apply

1. If objection in pursuance of the enactment conferring the power is made by excepted statutory undertakers or by a navigation authority.

2. If the power is exercised in relation to land of excepted statutory undertakers or land held by a local authority for the purpose of scheduled functions.

3. If the power is exercised in relation to the rights, or apparatus, or powers and duties of excepted statutory undertakers.

4. If the power is a power to make or confirm a compulsory purchase order and is exercised in relation to land belonging to the National Trust for Scotland which is inalienable under section 22 of the Order confirmed by the National Trust for Scotland Order Confirmation Act 1935.

DEFINITIONS
  " excepted statutory undertakers ": s. 81 (1).
  " navigation authority ": s. 81 (1).
  " scheduled functions ": s. 81 (1).

GENERAL NOTE
  This Schedule, which should be read along with s. 22 (3), was reshaped by a Government amendment during the Report stage in the Lords. As originally drafted, it listed the circumstances in which orders affecting reserved bodies would continue to be subject to the special parliamentary procedure by reference to particular enactments. In the form as enacted, it refers to specified circumstances. Thus, when an Act contains a provision for the special parliamentary procedure, it is necessary to check against this Schedule to see whether the special parliamentary procedure continues to apply. The purpose of the amendment was to achieve greater clarity: *Hansard*, H.L. Vol. 392, cols. 1474–6 (June 8, 1978).

Section 23   SCHEDULE 4

STATUTORY POWERS EXERCISABLE WITH CONCURRENCE OR SUBJECT TO CONSENT OR APPROVAL OF A MINISTER OF THE CROWN

Preliminary

  Where there is an entry in column 2 opposite an enactment listed in column 1 the exercise of the power conferred by the enactment requires consent only to the extent that it relates to the matter specified in that entry; and if the entry is or includes a condition, only if that condition is satisfied.

Enactment	*Limitation of requirement of consent*
The Public Health (Scotland) Act 1945, section 1 (1) (*b*).	
The National Health Service (Scotland) Act 1947, sections 34, 39, 40 and 42, and regulations made under any of those sections.	Terms and conditions of service.
The Fire Services Act 1947, section 26.	
The Fire Services Act 1947, section 36.	Terms and conditions of service.
The Superannuation (Miscellaneous Provisions) Act 1948, section 2.	
The Hospital Endowments (Scotland) Act 1953, section 3 (1) (*c*).	Terms and conditions of service.
The Mental Health (Scotland) Act 1960, section 90 (3).	Terms and conditions of service.
The Housing (Scotland) Act 1966, Schedule 7, paragraph 6.	
The Superannuation (Miscellaneous Provisions) Act 1967, section 7.	
The Police (Scotland) Act 1967, section 47 (1).	
The New Towns (Scotland) Act 1968, sections 10 (5), 26 (5), 26 (6) and 28 (4).	Excepted statutory undertakers or operational land of such undertakers.
The New Towns (Scotland) Act 1968, section 36.	Extension or modification of powers and duties of excepted statutory undertakers.
The Transport Act 1968, sections 7, 8 and 29.	The making of a scheme or order for the transfer of any property, rights or liabilities to or from the Scottish Transport Group or any of its subsidiaries.

Enactment	*Limitation of requirement of consent*
The Transport Act 1968, section 135 (6).	If the exercise of the power relates to a case where the Scottish Transport Group is a compensating authority.
The Roads (Scotland) Act 1970, section 28 (2).	Appliances or vehicles of excepted statutory undertakers.
The Hospital Endowments (Scotland) Act 1971, section 8 (2) (*c*).	Terms and conditions of service.
The Pensions (Increase) Act 1971, section 13 (2) to (5).	
The Superannuation Act 1972, sections 7, 8 and 10.	
The Superannuation Act 1972, section 24.	Provision for or in respect of persons in relation to whom the Firemen's Pension Scheme, or regulations under section 7 or 10 of the Act, may be made.
The Town and Country Planning (Scotland) Act 1972, section 219.	The making of an order against excepted statutory undertakers.
The Town and Country Planning (Scotland) Act 1972, section 222.	Powers and duties of excepted statutory undertakers.
The Town and Country Planning (Scotland) Act 1972, section 226 (4).	Excepted statutory undertakers.
The Town and Country Planning (Scotland) Act 1972, section 259.	
The National Health Service (Scotland) Act 1972, section 34A, Schedule 1, Part I, paragraphs 7 and 8, and Schedule 3, paragraphs 7 and 8 (*e*).	Terms and conditions of service.
The Local Government (Scotland) Act 1973, sections 219 and 220.	
The Community Land Act 1975, Schedule 4, paragraphs 17 and 18 (1) (*b*).	The making of an order against excepted statutory undertakers.
The Inner Urban Areas Act 1978, section 8 (1).	
Any enactment conferring power to make or confirm a compulsory purchase order.	If—

    (*a*) the land in respect of which the order is made, or an interest or right in the land, is held by excepted statutory undertakers for the purposes of their undertaking or by a local authority, or any body formed by local authorities, for the purposes of scheduled functions; and

    (*b*) the undertakers, authority or body have duly objected to the making of the order and have not withdrawn their objection.

DEFINITIONS
    " excepted statutory undertakers ": s. 81 (1).
    " property ": s. 81 (1).

GENERAL NOTE
    The enactments listed in this Schedule were subject to a considerable number of minor Government amendments during the passage of the Schedule through Parliament: *Hansard*, H.C. Vol. 944, col. 607 (February 15, 1978); H.L. Vol. 392, cols. 1476–1482 (June 8, 1978); Vol. 393, cols. 432–433 (June 29, 1978).
    See s. 23 (1) and (2), and notes thereon.

SCHEDULE 5

ENACTMENTS CONFERRING POWERS EXERCISABLE CONCURRENTLY

The Requisitioned Land and War Works Act 1945, section 52.
The Agriculture Act 1947, section 78.
The Criminal Justice (Scotland) Act 1949, section 75 (1) (*b*) and (3) (*f*).
The Salmon and Freshwater Fisheries (Protection) (Scotland) Act 1951, section 15.
The Historic Buildings and Ancient Monuments Act 1953, sections 4 to 6.
The Transport Act 1968, section 57.
The Local Authorities (Goods and Services) Act 1970, section 1 (5).
The Community Land Act 1975, section 18.
The Inner Urban Areas Act 1978, paragraph 2 of the Schedule.

GENERAL NOTE
   The enactments listed in this Schedule were subject to a number of minor Government amendments during the passage of the Schedule through Parliament; *Hansard*, H.C. Vol. 944, col. 607 (February 15, 1978); H.L. Vol. 392, cols. 1483–9 (June 8, 1978); Vol. 393, col. 433 (June 29, 1978).
   " *concurrently.*" See s. 23 and note thereon.

SCHEDULE 6

PROVISIONS IN ASSEMBLY BILLS REQUIRING CROWN'S CONSENT

1. Any provision affecting the Crown in its private capacity.
2. Any provision affecting the rules of law authorising or requiring the withholding of any document or the refusal to answer any question on the ground that the disclosure of the document or the answering of the question would be injurious to the public interest.
3. Any provision affecting property vested in a Minister of the Crown or property vested in Her Majesty in right of the Crown or of the Duchy of Lancaster or forming part of the Crown Estate or held in trust for Her Majesty, or affecting property belonging to the Duchy of Cornwall or the Principality and Stewartry of Scotland.
4. Any provision imposing duties on, or on officers or servants of, a Minister of the Crown, on members of the armed forces of the Crown or on any person whose remuneration is paid out of central United Kingdom funds.
5. Any provision—
   (*a*) conferring on any person any privilege or immunity of the Crown;
   (*b*) depriving any person of any such privilege or immunity;
   (*c*) requiring or enabling any person to exercise any functions on behalf of the Crown; or
   (*d*) securing that any functions exercisable by any person on behalf of the Crown are no longer so exercisable by him.
6. Any provision affecting the provisions of a Royal Charter.
7. Any provision relating to the care and preservation of, or access to, records in the custody of the Keeper of the Records of Scotland at the coming into operation of this paragraph, except court records and private records.

DEFINITION
   " property ": s. 81 (1).

GENERAL NOTE
   This Schedule contains details of the provisions which, if contained in an Assembly Bill, require the consent of the Crown to be signified in accordance with s. 24, which should be read along with this Schedule. It is not to be implied from this Schedule that the Assembly is necessarily competent to legislate on the matters to which the Schedule relates; it is likely that Assembly legislation will impinge upon Crown interests only in an indirect fashion; see Sched. 2, para. 8.
   Para. 1. This paragraph is concerned with the Crown in its personal or private capacity. The term " private capacity " is also to be found in the Crown Proceedings Act

1947, s. 40 (1). The Crown Private Estates, regulated by the Crown Private Estates Acts 1862 and 1873, fall within this paragraph.

Para. 2. The rules of law in question have, until relatively recently, been subsumed under the general heading of " Crown privilege," and are based on both statute law (see Crown Proceedings Act 1947) and common law (see, *e.g. Glasgow Corporation* v. *Central Land Board*, 1956 S.C. (H.L.) 1). The term " Crown privilege " has, however, been described as misleading (see *R.* v. *Lewes Justices, ex p. Home Secretary* [1973] A.C. 388 (H.L.), *per* Lord Reid at p. 400), and it is now recognised that the privilege which may attach to certain documents in court proceedings should be justified on the grounds of public interest, and not on a privilege of the Crown as such. The wording of this paragraph reflects this change in attitude, but as a result the paragraph appears to be out of place in this Schedule. Note, however, that it will be within the legislative competence of the Assembly to alter the rules of law referred to in this paragraph, for " evidence " is made a devolved matter by Sched. 10, Pt. I, Group 24.

Para. 3. This paragraph is concerned with provisions affecting Crown property of various types. Property vested in Her Majesty in right of the Crown includes the Palace of Holyrood House, and property held in trust for Her Majesty includes Balmoral Castle. Property forming part of the Crown Estate consists of a wide range of lands under the management of the Crown Estate Commissioners under the Crown Estate Act 1961. Property belonging to the Duchy of Cornwall or the Principality and Stewartry of Scotland vests in the Crown when it is not vested in the Prince of Wales.

Para. 4. While it may be assumed that Assembly Acts will regularly place duties on Scottish Secretaries and their staff, it is likely that on only very few occasions will the Assembly wish to place duties on Ministers and their staff, and on the other categories listed in the paragraph. In particular, the armed forces are not a devolved matter. The duties to be imposed by the Assembly legislation may, but need not necessarily, affect the prerogatives of the Crown. The most likely explanation is that the categories listed are intended to be exhaustive of the concept of " Crown servants " although the ambiguity of the last limb of the paragraph (despite the words " paid out of central United Kingdom funds ") leads to uncertainty on this point; *cf.* Crown Proceedings Act 1947, s. 2 (6). The paragraph does seem to go beyond the categories of provisions in parliamentary Bills for which Crown consent is required; it seems to have been assumed that it would not be proper for the Assembly (having no direct constitutional relationship with the Crown) to impose duties on servants of the Crown without Crown consent.

Para. 5. This paragraph requires the consent of the Crown to be signified where a provision in an Assembly Bill confers Crown status upon a new body, or takes Crown status away from a body. Whether a public body enjoys the immunities and privileges of the Crown has in the past caused difficulties in litigation (see, *e.g. Pfizer Corporation* v. *Minister of Health* [1965] A.C. 512 (H.L.); *British Broadcasting Corp.* v. *Johns* [1965] Ch. 32) although in Acts of Parliament which establish new public corporations it is now customary to make express provision for their status (see, *e.g.* Health and Safety at Work Act 1974, s. 10 (7), regarding the Health and Safety Commission and the Health and Safety Executive).

This paragraph was added by way of a Government amendment made during the Report stage in the Lords; *Hansard*, H.L. Vol. 392, cols. 1491–4 (June 8, 1978).

For the term " person," see Interpretation Act 1978, Sched. 1.

Para. 6. Royal charters are granted by the Queen in Council in response to a petition, and are normally amended by the same method. It will be competent for the Assembly to amend a provision in a charter by legislation, just as it is competent for Parliament to do so. However, the consent of the Crown will be required for any such legislation.

Para. 7. This relates directly to Sched. 10, Pt. I, Group 23.

Section 42   SCHEDULE 7

ENACTMENTS CONFERRING POWER RELATING TO THE DISPOSAL OF PREMISES OR OTHER LAND FOR INDUSTRIAL PURPOSES

The Highlands and Islands Development (Scotland) Act 1965, sections 2, 3 and 4.
The New Towns (Scotland) Act 1968, sections 4 and 18.
The Town and Country Planning (Scotland) Act 1972, section 113.

The Local Government (Scotland) Act 1973, sections 74 and 74A.
The Scottish Development Agency Act 1975, sections 4, 6 and 9.
The Community Land Act 1975, section 45.

GENERAL NOTE

This Schedule lists the enactments which confer the powers which in their exercise by a Scottish Secretary will be subject to guidelines made under s. 42 (1) (*c*); see note thereon.

Section 43

SCHEDULE 8

TERMS AND CONDITIONS OF SERVICE—DESCRIPTION OF PERSONS REFERRED TO IN SECTION 43

Description of persons

Pharmacists and opticians providing services under contract with health authorities.
Officers and servants of health authorities.
Staff employed at State hospitals (within the meaning of section 89 of the Mental Health (Scotland) Act 1960).
Officers and servants of the Scottish Hospital Trust.
Officers and servants of the Scottish Hospital Endowment Research Trust.

Definition

In this Schedule "health authority" means a health board established under the National Health Service (Scotland) Act 1972 or the Common Services Agency for the Scottish Health Service.

GENERAL NOTE

This Schedule should be read along with s. 43.

An amendment made during the Committee stage in the Lords removed from the Schedule the category of medical and dental practitioners providing services under contract with health authorities, on the argument that it would be damaging to these professions if their terms and conditions of service were dealt with separately in Scotland; *Hansard*, H.L. Vol. 391, cols. 241–52 (May 3, 1978).

Sections 60, 61

SCHEDULE 9

ENACTMENTS AUTHORISING THE LENDING OF MONEY

The Transport Act 1962.
The New Towns (Scotland) Act 1968.
The Housing (Financial Provisions) (Scotland) Act 1968.
The Transport Act 1968.
The Housing Act 1974.
The Scottish Development Agency Act 1975.

SCHEDULE 10

MATTERS WITHIN LEGISLATIVE COMPETENCE OF ASSEMBLY, AND WITHIN POWERS OF SCOTTISH EXECUTIVE

PART I

THE GROUPS OF DEVOLVED MATTERS

Preliminary

Subject to paragraphs (*a*) and (*b*) below, a matter is included in the Groups in this Part of this Schedule if, and only if, it falls within the subjects listed in them; but—

(*a*) the matters specified in Part II of this Schedule are not included in those Groups; and

(*b*) any question whether, or how far, the matters dealt with in the enactments listed in the first column of Part III of this Schedule are included in those Groups is to be determined in accordance with the second column of that Part.

GROUP 1 (*Health*)

Prevention, treatment and alleviation of disease or illness, including injury, disability and mental disorder. Family planning. Investigation of maladministration.

GROUP 2 (*Social welfare*)

Social welfare, including children and adoption.

GROUP 3 (*Education, etc.*)

Education, the arts, crafts, social, cultural and recreative activities. Libraries, museums and art galleries. Teaching profession.

GROUP 4 (*Housing*)

Housing. Regulation of rents. Rent allowances and rebates. Mobile homes and caravans.

GROUP 5 (*Local government and local finance*)

Constitution, area and general powers and duties of local authorities and similar bodies. Investigation of maladministration. Revenue and expenditure of local authorities and similar bodies. Rating and valuation for rating. Rate support grants and grants for specific purposes.

GROUP 6 (*Land use and development*)

Town and country planning. Building control. New towns. Industrial sites. Improvement of derelict land. Mitigation of the injurious effect of public works.

GROUP 7 (*Pollution*)

Control of pollution.

GROUP 8 (*Erosion and flooding*)

Protection of the coast against erosion and encroachment from the sea. Prevention or mitigation of flooding of land.

GROUP 9 (*Countryside*)

Development of the countryside for public enjoyment and the conservation and enhancement of its natural beauty and amenity.

GROUP 10 (*Transport*)

Provision of public passenger and freight transport services within Scotland. Payment of subsidies to operators of such services within Scotland. Aerodromes.

Insulation of nearby buildings from noise and vibration attributable to the use of aerodromes.

GROUP 11 (*Roads, etc.*)

Provision, improvement and maintenance of streets, roads and bridges.

GROUP 12 (*Marine works*)

Provision, improvement and maintenance of harbours and boatslips principally used or required for the fishing or agricultural industries or for the maintenance of communications between places in Scotland. Provision of financial assistance for the execution of works, in connection with any other harbours, for the benefit of the fishing industry.

GROUP 13 (*Agricultural land*)

Tenure and management of agricultural land. Grants, loans and subsidies payable in relation to landholders. Crofting, including grants, loans and subsidies payable primarily in relation to crofters, cottars and persons of substantially the same economic status.

GROUP 14 (*Fisheries*)

Protection, improvement and maintenance of salmon, migratory trout and fresh water fisheries in any waters, including any part of the sea up to a distance of 3 nautical miles from the low water mark of any part of the mainland or adjacent islands of Scotland (other than the Island of Rockall) or, where an estuarial limit fixed under the Salmon Fisheries (Scotland) Acts 1828 to 1868 extends beyond that distance, up to that estuarial limit.

GROUP 15 (*Water, etc.*)

Supply of water and safety of reservoirs. Inland waterways.

GROUP 16 (*Fire Services*)

Fire services and fire precautions.

GROUP 17 (*Tourism*)

Development of tourism.

GROUP 18 (*Ancient monuments, etc.*)

Ancient monuments and historic buildings.

GROUP 19 (*Registration services*)

Registration of births, deaths, marriages and adoptions. Population statistics.

GROUP 20 (*Miscellaneous*)

Charities, including collections for charities. Public holidays. Deer and sale of venison. Local regulation of trades. Provision or control by local authorities of facilities and local activities. Parks and open spaces. Markets and fairs. Lotteries. Liquor licensing. Local licensing. Shop hours. Allotments. Burial and cremation. Licensing of dogs and keepers of dogs. Control of stray dogs.

GROUP 21 (*Courts and legal profession, etc.*)

Courts, including juries. Court jurisdiction and procedure. Contempt of court. Vexatious litigation. Justices of the peace. Legal profession. Legal aid, advice and assistance.

GROUP 22 (*Tribunals and inquiries*)

Tribunals and inquiries related to matters included in other Groups in this Part of this Schedule. The Lands Tribunal for Scotland.

GROUP 23 (*Public records*)

Records of the Scottish Assembly, the Scottish Executive and the courts and of any body created by or under any Scottish Assembly Act or whose functions are matters which are wholly within the legislative competence of the Assembly. Private records. Any records in the custody of the Keeper of the Records of Scotland on the coming into force of this Group.

GROUP 24 (*Civil law matters*)

Natural and juristic persons and unincorporated bodies. Obligations, including voluntary and conventional obligations, obligations of restitution and obligations of reparation. Heritable and moveable property. Conveyancing. Trusts. Bankruptcy. Succession. Remedies. Evidence. Diligence. Recognition and enforcement of court orders. Arbitration. Prescription and limitation of actions. Private international law.

GROUP 25 (*Crime*)

Principles of criminal liability. Offences against the person. Sexual offences. Offences against property. Offences of dishonesty. Offences against public order, decency and religion. Offences against the administration of justice. Offences related to matters included in other Groups in this Part of this Schedule. Criminal penalties. Treatment of offenders (including children and young persons, and mental health patients, involved in crime). Compensation out of public funds for victims of crime. Criminal evidence. Criminal procedure, including arrest, search, custody and time limits for prosecutions. Recognition and enforcement of court orders. Criminal research.

PART II

MATTERS NOT INCLUDED IN THE GROUPS

1. Control of drugs, medicinal products, biological substances and food.

2. Social security and war pensions.

3. Universities, university staff and grants to universities. Career guidance.

4. Provision by private financial institutions of finance for housing.

5. Grants for specific purposes relating to scheduled functions.

6. Compensation in respect of the compulsory acquisition of land by bodies possessing statutory powers and in respect of depreciation caused to land by the activities of bodies possessing statutory powers of compulsory acquisition.

7. Control of pollution as respects motor vehicles, aircraft and dumping at sea and as respects vessels other than those in inland waters.

8. Provision of air services, provision of freight transport services by road (other than by the Scottish Transport Group or any body directly or indirectly replacing it) and provision of railway services by the British Railways Board. Payments, in respect of public freight services, of subsidies—

    (*a*) to operators (other than the Scottish Transport Group or any body directly or indirectly replacing it) of such services by road;

    (*b*) to operators (other than those providing services to or from places in the Highlands and Islands) of such services by air; and

    (*c*) to operators of such services by rail.

9. Any regulatory powers of the Civil Aviation Authority relating to aerodromes. Protection of aircraft and aerodromes against acts of violence.

10. The following, except in relation to the provision of financial assistance for the execution of works for the benefit of the fishing industry: harbours, ferries and boatslips vested in the British Transport Docks Board, the British Railways Board, the British Waterways Board or the National Freight Corporation or in any subsidiary (within the meaning of the Transport Act 1968) of any of those Boards or of that Corporation, or vested in any of the bodies specified in Schedule 3 to the Harbours, Piers and Ferries (Scotland) Act 1937.

11. Payment of grants and subsidies in relation to agricultural land other than those mentioned in Group 13 and those relating to arterial drainage works.

12. Plant health. Control of diseases of animals, including fish.

13. Taking of censuses of the population.

14. The continued existence of—

    (*a*) the High Court of Justiciary as a criminal court of first instance and of appeal;

(*b*) the Court of Session as a civil court of first instance and of appeal;

(*c*) the sheriff courts.

15. Judges of the High Court of Justiciary and the Court of Session, the Chairman and members of the Scottish Land Court, sheriffs principal, temporary sheriffs principal, sheriffs and temporary sheriffs.

The matters above do not extend to the number of such persons or to the determination of the territorial areas in respect of which sheriffs principal or sheriffs are to act.

16. The jurisdiction—

(*a*) of the High Court of Justiciary over any offence of a description which on the date of commencement of this paragraph was within its jurisdiction at first instance, and in respect of its *nobile officium*;

(*b*) of the sheriff court over any offence of a description which at that date was within its jurisdiction;

(*c*) of the Court of Session over any question of status, right or obligation of a description and value which at that date was within its jurisdiction at first instance, and in respect of its *nobile officium*;

(*d*) of the sheriff court over any question of status, right or obligation of a description and value which at that date was within its jurisdiction at first instance.

The matters above do not extend to the continued existence of the privative nature of any jurisdiction or to the determination of the territorial jurisdiction of the sheriff courts.

17. Appeals to the House of Lords against decisions of the Court of Session. Recourse to the High Court of Justiciary by any person found to have committed an offence by any court.

The matters above do not extend to the manner or grounds of recourse to the High Court of Justiciary.

18. The power of the High Court of Justiciary to regulate its own procedure and the procedure in criminal matters of all inferior courts. The power of the Court of Session to regulate its own procedure and the procedure in civil matters of the sheriff courts.

19. The following courts—

Courts-martial and the Courts-Martial Appeal Court;

and all matters of penalties, jurisdiction, evidence and procedure relating to those courts;

The Lyon Court;

Election Courts constituted under section 110 of the Representation of the People Act 1949;

Courts constituted under section 45 (9) (registration appeals) of the said Act of 1949;

The Restrictive Practices Court;

The Employment Appeal Tribunal;

and special matters of penalties, jurisdiction, evidence and procedure relating to those courts.

20. Corporate bodies other than public bodies related to devolved matters. Insurance. Banking. Legal tender. Intellectual property. Safety standards for goods. Restrictive trading practices and monopolies. Regulation of interest rates and credit.

21. Regulation of charges and prices other than those charged by—

(*a*) a Scottish Secretary; or

(*b*) a public body or person appointed by a Scottish Secretary or appointed under an enactment relating to a devolved matter; or

(*c*) a local authority in relation to a function which is not a scheduled function.

22. Trade unions and employers' associations. Trade disputes and labour relations.

23. Terms and conditions of employment and related statutory rights and duties of employment, but excluding regulation of terms and conditions of service in respect of a person who is paid—

(*a*) by a Scottish Secretary; or

(*b*) by a public body or person appointed by a Scottish Secretary or appointed under an enactment relating to a devolved matter; or

(*c*) by a local authority.

Paragraphs (*a*) and (*b*) above do not apply to a person who is a member of Her Majesty's Home Civil Service, including a person of a description designated under section 67 (5) of this Act; and paragraph (*c*) above does not apply to a person who is employed exclusively for the purpose of a scheduled function.

24. Any matter relating to the right to prosecute any offence, or to organisation, accommodation, appointments, qualifications or terms or conditions of service in relation to the prosecution of offences.

25. Any special matter of criminal penalties, evidence or procedure relating to matters not included in any Group in Part I of this Schedule. Deportation and extradition.

PART III

ENACTMENTS RELATING TO THE GROUPS IN PART I

Enactment	*Whether, or how far, matters dealt with are included in the Groups*
The Anatomy Acts 1832 and 1871.	Included.
The Harbours, Docks and Piers Clauses Act 1847 (c. 27), sections 28 and 102.	Not included.
The Salmon Fisheries (Scotland) Act 1863 (c. 50), section 4.	Not included.
The Congested Districts (Scotland) Act 1897 (c. 53), section 4 (1) (*e*).	Included, so far as relating to the erection and formation of fishermen's dwellings and holdings in congested districts.
The Development and Road Improvement Funds Act 1909 (c. 47), Part I.	Not included.
The Registration of Business Names Act 1916 (c. 58).	Not included.
The National Library of Scotland Act 1925 (c. 73).	The power to recommend to Her Majesty the appointment of members of the Board of Trustees is not included.
The Land Drainage (Scotland) Act 1930 (c. 20), sections 7 and 8.	Not included, except for the power of consent under section 7 which is included so far as it relates to land vested in the First Secretary or held for the purposes of a Scottish Secretary.
The Harbours, Piers and Ferries (Scotland) Act 1937 (c. 28), sections 5 (6), 9 (*a*) and (*d*) and 26.	Not included, except that section 5 (6) is included so far as it relates to matters other than works to be constructed below the high water mark of ordinary spring tides.
The Disabled Persons (Employment) Acts 1944 and 1958.	Not included.
The Hill Farming Act 1946 (c. 73).	Not included, except for the matters dealt with in sections 23 to 31.
The Statistics of Trade Act 1947 (c. 39).	Not included.

Enactment	Whether, or how far, matters dealt with are included in the Groups
The Acquisition of Land (Authorisation Procedure) (Scotland) Act 1947 (c. 42).	Not included.
The National Health Service (Scotland) Act 1947 (c. 27), Schedule 3, paragraph 6.	Not included.
The Radioactive Substances Act 1948 (c. 37), sections 5 (1) (*b*) and 7.	The power under section 5 (1) (*b*) is not included so far as it relates to sites and premises mentioned in section 2 (1) and (2) of the Radioactive Substances Act 1960 (c. 34); and the matters dealt with in section 7 are included only in relation to offences under regulations made by a Scottish Secretary.
The Agriculture (Scotland) Act 1948 (c. 45), Parts IV and V.	Included, except for the matters dealt with in sections 55 (*d*), 56 and 61 (2) so far as they relate to land used wholly or mainly for agricultural research or experiment.
The Civil Aviation Act 1949 (c. 67), Part III and section 56.	Included, except for the matters dealt with in section 37.
The Coast Protection Act 1949 (c. 74), Part I.	Included except that— (*a*) the powers of the Treasury under section 11 (2) (*b*) and the power to determine questions under section 32 are not included; (*b*) the powers to give directions under section 17 (5) and determine questions under section 17 (8) are not included so far as exercisable in relation to excepted statutory undertakers in cases where an objection is made by a coast protection authority; (*c*) the power to give consent under section 32 is included only so far as it relates to land vested in the First Secretary or held for the purposes of a Scottish Secretary; (*d*) the matters dealt with in section 46 are included only so far as relating to matters with respect to which a Scottish Secretary exercises functions.
The Agricultural Holdings (Scotland) Act 1949 (c. 75), section 86.	Included so far as it relates to land vested in the First Secretary or held for the purposes of a Scottish Secretary.
The National Parks and Access to the Countryside Act 1949 (c. 97).	The matters dealt with in Part VI are included so far as that Part is applicable to section 21; and the matters dealt with in section 101 are included so far as relating to land vested in the First Secretary or held for the purposes of a Scottish Secretary.

Enactment	*Whether, or how far, matters dealt with are included in the Groups*
The Shops Act 1950 (c. 28), section 67.	Included.
The Nurses (Scotland) Act 1951 (c. 55), Part III.	Included.
The Rivers (Prevention of Pollution) (Scotland) Act 1951 (c. 66), section 29.	Not included.
The Historic Buildings and Ancient Monuments Act 1953 (c. 49), section 7.	Not included.
The Clean Air Act 1956 (c. 52), section 22.	Not included, except so far as relating to property vested in the First Secretary or held for the purposes of a Scottish Secretary.
The Prevention of Fraud (Investments) Act 1958 (c. 45).	Not included.
The Opencast Coal Act 1958 (c. 69), section 2.	Not included.
The Building (Scotland) Acts 1959 and 1970.	The powers to give approval, directions and consent under section 26 of the Building (Scotland) Act 1959 (c. 24) (but not to determine questions) are included only so far as they relate to buildings or land vested in the First Secretary or held for the purposes of a Scottish Secretary.
The Weeds Act 1959 (c. 54).	Included.
The Road Traffic Act 1960 (c. 16).	The following matters are not included:— (a) those dealt with in section 120 so far as relating to the establishment of traffic commissioners and their power and duty of issuing licences; (b) those dealt with in section 135 (1) so far as relating to the authority having power to grant a road service licence; (c) those dealt with in section 137 (1); (d) the other matters dealt with in Part III, except so far as they relate to the two traffic commissioners other than the chairman and to road service licences or permits under section 30 of the Transport Act 1968 (c. 73); and (e) the matters dealt with otherwise than in Part III.
The Radioactive Substances Act 1960 (c. 34).	Included, except that— (a) the matters dealt with in section 2 (1) and (2) are not included; (b) the matters dealt with in sections 6 to 8 are not included so far as they relate to sites and premises mentioned in section 2 (1) and (2);

Enactment	*Whether, or how far, matters dealt with are included in the Groups*
The Radioactive Substances Act 1960 —*cont.*	(*c*) the powers under section 10 are not included so far as they relate to such sites and premises; (*d*) the powers under section 12 are not included, so far as they relate to premises mentioned in subsection (3) (*b*) of that section; (*e*) the powers under section 14 (3) are included only so far as they relate to premises vested in the First Secretary or held for the purposes of a Scottish Secretary.
The Mental Health (Scotland) Act 1960 (c. 61), section 2 (4).	The power to recommend to Her Majesty the appointment of Commissioners is not included.
The Flood Prevention (Scotland) Act 1961 (c. 41), section 14 (2).	The power to determine questions is not included.
The Human Tissue Act 1961 (c. 54).	Included.
The Transport Act 1962 (c. 46).	Not included, except that— (*a*) the matters dealt with in sections 62, 63 and 91 are included; (*b*) the matters dealt with otherwise than in sections 21 and 27 (6) are included so far as they relate to the Scottish Transport Group and its subsidiaries; (*c*) the matters dealt with in Parts I, II and III (except sections 21 and 27 (6) and Schedule 1) and sections 66, 86, 89 and 90 are included so far as they relate to the property and activities of the British Waterways Board and its subsidiaries.
The Education (Scotland) Act 1962 (c. 47).	The following matters are not included:— (*a*) so much of sections 49 and 75 (*f*) as relates to grants, bursaries, scholarships or other allowances to persons attending courses of initial teacher training, courses leading to a degree of a university or to a Higher National Diploma or courses of equivalent or higher standard; (*b*) any provision relating to the Carnegie Trust; (*c*) the power to recommend to Her Majesty the appointment of inspectors of schools (section 145 (24)).
The Pipe-lines Act 1962 (c. 58), section 5.	Not included.
The Protection of Depositors Act 1963 (c. 16).	Not included.

Enactment	*Whether, or how far, matters dealt with are included in the Groups*
The Land Compensation (Scotland) Act 1963 (c. 51).	Not included, except for the matters dealt with in Parts II and IV.
The Housing Act 1964 (c. 56), section 8.	Not included.
The Local Government (Development and Finance) (Scotland) Act 1964 (c. 67), section 7.	Not included, so far as relating to the erection of industrial buildings, within the meaning of section 64 of the Town and Country Planning (Scotland) Act 1972 (c. 52).
The Highlands and Islands Development (Scotland) Acts 1965 and 1968.	Not included.
The Science and Technology Act 1965 (c. 4).	Not included so far as relating to bodies which are Research Councils for the purposes of the Act.
The Rivers (Prevention of Pollution) (Scotland) Act 1965 (c. 13), section 8.	Not included.
The Law Commissions Act 1965 (c. 22).	Included so far as relating to the Scottish Law Commission.
The Registration of Births, Deaths and Marriages (Scotland) Act 1965 (c. 49), section 1 (1).	Included.
The Nuclear Installations Act 1965 (c. 57).	Not included.
The Housing (Scotland) Act 1966 (c. 49), section 25.	Not included.
The Local Government (Scotland) Act 1966 (c. 51).	The matters dealt with in section 11, and the power in section 18 (3) to determine questions (so far as it relates to excepted statutory undertakers), are not included.
The Forestry Act 1967 (c. 10), section 15.	Included.
The Parliamentary Commissioner Act 1967 (c. 13).	Included (subject to section 76 of this Act).
The Agriculture Act 1967 (c. 22), Part III.	Included, except for the matters dealt with in sections 43 and 44.
The Housing Subsidies Act 1967 (c. 29), Part II.	Not included.
The Countryside (Scotland) Act 1967 (c. 86).	The powers under section 73 are included only so far as exercisable in relation to land vested in the First Secretary or held for the purposes of a Scottish Secretary; and the matters dealt with in section 58 are not included.
The Abortion Act 1967 (c. 87).	Not included.

Enactment	*Whether, or how far, matters dealt with are included in the Groups*
The New Towns (Scotland) Act 1968 (c. 16), sections 4, 10 (3), 14 (2), 18, 19 (1) (proviso), 24, 28, 30 (1), (3) and (5), 38A, 47 (4) and Schedules 3, 4 and 8.	Not included, except that— (*a*) the matters dealt with in sections 4 and 18 are excluded only in relation to the disposal of premises or other land for industrial purposes; (*b*) those dealt with in section 28 are excluded only so far as they relate to representations made by excepted statutory undertakers; (*c*) those dealt with in sections 10 (3), 30 (1), (3) and (5), 47 (4) and Schedule 8 are excluded only so far as they relate to excepted statutory undertakers or operational land of such undertakers.
The Trade Descriptions Act 1968 (c. 29).	Not included.
The Housing (Financial Provisions) (Scotland) Act 1968 (c. 31), section 50.	Not included.
The Sewerage (Scotland) Act 1968 (c. 47).	The power to determine questions under section 55 (4) is not included.
The Civil Aviation Act 1968 (c. 61), sections 1 to 6, 8, 12, 21, 22 and 27.	Included.
The Transport Act 1968 (c. 73).	Not included except that— (*a*) the matters dealt with in sections 9 to 19, 20 (1) to (5) and (8), 21 to 23, 30, 31, 34, 36, 37, 56, 57, 110 and 138 are included; (*b*) the power to make regulations under section 135, by virtue of subsection (1) (*d*) of that section, is included; (*c*) the matters dealt with in section 26 (1) (*a*) are included so far as relates to passenger services within Scotland and passenger services by road outside Scotland; (*d*) the matters dealt with in section 162 are included except so far as subsection (2) provides for determination of disputes; (*e*) the powers under sections 116 to 119, 121 and 122 are included so far as exercisable in relation to bridges over inland waterways; (*f*) the powers under sections 157 and 158 are included so far as exercisable in relation to functions exercised by a Scottish Secretary; (*g*) the powers under sections 7, 8 and 29 are included so far as they relate to schemes or orders transferring property to or from the Scottish Transport Group or any of its subsidiaries;

Enactment	*Whether, or how far, matters dealt with are included in the Groups*
The Transport Act 1968—*cont.*	(*h*) the powers under section 135 (6) are included in cases where the Scottish Transport Group is the compensating authority; (*i*) the matters dealt with in the other provisions of the Act are included so far as they relate to the Scottish Transport Group and its subsidiaries; (*j*) the matters dealt with in Parts IV and VII are included so far as they relate to the British Waterways Board and its subsidiaries.
The Housing (Scotland) Act 1969 (c. 34), section 21.	Not included.
The Post Office Act 1969 (c. 48), Schedule 4, paragraph 93 (4).	Not included.
The Development of Tourism Act 1969 (c. 51).	Included, so far as relating to the Scottish Tourist Board and hotels and other establishments in Scotland, except that— (*a*) the matters dealt with in section 1 (2) and paragraph 18 of Schedule 1 are not included; (*b*) the matters dealt with in sections 19 and 20 are not included so far as they relate to grants or loans made under Part II.
The Roads (Scotland) Act 1970 (c. 20), section 44.	The power of the Treasury under subsection (4) is not included and the other matters dealt with are included only so far as relating to land vested in the First Secretary or held for the purposes of a Scottish Secretary.
The Chronically Sick and Disabled Persons Act 1970 (c. 44), sections 9, 21 and 23.	Not included.
The Radiological Protection Act 1970 (c. 46).	Not included.
The Fire Precautions Act 1971 (c. 40), sections 36 (4) to (6) and 41.	Not included.
The Prevention of Oil Pollution Act 1971 (c. 60).	Not included, except that the power in section 23 (*b*) is included so far as it relates to— (*a*) discharges from land in Scotland; and (*b*) discharges (otherwise than from land or vessels) into tidal waters in Scotland or other waters which are adjacent to Scotland and are controlled waters for purposes of Part II of the Control of Pollution Act 1974 (c. 40).

Enactment	*Whether, or how far, matters dealt with are included in the Groups*
The Tribunals and Inquiries Act 1971 (c. 62).	The matters dealt with in sections 1 to 4 (1) and 15 (1) and (5) are not included and the other matters dealt with in the Act are included only so far as they relate to matters with respect to which a Scottish Secretary exercises functions otherwise than under the Act.
The Civil Aviation Act 1971 (c. 75).	Not included, except so far as relating to the insulation of buildings near aerodromes against aircraft noise and vibration and except for— (a) the matters dealt with in sections 30 to 32; and (b) those dealt with in sections 6 to 11, 13, 14, 16 to 20, 34 and 36, so far as relating to the operation of aerodromes.
The Road Traffic Act 1972 (c. 20), sections 154 to 156.	Included.
The Town and Country Planning (Scotland) Act 1972 (c. 52).	The following matters are not included:— (a) those dealt with in sections 37, 47, 64 to 70, 103, 108 (2), 117 (1) (proviso), 121 (1), 209, 227 to 229, 240 and 241 and paragraph 70 of Schedule 22; (b) the powers conferred by sections 44, 45 and 46 (4), so far as they relate to the reference to a Planning Inquiry Commission of a proposal that a government department should give a direction under section 37 or that development should be carried out by or on behalf of a government department; (c) the power to decide any question under section 195 (6), where the appropriate authority is a government department or an excepted statutory undertaker; (d) the power to make orders under section 221, so far as exercisable in relation to notices served by excepted statutory undertakers; (e) the powers under sections 222 and 224 (and the supplementary powers under section 225), so far as exercisable by virtue of representations made by excepted statutory undertakers; (f) the powers under sections 253 and 254, except so far as exercisable in relation to land vested in the First Secretary or held for the purposes of a Scottish Secretary; (g) the power of the Treasury under section 253 (7);

Enactment	Whether, or how far, matters dealt with are included in the Groups
The Town and Country Planning (Scotland) Act 1972—*cont.*	(*h*) the power under section 266 (6) in respect of land held by excepted statutory undertakers; (*i*) the powers under section 275 (2), so far as exercisable in relation to excepted statutory undertakers; (*j*) the power under paragraph 4 (2) of Schedule 18, so far as exercisable in relation to excepted statutory undertakers.
The British Library Act 1972 (c. 54).	Not included.
The National Health Service (Scotland) Act 1972 (c. 58), section 55.	Included.
The Counter-Inflation Act 1973 (c. 9).	Not included.
The Fire Precautions (Loans) Act 1973 (c. 11), section 1 (3) and (4).	Not included.
The Employment Agencies Act 1973 (c. 35).	Not included.
The Social Security Act 1973 (c. 38).	Not included.
The Fair Trading Act 1973 (c. 41).	Not included.
The Employment and Training Act 1973 (c. 50).	Not included.
The Nature Conservancy Council Act 1973 (c. 54).	Not included.
The Land Compensation (Scotland) Act 1973 (c. 56).	Not included, except that the matters dealt with in Parts II and V and in sections 14 and 36 to 40 are included so far as they do not affect any Minister of the Crown in his capacity as a responsible authority.
The Local Government (Scotland) Act 1973 (c. 65).	The following matters are not included:— (*a*) those dealt with in sections 4 to 11, 20, 29 to 37, 59 and 197 (2) to (5); (*b*) the power to give consent under sections 71, 73, 74 and 74A, except in cases where the functions of the Minister concerned are exercisable by a Scottish Secretary; (*c*) the power under section 87, so far as it relates to scheduled functions and the power under section 94, so far as it relates to expenses for the purpose of scheduled functions; (*d*) the power under section 202 (9) to give a direction with respect to byelaws and the power under section 202 (10) to confirm byelaws, except in cases where the byelaws deal with matters within the legislative competence of the Assembly;

Enactment	*Whether, or how far, matters dealt with are included in the Groups*
The Local Government (Scotland) Act 1973—*cont.*	(*e*) the power under section 209 (2) and (3), except in so far as it relates to enactments dealing with matters within the legislative competence of the Assembly; (*f*) the powers under sections 199, 210, 211, 215, 225 and 233, except in so far as they relate to matters with which a Scottish Secretary (but no Minister of the Crown) is concerned.
The Prices Act 1974 (c. 24).	Not included.
The Health and Safety at Work etc. Act 1974 (c. 37).	Not included, except for section 75.
The Consumer Credit Act 1974 (c. 39).	Not included.
The Control of Pollution Act 1974 (c. 40).	The following matters are not included:— (*a*) those dealt with in section 21, except in so far as they relate to the production of heat from waste; (*b*) the power under section 56 (1) to prescribe in relation to controlled waters; (*c*) those dealt with in sections 75 to 77 and 100 to 103; (*d*) those dealt with in section 30 (5) so far as they relate to sites and premises mentioned in section 2 (1) and (2) of the Radioactive Substances Act 1960 (c. 34).
The Policing of Airports Act 1974 (c. 41).	Not included.
The Housing (Scotland) Act 1974 (c. 45), section 30.	Not included.
The Friendly Societies Act 1974 (c. 46).	Not included.
The Railways Act 1974 (c. 48), section 8.	Included.
The Criminal Procedure (Scotland) Act 1975 (c. 21), sections 5, 10, 11, 21, 35, 41, 76, 113 (4), 114, 245 (1) and 263.	Not included, except so far as section 35 relates to the High Court.
The Local Government (Scotland) Act 1975 (c. 30), Schedule 3, paragraphs 2 to 9 and 26.	Not included.
The Prices Act 1975 (c. 32).	Not included.
The Air Travel Reserve Fund Act 1975 (c. 36).	Not included.
The Safety of Sports Grounds Act 1975 (c. 52).	Included.

Enactment	*Whether, or how far, matters dealt with are included in the Groups*
The Remuneration, Charges and Grants Act 1975 (c. 57).	Not included.
The Social Security Pensions Act 1975 (c. 60).	Not included.
The Sex Discrimination Act 1975 (c. 65).	Not included.
The Scottish Development Agency Act 1975 (c. 69).	Not included, except for the matters dealt with in—

Not included, except for the matters dealt with in—

(*a*) section 2 (1) (*d*);

(*b*) section 2 (2) (*d*), (*e*), (*g*) and (*h*);

(*c*) section 2 (2) (*i*), (3), (4) (*a*) to (*e*) and (6), so far as relating to the functions specified in section 2 (2) (*d*), (*e*), (*g*) and (*h*);

(*d*) section 2 (4) (*g*) to (*m*);

(*e*) section 2 (4) (*f*) and (7) and section 3, so far as relating to the functions specified in section 2 (2) (*d*), (*e*), (*g*) and (*h*);

(*f*) section 2 (8) and (9);

(*g*) section 2 (10), so far as relating to the functions specified in section 2 (2) (*d*), (*e*), (*g*) and (*h*);

(*h*) section 4, so far as relating to the functions specified in the provisions as mentioned in (*a*) to (*g*) above;

(*i*) sections 6, 7, 8 (1) to (5), 9, 11 (1) to (5), 13 (2) to (5), 18, 21, 22 and 24;

(*j*) sections 12, 13 (1) and 19 and Schedule 2, paragraphs 3 to 5 and 7 to 9, so far as relating to the functions specified in section 2 (2), (*d*), (*e*), (*g*) and (*h*);

(*k*) section 10, so far as relating to matters other than excepted statutory undertakers;

(*l*) section 16, so far as relating to property held by any person for the purposes of a devolved matter;

(*m*) Schedule 2, paragraph 2 so far as it relates to administrative expenses and to functions other than those to which public dividend capital relates;

(*n*) sections 25 to 28, so far as relating to the provisions as mentioned in (*a*) to (*m*) above.

| The Community Land Act 1975 (c. 77). | Not included. |
| The Airports Authority Act 1975 (c. 78), section 7. | Not included. |

Enactment	Whether, or how far, matters dealt with are included in the Groups
The Lotteries and Amusements Act 1976 (c. 32).	The matters dealt with in Parts I and II are included, except for those dealt with in sections 5 (3) (d) (ii), 6 (2) (c), 9 and 12 (5) (a). The matters dealt with in section 18 (1) (e) and (2) are not included.
The Valuation and Rating (Exempted Classes) (Scotland) Act 1976 (c. 64).	Not included.
The Licensing (Scotland) Act 1976 (c. 66), sections 54 (3) (j), 87 (3) and 138 (1) (a).	Not included.
The Race Relations Act 1976 (c. 74).	Not included.
The Dock Work Regulation Act 1976 (c. 79).	Not included.
The Passenger Vehicles (Experimental Areas) Act 1977 (c. 21).	Included, except for— (a) the matters dealt with in section 2 (3); (b) the matters dealt with in section 2 (8) (other than those in respect of the imposition of conditions), so far as relating to the treatment of vehicles for the purposes of enactments dealing with matters which are not devolved matters.
The Minibus Act 1977 (c. 25).	Not included, except for— (a) the powers under section 1 to give directions and to make orders; and (b) the power under section 3 (1) (a) to prescribe matters to be taken account of under section 2 (2) (b).
The Price Commission Act 1977 (c. 33).	Not included.
The Refuse Disposal (Amenity) Act 1978 (c. 3), section 4 (2).	Not included.
The Civil Aviation Act 1978 (c. 8), sections 8 and 9.	Not included.
The Inner Urban Areas Act 1978 (c. 50).	Not included.
The Transport Act 1978 (c. 55).	Not included, except so far as relating to inland waterway transport and grants to assist the provision of facilities for freight haulage by rail and except for the matters dealt with in sections 5 (1) to (4) and 6 to 8 so far as relating to road service licences or permits under section 30 of the Transport Act 1968 (c. 73).

GENERAL NOTE

This Schedule states the matters which are to be within the legislative competence of the Assembly and *ipso facto* also within the powers of the Scottish Executive. As explained in the notes on s. 63, Pt. I classifies the matters devolved in 25 groups, but these must be read subject to the matters excluded from devolution by Pt. II. By reference to existing U.K. statutes, Pt. III then provides the " fine tuning " by stating expressly whether or not specified matters dealt with in those statutes are devolved. Some entries in Pt. III must have been included for the avoidance of doubt; others add to or subtract from what would otherwise be devolved by the operation of Pts. I and II. The order of the groups in Pt. I is not alphabetical and seems to be completely random, but it is followed broadly by the sequence of topics in Pt. II, and also in Sched. 11, which lists matters on which executive but not legislative powers are devolved. Note that the entries in Pt. II apply to all the matters mentioned in Pt. I, and not merely to the most relevant subject group. For example, the exclusion of universities in para. 3 of Pt. II applies not merely to Group 3 (Education) in Pt. I but also to the university aspects of any other group in Pt. I, *e.g.* Group 1 (Health), Group 21 (Courts and legal profession). Note also that the scheme of the Act does not require definite demarcation lines to be drawn between the different subject groups in Pt. I of the Schedule. For example, it is immaterial whether day nurseries and nursery schools for young children are regarded as falling with Group 2 (social welfare), or Group 3 (education); on either view they are devolved matters.

Sched. 10, Pt. I originally included a subject providing for the devolution of forestry and afforestation but this group was removed from the Bill by the House of Lords (*Hansard*, H.L. Vol. 391, cols. 873–890 (May 9, 1978)) and, despite a vote to the contrary in the Commons (*Hansard*, H.C. Vol. 954, col. 216 (July 17, 1978)), the Lords persisted in its view (*Hansard*, H.C. Vol. 954, col. 1666 (July 26, 1978)). The other major deletion from Sched. 10, Pt. I which was not reinstated was betting and gaming (*Hansard*, H.L. Vol. 393, cols. 116–136 (June 12, 1978)).

It would be impossible except at great length to provide detailed notes on all the matters dealt with in this Schedule. The main aim of the notes which follow is, by taking each subject group from Pt. I in turn, to indicate the scope of each group and to show the connection between that group and other provisions of the Act (in particular, Pts. II and III of this Schedule, Sched. 11 and Sched. 16).

Part I

Group 1 (*Health*)

The general words used (from " Prevention " to " disorder ") seem broad enough to cover all aspects of the public sector of medicine (see the National Health Service (Scotland) Acts 1947–72) and the private sector. Such related or ancillary services as nursing, dentistry, pharmaceutical services, the ambulance service, community health and osteopathy seem to be included. The context is obviously the health of human beings—animal health is not devolved (Sched. 10, Part II, para. 12).

" Family planning " is mentioned expressly since this is not related directly to disease or illness. " Abortion " was deleted from this group by an amendment to the Bill forced on the Government in the House of Lords (*Hansard*, H.L. Vol. 391, cols. 483–496 (May 4, 1978)).

" Investigation of maladministration " relates particularly to the Health Service Commissioner for Scotland (and see the notes on s. 76 and also the entry for the National Health Service (Scotland) Act 1972 in Sched. 16).

By contrast with Groups 3 and 21, which mention respectively the teaching and legal professions, Group 1 does not mention the medical profession. The Government's view is that Group 1 does not include power to regulate the medical and other health professions, and that the right to practise medicine must remain a matter for U.K. legislation. While the Government's intention may be clear, this approach to the interpretation of Group 1 raises questions about the scope of matters devolved by other subject groups. For example, does the inclusion of social welfare in Group 2, local government in Group 5, and fire services in Group 16 give to the Assembly power to legislate regarding the professional qualifications of (respectively) social workers, local government officers and fire officers?

Important exclusions from devolved health matters are made in Sched. 10, Pt. II: see para. 1 (control of drugs, medicinal products, biological substances and food) and para. 3 (universities). The exclusion of universities does not, however, apply to education for careers in health where this takes place outside the universities.

In Sched. 10, Pt. III, certain matters dealt with by the following Acts are devolved: Anatomy Acts 1832 and 1871 (use of bodies for medical teaching); Nurses (Scotland) Act 1951, Pt. III (control of nursing agencies); Human Tissue Act 1961 (use of parts of bodies for transplants or for medical education and research); National Health Service (Scotland) Act 1972, s. 55 (aid to overseas countries). Other entries in

Sched. 10, Pt. III exclude from devolution matters dealt with by the following Acts: National Health Service (Scotland) Act 1947, Sched. 3, para. 6 (interest rates regarding compensation for hospital property); Mental Health (Scotland) Act 1960, s. 2 (4) (power to recommend to the Crown appointments to the Mental Welfare Commission); Science and Technology Act 1965 (the Research Councils); Abortion Act 1967; Health and Safety at Work, etc. Act 1974 (occupational health).

On matters relating to the terms and conditions of service of N.H.S. staff, see also s. 23 and Sched. 4, s. 43 and Sched. 8 (and notes thereon).

Group 2 (*Social welfare*)

" Social welfare " is not defined but seems broad enough to cover the services provided by social work authorities under the Social Work (Scotland) Act 1968; they include probation and after-care of offenders; care of old people, the disabled, those suffering from alcoholism and drugs; urban and related personal services such as residential and day care, and social care work. Child care, protection and adoption are also within the group.

Social security and war pensions are not however devolved (Sched. 10, Pt. II, para. 2). Social security for this purpose must include benefits under the Supplementary Benefits Act 1976 as well as benefits paid under the Social Security Act 1975. Also excluded is the control of occupational pensions (Sched. 10, Pt. III, entries for Social Security Act 1973 and Social Security Pensions Act 1975). For other exclusions, see the entries in Sched. 10, Pt. III for the Disabled Persons (Employment) Acts 1944 and 1954, Chronically Sick and Disabled Persons Act 1970 (ss. 9, 21, 23) and Inner Urban Areas Act 1978.

Group 3 (*Education, etc.*)

The scope of this group is wide. As with health, power to legislate is devolved in respect of both the public (Education (Scotland) Acts 1939–76) and private sectors of education. " Education " means education at all levels, including tertiary education, but not university education and career guidance (see Sched. 10, Pt. II, para. 3; career guidance is excluded from devolution because of its close link with employment, which is not devolved). Ancillary matters are also devolved by implication, *e.g.* school transport, school clothing and educational endowments (other than university endowments).

" Recreative activities " are defined to include any form of sport (s. 81 (1)). On cultural and recreative activities, *cf.* the meaning given to " further education " in Education (Scotland) Act 1962, s. 4.

Although " universities, university staff and grants to universities " are excluded from devolution (Sched. 10, Pt. II, para. 3) payments to universities by education authorities are not affected by this exclusion (s. 81 (1)).

Relevant exclusions in Sched. 10, Pt. III include: National Library of Scotland Act 1925 (Secretary of State's power to recommend appointment of Board of Trustees); Education (Scotland) Act 1962 (specified matters, including provisions relating to the Carnegie Trust, by which is meant the Carnegie Trust for the Universities of Scotland: Education (Scotland) Act 1962, s. 135 (1) (*a*), and power to recommend appointment of school inspectors); Science and Technology Act 1965 (Research Councils); British Library Act 1972 (constitution and powers of British Library Board).

By Sched. 11, Group B, the Scottish Executive will have power to pay grants to universities, though universities are excluded from the devolution of legislative powers and the main source of university revenue will continue to be the University Grants Committee. For s. 75 (*b*) of the Education (Scotland) Act 1962, see Education (Scotland) Act 1969, s. 12.

Group 4 (*Housing*)

This group comprises the matters presently covered by the Housing (Scotland) Acts 1966 to 1977 and the Rent (Scotland) Acts 1971 to 1974. These include the provision of housing accommodation in the public and private sectors; the regulation of rents; rent allowances, rent rebates and subsidies to local authorities and housing associations; the Scottish Special Housing Association; housing standards and slum clearance. Power to legislate on caravans and mobile homes is also devolved.

The Housing Corporation may continue to exercise functions in Scotland but the Assembly may legislate in respect of its Scottish activities (subject to the restrictions concerning borrowing powers contained in Sched. 2, para. 3). The Assembly will have power to terminate the Housing Corporation's functions in Scotland; should it do so, the Assembly would be unable to dispose of the Housing Corporation's Scottish property (Sched. 2, para. 6) and an order by a U.K. Minister would be necessary providing for the transfer of the property (s. 72 (2)). The Housing Corporation is listed in Sched. 13, and therefore could be the subject of an order made under s. 69 by a U.K. Minister transferring its activities to the Scottish administration; such an order could include provision for apportioning the assets and liabilities of the Corporation and for requiring it to account to the Assembly in respect of its Scottish activities. The Housing Corporation is the sole body in Pt. I of Sched. 13; this means, *inter alia*, that the Scottish Assembly will be able to legislate about the Housing Corporation even before an order under s. 69 is made (Sched. 2, para. 5).

An important exclusion from the devolution of housing is made in Sched. 10, Pt. II, para. 4, namely provision by private financial institutions of finance for housing. Thus the Assembly will not be able to legislate regarding building societies. Plainly, the private financing of housing has important implications for national economic management and tax policy. For this reason, Sched. 10, Pt. III excludes from devolved matters the Housing Act 1964, s. 8 (building society loans to housing societies), and the Housing Subsidies Act 1967, Pt. II (option mortgage subsidy).

Also excluded from legislative devolution by Sched. 10, Pt. III, is the Housing (Financial Provisions) (Scotland) Act 1968, s. 50 (guarantees by local authorities in respect of loans by building societies; and see the restrictions on the Assembly imposed by Sched. 2, para. 3 (1)). But by Sched. 11, Group C, executive power to approve guarantees by local authorities under s. 50 of the 1968 Act is granted to the Scottish Executive. Also in Sched. 10, Pt. III, the entries for the Housing (Scotland) Acts of 1966 (s. 25), 1969 (s. 21) and 1974 (s. 30) exclude power to legislate regarding special compensation for well-maintained houses that are acquired under Housing Act powers. But power in respect of the erection of fishermen's dwellings in congested districts is devolved (Congested Districts (Scotland) Act 1897, s. 4 (1) (*e*)).

According to the Scotland and Wales Bill, 1976–77, the power to provide for rent rebates and rent allowances was devolved but had to be exercised in accordance with model schemes made by the Secretary of State (cls. 52–54). Although rent schemes could directly affect the U.K. Government's responsibility for income maintenance, and especially the supplementary benefits scheme, the Government decided that it was not necessary to retain this specific control in the Scotland Bill.

Group 5 (Local government and local finance)

This group entrusts the Assembly with legislative competence regarding the general structure and organisation of local government, as opposed to the specific services provided by local councils (*e.g.* education, housing, social work). The provision for local government in the Act would have been much simpler had not the Government decided that the Secretary of State for Scotland must retain responsibility for the supervision of several local government functions, namely those described in the Act as " scheduled functions " and listed in Sched. 15 (and see Sched. 10, Pt. II, para. 5). These " scheduled functions " range in importance from police and electoral registration to rodent control and protection of birds. In respect of " scheduled functions," the Secretary of State will exercise the powers of central government over the local authority. In respect of other local functions the Scottish Executive will exercise the relevant central tasks of supervision and control. Accordingly the entry for the Local Government (Scotland) Act 1973 in Sched. 10, Pt. III has to distinguish between central government powers in relation to " scheduled functions," which are not devolved, and the same powers in respect of other functions of local government, which are devolved. Assuming that it is within the legislative competence of the Assembly to reorganise the pattern of local government, this would be a most elaborate operation requiring the closest co-operation between the Scottish administration and the U.K. Government. But, by relying upon Sched. 2, para. 8, the Assembly could impinge upon the area of " scheduled functions " where this was necessary to make consequential adjustments to the administration of those functions.

The general words in the first sentence of Group 5 are broad enough to include the formation and pattern of local government areas, the constitution of local authorities, the meetings and internal organisation of local authorities (*e.g.* committees) and such general powers as the power to acquire land by agreement and the power to provide offices (Local Government (Scotland) Act 1973, ss. 70 and 79). But several exceptions and reservations are made. In addition to protection for the status of the Orkney and Shetland councils (s. 41), the entry for the Local Government (Scotland) Act 1973 in Sched. 10, Pt. III by para. (*a*) excludes entirely from the legislative competence of the Assembly a variety of matters; these include electoral arrangements for local councils, the initial review of local government boundaries authorised by s. 20 of the 1973 Act, qualifications and disqualifications of councillors, and the duty of local authorities to retain certain documents for inspection by the public. As explained above, paras. (*b*)–(*f*) of the same entry exclude from devolution various powers of central government so far as they are exercisable in respect of " scheduled functions."

" Investigation of maladministration " refers to the Commissioner for Local Administration in Scotland, set up by the Local Government (Scotland) Act 1975, Pt. II.

Financial matters within Group 5 are defined broadly. They include the regulation and control of local authority expenditure in respect of devolved functions, the calculation, assessment and payment of the rate support grant, control of the revenues of local authorities obtained from performing devolved services, accounting and audit of local finances, and the administration of the rating and valuation system. The financing of " scheduled functions " (see Sched. 15) is excluded, except that account may be taken of them in the calculation of the rate support grant to the extent and by the procedure indicated in s. 68 (2). Specific grants in respect of " scheduled functions " are excluded from devolution (Sched. 10, Pt. II, para. 5). The powers of the Scottish Executive in respect of capital expenditure and borrowing are restricted by Sched. 2, para. 3 (1), by s. 23 (1) (*b*) and by s. 52 (1). By Sched. 2, para. 4, the Assembly's legislative competence in respect of the rating system is limited. In Sched. 10, Pt. III, the entry for the Valuation and Rating (Exempted Classes) (Scotland) Act 1976 excludes from devolution the power to exempt from valuation lands and heritages lying on, over or under the sea bed.

Group 6 (*Land use and development*)

The broad devolution of town planning and other matters relating to use and development of land made by this group is considerably limited by other provisions in the Act. S. 71 and Sched. 14 provide for intervention in planning matters by the Secretary of State when he considers this desirable in the public interest. The devolution of powers regarding industrial sites is qualified by s. 42 (1) (*c*) and Sched. 7, by which the Secretary of State may issue guidelines to the Scottish Executive regarding disposal of such sites.

In Sched. 10, Pt. III, the entry for the Town and Country Planning (Scotland) Act 1972, ss. 64–70, excludes the issuing of industrial development certificates from devolution. Powers under the same Act are also reserved in respect of certain interests of " excepted statutory undertakers " (as defined in s. 81 (1) of the present Act). Power to appoint a Planning Inquiry Commission under the 1972 Act is devolved but subject to reservations protecting British interests (Sched. 10, Pt. III).

By Sched. 10, Pt. II, para. 6, compensation for the compulsory purchase of land and for depreciation to land caused by the exercise of statutory powers is excluded from legislative devolution. Similarly in Sched. 10, Pt. III, the entries for the Acquisition of Land (Authorisation Procedure) (Scotland) Act 1947, the Town and Country Planning (Scotland) Act 1972, ss. 277–8, and the Community Land Act 1975 exclude from devolution the power to legislate on such matters as the procedure for the compulsory purchase of land and the community land scheme.

The exclusion of legislative competence on these matters is offset by Sched. 11, Group E, which confers power on the Scottish Executive to administer matters contained in these statutes and in related legislation. The entry for the Community Land Act 1975 is however subject to the matters reserved in the entry for Group E on which the Government intend a uniform policy to be applied throughout Great Britain, *e.g.* s. 7 of the 1975 Act (power to fix the second appointed day, from which date the basis for compensation will change from market to current use value).

Power to guarantee loans made to new town development corporations is reserved to the Treasury (entry in Sched. 10, Pt. III for the New Towns (Scotland) Act 1968; and see Sched. 2, para. 3).

In Sched. 4, several entries qualify the exercise of executive powers under planning and other land use legislation, to protect the interests of " excepted statutory undertakers " (defined in s. 81 (1)) and of local authorities in respect of their " scheduled functions " (Sched. 15) : see in particular the last entry in Sched. 4 which provides in effect that the confirmation of orders for the compulsory purchase of land in the circumstances specified requires the consent of a U.K. Minister.

Relevant entries in Sched. 16 include those for the New Towns Act 1965, the New Towns (Scotland) Act 1968 and the Town and Country Planning (Scotland) Act 1972.

Building control, included in Group 6, is already the subject of separate legislation for Scotland (Building (Scotland) Acts 1959 and 1970; Health and Safety at Work, etc. Act 1974, s. 75). This control relates to the structure of buildings in the interests of health and safety, particularly when buildings are under construction, repair or demolition, but extends to aspects of building operations such as the deposit of building materials on streets. In Sched. 10, Pt. III, the entry for the Building (Scotland) Act 1959, s. 26 excludes from control by the Scottish Executive Crown buildings held for purposes which are not devolved.

The inclusion in Group 6 of industrial sites and improvement of derelict land brings the environmental and factory building functions of the Scottish Development Agency within the legislative competence of the Assembly (see s. 42 (1) and note thereon). The entry in Sched. 10, Pt. III for the Scottish Development Agency Act 1975 specifies the provisions of the Act which relate to these functions. The entry in Sched. 11, Group E, para. 9 sets out powers relating to the Agency's industrial investment programme which are to be within the administrative competence of the Scottish Executive, subject to guidelines issued under s. 42. See also Sched. 16, para. 51.

Group 7 (Pollution)

This succinctly phrased subject, read in conjunction with more detailed provisions of the Act, seems to bring within the legislative competence of the Assembly such matters as: (a) sewerage, sewage treatment and disposal; (b) pollution of water; (c) collection and disposal of waste and abandoned vehicles; (d) control of public health nuisances, including offensive trades; (e) environmental noise; (f) air pollution. But, while pollution may always have a local incidence, some forms of pollution may only be controlled effectively by national or international action. Accordingly Group 7 has to be read subject to Sched. 10, Pt. II, para. 7, which excludes from devolution certain forms of pollution.

Several relevant entries in Sched. 10, Pt. III exclude from devolution matters governed by existing legislation. Certain effects of these exclusions may be briefly noted, the relevant statute being stated in parenthesis. The Assembly will not have power to regulate the importation or use of injurious substances, *e.g.* sulphur in oil fuel and lead in petrol (Control of Pollution Act 1974, ss. 75–77, 100) nor to regulate the discharge of oil at sea, but it will have limited powers in respect of discharges from land in Scotland or into adjacent waters (Prevention of Oil Pollution Act 1971, s. 23 (*b*) for which see Petroleum and Submarine Pipe-lines Act 1975, s. 45 (2)). The Assembly will not have power to extend the present limits of waters for the control of pollution (Rivers (Prevention of Pollution) (Scotland) Acts 1951 and 1965; Control of Pollution Act 1974, s. 56 (1)). The Assembly will have no powers over aspects of waste disposal closely related to the production of energy, *e.g.* control of waste storage and disposal from nuclear sites and electricity generating stations (Radioactive Substances Act 1948 and 1960; Nuclear Installations Act 1965) and production by local authorities of heat or electricity from waste (Control of Pollution Act 1974, s. 21); but the Assembly will have power to control storage and use of radioactive substances for purposes not otherwise excluded. Control of industrial emissions is not devolved to the Assembly (Health and Safety at Work, etc. Act 1974, s. 5).

In Sched. 11, however, Group F (Pollution, etc.) confers on the Scottish Executive administrative powers on certain matters outside the competence of the Assembly. This has the effect (*inter alia*) of transferring to the Executive ministerial powers for the control of industrial emissions into the air under the Alkali etc. Works Regulation Act 1906 and the Health and Safety at Work, etc. Act 1974. Thus in Scotland the Health and Safety Executive will become responsible to the Scottish Executive for its industrial emission enforcement functions. By Sched. 16, paras. 44–47, consequential amendments are made to the Health and Safety at Work, etc. Act 1974.

Group 8 (Erosion and flooding)

For present legislation, see the Coast Protection Act 1949 and the Land Drainage (Scotland) Act 1958. The entry for the former Act in Sched. 10, Pt. III, makes certain reservations from the general devolution of coast protection matters. It is unclear whether the scope of Group 8 extends to erosion by wind.

Group 9 (Countryside)

The general words used have the effect of vesting in the Assembly legislative competence regarding such matters as the designation of country parks, access to the countryside and long-distance footpaths. The functions of the Countryside Commission for Scotland (established by the Countryside (Scotland) Act 1967, s. 1) seem to be wholly included within the group. The word "countryside" used in Group 9 does not seem to be limited to the countryside areas designated under s. 2 of the 1967 Act. By an entry in Sched. 10, Pt. III, however, the matters dealt with in the Nature Conservancy Act 1973 are wholly excluded from the legislative competence of the Assembly. Thus the Nature Conservancy Council, whose functions under the 1973 Act, s. 1, have a more scientific emphasis than those of the Countryside Commission, will remain responsible to the U.K. Government. Sched. 16, para. 43, extends the functions of the Nature Conservancy Council to include advice to the Scottish administration relating to "the conservation of features of geological or physiographical interest and of flora and fauna."

In Sched. 10, Pt. III, the entry for the National Parks and Access to the Countryside Act 1949 devolves responsibility for the nature conservation activities of local authorities in Scotland; the entry for the Countryside (Scotland) Act 1967 excludes powers in relation to certain Crown land, and the Forestry Commissioners.

Group 10 *(Transport)*

If read with Sched. 10, Pt. II, paras. 8 and 9, which exclude matters that would otherwise fall within Group 10, this devolves to the Assembly:

(a) provision of public passenger transport services by road, underground railway, inland water and sea transport between places in Scotland;

(b) provision of freight transport services by road in Scotland by the Scottish Transport Group (or any body replacing it);

(c) payment of subsidies to operators of all forms of public passenger transport services in Scotland (including British Railways);

(d) payment of subsidies for road freight services to the Scottish Transport Group (or any body replacing it);

(e) payment of subsidies to operators of air freight services to or from places in the Highlands and Islands;

(f) ancillary powers related to activities of the Scottish Transport Group, *e.g.* the Group's hotel interests; and other aspects of sea transport services (see Highlands and Islands Shipping Services Act 1960);

(g) powers in respect of aerodromes, other than regulatory powers of the Civil Aviation Authority and anti-terrorist protection (see note on aerodromes below).

Relevant entries in Sched. 10, Pt. III include those for Road Traffic Act 1960; Transport Acts 1962, 1968 and 1978; Policing of Airports Act 1974; Railways Act 1974, s. 8 (grants for local purposes to assist provision of facilities for freight haulage by rail); Passenger Vehicles (Experimental Areas) Act 1977; and Minibus Act 1977.

Regarding the Road Traffic Act 1960, road service licensing by the traffic commissioners in respect of routes, fares and frequency of bus services within Scotland is devolved; but public service vehicle licensing and licensing for freight services are not devolved. Because of his responsibility for the latter matters, appointment of the chairman of the traffic commissioners is not devolved. The reference to the Transport Act 1968, s. 26 (1) (a), devolves to the Assembly and Executive power in relation to cross-border bus services. The entry in Sched. 5 for the Transport Act 1968, s. 57, will enable ministerial powers concerning research and development of transport services to be exercised both by a Secretary of State and a Scottish Secretary. See also entries for the Transport Act 1968 in Sched. 4.

For the devolution of inland waterways, see Group 15.

Aerodromes. While the Act makes general provision for devolving responsibility for aerodromes to the Scottish Assembly and Executive, the Act will at first take effect only in respect of aerodromes which are owned privately or by local authorities. Since the British Airports Authority and the Civil Aviation Authority are listed in Sched. 13, Pt. II, it will be necessary for an order under s. 69 to be made by a U.K. Minister (after consultation with the body concerned and on the request of a Scottish Secretary) before legislative powers in respect of their aerodromes will be devolved (Sched. 2, para. 5); the necessary transfers of property will require an order under s. 72 (2) (Sched. 2, para. 6).

The entries in Sched. 10, Pt. III for the Civil Aviation Acts 1949, 1968, 1971 and 1978 govern in detail the powers devolved in respect of aerodromes. The entry for the Airports Authority Act 1975, s. 7, excludes from devolution the power of the Treasury to guarantee loans made to the British Airports Authority (and see Sched. 2, para. 3).

Group 11 (*Roads, etc.*)

This group is phrased in broad terms to devolve existing central government responsibility for trunk roads (including motorways) as well as existing local authority functions in relation to roads and bridges. Note that the emphasis in Group 11 is on the physical provision of the roads, bridges and related features (*e.g.* street lighting and cattle grids), not on the regulation of the traffic or vehicles which may use the roads or bridges: matters dealt with by road traffic legislation are mostly not within the legislative competence of the Assembly (*e.g.* see entries in Sched. 10, Pt. III for Road Traffic Acts 1960 and 1972), but certain powers under road traffic legislation are to be within the administrative competence of the Scottish Executive (see Sched. 11, Group G).

The entries in Sched. 10, Pt. III for the Development and Road Improvement Funds Act 1909 and the Roads (Scotland) Act 1970 do not materially affect the wide terms of Group 11. The entry in Sched. 4 for the Roads (Scotland) Act 1970, s. 28 (2) means that the power to make regulations governing the use of appliances or vehicles on footpaths may be exercised only with the consent of a U.K. Minister where the regulation might affect the vehicles or appliances of " excepted statutory undertakers " (defined in s. 81 (1)).

Group 12 (*Marine works*)

This group devolves to the Assembly powers in respect of harbours and boatslips principally used or required for the fishing or agricultural industries or for maintaining communications between places in Scotland; and also the power to provide financial assistance to other harbours where this will be for the benefit of the fishing industry. Thus no powers are devolved in respect of harbours principally used in connection with other industries such as North Sea oil. The terms of Group 12 could give rise to difficult questions regarding the main use being made of a particular harbour at any one time. But the scope for uncertainty is materially reduced by Sched. 10, Pt. II, para. 10 which, except in respect of financial assistance for works to benefit the fishing industry, excludes from the scope of Group 12 the harbours, ferries and boatslips owned by various public bodies (not including the Scottish Transport Group). See also Sched. 16, para. 17, which amends the Harbours Act 1964, s. 57 (1) by providing a new definition of " marine works " for the purposes of that Act: the effect is to enable harbours or boatslips which meet specified criteria to be designed as " marine works " by a Scottish Secretary, acting with the concurrence of the Secretary of State.

See also the entries in Sched. 10, Pt. III for Harbours, Docks and Piers Clauses Act 1847, Harbours, Piers and Ferries (Scotland) Act 1937 and Dock Work Regulation Act 1976.

Group 13 (*Agricultural land*)

Agriculture itself is not devolved and such matters as agricultural prices, subsidies, marketing and animal health will continue to be dealt with by the U.K. Government, in conformity with EEC policies (see Sched. 10, Pt. II, paras. 11 and 12). Group 13 devolves matters relating to the tenure and management of agricultural land. Existing legislation includes the Agricultural Holdings (Scotland) Act 1949 (which governs agricultural leases), the Small Landholders (Scotland) Acts 1886 to 1931 and the Land Settlement (Scotland) Act 1919 (which deal with acquisition of land for settlement, its management and disposal) and also, in the crofting countries, the Congested Districts (Scotland) Act 1897, the Crofters (Scotland) Acts 1955 and 1961 and the Crofting Reform (Scotland) Act 1976. The position of subsidies in respect of agricultural land was altered during the Bill's passage through the House of Lords. The Bill originally excluded all grants and subsidies in relation to agricultural land but Group 13 was amended to include a variety of grants, loans and subsidies paid to landholders and also to crofters (*Hansard*, H.L. Vol. 393, cols. 110–114 (June 12, 1978)). The expression " persons of substantially the same economic status " is derived from Crofters (Scotland) Act 1955, s. 31 (2) (*c*) and Crofters (Scotland) Act 1961, s. 14 (1) (*a*).

Relevant entries in Sched. 10, Pt. III include those for the Hill Farming Act 1946 (including within devolved matters the regulation of muirburn and the valuation of sheep stocks) the Agriculture (Scotland) Act 1948 (excluding from devolved matters the acquisition and management of land for agricultural research), the Agricultural Holdings (Scotland) Act 1949, the Weeds Act 1959 (devolving the control of injurious weeds) and the Agriculture Act 1967 (devolving the power to establish rural development boards).

In Sched. 5, the inclusion of the Agriculture Act 1947, s. 78, means that both the Scottish Executive and the U.K. Government will have power to obtain statistical information relevant to their respective agricultural functions.

Group 14 (*Fisheries*)

This group devolves legislative competence in respect of salmon, migratory trout (on which, see *Hansard*, H.L. Vol. 393, cols. 114–5 (June 12, 1978)) and fresh water fisheries, within geographical limits which resemble those within which by Scots law salmon fishing rights are recognised as a private heritable right of property and follow present limits of the district boards for salmon fishing set up under the Salmon Fisheries (Scotland) Acts 1828–1868. Fisheries beyond these limits have international and EEC implications and are not devolved. The power to fix estuarial limits is not devolved (Sched. 10, Pt. III, entry for Salmon Fisheries (Scotland) Act 1863, s. 4). In the case of the Tweed Estuary, the estuarial limit is fixed at five miles (*Hansard*, H.L. Vol. 393, cols. 115–6 (June 12, 1978)). Note that the matters devolved in Group 14 are governed by the terms " protection, improvement and maintenance."

See also in Sched. 5 the entry for Salmon and Freshwater Fisheries (Protection) (Scotland) Act 1951, s. 15, which, in relation to devolved fisheries matters, confers concurrent powers of research on the Scottish Executive.

Group 15 (*Water, etc.*)

The broad terms of this group devolved legislative competence in respect of all matters relating to the supply of water, the safety of reservoirs, and inland waterways. These include the conservation, protection and development of water resources; abstraction and supply of water; functions of water authorities; financing of water supply services (on which see the Water Act 1973).

The main statutes dealing with inland waterways are the Transport Acts 1962 and 1968, under which the British Waterways Board is responsible for inland waterways to the Secretary of State. Relevant provisions of those Acts are included in devolved matters by the entries in Sched. 10, Pt. III, which exclude from devolution the following powers under the Transport Act 1962: s. 21 (Treasury guarantee of loans); s. 27 (6) (direction in interests of national defence); Sched. 1 (constitution of British Waterways Board). The listing of the Board in Sched. 13 means that before the Assembly can legislate about the Board's affairs (Sched. 2, para. 5) an order under s. 69 will be needed, *e.g.* to transfer powers and duties from the Secretary of State to a Scottish Secretary. Should the Scottish Assembly wish to terminate the Board's activities in Scotland, the Board's Scottish property will have to be dealt with by order of a U.K. Minister under s. 72 (2) (Sched. 2, para. 6).

The National Water Council and the Inland Waterways Amenity Advisory Council are also listed in Sched. 13, Pt. II, with the same effects.

Group 16 (*Fire Services*)

The devolution of fire services includes the matters dealt with in the Fire Services Act 1947–59, the Fire Precautions Act 1971 and the Fire Precautions (Loans) Act 1973. The Crown's power under the Fire Services Act 1947, s. 24 to appoint inspectors of fire services is not devolved since it does not fall within the executive powers transferred by s. 21. The exercise by a Scottish Secretary of powers under s. 26 (firemen's pensions) and s. 36 (terms and conditions of service) of the 1947 Act will be subject to the consent of a U.K. Minister. (See entries for 1947 Act in Sched. 4.)

In Sched. 10, Pt. III, entries for the Fire Precautions Act 1971 and the Fire Precautions (Loans) Act 1973 exclude from devolution the powers of the Treasury to determine rates of interest on loans made by local authorities for expenditure for fire precautions (s. 36 (4)–(6) of the 1971 Act; s. 1 (3) of the 1973 Act) and the application of the 1971 Act to the U.K. Atomic Energy Authority (s. 41). Since matters dealt with in the Health and Safety at Work, etc. Act 1974 are not devolved (see Sched. 10, Pt. III), the power of the Secretary of State to make regulations on fire precautions is excluded from devolution (1974 Act, Sched. 3, para. 12).

The inclusion of the Fire Service College Board in Sched. 13, Pt. II, attracts to the Board the provisions of ss. 69 and 72 (2) and, in Sched. 2, paras. 5 and 6.

Group 17 (*Tourism*)

The development of tourism in Scotland is devolved. This group must be read together with s. 70; with the entry for the Development of Tourism Act 1969 in Sched. 10, Pt. III; and with the amendments to the 1969 Act made by Sched. 16, paras. 29–32. The effect of these provisions is to devolve existing ministerial powers under the 1969 Act in relation to the Scottish Tourist Board and hotels and other establishments in Scotland, and to make consequential amendments to the 1969 Act. The entry for the 1969 Act in Sched. 10, Part III was re-drafted during the Bill's passage through Parliament (*Hansard*, H.L. Vol. 391, cols. 1024–6 (May 10, 1978)).

The amendments made to the 1969 Act by the present Act will, *inter alia*, empower the Scottish Tourist Board to conduct activities outside the U.K. to encourage people to visit Scotland.

Group 18 (*Ancient monuments, etc.*)

This group must be read with the entry in Sched. 10, Pt. III for the Historic Buildings and Ancient Monuments Act 1953. That entry, which excludes s. 7 of the 1953 Act from the legislative competence of the Assembly, preserves the access of the Secretary of State to the National Land Fund, which may be used, *inter alia*, to meet the cost of acquiring historic buildings. The inclusion in Sched. 5 of ss. 4–6 of the same Act of 1953 has the effect of giving the Secretary of State and the Scottish Executive concurrent powers to make grants for the preservation of historic buildings, etc., to such bodies as the National Trust for Scotland.

See also Sched. 11, Group I, which transfers to the Scottish Executive the Secretary of State's responsibility for managing the two Royal Parks (Holyrood Park, Edinburgh and Linlithgow Park and Loch). But the Assembly will require Crown consent to legislate for the Crown property within Sched. 6, para. 3.

As well as powers under the 1953 Act, the general words in Group 18 devolve matters dealt with in other legislation affecting historic buildings, *e.g.* the Town and Country Planning (Scotland) Act 1972, ss. 52–56 (see also Sched. 10, Pt. I, Group 6 and Sched. 14).

Group 19 (*Registration services*)

The existing law is found mainly in the Register of Births, Deaths and Marriages (Scotland) Act 1965 and in the Population (Statistics) Acts 1938 and 1960. In Sched. 10, Pt. II, para. 12 excludes censuses of the population from the legislative competence of the Assembly so that, for this function alone, the Registrar General for Scotland will continue to be responsible to the Secretary of State for Scotland and will be financed by him. In Sched. 10, Pt. III, the entry for the above Act of 1965 confirms that appointment of the Registrar General for Scotland is a matter for the Scottish administration. See also s. 67 (2) (status of Registrar General and his staff).

Group 20 (*Miscellaneous*)

Most matters within this group are at present administered by local authorities under separate Scottish legislation.

" *Charities.*" Neither the jurisdiction of the Charity Commissioners nor registration of charities under the Charities Act 1960 extends to Scotland. Legislation on these matters will be within the competence of the Assembly, as will be the matters dealt with in the House to House Collections Act 1939, but the Assembly will not be able to alter the status of charities in tax law (Sched. 2, para. 4).

" *Public holidays.*" In Scotland, bank holidays are often not observed as public holidays. While the Scottish Executive will have power to designate bank holidays in Scotland (see Sched. 16, paras. 33–4, amending the Banking and Financial Dealings Act 1971) the Assembly will have power to legislate for public holidays, whether local or national.

" *Deer and sale of venison.*" For the present law regarding the conservation, control and killing of deer and for the Red Deer Commission, see the Deer (Scotland) Act 1959 and the Deer (Amendment) Act 1967. For the registration of dealers in venison, see the Sale of Venison (Scotland) Act 1968. In Sched. 10, Pt. II, para. 1, the exclusion of the control of food from devolution materially limits the scope of the powers devolved in respect of venison (see *Hansard*, H.L. Vol. 391, col. 1041 (May 10, 1978)).

" *Local regulation of trades. Provision or control by local authorities of facilities and local activities.*" Since various forms of licensing are mentioned later, this would seem to refer to powers of local authorities (by use of byelaws, registration, etc.) to regulate trades and activities carried on by others, as well as to action by local authorities themselves in providing facilities and undertaking activities. But the Assembly's powers will not extend to the " scheduled functions " of local government (Sched. 15).

" *Parks and open spaces. Markets and fairs.*" For existing law, see Burgh Police

(Scotland) Acts 1892 and 1903, Public Parks (Scotland) Act 1878 and the Markets and Fairs Clauses Act 1847.

" *Lotteries.*" For existing law, see Betting, Gaming and Lotteries Act 1963, Lotteries Act 1975, and Lotteries and Amusements Act 1976 (on which see entry in Sched. 10, Pt. III). The Scotland Bill originally referred to " Betting, gaming and lotteries " but betting and gaming were deleted from the Bill by the House of Lords; *Hansard*, H.L. Vol. 393, cols. 116–136 (June 12, 1978).

" *Liquor licensing. Local licensing.*" For existing law on liquor licensing, and the licensing of theatres, cinemas and places of public entertainment, see Licensing (Scotland) Act 1976, Theatres Act 1968 and Cinematograph Acts 1909 and 1952, and also Local Government (Scotland) Act 1973, Pt. XI. See also the entry for the Licensing (Scotland) Act 1976 in Sched. 10, Pt. III, which excludes from devolution canteens used in connection with non-devolved matters (*e.g.* for the armed forces) and the amendment to the same Act made in Sched. 16, para. 52, in respect of drinking by Assembly members and staff (*cf. R.* v. *Graham-Campbell, ex p. Herbert* [1935] 1 K.B. 594).

" *Shop hours.*" For existing law see Shops Act 1950, Shops (Airports) Act 1962 and Shops (Early Closing Days) Act 1965.

" *Allotments.*" See Allotments (Scotland) Acts 1892 to 1950.

" *Burial and cremation.*" For existing law see Burial Grounds (Scotland) Act 1855, Public Health (Scotland) Act 1897, and Cremation Acts 1902 and 1952.

" *Dogs.*" Police and local authorities have a variety of powers relating to dogs, see, *e.g.* Guard Dogs Act 1975. The powers devolved do not include control over the importation of dogs into the U.K.

Group 21 (*Courts and legal profession, etc.*)

The broad terms of this group must be read with paras. 14–19 of Sched. 10, Pt. II which exclude from the competence of the Assembly important matters that would otherwise be within Group 21. Thus the Assembly's power to legislate for the courts excludes power to abolish the superior courts and the sheriff courts (para. 14), power to legislate in respect of the judges, *e.g.* their appointment, tenure and conditions of service (para. 15), power to alter certain forms of jurisdiction existing at the commencement of the Act (para. 16), power to legislate regarding appeals to the House of Lords (para. 17) and power to legislate regarding the powers of the superior courts to regulate their own procedure (para. 18). Certain courts (mainly those with jurisdiction in non-devolved areas) are stated by para. 19 to be outside the competence of the Assembly. Even though the Assembly would not wish to take some of the more extreme measures denied it, such as abolishing the Court of Session, some of the restraints (*e.g.* in paras. 16 and 18) could exclude certain forms of law reform by the Assembly (*e.g.* relating to jurisdiction and procedure) that might be desirable. Divorce jurisdiction, for example, could be entrusted to the Sheriff Court but could not be taken from the Court of Session (*Hansard*, H.L. Vol. 391, col. 428 (May 4, 1978)).

Nonetheless substantial powers are devolved by Group 21 concerning such matters as the use of juries, contempt of court and justices of the peace. District courts are fully within the competence of the Assembly. So too is the legal profession, except that the exclusion of matters relating to the appointment of judges might prevent the Assembly having power to make radical changes in the Faculty of Advocates. While the Assembly will have power to legislate for the solicitors' branch of the profession, it will have no power to legislate on matters concerning the universities (Sched. 10, Pt. II, para. 3).

For an account of the application of the Act to the Secretary of State's existing powers under the Sheriff Courts (Scotland) Act 1971, see Lord McCluskey, Solicitor-General for Scotland, *Hansard*, H.L. Vol. 391, cols. 937–9 (May 9, 1978). The servicing of the courts by the Scottish Courts Administration will be amongst the matters devolved but, by an agency agreement under s. 35, the Secretary of State could continue to use that administration for the performance of functions regarding the courts and judges which are not devolved (*Hansard*, H.L. Vol. 391, col. 940 (May 9, 1978)).

" *Legal aid, advice and assistance.*" For existing law, see Legal Aid and Advice (Scotland) Acts 1967 and 1972. By Sched. 16, para. 26, the Legal Aid (Scotland) Act 1967, s. 4 (6) is amended to transfer from the Supplementary Benefits Commission to a Scottish Secretary the power to assess the disposable income and capital of an applicant for legal aid and the amount of his own contribution. But an agency agreement under s. 35 would enable the Commission to continue to administer these matters.

Group 22 (Tribunals and inquiries)

This group confers legislative competence on the Assembly regarding tribunals and inquiries so far as they are related to other devolved matters. The Lands Tribunal for Scotland is mentioned expressly because its present jurisdiction is not confined to devolved matters. This group must be read with the entry in Sched. 10, Pt. III for the Tribunal and Inquiries Act 1971, which excludes some matters from the Assembly's competence, namely those relating to the composition, status and jurisdiction of the Council on Tribunals and its Scottish Committee, which will continue to be appointed by, and report to, the Lord Chancellor and the Lord Advocate; other matters under the 1971 Act are devolved so far as they relate to devolved matters. The Annual Report of the Council on Tribunals for 1976–77 (H.C. 108, 1977–78) lists the tribunals under the supervision of the Council and its Scottish Committee in 1977. Some of the tribunals under the supervision of the Scottish Committee relate to devolved matters (*e.g.* Crofters Commission, N.H.S. committees, valuation appeal committees, rent assessment committees, children's hearings) but others do not (*e.g.* industrial tribunals, pensions appeal tribunal, general commissioners of income tax, VAT tribunals).

It seems that the Assembly will be able to create new tribunals in relation to devolved matters (provided it does not take jurisdiction away from the established courts: Sched. 10, Pt. II, para. 16) and that such tribunals could be placed by the Lord Chancellor and Lord Advocate under the supervision of the Council on Tribunals (1971 Act, s. 15 (1)). The Scottish Executive would then become subject to the requirements of the 1971 Act (*e.g.* s. 10). But it is doubtful if the Assembly could without abolishing them remove from the scope of the Tribunals and Inquiries Act 1971 existing tribunals already subject to the Council's powers.

Note the entry for the Council on Tribunals in Sched. 13, which makes necessary a ministerial order under s. 69 before any legislative powers relating to the Council on Tribunals are devolved (Sched. 2, para. 5).

Regarding public inquiries, in some cases the power of the Scottish Executive is limited to administering existing law which the Assembly cannot alter (*e.g.* the procedure for the compulsory purchase of land laid down by the Acquisition of Land (Authorisation Procedure) (Scotland) Act 1947, see Sched. 11, Group E) but in local government generally the Assembly has wider powers (see entry for Local Government (Scotland) Act 1973, s. 210 in Sched. 10, Pt. III).

Group 23 (Public records)

This group confers on the Assembly legislative competence in relation to five types of records: (a) records of the Assembly and Scottish Executive; (b) records of the courts; (c) records of any body (*e.g.* a public board or tribunal) created by the Assembly or whose functions are wholly within the legislative competence of the Assembly; (d) private records; (e) existing records in the custody of the Keeper of the Records of Scotland.

Two qualifications apply to group (e). First, by Sched. 6, para. 7, Crown consent will be required to any Assembly Bill relating to existing records (other than court records and private records) held by the Keeper of the Records when devolution takes effect. Thus the U.K. Government will be able to satisfy itself that any legislative proposals regarding pre-devolution records are acceptable. Second, by Sched. 16, para. 1, the Public Records (Scotland) Act 1937 is amended by the addition of a new power in a U.K. minister to withdraw pre-devolution records (other than court, justice of the peace and private records) from the custody of the Keeper of the Records.

Assuming that the Scottish Record Office will maintain adequate standards of care for the records entrusted to it, the U.K. Government may wish in the future to make an agency arrangement under s. 35, whereby records relating to non-devolved matters of Scottish government could be deposited in the Scottish Record Office.

Group 24 (Civil law matters)

The separate history, traditions and content of Scottish private law form one argument for the devolution of legislative powers. This group indicates those areas of private law on which the Assembly will have legislative competence, but it must be read subject to paras. 20–23 of Sched. 10, Pt. II which specify areas of law (mainly related to commerce, finance, the economy, industry and employment) reserved to the U.K. Parliament. The reservations made in Pt. II mean, for example, that many areas of the law of " natural and juristic persons and unincorporated bodies " will be outside the competence of the Assembly, *e.g.* registered companies (since these are " corporate bodies other than public bodies related to devolved matters "), trade unions and employers' associations. But the Assembly will be able to legislate on the law of husband and wife. Similarly, many aspects of the law of contractual obligations are reserved from devolution, *e.g.* insurance, banking, employment.

Moreover, other exclusions from Group 24 are made by entries in Sched. 10, Pt. III, which include the following: Registration of Business Names Act 1916, Prevention of Fraud (Investments) Act 1958, Protection of Depositors Act 1963, Trade Descriptions Act 1968, Employment Agencies Act 1973, Fair Trading Act 1973, Health and Safety at Work, etc. Act 1974, Consumer Credit Act 1974, Friendly Societies Act 1974. Recent anti-inflation legislation is also excluded: Counter-Inflation Act 1973, Prices Act 1974, Prices Act 1975, Remuneration, Charges and Grants Act 1975, Price Commission Act 1977. On some matters (Race Relations Act 1976, Sex Discrimination Act 1975) legislative competence is excluded but some matters relating to discrimination in education are placed within the power of the Scottish Executive (Sched. 11, Groups H and I).

Note however that some of the exclusions made by entries in Sched. 10, Pt. II (notably paras. 21 and 23) are subject to qualifications which permit the Assembly to legislate on certain matters relating to the devolved public sector.

The Scottish Law Commission, whose duties include making proposals for the reform of civil law, is devolved (Sched. 10, Pt. III, entry for Law Commissions Act 1965).

Group 25 (Crime)

This group devolves legislative competence relating to: principles of criminal law; various classes of particular offences; offences related to other devolved matters (so that the Assembly will be able to create new criminal offences when it is exercising its legislative competence on other matters); criminal penalties and treatment of offenders; compensation for victims of crime (so that the Assembly will be able to provide its own form of the criminal injuries compensation scheme); criminal evidence and procedure (including police powers of arrest and search); enforcement of court orders; and criminal research. But all this must be read subject to Sched. 10, Pt. II, paras. 24 and 25, which exclude from devolution any matter relating to the prosecution of offences; any special matter of criminal penalties, evidence or procedure relating to matters not included in Sched. 10, Pt. I (so that the Assembly will not be able to invoke its criminal law competence to amend " special " provisions of legislation on matters that are not devolved, *e.g.* Misuse of Drugs Act 1971, excluded by Sched. 10, Pt. II, para. 1); and deportation and extradition, which have international implications. Moreover, many entries in Sched. 10, Pt. III which exclude from devolution matters dealt with by specific statutes will also bar the Scottish Assembly from legislating on offences under those statutes (*e.g.* Fair Trading Act 1973).

The conferment of legislative competence in the areas of crime specified carries with it the devolution of executive competence: thus the Scottish penal system is devolved by reason of the reference in this group to " treatment of offenders." But responsibility for the police is not devolved (see Sched. 15) and will remain with the Secretary of State.

Criminal research, the last item in Group 25, includes the preparation and analysis of criminal statistics, collection of which is mainly a matter for the police. In Sched. 11, Group K devolves to the Scottish Executive the Secretary of State's power to give directions to the police regarding criminal statistics under the Police (Scotland) Act 1967, s. 47 (1), but an entry in Sched. 4 requires the consent of the Secretary of State before the power may be exercised. In Sched. 5, the entry for the Criminal Justice (Scotland) Act 1949 means that both the Secretary of State and the Scottish Executive will be able to finance criminal research in Scotland.

SCHEDULE 11

MATTERS WITHIN POWERS OF SCOTTISH EXECUTIVE BUT NOT
WITHIN LEGISLATIVE COMPETENCE OF ASSEMBLY

GROUP A (*Abortion*)

The powers under the Abortion Act 1967.

GROUP B (*Grants to universities*)

The powers under section 75 (*b*) of the Education (Scotland) Act 1962 to apply sums for the purpose of the payment of grants to universities and the powers under sections 76 and 144 (5) of that Act so far as relating to section 75 (*b*).

GROUP C (*Local authority guarantees of housing loans*)

The powers to approve guarantees by local authorities under section 50 of the Housing (Financial Provisions) (Scotland) Act 1968 and to undertake to make good up to one half of any loss sustained under the terms of such a guarantee.

GROUP D (*Grants for expenditure due to immigrant population*)

The powers under section 11 of the Local Government (Scotland) Act 1966.

GROUP E (*Land use and development*)

1. The powers under the Acquisition of Land (Authorisation Procedure) (Scotland) Act 1947, in cases where the compulsory purchase order is or would be made or confirmed by a Scottish Secretary, except—
    (*a*) in cases where the apparatus belongs to excepted statutory undertakers, those under section 3 (4); and
    (*b*) those under paragraph 18 of Schedule 1.
2. The powers under the Highlands and Islands Development (Scotland) Acts 1965 and 1968 except—
    (i) the powers to extend the area of the Highlands and Islands Development Board under section 1 of the Act of 1965; and
    (ii) the power under section 10 (4) of the Act of 1965 to authorise the carrying out of works, so far as exercisable in relation to excepted statutory undertakers.
3. The powers under paragraphs 2 and 5 to 7 of Schedule 3 to the Gas Act 1965.
4. The powers under sections 4 and 18 of the New Towns (Scotland) Act 1968 so far as they are not included in the Groups in Schedule 10 to this Act.
5. The powers under Schedules 3 and 4 to that Act.
6. The powers exercisable under section 37 of the Town and Country Planning (Scotland) Act 1972 in relation to sanctions granted by a Scottish Secretary.
7. The powers under section 121 (1) of that Act, so far as exercisable in relation to matters with respect to which a Scottish Secretary exercises functions.
8. The power under section 240 of that Act.
9. The following powers under the Scottish Development Agency Act 1975:—
    (i) the powers under section 1;
    (ii) the powers under section 2 (6) so far as exercisable in relation to the functions specified in section 2 (2) (*c*);
    (iii) the powers under section 2 (7) so far as exercisable in relation to the functions specified in section 2 (2) (*a*) to (*c*);
    (iv) the powers under section 4 so far as exercisable in relation to the functions specified in section 2 (2) (*a*) to (*c*);
    (v) the powers under section 4 so far as exercisable in relation to the powers specified in subsection (4) (*a*) to (*f*) of section 2 but so far only as that section relates to the functions in subsection (2) (*a*) to (*c*) of section 2;
    (vi) the powers under section 4 so far as exercisable in relation to the powers specified in section 3 but so far only as that section relates to the functions in section 2 (2) (*a*) to (*c*);
    (vii) the powers under section 12 so far as exercisable in relation to the functions specified in section 2 (2) (*a*) to (*c*) and (*f*);
    (viii) the powers under section 14;
    (ix) the power under section 19 so far as exercisable in relation to the functions specified in section 2 (2) (*c*);
    (x) the powers under Schedule 1;
    (xi) the powers under Schedule 2, except paragraph 6, so far as exercisable in relation to the functions specified in section 2 (2) (*a*) to (*c*) and (*f*).
10. The powers exercisable under the Community Land Act 1975 except—
    (i) the powers under section 3;
    (ii) the powers under section 5 (1) (*c*) and (4) (*b*), and the powers under section 5 (3) and (5) so far as exercisable in relation to excepted statutory undertakers;

(iii) the powers under section 7 and the power to vary or revoke any order made by the Secretary of State under section 18;

(iv) the powers to make, or consent to the making of, orders under section 26 (3);

(v) the powers under section 37;

(vi) the powers under section 39, save in so far as they are exercisable in relation to land vested in the First Secretary or held for the purposes of a Scottish Secretary;

(vii) the powers under section 40, save in so far as they are exercisable in relation to the acquisition from the First Secretary of any interest in land;

(viii) the powers under sections 43 and 44 (except section 44 (4));

(ix) the powers exercisable under paragraph 19 of Schedule 4 in relation to the apparatus of excepted statutory undertakers;

(x) the power under paragraph 21 (6) (*b*) of Schedule 4 to authorise works on land held by excepted statutory undertakers.

11. The following powers under the Inner Urban Areas Act 1978:—

(*a*) the powers under sections 1, 7 (1), 8 (1) and 9 (6) and paragraph 2 of the Schedule;

(*b*) the powers under section 3 (2), as applied to loans under section 5.

GROUP F (*Pollution etc.*)

1. The powers exercisable under the Alkali etc. Works Regulations Act 1906.

2. The power under section 1 (1) (*d*) of the Health and Safety at Work etc. Act 1974 to prescribe classes of premises, except so far as exercisable in relation to motor vehicles, aircraft, hovercraft or vessels.

3. The powers under sections 3 (3), 5, 11, 12, 14 (1) to (6), 15, 16, 18 (2), 20 (3), 27 (1), 44, 45, 50 and 80 of that Act so far as exercisable in relation to the control of emissions into the atmosphere of noxious or offensive substances otherwise than from motor vehicles, aircraft or hovercraft.

4. So far as they relate to vessels other than those in inland waters, the powers under:—

(*a*) sections 32 (1) to (3) and 36 (1) of the Public Health (Scotland) Act 1897;

(*b*) sections 6, 8, 146 (1), 148, 149 and 178 of that Act (so far as they relate to sections 16 to 27, 29 to 32 and 36 of that Act);

(*c*) section 1 (2) of the Clean Air Act 1956; and

(*d*) the Control of Pollution Act 1974 (other than those under sections 30 (5), 75 to 77 and 100 to 103).

GROUP G (*Road traffic*)

1. The power under section 13 of the Road Traffic Regulation Act 1967 to make regulations with respect to the use of particular special roads.

2. The power under section 23 of that Act to make regulations with respect to a particular crossing or particular crossings.

3. The power under subsection (2) of section 54 of that Act to authorise the erection or retention of signs which are not of a prescribed type.

4. The power under section 77 of that Act to prohibit, by order, the driving of motor vehicles—

(*a*) on all roads in any area specified in the order, or on any road so specified, at a speed greater than that so specified; or

(*b*) on any road so specified, at a speed less than that so specified.

5. The powers under the other sections of that Act except those in sections 55 (1), 59, 71, 78, 80, 81, 95 to 97, 99, 101, 103 and 104 (1B).

6. The powers under sections 15, 20, 26, 31 (5), 36A (3A), 36B (4), 38 and 39 of the Road Traffic Act 1972.

7. The powers under section 17 of the Road Traffic Act 1974.

GROUP H (*Race discrimination*)

The powers under sections 19 (3) and (5) and 57 (5) of the Race Relations Act 1976 so far as exercisable in relation to establishments falling within paragraphs 6 and 7 of the Table in section 17 of that Act.

GROUP I (*Sex discrimination*)

The powers under—
(*a*) sections 25 (3) and (5), 27 and 66 (5) of, and Schedule 2 to, the Sex Discrimination Act 1975, so far as exercisable in relation to establishments falling within paragraphs 6 and 7 of the Table in section 22 of that Act, and
(*b*) section 79, except so far as exercisable in relation to university endowments or the Carnegie Trust.

GROUP J (*Royal parks*)

The powers exercisable by virtue of section 22 of the Crown Lands Act 1851 and any provision of the Parks Regulation Acts 1872 to 1974.

GROUP K (*Criminal statistics*)

The power of the Secretary of State to give directions under section 47 (1) of the Police (Scotland) Act 1967.

GENERAL NOTE
The effect of this Schedule is accurately described by its title. Notes on the matters covered by the groups in this Schedule may be found above in the notes on the related groups in Sched. 10, Pt. I. As a guide to those notes, the following list of the groups in Sched. 11 indicates in parenthesis the appropriate group in Sched. 10, Pt. I: Group A, abortion (Group 1, health); Group B, grants to universities (Group 3, education); Group C, housing guarantees (Group 4, housing); Group D, grants for immigrant population (Group 5, local government); Group E, land use and development (Group 6, land use); Group F, pollution (Group 7, pollution); Group G, road traffic (Group 11, roads); Group J, royal parks (Group 20, miscellaneous); Group K, criminal statistics (Group 25, crime). Groups H (race discrimination) and I (sex discrimination) do not appear in the above list since they are not related closely to any particular group in Sched. 10, Pt. I. In general, race and sex discrimination are not devolved subjects but the effect of Groups H and I is that certain powers under the Race Relations Act 1976 and the Sex Discrimination Act 1975 relating to public sector educational establishments are devolved to the Scottish Executive; the reference in Group I to s. 79 of the Act of 1975 devolves power to modify educational endowments so as to benefit both sexes.
Note in relation to Group E (land use and development) that matters relevant to the Scottish Development Agency and the Highlands and Islands Development Board are dealt with in the notes on s. 42.
Note that Group G devolves administrative responsibility for certain powers related to road traffic management and regulation, and road safety publicity and training. But most powers related to the regulation of road traffic are not devolved, in the interest of maintaining national uniformity (*e.g.* Highway Code, traffic offences, motorway regulations, national speed limits, road signs, driver and vehicle licensing, vehicle construction).

Section 65

SCHEDULE 12

LEGAL PROCEEDINGS INVOLVING DEVOLUTION ISSUES

PART I

PRELIMINARY

1. In this Schedule "devolution issue" means a question—
    (*a*) whether a Scottish Assembly Act or any provision of a Scottish Assembly Act is within the legislative competence of the Assembly; or
    (*b*) whether a matter with respect to which a Scottish Secretary has purported to exercise or proposes to exercise a power is a devolved matter.
2. A devolution issue shall not be taken to arise in any legal proceedings by

reason only of any contention of a party to the proceedings which appears to the court or tribunal before which the proceedings take place to be frivolous or vexatious.

PART II

PROCEEDINGS IN SCOTLAND

Application of Part II

3. This Part of this Schedule applies with respect to devolution issues in proceedings in Scotland.

Institution of proceedings

4. Without prejudice to any power exercisable apart from this paragraph, proceedings for the determination of a devolution issue may be instituted by the Lord Advocate and defended by any person who, as a Scottish Secretary or assistant to a Scottish Secretary, performs functions corresponding to those performed by a Law Officer of the Crown.

Intimation of devolution issue

5. Where a devolution issue arises in any proceedings before a court or tribunal the court or tribunal shall order intimation of it to be given to the Lord Advocate and to any person who, as a Scottish Secretary or assistant to a Scottish Secretary, performs functions corresponding to those performed by a Law Officer of the Crown (unless the person to whom the intimation would be given is a party to the proceedings).

6. A person to whom intimation is given in pursuance of paragraph 5 above may take part as a party in the proceedings, so far as they relate to a devolution issue.

Reference of devolution issue to higher court

7. Where a devolution issue arises in civil proceedings, other than proceedings before the House of Lords or before any court consisting of three or more judges of the Court of Session, the court or tribunal before which the proceedings take place may refer the issue to the Inner House of the Court of Session.

8. Where a devolution issue arises in criminal proceedings, other than proceedings before any court consisting of three or more judges of the High Court of Justiciary, the court before which the proceedings take place may refer the issue to the High Court of Justiciary.

Appeals from superior courts to Judicial Committee of Privy Council

9. Where a devolution issue has been determined on a reference to the Inner House of the Court of Session under paragraph 7 above, an appeal against the determination shall lie to the Judicial Committee of the Privy Council.

10. Where a devolution issue has been determined by a court of three or more judges of the High Court of Justiciary, whether in the ordinary course of proceedings or on a reference under paragraph 8 above, an appeal against the determination shall lie to the Judicial Committee of the Privy Council, but only with leave of the High Court or, failing such leave, with special leave of the Judicial Committee.

PART III

PROCEEDINGS IN ENGLAND AND WALES

Application of Part III

11. This Part of this Schedule applies with respect to devolution issues in proceedings in England and Wales.

Institution of proceedings

12. Without prejudice to any power exercisable apart from this paragraph, proceedings for the determination of a devolution issue may be instituted by the Attorney General and defended by any person who, as a Scottish Secretary or assistant to a Scottish Secretary, performs functions corresponding to those performed by a Law Officer of the Crown.

Notice of devolution issue

13. Where a devolution issue arises in any proceedings before a court or tribunal, the court or tribunal shall order notice of it to be given to the Attorney General and to any person who, as a Scottish Secretary or assistant to a Scottish Secretary, performs functions corresponding to those performed by a Law Officer of the Crown (unless the person to whom the notice would be given is a party to the proceedings).

14. A person to whom notice is given in pursuance of paragraph 13 above may take part as a party in the proceedings, so far as they relate to a devolution issue.

Reference of devolution issue to Court of Appeal or High Court

15. Where a devolution issue arises in civil proceedings, other than proceedings before the House of Lords or the Court of Appeal, the court or tribunal before which the proceedings take place may refer the issue to the Court of Appeal.

16. Where a devolution issue arises in criminal proceedings, other than proceedings before the House of Lords or the Court of Appeal, the court before which the proceedings take place may refer the issue—

    (*a*) if the proceedings are summary proceedings, to the High Court; and

    (*b*) if they are proceedings on indictment, to the Court of Appeal.

Appeals from superior courts to Judicial Committee of Privy Council

17. Where a devolution issue has been determined on a reference to the High Court or to the Court of Appeal under paragraph 15 or 16 above, an appeal against the determination shall lie to the Judicial Committee of the Privy Council, but only with leave of the High Court or, as the case may be, of the Court of Appeal or, failing such leave, with special leave of the Judicial Committee.

Part IV

Proceedings in Northern Ireland

Application of Part IV

18. This Part of this Schedule applies with respect to devolution issues in proceedings in Northern Ireland.

Institution of proceedings

19. Without prejudice to any power exercisable apart from this paragraph, proceedings for the determination of a devolution issue may be instituted by the Attorney General for Northern Ireland and defended by any person who, as a Scottish Secretary or assistant to a Scottish Secretary, performs functions corresponding to those performed by a Law Officer of the Crown.

Notice of devolution issue

20. Where a devolution issue arises in any proceedings before a court or tribunal, the court or tribunal shall order notice of the issue to be given to the Attorney General for Northern Ireland and to any person who, as a Scottish Secretary or assistant to a Scottish Secretary, performs functions corresponding to those performed by a Law Officer of the Crown (unless the person to whom the notice would be given is a party to the proceedings).

21. A person to whom notice is given in pursuance of paragraph 20 above may take part as a party in the proceedings, so far as they relate to a devolution issue.

Reference of devolution issue to Court of Appeal

22. Where a devolution issue arises in any proceedings, other than proceedings before the Court of Appeal or Court of Criminal Appeal in Northern Ireland,

the court or tribunal before which the proceedings take place may refer the issue to the Court of Appeal in Northern Ireland.

Appeals from Court of Appeal to Judicial Committee of Privy Council

23. Where a devolution issue has been determined on a reference to the Court of Appeal in Northern Ireland under paragraph 22 above, an appeal against the determination shall lie to the Judicial Committee of the Privy Council, but only with leave of the Court of Appeal in Northern Ireland or, failing such leave, with special leave of the Judicial Committee.

PART V

GENERAL

Proceedings in the House of Lords

24. If a devolution issue arises in judicial proceedings in the House of Lords it shall be referred to the Judicial Committee of the Privy Council, unless the House considers it more appropriate, having regard to all the circumstances, that they should determine the issue.

Effect of decision of Judicial Committee on subsequent proceedings

25. A decision of the Judicial Committee of the Privy Council in proceedings under this Schedule shall be binding in all subsequent legal proceedings.

Expenses

26. Where it appears to the court or tribunal before which any proceedings take place that the participation of any person in pursuance of paragraph 6, 14 or 21 above has occasioned any party to the proceedings additional expense, the court or tribunal may take account of it in deciding any question as to costs or expenses and may, whatever the decision on the devolution issue, award the whole or part of the additional expense as costs or, as the case may be, expenses, to that party.

Procedure

27. Her Majesty may by Order in Council make rules for regulating the procedure with respect to proceedings under this Schedule before the Judicial Committee of the Privy Council.

28. Any power to make provision for regulating the procedure before any court or tribunal shall include power to make provision for the purposes of this Schedule including (without prejudice to the generality of the foregoing) provision—

(a) for prescribing the stage in the proceedings at which a devolution issue is to be raised;

(b) for the sisting or staying of proceedings for the purpose of any proceedings under this Schedule; and

(c) for determining the manner in which and the time within which any intimation or notice is to be given.

GENERAL NOTE

Sched. 12 first defines a "devolution issue" and then provides machinery by which such an issue may be decided in each jurisdiction within the U.K. Possibly the most notable aspect of this machinery is the role assigned to the Judicial Committee of the Privy Council (for a suggestion that a new constitutional court be created for this purpose, see Lord Wilberforce, *Hansard*, H.L. Vol. 390, cols. 1087 *et seq.* (April 18, 1978)). Devolution issues will not however reach the Judicial Committee except on an appeal from an appellate court (paras. 9, 10, 17, 23) or on a reference from the House of Lords (para. 24) so that particular devolution issues may be decided by other courts. The rôle here of the Judicial Committee complements its rôle under s. 19 (pre-assent review of Assembly bills), the main difference being that under s. 19 no other courts are involved. All proceedings under Sched. 12 are themselves subject to s. 19 (4), whereby a decision by the Judicial Committee that a provision of an Assembly bill is within the legislative competence of the Assembly " shall be binding in all legal proceedings."

Sched. 12 is confined to machinery and procedure. The substantive law governing the scope of devolved powers is to be found elsewhere in the Act (*e.g.* s. 18 and Sched. 2, ss. 63, 64 and Scheds. 10 and 11). The Act nowhere provides for the legal consequences of a judicial decision that a provision in an Assembly Act is void as being beyond the Assembly's competence (see the Solicitor-General for Scotland, Lord McCluskey, in *Hansard*, H.L. Vol. 391, cols. 1118–1125 (May 10, 1978), citing *Glasgow Corporation* v. *Lord Advocate*, 1959 S.C. 203).

Para. 1. The definition of " devolution issue " falls into two parts : (a) questions as to whether the whole of an Assembly Act or any provision of it is within the competence of the Assembly; (b) questions as to whether an act or proposed act of a Scottish Secretary relates to a devolved matter. If an act of a Scottish Secretary were to be challenged on other grounds (*e.g.* that it was not authorised by an Assembly Act; or that it had been made for improper purposes or in breach of natural justice), this would not raise a devolution issue. If, therefore, facts as in *Malloch* v. *Aberdeen Corporation*, 1974 S.L.T. 253 had arisen after devolution, and subordinate legislation by a Scottish Secretary had been challenged as being outside his powers under the Education (Scotland) Act 1962, this would not in itself have raised a devolution issue. If an Assembly Act were to be challenged on the ground that, although it was within the legislative competence of the Assembly, it had been passed by the Assembly in bad faith or for improper motives, it is uncertain whether this would raise a " devolution issue." But the uncertainty is academic since such a challenge would be unlikely to succeed in view of the principle in other jurisdictions that the good faith of a legislative body may not be reviewed by a court (*U.S.* v. *Constantine* (1935) U.S. 287, 299, and other authorities cited in *Arthur Yates and Co. Pty.* v. *Vegetable Seeds Committee* (1945) 72 C.L.R. 37).

Para. 2. Although para. 1 does not say so expressly, it seems from paras. 2, 5, 13 and 20 that a devolution issue may be raised in legal proceedings before any court or tribunal. Although there is no definition of court or tribunal for this purpose, all courts of civil and criminal jurisdiction are included and probably all the tribunals subject to the Tribunals and Inquiries Act 1971. There may also be other public bodies with judicial or quasi-judicial functions that are tribunals for this purpose, *e.g.* the Criminal Injuries Compensation Board (on which see *R.* v. *Criminal Injuries Compensation Board, ex p. Lain* [1967] 2 Q.B. 864) and certain professional tribunals with statutory powers. It is doubtful whether public inquiries, decisions by Ministers and miscellaneous licensing decisions of local authorities would fall within the notion of a tribunal for this purpose. Art. 177 of the EEC Treaty raises the question of what is a " court or tribunal " in a somewhat similar context; case law of the European Court of Justice might provide guidance in borderline cases under this Schedule.

The effect of this paragraph is that when a party in proceedings before a court or tribunal contends that a devolution issue is raised by the proceedings, the court or tribunal may reject the contention as frivolous or vexatious. Unless it does so, the court or tribunal must give notice of the issue to the appropriate law officer of the Crown (paras. 5, 13, 20).

Para. 3. Most devolution issues are likely to be raised in proceedings in Scotland, since it is mainly in Scotland that Assembly Acts will be enforced. But the Schedule properly provides for the eventuality of a devolution issue being raised in proceedings outside Scotland. It will usually be very easy to decide whether the proceedings before a court or tribunal are in Scotland or elsewhere. But difficult questions might arise in the case of U.K. or British tribunals which have jurisdiction both in Scotland and England and may sometimes hear Scottish cases in England or English cases in Scotland (*e.g.* the National Insurance Commissioners). Possibly the phrase " proceedings in Scotland " requires a geographical test to be applied to the location of the tribunal when a case is heard. A better approach might be to ask whether the Court of Session or the English High Court would have supervisory jurisdiction over the decision of the tribunal.

Para. 4. Although devolution issues may arise in the course of ordinary civil or criminal proceedings, this paragraph authorises the Lord Advocate to institute proceedings in Scotland against the Scottish administration expressly for the purpose of getting a devolution issue decided. Such an action will be raised against the Scottish Secretary or assistant Secretary with " law officer " functions (see s. 20 (6)). The paragraph confers on the Lord Advocate (who will continue to be a Minister in the U.K. Government) the requisite title and interest to sue. Para. 4 does not, however, prevent an action being raised for the same purpose by a private person who qualifies both title and interest in the matter (*cf. MacCormick* v. *Lord Advocate*, 1953 S.C. 396); and devolution issues may also be raised during the course of other litigation. Although para. 4 is primarily intended to give the Lord Advocate title and interest to sue, it would seem also to be implicitly authorising him to raise an action (probably for a declarator) on a devolution issue, even though, but for this statutory authority, the matter in dispute might have seemed too abstract or hypothetical to be the subject of a judicial decision. The court would probably be unable to review the Lord Advocate's decision to raise such an action (*cf.* in English law *Gouriet* v. *Union of Post Office Workers* [1978] A.C. 435 (H.L.) and *Att.-Gen.* v. *Harris* [1961] 1 Q.B. 74), but there might be circumstances in which the court could rule that a particular action was not a competent use of the authority conferred by para. 4.

Para. 4 does not authorise a Scottish Secretary to initiate proceedings for determination of a devolution issue, although in some situations he might wish to do so. Assuming that he could establish title and interest to sue, it might be difficult to find an appropriate defender.

Paras. 5 & 6. The court or tribunal before whom a devolution issue is raised must ensure that both the Lord Advocate and the Scottish Secretary with " law officer " functions are notified of the issue. Where the issue is raised as a defence to criminal proceedings, the Lord Advocate would as prosecutor already be a party. But in civil proceedings between two private parties, both the Lord Advocate and the Scottish Secretary would be notified and thereafter would be able to take part as parties. Once a devolution issue has been raised, further proceedings may need to be stayed or sisted until that issue is resolved (para. 28 (*f*)).

Paras. 7 & 8. Where either paragraph applies, the court or tribunal in question may in the exercise of a judicial discretion refer the devolution issue to the Inner House of the Court of Session, or to the High Court of Justiciary as the case may be. This discretion is similar to that conferred on courts and tribunals by art. 177 of the EEC Treaty enabling issues of Community law to be referred to the European Court of Justice. Before taking the decision, the court or tribunal would doubtless wish to hear the views of the parties.

Para. 9. Appeals from the Inner House of the Court of Session lie to the House of Lords; leave is not required, except for an appeal against a unanimous interlocutory decision. Where, under para. 7, a devolution issue has been referred to the Inner House, appeal will lie instead to the Judicial Committee of the Privy Council. Note that para. 9 does not provide for the appeal to lie to the Judicial Committee where a devolution issue has been decided by the Inner House other than on a reference under para. 7. In such a case the right of appeal lies to the House of Lords, and para. 24 will enable the House to refer the devolution issue to the Judicial Committee. The drafting of para. 10 is significantly different on this point because apart from the present Act there is no right of appeal beyond the High Court of Justiciary.

Para. 10. Hitherto the High Court of Justiciary has been the final court of appeal in criminal matters in Scotland. Para. 10 introduces a restricted right of appeal to the Judicial Committee on the devolution issue alone, but leave must be given before the appeal will lie.

Paras. 11–17. These paragraphs make corresponding provision for the determination of devolution issues that arise in proceedings in England and Wales. Thus para. 12 gives the Attorney-General the same right to institute proceedings against the Scottish Secretary with " law officer " functions as is given to the Lord Advocate by para. 4. Paras. 13–16 correspond to paras. 5–8, and para. 17 to paras. 8 and 10. By contrast with para. 9, para. 17 requires leave to be obtained for an appeal to the Judicial Committee in civil proceedings whenever a devolution issue has been determined on a reference to the Court of Appeal under para. 15, but this difference between paras. 9 and 17 arises because of the existing differences in the right of appeal to the House of Lords between the Court of Session and the English Court of Appeal. Appeal lies to the Judicial Committee only when the devolution issue has been determined on a reference made under para. 15 or 16. In other cases where a devolution issue has been determined, the normal rights of appeal are available.

Para. 19. This was added by an amendment accepted by the Government during the Report stage of the Scotland Bill. It had not been included earlier because of the Government's view that Law Officers of the Crown would not wish to raise devolution issues in Northern Ireland; *Hansard*, H.L. Vol. 392, cols. 138–141 (May 16, 1978); Vol. 393, cols. 237–239 (June 13, 1978).

Para. 24. Under earlier paragraphs (7, 8, 15, 16, 22) lower courts and tribunals have an unqualified discretion to refer devolution issues to the appropriate appellate court. But by para. 24, the House of Lords are required to refer a devolution issue to the Judicial Committee unless the House consider that in the circumstances they should determine the issue.

Para. 25. This paragraph was added to the Bill by a Government amendment during the Report stage in the Lords; *Hansard*, H.L. Vol. 393, cols. 239–241 (June 13, 1978). Its counterpart in respect of pre-assent proceedings before the Judicial Committee is s. 19 (4) (see note thereon). The effect of the paragraph is that decisions of the Judicial Committee bind all superior and inferior courts in the U.K., including both the House of Lords and, in the Government's view, the Judicial Committee itself; *Hansard*, H.L. Vol. 393, col. 240 (June 13, 1978). While a written constitution may need to be reinterpreted from time to time, the Scotland Act is in many ways less than a written constitution; it could be amended by the U.K. Parliament if this was necessary to overcome a decision of the Judicial Committee which placed an awkward interpretation upon the Act.

Although under para. 24 the House of Lords may decide devolution issues, these decisions do not come within the scope of para. 25. They would however appear to be binding on courts in the various hierarchies in which the House of Lords is the final court of appeal. But the decisions could be of no more than strong persuasive authority in respect of the High Court of Justiciary and the Judicial Committee of the Privy Council.

Para. 26. The effect of this is that where a Law Officer of the Crown or his equivalent in the Scottish Executive has intervened in proceedings involving a devolution issue, costs or expenses attributable to his intervention may be awarded against him, whatever the outcome. This makes only partial provision to meet the extra costs of a private litigant who finds himself unwillingly involved in a devolution issue. Possibly the effect on such a party of the additional expenses could be taken into account by a court in deciding whether to make a reference of the devolution issue as provided for by Sched. 12.

Section 69

SCHEDULE 13

PUBLIC BODIES

PART I

Name of body	Constituting enactment
The Housing Corporation.	The Housing Act 1964, section 1.

PART II

Name of body	Constituting enactment
The Advisory Committee for Scotland.	The Hill Farming Act 1946, section 32.
The Area Committee for Scotland.	The Transport Act 1962, section 56.
The British Airports Authority.	The Airports Authority Act 1975, section 1.
The British Waterways Board.	The Transport Act 1962, section 1.
The Civil Aviation Authority.	The Civil Aviation Act 1971, section 1.
The Council on Tribunals and its Scottish Committee.	The Tribunals and Inquiries Act 1971, sections 1 and 2.
The Fire Service College Board.	The Fire Services Act 1947, section 23 (2).
The General Practice Finance Corporation.	The National Health Service Act 1966, section 1.
The Health Services Board and its Scottish Committee.	The Health Services Act 1976, section 1.
The Housing Association Registration Advisory Committee.	The Housing Act 1974, section 14.
The Inland Waterways Amenity Advisory Council.	The Transport Act 1968, section 110.
The National Water Council.	The Water Act 1973, section 4.

General Note

This Schedule, which should be read along with s. 69, lists the public bodies in respect of which orders under that section may be made.

The British Waterways Board and the Inland Waterways Amenity Advisory Council were added to the Schedule by a Government amendment made during the Committee stage in the Commons; *Hansard*, H.C. Vol. 942, col. 1338 (January 24, 1978). Other amendments were made to remove the Forestry Commission, the Gaming Board, the Horserace Betting Levy Board and the Horserace Totalisation Board from the list in consequence of other amendments to the list of devolved matters in Sched. 10; *Hansard*, H.L. Vol. 392, cols. 241–2 (May 16, 1978); Vol. 393, cols. 306–8 (June 13, 1978).

Section 71

SCHEDULE 14

Intervention by Secretary of State in Planning Matters

Part I

Powers Affected

1. The powers exercisable under or by virtue of the following provisions of the Town and Country Planning (Scotland) Act 1972 (but subject to paragraph 2 below)—

sections 32 to 34

section 42

section 49

section 85

section 91

section 260 so far as it relates to sections 42, 49, 84 and 87.

2. The powers specified in paragraph 1 above do not include the powers under sections 32 and 91 to give directions in relation to applications other than particular applications.

Part II

Powers of Secretary of State

3. The Secretary of State may intervene in accordance with the following provisions of this Schedule in any case where—

(a) action is being or is capable of being taken by a Scottish Secretary in the exercise of a power specified in Part I of this Schedule; and

(b) it appears to the Secretary of State that any action so taken would or might affect, directly or indirectly, any matter which concerns Scotland (whether or not it also concerns any other part of the United Kingdom) but with respect to which a Scottish Secretary has no power to act and that it is desirable in the public interest that he should intervene.

4. Where the Secretary of State intervenes in a case under this Schedule—

(a) no action (or no further action) shall be taken in the case by a Scottish Secretary;

(b) any action previously taken in the case, whether by a Scottish Secretary or by any other person, shall be of no effect except to the extent (if any) that contrary provision is made in accordance with paragraph 6 below; and

(c) the Secretary of State shall in relation to the case have all the powers and duties that a Scottish Secretary would have if the Secretary of State had not intervened and no action (except action the effect of which is saved in accordance with paragraph 6 below) had previously been taken in the case.

5. An intervention by the Secretary of State under this Schedule shall be made by notice published in the Edinburgh Gazette.

6. A notice under paragraph 5 above may save the whole or part of the effect of any action previously taken, whether by a Scottish Secretary or by any other person, and may extend the time for the taking of any action by the Secretary of State or any other person, whether or not the time for taking it would otherwise have expired at the time the notice is published.

7. Where the Secretary of State has intervened in a case he shall, in addition to the notice under paragraph 5 above, give notice of the intervention—

(a) to a Scottish Secretary,

(b) to any planning authority concerned, and

(c) to any person who has previously been given notice of any action taken or proposed to be taken in the case;

and he shall also publish a notice in two successive weeks in one or more local newspapers circulating in the area concerned.

8.—(1) Before he determines an application or appeal or confirms or makes an order in a case in which he has intervened under this Schedule, the Secretary of State shall afford to a Scottish Secretary an opportunity of making representations at a hearing before a person appointed by the Secretary of State.

(2) Sub-paragraph (1) above does not apply to an intervention in relation to the powers exercisable under or by virtue of section 260 (5) of the Town and Country Planning (Scotland) Act 1972; but before exercising those powers in any case the Secretary of State shall consult a Scottish Secretary.

9.—(1) A notice under paragraph 5 or 7 above shall state the reason for the Secretary of State's intervention.

(2) Section 269 of the Town and Country Planning (Scotland) Act 1972 shall apply to notices given under paragraph 5 above as it applies to notices under that Act.

10.—(1) Where the Secretary of State has intervened, or is considering whether to intervene, in a case under this Schedule, he may require a Scottish Secretary or any planning authority concerned to supply him with information or copies of documents relating to the case.

(2) The Secretary of State may require a Scottish Secretary to make available to him the services of any of his officers for the purposes of any local inquiry held in respect of a case in which the Secretary of State has intervened under this Schedule.

11.—(1) The Secretary of State may by order require such planning authorities as may be prescribed by or under the order to give him such information as may be so prescribed with respect to applications for planning permission made to them (including information as to the manner in which any such application has been dealt with) and with respect to proposals for the development by them of land in respect of which they are the planning authority.

(2) A statutory instrument made under this paragraph shall be subject to annulment in pursuance of a resolution of either House of Parliament.

GENERAL NOTE

This Schedule determines the circumstances in which the Secretary of State can intervene in devolved planning matters where non-devolved interests are affected (paras. 1–3) and lays down the procedure to be followed when such intervention takes place (paras. 4–11). See s. 71 and note thereon.

Part I

The powers in question, all exercisable by virtue of the Town and Country Planning (Scotland) Act 1972, are as follows:

(i) the call-in of particular planning applications made to a planning authority (s. 32);

(ii) the determination of appeals against the decision of a planning authority (s. 33);

(iii) the determination of appeals where the planning authority has failed to decide an application within a prescribed period (s. 34);

(iv) the confirmation of orders for the revocation or modification of a planning permission already given by a planning authority (s. 42);

(v) orders for the discontinuance of a use of land or the alteration or removal of buildings or works (s. 49);

(vi) the determination of appeals against enforcement notices issued by a planning authority alleging a breach of planning control (s. 85);

(vii) the call-in of particular applications for an established use certificate (s. 91);

(viii) default powers, including the revocation or modification of planning permission, orders relating to (v) above, notices concerning appeals against enforcement notices ((vi) above) and stop notices (s. 260).

Each of these powers may involve a public inquiry leading ultimately to a decision at ministerial level and is concerned with planning processes set in motion by or against individuals; thus, for example, the power to call in *classes* of planning application, even though devolved to the Scottish administration, is not included.

Following discussion at the Committee stage, the House of Lords agreed at the Report stage to accept amendments which would have made planning powers concerning historic listed buildings subject to the possible intervention of the Secretary of State under this Schedule. Government spokesmen observed, however, that protection for historic buildings was already provided by the Historic Buildings and Ancient Monuments Act 1953, ss. 4–6 (see s. 23 and Sched. 5). The Commons later rejected the amendments; *Hansard*, H.L. Vol. 392, cols. 251–60 (May 16, 1978); Vol. 393, cols. 956–74 (June 20, 1978); H.C. Vol. 954, col. 404 (July 18, 1978).

Part II

Para. 3 sets out the circumstances in which the Secretary of State may intervene to exercise the powers listed in Pt. I. Intervention may take place when the Secretary of State is of the view that the exercise of the relevant power by a Scottish Secretary would or might affect a matter which concerns Scotland (whether or not it also concerns any other part of the U.K.) but with respect to which a Scottish Secretary has no power to act, and that intervention would be in the public interest. The wording of this paragraph is based on s. 39 (1) and (3); see notes thereon.

Paras. 4–11 set out the procedure to be followed once the Secretary of State has intervened. The Secretary of State is empowered to take over proceedings from the stage reached by the Scottish Secretary, or to start proceedings afresh. Individual rights under the legislation are protected, and the Secretary of State is obliged to follow the same procedure as the Scottish Secretary. The Scottish Secretary must be given an opportunity to make representations before a decision is reached, except in the case of default powers where consultation only is required (para. 8). The Secretary of State is empowered to require, by order, planning authorities to provide him with information regarding planning applications, to enable him to judge whether to use his powers of intervention (para. 11).

Section 81   SCHEDULE 15

LOCAL GOVERNMENT BODIES: SCHEDULED FUNCTIONS

Police (including police houses).
Diseases of animals.
Plant health.
Issue of game licences.
Licensing of game dealers.
Animal keeping, breeding and welfare.
Civil defence.
Fertilisers and feedingstuffs.
Careers service.
Sheltered employment.
Consumer protection (including weights and measures).
Rodent control.

Food, drugs and medicines.
Electoral registration.
Slaughter of animals.
Offices, shops and railway premises.
Factory inspection.
Protection of birds.
Traffic wardens.
Control of filling materials (rag flock, etc.).
Ports (other than marine works).
Motor and oil fuel standards.
Petroleum spirit licensing.

GENERAL NOTE

See note on the definition of " scheduled functions " in s. 81 (1). The heading of the Schedule refers to " local government bodies " rather than " local authorities " because some of the functions specified are in the hands of joint boards; *Hansard*, H.L. Vol. 393, cols. 141–142 (June 12, 1978). For the financing of scheduled functions, see note on s. 68.

Section 82 (2)   SCHEDULE 16

AMENDMENTS OF ENACTMENTS

THE PUBLIC RECORDS (SCOTLAND) ACT 1937

1. In section 5 of the Public Records (Scotland) Act 1937, there shall be inserted at the end the following subsection:—

" (4) Any record (other than a court, justice of the peace or private record) which was in the custody of the Keeper on the day on which Group 23 in Schedule 10 to the Scotland Act 1978 came into force may, by direction of a Minister of the Crown, be withdrawn from the Keeper's custody either temporarily or permanently; and the Keeper shall act in accordance with any direction given by a Minister of the Crown under this subsection.".

THE STATUTORY INSTRUMENTS ACT 1946

2. The Statutory Instruments Act 1946 shall be amended as follows.

3. At the end of section 1 there shall be added the following subsection:—

" (3) References in this section to a Minister of the Crown shall be construed as including references to a Scottish Secretary.".

4. At the end of section 4 there shall be added the following subsection:—

" (4) In relation to a statutory instrument required to be laid before the Scottish Assembly the foregoing provisions of this section shall have effect as if for any reference to Parliament or to each House of Parliament there were substituted a reference to the Scottish Assembly, and for the reference to the Lord Chancellor and the Speaker of the House of Commons a reference to the presiding officer of that Assembly.".

5. After section 5 there shall be inserted the following section:—

" **Statutory instruments subject to annulment by resolution of Scottish Assembly**

5A.—(1) Where any statutory instrument is subject to annulment in pursuance of a resolution of the Scottish Assembly the instrument shall be laid before the Assembly, and if the Assembly, within the period of forty days beginning with the date on which the instrument is laid before it, resolves that the instrument be annulled, no further proceedings shall be taken under the instrument, and a Scottish Secretary may by order made by a statutory instrument revoke the instrument, but without prejudice to the validity of anything previously done under it or to the making of a new statutory instrument.

(2) Where any such provision as is mentioned in section 5 (2) of this Act is made with respect to any instrument which is made in the exercise of a power exercisable, by virtue of section 22 of the Scotland Act 1978, by a Scottish Secretary, that instrument shall be subject to annulment in pursuance of a resolution of the Scottish Assembly and subsection (1) of this section shall apply to it accordingly in substitution for that provision.".

6. After section 6 there shall be inserted the following section:—

" **Statutory instruments of which drafts are to be laid before Scottish Assembly**

6A.—(1) Where any provision requires or has effect by virtue of section 22 of the Scotland Act 1978, as requiring the draft of any statutory instrument to be laid before the Scottish Assembly but the provision does not prohibit the making of the instrument without the approval of the Assembly, the instrument shall not be made until after the expiration of a period of forty days beginning with the day on which the draft is laid before the Assembly, and if within that period the Assembly resolves that the instrument be not made, no further proceedings shall be taken on it, but without prejudice to the laying of a new draft before the Assembly.

(2) Where any such provision as is mentioned in section 6 (2) of this Act is made with respect to the draft of any instrument to be made in the exercise of a power which, by virtue of section 22 of the Scotland Act 1978, is exercisable by a Scottish Secretary, a draft of any such instrument shall be laid before the Scottish Assembly and subsection (1) of this section shall apply accordingly in substitution for that provision.".

7. In section 7—

(*a*) in subsection (1) for the words "either of the last two foregoing sections" there shall be substituted the words "section 5 or 6 of this Act";

(*b*) in subsection (2) for the words "the last three foregoing sections" there shall be substituted the words "sections 4, 5 and 6 of this Act"; and

(*c*) at the end of the section there shall be inserted the following subsections:—

"(4) In reckoning for the purposes of sections 5A and 6A of this Act any period of forty days, no account shall be taken of any time during which the Scottish Assembly is adjourned for more than four days.

(5) The provisions of section 5A of this Act shall not apply to any statutory instrument which is an order subject to special parliamentary procedure and the provisions of that section and section 4 of this Act shall not apply to any other instrument which, by virtue of section 22 of the Scotland Act 1978, is required to be laid before the Scottish Assembly for any period before it comes into operation.".

8. In section 8 (1) (*b*) after the words "House of Commons" there shall be inserted the words "or by the Scottish Assembly".

THE STATISTICS OF TRADE ACT 1947

9.—(1) In section 1 (1) of the Statistics of Trade Act 1947 the reference to the discharge by government departments of their functions shall include a reference to the discharge by a Scottish Secretary of his functions.

(2) Section 9 (1) of that Act shall apply in relation to a Scottish Secretary as it applies in relation to a government department (or the Minister in charge of a government department).

THE COAST PROTECTION ACT 1949

10.—(1) The Coast Protection Act 1949 shall be amended as follows.

(2) In subsections (4) and (5) of sections 5 and 8 there shall be inserted, in each case at the beginning, the words "Subject to subsection (5A) below".

(3) After subsection (5) of each of those sections there shall be inserted the following subsection:—

"(5A) Where—

(*a*) notice of objection has been served under subsection (3) above by an excepted statutory undertaker (within the meaning of section 81 (1) of the Scotland Act 1978) and not withdrawn; and

(*b*) the coast protection authority proposing to carry out the work concerned is in Scotland;

the powers of the Minister under subsections (4) and (5) above shall be exercised by a Scottish Secretary with the consent of a Minister of the Crown.".

(4) In subsection (4) of section 17 there shall be inserted at the beginning the words "Subject to subsection (4A) below".

(5) After subsection (4) of that section there shall be inserted the following subsection:—

" (4A) Where—
  (a) the undertakers are an excepted statutory undertaker (within the meaning of section 81 (1) of the Scotland Act 1978); and
  (b) notice of objection has been served under subsection (3) above by a coast protection authority in Scotland and has not been withdrawn;

a Scottish Secretary, after affording to the undertakers and to the authority an opportunity of being heard by a person appointed for the purpose by him with the approval of the appropriate Minister, shall, subject to the consent of that Minister, determine the objection.".

THE DEFAMATION ACT 1952

11. In section 10 of the Defamation Act 1952 after the words " local government authority " there shall be inserted the words " to the Scottish Assembly ".

12. After paragraph 1 of the Schedule to that Act there shall be inserted the following paragraph:—
  " 1A. A fair and accurate report of any proceedings in public of the Scottish Assembly.".

13. In paragraph 13 of that Schedule—
  (a) after the words " Act of the Parliament of Northern Ireland " there shall be inserted the words " and a Scottish Assembly Act ", and
  (b) at the appropriate place there shall be inserted the words " ' Scottish Assembly ' includes any committee of the Assembly and any sub-committee of such a committee.".

THE DEFAMATION ACT (NORTHERN IRELAND) 1955

14. In section 10 (1) of the Defamation Act (Northern Ireland) 1955 after the words " local authority " there shall be inserted the words " to the Scottish Assembly ".

15. After paragraph 1 of the Schedule to that Act there shall be inserted the following paragraph:—
  " 1A. A fair and accurate report of any proceedings in public of the Scottish Assembly.".

16. In paragraph 13 of that Schedule—
  (a) after the words " Act of the Parliament of the United Kingdom " there shall be inserted the words " and a Scottish Assembly Act ", and
  (b) at the appropriate place there shall be inserted the words " ' Scottish Assembly ' includes any committee of the Assembly and any sub-committee of such a committee.".

THE OPENCAST COAL ACT 1958

17. After section 2 (1) of the Opencast Coal Act 1958 there shall be inserted the following subsection:—
  " (1A) The Minister shall not give a direction under this section in relation to land in Scotland unless—
  (a) he has, at least twenty-eight days previously, given notice of the proposed direction to a Scottish Secretary, or
  (b) a Scottish Secretary has informed him of his agreement to the giving of the proposed direction or to the giving of directions of a class that includes the proposed direction.".

THE PIPE-LINES ACT 1962

18. After section 5 (1) of the Pipe-lines Act 1962 there shall be inserted the following subsection:—
  " (1A) The Minister shall not give a direction under this section in relation to land in Scotland unless—
  (a) he has, at least twenty-eight days previously, given notice of the proposed direction to a Scottish Secretary, or

(*b*) a Scottish Secretary has informed him of his agreement to the giving of the proposed direction or to the giving of directions of a class that includes the proposed direction.".

THE HARBOURS ACT 1964

19.—(1) In section 57 (1) of the Harbours Act 1964 for the definition of "marine work" there shall be substituted the following:—

" 'marine work' means a harbour or boatslip in Scotland (other than a harbour or boatslip which is vested in any of the bodies specified in Schedule 3 to the Harbours, Piers and Ferries (Scotland) Act 1937 or which is vested in any of the Boards other than the Scottish Transport Group or a subsidiary, within the meaning of section 154 of the Companies Act 1948, of that Group)—

(*a*) which a Scottish Secretary, with the concurrence of the Secretary of State, determines is principally used or required for the fishing industry, or

(*b*) which, being situated in one of the areas mentioned in paragraph 19 (2) of Schedule 16 to the Scotland Act 1978, a Scottish Secretary, with the concurrence of the Secretary of State, determines is principally used or required for the fishing or agricultural industries or the maintenance of communications between any place in those areas and any other place in Scotland.".

(2) The areas referred to in the definition set out in sub-paragraph (1) above are, subject to sub-paragraph (3) below, the Highland Region, the islands areas of Orkney, Shetland and the Western Isles and the district of Argyll and Bute other than the former burgh of Rothesay and the former district of Bute.

(3) A Scottish Secretary may by order made by statutory instrument vary the description of any area in sub-paragraph (2) above or delete from that sub-paragraph any area for the time being specified in it or add any area to those so specified.

(4) An order made under sub-paragraph (3) above shall be subject to annulment in pursuance of a resolution of the Scottish Assembly.

THE HIGHLANDS AND ISLANDS DEVELOPMENT (SCOTLAND) ACT 1965

20. In section 3 of the Highlands and Islands Development (Scotland) Act 1965:—

(*a*) in subsections (1) (*b*) and (*d*) and (2) for references to the Secretary of State there shall be substituted references to a Scottish Secretary;

(*b*) for paragraph (*e*) of subsection (1) there shall be substituted the following paragraph:—

" (*e*) as soon as possible after the end of each calendar year to make a report as respects that year on the exercise and performance of their functions under this Act—

(i) relating to economic development, to a Scottish Secretary and the Secretary of State.

(ii) relating to social development, to a Scottish Secretary; each such report shall set out any directions given to the Board under section 2 (1) of this Act and a summary of any proposals submitted to a Scottish Secretary under paragraph (*b*) of this subsection, and where he has refused to approve any such proposals, a summary of his reasons for so refusing but shall not disclose any such information as is referred to in section 12 (1) of this Act without the consent referred to in that subsection.";

(*c*) after subsection (3) there shall be inserted the following subsection:—

" (3A) Every report made to a Scottish Secretary under subsection (1) (*e*) of this section shall be laid by him before the Scottish Assembly.".

THE NEW TOWNS ACT 1965

21.—(1) Section 43 of the New Towns Act 1965 shall not apply in relation to any sums advanced to or borrowed by development corporations in Scotland after the coming into force of this paragraph.

(2) A Scottish Secretary may by order impose a limit on the amount outstanding at any time in respect of the principal of any money so advanced to or borrowed by development corporations in Scotland; but no such order shall be made by a Scottish Secretary unless a draft of it has been laid before and approved by the Scottish Assembly.

The Parliamentary Commissioner Act 1967

22. In section 6 (1) (*b*) of the Parliamentary Commissioner Act 1967 after the word " department " there shall be inserted the words " by a Scottish Secretary " and at the end there shall be added the words " or sums payable out of the Scottish Consolidated Fund ".

23. In section 8 (4) of that Act after the word " Cabinet " in the second place, there shall be inserted the words " or of any body performing the functions of a secretariat of the Scottish Executive ", and after the words " Prime Minister " there shall be inserted the words " or, as the case may be, by the First Secretary.".

24. At the end of section 11 (4) of that Act there shall be added the words " and to a Scottish Secretary ".

25. In section 12 (1) of that Act for the definition of " enactment " there shall be substituted the following:—

> " ' enactment ' includes an enactment of the Parliament of Northern Ireland, a Measure of the Northern Ireland Assembly, an Order in Council under section 1 (3) of the Northern Ireland (Temporary Provisions) Act 1972 or paragraph 1 of Schedule 1 to the Northern Ireland Act 1974, a Scottish Assembly Act, and any instrument made by virtue of an enactment (as herein defined).".

The Legal Aid (Scotland) Act 1967

26. In section 4 (6) of the Legal Aid (Scotland) Act 1967, for the words " the Supplementary Benefits Commission, and the Commission " there shall be substituted the words " a Scottish Secretary and the Scottish Secretary ".

The New Towns (Scotland) Act 1968

27. Section 47 (4) of the New Towns (Scotland) Act 1968 shall have effect as if it provided for the appropriate Minister alone to determine the question whether land in Scotland of excepted statutory undertakers is operational land.

The Transport Act 1968

28. In the Transport Act 1968 the following shall be omitted:—
> (*a*) in sections 7 (2) and (7) and 8 (2) and (5) the words from " and in " to the end;
> (*b*) in sections 8 (2) (where they first occur) and 29 (5) (*b*), the words " and the Secretary of State acting jointly "; and
> (*c*) in section 135, subsection (7).

The Development of Tourism Act 1969

29.—(1) In section 1 of the Development of Tourism Act 1969, in paragraph (*a*) of subsection (2), for the word " five " there shall be substituted the word " two " and the word " and ", where it last occurs, shall be omitted.

(2) After paragraph (*b*) of that subsection there shall be inserted the following paragraphs:—
> " (*c*) a member of the English Tourist Board, appointed by the Secretary of State;
> (*d*) a member of the Scottish Tourist Board, appointed by a Scottish Secretary and
> (*e*) a member of the Wales Tourist Board, appointed by the person who, at the time of the appointment, is responsible for appointing members of that Board.".

30. Notwithstanding the provisions of subsection (3) of section 2 of that Act, the Scottish Tourist Board shall have power, by virtue of subsection (2) of that

section, to carry on activities outside the United Kingdom for the purpose of encouraging people to visit Scotland.

31. In section 3 of that Act—
- (a) subsection (1) shall have effect as if the reference to the Scottish Tourist Board were omitted and as if the reference to Great Britain did not include a reference to Scotland;
- (b) after subsection (1) there shall be inserted the following subsection:—
    " (A) The Scottish Tourist Board may prepare a scheme providing for the giving of financial assistance by it for the carrying out of projects of such classes as may be specified in the scheme, being projects which in the opinion of the Board will provide or improve tourist amenities and facilities in Scotland.";
- (c) in subsection (2) after the words " the Board of Trade " there shall be inserted the words " and any scheme prepared under subsection (1A) of this section shall be submitted to a Scottish Secretary ";
- (d) in subsection (6) the words " of the Board of Trade " shall be omitted and after the word " section ", in the third place where it occurs, there shall be inserted the words " relating to a scheme prepared by the British Tourist Authority ".

32. In sections 17 (1) and 18 (1) of that Act the words " in Great Britain " shall be omitted.

The Banking and Financial Dealings Act 1971

33. After section 1 (2) of the Banking and Financial Dealings Act 1971 there shall be inserted the following subsection:—
" (2A) Subsection (2) above does not apply to Scotland, but if it appears to a Scottish Secretary that, in the special circumstances of any year, it is inexpedient that a day specified in Schedule 1 to this Act should be a bank holiday in Scotland, the Scottish Secretary may by order declare that that day shall not in that year be a bank holiday and appoint another day in place of it; and the day appointed by the order shall, in that year, be a bank holiday under this Act instead of the day specified in Schedule 1.".

34. After section 1 (3) of that Act there shall be inserted the following subsection:—
" (3A) A Scottish Secretary may from time to time by order appoint a special day to be a bank holiday in Scotland under this Act.".

The Local Employment Act 1972

35.—(1) In relation to a development area or intermediate area in Scotland, subsection (1) of section 7 of the Local Employment Act 1972 shall have effect as if—
- (a) for the words " the Minister in charge of any Government department " there were substituted the words " a Minister of the Crown "; and
- (b) the words " for which the department is responsible " were omitted.

(2) After that subsection there shall be inserted—
" (1B) Where it appears to a Scottish Secretary that adequate provision has not been made for the needs of any development area or intermediate area in Scotland in respect of a basic service for which he is responsible, and that it is expedient with a view to contributing to the development of industry in that area that the service should be improved, he may make grants or loans towards the cost of improving it to such persons and in such manner as appear to him appropriate."

(3) In subsection (3) of that section before the words " to make " there shall be inserted the words " or of a Scottish Secretary ".

The Summer Time Act 1972

36.—(1) In sections 2 (1) (b), 4 (1) and 5 (1) and (2) of the Summer Time Act 1972, for the words " Great Britain " there shall be substituted, in each case, the words " England and Wales ".

(2) After section 2 of that Act there shall be inserted the following section:—

" 2A. *Modification for Scotland*.—Section 2 of this Act shall have effect in relation to Scotland as if for references in subsections (1) and (2) to an Order in Council there were substituted references to an order of a Scottish Secretary, as if for the reference in subsection (1) (*b*) to England and Wales there were substituted a reference to Scotland and as if for subsection (3) there were substituted the following subsection:—

' (3) No order under this section shall be made unless a draft thereof has been laid before and approved by resolution of the Scottish Assembly.' ".

The Finance Act 1972

37. In section 19 (4) of the Finance Act 1972 after the words " Minister of the Crown " there shall be inserted the words " or of a Scottish Secretary ".

The Town and Country Planning (Scotland) Act 1972

38. After section 37 (1) of the Town and Country Planning (Scotland) Act 1972 there shall be inserted the following subsection:—

" (1A) A government department shall not give a direction under this section in respect of development in Scotland unless—

(*a*) the department has, at least 28 days previously, given notice of the proposed direction to a Scottish Secretary, or

(*b*) a Scottish Secretary has informed the department of his agreement to the giving of the proposed direction or to the giving of directions of a class that includes the proposed direction.".

39. After section 241 of that Act there shall be inserted the following section:—

" Contributions by Scottish Secretaries towards compensation paid by local authorities

241A. Where compensation is payable by a local authority under this Act in consequence of any such decision or order as is mentioned in section 241 of this Act and the decision or order was given or made wholly or partly in the interest of a service provided by a Scottish Secretary, he may pay a contribution to that authority.".

The National Health Service (Scotland) Act 1972

40.—(1) In section 42 (3) of the National Health Service (Scotland) Act 1972 for the words from " in consequence " to " Parliament " there shall be substituted the words " if the Scottish Assembly resolves that the Secretary of State be requested to recommend his removal to Her Majesty ".

(2) In section 43 (1) of that Act for the reference to the House of Commons there shall be substituted a reference to the Scottish Assembly.

(3) In section 46 (1) of that Act for paragraph (*b*) there shall be substituted the following paragraph:—

" (*b*) any other authority or body whose members are appointed by Her Majesty or any Minister of the Crown or government department or Scottish Secretary or whose revenues consist wholly or mainly of moneys provided by Parliament or sums payable out of the Scottish Consolidated Fund.".

(4) In paragraphs (*a*) and (*b*) of section 55 (1) of that Act for the words " the Secretary of State " there shall be substituted the words " a Scottish Secretary ".

The European Communities Act 1972

41. The references in subsection (2) of section 2 of the European Communities Act 1972 to a Minister of the Crown or government department and to a statutory power or duty shall include references to a Scottish Secretary and to a power or duty arising under or by virtue of a Scottish Assembly Act; and " enactment " in subsection (4) of that section shall include a Scottish Assembly Act and any instrument made by virtue of a Scottish Assembly Act.

42. In relation to a statutory instrument made in the exercise of a power conferred on a Scottish Secretary paragraph 2 (2) of Schedule 2 to that Act shall have effect as if the references to each House of Parliament and either House were references to the Scottish Assembly.

The Nature Conservancy Council Act 1973

43. In section 1 (1) (*a*) of the Nature Conservancy Council Act 1973, after sub-paragraph (iv) there shall be inserted the following sub-paragraph:—

" (v) the provision of advice for any Scottish Secretary for the purposes of any functions exercised by him in relation to the conservation of features of geological or physiographical interest and of flora and fauna; and ".

The Health and Safety at Work etc. Act 1974

44. In relation to regulations made by a Scottish Secretary section 14 (4) of the Health and Safety at Work etc. Act 1974 shall have effect as if in paragraph (*c*) for the reference to a Minister of the Crown there were substituted a reference to a Scottish Secretary and as if it required the regulations to include provision for such an inquiry as is mentioned therein to be held otherwise than in public where or to the extent that a Minister of the Crown so directs.

45. In section 44 (1) of that Act at the end there shall be added the words " or, where a licence is required under regulations made by a Scottish Secretary, to a Scottish Secretary ".

46. In section 48 (4) of that Act after the words " this Part " there shall be inserted the words " or of regulations made under this Part by a Scottish Secretary ".

47. Any modification made by an Order in Council under section 84 (3) of that Act may include provisions conferring functions on a Scottish Secretary.

The Finance Act 1975

48. In paragraph 12 (1) of Schedule 6 to the Finance Act 1975, after the entry beginning " Any Government department " there shall be inserted the words " A Scottish Secretary ".

The House of Commons Disqualification Act 1975

49. In Part III of Schedule 1 to the House of Commons Disqualification Act 1975 the following shall be inserted at the appropriate place:—
" Scottish Comptroller and Auditor General "

The Northern Ireland Assembly Disqualification Act 1975

50. In Part III of Schedule 1 to the Northern Ireland Assembly Disqualification Act 1975 the following shall be inserted at the appropriate place:—
" Scottish Comptroller and Auditor General ".

The Scottish Development Agency Act 1975

51.—(1) In section 18 of the Scottish Development Agency Act 1975 for the words " the Secretary of State ", in both places, there shall be substituted the words " a Scottish Secretary ".

(2) In Schedule 2 to that Act, in paragraph 9—

(*a*) for sub-paragraph (1) there shall be substituted the following sub-paragraph:—

" (1) It shall be the duty of the Agency, as soon as possible after the end of each financial year, to make a report dealing with the operations of the Agency during that year—

(*a*) in pursuance of section 2 (2) (*a*) to (*c*) of this Act, to a Scottish Secretary and the Secretary of State;

(*b*) in pursuance of section 2 (2) (*f*) or 5 of this Act, to the Secretary of State; and

(*c*) in pursuance of any other provision of this Act, to a Scottish Secretary.".

(*b*) after sub-paragraph (2) there shall be inserted the following sub-paragraph:—

" (2A) It shall be the duty of a Scottish Secretary to lay before the Scottish Assembly a copy of each report received by him under this paragraph.".

(*c*) in sub-paragraph (3) for the words from " the Secretary of State " to the end there shall be substituted the words " —

(*a*) by the Secretary of State, in the case of a direction given by him,

(*b*) by a Scottish Secretary, in the case of a direction given by him." and the said subsection (2) shall not apply to the direction.".

The Licensing (Scotland) Act 1976

52. In section 138 (1) of the Licensing (Scotland) Act 1976, after paragraph (*a*) there shall be inserted the following paragraph:—

" (*aa*) trafficking in alcoholic liquor on premises used for the purposes of the Scottish Assembly while they are so used or, under the authority of the Assembly, at other times.".

The Patents Act 1977

53. Sections 55 to 59 of the Patents Act 1977 shall have effect as if references to a government department included references to a Scottish Secretary; and, in relation to any use of an invention by a Scottish Secretary or by any person authorised in writing by a Scottish Secretary, section 55 (4) of that Act shall have effect as if the words " with the approval of the Treasury " were omitted.

The Inner Urban Areas Act 1978

54.—(1) Section 2 (4) (*b*) of the Inner Urban Areas Act 1978 (power of Secretary of State to fix rate of interest for loan under section 2) shall have effect, in any case where—

(*a*) the loan is made by a designated district authority in Scotland; and

(*b*) a Scottish Secretary is satisfied that it is not for the acquisition, construction or alteration of a building intended for use for industrial or commercial purposes;

as if the reference to the Secretary of State were a reference to a Scottish Secretary.

(2) Paragraphs 1 (3) (*b*) and 3 (3) (*b*) of the Schedule to that Act shall have effect, in relation to any area within Scotland, as if the reference to the Secretary of State included a reference to a Scottish Secretary.

GENERAL NOTE

Throughout this Schedule for the term " Scottish Secretary " see s. 81 (1), referring to s. 20 (2), and for the term " Minister of the Crown," see s. 81 (1).

Para. 1. *The Public Records (Scotland) Act* 1937. This extends s. 5 of the Act to enable a minister to withdraw records (except those of courts or justices of the peace or private records) which are in the Keeper's custody when Sched. 10, Pt. I, Group 23 (Public Records) comes into operation.

Paras. 2–8. *The Statutory Instruments Act* 1946. The Statutory Instruments Act 1946, as amended, is to apply to instruments made by a Scottish Secretary under (i) powers conferred on a minister to make statutory instruments under existing Acts of Parliament and transferred to a Scottish Secretary by s. 22 (1); (ii) powers conferred on Her Majesty to make Orders in Council and transferred to a Scottish Secretary by an Order under s. 22 (6); (iii) powers conferred on a Scottish Secretary by a future Act of Parliament and expressed to be exercisable by statutory instrument. Paras. 3–8 therefore amend the 1946 Act so that it applies to Scottish Secretaries and procedures in the Assembly as well as to ministers and procedures in Parliament. It will be necessary for the Assembly to create its own procedures in respect of instruments made under Assembly Acts, either by applying the procedures of the 1946 Act or otherwise. Should the Assembly create new procedures of its own, it will be competent for the Assembly to repeal these paragraphs (see Sched. 2, para. 7) and to apply the new procedures to instruments covered by these paragraphs. See s. 22 and note thereon.

Para. 3. This extends s. 1 so that the expression " statutory instrument " covers an instrument made under a power expressed to be exercisable by statutory instrument and conferred on a Scottish Secretary by Act of Parliament (*i.e.* by this Act or by a future Act; see the 1946 Act, s. 1 (1)).

Para. 4. This converts references in s. 4 to laying before Parliament into references to laying before the Assembly. It also amends the proviso to s. 4 (1) by providing that where an instrument comes into force before being laid, the requisite notification and explanation should be sent to the presiding officer of the Assembly.

Para. 5. This creates a new s. 5A as the counterpart to s. 5 (statutory instruments which are subject to annulment by resolution of either House of Parliament). The new section provides for a resolution by the Assembly that the instrument be annulled, and empowers a Scottish Secretary then to revoke the instrument.

Para. 6. This creates a new s. 6A as the counterpart to s. 6 (statutory instruments of which drafts are to be laid before Parliament).

Para. 7. This relates to s. 7, which contains provisions supplementary to ss. 4–6. Sub-paras. (*a*) and (*b*) are supplementary to paras. 5 and 6 above. The new subsections (4) and (5) are added by sub-para. (*c*) as the counterpart to subs. (1) and (3) of s. 7. *Cf.* s. 77.

Para. 8. This makes a consequential amendment to s. 8, which empowers the making of regulations in relation to statutory instruments.

Para. 9 (1). *The Statistics of Trade Act* 1947. S. 1 (1) of the 1947 Act empowers competent authorities (defined in s. 17 (3) of that Act) to obtain statistical information for, *inter alia*, the discharge by government departments of their functions. The amendment permits such authorities to collect information for the discharge by a Scottish Secretary of his functions; it does not, however, permit a Scottish Secretary to gather such information himself; *cf.* s. 36 (Provision of information) and see note thereon.

Para. 9 (2). S. 9 (1) of the 1947 Act prevents the disclosure of information collected which concerns individual undertakings, except in accordance with directions given by a Minister for the purpose of his department's functions. The effect of the amendment is that a Scottish Secretary may be given access to such information in accordance with directions given by the Minister in charge of the department which possesses the information.

Note that by Sched. 10, Pt. III, the matters dealt with in the 1947 Act are not included in the Groups in Pt. I of that Schedule.

Para. 10. *The Coast Protection Act* 1949. This amends the procedure to be followed where objection is taken to the carrying out of coast protection work under ss. 5, 8 and 17 of the 1949 Act. Hitherto, where either a coast protection authority or a statutory undertaker have wished to carry out coast protection work to which the other has objected, the objections have been determined jointly by the Minister responsible for coast protection and the Minister responsible for the statutory undertaker. The effect of the amendment is that where an excepted statutory undertaker is involved, the decision will be taken by a Scottish Secretary subject to the consent of the Minister responsible for the excepted statutory undertaker in question. By Sched. 10, Pt. I, Group 8, coast protection is a devolved matter. See also s. 23 (Powers exercisable with consent or concurrently).

This paragraph was added by a Government amendment during the Committee stage in the Commons; *Hansard*, H.C. Vol. 943, col. 589–90 (February 1, 1978).

"*excepted statutory undertaker.*" See s. 81 (1).

Paras. 11–13. *The Defamation Act* 1952. Paras. 11–13 should be read along with s. 15; see note thereon.

Para. 11. This extends to Assembly elections the rule in s. 10 of the 1952 Act that a defamatory statement published by or on behalf of an election candidate is not entitled to privilege on the grounds that it is material to an election issue.

Paras. 12 *and* 13 (*b*). This extends qualified privilege to the publication in a newspaper, or a broadcast, of a fair and accurate report of any public proceedings of the Assembly, or of one of its committees or subcommittees; see 1952 Act, ss. 7 and 9.

Para. 13 (a). This extends the definition of " Act of Parliament " to include " Assembly Acts "; the amendment affects the Schedule to the 1952 Act.

Para. 16. *The Defamation Act* (*Northern Ireland*) 1952. This makes identical amendments to those made to the Defamation Act 1952; see above.

Para. 17. *The Opencast Coal Act* 1958. This amendment concerns " deemed planning permission," by which certain forms of ministerial authorisation carry with them planning permission for the development concerned. In cases where deemed planning permission is granted, it is not necessary for the body requiring ministerial authority to seek planning permission from the local planning authority. Most cases of deemed planning permission arise under the Town and Country Planning (Scotland) Act 1972, s. 37 (see para. 38 of this Schedule), but they can also arise under s. 2 of this Act and the Pipe-lines Act 1962, s. 5 (see para. 18 of this Schedule).

The general approach taken is that where the power to grant authorisation is retained by a U.K. Minister, so also is the power to grant deemed planning permission. However, the interest of the Scottish Executive in planning matters (see Sched. 10, Pt. I, Group 6) is recognised in that by this paragraph, the Department of Energy must notify a Scottish Secretary before granting deemed planning permission for authorised open cast operations, and the Scottish Secretary must give his agreement.

This paragraph, along with para. 18 below, was added to the Schedule by a Government amendment during the Committee stage in the Lords, in consequence of an amendment to Sched. 10, Pt. III; *Hansard*, H.L. Vol. 392, cols. 436–9 (May 17, 1978).

Para. 18. *The Pipelines Act* 1962. This paragraph is similar to para. 17 above; see note thereon.

Para. 19. *The Harbours Act* 1964. This paragraph amends the definition of " marine work " in s. 57 (1) of the 1964 Act. By Sched. 10, Pt. I, Group 12, " marine works " are a devolved matter. Hitherto the Secretary of State has had power to add to the categories of harbours for which he has been responsible, with the consent of the Minister of Transport, who remains responsible for ports, since they are not a devolved matter. The effect of the amendment is to empower a Scottish Secretary, with the concurrence of the Secretary of State, to define a harbour as a marine work if it meets the criteria set out in the definition; it also empowers a Scottish Secretary, with the same concurrence, to change by order the areas of Scotland within which marine works may be designated. The order is to be subject to the negative resolution procedure (see para. 5 above). The amendment ensures that a Scottish Secretary cannot defeat the intention that ports be a reserved matter by having them defined as marine works and so bringing them within his competence.

This paragraph was the subject of a Government amendment made during the Report stage in the Commons; *Hansard*, H.C. Vol. 944, col. 608 (February 15, 1978).

Para. 20. *The Highlands and Islands Development (Scotland) Act* 1965. The amendments made by this paragraph reflect the division of responsibility for the Board between the Secretary of State and the Scottish Executive which is created by this Act; see s. 42 and note thereon. Thus by sub-para. (*a*), development proposals and advice will now be submitted to a Scottish Secretary. The effect of sub-para. (*b*) is that the Board will now report to both the Secretary of State and a Scottish Secretary on economic development, and to a Scottish Secretary alone on social development. By sub-para. (*c*), reports made to a Scottish Secretary are to be laid before the Assembly.

See also para. 51 (amendments to Scottish Development Agency Act 1975).

Para. 21. *The New Towns Act* 1965. Hitherto s. 43 has operated to limit the total amount of money which can be advanced or borrowed by development corporations and the Commission for New Towns. The effect of the amendment is that the Scottish Executive is now empowered to set its own limits, subject to Assembly approval, on the borrowing activities of development corporations in Scotland.

Paras. 22–25. *The Parliamentary Commissioner Act* 1967. Paras. 22–25 should be read together with s. 76 (Complaints of maladministration), but the amendments which they make to the 1967 Act could operate independently of s. 76 and will in fact do so unless the amended provisions are among those applied by Order in Council under s. 76 (2) to the investigation of maladministration on the part of a Scottish Secretary and the other bodies to which s. 76 applies.

Para. 22. S. 6 (1) (*a*) and (*b*) determine the categories of authorities or bodies who may not make complaints to the Parliamentary Commissioner for Administration (P.C.A.). This paragraph maintains the principle that one public body should not make complaints of maladministration against another by adding to these categories authorities or bodies whose members are appointed by a Scottish Secretary, and those whose revenues consist wholly or partly of sums payable out of the Scottish Consolidated Fund (for which see Pt. III of this Act). *Cf.* para. 40 (3).

Para. 23. This paragraph extends s. 8 (4) by preventing the disclosure to the P.C.A. of any documents or information relative to the proceedings of a secretariat of the Scottish Executive; it also provides a certification procedure, similar to that operating in respect of the Cabinet, for material falling into that category. The reference to " any body performing the functions of a secretariat of the Scottish Executive " seems to envisage that the Scottish Executive will be a Cabinet-style government, but the formulation is extremely vague, and there is no corresponding reference to such a body elsewhere in the Act; *cf.* especially s. 20.

Para. 24. This extends the description of " Minister of the Crown " in s. 11 (4) to include a Scottish Secretary. The effect of the amendment is to enable a Scottish Secretary to prevent, under s. 11 (3), the P.C.A. from disclosing a document or information which he considers would be prejudicial to the safety of the State or otherwise contrary to the public interest.

Para. 25. This extends the definition of " enactment " in s. 12 (1) to include an Assembly Act and an instrument made under such an Act; *cf.* definition of " enactment " in s. 81 (1).

Para. 26. *The Legal Aid (Scotland) Act* 1967. By Sched. 10, Pt. I, Group 21, legal aid, advice and assistance are devolved matters. For the effect of this paragraph, see note thereon.

Para. 27. *The New Towns (Scotland) Act* 1968. This is consequential upon an amendment made to the entry for this Act in Sched. 10, Pt. III. Hitherto such questions have been decided jointly by the Secretary of State and the appropriate minister. The paragraph was added by a Government amendment during the Report stage in the Lords; *Hansard,* H.L. Vol. 393, col. 1053 (June 20, 1978).

" *excepted statutory undertakers.*" See s. 81 (1).

Para. 28. *The Transport Act* 1968. This is consequential upon an amendment made to the entry for this Act in Sched. 10, Pt. III. The paragraph was added by a Government amendment during the Report stage in the Lords; *Hansard,* H.L. Vol. 393, col. 1053 (June 20, 1978).

Paras. 29–32. *The Development of Tourism Act* 1969. Paras. 29–32 should be read along with s. 70 (Tourism); see note thereon. They make alterations to the constitution and powers of the British Tourist Authority and the Scottish Tourist Board. Para. 29 was amended during the Report stage in the Lords, following discussion at the Committee stage; *Hansard,* H.L. Vol. 392, cols. 439–50 (May 17, 1978); Vol. 393, cols. 1054–5 (June 20, 1978).

Paras. 33 *and* 34. *The Banking and Financial Dealings Act* 1971. By Sched. 10, Pt. I, Group 20, public holidays are devolved matters. Para. 33 : s. 1 (2) of the 1971 Act empowers Her Majesty, by proclamation, to designate a day as a bank holiday in place of one listed in Sched. 1. The effect of this paragraph is that the subsection is no longer to apply in Scotland; instead, by the new subs. (2A), the power is to be conferred on a Scottish Secretary and exercisable by order. Para. 34 : the new subs. (3A) empowers a Scottish Secretary, by order, to declare a day as an extra bank holiday for Scotland. By contrast with the amendment made by para. 33 above, this amendment does not affect the power exercisable under s. 1 (3) by Her Majesty to declare extra bank holidays by proclamation.

Para. 34. *The Local Employment Act* 1972. S. 7 of the 1972 Act is concerned with the improvement of basic services in development and intermediate areas (for which see s. 1). It empowers the Minister in charge of any government department to make grants or loans for the improvement of such services (*i.e.* transport, power supply, lighting, heating, water, sewerage and sewage disposal) in these areas. The amendments made by this paragraph are necessary to give effect to the fact that some basic services (*e.g.* roads and sewers) become devolved matters by this Act; in respect of such services, the power created by s. 7 is to be exercisable by a Scottish Secretary. This paragraph was added to the Schedule by a Government amendment during the Report stage in the Lords; *Hansard,* H.L. Vol. 392, cols. 1484–9 (June 8, 1978); Vol. 393, cols. 1055–6 (June 20, 1978).

Para. 36. *The Summer Time Act* 1972. Sub-para. (1) converts references to Great Britain in the Act into references to England and Wales. The new s. 2A, created by sub-para. (2), empowers a Scottish Secretary, by order (subject to the approval of the Assembly), to designate the period of summer time for Scotland.

Para. 37. *The Finance Act* 1972. The effect of this amendment is that the supply of goods and services by a Scottish Secretary will be liable to VAT to the same extent as the supply of goods and services by a U.K. department. This paragraph was added by a Government amendment during the Report stage in the Commons; *Hansard,* H.C. Vol. 944, col. 608 (February 15, 1978).

Para. 38. *The Town and Country Planning (Scotland) Act* 1972. This amendment concerns deemed planning permission; see note on para. 17 (Opencast Coal Act 1958). The effect of the amendment is that where the body which is seeking ministerial authorisation operates for purposes which are not devolved, the U.K. department in question must notify a Scottish Secretary and obtain his consent before granting deemed planning permission.

Para. 39. S. 241 of the 1972 Act provides that where compensation is payable by a local authority under the Act as the result of a decision or order made wholly or partly in the interests of a service provided by a U.K. department, the appropriate Minister may pay a contribution towards the amount of the compensation. The effect of the new s. 241A created by this paragraph is to give a Scottish Secretary equivalent power where the decision or order is made in the interests of a service provided by the Scottish Executive.

Para. 40. *The National Health Service (Scotland) Act* 1972. By Sched. 10, Pt. I, Group 1, the investigation of maladministration within the Health Service in Scotland is made a devolved matter, and para. 40 (1)–(3) make consequential amendments to the 1972 Act.

Para. 40 (1). Hitherto an address from both Houses of Parliament has been required before the Health Service Commissioner can be removed from office by the Crown. The effect of the amendment is that the Commissioner may be removed from office by the Crown if the Assembly resolves that the Secretary of State be requested to recommend his removal. Note that this amendment is so formulated as to avoid a direct link between the Assembly and the Crown.

Para. 40 (2). The effect of this amendment is that the Commissioner's salary will be determined by the Assembly and not by the House of Commons as hitherto.

Para. 40 (3). S. 46 (1) (*a*) and (*b*) of the 1972 Act determine the categories of authorities or bodies who may not make complaints to the Commissioner. The effect of the amendment is to add to these categories authorities or bodies whose members are appointed by a Scottish Secretary, or whose revenues consist wholly or mainly of sums payable out of the Scottish Consolidated Fund (for which see Pt. III of this Act). *Cf.* para. 22.

Para. 40 (4). S. 55 of the 1972 Act is concerned with the furnishing of overseas aid by Health Boards and the Common Services Agency. The effect of the amendment is, as regards s. 55 (1) (*a*), that arrangements between Health Boards or the Common Services Agency and the Minister of Overseas Development are to be subject to the consent of a Scottish Secretary, and, as regards s. 55 (1) (*b*), that arrangements made directly between Health Boards or the Common Services Agency and any authority outside the U.K. are to be subject to the separate consent of a Scottish Secretary and the Ministry of Overseas Development. *Cf.* para. 51 (1).

Para. 41. *The European Communities Act* 1972. This amendment extends the reference in s. 2 (2) of the 1972 Act to a minister or department to include a Scottish Secretary. Its effect is to enable a Scottish Secretary to be designated by Order in Council to make regulations for the purposes set out in s. 2 (2) (*a*) and (*b*); these purposes include the implementation of Community obligations of the U.K.

S. 2 (2) also contains a general provision enabling regard to be had to Community objects in the exercise of any statutory power or duty; this is extended by this paragraph to include powers or duties arising under, or by virtue of, Assembly Acts.

S. 2 (4) is in part intended to make future enactments subject to the provisions of s. 2 (1)–(3), with a view to ensuring that Community law should prevail over U.K. law to the extent required by the Treaty; this paragraph accordingly extends the term " enactment " (which is not defined in the 1972 Act) to include Assembly Acts.

Para. 42. The exercise by a Scottish Secretary of the power to make regulations under s. 2 (2) will, as in the case of a U.K. Minister, be subject to the provisions of Sched. 2. This paragraph accordingly amends Sched. 2, para. 2 (2), to ensure that regulations made under s. 2 (2) by a Scottish Secretary will be subject to either an affirmative or negative resolution procedure in the Assembly.

Para. 43. *The Nature Conservancy Council Act* 1973. Although by Sched. 10, Pt. I, Group 9 (see note thereon) the countryside is in general made a devolved matter, the Nature Conservancy Council will continue to be responsible to the U.K. Government (see Sched. 10, Pt. III). By this amendment, however, the Council's responsibilities are increased to include the provision of advice to the Scottish Executive on nature conservation.

Paras. 44–47. *The Health and Safety at Work, etc. Act* 1974. Although by Sched. 10, Pt. I, Group 7, pollution control is in general made a devolved matter, the matters covered in the 1974 Act, with the exception of s. 75, are not devolved to the Assembly. However, a number of powers under the 1974 Act are devolved to the Scottish Executive by Sched. 11, Group F, paras. 2–3, insofar as they relate to the control of emissions into the atmosphere otherwise than from vehicles, aircraft or hovercraft, and these amendments are consequential upon those paragraphs.

Para. 44. S. 14 of the 1974 Act empowers the Health and Safety Commission to direct the Health and Safety Executive to investigate, or, with the consent of the Secretary of State, to direct an inquiry to be held into, any accident, occurrence, etc. which it considers necessary or expedient to investigate for any of the general purposes set out in s. 1 (see especially s. 1 (1) (*d*)) or with a view to making regulations for these purposes. While normally such inquiries are held in public, regulations may provide for them to be held in private where, or to the extent that, the Minister directs.

The power under s. 14 (4) to make regulations governing the conduct of such inquiries is devolved to the Scottish Executive by Sched. 11, but the effect of the amendment is that either a Scottish Secretary or a U.K. Minister may direct that an inquiry be held in private.

Para. 45. S. 44 is concerned with appeals against the refusal of licences. Where a licence is required under regulations made by a Scottish Secretary, appeals will now be determined by a Scottish Secretary and not the Secretary of State as hitherto.

Para. 46. S. 48 is concerned with the application of the provisions of the Act to the Crown. The effect of the amendment is to enable the Secretary of State to secure Crown exemption (in the interests of the safety of the State or the safe custody of prisoners) from any regulations made by a Scottish Secretary in the exercise of a devolved power.

Para. 47. S. 84 (3) enables the provisions of Pts. I and II of the Act to be applied by Order in Council outside Great Britain (*e.g.* in territorial waters). This power is not devolved, except that by this amendment it will be competent when extending the scope of the Act to permit the Scottish Executive to exercise powers in new geographical areas.

Para. 48. *The Finance Act* 1975. The effect of this amendment is that gifts of property made to a Scottish Secretary will be exempt from capital transfer tax in the same way as gifts to a U.K. department. This paragraph was added by a Government amendment during the Report stage in the Commons; *Hansard*, H.C. Vol. 944, col. 609 (February 15, 1978).

Para. 49. *The House of Commons Disqualification Act* 1975. This amendment adds the Scottish Comptroller and Auditor General (see s. 54) to the list of offices which disqualify for membership of the House of Commons.

Para. 50. *The Northern Ireland Assembly Disqualification Act* 1975. This amendment adds the Scottish Comptroller and Auditor General (see s. 54) to the list of offices which disqualify for membership of the Northern Ireland Assembly.

Para. 51. *The Scottish Development Agency Act* 1975. The amendments made by this paragraph reflect the division of responsibility for the Agency which is created by this Act; see s. 42 and note thereon.

Para. 51 (1). S. 18 empowers the Agency to act on behalf of the Minister of Overseas Development to provide technical assistance to overseas countries. The effect of the amendment is that such arrangements will now require the consent of a Scottish Secretary and not the Secretary of State as hitherto. *Cf. para.* 40 (4).

Para. 51 (2). Sched. 2, para. 9, is concerned with reporting arrangements. The broad effect of the amendments is that the Agency will report to the Secretary of State on its reserved functions, and to a Scottish Secretary on its devolved functions. Reports submitted to a Scottish Secretary will be required to be laid before the Assembly.

Para. 52. *The Licensing (Scotland) Act* 1976. The effect of this amendment is that the sale and consumption of alcoholic liquor on premises used for the purposes of the Assembly, either while the Assembly is in session or, with the Assembly's authority, at other times, will not be contrary to the 1976 Act. This paragraph was added by a Government amendment during the Report stage in the Commons; *Hansard*, H.C. Vol. 944, col. 609 (February 15, 1978).

Para. 53. *The Patents Act* 1977. Ss. 55–9 of the 1977 Act are concerned with the use of patented inventions for the services of the Crown. The effect of this amendment is to extend the use of patented inventions for these purposes to a Scottish Secretary.

Para. 54. *The Inner Urban Areas Act* 1978. The purpose of this Act is to enable local authorities in inner areas with acute social and economic problems to develop their local economies by making grants and loans available for works and by setting up industrial improvement areas. By Sched. 10, Pt. III, the matters covered by the Act are not devolved to the Assembly, but a number of powers under the Act are devolved to the Scottish Executive by Sched. 11, Group E, para. 11. S. 2 of the Act empowers local authorities which are designated for the purposes of the Act by s. 1 to offer loans for the acquisition of land or for works on land, and the effect of the amendment is that the rates of interest on such loans will be fixed by a Scottish Secretary, and not by the Secretary of State as originally provided in the Act.

Section 85   SCHEDULE 17

REFERENDUM

Date of referendum

1. The referendum shall be held on such day, not less than six weeks after the making of the Order, as Her Majesty may by Order in Council appoint.

Persons eligible to vote

2. Those entitled to vote in the referendum shall be—
   (a) the persons who, at the date of the referendum, would be entitled to vote as electors at a parliamentary election in any constituency in Scotland; and
   (b) peers who at that date would be entitled to vote as electors at a local government election in any electoral area in Scotland.

Question to be asked and form of ballot paper

3. The question to be asked in the referendum and the front of the ballot paper to be used for that purpose shall be in the form set out in the Appendix to this Schedule.

Conduct of referendum

4. Subject to the following provisions of this Schedule, Her Majesty may by Order in Council make provision as to the conduct of the referendum and apply in relation to it, with such modifications or exceptions as may be specified in the Order, any provision of the Representation of the People Acts, any provision of the enactments relating to returning officers and any provision made under any enactment.

5. An Order in Council under this Schedule shall not charge any sum on the Consolidated Fund but may provide for the expenses of the returning officers to be defrayed as administrative expenses of the Secretary of State.

6. The functions which, in relation to a parliamentary election, are conferred on returning officers by any provision applied by an Order in Council under this Schedule shall in relation to the referendum be discharged by the persons who, under section 6 of the Local Government (Scotland) Act 1973 are, or may discharge the functions of, returning officers, at elections of councillors for regional or islands councils.

7. The Secretary of State shall appoint a Chief Counting Officer, who shall appoint a counting officer for each region and islands area, and each counting officer shall conduct the counting of votes cast in the area for which he is appointed in accordance with any directions given to him by the Chief Counting Officer.

8. The counting officer for each area shall certify the number of ballot papers counted by him and the number of respective answers given by valid votes; and the Chief Counting Officer shall certify the total of the ballot papers and the respective answers for the whole of Scotland.

9. Every regional and islands council shall place the services of its officers at the disposal of the counting officer for its area; and if the council of any region or

the counting officer for any region so requests, the council of any district situated in that region shall place the services of its officers at the disposal of the counting officer for that region.

Exclusion of legal proceedings

10. No court shall entertain any proceedings for questioning the numbers, as certified by the Chief Counting Officer or any counting officer, of any ballot papers counted or answers given in the referendum.

Orders in Council

11. No recommendation shall be made to Her Majesty in Council to make an Order under this Schedule until a draft of the Order has been laid before Parliament and approved by resolution of each House of Parliament.

APPENDIX

FORM OF BALLOT PAPER

Parliament has decided to consult the electorate in Scotland on the question whether the Scotland Act 1978 should be put into effect.

DO YOU WANT THE PROVISIONS OF THE SCOTLAND ACT 1978 TO BE PUT INTO EFFECT?

Put a cross (**X**) in the appropriate box.

YES	
NO	

GENERAL NOTE

This Schedule makes detailed provision for the conduct of the referendum to be held under s. 85. A number of its provisions are derived from the Referendum Act 1975.

The Government's intention is that only one order be made under this Schedule; Lord Kirkhill, Minister of State at the Scottish Office, *Hansard*, H.L. Vol. 393, 1024 (June 20, 1978). This Order will, therefore, specify the date of the referendum (para. 1), make further provision for the conduct of the referendum (including the application of the Representation of the People Acts and other legislation) (para. 4), and make provision for the expenses of returning officers (para. 5). The Order is to be laid in draft before Parliament and must be approved by each House before it can be made (para. 11).

Para. 1. "*not less than six weeks after the making of the Order*": these words were added by an amendment made during the Report stage in the Lords. At the time the Government opposed the amendment on the grounds that it would create an undesirable lack of flexibility, but later withdrew its objection; *Hansard*, H.L. Vol. 393, cols. 1021–34 (June 20, 1978); H.C. Vol. 954, cols. 404–5 (July 18, 1978). The six-week period specified is a minimum period, and the period between the laying of the draft before Parliament and the making of the Order will in practice permit additional time for campaigning.

Para. 2. This paragraph provides that those entitled to vote in the referendum will be persons who are entitled to vote at parliamentary elections in any Scottish constituency, and peers who are entitled to vote at local government elections in Scotland; see s. 4 of this Act, and Referendum Act 1975, s. 1 (3).

Although this Act is a U.K. Act, Scottish voters only are to be consulted in the referendum, on the argument that they would be directly affected by the provisions of the Act; Lord McCluskey, Solicitor-General for Scotland, *Hansard*, H.L. Vol. 392, cols. 410, 414 (May 17, 1978). While sympathetic to the problem of expatriate Scots, the Government resisted attempts to make Scottish domicile the criterion for a vote in the referendum on the grounds that it would be unfair for the vote of an expatriate, who might have no intention of ever returning to Scotland, to count equally with the vote of a Scottish resident, and that a domicile test would create awkward problems in practice; *Hansard*, H.L. Vol. 392, cols. 390–6 (May 17, 1978); Vol. 393, cols. 1035–9 (June 20, 1978). The referendum on the Wales Act 1978 is to be governed by the same principle. See also Northern Ireland (Border Poll) Act 1972, s. 1 (1) (*a*).

In contrast to the Referendum Act 1975 (see s. 1 (5)), no special provision is made for service voters; their position is now covered by the Representation of the People (Service Voters) Act 1976. Crown servants and British Council employees working overseas will be able to vote provided that they are registered in a Scottish constituency.

Para. 5. The first limb of this paragraph provides that the Order made under this Schedule may not charge any sum on the Consolidated Fund. No government funds will therefore be made available to any organisation for the purposes of the referendum campaign; *cf.* Referendum Act 1975, s. 3. The Government have, however, announced that since devolution forms part of their policy, the normal resources will be available to ministers in furthering that policy; Lord Kirkhill, Minister of State at the Scottish Office, *Hansard*, H.L. Vol. 394, cols. 457–8 (June 29, 1978). During the Third Reading stage in the Lords, the paragraph was amended so that no charge could be made on the Consolidated Fund for the purposes of the referendum, whether by the order made under this Schedule or otherwise; the object of the amendment was to prevent the use of the Civil Service and its facilities in the campaign. The amendment was rejected by the Commons; *Hansard*, H.L. Vol. 394, cols. 448–62 (June 29, 1978); H.C. Vol. 954, cols. 405–33 (July 18, 1978).

By the second limb of the paragraph, the order may provide for the expenses of returning officers (see para. 6) to be defrayed as administrative expenses of the Secretary of State. This relates to s. 80, which provides that administrative expenses incurred by a minister under this Act shall be paid out of money provided by Parliament. Unlike counting officers (see para. 7), returning officers exist for purposes other than the referendum, and the purpose of this provision is to ensure that their expenses will fall under s. 80.

Para. 6. This follows the Referendum Act 1975, s. 2 (1) (*b*).

Para. 7. This follows the Referendum Act 1975, s. 2 (4) (first limb).

Para. 8. This follows the Referendum Act 1975, s. 2 (6). Although the paragraph does not specify how the results are to be announced, the Government's intention is to publish the results for each region and islands area and for the whole of Scotland; Lord Kirkhill, Minister of State at the Scottish Office, *Hansard*, H.L. Vol. 393, col. 1044 (June 20, 1978).

Para. 9. This paragraph is similar to the Referendum Act 1975, s. 2 (2) and (4) (second limb). It was the subject of a Government amendment made during the Committee stage in the Commons; *Hansard*, H.C. Vol. 942, col. 1553 (January 25, 1978).

Para. 10. This follows the Referendum Act 1975. s. 4.

Appendix: The ballot paper (see para. 3) will follow the general pattern of that used in the EEC referendum (see Referendum Act 1975, Sched.). The preamble on the paper was considerably shortened by a Government amendment made during the Committee stage in the Commons; *Hansard*, H.C. Vol. 942, col. 1553 (January 25, 1978). The preamble now provides minimal information on the issue, but the Government have decided not to issue any explanatory literature of their own; Lord Kirkhill, Minister of State at the Scottish Office, *Hansard*, H.L. Vol. 393, cols. 1042–3 (June 20, 1978).

Wales Act 1978 *

(1978 c. 52)

ARRANGEMENT OF SECTIONS

PART I

THE WELSH ASSEMBLY

* Annotations by David Foulkes, Reader in Law, University of Wales, UWIST, Cardiff.

PART V

GENERAL AND SUPPLEMENTARY

General Note

The Act in brief

The Act provides for the creation of a Welsh Assembly, a body of some 80 members, elected initially on the basis of parliamentary, later of Assembly, constituencies. The Assembly is a Crown body, staffed by civil servants. It will exercise, as regards Wales, certain functions hitherto exercised by Ministers. It will therefore be exercising administrative (or executive) functions, including the making of statutory instruments, but not powers of primary legislation. The functions it will exercise are marked out with precision. This is done by listing (in the first column of Sched. 2 to the Act) the Acts (or sections of Acts) the functions under which are to be exercised by the Assembly. The functions thought suitable for transfer to the Assembly were, generally speaking, those hitherto exercised by the Secretary of State for Wales—education, local government, housing, town and country planning, highways, the health service, etc. Ministerial functions not transferred or reserved include taxation, social security, defence, industrial and energy policy, summer time, certain statutory undertakers, the University, etc. Where the exercise of a devolved power would or might affect a reserved area the Act withdraws the exercise of the power from the Assembly, or gives the Secretary of State power to intervene. This power of intervention can be exercised in different circumstances in different ways, for example by directing the Assembly to take or not to take certain action, by revoking statutory instruments, by intervening in planning decisions, etc. One thing the Assembly is expressly forbidden to do is to conduct relations with any country outside the United Kingdom. The functions of certain nominated bodies operating in Wales (not including the nationalised industries) may be transferred to the Assembly by ministerial order made with parliamentary approval.

The Act contains provisions about the holding of elections and who may vote; about disqualification for membership of the Assembly, and members' remuneration. It requires the Assembly to work through a committee structure similar to that in local government—it must appoint committees which between them must cover all the areas of government it is concerned with. The membership of these committees must as far as practicable reflect the party-balance in the Assembly. A central role in giving political leadership to the Assembly is given to the Executive Committee which also has a number of important functions in the realm of finance. (The party-balance rule does not apply to this committee).

As to the Assembly's financial arrangements, it has no taxing power. It will get its money from central government by way of a block grant. The Act's provisions parallel central institutions by providing the equivalent in Wales of the Consolidated Fund, National Loans Fund, Public Accounts Committee and Comptroller and Auditor General. As the Assembly succeeds to ministerial functions in relation to local government, it will be responsible for the calculation of and the distribution of the rate support grant. This will come out of and be a substantial proportion of, the block grant. The Assembly has also had put on it the duty to review the structure of local government in Wales and report its conclusions to the Secretary of State.

As to the judicial review and control of the Assembly's acts, it must be remembered that it is the successor to ministerial functions and is a Crown body: thus it will be in the same position in law as ministers from whom its functions were transferred, subject to the same controls as them, entitled to the same immunities. In addition the Attorney-General is specially empowered to take action against the Assembly to test the *vires* of its acts.

However, none of this will come about unless the electorate in Wales are in favour of it and even if they are in favour of it, in sufficient numbers, as if less than 40 per cent. of those entitled to vote say " yes " in the referendum, an order for the repeal of the Act will be laid before Parliament. The referendum will be held on March 1, 1979. At the time of the passing of the Act this seems a formidable hurdle. The timing of the referendum is in the Government's hands, unless a general election is held before then, in which case at least three months must elapse before the referendum is held.

The creation of the Assembly is a contentious political issue in Wales. The notes which follow refer to the politics of the matter where it seemed desirable for an understanding of the significance of various provisions. As this Act seeks to make a significant change in our constitutional arrangements some background notes on the law and administration of Wales are provided.

A brief history

The Act of Union of 1536 was " an Act for Laws and Justice to be administered in Wales in like form as it is in this Realm." It brought Wales within the realm of England and under the authority of Acts of Parliament. It was, however, but the last stage in a process of assimilation that had been taking place for over two centuries. It took a further six years for the administrative machinery necessary for full incorporation with England to be set up. This was accomplished by the Act of Union of 1542. " Broadly therefore it may be said that the Act of 1536 enunciates the general principles governing the Union and that of 1542 the details. Together they form the constitution under which Wales was henceforth to be governed " (W. Rees, *The Union of England and Wales*).

The most important immediate cause for the Union lay in the breach with Rome. Ecclesiastically, Wales lay within England as part of the province of Canterbury, but was not subject to the English Parliament. The establishment of a State Church required that the ecclesiastical and civil boundaries should coincide; the legal changes involved in the Reformation required Wales to be put on the same footing as England. And the justified fear of foreign invasion made urgent a unified defence system for England and Wales.

Under the Union the counties and boroughs henceforth sent representatives to Parliament. Welshmen were granted equality with Englishmen before the law: the severe disabilities previously applied to them were abolished. The English system of land tenure was introduced, and gavelkind where it still obtained in Wales was over a period displaced.

The English system of local government was applied to Wales. The country was divided into twelve counties, grouped into four areas each with three counties. Sheriffs, coroners and other officers were appointed, and eight Justices of the Peace for each county. " Local administration was now placed in the hands of men drawn from local families and the energies of these families were now directed to the prevention of disorder rather than its perpetration as hitherto " (David Williams, *A History of Modern Wales*, p. 44).

However, the system of government differed in some respects from that of England. Wales was given its own system of courts, the Courts of Great Session, largely independent of the courts at Westminster: in effect the system which had operated in North Wales for two and a half centuries was extended to the whole country. In these courts English law was administered—and in English, for the Act of Union required all official business to be in that tongue (out of a concern for administrative simplicity). Wales also had a separate organisation for revenue purposes, each group of three counties serving also as a fiscal unit with its own exchequer and system of audit. " Wales thus became a special administrative area " (Rees, *op. cit.* p. 49).

The Council of the Marches of Wales, formerly a prerogative court, was continued by the Act of Union as a permanent administrative body responsible to the Privy Council. It was abolished in 1641.

Apart from the abolition of the Courts of Great Session in 1830, little of direct relevance to the story happened until the latter half of the nineteenth century. It has been shown how the General Election of 1868 following the extension of the franchise in the previous year, marked the beginning of 50 years of " Welsh political nationalism as a major force in British public life," how the distinctive needs of Wales were brought " into the general context of British politics after the obscurity and isolation of centuries " (K. O. Morgan, *Wales in British Politics*, p. 297). The Sunday Closing (Wales) Act 1881 (referring to the closing of public houses) was the first Act to apply to Wales a legislative principle that did not apply to England. Even at that time it did not escape notice that the principle of treating Wales as a national unit could be extended to matters other than liquor licensing. (The present statutory provisions will be found in the Licensing Act 1964, ss. 66, 67 (as amended by the Local Government Act 1972, Sched. 25, paras. 3, 4) which give a local option exercised by plebiscite organised on a district council basis. The 1881 Act had recited that the people of Wales were desirous of the measure).

Another important issue was the provision and administration of education. The Welsh Intermediate Education Act 1889 required each new county and county borough, established by the legislation of 1888, to appoint an education committee which was to submit to the Charity Commissioners schemes for intermediate (that is secondary) and technical education; and empowered them to levy a $\frac{1}{2}$d. rate for that purpose. (It thus preceded, though it did not provide the pattern for, the Education Act 1902 which created the county and county borough councils as local education authorities and applied to England and Wales). In 1896 the Central Welsh Board was established under the 1889 Act as an examining and inspecting board for those schools. Suggestions for a National Council for Education in Wales were made from time to time. An Education Bill of 1907 originally contained a clause for establishing a " central education authority in Wales." One of the arguments against it was the difficulty of ensuring fair representation and national body for the rest of Wales as against the heavily populaced South —an issue that is not infrequently raised today. The clause and then the Bill was lost. But as a consolation prize the Welsh Department of the Board of Education was set up.

The creation of the University of Wales (1893)—the first College at Aberystwyth, was founded in 1872—of the National Library (1907) and the National Museum (1907) dates from this period.

A third issue, and one which was at the forefront of political life in Wales during this period, was the demand for the Disestablishment of the Church in Wales or, as it was seen, of the Church of England in Wales. As with any other issue affecting Wales, the Welsh interest in Parliament had to persuade a major British political party to its view—at this time this could of course only be the Liberal Party. Disestablishment was eventually provided for by the Welsh Church Act 1914, but did not take place until 1920.

Wales was chosen as a " special administrative area " in other legislation. The National Insurance Act 1911 provided in s. 82 for the appointment of Welsh Insurance Commissioners for the purpose of carrying Pt. I of the Act (relating to health insurance) into effect in Wales. The Ministry of Health Act 1919, which created that Ministry, provided in s. 5 that the Minister was to constitute a Welsh Board of Health " through whom he may exercise and perform in Wales in such manner as he may think fit any of his powers and duties." The (three) Board members were civil servants. The Board was in effect a local office of the Ministry. The same year, 1919, also saw the creation administratively of the Welsh Department of the Ministry of Agriculture responsible for a limited range of functions in Wales.

The Home Rule movement which, in relation to Ireland, so dominated English politics at that time, flickered uncertainly in Wales. There were a number of legislative suggestions. Perhaps the most remarkable was the National Institutions (Wales) Bill of 1891. The long title spoke of it as " a Bill to appoint a Secretary for Wales, to constitute a Welsh Education Department, to make further provision for local government and to create a National Council for Wales ". Of particular interest in the light of the Wales Act was the proposal that there was to be vested in the Secretary for

Wales the powers and duties of the principal Secretaries of State (except of that for War), the Local Government Board, Commissioners for Works and the Charity Commissioners " so far as such powers and duties relate to Wales." The National Council, representative of County and County Borough Councils, was " to discuss and inquire into such matters as they deem of common interest to Wales " and was to be empowered " to pass Bills in the nature of Private Bills " relating to public works in Wales and also to confirm provisional orders made by the Secretary. The Secretary could also transfer to the Council any statutory functions of a government department of an administrative character relating to matters " arising within Wales."

The Bill aroused little interest in Wales or Westminster. Attempts to gain support for Bills for the creation of the office of Secretary for Wales were made between 1908 and 1921 but again without success.

This is not the place to consider why the Home Rule movements never got off the ground in Wales. To do so one would have to take into account such matters as the party affiliation of Welsh M.P.s (overwhelmingly Liberal during this period), the relationship between each Welsh Parliamentary party and its United Kingdom party, the concern for and the effect of success in particular issues such as disestablishment, internal dissensions within the country etc. This matter is discussed at length in Morgan, *op. cit.*

In the 1920s and 1930s there were no significant changes in the law or administrative practice affecting Wales. " The quarter of a century which preceded the outbreak of the Great War was, thus, a period of great achievement in Welsh life, and is in strong contrast to the ineffectiveness of the quarter of a century which followed " (David Williams, *op. cit.* p. 284). Politically the Liberal party was replaced by Labour. In the 1905 general election Wales returned 29 Liberals, six Labour and no Conservatives; in the 1929 election 25 Labour, nine Liberals, one Conservative. In 1925 the Welsh Nationalist Party (now Plaid Cymru—Welsh Party) was formed. Its aim then was Dominion status; now independence. Attempts during this period to introduce Bills for a Secretary of State for Wales were as complete failures as the earlier.

Administrative decentralisation to the regions that was found necessary during the 1939–45 war included decentralisation to Wales as a unit. Under the Regional Commissioner scheme Wales was a region. In 1940 the Welsh Board of Health assumed within Wales the Ministry of Health's responsibility for housing, sewerage, water supplies, loan sanction, provisional orders and other local government services. By the end of the war 15 departments had established regional offices in Wales.

There was little enthusiasm in the Labour Government of 1945–51 for the creation of a separate government department—a Welsh Office, headed by a Secretary of State— to deal with the affairs of Wales. Significantly Bevan feared that " devolution of authority would divorce Welsh political activity from the main stream of British politics, as he felt was already happening in Scotland " (James Griffiths, *Pages from Memory*, pp. 161–163).

However, co-ordination between the various Government departments was sought to be achieved by a Conference of Heads of Departments. Thus " in the absence of a Department for Wales the Government evolved the necessary machinery to fill the gap, so that when the Welsh Office was created it did not have to work in a vacuum " (Gowan in *Welsh Studies in Public Law*, ed. Andrews, p. 53). And Wales was created as an administrative unit by the National Health Service Act 1946 (the Welsh Regional Hospital Board) and the Gas Act 1948 (the Wales Gas Board—not at all convenient administratively); but not by the Electricity Act 1947 (South Wales Electricity Board and Merseyside and North Wales Electricity Board).

The most the Labour Government was willing to do was to set up in 1948 the Council for Wales and Monmouthshire, a nominated body, whose function was to meet (in private) for the exchange of views and information, and to ensure that the Government was adequately informed on the impact of government action on the general life of the country.

It was a Conservative Government which created in 1951 the office of Minister for Welsh Affairs, but it was a curious arrangement, as the post, which existed until 1964, was always held in conjunction with another office—until 1957 by the Home Secretary, and from then until 1964 by the Minister of Housing and Local Government. In 1957 the Office of Minister of State for Welsh Affairs was created as a junior office in that Ministry. In 1951 the Welsh Office of that Ministry had been created; the Permanent Secretary of the Welsh Department of Education whose office had until then been in London was also given an office in Cardiff; and the office of the civil servant in charge of the Welsh Department of the Ministry of Agriculture was upgraded.

The Annual Report on Government Action in Wales was first published in 1957, and the Annual Digest of Welsh Statistics in 1954.

In 1957 the Council of Wales produced a memorandum which set out the case for a Secretary of State for Wales and a Welsh Office. The Government remained unconvinced (its response included the appointment of the Minister of State referred to) but the report must have added weight to those in the Labour Party who had been arguing the case for some time. An undertaking to appoint a Secretary of State was given by the Labour Party in its manifesto for the 1959 general election and reaffirmed in the 1964 manifesto. The office was therefore created when a Labour Government was returned in 1964. It has been pointed out that " the underlying case for the existence of a department of state is that it handles a specialised function, or a closely related group of functions. In the case of the Scottish Office and the Welsh Office, however, the role of the departments concerned is the government of part of the territory of Great Britain. Despite the fact that this principle had been accepted for Scotland in the nineteenth century, its extension to Wales met a great deal of resistance in Whitehall." (Gowan, *op. cit.* p. 56). And the first Secretary of State was later to write, " There were some who held the view that it would be best to begin without any specific transfer of powers and that we would serve Wales the better by acting as watchdog over the work of all departments. I did not share this view." (Griffiths, *op. cit.* p. 166).

The Secretary of State first took over executive responsibilities of the Ministry of Housing and Local Government in Wales and thus became responsible there for housing, town and country planning, new towns, local government, etc.

Over the years other functions were transferred to him. The written evidence submitted by the Welsh Office to the Commission on the Constitution explained the general principles applicable when that was done:

(i) the legislation itself applied alike to England and Wales. The Secretary of State for Wales would participate in the formulation of new policies and in the preparation of new legislation applying alike to England and Wales, though in practice the preparatory work was done mainly by the larger Whitehall department. Likewise responsibility for making major regulations affecting alike both countries rested with the appropriate Minister who would make them after consulting the Secretary of State.

(ii) The application of such legislation would be the responsibility in England of the appropriate Minister, in Wales of the Secretary of State. For example, under the Town and Country Planning Act the Welsh Secretary was responsible for the approval of structure plans, for calling-in planning applications and for deciding planning appeals. And in the housing field the different approach adopted by the Welsh Secretary to local authority refusal to implement the Housing Finance Act 1972 is shown in *Asher* v. *Secretary of State* [1974] Ch. 208.

With reference to the work of other government departments, where executive responsibilities have not been transferred to the Secretary of State, " the application of national policies in Wales will be for the Ministers centrally responsible, but [the Secretary of State] will have oversight within Wales of the execution of national policy by [them] " This was sought to be clarified by saying that the Welsh Secretary had " real powers to oversee the activity of all Government Departments in Wales and to see that they coordinate." An important field in this connection is that of economic and regional planning. The mechanics of this are explained in the Welsh Office Written Evidence to the Commission on the Constitution (paras. 33 to 37) and in Minutes of Evidence, Vol. 1, p. 91–111.

The most recent transfer of powers to the Secretary of State took place on April 1, 1978 (S.I. 1978 Nos. 272, 274).

Monmouthshire

Before the Act of Union the area later known as Monmouthshire was part of Wales. The shire of Monmouth was created by that Act, but the 12 shires into which the Wales created by the Act was divided did not include Monmouth. And the judicial and administrative arrangements made for that shire differed in a number of ways from those made for the 12 counties. It did not fall within the Courts of Great Session nor within the fiscal arrangements referred to above. In these matters it was administered in the same way as the English shires. Later, it was included in the Oxford, not the Wales, Assize circuit. On the other hand the Acts of Union nowhere expressly state that Monmouthshire was to be separated from Wales and added to England. But as against that, as the 12 counties and Monmouthshire were annexed to England, and the 12 declared to be Wales, it might be said that Monmouthshire was, in law, English. (Rees, *op. cit.* p. 51, says, that it would be difficult to assign an adequate reason why Monmouthshire was singled out for special treatment). The Local Government Act 1933 included Monmouthshire in the list of English Counties (see Sched. 1). When it was desired to apply an Act to Monmouth as well as to Wales, it was necessary to say " This Act shall apply to Wales and Monmouthshire."

The position now is that the Local Government Act 1972, s. 269 provides that in Acts passed on or after April 1, 1974, " Wales " means the area consisting of the counties established by s. 20 of the Act; and by Pt. 1 of Sched. 4 to the Act, this includes the new county of Gwent which embraces, in effect, the former county of Monmouthshire (and the county borough of Newport).

Local government in Wales

It is desirable to say something on this topic for two connected reasons, first, because of the discussion on s. 12 of the Act, and secondly because proposals for reform of local government in Wales have for long been entangled with proposals for devolution, particularly in connection with suggestions for the creation of an all-Wales authority of some kind. (See, *e.g.* the reference above to the National Institutions (Wales) Bill, and Trice, " Welsh Local Government Reform " [1970] P.L. 277–297.)

The structure of local government in Wales is basically the same as that of England as established by the Local Government Acts of 1888 and 1894. Under the Local Government Act 1972 there is the two-tier system as in England, with eight counties and 37 districts (there are no metropolitan counties). These replaced the 13 counties, four county boroughs and 164 county districts previously in existence. However, the structure of local government in Wales has been under separate consideration from that in England since the end of the 1939–45 War. Under the Local Government Act 1958 separate Commissions were created for England and Wales to make recommendations on the boundaries of county and county boroughs. The Welsh Commission's draft proposals for, *inter alia*, a reduction to five counties met with hostility. Revised proposals were no more favoured, and were rejected by the Government.

In 1965 the Secretary of State for Wales set up an Interdepartmental Working Party of senior officials of relevant departments to look at the problem again. The Working Party consulted informally a number of people experienced in local government in Wales. The three broad lines of thought which the Working Party noted in the views of those informal advisers were:

(a) that the then existing two-tier structure should be retained but with fewer and stronger authorities;

(b) that that structure should be replaced by a single tier of all-purpose authorities;

(c) that some kind of regional or sub-regional authority should be formed.

Those who favoured a single tier system (they proposed 16 authorities) also, it seems, took the view that some functions could be exercised more efficiently on an all-Wales level and were therefore in favour of an elected all-Wales council. The Government, having considered the report of its Working Party opted for a two-tier system, rejected the single tier proposal and with it proposals for a new all-Wales body (*Local Government in Wales*, Cmnd. 3340 of 1967). They said, " Some far-reaching suggestions have been put forward for an elected council to take over the administration of certain central government services such as trunk roads and hospitals and also of certain services such as parts of the educational and health and welfare services, town and country planning . . . now run by the counties and county boroughs or by joint authorities. So far as present central government services are concerned, such a change would require extensive alterations in existing legislation and national administrative machinery and would require decisions on wider issues than can be properly decided in the context of *the present reorganisation* of local government in Wales " (para. 47). As for such a council taking over the work done by joint authorities, it would not be appropriate on the one hand to alter the structure of local government so as to strengthen local authorities for the better discharge of their functions, and on the other to transfer some of those functions elsewhere. There was, however, the White Paper said, a need to improve the then existing machinery in Wales for advisory and promotional work. The Council for Wales which had been set up in 1949 had, on the creation of the Welsh Economic Council in 1965, been discontinued. The Government therefore proposed, and later proceeded to the creation of, the Welsh Council which provides a forum for the interchange of errors and information, assists in the formulation of plans, advises the Secretary of State on major land use matters, etc.

The phrase italicised in the above paragraph will be noted. The White Paper contained proposals for legislative action. In the previous year, 1966, the Redcliffe Maud Commission on Local Government in England had been appointed. The Government decided, however, " to proceed with this reorganisation instead of including Wales within the terms of reference " of that Commission. It did so for two reasons, first the need for early action was particularly urgent in Wales, and secondly, consideration of the reorganisation of local government in Wales was already well advanced at the time the Commission was set up (para. 2).

The White Paper proposals of 1967 (Cmnd. 3340) were in brief for five counties, three county boroughs in South Wales (one of the four was to be abolished) and 36 districts. Following consultations these were amended slightly in November 1968. In June 1969 the Redcliffe Maud Commission on Local Government reported (Cmnd. 4040). In the light of that the Government reconsidered the proposed retention of county boroughs and in March 1970 a White Paper (Cmnd. 4310) proposed three unitary authorities for the area of the former counties of Glamorgan and Monmouthshire. The incoming Conservative Government of 1970 thought that it was wrong to treat that area differently from the rest of Wales, and proposed a two-tier system for the whole of Wales, with seven county councils and 36 district councils. In the result the Local Government Act 1972 provided for eight county councils. (The originally proposed East Glamorgan county was split into two—Mid and South Glamorgan. The opposition regarded this as gerrymandering, the aim being to ensure that at least one county in Wales—South Glamorgan, where Cardiff predominates—might be Conservative controlled. (It was not from 1973 to 1977, but is now.))

The 1972 Act created separate Local Government Boundary Commissioners for England and Wales (see Pt. IV of the Act).

Nominated bodies in Wales

It is relevant to refer to these in the context of the devolution discussions and legislation.

(i) The nationalised industries. For the most part these operate on a United Kingdom basis. For internal administrative purposes they may recognise Wales as a unit (e.g. Wales Gas, a division of the British Gas Corporation, but not, e.g. British Rail Western Region). The water industry (assuming that this can properly be regarded as " nationalised ") presents particular problems. It is dealt with in the note to s. 63 of the Act.

(ii) The Health Service. The organisation of the Health Service in Wales differs from that in England in that in Wales there are no Regional Health Authorities, only Area Health Authorities. In the absence of R.H.A.s, Welsh A.H.A.s are responsible for certain functions additional to those vested in English A.H.A.s. In addition there is in Wales a special health authority created by the Secretary of State, to provide various services on an all-Wales basis for the N.H.S. in Wales including design and construction of major capital works, and computers. (See Welsh Health Technical Services Organisation (Establishment and Constitution) Order 1973 (S.I. 1973 No. 1624).)

(iii) The Welsh Development Agency. This was created by an Act of that name of 1975. Its functions are to promote Wales as a location of industrial development, to provide finance for persons intending to carry on industrial undertakings and to provide or manage sites for them, to bring derelict land into use, etc. (s. 1 (3)). It is to exercise those functions for the purpose of furthering economic development, promoting industrial efficiency, safeguarding employment, etc. (s. 1 (2)). It is a non-Crown body subject to ministerial direction.

(iv) Community Land Act 1975: the Land Authority for Wales. The Act enables certain public authorities to acquire land suitable for development. In England and Scotland these authorities are the local authorities and New Town authorities. The White Paper, Land (Cmnd. 5730), which introduced the scheme, stated that the creation of one central agency for the United Kingdom for this purpose had been rejected on the ground that it would be too remote—hence the conferment of powers in England and Scotland on the bodies mentioned. However, this argument, it was said, did not apply to Wales because of the size of the country and of its population. The Act therefore created the Land Authority for Wales to exercise there those functions which elsewhere are exercised by local authorities. In the debate on the Bill a Minister stated in response to criticisms of the exclusion of local authorities from the scheme in Wales, that he hoped the Authority was " an interim measure in the context of future devolution " (Standing Committee G, June 12, 1975, col. 993). The Authority is a non-Crown body subject to detailed Secretary of State directions. It may arrange for the discharge of any of its functions by a local authority.

(v) New Towns and the Rural Development Board. The New Towns Act 1965, s. 2, empowers the creation in the United Kingdom of development corporations by ministerial order. There is one such in Wales (Cwmbran). The Development of Rural Wales Act 1976 created the Development Board for Rural Wales. Its general function is to prepare and undertake measures for the economic and social development of the area for which it is responsible, and in particular for the development of any area of a new town within its area (any development corporation established under the New Towns Act within its area was to be dissolved—there was one, at Newtown). In carrying out that general function it has to submit proposals to the Secretary of State and carry out those which are approved by him (s. 3). It must also give effect to such directions as the Secretary of State may give it (s. 2). It may appoint any public body to act on its behalf and may itself act as agent for the Welsh Development Agency in some matters (ss. 4 (1), 8).

(vi) Miscellaneous. (a) The Development of Tourism Act 1969 created the English, Scottish and Wales Tourist Boards for the promotion of that industry. Ministerial functions in relation to the Wales Board were allocated by the Act (s. 1 (6)) to the Secretary of State for Wales.

(b) The Countryside Commission, created by the Countryside Act 1968, was required to appoint a Committee for Wales to which the Commission was empowered, after consulting the Secretary of State, to delegate any of its functions in Wales (s. 3).

(c) The Welsh Consumer Council carries on within Wales the work of the National Consumer Council (they are both non-statutory).

(d) The Sports Council for Wales was created by Charter in 1972.

(e) The Welsh Arts Council is a Committee of the Arts Council of Great Britain receiving all its money from the Council.

(f) One of the members of the Independent Broadcasting Authority has to be someone who is suited to make the interests of Wales his special care (Independent Broadcasting Authority Act 1973, Sched. 1, para. 1 (1)). Responsibility for the policy and content of B.B.C. Wales programmes is vested in the (non-statutory) National Broadcasting Council for Wales.

(g) There are separate Historic Buildings Councils for England, Scotland and Wales (Historic Buildings and Ancient Monuments Act 1953, ss. 1–3).

(vii) Other provisions concerning government and public administration in Wales.

(a) The Ombudsmen

—Parliamentary. The Welsh Office is of course listed in the Parliamentary Commissioner for Administration Act 1967 as one of the Departments subject to the Commissioner's jurisdiction. Matters arising in Wales which are the responsibility of other Departments are also investigatable in the usual way.

—Health Service. By s. 31 (1) of the National Health Service Reorganisation Act 1973 there is a Health Service Commissioner for England and one for Wales. Both offices are currently held by the same person (the Parliamentary Commissioner). For delineation of jurisdiction between the two Commissioners, see s. 34 (2). (see now the corresponding sections of the National Health Service Act 1977).

—Local Government. For the purpose of investigating complaints against local authorities, the Local Government Act 1974 created two Commissions for Local Administration, one for England, one for Wales. Each Commission consists of the Parliamentary Commissioner and such other persons—"Local Commissioners"—as may be appointed. One full time Commissioner has been appointed for Wales. The Land Authority for Wales has been added to the authorities (listed in s. 25 of the 1974 Act) subject to investigation.

(b) The Council on Tribunals. The Tribunals and Inquiries Act 1971 provides that there shall be a Scottish Committee of the Council. There is no such Committee for Wales, but in making appointments to the Council the Lord Chancellor is required to have regard to the need for representation of the interests of persons in Wales (s. 2 (4)).

The Welsh Language

It would not be appropriate to attempt to provide here an account of the significance of the Welsh language in Welsh politics and in the devolution discussions. (See for example A. H. Birch, *Political Integration and Disintegration in the British Isles*; Tom Nairn, *The Break-up of Britain*. For the view of the Welsh Nationalist Party see Commission on the Constitution, Minutes of Evidence V, Wales, pp. 79–91). A relevant provision of the Act of 1536 has been referred to. It was repealed by the Welsh Courts Act 1942. The Elections (Welsh Forms) Act 1964 authorised the use in connection with elections in Wales of translations of statutory forms into Welsh. The Committee on the Legal Status of the Welsh Language (Cmnd. 2785) recommended in 1964 that there should be a "clear, positive, legislative declaration of general application, to the effect that any act, writing or thing done in Welsh in Wales or Monmouthshire should have the like legal force as if it had been done in England." It was followed by the Welsh Language Act 1967 which authorised the use of Welsh in any legal proceedings in Wales by anyone who desires to use it, and provided for Welsh versions of statutory forms. One in five of those living in Wales is able to speak, and one in six is able to read, Welsh.

The Commission on the Constitution

It is generally believed that the announcement in October 1968 by the Labour Government of the appointment of the Commission was not unconnected with the earlier electoral progress of the Scottish and Welsh Nationalist Parties. In a by-election in the Carmarthen constituency in 1966 the Nationalist candidate converted a Labour majority of 9,200 in the 1966 general election into a Labour minority of 2,400. At the Hamilton by-election in Scotland in 1967 the Nationalist candidate converted a Labour majority of 16,800 into a minority of 1,800. In the 1966 general election the 20 Welsh Nationalists who stood collected a total of 61,071 votes. In 1970, 36 candidates got 175,016 votes. In the 1974 elections the total vote for 36 candidates was 171,364 in February and 166,321 in October. This was 11·4 per cent. and 10·8 per cent. of the total vote in Wales respectively. In Scotland in the October 1974 election the nationalist vote was a substantial increase on the February vote and was some 30 per cent. of the total vote. At present (Summer 1978) there are three Welsh nationalist and 11 Scottish nationalist M.P.s.

The terms of reference of the Commission required it "to examine the present functions of the central legislature and government in relation to the several countries ... of the United Kingdom; to consider having regard, *inter alia*, to developments in local Government organisation ... whether any changes are desirable in those functions...." The Commission's report was published in 1973 in two volumes (Cmnd. 5460) the first being the Report (by 11 members) the second the Memorandum of Dissent (by two members).

The Report said "We have no doubt that the main intention behind our appointment was that we should investigate the case for transferring or devolving responsibility for the exercise of government functions from Parliament and the central government to new institutions of government in the various countries and regions of the United Kingdom" (para. 13). They also believed that what they regarded as the obvious discontent with workings of government was particularly strong amongst those living furthest from London.

All the 11 members who signed the Report agreed that executive functions should where practicable be devolved to newly constituted authorities; that Scotland and Wales should have directly-elected Assemblies; that in England there should be no regional Assemblies. But beyond this there was disagreement. Nine of the 11 thought it was not necessary to have a uniform system of government in all parts of Great Britain: two thought it was, so that if any region had an assembly, every region should. These two favoured a scheme of executive devolution so that there would be in Wales an elected assembly with responsibility for policy-making and administration within the framework of Acts of Parliament, with similar assemblies for Scotland and the various regions of England. Of the other nine, six favoured a scheme of legislative devolution so that there would be a transfer to a Welsh legislature of responsibility for a number of specific matters, *e.g.* town and country planning. Two of the nine favoured a Welsh Advisory Council, directly elected to replace the existing Welsh Council. The subscribers to the Memorandum of Dissent, who disagreed with the view taken by the Report of the Commission's terms of reference, proposed seven elected assemblies and governments, one for Wales, one for Scotland, and one for each of five English regions.

Appointed by a Labour Government, the Commission reported to a Conservative Government. The Conservative Party was the only major party which did not submit evidence to the Commission. Labour were returned in the 1974 general elections.

It is convenient at this point to look at some of the evidence presented to the Commission in the light of the form the Wales Bill eventually took, and of the debates that took place on it. On the first day of oral evidence the Permanent Under Secretary at the Welsh Office said, "The essential feature of a Parliament of Wales is that you have a body of elected representatives of the people with responsibilities taken *from the Parliament in Westminster and from United Kingdom Ministers*. An alternative ... is to ... take responsibilities not from that quarter nor indeed *from local government*, but from the large and growing field in between covered by *nominated bodies*." (Minutes of Evidence I, p. 9, Q. 7: italics added: note the three possible sources).

The evidence submitted by the Welsh Council of Labour (as representing the Labour Party in Wales) must be of particular interest. (The Secretary of State was later to say "The policy in the Bill has sprung from the endeavours of the Labour movement in Wales. No one else is answerable for it" (H.C. Vol. 945, col. 798). That evidence rejected separatism and federalism (as the Report itself was to do) and the grant of legislative powers to a Welsh Assembly. At the time (1970) it will be remembered, local government had not been refashioned by the Act of 1972, and the latest pronouncement had been the White Paper of 1967 (as amended in respect of Wales in the way referred to above). In suggesting an elected Assembly the party had in mind some " fundamental considerations." The first was the value of an all-Wales authority *as the top tier of local government.* Some local authority functions could better be carried out, the evidence said, on an all-Wales basis. Local government reorganisation should be looked at again to provide for an all-Wales authority which would therefore to that extent take away functions from local authorities. Beneath that authority there would be a single tier of local authorities. A second fundamental consideration was the need to extend democratic control over as many *nominated bodies* as possible. In some cases this could be done by transferring the function of the body to the Assembly (*e.g.* the Regional Hospital Board); in some other cases the Assembly would take over the function of nominating to the body (*e.g.* the Arts Council). Third but rather more tentatively, more powers should be transferred to the Welsh Office, and in due course some of the *Welsh Office* functions could be given to the Assembly. The witnesses were clear that while central and local government had to be considered together in the context of devolution, their proposal for an elected Assembly had a validity of its own, though it was not possible to be specific about its powers until they knew what the final proposals for local government reorganisation were to be (Minutes of Evidence I, p. 26, Q. 31–38). Thus when during the deliberations of the Commission the Government produced the Bill which became the Local Government Act 1972, the Labour Party in Wales requested the Commission to ask the Government to halt consideration of local government reorganisation until the Commission had reported. An all-Wales authority, they reiterated, must "grow naturally out of" local government. They added that it would be undesirable to slot in a regional authority between central and local government.

The evidence given by Mr. G. P. Davies contains, in retrospect, much of interest. This witness had been a Labour Parliamentary candidate, was at the time Chairman of the Welsh Hospital Board and later was appointed special (political) adviser to the Secretary of State. The changes he considered were (a) the transfer of more functions to the Secretary of State—this by itself would not be enough; (b) a directly elected Assembly which would be empowered to enact legislation in certain specified fields subordinate to Westminster legislation—a quasi-federal solution he called it: this, he thought would not carry enough support; (c) an Assembly to which specific executive powers would be transferred from central government departments or from existing administrative or statutory bodies, which could co-ordinate the activities of local authorities and which could take over the functions of the Welsh Council and of other advisory bodies: there was he thought, substantial support for such a body, adding significantly "although hitherto it has been conceived of as the top tier of a reformed Welsh local government structure" (Minutes of Evidence I, p. 68).

The evidence of D. M. Evans and J. Reynolds is also of particular interest. (See *Political Quarterly* Vol. 42 (1971), p. 191.)

The nationalist party argued for "a Welsh state endowed with all the powers of a modern state ... This involves the ultimate transfer of the whole range of government to the new State ... The powers now exercised by the U.K. Parliament in relation to Wales will be transferred to the Parliament of Wales and the functions now exercised by the U.K. Government in Wales will be exercised by the Government of Wales." (Mr. (now Judge) Powell, Minutes of Evidence I, p. 33). "We want a separate state, a separate government and a separate administration ... It is essential to have control of our defence policy [and hence we reject federalism]." (Mr. G. Evans, M.P., *op. cit.* p. 85).

The Liberal Party favoured a federal system. (*op. cit.* pp. 44–58).

The Scotland and Wales Bill

In June 1974 the Government published *Devolution within the United Kingdom: Some alternatives for discussion*, and in November 1975 its proposals in *Our Changing Democracy: Devolution to Scotland and Wales* (Cmnd. 6348). In April 1976 the Government started to incur expenditure on accommodation, in Edinburgh and Cardiff, for the two proposed Assemblies. It was originally intended that a Bill would be presented in the spring of that year, for discussion only, perhaps on a " take note " motion, but this was abandoned. In May the Lord President outlined in the House the decisions taken on the Scotland and Wales Bill (H.C. Vol. 912, col. 270), and in August the Government issued a further White Paper setting out amended proposals (Cmnd. 6585). The Bill was presented in November 1976. It was approved on Second Reading by 35 votes (H.C. Vol. 922, col. 974). Progress in Committee (on the floor of the House, it being a constitutional measure) was so slow that the Government sought to impose a " guillotine." This being rejected (H.C. Vol. 926, col. 1362) the Bill was dropped. The House had spent 15 days discussing it. Separate Bills for Scotland and Wales were presented in November 1977. In the meantime in 1976 the Government published a consultative document, *Devolution: The English Dimension* in which it rejected the idea of an English Assembly and of regional legislative assemblies.

A detailed account of the Scotland and Wales Bill is not necessary, but the following comments are relevant at this point in the light of later developments.

(i) The Government had decided against having separate Bills as to do so " would demand too much Parliamentary time for both to pass in a single session " (H.C. Vol. 912, col. 271). The Opposition case for separate Bills was that the problems of the two countries were very different, but the Government suspected the real reason was to prevent devolution to Wales from taking place at all. Whatever the motives were on both sides, the subsequent joint Act would have been inconvenient in use, with differing provisions for Scotland and Wales not infrequently dealt with in the same section (see, *e.g.* cl. 78, rate support grants). The Government conceded that it would be very difficult to split the Bill so that the clauses effecting only Scotland or Wales should be discussed in the respective Grand Committee (H.C. Vol. 912, col. 281).

(ii) The Government decided against a referendum, which had been much mooted. There would be " great difficulties in putting any devolution proposals to the public in the form of a referendum " (H.C. Vol. 912, col. 276). The Welsh Labour Party supported this in September 1976, asking whether those in the Party who argued for it were prepared to see the extension of public ownership and the abolition of the eleven-plus to be made subject to referendum. However, support for the Bill amongst Labour M.P.s, and elsewhere, was less than solid. Parliamentary arithmetic was such that the support of the former was necessary to ensure the passage of the Bill. The Government therefore gave way to their demands for a referendum, and provision for one was made by the Government in the Wales Bill.

(iii) Opposition also came from within Labour ranks on the ground that the Assembly would be seen to be another tier of the Government. The proposals would therefore, it was argued, be made more palatable if a firm commitment to local government reorganisation was given. The Secretary of State's view (expressed at the time when the Scotland and Wales Bill was being drafted) was that while there might be a case for such reorganisation, there was no general agreement as to what should be done, and nothing could be allowed to hold up the Assembly. To provide a Bill at that time specifically for local government reorganisation, or to put powers for that purpose into the proposed Bill would both involve unacceptable delay. Nor would it be possible to give the Assembly power to reform local government, as it was not intended that it should have powers of primary legislation (which would of course be necessary for that purpose). Nor would it be practicable to give the Assembly powers of primary legislation on local government matters alone. The Assembly would of course be free to express its view on local government reorganisation. In the result the Scotland and Wales Bill contained no provisions concerning local government.

(iv) An official Opposition attempt to exclude Wales from the Scotland and Wales Bill failed by 24 votes.

Wales at Westminster

Under the House of Commons (Redistribution of Seats) Act 1949, the minimum number of seats for Wales is specified as 35; there are at present 36. Were the average electorate to be the same throughout the United Kingdom, Wales would have 31 seats. Electorates in Wales range in size from 26,722 (Merioneth) to 76,089 (Wrexham) (October 1974 figures).

Government action taken in Wales, whether by the Secretary of State for Wales or any other Minister, is subject to parliamentary scrutiny in the same way as action taken elsewhere. With regard to parliamentary questions, Welsh Office questions are answered first once every five weeks.

Very few public Bills deal exclusively with Wales. Such as do may, by Standing Order, be dealt with by a committee that includes all Welsh constituency members. This device has rarely been used.

In 1960 the Welsh Grand Committee was established. It consists of all Welsh constituency members together with not more than five others. It has power only to " consider such specified matters relating exclusively to Wales as may be referred to them " by agreement through the " usual channels." The committee are to " report only that they have considered the said matters." Votes are not taken. The committee meets about three times a session. It does not consider estimates or Bills.

In addition one day a session (about six hours) is given by the House to the discussion of Welsh business. (See Commission on the Constitution, Research Paper No. 5. Welsh Committees in the House of Commons, by Borthwick.)

The effect of the devolution measures on the role and number of Welsh (and Scottish) M.P.s and hence on Parliament itself was much discussed. Under the Wales Act many functions exercised by Ministers, principally the Secretary of State, are transferred to the Assembly. A member of the public with a complaint about the exercise of those functions will have to raise it with a member of the Assembly, not with his M.P. A Minister no longer being responsible to Parliament, a member will have no special role in the matter. If, as is frequently the case, the complaint to the M.P. is not about central but about local government, *e.g.* education, housing, there may have been before devolution scope for intervention by the central government, *e.g.* s. 68 of the Education Act 1944, and therefore for effective intervention by an M.P. After devolution, where such intervention is by the Assembly, *e.g.* s. 68 of the Education Act 1944, scope for intervention by an M.P. is drastically reduced. There seems no doubt therefore that following devolution the role of Welsh M.P.s must be considerably diminished. Of course, many matters affecting Wales remain to Parliament and therefore M.P.s—trade and industry, taxation, social security, industrial relations, EEC, defence policy, but many constituency matters will be lost.

This brings us to the related " West Lothian " question, named after the constituency of the (anti-devolution, Labour) member Mr. Dalyell, who persistently raised it. The argument is that although English (and Scottish) members will not be able to vote on Scottish housing, education, etc. (these being within the legislative competence of the Scottish Assembly), Scottish members will be able to vote on those matters as they affect England. The argument is not so strong as it affects Wales, as administrative power only and not legislative power is to be devolved there and thus English (and Welsh) M.P.s have retained legislative powers over Wales. The problem is not new. In the debates on various Irish Home Rule Bills the adoption of an in-out procedure was considered to deal with it, but was abandoned. In the context of the present devolution measures it would have involved Scottish M.P.s not voting on matters affecting England which English M.P.s could not vote on in respect of Scotland. This was generally regarded in debates on the Wales Bill as quite unworkable and unacceptable. For example, financial measures affecting one part of the Kingdom would be bound to have some effect on other parts. And the House would consist of three groups of Members—English, Scottish and Welsh M.P.s—whose rights would depend on the constituency they represented.

At early stages in the debate the possibility was raised of the reduction at some time in the future in the number of Welsh (and Scottish) M.P.s in recognition of their diminished role. The Commission on the Constitution had referred to the problem, and a White Paper (Cmnd. 5732) had dismissed the possibility. As stated above, there are at present 36 Welsh constituencies, and if Wales was treated on a parity with the United Kingdom as a whole there would be 31. The average electorate in England is 66,056, in Wales 57,088, in Scotland 53,336. This over-representation for Wales has long been accepted for such reasons as the geographical size of some constituencies and the need to balance the interests of various regions of the country. It is the case, of course, that the majority of Welsh (as of Scottish) seats are held by Labour, and that a reduction in the number of these seats might be likely to reduce the number of Labour M.P.s. It was therefore out of a desire to provide for a full discussion of the matter for instructional purposes that the Opposition moved a new clause to the Bill, providing that a Speaker's conference might be convened " with the function of considering and making recommendations to the House of Commons relating to the appropriate number of Members of that House representing Welsh constituencies after the enactment of this Act.'' (An identical clause was moved without success on the Scotland Bill). The arguments for retaining the full complement of Welsh seats after devolution are respectable: (i) as sovereignty remains in Parliament, it is right that all parts of Great Britain should be fully represented in that Parliament; (ii) Parliament retains oversight of the '' over-riding '' provisions of the devolution Acts: those areas subject to those provisions should therefore be fully represented; (iii) the collection and distribution of taxes is done on a central government basis, with parliamentary approval. All parts of the country should therefore be fully represented. If either Assembly had taxing powers, it would be necessary to reconsider the position; (iv) future legislation would have to be very carefully examined to see whether it should apply to Wales, and what the powers of the Assembly should be. This required a full complement of Welsh M.P.s to undertake that scrutiny.

While recognising the force of the arguments for the retention of Welsh over-representation, the Opposition thought that it would be an inevitable consequence of devolution that, however regrettable, there would be a demand for a re-consideration of the position. This was '' for the simple reason that the impact on England will in the end prove to be untenable ''—untenable for the reason, for example, that when Parliament was concerned with subordinate legislation effective in England, Welsh and Scottish M.P.s would be involved, so that English electors would only have 83 per cent. control over their destiny, whereas the Welsh and Scots would have through their devolved constitutions 100 per cent. control over their destiny (H.C. Vol. 948, col. 1295, Mr. Pym). Hence this clause. (For the Opposition to seek to provide in the Bill for a reduction in the number of Welsh constituencies might have been out of order.) The outcome might be not merely a reduction to parity (31 seats) but below it. As this would be abhorrent to the Opposition—so much so that the chief Opposition spokesman said that it was precisely for this reason that they were fighting the Bill (H.C. Vol. 948, col. 1249)—the remedy, they said, was to drop the Bill which was creating the problem.

The Unity of the Kingdom

Cl. 1 of the Bill as laid read: '' The following provisions of this Act make changes in the government of Wales as part of the United Kingdom. They do not affect the unity of the United Kingdom or the supreme authority of Parliament to make laws for the United Kingdom or any part of it.'' The same clause (*mutatis mutandis*) appeared as cl. 1 of the Scotland and Wales Bill and of the Scotland Bill and indeed comprised the whole of Pt. 1 of each Bill.

The Government's view was that this Bill and others just referred to not only maintained but strengthened the unity of the Kingdom by meeting demands for change. This political judgment was of course challenged by the Bill's opponents, who were not only from the Opposition. Of the nine Labour back-benchers who spoke in the second reading debate, five were against the Bill. Of those five, three voted for it, one against, and one abstained. (The Bill was given a second reading by 294 votes to 264). Cl. 1 of the Scotland Bill had in fact been deleted by the Commons at the Committee stage and when the Wales Bill later went into Committee the Government announced that it was '' not seeking to retain '' cl. 1. The Opposition suggested that this withdrawal was a recognition that the Bill did indeed affect the unity of the Kingdom. The Government said that the Bill was consistent with that unity, that the clause was accurate and a useful declaratory provision, but that as the Committee on the Scotland Bill had disagreed with it, '' it might assist the Committee and speed up the debate if the Government made their position clear at the outset '' (H.C. Vol. 945, col. 591). (There then followed a six-hour debate on the withdrawn clause, with the result that one hour was left for a debate on the method of voting for Assembly members, and that there was no discussion at all on seven clauses or on Sched. 1).

Other views were that the clause accurately stated the position, but was surplusage; and that it broke a basic rule of drafting, that when introducing an Act one does not make expressions of opinion (Sir D. Renton). (The Government might have got itself in less difficulty if it had made use of a preamble).

In the second reading debate and at later stages, the opponents argued that the Assembly would provide a stage for the nationalists to seek their goal of independence. (The Welsh nationalists said they regarded the Bill as a step in the direction of placing Wales amongst the free nations of Europe, for as yet the Welsh are '' totally unfree '' (H.C. Vol. 939, col. 405). The Assembly, it was argued, would be a focus of discontent.

As it was to be dependent for its finance on central government any shortcomings could be laid at the door of central government in England. A national assembly of elected persons would be bound to seek to increase its powers. All these factors would tend to the disunity of the Kingdom. One rather different view was that the demand for separatism would come not from Wales, but from England. The argument was that the economic and social conditions of Wales are such that there is necessarily a greater call there on public resources than in England. (For identifiable public expenditure per head in England and Wales, see H.C. Vol. 947, col. 309 *et seq.*) The method of financing the Assembly would, it was argued, make this clear. The English could not be expected to be perpetually tolerant, and would seek to cast Wales and Scotland adrift: with their own Assemblies they could look after themselves, it would be said, or at the least the Government was likely, after the referendum, to welcome giving taxing powers to the Assembly to silence the demands for increases in the block grant. Neither of those developments would be to the benefit of Wales.

The Opposition argued that if the Government saw the Bill as a measure of administrative reform, democraticising government, why were not its advantages being extended to the Kingdom as a whole? It would not then be seen to be a sop to nationalism. Based as it was on nationalism it would be likely to advance fissiparous tendencies within the Kingdom. Given that some political response to nationalism was required the solution provided was unstable. Only some form of federalism, it was suggested, might be the answer but there was no evidence of public demand for it.

No detailed alternative proposals for administrative or constitutional reform came from the Conservative Opposition, nor should they have been expected, for the party did not submit evidence to the Commission on the Constitution. There were occasional references from that quarter and elsewhere to the possibility of the amendment of House of Commons procedures to deal more fully with Welsh Affairs by for example the appointment of a Welsh Select Committee which might meet elsewhere than at Westminster.

Parliamentary Debates

The Scotland and Wales Bill (referred to above) had been discussed for 15 days before the failure of the " guillotine " motion. After the one-day debate on the Second Reading of the Wales Bill a " guillotine " motion was approved. This allowed 11 days for the Committee Stage, Report and Third reading on the Bill. Following a further " guillotine " motion two days were allowed for the consideration of Lords' amendments, and a further two and a half hours for consideration of Lords' amendments moved in lieu of amendments to which the Commons had disagreed. The Lords spent one day on the Second Reading, nine days on Committee, Report and third reading (there are no " guillotines " in the Lords) and two days on consideration of Commons Reasons.

For parliamentary debates, see *Hansard*, H.C. Vol. 939, cols. 357, 655; Vol. 945, cols. 465, 467, 675, 1235 and 1430; Vol. 947, cols. 255, 463; Vol. 948, col. 1201; Vol. 949, cols. 249, 995; Vol. 954, cols. 434, 583, 802, 1671; H.L. Vol. 392, cols. 828, 857, 1072, 1075, Vol. 393, cols. 324, 515, 1126, 1387; Vol. 394, cols. 989, 1007, 1174, 1700; Vol. 395, cols. 651, 968.

Commencement

The Act shall come into force on a day to be appointed by the Secretary of State.

PART I

THE WELSH ASSEMBLY

Establishment and membership

The Welsh Assembly

1.—(1) There shall be a Welsh Assembly.

(2) The initial members of the Assembly shall be returned for the areas which, at the time of their election, are constituencies for parliamentary elections in Wales, and there shall be—

(*a*) three initial members for each of those areas of which the electorate is more than 125 per cent. of the electoral quota; and

(*b*) two initial members for each of the others.

(3) The members of the Assembly other than the initial members shall be returned for the Assembly constituencies for the time being specified in an Order in Council under Schedule 1 to this Act, and there shall be one member for each such constituency.

(4) The Assembly shall be a body corporate.

(5) In this section and Part III of Schedule 1 to this Act " initial members " means members elected before an election to which an Order in Council under Part I of that Schedule applies, and " electorate " and " electoral quota " have the meanings assigned to them by paragraph 14 of that Schedule.

DEFINITION

" Wales ": by the Local Government Act 1972, s. 269, Wales comprises the eight counties created by that Act, including Gwent, formerly Monmouthshire.

GENERAL NOTE

The Act provides for the creation of a Welsh Assembly and for the exercise by it of the functions conferred on it by the Act. These functions being functions hitherto exercised by Ministers may be classified as executive or administrative. (In contrast the Scotland Act 1978 creates a Scottish Assembly with legislative powers and an Executive whose members are appointed from among the members of the Assembly). The Welsh Assembly is thus to be a body corporate (s. 1 (4)) capable of holding property, of suing and being sued, etc. (The Scottish Assembly on the other hand is not a body corporate.) In this and certain other respects the Welsh Assembly resembles a local authority.

The Assembly is a Crown body. This is not expressly stated in the Act, but the functions conferred on it are Crown functions, and its staff are civil servants (s. 65 (1)). Further the phrase in s. 70 (1) " notwithstanding that each of them [*i.e.*, the Attorney-General and the Assembly] acts on behalf of the Crown " clearly indicates the Assembly's status. (That phrase was not in the Bill as laid but was part of a Government amendment to that section.) In addition a number of amendments to enactments in Sched. 11 equate the Assembly with a Government department, *e.g.* para. 85 applying ss. 55 to 59 of the Patents Act 1977 to the Assembly (use of patented inventions for Crown services). As the Assembly is a Crown body the usual consequences flow, *e.g.* it is not bound by statute unless the statute so provides.

Although it is a Crown body, the Assembly's access to the Crown is through the Secretary of State. For example, although education is a devolved area, the appointment of H.M. Inspectors of Education is reserved to the Secretary of State. This is because these are Crown appointments and the proper constitutional channel to Her Majesty is through her Secretary of State. This power of appointment is reserved " solely to deny direct access to the Crown by the Assembly—an essential provision " (H.L. Vol. 395, col. 729—Lord Goronwy-Roberts. And see col. 709). If the Assembly wished to recommend the amendment of a Charter of a body operating wholly in Wales, for example the Sports Council, the recommendation would be via the Secretary of State.

The Assembly is a public body for the purposes of the Prevention of Corruption Acts 1889 to 1916 (s. 69).

All members of the Assembly are to be elected. The Act distinguishes between initial and other members. Initial members are to be returned for the areas which are Parliamentary constituencies in Wales. There are to be two initial members for each such constituency except that where the electorate of a constituency is more than 125 per cent. of the electoral quota, that constituency will return three members. This will produce an Assembly of some 80 members. (" Electoral quota " is defined in para. 14 of Sched. 1 to the Act.) The rationale of these proposals is stated at H.L. Vol. 392, col. 1116: in particular a White Paper proposal that a constituency with less than 75 per cent. of the electorate should return one member was dropped.

After the election of the initial members (by reference to Parliamentary constituencies), Assembly constituencies are to be specified by Order in Council. For such constituencies there will be one member. Proposals for the creation of Assembly constituencies will be made by the Boundary Commission for Wales in accordance with the principles set out in Pt. 2 of Sched. 1 to the Act. In particular each Assembly constituency shall be wholly comprised in one parliamentary constituency.

Time of election and term of office of members

2.—(1) The first ordinary election of members of the Assembly shall be held on a day appointed by order of the Secretary of State and, subject to subsection (2) below, any subsequent ordinary election shall be held on the third Thursday in March in the fourth year following that in which the previous ordinary election was held.

(2) The Secretary of State may, by order made with respect to the second or any subsequent ordinary election of members of the Assembly, appoint as the day for the holding of the election a day not more than two months earlier nor more than two months later than the day on which the election would be held apart from the order.

(3) The term of office of any member of the Assembly, whether elected at an ordinary election or elected to fill a casual vacancy, shall begin on the day on which he is elected and end on the eve of the ordinary election next following that day.

(4) No order under this section shall be made unless a draft of it has been laid before, and approved by resolution of, each House of Parliament.

GENERAL NOTE

The first ordinary election of members will be held on a day appointed by order of the Secretary of State. Any subsequent ordinary election will be held on the third Thursday in March in the fourth year following that in which the previous ordinary election is held. (Assuming that the Act is brought into force the time-table might be that the first elections will be held in, say, May 1979, the second on the third Thursday in March 1983, then 1987 and so on).

But in respect of the second or any subsequent ordinary election the Secretary of State may by order appoint as election day a day not more than two months earlier nor more than two months later than the day on which the election would otherwise have been held. The Opposition agreed that there might be good reasons for postponing an election—a national disaster or a clash with a general election for example—but could not see how it could be necessary to advance the date by up to two months. The only circumstances the Government could suggest in which it might be necessary were where Parliament was going to the end of a five-year term which was due to expire in the period of two months following the third Thursday in March.

Two points will be noted. (i) Ordinary elections will be for all Assembly seats: there is no provision for, *e.g.* retirement by thirds. (ii) There is no provision for dissolution of the Assembly before its four-year term runs out, though political control of the Assembly may change during its term: but so of course may control of a local authority, and there is no such provision in that case. (Contrast the Scottish Assembly, where, however, the Executive is dependent on the support of the Assembly.)

The " first past the post " electoral system will be used as in parliamentary and local government elections. A Lords' amendment provided for a system of proportional representation, but this was rejected by the Commons.

Elections

3.—(1) The persons entitled to vote as electors at an Assembly election in any Assembly constituency shall be—

(*a*) those who, at the date of the election,

(i) have their names on such parts of the register of parliamentary electors as relate to the Assembly constituency; and

(ii) would be entitled to vote as electors at a parliamentary election in the parliamentary constituency comprising the Assembly constituency; and

(*b*) peers who, at that date,

(i) have their names on such parts of the register of local government electors as relate to the Assembly constituency; and

(ii) would be entitled to vote at a local government election in an electoral area comprised in or wholly or partly coinciding with the Assembly constituency.

(2) Subsection (1) above applies with the necessary modifications to the election of initial members (within the meaning of section 1 above).

(3) The Secretary of State may by order make provision—

(*a*) as to the conduct of elections of members of the Assembly (including the registration of electors); and

(*b*) as to the questioning of such an election and the consequences of irregularities.

(4) An order under this section may—

(*a*) apply, with such modifications or exceptions as may be specified in it, any provision of the Representation of the People Acts, any provision of the enactments relating to returning officers, and any provision made under any enactment; and

(*b*) so far as may be necessary in consequence of any provision made by it for the registration of electors, amend any provision made by or under the Representation of the People Acts as to the registration of parliamentary electors or local government electors.

(5) An order under this section may provide for the charging of any sum on the Welsh Consolidated Fund.

(6) No election of a member of the Assembly shall be questioned except under the provisions of Part III of the Representation of the People Act 1949 as applied by an order under this section.

(7) A statutory instrument made under this section shall be subject to annulment in pursuance of a resolution of either House of Parliament.

GENERAL NOTE

By s. 3 (1) the persons entitled to vote as electors at an Assembly election in any Assembly constituency are those persons who, at the date of the election (i) have their names on such parts of the register of parliamentary electors as relate to the Assembly constituency; and (ii) would be entitled to vote as electors at a parliamentary election in the parliamentary constituency comprising the Assembly constituency.

Peers (they can vote in local authority elections) can vote if they have their names on the register, etc.

Notice that the above rules concern entitlement to vote in an Assembly constituency: the election of initial members (as to which see s. 1 (5)) is, however, in parliamentary constituencies. The Act therefore provides in s. 3 (2) that s. 3 (1) " applies with the necessary modifications to the election of initial members ..." The minister said, " ... the necessary modifications will relate only to the description of the constituencies and will not in any way affect a person's entitlement to vote " (H.L. Vol. 392, col. 1155).

The Secretary of State is empowered (by s. 3 (3) (4)) to make orders as to the conduct of elections, etc. Such orders may apply, with modifications, the provisions of Representation of the People Acts, of the enactments relating to returning officers, and any provision made under any enactment. (Examples of the latter would be reg. 9 of the Town and Country Planning (Control of Advertisements) Regulations 1969 (S.I. 1969, No. 1532); and the Representation of the People Regulations 1974 (S.I. 1974 No. 648)).

There is also power by such an order to amend statutory requirements as to the registration of electors.

Concerning s. 3 (5), the Government view was that it was more appropriate for the cost to fall on the United Kingdom Consolidated Fund as electoral arrangements are reserved to the United Kingdom authorities. The Lords amendment inserting "Welsh" was not challenged in the Commons: it is in any event a matter of indifference to the taxpayer. For Welsh Consolidated Fund, see s. 40.

Subs. (6)

Pt. III of the Representation of the People Act 1949 contains the provisions for questioning, by election petition, Parliamentary and local elections.

By-elections

4.—(1) Subject to subsection (4) below, where the seat of a member of the Assembly is vacant an election shall be held to fill the vacancy.

(2) The date of the election shall be fixed by the presiding officer of the Assembly in accordance with subsection (3) below.

(3) The date of the election shall be not later than three months after the occurrence of the vacancy, except that if the vacancy does not come to the notice of the presiding officer within one month of its occurrence the date of the election shall be not later than three months after the vacancy comes to his notice.

(4) The election shall not be held if the latest date for holding it would fall within the three months preceding the next ordinary election of members of the Assembly.

(5) For the purposes of this section a vacancy shall be deemed to have occurred on such date as may be determined under the standing orders of the Assembly, and references in this section to the presiding officer include references to any person for the time being performing the functions of presiding officer.

DEFINITION

" Ordinary election "—see s. 2.

GENERAL NOTE

For " presiding officer," see s. 15 (2).

Contrast the provisions of local government electoral law, where an election can be requisitioned by a certain number of the electorate.

A vacancy will occur on disqualification (s. 5), resignation or death of a member.

Disqualification for membership

5.—(1) Subject to section 6 below, a person is disqualified for membership of the Assembly if—

(a) he is disqualified for membership of the House of Commons under paragraphs (a) to (e) of section 1 (1) of the House of Commons Disqualification Act 1975; or

(b) he is disqualified otherwise than under that Act for membership of that House or for sitting and voting in it; or

(c) he is a Lord of Appeal in Ordinary; or

(d) he holds any of the offices for the time being designated by Order in Council as offices disqualifying for membership of the Assembly; or

(e) he is a member of the House of Commons; or

(f) he has been convicted in the United Kingdom, the Channel Islands, the Isle of Man or the Irish Republic of any offence and has had passed on him a sentence of imprisonment (whether suspended or not) for a period of not less than three months without the option of a fine and a period of less than five years has elapsed since the date of that conviction.

(2) A person who holds office as lord-lieutenant, lieutenant or high sheriff of a county in Wales is disqualified for membership of the Assembly for any Assembly constituency comprising the whole or part of that county.

(3) For the purposes of subsection (1) (*f*) above the ordinary date on which the period allowed for appealing against the conviction expires or, if an appeal against the conviction is made, the date on which the appeal is finally disposed of or abandoned, shall be deemed to be the date of the conviction.

(4) Subsection (2) above applies with the necessary modification to membership of the Assembly before an election to which an Order in Council under Part I of Schedule 1 to this Act applies.

(5) No recommendation shall be made to Her Majesty in Council to make an Order under this section unless a draft of the Order has been laid before and approved by a resolution of each House of Parliament, but this does not apply to an Order varying or revoking a previous Order if the Assembly has resolved that the Secretary of State be requested to recommend the making of the Order.

GENERAL NOTE

Subs. (1) (*a*)

By paras. (*a*) to (*e*) of s. 1 (1) of the House of Commons Disqualification Act 1975 a person is disqualified for membership of the Commons if he:
(a) holds any of the judicial offices specified in Pt. I of Sched. 1 to the 1975 Act;
(b) is employed, whether for the whole or the part of his time, in the civil service of the Crown;
(c) is a member of any of the regular armed forces of the Crown;
(d) is a member of any police force maintained by a police authority;
(e) is a member of the legislature of any country or territory outside the Commonwealth.

Notice that the disqualification in para. (*f*) of s. 1 (1) of the 1975 Act is not included here. That paragraph disqualifies a person holding an office described in Pt. II or Pt. III of Sched. 1 to that Act, including, for example, membership of the Boards of nationalised industries and of the Commission for Local Administration (Ombudsman). The Government view was that not all the offices listed justified disqualification—but see s. 5 (1) (*d*) below.

Subs. (1) (*b*)

By this paragraph the following are disqualified for membership of the Assembly:
(a) aliens, but not citizens of the Republic of Ireland;
(b) persons under 21;
(c) mental patients;
(d) bankrupts;
(e) persons guilty of corrupt or illegal practices;
(f) a person convicted of treason.
For details, see Erskine May, *Parliamentary Practice*, Chap. 3.

Subs. (1) (*c*).

Peers as such are not disqualified, see s. 6 (1) (*a*).

Subs. (1) (*d*).

Referring to the reference above to s. 1 (1) (*f*) of the 1975 Act, clearly some of the offices listed in Pt. II and Pt. III of the Sched. to the 1975 Act will be designated by Order in Council (including, doubtless, those mentioned above). The Opposition would have listed the disqualifying offices in a Schedule to the Wales Act, but the Government thought that the matter was appropriate for subordinate legislation. Paid appointments will carry disqualification.

Subs. (1) (*e*).

This was not in the Bill as laid, but was inserted by the Lords. It was agreed to by the Commons by 293 to 260 votes.

Subs. (1) (*g*).
Compare Local Government Act 1972, s. 80 (1) (*d*) (2) (5).

Subs. (2).
" *Assembly constituency* " For membership for a Parliamentary constituency as an initial member, see s. 5 (4).

The Lords inserted a provision that would in effect have disqualified for membership persons not resident in Wales. This was rejected by the Commons, and not insisted on by the Lords.

There is no requirement that an Assembly member shall have a local connection with the constituency he represents (*cf.* Local Government Act 1972, s. 79).

Exceptions and power to grant relief from disqualification

6.—(1) A person is not disqualified for membership of the Assembly by reason only—

(*a*) that he is a peer, whether of the United Kingdom, Great Britain, England, Scotland or Ireland; or

(*b*) that he has been ordained or is a minister of any religious denomination.

(2) Where a person was, or is alleged to have been, disqualified for membership of the Assembly, either generally or for any Assembly constituency, on any ground other than one falling within section 5 (1) (*b*) or (*f*) of this Act and it appears to the Assembly—

(*a*) that that ground has been removed; and

(*b*) that it is proper to do so;

it may resolve that any disqualification incurred by that person on that ground shall be disregarded.

(3) A resolution under subsection (2) above shall not affect any proceedings under Part III of the Representation of the People Act 1949 as applied by an order under section 3 above or enable the Assembly to disregard any disqualification which has been established in such proceedings under section 8 below.

GENERAL NOTE
Subs. (1) (*a*)
For Lord of Appeal in Ordinary, see s. 5 (1) (*c*).
Notice that the Assembly may not grant relief from disqualification where disqualification arises from those disabilities which disqualify for membership of the Commons (other than those arising under the House of Commons Disqualification Act 1975) (s. 5 (1) (*b*) above) or from criminal conviction (s. 5 (1) (*f*) above). Thus disregard of disqualification is in effect justifiable only where a person inadvertently held an *office* incompatible with membership.

Effect of disqualification

7.—(1) Subject to any resolution of the Assembly under section 6 above,—

(*a*) if a person disqualified for membership of the Assembly, or for membership for a particular Assembly constituency, is elected as a member of the Assembly or, as the case may be, as a member for that constituency, his election shall be void; and

(*b*) if a member of the Assembly becomes disqualified for membership of the Assembly or for membership for the Assembly constituency for which he is sitting, his seat shall be vacated.

(2) Subsection (1) above applies with the necessary modifications to membership of the Assembly before an election to which an Order in Council under Part I of Schedule 1 to this Act applies.

(3) The validity of any proceedings of the Assembly shall not be affected by the disqualification of any person for membership of the Assembly or for membership for any Assembly constituency.

GENERAL NOTE

For disqualification for a particular Assembly constituency, see s. 5 (2) above.

S. 7 (2) is necessary because initial elections will be for parliamentary not Assembly constituencies (see s. 1 above).

Judicial proceedings as to disqualification

8.—(1) Any person who claims that a person purporting to be a member of the Assembly is disqualified or has been disqualified at any time since his election may apply to the High Court for a declaration to that effect, and the decision of the court on the application shall be final.

(2) On an application under this section the person in respect of whom the application is made shall be the respondent; and the applicant shall give such security for the costs of the proceedings, not exceeding £200, as the court may direct

(3) An application under this section in respect of any person may be made whether the grounds on which it is made are alleged to have subsisted at the time of his election or to have arisen subsequently; but no declaration shall be made under this section in respect of any person—

(a) on grounds which subsisted at the time of his election, if an election petition is pending or has been tried in which his disqualification on those grounds is or was in issue; or

(b) on any ground, if a resolution under section 6 above requires that the ground shall be disregarded.

(4) In this section " disqualified " means disqualified for membership of the Assembly or for any Assembly constituency.

REFERENCE

For election petition, see Pt. III of the Representation of the People Act 1949 as applied to this Act by s. 3 (6) above.

Principal functions

Existing statutory functions

9.—(1) The Assembly shall exercise as regards Wales the functions given to Ministers of the Crown by or under the enactments specified in the first column of Schedule 2 to this Act, with the exception of the functions specified in the second column.

(2) Any function given to a Minister of the Crown by or under an enactment listed in Schedule 3 to this Act shall continue to be exercisable by him as regards Wales notwithstanding that it is exercisable by the Assembly by virtue of subsection (1) above.

DEFINITIONS

" Functions ": this is not defined nor is any definition needed, for whatever Ministers do under the relevant statutory provisions the Assembly is to do.

" Ministers of the Crown ": includes the Treasury (s. 78).

" Wales ": by s. 269 of the Local Government Act 1972 Wales consists of the eight counties listed in Pt. I of Sched. 4 to that Act.

GENERAL NOTE

The functions transferred

This is the main section to confer functions on the Assembly. By it there is transferred to the Assembly a wide range of functions presently exercised by Ministers. The following points will be noted :

(i) The functions transferred are those *precisely identified* in Sched. 2 by reference to the Acts by which they were given to Ministers. Thus the transfer of functions is not by means of granting competence in certain general areas;

(ii) The devolved functions being those exercised by Ministers, powers of *primary legislation* are not, but powers of making subordinate legislation are, conferred on the Assembly (the latter are referred to in the note on s. 20 below);

(iii) Only functions exercised by *Ministers* are by this section transferred (" Ministers " includes the Treasury: s. 78). Functions exercised by persons or bodies other than Ministers are not therefore transferred;

(iv) Only *statutory* functions are transferred by this section not therefore powers exercisable under the prerogative (as to these, see ss. 10 and 11);

(v) Only functions under *statutes in existence* before the passing of this Act are transferred. There is nothing in the Act authorising Ministers to transfer functions under future legislation to the Assembly. Future legislation dealing with devolved matters will therefore have to make special provision for the Assembly;

(vi) Functions are exercisable " as regards Wales." This causes particular difficulty in connection with the water industry (see s. 63).

The scheme of the Act therefore required, first, ministerial decisions as to which areas of administration should in general be devolved to the Assembly and then detailed examination of the relevant statutes to pinpoint those provisions which conferred the functions in questions on Ministers. Those provisions are listed in the first column of Sched. 2. If it was desired to exclude certain functions from those which would other-wise be transferred by an entry in the first column, an entry is made of the relevant statutory provisions in the second column. But if it was desired not to devolve an area of administration at all (*e.g.* defence), there will be no entry relating to that area in the first column. An area of administration is excluded or reserved by omission.

The Schedule lists 176 Acts or groups of Acts. It is divided into 18 Parts—education, planning, pollution, etc. Within each Part Acts are listed chronologically. Where only the title of the Act is given all ministerial functions under that Act are transferred. Where only certain functions under an Act are to be transferred, the relevant sections or Parts of the Act will be listed in the first column. (The Road Traffic Act 1960 is in Pt. XIV (Transport), the Road Traffic Acts 1972 and 1974 in Pt. XVI (Road Traffic).)

The whole of one Part of the Schedule was deleted by the Lords, that dealing with forestry. Agriculture is not devolved, but planning and land use, rural development, countryside and tourism are. The Government's view was that on balance it was better for forestry to be treated along with the devolved matters just mentioned. However, the Commons did not disagree with the Lords deletion of forestry from the Schedule. Again, agriculture is not devolved but housing is. Should the ministerial functions in respect of agricultural dwelling-house advisory committees be devolved or not? The Government's view was that although there is an agricultural element, the housing element in the work of those committees is the more important, the relevant functions are therefore devolved (Rent (Agriculture) Act 1976) (H.L. Vol. 394, col. 1022).

It will be appreciated that various parts of what might be thought of as one adminis-trative scheme may be authorised or required by differing statutory provisions. Take town planning. Appeals against refusal by a local authority of planning permission lie by s. 36 of the Town and Country Planning Act 1971 to the Secretary of State. The (whole of the) 1971 Act is listed in the first column of Sched. 2. S. 36 is not listed in the second column. Appeal will therefore lie, on the coming into force of the Wales Act, to the Assembly, which, succeeding to the functions of the Secretary of State, shall, by s. 36 (4) of the 1971 Act, before determining the appeal, afford to either party an opportunity of appearing before a person appointed by the Assembly whose decision shall, by s. 36 (6) be final (subject to application for the High Court under s. 245). What of the procedure at the appeal? Can this also be determined by the Assembly? That procedure is governed by the Town and Country Planning Appeals (Inquiry Procedure) Rules 1974 (S.I. 1974 No. 419). These Rules are made, not under the Town and Country Planning Act but by the Lord Chancellor under s. 11 of the Tribunals and Inquiries Act 1971. That latter Act is listed in Pt. XIX of Sched. 2, but only ss. 5 (1) and 12 thereof. The Assembly cannot therefore amend or repeal the Inquiry Procedure Rules.

A particularly complex case is the Mental Health Act 1959, which contains a wide variety of ministerial functions. The principle on which the Government acted in deciding which functions should be devolved and which left with Ministers are explained at H.L. Vol. 394, cols. 1023–1027.

The excepted functions

As stated, the principle of the Act is to devolve ministerial functions in certain areas (what we may call devolved areas)—local government, town and country planning, housing, education, etc., but not in others (which we may call reserved areas)—industrial and energy policy, defence, national taxation, social security, sea fisheries, etc., and those matters where on other grounds uniformity throughout England and Wales is thought desirable. Where therefore responsibility for a devolved area of administration would involve the exercise of a function in the reserved area, the exercise of that function is excluded by an entry in the second column of Sched. 2. Some examples will show how this works. Education is a devolved area, but functions in respect of teachers' pay (but not teacher training) and of the appointment of H.M. Inspectors are amongst those excluded. (Public service pay generally is excluded. For exclusion of H.M.I.s, see note on s. 1.) In another area, pollution, wide powers are transferred to the Assembly, including environmental noise and air pollution. However, ministerial functions relating to the control of pollution from motor vehicles, aircraft, etc., are amongst those reserved as this type of control has implications for design, trade requirements and safety, and international conventions may be involved. As to the Health and Safety Act 1974, most functions are reserved. There is, for example no devolution in relation to the safety of factory machinery. But the Act also deals with the pollution of the atmosphere: functions which bear on this are therefore transferred, including the power to prescribe premises, to make regulations and to provide for enforcement. But those powers are reserved so far as they apply to every other aspect of the Act. Functions under the National Health Service Act 1977 are transferred. Amongst excluded functions is that under s. 23 (4), which empowers the Secretary of State to modify the terms of the Vehicles (Excise) Act 1971: this touches on the reserved subject of national taxation. Another devolved Act is the Nursing Homes Act 1975, but s. 11, which provides that proceedings in respect of certain offences cannot be brought without the written consent of the Attorney-General, is excluded: Attorney-General functions are all reserved and although the Treasury is included in the definition of Ministers, Treasury functions are excluded from transfer in many cases.

A group of excluded functions are those affecting " excepted statutory undertakers," defined in s. 78. For these, central government retains responsibility. For example, under s. 39 (6) of the Opencast Coal Act 1958, the National Coal Board is given power to enter land for the purpose of establishing whether it would be suitable for the excavation of coal. Subs. (6) provides that where land is held by a statutory undertaker, ministerial consent is necessary. This ministerial function is transferred to the Assembly, but an exception is made where the function is exercisable in relation to excepted statutory undertakers—for example British Rail. Where the statutory undertaker is not an excepted statutory undertaker within the meaning of the Wales Act, for example a water authority, the function remains with the Assembly. (For further reference to excepted statutory undertakers, see s. 36.)

Another ground for the exclusion of functions is where they relate to " reserved local matters," listed in Sched. 5. These are matters in respect of which local authorities remain responsible to United Kingdom Ministers, not to the Assembly. For example, the ministerial power under the Local Government Act 1972 to confirm by-laws is transferred, but not the exercise of that power as it affects the matters listed in Sched. 5. (For further reference to reserved local matters, see ss. 36 and 58.)

Functions exercisable only with ministerial consent

Some powers transferred by s. 9 (1) are exercisable only with ministerial consent. See s. 36.

Functions exercisable by Ministers despite transfer to Assembly

Certain powers transferred under s. 9 (1) continue by s. 9 (2) to be exercisable by relevant Ministers despite their exercise within Wales by the Assembly. They are exercisable concurrently. The 10 relevant statutes are listed in Sched. 3. Why this duality? The first entry is the Commissioners of Works Act 1852, devolved to the Assembly in Sched. 2, Pt. XVIII. The Act empowers the acquisition of land by agreement for the public service. Thus the Assembly can use that power to acquire land for devolved purposes. The inclusion of the entry in Sched. 3 means that the Government can exercise that power in Wales (even though the Assembly can also use it there) and can do so for devolved or non-devolved functions. Another entry, s. 113 of the Town and Country Planning Act 1971, empowers the Secretary of State for the Environment to acquire land compulsorily for the public service. This power is not devolved to the Assembly except " in connection with the part of the public service with respect to which the powers of the Assembly are exercisable " (Sched. 2, Pt. VIII). By this entry in Sched. 3 the whole of the power in s. 113 is exercisable by the Secretary of State, that is, in respect of devolved or non-devolved functions.

Another entry is the Transport Act 1968, s. 57. This contains a power to make grants for research into transport services. Some transport functions have been devolved, others have not. Thus both the Government and the Assembly need to be able to exercise the power in question. The entry for the Historic Buildings and Ancient Monuments Act 1953 in Scheds. 2 and 3 means that while payment for the acquisition of buildings will normally be the responsibility of the Assembly, the Secretary of State will be able to make grants, etc., out of the National Land Fund, to which the Assembly has no access. S. 9 (2) is thus " a device for coping with a very few, relatively marginal, powers which cannot be dealt with by the more usual mechanisms in the Bill," each of which is justified by the particular circumstances as the above examples show (H.L. Vol. 394, col. 1010).

By s. 29, concurrent powers to make subordinate instruments are exercisable to ensure the implementation of international obligations. This is explained below in the note on that section.

Sched. 11: *amendments to enactments*

Sched. 11 to the Act contains amendments to enactments which have a bearing on the Assembly's functions. That is, certain functions are given to the Assembly by such amendments rather than by a transfer of functions under s. 9 or any other section. For example, by para. 37 the Assembly may appoint a special day to be a Bank Holiday in Wales. Important duties in respect of the water industry are imposed by amendments to the Water Act (para. 42). Detailed amendments to the Local Government Act 1974 are made so as to apply the provisions of that Act concerning the payment of rate support grants by the Assembly (paras. 49 to 67). In addition, third parties may have obligations imposed on them, *e.g.* Ministers (see *e.g.* paras. 21 and 23), and the Development Board for Rural Wales (para. 83). The powers of third parties where they have reference to Wales may be extended, *e.g.* the Wales Tourist Board (para. 30). The importance of referring to Sched. 11 in understanding the working of the devolved administration can be illustrated by reference to the N.H.S. in Wales—which in any case deserves further comment (for a brief note on the present position, see " Nominated Bodies in Wales " above). By Pt. VI of Sched. 2 to the Act this is a devolved area, and the National Health Service Act 1977 is listed in the first column. Thus, as regards Wales, it is the Assembly's, not the Secretary of State's, duty to continue the promotion of a comprehensive health service (s. 1 of the 1977 Act), to provide, to such extent as it considers necessary to meet all reasonable requirements, hospital accommodation, medical, dental, nursing and ambulance services, etc. (s. 3), to establish A.H.A.s, etc. (s. 8). However, the Government decided that the power to determine the remuneration of general practitioners should be reserved. Accordingly, in the Bill as originally laid the relevant sections of the 1977 Act were listed in the second column of Sched. 2. But it was realised that that would not do, as there was thereby excluded from the competence of the Assembly the power to make regulations on related matters. " The interrelationship between pay and other matters is close. For example, disciplinary action against a general practitioner is possible by way of withholding part of his remuneration. So it is not possible to draw a clear distinction between these matters concerned with remuneration and those which are not. Nor can the split be achieved by reference to existing regulations as they may change over the years, whereas the approach adopted in the Wales Bill must be such that it can withstand such changes " (H.L. Vol. 393, col. 565, and H.C. Vol. 954, col. 884). Accordingly formal amendments were made to the Bill to devolve all the regulation-making powers in question, and an amendment was made to the 1977 Act by Sched. 11, para. 86, to the Wales Act giving the Secretary of State power to direct the Assembly about the exercise of those functions. " The Secretary of State can therefore determine the aspects of any Assembly regulations which are concerned essentially with remuneration, and then direct the Assembly as to what the regulations should contain in this respect. A further complication is that the Statement of Fees and Allowances, which lays down the precise sums to be charged for medical services, is made under the terms of the regulations [rather than contained in the regulations themselves]. The Statement is closely concerned with remuneration so it is essential that the Secretary of State should be able to fix the fees and allowances

... this is achieved by including in the Secretary of State's directing powers the power to direct the Assembly to confer functions on him " (H.L. Vol. 393, col. 599). (See Sched. 11, para. 86 (2)).

A similar complication arose concerning N.H.S. employees (*e.g.* hospital doctors). In the Bill as presented the provisions of the 1977 Act dealing with their conditions of service (*viz.* paras. 10 (1) and 11 (1) of Sched. 5) were excluded from the competence of the Assembly. But this exclusion also prevented the Assembly from making regulations about the appointment of any A.H.A. staff. Those exclusions from the Assembly's competence were therefore excised from the second column of Sched. 2 and a further amendment made in Sched. 11 to the 1977 Act to give the Secretary of State the power of direction over the Assembly's regulations. A particularly delicate matter involved here was the composition of committees for the appointment of consultants: the power of direction will ensure that the Assembly cannot go its own way in altering the structure of these committees, which is of much concern to the consultants.

Another tier?

One of the arguments against the Assembly was that it would be yet another tier of government, so that Wales would be administered by community councils (in most areas), district councils, county councils, the Assembly, the Secretary of State and the EEC organisations. The Secretary of State was most insistent throughout that there would not be another tier. For example, " In a nutshell, what we are dealing with is the transfer of existing functions, not the creation of a new tier of government. Hon. Members who say that we are creating a new tier of government are living in cloud-cuckoo-land, because the tier already exists. It is there because some of the functions [of the Assembly] are those that I exercise and some of the functions are those exercised by the nominated bodies in Wales " (H.C. Vol. 945, col. 796). However, the Secretary of State is given by the Act certain powers over the Assembly: he can in certain circumstances direct it to take or not to take certain action, can revoke its statutory instruments, intervene in planning matters, give it directions in certain N.H.S. matters, etc. Does this relationship constitute a tier that did not previously exist? What is undisputed is that by government calculations the Assembly will mean some extra 1,150 civil servants: perhaps this is the objection, rather than the existence of another tier. Another view was that whether or not there is a new tier, there is a new form of administration, an extra part of government, another body to deal with. See also Bogdanor, *Parliamentary Affairs* (1978), p. 258.

Cultural and recreative activities

10. The Assembly may do anything it considers appropriate to support museums, art galleries, libraries, the Welsh language, the arts, crafts, sport and other cultural and recreative activities.

GENERAL NOTE

This section confers on the Assembly powers previously exercised by Ministers under the prerogative (whereas s. 9 confers statutory powers). They are thus, in relation to the Assembly, converted into formal statutory powers.

The word " anything " is to be read in the context of the Assembly's powers, so does not give powers to take action for which legislation would be necessary, *e.g.* powers of compulsory purchase.

An effect of the section is that the Assembly will be responsible for museums and galleries in Wales, which will be funded out of the block grant (as to which, see s. 48). If it was desired to purchase an extremely expensive item costing more than the block fund could be expected to bear, the issue " might well take on a Great Britain dimension," that is, the Government might be prepared to assist (H.L. Vol. 394, col. 1055). The word " may " empowers the Assembly to act; it does not disable the Government from continuing to do so in the matters in question.

It would seem that the Assembly is not limited to actions in Wales in the matters in question (*cf.* s. 11). Thus it could give financial support to the teaching of Welsh in England.

Concerning the support of the Welsh language, a number of amendments were put down to this section and to s. 25 which sought to protect the interests of those who do or do not speak that language.

Other non-statutory powers

11. The Assembly may—

   (*a*) make arrangements for the provision in Wales of services for the war disabled, and

   (*b*) make grants towards the carrying on of public passenger transport undertakings in Wales.

DEFINITION

" Wales ": by the Local Government Act 1972, s. 269, Wales comprises the eight counties created by that Act, including Gwent, formerly Monmouthshire.

GENERAL NOTE

This section confers powers previously exercised by Ministers under the prerogative (*cf.* s. 10; *cf.* s. 9).

Review of local government structure

12. The Assembly shall review the structure of local government in Wales and shall report its conclusions to the Secretary of State.

DEFINITION

" Structure " is not defined but must include the functions of authorities: the one cannot be considered without the other. Could the review consider the financing of local government? A meaningful view of local government requires consideration of its financing, including its relationship to central government, but it is not clear beyond all doubt that it falls within " structure."

GENERAL NOTE

In the Introductory Notes to the Act (above) the recent history of local government in Wales was outlined. We saw how the need for local government reform was part of the case for some new administrative machinery in Wales, and how the Scotland and Wales Bill did not attempt to meet that need. Following the demise of that Bill, discussions within the Labour Party continued on the relationship between local government reform and devolution. This section was the outcome. It was discussed many times in Parliament. Whatever its pros and cons it is clear, first, that even without this section the Assembly could have done what by the section it is required to do, and secondly, that the structure of local government in Wales can be altered only by Parliament, not by the Assembly. For the clause, it was said that there is substantial dissatisfaction with the present system of local government in Wales; that any proposals the Assembly would come up with would, by reason of the fact the Assembly is an elected body, be more likely to be acceptable than anything suggested or done in the past; that the Assembly would have many members experienced in local government, and that it would have an interest in a successful reform as it would be taking over Ministers' supervisory responsibilities for local government. Against the clause it was said that there would have been dissatisfaction with local government whatever form the (necessary) reorganisation had taken; that what was needed was not another 1974-type upheaval but a period of stability, or at most some readjustment of functions, *e.g.* in town and country planning; that the Assembly, inevitably anxious to increase its powers, was not the right body to make recommendations which might well include proposals to transfer powers to it; that if the (perhaps Conservative) government rejected the proposals of a (perhaps Labour) Assembly, this would cause friction; that the purpose of the section was to buy parliamentary and public support for the Bill. It is of interest that the Welsh County Councils were against the clause. The District Councils on the other hand were in favour—in their view the creation of the Assembly would mean that Wales would be overgoverned, that in consequence local government should be reviewed with a view to the abolition of both existing tiers and the creation of all-purpose authorities strong enough to avoid powers passing from local government to the Assembly.

A perhaps minor point is that the section does not state the time within which the report is to be submitted to the Secretary of State.

The clause was deleted from the Bill by the Lords but restored by the Commons by 278 votes to 277. On the return of the Bill to them the Lords did not insist on their amendment but instead inserted a provision requiring the approval of the Secretary of State and of Parliament to the initiation of a review. The Commons in its turn rejected that amendment by 292 to 271 votes and the Lords did not further insist.

Powers under local Acts

13.—(1) The Assembly shall exercise such functions given to Ministers of the Crown by or under local Acts as the Secretary of State may by order specify.

(2) An order under this section may contain such consequential, incidental and supplementary provisions (including provisions for the exercise of the powers with the concurrence or subject to the consent or approval of, or after consultation with, a Minister of the Crown) as appear to the Secretary of State to be necessary or expedient.

(3) A statutory instrument under this section shall be subject to annulment in pursuance of a resolution of either House of Parliament.

GENERAL NOTE

The Act does not transfer to the Assembly functions presently exercised by Ministers under local Acts. This section therefore empowers the Secretary of State to confer such functions on the Assembly. Local Acts do not frequently confer functions on Ministers. The Government's intention is that those functions will be transferred which are analogous to functions under public Acts transferred under Sched. 2 (H.L. Vol. 393, col. 394).

Conduct of business

First meeting

14. The first meeting of the Assembly shall be held on such day and at such time and place as the Secretary of State may direct.

Standing orders

15.—(1) The procedure of the Assembly shall be regulated by standing orders of the Assembly; but the Secretary of State may give directions for regulating its procedure pending the making of standing orders.

(2) The standing orders shall include provision for the election of a presiding officer from among the members of the Assembly and for his tenure of office.

(3) The standing orders shall include provision for preserving order in the proceedings of the Assembly, and any standing order made by virtue of this subsection may include provision for excluding a member from such proceedings.

(4) The standing orders shall include provision for the publication of a report of the proceedings of the full Assembly as soon as practicable after the day on which they take place.

(5) The standing orders shall include provision as to the circumstances in which the public may be admitted to meetings of the Assembly and of its committees.

DEFINITION

" The procedure of the Assembly ": by s. 7 (2) this includes, except where the context otherwise requires, reference to proceedings of Assembly committees and sub-committees.

GENERAL NOTE

By this and other sections standing orders are to include provision:
(i) for regulating the procedure of the Assembly and its committees (s. 15 (1));

(ii) for the election of a presiding officer from among the members of the Assembly and for his term of office. (The Act does not require that the person performing the function of presiding officer shall have that title: that is for the Assembly to decide) (s. 15 (2));

(iii) for the publication of a report of the proceedings of the full Assembly (s. 15 (4)). This was a Lords amendment agreed to by the Commons except that the Commons deleted "verbatim" from before "report" and added "full" before "Assembly." Thus a Hansard-type report is not required; and a report of Assembly committees is not required (see Definition above);

(iv) for securing that members with pecuniary interests in any matter as defined in standing orders (or such other interests if any as may be specified in standing orders) shall disclose them before taking part in any proceedings dealing with that matter; provision for preventing or restricting participation of such members in such proceedings may be included (s. 16 (1));

(v) for preserving order in Assembly (including committee) proceedings: provision for excluding a member from those proceedings may be included. The standing orders concerning pecuniary interests may include provision for excluding members contravening them: exclusion is not of course expulsion (ss. 15 (3), 16 (2));

(vi) for determining the date on which a vacancy in a membership of the Assembly is deemed to have occurred (s. 4 (5));

(vii) requiring the recommendation of the Executive Committee for the exercise of any power conferred by Act of Parliament and exercisable by the Assembly to make a general instrument involving the payment of any sum out of the Welsh Consolidated Fund or the Welsh Loans Fund (s. 19);

(vii) stating the grounds on which the Scrutiny Committee is to draw the attention of the Assembly to instruments considered by the Committee (s. 21 (1));

(ix) specifying the cases of urgency in which a committee may make certain categories of subordinate legislation, where it is desired to give a committee that function (s. 20 and para. 40 (2) of Sched. 11);

(x) as to the circumstances in which the public may be admitted to meetings of the Assembly and its committees. This was not in the Bill as laid. Ministers said there was no need for such provision. Various attempts were made to amend the Bill to provide for public admission; this provision is the result of a Lords amendment which would however have required standing orders to include provision "for the admission of the public." The Government said there might well be circumstances in which it would be quite proper for the public to be excluded from committee meetings, and therefore moved an amendment which had the effect of putting the provision in its present form (s. 15 (5)).

Members' interests

16.—(1) The standing orders of the Assembly shall include provision for securing that members with pecuniary interests, as defined by the standing orders, or such other interests (if any) as may be specified in the standing orders in any matter disclose them before taking part in any proceedings dealing with that matter, and may include provision for preventing or restricting participation of such members in such proceedings.

(2) Standing orders made in pursuance of subsection (1) above may include provision for excluding members contravening them from the proceedings of the Assembly.

(3) If a member of the Assembly takes part in any proceedings of the Assembly in contravention of any provision made in pursuance of this section he shall be liable on summary conviction to a fine not exceeding £500.

(4) A prosecution for an offence under this section shall not be instituted except by or with the consent of the Director of Public Prosecutions.

GENERAL NOTE

See note on s. 15 for contents of standing orders.

Subject committees

17.—(1) Without prejudice to its powers to appoint other committees, the Assembly shall appoint committees in accordance with the following provisions of this section with functions relating to all the areas of government with which the Assembly is concerned.

(2) Subject to the provisions of this Act,—

(*a*) the Assembly may charge any of its committees appointed under this section with the exercise, to such extent as the Assembly may determine, of any of its powers, but shall not thereby be prevented from exercising those powers itself; and

(*b*) where any committee appointed under this section is charged with the exercise of any powers it may arrange for all or any of them to be exercised by the leader of the committee or by a sub-committee, but shall not thereby be prevented from exercising them itself.

(3) Subject to section 18 below, a committee appointed under this section shall consist of such number of members of the Assembly as the Assembly may determine; and the Assembly shall name one of the members of each such committee as its chairman and another as leader of the committee, and the leader of a committee shall be known as its executive member.

GENERAL NOTE

For general note, see note on s. 18.

The Executive Committee

18.—(1) One of the committees appointed under section 17 above shall be known as the Executive Committee and shall consist of the leaders of the other committees so appointed and no greater number of other members of the Assembly than one-third of the number of those leaders; and the person named by the Assembly as chairman of the Executive Committee shall also be its leader.

(2) Except where the context otherwise requires, references in this Act to the Executive Committee include references to its leader acting on the authority of the Executive Committee.

GENERAL NOTE
Subject committees

By s. 17 the Assembly is required to appoint committees with functions relating to all the areas of government with which the Assembly is concerned. (The side-note refers to these as subject committees.) Exactly how many such committees will be appointed and how subjects will be grouped together for that purpose will be for the Assembly to decide but between them they must deal with all the Assembly's areas of government. There is nothing to prevent the Assembly and therefore a committee from discussing a matter in respect of which the Assembly has no executive power, for example, relations with the EEC.

Committees appointed under this section shall consist of such number of members of the Assembly as the Assembly may determine. There is no power to co-opt members but it seems that advisers could be appointed. They could be paid (under s. 27) but would be non-voting. The Assembly (and by inference not the committee) is to name one of the members of each such committee as its *chairman* and *another* as leader of the committee: the leader is to be known as the committee's Executive Member.

The Executive Committee (s. 18)

One of the committees appointed under s. 17 is to be known as the Executive Committee. This is to consist of the leaders (executive members) of all the other committees appointed under s. 17, together with no greater number of other members of the Assembly than one-third of the number of those leaders. It seems that there is no obligation to appoint such additional members as " nil " is " no greater than." The person named by the Assembly as the chairman of the Executive Committee is also to be its leader. In the Bill as originally presented the leader was required to be called the Chief Executive. Many were unhappy with this, as in local government it signifies the senior employee of an authority. The Lords deletion of the title was agreed to by the Commons. (The necessary repeal of para. 27 of Sched. 11 was overlooked.)

The Executive Committee is given specific functions under the following provisions of the Act—s. 19 (payment out of Welsh Consolidated and Welsh Loans Funds); s. 34 (4) (direction to Assembly by Secretary of State by communication to Executive member); s. 40 (2) (transfer of sums to and from Welsh Funds); s. 41 (2) (credits on Welsh Consolidated Fund on request of Executive Committee); s. 42 (2) (appropriation of sums from Welsh Consolidated Fund on recommendation of Executive Committee); s. 52 (1) (*b*) (preparation of accounts.)

The party-balance rule

In naming persons to be members of a committee appointed under s. 17 the Assembly " shall secure that the balance of parties in the Assembly is, so far as practicable, reflected in the membership of the committee " (s. 22). An exact reflection is likely to be impossible to achieve, but it seems that it must be as accurate a reflection as mathematics allows. A very small minority party could not expect representation on every committee.

This party-balance rule does not apply to the Executive Committee. A Lords amendment which had the effect of applying it was disagreed by the Commons.

Assuming one party has overall control (i) it will not be able to take more than its arithmetic share on s. 17 committees; (ii) it will doubtless take the leadership of each committee, having a majority on each; (iii) it may think it right to take its arithmetic share of the chairmanships, but no more, the function of chairmanship being separated from that of political leadership.

A majority of the Executive Committee will then consist of members of the ruling party; indeed they all might be, as there is nothing in the Act to prevent the additional members being from that party. Some will argue that they all should be, that the Executive Committee is as it were the " Cabinet," whose chairman (unlike other committees) is also its leader and thus " Prime Minister ": minority parties are not represented in the Cabinet (see H.C. Vol. 954, col. 642).

There is not, of course, a party-balance rule in local government, and it is of interest that the government thought it necessary to insert such a rule here.

For standing orders relating to Committee procedures, see note on s. 15.

Delegation to s. 17 committees

The Assembly may charge any of its committees appointed under s. 17 with the exercise to such an extent as it determines of any of its powers, but it is not thereby prevented from exercising any of those powers itself. Where a committee is thus charged with the exercise of any powers, it may arrange for all or any of them to be exercised by the leader or a sub-committee, but it is not thereby prevented from exercising these powers itself. (*Cf.* Local Goverment Act 1972, s. 101 (4).)

The Act thus permits extensive delegation to individual members (leaders). Will the Assembly delegate the determination of planning appeals to the leader of the Planning Committee? (An Opposition member suggested that it would be inconsistent with the transfer of powers from the Secretary of State to an elected *body* if this were done, but that appointments by the Assembly to various public bodies should be delegated to one person.) An Opposition amendment which would have required the exercise of powers by a leader or sub-committee to be reported to the next meeting of the committee was withdrawn. (H.L. Vol. 394, col. 1105.)

The power to delegate decision-making to a committee appointed under s. 17 is " subject to the provisions of this Act " (s. 17 (2)). See ss. 20 (1) and 42 (2). Sched. 11 to the Act (amendment of enactments) provides that functions under the following provisions cannot be delegated to committees:

(i) Ancient Monuments Consolidation and Amendment Act 1913, s. 15 (2) (para. 2 of the Schedule).

(ii) New Towns Act 1965, s. 43 (para. 24 (3)).

(iii) Development of Tourism Act 1969, s. 3 (7) (para. 31 (*e*)).

(iv) European Communities Act 1972, s. 2 (2) (para. 40) and ss. 17 and 18 (para. 32 (2)).

(v) Water Act 1973, s. 3 (10) (para. 46).

(vi) Local Government Act 1974, ss. 3, 4 (1), 5 (2), 10 (3), Sched. 1, para. 11 (para. 67).

Other Committees

The obligation to appoint committees under s. 17 is without prejudice to the Assembly's powers to appoint other committees. Thus it would probably wish to appoint a committee to deal with its domestic (catering, etc.) affairs. This is not an " area of government " (see s. 17 (1)). The party-balance rule does not apply.

The Accounts Committee

By s. 53 the Assembly is required to appoint an Accounts Committee. The party-balance rule applies, but the committee is not to include more than one member of the Executive Committee. The section (s. 17 (2)) which empowers a committee to sub-delegate does not apply to this committee.

The Scrutiny Committee

By s. 21 the Assembly is required to appoint a committee to scrutinise subordinate legislation (but it may have other functions—subs. (2)). The party-balance rules applies, but the committee is not to include any member of the Executive Committee. The section (s. 17 (2)) which empowers a committee to sub-delegate does not apply to this committee as it is not appointed under s. 17.

Financial initiative

19. The standing orders of the Assembly shall include provision requiring the recommendation of the Executive Committee for the exercise of any power conferred by Act of Parliament and exercisable by the Assembly to make a general instrument involving the payment of any sum out of the Welsh Consolidated Fund or the Welsh Loans Fund.

GENERAL NOTE

For further provisions relating to standing orders, see note on s. 15.
For further reference to Executive Committee, see note on s. 18.
For further reference to Welsh Funds, see note on s. 48.

Exercise of certain powers of subordinate legislation

20.—(1) Subject to subsection (3) below, the Assembly shall not charge a committee with the exercise of a power to which subsection (2) below applies.

(2) This subsection applies to any power exercisable by the Assembly by virtue of section 9 above to make, confirm or approve orders, rules, regulations or other subordinate legislation if (disregarding section 75 below) the power is subject to a provision—

(a) for the annulment or approval by or in pursuance of a resolution of either or both Houses of Parliament of any instrument made in the exercise of the power, or a draft of any such instrument, or

(b) prohibiting the making of such an instrument without that approval, or

(c) for any such instrument to be a provisional order, that is to say an order which requires to be confirmed by Act of Parliament, or

(d) requiring any order (within the meaning of the Statutory Orders (Special Procedure) Act 1945) to be subject to special parliamentary procedure.

(3) In such cases of urgency as may be specified for the purposes of this section by the standing orders of the Assembly, a committee may be charged with the exercise of a power to which subsection (2)

above applies by virtue of paragraph (*a*) or (*b*) of that subsection; but in such cases a committee shall not arrange for the exercise of the power by the leader of the committee or by a sub-committee.

GENERAL NOTE
    See note on s. 21.

Scrutiny of subordinate legislation

21.—(1) The Assembly shall appoint a committee to consider instruments of a general character made or proposed to be made by the Assembly under powers conferred by an Act of Parliament, with a view to determining whether the special attention of the Assembly should be drawn to the instrument or proposed instrument on such grounds as may be specified in the standing orders; and those grounds shall include the following—

(*a*) that the instrument purports to impose a charge without due authority;

(*b*) that it purports to have retrospective effect when no express power is conferred to give it retrospective effect; and

(*c*) that there appears to be a doubt whether it is within the powers under which it purports to be made or that it appears to make some unusual or unexpected use of those powers.

(2) The Assembly may confer on the committee appointed under this section such other functions as the Assembly may determine.

(3) The committee appointed under this section shall not include any member of the Executive Committee.

GENERAL NOTE
Statutory Instruments
    Powers exercisable by the Welsh Assembly include powers previously given to Ministers to make orders, rules and regulations, to give approvals, directions, consents, etc. Included is the power to make statutory instruments where the Minister's power was previously exercisable in that form. Accordingly by s. 77 of and para. 4 of Sched. 11 to the Act, the Statutory Instruments Act 1946 is amended so that references to a Minister of the Crown in s. 1 of the Act are to be construed as references to the Assembly. S. 1 of the 1946 Act can accordingly be read, in part, as follows " Where ... power to make, confirm or approve orders, rules, regulations or other subordinate legislation is conferred on the Welsh Assembly then if the power is expressed ... to be exercisable by statutory instrument, any document by which that power is exercised shall be known as a statutory instrument . . . ." (paras. 1, 2 and 40 (1) of Sched. 11 to the Wales Act should also be noted).
    The requirements of ss. 2 and 3 of the Statutory Instruments Act 1946 concerning numbering, publication, etc. of statutory instruments thus apply to statutory instruments made by the Assembly.
    An Act which empowers a Minister to make subordinate legislation commonly requires it to undergo some form of parliamentary process—laying, annulment, approval, etc. On the transfer of such a power to the Assembly it would not be appropriate to subject the subordinate legislation to parliamentary process. S. 75 in effect provides that it shall not be (and see para. 40 (3) of Sched. 11).
    However, provisions in a parent Act empowering Ministers to make subordinate legislation subject to some form of parliamentary process remain relevant in the context of the *making* of subordinate legislation by the Assembly. S. 20 provides that where by a parent Act the power to make subordinate legislation is subject to any of the parliamentary processes there specified, the making of the subordinate legislation can be done only by the Assembly, not by a committee of the Assembly (s. 20 (1)). What this amounts to is that where the parent Act requires only the laying of an instrument, the instrument can be made by a committee of the Assembly (paras. (*a*) to (*d*) of s. 20 (2) correspond to paras. (*b*) to (*e*) of s. 75 (1)).
    But (by s. 20 (3)) in cases of urgency (as specified by the Assembly in standing orders) a committee (but not its leader or a sub-committee) may make subordinate legis-

lation which (or a draft of which) by the parent Act which empowered the Minister to make it, (a) was subject to parliamentary annulment or to subsequent approval; or (b) could not be made without such prior approval (s. 20 (2) (*a*) (*b*)). This exception, permitted in the case of urgency, does not apply to an instrument which by the parent Act is a provisional order, or is subject to special parliamentary procedure (*i.e.* is a special procedure order). These are the two categories of orders referred to in s. 20 (2) (*c*) (*d*).

For the Secretary of State's power to revoke instruments made by the Assembly, see the note to s. 35.

The committee to scrutinise subordinate legislation

The Assembly is required to appoint a committee to scrutinise subordinate legislation: s. 21. This is to be a reflection of the Parliamentary Joint Committee on Statutory Instruments. The committee is, as the section puts it, to consider " instruments of a general character made or proposed to be made by the Assembly " under statutory powers.

" Instruments of a general character " is not defined but two points can be made, first, the committee's consideration is not expressed to be confined to statutory instruments; secondly, statutory instruments are themselves classified (for the purposes of publication) as general or local: this suggests the view that might be taken of " general " here.

" Made or proposed to be made " cannot mean that the committee can consider either instruments made or those proposed to be made. It can consider both.

The committee decides " whether the special attention of the Assembly should be drawn " to the instrument or proposed instrument on certain grounds. This is the same language as that used in the terms of reference of the Parliamentary Scrutiny Committee. The grounds on which the Assembly's attention may be drawn to an instrument are such as may be specified in standing orders. Those grounds must include those specified in paras. (*a*), (*b*) and (*c*) of s. 21 (1). These reproduce three of the eight grounds on which the Parliamentary Scrutiny Committee may draw the attention of Parliament to instruments within its jurisdiction. The Assembly will doubtless consider the relevance of the other grounds to the work of its Scrutiny Committee. However, an important limitation on the work of the Parliamentary Committee is that it cannot concern itself with the merits of an instrument or with the policy behind it. These matters are the concern of the House of Commons Standing Committees on Statutory Instruments. There is no constitutional reason why the Assembly Committee should be limited to the terms of reference of the Parliamentary Scrutiny Committee.

The Assembly may confer other functions on this committee (s. 21 (2)).

As to membership, the party-balance rule applies (s. 22), and no member of the Executive Committee is to be appointed to it (s. 21 (3)).

The conferment of powers of subordinate legislation on the Assembly deserves a brief general comment. The creation of primary and secondary legislation can be regarded as part of a single process of creating laws to regulate the matter in question. The Bill is drafted on the Department's instructions. Where resort to delegated legislation is thought by the Department to be necessary to achieve the aim of the legislative scheme, the regulations will be made by the Department itself, normally after consultation with affected interests. In some cases the Department responsible for the Bill will have to study the matter in greater detail before the regulations can be made. Having made the regulations, the Department is well placed from its experience of their effect and the functioning of the scheme in question to decide whether amendment of the Act itself is necessary. It is a criticism of this scheme of devolution therefore that this overall responsibility for legislation and administration is to be divided between Whitehall and Cardiff. Furthermore, in the operation of this scheme a good deal of inconsistency will doubtless be found between Acts in the extent to which powers of subordinate legislation are devolved to the Assembly. Acts of Parliament were not of course drafted with a sensible distribution of functions between Whitehall and Cardiff in mind. Probably some amendments will be found necessary. Certainly future Acts will have to be drafted with the role of the Assembly in making subordinate legislation in mind.

Party balance in committees

22. In naming persons to be members of a committee appointed under section 17, 21 or 53 of this Act, other than the Executive Committee, the Assembly shall secure that the balance of parties in the Assembly is, so far as practicable, reflected in the membership of the committee.

GENERAL NOTE

The implications of this section are considered in the note on s. 18.

Defamation

23.—(1) For the purposes of the law of defamation in any part of the United Kingdom—

> (*a*) any statement (whether oral or written) made in proceedings of the Assembly, and
>
> (*b*) the publication under the authority of the Assembly of any document,

shall be absolutely privileged.

(2) Where the publication of a document is privileged by virtue of subsection (1) (*b*) above, the publication of any abstract from or summary of it which is fair and accurate is also privileged, unless the publication is proved to be made with malice.

DEFINITION

" Proceedings of the Assembly ": see s. 78 (2).

GENERAL NOTE

The Opposition doubted whether it was right to confer absolute privilege; it was argued that qualified privilege would give adequate protection, as for local authorities. The Government view was that the status of the Assembly, as a national Assembly, and the kinds of matters it would discuss called for absolute privilege even though, unlike Parliament, it had no legislative functions. But there was no reason to think that members would act irresponsibly (H.L. Vol. 393, col. 1262, Vol. 394, col. 115).

Note that consequential amendments are made to the Defamation Act 1952 and the Defamation Act (Northern Ireland) 1955 by Sched 11, paras. 11 to 13, and 18 to 20 of this Act.

Ancillary powers

Staff

24. The Assembly may appoint such officers and servants as it considers appropriate.

GENERAL NOTE

This section is to be read in conjunction with s. 65 (1) " Service as an official or servant of the Assembly . . . shall be service in Her Majesty's Home Civil Service, and appointments to any position as such officer or servant shall be made accordingly. . . ."

This means that there is to be no separate Welsh civil service, and that employees of the Assembly, though technically appointed by it will be recruited strictly according to the standard procedures applying to recruitment to the home civil service, including the need to be certified by the Civil Service Commissioners. The Act does not provide for any kind of direct government control over the total number of Assembly employees. Such control would imply that the Government could frustrate the policies of the Assembly and would be, in the Government's view, an unwarranted interference in its affairs.

The two Houses of Parliament employ in various departments permanent employees who are not civil servants. This will not be the case with the Assembly: as a body with executive and not legislative functions all its staff will be civil servants.

Various amendments which sought to ensure that (a) a person is not to be disqualified from being an Assembly officer or servant by reason only of inability to speak Welsh; and (b) the Assembly should not solely prefer a person by reason of his being a civil servant over a person who is a local government official, were withdrawn.

Inquiries

25.—(1) The Assembly may cause an inquiry to be held into any matter relevant to the performance of any of its functions.

(2) Subsections (2) to (5) of section 250 of the Local Government Act 1972 shall apply in relation to such an inquiry as if it were a local inquiry held under that section and the Assembly were the Minister causing it to be held.

GENERAL NOTE

S. 250 (1) of the Local Government Act 1972 empowers Ministers to cause a local inquiry to be held in certain circumstances. Subs. (2) to (5) empower the person appointed to hold the inquiry to require any person to attend to give evidence, etc., to take evidence on oath, etc., imposes criminal penalties for failure to attend, etc., and deal with the payment of costs. Subs. (6) is not relevant.

Civil proceedings

26. Where it considers it expedient for the promotion or protection of the public interest, the Assembly may institute in its own name, or appear in, any civil proceedings relating to matters with respect to which the powers of the Assembly are exercisable.

GENERAL NOTE

See the note to s. 70. There were no parliamentary debates on this section.

This section may be compared with s. 222 of the Local Government Act 1972 which is however wider.

The power given by this section is of course in addition to such other rights of suit as the Assembly may have under functions transferred to it, *e.g.* to enforce obligations owed to it by a local authority.

Supplementary powers

27. Subject to the provisions of this Act, the Assembly may do anything (whether or not involving the acquisition or disposal of property) which is calculated to facilitate, or is conducive or incidental to, the discharge of its functions.

GENERAL NOTE

Some Opposition members expressed suspicion, but the Government pointed out that the purpose of the section is to make sure that the Assembly will have adequate powers to carry out its devolved functions on such matters as furnishing offices, providing members with stationery, facilities for the media to report debates, etc. It was, in brief, a " paper-clips " clause. It gives no extra devolved functions (H.L. Vol. 393, col. 1302). Compare Local Government Act 1972, s. 111.

International affairs

International relations

28. The Assembly shall not in the exercise of its functions conduct relations with any country outside the United Kingdom.

GENERAL NOTE

The Assembly may conduct relations with Scotland. What of the Isle of Man? (H.C. Vol. 945, col. 1538). The Assembly is not by this section prevented from discussing at Assembly proceedings relations with other countries: what it is not to do is to conduct them with those countries.

For Wales and the EEC, see note on s. 36.

International obligations

29. If it appears to a Minister of the Crown—

(*a*) that the implementation of a Community obligation or any other international obligation of the United Kingdom requires the exercise of any power to make a subordinate instrument, and

(*b*) that it is desirable that the power should be exercised by him,

he may exercise the power notwithstanding that it is exercisable by the Assembly by virtue of section 9 above.

Definition
"Community obligation": see European Communities Act 1972, Sched. 1, Pt. II.

General Note
See the note on s. 35.

Further provisions as to members

Oath of allegiance

30.—(1) A member of the Assembly shall, as soon as may be after his election, and at a meeting of the Assembly, take the oath of allegiance set out in section 2 of the Promissory Oaths Act 1868 or make the corresponding affirmation and shall not, until he has done so, take part in any other proceedings of the Assembly.

(2) If a member has not taken the oath or made the affirmation required by this section within two months of his election, or such longer period as the Assembly may have allowed before the expiration of the second month, he shall cease to be a member at the expiration of that month or longer period.

General Note
Remuneration to which a member may be entitled under s. 32 will not be paid to him unless he has taken the oath or made the affirmation (see s. 32 (4)).

Resignation

31. A member of the Assembly may at any time resign his seat by giving notice in writing to the presiding officer or to any person authorised by the standing orders of the Assembly to receive the notice.

General Note
A member may also cease to be such by disqualification (s. 5), and failure to take the oath within the period required (s. 30). There is no provision in the Act that a person shall cease to be a member by reason of failure to attend meetings. There was such a provision in the Scotland and Wales Bill (cl. 14) (and see the Local Government Act 1972, s. 85).

Remuneration

32.—(1) There shall be paid to members of the Assembly such salaries and allowances as the Assembly may from time to time determine or, pending the first determination, as the Secretary of State may direct.

(2) The Assembly may make provision for the payment of pensions, gratuities or allowances to or in respect of persons who have ceased to be members.

(3) Different provision may be made under this section for different cases.

(4) Without prejudice to the period for which any salaries or allowances are payable under this section, no payment shall be made under this section to or in respect of a person required by section 30 above to take an oath or make an affirmation unless he has done so.

(5) Payments under this section shall be made out of the Welsh Consolidated Fund.

GENERAL NOTE

The House of Lords amended this section so as to provide that members' remuneration should be fixed by the Secretary of State. The Commons disagreed and the Lords did not insist on its amendment. The Secretary of State's view is that members should be paid less than members of the Commons (H.C. Vol. 945, col. 613). In the Lords the Opposition moved an amendment, which they later withdrew, the effect of which would have been that members would get a salary of about £10,000 per annum (H.L. Vol. 393, col. 1323).

By s. 32 (3) it would be possible, for example, for leaders and chairmen to be paid at different rates from other members.

Subs. (4)

For the oath of allegiance, see s. 30.

Subs. (5)

For the Welsh Consolidated Fund, see note on s. 48.

Jury service

33.—(1) In Part III of Schedule 1 to the Juries Act 1974 (excusal of certain persons from jury service) after the entries under the heading " Parliament " there shall be inserted—

" *Welsh Assembly*
Member of the Welsh Assembly."

(2) A member of the Assembly shall not be liable to serve on any jury in Scotland.

GENERAL NOTE

By Pt. I of Sched. 1 to the Juries Act certain persons are ineligible for jury service. By Pt. II others are disqualified. By Pt. III members of the Commons, peers and peeresses entitled to receive writs of summons to attend the House of Lords, officers of both Houses, and full-time members of the armed forces, are " excusable as of right." To that list is added members of the Assembly. The excusal of other persons is discretionary.

PART II

RELATIONS WITH UNITED KINGDOM AUTHORITIES

Supplementary and reserve powers

Power of Secretary of State to prevent or require action

34.—(1) If it appears to the Secretary of State—

    (*a*) that any action proposed to be taken by the Assembly would or might affect a reserved matter, whether directly or indirectly, or

    (*b*) that any action capable of being so taken is not proposed to be taken and that failure to take it would or might affect a reserved matter, whether directly or indirectly;

then, if it appears to him desirable in the public interest to use his powers under this subsection, he may direct that the proposed action shall not be taken or, as the case may be, that the action capable of being taken shall be taken.

(2) If it appears to the Secretary of State—

    (*a*) that any action proposed to be taken by the Assembly would be incompatible with Community obligations or any other international obligations of the United Kingdom, or

    (*b*) that any action capable of being so taken is required for the purpose of implementing any Community obligation or any other international obligation of the United Kingdom,

he may direct that the proposed action shall not be taken or, as the case may be, that the action capable of being taken shall be taken.

(3) For the purposes of this section a reserved matter is one—

    (*a*) which concerns Wales (whether or not it also concerns any other part of the United Kingdom); but

    (*b*) with respect to which the Assembly has no power to act.

(4) A direction under this section may be varied or revoked by a further direction; and any such direction shall be taken to be given as soon as it is communicated to a member of the Executive Committee.

(5) A direction under this section shall be binding on the Assembly.

(6) A direction under subsection (1) above shall cease to have effect at the expiration of a period of twenty-eight days beginning with the day on which it is given unless before the end of that period a resolution approving it is passed by each House of Parliament; and if at any time before the end of that period either House rejects a motion approving the direction, the direction shall cease to have effect at that time.

DEFINITION

    " Community obligations ": see European Communities Act 1972, Sched 1, Pt. II.

GENERAL NOTE

    See note on s. 35.

Power of Secretary of State to revoke subordinate instruments

35.—(1) If it appears to the Secretary of State—

    (*a*) that an instrument made by the Assembly under any Act of Parliament affects a reserved matter, whether directly or indirectly, and

    (*b*) that the public interest makes it desirable that he should use his powers under this subsection,

he may by order revoke the instrument.

(2) If it appears to the Secretary of State that an instrument made by the Assembly under any Act of Parliament is incompatible with Community obligations or any other international obligations of the United Kingdom or provides for any matter which is or ought to be provided for in an instrument made by the Secretary of State and implementing such an obligation, he may by order revoke the instrument.

(3) For the purposes of this section a reserved matter is one which is a reserved matter for the purposes of section 34 above.

(4) An order under this section may contain such consequential provisions as appear to the Secretary of State to be necessary or expedient.

(5) An order under subsection (1) above revoking an instrument shall not be made unless either—

    (*a*) a draft of the order has, within the period of twenty-eight days beginning with the day on which the instrument was made, been approved by resolution of each House of Parliament; or (*b*) the order is laid before Parliament with a statement by the Secretary of State that the public interest requires it to be made without delay;

but an order made in pursuance of paragraph (*b*) above shall cease to have effect at the expiration of the period of twenty-eight days mentioned in paragraph (*a*) above unless before the end of that period a resolution approving it is passed by each House of Parliament; and if at any time before the end of that period either House rejects a motion approving the order, the order shall cease to have effect at that time.

(6) Where an order under subsection (1) above revoking an instrument ceases to have effect at any time the instrument shall after that time again have effect as if the order had not been made.

Definition

" Community obligations ": see the European Communities Act 1972, Sched. 1, Pt. II.

General Note

S. 9 (1) of the Act transfers certain ministerial functions to the Assembly; s. 9 (2) empowers Ministers to exercise certain of these functions even though they have by s. 9 (1) been transferred to the Assembly; s. 36 requires the Assembly to obtain ministerial consent to the exercise of certain of its powers; s. 37 requires it to give effect to ministerial guidelines in the exercise of certain other powers; and by ss. 63 and 64 respectively the Secretary of State is given power to intervene in the exercise by the Assembly of its powers in relation to water and planning.

Ss. 34 and 35 give the Secretary of State certain general powers of intervention in relation to two matters, reserved matters and Community and international obligations; s. 29 is also referred to here in that context.

Reserved Matters

(a) Power to prevent or require action by the Assembly by s. 34 (1). If it appears to the Secretary of State that any action proposed to be taken by the Assembly would or might affect a reserved matter directly or indirectly, and if it appears to him desirable in the public interest to use his power in this matter, he may direct that that proposed action shall not be taken. A reserved matter is defined (in s. 34 (3)) as one (i) which concerns Wales (whether or not it concerns any other part of the United Kingdom), but (ii) with respect to which the Assembly has no power to act.

By the use of its devolved powers the Assembly could affect a matter which is not devolved—defence, trade, energy policy, etc. The function of these ministerial powers is therefore to protect matters which are not devolved against action prejudicial to them by the Assembly in the exercise of a devolved function. In the Scotland and Wales Bill the reserve powers were more widely drafted, with the effect that the Secretary of State could intervene if the Assembly in the exercise of a devolved function, say education, adversely affected an English interest *in education*. This is not now the case. Education is a matter in respect of which the Assembly has power to act and is not therefore a reserved matter (see (ii) above). The Opposition in both Lords and Commons sought unsuccessfully to amend the Bill so as to bring the reserve powers into line with what had been proposed in the Scotland and Wales Bill.

In addition to his power to direct that action shall *not* be taken, the Secretary of State has power to *require* action to be taken. Where it appears to him that any action capable of being taken by the Assembly is not proposed to be taken and that failure to take it would or might affect a reserved matter, whether directly or indirectly, he may (where it appears to him desirable in the public interest to do so) direct that the action capable of being taken shall be taken (s. 34 (1)).

By s. 34 (5) a direction given under the section is stated to be binding on the Assembly; and s. 34 (4) states when a direction is to be taken as given to the Assembly. A direction under s. 34 (1) is a " twenty-eight day " order (s. 34 (6)).

(b) Revoking subordinate instruments made by the Assembly. By s. 35 (1), if it appears to the Secretary of State that an instrument made by the Assembly under any Act of Parliament affects a reserved matter, whether directly or indirectly, and that the public interest makes it desirable that he should use this power, he may by order revoke the instrument. The definition of " reserved matter " is the same as for s. 34 (above). Notice the provision in s. 35 (5) for parliamentary consideration of the Secretary of State's order.

Community and international obligations

(a) Power to prevent or require action by the Assembly. By s. 34 (2) the Secretary of State may direct the Assembly not to take action it proposes to take which would be incompatible with Community obligations or any other international obligations of the United Kingdom. Likewise, he may direct it to take action capable of being taken by it where such action is required for the purpose of implementing any Community obligation, etc. See also s. 34 (4) (5) and (6).

(b) Power to revoke subordinate instruments made by the Assembly. S. 35 (2) gives the Secretary of State a power to revoke an instrument made by the Assembly under any Act of Parliament which appears to him to be incompatible with Community obligations, etc., or which provides for any matter which is or ought to be provided for in an instrument made by the Secretary of State and implementing such an obligation. An order made under s. 35 (2) is not subject to the parliamentary procedures required by s. 35 (5).

It will be noted that before exercising the power to prevent or require action or to revoke subordinate instruments which affect a reserved matter, it must appear to the Secretary of State that it is desirable in the public interest to exercise that power. There is no such requirement in the case of the exercise of the power where there is incompatibility with Community obligations. The meaning of the " public interest " requirement was queried in Parliament. The Lord Chancellor said that " it means that the Secretary of State need not take action if he thinks that it would not be in the public interest to do so " (H.L. Vol. 393, col. 1335). A major consideration in his mind would presumably be that he would be overriding, subject to parliamentary consideration (ss. 34 (6), 35 (5)), a national elected body. Incompatibility with Community obligations on the other hand, does not involve a balancing of such interests.

For the reckoning of periods mentioned in ss. 34 and 35, see s. 71.

(c) Power to make subordinate instruments. We have seen that the transfer by s. 9 of the Act to the Assembly of functions under the Act listed in Sched. 2 to the Act includes in principle the power to make subordinate legislation. (In addition, by para. 40 of Sched. 11 the references in s. 2 (2) of the European Communities Act 1972 to Ministers and government departments include reference to the Assembly which can therefore make subordinate legislation for the purpose of implementing any Community obligation of the United Kingdom.) However, as final responsibility for implementing Community and other international obligations rests with the Government, s. 29 of the Act gives Ministers the power to exercise, for the purpose of implementing these obligations, any ministerial power to make a subordinate instrument even though the power is exercisable by the Assembly by virtue of having been transferred to it by s. 9 of the Act. " This clause is deliberately drawn widely, and must be interpreted widely, so that the United Kingdom Government . . . will be in no way inhibited from taking action in this field to make good a deficiency in the devolved executive function . . . by the Assembly " (H.L. Vol. 393, col. 1307, Lord Goronwy-Roberts).

The Government had proposed, in the 1975 White Paper, to take power, where the Assembly declined to put any matter right, to resume responsibility for any devolved matter and to require and direct the use of Assembly staff for this purpose (Cmnd. 6348, para. 208c). This proposal was dropped.

The following note may be of interest. Directions given under s. 34 (1) and orders made under s. 35 (1) (but not directions or orders under s. 34 (2) or 35 (2)) (concerning compatibility with Community obligations) are subject to the approval in some form of both Houses. The Bill as laid contained a clause (cl. 73) enabling the Commons to override the Lords on this matter. (The Parliament Act 1911 enabling the Commons to override the Lords does not apply to ministerial orders.) A similar clause had been deleted from the Scotland Bill by the Lords, and its deletion from the Wales Bill was not contested. (A precedent for the clause will be found in the Parliament Bill (No. 2) 1968.)

Sched. 8 to this Act gives the Secretary of State powers to intervene in the exercise by the Assembly of its powers in relation to water authorities. Where the Secretary of State has such a power of intervention, ss. 34 and 35 do not apply (see s. 63).

Requirement of consent

36.—(1) The Assembly shall not without the consent of a Minister of the Crown exercise, under an enactment specified in column 1 of Schedule 4 to this Act, any power specified in relation to that enactment in column 2 of that Schedule.

(2) The Assembly shall not without the consent of a Minister of the Crown make or confirm a compulsory purchase order if the land in respect of which the order is made or an interest or right in it—

(a) is held by excepted statutory undertakers for the purposes of their undertaking, or

(b) is held by a local authority (or by a body formed by local authorities) for the purposes of any of the matters listed in Schedule 5 to this Act,

and the undertakers, authority or body have duly objected to the making of the order and have not withdrawn their objection.

DEFINITION

" Excepted statutory undertakers ": see s. 79 (1) (4).

GENERAL NOTE

By s. 36 (1), some of the powers transferred by s. 9 (1) of the Act to the Assembly are exercisable only with ministerial consent. They are listed in Sched. 4. Of the 14 entries, eight relate to excepted statutory undertakers, one (Town and Country Planning Act 1971, s. 273) relates to the National Coal Board, one (Control of Pollution Act 1974) to water authorities. The first entry (Public Health Act 1936, ss. 2 and 6) relates to the constituting of port health district and united districts; the second (s. 143 of the same Act) to a power to make regulations for preventing infectious diseases affecting vessels and aircraft.

By s. 36 (2) the interests of " excepted statutory undertakers " and of local authorities' " reserved local matters " are safeguarded against compulsory purchase orders. " These controls are not concerned with safeguarding any particular land uses but with safeguarding the carrying out of their statutory functions by the bodies operating in those reserved areas " (H.L. Vol. 393, col. 1340). For further reference to excepted statutory undertakers and to reserved local matters, see note on s. 9 (1) above.

Industrial and economic guidelines

Industrial and economic guidelines

37.—(1) The Secretary of State shall with the approval of the Treasury prepare guidelines as to the exercise by the Assembly of its powers with respect to—

(a) such of the functions of the bodies mentioned in subsection (2) below as relate to the disposal of premises or other land for industrial purposes,

(b) any other functions of the Welsh Development Agency relating to the promotion, financing, establishment, carrying on, growth, reorganisation, modernisation or development of industrial or commercial activities or undertakings, and

(c) any other functions of the Development Board for Rural Wales relating to economic development.

(2) The bodies referred to in subsection (1) above are—

(a) the Welsh Development Agency;

(b) a county or district council;

(c) a development corporation within the meaning of the New Towns Act 1965;

(d) the Land Authority for Wales;

(e) the Development Board for Rural Wales.

(3) The Assembly shall exercise its powers so as to give effect to guidelines prepared under this section.

(4) Guidelines under this section shall be contained in or determined under an order of the Secretary of State.

(5) A statutory instrument made under this section shall be subject to annulment in pursuance of a resolution of either House of Parliament.

General Note

By Pt. VIII of Sched. 2, "development" is a devolved area. Thus, subject to exceptions, Secretary of State powers in relation to the Welsh Development Agency, the Land Authority for Wales and the Development Board for Rural Wales are transferred (for a brief account of these bodies, see the section " Nominated Bodies in Wales " in the introductory notes on this Act). The Lords deleted this Part from the Schedule but the Commons disagreed. The Lords' response was to exclude the W.D.A. and the D.B.R.W. from the Assembly's powers, but not to insist on the exclusion of the L.A.W. They sought to distinguish between them by saying that as the L.A.W. deals specifically with housing and land development it would not be inconsistent to devolve functions in relation to it, whereas the work of the other two bodies could not be considered in isolation from the economic development of the United Kingdom. The Government view was that the W.D.A. and D.B.R.W. were purely Welsh, and to deprive the Assembly of responsibility for them would be to divorce them from an important aspect of life in Wales. Further they both have a number of planning and environmental functions which are devolved under other provisions of the legislation.

But the Bill acknowledged that the exercise by all three bodies of certain of their functions might impinge on government economic or industrial policy. This section seeks to ensure that they can be kept in line with that policy by requiring the Secretary of State to prepare guidelines as to the exercise by the Assembly of its powers with respect to certain functions of the three bodies and also of a New Town Corporation and of county and district councils. The guidelines will be contained in or determined under a statutory instrument made by the Secretary of State. Guidelines, as a Minister put it, are a well-established administrative tool. Normally the obligation is to "have regard to" guidelines, but in this case the Assembly "shall exercise its powers so as to give effect to them." With regard to the W.D.A., for example, the Assembly can give it directions, to which it must give effect. If the Assembly failed to give effect to the guidelines the Government could act under s. 34 or 70.

Reference is made to the W.D.A. in the note to s. 60.

For devolved functions in relation to New Towns, see Sched. 2, Pt. VIII. For disposal of land by county and district councils, see Local Government Act 1972, ss. 123 and 123A.

Agency arrangements and information

Agency arrangements and provision of services

38.—(1) Arrangements may be made between the Assembly and any relevant authority for any functions of one of them to be discharged by, or by officers of, the other, and for the provision by one of them for the other of administrative, professional or technical services.

(2) No such arrangements for the discharge of any functions shall affect the responsibility of the authority on whose behalf the functions are discharged.

(3) In this section " relevant authority " means any department of the Government of the United Kingdom and any public or local authority or public corporation.

General Note

In the arrangements authorised by this section, the Assembly may be principal or agent.

Subs. (3) is not to be read as though it ended with the words "in Wales."

Compare the Northern Ireland Constitution Act 1973, s. 11.

Provision of information

39. Where it appears to the Secretary of State that any information relating to the exercise of functions by the Assembly is required for the exercise of functions by a Minister of the Crown he may request the Assembly to supply the information and the Assembly shall comply with the request.

GENERAL NOTE

A Minister explained that the sort of information the Government might need for United Kingdom purposes was information about devolved matters which is relevant to non-devolved matters or required for the proper discharge of non-devolved responsibilities, *e.g.* information about trends in secondary education (devolved) which would affect planning of university provision (non-devolved); or information which needs to be produced on a consistent United Kingdom basis, *e.g.* for the EEC (H.L. Vol. 393, col. 1356). Note that whichever Minister needs the information it must appear to the Secretary of State that it is required for that Minister's functions, and only the Secretary of State may require the Assembly to supply it.

PART III

FINANCIAL PROVISIONS

Establishment and management of Welsh Funds

Welsh Consolidated Fund and Loans Fund

40.—(1) There shall be a Welsh Consolidated Fund and a Welsh Loans Fund.

(2) The Executive Committee of the Assembly may from time to time cause sums to be transferred from one to the other of those Funds.

REFERENCES

For the Executive Committee, see s. 18.

For a general note on the financial provisions of the Act, see s. 48.

Payments out of Welsh Consolidated Fund

41.—(1) No payment shall be made out of the Welsh Consolidated Fund except in accordance with credits granted on the Fund by the Welsh Comptroller and Auditor General; but this subsection does not apply to transfers under section 40 (2) above.

(2) The Welsh Comptroller and Auditor General shall grant credits on the Welsh Consolidated Fund at the request of the Executive Committee of the Assembly, but shall not grant any such credit for the payment of any sum unless that sum—

(*a*) has been charged on the Fund by or under any Act of Parliament, or

(*b*) is part of the sums appropriated for any purpose by an order of the Assembly;

and no sum issued out of the Welsh Consolidated Fund on credits granted under paragraph (*a*) or (*b*) above shall be applied for any purpose other than that for which it is charged or appropriated as mentioned in that paragraph.

REFERENCES

For Welsh Comptroller and Auditor General, see s. 49.

For Executive Committee, see s. 18.

For general note on the financial provisions of the Act, see s. 48.

Appropriation of sums forming part of Welsh Consolidated Fund and destination of receipts

42.—(1) Sums forming part of the Welsh Consolidated Fund may be appropriated only for a purpose for which the Assembly may exercise its powers or a purpose for which they are payable out of that Fund under this Act or any other Act of Parliament.

(2) The Assembly shall not charge a committee with the exercise of the power to make orders appropriating sums from the Welsh Consolidated Fund and shall not itself make such an order except on the recommendation of the Executive Committee.

(3) An order appropriating sums forming part of the Welsh Consolidated Fund may provide for the disposal of or the accounting for sums forming part of the receipts of the Assembly; and so far as those receipts are not so disposed of or accounted for and are not payable into the Welsh Loans Fund they shall be paid into the Welsh Consolidated Fund.

REFERENCES

For Executive Committee, see s. 18.

For general note on financial provisions of the Act, see s. 48.

Payments out of Welsh Loans Fund

43.—(1) No payment shall be made out of the Welsh Loans Fund except in accordance with credits granted on the Fund by the Welsh Comptroller and Auditor General; but this subsection does not apply to transfers under section 40 (2) above.

(2) The Welsh Comptroller and Auditor General shall grant credits on the Welsh Loans Fund at the request of the Executive Committee of the Assembly, but shall not grant any such credit for the payment of any sum unless—

(a) the Assembly has power to lend that sum; or

(b) the sum is required for the payment of interest on, or the repayment of, sums paid into the Fund under section 45 or 46 below or amounts deemed under any provision of this Act to be amounts of advances made to the Assembly; or

(c) the sum is required for a purpose incidental to any for which credits may be granted under paragraph (a) or (b) above;

and no sum issued out of the Welsh Loan Fund on credits granted under paragraph (a) above shall be applied for any purpose other than the lending of money by the Assembly.

REFERENCES

For Welsh Comptroller and Auditor General, see s. 49.

For Executive Committee, see s. 18.

For general note on financial provisions of the Act, see s. 48.

Payments into Welsh Funds out of United Kingdom Funds

Payments into Welsh Consolidated Fund out of moneys provided by Parliament

44.—(1) The Secretary of State shall from time to time make out of moneys provided by Parliament payments into the Welsh Consolidated Fund of such sums as he may determine by order made with the consent of the Treasury.

(2) No order under this section shall be made unless a draft of it has been laid before the House of Commons and approved by a resolution of that House; and there shall be laid before that House, together with

the draft, a statement of the considerations leading to the determination to be made by the order.

GENERAL NOTE

The Assembly thus gets its money from central government. It has no taxing powers.

For a general note on the financial provisions of the Act see s. 48.

" Out of moneys provided by Parliament " means that an estimate must be presented to Parliament in each year that the expenditure is to be incurred and payment appropriated to it by an Appropriation Act (Wade & Phillips, *Constitutional and Administrative Law* (9th ed.) p. 273).

Payments into Welsh Loans Fund out of National Loans Fund

45.—(1) The Secretary of State shall from time to time pay into the Welsh Loans Fund such sums as he may with the consent of the Treasury determine.

(2) The Treasury may issue to the Secretary of State such sums out of the National Loans Fund as are required to enable him to make payments under this section.

(3) Payments under this section into the Welsh Loans Fund shall be deemed to be advances made to the Assembly and shall be repayable at such times and with interest at such rates as may be determined by the Treasury; and any sums received by the Secretary of State by way of repayment or interest shall be paid into the National Loans Fund.

(4) The aggregate outstanding in respect of the principal of sums paid under subsection (1) above shall not exceed £250 million.

(5) The Secretary of State may from time to time by order made with the consent of the Treasury substitute for the amount specified in subsection (4) above such increased amount as may be specified in the order.

(6) No order shall be made under this section unless a draft of it has been laid before the House of Commons and approved by a resolution of that House.

REFERENCES

For a general note on the financial provisions of the Act see s. 48.

Borrowing and capital expenditure

Short term borrowing

46.—(1) The Assembly may borrow in sterling temporarily, either by way of overdraft or otherwise, such sums as may appear to the Assembly to be required for the purpose of meeting a temporary excess of sums paid out of the Welsh Consolidated Fund or the Welsh Loans Fund over sums paid into that Fund or for the purpose of providing a working balance in either Fund.

(2) Sums borrowed by the Assembly shall be paid into the Welsh Loans Fund or the Welsh Consolidated Fund.

(3) So far as sums required for the repayment of, or the payment of interest on, sums borrowed under this section are not paid out of the Welsh Loans Fund they shall be charged on the Welsh Consolidated Fund.

(4) The aggregate outstanding in respect of the principal of sums borrowed by the Assembly shall not exceed £35 million.

(5) The Secretary of State may from time to time by order made with the consent of the Treasury substitute for the amount specified in

subsection (4) above such increased amount as may be specified in the order.

(6) A statutory instrument made under this section shall be subject to annulment in pursuance of a resolution of the House of Commons.

REFERENCES

For a general note on the financial provisions of the Act, see s. 48.

Treasury guarantee of sums borrowed by Assembly

47.—(1) The Treasury may guarantee, in such manner and on such conditions as they think fit, the repayment of the principal of and the payment of interest on any sums borrowed by the Assembly.

(2) Immediately after a guarantee is given under this section the Treasury shall lay a statement of the guarantee before each House of Parliament; and where any sum is issued for fulfilling such a guarantee the Treasury shall as soon as possible after the end of each financial year (beginning with that in which the sum is issued and ending with that in which all liability in respect of the principal of the sum and in respect of interest thereon is finally discharged) lay before each House of Parliament a statement relating to that sum.

(3) Any sums required by the Treasury for fulfilling a guarantee under this section shall be charged on the Consolidated Fund.

(4) If any sums are issued in fulfilment of a guarantee given under this section, the Assembly shall make to the Treasury, at such time and in such manner as the Treasury may from time to time determine, payments of such amounts as the Treasury may determine in or towards repayment of the sums so issued and payments of interest, at such rate as the Treasury may from time to time determine, on what is outstanding for the time being in respect of sums so issued.

(5) Any sums payable to the Treasury under subsection (4) above shall be charged on the Welsh Consolidated Fund and any sums received by the Treasury under that subsection shall be paid into the Consolidated Fund of the United Kingdom.

REFERENCES

For a general note on the financial provisions of the Act, see s. 48.

Limitation of capital expenditure financed by borrowing

48.—(1) In exercising its powers in relation to the bodies specified in subsection (3) below and its powers under Schedule 13 to the Local Government Act 1972 (loans and other financial provisions) the Assembly shall endeavour to secure that the aggregate of the expenditure incurred in any financial year which is relevant capital expenditure does not exceed such amount as the Secretary of State may by order made with the consent of the Treasury determine as the limit of such expenditure for that year.

(2) For the purposes of this section relevant capital expenditure is capital expenditure—

    (a) met out of borrowed money by any body specified in paragraphs
        (b) to (h) of subsection (3) below, or

    (b) incurred by the Housing Corporation, the Severn-Trent Water
        Authority or the Welsh Water Authority and met out of money
        borrowed from, or with the consent of, the Assembly, or

    (c) incurred by (or by bodies formed by) local authorities in Wales,
        and met out of money borrowed with the consent of the Assembly;
and " expenditure " includes the making of loans.

(3) The bodies referred to in subsection (1) above are—

    (*a*) the Housing Corporation;

    (*b*) the Land Authority for Wales;

    (*c*) the Welsh Development Agency;

    (*d*) the Development Board for Rural Wales;

    (*e*) any development corporation (within the meaning of the New Towns Act 1965) in Wales;

    (*f*) any port health authority in Wales;

    (*g*) any internal drainage board (within the meaning of the Land Drainage Act 1976) for a district which is wholly in Wales or is within the area of the Welsh Water Authority and partly in Wales;

    (*h*) the Wales Tourist Board;

    (*i*) the Severn-Trent Water Authority; and

    (*j*) the Welsh Water Authority.

(4) No order under subsection (1) above shall be made unless a draft of it has been laid before the House of Commons and approved by a resolution of that House; and there shall be laid before that House, together with the draft, a statement of the considerations leading to the determination to be made by the order.

GENERAL NOTE

The Block Grant

The Assembly has no taxing powers. Where then does it get its money from? From the Secretary of State in the form of a block grant. (It may also receive fees for various services but these will be insignificant). The Assembly is thus a spending and not a revenue-raising body. It is argued that it thereby infringes the principle that the body which spends should be one which has the odium of raising the money—a principle infringed, however, to some considerable degree by local authorities some 61 per cent. of whose total expenditure is derived from the rate support grant. The possible political consequences of the 100 per cent. block grant for the Assembly on the future unity of the Kingdom were referred to in the debates. (See Introductory Notes to the Act: The unity of the Kingdom).

The devolved services are thus financed on an expenditure basis: the expenditure requirements of the devolved services are measured and the devolved administration is furnished with the income needed to meet them. The alternative, rejected, method of finance is the revenue basis: the Assembly would be given certain sources of revenue and would be obliged to finance the devolved services out of the income those services provided. The Government's reasons for adopting the expenditure basis are explained in the 1977 White Paper, *Devolution: Financing the Devolved Services* (Cmnd. 6890). Basically they are that traditionally the allocation of public expenditure between different areas of Great Britain has not been determined by the amount of revenue raised in them but by their needs; and that the economic unity of the United Kingdom requires the continued pooling of all United Kingdom resources (including for example, revenue from off-shore oil) and the consideration of expenditure needs of the United Kingdom as a whole. In the Government's view the adoption of the expenditure basis did not rule out altogether giving the Assemblies power to levy limited additional taxation to finance extra expenditures which they might think especially important. However, its proposal to give them power to levy a surcharge on local rates for that purpose was dropped, and no other way of revenue-raising was found possible.

The block-grant made over to the Assembly by the Secretary of State will of course be only part of the total sum made available to the Welsh Office annually for its purposes and arrived at as a result of the usual negotiations within central government. That is to say the Welsh Office claims on total public expenditure for any year will include a sum in respect of the block grant. The Assembly will of course before that have urged its claims on the Welsh Office.

We have noted that Wales is in public expenditure deficit with the rest of the United Kingdom. If the block grant were to be calculated on a per capita basis, Wales would clearly be poorer than it is now. But as explained above the Government gave as a reason for deciding on the block grant expenditure-based financing of the Assembly the desirability of ensuring that Wales' needs will continue to be met. How then are those needs to be assessed? How is the block grant to be calculated? The Act does not say. All it does say (s. 44) is that " the Secretary of State shall from time to time make out of moneys provided by Parliament payments into the Welsh Consolidated Fund of such sums as he may determine by order made with the consent of the Treasury." The Government acknowledged, however, that the assessment of needs and hence the calculation of the block grant, should be made as objective and as generally acceptable as it is possible to make it but insisted that the decision must be a matter of political judgment. The remarkable proposal of the Commission on the Constitution for expenditure to be allocated by an independent (*i.e.* politically unaccountable) Exchequer Board, was rightly rejected. Nevertheless the Government thought that the provision of a basis of information about needs and standards of public services could be assisted by the creation of an independent advisory and research board. The creation of such a body would be discussed with the Assemblies (there is therefore nothing in the Act about it) (Cmnd. 6890, para. 72).

The Government acknowledged that the annual discussion of levels of devolved expenditure might well lead to detailed central government involvement in the work of the Assembly, and might make it difficult for the Assembly to determine its own plans on a satisfactory basis. The Government has therefore also proposed for discussion with the Assemblies a *formula-based system*. The total of devolved public expenditure in Wales (and Scotland) would be related to comparable expenditure elsewhere in the country on the basis of relative needs. This would be expressed as a percentage of comparable expenditure in the country as a whole. This percentage would be maintained over a stated period (which might be four years—the term of the Assembly), but changes in the level of comparable expenditure outside Wales (and Scotland) would automatically lead to corresponding increases or decreases in devolved expenditure. There is nothing of this in the Act: in the Government's view to deal with the matter on a statutory basis would lead at best to " extremely cumbersome provisions of doubtful validity and effectiveness " (Cmnd. 6890, para. 77). It will be noted that the purpose is to maintain an agreed percentage over a period. This does not mean that the block grant will be maintained at a certain level over any particular period. Like every other item of public expenditure it is bound to be subject to review in the light of prevailing economic circumstances.

The Assembly will allocate the block grant amongst the devolved services in accordance with its own priorities. Thus though the grant will be calculated on the basis of comparable needs in various services, the Assembly will not be required to allocate expenditure in accordance with that view of needs. (The same applies of course to the use of rate support grant by local authorities.)

Although the block grant will be the only effective source of finance for the Assembly, it will not be the only source of finance for devolved services. For example, housing and education are devolved services. Part of the Assembly's block grant will be expended on them as at present is part of central government's expenditure. In addition of course, local authorities raise money by way of rates and borrowing to help pay for these as for other devolved services. In determining the amount of the block grant it will be necessary to take account of this and other sources of finance for devolved services. The Government will therefore have to determine two sets of figures: the amount of the block fund, and the limit on capital expenditure on devolved services by local authorities and public corporations which is financed from borrowing and require authorisation by the Assembly. Both figures will require parliamentary approval (ss. 44 & 48). As for rates, a contribution from rates will be assumed. The Government will have to decide whether by comparison with rate income in England this is fair, for a lower rate would mean the need for a higher block grant to provide services to the desired level.

The Welsh Funds

The scheme of the Act is to reflect on a smaller scale the United Kingdom arrangement of a Consolidated Fund and a National Loans Fund.

Thus the Act provides (s. 40) that there is to be a Welsh Consolidated Fund. As we have noted, payments into this Fund are to be made by the Secretary of State: this is the bank account into which the block grants are paid. (Payments will be made in instalments, perhaps weekly).

No payment is to be made out of the Fund except in accordance with credits granted by the Welsh Controller and Auditor General (an office created by the Act—see s. 49). The Welsh C. & A. G. grants credits on the Fund at the request of the Executive Committee of the Assembly but is not to grant credit for payment of any sum unless that sum (a) has been *charged on* the Fund by or under any Act of Parliament—see for example s. 50 (5); or (b) is part of the sums appropriated for any purpose by an order of the Assembly (s. 41 (2)). For what purpose may sums be appropriated? By s. 42 (1) sums forming part of the Fund may be appropriated only for a purpose (i) for which the Assembly may exercise its powers; or (ii) for which they are payable out of that Fund under the Act or any other Act. The need for (ii) is that the purpose of payment may be one for which the Assembly does not exercise its powers, but which is nevertheless one for which sums may by statute be payable out of (but not charged on—(a) above) the Fund—see for example s. 49 (8).

No sum issued out of the Fund on credits granted under para. (a) or (b) above is to be applied for any purpose other than that for which it is charged or appropriated (s. 41 (2)).

The Act also provides (s. 40 (1)) that there is to be a Welsh Loans Fund. Payments into this are to be made from time to time by the Secretary of State of such sums as he with Treasury consent determines (s. 45 (1)). The Treasury issues to the Secretary of State such sums out of the National Loans Fund as are required to enable the Secretary of State to make payments to the Welsh Loans Fund. (For the National Loans Fund see National Loans Act 1968).

Payments into the Welsh Loans Fund are deemed to be advances made to the Assembly, and are repayable at such times and with interest at such rates as the Treasury determines. Any sums received by the Secretary of State by way of repayment or interest are to be paid into the National Loans Fund (s. 45 (3)).

The maximum amount outstanding in respect of the principal of sums advanced to the Assembly under these provisions is fixed by the Act at £250 million but this may be increased by ministerial order with the approval of the House of Commons (s. 45 (4), (5), (6)).

As with the Welsh Consolidated Fund, no payment is to be made out of the Loans Fund except in accordance with credits granted on the Fund by the Welsh C. & A.G. He is to grant credits at the request of the Executive Committee, but is not to grant any such credit for the payment of any sum unless (a) the Assembly has power to lend that sum, (and such sum is not to be applied for any purpose other than the lending of money by the Assembly); or (b) the sum is required for certain other specified purposes (s. 43 (2)).

A Treasury Minister explained the need for the Loans Fund in this way (H.C. Vol. 947, col. 317): there are certain public bodies which borrow with the Secretary of State's consent from the National Loans Fund. The functions of the Secretary of State over the bodies in question are transferred by the Act to the Assembly. It is not appropriate for those bodies to borrow directly from the National Fund. Thus since control over their borrowing is to be exercised by the Assembly, the Assembly itself borrows from the Welsh Loans Fund (which is fed from the National Fund). (The bodies in question are listed in s. 48 (3) of the Act). By s. 48 (1) the Assembly is to try to ensure that the amount of capital expenditure financed by borrowing by those bodies and by local authorities does not exceed such amounts as is fixed by ministerial order, which requires Parliamentary approval (s. 48 (3)).

We refer now to *short-term borrowing*. By s. 46 the Assembly may borrow temporarily (which in Treasury terms means less than 12 months) in sterling by way of overdraft or otherwise, such sums as may appear to the Assembly to be required to meet a shortfall in either Consolidated or Loans Fund or in order to maintain a working balance in either Fund. The amount outstanding is not to exceed £35 million, but this figure can be increased by ministerial order (subss. (5), (6)). The Treasury may guarantee the repayment of sums borrowed (s. 47).

The Act provides (s. 40 (2)) for *transfer between the Funds*. The Executive Committee of the Assembly may cause sums to be transferred from one to the other of the Funds. The requirement (referred above), that no payment is to be made out of either Fund except in accordance with credits granted by the Welsh C. & A.G., does not apply to transfer between the Funds (ss. 41 (1), 43 (1)). This is because the Welsh C. & A.G.'s consent is necessary for payment out of the Funds, and transfer between the Funds is not payment out of them to a third party.

What is the reason for authorising this transfer between the funds? It is to enable the Assembly to deal with the situation where one fund is in surplus, the other in deficit. In such a case the fund in deficit could get an overdraft from the bank (see above). If it did that, interest would of course be payable. The transfer of the surplus of one fund to reduce the deficit of the other is therefore simply to avoid interest charges.

In the course of the debate a Treasury Minister said a number of times that money paid into one fund but transferred to another could be used only for the purpose of the first fund. He later acknowledged (in a letter to the chief Opposition Spokesman on devolution) that this was incorrect, that "money can be paid out of either fund, no matter what its source, upon a decision by the Assembly to do so and subject only to a certificate from the Welsh C. & A.G.; a certificate which would be forthcoming if the Assembly were acting within its powers in making its spending decision." However he gave an assurance that the section permitting transfer (s. 40 (2)) would not permit evasion of the limitations laid down in the Act on the use of Assembly Funds. Thus payments by the Secretary of State into the Welsh Consolidated Fund cannot exceed the block fund (the total of which is agreed by the House), and the size of that fund would not be affected by a decision to transfer sums from the Consolidated to the Loans Fund. Secondly, payments from the National to the Welsh Loans Fund are subject to the limits specified in s. 45 (4) and (5), and would have to remain within the s. 45 (4) limit whether employed for lending or transferred to the Consolidated Fund. Thus there is control over the two funds taken together, with freedom to the Assembly within that control to spend the money allocated to it. The Minister added, "An additional safeguard in both cases is that payments into the Welsh Consolidated and Loans Fund are subject to the discretion of the Secretary of State who would have the power to reduce or delay the payment if some situation arose for which the arrangements in the Bill had not adequately provided."

Various Acts of Parliament charge sums on the Consolidated Fund, or require or authorise the payment of sums into or out of the Fund or out of moneys provided by Parliament. By s. 55 of the Wales Act 1978 such Acts have effect so far as they relate to the exercise of functions by the Welsh Assembly as if they provided for the sum to be charged on or paid into or out of the Welsh Consolidated Fund.

Likewise where the power to advance money under certain enactments is exercisable by the Assembly, the Welsh Loans Fund is substituted for the National Loans Fund, the rate of interest is specified, and provision is made for the auditing of the relevant accounts by the Welsh C. & A.G. (referred to below) (s. 51). Provision is also made for the repayment into the Welsh Loans Fund of advances previously made under those enactments by the Secretary of State, and for subsequent adjustments (s. 56).

For each financial year (that is, each year ending with March 31) the Assembly has to prepare appropriation accounts of sums paid and received by it; and the Executive Committee has to prepare an account of payments into and out of the Welsh Consolidated Fund and an account of payments into and out of the Welsh Loans Fund (s. 52). The Assembly has to publish those accounts and the reports made on them by the Welsh C. & A.G. and by its Accounts Committee (see below, s. 54).

Accounts and audit

Welsh Comptroller and Auditor General

49.—(1) There shall be a Welsh Comptroller and Auditor General.

(2) The Welsh Comptroller and Auditor General shall be appointed by Her Majesty and, subject to subsection (3) below, shall hold office during good behaviour.

(3) A person appointed under this section—

(a) may be relieved of office by Her Majesty at his own request; and

(b) may be removed from office by Her Majesty if the Secretary of State, after consultation with the Assembly, recommends the removal to Her Majesty.

(4) The Welsh Comptroller and Auditor General shall not be a member of the House of Commons or of the Scottish or Welsh or Northern Ireland Assembly.

(5) The Welsh Comptroller and Auditor General may appoint officers and servants, subject to the consent of the Assembly as to numbers.

(6) Subject to subsection (7) below, any functions of the Welsh Comptroller and Audit General may be performed by an officer of his authorised by him for that purpose.

(7) An authority given under subsection (6) above to certify and report on accounts for the Assembly—

(a) shall extend only to accounts in respect of which the presiding officer of the Assembly has certified to the Assembly that the Welsh Comptroller and Auditor General is unable to do so himself; and

(b) shall cease on a vacancy arising in the office of the Welsh Comptroller and Auditor General.

(8) The expenses of the Welsh Comptroller and Auditor General shall be defrayed out of the Welsh Consolidated Fund.

GENERAL NOTE

The office and functions of the Welsh C. & A.G. are of course based on that of the U.K. C. & A.G. The Assembly being a Crown body this is a Crown appointment. In the Bill as originally presented the C. & A.G. could be removed if the Assembly resolved that the Secretary of State be requested to recommend his removal to Her Majesty. A Lords amendment was accepted by the Commons (see s. 49 (3) (b)).

Some members queried the need for a separate office of Welsh C. & A.G. Would it not be preferable, they asked, for the existing office of C. & A.G. to do the work? As the Assembly is not a taxing body, but spends money provided by Parliament why should not the Assembly's spending be audited by the same officer who audits other expenditure approved by Parliament? Was sufficient expertise available for the two bodies? How would the two career structures be related? The Government's view was that the new institution of the Assembly required its own internal audit office; that the Welsh C. & A.G. would not necessarily work in the same way as the present office, but would perhaps look to what was done in other countries; that the C. & A.G. had been consulted on the proposals in the Bill; that the career structures would be for discussion.

The Opposition moved in both the Commons and the Lords a new clause which would have applied s. 161 of the Local Government Act 1972 to the Assembly: that is to say, it would have given the Welsh C. & A. G. the powers of the district auditor and subjected Assembly members to possible surcharge and disqualification. The government view was that as the Assembly is to act on behalf of the Crown, central rather than local government arrangements provided the more apt analogy. The clause was rejected in the Commons and withdrawn in the Lords.

Salary and pension of Welsh Comptroller and Auditor General

50.—(1) There shall be paid to the Welsh Comptroller and Auditor General such salary as the Assembly may from time to time determine.

(2) There shall be paid to or in respect of a person who ceases to hold office as Welsh Comptroller and Auditor General such amounts by way of pensions, allowances or gratuities or by way of provision for any such benefits as the Assembly may from time to time determine.

(3) Any determination under the preceding provisions of this section may take effect from the date on which it is made or such other date as the Assembly may specify, but not so as to diminish the sums payable for any period preceding the determination.

(4) If a person ceases to be Welsh Comptroller and Auditor General and it appears to the Assembly that there are special circumstances which make it right that he should receive compensation there shall be paid to him such amount as the Assembly may determine.

(5) Any sums payable under this section shall be charged on the Welsh Consolidated Fund.

GENERAL NOTE

The sums payable under the section (the Welsh C. & A.G.'s salary, etc.) are charged on the Welsh Consolidated Fund, whereas (by s. 49 (8)) the expenses of the office are merely to be defrayed out of that Fund.

For a general note on the Welsh C. & A.G. see s. 49.

Access of Welsh Comptroller and Auditor General to books and documents

51. The Welsh Comptroller and Auditor General shall have free access, at all convenient times, to the books of account and other documents relating to the accounts of the Assembly and may require the Assembly to furnish him from time to time, or at regular periods, with accounts of its transactions.

GENERAL NOTE

For a note on the Welsh C. & A.G. see s. 49.

Appropriation and other accounts and audit

52.—(1) For each financial year—
　　(a) the Assembly shall prepare appropriation accounts of sums paid and received by it; and
　　(b) the Executive Committee shall prepare an account of payments into and out of the Welsh Consolidated Fund and an account of payments into and out of the Welsh Loans Fund.

(2) The accounts prepared under this section shall be sent to the Welsh Comptroller and Auditor General not later than the end of November following the end of the financial year to which they relate; and he shall examine, certify and report on them and send copies of them, together with his reports, to the Assembly.

DEFINITION

" Financial year ": means a year ending with March 31 (s. 78 (1)).

REFERENCES

For Executive Committee see s. 18.
For Welsh C. & A.G. see s. 49.

Accounts Committee

53.—(1) The Assembly shall appoint an Accounts Committee, which shall examine and report to the Assembly on the accounts and reports sent to the Assembly by the Welsh Comptroller and Auditor General.

(2) The Accounts Committee may include one but shall not include more than one member of the Executive Committee.

GENERAL NOTE

This Committee is intended to parallel the Public Accounts Committee of the House of Commons. Its membership must reflect the party balance in the Assembly (see s. 21) and may include one, but shall not include more than one, member of the Executive Committee, as to which see s. 18.

For an account of other Assembly committees, see s. 18.

Publication of accounts and reports

54. The Assembly shall publish the accounts prepared and reports made under section 52 and 53 above.

Modification of existing enactments

Modification of enactments providing for payments into or out of Consolidated Fund or authorising advances from National Loans Fund

55.—(1) Any Act passed before this Act which—
　　(a) charges any sum on the Consolidated Fund; or

(*b*) requires or authorises the payment of any sum into or out of the Consolidated Fund; or

(*c*) requires or authorises the payment of any sum out of moneys provided by Parliament;

shall have effect so far as it relates to the exercise of functions by the Assembly as if it provided for the sum to be charged on or, as the case may be, paid into or out of the Welsh Consolidated Fund.

(2) So far as any power to advance money conferred by the enactments mentioned in Schedule 6 to this Act is exercisable by the Assembly—

(*a*) any sums which for the purpose or as the result of the exercise of the power are required to be issued or paid shall, instead of being issued to a Minister of the Crown out of the National Loans Fund or paid to a Minister of the Crown or into that Fund, be issued to the Executive Committee out of the Welsh Loans Fund or, as the case may be, paid to the Assembly or into that Fund; and

(*b*) the rate of interest on any advance made in the exercise of the power shall be not less than the lowest rate determined by the Treasury under section 5 of the National Loans Act 1968 in respect of similar advances made out of the National Loans Fund on the day the advance is made; and

(*c*) any account relating to the sums mentioned in paragraph (*a*) above shall be sent to and audited and reported on by the Welsh Comptroller and Auditor General and his report shall be sent to and published by the Assembly.

REFERENCES

For an account of the financial provisions of the Act and a reference to this section, see note on s. 48.

Existing debt

Existing and advances from National Loans Fund

56. Where any power to advance money conferred by the enactments mentioned in Schedule 6 to this Act is exercisable by the Assembly but was, before it became so exercisable, exercised by the Secretary of State—

(*a*) any amount payable by way of repayment of or interest on the sum advanced by the Secretary of State in the exercise of that power shall, instead of being paid to the Secretary of State and into the National Loans Fund, be paid to the Assembly and into the Welsh Loans Fund; and

(*b*) amounts equal to those which, by virtue of this section, are to be received by the Assembly in repayment of principal shall be deemed to be amounts of advances made at the coming into operation of this section to the Assembly by the Secretary of State and repayable at such times and with interest at such rates as may be determined by the Treasury; and

(*c*) any sums received by the Secretary of State by virtue of paragraph (*b*) above shall be paid into the National Loans Fund.

REFERENCES

For an account of the financial provisions of the Act and reference to this section, see s. 48.

Accounts by Secretary of State

57. The Secretary of State shall for each financial year prepare an account in such form and manner as the Treasury may direct of sums paid and received by him under section 45 or 56 above and send it to the Comptroller and Auditor General not later than the end of November following the end of the year; and the Comptroller and Auditor General shall examine, certify and report on the account and lay copies of it, together with his report, before each House of Parliament.

DEFINITION

" Financial year ": means a year ending with March 31 (s. 79 (1)).

GENERAL NOTE

The Comptroller and Auditor General is of course the United Kingdom not the Welsh officer.

PART IV

MISCELLANEOUS

Rate support and other grants

58.—(1) Grants for any financial year which, after the coming into force of this section, fall to be made under Part I of the Local Government Act 1974, except section 8 (2), to local authorities in Wales shall be made by the Assembly out of the Welsh Consolidated Fund instead of by the Secretary of State out of moneys provided by Parliament.

(2) In taking into consideration the matters mentioned in paragraphs (a) to (d) of subsection (3) of section 1 of the Local Government Act 1974 the Assembly shall have regard to such considerations affecting the matters listed in Schedule 5 to this Act as the Secretary of State may bring to its notice after consulting such associations of local authorities as appear to him to be concerned and before the conclusion of the consultations required by that subsection.

GENERAL NOTE

By s. 1 (1) of the Local Government Act 1974 the Secretary of State (for the Environment) is to make rate support grants to local authorities in England and Wales. By s. 58 of the Wales Act 1978 such grants are in future to be made to local authorities in Wales by the Assembly out of the Welsh Consolidated Fund, that is, out of the block grant, and not by the Secretary of State.

S. 1 of the 1974 Act goes on to specify how the Secretary of State is to fix the estimated aggregate amount of the rate support grant for any year, provides for consultation with local authority interests, and the matters he must take into account. S. 2 requires the Secretary of State to divide the aggregate amount of rate support grant into various elements, to state to which class of authority payments in respect of the various elements are to be made, etc. By the Wales Act 1978 (Sched. 11, para. 52) the Wales Assembly is substituted in those matters for the Secretary of State—but see s. 58 (2) for certain considerations to be taken into account affecting " reserved local matters " referred to below.

S. 3 of the 1974 Act requires the estimated aggregate amounts of rate support grant to be fixed and prescribed by a rate support grant order made by the Secretary of State with the consent of the Treasury and after consulting local authority interests. Under the Wales Act 1978 the order is of course to be made by the Welsh Assembly after consultation, but Treasury consent is not required. The Assembly is to publish the rate support grant order together with a report setting out the considerations stated in s. 3 (3) of the 1974 Act.

S. 4 powers referring to the variation of rate support grant orders are exercisable by the Assembly. The s. 5 power of reducing the grants in case of default is also exercisable by the Assembly (though references in s. 5 (1) to Parliament are of course deleted in their application to the Assembly). Under s. 5 (2) the appropriate Minister may make regulations for prescribing standards and general requirements in relation to any function of a local authority. (A number of educational regulations are deemed by s. 5 (3) to have been made under that subsection.) This regulation-making power is now exercisable by the Assembly, but " reserved local matters " (listed in Sched. 5 and referred to below) are excluded (Sched. 11, para. 59).

Ss. 6, 7, 8 and 9 of the 1974 Act provide for the payment of certain additional grants by the Secretary of State. These are now payable by the Assembly except those specified in s. 8 (2) of the Act, *viz.* grants paid in respect of university and teacher training grants. These remain payable by local authorities and reimbursable by the Secretary of State.

Thus the general position as far as Welsh local authorities is concerned is that the Assembly is substituted for the Secretary of State. They will look to and negotiate with the Assembly for the payment of their rate support grant as in the past they looked to central government. The Assembly will of course pay the R.S.G. out of the block grant, of which it will in fact form a considerable proportion—about 50 per cent. Thus the amount payable by the Assembly to local authorities by way of R.S.G. will form a major element in the Assembly's claim to the Secretary of State for the block grant. Thus when the amount of the block fund is being worked out, assumptions will be made as to the needs of R.S.G. (or any other major expenditure by the Assembly) " but such assumptions would cease to have any validity once the total amount was fixed. . . . Whatever assumptions it may be necessary to make when the block fund is settled, the amount of the statutory rate support grant settlement must be left to the discretion of the Assembly " (H.L. Vol. 394, col. 1144—Lord Harris). Thus it will not be obligatory for the Assembly, when it receives the block grant, to pay out of it by way of R.S.G. the amount that was negotiated for that purpose as part of the block grant. Theoretically, the Assembly could use some of the R.S.G. element for some other lawful purpose leaving it to local authorities to meet their financial needs by putting up the rates. (Central government can of course do this at present by providing less by way of R.S.G.)

If the Assembly were to come into existence during the currency of a financial year it would take over from the Secretary of State responsibility for the payment during the rest of that year of the R.S.G. already agreed by the Secretary of State to be paid to Welsh local authorities, and would be put in funds by the Secretary of State to do so. This is the effect of the phrase in s. 58 (1) " after the coming into force of this section " which replaced the phrase in the original Bill " beginning after the coming into force of this section."

Reserved local matters

By the Local Government Act 1974, s. 1 (3), before determining the amount available for grants (which is the first step towards determining the amount of rate support grants) the Secretary of State is required to take into account various matters relating to expenditure, the demand for services, future costs, etc. When exercising its functions in this matter in relation to Welsh local authorities, the Assembly is required to have regard to such considerations affecting reserved local matters as the Secretary of State may bring to its attention (after he has consulted local authority associations). This means that the level of expenditure on reserved local matters will be subject to consultation between the Secretary of State and Welsh local authorities, and the Secretary of State will indicate to the Assembly what should be included in the total of the relevant expenditure for rate support grant purposes, and the Assembly " shall have regard " to it.

The 27 reserved local matters are listed in Sched. 5. They include police, mandatory awards to students, smallholdings, protection of birds, etc. Some 85 per cent. of expenditure on reserved services is in respect of police and mandatory student awards. The specific grants local authorities receive for those services—50 per cent. and 90 per cent. respectively—will continue, and will be paid by the appropriate Secretary of State, not the Assembly, the first being provided under the Police Act 1964, no powers of which are devolved, the second being reserved by s. 8 (2) of the Local Government Act 1974.

(Further reference to reserved local matters will be found in the notes to ss. 9 and 36.)

Power to make new provision as to certain bodies

59.—(1) In relation to any body listed in Schedule 7 to this Act, a Minister of the Crown may by order make any such provision as is mentioned in subsection (3) below.

(2) In relation to a body listed in Part I of Schedule 7 to this Act, a Minister of the Crown may by order modify or exclude any provision of this Act.

(3) The provisions that may be made in relation to a body by an order under subsection (1) above are provisions—

(a) enabling powers to be exercised or requiring duties to be performed by the Assembly instead of by a Minister of the Crown, or by the one or by the other, or by the Assembly with the consent of a Minister of the Crown;

(b) requiring or authorising the appointment of additional members;

(c) apportioning any assets or liabilities;

(d) imposing, or enabling the imposition of, any special limits in addition to or in substitution for existing limits;

(e) providing, in the case of a body listed in Part II of Schedule 7 to this Act, for the application of section 48 above;

(f) requiring or authorising payments into or out of the Welsh Consolidated or Loans Fund (instead of or in addition to payments into or out of the Consolidated Fund of the United Kingdom or the National Loans Fund or out of moneys provided by Parliament);

(g) requiring payments, with or without interest, to a Minister of the Crown or into the Consolidated Fund or National Loans Fund;

and such provisions, including provisions relating to the keeping, auditing and certification of accounts and the making of reports and provisions modifying any enactment, as appear to the Minister making the order necessary or expedient in consequence of other provisions of the order or incidental or supplementary thereto.

(4) Before making an order under this section relating to any body the Minister making the order shall consult the body; and if the body is listed in Part II of Schedule 7 to this Act the order shall not be made except at the request of the Assembly.

(5) No order shall be made under this section unless a draft of the order has been laid before and approved by a resolution of each House of Parliament.

GENERAL NOTE

In the Introductory Notes to this Act we saw that one of the strands in the argument for an elected Assembly was the dislike of nominated bodies. The Secretary of State put it this way at Second Reading, " [It] is through the nominated bodies in Wales that the Conservative Party seeks to perpetuate its power and influence because it has been in a minority in Wales ever since the last century. This is one of the fundamental reasons why there is deep concern in Wales about the lack of democracy " (H.C. Vol. 945, col. 796).

The principle of the Act is to devolve certain ministerial functions to the Assembly, not those of other bodies. What can therefore be devolved to the Assembly in respect of nominated bodies is not their functions, but ministerial functions in relation to them —appointments, financial oversight, etc. Ss. 59 and 60 have to be considered in that context.

The policy of the Act is to devolve ministerial functions to the Assembly including where appropriate the function of appointing to nominated bodies. But where such a body operates on an England and Wales basis (or more broadly on a United Kingdom basis) ministerial functions over it cannot be devolved to an Assembly operating only in Wales without some adjustment to ensure that the body, while continuing to operate on an England and Wales basis, is responsible for its activities in England to the Minister, and for its activities in Wales to the Assembly.

It is with this situation that s. 59 deals. The essence of the section is that it empowers a Minister to confer on the Assembly functions previously exercised by himself in relation to the public bodies listed in the two Parts of Sched. 7, all of which operate on a Great Britain or United Kingdom basis: " so that we have to have provision to divide their responsibilities so that they can account satisfactorily to and be responsible to the Welsh Assembly for what are their activities in Wales while they remain responsible to Government in the United Kingdom for their other operations. . . . If we had made detailed arrangements, we should have burdened the Bill with immense and unnecessary detail about accounts, appointments, finance and other matters which are normally best dealt with by orders " (H.L. Vol. 393, col. 1417).

It is of course a Minister who makes an order under the section not the Assembly. Before making an order the Minister must consult the body in question; and a draft of an order has to be approved by Parliament (the Bill as originally drafted provided only for the negative procedure); and in respect of a body listed in Pt. II of the Schedule an order is not to be made except at the request of the Assembly (and cannot therefore be made before the Assembly comes into existence). The bodies listed in Pt. I are, however, according to the Government, those " whose devolution is so central to the devolution of functions in the field in which they operate [housing, water, forestry] that provision must be made for them from day one." Many functions relating to them have thus been transferred to the Assembly under Sched. 2. However, " some of the functions which need to be divided between England and Wales are at present expressed in a way which makes them ' unsplittable '. . . without some modification. The effect of the order will be to re-express the functions in a way which makes them operable separately by both the Assembly and the Minister " (H.L. Vol. 393, col. 1418). By s. 59 (2) an order in relation to a Pt. II body may modify or exclude (but not extend?) any provision of the Wales Act.

Reference is made in the preceding paragraph to forestry. This function was deleted from the Bill by the Lords, and the Commons did not dispute the deletion.

Power to transfer functions to certain bodies to Assembly

60.—(1) Where, under the provisions of this Act, all powers conferred by any enactment on a Minister of the Crown to appoint members of a body established by any enactment are exercisable by the Assembly, a Minister of the Crown may by order provide for the exercise by the Assembly or all or any of the functions of that body and, if he so provides as to all those functions, for the dissolution of that body.

(2) An order under this section may contain such consequential, incidental or supplementary provisions, including the modification of any enactment, as appear to the Minister making the order to be necessary or expedient.

(3) An order under this section shall not be made except at the request of the Assembly and after the Assembly has consulted the body to which it relates.

(4) No order shall be made under this section unless a draft of it has been laid before and approved by resolution of each House of Parliament.

General Note

This section, like s. 59, deals with the relationship between the Assembly and nominated bodies. Where a Minister has statutory powers to appoint members of a statutory body, and *all* these powers are, by the Wales Act, exercisable by the Assembly, a Minister may by order provide for the exercise by the Assembly of all or any of the functions of the body. Where all the functions are taken over, the order may provide for the dissolution of the body in question.

Note that (i) the section applies only to statutory powers to appoint to statutory bodies and not therefore, for example, to the Welsh Consumer Council which is non-statutory.

(ii) The section does not require that all powers of appointment are to be vested in the Assembly for this power to be exercisable, but that all ministerial powers of appointment are to be vested in it. Thus, if a Minister retains any power of appointment, the s. 60 power is not exercisable (this is the case with the Welsh Water Authority: see Wales Act 1978, Sched. 11, para. 46). But if appointment to a body is made by someone other than a Minister as well as by a Minister, then if the totality of the ministerial power of appointment is devolved, the power is exercisable (an example is Area Health Authorities, some members of which are, and will continue to be, appointed by local authorities).

(iii) Until such time as the s. 60 power is exercised, the Assembly in exercising a power of appointment could appoint its own members to the body in question, subject to the rules about disqualification for membership of the Assembly under s. 5 (1) (c).

(iv) An order made under the section could, by subs. (2) delete a provision in any enactment for the appointment to the body in question by some other body (*e.g.* the appointment by local authorities of members of A.H.A.s). Such a deletion would have to be made if all the functions of the body in question were taken over by the Assembly.

In a written answer the Secretary of State stated: " The following are the principal statutory bodies which would fall within the scope of [s. 60]—The Ancient Monuments Board for Wales, the Area Health Authorities, The Central Advisory Council for Education (Wales), the Development Board for Rural Wales, the Historic Buildings Council for Wales, New Town Development Corporations, the Wales Tourist Board, the Welsh Development Agency, and the Library Advisory Council (Wales)." (H.C. Vol. 946, col. 339). The Land Authority for Wales also falls within it. (See also s. 62 (13).)

This clause was subject to a good deal of discussion in Parliament. In the Bill as laid, it provided that the order transferring functions to the Assembly could be made by the Assembly itself (and did not therefore contain what is now subs. (4) as such provision would have been inappropriate), but could only be made with the approval of the Secretary of State. The clause was deleted from the Bill by the Lords. The Commons reinstated it " because it is appropriate that the functions of the bodies concerned should be capable of being assumed by the Assembly " (Commons reasons for disagreeing to certain Lords amendments). The Lords did not insist on the deletion, but suggested two amendments. One was agreed to, the other not. The clause took its final shape as a result of government amendments in the Commons (including the provision that the order transferring functions is to be made by a Minister, not the Assembly), which the Lords accepted (H.L. Vol. 395, col. 979).

Tourism

61. The Assembly may make arrangements with the British Tourist Authority for that Authority to undertake activities outside the United Kingdom for the purpose of encouraging people to visit Wales.

GENERAL NOTE

The Development of Tourism Act 1969 created the British Tourist Authority, the English, Scottish and Wales Tourist Boards. Under it only the B.T.A. can carry on activities outside the United Kingdom for the purpose of encouraging people to visit Great Britain (though the Boards can engage in such activities on behalf of the B.T.A.). By Sched. 11, para. 30 of the Wales Act the Wales Tourist Board is authorised to carry on activities outside the United Kingdom for encouraging people to visit Wales. By s. 61 the Assembly can arrange with the B.T.A. for it to carry out promotional activities abroad in relation to Wales. The financing of the B.T.A. is in no way affected by the Wales Act: the Assembly will doubtless make payment (out of its block grant) to the B.T.A. for s. 61 arrangements. Any such arrangements made by the Assembly will doubtless be made in conjunction with the Wales Tourist Board. (See s. 60 of the Wales Act for the Assembly's powers to assume the functions of that Board).

Note the further amendments by Sched. 11, paras. 31 and 32, to the Development of Tourism Act 1969. In particular, general schemes for assistance for tourist projects (s. 3) are to be made in relation to Wales by the Wales Tourist Board subject to confirmation by the Assembly, not as before, by the B.T.A. after consultation with the Wales Board and subject to government confirmation.

Countryside Commission for Wales

62.—(1) There shall be a Countryside Commission for Wales (in this section referred to as " the Welsh Commission ") which shall exercise the functions conferred on them by the following provisions of this section for the conservation and enhancement of the natural beauty and amenity of the Welsh countryside, particularly in areas designated under the National Parks and Access to the Countryside Act 1949 as National Parks or as areas of outstanding natural beauty; and for the encouragement of the provision and improvement, for persons resorting to the countryside, of facilities for the enjoyment of the countryside and of open air recreation in the countryside.

(2) So far as the functions under the provisions specified in subsection (9) below are exercisable as regards Wales they shall be exercised by the Welsh Commission instead of by the Countryside Commission.

(3) The Welsh Commission shall be a body corporate and shall consist of such number of members appointed by the Assembly as the Assembly may determine; and the Assembly shall appoint one of them to be chairman.

(4) The Assembly may pay to any of the members of the Welsh Commission such remuneration (whether by way of salary or by way of fees) and such reasonable allowances as the Assembly may determine in respect of—

(a) expenses properly incurred in the performance of their duties,

(b) loss of remunerative time, or

(c) additional expenses necessarily incurred by them for the purpose of enabling them to perform their duties, being expenses to which they would not otherwise have been subject.

(5) The Welsh Commission may with the approval of the Assembly appoint a secretary to the Commission and may appoint such number of other officers and servants as the Assembly may determine.

(6) The functions of the Welsh Commission and of their officers and servants shall be exercised on behalf of the Crown.

(7) The procedure (including the quorum) of the Welsh Commission shall be such as the Commission may determine.

(8) The validity of any proceeding of the Welsh Commission shall not be affected by any vacancy among their members or by any defect in the appointment of any of their members.

(9) The provisions mentioned in subsection (2) above are—

(a) section 4 and Parts II, IV, V and VI of the National Parks and Access to the Countryside Act 1949;

(b) the Countryside Act 1968;

(c) paragraphs 9 to 13, 15, 17 and 19 of Schedule 17 to the Local Government Act 1972;

(d) section 49 of the North Wales Hydro Electric Power Act 1973.

(10) The Assembly may give to the Welsh Commission such directions of a general character as appear to it expedient in relation to the exercise of the Commission's functions and the Commission shall comply with the directions.

(11) As soon as may be after giving a direction under subsection (10) above the Assembly shall cause a notice setting out the directions to be published in such manner as appears to it to be requisite for notifying persons concerned.

(12) The Committee for Wales appointed under section 3 of the Countryside Act 1968 shall be dissolved and that section shall cease to have effect.

(13) Section 60 above shall apply in relation to the Welsh Commission as it applies in relation to the bodies there referred to.

(14) The reference in subsection (1) above to the conservation of the natural beauty of the Welsh countryside shall be construed as including a reference to the conservation of its flora, fauna and geological and physiographical features.

The Countryside Act 1968, s. 1 created the Countryside Commission with functions for England and Wales. S. 3 of the Act provided for the appointment of a Committee for Wales. This section of this Act creates (as a body corporate) a Countryside Commission for Wales, and dissolves the Committee. The Commission's functions are those referred to in subs. (9); in respect of those matters it acts in Wales instead of the Countryside Commission. The purposes for which it is to exercise its functions are set out in subs. (1) and (14).

The relationship between the Assembly and the Commission is as follows:

(i) the Assembly determines the number of members, appoints them and appoints one of them to be Chairman;

(ii) it determines members' remuneration and pays it;

(iii) it determines the number of staff the Commission may employ;

(iv) its approval of the appointment of the Commission's Secretary is required;

(v) it can give the Commission directions of a general character (which the Assembly is to publish and the Commission is to comply with);

(vi) it can take over the Commission's functions under s. 60 above.

Note also the amendments to the relevant statutes in Sched. 11 at paras. 9, 10, 29, 41, 48, 60 and 62.

Water and land drainage

63.—(1) For the purposes of section 9 above any power which, by any provision specified in Part I of Schedule 8 to this Act, is conferred on a Minister of the Crown shall be deemed—

(*a*) so far as it is exercisable in relation to the Welsh Water Authority, to be a power exercisable as regards Wales; and

(*b*) so far as it is exercisable in relation to the Severn-Trent Water Authority, not to be a power exercisable as regards Wales.

(2) The Secretary of State may, with respect to any statutory water company (within the meaning of the Water Act 1973) which supplies water to an area most of which is within Wales, by order make provision similar to the provision made by this Act with respect to the Welsh Water Authority but no such order shall be made unless a draft of it has been laid before and approved by resolution of each House of Parliament.

(3) The powers of the Assembly under any of the provisions specified in Part III or IV of Schedule 8 to this Act shall be subject to the provisions of Part II of that Schedule and sections 34 and 35 above shall not apply in any case where, under that Schedule, the Secretary of State has power to intervene.

(4) For the purposes of section 9 above, any power conferred on a Minister of the Crown by sections 7 (3), 23, 68 to 78, 84 to 87 and 94 of and Schedule 2 to the Land Drainage Act 1976 shall be deemed—

(*a*) so far as it is exercisable in relation to a drainage board for an internal drainage district which is within the area of the Welsh Water Authority and partly in Wales, to be a power exercisable as regards Wales; and

(*b*) so far as it is exercisable in relation to a drainage board for an internal drainage district which is within the area of the Severn-Trent Water Authority and partly in England, not to be a power exercisable as regards Wales.

The Water Act 1973 created nine Regional Water Authorities and the Welsh National Water Development Authority, now the Welsh Water Authority (hereafter the Welsh Authority). The areas within which the authorities exercise their functions are defined by reference to the previously existing areas of river authorities, and these were determined by river drainage areas. The boundaries of these are not coincident with political boundaries. A part of Wales is within the area of the Severn-Trent Authority

(Wales is an important supplier of water to England), and parts of England are within the area of the Welsh Authority.

Water is a devolved area of administration, and most ministerial functions in that area are transferred to the Assembly by s. 9 and Sched. 2 (Pts. VII, IX and X are relevant). The Assembly can of course exercise its functions only " as regards Wales " (s. 9) but as part of the area of the Welsh Authority is in England and parts of the Severn-Trent Authority are in Wales s. 63 (1) provides that certain ministerial powers (the relevant enactments are in Sched. 8, Pt. I), so far as they are exercisable in relation to the Welsh Authority, are deemed to be exercisable as regards Wales (even though they in fact affect part of England), and so far as they are exercisable in relation to the Severn-Trent Authority are deemed not to be exercisable as regards Wales (even though they in fact affect part of Wales). The former are thus exercisable by the Assembly, the latter by central government. The powers in question relate to the constitution, etc., of the two water authorities, their financial duties, and charges; and to appointments to regional land drainage committees, etc.

A similar adjustment is made by s. 63 (4) in respect of certain powers under the Land Drainage Act.

As to the constitution of the two authorities, the Wales Act does not alter the provisions of the Water Act 1973 as to the constitution of the Severn-Trent Authority. As a result of Opposition amendments to the Bill there is no provision for Assembly appointments to that Authority, but the Government intend to provide for it by an order under s. 59 (H.L. Vol. 394, col. 1247). The constitution of the Welsh Authority is, by the Water Act 1973, to be determined by ministerial order—now by an order of the Assembly, but the Wales Act requires that a certain number of members shall be appointed by the relevant English local authorities (see Sched. 11, para. 46). (For the constitution of regional land drainage committees, see H.L. Vol. 394, col. 1252.)

The Assembly may give directions to the Severn-Trent Authority in respect of the exercise of its functions in Wales, as well as to the Welsh Authority. (See Sched. 11, para. 47, amending s. 5 (3) of the Water Act 1973.)

By s. 1 of the Water Act 1973, as amended by para. 42 of Sched. 11 to the Wales Act 1978, it is the duty of Ministers to promote jointly a national policy for water in England and Wales. As Wales is an important source of water for England, decisions there could affect a policy for England and Wales. The overall effectiveness of a national water policy is therefore sought to be safeguarded by s. 1 (1) (c) of the Water Act 1973 (see Sched. 11, para. 42, to the Wales Act 1978), by which the Assembly is required to promote a water policy for Wales in harmony with the national policy for England and Wales.

In addition, the Wales Act empowers the Secretary of State to " intervene " in the exercise of certain powers by the Assembly which might adversely affect the national policy for water, or certain statutory interests in England. Where he does so intervene it is as though the power in question were not exercisable by the Assembly, and shall be exercisable by the Secretary of State (s. 63 (3) and Sched. 8, Pts. II, III and IV).

The powers of " intervention " under ss. 34 and 35 of this Act (see above) do not apply where the Secretary of State has power to intervene under Sched. 8. (Thus the powers of intervention under ss. 34 and 35 do apply in respect of the exercise by the Assembly of any powers other than those under enactments listed in Pt. III or IV of Sched. 8.)

It was the view of the Severn-Trent Authority that these procedures are inadequate to protect national policy (memorandum sent to members of the Lords). Strenuous efforts were made in the Lords by the water interests to extend the ministerial control over the exercise by the Assembly of its water functions. An amendment which provides that either of the two water authorities can apply to the Secretary of State to use his intervention powers under Pt. II of Sched. 8 was agreed to on a division and agreed to by the Commons (see Sched. 8, para. 8).

Powers under the Water Acts which are exercisable in relation to statutory water companies are excluded from transfer to the Assembly.

Planning

64. Section 34 above shall not apply to any action proposed to be taken or capable of being taken by the Assembly in the exercise of any of the powers specified in Part I of Schedule 9 to this Act; but the provisions of Part II of that Schedule shall have effect in relation to those powers.

Planning and land use is a devolved area. Pt. VIII of Sched. 2 transfers to the Assembly most ministerial functions relating to planning applications and enforcement, call-ins and appeals, structure and local plans, listed buildings, caravan control, coast protection, compulsory purchase, new towns, etc. Not transferred are industrial and office development controls (instruments of regional policy for which the Government retains responsibility), the interests of the excepted statutory undertakers, and the Treasury function of guaranteeing loans to public bodies.

Under s. 34 of this Act, the Secretary of State can prevent or require action by the Assembly which could or might affect a "reserved matter." S. 64 gives the Secretary of State power to intervene in certain circumstances in the exercise by the Assembly of certain planning functions: the power of intervention under s. 34 does not then apply.

For the power of intervention to be exercisable under s. 64 the following circumstances must exist:

(i) Action is being or is capable of being taken by the Assembly in the exercise of a power specified in Pt. I of Sched. 9. This lists eight sections of the Town and Country Planning Act 1971.

(ii) It must appear to the Secretary of State that any action so taken by the Assembly (under (i) above) would or might affect, directly or indirectly, any matter which concerns Wales (whether or not it also concerns any other part of the United Kingdom) but with respect to which the Assembly has no power to act, and that it is desirable in the public interest that he should intervene (compare the circumstances in which the s. 34 power can be used). As to the procedure for and effect of intervention, see Sched. 9, Pt. II, paras. 2 to 9.

A Minister said "[T]he Assembly might call in or determine an appeal on a planning application for housing adjacent to a defence base, which might pose security problems. Clearly some intervention power is required to safeguard the Government's interests. . . . But equally it would be wrong to make use of the general intervention powers under cl. 34, because the procedures under that clause would effectively remove established planning procedures under which interested parties have certain rights to be heard. So for that reason Sched. 9 contains special intervention powers by which the Secretary of State will be able to protect the Government's interests in certain planning matters without reducing the existing rights of the parties to the case " (H.L. Vol. 393, col. 622).

Status and remuneration of certain officers and servants

65.—(1) Service as an officer or servant of the Assembly or of the Welsh Comptroller and Auditor General shall be service in Her Majesty's Home Civil Service, and appointments to any position as such an officer or servant shall be made accordingly; but any salary and allowances in respect of such service (including contributions to any pension scheme) shall be payable out of the Welsh Consolidated Fund.

(2) The Assembly shall pay to the Minister for the Civil Service out of the Welsh Consolidated Fund such sums in respect of each financial year as the Minister for the Civil Service may determine, subject to any directions of the Treasury, as being equivalent to—

(a) the increase during that year of such of his liabilities as are attributable to the provision of pensions, allowances or gratuities to or in respect of persons who are or have been such officers or servants as are mentioned in subsection (1) above, in so far as that increase results from their service, their ceasing to serve or their suffering diminution of emoluments during that financial year; and

(b) the increase during that year of such of his liabilities as are attributable to the expenses to be incurred in administering those pensions, allowances or gratuities.

REFERENCES
For reference to the status of Assembly staff, see note on s. 24.
For reference to Welsh Consolidated Fund, see s. 40 and note on s. 48.

Transfer of property

66.—(1) The Secretary of State shall by order provide—

(*a*) for the transfer to and vesting in the Assembly of property vested in him and appearing to him to be property used or to be used solely or mainly for or in connection with the exercise of functions which by virtue of this Act have become or will become functions of the Assembly; and

(*b*) for the exercise by the Assembly of rights specified in or determined under the order to use property vested in him and appearing to him to be property used or to be used as mentioned in paragraph (*a*) above but not solely or mainly so used or to be used.

(2) An order under subsection (1) above may be made with respect to any property, notwithstanding any provision (of whatever nature) which would prevent or restrict its transfer or, as the case may be, the granting of the rights concerned by other means.

(3) An order under this section may be made subject to any exceptions or reservations specified in or determined under the order and may contain such consequential, incidental or supplementary provisions (including provisions for the transfer of liabilities connected with the property concerned) as appear to the Minister making the order to be necessary or expedient.

(4) A statutory instrument made under this section shall be subject to annulment in pursuance of a resolution of either House of Parliament.

Stamp duty

67. No stamp duty shall be chargeable on any instrument made by, to or with the Assembly.

Complaints of maladministration

68.—(1) Her Majesty may by Order in Council make provision for the investigation by the Parliamentary Commissioner for Administration of administrative action taken by or on behalf of the Assembly.

(2) An Order in Council under this section may apply, with such exceptions and modifications as appear to Her Majesty to be necessary or expedient, any of the provisions of the Parliamentary Commissioner Act 1967.

(3) A statutory instrument made under this section shall be subject to annulment in pursuance of a resolution of either House of Parliament.

GENERAL NOTE

The Scotland and Wales Bill provided for the appointment of a Welsh Assembly Commissioner as an addition to the team of Parliamentary, Local and National Health Service Commissioners. However, on second thoughts, the need for yet another Ombudsman was doubted, hence this section providing for investigation of administrative action by the Assembly to be undertaken by the Parliamentary Commissioner. For this purpose an Order in Council will apply, with exceptions and modifications, the Parliamentary Commissioner Act 1967.

The creation of the Assembly necessitates a number of amendments to the legislation creating the Ombudsmen. In particular, in each case there is added to the category of those who cannot complain to the relevant Commissioner any body whose members are appointed by the Assembly or whose revenues consist wholly or mainly of moneys payable out of the Welsh Consolidated Fund; and the Local Commissioner cannot investigate action in respect of which the person aggrieved has a right of appeal to the Assembly (see Sched. 11, paras. 26, 27; 68 to 73; 87 to 89).

With reference to the word "administrative" in subs. (1), it will be noted that the Parliamentary Commissioner can investigate only action taken by Departments "in the exercise of administrative functions" (Parliamentary Commissioner Act 1967, s. 5 (1)). A distinction has been drawn between legislative and administrative functions. In particular the Commissioner will not investigate complaints about the making or the procedure leading up to the making of statutory instruments, as that is a legislative function (though he will inquire whether, following a complaint, a Department has taken the proper steps to review the working of such instruments). It is arguable that the same view need not be taken of statutory instruments made by the Assembly. The making of statutory instruments by Ministers can be said to be legislative because it is part of the whole process of legislation for which Ministers are responsible: the drafting of the Bill, getting it through Parliament and implementing the resulting Act by means of regulations. In respect of regulations made by the Welsh Assembly, this unity is fractured: indeed in certain circumstances regulations made by the Assembly may be revoked by the Secretary of State (see s. 35). This argument does not render the word "administrative" otiose: it would exclude investigation of judicial action taken by the Assembly.

Corrupt practices

69. The Assembly shall be a public body for the purposes of the Prevention of Corruption Acts 1889 to 1916.

GENERAL NOTE

By s. 4 (2) of the Prevention of Corruption Act 1916, that Act together with the Public Bodies Corrupt Practices Act 1889 and the Prevention of Corruption Act 1906 may be cited together as the Prevention of Corruption Acts 1889 to 1916.

On the application of those Acts to Parliament and to Members of Parliament, see the Report of the Royal Commission on Standards of Conduct in Public Life, Cmnd. 6524, para. 307.

PART V

GENERAL AND SUPPLEMENTARY

Determination of issues as to Assembly's powers

70.—(1) Without prejudice to any power exercisable apart from this section, the Attorney General may institute against the Assembly proceedings of the kind specified in subsection (2) below notwithstanding that each of them acts on behalf of the Crown.

(2) The proceedings referred to in subsection (1) above are proceedings for a declaration as to—

(a) whether a power conferred or duty imposed by or under any enactment is exercisable or falls to be discharged by the Assembly;

(b) whether anything done or proposed to be done by the Assembly is within its powers; or

(c) whether the Assembly has failed to discharge a duty imposed on it.

GENERAL NOTE

As originally presented to Parliament the Bill contained the following clause (cl. 72): "Without prejudice to any power exercisable apart from this section, the Attorney-General may institute, and the Assembly may defend proceedings for the determination of any question whether anything done or proposed to be done by the Assembly is within its powers." A Government amendment was moved in the Lords (H.L. Vol. 393, col. 1515) to put the clause in the form of what is now this section. The following points will be noted about the section:

(i) It is not about the rights and duties of the individual citizen against the Assembly, but enables the Attorney-General to institute proceedings against the Assembly to determine the extent of its powers. The constitutional difficulty in this is indicated by the phrase in the section "notwithstanding that [the Attorney-General and the Assembly both act] on behalf of the Crown." The Attorney-General as legal adviser to the Crown does not sue his client, and the Assembly is a Crown body. "The creation of a separate Executive in the Welsh Assembly affects this aspect of our Constitution. There will be two arms of the Crown which may receive conflicting advice as to their duties or the extent of their powers" (*ibid.*).

(ii) Proceedings may be brought only for a declaration. There is no power of enforcement in proceedings under this section. The theory is that having been informed what the law is, the Assembly will observe it.

(iii) A declaration may be sought on the questions referred to in paras. (*a*) (*b*) and (*c*) in subs. (2). Para. (*a*) deals with the question as to where a particular function lies, with the Assembly or a Minister. The scheme of the Acts is to identify precisely the functions which the Assembly is to exercise, but it would be surprising if no loopholes or overlap were ever to be discovered; para. (*b*) deals with the vires of an act done or proposed to be done; para. (*c*) was included as it was suggested that the original clause did not cover acts of omission.

What then of the rights of the individual against the Assembly? As a body corporate the Assembly may sue and be sued. As a Crown body it will in principle be entitled to such immunities and privileges as the Crown enjoys and can be sued only so far as the Crown Proceedings Act 1947 permits. If nothing further were done, the Attorney-General could be sued under s. 17 (3) of that Act for the acts of the Assembly. However the Government did not think it desirable that that arrangement should continue indefinitely. It is therefore its intention to use the power given by s. 77 (2) of the Wales Act to make the necessary amendments to the Crown Proceedings Act. "The intention is that the Assembly will be placed in substantially the same position as regards the Crown Proceedings Act as is a Minister of the Crown" (H.C. Vol. 954, col. 851, Att.-Gen.). The Attorney-General gave an undertaking that an order applying the Crown Proceedings Act can be made to have effect from the time when the Assembly has effectively come into existence (that is immediately after the first elections) and that it was his intention to make such an order (H.C. Vol. 954, col. 856). The amendments to the Crown Proceedings Act "will not and could not change the essential nature of the citizens' rights against the Crown" (H.L. Vol. 393, col. 1518); "could not," as s. 77 (2) empowers only amendments necessary or expedient in consequence of the Wales Act. Thus a citizen will have the same recourse against the Assembly as he has against Ministers whether at common law or by virtue of a statutory procedure such as s. 245 of the Town and Country Planning Act 1971.

The Lords added a sub-clause which would have done two things. It would have (a) empowered the Attorney-General to institute proceedings against the Assembly seeking a determination against the Assembly whether the Assembly was in default of any duty (this was repetitive of subs. (2)) and seeking an order requiring the fulfilment of such a duty; and (b) empowered "any other person" to have instituted such proceedings provided he was aggrieved by such default or had an interest in the fulfilment of the duty. The Government's view was that the order proposed to be made under s. 77 (2) (referred to above) would ensure the individual's right of action against the Assembly, and that it would "make a fundamental change to our system of administrative law ... to enable either the Attorney-General or an individual to obtain not merely a declaratory judgment as to the vires or the law . . . but also a coercive judgment against an emanation of the Crown" (H.C. Vol. 954, col. 853, Att.-Gen.). The Government always accepted a court's pronouncement as to what the law was, and the Attorney-General was not prepared to assume that the Crown, through its emanation as the Welsh Assembly, would adopt a lower standard than a Minister. If it did, the power still resided at Westminster to deal with the matter. On the political side it would in his view be quite wrong to treat the Assembly as though it were not an emanation of the Crown, but a mere local authority. The Opposition thought that the question of individual rights against the Assembly was so important that the draft amendment of the Crown Proceedings Act should have been produced. On the question of coercive action the language about emanation of the Crown ("constitutional gobbledegook") obscurred the reality of the situation. True, they said, one cannot have one part of the government suing another, but in effect, two separate governments had been created, elected on a different basis and with nothing in common. And s. 70 (1) itself breached the principle relied on by the Attorney-General by permitting him to take action against the Assembly even though each acts on behalf of the Crown. The Lords amendment was disagreed to by the Commons and not insisted on.

Further, on the Assembly and the courts, see s. 25.

Reckoning of time for certain purposes

71. In reckoning any period for the purposes of section 34 or 35 above, no account shall be taken of any time during which Parliament is dissolved or prorogued or during which both Houses are adjourned for more than four days.

Orders

72.—(1) Any power to make orders conferred by this Act on a Minister of the Crown shall be exercisable by statutory instrument.

(2) Any order made under any provisions of this Act may be varied or revoked by a subsequent order made under that provision.

REFERENCES

For statutory instruments, see Statutory Instruments Act 1946.

Expenses

73. There shall be paid out of moneys provided by Parliament any administrative expenses incurred by a Minister of the Crown under this Act and any increase attributable to this Act in the sums so payable under any other Act.

REFERENCES

For meaning of " out of moneys provided by Parliament," see note on s. 44.

Construction of references to Ministers, etc.

74.—(1) So far as may be necessary for the purpose or in consequence of the exercise by the Assembly of any of its functions, any enactment or other document passed or made before the passing of this Act shall be construed as if references to a Minister of the Crown were or included references to the Assembly.

(2) References in any such enactment to property vested in or held for the purposes of a Government department shall be construed as including references to property vested in or held for the purposes of the Assembly; and in relation to land so vested or held the Assembly shall be deemed to be a Government department for the purposes of any such enactment.

Statutory references to Parliament in connection with subordinate legislation

75.—(1) Where a power conferred on a Minister of the Crown to make, confirm or approve orders, rules, regulations or other subordinate legislation is subject to a provision—

  (*a*) requiring any instrument made in the exercise of the power, or a draft of any such instrument, to be laid before Parliament or either House of Parliament, or

  (*b*) for the annulment or approval of any such instrument or draft by or in pursuance of a resolution of either or both Houses of Parliament, or

  (*c*) prohibiting the making of such an instrument without that approval, or

  (*d*) for any such instrument to be a provisional order, that is to say an order which requires to be confirmed by Act of Parliament, or

(e) requiring any order (within the meaning of the Statutory Orders (Special Procedure) Act 1945) to be subject to special parliamentary procedure,

then, in relation to an exercise of the power by the Assembly by virtue of section 9 above, that provision shall not have effect.

(2) Subsection (1) above shall not have effect so as to prevent a provision for special parliamentary procedure from applying in relation to a power exercisable under an enactment specified in the first column of Schedule 10 to this Act if it is exercised in circumstances specified in the second column.

REFERENCE
For reference to this section, see note on s. 21.

Modification of enactments requiring the laying of reports before Parliament

76.—(1) Where any enactment passed or made before the passing of this Act makes provision for any report to be laid before Parliament or either House of Parliament and the report relates exclusively to matters with respect to which the Assembly exercises functions, it shall instead be sent to and published by the Assembly, but subject to subsection (2) below.

(2) If the report is one which, by virtue of this Act, is to be made by the Assembly instead of by a Minister of the Crown, the provisions shall not have effect but the Assembly shall publish the matter which would have been contained in the report had the provision had effect.

(3) In this section " report " includes any statement.

DEFINITION
" Enactment ": see s. 78 (1).

Amendment of enactments

77.—(1) The enactments mentioned in Schedule 11 to this Act shall have effect subject to the amendments specified in that Schedule.

(2) A Minister of the Crown may by order make such amendments in any Act passed before or in the same session as this Act and in any other enactment passed or made before the passing of this Act as appear to him necessary or expedient in consequence of this Act.

(3) A statutory instrument made under subsection (2) above shall be subject to annulment in pursuance of a resolution of either House of Parliament.

DEFINITION
" Enactment ": see s. 78 (1).

GENERAL NOTE
Subs. (1)
For the significance of Sched. 11 on the conferment of powers on the Welsh Assembly, see the note on s. 9 above.

Interpretation

78.—(1) In this Act, except where the context otherwise requires—
" enactment " includes an enactment of the Parliament of Northern Ireland, a Measure of the Northern Ireland Assembly, an Order in Council under section 1 (3) of the Northern Ireland (Temporary Provisions) Act 1972 or paragraph 1 of Schedule 1 to the Northern Ireland Act 1974, a Scottish Assembly Act, any instrument made by virtue of an enactment (as defined herein) and a Royal Warrant;

" excepted statutory undertakers " means—

  (a) persons authorised by any enactment to carry on any road transport, dock, harbour, pier or lighthouse undertaking or any undertaking for the supply of electricity, gas or hydraulic power; and

  (b) the Post Office, the British Railways Board and the National Coal Board;

but subject to subsection (4) below;

" financial year " means a year ending with 31st March;

" Minister of the Crown " includes the Treasury;

" property " includes rights and interests of any description;

" road transport undertaking " does not include a passenger transport undertaking.

(2) Except where the context otherwise requires, references in this Act to the proceedings of the Assembly include references to proceedings of any committee of the Assembly or of any sub-committee of such a committee.

(3) Except where the context otherwise requires, any reference in this Act to an enactment is a reference to that enactment as amended, and includes a reference to it as applied, by any other enactment.

(4) The Secretary of State may by order provide that any persons specified in the order shall be treated as being, or as ceasing to be, excepted statutory undertakers for the purposes of this Act or for such of those purposes as may be so specified; and a statutory instrument made under this subsection shall be subject to annulment in pursuance of a resolution of either House of Parliament.

Commencement

79.—(1) The preceding provisions of this Act shall not come into operation until such day as the Secretary of State may by order appoint.

(2) Different days may be appointed under this section for different provisions of this Act and for different purposes of the same provision.

(3) An order under this section may contain such transitional and supplementary provisions as appear to the Secretary of State to be necessary or expedient, including provision for expenses to be defrayed out of moneys provided by Parliament.

(4) The first order under this section shall not be made unless a draft of it has been laid before and approved by resolution of each House of Parliament.

GENERAL NOTE
 See note on s. 81.

Referendum

80.—(1) Before a draft of the first order to be made under section 79 above is laid before Parliament a referendum shall be held in accordance with Schedule 12 to this Act on the question whether effect is to be given to the provisions of this Act.

(2) If it appears to the Secretary of State that less than 40 per cent. of the persons entitled to vote in the referendum have voted " Yes " in reply to the question posed in the Appendix to Schedule 12 to this Act or that a majority of the answers given in the referendum have been " No " he shall lay before Parliament the draft of an Order in Council for the repeal of this Act.

(3) If a draft laid before Parliament under this section is approved by resolution of each House, Her Majesty in Council may make an Order in the terms of the draft.

GENERAL NOTE
   See note on s. 81.

Period between general election and referendum

   81. If a proclamation summoning a new Parliament is made before
a referendum is held in pursuance of section 80 above, the referendum
shall not be held earlier than three months after the date of the poll at
the election of members of the new Parliament; and if an earlier date
has been appointed by Order in Council under paragraph 1 of Schedule 12
to this Act, the Order shall not take effect, but without prejudice to the
making of a new Order under that paragraph.

GENERAL NOTE
   The Act received the Royal Assent on July 31, 1978. By s. 79 it is not to come into
operation until such day as the Secretary of State by order appoints. Different days
may be appointed for different provisions of the Act. The first such order is not to be
made unless a draft has been laid before and approved by Parliament. However, before
a draft of the first order is laid a referendum must be held. (Attempts to have the
referendum at an earlier stage, *e.g.* after Second Reading, failed.) The date of the
referendum will be fixed by the Government (Sched. 12, para. 1) but may be limited by
s. 81. This provides that if there is a general election before the referendum, the referendum is not to be held earlier than three months after the date of the election. But if
an Order in Council had been made fixing a date for the referendum earlier than the
expiry of the three months, the Order in Council is not to take effect, that is, the
referendum will not be held on that date, but another date for the referendum may be
fixed. This section (s. 81) was added to the Bill on a Government motion during the
committee stage. A similar clause had been added to the Scotland Bill by the Commons
(against the Government's advice), and the Government accepted that it was desirable
that the two Bills should contain the same provision. The thinking behind the section
was that the two questions " which party is to form the Government?" and " shall there
be devolved administrations in Scotland and Wales?" should be kept separate. Some
feared that the referendum might even be held on the same day as a general election.
(At the time these matters were being discussed—summer 1978—it seemed likely that
a general election would be held in the autumn.) The Government stated a number of
times that it is their intention that the referendums in Scotland and Wales will be held
on the same day but recommended against a legislative provision to that effect in case
of some totally unforeseeable circumstances arising. (The known result of one referendum
could affect the outcome of the other.) The Conservative Opposition have stated that
though opposed to the Bill they would, as a Government, hold and give effect to the
result of the referendums. The referendum is to be held on March 1, 1979.

Who can vote?

   Those entitled to vote are electors at a parliamentary election in any constituency in
Wales, and peers entitled to vote at a local government election in Wales (Sched. 12,
para. 2). (Electors in England are thus excluded.) Electoral law requires that to be
entitled to vote one's name must be on the electoral register, and one must not be disqualified for voting by reason, for example, of age.

The effect of the referendum

   The form of the ballot paper to be used in the referendum is set out in the Appendix
to Sched. 12. If a majority of the answers to the question posed in the referendum is
" no "; or if a majority of the answers is " yes " but nevertheless fewer than 40 per
cent. of those entitled to vote have said " yes " (or rather if it appears to the Secretary
of State that either of those situations exists), the Secretary of State shall lay before
Parliament the draft of an order for the repeal of the Act—which Parliament may or
may not approve. The referendum is in that sense consultative. (If, say, 38 per cent.
of those entitled to vote say " yes," 15 per cent. say " no " and 47 per cent. abstain—
admittedly an unlikely outcome—what would Parliament do?) If the necessary number
say " yes," the draft of the first order bringing the Act into force will then be laid for
approval. Here again parliamentary approval is necessary. The Lords added a sub-clause
to s. 80 the effect of which was that if Parliament did not approve the draft order
the Secretary of State had to lay a draft order for the repeal of the Act. This was

presented by the Opposition as a tidying-up operation. The sub-clause was disagreed to by the Commons and not insisted on.

The 40 *per cent. requirement* (*s.* 80 (2))

This is the " Cunningham " amendment, named after the M.P. who successfully moved the addition of the parallel provision to the Scotland Act. A motion to add the subsection to the Wales Bill was carried by the Commons by 72 votes (April 19, 1978). The 40 per cent. is of those entitled to vote—" x." It seems from what is said above that to arrive at " x " one deducts from the total number of entries on the relevant registers in Wales the number of those disqualified for voting. However (i) no figures can be available of those so disqualified; (ii) some people will have their names on more than one electoral register in Wales, *e.g.* students whose home is in and who are at University in Wales: no figures of these are available; (iii) even between the qualifying date and the coming into force of a register some 12,000 people old enough to be on the electoral register will have died (H.C. Vol. 945, col. *233* (written answer)). No figures are kept. It follows that the number of names on the register must be greater than that of the persons entitled to vote. However, in view of the impossibility of making the necessary deductions it seems that " x " is the total number of names on the registers: the figure required by the 40 per cent. rule will be proportionately increased. The Government has rejected the idea of bringing the electoral register in Scotland (and therefore Wales) up to date to ensure that the dead will be excluded from " x." It also rejected the proposal that it seek powers to allow next-of-kin of dead voters " to vote as they think the dead person would have wished " (probably the most bizarre idea thrown up in the devolution debates—H.C. Vol. 945, col. *215* (written answer)). The choice of March 1 for the referendum means that a very up-to-date electoral register will be in force.

It is up to the Secretary of State to say whether the requirements of s. 80 (2) have been met. However, even the subjective terms of the subsection (" If it appears to the Secretary of State . . .") do not allow him to ignore the limitations of arithmetic. But does the wording give him some elbow-room in deciding the total number entitled to vote and therefore what the 40 per cent. requirement is? It is of interest that in the EEC referendum the totals of the electoral lists were reduced by 2 per cent. to take account of the factors mentioned above.

The Opposition moved at the Report Stage in the Lords an amendment to Sched. 12 which sought to prevent the Government doing anything which involved the use of public funds to secure a result one way or the other in the referendum. The Government stated that they did not intend to provide public funds for campaigning organisations, and had no plans themselves to issue any leaflet, etc., explaining the provisions of the devolution legislation. However, devolution being government policy, the normal facilities available to Ministers in furthering government policy should be available. The Opposition amendment would have forbidden this. It was agreed to by the Lords but disagreed by the Commons and is not in the Act. A similar provision had been inserted in the Scotland Bill with the same result (H.L. Vol. 394, col. 1226).

Short title

82. This Act may be cited as the Wales Act 1978.

SCHEDULES

SCHEDULE 1

Assembly Constituencies

Part I

Reports of Boundary Commission and Orders in Council

1. Where the Boundary Commission for Wales submit to the Secretary of State a report under subsection (1) of section 2 of the Act of 1949 they shall submit with it a supplementary report showing into what Assembly constituencies Wales should be divided in accordance with the provisions of Part II of this Schedule; and where, after

the first supplementary report submitted under this paragraph, they submit a report under subsection (3) of that section, they shall submit with it a supplementary report showing into what Assembly constituencies the area to which the report relates should be divided in accordance with the provisions of Part II of this Schedule.

2. Sections 2 (4), 2 (5) and 3 of the Act of 1949 (notice of proposed report of Boundary Commission and implementation of recommendations in report) paragraphs 3 and 4 of Part III of Schedule 1 to that Act (notice of proposed recommendation and local inquiries) and section 4 of the Act of 1958 (procedure) shall apply in relation to a supplementary report made under this Schedule and a recommendation made or proposed to be made in such a report; and in those provisions as they apply by virtue of this paragraph references to constituencies shall be construed as references to Assembly constituencies and references to electors as references to electors for the Assembly.

3. Subsections (2) and (3) of section 250 of the Local Government Act 1972 (attendance of witnesses at inquiries) shall apply in relation to an inquiry held in pursuance of paragraph 2 above.

4. Nothing in paragraph 2 above shall be taken as enabling the Secretary of State to modify any recommendation or draft Order in Council in a manner conflicting with the provisions of Part II of this Schedule.

5. An Order in Council under the provisions applied by paragraph 2 above shall apply to the first ordinary election for the Assembly held after the Order comes into force and (subject to any further Order in Council) to any subsequent election for the Assembly, but shall not affect any earlier election or the constitution of the Assembly before the expiry of the term of office of the members holding office at the time the Order comes into force.

PART II

Division of Wales into Assembly Constituencies

6. Each Assembly constituency shall be wholly comprised in one parliamentary constituency.

7. The electorate of any Assembly constituency shall be as near the electorate of any other Assembly constituency comprised in the same parliamentary constituency as is practicable, having regard to paragraph 8 below.

8. Regard shall be had, so far as practicable, to the boundaries of local government areas.

9. A parliamentary constituency the electorate of which is more than 125 per cent. of the electoral quota shall comprise three Assembly constituencies and any other parliamentary constituency shall comprise two Assembly constituencies.

10. The Boundary Commission may depart from the strict application of paragraph 8 above if it appears to them that the departure is desirable to avoid an excessive disparity between the electorates of Assembly constituencies comprised in the same parliamentary constituency.

11. The Boundary Commission may depart from the strict application of paragraph 7 or 8 above—

(a) if special geographical considerations, including in particular the size, shape and accessibility of an Assembly constituency, appear to them to render the departure reasonable; or

(b) if, taking account, so far as they reasonably can, of the inconvenience resulting from alterations of Assembly constituencies, and of any local ties which would be broken by such alterations, a departure appears to them desirable.

PART III

Return of Initial Members

12. The Secretary of State shall by order specify the areas for which, in accordance with section 1 (2) of this Act, the initial members of the Assembly are to be returned, and the order shall indicate the electoral quota and, for each of those areas, the electorate and the number of initial members to be returned.

Wales Act 1978

PART IV

INTERPRETATION

13. In Parts I and II of this Schedule—
   " electoral quota " means the number obtained by dividing the electorate by the
      number of parliamentary constituencies into which Wales would be divided
      if effect were given to the recommendations of the Boundary Commission;
   " electorate " means the number of persons whose names, on the date specified
      for the purposes of this paragraph in the supplementary report of the Boundary
      Commission, appear on the registers of electors for the Assembly, or as the
      case may require, such parts of those registers as relate to the constituency
      or proposed constituency concerned;
   " the Act of 1949 " means the House of Commons (Redistribution of Seats) Act
      1949;
   " the Act of 1958 " means the House of Commons (Redistribution of Seats) Act
      1958.

14. In Part III of this Schedule, this paragraph and section 1 of this Act—
   " electoral quota " means the number obtained by dividing the electorate (as
      defined in this paragraph) of Wales by the number of parliamentary con-
      stituencies there at the time of the election of initial members; and
   " electorate " means the number of persons whose names appear on the relevant
      registers of parliamentary electors last published before the date on which the
      order under paragraph 12 above was made, the relevant registers being, as
      the case may require, those for the constituency concerned or those for all
      constituencies in Wales.

Section 9 (1) SCHEDULE 2

EXISTING STATUTORY FUNCTIONS

PART I

LOCAL GOVERNMENT

Enactment	*Excluded functions*
The Local Government (Miscellaneous Provisions) Act 1953 (c. 26).	The function under section 5 (3) (*b*) of determining disputes between a local authority and excepted statutory undertakers.
The Public Bodies (Admission to Meetings) Act 1960 (c. 67).	
The Local Government (Records) Act 1962 (c. 56).	
The Local Authorities (Land) Act 1963 (c. 29).	The power to fix rates of interest in respect of advances made under section 3 or 4 for the erection of industrial buildings (within the meaning of section 66 of the Town and Country Planning Act 1971 (c. 78)).
The Local Government Act 1966 (c. 42).	The functions under section 35 (2) so far as exercisable in relation to matters listed in Schedule 5 to this Act.
The Local Authorities (Goods and Services) Act 1970 (c. 39).	
The Local Government Act 1972 (c. 70) sections 55, 68 (1) to (7) and 74 and Parts V to IX, XI and XII.	The functions under section 103 as modified by section 107 (7).
	The functions under sections 110 (5), 141 and 230 so far as exercisable in relation to matters listed in Schedule 5 to this Act.
	The powers under section 119.

Enactment	*Excluded functions*
The Local Government Act 1972—*cont.*	The functions under sections 121 (1), 122 (3), 123 (4) and 123A so far as exercisable in relation to land which is to be acquired or is held for purposes relating to matters listed in Schedule 5 to this Act.
	The functions under sections 171, 198, 200 and 201.
	The power under section 236 to confirm byelaws relating to matters listed in Schedule 5 to this Act.
	The functions under section 244.
	The powers under section 250 so far as their exercise is incidental to functions which remain exercisable by a Minister of the Crown.
	The functions under sections 254 and 262 except so far as exercisable in relation to matters with respect to which the powers of the Assembly are exercisable.
	The functions under sections 259 and 260.
	The functions under Schedule 12.
	The powers of the Treasury under paragraphs 2 (1) (*g*) and 3 to 6 of Schedule 13 and, so far as they relate to borrowing for purposes relating to matters listed in Schedule 5 to this Act, the powers under paragraph 1 of Schedule 13.
The Local Government Act 1974 (c. 7) sections 11 to 13, 23 (7), 24, 35 (3) and 40 (1), and paragraph 9 of Schedule 4.	The powers under section 35 (3) so far as they relate to any control which remains exercisable by a Minister of the Crown.
The Housing Finance (Special Provisions) Act 1975 (c. 67).	
The Local Government (Miscellaneous Provisions) Act 1976 (c. 57) Parts I and III.	The functions under section 11.
	The functions under section 13 so far as exercisable in relation to the acquisition of rights for purposes relating to matters listed in Schedule 5 to this Act.
	The functions under section 14 so far as exercisable in relation to interests held for purposes relating to matters listed in Schedule 5 to this Act.
	The powers under section 15 (3) (*e*) and (*f*) so far as exercisable in relation to land held by excepted statutory undertakers.
	The powers under section 26 (6) (*b*).

PART II

LOCAL MATTERS

Enactment	*Excluded functions*
The Markets and Fairs Clauses Act 1847 (c. 14) section 44.	
The Burial Act 1853 (c. 134).	
The Burial Act 1855 (c. 128).	
The Burial Act 1857 (c. 81).	
The Burial Act 1859 (22 Vict. c. 1).	
The Fairs Act 1871 (c. 12).	
The Fairs Act 1873 (c. 37).	
The Public Health Act 1875 (c. 55) section 184 and Part IX.	The functions under Part IX so far as exercisable in relation to matters listed in Schedule 5 to this Act.
The Cremation Act 1902 (c. 8).	The powers under section 7 to make regulations in connection with the burning of human remains.

Enactment	*Excluded functions*
The Public Health Acts Amendment Act 1907 (c. 53) section 82.	
The Cinematograph Act 1909 (c. 30).	
The Fees (Increase) Act 1923 (c. 4) section 7.	
The Theatrical Employers Registration Act 1925 (c. 50).	
The Welsh Church (Burial Grounds) Act 1945 (c. 27).	
The Shops Act 1950 (c. 28) Part I, section 43, Part IV and section 69.	The power under section 69 so far as exercisable in relation to functions other than those under Part I, section 43 and Part IV.
The Cremation Act 1952 (c. 31).	
The Food and Drugs Act 1955 (4 and 5 Eliz. 2 c. 16) section 125 (1) (*b*).	The powers under that section so far as relating to byelaws other than those under section 61.
The Shops (Airports) Act 1962 (c. 35).	
The Licensing Act 1964 (c. 26).	
The Theatres Act 1968 (c. 54) section 19 (3) and Schedule 1, paragraph 3.	
The Mines and Quarries (Tips) Act 1969 (c. 10) Part II.	

PART III

EDUCATION, ETC.

Enactment	*Excluded functions*
The School Sites Acts 1841 to 1852.	
The School Grants Act 1855 (c. 131).	
The Technical and Industrial Institutions Act 1892 (c. 29).	
The Physical Training and Recreation Act 1937 (c. 46).	
The Education Acts 1944 to 1976.	The function under section 45 (4) of the Education Act 1944 (c. 31) of issuing instructions to local offices of the Department of Employment.
	The functions under section 75 (1) of that Act.
	The function under section 77 of that Act of making recommendations to Her Majesty on the appointment of inspectors.
	The powers under section 93 of that Act so far as their exercise is incidental to functions which remain exercisable by a Minister of the Crown.
	The functions under section 100 (1) (*b*) of that Act so far as relating to terms and conditions of service, pensions, gratuities or allowances payable on retirement or death, or compensation for loss of office or employment or loss or diminution of emoluments.
	The function of giving certificates under section 115 of that Act,
	The functions of the Lord Chancellor under Schedule 6 to that Act.
	The functions under section 6 of the Education (Miscellaneous Provisions) Act 1948 (c. 40) except those exercisable under subsection (1) in cases involving two authorities in Wales.

Enactment	Excluded functions
The Education Acts 1944 to 1976—*cont.*	The functions under section 7 of the Education (Miscellaneous Provisions) Act 1953 (c. 33) except those exercisable under subsection (1) in cases involving two authorities in Wales.
	The functions under the Education Act 1962 (c. 12) except section 3 (*a*), (*c*) and (*d*).
	The functions under the Remuneration of Teachers Act 1965 (c. 3).
	The functions under sections 3 and 4 of the Education Act 1973 (c. 16).
The Public Libraries and Museums Act 1964 (c. 75).	
The Sex Discrimination Act 1975 (c. 65) sections 24, 25 (2), 27, 66 (5) and 78.	The functions under section 78 and Schedule 2 so far as exercisable in relation to establishments falling within paragraph 4 of the Table in section 22.
The Race Relations Act 1976 (c. 74) sections 19 (2) and 57 (5).	

PART IV

LANDLORD AND TENANT AND HOUSING

Enactment	Excluded functions
The Small Dwellings Acquisition Act 1899 (c. 44).	The function under section 5 (2) (*b*).
The Housing Act 1914 (c. 31).	
The Landlord and Tenant Act 1927 (c. 36) section 20.	
The Housing (Emergency Powers) Act 1939 (c. 73).	
The Repair of War Damage Act 1941 (c. 34).	
The Landlord and Tenant Act 1954 (s. 56).	The functions under sections 58, 60 and 63.
	The functions under section 57, except so far as exercisable in relation to property in which the interest of the landlord or of any superior landlord belongs to or is held for the purposes of the Assembly.
The Housing Acts 1957 to 1977.	The function under section 85 (1) of the Housing Act 1957 (c. 56).
	The function under paragraph 1 (1) of Schedule 2 to that Act (as set out in Schedule 4 to the Housing Act 1969 (c. 33)).
	The power of the Treasury under paragraph 6 of Schedule 8 to the Housing Act 1957.
	The functions under the House Purchase and Housing Act 1959 (c. 33) except section 29 (3).
	The functions under Part II of the Housing Subsidies Act 1967 (c. 29).
	The functions under section 23 of the Housing Finance Act 1972 (s. 47).
	The functions under Part II of Schedule 4 to that Act.
	The powers of the Treasury under section 7 (3) and (4) of the Housing Act 1974 (c. 44) so far as relating to borrowing outside the United Kingdom or in a currency other than sterling.
	The functions under section 14 of that Act.
	The functions under section 99 (1) of that Act, except so far as exercisable in relation to land belonging to or held for the purposes of the Assembly.

Enactment	*Excluded functions*
The Housing Acts 1957 to 1977—*cont.*	The functions under sections 99 (5) and 119 of that Act. The functions under section 11 of the Housing Rents and Subsidies Act 1975 (c. 6).
The Landlord and Tenant Act 1962 (c. 50).	
The Leasehold Reform Act 1967 (c. 88).	The functions under sections 22 (2), 28 (7) and 29 (6). The functions under section 33 and paragraph 14 of Schedule 1, except so far as exercisable with respect to land in which there is or has been an interest belonging to or held for the purposes of the Assembly. The functions under paragraphs 4 and 5 of Schedule 4.
The Defective Premises Act 1972 (c. 35) section 2.	
The Rent (Agriculture) Act 1976 (c. 80).	The powers under section 26 (5). The powers under section 29. The powers under paragraph 12 of Schedule 3.
The Rentcharges Act 1977 (c. 30).	The powers under that Act so far as exercisable in relation to any rentcharge (or legally apportioned part) that affects both land in England and land in Wales.
The Rent Act 1977 (c. 42).	The powers under section 142. The powers of the Lord Chancellor under paragraph 2 of Schedule 10.
The Protection from Eviction Act 1977 (c. 43) section 5.	
The Home Purchase Assistance and Housing Corporation Guarantee Act 1978 (c. 27) sections 1 and 2 (2) to (4).	The functions under those sections so far as exercisable otherwise than in relation to advances to or loans by the institutions specified in paragraphs 2, 3 and 5 of the Schedule.

PART V

FIRE SERVICES

Enactment	*Excluded functions*
The Fire Services Act 1947 (c. 41).	The functions under sections 23, 26 and 29.
The Fire Services Act 1959 (c. 44).	
The Fire Precautions Act 1971 (c. 40).	The functions under section 36.
The Fire Precautions (Loans) Act 1973 (c. 11).	The functions under section 1 (4).

PART VI

HEALTH AND SOCIAL SERVICES

Enactment	*Excluded functions*
The Children and Young Persons Act 1933 (c. 12) sections 10 (4), 18, 27, 93 and 103.	
The National Assistance Act 1948 (c. 29).	
The Children Act 1948 (c. 43).	The functions under sections 30 (4) and 43. The powers of the Lord Chancellor under Part I of Schedule 1.
The Nurses Agencies Act 1957 (c. 16).	
The Children Act 1958 (c. 65).	
The Adoption Act 1958 (7 & 8 Eliz. 2 c. 5) sections 30, 32, 34A and 50.	

Enactment	*Excluded functions*
The Mental Health Act 1959 (c. 72) section 3 (4), Part IV, sections 64, 81, 85, 99, 133, 142 and 143 and Schedule 1.	The powers under section 39 (1) and (4) and the powers of consent under sections 41 and 47 (being powers conferred by virtue of section 65 (3)). The functions under sections 81 and 85 so far as relating to a patient subject to an order or direction restricting his discharge. The powers under section 99 other than the powers to direct transfers between hospitals in Wales. The powers under sections 142 and 143 so far as exercisable otherwise than in relation to matters with respect to which the powers of the Assembly are exercisable. The functions of the Lord Chancellor under Schedule 1.
The Health Visiting and Social Work (Training) Act 1962 (c. 33) section 5.	
The Children and Young Persons Act 1963 (c. 37) sections 37, 39 and 45.	
The Emergency Laws (Re-enactments and Repeals) Act 1964 (c. 60) section 4 and Schedule 1 so far as applicable for the purposes of that section.	
The Abortion Act 1967 (c. 87).	
The Health Services and Public Health Act 1968 (c. 46).	
The Local Government Grants (Social Need) Act 1969 (c. 2).	
The Children and Young Persons Act 1969 (c. 54) sections 1, 11A, 19, 24 to 26, 27 (3) and (5), 31, 35 to 37, 39, 40, 43, 45, 47, 48, 58, 63 (1), (2), (4) and (5), 64, 64A and 65 (1) and (2).	
The Local Authority Social Services Act 1970 (c. 42).	The functions under section 9.
The Chronically Sick and Disabled Persons Act 1970 (c. 44) sections 17, 18 (1) and (3) and 25 to 27.	
The Employment of Children Act 1973 (c. 24).	
The National Health Service Reorganisation Act 1973 (c. 32).	The powers under section 44.
The Nursing Homes Act 1975 (c. 37).	The power of consent under section 11.
The Children Act 1975 (c. 72).	The functions relating to Convention adoption orders under section 24. The functions under sections 69, 98 (1) (*e*), 107 (1) and 108.
The Adoption Act 1976 (c. 36) sections 3, 4, 5, 8, 9, 28 (10) and 57.	
The National Health Service Act 1977 (c. 49).	The functions under section 5 (4) and (5). The functions under sections 6 and 7. The power under section 23 (4). The powers under section 24 so far as relating to the Public Health Laboratory Service Board, and the power of consent under that section other than that of the Secretary of State. The power under section 27 (5). The functions under sections 31 and 32. The functions under section 34 except the function of providing by regulations for the making and determination of appeals to the Assembly under section 33 and for persons to be informed of decisions on those appeals.

Enactment	*Excluded functions*
The National Health Service Act 1977— *cont.*	The functions under section 37.
	The functions under sections 46, 47 and 49.
	The powers under section 57.
	The powers under section 84 so far as exercisable otherwise than in relation to matters with respect to which the powers of the Assembly are exercisable.
	The powers under section 85 so far as exercisable in relation to the Dental Estimates Board and the Medical Practices Committee.
	The powers under section 86 so far as exercisable otherwise than in relation to an Area Health Authority or a special health authority.
	The functions under sections 98 and 99 so far as exercisable in relation to the Dental Estimates Board.
	The powers under section 100.
	The powers under section 102 so far as exercisable in relation to the bodies referred to in subsection (1) (*a*).
	The powers under section 104.
	The powers under sections 107 and 108.
	The functions under section 119.
	The power under section 124 (6).
	The power of the Treasury under section 126 (2) so far as relating to any power which remains exercisable by the Secretary of State.
	The functions under section 127 so far as their exercise is incidental to functions which remain exercisable by a Minister of the Crown or relates to the bodies referred to in section 5 (4) and 102 (1) (*a*).
	The power under paragraph 5 of Schedule 7 and, so far as exercisable in connection with any body established under that paragraph, the power under paragraph 6 of that Schedule.
	The power under paragraph 1 (3) of Schedule 10.
	The powers under Schedule 13.
	The power under paragraph 8 of Schedule 14.

Part VII

Pollution

Enactment	*Excluded functions*
The Alkali, etc. Works Regulation Act 1906 (c. 14).	
The Public Health Act 1936 (c. 49).	The functions under sections 53 and 61 to 71.
	The powers of consent under the proviso to section 143 (3).
	The powers under sections 291 and 340.
	The power under section 341 except so far as exercisable in relation to land vested in or held for the purposes of the Assembly.
The Radioactive Substances Act 1948 (c. 37).	
The Public Health (Drainage of Trade Premises) Act 1937 (c. 40).	The functions under sections 2 and 5 (2) and, so far as exercisable in relation to those functions, the functions under sections 7 and 9.

Enactment	*Excluded functions*
The Radioactive Substances Act 1948—*cont.*	The functions under section 5 (1) (*b*) in relation to sites and premises mentioned in section 2 (1) and (2) of the Radioactive Substances Act 1960.
The Rivers (Prevention of Pollution) Acts 1951 to 1961.	The powers under section 6 of the Rivers (Prevention of Pollution) Act 1951 (c. 64).
	The powers under section 9 (6) of the Rivers (Prevention of Pollution) Act 1961 (c. 50).
The Clean Air Act 1956 (c. 52).	The functions under section 22 so far as exercisable otherwise than in relation to land vested in or held for the purposes of the Assembly.
	The functions under section 23.
The Radioactive Substances Act 1960 (c. 34).	The functions under sections 6 (1), 8 to 12 and 15 so far as exercisable in relation to premises mentioned in section 8 (1) or radioactive waste on or from such premises.
The Clean Air Act 1968 (c. 62).	The functions under section 18 (6).
The Deposit of Poisonous Waste Act 1972 (c. 21).	
The Health and Safety at Work, etc. Act 1974 (c. 37) sections 1 (1) (*d*), 3 (3), 5, 11, 12, 14, 15, 16, 18 (2), 20 (3), 27 (1), 44, 45, 50 and 80.	The functions under those sections so far as exercisable in relation to matters other than the control of emissions into the atmosphere of noxious or offensive substances.
	The functions under those sections so far as exercisable in relation to the control of emissions from vehicles, aircraft or hovercraft.
	The power to prescribe vehicles, vessels, aircraft or hovercraft for the purposes of section 1 (1) (*d*).
The Control of Pollution Act 1974 (c. 40).	The functions under sections 21 (2) and (5), 30 (5) and 31 (9).
	The power under section 39 (2) to issue a certificate.
	The power to prescribe parts of the territorial sea for the purposes of the definition of " controlled waters " in section 56 (1).
	The functions under section 56 (4).
	The powers under section 70 to make regulations as to appeals to magistrates' courts.
	The functions under sections 73 (2) (*a*), 75 and 76.
	The functions under section 80 except so far as exercisable in relation to premises used for the purposes of the Assembly and to its officers and servants.
	The functions under sections 91 (1), 92 (5), 93 (1), 96, 104, 108 and 109 except so far as exercisable in relation to matters with respect to which the powers of the Assembly are exercisable.
	The powers under sections 100 to 103.
The Refuse Disposal (Amenity) Act 1978 (c. 3).	The power under section 13 so far as exercisable in relation to section 4 (2).

PART VIII

LAND USE AND DEVELOPMENT

Enactment	*Excluded functions*
The Inclosure Acts 1845 to 1882.	The functions under section 12 of the Inclosure Act 1845 (c. 118).
The Poor Allotments Management Act 1873 (c. 19) section 9.	
The Law of Commons Amendment Act 1893 (c. 57).	
The Commons Act 1899 (c. 30).	
The Allotments Acts 1908 to 1950.	
The Commons Act 1908 (c. 44).	
The Law of Property Act 1925 (c. 20) sections 193 and 194.	
The Acquisition of Land (Authorisation Procedure) Act 1946 (c. 49) sections 3 and 5 and paragraphs 10, 11 and 12 of Schedule 1.	The functions under section 3 (1) so far as exercisable where the compulsory purchase order is or would be made or confirmed by a Minister of the Crown. The functions under section 3 (4) so far as exercisable where the apparatus belongs to excepted statutory undertakers. The functions under section 5 so far as their exercise is incidental to functions which remain exercisable by a Minister of the Crown. The functions under paragraph 10 of Schedule 1 so far as exercisable in relation to excepted statutory undertakers.
The Coast Protection Act 1949 (c. 74).	The functions under sections 11 (2) (*b*), 34 and 36. The functions under section 17 (5) so far as exercisable in relation to excepted statutory undertakers, and the function conferred on the Treasury by section 17 (8). The functions under section 32 except so far as exercisable in relation to land vested in or held for the purposes of the Assembly. The functions under section 46 except so far as exercisable in relation to matters with respect to which the powers of the Assembly are exercisable.
The Town Development Act 1952 (c. 54).	
The Opencast Coal Act 1958 (c. 69) section 39 (6).	The functions under that section so far as exercisable in relation to land of excepted statutory undertakers.
The Town and Country Planning Act 1959 (c. 53), sections 23, 24, 26 and 27.	The functions under sections 23 (2) (*b*) and (in a case within subsection (2) (*b*)), 26 (2) so far as exercisable in relation to land acquired for purposes relating to matters listed in Schedule 5 to this Act.
The Caravan Sites and Control of Development Act 1960 (c. 62).	The function under paragraph 6 of Schedule 2, except so far as exercisable in relation to land vested in or held for the purposes of the Assembly.
The Land Compensation Act 1961 (c. 33) sections 18 and 37 and paragraph 2 of Schedule 2.	The powers under section 37 so far as their exercise is incidental to functions which remain exercisable by a Minister of the Crown.
The Public Health Act 1961 (c. 64).	The functions under sections 4 to 9.
The Pipe-lines Act 1962 (c. 58) section 13 (7) and paragraph 8 of Schedule 2.	The functions under those provisions so far as exercisable in relation to land of excepted statutory undertakers.
The Harbours Act 1964 (c. 40) Schedule 3, paragraph 6 and Schedule 5, paragraph 6.	The functions relating to certificates in respect of land of excepted statutory undertakers.

Enactment	*Excluded functions*
The Gas Act 1965 (c. 36) Schedule 3, paragraphs 2 and 5 to 7.	
The New Towns Act 1965 (c. 59).	The functions under section 10 (3) so far as exercisable in relation to excepted statutory undertakers.
	The functions under sections 28 to 30 and Schedule 8 so far as exercisable by virtue of representations made by excepted statutory undertakers.
	The functions under sections 36, 37, 41, 42 (3A) to (5) and 43 to 45.
	The functions exercisable in relation to the Commission for the New Towns under sections 42A and 46.
	The power of the Treasury under section 42A so far as relating to borrowing outside the United Kingdom or in a currency other than sterling.
	The powers under section 50 so far as their exercise is incidental to functions which remain exercisable by a Minister of the Crown.
	The functions under section 54 (4) so far as exercisable by the Treasury or in relation to excepted statutory undertakers.
	The functions under Schedules 9 to 11.
The Commons Registration Act 1965 (c. 64) section 19.	The power to make regulations for the purposes specified in paragraphs (*e*) and (*g*) of subsection (1).
The Caravan Sites Act 1968 (c. 52).	
The Town and Country Planning Act 1971 (c. 78).	The function exercisable under section 40 in relation to authorisations granted by government departments.
	The functions conferred by sections 47, 48 and 49 (4) and (7), so far as they relate to the reference to a Planning Inquiry Commission of a proposal that a government department should give a direction under section 40 or that development should be carried out by or on behalf of a government department.
	The functions under sections 67 to 70, 73 to 77 and 84.
	The functions under section 113 so far as exercisable otherwise than in connection with the part of the public service with respect to which the powers of the Assembly are exercisable.
	The function of deciding any question under section 206 (6) where the appropriate authority is a government department or an excepted statutory undertaker.
	The function of making orders under section 232, so far as exercisable in relation to notices served by excepted statutory undertakers.
	The functions under sections 233 to 236 so far as exercisable by virtue of representations made by excepted statutory undertakers.
	The powers under section 254.
	The functions under sections 266 and 267, except so far as exercisable in relation to land belonging to or held for the purposes of the Assembly.
	The powers of the Treasury under section 266 (7).

Enactment	*Excluded functions*
The Town and Country Planning Act 1971 —*cont.*	The functions under sections 280, 282 and 284, so far as their exercise is incidental to functions which remain exercisable by a Minister of the Crown.
	The function under section 281 (6) in respect of land held by excepted statutory undertakers.
	The functions under section 287 except so far as exercisable in relation to matters with respect to which the powers of the Assembly are exercisable.
	The function conferred on the Treasury by section 290 (2) and the power under that provision to determine whether land is operational land of an excepted statutory undertaker.
	The function under paragraph 4 (2) of Schedule 20, so far as exercisable in relation to excepted statutory undertakers.
	The function under paragraph 84 of Schedule 24.
The Town and Country Planning (Amendment) Act 1972 (c. 42) section 10.	
The Land Compensation Act 1973 (c. 26) sections 15 (2), 20, 22 (5), 41 (2), 42 (5), 51 and 72.	
The Mobile Homes Act 1975 (c. 49).	
The Safety of Sports Grounds Act 1975 (c. 52).	
The Welsh Development Agency Act 1975 (c. 70).	The power under section 1 (9) to give directions as to the function described in section 1 (3) (*e*).
	The functions under section 3 of the Minister of Overseas Development.
	The functions under sections 12 and 13.
	The functions under section 14 except so far as exercisable in relation to property held by or on behalf of the Assembly or by a company all of whose shares are so held or by a wholly owned subsidiary of such a company.
	The functions under section 19 (7) and (8).
	The function under section 23 (5) so far as exercisable in relation to excepted statutory undertakers.
	The function under section 26 except so far as exercisable in relation to land vested in or held for the purposes of the Assembly.
	The functions under Schedule 2.
	The power of the Treasury under paragraph 3 of Schedule 3 so far as relating to borrowing outside the United Kingdom or in a currency other than sterling.
	The powers under paragraph 6 of Schedule 3.
The Community Land Act 1975 (c. 77).	The functions under section 3.
	The functions under section 5 (1) (*c*) and (4) (*b*).
	The functions under section 5 (3) and (5) so far as exercisable in relation to excepted statutory undertakers.
	The functions of the Treasury under section 5 (5).
	The powers under section 7.

Enactment	*Excluded functions*
The Community Land Act 1975—*cont.*	The powers of the Treasury under section 10 (1) to (3) so far as relating to borrowing outside the United Kingdom or in a currency other than sterling. The powers under section 11. The function of varying or revoking any order made by the Secretary of State under section 18. The function of making, or consenting to the making of, orders under section 26 (3). The powers under section 37, except so far as exercisable in connection with the part of the public service with respect to which the Assembly exercises functions or in relation to land held by the Assembly. The functions under section 39, except so far as exercisable in relation to land vested in or held for the purposes of the Assembly. The functions under section 40, except so far as exercisable in relation to the acquisition from the Assembly of any interest in land. The functions under sections 43 and 44 (except section 44 (4)). The functions exercisable under paragraph 19 of Schedule 4 in relation to the apparatus of excepted statutory undertakers. The functions under paragraph 21 (6) (*b*) of Schedule 4 of authorising works on land held by excepted statutory undertakers.
The New Towns (Amendment) Act 1976 (c. 68).	The functions under sections 13 (4) and 14.
The Development of Rural Wales Act 1976 (c. 75).	The powers under section 1 (2) to (4) and (8). The functions of the Minister of Overseas Development under section 7. The powers of the Treasury under section 9 so far as relating to borrowing outside the United Kingdom or in a currency other than sterling. The functions under section 10. The functions under section 15 (6) so far as exercisable in relation to excepted statutory undertakers. The functions under section 30, except so far as exercisable in relation to land belonging to or held for the purposes of the Assembly. The functions under paragraph 16 (3) of Schedule 3, so far as exercisable in relation to excepted statutory undertakers. The functions under paragraphs 46 to 50 of Schedule 3 so far as exercisable by virtue of representations made by excepted statutory undertakers. The powers under paragraph 53 of Schedule 3 so far as their exercise is incidental to functions which remain exercisable by a Minister of the Crown. The functions under paragraph 56 (2) of Schedule 3, so far as exercisable in relation to land of excepted statutory undertakers.

Enactment	*Excluded functions*
The Development of Rural Wales Act 1976 —cont.	The functions under paragraph 56 (5) of Schedule 3.
The Inner Urban Areas Act 1978 (c. 50) section 1, section 2 (4) (*b*) as applied by section 9, section 3 (2) as applied by section 5 (3), sections 7, 8, 9 (6) and 12, and paragraph 2 of the Schedule.	

Part IX

Water and Land Drainage

Enactment	*Excluded functions*
The Agriculture (Miscellaneous War Provisions) Act 1940 (c. 14) section 15 (1).	
The Rural Water Supplies and Sewerage Acts 1944 to 1955.	
The Water Acts 1945 and 1948.	The functions under those Acts so far as exercisable in relation to statutory water companies.
	The power of the Attorney General to give consent under section 46 of the Water Act 1945 (c. 42).
The Water Resources Acts 1963 to 1971.	The functions under paragraphs (*a*) and (*b*) of section 82 (1) of the Water Resources Act 1963 (c. 38) and, in so far as exercisable in relation to those paragraphs, the functions under section 106 of and Schedule 10 to that Act.
	The functions under section 91 (3) of that Act.
	The powers under section 111 (2) so far as their exercise is incidental to functions which remain exercisable by a Minister of the Crown.
The Water Act 1973 (c. 37).	The powers under sections 2 (5), 5 and 8 (3) (*a*).
	The functions under section 4.
	The functions under section 12 (4), (5) and (6).
	The powers under section 13 (4) so far as exercisable in relation to statutory water companies.
	The powers under section 17 (5).
	The functions under section 27.
	The functions under paragraphs 4, 5, 7 and 14 to 19 of Schedule 2.
	The functions under Part II of Schedule 3.
	The functions under Part III of that Schedule so far as exercisable in relation to the National Water Council.
	The power of the Treasury under paragraph 34 of that Schedule, so far as relating to borrowing outside the United Kingdom or in a currency other than sterling.
	The functions under paragraphs 34 (5) and 36 of that Schedule.
The Reservoirs Act 1975 (c. 23).	
The Drought Act 1976 (c. 44).	
The Land Drainage Act 1976 (c. 70).	The power under section 27.
	The functions under sections 42 and 64.
	The functions under sections 95 and 96 and Schedule 3 so far as their exercise is incidental to functions which remain exercisable by a Minister of the Crown.

Enactment	*Excluded functions*
The Land Drainage Act 1976—*cont.*	The power under section 115 (2) (*c*) (ii).
	The power under section 115 (2) (*c*) (iii) so far as exercisable otherwise than in relation to land belonging to the Assembly.

PART X

FRESHWATER FISHERIES

Enactment	*Excluded functions*
The Salmon and Freshwater Fisheries Act 1975 (c. 51).	The functions under section 38.

PART XI

COUNTRYSIDE

Enactment	*Excluded functions*
The National Parks and Access to the Countryside Act 1949 (c. 97) Parts II, IV, V and VI.	The functions under section 31 (2). The functions under Part VI so far as relating to the functions of the Nature Conservancy Council under Part III. The functions under section 101 except so far as exercisable in relation to land vested in or held for the purposes of the Assembly.
The Countryside Act 1968 (c. 41).	The functions under section 47 except so far as exercisable in relation to land vested in or held for the purposes of the Assembly.

PART XII

ANCIENT MONUMENTS AND HISTORIC BUILDINGS

Enactment	*Excluded functions*
The Ancient Monuments Acts 1913 to 1974.	
The Historic Buildings and Ancient Monuments Act 1953 (c. 49) Part I.	The functions under section 7.
The Coal-Mining (Subsidence) Act 1957 (c. 59) section 9.	
The Civic Amenities Act 1967 (c. 69) section 4 (2).	The powers under that provision so far as exercisable in relation to loans made by a Minister of the Crown.

PART XIII

TOURISM

Enactment	*Excluded functions*
The Development of Tourism Act 1969 (c. 51).	The functions under that Act so far as exercisable otherwise than in relation to the Wales Tourist Board and hotels and other establishments in Wales. The functions under Part II and, so far as they relate to grants or loans under that Part, sections 19 and 20.

PART XIV

TRANSPORT

Enactment	*Excluded functions*
The Civil Aviation Act 1949 (c. 67) Part III and section 56.	The functions under section 37.
The Transport Charges, &c. (Miscellaneous Provisions) Act 1954 (c. 64) section 6.	The power under subsection (1). The functions under that section so far as exercisable in relation to undertakings other than inland waterway undertakings.
The Road Traffic Act 1960 (c. 16) sections 120, 121, 123, 125 (2), 143, 149, 155, 159 and 160.	The functions under sections 120, 143, 155, 159 and 160 so far as exercisable in relation to matters other than road service licences and permits under section 30 of the Transport Act 1968. The functions under sections 121, 123 and 125 (2), so far as exercisable in relation to the chairman of the Commissioners or his deputy. The power under section 160 so far as exercisable for the purposes of section 5 of the Transport Act 1978 (c. 55).
The Civil Aviation Act 1968 (c. 61) sections 1, 2, 3 (2) and (4) 4, 6 (5), 8 (1) and 12 (1) and (3).	The functions under sections 2, 3 (2) and 4 (2) so far as exercisable in relation to byelaws made by virtue of section 8 of the Civil Aviation Act 1978 (c. 8).
The Transport Act 1968 (c. 73) Part II and sections 56, 57, 112, 113, 135 (1) (*d*) and 158.	The functions under sections 17 (3) and 20 (6). The powers under section 112 so far as exercisable in relation to a canal forming part of a harbour. The powers under section 113 so far as exercisable in relation to a waterway forming part of a harbour or owned or managed by excepted statutory undertakers. The powers under section 158 so far as their exercise is incidental to functions which remain exercisable by a Minister of the Crown.
The Civil Aviation Act 1971 (c. 75) sections 29 (7) and (8) and 29A. The Railways Act 1974 (c. 48) section 8. The Passenger Vehicles (Experimental Areas) Act 1977 (c. 21). The Minibus Act 1977 (c. 25).	The power under section 1 (3) except so far as exercisable in connection with the grant of permits in respect of vehicles ordinarily kept in Wales. The functions under section 3 except the power under subsection (1) to prescribe the matter to be taken into account in determining the conditions of permits granted in respect of vehicles ordinarily kept in Wales.
The Transport Act 1978 (c. 55) section 3 (5) (*b*).	

PART XV

HIGHWAYS

Enactment	*Excluded functions*
The Highways and Locomotives (Amendment) Act 1878 (c. 77). The Locomotives Act 1898 (c. 29).	

Enactment	*Excluded functions*
The Ministry of Transport Act 1919 (c. 50) sections 11 and 20.	
The Ferries (Acquisition by Local Authorities) Act 1919 (c. 75).	The functions of the Secretary of State under section 3.
The Roads Act 1920 (c. 72) section 3.	
The Trunk Roads Act 1936 (1 Edw. 8 & 1 Geo. 6 c. 5).	
The War Damage Act 1943 (c. 21) section 71.	
The Requisitioned Land and War Works Act 1945 (c. 43) sections 15 to 20 and 52.	
The Requisitioned Land and War Works Act 1948 (c. 17) section 3.	
The Public Utilities Street Works Act 1950 (c. 39).	The functions under section 4 (8). The functions under section 22 (2) (iii). The functions under section 30 (2).
The Parish Councils Act 1957 (c. 42) section 5.	
The Land Powers (Defence) Act 1958 (c. 30) sections 9 (1) to (3) and 21.	The powers under section 21 so far as their exercise is incidental to functions which remain exercisable by a Minister of the Crown.
The Highways Act 1959 (c. 25).	The function of the Secretary of State under section 6 so far as exercisable in relation to a bridge part of which is in a county in England and part in a county in Wales. The function under section 12 (3). The function of making determinations under section 113 (4) in relation to excepted statutory undertakers. The functions under sections 136 (7) and 271. The function of the Treasury under section 198 (2) of fixing interest rates. The functions under section 279 except so far as exercisable in relation to matters with respect to which the powers of the Assembly are exercisable. The functions under section 287 except so far as exercisable in relation to land vested in or held for the purposes of the Assembly.
The Highways (Miscellaneous Provisions) Act 1961 (c. 63).	
The Highways Act 1971 (c. 41).	The function under section 65 (7) so far as exercisable in relation to excepted statutory undertakers.

PART XVI

ROAD TRAFFIC

Enactment	*Excluded functions*
The Road Traffic Regulation Act 1967 (c. 76).	The powers under section 13, except the powers to make regulations with respect to particular special roads. The powers under section 23, except the powers to make regulations applying to particular crossings.

Enactment	*Excluded functions*
The Road Traffic Regulation Act 1967—*cont.*	The power to make regulations under section 54, except the power to prescribe a variant of any sign of a type prescribed by regulations made by a Minister of the Crown and carrying words in English, being a variant identical with a sign of that type except for the substitution or addition of words in Welsh (and any increase in size needed to accommodate the substituted or added words).
	The power under section 55 (1) to give general directions other than directions as to the placing of signs of a type prescribed by regulations made by the Assembly under section 54.
	The powers under sections 59 and 71.
	The powers under section 77, except so far as they relate to speed limits on any road specified in an order or on all roads in any area so specified.
	The functions under sections 78, 80, 81, 95, 96, 97, 99, 101, 103 and 104 (1B).
The Road Traffic Act 1972 (c. 20) sections 15, 20, 26, 31 (5), 36A (3A), 36B (4), 38 and 39.	
The Road Traffic Act 1974 (c. 50) section 17.	

PART XVII

REGISTRATION SERVICES

Enactment	*Excluded functions*
The Marriages Validity (Provisional Orders) Acts 1905 and 1924.	
The Census Act 1920 (c. 41) section 2 (2).	The functions under that section so far as exercisable otherwise than in relation to the duty imposed by section 5.
The Births and Deaths Registration Act 1926 (c. 48) section 12.	The power to concur in regulations not exclusively made in connection with burials in Wales or the notification of registrars in Wales.
The Population (Statistics) Act 1938 (c. 12) section 2 (2).	
The Marriage Act 1949 (c. 76) section 74.	The power to approve regulations not exclusively made in connection with marriages in Wales or notices given to, or certificates or licences issued by persons in Wales.
The Births and Deaths Registration Act 1953 (c. 20) section 39.	The power to approve regulations made for the purposes of section 3A or 14 and regulations not exclusively made in connection with births or deaths in Wales or registration in Wales.
The Registration Service Act 1953 (c. 37) sections 10 (3), 14, 19 and 20 (a), (b) and (d).	The power under section 20 to approve regulations not exclusively made in connection with the registration service in Wales.
The Marriage (Registrar General's Licence) Act 1970 (c. 34) section 18.	The power to approve regulations not exclusively made in connection with marriages in Wales.

PART XVIII

GENERAL

Enactment	*Excluded functions*
The Commissioners of Works Act 1852 (c. 28) section 2.	The functions under that section so far as exercisable otherwise than in connection with the part of the public service with respect to which the powers of the Assembly are exercisable.
The Tribunals and Inquiries Act 1971 (c. 62) sections 5 (1) and 12.	The functions under section 5 (1) so far as they relate to appointments not made by the Assembly. The functions under section 12 so far as they relate to decisions taken by Ministers of the Crown. The powers under section 12 (6).

Section 9 (2)   SCHEDULE 3

ENACTMENTS CONFERRING POWERS EXERCISABLE CONCURRENTLY

The Commissioners of Works Act 1852 (c. 28) section 2.
The Requisitioned Land and War Works Act 1945 (c. 43) section 52.
The Historic Buildings and Ancient Monuments Act 1953 (c. 49) sections 4 to 6.
The Transport Act 1968 (c. 73) section 57.
The Local Authorities (Goods and Services) Act 1970 (c. 39) section 1 (5).
The Civil Aviation Act 1971 (c. 75) section 29 (7) and (8).
The Town and Country Planning Act 1971 (c. 78) section 113.
The Local Government Act 1972 (c. 70) section 177 (1) (*f*) and (2) (*c*).
The Community Land Act 1975 (c. 77) sections 18 and 37.
The Inner Urban Areas Act 1978 (c. 50) paragraph 2 of the Schedule.

Section 36 (1)   SCHEDULE 4

POWERS EXERCISABLE ONLY WITH CONSENT OF A MINISTER OF THE CROWN

Enactment	*Powers*
The Public Health Act 1936 (c. 49) sections 2 and 6.	All powers under the sections.
The Public Health Act 1936 (c. 49) section 143.	The power to make regulations for the purposes specified in paragraphs (*b*) and (*c*) of subsection (1).
The Coast Protection Act 1949 (c. 74) sections 5 and 8.	The powers exercisable under subsections (4) and (5) where notice of objection is served by excepted statutory undertakers.
The Coast Protection Act 1949 (c. 74) section 17.	The powers exercisable under subsection (4) where the undertakers are excepted statutory undertakers.
The New Towns Act 1965 (c. 59) section 10 (5).	The power to make an order in respect of land of excepted statutory undertakers.
The New Towns Act 1965 (c. 59) sections 26 (5), 26 (6) and 28 (4).	The powers to make orders in respect of the rights or apparatus, or powers and duties, of excepted statutory undertakers.
The Town and Country Planning Act 1971 (c. 78) sections 230 (4) and (5) and 233 (4).	The powers to make orders in respect of the rights or apparatus, or powers and duties, of excepted statutory undertakers.
The Town and Country Planning Act 1971 (c. 78) section 237 (4).	The powers relating to excepted statutory undertakers.
The Town and Country Planning Act 1971 (c. 78) section 273.	All powers under the section.
The Control of Pollution Act 1974 (c. 40) section 39 (2).	The power to make a determination.

Enactment	*Powers*
The Community Land Act 1975 (c. 77) Schedule 4, paragraph 17.	The powers to make orders in respect of the rights or apparatus of excepted statutory undertakers.
The Land Drainage Act 1976 (c. 70) section 23.	The power of approval under subsection (2).
The Development of Rural Wales Act 1976 (c. 75) Schedule 3, paragraphs 44 (6) and (7) and 46 (4).	The powers to make orders in respect of the rights or apparatus, or powers and duties, of excepted statutory undertakers.
The Inner Urban Areas Act 1978 (c. 50) section 8.	All powers under the section.

Section 36 (2) etc.   SCHEDULE 5

RESERVED LOCAL MATTERS

Police (including police houses).
Diseases of animals.
Plant health.
Animal keeping, breeding and welfare.
Smallholdings.
Food, drugs and medicines.
Electoral registration.
Slaughter of animals.
Consumer protection (including weights and measures).
Rodent control.
Traffic wardens.
Control of filling materials (rag flock, etc.).
Statutory harbour undertakings.
Building regulations.

Offices, shops and railway premises.
Factory inspection.
Protection of birds.
Civil defence.
Fertilisers and feedingstuffs.
Careers service.
Sheltered employment.
Motor and oil fuel standards.
Services and facilities for magistrates' courts.
Probation and after-care.
Appointment of coroners.
Mandatory awards to students.
Petroleum spirit licensing.

REFERENCE
    For reference to reserved local matters, see notes on ss. 9 (1) 36 (2) and 58.

Sections 55 (2) and 56   SCHEDULE 6

ENACTMENTS AUTHORISING THE LENDING OF MONEY
The New Towns Act 1965 (c. 59).
The Transport Act 1968 (c. 73).
The Water Act 1973 (c. 37).
The Housing Act 1974 (c. 44).
The Welsh Development Agency Act 1975 (c. 70).
The Community Land Act 1975 (c. 77), Part II.
The Development of Rural Wales Act 1976 (c. 75).

Section 59   SCHEDULE 7

PUBLIC BODIES

PART I

Name of Body	*Constituting enactment*
The Housing Corporation.	The Housing Act 1964 (c. 56) section 1.
The Severn-Trent Water Authority.	The Water Act 1973 (c. 37) section 2.
The Welsh Water Authority.	The Water Act 1973 (c. 37) section 2.

PART II

Name of Body	*Constituting enactment*
The Advisory Council on Child Care.	The Children Act 1948 (c. 43) section 43.
The Advisory Committee on Rent Rebates and Rent Allowances.	The Housing Finance Act 1972 (c. 47) section 23.
The British Waterways Board.	The Transport Act 1962 (c. 46) section 1.

Name of Body	*Constituting enactment*
The Central Fire Brigades Advisory Council for England and Wales.	The Fire Services Act 1947 (c. 41) section 29.
The Central Health Services Council and standing advisory committees.	The National Health Service Act 1977 (c. 49) section 6.
The Clean Air Council.	The Clean Air Act 1956 (c. 52) section 23 (1).
The Council on Tribunals.	The Tribunals and Inquiries Act 1971 (c. 62) section 1.
The Dental Estimates Board.	The National Health Service Act 1977 (c. 49) section 37.
The Fire Service College Board.	The Fire Services Act 1947 (c. 41) section 23 (2).
The General Practice Finance Corporation.	The National Health Service Act 1966 (c. 8) section 1.
The Health Services Board and the Welsh Committee of that Board.	The Health Services Act 1976 (c. 83) section 1.
The Housing Association Registration Advisory Committee.	The Housing Act 1974 (c. 44) section 14.
The Inland Waterways Amenity Advisory Council.	The Transport Act 1968 (c. 73) section 10.
The Medical Practices Committee.	The National Health Service Act 1977 (c. 49) section 7.
The National Water Council.	The Water Act 1973 (c. 37) section 4.
The New Towns Staff Commission.	The New Towns (Amendment) Act 1976 (c. 68) section 14.
The Public Health Laboratory Service Board.	The National Health Service Act 1977 (c. 49) section 5.

Section 63

SCHEDULE 8

WATER

PART I

ENACTMENTS CONFERRING POWERS DEEMED TO BE EXERCISABLE WHOLLY IN ENGLAND OR WHOLLY IN WALES

The Water Act 1973 (c. 37) sections 2 (4), 3 (1), (2), (3) and (9) and 29 to 31 and Schedule 3 paragraph 11.

The Control of Pollution Act 1974 (c. 40) section 52.

The Land Drainage Act 1976 (c. 70) sections 2, 3 (1) to (8), 4, 23, 49 (1) (*b*), 60 (5), 62 and 94 and Schedule 1.

PART II

INTERVENTION BY SECRETARY OF STATE

1. In any case where—
   (*a*) a power under any enactment specified in Part III or Part IV of this Schedule is capable of being or has been exercised by the Assembly; and
   (*b*) it appears to the Secretary of State that the condition stated in paragraph 2 below is satisfied,

the Secretary of State may intervene in accordance with the following provisions of this Schedule; and in any case in which he does so the same consequences shall follow, subject to the following provisions of this Schedule, as if the power were not exercisable by the Assembly; and the power shall be exercisable by the Secretary of State accordingly, and any previous exercise of it by the Assembly shall be of no effect except to the extent, if any, that it is saved under paragraph 4 below.

2. The condition referred to in paragraph 1 above is—
   (*a*) where the power is one conferred by an enactment specified in Part III of this Schedule, that the intervention is required in the interests of the national policy for water in England and Wales; and
   (*b*) where the power is one conferred by an enactment specified in Part IV of this

Schedule, that the intervention is required for the protection of such interests with respect to land or water in England as are specified in paragraph 3 below.

3.—(1) The interests referred to in paragraph 2 (*b*) above are—

  (*a*) the interests of any person as the owner, lessee or occupier of land in England which is covered by or contiguous to an inland water;

  (*b*) the interests of any person as the owner of fishing rights in respect of an inland water in England;

  (*c*) the interests of any person as the holder of a licence under the Water Resources Act 1963 to abstract water in England; and

  (*d*) the interests of persons entitled to a public right of fishing in tidal waters and parts of the sea in England or adjoining the coast of England.

(2) In this paragraph expressions defined in section 135 of the Water Resources Act 1963 have the same meaning as in that Act and " fishing rights " has the same meaning as in section 47 of that Act.

4. An intervention by the Secretary of State under this Schedule shall be made by notice published in the London Gazette; and the notice may save the whole or part of the effect of any steps previously taken, whether by the Assembly or by other persons, and may extend the time for the taking of any steps by the Secretary of State or any other persons, whether or not the time for taking them would otherwise have expired at the time the notice is published.

5. Where the Secretary of State has made an intervention in a case he shall, in addition to the notice under paragraph 4 above, give notice of the intervention to the Assembly and the water authority concerned and publish a further notice in two successive weeks in one or more local newspapers circulating in the area concerned; and the Assembly shall give notice of the intervention to any person who has previously been given notice of any steps taken or proposed to be taken in the case.

6. A notice under paragraph 4 or 5 above shall state the reason for the Secretary of State's intervention and shall further state that, before determining how to exercise any power which, but for the intervention, would be exercisable by the Assembly, he will consider representations in writing received by him within a time specified in the notice which, if the powers to be exercised are or include powers under the Drought Act 1976, shall be not less than one week from the first publication in pursuance of paragraph 5 above of the further notice mentioned therein and, in any other case, shall be not less than three weeks from the publication.

7. Where a notice under paragraph 4 above saves the whole or part of any steps previously taken, the Assembly shall, if requested to do so by the Secretary of State, supply him with the documents or copies of the documents by which any of the steps were taken; and if any person has, in connection with such a step, exercised a right to be heard the Secretary of State shall, if so requested by that person within the time limited by the notice, give him an opportunity to be heard by a person appointed by the Secretary of State.

8. Where it appears to a water authority whose area lies wholly or partly in England that circumstances exist which would enable the Secretary of State to intervene under paragraph 1 above, the water authority may make application to the Secretary of State, requesting him to intervene under that paragraph.

9. An application under paragraph 8 above shall be made by notice published in the London Gazette and not later than the date on which the notice is published the water authority shall give notice of the application to the Secretary of State and the Assembly.

10. A notice under paragraph 9 above shall state the reason for requesting the Secretary of State's intervention.

11. If upon considering an application under paragraph 8 above, the Secretary of State decides not to intervene under paragraph 1 above, he shall publish his decision and his reason for it by notice in the London Gazette.

12.—(1) The Secretary of State may cause a local inquiry to be held for the purposes of this Part of this Schedule, and subsections (2) to (5) of section 250 of the Local Government Act 1972 shall apply to any such inquiry subject to any necessary modifications and, in particular, with the substitution in subsection (4) for the reference to a local authority of a reference to a water authority.

(2) The Assembly shall, if requested by the Secretary of State, make available to him the services of any of its officers for the purposes of any inquiry under this paragraph.

PART III

ENACTMENTS CONFERRING POWERS SUBJECT TO INTERVENTION
UNDER NATIONAL POLICY FOR ENGLAND AND WALES

The Water Act 1945 (c. 42) sections 9, 12 (5), 13, 23 and 24, so much of Schedule 1 as relates to orders under any of those sections, and Schedule 2.

The Water Act 1948 (c. 22) section 8.

The Water Resources Act 1963 (c. 38) sections 21, 25, 38, 65 to 67 and 108, and so much of Schedules 7 and 8 as relates to orders under any of those sections.

The Water Resources Act 1971 (c. 34) section 1.

The Water Act 1973 (c. 37) so much of Part II of Schedule 4 as relates to orders under sections 12 (5) and 13 of the Water Act 1945.

The Drought Act 1976 (c. 44).

PART IV

ENACTMENTS CONFERRING POWERS SUBJECT TO INTERVENTION
FOR PROTECTION OF INTERESTS IN ENGLAND

The Water Act 1945 (c. 42) sections 10, 12 (5), 18, 19, 23 and 33 and so much of Schedule 1 as relates to orders under any of those sections.

The Water Resources Act 1963 (c. 38) sections 21, 39, 40, 44, 47, 72, 74, 78, 82 and 108, and so much of Schedule 7 as relates to statements or draft statements under sections 19 to 21.

The Water Resources Act 1971 (c. 34) section 1.

The Control of Pollution Act 1974 (c. 40) sections 35, 37, 39, 42, 49, 51 and 97.

The Salmon and Freshwater Fisheries Act 1975 (o. 51) sections 26 and 28 and Schedule 3.

The Drought Act 1976 (c. 44).

Section 64　　　　　　SCHEDULE 9

INTERVENTION BY SECRETARY OF STATE IN PLANNING MATTERS

PART I

POWERS AFFECTED

The powers exercisable under or by virtue of any of the following provisions of the Town and Country Planning Act 1971—

　　　sections 35 to 37,
　　　section 45,
　　　section 51,
　　　section 88,
　　　section 95,
　　　section 276 so far as it relates to sections 45, 51, 87 and 90,

except the powers under sections 35 and 95 to give directions in relation to applications other than particular applications.

PART II

POWERS OF SECRETARY OF STATE

1. The Secretary of State may intervene in accordance with the following provisions of this Schedule in any case where—

(a) action is being or is capable of being taken by the Assembly in the exercise of a power specified in Part I of this Schedule; and

(b) it appears to the Secretary of State that any action so taken would or might affect, directly or indirectly, any matter which concerns Wales (whether or not it also concerns any other part of the United Kingdom) but with respect to which the Assembly has no power to act, and that it is desirable in the public interest that he should intervene.

2. Where the Secretary of State intervenes in a case under this Schedule—

    (*a*) no action (or no further action) shall be taken in the case by the Assembly;

    (*b*) any action previously taken in the case, whether by the Assembly or by any other person, shall be of no effect except to the extent (if any) that contrary provision is made in accordance with paragraph 4 below; and

    (*c*) the Secretary of State shall in relation to the case have all the powers and duties that the Assembly would have if the Secretary of State had not intervened and no action (except action the effect of which is saved in accordance with paragraph 4 below) had previously been taken in the case.

3. An intervention by the Secretary of State under this Schedule shall be made by notice published in the London Gazette.

4. A notice under paragraph 3 above of an intervention by the Secretary of State in a case may save the whole or part of the effect of any action previously taken, whether by the Assembly or by any other person, and may extend the time for the taking of any action by the Secretary of State or any other person, whether or not the time for taking it would otherwise have expired at the time the notice is published.

5. Where the Secretary of State has intervened in a case he shall, in addition to the notice under paragraph 3 above, give notice of the intervention—

    (*a*) to the Assembly,

    (*b*) to any local planning authority concerned, and

    (*c*) to any person who has previously been given notice of any action taken or proposed to be taken in the case;

and he shall also publish a notice in two successive weeks in one or more local newspapers circulating in the area concerned.

6.—(1) Before he determines an application or appeal or confirms or makes an order in a case in which he has intervened under this Schedule, the Secretary of State shall afford to the Assembly an opportunity of making representations at a hearing before a person appointed by the Secretary of State.

(2) Sub-paragraph (1) above does not apply to an intervention in relation to the powers exercisable under or by virtue of section 276 (5) of the Town and Country Planning Act 1971; but before exercising those powers in any case the Secretary of State shall consult the Assembly.

7.—(1) A notice under paragraph 3 or 5 above shall state the reason for the Secretary of State's intervention.

(2) Section 283 of the Town and Country Planning Act 1971 shall apply to notices given under paragraph 5 above as it applies to notices under that Act.

8.—(1) Where the Secretary of State has intervened, or is considering whether to intervene, in a case under this Schedule, he may require the Assembly or any local planning authority concerned to supply him with information or copies of documents relating to the case.

(2) The Secretary of State may require the Assembly to make available to him the services of any of its officers for the purposes of any local inquiry held in respect of a case in which the Secretary of State has intervened under this Schedule.

9.—(1) The Secretary of State may by order require such local planning authorities as may be prescribed by or under the order to give him such information as may be so prescribed with respect to applications for planning permission made to them (including information as to the manner in which any such application has been dealt with) and with respect to proposals for the development by them of land in respect of which they are the local planning authority.

(2) A statutory instrument containing an order under this paragraph shall be subject to annulment in pursuance of a resolution of either House of Parliament.

Section 75   SCHEDULE 10

POWERS OF ASSEMBLY TO MAKE OR CONFIRM ORDERS SUBJECT
TO SPECIAL PARLIAMENTARY PROCEDURE

Enactment conferring power	*Circumstances in which S.P.P. applies or may apply*
The Coast Protection Act 1949 (c. 74) sections 2, 18 and 31.	If objection is made by excepted statutory undertakers.
The Public Utilities Street Works Act 1950 (c. 39) Schedule 6, paragraph 1.	If objection is made by excepted statutory undertakers.

Enactment conferring power	*Circumstances in which S.P.P. applies or may apply*
The Highways Act 1959 (c. 25) sections 7, 9, 11, 13 and 20.	If objection is made by a person authorised by any enactment (within the meaning of that Act) to work, maintain, conserve, improve or control any estuary, harbour or dock.
The Highways Act 1959 (c. 25) sections 28, 110 and 111.	If objection is made by excepted statutory undertakers.
The Highways (Miscellaneous Provisions) Act 1961 (c. 63) section 3.	If objection is made by a person authorised by any enactment (within the meaning of that Act) to work, maintain, conserve, improve or control any estuary, harbour or dock.
The New Towns Act 1965 (c. 59) sections 7, 8 and 10 (5).	If exercised in relation to land of excepted statutory undertakers or land held by a local authority (or by a body formed by local authorities) for the purposes of any of the matters listed in Schedule 5 to this Act.
The New Towns Act 1965 (c. 59) sections 26 and 28.	If exercised in relation to the rights or apparatus, or powers and duties, of excepted statutory undertakers.
The Highways Act 1971 (c. 41) section 1.	If objection is made by a person authorised by any enactment (within the meaning of that Act) to work, maintain, conserve, improve or control any estuary, harbour or dock.
The Town and Country Planning Act 1971 (c. 78) section 233.	If exercised in relation to the powers and duties of excepted statutory undertakers.
The Town and Country Planning Act 1971 (c. 78) Schedule 20 paragraph 3.	If objection is made by excepted statutory undertakers.
The Land Drainage Act 1976 (c. 70) sections 11 (4) and 88 (1).	If the order is opposed by a harbour authority or conservancy authority.
The Land Drainage Act 1976 (c. 70) section 62.	All circumstances.
The Development of Rural Wales Act 1976 (c. 75) section 6 (2) (a) and paragraphs 2 and 16 of Schedule 3.	If exercised in relation to land of excepted statutory undertakers or land held by a local authority (or by a body formed by local authorities) for the purposes of any of the matters listed in Schedule 5 to this Act.
The Development of Rural Wales Act 1976 (c. 75) Schedule 3, paragraphs 44 and 46.	If exercised in relation to the rights or apparatus, or powers and duties, of excepted statutory undertakers.
Any enactment conferring power to make or confirm a compulsory purchase order.	If exercised in relation to land held inalienably by the National Trust.

Section 75

SCHEDULE 11

AMENDMENTS OF ENACTMENTS
THE BURIAL ACTS 1853, 1855 AND 1857

1.—(1) The powers conferred on Her Majesty in Council by—
  (a) section 1 of the Burial Act 1853;
  (b) section 1 of the Burial Act 1855;
  (c) section 10 of the Burial Act 1857;
  (d) section 23 of the Burial Act 1857;
shall as regards Wales be exercisable instead by the Assembly by order made by statutory instrument; and except where the context otherwise requires references in any enactment to Orders in Council made under any of those sections shall be construed as including references to orders so made by the Assembly.

(2) The provisions of section 1 of the Burial Act 1853 and sections 10 and 23 of the Burial Act 1857 concerning representations shall not have effect in relation to orders of the Assembly; but the like notices shall be given of a proposal that an order be made by the Assembly under any of those sections as is required in the case of a representation under that section.

THE ANCIENT MONUMENTS CONSOLIDATION AND AMENDMENT ACT 1913

2. The powers conferred on Her Majesty in Council by section 14 (4) and 15 (2) of the Ancient Monuments Consolidation and Amendment Act 1913 shall in relation respectively to monuments in Wales and the Ancient Monuments Board for Wales be exercisable instead by the Assembly by order made by statutory instrument; but the Assembly shall not charge a committee with the exercise of its powers under section 15 (2).

THE BIRTHS AND DEATHS REGISTRATION ACT 1926

3. In prescribing anything for the purposes of section 1 of the Births and Deaths Registration Act 1926, the Registrar General may make separate provision in connection with burials in Wales and burials in England; and in prescribing anything for the purposes of section 3 of that Act he may make separate provision in relation to the notification of registrars in Wales and the notification of registrars in England.

THE STATUTORY INSTRUMENTS ACT 1946

4. References to a Minister of the Crown in section 1 of the Statutory Instruments Act 1946 shall be construed as including references to the Assembly.

THE ACQUISITION OF LAND (AUTHORISATION PROCEDURE) ACT 1946

5. In paragraph 7B of Schedule 1 to the Acquisition of Land (Authorisation Procedure) Act 1946—
   (a) in sub-paragraph (2) (a) and (3) (a) after the word " powers " there shall be inserted the words " in respect of land in England "; and
   (b) in sub-paragraph (6), the words " or Wales, as the case may be " shall be omitted.

THE STATISTICS OF TRADE ACT 1947

6. In section 1 (1) of the Statistics of Trade Act 1947 the reference to the discharge by government departments of their functions shall include a reference to the discharge by the Assembly of its functions.

7. Section 9 (1) of that Act shall apply in relation to the Assembly as it applies in relation to a government department (or the Minister in charge of a government department).

THE MARRIAGE ACT 1949

8. At the end of section 74 of the Marriage Act 1949 there shall be added the words " and may make separate provision in connection with marriages in Wales or notices given to, or certificates or licences issued by, persons in Wales ".

THE NATIONAL PARKS AND ACCESS TO THE COUNTRYSIDE ACT 1949

England

9. In the application of the National Parks and Access to the Countryside Act 1949 to England—
   (a) the words " and Wales " in sections 1, 5 and 6 shall be omitted;
   (b) the words " or Wales " in sections 51 and 87 shall be omitted.

Wales

10.—(1) The following amendments shall have effect in the application of that Act to Wales.

(2) References to the Countryside Commission shall be construed as references to the Countryside Commission for Wales.

(3) Sections 1 to 3 shall be omitted.

(4) In section 4—
   (a) in subsection (1) for the words from " thirtieth " to " Minister " there shall be substituted the words " 31st March in each year, make to the Welsh Assembly ";

(*b*) in subsection (3) for the words from " Minister " where first occurring to " his " there shall be substituted the words " Welsh Assembly during that period under section 62 of the Wales Act 1978 unless the Welsh Assembly has notified to the Commission its "; and

(*c*) for subsection (4) there shall be substituted—

" (4) The Welsh Assembly shall publish every report of the Commission under this section ".

(5) In sections 5 and 6 the words " England and " shall be omitted, and in section 6—

(*a*) in subsection (3) (*b*) for the words " the Minister " there shall be substituted the words " the Welsh Assembly " and for the words " any other Minister " there shall be substituted the words " any Minister "; and

(*b*) in subsection (4)—

(i) in paragraph (*e*) for the words " any Minister " there shall be substituted the words " the Welsh Assembly or any Minister ";

(ii) in paragraph (*f*) for the words " the Minister " there shall be substituted the words " the Welsh Assembly " and for the words " other Ministers " there shall be substituted the words " any Minister "; and

(iii) in paragraph (*g*) for the words " the Minister ", in the first place, there shall be substituted the words " the Welsh Assembly ", for the words " other Ministers " there shall be substituted the words " any Minister " and for the words " the Minister ", in the second place, there shall be substituted the words " the Welsh Assembly or the Minister ".

(6) In sections 51 and 87 the words " England or " shall be omitted.

The Defamation Act 1952

11. In section 10 of the Defamation Act 1952 before the words " or to Parliament " there shall be inserted the words " to the Welsh Assembly ".

12. In the Schedule to that Act before paragraph 2 there shall be inserted—

" 1B. A fair and accurate report of any proceedings in public of the Welsh Assembly ".

13. In paragraph 13 of that Schedule there shall be inserted at the appropriate place—

" ' Welsh Assembly ' includes any committee of the Assembly and any sub-committee of such a committee ".

The Births and Deaths Registration Act 1953

14. Section 39 of the Births and Deaths Registration Act 1953 shall become section 39 (1) and at the end of it there shall be added—

" (2) The power to make regulations under this section includes power to make separate provision in connection with births or deaths in Wales or registration in Wales."

The Registration Service Act 1953

15.—(1) The Registrar General shall for the purposes of section 19 of the Registration Service Act 1953 prepare separate general abstracts relating to registrations in England and registrations in Wales.

(2) So much of that section as provides for an abstract to be laid before each House of Parliament shall not apply to an abstract relating to registrations in Wales; but the Assembly shall publish every abstract that it receives under that section.

16. At the end of section 20 of that Act there shall be added the words " and the power to make regulations under this section includes power to make separate provision in connection with the registration service in Wales ".

The Historic Buildings and Ancient Monuments Act 1953

17.—(1) Section 1 (3) of the Historic Buildings and Ancient Monuments Act 1953 shall have effect in its application (by virtue of section 3 (2)) to the Historic Buildings Council for Wales as if the second reference to the House of Commons included a reference to the Assembly.

(2) The expenses referred to in section 7 of that Act do not include expenses incurred by the Assembly.

THE DEFAMATION ACT (NORTHERN IRELAND) 1955

18. In section 10 (1) of the Defamation Act (Northern Ireland) 1955 after the words " in any election " there shall be inserted the words " to the Welsh Assembly ".

19. In the Schedule to that Act before paragraph 2 there shall be inserted—

" 1B. A fair and accurate report of any proceedings in public of the Welsh Assembly ".

20. In paragraph 13 of that Schedule there shall be inserted at the appropriate place—

" ' Welsh Assembly ' includes any committee of the Assembly and any sub-committee of such a committee ".

THE OPENCAST COAL ACT 1958

21. After subsection (1) of section 2 of the Opencast Coal Act 1958 there shall be inserted—

" (1A) The Minister shall not give a direction under this section in relation to land in Wales unless—

(a) he has, at least 28 days previously, given notice of the proposed direction to the Welsh Assembly, or

(b) the Welsh Assembly has informed him of its agreement to the giving of the proposed direction or to the giving of directions of a class that includes the proposed direction ".

THE MENTAL HEALTH ACT 1959

22. In section 28 (2) of the Mental Health Act 1959 after the words " Secretary of State " there shall be inserted the words " or the Welsh Assembly ".

THE PIPE-LINES ACT 1962

23. After subsection (1) of section 5 of the Pipe-lines Act 1962 there shall be inserted—

" (1A) The Minister shall not give a direction under this section in relation to land in Wales unless—

(a) he has, at least 28 days previously, given notice of the proposed direction to the Welsh Assembly, or

(b) the Welsh Assembly has informed him of its agreement to the giving of the proposed direction or to the giving of directions of a class that includes the proposed direction ".

THE NEW TOWNS ACT 1965

24.—(1) Section 43 of the New Towns Act 1965 shall not apply in relation to any sums advanced to or borrowed by development corporations in Wales after the coming into force of this paragraph.

(2) The Assembly may by order impose a limit on the amount outstanding at any time in respect of the principal of any money so advanced to or borrowed by development corporations in Wales.

(3) The Assembly shall not charge a committee with the exercise of the power to make such an order.

25. Section 54 (4) of that Act shall have effect as if it provided for the appropriate Minister alone to determine the question whether land in Wales of excepted statutory undertakers is operational land.

THE PARLIAMENTARY COMMISSIONER ACT 1967

26. In section 61 (1) (b) of the Parliamentary Commissioner Act 1967 before the words " or those " there shall be inserted the words " or by the Welsh Assembly " and at the end there shall be added the words " or sums payable out of the Welsh Consolidated Fund ".

27. At the end of section 11 (4) of that Act there shall be added the words " and to the Chief Executive of the Welsh Assembly ".

The Welsh Language Act 1967

28. In section 2 of the Welsh Language Act 1967—
(*a*) in subsections (1) and (3) for the words " the appropriate Minister " there shall be substituted the words " the appropriate authority "; and
(*b*) in subsection (3), before paragraph (*a*) there shall be inserted—
(*aa*) in the case of an enactment for the execution of which in Wales the Welsh Assembly is responsible, that Assembly; and ".

The Countryside Act 1968

29. In the application of the Countryside Act 1968 to Wales—
(*a*) section 1 (1) and (2) shall be omitted;
(*b*) references to the Countryside Commission, except in section 1 (4) and (5), shall be construed as references to the Countryside Commission for Wales; and
(*c*) in section 2—
(i) in subsection (4) for the words " any Minister having functions under this Act or any other Minister " there shall be substituted the words " the Welsh Assembly or any Minister "; and
(ii) in subsection (5) for the words " section 1 (2) of this Act " there shall be substituted the words " section 62 of the Wales Act 1978 " and for the word " Minister " there shall be substituted the words " Welsh Assembly ".

The Development of Tourism Act 1969

30. Notwithstanding the provisions of subsection (3) of section 2 of the Development of Tourism Act 1969, the Wales Tourist Board shall have power, by virtue of subsection (2) of that section, to carry on activities outside the United Kingdom for the purpose of encouraging people to visit Wales.

31. In section 3 of that Act—
(*a*) subsection (1) shall have effect as if the reference to the Wales Tourist Board were omitted and the reference to Great Britain did not include a reference to Wales;
(*b*) before subsection (2) there shall be inserted—
" (1B) The Wales Tourist Board may prepare a scheme providing for the giving of financial assistance by it for the carrying out of projects of such classes as may be specified in the scheme, being projects which in the opinion of the Board will provide or improve tourist amenities and facilities in Wales ";
(*c*) in subsection (2) before the word " who " there shall be inserted the words " and any scheme prepared under subsection (1B) of this section shall be submitted to the Welsh Assembly ";
(*d*) in subsection (6) the words " of the Board of Trade " shall be omitted and after the word " section ", in the third place where it occurs, there shall be inserted the words " relating to a scheme prepared by the British Tourist Authority "; and
(*e*) after subsection (6) there shall be added—
" (7) The Welsh Assembly shall not charge a committee with the exercise of its power to make orders under this section ".

32.—(1) The powers conferred on Her Majesty in Council by sections 17 and 18 of that Act shall in relation to establishments in Wales be exercisable instead by the Assembly by order made by statutory instrument.

(2) The Assembly shall not charge a committee with the exercise of its powers under those sections.

(3) Those sections shall have effect in relation to orders made by the Assembly as if—
(*a*) references to the Wales Tourist Board were substituted in paragraph (*a*) of section 17 (3) for the references to the British Tourist Authority;
(*b*) the consultation referred to in that paragraph did not include consultation with other Tourist Boards; and
(*c*) the provisions of section 17 (4) relating to regulations, and the provision for annulment made by section 17 (6), were omitted.

The Marriage (Registrar General's Licence) Act 1970

33. At the end of section 18 (2) of the Marriage (Registrar General's Licence) Act 1970 there shall be added the words " and power to make separate provision in connection with marriages in Wales ".

The Town and Country Planning Act 1971

34. After section 40 (1) of the Town and Country Planning Act 1971 there shall be inserted—

" (1A) A government department shall not give a direction under this section in respect of development in Wales unless—

(a) the department has, at least 28 days previously, given notice of the proposed direction to the Welsh Assembly, or

(b) the Welsh Assembly has informed the department of its agreement to the giving of the proposed direction or to the giving of directions of a class that includes the proposed direction ".

35. After section 254 of that Act there shall be inserted—

" Contributions by Welsh Assembly towards compensation paid by local authorities

254A. Where compensation is payable by a local authority under this Act in consequence of any such decision or order as is mentioned in section 254 of this Act and the decision or order was given or made wholly or partly in the interest of a service provided by the Welsh Assembly, the Assembly may pay a contribution to that authority ".

The Banking and Financial Dealings Act 1971

36. In section 1 of the Banking and Financial Dealings Act 1971 before subsection (3) there shall be inserted—

" (2B) Subsection (2) above does not apply to Wales, but if it appears to the Welsh Assembly that, in the special circumstances of any year, it is inexpedient that a day specified in Schedule 1 to this Act should be a bank holiday in Wales, the Welsh Assembly may by order declare that that day shall not in that year be a bank holiday and appoint another day in place of it; and the day appointed by the order shall, in that year, be a bank holiday under this Act instead of the day specified in Schedule 1 ".

37. Before subsection (4) of that section there shall be inserted—

" (3B) The Welsh Asembly may from time to time by order appoint a special day to be a bank holiday in Wales under this Act ".

The Local Employment Act 1972

38.—(1) In relation to a development area or intermediate area in Wales, subsection (1) of section 7 of the Local Employment Act 1972 shall have effect as if—

(a) for the words "the Minister in charge of any Government department " there were substituted the words " a Minister of the Crown "; and

(b) the words " for which the department is responsible " were omitted.

(2) After that subsection there shall be inserted—

" (1A) Where it appears to the Welsh Assembly that adequate provision has not been made for the needs of any development area or intermediate area in Wales in respect of a basic service for which the Assembly is responsible, and that it is expedient with a view to contributing to the development of industry in that area that the service should be improved, the Assembly may make grants or loans towards the cost of improving it to such persons and in such manner as appear to the Assembly appropriate ".

(3) In subsection (3) of that section after the words " Minister of the Crown " there shall be inserted the words " or of the Welsh Assembly ".

The Finance Act 1972

39. In section 19 (4) of the Finance Act 1972 before the words " and any part " there shall be inserted the words " or of the Welsh Assembly ".

The European Communities Act 1972

40.—(1) The references in section 2 (2) of the European Communities Act 1972 to a Minister of the Crown or government department shall include references to the Assembly.

(2) The Assembly shall not charge a committee with the exercise of a power to make regulations under that section except in such cases of urgency as may be specified for the purposes of this paragraph by the standing orders of the Assembly, and in such cases a committee shall not arrange for the exercise of the power by the leader of the committee or by a sub-committee.

(3) Paragraph 2 (2) of Schedule 2 to that Act shall not have effect in relation to regulations made by the Assembly.

The Local Government Act 1972

41. In the application of Schedule 17 to the Local Government Act 1972 to Wales, the references to the Countryside Commission in paragraphs 9 to 13, 15, 17 and 19 shall be construed as references to the Countryside Commission for Wales.

The Water Act 1973

42. For subsection (1) of section 1 of the Water Act 1973 there shall be substituted—

" (1) It shall be the duty of the Secretary of State and the Minister of Agriculture, Fisheries and Food (in this Act referred to as " the Minister ") to promote jointly a national policy for water in England and Wales and—
- (a) it shall be the duty of the Secretary of State to secure the effective execution in England of so much of that policy as relates to matters mentioned in subsection (2) below by the bodies responsible for them; and
- (b) it shall be the duty of the Minister to secure the effective execution in England of so much of that policy as relates to the matters mentioned in subsection (3) below by the bodies responsible for them; and
- (c) it shall be the duty of the Welsh Assembly to promote a national policy for water in Wales in harmony with the national policy for water in England and Wales and to secure its effective execution by the bodies responsible for the matters mentioned in subsections (2) and (3) below ".

43. In subsection (2) of that section, for the words preceding the paragraphs there shall be substituted the words " The matters referred to in subsection (1) (a) above are— ".

44. For subsection (3) of that section there shall be substituted—

" (3) The matters referred to in subsection (1) (b) above are land drainage and fisheries in inland and coastal waters ".

45. In subsection (7) of that section after the words " The Secretary of State " there shall be inserted the words " and the Welsh Assembly ", for the words " he considers " there shall be substituted the words " he or it considers " and for the words " England and Wales " there shall be substituted the words " England or Wales ".

46. For subsection (10) of section 3 of that Act there shall be substituted—

" (10) The constitution of the Welsh authority shall be prescribed by the order establishing it under section 2 above and any order establishing or varying the constitution of the Welsh authority shall make provision for twenty-one of its members to be appointed as mentioned in subsection (10A) below; and the Welsh Assembly shall not charge any committee of the Assembly with the exercise of the power to make an order varying that constitution.

(10A) Of the twenty-one members mentioned in subsection (10) above one each shall be appointed by the following, that is to say :—
- (a) the county council of each county in Wales;
- (b) the councils of the districts within each county in Wales;
- (c) the Cheshire county council;
- (d) the Hereford and Worcester county council;
- (e) the councils of the districts within the county of Cheshire;
- (f) the councils of the districts within the county of Hereford and Worcester; and
- (g) the Secretary of State and the Minister acting jointly ".

47. At the end of subsection (3) of section 5 of that Act there shall be added—

" (4) In relation to any functions exercisable by the Welsh authority or the Severn-Trent Water Authority in Wales subsections (1) and (2) of this section shall have effect as if for the references to the Minister and the Secretary of State there were substituted references to the Welsh Assembly ".

THE NATURE CONSERVANCY COUNCIL ACT 1973

48. In section 1 (1) (*a*) of the Nature Conservancy Council Act 1973 after sub-paragraph (ii) there shall be inserted—

" (ii*a*) the provision of advice for the Welsh Assembly for the purposes of any functions exercised by it in relation to the conservation of features of geological or physiographical interest and of flora and fauna; and ".

THE LOCAL GOVERNMENT ACT 1974

England

49. In the application of Part I of the Local Government Act 1974 to England the words " and Wales " in section 1 (1) and (3) (*b*) shall be omitted.

Wales

50. Paragraphs 51 to 67 below shall have effect in the application of that Part of Wales.

51. The words " England and " in section 1 (1) and (3) (*b*) shall be omitted.

52. For references to the Secretary of State, wherever they occur (except in section 8 (2) and (3) and in paragraphs 8 (1) (*b*), 9 and 11 of Schedule 1) there shall be substituted references to the Welsh Assembly; and references to the consent of the Treasury, except in section 8, shall be omitted.

53. Any reference to a local authority for an area in England (but not the reference in paragraph 3 (4) of Schedule 2) shall be omitted.

54. In section 1 (2) after the words " out of money provided by Parliament " there shall be inserted the words " or out of the Welsh Consolidated Fund ".

55. In section 1 (6), paragraph (*a*) and the words from " of the Receiver " to " District or " shall be omitted.

56. In section 1 (7) the words " out of money provided by Parliament " shall be omitted.

57. In section 3, subsection (2) shall be omitted and, in subsection (3), for the words from the beginning to " report " there shall be substituted the words " Every rate support grant order shall be published by the Welsh Assembly together with a report ".

58. In section 5 (1), for references to the appropriate Minister there shall be substituted references to the Welsh Assembly, and the words from " make and cause " to " may " shall be omitted.

59. In section 5 (2) a reference to the Assembly shall be substituted for the reference to the appropriate Minister except in relation to functions relating to matters listed in Schedule 5 to this Act.

60. In section 7 (3) for the reference to the Countryside Commission there shall be substituted a reference to the Countryside Commission for Wales.

61. In section 8 (3) for the words from the beginning to " subsection (1) or " there shall be substituted the words " Payments of grants under subsection (1) above shall be made at such times as the Welsh Assembly may determine and payments of grants under ".

62. In section 9 for the references to the Countryside Commission there shall be substituted references to the Countryside Commission for Wales.

63. In section 10 (4) the words from " which " to the end shall not have effect in relation to regulations made by the Assembly.

64. In paragraph 6 of Schedule 1, for the words from " except " to " that " there shall be substituted the words " but the Welsh Assembly may make such advances or grants out of the Welsh Consolidated Fund in cases where it appears to the Welsh Assembly that ".

65. In paragraph 8 (1) of Schedule 1, for the words from " then " to " section " there shall be substituted the words " the Welsh Assembly may make to that person, out of the Welsh Consolidated Fund ".

66. The powers conferred on the Secretary of State by paragraph 11 of Schedule 1 shall, in relation to grants payable by the Assembly, be exercisable by the Assembly; and subparagraph (4) of that paragraph shall not have effect in relation to an order made by the Assembly.

67. The Assembly shall not charge a committee with the exercise of a power to make an order under section 3 or 4 (1) or paragraph 11 of Schedule 1 or to make regulations under section 5 (2) or 10 (3).

Local government administration

68. In section 23 (12) of that Act, after the words " section 24 below) " there shall be inserted the words " to the Welsh Assembly ".

69. In section 26 (6) (*b*) of that Act, after the word " Crown " there shall be inserted the words " or to the Welsh Assembly ".

70. In section 27 (1) of that Act, for paragraph (*b*) there shall be substituted—

" (*b*) any other authority or body—

(i) whose members are appointed by Her Majesty, by any Minister of the Crown or government department or by the Welsh Assembly; or

(ii) whose revenues consist wholly or mainly of moneys provided by Parliament or sums paid out of the Welsh Consolidated Fund ".

71. In section 29 (3) of that Act, after the words " Government department " there shall be inserted the words " or the Welsh Assembly ".

72. In section 32 (3) of that Act—

(*a*) after the words " Minister of the Crown " there shall be inserted the words " or the Welsh Assembly ";

(*b*) after the words " the Minister " there shall be inserted the words " or the Assembly "; and

(*c*) after the words " Secretary of State " there shall be inserted the words " or by the Welsh Assembly ".

73. In section 32 (5) of that Act—

(*a*) after the words " from a government department " there shall be inserted the words " or the Welsh Assembly ";

(*b*) after the words " the government department " there shall be inserted the words " or the written consent of the Assembly "; and

(*c*) after the words " the department " there shall be inserted the words " or Assembly ".

The Health and Safety at Work etc. Act 1974

74. Regulations made by the Assembly for the purposes of subsection (3) of section 14 of the Health and Safety at Work etc. Act 1974 shall include provision for an inquiry to be held otherwise than in public where or to the extent that a Minister of the Crown so directs; and in relation to such regulations paragraph (*c*) of subsection (4) shall have effect as if it referred to the Assembly instead of to a Minister of the Crown.

75. In section 44 (1) of that Act at the end there shall be added the words " or, where a licence is required under regulations made by the Welsh Assembly, to the Welsh Assembly ".

76. In section 48 (4) of that Act before the word " which " there shall be inserted the words " or of regulations made under this Part by the Welsh Assembly ".

77. Any modification made by an Order in Council under section 84 (3) of that Act may include provision conferring functions on the Assembly.

The Finance Act 1975

78. In paragraph 12 (1) of Schedule 6 to the Finance Act 1975, before the entry beginning " Any university " there shall be inserted the words " The Welsh Assembly ".

The House of Commons Disqualification Act 1975

79. In Part III of Schedule 1 to the House of Commons Disqualification Act 1975 the following shall be inserted at the appropriate places—

Any member of the Countryside Commission for Wales in receipt of remuneration.

Welsh Comptroller and Auditor General.

THE NORTHERN IRELAND ASSEMBLY DISQUALIFICATION ACT 1975

80. In Part III of Schedule 1 to the Northern Ireland Assembly Disqualification Act 1975 there shall be inserted at the appropriate place—

Welsh Comptroller and Auditor General.

THE WELSH DEVELOPMENT AGENCY ACT 1975

81. For paragraph 9 of Schedule 3 to the Welsh Development Agency Act 1975 there shall be substituted—

" 9.—(1) It shall be the duty of the Agency, as soon as possible after the end of each accounting year, to make a report dealing with the operations of the Agency during that year—

    (a) in pursuance of section 1 (3) (b) to (d) of this Act, to the Assembly and the Secretary of State;

    (b) in pursuance of section 1 (3) (e) or 12 of this Act, to the Secretary of State; and

    (c) in pursuance of any other provision of this Act, to the Assembly.

(2) It shall be the duty of the Secretary of State to lay before each House of Parliament a copy of each report received by him under this paragraph.

(3) The Welsh Assembly shall publish each report received by it under this paragraph."

THE DEVELOPMENT OF RURAL WALES ACT 1976

82.—(1) In subsection (1) (e) of section 3 of the Development of Rural Wales Act 1976, the words " to the Secretary of State " shall be omitted and for the words " a report " there shall be substituted the word " reports ".

(2) At the end of subsection (8) of that section there shall be added the words " and the Welsh Assembly shall publish every report made to it under that provision ".

83. For paragraph 17 of Schedule 1 to that Act there shall be substituted—

" 17.—(1) The reports to be made by the Board under section 3 (1) (e) of this Act are—

    (a) a report as to its functions relating to economic development, which shall be made to the Welsh Assembly and the Secretary of State; and

    (b) a report as to its remaining functions, which shall be made to the Welsh Assembly.

(2) A report made in accordance with sub-paragraph (1) (b) above shall set out—

    (a) any directions given to the Board under section 2 of this Act; and

    (b) a summary of any proposals submitted under section 3 (1) (b) of this Act."

THE HEALTH SERVICES ACT 1976

84. In section 14 (5) of the Health Services Act 1976, the references to the Secretary of State, in relation to functions exercisable by the Assembly, shall be construed as references to the Assembly.

THE PATENTS ACT 1977

85. Sections 55 to 59 of the Patents Act 1977 shall have effect as if references to a government department included references to the Assembly; and, in relation to any use of an invention by the Assembly or by any person authorised in writing by the Assembly, section 55 (4) of that Act shall have effect as if the words " with the approval of the Treasury " were omitted.

THE NATIONAL HEALTH SERVICE ACT 1977

86.—(1) The Secretary of State may give directions to the Assembly as to the exercise of any of its functions under sections 29 and 34 to 43 of, and paragraph 10 (1) of Schedule 5 to, the National Health Service Act 1977, and the Assembly shall give effect to any such directions.

(2) The power of the Secretary of State under this paragraph includes power to require functions to be conferred on him by or under regulations made by the Assembly.

87. In section 111 (1) of that Act, for paragraph (b) there shall be substituted—

" (b) any other authority or body—
  (i) whose members are appointed by Her Majesty, by any Minister of the Crown or government department or by the Welsh Assembly; or
  (ii) whose revenues consist wholly or mainly of money provided by Parliament or sums paid out of the Welsh Consolidated Fund ".

88.—(1) In section 119 of that Act, at the end of subsection (1) (d) there shall be inserted the words " or, if the investigation was conducted by the Health Service Commissioner for Wales, to the Welsh Assembly ".

(2) Subsections (3) and (4) of that section shall have effect as if they provided for reports of the Health Service Commissioner for Wales to be made to and published by the Assembly (instead of providing for them to be laid before each House of Parliament or made to the Secretary of State).

89. In paragraph 17 of Schedule 13 to that Act—
  (a) after the words " Minister of the Crown " there shall be inserted the words " or the Welsh Assembly "; and
  (b) for the words " Minister's opinion " there shall be substituted the words " opinion of the Minister or Assembly ".

The Inner Urban Areas Act 1978

90.—(1) Section 2 (4) (b) of the Inner Urban Areas Act 1978 shall have effect, in any case where—
  (a) the loan is made by a designated district authority in Wales; and
  (b) the Assembly is satisfied that it is not for the acquisition, construction or alteration of a building intended for use for industrial or commercial purposes,
as if the reference to the Secretary of State were a reference to the Assembly.

(2) Paragraphs 1 (3) (b) and 3 (3) (b) of the Schedule to that Act shall have effect, in relation to any area in Wales, as if the reference to the Secretary of State included a reference to the Assembly.

Reference

For a note on the significance of and on some of the provisions of this Schedule, see note on s. 9.

General Note

Para. 26. There is no s. 61 in the Parliamentary Commissioner Act 1967; it seems that the reference should be to s. 6 (1) (b) of that Act.

There is no " or those " in s. 6 (1) (b) of that Act; it seems that the reference should be to " or whose."

Para. 27. There is no reference in the Wales Act to a " Chief Executive of the Welsh Assembly." Those words were deleted from the Bill, and this paragraph should also have been deleted.

Section 80   SCHEDULE 12

Referendum

Date of Referendum

1. The referendum shall be held on such day, not less than six weeks after the making of the Order, as Her Majesty may by Order in Council appoint.

Persons eligible to vote

2. Those entitled to vote in the referendum shall be—
  (a) the persons who, at the date of the referendum, would be entitled to vote as electors at a parliamentary election in any constituency in Wales; and
  (b) peers who at that date would be entitled to vote as electors at a local government election in any electoral area in Wales.

Question to be asked and form of ballot paper

3. The question to be asked in the referendum and the front of the ballot paper to be used for that purpose shall be in the form set out in the Appendix to this Schedule.

Conduct of referendum

4. Subject to the following provisions of this Schedule, Her Majesty may by Order in Council make provision as to the conduct of the referendum and apply in relation to it, with such modifications or exceptions as may be specified in the Order, any provision of the Representation of the People Acts, any provision of the enactments relating to returning officers and any provision made under any enactment.

5. An Order in Council under this Schedule shall not charge any sum on the Consolidated Fund but may provide for the expenses of the returning officers to be defrayed as administrative expenses of the Secretary of State.

6. The functions which, in relation to a parliamentary election, are conferred on returning officers by any provision applied by an Order in Council under this Schedule shall in relation to the referendum be discharged by the persons who under section 41 of the Local Government Act 1972 are, or may discharge the functions of, returning officers at elections of councillors of districts.

7. The Secretary of State shall appoint a Chief Counting Officer, who shall appoint a counting officer for each county in Wales; and each counting officer shall conduct the counting of votes cast in the area for which he is appointed in accordance with any directions given to him by the Chief Counting Officer.

8. The counting officer for each area shall certify the number of ballot papers counted by him and the number of respective answers given by valid votes; and the Chief Counting Officer shall certify the total of the ballot papers and the respective answers for the whole of Wales.

9. The council of each county in Wales shall place the services of its officers at the disposal of the counting officer for the county; and if the council or the counting officer for a county so requests, the council of any district in the county shall place the services of its officers at the disposal of the county officer for the county.

10. Section 2 (1) of the Welsh Language Act 1967 (power to prescribe Welsh version) shall apply in relation to an Order in Council under this Schedule as if the Order were an enactment within the meaning of that Act.

Exclusion of legal proceedings

11. No court shall entertain any proceedings for questioning the numbers, as certified by the Chief Counting Officer or any counting officer, of any ballot papers counted or answers given in the referendum.

Orders in Council

12. No recommendation shall be made to Her Majesty in Council to make an Order under this Schedule until a draft of the Order has been laid before Parliament and approved by resolution of each House of Parliament.

APPENDIX

FORM OF BALLOT PAPER

Parliament has decided to consult the electorate in Wales on the question whether the Wales Act 1978 should be put into effect.

Mae'r Senedd wedi penderfynu ymgynghori ag etholwyr
Cymru ynglyn â ddylid gweithredu Deddf Cymru 1978.

DO YOU WANT THE PROVISIONS OF THE WALES ACT 1978
TO BE PUT INTO EFFECT?
A YDYCH AM I DDARPARIAETHAU DEDDF CYMRU 1978
GAEL EU GWEITHREDU?

Put a cross (X) in the appropriate box
Rhowch groes (X) yn y blwch cymwys

YES YDWYF	
NO NAC YDWYF	

Chronically Sick and Disabled Persons (Northern Ireland) Act 1978

(1978 c. 53)

ARRANGEMENT OF SECTIONS

An Act to make further provision with respect to the welfare of chronically sick and disabled persons in Northern Ireland; and for connected purposes.   [31st July 1978]

General Note

This Act makes further provision for the welfare of chronically sick and disabled persons in Northern Ireland.

S. 1 relates to information as to the need for, and existence of, social welfare services; s. 2 enumerates various kinds of social welfare provision available; s. 3 directs the Northern Ireland Housing Executive to have regard to the special needs of the chronically sick and disabled; s. 4 concerns access to, and facilities at, premises open to the public; ss. 5 and 6 relate to the provision of public sanitary conveniences; s. 7 directs the display of signs at buildings complying with ss. 4–6; s. 8 concerns access to, and facilities at, university and school buildings; s. 9 relates to the appointment of advisory committees; s. 10 deals with the co-option of chronically sick or disabled persons by committees of Health and Social Services Boards; s. 11 similarly relates to committees of district councils; s. 12 deals with the separation of younger from older patients; s. 13 concerns the dissemination of information as to accommodation of younger and older persons; s. 14 directs the issue of badges for display on motor vehicles used by disabled persons; s. 15 relates to information about special educational treatment for the deaf-blind; s. 16 does likewise for autistic and certain other children; s. 17 similarly relates to the provision of special educational treatment for dyslexic children; s. 18 empowers the Department of Health and Social Services for Northern Ireland to define certain expressions used in this Act; s. 19 provides for the enactment of secondary legislation; s. 20 is the interpretation section; s. 21 gives the short title, and states that the Act extends to Northern Ireland only.

The Act received the Royal Assent on July 31, 1978, and shall come into force on such day or days as the Secretary of State may by order appoint.

For parliamentary debates, see *Hansard*, H.C. Vol. 943, col. 1681; Vol. 944, col. 1959; Vol. 953, col. 2018; H.L. Vol. 395, cols. 10, 390 and 984.

Information as to need for and existence of social welfare services

1.—(1) The Department of Health and Social Services for Northern Ireland shall inform itself of the number of and, so far as reasonably practicable, the identity of persons who are blind, deaf or dumb, and other persons who are substantially handicapped by illness, injury or congenital deformity and whose handicap is of a permanent or lasting nature or are suffering from a mental disorder within the meaning of the Mental Health Act (Northern Ireland) 1961, and of the need for the making by that Department of arrangements for promoting the social welfare of such persons under Articles 4 (*b*) and 15 of the Health and Personal Social Services (Northern Ireland) Order 1972.

(2) The Department of Health and Social Services for Northern Ireland—

(*a*) shall cause to be published from time to time at such times and in such manner as that Department considers appropriate general information as to the services provided under such arrangements which are for the time being available under Articles 4 (*b*) and 15 of the Health and Personal Social Services (Northern Ireland) Order 1972; and

(*b*) shall ensure that any such person as aforesaid who uses any of those services is informed of any other services provided under the Health and Personal Social Services (Northern Ireland) Order 1972 and of services provided by other government departments, public bodies and voluntary organisations which in the opinion of the Department are relevant to his needs.

Provision of social welfare services

2. Where the Department of Health and Social Services for Northern Ireland is satisfied in the case of any person to whom section 1 above applies that it is necessary in order to meet the needs of that person for that Department to make arrangements under Articles 4 (*b*) and 15 of the Health and Personal Social Services (Northern Ireland) Order 1972 for all or any of the following matters namely—

(*a*) the provision of practical assistance for that person in his home;

(*b*) the provision for that person of, or assistance to that person in obtaining, wireless, television, library or similar recreational facilities;

(*c*) the provision for that person of lectures, games, outings or other recreational facilities outside his home or assistance to that person in taking advantage of educational facilities available to him;

(*d*) the provision for that person of facilities for, or assistance in, travelling to and from his home for the purpose of participating in, any services provided under arrangements made by that Department under the said Articles 4 (*b*) and 15 for promoting the social welfare of such persons or, with the approval of that Department, in any services provided otherwise than as aforesaid which are similar to services which could be provided under such arrangements;

(*e*) the provision of assistance for that person in arranging for the carrying out of any works of adaptation in his home or the provision of any additional facilities designed to secure his greater safety, comfort or convenience;

(*f*) facilitating the taking of holidays by that person, whether at holiday homes or otherwise and whether provided under arrangements made by that Department or otherwise;

(*g*) the provision of meals for that person whether in his home or elsewhere;

(*h*) the provision for that person of, or assistance to that person in obtaining, a telephone and any special equipment necessary to enable him to use a telephone,

then, that Department shall make those arrangements.

Duties of Housing Executive

3. The Northern Ireland Housing Executive when considering the needs of any district with respect to the provision of further housing accommodation shall have regard to the special needs of chronically sick and disabled persons; and any proposals for the provision of new housing shall distinguish any houses which the Executive proposes to provide which make special provision for the needs of those persons.

Access to and facilities at premises open to the public

4.—(1) Any person undertaking the provision of any building or premises to which the public are to be admitted, whether on payment or otherwise, shall, in the means of access both to and within the building or premises, and in the parking facilities and sanitary conveniences to be available (if any), make provision, in so far as it is in the circumstances both practicable and reasonable, for the needs of members of the public visiting the building or premises who are disabled.

(2) This section shall not apply to any building or premises intended for purposes mentioned in subsection (2) of section 8 of this Act or any such premises as are mentioned in subsection (3) of that section.

Provision of public sanitary conveniences

5.—(1) Where any district council undertakes the provision of a public sanitary convenience, it shall be the duty of the council, in doing so, to make provision, in so far as it is in the circumstances both practicable and reasonable, for the needs of disabled persons.

(2) Any district council which in any public sanitary convenience provided by it makes or has made provision for the needs of disabled persons shall take such steps as may be reasonable, by sign-posts or similar notices, to indicate the whereabouts of the convenience.

Provision of sanitary conveniences at certain premises open to the public

6. Any person upon whom a notice is served with respect to any premises under section 44 of the Public Health Acts Amendment Act 1907 (under which a district council may serve a notice requiring the provision of urinals or sanitary conveniences on certain premises) shall in complying with that notice make provision, in so far as it is in the circumstances both practicable and reasonable, for the needs of persons frequenting those premises who are disabled.

Signs at buildings complying with sections 4 to 6

7.—(1) Where any provision required by or under section 4, 5 or 6 of this Act is made at a building in compliance with that section, a notice or sign indicating that provision is made for the disabled shall be displayed outside the building or so as to be visible from outside it.

(2) This section applies to a sanitary convenience provided elsewhere than in a building, and not itself being a building, as it applies to a building.

Access to and facilities at university and school buildings

8.—(1) Any person undertaking the provision of a building intended for purposes mentioned in subsection (2) below or of premises mentioned in subsection (3) below shall, in the means of access both to and within the building or premises, and in the parking facilities and sanitary conveniences to be available (if any), make provision, in so far as it is in the circumstances both practicable and reasonable, for the needs of persons using the building or premises who are disabled.

(2) The purposes referred to in subsection (1) above are the purposes of any of the following: —

  (a) universities;

  (b) schools within the meaning of the Education and Libraries (Northern Ireland) Order 1972, colleges of education or other establishments for the training of teachers maintained in pursuance of Article 55 of that Order or in respect of which grants are paid under that Article and other institutions providing further education under Article 23 of that Order;

  (c) the Ulster College.

(3) The premises referred to in subsection (1) above are—

  (a) office premises and shop premises within the meaning of the Office and Shop Premises Act (Northern Ireland) 1966;

  (b) premises which are treated as such premises for the purposes of that Act;

  (c) factories within the meaning of the Factories Act (Northern Ireland) 1965,

being (in each case) premises in which persons are employed to work.

Advisory committees, etc.

9. Where an advisory committee is appointed under any statutory provision as defined by section 1 of the Interpretation Act (Northern Ireland) 1954, regard shall be had, in the appointment of persons to be members of that committee, to the desirability of the committee including one or more persons with experience of work among, and the special needs of, disabled persons and of the person or persons with that experience being or including a disabled person or persons.

Co-option of chronically sick or disabled persons by committees of Health and Social Services Board

10. Where a Health and Social Services Board appoints a committee or sub-committee of the Board and the members of the committee or sub-committee include or may include persons who are not members of the Board, then in considering the appointment to the committee or sub-committee of such persons regard shall be had, if the committee or sub-committee is concerned with matters in which the chronically sick or disabled have special needs, to the desirability of appointing to the committee or sub-committee persons with experience of work among and of the needs of the chronically sick and disabled, and of the person or persons with that experience being or including a chronically sick or disabled person or persons.

Co-option of chronically sick or disabled persons to committees of district council

11. Where a district council appoints a committee of the council under any statutory provision as defined by section 1 of the Interpretation Act (Northern Ireland) 1954, and the members of the committee include or may include persons who are not members of the council, then in considering the appointment to the committee of such persons regard shall be had, if the committee is concerned with matters in which the chronically sick or disabled have special needs, to the desirability of appointing to the committee persons with experience of work among and of the needs of the chronically sick and disabled, and of the person or persons with that experience being or including a chronically sick or disabled person or persons.

Separation of younger from older patients

12.—(1) The Department of Health and Social Services for Northern Ireland shall use its best endeavours to secure that, so far as practicable, in any hospital for which it is responsible a person who is suffering from a condition of chronic illness or disability and who—

(*a*) is in the hospital for the purpose of long-term care for that condition; or

(*b*) normally resides elsewhere but is being cared for in the hospital because—

(i) that condition is such as to preclude him from residing elsewhere without the assistance of some other person; and

(ii) such assistance is for the time being not available,

is not cared for in the hospital as an in-patient in any part of the hospital which is normally used wholly or mainly for the care of elderly persons, unless he is himself an elderly person.

(2) The Head of the Department of Health and Social Services for Northern Ireland shall in each year lay before the Northern Ireland Assembly a statement in such form as he considers appropriate of information as to any persons to whom subsection (1) of this section applies who, not being elderly persons, have been cared for in any hospital for which that Department is responsible in such a part of the hospital as is mentioned in that subsection.

(3) In this section " elderly person " means a person who is aged sixty-five or more or is suffering from the effects of premature ageing.

Information as to accommodation of younger and older persons

13. The Head of the Department of Health and Social Services for Northern Ireland shall in each year lay before the Northern Ireland Assembly a statement in such form as he considers appropriate of the number of persons under the age of sixty-five appearing to that Department to be persons to whom section 1 above applies for whom residential accommodation is from time to time provided, whether by that Department or in accordance with arrangements made under Article 36 of the Health and Personal Social Services (Northern Ireland) Order 1972 (being accommodation for persons in need within the meaning of Article 2 of that Order) at any premises in a part of those premises in which such accommodation is so provided for persons over that age.

Badges for display on motor vehicles used by disabled persons

14.—(1) There shall be a badge of a prescribed form to be issued by the Department of the Environment for Northern Ireland (in this section referred to as " the Department ") for motor vehicles driven by, or used for the carriage of, disabled persons; and—

(*a*) subject to the provisions of this section, the badge so issued for any vehicle or vehicles may be displayed on it or on any of them; and

(*b*) the Department may by regulations exempt vehicles displaying such badges from the requirements of orders, byelaws and regulations made, or having effect as if made, under section 19 or 90 of the Road Traffic Act (Northern Ireland) 1970.

(2) A badge may be issued to a disabled person of any prescribed description for one or more vehicles which he drives and, if so issued, may be displayed on it or any of them at times when he is the driver.

(3) In such cases as may be prescribed, a badge may be issued to a disabled person of any prescribed description for one or more vehicles used by him as a passenger and, if so issued, may be displayed on it or any of them at times when the vehicle is being used to carry him. A badge may be issued to the same person both under this subsection and under subsection (2) above.

(4) A badge may be issued to an institution concerned with the care of the disabled for any motor vehicle or, as the case may be, for each motor vehicle used by or on behalf of the institution to carry disabled persons of any prescribed description; and any badge so issued may be displayed on the vehicle for which it is issued at times when the vehicle is being so used.

(5) The Department shall maintain a register showing the holders of badges issued by it under this section, and the vehicle or vehicles for which each of the badges is held; and in the case of badges issued to disabled persons the register shall show whether they were, for any motor vehicle, issued under subsection (2) or under subsection (3) or both.

(6) A badge issued under this section shall remain the property of the Department, shall be issued for such period as may be prescribed, and shall be returned to the Department in such circumstances as may be prescribed.

(7) Anything which is under this section to be prescribed shall be prescribed by regulations made by the Department; and regulations so made may make provision—

(a) as to the cases in which the Department may refuse to issue badges, and as to the fee (if any) which the Department may charge for the issue or re-issue of a badge; and

(b) as to the continuing validity or effect of badges issued before the coming into force of this section in pursuance of any arrangements made by Health and Social Services Boards or the Department for the welfare of disabled persons; and

(c) as to any transitional matters, and in particular the application to badges issued under this section of orders, byelaws or regulations made, or having effect as if made, under the Road Traffic Act (Northern Ireland) 1970 before the coming into force of this section and operating with reference to any such badges as are referred to in paragraph (b) above.

(8) In this section " motor vehicle " has the same meaning as in section 190 (1) of the Road Traffic Act (Northern Ireland) 1970.

Special educational treatment for the deaf-blind

15.—Every Education and Library Board shall provide the Department of Education for Northern Ireland at such times as that Department may direct with information on the provision made by that Board of special educational facilities for children who suffer the dual handicap of blindness and deafness.

Special educational treatment for children suffering from autism, etc.

16.—(1) Every Education and Library Board shall provide the Department of Education for Northern Ireland at such times as that Department may direct with information on the provision made by that Board of special educational facilities for children who suffer from autism or other forms of early childhood psychosis.

(2) The arrangements made by an Education and Library Board for the special educational treatment of children suffering from autism and

other forms of early childhood psychosis shall, so far as is practicable, provide for the giving of such education in any grant-aided school within the meaning of the Education and Libraries (Northern Ireland) Order 1972.

Special educational treatment for children suffering from dyslexia

17.—(1) Every Education and Library Board shall provide the Department of Education for Northern Ireland at such times as that Department may direct with information on the provision made by that Board of special educational facilities for children who suffer from severe specific language learning disabilities.

(2) The arrangements made by an Education and Library Board for the special educational treatment of children suffering from severe specific language learning disabilities shall, so far as is practicable, provide for the giving of such education in any grant-aided school within the meaning of the Education and Libraries (Northern Ireland) Order 1972.

Power to define certain expressions

18. Where it appears to the Department of Health and Social Services for Northern Ireland to be necessary or expedient to do so for the proper operation of any provision of this Act that Department may by regulations make provision as to the interpretation for the purposes of that provision of any of the following expressions appearing therein, that is to say " chronically sick ", " chronic illness ", " disabled " and " disability ".

Regulations and orders

19.—(1) Regulations and orders made under this Act shall be statutory rules for the purposes of the Statutory Rules Act (Northern Ireland) 1958.

(2) Regulations made under this Act shall be subject to negative resolution.

Interpretation

20. The Interpretation Act (Northern Ireland) 1954 shall apply to this Act as it applies to a measure of the Northern Ireland Assembly.

Short title and commencement

21.—(1) This Act may be cited as the Chronically Sick and Disabled Persons (Northern Ireland) Act 1978.

(2) This Act shall come into operation on such day or days as the Secretary of State may by order appoint.

(3) This Act extends to Northern Ireland only.

Dividends Act 1978

(1978 c. 54)

An Act to provide for section 10 of the Counter-Inflation Act 1973 to continue in force until the end of July 1979.

[31st July 1978]

General Note

This Act extends the duration of s. 10 of the Counter-Inflation Act 1973 (c. 9).

S. 1 provides that s. 10 of the Counter-Inflation Act 1973, which enables the Treasury to restrict the declaration and payment of ordinary dividends by companies at any time when that section is in force, shall be extended in duration until July 31, 1979, and shall then expire; s. 2 contains the short title, and extends the Act to Northern Ireland.

The Act received the Royal Assent on July 31, 1978, and came into force on that date.

For parliamentary debates, see *Hansard*, H.C. Vol. 954, cols. 1035, 1377, 1802, 2010; H.L. Vol. 395, cols. 1072, 1127.

Continuation in force of 1973 s. 10

1.—(1) Section 10 of the Counter-Inflation Act 1973 (which enables the Treasury to restrict the declaration or payment of ordinary dividends by companies at any time when that section is in force and which will not be in force after 31st July 1978 unless its duration is extended) shall continue in force until the end of July 1979 and shall then expire.

(2) Accordingly in paragraph 2 of Schedule 2 to the Price Commission Act 1977 (which among other things provides for the said section 10 to cease to be in force at the expiration of periods mentioned in that paragraph) the words from " and section 10 " to " dividends) " and the word " severally " are hereby repealed.

Short title and extent

2.—(1) This Act may be cited as the Dividends Act 1978.

(2) This Act extends to Northern Ireland.

Transport Act 1978

(1978 c. 55)

ARRANGEMENT OF SECTIONS

An Act to provide for the planning and development of public
passenger transport services in the counties of England and
Wales; to make further provision about public service vehicle
licensing, the regulation of goods vehicles and parking and
about inland waterway transport; to make amendments about
British Rail and railways, and about Freightliners Limited and
the finances of the National Freight Corporation and other
transport bodies in the public sector; and for purposes connected with those matters.　　　　　　　　　　[2nd August 1978]

General Note

This Act governs public passenger transport services in England and Wales, and further regulates certain public sector transport bodies.

S. 1 sets out new passenger transport policies to be implemented in county areas; s. 2 requires the publication of a five-year plan for each non-metropolitan county council's public transport system; s. 3 relates to agreements with transport operators; s. 4 requires details of concessionary fare schemes to be included in such plans; s. 5 is concerned with the authorisation of community bus services; s. 6 governs car-sharing for social and other purposes; s. 7 amends the law relating to road service licences and permits; s. 8 amends the law governing lorries; s. 9 modifies drivers' hours as a result of European Community rules; s. 10 affects bicycles; s. 11 states the duty of the British Railways Board; s. 12 has to do with British Rail's public service obligations; s. 13 arranges for the transfer of the controlling interest in Freightliners Limited from the National Freight Corporation to the British Railways Board; s. 14 amends the Railways Act 1974 (c. 48), s. 8; s. 15 directs the reduction of the capital debt of the National Freight Corporation; s. 16 permits the making of capital grants to the Corporation; s. 17 provides for the funding of pension obligations; s. 18 makes supplementary provisions to s. 17; s. 19 directs travel concessions for transferred employees; s. 20 contains amendments to transport supplementary grants; s. 21 makes general financial provisions; s. 22 concerns commencement, interpretation and repeals; s. 23 gives the short title, and states that the Act does not extend to Northern Ireland except for ss. 13, 15–19, and 21–23, but does not extend to Scotland with the exception of ss. 1–4, and 20.

The Act received the Royal Assent on August 2, 1978, and ss. 15, 17, 18, 21, 23, 24 (part) and Sched. 4 (part) came into force on August 4, 1978 (S.I. 1978 No. 1150 (C. 32)).

Ss. 1–4, 7, 8 (part), 10–14, 16, 22, 24 (part), and Scheds. 1, 2 (part) and 4 (part) came into force on September 1, 1978 (S.I. 1978 No. 1187 (C. 32)); ss. 5, 6, 8 (part), 9, 24 (part) and Scheds. 2 (part), 3 and 4 (part) came into force on November 1, 1978 (S.I. 1978 No. 1187 (C. 32)); ss. 19 and 20 came into force on October 1, 1978 (S.I. 1978 No. 1289 (C. 34)).

For parliamentary debates, see *Hansard*, H.C. Vol. 941, col. 496; Vol. 942, col. 691; Vol. 950, col. 603; H.L. Vol. 392, cols. 648, 1556; Vol. 395, col. 352.

County transport planning (England and Wales)

Passenger transport policies in county areas

1.—(1) In each non-metropolitan county of England and Wales, it shall be the duty—

(a) of the county council, acting in consultation with public passenger transport service operators and district councils within the county—

(i) to develop policies which will promote the provision of a co-ordinated and efficient system of public passenger transport to meet the county's needs, and

(ii) for that purpose to take such steps as the council think appropriate for promoting the co-ordination, amalgamation and re-organisation of road passenger transport undertakings in the county;

(b) of each of the district councils in the county who provide any public passenger transport service to operate the service in accordance with policies developed by the county council as mentioned in paragraph (a) above; and

(c) of public passenger transport service operators, and the county and district councils—

(i) to co-operate with one another in the exercise and performance of their respective functions for the purpose of co-ordinating public passenger transport services within the county, and

(ii) to afford to one another such information as may be reasonably required for that purpose.

(2) In this section and sections 2 and 4 below, " public passenger transport services " means all those services (whether publicly or privately operated) on which members of the public rely for getting from place to place, when not relying on private facilities of their own, including school transport but not—

(a) services provided in accordance with permits under the Minibus Act 1977 (carriage of passengers by bodies concerned with education, social welfare etc.); or

(b) excursions or tours within the meaning of the 1968 Act.

(3) For the purpose of such co-operation as is referred to in subsection (1) (c) above, all those mentioned in that subsection shall have power to enter into such arrangements with one another with respect to the exercise and performance of their respective functions on such terms as may appear to them to be expedient.

(4) Those who provide public passenger transport services may under subsection (3) enter into arrangements between themselves for the establishment under the Companies Acts of companies controlled (jointly or severally) by the parties to the arrangements and for—

(a) the transfer of assets to such companies; and

(b) facilitating the voluntary transfer of employees.

(5) The council of a non-metropolitan county or non-metropolitan district may make grants towards any costs incurred by persons carrying on public passenger transport undertakings wholly or partly in the county or district, as the case may be, and may also make grants—

(a) to persons providing community bus services; and

(b) in cases where local authorities and traffic commissioners have consented, under paragraph 5 of Schedule 12 to the 1960 Act, to the advertisement of facilities as being provided under a social car scheme, to persons arranging those facilities.

(6) Where, in carrying out their duty under subsection (1) (b) above, a district council incur expenditure which they would not otherwise have incurred or receive less revenue than they would otherwise have done, the district council may, by notice to the county council, require the county council to reimburse the amount of that expenditure or of that reduction in revenue.

(7) If any amount which, in accordance with the notice under subsection (6) above, a county council are required to reimburse to a district council is not determined by agreement between these councils within 6 months of the receipt of the notice or such longer period as may be agreed between them, the amount shall be determined by an arbitrator appointed either by agreement between those councils or, in default of such agreement, by the President of the Chartered Institute of Public Finance and Accountancy.

County public transport plans

2.—(1) Every non-metropolitan county council shall—

(a) not later than 31st March 1979, prepare and publish a public passenger transport plan for the succeeding period of 5 years; and

(b) revise and re-publish the plan every 12 months (which means not later than 31st March in each year after 1979), relating its contents always to the next 5 years after re-publication.

(2) The plan shall contain—

(a) a review of the county's needs, and the needs of communities comprised in it, in respect of public passenger transport services, and the extent to which those needs are met by existing services (this review to be accompanied by an account of the criteria applied to determine need);

(b) a description of—

(i) the council's policies and objectives for public passenger transport, and the services and facilities they consider to be needed by the county; and

(ii) the measures proposed for securing them in the short, and also in the longer, term;

(c) estimates of the financial resources required for the realisation of those policies and objectives, with proposals for obtaining such resources; and

(d) an account of how far forecasts in earlier plans have been, and are being, realised as regards the availability and use of such resources.

(3) When preparing or revising the plan, and when considering from time to time the way in which they are to discharge their responsibilities under section 1 above, the council shall enter into consultations with—

(a) public passenger transport service operators in the county, or their representatives;

(b) district councils in the county; and

(c) the following, if they or their areas may be affected by the policies described in the plan—

(i) other county councils,

(ii) the Greater London Council, and

(iii) joint planning boards set up under section 1 of the Town and Country Planning Act 1971.

(4) To all those mentioned in paragraphs (a) to (c) of subsection (3), and also to—

(a) the county's parish and (in Wales) community councils; and

(b) trade unions, transport user organisations and others appearing to the county council to be especially concerned with public passenger transport matters,

there shall be afforded an opportunity of commenting on a preliminary draft of the plan, and of making representations with respect to its contents.

(5) Particulars shall be given in the plan of the county council's consultations entered into in compliance with subsection (3) and of the consideration which has been given to views expressed in the consultations.

(6) When the plan or revised plan has been published, the county council shall cause it to be made available for inspection (at all reasonable hours)—

(a) at the council offices; and

(b) at the offices of each of the district councils in the county; and

(c) at such other places as are considered suitable, having regard to the convenience of members of the public.

(7) The council shall give notice, by such means as they think expedient for bringing it to the attention of the public, about where the plans can be inspected, and as to the way in which copies of the plan (and if practicable, parts of it) can be purchased or otherwise obtained.

Agreements with operators

3.—(1) A non-metropolitan county council shall from time to time, with a view to implementation of their public passenger transport plan, enter into agreements with persons carrying on public passenger transport undertakings wholly or partly in the county for the provision or retention and financing of services and facilities which are required by the plan but would not, apart from such agreements, be available.

(2) The council may enter into similar agreements with persons within section 1 (5) (*a*) and (*b*) above.

(3) Agreements under subsection (1) above shall be made so as to remain in force for a period of 3 years, except in cases where, having regard to the nature of the services and facilities to be provided, a longer or shorter period is determined by the parties to be expedient.

(4) Whenever the public passenger transport plan is published or re-published, it shall include particulars of such agreements made by the council as are referred to in subsections (1) and (2) above and are then in force or to be in force during the period of 12 months immediately following.

(5) When preparing or revising their plan and deciding whether any, and if so what, agreements should be made under this section, the council may require any of the persons referred to in section 1 (5) above to furnish such information concerning their services (including the cost of providing them) as is reasonably required by the council for those purposes; and—

(*a*) the information shall be formulated in such a manner as may be specified in the council's requirement; and

(*b*) the council shall, when framing the requirement, have regard to any directions given by the Secretary of State to county councils about the form and content of the information which ought to be obtained by them from persons qualifying for grant under section 1 (5).

(6) Any requirement under subsection (5) above shall be complied with by the persons to whom it is addressed, subject to the council giving, and complying with, such written undertakings of confidentiality as may be requested by those persons as a condition of the information being furnished; but nothing in subsection (4) or (5) above requires or authorises the council to include anything in their plan whose disclosure may adversely affect the business interests or commercial security of any person.

Concessionary fare schemes

4.—(1) All those county councils who have under this Act to prepare and publish an annual public passenger transport plan shall include in the plan, whenever it is published or re-published, the following matters relating to travel concession schemes (meaning schemes for the reduction or waiver of fares or charges on public passenger transport services in favour of special categories of persons).

(2) The matters to be included in the plan are—

(*a*) an account of what (if any) travel concession schemes are operative in the county or planned for early introduction, being schemes which are wholly or partly financed, or the subject of financial contribution, by the council themselves or by any of the district councils in the county;

(*b*) the nature and extent of the concessions available under those schemes;

(*c*) proposals for introducing new travel concession schemes such as are mentioned in paragraph (*a*) above, or for extending or improving existing schemes; and

(*d*) the reasons why (if it be the case) in any part of the county either no such schemes are operative or existing schemes are inadequate.

Public service vehicle licensing

Community bus services

5.—(1) Subject to the provisions of this section, the traffic commissioners for any traffic area may grant—

(*a*) a road service licence under Part III of the 1960 Act, authorising the use of a vehicle as a stage carriage or an express carriage; or

(*b*) a permit under section 30 of the 1968 Act, authorising the use of a vehicle as a stage carriage,

in either case so as to provide a community bus service (to be specified in the licence or permit) using volunteer drivers.

(2) The vehicles to be so used by virtue of this section are those, and those only, adapted to carry at least 8 and at most 16 passengers.

(3) A community bus service may extend to the provision of excursions and tours as defined by section 159 of the 1968 Act.

(4) The commissioners shall not by virtue of this section grant a licence or permit unless they are satisfied that the applicants for it—

(*a*) are a body of persons (whether corporate or unincorporate) who in making the application are concerned for the social and welfare needs of one or more communities; and

(*b*) propose to provide the bus service without profit either to themselves or to anyone else;

and this, in the case of an application for a permit under section 30, is in addition to the requirement in subsection (2) of that section that the traffic commissioners must, before granting the permit, be satisfied that there are no other transport facilities available to meet the reasonable needs of the proposed route.

(5) In the case of a vehicle used in providing a community bus service, there shall be no requirement under section 127 of the 1960 Act for any person to be the holder of a public service vehicle licence authorising that use; and at any time when a vehicle is so used, the person driving it need not be the holder of a public service vehicle driver's licence under section 144 of that Act.

(6) But at any such time—

(*a*) the driver must be a volunteer and, if not the holder of a public service vehicle driver's licence, must fulfil such conditions as may be prescribed for drivers of community buses;

(*b*) the vehicle must (unless there is a public service vehicle licence in force in respect of it) fulfil such conditions as may be prescribed with respect to fitness for use as a community bus; and

(*c*) there must be displayed on the vehicle such disc or other document issued by the traffic commissioners as may be prescribed for a vehicle used as a community bus;

and compliance with paragraphs (*a*) to (*c*) of this subsection is a condition of the use of the vehicle being treated as authorised by the road service licence or section 30 permit.

(7) For the purposes of subsection (6) (*a*) above, " volunteer " means that the driver is not paid for driving the vehicle on the particular journey, disregarding—

(*a*) any payment of reasonable expenses incurred by him in making himself available to drive; and

(*b*) any payment representing earnings lost as a result of making himself available to drive in exceptional circumstances.

(8) The traffic commissioners may by virtue of this section grant a licence or permit for a community bus service to be provided wholly or partly in Greater London and the service shall not be regarded as a

London bus service within section 23 of the Transport (London) Act 1969 (which provides exclusivity for the London Transport Executive); but the commissioners—

(a) before granting or renewing such a licence or permit, shall satisfy themselves that the application for the grant or renewal is approved by that Executive; and

(b) before varying the conditions attached to such a licence or permit, shall consult the Executive about the proposed variation.

(9) This section and Part III of the 1960 Act shall be construed and have effect as if this section were contained in that Part of that Act.

(10) In section 44 of the 1972 Act (requirement of M.O.T. test certificate), at the end of subsection (4) (exclusion of public service vehicles) there shall be inserted—

" but shall apply (except in prescribed cases) to a vehicle which is used in providing a community bus service under section 5 of the Transport Act 1978, if no public service vehicle licence is in force in respect of the vehicle.".

Use of community bus for contract work

6.—(1) A road service licence or section 30 permit authorising the provision of a community bus service may be granted so as to authorise the use of the community bus as a contract carriage, subject to such restrictions (if any) as the traffic commissioners think fit to impose.

(2) " The community bus " means any vehicle (being adapted to carry at least 8 and at most 16 passengers) which, whether or not belonging to the holders of the applicable road service licence or permit, is used on a regular basis for the purposes of the service.

(3) The licence or permit shall not be granted with an authorisation under subsection (1) unless the commissioners are satisfied that it is reasonable in all the circumstances with a view to financial support of the service.

(4) Section 5 (5) and (6) of this Act apply to any use of the community bus as a contract carriage in the same way as they apply to any other use of it.

(5) This section and Part III of the 1960 Act shall be construed and have effect as if this section were contained in that Part of that Act.

Car-sharing for social and other purposes

7.—(1) For Part II of Schedule 12 to the 1960 Act (which regulates the use of smaller vehicles carrying passengers at separate fares) there shall be substituted the Part II set out in Schedule 1 to this Act (which consists of new or altered provisions as to the number of passengers carried, notices and advertisement, arrangements by local authorities for social purposes, etc.).

(2) In Part V of Schedule 12, at the end of paragraph 13 (advertisements to be disregarded for certain purposes of the Schedule), there shall be added " or

(c) a notice displayed or announcement made in or at any place of work with regard to journeys to be made to or from that place by people who work there, or

(d) a notice displayed or announcement made by a club or other voluntary association which—

(i) relates only to journeys arranged incidentally in connection with activities of the club or association (but they must not be activities directed to the provision of road transport facilities, whether for members of the club or association, or for others), and

(ii) is displayed or made in premises occupied or used by the club or association or contained in any periodical issued by it ".

(3) At any time when a vehicle would, apart from—

    (a) section 118 of the 1960 Act (exemption from licensing system of vehicles adapted to carry no more than 7 passengers); or

    (b) section 1 (1) of the Minibus Act 1977 (corresponding exemption for 8 to 16-seaters used by educational and other bodies),

be a public service vehicle, it shall continue to be treated as such for the purpose only of provisions contained in a local Act, in section 270 or 271 of and Schedule 5 to the Burgh Police (Scotland) Act 1892 or in Part II of the Local Government (Miscellaneous Provisions) Act 1976, which regulate the use of private hire vehicles provided for hire with the services of a driver for the purpose of carrying passengers and exclude public service vehicles from the scope of that regulation.

Road service licences and permits

8.—(1) The provisions of Part III of the 1960 Act and of the 1968 Act specified in Schedule 2 to this Act (being provisions about grant, refusal and variation of road service licences and permits in lieu of road service licences; duration of licences; attachment of conditions to licences and permits; procedure of traffic commissioners and related matters) shall be amended as shown in that Schedule.

(2) But the amendments of section 135 of the 1960 Act (criteria for grant etc. of road service licences and attachment of conditions) do not operate in relation to—

    (a) an application to traffic commissioners for, or for the backing of, a road service licence, or for the variation of the conditions attached to such a licence, if the application is made before those amendments come into force; or

    (b) a proposal by traffic commissioners to vary the conditions attached to a road service licence (otherwise than on an application falling within paragraph (a) above) if notice of the proposal is given before those amendments come into force; or

    (c) any appeal arising out of an application or proposal in relation to which, by virtue of paragraph (a) or paragraph (b) above, those amendments do not operate.

Road traffic regulation

Lorries

9.—(1) Sections 56 to 58, 82, 83 and 160 of, and Schedule 4 to, the 1972 Act and sections 1, 2 and 7 of the Road Traffic (Foreign Vehicles) Act 1972 shall be amended as shown in Schedule 3 to this Act (the amendments being to extend powers of inspection and control of vehicles by means of spot checks for mechanical defect or overload and restrictions on further use of a vehicle found in breach of the relevant Acts and regulations).

(2) In section 45 of the 1972 Act (regulations for checking condition of goods vehicles, determining plated weights, etc.), in subsection (6) (scope of regulation-making power), the following shall be added at the end of paragraph (a)—

" and

    (iii) require any such vehicle to be submitted for examination or re-examination for any purpose of plating or certification ".

Drivers' hours (EEC Rules)

10. In section 96 of the 1968 Act (restrictions on drivers' hours), after subsection (11A) (added by the European Communities Act 1972, with a view to penalising contraventions of the applicable Community rules), there shall be inserted—

" (11B) But a person shall not be liable to be convicted under subsection (11A) if—

(a) he proves the matters specified in paragraph (i) of subsection (11); or

(b) being charged as the offender's employer or a person to whose orders the offender was subject, he proves the matters specified in paragraph (ii) of that subsection ".

Control of off-street parking

11.—(1) With a view to providing further means of regulating traffic in urban areas, Her Majesty may by Order in Council, provide for enabling the operation of public off-street parking places to be regulated—

(a) in English and Welsh counties, by the county council; and

(b) in Scottish regions and islands areas, by the regional or islands council.

(2) An Order in Council under this section may make any such provision for the remainder of England and Wales, or for Scotland as the case may be, as is made for Greater London by section 36 of, and Schedule 5 to, the Transport (London) Act 1969 and shall be so framed as to conform with the 1969 provisions as respects all matters there dealt with, subject only to the modifications permitted or required by the following subsection and other minor and incidental modifications.

(3) The modifications referred to above are that the Order—

(a) shall provide for controlled areas to be so designated that they comprise only premises to which there is no road access otherwise than (directly or indirectly) from one or more urban roads;

(b) may in relation to Scotland substitute the regional or islands council for local authorities (which in the 1969 provisions are London borough councils and in the corresponding provisions to be made under this section for England and Wales are district councils);

(c) may take account of the repeal, amendment or replacement since 1969 of enactments then in force and also take account of Scottish legislation corresponding to legislation for England and Wales; and

(d) may include, in place of references and requirements which are apposite only for London, corresponding references and requirements apposite for other areas of Great Britain.

(4) Any such Order shall also require councils—

(a) to consult organisations representative of the disabled before deciding to propose the designation of a controlled area under the Order; and

(b) if representations are received from such organisations about the proposal, to send to the Secretary of State (together with copies of representations received from other organisations consulted) a statement of how parking requirements of the disabled arising from implementation of the proposal are met by existing facilities or, if in the opinion of the council they are not already so met, how it is intended to meet them.

(5) In this section—

(a) " public off-street parking place " means a place, whether above or below the ground and whether or not consisting of or including buildings, where parking space for motor vehicles off the highway is made available to the public for payment;

(*b*) the reference to the operation of such a parking place is to making such parking space at a parking place so available;

(*c*) " urban road " means a road which—

(i) is a restricted road for the purposes of section 71 of the Road Traffic Regulation Act 1967 (30 m.p.h. speed limit), or

(ii) is subject to an order under section 74 of that Act imposing a speed limit of not more than 40 'm.p.h.; and

(*d*) " the 1969 provisions " means section 36 of, and Schedule 5 to, the Transport (London) Act 1969.

(6) An Order in Council made under this section may be varied or revoked by a subsequent Order so made, and shall be subject to annulment by resolution of either House of Parliament.

Bicycles

12. The powers of any authority under the Road Traffic Regulation Act 1967 to provide parking places shall extend to providing, in roads and elsewhere, stands and racks for bicycles.

Waterway transport and railways

National policy for inland waterway transport

13. It shall be the duty of the Secretary of State to promote a national policy for the use of inland waterways for commercial transport.

British Rail public service obligations

14.—(1) In section 3 (4) of the Railways Act 1974 (financial limit governing Secretary of State's power to impose public service obligations on British Rail), after the words " shall not " there shall be inserted " for periods up to the end of 1978 ".

(2) The Secretary of State's power of giving directions under section 3 (1) of the Act shall be so exercised that the aggregate amount of any compensation payable under the relevant transport regulations of the European Communities in respect of all obligations imposed by directions for the time being in force under that subsection shall not, for periods after the end of 1978, exceed £1,750 million or such greater sum not exceeding £3,000 million as may be specified by Order in Council.

(3) Her Majesty shall not be recommended to make such an Order unless a draft of it has been approved by resolution of the House of Commons.

(4) " The relevant transport regulations " means the same as in the Railways Act 1974.

Transfer of controlling interest in Freightliners Limited

15.—(1) On the appointed day there shall be transferred to, and vested in, the British Railways Board all those securities (within the meaning of the 1968 Act) of Freightliners Limited which immediately before that day are vested in the National Freight Corporation.

(2) On that day—

(*a*) any liabilities of N.F.C. under guarantees given by them in respect of obligations of Freightliners Limited shall be transferred to, and become liabilities of, that Board; and

(*b*) the rights and liabilities of N.F.C. under contracts of employment with persons employed by them wholly or mainly in connection with the undertaking of Freightliners Limited shall be transferred to, and become rights and liabilities of, the Board.

(3) The following provisions of the 1968 Act—

(a) section 135 (1) (regulations as to compensation of employees); and

(b) Schedule 4 (supplementary provisions about transfers of property etc.),

and also any regulations made under section 135 (1) of the 1968 Act before the coming into force of this section, apply as if the transfers effected by subsections (1) and (2) above were transfers under section 8 (4) of that Act (the appointed day counting as the " first material date " for the purposes of the British Transport (Compensation to Employees) Regulations 1970, instead of the date shown in the second column of Schedule 1 to the Regulations).

(4) Section 136 (2) and (4) of the 1968 Act (transfers in connection with pension schemes and preservation of pension rights) apply in the same way; and for the purposes of section 136 (4) (c), Freightliners Limited is to be treated (despite section 51 (5) of that Act, which made it a joint subsidiary both of the British Railways Board and N.F.C.) as having become a subsidiary of the British Railways Board only on the appointed day.

(5) The 1968 Act shall be amended as follows—

(a) in section 7 (4) (b) (restriction on alteration of proportion of interests in Freightliners Limited by means of a scheme), for the words from the beginning to " entitled in " substitute " for transferring any interest in securities of ";

(b) in section 42 (3) (power of Secretary of State to vary amount of commencing capital debt of British Railways Board), for the words " specified in subsection (2) (b) of this section " onwards substitute " of the commencing capital debt of the Board as determined by or under any enactment for the time being in force, where that appears to him expedient to take account of any transfer of property, rights or liabilities under section 7 (5) or (6) or 8 (4) of this Act "; and

(c) in paragraph 3 of Schedule 2 (power of Secretary of State to vary commencing capital debt of N.F.C. etc.), for the words from " where that appears " to " of this Act; or " substitute " or, in the case of the Freight Corporation, its commencing capital debt as determined by or under any enactment for the time being in force, where that appears to him expedient to take account ".

(6) It shall be within the powers of the British Railways Board—

(a) where it appears to them expedient with a view only to achieving the more productive use of road vehicles predominantly used for the carriage of containers which have been or are to be carried by rail, to use such vehicles for any carriage of containers; and

(b) where they have entered into a contract for the carriage of containers or goods in containers (with or without provisions in the contract specifying whether the carriage is to be by road or by rail), and the contract is to be performed predominantly by rail carriage, to use any road vehicles in partial discharge of their obligations under the contract;

and " containers " means high capacity containers of a kind capable of being carried by freightliner rail vehicles.

(7) The annual report made by the Board under section 4 of the Railways Act 1974 shall include, in addition to the matters there mentioned, such information about the Board's exercise of their powers under subsection (6) above as may be called for by the Secretary of State.

(8) In this section "the appointed day" means the day appointed under section 24 (1) below for the coming into force of this section.

Amendment of Railways Act 1974, s. 8

16. Section 8 of the Railways Act 1974 (grants to assist provision of facilities for freight haulage by rail) shall be amended as follows—

(*a*) in subsection (1), after "for or in connection with" insert "the carriage of freight by rail or";

(*b*) in subsection (2), after "include" insert "rolling stock", and before "loading or unloading" insert "carriage".

National Freight Corporation (finance)

Reduction of capital debt

17.—(1) On the day appointed under section 24 (1) below for the coming into force of this section, there shall be extinguished so much of the liability of the National Freight Corporation on that day in respect of—

(*a*) the commencing capital debt of the Corporation under section 3 (2) of, and Schedule 2 to, the 1968 Act; and

(*b*) the principal of money borrowed by the Corporation from the Secretary of State under section 19 of the 1962 Act as applied by section 3 (1) (*b*) of the 1968 Act,

as is necessary to reduce that liability to £100 million.

(2) Of the amount in respect of which the Corporation's liability is extinguished by subsection (1) above, such part as the Secretary of State may, with the approval of the Treasury, direct shall be treated as reducing the commencing capital debt of the Corporation and the remainder shall be treated as reducing the principal of money borrowed as mentioned above.

(3) The assets of the National Loans Fund shall accordingly be reduced by the amount in respect of which the Corporation's liability is so extinguished.

Capital grants

18.—(1) The Secretary of State may, with the approval of the Treasury, out of money provided by Parliament make grants to the National Freight Corporation in respect of any expenditure of a capital nature incurred or to be incurred during the period 1st July 1978 to 31st December 1981 by National Carriers Limited or any of its subsidiaries.

(2) Any grants under this section shall be made on such terms and conditions as the Secretary of State may with the approval of the Treasury determine; and the amounts of the grants shall be determined so that—

(*a*) the amount for the year 1980 is less than for the year 1979, and the amount for the year 1981 is less than that for the year 1980; and

(*b*) the aggregate amount of the grants does not exceed £15 million.

Funding of pension obligations

19.—(1) The National Freight Corporation shall, subject to the following provisions of this section, provide the money for funding such of the obligations mentioned in subsection (2) below as may be prescribed, in so far as those obligations have not been funded before the appointed day.

(2) The obligations mentioned in subsection (1) are obligations of N.F.C., N.C.L. and Freightliners Limited which are owed, in connection with any prescribed relevant pension scheme in force on the appointed day, to or in respect of persons who are or have been employed by any of those bodies.

(3) But the obligations which may be prescribed under subsection (1) above shall not include—

(a) any obligation imposed on N.F.C., N.C.L. or Freightliners Limited and resulting from an amendment of a pension scheme made after 1st April 1975, other than an amendment made by virtue of section 74 of the 1962 Act; or

(b) any obligation of N.F.C., N.C.L. or Freightliners Limited arising after that date to pay increases of pensions in excess of those payable, in the case of official pensions, under the Pensions (Increase) Act 1971 and section 59 of the Social Security Pensions Act 1975.

(4) The Secretary of State may by order made with the consent of the Treasury prescribe—

(a) the aggregate amount to be provided by the Corporation for funding the prescribed obligations in any prescribed period; and

(b) the manner in which the prescribed aggregate amount is to be apportioned between pension schemes.

(5) The amounts so apportioned shall be debts of N.F.C. to the persons administering the pension scheme in question; and the Secretary of State may by order made with the consent of the Treasury prescribe—

(a) the instalments by which and the dates on which the debts are to be paid off; and

(b) the rate at which and dates on which interest on the debts is to be paid.

(6) An order made under subsection (5) (a) above may make different provisions for different debts; but no order shall be made under that paragraph unless a draft of the order has been laid before, and approved by, the House of Commons.

(7) The Secretary of State shall reimburse the Corporation in respect of any sums paid under this section in respect of the principal of or interest on the debts due by virtue of this section, and any sums required by him for that purpose shall be paid out of money provided by Parliament.

Provisions supplementary to s. 19

20.—(1) In section 19 above and this section—

" the appointed day " means a day appointed for the purposes of that section and this section by an order made by the Secretary of State;

" prescribed " means prescribed by an order made by the Secretary of State with the consent of the Treasury;

" pension " and " pension scheme " mean the same as in the 1962 Act and " relevant pension scheme " means—

(a) a pension scheme in relation to which rights,

liabilities and functions were conferred or imposed on N.F.C., N.C.L., or Freightliners Limited by an instrument made under or by virtue of any provision of the 1962 Act; or

(b) a pension scheme established by N.F.C., N.C.L., or Freightliners Limited for the provision of pensions for or in respect of persons who are or have at any time been employed by any of those bodies;

and a reference to N.C.L. or to Freightliners Limited shall be read as including a reference to its subsidiaries.

(2) Where at any time, whether before or after the appointed day, N.F.C., N.C.L., or Freightliners Limited make payments in respect of pensions payable under a prescribed pension scheme or increases in such pensions, the body making the payments shall be treated for the purposes of section 19 as being under an obligation at that time to make those payments.

(3) The funding of an obligation under section 19 shall not discharge the obligation so far as it is one to pay pensions or increases of pensions under the relevant pension scheme owed to the person to whom pensions or increases of pensions are or may become payable under the scheme or is an obligation to secure the payment of those pensions or increases.

(4) If the persons administering a prescribed pension scheme have no power to amend the scheme apart from this subsection, they may amend it by instrument in writing for the purpose of bringing it into conformity with any provision of section 19 or this section, or any order under either section; and the power of amending any such scheme apart from this subsection may for that purpose be exercised without regard to any limitations on the exercise of the power and without compliance with any procedural provisions applicable to its exercise.

(5) Where it appears to N.F.C. that there is a doubt as to who are the persons administering a pension scheme, N.F.C. may by instrument in writing specify the persons who are to be treated for the purposes of section 19 and this section as the persons administering it.

(6) Where any obligation of N.F.C., N.C.L. or Freightliners Limited is funded under section 19, or any obligation of the British Railways Board is funded under section 5 of the Railways Act 1974—

(a) any right of N.F.C., N.C.L. or Freightliners Limited to be indemnified by B.R. in respect of the funded obligation or part of it; or

(b) any right of B.R. to be so indemnified by N.F.C., N.C.L. or Freightliners Limited,

shall be extinguished in proportion to the funding of the obligation.

(7) For the purposes of section 19 (3) above and section 5 (2) of the Railways Act 1974 (equivalent provision as to British Rail pension schemes), a scheme shall not be taken to be amended by virtue only of the transfer effected by section 15 (1) above or by any provision made by virtue of section 15 (3) in consequence of the transfer.

(8) Any power to make an order conferred by section 19 or this section shall be exercisable by statutory instrument; and any such instrument (other than one containing an order made by virtue of section 19 (5) (a) or one appointing a day for the purposes of section 19 and this section) shall be subject to annulment by a resolution of the House of Commons.

(9) An order under section 19 or this section may be varied or revoked by a subsequent order so made, but no order shall be made under section 19 (4) after the end of 1979, except a varying or revoking order under that subsection.

Travel concessions for transferred employees

21. The Secretary of State may, with Treasury approval, out of money provided by Parliament reimburse the National Freight Corporation to such extent as he considers appropriate, and on such terms as he may with that approval determine, in respect of amounts paid by N.F.C., N.C.L. or any subsidiary of N.C.L. to the British Railways Board and the London Transport Executive in connection with travel concessions afforded by them to employees transferred from the employment of the Board under the 1968 Act, or to widows or dependants of such employees.

General

Transport supplementary grant

22. Section 6 (1) of the Local Government Act 1974 (transport supplementary grants to county councils and the G.L.C.) shall be amended as follows—

(*a*) omit " and " at the end of paragraph (*c*);

(*b*) at the end of paragraph (*d*) add—

" and

(*e*) compensation payable under Part IV of Schedule 5 to the Transport (London) Act 1969 (control of off-street parking in Greater London) or any corresponding provisions in an Order in Council under section 11 of the Transport Act 1978 (provision to the same effect for the remainder of Great Britain) "; and

(*c*) for " (*a*) to (*d*) " substitute " (*a*) to (*e*) ".

Finance (general)

23. There are hereby authorised—

(*a*) all such charges or increased charges on public funds as may result from sections 1 (5), 3 (1), 15 and 17 of this Act;

(*b*) increased payments out of money provided by Parliament attributable to sections 16 and 22 of this Act;

(*c*) such other increased payments out of money so provided as may result from provisions of this Act which increase the administrative expenses of local authorities and government departments; and

(*d*) any increase attributable to this Act in the sums payable into the Consolidated Fund under any other enactment.

Commencement; interpretation; repeals

24.—(1) This Act shall come into force on a day appointed by the Secretary of State by order in a statutory instrument; and different days may be so appointed for different provisions and different purposes.

(2) In this Act—

" the 1960 Act " means the Road Traffic Act 1960;

" the 1962 Act " means the Transport Act 1962;

" the 1968 Act " means the Transport Act 1968;

" the 1972 Act " means the Road Traffic Act 1972;

" B.R." means the British Railways Board;

" N.C.L." means National Carriers Limited;

" N.F.C." means the National Freight Corporation; and

" subsidiary " means the same as in the 1962 Act.

(3) A reference in this Act to any enactment shall be construed as a reference to that enactment as amended, extended or applied by or under any other enactment, including this Act.

(4) The enactments specified in Schedule 4 to this Act are repealed to the extent specified in the third column of the Schedule.

Citation and extent

25.—(1) This Act may be cited as the Transport Act 1978.

(2) Sections 1 to 4 and 22 of this Act do not extend to Scotland.

(3) This Act, except sections 15, 17 to 21 and 23 to 25, does not extend to Northern Ireland.

SCHEDULES

Section 7 (1)   SCHEDULE 1

RE-STATEMENT OF ROAD TRAFFIC ACT 1960, SCHEDULE 12, PART II

" PART II

CONDITIONS RELATING TO CERTAIN JOURNEYS WITH VEHICLES ADAPTED TO CARRY AT MOST SEVEN PASSENGERS

2. The number of passengers carried must not exceed 7; and if any passengers are carried in the course of a business of carrying passengers, the number carried must not exceed 4.

3. Where the passengers are carried in the course of a business of carrying passengers, the making of the agreement for the payment of separate fares must not have been initiated by the driver or by the owner of the vehicle, by the person who has let the vehicle for hire by any hiring agreement or hire-purchase agreement, or by any person who receives any remuneration in respect of the arrangements for the journey.

4. The journey must be made without previous advertisement to the public of facilities for its being made by passengers to be carried at separate fares.

5.—(1) The facilities for the journey may have been previously advertised if the conditions of this paragraph are satisfied.

(2) Those conditions are that—

    (a) the local authorities and traffic commissioners concerned have consented to the advertisement of the facilities as being provided under a social car scheme, and their consents remain in force; and

    (b) the advertisement in each case contains a statement that the consents required by this paragraph have been given.

(3) Local authorities and traffic commissioners shall not give consent for the purposes of this paragraph where it appears that arrangements for provision of the facilities in question are, or are to be, made for any commercial purpose or with a view to profit; and consent shall be given only if the facilities are to be provided with a view to meeting the social and welfare needs of one or more communities.

(4) Before a local authority or traffic commissioners withdraw their consent, they shall consult with others by whom it was also given for the facilities in question; and withdrawal of consent shall be signified by notice in writing to those arranging the facilities.

(5) In relation to any such journey, the local authorities and traffic commissioners concerned for the purposes of this paragraph are those in whose area any part of the journey is to be made; and " local authority " means—

    (a) in Greater London, the Greater London Council;

    (b) elsewhere in England and Wales, the county council; and

    (c) in Scotland, the regional or islands council.

6. The journey must not be made in conjunction with, or in extension of, a service provided under a road service licence if the vehicle is owned by, or made available under any arrangement (including a hiring agreement or hire-purchase agreement) with, the holder of the licence or any person who receives any remuneration in respect of the service provided under it or in respect of arrangements for that service.".

Section 8 (1)   SCHEDULE 2

AMENDMENTS ABOUT ROAD SERVICE LICENCES AND PERMITS

A. ROAD TRAFFIC ACT 1960 (C. 16) PART III

1. In section 135 (criteria for grant, variation or refusal of, or attaching of conditions to, road service licences) for subsection (2) substitute—

" (2) Traffic commissioners shall not grant a road service licence in respect of a route if it appears to them from the particulars furnished on the application for the licence that section 78 of the Road Traffic Regulation Act 1967 (speed limits) is likely to be contravened.

(2A) In exercising their discretion to grant, refuse or vary a road service licence in respect of any routes and their discretion to attach conditions to any such licence, the traffic commissioners shall have regard to the interests of the public and (subject to subsection (2D) below) in particular to—

(a) any transport policies or plans which have been made by the local authorities concerned and have been drawn to the commissioners' attention by those authorities;

(b) the transport requirements of the area as a whole (including both the commissioners' own traffic area and, so far as relevant, adjoining traffic areas) and of particular communities in the area;

(c) the need to provide and maintain efficient services to meet those requirements;

(d) the suitability of the routes on which a service may be provided under the licence; and

(e) the convenience of persons who are disabled.

(2B) In subsection (2A) above " the local authorities concerned " means—

(a) in Greater London, the Greater London Council;

(b) elsewhere in England and Wales, county councils; and

(c) in Scotland, regional and islands councils.

(2C) The commissioners shall further take into consideration any representations made to them by persons who are already providing transport facilities along or near to the routes or any part of them or by a local authority in whose area any part of the route is situated; and in this subsection " local authority " means—

(a) in Greater London, the Greater London Council, the council of a London borough or the Common Council of the City of London;

(b) elsewhere in England and Wales, a county or district council;

(c) in Scotland, a regional, islands or district council.

(2D) Traffic Commissioners are not required, in relation to excursions or tours (within the meaning of the Transport Act 1968) for which each fare includes a charge for overnight accommodation in the course of the journey, to take into account the matters specified in subsection (2A) (a) to (c) above.".

2. In section 135 (4) (power to attach conditions to road service licence)—

(a) in paragraph (b) after " public interest " insert " having regard to the nature of the service ";

(b) after paragraph (d) insert—

" (e) in appropriate cases passengers are enabled to continue their journey by another means of transport ".

3. After section 139 insert—

"139A.—(1) A road service licence may be granted by the traffic commissioners to be in force for a period of six months or less, the date of expiration to be shown on the face of the licence; but section 139 (2) above applies as it does to any other road service licence.

(2) On an application for a licence of longer duration under section 139 (1) to replace a short-term licence under this section, the traffic commissioners may take into account any matters arising out of the operation of the road service under the short-term licence.".

4. In section 153 (2) (cases in which traffic commissioners need not hold public sittings) after the words " determination of an application for " insert " (a) ", and at the end add—

" or

(b) the grant of a short-term road service licence under section 139A above.".

5. In section 160 (1) (general power to make regulations for purposes of Part III of the Act), after paragraph (c) insert—

" (cc) applications for, and issue of, the disc or other document required, under section 5 (6) of the Transport Act 1978, in connection with a community bus service ".

B. TRANSPORT ACT 1968 (c. 73)

6. In section 30 (permits in lieu of road service licences), in subsection (1) (a) (permits for road services by vehicles adapted to carry not more than 12 passengers), omit the words from " by means of vehicles " to " passengers ".

7. In section 21 (1) (representations by Executive of designated area) for " section 135 (2) " substitute " section 135 (2C) ".

Section 9 (1)   SCHEDULE 3

AMENDMENTS ABOUT LORRIES

A. ROAD TRAFFIC ACT 1972 (c. 20)

1. In section 56 (4) (power of examiner to divert vehicles for inspection, but not more than one mile away) for " one mile " substitute " five miles ".

2.—(1) In section 57 (prohibition of further use on road), after subsection (4) insert—

" (4A) A prohibition under subsection (1) above may be imposed with a direction making it irremovable unless and until the vehicle has been inspected at an official testing station.".

(2) In section 57 (7) (suspected overload)—

(a) omit " and " at the end of paragraph (a), and paragraph (b);

(b) for " and, if the vehicle is a heavy commercial vehicle, he " substitute—

" and official notification has been given to whoever is for the time being in charge of the vehicle that it is permitted to proceed.

The person to whom it so appears "

(c) for subsection (7A) substitute—

" (7A) Official notification for the purposes of subsection (7)—

(a) must be in writing and be given by a goods vehicle examiner, a person authorised as mentioned in that subsection or a constable authorised as so mentioned; and

(b) may be withheld until the vehicle has been weighed or re-weighed in order to satisfy the person giving the notification that the weight has been sufficiently reduced.".

3. In section 58 (removal of prohibition imposed under section 57)—

(a) after subsection (2) insert—

" (2A) If the prohibition has been imposed with a direction under section 57 (4A), neither a goods vehicle examiner nor a certifying officer shall remove it unless and until the vehicle has been inspected at an official testing station ";

(b) after subsection (5) insert—

" (5A) In the case of vehicles brought to an official testing station for inspection with a view to removal of a prohibition, the Secretary of State may require the payment of fees for inspection, in accordance with prescribed scales and rates; and (*a*) payment of the fee may be required to be made in advance;

    (*b*) the Secretary of State shall ensure that the scales and rates prescribed for the purposes of this subsection are reasonably comparable with the fees charged under section 45 (6) of this Act in respect of the periodic examination of goods vehicles ";

    (*c*) in subsection (6), after " subsection (3) ", insert " or (5A) ", and for " that subsection " substitute " subsection (3) ".

4. In section 82 (interpretation for Part II of the Act) after the definition of " Minister's approval certificate " insert—

    " " official testing station " means a testing station maintained by the Secretary of State under section 58 (5) of this Act.".

5. In section 83 (5) (destination of fees), after " 50 " insert " 58 (5A) ".

6.—(1) In section 160 (2) (compensation for diversion of vehicles to be inspected for overload but found within limits), for " one mile " substitute " five miles ".

    (2) After section 160 (2) of the 1972 Act insert—

    " (2A) The Secretary of State may by order designate areas in Great Britain where subsection (2) above is to have effect, in such cases as may be specified by the order, with the substitution for five miles of a greater distance so specified.

    An order under this subsection shall be made by statutory instrument subject to annulment by a resolution of either House of Parliament, and may be varied or revoked by another such order."

7. In Part I of Schedule 4, in column 2 of the entry relating to section 57 (9) of the Act, for " dangerous heavy commercial vehicle " substitute " goods vehicle found overloaded ".

B. Road Traffic (Foreign Vehicles) Act 1972 (c. 27)

8. In section 1 (stopping and checking foreign vehicles for mechanical defect, overload, etc.), after subsection (5) insert—

    " (6) In the case of a goods vehicle—

    (*a*) a prohibition under subsection (2) (*b*) above, by reference to a supposed contravention of—

        (i) section 40 of the Road Traffic Act 1972 (construction, weight, equipment etc. of motor vehicles and trailers),

        (ii) any of sections 68 to 73 and 76 to 79 of that Act (lights, overhanging or projecting load, etc.), or

        (iii) regulations under any of the sections of that Act referred to above in this paragraph,

    may be imposed with a direction making it irremovable unless and until the vehicle has been inspected at an official testing station;

    (*b*) a prohibition imposed under subsection (3) above may be against driving the vehicle on a road until the weight has been reduced and official notification has been given to whoever is for the time being in charge of the vehicle that it is permitted to proceed.

    (7) Official notification for the purposes of subsection (6) (*b*) above must be in writing and be given by an authorised person and may be withheld until the vehicle has been weighed or reweighed in order to satisfy the person giving the notification that the weight has been sufficiently reduced ".

9. In section 2 (enforcement etc. of prohibitions under section 1 of the Act), after subsection (3) insert—

    " (3A) If the prohibition under section 1 of this Act has been imposed with a direction under subsection (6) (*a*) of that section, the prohibition shall not then be removed under subsection (3) above unless and until the vehicle has been inspected at an official testing station.

    (3B) In the case of vehicles brought to an official testing station for inspection with a view to removal of a prohibition, section 58 (5A) of the Road Traffic Act 1972 (fees for inspection) applies.".

10. In section 7 (1) (interpretation) after the definition of " goods vehicle " insert—

    " " official testing station " means a station maintained by the Secretary of State under section 58 (5) of the Road Traffic Act 1972 ".

Section 24 (4)   SCHEDULE 4

REPEALS

Chapter	Title	Extent of repeal
1967 c. 76.	Road Traffic Regulation Act 1967.	In Schedule 6, the amendment of section 135 (2) of the Road Traffic Act 1960.
1968 c. 73.	Transport Act 1968.	In section 30 (1) (*a*), the words from " by means of vehicles " to " passengers ". In paragraph 3 of Schedule 2, the words from " but no order" onwards.
1969 c. 35.	Transport (London) Act 1969.	In section 24 (4), paragraph (*a*).
1972 c. 20.	Road Traffic Act 1972.	In section 57 (7), the word " and " at the end of paragraph (*a*), and paragraph (*b*).
1972 c. 70.	Local Government Act 1972.	Section 203.
1973 c. 65.	Local Government (Scotland) Act 1973.	In Schedule 18, paragraph 31.
1974 c. 7.	Local Government Act 1974.	In section 6 (1), the word " and " at the end of paragraph (*c*).
1977 c. 25.	Minibus Act 1977.	Section 1 (5).

Parliamentary Pensions Act 1978

(1978 c. 56)

Arrangement of Sections

An Act to make further provision with respect to the contributory pensions schemes for Members of the House of Commons and for the holders of certain Ministerial and other offices.

[2nd August 1978]

General Note

This Act further regulates the contributory pension schemes for Members of the House of Commons and certain other office-holders.

S. 1 directs the payment of pensions to Members on early retirement; s. 2 relates to ill-health pensions based on service as a Member; s. 3 deals with ill-health pensions based on service as an office-holder; s. 4 is concerned with ill-health pensions for those no longer Members or office-holders; s. 5 deals with medical evidence for purposes of ss. 2–4; s. 6 relates to widowers' pensions; s. 7 makes further provision with respect to widows', widowers' and children's pensions; s. 8 provides for short-term pensions for widows, widowers and children; s. 9 has to do with children's pensions; s. 10 directs the method of payment of gratuities on the death of a Member or office-holder; s. 11 arranges for the purchase of added years; s. 12 amends the provisions for calculating reckonable service; s. 13 relates to participation by holders of qualifying offices; s. 14 directs an increase of contributions from Parliamentary remuneration; s. 15 sets out future changes in the basis of contributions to, and payments out of, the Fund; s. 16 reduces the reckonable service needed for a pension under s. 9 of the Parliamentary and Other Pensions Act

1972 (c. 48); s. 17 relates to the duration of pensions, and makes provision for partial abatement; s. 18 deals with transfers to and from overseas pension schemes; s. 19 amends s. 30 (3) of the Parliamentary and Other Pensions Act 1972; s. 20 stipulates the rate of interest for the purposes of the 1972 Act; s. 21 makes certain financial provisions; s. 22 deals with the citation and construction of this Act, and makes minor and consequential repeals and amendments.

The Act received the Royal Assent on August 2, 1978, and came into force on that date.

For parliamentary debates, see *Hansard*, H.C. Vol. 951, col. 658; Vol. 952, cols. 615, 1289; H.L. Vol. 394, cols. 474, 1595; Vol. 395, col. 799.

Pensions for Members on early retirement

Pensions for Members on early retirement

1.—(1) Section 7 (pensions of Members) of the Parliamentary and other Pensions Act 1972 (hereafter in this Act referred to as " the Act of 1972 ") shall be amended as follows.

(2) After subsection (4) there shall be inserted as subsection (4A)—
> " (4A) Where, in the case of any dissolution of Parliament occurring after the passing of the Act of 1978, a person who—
>
> > (a) immediately before the dissolution was a Member of the House of Commons;
> >
> > (b) at the dissolution had attained the age of sixty-two years and had been a Member of that House for a period of not less than twenty-five years, or for two or more periods amounting in the aggregate to not less than twenty-five years; and
> >
> > (c) is not a candidate for election to that House,
>
> applies to the Trustees, before the end of the day of the poll in the general election consequent upon the dissolution, for a pension under this section payable from the time when the salary payable to him as a Member of that House ceases to be payable, then, if the Trustees are satisfied that he does not intend to stand for re-election to that House, he shall be entitled to receive a pension under this section as from the time when that salary ceases to be payable, calculated (subject to sections 11 and 31 of this Act) in accordance with subsection (3) of this section.".

Ill-health pensions

Ill-health pensions based on service as a Member

2.—(1) A person who because of ill-health—
> (a) has after the passing of this Act ceased to be a Member of the House of Commons before attaining the age of sixty-five years; or
>
> (b) having been at any time a Member of that House has, after the passing of this Act and while not a Member of that House, ceased to hold a qualifying office before attaining that age,

may apply to the Trustees for an early pension under section 7 of the Act of 1972 if at the time when he so ceased (" the material time ") he would have become entitled to receive a pension under that section but for his not having attained the age of sixty-five years.

(2) If on an application under this section the Trustees are satisfied—
> (a) that the applicant does not intend to seek re-election to the House of Commons or to accept any future offer of a qualifying office;

(*b*) that his ceasing as mentioned in subsection (1) (*a*) or (*b*) above was a direct consequence of his ill-health; and

(*c*) that his ill-health is such as would prevent him from performing adequately the duties of a Member of the House of Commons,

the applicant shall be entitled to receive a pension under section 7 of the Act of 1972 as from the material time.

(3) A person who, if he were to cease as mentioned in paragraph (*a*) or (*b*) of subsection (1) above at a particular time in the future because of ill-health, would become entitled to make an application under that subsection may make such an application before that time, specifying in it the time when he proposes to so cease; and where on such an application the Trustees are satisfied that, if the applicant so ceases at the time specified therein, he will be entitled under subsection (2) above to receive a pension under section 7 of the Act of 1972 as from that time, they shall give him notice in writing to that effect.

(4) The annual amount of a pension payable under section 7 of the Act of 1972 to a person by virtue of this section shall (subject to sections 11 and 31 of that Act) be calculated in accordance with section 7 (3) of that Act; but for the purposes of that calculation his aggregate period of reckonable service as a Member shall, subject to subsection (5) below, be increased by whichever of the following periods applies in his case, namely—

(*a*) if, apart from this subsection, his aggregate period of reckonable service as a Member at the material time was less than ten years, a period equal to that aggregate period;

(*b*) if, apart from this subsection, his aggregate period of reckonable service as a Member at that time was ten years or more but less than twenty years, a period equal to the difference between that aggregate period and twenty years or a period of six years and eight months, whichever is the longer;

(*c*) in any other case, a period of six years and eight months.

(5) A person's aggregate period of reckonable service as a Member—

(*a*) shall in no case be increased under subsection (4) above by a period longer than the period between his ceasing as mentioned in subsection (1) (*a*) or (*b*) above and the time when he would attain the age of sixty-five years; and

(*b*) as increased under subsection (4) above shall in no case exceed forty years.

(6) References in subsection (4) and (5) above to a person's aggregate period of reckonable service as a Member are references to that period as increased by or under any provision of the Act of 1972 or this Act other than subsection (4) above, and include any additional period of reckonable service which, in accordance with any provision made by order under section 11 of this Act, he has undertaken to purchase by way of periodical deductions from salary.

(7) In relation to a person who—

(*a*) was a Member of the House of Commons at any time before 1st January 1972 but has not been a Member of that House on or after that date; and

(*b*) because of ill-health has after the passing of this Act ceased to hold a qualifying office before attaining the age of sixty-five years,

subsections (1) to (5) above shall have effect with the following modifications, that is to say—

(i) references to section 7 of the Act of 1972 shall be read as references to Part II of the Act of 1965;

(ii) references to a person's aggregate period of reckonable service as a Member shall be read as references to the aggregate of his periods of reckonable service within the meaning of the said Part II; and

(iii) in subsection (4), paragraph (a) and the reference to section 11 of the Act of 1972 shall be omitted, and the reference to section 7 (3) of that Act shall be read as a reference to section 7 (3) of the Act of 1965.

(8) For the purposes of this section—

(a) a person who has ceased to be a Member of the House of Commons in consequence of the dissolution of Parliament shall be treated as having so ceased because of ill-health if, but only if, he satisfies the Trustees that as a direct consequence of his ill-health he did not seek re-election to that House after the dissolution; and

(b) a person who has, while not a Member of that House, ceased to hold a qualifying office because of the result of a general election consequent upon the dissolution of Parliament shall be treated as having so ceased as a direct consequence of his ill-health if, but only if, he satisfies the Trustees than on the day of the poll in that election his ill-health was such as would prevent him from performing adequately the duties of a Member of the House of Commons.

Ill-health pensions based on service as an office-holder

3.—(1) A person who because of ill-health—

(a) has after the passing of this Act ceased to be a Member of the House of Commons before attaining the age of sixty-five years; or

(b) has, after the passing of this Act and while not a Member of that House, ceased to hold a qualifying office before attaining that age,

may apply to the Trustees for an early pension under section 9 of the Act of 1972 if at the time when he so ceased (" the material time ") he would have become entitled to receive a pension under that section but for his not having attained the age of sixty-five years.

(2) If on an application under subsection (1) above the Trustees are satisfied as mentioned in paragraph (a) (so far as applicable) and paragraphs (b) and (c) of section 2 (2) of this Act, the applicant shall be entitled to receive a pension under section 9 of the Act of 1972 as from the material time.

(3) Subsection (3) of section 2 of this Act shall apply in relation to subsections (1) and (2) above as it applies in relation to subsections (1) and (2) of that section, the reference to a pension under section 7 of the Act of 1972 being for this purpose read as a reference to a pension under section 9 of that Act.

(4) The annual amount of a pension payable under section 9 of the Act of 1972 by virtue of this section shall (subject to sections 11 and 31 of that Act) be calculated in accordance with section 10 (1) to (3) of that Act.

(5) Section 2 (8) of this Act shall apply for the purposes of this section.

Ill-health pensions for those no longer Members or office-holders

4.—(1) A person who because of ill-health has, after the passing of this Act and while neither a Member of the House of Commons nor a candidate for election to it nor the holder of a qualifying office, retired from gainful work before attaining the age of sixty-five years may apply to the Trustees for an early pension under section 7 of the Act of 1972, or under section 9 of that Act, or under Part II of the Act of 1965 if at the time when he so retired he would have become entitled to receive a pension under that section or Part but for his not having attained the age of sixty-five years.

(2) If on an application under this section the Trustees are satisfied—

(a) that the applicant does not intend to seek election to the House of Commons or to accept any future offer of a qualifying office;

(b) that his retirement from gainful work was a direct consequence of his ill-health; and

(c) that his ill-health is such as would prevent him from performing adequately the duties of a Member of the House of Commons,

the applicant shall, as from the date on which the Trustees are so satisfied, be entitled to receive a pension under, or under each of, whichever one or more of the following provisions is or are applicable to him, namely sections 7 and 9 of the Act of 1972 and Part II of the Act of 1965.

(3) Where an application is made under this section, the Trustees shall by notice in writing inform the applicant whether they are satisfied as mentioned in subsection (2) above and, if they are so satisfied, shall state the date as from which the pension or pensions payable to him by virtue of this section is or are payable in accordance with that subsection.

(4) In this section " gainful work " means work under a contract of employment, or as the holder of an office, or as a self-employed person engaged in a business or profession, being in any case work from which the person concerned gains the whole or a substantial part of his income.

Medical evidence for purposes of ss. 2 to 4.

5.—(1) Every application under section 2, 3 or 4 of this Act must be accompanied by medical evidence of the applicant's state of health.

(2) In the case of any such application, the Trustees may require the applicant to undergo a medical examination by a medical practitioner nominated by them for the purpose; and the fees for any such examination shall be borne by the Trustees or the applicant, as the Trustees may determine.

Widows, widowers and children

Widowers' pensions

6.—(1) In section 14 of the Act of 1972 (pensions for certain widowers), after subsection (1) (qualifying conditions) there shall be inserted as subsection (1A)—

" (1A) Subject to the following provisions of this section the widower of a woman who was a Member of the House of Commons at any time after the passing of the Act of 1978 shall, if at the time of her death she fulfilled any of the conditions specified in paragraphs (a) and (b) of subsection (1) above (as it applies in her case), be entitled to receive a pension under this section—

(a) as from the day following the date of her death if at the time of her death he had attained the age of sixty-five years or was incapable by reason of bodily or mental infirmity of earning his own living; or

(b) where the preceding paragraph does not apply, as from the time when he attains the age of sixty-five years or, before attaining that age, becomes incapable as mentioned in that paragraph;

and subsection (1) above shall not apply in the case of a widower to whom this subsection applies."

(2) In the case of a widower to whom subsection (1A) of section 14 of the Act of 1972 applies, subsections (3) and (4) of that section (Trustees' power to terminate or restore pension in certain events) shall have effect with the following modifications, that is to say—

(a) the references to subsection (1) of that section shall be read as references to subsection (1A) thereof; and

(b) so much of subsection (3) as relates to the termination of a widower's pension in the event of his ceasing to be incapable as there mentioned shall not apply after the widower has attained the age of sixty-five years;

and where his pension has been terminated under subsection (3) of that section on his ceasing to be incapable as there mentioned before attaining the age of sixty-five, that fact shall not affect his entitlement to the pension as from the time when he attains that age.

Widows', widowers' and children's pensions

7.—(1) Where the widow of a man who—

(a) has been a Member of the House of Commons at any time since the passing of this Act; and

(b) was at the time of his death entitled to receive a pension under section 7 of the Act of 1972,

is entitled to receive a pension under section 13 of that Act, subsections (2) and (3) below shall apply.

(2) If, for any part of the three-month period, the aggregate of the following amounts, namely—

(a) the amount payable to her by way of pension under section 13 of the Act of 1972 apart from this subsection; and

(b) any amount which (by direction of the Trustees under section 15 (5) of that Act) is payable to her by way of pension under section 15 of that Act for the benefit of any relevant child or children of the deceased,

is less than the amount mentioned in subsection (3) below, then for that part of that period the amount payable to her by way of pension under the said section 13 shall be increased by the difference.

(3) The said amount is the amount or aggregate amount which, if the deceased had lived, would have been payable to him for the part of the three-month period in question by way of pension under one or both of sections 7 and 9 of the Act of 1972.

(4) Where a man has died after the passing of this Act and, at the time of his death, he—

(a) was a Member of the House of Commons; and

(b) was not entitled to receive a pension under section 7 of the Act of 1972 but had an aggregate period of reckonable service (whether as a Member or otherwise) of not less than four years,

subsections (5) to (7) below (so far as applicable) shall apply if his widow is entitled to receive a pension under section 13 of that Act or if a children's pension under section 15 of that Act is payable for the benefit of any relevant child or children of his.

(5) If the deceased died before attaining the age of sixty-five years, the annual amount of any pension payable to his widow under section 13

of the Act of 1972 or for the benefit of any relevant child or children of his under section 15 of that Act shall be calculated as if he had immediately before his death ceased to be a Member of the House of Commons because of ill-health and had by virtue of section 2 of this Act been entitled to receive a pension under section 7 of the Act of 1972 as from the time when he so ceased.

(6) If, for any part of the three-month period, the aggregate of the following amounts, namely—

    (*a*) the amount payable to the deceased's widow by way of pension under section 13 of the Act of 1972 apart from this subsection; and

    (*b*) any amount which (by direction of the Trustees under section 15 (5) of that Act) is payable to her by way of pension under section 15 of that Act for the benefit of any relevant child or children of the deceased,

is less than the amount mentioned in subsection (7) below, then for that part of that period the amount payable to her by way of pension under the said section 13 shall be increased by the difference.

(7) The said amount is the amount which, if—

    (*a*) the deceased had lived and had at the material time become entitled to a pension under section 7 of the Act of 1972; and

    (*b*) the annual amount of that pension had been (subject to section 31 of that Act) a sum equal to a Member's ordinary salary at the rate in force at the material time,

would have been payable to him for the part of the three-month period in question by way of that pension.

In this subsection " the material time " means the time when the deceased in fact died.

(8) The preceding provisions of this section are without prejudice to subsections (3) to (5) of section 13 of the Act of 1972 (duration of widow's pension, and restrictions on payment).

(9) The preceding provisions of this section shall apply in relation to a woman who has died after the passing of this Act and her widower as they apply in relation to a man who has so died and his widow, subject to the modifications that any reference to section 13 of the Act of 1972 shall be read as a reference to section 14 of that Act, the reference to subsections (3) to (5) of section 13 of that Act shall be read as a reference to the following provisions of that Act, namely section 14 (3) and (4) and section 13 (4) and (5) as applied by section 14 (5), and subsections (2) and (6) above shall not apply where the widower is entitled to a pension by virtue of section 14 (1A) (*b*) of that Act.

(10) In this section—

    " a Member's ordinary salary " has the same meaning as in section 3 (6) of the Act of 1972;

    " relevant child " has the same meaning as in section 15 of the Act of 1972;

    " the three-month period ", in relation to a person who has died, means the period of three months beginning with the day following the date of his death.

Short-term pensions for widows, widowers and children

8.—(1) Where a person has died after the passing of this Act and, at the time of his death, he—

    (*a*) was a Member of the House of Commons; and

    (*b*) had an aggregate period of reckonable service (whether as a Member or otherwise) of less than four years; and

(c) was not entitled to receive a pension under section 7 of the Act of 1972,

the following provisions of this section (so far as practicable) shall apply.

(2) Subject to subsections (6) to (8) below, if the deceased was a man and left a widow, she shall be entitled to receive a pension under this subsection for the relevant period beginning with the day following the date of the deceased's death, that is to say—

(a) if there is no relevant child of the deceased, three months;

(b) if there is only one relevant child of the deceased, four months and fifteen days;

(c) if there are two or more relevant children of the deceased, six months;

and, subject to section 31 of the Act of 1972, a pension under this subsection shall be payable at a rate equal to what was the rate of a Member's ordinary salary at the time of the deceased's death.

(3) If the deceased was a woman and left a widower who, at the time of her death, was incapable by reason of bodily or mental infirmity of earning his own living or had attained the age of sixty-five years, subsection (2) above shall apply in relation to the deceased and her widower as it applies in relation to a man who has died and his widow.

(4) Subject to subsections (5) and (6) below (and whether the deceased was a man or a woman), a pension under this subsection shall be payable for the benefit of any relevant child or children of the deceased for the relevant period beginning with the day following the date of the deceased's death, that is to say—

(a) if there is only one relevant child, two months;

(b) if there are two or more relevant children, four months;

and, subject to section 31 of the Act of 1972, a pension under this subsection shall be payable at a rate equal to what was the rate of a Member's ordinary salary at the time of the deceased's death.

(5) So much of any pension under subsection (4) above as would otherwise (by direction of the Trustees under section 15 (5) of the Act of 1972 as applied by subsection (9) below) be payable to the widow or widower of the deceased for the benefit of any relevant child or children of the deceased shall not be payable for any period for which a pension under subsection (2) above is payable.

(6) A pension payable under subsection (2) above to a widow shall cease to be payable if she remarries, unless the Trustees direct otherwise; and the Trustees may, if they think fit, so direct, if satisfied that there are exceptional reasons for continuing to pay the pension notwithstanding her remarriage.

(7) A pension payable under subsection (2) above to a widower—

(a) may be terminated by direction of the Trustees in the event of his remarriage or of his ceasing to be incapable as mentioned in subsection (3) above; and

(b) if so terminated, may be restored by direction of the Trustees if the pensioner again becomes incapable as mentioned in subsection (3) above, or if the Trustees are satisfied that for exceptional reasons it is proper to restore the pension.

(8) Subsections (4) and (5) of section 13 of the Act of 1972 (provisions as to cohabitation, and as to marriage in the year preceding death) shall apply for the purposes of subsection (2) above with the necessary modifications, references to that section or to a widow's pension being for this purpose read as referring to subsection (2) above or, as the case may be, to a pension thereunder.

(9) Subsections (4) and (5) of section 15 of the Act of 1972 (restrictions on, and payment and application of, children's pension) shall apply

in relation to a pension under subsection (4) above as they apply in relation to a pension under that section subject, in the case of subsection (4) of the said section 15, to the modifications that—

    (*a*) the reference to a pension under section 13 or 14 of that Act shall be read as a reference to a pension under subsection (2) above;

    (*b*) the references to the provision as to cohabitation shall be read as references to section 13 (4) of that Act as applied by subsection (8) above.

    (10) In this section—

        " a Member's ordinary salary " has the same meaning as in section 3 (6) of the Act of 1972;

        " relevant child " has the same meaning as in section 15 of the Act of 1972.

Children's pensions

    9.—(1) Subject to subsection (5) below, section 15 of the Act of 1972 (amount and payment of children's pension) shall be amended as follows:

    (2) In subsection (2) (children's pension to be sum equal to one-eighth of deceased's pension for each child not exceeding four) the words " to the next following subsection and " shall cease to have effect, and for the words " one-eighth " and " four " there shall be substituted the words " one-quarter " and " two " respectively.

    (3) Subsection (3) (children's pension, where no widow or widower, to be one-quarter of the deceased's pension if only one child or one-half of that pension in the case of two or more children) and, in subsection (4), the words from " and if " to the end of the subsection shall cease to have effect.

    (4) In subsection (6) (*a*) (age at which child not in full-time education or dependent on deceased ceases to be a relevant child) for the word " sixteen " there shall be substituted the word " seventeen ".

    (5) Subsections (2) to (4) above and the repeals in section 15 of the Act of 1972 provided for in Schedule 2 to this Act shall not apply for the determination of the annual amount of a children's pension payable for the benefit of a relevant child or children (within the meaning of section 15 of the 1972 Act) of a person who has not been a Member of the House of Commons or the holder of a qualifying office since the passing of this Act.

Gratuity on death of Member or office-holder

    10.—(1) Subject to subsection (5) below, section 16 of the Act of 1972 (gratuity on death of Member or office-holder) shall be amended as follows.

    (2) In subsection (1) (discretion to grant gratuity to personal representatives) the words " (subject to the next following subsection) " and " to his personal representatives " shall be omitted, and at the end there shall be added the words " in respect of him ".

    (3) After subsection (1) there shall be inserted as subsections (1A) and (1B)—

        " (1A) A gratuity granted under this section in respect of a person shall be granted—

        (*a*) to the person nominated in any nomination made by him for the purposes of this section which was in force at the time of his death; or

        (*b*) if no such nomination was in force at that time, to his personal representatives.

(1B) Only the wife or husband of a person ("the nominator") making a nomination for the purposes of this section may be nominated in it, and any such nomination—

    (*a*) must be made by notice in writing given to the Trustees;

    (*b*) may be revoked by a subsequent notice in writing so given by the nominator; and

    (*c*) shall cease to have effect if in the lifetime of the nominator the person nominated ceases to be the nominator's wife or husband, as the case may be."

(4) Subsection (2) (which precludes the grant of a gratuity if the deceased had insufficient reckonable service) shall cease to have effect.

(5) This section, and the repeals in section 16 of the Act of 1972 provided for in Schedule 2 to this Act, shall not apply in the case of a person who died before the passing of this Act.

Other provisions

Purchase of added years

11.—(1) The Lord President of the Council may by order made by statutory instrument make provision for enabling Members of the House of Commons, subject to compliance with any specified conditions, to purchase additional periods of reckonable service as a Member; and the aggregate period of reckonable service as a Member of a person who purchases an additional period in pursuance of an order under this section shall be treated as increased by that additional period.

(2) Without prejudice to the generality of subsection (1) above, an order under that subsection may—

    (*a*) enable Members to purchase additional periods of reckonable service either by way of periodical deductions from salary or by payment of a lump sum;

    (*b*) specify different conditions in relation to different methods of payment; and

    (*c*) be framed by reference to the opinion of the Trustees or to their approval, or require any matter to be established to their satisfaction.

(3) An order under subsection (1) above may enable persons who are Members of the House of Commons at the passing of this Act but who cease to be Members before the date on which an order under this section is first made to purchase additional periods of reckonable service as a Member.

(4) An order made under subsection (1) above may be revoked or varied by a subsequent order made under that subsection.

(5) A statutory instrument containing an order made under this section shall be subject to annulment in pursuance of a resolution of the House of Commons.

Reckonable service

12.—(1) Subject to subsections (7) and (8) below, section 6 of the Act of 1972 (reckonable service) shall be amended as follows.

(2) In subsection (1), after the word "means" there shall be inserted the words "(subject to subsection (2A) of this section)".

(3) In subsection (2) (*b*) (maximum reckonable service before 16th October 1964), after the words "ten years" there shall be inserted the words "or, in the case of a person who is or was a Member of the House of Commons after the passing of the Act of 1978, fifteen years".

(4) After subsection (2) there shall be inserted as subsection (2A)—

" (2A) In calculating for the purposes of this Part of this Act a person's aggregate period of reckonable service as a Member, a period during which he was a Member of the House of Commons shall be disregarded—

(*a*) in so far as it fell after the time when his aggregate period of reckonable service as a Member reached forty years and before the time when he attains or attained the age of sixty-five years; and

(*b*) in so far as it fell after the time when he attained that age and would, apart from this paragraph, cause his aggregate period of reckonable service as a Member to exceed forty-five years.".

(5) In subsection (3), after the word " means " there shall be inserted the words " (subject to subsection (3A) of this section) ".

(6) After subsection (3), there shall be inserted as subsection (3A)—

" (3A) In calculating for the purposes of this Part of this Act a person's aggregate period of reckonable service as an office-holder, his period or periods of reckonable service as an office-holder shall be disregarded—

(*a*) so far as may be necessary to prevent his aggregate period of reckonable service as an office-holder from exceeding forty years at or before the time when he attains or attained the age of sixty-five years; and

(*b*) so far as may be necessary to prevent his aggregate period of reckonable service as an office-holder from exceeding forty-five years at any time;

and, in the case of any person, the particular part or parts of his period of reckonable service as an office-holder to be disregarded in pursuance of this subsection or, if there are two or more such periods, the particular periods or parts of periods (or both) to be so disregarded shall be that or those which, being disregarded, will make the aggregate of the contribution credits calculated in his case under section 10 (3) of this Act as large as possible consistently with this subsection.".

(7) Subsections (2) and (4) above shall not apply in relation to a person who became entitled to receive a pension under section 7 of the Act of 1972 before the passing of this Act; and subsections (5) and (6) above shall not apply in relation to a person who became entitled to receive a pension under section 9 of that Act before the passing of this Act.

(8) For the purpose of calculating the annual amount of—

(*a*) a pension payable under section 13 of the Act of 1972 to the widow of a man whose aggregate period of reckonable service (whether as a Member or otherwise) comprises no period which began before 6th April 1978; or

(*b*) a pension payable under section 14 of that Act to the widower of a woman whose aggregate period of reckonable service (whether as a Member or otherwise) comprises no period which began before that date,

subsections (2), (4), (5) and (6) above shall be disregarded; and where to do so would increase the annual amount of a pension payable under the said section 13 or 14, there shall be disregarded, both for the purposes of this subsection and for the purpose of calculating that annual amount, all periods before 6th April 1978 during which the deceased was a Member of the House of Commons or held a qualifying office.

Participation by holders of qualifying offices

13.—(1) Section 2 of the Act of 1972 (participation by holders of qualifying offices) shall be amended as follows.

(2) In subsection (2), for the words " he may elect to be, or not to be, a participant under this section." there shall be substituted the words " he shall be a participant under this section unless he has elected otherwise in accordance with subsection (3) of this section.".

(3) In subsection (3)—

(a) in paragraph (b), for the words " in any other case " there shall be substituted the words " if the period of tenure of a qualifying office in question began after the passing of this Act but before the passing of the Act of 1978," and at the end of the paragraph there shall be added the word " and "; and

(b) for the words from " and any person who " onwards there shall be substituted as paragraph (c)—

" (c) in any other case, such an election must be made by notice in writing given to the Trustees before the end of the period of twelve months beginning—

(i) if a salary is payable to the holder of the office as from the date on which his period of tenure of that office began, with that date;

(ii) if a salary becomes payable to the holder of the office as from a date later than the date on which his period of tenure of that office began, with that later date,

or, in any case within this paragraph, before the end of such further period as the Trustees, having regard to the circumstances of the case, may allow.".

(4) The following subsections shall be substituted for subsection (4)—

" (3A) An election made under this section after the passing of the Act of 1978 shall be irrevocable and shall have effect from the date on which the period in question began.

(4) Notwithstanding the preceding provisions of this section, where before the passing of the Act of 1978 a person has elected to be a participant under this section in respect of a period of tenure of a qualifying office, he shall continue to be a participant under this section in respect of that period.".

Increase of contributions from Parliamentary remuneration

14.—(1) In section 3 of the Act of 1972 (contributions from Parliamentary remuneration), in subsection (2) (contributions to be at the rate of five per cent. of a Member's pensionable salary) for the words " five per cent." there shall be substituted the words " six per cent.".

(2) In the case of the payment of salary made in respect of a period falling partly before and partly after the passing of this Act, the amendment made by subsection (1) above shall not apply in relation to so much of the payment as is attributable to the part of the period which falls before the passing of this Act.

Future changes in basis of contributions to any payments out of the Fund

15.—(1) For subsection (7) of section 3 of the Act of 1972 (which was inserted by section 1 of the Parliamentary and other Pensions and Salaries Act 1976) there shall be substituted the following subsection—

" (7) Any reference in this Part of this Act to a resolution of the House of Commons relating to the remuneration of Members shall be construed as a reference to an effective resolution of the House of Commons relating to the remuneration of Members and, where there are two or more such resolutions in force, as a reference to those resolutions taken together."

(2) In section 35 (1) (interpretation) of the Act of 1972 the following shall be inserted after the definition of " contribution "—

" ' effective resolution ' means a resolution which is not framed as an expression of opinion ".

(3) This section shall not affect the operation under the Act of 1972 of any resolution passed by the House of Commons before the commencement of this Act.

Reduction of reckonable service needed for pension under s. 9 of Act of 1972.

16.—(1) The minimum aggregate period of reckonable service (whether as a Member or otherwise) needed to qualify for a pension under section 9 of the Act of 1972 shall be reduced from four years to three years; and accordingly in subsection (1) of that section there shall be added at the end of the words " , paragraph (*c*) of the said section 7 (1) being for this purpose read as if it mentioned an aggregate period of reckonable service (whether as a Member or otherwise) of not less than three years (instead of four).".

(2) This section, and the repeal in section 25 of the Act of 1972 provided for in Schedule 2 to this Act, shall not apply in the case of a person who has held no qualifying office since the passing of this Act.

Duration of pensions and provision for partial abatement

17.—(1) The provisions of section 12 of the Act of 1972 (duration of pension under section 7 or section 9 of that Act) shall be amended as follows and, as so amended, shall apply to any such pension under Part II of the Act of 1965 as is mentioned in section 36 (2) (*c*) of the Act of 1972 as they apply to a pension under the said section 7.

(2) In subsection (2) of the said section 12 (periods in respect of which pension is not payable)—

    (*a*) at the beginning there shall be inserted the words " Subject to subsection (2A) of this section "; and

    (*b*) after the words " or in respect of any part of a period of tenure of a qualifying office " there shall be added the words " other than a part in respect of which no salary is payable in respect of which no salary is drawn.".

(3) After subsection (2) of the said section 12 there shall be inserted as subsection (2A)—

" (2A) Where, in the case of any person, a pension under section 7 or section 9 of this Act or a pension under each of those sections would, but for subsection (2) of this section, be payable to him in respect of a period of tenure of a qualifying office during which he is neither a Member of the House of Commons nor a candidate for election to that House—

    (*a*) that subsection shall not apply to that pension or either of those pensions in respect of any part of that period; but

    (*b*) the amount or aggregate amount payable to him in right of that pension or those pensions for any part of that period shall not exceed the amount, if any, by which the total salary payable to him for that part of that period falls short of the amount which, in accordance with the relevant resolution or resolutions of the House of Commons relating to the remuneration of Members, would be payable to a

Member for that part of that period by way of a Member's ordinary salary as defined in section 3 (6) of this Act; and

(c) if he is a participant under section 2 of this Act in respect of that period then, for the purpose of calculating the amount, if any, which apart from the preceding paragraph would be payable to him in right of a pension under the said section 9 for any part of that period (but not for any other purpose, and in particular not for the purpose of recalculating at the end of that period the annual amount of the pension, if any, to which apart from the preceding paragraph he is entitled under the said section 9), that period shall be deemed not to be period of reckonable service as an office-holder.

In this subsection ' salary ' (except in the expression ' a Member's ordinary salary ') means salary payable to the holder of a qualifying office in respect of his tenure of that office.''.

Transfers to and from overseas pensions schemes

18.—(1) In section 21 (2) of the Act of 1927 (transfers to other pension schemes)—

(a) in paragraph (a), after the words " any scheme " there shall be inserted the words " (other than an overseas fund or scheme) '';

(b) in paragraph (b), after the words " any fund or scheme " there shall be inserted the words " (other than an overseas fund or scheme) ''; and

(c) at the end of paragraph (b) there shall be added the words " and

(c) to any overseas fund or scheme which is recognised by the Trustees and approved by the Commissioners of Inland Revenue and the Occupational Pensions Board for the purposes of this section.

In this section ' overseas fund or scheme ' means a fund or scheme which is established outside the United Kingdom or wholly or primarily administered outside the United Kingdom.''.

(2) At the request of any person—

(a) in respect of whom any sum has been paid under section 21 of the Act of 1972 into or for the purposes of an overseas fund or scheme (within the meaning of subsection (2) of that section); and

(b) who is not at the time the request is made a Member of the House of Commons or a participant under section 2 of that Act,

the Trustees may receive a sum, out of, or out of moneys held for the purposes of, that fund or scheme, equal to the sum paid under section 21 of that Act together with interest thereon from the date of that payment at such rate as may be agreed by the Trustees.

(3) The following provisions of the Act of 1972 shall not apply in relation to any person in respect of whom a sum is received by the Trustees under subsection (2) above, namely—

(a) paragraph (c) of section 7 (1) (minimum qualifying period for pension), including that paragraph as applied by section 9 (1) of that Act; and

(b) section 21 (4) (a) (discounting of reckonable service in period before date of payment under section 21 of the Act of 1972).

Amendment of s. 30 (3) of the Act of 1972

19. In section 30 (3) of the Act of 1972 (refund of contributions paid by former holders of certain offices)—

(*a*) after the words " equal to " there shall be inserted the words " the amount obtained by reducing by the appropriate percentage the following amount, namely "; and

(*b*) at the end there shall be added—

" For the purposes of this subsection the appropriate percentage is a percentage equal to the rate of tax for the time being in force under paragraph 2 (2) of Part II of Schedule 5 to the Finance Act 1970 (tax on repayment of employee's contributions).".

Rate of interest for purposes of Act of 1972.

20. In section 35 (1) of the Act of 1972 (interpretation) in the definition of " interest ", after the words " three per cent. per annum " there shall be inserted the words " in respect of any period falling before the passing of the Act of 1978 and at the rate of four per cent. per annum in respect of any later period, and, in either case, the interest shall be ".

Financial provisions

21. There shall be paid out of money provided by Parliament, or paid into or out of the Consolidated Fund, any increase attributable to this Act in the sums payable under the Act of 1972.

Citation, construction, minor and consequential amendments and repeals

22.—(1) This Act may be cited as the Parliamentary Pensions Act 1978.

(2) In this Act " the Act of 1972 " means the Parliamentary and other Pensions Act 1972.

(3) This Act and the Act of 1972 shall have effect as if this Act (except section 20 and paragraphs 8 and 9 of Schedule 1) were contained in Part I of that Act, and any reference to Part I of the Act of 1972 in any other enactment shall be construed accordingly.

(4) The provisions of the Act of 1972 specified in Schedule 1 to this Act shall have effect subject to the amendments there specified, being minor amendments and amendments consequential on the preceding provisions of this Act.

(5) Subject to the transitional provisions contained in this Act, the enactments specified in Schedule 2 to this Act are hereby repealed to the extent specified in the third column of that Schedule.

SCHEDULES

Section 22 (4)   SCHEDULE 1

Minor and Consequential Amendments of Act of 1972

1. The provisions of the Act of 1972 which refer to a person who has or had elected to be a participant under section 2 of that Act shall be amended as follows—

(*a*) in section 4 (1), 6 (3), 9 (1), 18 (3) (*a*), 22 (1) and 23 (*b*) for " has elected to be " substitute " is ";

(*b*) in sections 16 (1) (*b*), 19 (*a*) and 25 (2) (*b*), for " had elected to be " substitute " had been ";

(*c*) in sections 18 (3) (*b*) and 22 (2) (*a*), for " he elects to be " substitute " he is "; and

(*d*) in section 21 (1), for paragraph (*b*) substitute—
    " (*b*) is a participant under section 2 of this Act in respect of a period of tenure of a qualifying office but has ceased to be the holder of a qualifying office,".

2. In section 7 (pensions of Members), after subsection (5) add—
    " (6) For the purposes of paragraph 4 of Schedule 16 to the Social Security Act 1973 (meaning of " normal pension age " in relation to an occupational pension scheme) subsections (4) and (4A) of this section shall be disregarded.".

3. In section 10 (pensions of office-holders), after subsection (6) add—
    " (7) For the purposes of paragraph 4 of Schedule 16 to the Social Security Act 1973 (meaning of " normal pension age " in relation to an occupational pension scheme) subsection (4) of this section shall be disregarded.".

4. Subject to paragraph 10 below, in sections 13 (1) (*b*) and 14 (1) (*b*) (reckonable service needed for widow's or widower's pension) for the words from " was not so entitled " onwards substitute " was not so entitled, but either—
    (i) had been a Member of the House of Commons on or after 1st January 1972 and had an aggregate period of reckonable service (whether as a Member or otherwise) of not less than four years; or
    (ii) had been a participant under section 2 of this Act in respect of one or more periods of tenure of a qualifying office and had an aggregate period of reckonable service (whether as a Member or otherwise) of not less than three years.".

5. Subject to paragraph 10 below, in section 18 (refund of contributions to contributor)—
    (*a*) in subsection (2), after " person " insert " under section 5 of the Act of 1965 or under section 3 or section 4 of this Act "; and
    (*b*) in subsection (3) (*c*), after " four years " insert " or, in the case of contributions paid under section 4 of this Act, less than three years ".

6. In section 22 (2) (transfers from other pension schemes), for " three months " substitute " twelve months ".

7.—(1) Subject to paragraph 10 below, section 25 (interpretation of Part I) shall be amended as follows.
    (2) In subsection (2) (meaning of " basic or prospective pension or pensions ")—
    (*a*) after " means ", where it first occurs, insert " (subject to subsection (2A) of this section) ";
    (*b*) omit the words from " but had " to " four years "; and
    (*c*) in paragraph (*b*), for " mentioned in the preceding paragraph " substitute " specified in paragraphs (*a*) to (*d*) of section 7 (1) of this Act, paragraph (*c*) of the said section 7 (1) being for this purpose read as provided in section 9 (1) of this Act.".
    (3) After subsection (2) insert—
    " (2A) Where, in the case of a person who has died and who at the time of his death was entitled to receive a pension under section 7 or section 9 of this Act, the annual amount of that pension resulted from one or more reductions made under section 7 (4), 10 (4) or 11 (2) of this Act, no such reduction shall be made in calculating the annual amount of that pension for the purposes of subsection (2) of this section.".

8. In section 31 (4) (construction of references to Pensions (Increase) Act 1971) after " as amended by this section " insert " and by section 22 (3) of the Act of 1978 ".

9. In section 35 (1) (interpretation), after the definition of " the Act of 1965 " insert—
    " ' the Act of 1978 ' means the Parliamentary Pensions Act 1978;".

10. Paragraphs 4, 5 and 7 (2) (*b*) and (*c*) above shall not apply in the case of a person who has held no qualifying office since the passing of this Act.

Section 22 (5)

SCHEDULE 2

REPEALS

Chapter	Short title	Extent of repeal
1965 c. 11.	Ministerial Salaries and Members' Pensions Act 1965.	Section 7 (4), as far as unrepealed.
1972 c. 48.	Parliamentary and other Pensions Act 1972.	In section 15, in subsection (2), the words " to the next following subsection and ", subsection (3) and, in subsection (4), the words from " and if " to the end of the subsection. In section 16, in subsection (1), the words " (subject to the next following subsection) " and " to his personal representatives ", and subsection (2). In section 25 (2), the words from " but had " to " four years ".

Appropriation Act 1978

(1978 c. 57)

An Act to apply a sum out of the Consolidated Fund to the service
of the year ending on 31st March 1979, to appropriate the
supplies granted in this Session of Parliament, and to repeal
certain Consolidated Fund and Appropriation Acts.

[2nd August 1978]

General Note

This Act received the Royal Assent on August 2, 1978.
The Schedules to the Act have not been reproduced here as they are of little or
no legal interest.

GRANT OUT OF CONSOLIDATED FUND

Issue out of the Consolidated Fund for the year ending 31st March 1979

1. The Treasury may issue out of the Consolidated Fund of the
United Kingdom and apply towards making good the supply granted to
Her Majesty for the service of the year ending on 31st March 1979 the
sum of £26,236,313,000.

APPROPRIATION OF GRANTS

Appropriation of sums voted for supply services

2. All sums granted by this Act and the other Acts mentioned in
Schedule (A) annexed to this Act out of the said Consolidated Fund
towards making good the supply granted to Her Majesty amounting,
as appears by the said schedule, in the aggregate, to the sum of
£46,985,853,295·71 are appropriated, and shall be deemed to have been
appropriated as from the date of the passing of the Acts mentioned in
the said Schedule (A), for the services and purposes expressed in
Schedule (B) annexed hereto.

The abstract of schedules and schedules annexed hereto, with the
notes (if any) to such schedules, shall be deemed to be part of this Act
in the same manner as if they had been contained in the body thereof.

In addition to the said sums granted out of the Consolidated Fund,
there may be applied out of any money directed, under section 2 of the
Public Accounts and Charges Act 1891, to be applied as appropriations
in aid of the grants for the services and purposes specified in Schedule (B)
annexed hereto the sums respectively set forth in the last column of the
said schedule.

Repeals

3. The enactments mentioned in Schedule (C) annexed to this Act are
hereby repealed.

Short title

4. This Act may be cited as the Appropriation Act 1978.

Pensioners Payments Act 1978

(1978 c. 58)

An Act to make provision for lump sum payments to pensioners, and for connected purposes.   [23rd November 1978]

General Note

This Act provides for lump sum payments to pensioners.

S. 1 provides for payments to be made to pensioners corresponding to those made by the Pensioners Payments Act 1977; s. 2 contains the short title.

The Act received the Royal Assent on November 23, 1978, and came into force on that date.

For parliamentary debates, see *Hansard,* H.C. Vol. 957, col. 198; Vol. 958, col. 127; H.L. Vol. 396, cols. 702 and 899.

Lump sum payments to pensioners

1.—(1) For the purpose of making, in relation to the week beginning with 4th December 1978, provision corresponding to that made, in relation to the week beginning with 5th December 1977, by the Pensioners Payments Act 1977 (lump sum payments to pensioners), that Act shall have effect as if—

(*a*) references in that Act to the relevant week and the passing of that Act were respectively references to the week beginning with 4th December 1978 and the passing of this Act; and

(*b*) any reference in that Act to a provision of the Supplementary Benefits &c. Act (Northern Ireland) 1966 were a reference to the corresponding provision of the Supplementary Benefits (Northern Ireland) Order 1977.

(2) Nothing in subsection (1) above shall be taken as prejudicing the right of any person to receive a payment under the said Act of 1977 as originally enacted.

Short title

2. This Act may be cited as the Pensioners Payments Act 1978.

Consolidated Fund (No. 2) Act 1978

(1978 c. 59)

An Act to apply certain sums out of the Consolidated Fund to the service of the years ending on 31st March 1979 and 1980.

[14th December 1978]

General Note

This Act provides for the issue of certain moneys out of the Consolidated Fund. The Act received the Royal Assent on December 14, 1978, and came into force on that date.

Issue out of the Consolidated Fund for the year ending 31st March 1979

1. The Treasury may issue out of the Consolidated Fund of the United Kingdom and apply towards making good the supply granted to Her Majesty for the service of the year ending on 31st March 1979 the sum of £2,108,662,000.

Issue out of the Consolidated Fund for the year ending 31st March 1980

2. The Treasury may issue out of the Consolidated Fund of the United Kingdom and apply towards making good the supply granted to Her Majesty for the service of the year ending on 31st March 1980 the sum of £20,628,376,900.

Short title

3. This Act may be cited as the Consolidated Fund (No. 2) Act 1978.

Dioceses Measure 1978

(1978 No. 1)

ARRANGEMENT OF SECTIONS

A MEASURE passed by the General Synod of the Church of England to make provision for enabling alterations to be made in the diocesan structure of the provinces of Canterbury and York; to make further provision for enabling certain functions of diocesan bishops to be discharged by suffragan bishops; to abolish the power to commission suffragan bishops; to make provision for constituting separate synods for areas of a diocese; to make further provision with respect to the nomination of suffragan bishops; to make provision with respect to the discharge of the functions of certain diocesan bodies; and for purposes connected with those matters.

[2nd February 1978]

General Note

This Measure makes provision for enabling alterations to be made in the diocesan structure of the provinces of Canterbury and York and for the discharge of functions of certain diocesan bodies and for enabling certain functions of diocesan bishops to be discharged by suffragan bishops: it abolishes the power to commission suffragan bishops, and makes further provisions for their nomination, and provides for constituting separate synods for areas of a diocese.

S. 1 deals with the appointment of a Dioceses Commission by the Standing Committee of the General Synod; s. 2 lays down the advisory functions of the Commission in respect of the diocesan structure of Canterbury and York and the episcopal administration of any diocese; s. 3 allocates to the Commission the preparation, etc., of "reorganisation schemes"; s. 4 deals with procedures for proposing schemes to the commission; s. 5 relates to the Commission's preparation of draft schemes; s. 6 provides for the approval by the General Synod of such schemes; s. 7 deals with the confirmation of such schemes by Order of Her Majesty in Council; s. 8 makes supplementary provisions in respect of reorganisation schemes; s. 9 confers power on the General Synod to make temporary provision in respect of membership of certain Convocations; s. 10 provides for the temporary delegation, by a diocesan bishop, of certain functions to a suffragan bishop; s. 11 instigates permanent schemes for the discharge of episcopal functions within each area of a diocese; s. 12 lays down procedures for submission of such schemes to the Commission; s. 13 relates to variations of such schemes; s. 14 makes special provision as regards rights of collation; s. 15 abolishes the power to commission a suffragan bishop; s. 16 makes provision with respect to Acts and Measures conferring functions on diocesan bishops; s. 17 deals with the creation of area synods for episcopal areas; s. 18 relates to the creation or revival of suffragan sees; s. 19 instigates schemes for the discharge of functions of diocesan bodies corporate; s. 20 makes further provision with respect to these schemes; s. 21 empowers the Commission to pay stipends to certain bishops; s. 22 relates to cathedral churches of new dioceses created by the aforesaid schemes; s. 23 permits amendment of reorganisation schemes by other schemes; s. 24 contains definitions; s. 25 contains the short title, and deals with commencement and extent.

The Measure received the Royal Assent on February 2, 1978, and came into force on May 2, 1978.

Dioceses Commission

Dioceses Commission

1.—(1) The Standing Committee of the General Synod (hereafter referred to as " the Standing Committee ") shall appoint a Commission to be known as the Dioceses Commission (hereafter referred to as " the Commission "), and the Commission shall have such functions as are conferred or imposed on it by or under this Measure.

(2) The Commission may appoint committees consisting of such of its members as it may designate and may delegate to any such committee such of the functions of the Commission as it thinks fit.

(3) The Commission shall present annually to the General Synod a report of its activities during the preceding year.

Advisory functions of the Commission

2.—(1) It shall be the duty of the Commission, on the instructions of the General Synod, the Standing Committee, or the House of Bishops of the General Synod, to advise on matters affecting the diocesan structure

of the provinces of Canterbury and York or on the action which might be
taken under this Measure to improve the episcopal oversight of any
diocese therein or the administration of its affairs.

(2) Where it appears to the Commission that there is any such matter
as is mentioned in subsection (1) above on which it might usefully advise,
it may bring that matter to the attention of the General Synod or the
Standing Committee with a view to receiving instructions under that
subsection.

(3) The Commission shall be available to be consulted by any
diocesan synod or the bishop of any diocese on any action which might
be taken under this Measure in relation to the diocese.

Preparation, etc. of reorganisation schemes by the Commission

3.—(1) It shall be the duty of the Commission to prepare and make
schemes in accordance with sections 5 and 6 of this Measure, and a
scheme made under the said section 6 and confirmed by Order in Council
under section 7 is referred to in this Measure as a " reorganisation
scheme ".

(2) A reorganisation scheme may make provision for one or more of
the following purposes—

(*a*) the foundation of a new bishopric with a diocese constituted from
existing dioceses and, if necessary, the dissolution of an existing
diocese and the abolition of the bishopric thereof;

(*b*) the transfer of the whole of the area of any diocese to another
diocese and the dissolution of the first mentioned diocese and
the abolition of the bishopric thereof;

(*c*) the transfer of parts of the area of any diocese to other dioceses
and, if necessary, the dissolution of the first mentioned diocese
and the abolition of the bishopric thereof;

(*d*) the transfer of a diocese from one province to the other.

(3) The Schedule to this Measure, which sets out the provisions which
must or may be made by a reorganisation scheme, shall have effect.

Procedure for making reorganisation schemes

Application for reorganisation scheme

4.—(1) Subject to the provisions of this section, the bishop of a
diocese may, with the consent of the Standing Committee, submit to the
Commission proposals to be implemented by a reorganisation scheme
relating to that diocese.

(2) The proposals referred to in subsection (1) above shall be prepared
by the bishop of the diocese concerned after preliminary consultation
with the diocesan synod of that diocese, and an application by him for
consent under that susbsection shall set out the proposals which have
been so prepared.

(3) Where such proposals would, if implemented, affect two or more
dioceses, the proposals shall be prepared by the bishops of those dioceses
after preliminary consultation by each of them with the diocesan synod
of his diocese, and an application for consent under subsection (1) above
shall be made by the said bishops acting jointly.

(4) Section 4 (4) of the Synodical Government Measure 1969 shall not
be taken as permitting the consultative functions of a diocesan synod
under this section to be discharged on its behalf by the bishop's council
and standing committee of that synod.

Preparation of draft scheme by the Commission

5.—(1) In this section " interested parties ", in relation to any draft scheme, means—

(a) the bishop of every diocese which would be affected by the implementing of such scheme and the archbishop of the province in which that diocese is;

(b) every suffragan bishop, and every archdeacon, of every such diocese;

(c) the diocesan synod of every such diocese;

(d) the Commissioners;

(e) the Charity Commissioners;

(f) the body which for the purposes of the Cathedrals Measure 1976 is the consenting body of the cathedral church of each of the dioceses which would be affected by the implementing of such scheme;

(g) where the implementing of such scheme would result in the transfer of a diocese from one province to the other, the archbishop of that other province;

(h) the deanery synod of any deanery which would be particularly affected by the implementing of any provision of such scheme;

(i) the incumbent or priest in charge, and the parochial church council, of any parish or conventional district which would be particularly affected by the implementing of any such provision;

(j) such other persons, if any, who would be so affected as the Commission thinks fit.

(2) On receiving proposals submitted to it under section 4 of this Measure the Commission shall, in consultation with the Commissioners, first prepare a detailed estimate of the financial effect of the proposals (" the financial estimate ") and shall then, as it thinks fit, either—

(a) prepare a draft scheme to give effect to the proposals with such amendments, if any, as the Commission thinks should be made therein; or

(b) report to the Standing Committee and to the bishop of every diocese concerned that it has decided not to proceed with the preparation of such a scheme, giving the reasons for that decision.

(3) Where the Commission decides to proceed under subsection (2) (a) above it shall send a copy of the draft scheme and of the financial estimate to every interested party together with a notice stating that written representations with respect to the draft scheme may be made to the Commission not later than a date specified in the notice, being a date not less than three, nor more than six, months after the service of the notice.

(4) After considering any representations made to it under subsection (3) above the Commission shall, as it thinks fit, either proceed under subsection (5) below or report to the Standing Committee and to the bishop of every diocese concerned that it has decided not to proceed further with the scheme in question, giving the reasons for that decision.

(5) Where the Commission decides to proceed under this subsection, it shall make such amendments, if any, in the draft scheme as it thinks fit as a result of such representations, and such amendments, if any, in the financial estimate as, after consultation with the Commissioners, it thinks necessary, and shall then submit the draft scheme to the diocesan synod of every diocese which would be affected by the implementing of that scheme for its consent.

(6) A copy of the draft scheme and of a report thereon by the

Commission shall be sent to every member of every such synod at least six weeks before the session at which the draft scheme is considered.

(7) The report referred to in subsection (6) above shall include the financial estimate, as amended (if at all) under subsection (5) above, and a summary of any representations made to the Commission under subsection (8) above which the Commission thinks should be brought to the attention of the diocesan synod.

Making of reorganisation scheme

6.—(1) Subject to subsection (2) below, if the diocesan synod of every diocese affected by a draft scheme prepared under section 5 of this Measure gives its consent under subsection (5) thereof, the Commission shall lay the draft scheme before the General Synod for its approval.

(2) If, in the case of a draft scheme which affects two or more dioceses, the diocesan synod of any of those dioceses does not give its consent under the said section 5 (5) and it appears to the Standing Committee, on an application made to it by the Commission, that the interest of that diocese in the scheme is so small that the withholding of consent by the diocesan synod thereof should not prevent the submission of the draft scheme to the General Synod, the Standing Committee may authorise the Commission to lay the draft scheme before the General Synod.

(3) A copy of the draft scheme and of the report referred to in section 5 (6) of this Measure shall be sent to every member of the General Synod at least fourteen days before the beginning of the group of sessions at which the draft scheme is considered.

(4) If the General Synod approves such a scheme a copy of the draft scheme shall be signed in accordance with subsection (5) below and the Commission shall thereby make the scheme.

(5) A copy of the draft scheme shall be signed by the chairman of the Commission on its behalf or, in the case of the absence or incapacity of the chairman, by two other members of the Commission nominated by the Commission for that purpose; and the signing of the copy of the draft scheme by the chairman or by two members nominated as aforesaid shall be conclusive evidence that the provisions of this Measure relating to the draft scheme have been complied with.

Confirmation of scheme by Order in Council

7.—(1) As soon as possible after a scheme is made under section 6 of this Measure the Commission shall submit the scheme for confirmation by Her Majesty in Council, who may confirm the scheme by Order in Council.

(2) As soon as possible after a scheme is confirmed by Order in Council under this section there shall be published in the London Gazette a notice sufficiently identifying the scheme and stating that it has been confirmed and where a copy of the Order in Council may be obtained.

(8) The Commission shall send a copy of every such Order in Council to the Commissioners and to the registrar of every diocese affected by the scheme, and the registrar shall file it in the diocesan registry.

Supplementary provisions with respect to reorganisation schemes

8.—(1) Except in so far as a reorganisation scheme, or any provision therof, is expressed to come into operation on a date, event or contingency specified therein, it shall come into operation on the first day of the month next following the confirmation of the scheme by Order in Council under section 7 of this Measure.

(2) A reorganisation scheme may be varied or revoked by a subsequent reorganisation scheme.

(3) Any Order in Council confirming a reorganisation scheme under this Measure may revoke any Order in Council confirming such a scheme made thereunder.

*Temporary provisions with respect to membership of Convocations, etc.
after coming into force of reorganisation scheme*

Power of General Synod to make temporary provision with respect to membership of Convocations, etc.

9.—(1) The General Synod may, by resolution, make provision with respect to—

    (a) the representation in the Convocations of Canterbury and York or either of them, as the circumstances require, during the transitional period of any new diocese created by a reorganisation scheme, any diocese the area of which is altered by such a scheme or any diocese transferred by such a scheme from one province to the other; and

    (b) the representation in the House of Laity of the General Synod during that period of any such diocese.

(2) In exercising its powers under subsection (1) above the General Synod—

    (a) shall, as respects any new diocese created by the scheme, determine the number of elected members who are to represent that diocese in a Convocation or in the House of Laity;

    (b) may, as respects any diocese the area of which is altered by the scheme, alter the number of elected members fixed for that diocese by a determination of the General Synod in force at the passing of a resolution under this section;

but the General Synod shall not have power by virtue of this subsection to increase, as respects the Convocations, the total number of proctors elected for all the dioceses, or, as respects the House of Laity, the total number of members elected by the diocesan electors of all the dioceses, being the numbers fixed by a determination of the General Synod in force at the passing of the said subsection.

(3) In exercising its powers under subsection (1) above the General Synod may allocate any members of a Convocation, or of the House of Laity, who were originally elected by the diocesan electors of—

    (a) a diocese dissolved by the scheme or an electoral area thereof, or

    (b) a diocese part of which is by virtue of the scheme to become part of another diocese or an electoral area of the first-mentioned diocese,

to such diocese, being a new diocese created by the scheme or a diocese the area of which is altered by the scheme, as the Synod may determine.

(4) Any member of a Convocation or of the House of Laity allocated to a diocese in accordance with a determination of the General Synod under subsection (3) above shall be in the same position as if he had been elected by the diocesan electors of that diocese.

(5) A resolution under this section may make provision with respect to any matter incidental to, or consequential on, the other matters with respect to which provision may be made by such a resolution.

(6) The power of the General Synod to make provision in pursuance of this section shall be exercisable on or after the date on which the reorganisation scheme in question is approved by the Synod under section 6 of this Measure.

(7) In this section " transitional period " means the period beginning with the date of the commencement of the relevant provision of the reorganisation scheme in question and ending with the date of the dissolution of the General Synod which is in being on the first mentioned date, and " relevant provision " means the provision creating a new diocese, altering the area of a diocese or transferring a diocese from one province to the other, as the circumstances require.

(8) The New Dioceses (Transitional Provisions) Measure 1927 is hereby repealed.

Provisions with respect to the discharge of episcopal functions

Temporary delegation by instrument of certain functions to suffragan bishop

10.—(1) Subject to the provisions of this section, the bishop of a diocese may by an instrument under his hand delegate to a suffragan bishop of the diocese such of his functions as may be specified in the instrument.

(2) Such instrument may provide for the discharge of any function specified therein to be subject to such conditions as may be so specified.

(3) Such instrument may provide that the functions thereby delegated may be discharged by the suffragan bishop throughout the diocese or only in a particular area thereof specified in the instrument.

(4) Such instrument may provide that any function specified therein shall be discharged by the bishop of the diocese and the suffragan bishop acting jointly.

(5) Such instrument may provide for the delegation to be for a period specified in the instrument, but if the instrument so provides, it shall not prevent the making of a fresh instrument at the expiration of that period.

(6) Subject to subsection (7) below, such instrument shall cease to have effect on the date on which—

(*a*) the period, if any, specified in the instrument in accordance with subsection (5) above expires, or

(*b*) the bishop of the diocese ceases to hold that office, or

(*c*) the suffragan bishop to whom functions are delegated by the instrument ceases to hold that office,

whichever first occurs.

(7) Where but for this subsection such instrument would cease to have effect on the date on which the bishop of the diocese ceases to hold that office, it shall, except as provided by section 14 of this Measure, continue to have effect until the date of the expiration of a period of two monhs beginning with the date on which another person becomes the bishop of that diocese or the date on which the suffragan bishop to whom functions are delegated by the instrument ceases to hold that office, whichever first occurs.

(8) Subject to subsection (9) below, the bishop of a diocese may vary or revoke an instrument made by him under this section by a subsequent instrument made thereunder.

(9) Subject to subsection (10) below, the bishop shall not make an instrument under this section without the consent of the diocesan synod.

(10) Where either or both of the following functions, namely, the administration of the rite of confirmation and the holding of ordinations, is or are the only functions to be specified in an instrument under this section, the bishop may make the instrument without the consent of the diocesan synod.

(11) An instrument under this section shall come into operation on

the day after the day on which it is made or on such later date as may be specified therein.

(12) On making an instrument under this section the bishop shall send a copy of the instrument to the Commissioners and to the registrar of the diocese, and the registrar shall file it in the diocesan registry.

(13) The making of an instrument under this section shall not be taken as divesting the bishop of the diocese of any of his functions.

Permanent provision by scheme with respect to discharge of episcopal functions

11.—(1) A scheme under this section shall provide for the division of a diocese into areas and for specifying the bishop, either the bishop of the diocese or a suffragan bishop thereof, or the bishops, being the bishop of the diocese and a suffragan bishop thereof, who is to have, or are to share, the episcopal oversight of each such area.

(2) A scheme under this section shall provide that any suffragan bishop who under the scheme is to have, or is to share with the bishop of the diocese, the episcopal oversight of an area of the diocese shall, in relation to that area, discharge such of the functions of the bishop of the diocese as may be specified in the scheme.

(3) A scheme under this section may provide for the discharge of any function specified therein to be subject to such conditions as may be so specified.

(4) A scheme under this section may provide that any function specified therein shall be discharged by the bishop of the diocese and a suffragan bishop acting jointly.

(5) Where by virtue of such a scheme the episcopal oversight of a diocese will be shared by more than two bishops, the scheme may require those bishops to meet together periodically as an episcopal chapter.

(6) Subject to section 13 (1) of this Measure, a scheme under this section shall bind the person who when the scheme is made is the bishop of the diocese to which the scheme relates and his successors in that office.

(7) The making of a scheme under this section shall not be taken as divesting the bishop of the diocese to which the scheme relates of any of his functions.

Making of scheme under s. 11

12.—(1) The bishop of a diocese may, with the consent of the Standing Committee, prepare a draft of a scheme under section 11 of this Measure and submit it to the Commission for it to report thereon.

(2) On receiving a draft scheme submitted to it under subsection (1) above the Commission shall, in consultation with the Commissioners, prepare an estimate of the financial effect of the scheme and shall include that estimate in its report on the scheme.

(3) The bishop shall consider the report of the Commission on the draft scheme, and if he decides to proceed with the scheme he may either—

(*a*) lay the draft scheme before the diocesan synod for its approval; or

(*b*) make such amendments in that scheme as he thinks fit and submit the amended draft scheme to the Commission for it to make a further report thereon.

(4) On receiving an amended draft scheme submitted to it under subsection (3) above the Commission shall, in consultation with the Commissioners, make such amendments, if any, in the estimate of the financial effect of the scheme as it thinks necessary and shall include that estimate as amended (if at all) in its report on the draft scheme.

(5) Where the bishop has proceeded under subsection (3) (*b*) above, he shall consider the report of the Commission on the draft scheme, as amended by him, and if he decides to proceed with the scheme he shall lay the draft scheme as so amended before the diocesan synod for its approval.

(6) A copy of the draft scheme and of the report of the Commission thereon shall be sent to every member of the diocesan synod at least six weeks before the session at which the draft scheme is considered.

(7) If the draft scheme is approved by the diocesan synod, the draft scheme shall be laid before the General Synod.

(8) A copy of the draft scheme and of the report of the Commission thereon shall be sent to every member of the General Synod at least fourteen days before the beginning of the group of sessions at which it is laid.

(9) If the General Synod resolves that such scheme be not made no further proceedings shall be taken thereon, but without prejudice to the laying before the General Synod of a new draft.

(10) If—

> (*a*) no resolution under subsection (9) above is tabled before the end of the group of sessions during which the draft scheme was laid before the Synod; or
>
> (*b*) such a resolution is so tabled but is defeated or withdrawn during the group of sessions during which it is considered,

a copy of the draft scheme shall be signed by the bishop of the diocese who shall thereby make the scheme.

(11) A scheme under section 11 of this Measure shall come into operation on the day after the day on which it is made or on such later date as may be specified in the scheme.

(12) On making a scheme under the said section 11 the bishop shall send a copy of the scheme to the Commissioners and to the registrar of the diocese, and the registrar shall file it in the diocesan registry.

Variation, etc. of scheme under s. 11

13.—(1) Subject to the provisions of this section, a scheme under section 11 of this Measure may be varied or revoked by a subsequent scheme made thereunder.

(2) If, on the application of the bishop of a diocese, the Commission so directs, subsections (4) to (6) below shall apply in relation to a scheme which the bishop proposes to make under the said section 11 (hereinafter referred to as " the amending scheme ") and the purpose of which is to make minor amendments of a scheme under that section (hereinafter referred to as " the original scheme "), and section 12 of this Measure, except subsections (6), (11) and (12), shall not so apply.

(3) An application for a direction under subsection (2) above shall specify the amendments which it is proposed should be made by the amending scheme, and the Commission shall issue the direction if, but only if, it is satisfied that none of the amendments is of substantial importance and that the effect of the amendments, if made, will be neither—

> (*a*) to alter the areas into which the diocese was divided by the original scheme, nor
>
> (*b*) to increase significantly the cost of operating that scheme.

(4) The bishop of the diocese concerned shall prepare a draft of the amending scheme to which a direction under subsection (3) above relates and submit it to the Commission for it to report thereon.

(5) The bishop shall consider the report of the Commission on the draft scheme and if he decides to proceed with the scheme he shall lay the draft scheme before the diocesan synod for its approval.

(6) If the draft scheme is approved by the diocesan synod, a copy thereof shall be signed by the bishop of the diocese who shall thereby make the scheme.

(7) In this section " amendment " includes revocation.

Special provision with respect to rights of collation

14. Where by virtue of any provision of an instrument made under section 10 of this Measure, or of a scheme made under section 11 thereof, or of a reorganisation scheme, the right to collate to any benefice upon a vacancy is exercisable by a suffragan bishop of the diocese to which the instrument or scheme relates, that provision shall be of no effect during a vacancy in the see of the bishop of that diocese.

Abolition of power to commission suffragan bishop

15.—(1) The power of the bishop of a diocese to give a commission to a suffragan bishop is hereby abolished.

(2) The following provision of the Suffragan Bishops Act 1534, that is to say,—

(a) in section 2 (powers of suffragan bishops), the words from " and have such capacitie " to the end, and

(b) in section 4 (authority, etc. of suffragan bishops limited by their commissions), the words from " nor use " to the end,

are hereby repealed.

(3) Neither the abolition by subsection (1) above of the power mentioned therein nor any repeal effected by subsection (2) above shall invalidate any commission given to a suffragan bishop which is in force immediately before the commencement of this Measure.

(4) Where but for this subsection any such commission would cease to have effect, that commission shall continue in force until—

(a) the date on which the suffragan bishop to whom the commission was given ceases to hold that office, or

(b) the date on which the commission is revoked by the bishop of the diocese, whichever first occurs.

(5) So long as any such commission remains in force so much of section 2 of the said Act of 1534 as is repealed by subsection (2) above shall, notwithstanding the repeal, continue to apply to the suffragan bishop to whom the commission was given.

(6) In section 6 of the said Act of 1534 (residence of suffragan bishops), for the words " where he shall have comyssyon " there shall be substituted the words " of the bishop to whom he shall be suffragan ".

Provision with respect to Acts, etc. which confer functions on diocesan bishop

16. Any Act, Measure or Canon which confers or imposes on the bishop of a diocese any functions which by virtue of an instrument made under section 10 of this Measure, a scheme made under section 11 thereof or a reorganisation scheme may be discharged by a suffragan bishop shall have effect in any diocese subject to the provisions of any such instrument or scheme relating to that diocese and for the time being in force, and references in that Act, Measure or Canon to the bishop of a diocese shall be construed accordingly.

Area Synods

Provision for constituting area synods for episcopal areas

17.—(1) In this section '' episcopal area '', in relation to a diocese, means any of the areas into which the diocese is to be, or is for the time being, divided by a provision included in a reorganisation scheme by virtue of paragraph 7 (1) of the Schedule to this Measure or by a scheme under section 11 thereof.

(2) Any of the following schemes, that is to say, a reorganisation scheme, a scheme under the said section 11 and a scheme under this section, may make provision—

(a) for constituting an area synod for each of the episcopal areas of a diocese; and

(b) for empowering the diocesan synod from time to time to delegate to each area synod so constituted such of its functions in respect of the episcopal area for which that synod is to act as may be specified in a resolution of the diocesan synod.

(3) Part IV of the Church Representation Rules as for the time being in force and any other provisions of those rules relating to diocesan synods, the election of members of such synods and the vacation of the seats of those members shall apply in relation to an area synod constituted by any such scheme as is mentioned in subsection (2) above, the election of members thereof and the vacation of the seats of those members with such modifications, adaptations and exceptions as the scheme may provide.

(4) The bishop's council and standing committee of a diocesan synod may with the consent of the bishop of the diocese delegate to the bishop's council and standing committee of an area synod constituted for an episcopal area of the diocese such of its functions in respect of that area as it may from time to time determine.

(5) Sections 11 (6), 12 and 13 of this Measure shall apply in relation to a scheme under this section as they apply in relation to a scheme under the said section 11.

Creation or revival of suffragan sees

Provisions with respect to creation or revival of suffragan sees

18.—(1) No bishop of a diocese shall—

(a) petition Her Majesty in Council under the Suffragans Nomination Act 1888 to direct that a town in his diocese shall be taken and accepted for a see of a suffragan bishop as if it had been included in the Suffragan Bishops Act 1534, or

(b) petition Her Majesty to make an appointment under the said Act of 1534 to a see in his diocese which has been vacant and to which no appointment has been made thereunder during at least the preceding five years,

unless his proposal to do so is approved by the diocesan synod and the General Synod under this section.

(2) After consulting (if the bishop is not also an archbishop) the archbishop of the province the bishop shall, with the consent of the Standing Committee, send a copy of his proposal, together with a statement of his reasons for making it, to the Commission for it to report thereon.

(3) On receiving such proposal, the Commission shall, in consultation with the Commissioners, prepare an estimate of the financial effect of the proposal, if implemented, and shall include the estimate in its report.

(4) The bishop shall consider the report of the Commission on the proposal and if he decides to proceed with it he shall lay the proposal before the diocesan synod for its approval.

(5) A copy of the proposal and of the report of the Commission thereon shall be sent to every member of the diocesan synod at least six weeks before the session at which the proposal is considered.

(6) If the proposal is approved by the diocesan synod, the bishop shall lay the proposal before the General Synod for its approval.

(7) A copy of the proposal and of the report of the Commission thereon shall be sent to every member of the General Synod at least fourteen days before the beginning of the group of sessions at which the proposal is considered.

Provisions with respect to discharge of functions of certain bodies corporate, etc.

Schemes with respect to discharge of functions of diocesan bodies corporate, etc.

19.—(1) In this and the next following section " diocesan body " means any body corporate or committee established for a diocese or any part thereof, other than a diocesan synod or the bishop's council and standing committee of a diocese.

(2) A scheme under this section may make provision for one or more of the following purposes: —

(a) for constituting a body corporate or committee to discharge in respect of such dioceses as are specified in the scheme the functions previously discharged in respect of each of those dioceses by such diocesan body as is so specified and for winding up or dissolving each such body;

(b) for empowering such diocesan bodies for such dioceses, or such parts of such dioceses, as are so specified to discharge any of their functions jointly and, in particular, to establish a joint committee to discharge any of the functions of each such body;

(c) for empowering such a diocesan body for such diocese as is so specified to arrange for any of its functions to be discharged by the corresponding diocesan body for such other diocese as is so specified or by a committee or sub-committee of that body.

(3) The bishops of the dioceses to which a scheme under this section is to apply (" the participating dioceses ") shall prepare a draft of such scheme and shall, with the consent of the Standing Committee, send copies of the draft to the Commission and the Commissioners for them to advise and comment thereon.

(4) If the draft scheme would, if implemented, affect a charity established for ecclesiastical purposes of the Church of England, not being an exempt charity within the meaning of the Charities Act 1960, the bishops of the participating dioceses shall cause a copy of the draft to be sent to the Charity Commissioners.

(5) After any comments made by the Commission or the Commissioners on the draft scheme have been received by the bishops of the participating dioceses and such amendments, if any, as the said bishops think fit have been made therein, the draft scheme shall be laid before the diocesan synod of every participating diocese for its approval.

(6) A copy of the draft scheme and of any comments thereon made by the Commission or the Commissioners shall be sent to every member of the diocesan synod of every participating diocese at least six weeks before the session at which the draft scheme is considered.

(7) If the draft scheme is approved by the diocesan synod of every

participating diocese, a copy of the draft scheme shall be signed by the bishops of the participating dioceses who shall thereby make the scheme.

(8) A scheme under this section shall come into operation on the first day of the month next following the making of the scheme or on such later date as may be specified therein.

(9) The bishop of each participating diocese shall send a copy of the scheme to the Commissioners and to the registrar of his diocese, and the registrar shall file it in the diocesan registry.

Further provisions with respect to schemes under s. 19

20.—(1) A scheme under section 19 of this Measure which makes provision for either of the purposes mentioned in subsection (2) (*a*) or (*b*) thereof may provide for regulating the term of office of members of the body corporate or committee referred to therein, for regulating the proceedings of that body or committee and for determining the manner in which its expenses are to be defrayed.

(2) A scheme under the said section 19 may contain such incidental, consequential and supplementary provisions as appear to the bishops by whom the scheme is to be made to be necessary or expedient for bringing the scheme into operation and giving full effect thereto and, in particular, but without prejudice to the generality of the foregoing words, provisions—

(*a*) for the transfer of property and liabilities;

(*b*) for the adjustment of accounts and apportionment of liabilities; and

(*c*) for the settlement of any differences arising in consequence of the operation of the scheme.

(3) Where a scheme under the said section 19 is in force, any enactment relating to the functions to which the scheme applies or the diocesan bodies by which or the dioceses in respect of which they are to be discharged shall have effect subject to all necessary modifications in its application in relation to those functions and the persons by whom and the dioceses in respect of which (whether in pursuance of the scheme or otherwise) they are to be discharged.

(4) A scheme under the said section 19 may be varied or revoked by a subsequent scheme made thereunder.

Miscellaneous and Supplemental

Power of Commissioners to pay stipend, etc. of certain bishops

21. Where a new bishopric is founded and a new diocese created by a reorganisation scheme, the Commissioners shall have power—

(*a*) to pay out of their general fund to the bishop of that diocese, and to any suffragan bishop thereof, such a stipend and such annual sum in respect of the expenses incurred by him in connection with the performance of the duties attaching to his office as they think fit; and

(*b*) to provide the bishop of that diocese with a suitable residence; but before exercising the power conferred on them by paragraph (*b*) above the Commissioners shall consult the bishop's council and standing committee of that diocese.

Provisions with respect to cathedral church of new diocese

22.—(1) The Cathedrals Measures 1963 and 1976, with any necessary modifications, shall apply to a church which in accordance with a reorganisation scheme is to be or has become the cathedral church of a new diocese created by that scheme as if it—

  (*a*) were a cathedral church to which those Measures apply and a cathedral church within the meaning of those Measures; and

  (*b*) were a dean and chapter cathedral or a parish church cathedral within the meaning of those Measures, as that scheme determines in accordance with paragraph 4 (1) of the Schedule to this Measure.

(2) Sections 16 and 17 of the said Measure of 1963 (which respectively relate to property vested in provosts of parish church cathedrals and to property of benefices of such cathedrals) shall have effect in relation to a church to which by virtue of subsection (1) above that Measure applies as if it were a parish church cathedral within the meaning thereof, and section 27 thereof (plans for inspection and care of cathedral property) shall have effect in relation to a cathedral church to which by virtue of that subsection that Measure applies, subject, in each case, to the following modification, that is to say, for any reference therein to the passing of that Measure there shall be substituted a reference to the coming into force of the constitution and statutes provided for the church in question by virtue of paragraph 4 (1) of the Schedule to this Measure.

Amendment of certain provisions of reorganisation scheme by other schemes

23.—(1) Sections 11 (6) and 13 of this Measure shall apply to provisions included in a reorganisation scheme by virtue of paragraph 7 of the Schedule to this Measure as if those provisions were a scheme made under section 11 by the bishop of the diocese concerned who is in office at the date on which those provisions come into operation.

(2) Section 40 of the Pastoral Measure 1968 (amendment and revocation of pastoral schemes and orders) shall apply to provisions included in a reorganisation scheme by virtue of paragraph 8 of the said Schedule as if those provisions were a pastoral scheme or pastoral order made under that Measure.

Interpretation

24.—(1) In this Measure the following expressions have the meanings hereby respectively assigned to them:—

  " the Commission " has the meaning assigned by section 1 (1) of this Measure;

  " the Commissioners " means the Church Commissioners;

  " functions " include powers and duties;

  " reorganisation scheme " has the meaning assigned by section 3 (1) of this Measure;

  " Standing Committee " has the meaning assigned by section 1 (1) of this Measure.

(2) Any reference in this Measure to any enactment shall be construed as a reference to that enactment as amended by any subsequent enactment.

Short title, commencement and extent

25.—(1) This Measure may be cited as the Dioceses Measure 1978.

(2) This Measure shall come into operation at the expiration of a period of three months beginning with the date on which it is passed.

(3) This Measure shall extend to the provinces of Canterbury and York except the Channel Islands, but may be applied to the Channel Islands or either of them, as defined in the Channel Islands (Church Legislation) Measures 1931 and 1957, in accordance with those Measures.

SCHEDULE

CONTENTS OF REORGANISATION SCHEMES

Preliminary

1. In this Schedule, except where the context otherwise requires, " a scheme " means a reorganisation scheme.

Provisions relating to bishopric

2. A scheme by which a new bishropric is to be founded and a new diocese created shall provide for—
   (a) constituting the bishop of the diocese a corporation sole and investing him with all such rights, privileges and jurisdictions as are possessed by any other bishop in England;
   (b) subjecting the bishop of the diocese to the metropolitan jurisdiction of one of the archbishops;
   (c) designating the church which is to be the cathedral church of the diocese;
   (d) empowering Her Majesty, until a cathedral chapter for the cathedral church of the diocese is established, to grant to a body constituted by the scheme and styled the provisional chapter of the diocese a licence under the Great Seal to proceed to the election of a bishop of the diocese with a letter missive as provided by the Appointment of Bishops Act 1533 and conferring on the last mentioned chapter the right of proceeding to an election in manner provided by that Act.

(3) The Schedule to this Measure, which sets out the provisions for abolishing the bishopric and conferring rights to compensation on the bishop of the diocese.

Provisions relating to cathedral church, etc.

4.—(1) A scheme by which a new diocese is to be created shall determine whether the church which is to be the cathedral church of the diocese shall be a dean and chapter cathedral or a parish church cathedral for the purposes of the Cathedrals Measures 1963 and 1976 and shall provide—
   (a) for applying those Measures to that church with such modifications specified in the scheme as are necessary to enable a constitution and statutes to be provided for that church by a scheme under the said Measure of 1976; and
   (b) for constituting a body to be the consenting body of that church for the purposes of that Measure unless and until a scheme thereunder provides that some other body shall be the consenting body thereof for those purposes.

(2) A scheme by which a new diocese is to be created may provide for founding honorary canonries in the cathedral church of the diocese with power to dispense with the consent of the cathedral chapter of that church so long as there is no such chapter and, if necessary, altering the number of such canonries in the cathedral church of any other diocese affected by the scheme.

5.—(1) A scheme by which a diocese is to be dissolved shall provide for—
   (a) altering the status of the cathedral church of the diocese and abolishing the dean and chapter or cathedral chapter of that church and any other body, dignity or office therein;
   (b) conferring rights to compensation on the dean or provost of that church and any residentiary canon holding office in it;
   (c) transferring any property (including rights of patronage) vested in the dean and chapter, or cathedral chapter, of that church to such persons as may be specified in the scheme and vesting such property in those persons without any conveyance or other assurance.

(2) Without prejudice to sub-paragraph (1) (c) above, a scheme may provide for transferring any property (including rights of patronage) vested in the dean and chapter, or cathedral chapter, of the cathedral church of any diocese affected by the scheme to such persons as may be specified in the scheme and vesting such property in those persons without any conveyance or other assurance.

(3) A scheme by which a diocese is to be dissolved may provide that any moneys held by the Commissioners on behalf of the dean and chapter, or the cathedral chapter, of the cathedral church of the diocese shall be held by them on behalf of such other persons as may be specified in the scheme.

Provisions relating to suffragan bishoprics, etc.

6. A scheme may provide for vacating thes office of a suffragan bishop, and a scheme which does so shall also provide for conferring rights to compensation on the holder of that office.

7.—(1) A scheme may make the like provision as may be made by a scheme under section 11 of this Measure.

(2) A scheme may provide for abolishing or altering an episcopal area and may accordingly revoke or amend a scheme under the said section 11.

(3) In this paragraph "episcopal area" means any of the areas into which a diocese is divided by a scheme under the said section 11 or by any provision included in a scheme by virtue of sub-paragraph (1) above.

Provisions relating to archdeaconries and deaneries

8.—(1) A scheme by which a new diocese is to be created shall make provision, by the creation of new archdeaconries or otherwise, for the archidiaconal supervision of the parishes comprised in the diocese.

(2) A scheme may provide for creating, altering or dissolving an archdeaconry or deanery, and shall name any new archdeaconry or deanry created by the scheme.

9. A scheme by which a diocese or archdeaconry is to be dissolved shall make provision for conferring rights to compensation on an archdeacon whose office is to be abolished by the scheme.

Provisions relating to patronage

10. A scheme shall provide for transferring to the bishop of a diocese, or to the diocesan board of patronage thereof, any right of patronage of a benefice or canonry which by virtue of the scheme is to become a benefice or canonry in that diocese, being a right which immediately before the commencement of the scheme was vested in the bishop, or the diocesan board of patronage, of another diocese affected by the scheme, and for preventing the Benefices (Transfer of Rights of Patronage) Measure 1930 from applying to such a transfer.

Provisions relating to diocesan synods and other bodies

11.—(1) A scheme by which a new diocese is to be created shall make provision with respect to the membership of the diocesan synod of the new diocese during the transitional period.

(2) Any other scheme may make provision for altering the numbers of elected members of the diocesan synod of a diocese affected by the scheme, the alteration to have effect only during the transitional period.

(3) Where a diocese is to be dissolved by a scheme, the provision to be made under this paragraph shall include such provision as is necessary to ensure that all persons who immediately before the transitional period begins were members of the diocesan synod of that diocese, having been elected thereto by the houses of clergy or the houses of laity of the deanery synods in that diocese, will during the transitional period be members of the appropriate house of the diocesan synod of a diocese created or affected by the scheme.

(4) In this paragraph "transitional period" means the period beginning with the date of the commencement of the scheme in question and ending with the 1st September next following the election of members of diocesan synods next held after the first mentioned date in accordance with the Church Representation Rules as for the time being in force.

12. A scheme by which a new diocese is to be created shall make provision—

(a) requiring the diocesan synod thereof, at its first meeting, to appoint the bishop's council and standing committee of the synod and to constitute the diocesan board of finance for the diocese in accordance with the Diocesan Boards of Finance Measure 1925 and, at that or the next following meeting, to appoint every other board, committee or panel which such a synod is required by any Measure to appoint;

(b) authorising those persons who were members of that bishop's council and standing committee of any diocese any part of the area of which is to be comprised in the new diocese to act as bishop's council and standing committee of the diocesan synod of the new diocese until such a council and committee is appointed in accordance with a provision made by virtue of sub-paragraph (a) above;

(c) requiring the persons referred to in sub-paragraph (b) above to make the necessary arrangements for the first meeting of such synod and to settle the agenda for that meeting.

13. A scheme by which a diocese is to be dissolved shall provide for the winding up or dissolution of every diocesan body for the diocese.

In this paragraph " diocesan body " has the same meaning as in section 19 of this Measure.

Provisions relating to chancellors and registrars

14. A scheme by which a diocese is to be dissolved shall provide for conferring rights to compensation on the chancellor of the diocese and the registrar thereof.

Provisions relating to property

15.—(1) A scheme by which a new diocese is to be created shall provide for transferring any property vested in or held by a diocesan body for a former diocese to the corresponding body for the new diocese, when constituted, and vesting such property in that body without any conveyance or other assurance.

In this sub-paragraph " diocesan body " has the same meaning as in section 19 of this Measure.

(2) Without prejudice to the provisions of the Bishops Trusts Substitution Act 1858, such a scheme may provide for the trusts of any charity established for ecclesiastical purposes of the Church of England the property of which is vested in, or under the management or control of,—

(a) any of the following persons, that is to say, the bishop of a former diocese, any archdeacon of a former diocese and any rural dean thereof, or

(b) any of the following bodies, that is to say, the dean and chapter or cathedral chapter of the cathedral church of a former diocese, the diocesan board of finance therefor and any other diocesan authority therefor,

with or without, in any case other persons, to have effect with the substitution, for that person, of the person holding the corresponding office in the new diocese and, for that body, of the corresponding body in that diocese, and for any change under any such provision in the vesting of property to have effect without any conveyance or other assurance.

(3) In this paragraph " diocesan authority " has the same meaning as in the Parochial Church Councils (Powers) Measures 1956 and " former diocese " means a diocese any part of the area of which is to be comprised in the new diocese.

16. A scheme by which a new diocese is to be created shall provide for authorising the Commissioners to hold for the new diocese any fund held by them for a former diocese or to make such apportionment of that fund as between the new diocese and a former diocese as they think fit.

In this paragraph " former diocese " has the same meaning as in paragraph 15 above.

17. Paragraphs 15 and 16 above shall apply to a scheme by which the boundaries between dioceses are to be altered without creating a new diocese as if the diocese in which any part of the area of another diocese is to be comprised were the new diocese.

Provisions relating to records

18. A scheme may make provision for the transfer to the registrar of a diocese of the records and other documents relating to the benefices or parishes which by virtue of the scheme are to be comprised in that diocese and to the clergy who are to hold office therein.

Provisions relating to compensation

19. A scheme which provides for conferring rights to compensation on any person shall make provision with respect to—

(a) the persons by whom, and the manner in which, claims to, and the amount of, such compensation are to be determined;

(b) the matters to be taken into account in determining whether any claimant has suffered loss giving a right to compensation;

(c) the circumstances in which payment of such compensation consisting of periodical payments may be suspended, renewed or terminated or the amount thereof increased or reduced;

(*d*) the body by which, and the resources from which, such compensation is to be paid;

and different provision may be made in relation to different cases.

Provisions relating to proceedings in consistory court

20. A scheme by which a diocese is to be dissolved may make provision for enabling any proceedings in the consistory court of that diocese or any proceedings under the Faculty Jurisdiction Measure 1964 before an archdeacon of that diocese, being proceedings which are pending at the commencement of the scheme, to be heard and determined notwithstanding the dissolution of the diocese.

Provisions relating to supplementary, etc. matters

21.—(1) A scheme may make such supplementary, incidental, consequential or transitional provisions as appear to the Commission to be necessary or expedient for giving effect to the purposes of the scheme.

(2) Without prejudice to the generality of sub-paragraph (1) above, a scheme may make provision for preserving the effect of any thing of whatever nature done by a body established for a diocese which is to be dissolved by the scheme or any part of which is to be transferred to another diocese or by the holder of an office in such a diocese in his capacity as such.

(3) A scheme may amend or repeal any provision of any Order in Council made under any Act or Measure which provided for the foundation of a bishopric if it appears to the Commission that that provision is inconsistent with or rendered unnecessary by the provisions of the scheme.

(4) A scheme shall, where the Commission considers it appropriate, have annexed thereto a map showing the changes to be made by the scheme.

(5) A scheme may provide that the scheme shall come into operation on a specified date, or on the happening of a specified event or contingency and different dates, events or contingencies may be specified for different provisions.

Parochial Registers and Records Measure 1978

(1978 No. 2)

ARRANGEMENT OF SECTIONS

A MEASURE passed by the General Synod of the Church of England to consolidate with amendments certain enactments relating to the registration of baptisms and burials and to repeal some of those enactments without re-enactment; to make fresh provision in place of the Parochial Registers and Records Measure 1929 with respect to diocesan record offices, the deposit therein of certain parochial registers and other records in ecclesiastical custody and the care of such registers and records; and for purposes connected therewith.

[2nd February 1978]

General Note

This Measure consolidates with amendments certain enactments relating to the registration of baptisms and burials and repeals some of those enactments; it also makes fresh provision with respect to diocesan record offices.

S. 1 states that every parish shall have a register book of public and private baptisms, and sets out the format of such book; s. 2 provides for the registration of baptisms in the register book; s. 3 provides for the registration of burials in the register book; s. 4 gives the procedure to be followed when errors are discovered in the register book of baptisms or burials; s. 5 applies ss. 1–4 to cathedrals and collegiate churches, and other non-parochial churches; s. 6 states that the incumbent of the benefice shall have custody of the register books of baptisms, confirmations, banns of marriage, marriage, burials or services provided for any church in his parish; s. 7 deals with the provision of diocesan record offices; s. 8 states that a diocesan record office may be used as a place of deposit for manorial documents; s. 9 provides for the periodic inspection of register books and records in parochial custody; s. 10 sets out the circumstances in which register books should be deposited in the diocesan record office; s. 11 deals with the safe-keeping, care and preservation of register books and records in parochial custody; s. 12 empowers the bishop to make an order for the deposit of register books in the diocesan record office; s. 13 relates to the return to parochial custody of register books deposited in the diocesan record office; s. 14 states that the chief officer of a diocesan record office shall custody of any register books or records deposited in that office; s. 15 provides for the transfer of certain books and records from one record office to another; s. 16 states that register books and records may be deposited in a diocesan record office or other suitable safe place for the purpose of exhibition or research; s. 17 provides for certain records and register books in diocesan record offices to be made available for exhibition or research; s. 18 sets out provisions ancillary to ss. 16 and 17; s. 19 provides for the disposal of register books and records on the dissolution of a parish; s. 20 relates to searches of certain register books; s. 21 empowers the bishop of a diocese to apply to the county court for an order that an unauthorised person do return register books in his possession; s. 22 makes special provision as to marriage registers; s. 23 applies s. 3 of the Church of England (Miscellaneous Provisions) Measure 1976 to the functions of a diocesan bishop in relation to matters arising under this Measure; s. 24 relates to the service of notices and orders; s. 25 contains definitions; s. 26 contains amendments, repeals and transitional provisions; s. 27 gives the short title and extent.

The Measure received the Royal Assent on February 2, 1978, and shall come into force on such day as the Archbishops of Canterbury and York may jointly appoint.

Registration of baptisms and burials

Provision of register books of baptisms and burials

1.—(1) A register book of public and private baptisms shall be provided for every parish or, in the case of a parish which has more than one parish church, for each such church, and a register book of burials shall be provided for every parish which has a burial ground in use or, in the case of a parish which has more than one such ground, for each such ground.

(2) The register books referred to in subsection (1) above shall be provided by, and shall be deemed to belong to, the parochial church council of the parish.

(3) Such register books shall be of durable material and the heads of information required by this Measure to be entered therein shall in the case of every such book provided after the commencement of this Measure be printed on every leaf thereof.

(4) Every place of entry in every such register book shall be numbered progressively from the beginning to the end of the book, beginning with the number one, and every entry shall be divided from the following entry by a printed line.

Registration of baptisms

2.—(1) Where the ceremony of baptism according to the rites of the Church of England is performed—

(a) in the parish church of a parish or, in the case of a parish having more than one such church, any parish church thereof, or

(b) in any other place in a parish by a minister of the parish,

the person by whom the ceremony was performed shall as soon as possible thereafter enter in the appropriate register book of baptisms the particulars required in Form No. 1 in Schedule 1 to this Measure and shall sign the register in the place provided.

(2) Where the ceremony of baptism according to the said rites is performed in any place in a parish other than a parish church by a person who is not a minister of the parish, the person by whom the ceremony was performed shall as soon as possible thereafter send to the incumbent or priest in charge of the parish a certificate signed by him certifying when and where the ceremony was performed and containing the other particulars required in Form No. 1 in the said Schedule 1.

(3) Where the ceremony of baptism according to the said rites is performed in an extra-parochial place, then, unless the ceremony is performed in a church or chapel for which a register book of baptisms has been provided by virtue of section 5 of this Measure or any enactment repealed by this Measure, the person by whom the ceremony was performed shall as soon as possible thereafter send to the incumbent or priest in charge of such of the adjoining parishes as the bishop in whose diocese that place is may direct a certificate signed by him certifying when and where the ceremony was performed and containing the other particulars required in Form No. 1 in the said Schedule 1.

(4) On receiving a certificate under subsection (2) or (3) above the incumbent or priest in charge shall enter particulars of the baptism to performed in a church or chapel for which a register book of baptisms and shall add to the entry the following words " According to the certificate of   received by me on the   day of   ".

(5) In this section " minister ", in relation to a parish, means the incumbent of the benefice to which the parish belongs, a vicar in a team ministry for the area of that benefice, the priest in charge of the parish and any curate licensed to officiate in the parish.

Registration of burials

3.—(1) Subject to subsection (4) below, the minister officiating at a burial according to the rites of the Church of England shall as soon as possible after the burial has taken place enter in the appropriate register book of burials the particulars required in Form No. 2 in Schedule 1 to this Measure and shall sign the register in the place provided.

(2) Subject to subsection (4) below, where a burial according to the said rites takes place in an extra-parochial place, then, unless the burial

takes place in the burial ground of a church or chapel for which a register book of burials has been provided by virtue of section 5 of this Measure or any enactment repealed by this Measure, the minister officiating at the burial shall as soon as possible after the burial has taken place send to the incumbent or priest in charge of such of the adjoining parishes as the bishop in whose diocese that place is may direct a certificate signed by him certifying when and where the burial took place and containing the other particulars required in Form No. 2 in the said Schedule 1.

(3) On receiving such certificate the incumbent or priest in charge shall enter particulars of the burial to which the certificate relates in the appropriate register book of burials and shall add to the entry the following words " According to the certificate of   received by me on the   day of   ".

(4) Subsections (1) and (2) above shall not apply in relation to a burial which takes place in a cemetery to which an Act incorporating the Cemeteries Clauses Act 1847 applies or in a cemetery provided and maintained by a burial authority within the meaning of section 214 of the Local Government Act 1972.

(5) In this section " minister " means any person who is authorised to bury the dead according to the rites of the Church of England.

Corrections of errors in register book of baptisms or burials

4.—(1) A person required to register a baptism or a burial under this Measure who discovers an error in the form or substance of an entry made in the register book of baptisms or burials, as the case may be, shall not be liable to any penalty under the Forgery Act 1913 by reason only that within one month after the discovery of the error he corrects the erroneous entry in the presence of the persons specified in subsection (2) below by entry in the margin of the register book, without any alteration of the original entry.

(2) The persons referred to in subsection (1) above are—

    (*a*) in the case of an erroneous entry in a register book of baptisms, either or both of the parents of the child to whom the entry relates or, in the case of the death or absence of both of them, the churchwardens of the parish to which the register book belongs; and

    (*b*) in the case of an erroneous entry in a register book of burials, two persons who were present at the burial to which the entry relates or the churchwardens of the parish to which the register book belongs.

(3) Any such marginal entry as is referred to in subsection (1) above shall be signed by the person by whom the entry is made and shall be attested by the persons in whose presence the entry is required to be made, and the person by whom the entry is made shall add the date when it is made.

Application of ss. 1 to 4 to cathedrals, etc.

5. The preceding provisions of this Measure shall, so far as applicable and with the necessary modifications, apply in relation to the provision of register books of baptisms or burials for any cathedral or collegiate church or any other church or chapel which does not belong to a parish, the registration of baptisms performed in any such church or chapel and the registration of burials which take place in any burial ground belonging to any such church or chapel.

Custody of register books in parochial custody

Custody of register books in parochial custody

6.—(1) The incumbent of the benefice to which a parish belongs shall have the custody of the register books of baptisms, confirmations, banns of marriage, marriages, burials or services which in accordance with any enactment or Canon are provided for any parish church or other place of public worship in the parish.

(2) During a vacancy in a benefice the churchwardens of the parish, or of each of the parishes, belonging to the benefice shall, subject to subsection (3) below, have the custody of the register books mentioned in subsection (1) above.

(3) Where the bishop appoints a priest in charge for any benefice to which a suspension period within the meaning of the Pastoral Measure 1968 applies, the priest in charge shall during that period have the custody of the said books.

(4) The preceding provisions do not apply to any register books which are for the time being deposited in a diocesan record office.

Diocesan record offices

Provision of diocesan record offices

7.—(1) Subject to subsection (2) below, there shall be a diocesan record office for every diocese.

(2) If the bishop of a diocese considers it necessary for the diocese to have more than one diocesan record office, he shall divide the diocese into parts for the purpose of this section, and there shall be a diocesan record office for each part.

(3) The diocesan record office for a diocese or part thereof shall be the place which is for the time being designated by the bishop of the diocese as such an office by an instrument in writing.

(4) The bishop of a diocese shall not designate a place as a diocesan record office unless that place—

    (*a*) is a depository provided by a local authority under the Local Government (Records) Act 1962 or the Local Government Act 1972 for documents deposited with or belonging to that authority; or

    (*b*) is a place of deposit appointed under the Public Records Act 1958; or

    (*c*) is in the opinion of the bishop a suitable place to be appointed as a place of deposit under that Act;

and before he designates any such place as a diocesan record office he shall obtain the agreement of the authority who will be responsible for register books and records deposited in that place under this Measure.

(5) Where the bishop of a diocese makes an instrument under this section, he shall notify the diocesan synod that he has done so and of the effect of the instrument.

(6) Where a diocese has more than one diocesan record office, any question which arises under this Measure by reason of that fact shall be determined by the bishop of the diocese.

(7) Any place which immediately before the commencement of this Measure is the diocesan record office for a diocese or part thereof under the Parochial Registers and Records Measure 1929 shall be deemed to have been duly designated by the bishop of the diocese under this section as such office; but the preceding provision shall not be taken as affecting the right of the bishop of the diocese to withdraw the designation or the

right of the authority responsible for register books and records deposited in such office to withdraw its agreement to the designation.

Use of diocesan record office as place of deposit for manorial documents, etc.

8.—(1) A diocesan record office may be used as a place of deposit for manorial documents within the meaning of section 144A of the Law of Property Act 1922 or documents to which section 36 (2) of the Tithe Act 1936 applies if it has been approved by the Master of the Rolls under any rules made by him under the said section 144A or the said section 36, as the case may be, as a place of deposit for such documents.

(2) Without prejudice to subsection (1) above nothing in this Measure shall be taken to affect the provisions of the said section 144A or of section 36 (2) of the Tithe Act 1936 (which respectively provide that manorial documents and sealed copies of certain documents made pursuant to the Tithe Acts 1836 to 1951 shall be under the charge and superintendence of the Master of the Rolls) or of any rules made under either of those sections.

*Preservation and care of register books and records in
parochial custody*

Inspection of register books and records in parochial custody

9.—(1) The bishop of a diocese shall cause the register books and records in parochial custody in his diocese, including register books in use for the purpose of making entries therein, to be inspected and reported on periodically by such person or persons as he may appoint.

(2) Before making an appointment under subsection (1) above the bishop shall consult the chief officer of the diocesan record office or, where the diocese has more than one such office, the chief officer of the appropriate office.

(3) The bishop of a diocese shall cause the first inspections under this section of all register books and records in parochial custody in his diocese to be begun within five years after the commencement of this Measure and every subsequent inspection thereunder affecting a particular parish to be begun not more than six years after the date on which the immediately preceding inspection affecting that parish was completed.

(4) A report under this section shall be made to the bishop of the diocese or to such person as he may designate for the purpose.

(5) The person carrying out an inspection under this section shall compile a list of the register books, and a list describing the records, which have been inspected by him under this section.

(6) In the case of any inspection affecting a particular parish under this section, except the first, the person carrying out the inspection may comply with subsection (5) above by certifying in writing that any such list previously compiled under that subsection on an inspection affecting that parish, with such additions or omissions, if any, as are specified in the certificate is a list of the register books or a list describing the records, as the case may be, which have been inspected by him under this section.

(7) The person in whose custody such books or records are shall allow the person carrying out an inspection under this section to have access to those books and records at any reasonable time and shall give him such facilities as he may reasonably require to enable him to carry out his functions under this section.

(8) The person carrying out an inspection under this section shall send a copy of any list or certificate compiled or issued by him thereunder to—

(a) the bishop or such person as he may designate for the purpose,
(b) the chief officer of the diocesan record office or, where the diocese has more than one such office, the chief officer of the appropriate office,
(c) the minister concerned, and
(d) the parochial church council of the parish affected,

with, in the case of the copy sent to such council, an instruction that it is to be kept with the registers and records to which the list relates.

In this subsection " minister " means an incumbent or priest in charge.

(9) Any expenses incurred by a person carrying out an inspection under this section in complying with the provisions thereof shall be paid by the parochial church council of the parish affected.

Deposit of register books, etc. in diocesan record office

10.—(1) Subject to section 11 (3) of this Measure, every person—
(a) who by virtue of section 6 of this measure has the custody of any register book belonging to a parish in a diocese, being a register book to which this subsection applies, or
(b) who has the custody of any record in parochial custody in such a parish, being a record to which this subsection applies,

shall as soon as practicable after the first and each subsequent inspection under section 9 of this Measure affecting that parish is begun deposit that book or record in the diocesan record office or, where the diocese has more than one such office, in such of those offices as the bishop of the diocese may specify.

(2) Subsection (1) above applies to—
(a) any register book wherein the date of the latest entry is one hundred years or more earlier than the relevant date, other than a book in use for the purpose of making entries therein, and
(b) any record which was completed one hundred years or more before the relevant date.

In this subsection " relevant date " means the date on which each of the inspections referred to in subsection (1) above is begun.

(3) Without prejudice to subsection (1) above, any person—
(a) who by virtue of section 6 of this Measure has the custody of any register books belonging to a parish in a diocese, or
(b) who has the custody of any records in parochial custody in such a parish,

may, with the consent of the parochial church council of the parish, deposit any of those books or records, except a register book in use for the purpose of making entries therein, in the diocesan record office for the diocese or, where the diocese has more than one such office, in such of those offices as the bishop of the diocese may specify.

(4) Any deposit under this section shall be accompanied by—
(a) a list of the register books, and a list describing the records, which are being deposited; and
(b) a list of the register books, and a list describing the records, which are being retained in parochial custody, other than register books in use for the purpose of making entries therein.

(5) Each of the lists referred to in subsection (4) (b) above shall specify the usual place of custody of the books or records to which the list relates.

(6) A copy of each of the lists referred to in subsection (4) above shall be sent to the bishop of the diocese concerned or to such person as he may designate for the purpose.

(7) Any person who under this section deposits any register books or records in a diocesan record office shall obtain from the chief officer of that office a receipt for the books or records deposited, and that receipt shall be kept with the register books and records retained in parochial custody.

Care, etc. of register books and records in parochial custody

11.—(1) Every person having the custody of any register books or records in parochial custody shall be responsible for their safe-keeping, care and preservation.

(2) The provisions contained in Schedule 2 to this Measure shall apply to any register book or record which is retained in parochial custody under an authorisation issued under subsection (3) below.

(3) Where the bishop of a diocese issues an authorisation in writing to that effect, any register book or record which is required by section 10 (1) of this Measure to be deposited in a diocesan record office for the diocese and is specified in the authorisation may be retained in parochial custody.

(4) An application for an authorisation under subsection (3) above shall be made in writing by the person or persons having the custody of the book or record in question, and the bishop shall issue the authorisation if he is satisfied that the provisions of the said Schedule 2 are being and will be complied with as respects that book or record.

(5) If it appears to the bishop of a diocese that any such provisions are not being complied with as respects any book or record to which an authorisation issued by him or a predecessor in office of his under subsection (3) above relates, he shall revoke the authorisation.

(6) The bishop of a diocese shall from time to time issue directions with respect to the safe-keeping, care and preservation of the other register books and records in parochial custody in his diocese; and all persons concerned shall comply with such directions.

(7) Subject to subsection (8) below, directions under subsection (6) above shall require the register books and records to which the directions apply to be kept in the appropriate parish church or other place of public worship and shall include directions with respect to the type of container in which those books and records are to be kept.

(8) The bishop may if he thinks it necessary to do so issue further or different directions under subsection (6) above to a particular incumbent, priest in charge or parochial church council or to particular churchwardens or with respect to particular registers or records in parochial custody.

(9) The expense of complying with directions issued under this section and with the provisions of the said Schedule 2 (if applicable) shall be met by the parochial church council concerned.

Order for deposit of register books, etc. in diocesan record office

12.—(1) If it appears to the bishop of a diocese—

    (*a*) that section 10 (1) of the Measure has not been complied with as respects any register book or record in parochial custody in the diocese to which that subsection applies, or

    (*b*) that the provisions of Schedule 2 to this Measure have not been complied with as respects any such book or record to which those provisions apply by virtue of section 11 (2) of this Measure, or (*c*) that directions issued by him under the said section 11 with respect to register books and records in parochial custody in the diocese have not been complied with, or

(*d*) that any such books or records are for any other reason exposed to danger of loss or damage,

he shall notify the persons who have the custody of that book or record or those books or records, as the case may be, and the parochial church council concerned of the facts as they appear to the bishop and inform them that he will consider any written representations made to him by any of them before a date specified in the notice, being a date not less than twenty-eight days after service of the notice.

(2) Where any such matters as are mentioned in subsection (1) above have become known to the bishop in consequence of a report under section 9 of this Measure, the notice under that subsection shall be accompanied by a copy of the report.

(3) If after considering any representations duly made to him under subsection (1) above the bishop is of opinion that the matter is urgent and the circumstances are such that delay must be avoided, then, subject to subsection (6) below, he may order that such of those books or records as are specified in the order shall be deposited in the diocesan record office within the period of seven days beginning with the date of service of the order.

(4) If after considering any such representations the bishop is of opinion that action by him under subsection (3) above is unnecessary but that he should proceed under this subsection, he shall serve a further notice on the persons referred to in subsection (1) above informing them that he will make an order under subsection (5) below unless within such period as may be specified in the notice they satisfy him—

(*a*) that section 10 (1) of this Measure has been complied with as respects any register book or record in their custody to which that subsection applies, or

(*b*) that the provisions of Schedule 2 to this Measure, so far as applicable, and the directions issued by him under section 11 thereof are being and will be complied with, or

(*c*) that adequate steps have been taken to remove the danger of loss of, or damage to, the register books or records in their custody,

as the circumstances of the case require.

(5) If at the expiration of the period specified in a notice served by him under subsection (4) above the bishop is not satisfied as to the matters so specified then, subject to subsection (6) below, he shall order that such of the register books or records in parochial custody as are specified in the order shall be deposited in the diocesan record office within the period of seven days beginning with the date of service of the order.

(6) No orders shall be made under this section in relation to register books which are in use for the purpose of making entries therein.

(7) An order under this section shall be directed to, and served on, the person or persons having the custody of the register books or records specified in the order.

(8) Where a diocese has more than one diocesan record office, an order under this section shall specify the office in which any register books or records are to be deposited in accordance with the order.

(9) If any person on whom an order made by the bishop of a diocese under this section is served refuses or fails to comply with the order, the bishop of that diocese may apply to the county court for the district in which the register books or records to which the order relates are for

an order that that person do deliver those books or records to the diocesan record office specified in the first-mentioned order, and the court, if satisfied that that order was made in accordance with the provisions of this section, may make an order accordingly.

Return to parochial custody of register books, etc. deposited in diocesan record office

13.—(1) Where any register books or records have been deposited in the diocesan record office for a diocese or any part thereof in pursuance of this Measure, then, subject to subsection (2) below, if an application in that behalf is made to the bishop of the diocese by any person who would have been entitled to have the custody of them had they not been so deposited, the bishop shall order that those books or records or such of them as may be specified in the order shall be returned to and placed in the custody of that person.

(2) A bishop shall not make an order under this section unless he is satisfied—

    (*a*) in the case of a register book or record the retention of which in parochial custody requires his authorisation under section 11 (3) of this Measure, that the provisions of Schedule 2 to this Measure, and

    (*b*) in the case of any other such book or record, that the directions issued by him under that section,

will be complied with by the applicant for the order.

(3) At least one month before making an order under this section the bishop shall give to the chief officer of the diocesan record office in which the register books or records in question were deposited written notice of his intention, containing particulars of such books or records and stating the name and address of the person into whose custody they are to be returned.

(4) The making of an order under this section with respect to any books or records shall not be taken as preventing the subsequent deposit of those books or records in a diocesan record office under section 10 of this Measure or as affecting the power to make an order under section 12 thereof with respect to them.

*Custody, care, etc. of certain books and records held in
diocesan record office*

Custody, care, etc. of certain books and records held in diocesan record office

14. The chief officer of a diocesan record office shall have the custody of any register books or records which are deposited in that office in pursuance of this Measure and shall be responsible for their safe-keeping, care and preservation.

Transfer of certain books and records from one record office to another

15.—(1) Where in consequence of the foundation of a new diocese or an alteration in the areas of dioceses any part of a diocese becomes part of another diocese, any register books or records belonging to parishes in that part which have been deposited in a diocesan record office may be transferred to the diocesan record office for that other diocese.

(2) Where a diocesan record office is established for part of a diocese, any register books or records belonging to parishes in that part which have been deposited in another such office may be transferred to the office for that part.

*Making register books and records available for purposes of
exhibition, research, etc.*

**Making register books and records in parochial custody available for certain
purposes**

16.—(1) Subject to subsection (2) below, any person having the
custody of any register books or records in parochial custody may
deposit any of them for a limited period in a diocesan record office or
other suitable and safe place approved by the bishop of the diocese in
which they are for the purpose of exhibition or research or for the
purpose of enabling copies or lists to be made of them or copies of any
part thereof.

(2) The power conferred by subsection (1) above on a person having
the custody of such books or records may be exercised at the request of
any other person, but, whether or not any such request is made, the first
mentioned person, if not the parochial church council concerned, may
exercise that power only with the consent of that council.

(3) Where a request for the deposit in accordance with subsection (1)
above of any such books or records is made to the person having the
custody of them, then—

(*a*) if that person refuses or fails to comply with the request, or
(*b*) where subsection (2) above applies, the parochial church council
    refuses to consent to the deposit being made,

the bishop of the diocese in which such books or records are, on the
application of the person who made the request and after giving the
parochial church council concerned and any other person who has
the custody of them an opportunity to make representations to him,
may order them to be deposited for a period specified in the order in a
diocesan record office or other suitable and safe place approved by him
for any of the purposes mentioned in subsection (1) above.

(4) Before approving a place as a suitable and safe place for the
purposes of this section the bishop of a diocese shall consult the chief
officer of the diocesan record office or, where the diocese has more than
one such office, the chief officer of the appropriate office.

**Making certain books and records in diocesan record office available for
exhibition or research**

17.—(1) Subject to the provisions of this section and of section
18 (1), where a request in that behalf is made to the chief officer of a
diocesan record office, he may authorise such of the register books or
records in his custody by virtue of this Measure as may be specified in
the authorisation to be transferred to, and deposited for such period as
may be so specified in, a suitable and safe place for the purpose of
exhibition or research.

(2) Where a request under this section is made by the parochial
church council of the parish to which the register books or records in
question belong, the chief officer shall issue the authorisation requested
if he is satisfied that the place of deposit specified in the request is a
suitable and safe place.

(3) Where a request under this section is made by any person other
than the parochial church council of the parish to which the register
books and records in question belong, the chief officer may issue the
authorisation requested only with the consent of that council.

Provisions ancillary to ss. 16 and 17

18.—(1) The period during which any register books or records may
be deposited in any place by virtue of any provision of section 16 or 17

of this Measure shall not exceed one year; but the person by whom that period was fixed shall have power, exercisable with the consent of the parochial church council concerned, to extend that period for a further period, not exceeding one year; and the said power may be exercised from time to time before or after the expiration of any extension of a period of deposit.

(2) The expenses arising out of the transfer, deposit and return of register books and records in pursuance of any provision of the said section 16 or 17 shall be paid by the person at whose request the deposit is made.

(3) Before—

(*a*) any person agrees to comply with a request for the deposit in accordance with section 16 (1) of this Measure of any such register books or records as are referred to therein, or

(*b*) a bishop makes an order under section 16 (3) of this Measure on the application of the person who made such request, or

(*c*) the chief officer of a diocesan record office issues an authorisation under section 17 of this Measure at the request of any person other than the parochial church council of the parish to which the books and records described in the request belong,

he may require the person who made the request to effect with the Ecclesiastical Insurance Office Ltd. or such other insurance office as may be agreed between that person and that council insurance against risks of loss of, or damage to, the register books and records while in transit to or from the place in which they are to be deposited in accordance with the request, order or authorisation, as the case may be, or while so deposited in that place, for such sum as may be so agreed.

Miscellaneous

Disposal of register books and records on dissolution of parish, etc.

19.—(1) Where a parish is dissolved by a pastoral scheme, whether in consequence of a union of parishes or otherwise, then, subject to the provisions of that scheme, the register books belonging to that parish and any record in parochial custody therein shall be dealt with in such manner as the bishop of the diocese concerned may direct.

(2) Subject to the provisions of section 62 of the Marriage Act 1949 (disposal of register books of marriage on church ceasing to be used for solemnisation of marriages), where a church within the meaning of the Pastoral Measure 1968 ceases to be used as such, whether by reason of a declaration of redundancy, demolition or otherwise, then, unless the bishop of the diocese in which that church is otherwise directs or any pastoral scheme otherwise provides, the register books and records kept in or relating to that church shall be deposited in the diocesan record office for the diocese or part thereof in which the church is situated.

(3) Subsections (1) and (2) above are without prejudice to the power of the bishop of the diocese referred to therein to make an order under section 12 of this Measure with respect to such books or records, and section 13 thereof, with the omission of subsection (3), shall apply in relation to any such books or records which in compliance with the direction of the bishop have been deposited in a place which is not a diocesan record office.

(4) In subsection (6) of section 27 of the Pastoral Measure 1968 (provisions in pastoral schemes as to parish churches, etc.) the words from " and a pastoral scheme " to " scheme " shall be omitted and after that subsection there shall be inserted the following subsection:

" (7) A pastoral scheme may provide for transferring to a church designated by such a scheme as a parish church or becoming a parish church under this section register books or records from any other church ceasing to be a parish church or otherwise affected by or in pursuance of that or any other pastoral scheme or for those books or records to be dealt with as the bishop of the diocese in which that other church is may direct under section 19 of the Parochial Registers and Records Measure 1978.

In this subsection " register books " and " records " have the same meanings respectively as in the said Measure of 1978."

Searches of certain register books

20.—(1) Every person having the custody of any register book of baptisms or burials, being an incumbent, priest in charge or church-warden, shall at all reasonable hours allow searches to be made in that book on payment of such fee, if any, as may be prescribed by any order for the time being in force made under the Ecclesiastical Fees Measure 1962 and shall, if requested to do so, give a copy certified under his hand of any entry in that book on payment of such fee, if any, as may be so prescribed.

(2) Where any register books of baptisms or burials are deposited in a diocesan record office—

(a) the chief officer of that office shall at all reasonable hours allow searches to be made in any such book and shall, if requested to do so, give a copy certified under his hand of any entry therein; and

(b) the authority under whose control that office is may charge such fees, if any, as it thinks proper for the making (whether by it or any other person) of searches in any such book and the provision by it of certified copies of entries therein.

(3) Where any register books of marriages are deposited in a diocesan record office, section 63 of the Marriage Act 1949 (searches in marriage register books) shall have effect as if for references therein to an incumbent there were substituted references to the chief officer of that office.

(4) No part of any fee paid to the chief officer of a diocesan record office by virtue of this section shall be payable by him to any person who would have had the custody of any register book had it not been deposited in that office.

(5) Nothing in subsection (1) above shall be taken as affecting section 2 (6) of the Ecclesiastical Fees Measure 1962 (during vacancy in benefice certain fees to be paid to the sequestrators).

Recovery of register books in possession of unauthorised persons

21.—(1) Where any register books which were originally in parochial custody in a diocese are in the possession of any other person who has no title to or right to the possession of them, the bishop of the diocese in which the parish in question is situated may apply to the county court for the district in which those books are for an order that that person do deliver those books to him, and the court if satisfied that that person has no title to or right to the possession of them may order him to deliver them to the bishop.

(2) Register books delivered to a bishop in accordance with an order of the court under subsection (1) above may, as he thinks fit, be placed by him in the custody of the person who would have had the custody of

them had they remained in parochial custody or be deposited by him in the diocesan record office for his diocese.

(3) For the removal of doubt it is hereby declared that subject to the provisions of this Measure and of the Marriage Act 1949 the title to or right to the possession of register books in the custody of any person by virtue of this Measure is incapable of assignment whether for value or otherwise.

Special provisions as to marriage registers

22.—(1) The chief officer of every diocesan record office who under this Measure has in his custody any register book of marriages solemnised after the passing of the Births and Deaths Registration Act 1836 shall—

    (a) furnish the Registrar General with particulars of such books; and

    (b) if any such book is required for the purpose of correcting any erroneous entry therein in accordance with section 61 of the Marriage Act 1949, deliver that book to the minister concerned and permit him to retain it for such period as may be necessary for that purpose.

(2) Nothing in this Measure shall authorise the deposit in a diocesan record office of any duplicate register book of marriages which, when filled, is to be delivered to a superintendent registrar in accordance with section 60 of the said Act of 1949.

Supplemental

Appointment of deputy to perform functions of bishop

23. Section 3 of the Church of England (Miscellaneous Provisions) Measure 1976 (appointment of deputy to perform certain functions of a diocesan bishop in certain circumstances) shall apply to the functions of the bishop of a diocese in relation to matters arising under this Measure as it applies to functions of such a bishop in relation to matters arising under the enactments specified in subsection (7) of that section.

Service of notices and orders

24.—(1) Any notice or order required or authorised by this Measure to be served on or sent or given to any person may be served, sent or given by delivering it to him, or by leaving it at his proper address, or by post.

(2) Any such notice or order required or authorised to be served on, sent or given to, a parochial church council shall be duly served, sent or given if it is served on or sent or given to the secretary of that council.

(3) For the purposes of this section and of section 26 of the Interpretation Act 1889 in its application to this section, the proper address of the person on or to whom any such notice or order is required or authorised to be served, sent or given shall be the last known address of that person.

Interpretation

25.—(1) In this Measure, except in so far as the context otherwise requires, the following expressions have the meanings hereby respectively assigned to them, that is to say—

    " records " means materials in written or other form setting out facts or events or otherwise recording information, other than register books, and " records in parochial custody " means records in the custody of an incumbent or priest in charge or of churchwardens or of a parochial church council or in the joint custody of any of them;

" register books " means the register books mentioned in section 6 (1) of this Measure and " register books in parochial custody " means register books in the custody of an incumbent or priest in charge or of churchwardens.

(2) In this Measure references to any enactment shall be construed as references to that enactment as amended, extended or applied by or under any other enactment.

Amendments, repeals and transitional provisions

26.—(1) The enactments specified in Schedule 3 to this Measure shall have effect subject to the amendments specified in that Schedule, being amendments consequential upon the provisions of this Measure.

(2) The enactments specified in Schedule 4 to this Measure (which include enactments which were obsolete, spent or unnecessary before the passing of this Measure) are hereby repealed to the extent specified in column 3 of that Schedule.

(3) Any registration effected, certificate or directions issued, order made, or other thing done under any enactment repealed by this Measure shall not be invalidated by the repeal effected by subsection (2) above but shall have effect as if effected, issued, made or done under the corresponding provision of this Measure.

(4) Without prejudice to subsection (3) above, any reference in this Measure to a thing done under or for the purposes of a provision of this Measure shall, in so far as the context permits, be construed as including a reference to the corresponding thing done under or for the purposes of the corresponding provision of the enactments repealed by this Measure.

(5) Nothing in subsection (1), (3) or (4) above shall be taken as prejudicing the operation of section 38 of the Interpretation Act 1889 (which relates to the effect of repeals) as applied by the Interpretation Measure 1925.

Short title, commencement and extent

27.—(1) This Measure may be cited as the Parochial Registers and Records Measure 1978.

(2) This Measure shall come into operation on such day, being a day which falls within the period of one year beginning with the date on which the Measure is passed, as the Archbishops of Canterbury and York may jointly appoint.

(3) This Measure shall extend to the whole of the provinces of Canterbury and York, except the Channel Islands and the Isle of Man, but may be applied to the Channel Islands, or either of them, as defined in the Channel Islands (Church Legislation) Measures 1931 and 1957, in accordance with those Measures and may by Act of Tynwald be extended to the Isle of Man, with such exceptions, adaptations and modifications, if any, as may be specified in such Act.

SCHEDULES

SCHEDULE 1

FORMS

No. 1

REGISTER OF BAPTISMS ADMINISTERED IN THE PARISH OF

In the †

IN THE DIOCESE OF

Entry No.	Date of birth	Date of baptism	Christian name and surname*	Father's Christian name and surname*	Mother's Christian name and surname*	Address	Father's occupation	Mother's occupation	Godparents	Officiating minister

† *Insert appropriate local government area.*
* *In block capitals.*

No. 2

REGISTER OF BURIALS IN THE PARISH OF

IN THE DIOCESE OF

IN THE †   OF

Entry No.	Christian name and surname *	Address	Age	Date of burial	Officiating minister

† *Insert appropriate local government area*
* *In block capitals*

SCHEDULE 2

PROVISIONS WHICH APPLY TO REGISTER BOOKS AND RECORDS RETAINED IN PAROCHIAL CUSTODY UNDER SECTION 11 (3)

1. Every register book or record to which this Schedule applies shall be kept in a rust-proofed, vented steel cupboard, the door of which is fitted with a multi-lever lock, and the cupboard shall be kept in the appropriate parish church or other place of public worship.

2. The place in the church or other place of public worship in which the cupboard is kept shall be the place where there is least risk of damage to any such book or record in the event of a flood or an outbreak of fire.

3. The temperature and relative humidity in such cupboard shall be checked at least once a week by means of a maximum-minimum thermometer and a hygrometer, each of which shall be kept in the cupboard.

The hygrometer shall be one conforming to British Standard Specification Number 3292 or any new British Standard which supersedes it.

4. The difference between the maximum and the minimum temperatures in the cupboard during any week shall not be allowed to exceed 10 degrees Celsius.

5. The relative humidity in the cupboard shall not be allowed to fall below 50 per cent. nor to rise above 65 per cent.

6. Subject to paragraph 3 above, nothing, except books or other documents, shall be kept in the cupboard in which any register book or record to which this Schedule applies is for the time being kept.

7. Without prejudice to the preceding provisions, the person or persons having the custody of any such book or record shall take all such steps as are reasonably practicable to ensure that the book or record is protected against theft, loss and damage.

SCHEDULE 3   **Section 26 (1)**

CONSEQUENTIAL AMENDMENTS

The Cemeteries Clauses Act 1847 (c. 65)

1. For section 33 of the Cemeteries Clauses Act 1847 there shall be substituted the following section:—

" 33. Section 35 of the Births and Deaths Registration Act 1836 (searches in register books of baptisms or burials), as in force immediately before the passing of the Ecclesiastical Fees Measure 1962, shall apply in relation to the register books kept under section 32 of this Act with the substitution for the reference to a rector, vicar or curate of a reference to the chaplain by whom the said books are kept."

The Registration of Burials Act 1864 (c. 97)

2. For section 6 of the Registration of Burials Act 1864 there shall be substituted the following section:—

" 6. Section 35 of the Births and Deaths Registration Act 1836 (searches in register books of baptisms or burials), as in force immediately before the passing of the Ecclesiastical Fees Measure 1962, shall apply in relation to the register books kept under this Act with the substitution for the reference to a rector, vicar or curate of a reference to the officer or person by whom the said books are kept."

The City of London (Guild Churches) Act 1952 (*o. xxxviii*)

3. In section 23 (2) of the City of London (Guild Churches) Act 1952 for the words " section 5 of the Parochial Registers Act 1812 " there shall be substituted the words " the Parochial Registers and Records Measure 1978 ".

4. In section 25 of the said Act for the words " Parochial Registers and Records Measure 1929 " there shall be substituted the words " Parochial Registers and Records Measure 1978 with any necessary modifications ".

The Baptismal Registers Measure 1961 (No. 2)

5. In section 1 (1) of the Baptismal Registers Measure 1961 for the words " section 3 of the Parochial Registers Act 1812 " there shall be substituted the words " section 2 of the Parochial Registers and Records Measure 1978 ".

6. In section 3 of the said Measure for the words from " rector " to " such registers " there shall be substituted the words " person who by virtue of section 6 or 14 of the Parochial Registers and Records Measure 1978 has the custody of registers of baptisms ".

SCHEDULE 4   **Section 26 (2)**

REPEALS

Session and Chapter	Short Title	Extent of Repeal
52 Geo. 3. c. 146.	The Parochial Registers Act 1812.	The whole Act.
11 Geo. 4 & 1 Will. 4. c. 66.	The Forgery Act 1830.	Section 21.
6 & 7 Will. 4. c. 86.	The Births and Deaths Registration Act 1836.	Section 35 except as applied by any enactment.
10 & 11 Vict. c. 65	The Cemeteries Clauses Act 1847.	In section 32, the words from ''and copies '' to the end.
27 & 28 Vict. c. 97.	The Registration of Burials Act 1864.	Section 3.
19 & 20 Geo. 5. No. 1.	The Parochial Registers and Records Measure 1929.	The whole Measure.

Church of England (Miscellaneous Provisions) Measure 1978

(1978 No. 3)

ARRANGEMENT OF SECTIONS

A MEASURE passed by the General Synod of the Church of England to make further provision with respect to the special majorities required for the final approval of certain Measures; to make further provision with respect to the continuance in certain offices of persons in office at the commencement of the Ecclesiastical Offices (Age Limit) Measure 1975; to make provision for altering the financial year of the Church Commissioners; to amend Schedule 1 to the Church Commissioners Measure 1947; to provide for an additional member of diocesan boards of finance; to amend section 20 of the Parochial Registers and Records Measure 1978; to extend section 17 of the New Parishes Measure 1943; to make provision for facilitating the conveyance of ecclesiastical property in certain circumstances; to make provision for extending the Inspection of Churches Measure 1955 and schemes made thereunder; to amend section 43 of the Cathedrals Measure 1963 and sections 3 and 43 of the Endowments and Glebe Measure 1976, to repeal so much of section 21 of the Queen Anne's Bounty Act 1714 as requires certain documents to be enrolled in the High Court.   [30th June 1978]

Special majorities required for certain Measures

1. In Article 8 of the Constitution of the General Synod of the Church of England set out in Schedule 2 to the Synodical Government Measure 1969, which Article lays down certain requirements for the final approval of the General Synod for, among other things, a Measure or Canon providing for permanent changes in the Services of Baptism or Holy Communion or in the Ordinal, the following paragraph shall be inserted after paragraph (1B):

" (1C) A motion for the final approval of a Measure providing for permanent changes in any such Service or in the Ordinal shall

not be deemed to be carried unless it receives the assent of a majority
in each House of the General Synod of not less than two-thirds of
those present and voting.".

Provisions with respect to certain persons in office at commencement of Ecclesiastical Offices (Age Limit) Measure 1975

2.—(1) Section 1 (1) of the Ecclesiastical Offices (Age Limit)
Measure 1975 (no person to be capable of being appointed or presented
to certain offices if he has attained the age of seventy) shall not be taken
as invalidating any provision made by a pastoral scheme or order for
designating as the holder of an office listed in the Schedule to that
Measure a person who on the date of the coming into operation of the
scheme or order had attained the age of seventy years if immediately
before that date, and at the commencement of that Measure, he was the
incumbent of a benefice affected by the scheme or order.

(2) Where—

    (*a*) by a pastoral scheme or order a person is designated as the
holder of an office listed in the Schedule to the said Measure,
and

    (*b*) that person was at the commencement thereof, and continued
until the coming into operation of the scheme or order to be,
the incumbent of a benefice affected by the scheme or order,

then, for the purposes of section 1 (4) (*d*) of that Measure (requirement
to vacate office on attaining age of seventy not to apply to person who
held the office at the said commencement), he shall be deemed to have
held the first mentioned office at the said commencement.

(3) Where by virtue of subsection (2) above a person is deemed to
have been at the said commencement the holder of the office of rector
or vicar in a team ministry established by a pastoral scheme and the
office is to be held for a term of years specified by or under the scheme,
the term of years for which that person is entitled by virtue of the scheme
to hold the office may, notwithstanding anything in the said Measure,
be extended in accordance with section 19 (5) of the Pastoral Measure
1968.

(4) The provisions of this section shall apply in relation to a pastoral
scheme or order which came into operation before, or comes into operation after, the commencement of this Measure, and in this section
" pastoral scheme " and " pastoral order " have the same meanings
respectively as in the Pastoral Measure 1968.

Provision for altering financial year of Church Commissioners

3.—(1) As from such year as the Board of Governors of the Church
Commissioners may determine the financial year of the Church Commissioners shall commence on 1st January instead of 1st April and,
accordingly, on and after the making of a determination under this
subsection, section 10 (1) of the Church Commissioners Measure 1947
shall have effect as if for the word " April " there were substituted the
word " January ".

(2) The financial year of the Church Commissioners which is current
when a determination is made by the said Board under subsection (1)
above shall end on 31st December.

Amendments relating to constitution of Church Commissioners

4.—(1) In that part of paragraph 1 of Schedule 1 to the Church
Commissioners Measure 1947 (constitution of the Church Commissioners)
which provides that of the eight Commissioners, four of whom are

nominated by Her Majesty and four by the Archbishop of Canterbury, at least two shall be, or shall have been, of counsel to Her Majesty, for the word " two " there shall be substituted the word " one ".

(2) In paragraph 2 of the said Schedule 1 for the words from the beginning to " determine ", where first occurring, there shall be substituted the following words:—

" Commissioners appointed by the General Synod (who need not be members thereof) shall be appointed for five years at such time and in such manner as the Synod may from time to time determine, but if the Synod alters the time at which they are to be appointed the period of office of the Commissioners so appointed who are then in office shall be extended or reduced accordingly, as the circumstances require ".

(3) In the said Schedule 1, the following paragraph shall be inserted after paragraph 5:—

" 5A.—(1) Without prejudice to paragraph 5 above, if an appointed Commissioner, being a Commissioner appointed by the General Synod, was at the time of his appointment a member of that Synod, then, subject to sub-paragraph (2) below, he shall on ceasing to be a member thereof thereby vacate his membership.

(2) Where a Commissioner to whom sub-paragraph (1) above applies ceases to be a member of the General Synod by reason of the dissolution of that Synod he may continue to act during the period of the dissolution as a Commissioner, but if he does not stand for re-election to the General Synod or is not re-elected, the preceding provision shall cease to apply to him with effect from the date on which the appointment of his successor is announced by the presiding officer.".

Additional member of diocesan boards of finance

5. The diocesan board of finance for each diocese shall take such action as it thinks appropriate to ensure that the diocesan member of the Central Board of Finance shall, unless he is also the secretary of the board, be a member of the board entitled to vote at meetings of the board.

In this section " diocesan member of the Central Board of Finance " means in relation to a diocese the member for that diocese elected in accordance with the articles of association of the Central Board of Finance.

Restriction on power to charge fees for searches, etc. of certain registers in certain diocesan record offices

6. In section 20 (2) of the Parochial Registers and Records Measure 1978 (searches, etc. of register books of baptisms or burials deposited in a diocesan record office), for paragraph (b) thereof there shall be substituted—

" (b) the authority under whose control that office is, not being a local authority, may charge such fees, if any, for allowing a search to be made in any such book or for providing a copy of an entry therein as is payable to an incumbent for the same service by virtue of any order for the time being in force made under the Ecclesiastical Fees Measure 1962 ";

and at the end of subsection (5) of the said section 20 there shall be inserted the words " and nothing in subsections (2) and (3) above shall be taken as affecting the powers of local authorities under section 1 of the Local Government (Records) Act 1962 (power to promote adequate use of records) ".

Extension of power to dispose of land no longer required for purpose for which acquired

7. Section 17 (1) of the New Parishes Measure 1943 (powers of the Church Commissioners and other persons to sell, exchange, etc. land or a building no longer required for the purpose for which it was acquired) shall apply in relation to land acquired by the Church Commissioners for any of the purposes mentioned in section 13 (1) (*e*) of that Measure, that is to say, for providing access to or improving the amenities of a church, churchyard or burial ground or a house of residence of an incumbent, as it applies in relation to any land or building acquired for any of the purposes mentioned in paragraphs (*a*) to (*c*) of the said section 13 (1) and, accordingly, in the said section 17 (1) for the words " or (*c*) " there shall be substituted the words " (*c*) or (*e*) ".

Church, etc. to be vested in Church Commissioners for certain purposes where fee simple is in abeyance

8.—(1) Where the fee simple of any ecclesiastical property is in abeyance, the fee simple shall for the purposes of a compulsory acquisition of the property under any enactment be treated as being vested in the Church Commissioners, and any notice to treat shall be served, or be deemed to have been served, accordingly.

(2) In this section " ecclesiastical property " means land being or forming part of a church subject to the jurisdiction of a bishop of any diocese (other than the diocese of Sodor and Man) or the site of such a church, or being or forming part of a burial ground subject to such jurisdiction, and " land " includes anything falling within any definition of that expression in the enactment under which the purchase is authorised.

Power to extend Inspection of Churches Measure 1955

9.—(1) Where the bishop of a diocese has licensed a building for public worship and he considers it desirable that the Inspection of Churches Measure 1955, and any scheme established by the diocesan synod of the diocese under section 1 of that Measure and for the time being in force, should apply to that building, he may by order direct that that Measure and scheme shall apply to that building with such modifications, if any, as may be specified in the order.

(2) Any order under this section may be varied or revoked by a subsequent order made thereunder.

(3) In this section " building " includes a part of a building.

Vacation of office by non-residentiary canons in Christ Church Cathedral

10.—(1) In subsection (1) of section 43 of the Cathedrals Measure 1963 (power of Bishop of Oxford to appoint non-residentiary canons) the words from " and any such " to the end shall be omitted and after that subsection there shall be inserted:—

" (2) Subject to subsection (3) of this section, a non-residentiary canon in the said cathedral church shall, unless the bishop otherwise determines, vacate that office—

(*a*) on ceasing to be beneficed, or licensed to serve, in the diocese of Oxford, or

(*b*) on attaining the age of seventy years,

whichever event first occurs.

(3) Subsection (2) of this section shall not apply to any person who held the office of non-residentiary canon in the said cathedral church at the commencement of the Church of England (Miscellaneous Provisions) Measure 1978, but, unless the bishop otherwise determines, that person shall vacate that office on ceasing to reside in the diocese of Oxford.

(4) The bishop may confer the title of canon emeritus in the said cathedral church on any person who vacates the office of non-residentiary canon in that church in accordance with subsection (2) or (3) of this section or in accordance with subsection (1) thereof, as originally enacted."

(2) Subsection (2) of the said section 43 shall be re-numbered (5) and in that subsection (rights and duties of non-residentiary canons to be determined by the dean and canons) after the words " non-residentiary canons " there shall be inserted the words " and of canons emeriti ".

Minor corrections of Endowments and Glebe Measure 1976

11.—(1) In section 3 (3) of the Endowments and Glebe Measure 1976 (amount of annual personal grant of incumbent of benefices held in plurality if one or more but not all of those benefices is declared vacant under the Incumbents (Vacation of Benefices) Measure 1975) for the words " 1975 " there shall be substituted the words " 1977 ".

(2) In section 43 of the said Measure of 1976 (delegation of functions of bishops) for the words " Section 85 of the Pastoral Measure 1968 " there shall be substituted the words " Section 3 of the Church of England (Miscellaneous Provisions) Measure 1976 ".

Abolition of requirement to enrol certain deeds, etc. in High Court

12. In section 21 of the Queen Anne's Bounty Act 1714 (which empowers the Church Commissioners by deed or instrument to allot land, etc. vested in them to any church or chapel and provides that such augmentation so made shall be effectual provided such deed or instrument be enrolled in the High Court within the period therein specified) the words from " provided such " to the end are hereby repealed.

Citation, construction, commencement and extent

13.—(1) This Measure may be cited as the Church of England (Miscellaneous Provisions) Measure 1978.

(2) The Synodical Government Measures 1969 to 1974 and section 1 of this Measure may be cited together as the Synodical Government Measures 1969 to 1978.

(3) Any reference in this Measure to any enactment shall be construed as a reference to that enactment as amended by any subsequent enactment.

(4) This Measure shall come into operation at the expiration of a period of one month beginning with the day on which it is passed.

(5) This Measure shall extend to the provinces of Canterbury and York except the Channel Islands and the Isle of Man, but sections 2, 7 and 11 thereof may be applied to the Channel Islands as defined in the Channel Islands (Church Legislation) Measures 1931 and 1957, or either of them, in accordance with those Measures.

INDEX

References, e.g. 3/56, are to the Statutes of 1978, Chapter 3, section 56.

[1]

Index

COMPULSORY PURCHASE,
refuse disposal, 3/7

Community Service by Offenders (Scotland) Act 1978 (c. 49)

COMPANY LAW,
Corporation tax. *See* CORPORATION TAX.
criminal law, 37/3
dividends, 54/1, 2
profit sharing schemes, 42/53–61
State immunity, 33/9

Consolidated Fund Act 1978 (c. 7)

Consolidated Fund (No. 2) Act 1978 (c. 59)

CONSTITUTIONAL LAW,
devolution, 51/1–87, schs. 1–17, 52/1–82, schs. 1–12
European Assembly, elections to, 10/1–9, schs.
European Assembly, increase in powers of, 10/6
Scotland, 52/1–87, schs. 1–17
Solomon Islands, 15/1–10, sch.
Tuvalu, 20/1–6, schs. 1, 2
Wales, 52/1–82, schs. 1–17

Consumer Safety Act 1978 (c. 38)

CONTRACT,
assignment, 23/87
employment, contracts of, 44/1–11, 45, 48–53, 78, 93, 131
industrial tribunal, jurisdiction, 44/131
restrictive trade practices, 1/1
time not of the essence, 23/88

CONTRIBUTION, 47/1–10
Crown, 47/5
carriage of goods, 47/sch. 1
limitation, period for, 47/sch. 1
Northern Ireland, 47/8

Co-operative Development Agency Act 1978 (c. 21)

CORPORATION TAX,
advance corporation tax, 42/16
capital allowances, 42/37–40
charge, 42/15–17
close companies, 42/35, 36
community land transactions, 42/34
interest relief, 42/18
investment trusts, 42/18
rate, 42/15–17
unit trusts, 42/17

COUNTY COURTS,
matrimonial proceedings: magistrates' courts, 22/28
Northern Ireland, 23/95–100, 102
remittal or removal to, 23/31

COSTS,
Northern Ireland, 23/57–61

COURT OF APPEAL,
Northern Ireland. *See* NORTHERN IRELAND.

CRIMINAL LAW,
appeals, 23/34, 36–41, 44, 45
arrest, 5/11
bail, 5/2, 4, 5
children, protection of, 37/1–9
collection of information, 5/22
community service orders, [S] 49/1–15
community service orders, England and Wales, 49/6, sch. 1
contempt of court, 23/44
Crown Court. *See* CROWN COURT.

CRIMINAL LAW—*cont.*
deception, offences of, 31/1–4
dishonesty, offences of, 31/1–4
duplicated offences: statutory interpretation, 30/18
emergency provisions, 5/1–35, schs. 1–6
evasion of liability by deception, 31/2
extradition, 17/3, 26/1–8
failure to disperse, 5/24
firearms and explosives, 5/9, 15, 16, 23, 9/2, sch. 1.
forfeiture, 37/5
internationally protected persons, 17/1–5 26/4
jurisdiction, offences outside U.K., 17/1–5, 26/4
non-political crimes, what are, 26/1
Northern Ireland, 23/4, 34, 36–41, 44–53, 26/6, 31/6
obtaining services by deception, 31/1
pornography, 37/1–9
probation orders, conditions, 49/7
prohibition orders and notices, 38/3
proscribed organisations, 5/21, 25, 26
rights of audience, 23/50
safety regulations, 38/2
scheduled offences (emergency provisions), 5/1–10
terrorism, suppression of, 26/1–9
theft and associated offences, 31/1–4
young persons. *See* MINORS.

CROWN,
contribution proceedings, 47/5
employment, 44/95, 138
Scottish Assembly, 51/24

CROWN COURT,
appearance, compelling, 23/51
Crown Court Rules, 23/52
Northern Ireland, 23/4, 44–53
rights of audience, 23/50
sentence, 23/49

CUSTODY. *See* HUSBAND AND WIFE, MINORS, *and* MAGISTERIAL LAW.

CUSTOMS AND EXCISE,
anti-dumping measures, 42/6
customs and excise Acts, amendment and consolidation, 42/79
excise duty on beer, 42/2
gaming licence duty, 42/7
goods, control on movement of, 42/4
seals, removal of, 42/5
tobacco products duty, 42/1
vehicle excise duty, 42/8
warehousing regulations, 42/3

DAMAGES,
judicial review, in lieu of, 23/20

DEFAMATION,
Scottish Assembly, 51/15, sch. 16
Welsh Assembly, 52/23

DEFINITIONS,
1927 Act, 12/4
1949 Act, 10/sch. 2
1958 Act, 10/sch. 2
1960 Act, 55/24
1962 Act, 55/24
1967, scheme, 44/145
1968 Act, 8/15. 55/24

[2]

Index

DEFINITIONS—*cont.*

county court, **23**/120, **30**/schs. 1, 2
court, **12**/9, **23**/44, **33**/22, **36**/sch. 2, **44**/139
Court of Appeal, **30**/sch. 1
court of assize, **23**/120
Court of Criminal Appeal, **23**/120
Court of summary jurisdiction, **30**/sch. 1
Court Service, **23**/69
court-martial enactments, **19**/7
credit-sale agreement, **38**/9
Criminal Appeal Act, **23**/120
cross-boundary petroleum field, **44**/137, **46**/2
Crown, **23**/31
Crown Court, **30**/sch. 1
Crown Court Rules, **23**/52
Crown Estate Commissioners, **30**/sch. 1
current specified cost, **29**/sch. 11
custody, **22**/36
customs Acts, **42**/sch. 12
customs and excise Acts, **42**/sch. 12
date of dismissal, **44**/62, 77
deception, **31**/5
defendant, **23**/120
Dental Estimates Board, **29**/108
dental practitioner, **29**/108
dependants, **47**/6
dependent territory, **2**/17, **33**/22
designated area, **42**/29, **46**/2
designated district, **50**/17
designated district authority, **50**/1, 17
designated medical officer, **29**/108
determination, **28**/48
development corporation, **14**/18, sch. 2
devolution issue, **51**/65
devolved matter, **51**/81
diminish, **44**/81
direction, **5**/4
director, **29**/sch. 10, **44**/120
disabled, **53**/18
disabled occupant, **14**/sch. 2
disabled person, **14**/sch. 2, **40**/18
disability, **53**/18
disciplinary case, **12**/6, sch. 3
dismiss, **44**/33, 55, 83
dismissal, **44**/33, 55, 83, 153
dismissal procedures agreement, **44**/153, sch. 17
dispensing optician, **29**/108
disqualified, **10**/sch. 1, **51**/11, 8
district, **50**/14, 17
division, **23**/120
dock work, **44**/145
domestic proceedings, **22**/79, 88
dwelling-house, **5**/31
education authority, **29**/108
Education committee, **12**/sch. 6
effective date of termination, **44**/55, 153
effective resolution, **56**/15
eggs, **35**/1
elderly person, **53**/12
elected member, **12**/1, 30, sch. 6
electoral quota, **10**/sch. 2, **51**/1, sch. 1, **52**/1, sch. 1
electorate, **10**/sch. 2, **51**/1, sch. 1, **52**/1, sch. 1
eligible expenditure, **14**/1
employee, **44**/153
employer, **44**/153
employer for the time being, **36**/sch. 2
employers' association, **44**/153
employer's payment, **44**/153

DEFINITIONS—*cont.*

employment, **44**/153
enactment, **5**/31, **10**/8, **26**/8, **51**/81, sch. 16, **52**/78
enforcement, **38**/sch. 2
England, **28**/65, **30**/schs. 1, 2
enumeration date, **10**/sch. 2
equipment, **29**/108
equity share capital, **11**/1
European Convention on State Immunity, **33**/22
excepted ship or aircraft, **29**/sch. 10
excepted statutory undertakers, **51**/81, **52**/78
excise Acts, **42**/sch. 12
excise licence trade, **42**/sch. 12
excise trade, **42**/sch. 12
excise trader, **42**/sch. 12
exempt body, **42**/69
expected week of confinement, **44**/153
expected orders, **22**/16, 17
expenditure, **51**/52, **52**/48
explosive, **5**/31
explosive substance, **5**/31
export contracts, **18**/15
facility, **25**/2
family company, **42**/46
film, **37**/7
financial provision, **22**/6
financial year, **30**/sch. 1, **51**/81, **52**/78
firearm, **5**/31
fish, **35**/1
foreign currency, **18**/15
foreign currency liabilities, **18**/15
foreign sector of the continental shelf, **44**/137, **46**/2
freshwater fish, **35**/1
full-time education in a school, **29**/108
fully registered, **12**/30, schs. 5, 6
fully registered person, **12**/30, schs. 5, 6
functions, **29**/108
fund, **44**/103
General Council, **12**/30, sch. 6
general dental services, **29**/25
general ophthalmic services, **29**/26
goods, **38**/1, 9, 11
governing body, **29**/108
government department, **44**/153
Government of overseas territory, **44**/114
Governor-General, **30**/sch. 1
grants to universities, **51**/81
group, **42**/49
group scheme, **42**/61
guarantee, **18**/15
guarantee payment, **44**/12, 153
guardian, **28**/65
harbour, **4**/2
Health Board, **29**/108
health service, **29**/108
health service for England and Wales, **29**/27
health service hospital, **29**/108
Health Services Board, **29**/108
health service ophthalmic list, **29**/sch. 16
health service tribunal, **29**/sch. 16
heretofore, **23**/120
High Court, **23**/1, **30**/sch. 1
Highlands and Islands, **51**/81
highway, **3**/11
hire-purchase agreement, **38**/9
holiday, **42**/sch. 12
holiday pay, **44**/127

[4]

HOUSE OF LORDS,
  appeals, Northern Ireland, **23**/39–44, sch. 1

HOUSING,
  building societies, **27**/3
  chronically sick persons, **53**/3
  disabled persons, **53**/3
  Exchequer payments, termination of, [S] **14**/7, sch. 1.
  home purchases, assistance with, **27**/1
  Housing Corporation, **27**/5
  housing revenue account, [S] **14**/11, sch. 2
  housing support grants, [S] **14**/1–3
  improvement of houses, **14**/10, sch. 2.
  insulation, grants for, **48**/1–4
  rent allowances, [S] **14**/12, 13, sch. 2
  rent limits, [S] **14**/14, 15
  rent rebates, [S] **14**/12, 13, sch. 2
  repairs grant, [S] **14**/8, sch. 2
  repairs, loans for, [S] **14**/9, sch. 2
  Scottish Special Housing Association, [S] **14**/4
  voluntary organisations, grants to, [S] **14**/5

Housing (Financial Provisions) (Scotland) Act 1978 (c. 14)

HUSBAND AND WIFE,
  access, **22**/14, 40
  arrest, powers of, **22**/18
  compellability as a witness, **37**/2
  custodianship order, **22**/64, 68, 69
  custody, **22**/8–15, 19, 21, 23–25, 33, 34, 36–38
  custody, definition of, **22**/36
  disputes between persons holding parental rights, **22**/13
  divorce: period of separation, calculation of, **22**/62
  divorce, validity of, **22**/58, 59
  enforcement, reciprocal, **22**/54–61
  expedited order, **22**/16, 17
  financial provision, **22**/1–8, 11, 19, 20, 22–25, 32, 35, 41–45, 54–61, 63–68, 76, 77, 85
  interim orders, **22**/19, 45, 59
  living together, effect of, **22**/25, 46
  lump sum orders, *see above under* financial provision.
  maintenance, *see above under* financial provision.
  matrimonial home, **22**/16–18, 62
  opportunity to make representations, **22**/12
  periodical payments, *see above under* financial provision.
  protection, order for, **22**/16
  reconciliation, **22**/26
  repayment of sums, **22**/35
  reports in proceedings, **22**/12, 83
  restriction on removal of child, **22**/34, 39, 70
  revocation of orders, **22**/17, 20, 21, 23–25, 66
  variation of orders, **22**/17, 20–25, 43, 63, 66, 76
  welfare of children, first and paramount consideration, **22**/15

Import of Live Fish (Scotland) Act 1978 (c. 35)

INCOME TAX,
  benefits in kind, **42**/23
  capital allowances, **42**/37–40
  charge, **42**/13, 14
  child allowances, **42**/20

INCOME TAX—*cont.*
  child benefits, **42**/20
  commodity dealings, **42**/31
  date for payment, **42**/41
  divers and diving supervisors, **42**/29
  farming: capital allowances, **42**/39
  farming: reliefs, **42**/28
  interest payments, deduction of, **42**/42
  interest relief, **42**/18
  life policies, **42**/25
  losses, **42**/30, 31
  loss of employment, payments for, **42**/24
  maintenance payments, **42**/21
  market gardening: reliefs, **42**/28
  P.A.Y.E., **42**/59
  personal reliefs, **42**/19
  police, **42**/43
  profit sharing schemes, **42**/53–61
  rate, **42**/13, 11
  relief for individuals carrying on trade abroad, **42**/27
  retirement annuities, **42**/26
  sale of land, **42**/32
  sub-contractors in the construction industry, **42**/33
  trustees, payments to, **42**/60
  wives, tax repayments, **42**/22

Independent Broadcasting Authority Act 1978 (c. 43)

Industrial and Provident Societies Act 1978 (c. 34)

INDUSTRIAL TRIBUNALS,
  appeal, **44**/135, 136
  breach of contract, **44**/131
  burden of proof, **44**/57
  compensation, **44**/72–76
  damages, jurisdiction in respect of, **44**/131
  Employment Appeal Tribunal, **44**/135, 136
  establishment, **44**/128
  guarantee payments, **44**/17
  insolvency of employer, **44**/124
  maternity, **44**/36, 43
  procedure, **44**/sch. 9
  redundancy, **44**/91, 108, 112
  referees, jurisdiction of, **44**/130
  remedies, **44**/67–79, 129
  suspension of work on medical grounds, **44**/22
  terms of employment, **44**/11
  time off work, **44**/30
  trade union membership and activities, **44**/24, 30
  unfair dismissal, 67–79, 133
    burden of proof, **44**/57
    interim relief, **44**/77, 79

Inner Urban Areas Act 1978 (c. 50)

INSURANCE,
  adopted child, [S] **28**/37, 43
  protected child, interest in, [S] **28**/37

INTERNATIONAL LAW,
  adoption, **28**/17, 40, 47, 49, 50, 53, 63, 64
  citizenship, [S] **28**/40
  contracts of employment, **33**/4
  divorce, validity of, **22**/58, 59
  enforcement of maintenance orders, **22**/53–61
  extradition, **17**/3, **26**/1–8, **37**/1
  Heads of State, **33**/20
  internationally protected persons, **17**/1–5, **26**/4

[9]

Index

Refuse Disposal (Amenity) Act 1978 (c. 3)

RENT RESTRICTION,
  rent limits, [S] 14/14, 15
Representation of the People Act 1978 (c. 32)

RESTRICTIVE PRACTICES,
  British National Oil Corporation, 1/1

REVENUE AND FINANCE,
  Aviation Security Fund, 8/3
  British Airways Board, 8/5
  British Steel Corporation, 41/1
  Capital Gains Tax. *See* CAPITAL GAINS TAX.
  Capital Transfer Tax. *See* CAPITAL TRANSFER TAX.
  Civil Aviation Authority, 8/5, 6
  Commonwealth Development Corporation, 2/9–13
  Co-operative Development Agency, 21/1, schs. 1, 2
  Corporation Tax. *See* CORPORATION TAX.
  Customs and Excise, 42/1–10. *See* CUSTOMS AND EXCISE.
  Development Land Tax, 42/76
  disclosure of information, 42/77
  employment subsidies, 6/1–4
  export guarantees, 18/1–10
  home purchases, 27/1
  housing, [S] 14/1–19, schs.
  Housing Corporation, 27/5
  Income Tax. *See* INCOME TAX.
  Maternity Pay Fund, 44/37
  national insurance surcharge, 42/75
  National Loans Fund, 44/38
  overseas investment: non-commercial risks, 18/11
  profit sharing schemes, 42/53–61
  rate support grant, 51/68, 52/58
  Scotland: devolution, 51/44–62
  shipbuilding: redundancy payments, 11/1–4
  stamp duty: N.H.S., [S] 29/104
  supply, 7/1–3, 57/1–3, schs. 59/1–3
  Value Added Tax, 42/11, 12. *See* VALUE ADDED TAX.
  Wales: devolution, 52/40–57

ROAD TRAFFIC,
  bicycles, 55/12
  car-sharing, 55/7
  disabled persons, 53/14
  drivers' hours, 55/10
  lorries, checks on, 55/9
  off-street parking, 55/11
  public service vehicle licences, 55/5–8
  transport, 55/1–25, schs.
  vehicle excise duty, 42/8, 9

SAFETY,
  civil liability, 38/6
  goods, 38/1–11
  offences, 38/2
  prohibition orders and notices, 38/3
  safety regulations, 38/1–11

SALE OF GOODS,
  civil liability, 38/6
  prohibition notices and orders, 38/3
  safety regulations, 38/1–12, schs.

SCOTLAND,
  adoption, [S] 28/1–67, schs.
  civil servants, 51/67

SCOTLAND—*cont.*
  community service orders, 49/1–15
  devolution, 51/1–87, schs. 1–17
  devolved matters, what are, 51/63–65
  economic guidelines, 51/42
  existing enactments, interpretation, 51/82
  financial provisions, 51/44–62
  fish, import of, 35/1–4
  gaming licence duty, 42/7
  housing, 14/1–19, schs. *See* HOUSING.
  industrial guidelines, 51/42
  legal aid, 22/61
  local government, 4/1–8, sch.
  maintenance orders, reciprocal enforcement of, 22/60, 61
  maladministration, 51/76
  National Health Service, 29/1–110, schs., 53/43, sch. 8
  Orkney, 51/41, 84
  planning, 51/71
  probation orders, conditions, 49/7
  public bodies, 51/69
  rate support grants, 51/68
  rating: disabled persons, 40/4–7
  referendum, 51/85, 86
  rent limits, 14/14
  Scottish Assembly, 51/1–19, 24–34
  Scottish Executive, 51/20–23
  Shetland, 51/41, 84
  subordinate legislation, 51/22, 40
  supplementary benefits, 14/12, 13
  Theatres Trust, 24/1, 2
  tourism, 51/70
  United Kingdom Authorities, relations with, 51/35–43

Scotland Act 1978 (c. 51)

SEARCH, POWERS OF,
  child pornography, 37/4
  munitions and radio transmitters, for, 5/15
  persons unlawfully detained, 5/17

SETTLEMENTS AND TRUSTS,
  Capital Transfer Tax. *See* CAPITAL TRANSFER TAX.
  income tax. *See* INCOME TAX.

Shipbuilding (Redundancy Payments) Act 1978 (c. 11)

SOCIAL SECURITY,
  chronically sick persons, 53/1–12
  disabled persons, 1–21
  Northern Ireland, 53/1–21
  recoupment of benefits, 44/132
  rent rebates and allowances, [S] 14/12, 13

SOLICITORS,
  Northern Ireland, 23/50,105, 106, 107
  rights of audience, 23/50, 106

Solomon Islands Act 1978 (c. 15)

State Immunity Act 1978 (c. 33)

STATUTES,
  amendment, 30/2, 14
  commencement, time of, 30/4
  continuity of powers and duties, 30/12
  Customs and Excise Acts, 42/79
  duplicated offences, 30/18
  employment legislation, 44/137
  implied power to amend, 30/14
  interpretation,
    citation of other Acts, 30/19
    definitions, 30/5

[13]

PRINTED IN GREAT BRITAIN
BY
THE EASTERN PRESS LTD.
OF LONDON AND READING